DATE DUE

DEMCO 38-296

ILLUSTRATED HISTORY OF SOUTH AFRICA

READER'S DIGEST

ILLUSTRATED HISTORY OF SOUTH AFRICA

The Real Story

Expanded third edition: completely updated

The Reader's Digest Association Limited
Cape Town, London, New York, Sydney, Montreal

ILLUSTRATED HISTORY OF SOUTH AFRICA –
THE REAL STORY
was edited and designed by
The Reader's Digest Association South Africa (Pty) Ltd,
130 Strand Street, Cape Town, 8001, South Africa

Editor Dougie Oakes
Art Editor Christabel Hardacre
Contributing Editor Alfie Steyn
Special Contributors Michael Kantey, John Linnegar
Picture Researchers Vivian Baard, Dominique Davis,
Henry Ludski, Rose-Ann Myers, David Rogers
Indexer Sandie Vahl

ISBN 1-874912-27-0

Consultant Editor
Christopher Saunders, Associate Professor of History,
University of Cape Town

Historical Advisor
Colin Bundy, Director, Institute for Historical Research,
University of the Western Cape

Writers
Brian Johnson Barker, Paul Bell, Bruce Cameron,
Chiara Carter, Allan Duggan, Vivien Horler,
Vincent Leroux, Portia Maurice, Cecile Reynierse,
Hugh Roberton, Peter Schafer, Lee-Ann Smith

Researchers
Judy Beyer, Tracy Neville, Chérise Pledger,
Thecla Schreuders, Peta Scop

'I never thought it could happen here'

In 1919, only nine years after the formation of the Union of South Africa, an 18-year-old girl made the long journey from her birthplace in the Transkei to settle among the small African community living around Cape Town. For the next 75 years Miriam Mqomboti lived through some of the most important dates in South African – and world – history: the Rand Rebellion, the Great Depression, the Second World War, Sharpeville, the Treason Trial, the rise and fall of apartheid ....

Then, on 26 April 1994, Mqomboti herself made history: for the first time in her 93 years she voted.

Leaning on the arm of an election monitor, the spirited old woman walked into a polling station in the sprawling Cape Town suburb of Guguletu – and drew an X against the political party of her choice. 'I am happy this day has come,' she told a reporter outside, 'I never thought it could happen here.'

And yet, almost incredibly, it had. In a few, frightening, tense and ultimately exhilarating days the old South Africa that Mqomboti had known for all her long life ended – and a new South Africa was born. Millions of Mqomboti's compatriates queued for up to eight hours in what one voter described as the 'hurry up and wait election' – an election that only four years previously had seemed impossibly beyond reach.

THE VOTE *for Africans was a long time coming, but for these pensioners in Soweto, near Johannesburg, the chance to make their mark came on 26 April 1994.*

A FOUR-YEAR JOURNEY *from political prisoner to president began for Nelson Mandela on 11 February 1990. He addressed a huge crowd at the Cape Town City Hall just hours after his release.*

The first ray of light

The man chosen to lead the new South Africa, Nelson Rolihlahla Mandela, also spent a large slice of his life within sight of Table Mountain – as a prisoner on Robben Island. It was his release on 11 February 1990 that planted the seed for the final handover of power from a government based solely on skin colour to a government based on what Mandela himself described in his inauguration speech as the 'rainbow nation'.

When Mandela walked to freedom on that fateful day, most South Africans saw him for the first time. For 27 years his face was hidden from South Africans – his photograph banned from newspapers, magazines, television and history books by a government fearful of freedom, and proprietors fearful of prosecution. He remained a mystery, an enigma.

This veil of darkness around Mandela was just one symptom of a malaise that gripped the teaching and understanding of history during the years of apartheid – and before. An obsession with so-called Christian nationalism that favoured the strong at the expense of the weak; that unashamedly rigged the facts in order to propagate the social engineering policies of the country's rulers.

History and nationalism are, perhaps, natural bedfellows, an almost daily reaffirmation of the right to be proud to exist. But history has many memories and many versions; one person's beliefs may be another's lies; today's truth may be tomorrow's fiction. So that, while every schoolchild learned about Union, how many learned of the desperate efforts by blacks to be part of it? And while we all know about the bravery (and bravery it undoubtedly was) of the trekkers, what do we really know of that other great trek – when millions of black people were uprooted from their homes by apartheid legislation?

The real story

It was this extraordinary inequality in South African history that prompted the publication in 1988 of the first edition of the 'Reader's Digest Illustrated History of South Africa – the Real Story'. At last ordinary South Africans were able to access the vast amount of new academic research into the nation's past that had been accumulating in our universities over recent years.

This research asserted that South African history did not begin with the 'discovery' of the country by the Portuguese. What about the people who had lived on the shores of Table Bay for centuries? How could Europeans have 'discovered' a land that was already settled? In the quest for truth nothing was taken for granted, and one by one many of the beliefs that were central to the traditional view of South African history came under the spotlight; and if they did not fit the facts, out they went. Even the vow that the Voortrekkers were believed to have made before their victory over the Zulu at the Battle of Blood River, celebrated for more than a century as a public holiday, was called into question.

The 'Reader's Digest Illustrated History of South Africa – the Real Story' was an immediate bestseller – a publishing sensation that sold out its first print run within a couple of months, revealing a thirst for the truth on the part of thousands of ordinary South Africans who clearly did not believe the old versions of history they had been taught at school.

Nearly every page broke new ground – not least because the book was the first local popular publication in nearly 30 years to feature photographs of Nelson Mandela – albeit taken when he was still a young man.

A second edition followed in 1992, detailing the already remarkable changes that had taken place in South Africa since the change in leadership of the National Party from P W Botha to F W de Klerk – and the decision to release Mandela and unban the African National Congress, the Pan-Africanist Congress and the South African Communist Party.

Since then much more has changed. The old gridlock of apartheid has finally crumbled and De Klerk's face has been replaced by Mandela's at the head of a new government. Men who once dominated the political arena have now melted into obscurity. A new set of challenges has taken the place of the old uncertainties. Time has moved on – and become history.

Third edition

The third edition reflects probably the most fundamental change that has affected South Africa this century: the fall of apartheid and the establishment of a democratically elected government.

In order to reflect these changes, a new chapter has been added dealing with the negotiating process that led to the election – and the violence and uncertainty that accompanied it. In addition, the entire text has been rechecked by our consultants and new research incorporated where appropriate.

Inevitably, in presenting a broader, more balanced view of South African history, this book will question, and in many cases overturn, long-held beliefs and cherished myths. We make no apology for this; a better understanding of our past will surely help us to interpret our present, and prepare us to face the continuing challenges of South Africa's future.

Contents

The 'Illustrated History of South Africa – the Real Story'
is divided into seven parts, each broken down into
several chapters following a broadly chronological
theme. The chapter heading will be found at the top
outside corner of each page. Special features entitled
'Life of the times', which deal with aspects of
social history, are included in five of the seven sections.

The peopling of southern Africa to 1652

'It is . . . probable that our early progenitors lived on the African continent . . . .'
Charles Darwin (1809-82), author of 'On the Origin of Species'.

When a horrified Victorian world read these words in the middle of the last century, the very idea that man could have originated in such an outlandish spot as Africa was generally dismissed as nonsense, especially by those who already regarded Darwin's evolutionary theories as rank heresy. Man, it was felt, was altogether too grand for Africa; his cradle must surely lie somewhere in Asia, where the first written records of human society had their origins.

Darwin was not a man to write or speak lightly; when he came up with an idea, he based it on the most careful observations and research. But it was to be many, many years before this particular theory began to make sense . . . not until 1924, when a fossilised skull, with features intermediate between ape and human, was found in the northern Cape. It was given the name *Australopithecus africanus*, the southern ape of Africa, which had lived between one and three million years ago – older than any similar hominid fossil ever found.

More discoveries followed, helping to fill in the gaps between the *australopithecines* and modern man, *Homo sapiens sapiens*, who first appeared about 100 000 years ago. This was the ancestor of the San, who flourished over a wide area of southern Africa for thousands of years, their descendants still living on in some of the more remote parts of the Kalahari. If any single group can claim to be the original inhabitants of this land, it must surely be they. These Stone Age people neither domesticated animals nor grew crops; everything they needed they took from nature: hunting with small bows and arrows and eating edible roots and berries. For this reason they are known to archaeologists as 'hunter-gatherers', living in rock shelters, or even in the open, sometimes erecting crude shelters from twigs or animal skins. They made no pottery, instead using ostrich eggshells for storing and holding liquids.

For tens of thousands of years this lifestyle remained little changed, until about 2 000 years ago when a revolution began among some of the San communities in the northern part of present-day Botswana – the acquisition of domestic stock – sheep and cattle (and goats in the case of the Nama) from the Bantu-speaking peoples who were moving into the region. They called themselves Khoikhoi, which is thought to mean 'men of men' or 'real people'.

Those same Bantu-speakers encountered by the early pastoralists in northern Botswana were also establishing themselves within the borders of present-day South Africa; and there is ample evidence of their occupation of the northern

Transvaal as early as 1500 years ago, while recent discoveries indicate that they coexisted with the Khoikhoi in the eastern Cape region as long ago as 1000 years. The rearing of cattle was not their only evolutionary success; they also cultivated crops and worked in iron – the first Iron Age men in southern Africa. Indications are that there was a fair amount of mingling between the Khoikhoi and the Bantu-speakers, although the hunter-gatherers, left out of the agricultural revolution brought about by cattle rearing and crop cultivation, began to dwindle in number, even though Khoikhoi sometimes lost their herds and were forced to fall back on hunting and gathering for sustenance. By all accounts there was little physical difference between the appearance of the Khoikhoi herders and the San hunter-gatherers.

This, then, was the situation when, about four centuries ago, a new wave of people began appearing in southern Africa, this time not overland, but from the sea. At first they came, they looked and they left; then they came more often, trading pieces of iron for cattle and sheep from the Khoikhoi; and finally, over three centuries ago, they came to stay. These new arrivals brought with them new technologies and a ruthless quest for land hitherto unknown in the region. But what made them significantly different from the San, the Khoikhoi and the Bantu-speakers was the colour of their skin . . . it was white.

Man in southern Africa

2,5- to 3-million years ago	Early Stone Age begins.
1- to 3-million years ago	*Australopithecus africanus* lives.
90 000 to 1-million years ago	*Homo erectus* lives in Africa, Europe and Asia; learns to shape implements; first to use fire; begins to resemble modern man. Earlier Stone Age people at Makapansgat possibly first Africans to harness fire.
100 000-50 000 years ago	*Homo sapiens sapiens* lives.
35 000 to 70 000 years ago	Neanderthal Man lives in Europe.
28 000 years ago	Castle Cavern in Swaziland first mined for specularite.
25 000 to 27 000 years ago	Earliest dated rock art being painted in Namibia.
20 000 years ago	Middle Stone Age in Africa replaced by Later Stone Age.
14 000 years ago	San hunter-gatherers widely distributed.
3 000 years ago	Iron Age man emerging in North Africa.
2 500 years ago	First settled communities in sub-Saharan Africa practising agriculture, metal-working and pottery.
2 300 years ago	Some San bands in northern Botswana acquire domestic stock and become pastoralists now known as Khoikhoi.
1 750 years ago	Iron-using farmers, ancestors of present Bantu-speaking peoples, established south of the Limpopo River.
c1 400 years ago	'Lydenburg Heads' indicate the use of rituals among Early Iron Age peoples.
c1 000 years ago	Site K2 (Bambandyanalo) settled, abandoned about 200 years later. Mapungubwe settled c700 years ago by people from K2.
800 to 900 years ago	Later Iron Age begins in southern Africa.
700 years ago	Gradual change occurs in pottery, related to arrival of Nguni and Sotho-Tswana immigrants.
c600 years ago	Mapungubwe abandoned.
500 years ago	Last Stone Age people, Khoisan (Khoikhoi and San) establish themselves as dominant society of the Cape; come into contact with Europeans on southern African coast.
400 years ago	Iron Age farmers come into contact with Europeans on southern African coast.

Enter the Europeans

By 1400s	Compass with 32 points in use.
1450-1500	First Europeans visit eastern and southern African coasts. Portuguese establish trade monopoly with East.
1460	Portuguese explorers reach coast of Guinea.
1462	First recorded calculation of latitude from European ship, using the Pole Star.
1483	Diego Cão reaches mouth of Zaïre (Congo) River.
1484	Portuguese astonomers first calculate latitude, using sun's position at midday.
1486	Cão dies at Cape Cross, north of Swakopmund.
1488	Bartolomeu Dias arrives at *Baia dos Vaqueiros* (Mossel Bay), comes into contact with Khoikhoi. By rounding the Cape, he opens sea route to the East to Europeans.
c1490	Dias erects *padrão* at Kwaaihoek, names Cape of Good Hope.
1495	Manuel I ascends to Portuguese throne, continues exploration.
1498	Da Gama rounds Cape of Good Hope, continues to Mossel Bay, *Terra do Natal* and India.
By 1500	Demise of Portuguese power under Spain's Philip II.
1500	Dias dies in storm off Cape of Good Hope after erecting cross at *Porto Fragoso* (Hout Bay).
1503	Portuguese navigator De Saldanha enters Table Bay.
1510	Portuguese India's Viceroy De Almeida dies in clash with Khoikhoi on shores of Table Bay.
1589	*São Tome* wrecked off Mozambique coast.
1594-1601	English navigator James Lancaster barters with Cape Khoikhoi.
1608	Dutch Admiral Cornelis Matelief barters for sheep in Table Bay.
1613	Khoikhoi named Gorachouqua (Goree) kidnapped, taken to London, returns to Cape as 'trading agent', demanding higher prices for cattle.
1616	Group of Dutchmen assist Gorachouqua plunder inland Cochoqua.
1626	Gorachouqua killed by Dutch sailors for refusing to trade with them.
1631	Strandloper leader Autshumao (Harry) sails to Java, to return as interpreter; unofficial postmaster for English sailors.
1647	*Haerlem* wrecked in Table Bay; crew under Leendert Jansz builds fortress on beach.
1650s	Inland trade reopened between Peninsular Khoikhoi and up-country chiefdoms; former maintain monopoly on trade with Dutch.
1652	Cape refreshment station established by the Dutch.

Unlocking the earliest past

1897	Attention first drawn to profusion of fossilised bones found in Sterkfontein caves near Krugersdorp.
1913	Fragments of a skull, possibly of an archaic form of *Homo sapiens*, found at Boskop, eastern Transvaal.
1920s	Dorothea Bleek compiles extensive photographic record of San life in Namibia.
1924	*Australopithecus africanus* found in northern Cape lime deposits at Taung; features midway between man and ape. M de Bruyn finds brain-cast and face embedded in rock matrix; site studied by Prof R B Young.
1925	Dr Robert Broom examines Taung skull.
1930s	University of Denver, USA, study tour of San populations in Cape and Namibia.
1932	Mapungubwe remains are uncovered by E S van Graan.
1934	Broom appointed as palaeontologist to Transvaal Museum; Publishes reconstruction of adult *Australopithecus*.
1936	Broom commences excavation at Sterkfontein.
By 1939	Broom discovers 19 specimens closely related, yet different to Taung child.
Post-1945	Dart researches Makapansgat limeworks and discovers remains of *Australopithecus africanus*. Gert Terblanche shows Broom site of palate find in lime-filled caves at Kromdraai: named *Paranthropus robustus* (*Australopithecus robustus*).
1947	Mrs Ples excavated at Sterkfontein.
1948	Broom and J T Robinson begin excavations at Swartkrans, discovering many specimens of *Australopithecus robustus* since. Subsequently discover *Telanthropus capensis*, which lived at the same time, having more human features.
1949	Willard Libby perfects radio-carbon dating.
1950s	Radio-carbon dating verifies age of Bambandyanalo.
1960s	Swartkrans excavations uncover a more human-like skull: *Homo erectus*; slightly earlier *Homo habilis* had almost certainly fashioned crude stone tools.
1969-73	De (Die) Kelders (east of Hermanus) yields the then earliest dated evidence of the presence of Khoikhoi herders in the south-western Cape during the Stone Age.

Riddle of a face in the rock

In his 'Naturalis Historia', Pliny the Elder, who lived during the 1st century AD, wrote:
'... It is commonly said among the Greeks that "Africa always offers something new".'
Of course, in making this observation, Pliny was unaware of what was possibly
Africa's most sensational offering – man himself.

WITH INCREASING CONFIDENCE, scientists are today claiming that it was perhaps in what is now South Africa, and certainly somewhere on the African continent, that modern man's ancestors first appeared.

Somewhere on the veld, where the vegetation was probably little changed from what it is today, man cowered in the immensity of a ferocious world. He cowered because he was puny. His claws were fragile, unable to rend the throats of the victims he might select as his food. His fangs and his jaws were feeble things, too, and his thin hide could be penetrated by the bite of the smallest rodent. His muscles were weak when contrasted with those of a leopard or lion, and he moved too slowly ever to catch the buck that bounded away across the plains. But the size and complexity of his brain, and the arrangement of his fingers, invested him with the power to conquer and destroy all that he saw before him.

A long process of evolution lay behind him, its record preserved as enduring fossils over a period of more than 3,5-million years. Fossilisation of bone involves replacement of the bone's protein content by percolated matter from the moisture in the soil in which the bone lies. Over many years, the bone is converted into a stone replica known as a fossil.

Man belongs to the class of animals known as mammals, which are distinguished by being warm-blooded, giving birth to live young which they are able to suckle, and by having hair, and two sets of teeth – deciduous and permanent. Man is further classified as belonging to the order of mammals called primates, which includes apes and monkeys. Classification is based on physical structure, and ultimately defines a species, which is a group of animals capable of breeding to produce fertile offspring similar to the parents. Man may be classified as follows: Class – Mammalia; Order – Primates; Family – Hominidae; Genus – *Homo* (man); Species – *sapiens* (wise).

Although a few forms of fossil man had been found in Europe, such as the Neanderthal and Cro-Magnon types, scientists expected to uncover the real 'cradle' of man somewhere in Asia, since in the 19th century it was assumed that the most advanced early civilisations had been Middle Eastern or Asian. This was despite the prediction of Charles Darwin, propounder of the theory of evolution, that 'it is somewhat more probable that our early progenitors lived on the African continent than elsewhere'. Darwin's prediction, made at a time when no hominid fossils had been discovered in Africa, was spectacularly vindicated in 1924.

The Taung baby

In that year, the professor of anatomy at the University of the Witwatersrand was Australian-born Raymond Dart. He had been appointed just 22 months earlier and, finding that his department had very few examples of human or

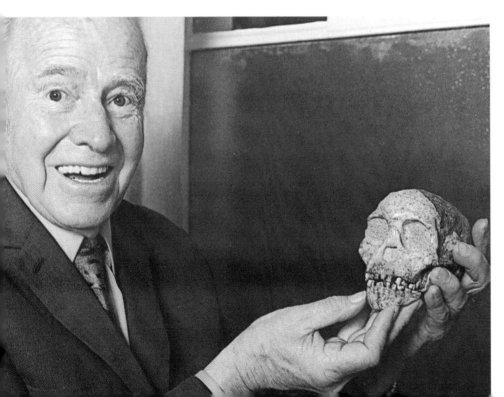

FIFTY YEARS AFTER *their paths had first crossed, 81-year-old Professor Raymond Dart renews his acquaintance with the Taung child – the skull which provided the most valuable clues yet to the origins of man. The 'reunion' took place in 1974 when the Museum of Man and Science commemorated the 50th anniversary of the discovery of the tiny skull at Taung in the northern Cape.*

animal skeletal material, he encouraged his students to bring in any interesting bone or fossil that they might find. About the same time, far away in the dry northern Cape, at the works of the Northern Lime Company near Taung (formerly Taungs), the first link in the chain of discovery was being forged.

In May 1924, a Johannesburg-based director of the company, E G Izod, was visiting the limeworks when he was shown a 'fossilised monkey' that had come to light during blasting operations. Thinking it would make a novel paperweight, he took the skull home with him, and left it on his desk. Its journey might have stopped right there, had not his son, Pat, thought it might interest his student friends at the university and taken it onto the campus. There it was seen by Josephine Salmons, who was in her third year of a medical BSC. She thought the fossilised skull might be that of an extinct baboon, and asked her professor for confirmation. His name was Raymond Dart.

Dart agreed that the skull did indeed represent an extinct species of baboon, and noted that a hole in the skull suggested that the baboon had been killed by a blow from a sharp instrument. If this was so, it raised the exciting possibility of the existence, contemporary with the extinct baboon species, of a creature sufficiently intelligent to make purposeful use of some sort of tool or weapon. And possibly intelligent enough to have actually made that tool for a specific purpose. A colleague of Dart, Professor R B Young of the geology department, was about to leave for Taung to study the lime deposits, and Dart asked him to keep an eye open for more specimens.

In November, one of the quarry-men at Taung, M de Bruyn, was blasting limestone that had filled an ancient cave, when he noticed a small brain-cast with, beside it, a face embedded in another piece of rock matrix. Although he was no anatomist, De Bruyn immediately recognised that this was no fossil baboon, and even argued with the quarry manager that it might be a fossil San (Bushman) type. A few days later, Young arrived and, when his work was complete, examined the site where the mysterious skull had been found. There, he selected additional fragments of fossil-bearing rock before returning to Johannesburg with the skull that was destined to become one of the most famous fossils ever discovered.

Dart was elated, and recognised that the skull showed features midway between man and the apes, even though no similar specimen had ever been recorded before. For the next four weeks, he worked in every spare moment to remove the adherent rock matrix from the bone which, itself, had absorbed the components of the rock. At first he used a light hammer and chisel, and then, as the work became finer, a steel knitting-needle.

What he had received on 28 November 1924 as mere lumps of rock was revealed just before Christmas to be the face – including upper and lower jaws and all teeth, as well as the brain-case and endocranial cast – of a creature hitherto unknown to science. Working with remarkable speed and accuracy, Dart wrote a preliminary report which he posted to the British scientific journal 'Nature' on 6 January 1925. The report struck the editor of the journal as so sensational that, before daring to publish, he sent copies

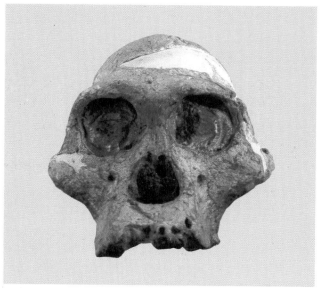

HER FULL NAME *was Plesianthropus transvaalensis, but her discoverer, Dr Robert Broom, called her Mrs Ples. Later she was found to be of the same species as the Taung child.*

to four of the leading British experts who, although they advised him to publish, were generally sceptical.

The Taung baby, so named because the state of development of its teeth revealed that it had died at the age of three or four years, had walked upright, almost like man. And its canine teeth, like those of man, were small. The brain, although small, showed human-like features. The forehead was smooth and vertical, and the mouth did not jut forward. In his report, Dart suggested that the skull belonged to a member of an extinct ape family with characteristics similar to those of man. He named it *Australopithecus africanus* – the southern ape of Africa.

The discovery, and Dart's conclusions, received prominence in the world's Press, evoking a flood of letters – all of them uncomplimentary. They ranged from the view that Dart was destined for 'the quenchless fires of Hell' to the hope that he would be 'placed in an institution for the feeble-minded'. But Dart stood firm. A major factor accounting for the virtual rejection of Dart's propositions was that the skull was that of a juvenile, whose physical characteristics had not developed fully. If an adult specimen could be obtained, said the experts, they might be persuaded to change their views that what Dart had described was just another extinct ape and had nothing to do with the line of man's ancestry.

Mrs Ples and others

One of Dart's few supporters was Dr Robert Broom, a colourful medical practitioner who was more interested in palaeontology and anthropology than in the straightforward practice of medicine. Broom had been the first scientific visitor to examine the Taung skull, and had dropped to his knees to study it more closely, saying cheerily: 'I am kneeling in adoration of our ancestor.'

Born in Scotland, Broom arrived in South Africa in 1897, and practised medicine in several places before being appointed professor of zoology and geology at Victoria College, Stellenbosch (the forerunner of Stellenbosch University), a post he held for some five years. He enthusiastically collected, described and named many Karoo fossils of reptiles and mammal-like reptiles and, on his partial retirement from medical practice in 1928, wrote three major scientific books. In 1934, at the age of 66 and with energy undiminished, he was appointed palaeontologist to the Transvaal Museum, Pretoria. At an age when many consider retirement, Broom was about to embark on an energetic and successful new career.

Determined to vindicate Dart's proposals, Broom published a reconstruction of what he thought an adult *Australopithecus* would look like and, in 1936, he began to work at excavations at Sterkfontein near Krugersdorp. As early as 1897 attention had been drawn to the profusion of fossilised bones contained in the breccia (a mass of consolidated stone particles) that filled the cave there, but no scientific work had been done. Instead, the rich cave-deposits were being quarried and burnt in lime kilns.

When Broom arrived at Sterkfontein, he found a small tea room, with a number of interesting fossils laid out on a table. Thinking this was an informal museum, he went ahead with his inspection of the quarry face, discovering only later that the public visited Sterkfontein on Sundays, and that the fossils were for sale. In a little booklet on Johannesburg and surroundings, the public was even invited to 'come to Sterkfontein and find the missing link'. This was soon stopped, but much invaluable material must have been lost.

THE YEAR IS 1947 – *and at the Sterkfontein excavation site near Krugersdorp in the Transvaal, Robert Broom (with waistcoat) and J T Robinson (crouching) unearth Mrs Ples, the fossilised skull which proved that a species of man existed on the African continent millions of years ago.*

As if to compensate, however, Broom found his adult skull within nine days. By the outbreak of war in 1939, when his work was suspended, he had discovered 19 specimens at Sterkfontein. They were clearly related to the Taung baby, but he felt that certain differences, particularly of the teeth, justified placing them in a different genus, which he named *Plesianthropus transvaalensis*. It was after the war that he found the almost perfectly preserved cranium of a female specimen, nicknamed 'Mrs Ples', that had lived some 2,5-million years ago. Later, Mrs Ples and others of her genus were to be reclassified as *Australopithecus africanus*.

Gert Terblanche's teeth

One day the quarry foreman at Sterkfontein handed Broom a part of a fossilised palate, with one molar tooth still in position. When Broom examined it closely, he noticed that two teeth had recently been broken off, and that the adherent rock matrix was different from that of Sterkfontein. Broom hurried back, to be told that the palate had been found by a schoolboy named Gert Terblanche, who worked in the cave as a guide on Sundays. He immediately drove to Gert's home, to find the boy was still in school. However, he was shown by Mrs Terblanche the spot where she thought Gert had found the palate. There, Broom found more pieces of skull, as well as more teeth. Convinced that Gert might know of the whereabouts of still more fragments, Broom drove towards the school and, when the road became too bumpy, continued on foot for some 1,5 kilometres. Gert was soon tracked down in his classroom, 'and drew from the pocket of his trousers four of the most wonderful teeth ever seen in the world's history'. All these pieces had been found in the lime-filled caves at nearby Kromdraai.

Because the skull seemed to show a bigger-toothed and more heavily built individual than *Australopithecus* and *Plesianthropus*, Broom named his latest find *Paranthropus robustus*. It is now considered, though, that this large ape-man belonged to the same genus as the smaller *Australopithecus*, but to a different species. Broom's *Paranthropus*, therefore, is now known as *Australopithecus robustus*. It has been proposed that the difference in size between *A. robustus* and *A. africanus* is due to the fact that *A. robustus* was a vegetarian, whereas *A. africanus* was omniverous, but this has not been generally accepted.

In the Sterkfontein valley, yet another lime-filled cave awaited exploration. This was Swartkrans, only 1,6 kilometres from the original discovery-site at Sterkfontein cave. Broom and J T Robinson began work at Swartkrans in 1948 and since then, many individuals of *A. robustus* have been discovered there. More significant was the discovery of the remains of a creature which they originally named *Telanthropus capensis*. Fossilised teeth, limb bones and skull fragments seemed to the investigators to be human, or very nearly so, and they were able to show that it had lived at the same time as *A. robustus* and, very likely, had preyed on the 'robust ape-man'.

Twenty years later, more pieces were excavated at Swartkrans which, when assembled, produced a striking-

The family tree of man

The crucial breakthrough in the evolution of man came when creatures became adapted to standing and walking upright. This freed the hands to develop a distinctively human skill: the ability to use, and to make tools.

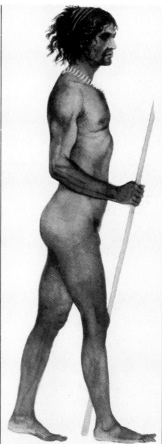

Australopithecus africanus inhabited eastern and southern Africa between 1- and 3-million years ago. The Taung child is a member of this species.

 Although A. africanus had human-like teeth, its brain was no larger than an ape's.

Homo habilis (handy man) was the first true human being. He fashioned crude tools from stone in order to hunt animals.

 His teeth were similar to A. africanus, but his brain was 50 percent bigger.

Remains of Homo erectus (erect man), who lived about 1-million years ago, were first excavated at Swartkrans, near Krugersdorp in the Transvaal, in 1948.

 His brain was 25 percent bigger than that of handy man.

Homo sapiens sapiens, or modern man, is thought to have first appeared approximately 50 000 years ago in parts of Africa and western Asia.

 The skull of modern man has space for a brain of about 1 400 milli-litres.

ly more human-like skull than had been thought at first. So far removed was it from the ape-like creatures with which the scientists were by now familiar, that it was placed within the human family, and given the name of *Homo erectus* – erect man. Another slightly earlier type was named *Homo habilis* (handy man), and had almost certainly fashioned crude tools from stone.

Discoveries at Makapansgat limeworks in the northern Transvaal in 1945 brought Professor Dart, heavily occupied with administrative duties, back to palaeontological research. The skulls of fossil baboons had been discovered, most of them showing the type of fracture present in the first skull brought to Dart by Josephine Salmons 20 years earlier. Soon the remains of *A. africanus* also began to emerge and, from the remains of pelvic bones, it was possible to prove what Dart had deduced from the skull of the Taung baby – *A. africanus* had indeed walked upright, almost like man.

Dart then investigated, with the help of a professor of forensic medicine, the likely cause of the skull fractures of the baboons, and came to the conclusion that they were caused by a blow from an antelope leg-bone, probably wielded by *A. africanus*. He went further to suggest that the little, small-brained australopithecines had used, as weapons and tools, the bones and horns of animals they had killed. While this is regarded by some as unproven, it is possible that australopithecines may have picked up razor-sharp flakes of naturally fractured rock, used them as a cutting tool, and so commenced the advance into the Stone Age.

The tool-makers

Most people have basic tool kits. The householder may possess a few elementary items, such as hammer and pliers; the motor-enthusiast's kit may be slightly more specialised, and that of the surgeon specialised to the point of high sophistication. The tools of australopithecines and early man fall into the same categories, although the variety of source materials was strictly limited and consisted of no more than stone, wood and bone.

Unworked stones were probably used as missiles, either to bring down a quarry or to frighten scavengers from a kill abandoned by one of the predatory carnivores. Stones that can be adapted to a variety of purposes are produced under natural conditions, and are referred to as 'eoliths' (dawn stones) to distinguish them from man-made artefacts. Sometimes the distinction is difficult to make. Alternating heat and cold can cause rock to splinter into flakes that have a sharp cutting-edge, while stones that are tumbled in a rocky riverbed may resemble smooth grindstones or be shaped to a point. There can be little doubt that these were the first tools, although Homo erectus very soon learnt that, by knocking two stones together in a variety of ways, he could control the splitting off of flakes, and also the shape of the implement.

The first type of shaped implement, apart from bones or horns, was probably the simple tool known as a 'pebble chopper', associated with the earlier Homo habilis. A rounded, water-worn pebble was battered against another stone until a few flakes split off from one aspect, leaving one or more cutting-edges. At first, such a tool was probably made on site. Only specialised, light tools were carried from place to place. This meant that man no longer encumbered himself as he moved about, but simply made a new implement where and when he required it, accounting in part for the tremendous profusion of stone implements to be found today.

Radio-carbon dating

In 1949, an American scientist, Willard Libby, perfected a process which enabled archaeologists to establish chronological dates with remarkable precision.

Libby discovered that although a living organism absorbed various types of carbon from the atmosphere, once such matter died, the amount of ordinary carbon (carbon-12) remained constant while the amount of radioactive carbon (carbon-14) decayed at a known rate.

Carbon-14 is absorbed by plants, and then in turn by herbivores and carnivores, including man. When the organism dies the store of carbon-14 is reduced by half every 5 730 years (accurate to 30 years either way). By using a Geiger counter to measure the proportion of carbon-14 remaining, it becomes possible to establish an approximate date of death.

However, this method is suitable only for dating remains up to 40 000 years old. The most commonly used system to date older archaeological finds is the potassium-argon method which works on the same principle as radio-carbon dating. Effective only in areas where volcanoes are present, this method relies on radioactive potassium which is trapped in volcanic lava and which decays (to form the inert gas, argon) at a much slower rate than carbon. Age is calculated by determining the percentage of radioactive potassium and argon present in the fossil. Archaeological finds in non-volcanic areas are dated by matching them with similar fossils discovered in regions where volcanoes are present.

Homo erectus was the first to use fire. Perhaps he made it himself, albeit accidentally, by means of sparks generated by his tool-making process, but it seems more likely that lightning would have been the source. These naturally caused fires must have gone out many times before man learnt to keep supplies of fuel on hand, or how to keep the blaze going and move it from place to place as he desired. It would not have taken long for him to realise that it would bring comfort to his cold cave, and successive layers of ash in the Cave of Hearths at Makapansgat show that it was much appreciated. There is no way of knowing when man began to cook meat, but it probably began by accident – a piece of flesh that fell into a fire and was retrieved with difficulty.

Unlike Australopithecus who, although he walked upright, had an awkward gait with his out-splayed feet, Homo erectus walked well, and had leg-bones scarcely distinguishable from those of modern man. In appearance, he had a very broad, flat nose, a sloping forehead above prominent eyebrow ridges, and almost no discernable chin. The brain, although very much larger than that of Australopithecus, was still, on average, smaller than that of modern man – a volume between 750 and 1 300 millilitres compared with a range between 1 200 and 2 000 millilitres. It is not possible to determine from fossil casts of his brain whether Homo erectus could speak, but the range of his activities suggests that he was able to convey thoughts through some form of articulate speech. Although his brain's frontal lobe was much smaller than modern man's, he was capable of some degree of thought.

How early man hunted

Homo erectus was a hunter, working in groups of various sizes, and evidence from Spain suggests that he may have lit fires to drive animals towards a certain area. In this case, elephants of a now-extinct variety had been driven into deep mud, where they had floundered helplessly. Fossilised bones showed evidence of having been smashed open, presumably for the marrow within, and entire portions of carcasses were missing. Thin layers of ash indicated burning for a short period over a wide area – suggesting a grass or bush fire. Mixed with the bones were stone tools of the type associated with Homo erectus in Africa, and the evidence appears to indicate that, once helpless, the elephants were butchered with elementary stone tools.

The main tools of Homo erectus were the hand-axe and cleaver belonging to the Acheulian 'industry', named after St Acheul in France, where the type was first described. In South Africa, similar tools were first discovered at a site in Stellenbosch, and were originally classified as the Stellenbosch industry (or 'culture'). The typical hand-axe made by Homo erectus has been trimmed until it is roughly pear-shaped, and may be about 20 centimetres long, or even longer. It is worked to a point and usually has fairly sharp edges. Although labelled as an 'axe', it probably served a variety of purposes, from cutting through the skin of an animal to smashing bone, or even for digging. In terms of modern equipment, the cleaver more closely resembles an axe-head. Chips, or flakes, struck from the stone being shaped as a tool may themselves have been

The first tools of early man

During the Early Stone Age, man had a small range of tools which had limited shape. The tools were usually between 8 and 20 centimetres in length, but were occasionally larger (see axe second from the right). Tools were multipurpose. With time the size of the tools decreased, while the range increased. The specialised and refined tools of the Khoisan belong to the Later Stone Age.

EOLITH   PEBBLE CHOPPER   AXE   AXE   CLEAVER

used as cutting-blades or scrapers. Later, more refined tools were produced by the early San and Khoikhoi, and many of these implements are fine examples of an art form and a skill that came to be taken for granted by these people and, ultimately, quite forgotten by modern man.

Homo erectus evolved, via *Homo habilis*, from *Australopithecus*, and lived from about 90 000 to 1-million years ago, ranging far over Africa, Europe and Asia. Fairly late during this period, various groups changed still more, and in the end, resembled modern man much more closely. A number, though, appear to have branched out along lines that became extinct.

New perspectives

For many years, experts in physical anthropology firmly believed that race and culture went hand in hand and that language and custom could be deduced by a simple classification of a skull.

This was the approach adopted in 1913 when workers dug up a skull on a farm close to the village of Boskop, near Potchefstroom. By piecing together fragments of skulls from other archaeological sites in the area, experts reconstructed a 'typical' skull complete with what they referred to as 'Boskopoid' features.

According to the researchers, the 'Boskop race' was uniquely southern African, and by the middle 1900s at least seven distinct races, each with their own particular traits and cultures, had been identified as being ancestors of 'Boskop' man.

However, this approach to the study of physical differences in humans has now fallen into disfavour.

Today, most experts are in agreement that the physical variations found in man are far more complex than simply the differences in colour, hair form and cranial structure. Indeed, latest studies indicate that only about 10 percent of mankind's genetic variability can be attributed to the 'race' factors on which most of the earlier classifiers based their findings.

Consequently, the search for conformity in skeletons has been largely ditched in favour of the study of the geographical distribution of groups, who through long contact share a common 'pool' of genes.

Although much work still has to be done in this field, many long-held beliefs have already been called into question: some researchers are now saying that there is little evidence to either support or reject the contention that a 'Stone Age race' once found over a large part of Africa, was replaced by a 'Negro' invasion from the north.

Indeed, they claim that although the San populations of Namibia and the Kalahari desert have been more genetically isolated than other groups, they nevertheless share many characteristics with other 'breeding populations'.

Also being called into question, as a result of this method of study, is the theory that first the San, and later, Bantu-speaking people migrated to southern Africa from the north. Comparison of skeletal remains excavated in northern and southern Africa has confirmed the presence, at a far earlier period, in the southern skeletons of 'gene pools' characteristic of inhabitants of the sub-continent.

If this is true, it would mean, in effect, that man formed part of the southern African landscape for an even longer period than was first thought.

All the experts agree that the origin of humankind is an enormously complex subject – far more complex than Dart, Broom and the other pioneers first imagined when they started trying to piece together the history of early man in southern Africa.

Although it is widely accepted that physical anthropology does provide invaluable information about the past, scientists now increasingly believe that the key to unlocking the distant past lies with the reconstruction of the distribution and dating of 'gene pools'.

But for this to happen, the careful study of large collections of skeletal remains is imperative. Unfortunately, up to now far too little work in this area has been done in southern Africa.

'A way of life perfected...'

For millennia, the southern end of Africa was occupied by small groups of aboriginal hunters whose enduring legacy consists of thousands of beautiful and often enigmatic rock paintings. Then, about 2 000 years ago, pastoralists from the north arrived, bringing with them a totally new way of life – the herding of stock – into the hunting grounds of the San. This caused a major disruption of the traditional hunter-gatherer way of life.

IF YOU WERE ABLE to part the mists of time and gaze out over South Africa as it existed about 20 000 years ago, the coastal outline of the country would come as a surprise. With the sea level more than 100 metres lower than it is today, the southern African coast extended further outwards, especially around the Cape, which was surrounded by additional thousands of square kilometres of open plains. Furthermore, with the world still in the grip of the last Ice Age, it was also a much colder and less hospitable place than it is today.

Yet, despite the chillier climate, the area nevertheless teemed with a multitude of reptiles, insects, birds, mammals – and *Homo sapiens*, who had long since split off from his hominoid ancestors and was present through much of sub-Saharan Africa. The descendants of those who lived in what is now South Africa, and who are believed to have been the area's original human inhabitants, are now usually known as the San.

The San were hunter-gatherers whose last remnants, the so-called 'Bushmen', still survive in small numbers in the Kalahari Desert. Their physical appearance – and that of the closely related Khoikhoi people (called 'Hottentots' by early Dutch settlers) – is different from the Bantu-speakers. Their smaller stature, lighter skin pigmentation and unique 'click' languages, are probably due to their having evolved for thousands of years in relative isolation, in the southern part of the sub-continent.

The San hunter-gatherers of southern Africa were a Stone Age people until they came into contact with other people. They did not use metals, their weapons being made of wood, bones and stone; they did not domesticate animals, and they did not cultivate crops. Furthermore, they did not make any pottery, instead using ostrich egg-shells for storing and holding liquids.

Always on the move

Because they were essentially migratory – moving round their territories in search of game and plant foods – the San did not build permanent settlements. Archaeological research has revealed that they used rock shelters as temporary living sites, although open encampments have also been located. It is probable that weather conditions dictated the choices of open or closed sites.

Unlike the Bantu-speakers, the San did not normally form sizeable groupings, but existed in small family groups of about 15-25 people. They were in fact the ultimate egalitarian society, having only a nominal chief who controlled their resources on behalf of the group.

However, the medicine man – who was responsible for divination and curing the sick – played a pivotal role in these small communities.

The San lived off a wide variety of animals, birds, plants, fish and shellfish. Bones dug from caves once occupied by the San reveal that their diet included a wide range of animals, such as dassies, tortoises, antelope and even occasionally the larger, more dangerous animals – such as hippo, elephant and rhino. (Large animals were probably scavenged or caught by means of pit-fall traps with stakes lining the bottom.)

FOR HUNDREDS OF YEARS, *the San people of southern Africa have used ostrich egg shells as water containers. In this picture they are making use of tortoise shells to transport the water to the containers.*

During the times when the San lived at the coast, mussels, perlemoen, alikreukel, crayfish and seals were basic foods, and the large number of fish bones found in coastal caves inhabited by the San indicate that they were accomplished fishermen. Slivers of bone or wood, sharpened at each end, were used to hook fish, which were also caught by means of tidal traps made with walls constructed from stacked stones.

While the San men were responsible for hunting and fishing, it was the women who did most of the gathering of plant foodstuffs. These included wild fruits and berries, as well as the leaves, stems, bulbs, corms and roots of a variety of plants. Underground foods were dug out by means of a sharpened, fire-hardened stick, which was sometimes weighted near one end with a bored stone to increase its penetration.

The pastoral revolution

For tens of thousands of years, the lifestyle of the San hunter-gatherers in southern Africa remained undisturbed. However, about 2 000 years ago there began a gradual but far-reaching revolution in the economic and social system of some of the groups in the northern part of what is now Botswana, namely the acquisition and rearing of livestock.

It is thought that these hunter-gatherers acquired their sheep from Sudanic people from the north, and cattle from Bantu-speakers to the east. The fat-tailed sheep that were acquired by the Khoikhoi were in fact known in the Middle East about 4 000 years before, where they were tended by Semitic-speaking people.

What was particularly significant about this 'pastoral revolution' was the development of the idea of individual ownership, a concept in marked contrast to the tradition of the San that all the resources of their territory – water, animals and plants – were the common property of the community. This inevitably gave rise to a degree of conflict between the hunter-gatherers and the pastoralists, the latter being seen as invaders into the territories of the hunter-gatherers, and their livestock as part of the territories' natural resources.

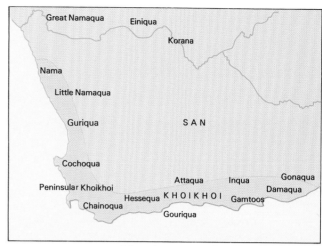

BEFORE THE ARRIVAL *of the white man, Khoikhoi clans along the coastline, and San hunters throughout the region, were undisputed masters of the western part of southern Africa.*

The pastoralists, or 'Khoikhoi' (the name is believed to mean 'men of men'), came to perceive themselves as superior to those who did not own domestic stock. Gone were the hunter-gathering days when everyone was essentially equal and shared what they had with one another. Ownership of livestock, which were often inherited by sons from their fathers, led to the evolvement of a social hierarchy in which the status of a person was determined by wealth in cattle and sheep.

Just as the acquisition of a few cattle or sheep could raise a person on the social level, so could the loss of this stock force him to become the servant of another stock-owner – or result in him leaving the group and reverting to a hunting and gathering existence with others in the same 'stockless' predicament.

The pastoralists move south

As the territorial requirements of the herders increased, so they began to move toward the south in search of new pastures. At one stage in the southerly migration of the Khoikhoi, the confluence of the Orange and Vaal rivers be-

THIS IS DE KELDERS, *an archaeological digging east of the Cape coastal resort of Hermanus. A Stone Age site, the potsherds and sheepbones recovered here between 1969 and 1973 provided the then earliest evidence of Khoikhoi herders in the south-western Cape.*

The two men in the centre are using crowbars to remove rockfall overlying the Middle Stone Age deposits, while the man at the back is studying archaeologically 'sterile' deposits which separate Middle Stone Age from Later Stone Age.

21

MANY OF THE EARLY PAINTINGS *of the Cape of Good Hope tend-* *ed to push artistic licence to the limit – and this early 19th* *century engraving of a 'Hottentot' man and woman with Table* *Mountain (shaped like a volcano) in the background, was no* *exception. The reason for this was that Cape scenes were often* *painted by artists who had never been to southern Africa.*

came an important area of settlement. According to one Khoikhoi oral tradition, the settlement split into three groups following a major quarrel. One group (the Korana) remained, another (the Namaqua) moved south-west towards the Cape Peninsula, and the third group (the Einiqua) followed the course of the Orange River westwards. The inevitable result of the split was rapid expansion. The Namaqua, the advance guard of the western movement, finally reached the arid area of the west coast and subsequently split into two groups in search of pasture. One group moved into what is now Namibia, while another moved south through Little Namaqualand down into the south-western Cape.

The spread of the Khoikhoi pastoralists into the Cape inevitably resulted in a conflict of interests with the aboriginal San hunter-gatherer inhabitants of the area. A major source of conflict was competition for game. Although the Khoikhoi were herders, they relied heavily on the spoils of the hunt for their daily nourishment. Despite the obvious source of protein that their herds represented, the Khoikhoi usually slaughtered their cattle only on special ceremonial occasions. Also, despite the fact that milk from their herds was an important supplement to their diet, its production was often irregular and, moreover dependent on the state of the pasture and the presence of new-born calves in the herds.

But while the Khoikhoi started competing with the San for game, their sheep and cattle were exacerbating the problem even further by denuding the pastures on which the indigenous game – such as zebra, antelope and wildebeest – was dependent. Consequently, as the San watched the vast herds of wild game dwindle, they felt increasingly justified in killing or stealing the alien animals that had displaced their traditional quarry. This in turn set up a deadly cycle of raid and counter-raid, sometimes culminating in full-scale warring between these groups – all of which lasted for many centuries.

Finally, the contact and conflict between the Khoikhoi and San had far-reaching effects on both cultures. On the one hand, the Khoikhoi began to form themselves into larger and better organised groups in order to form a united, stronger front against the cattle-raiding San. The San, in turn, were faced with three alternatives: some fled the continual fighting and retreated into less hospitable mountain and desert areas; others established themselves into robber bands which subsequently preyed on the herds of the Khoikhoi; while others made their peace with the Khoikhoi and entered their society as servants, hunters, herders and warriors. Many who chose the third option gradually acquired stock, and later, when they married Khoikhoi women, they were gradually accepted as fully fledged members of these communities.

If only rocks could talk . . .

Although the vast proportion of rock paintings and engravings which abound in southern Africa are the work of the San, some elements such as handprints are thought to be the work of the Khoikhoi.

It was originally believed that the reasons for these numerous paintings and engravings were to be found in man's innate desire to express himself in some way – art for art's sake – or in the need to exert some form of magical control over the animals portrayed in the art. Current research has shown that a great deal of this art is related to the trance-dancing which formed, and indeed still forms, an important part of the San response to environmental pressures.

The medicine man in trance was the important link between the world of the spirits and the everyday world in which the people lived. During trance, many duties such as healing of the sick, communication with the spirit world, information gathering and divination, were carried out and were formally communicated to the group through the medium of painting or engraving.

The images which the medicine man saw during the trance state were painted on the rock face and do not represent reality in many cases. Thus we find illustrations of men with animal attributes such as horns or hoofs. These do not portray a man in animal-skin disguise but represent the imagined change which the medicine man undergoes while in the

THE SAN *regarded the eland (right) as being beneficial to their society. It was a valuable source of food.*

trance state. Generally, medicine men involved in good deeds were said to adopt the form of one of the antelope – usually the eland, hartebeest or rhebok, while those bent on harming others would adopt the form of one of the large predators.

As the way of life changed after the arrival of black farmers and white settlers, the San artists incorporated the new arrivals into their art. As a result cattle began to replace the eland as the 'good' symbols and, towards the end, guns started replacing predators as symbols of aggression.

It is thought that the earliest paintings were monochromes (single colour), then two colours and finally the multi-coloured, often shaded works found in the Drakensberg. However, this development was probably inspired by the growing complexity of the rituals needed to

cope with an increasingly stressful existence forced on the San by the arrival of other people.

The pigments used were oxides of iron for the range of reds and yellows, manganese dioxide for black, and various compounds of calcium or magnesium for white. To produce paint, the Khoikhoi probably mixed these pigments with a binding agent such as albumen (egg white), plant sap, urine or even blood. The paint was applied in a variety of ways using feathers, sticks or even fingers to produce the desired result.

It is almost impossible to date rock art but research has shown that the earliest paintings recovered from an excavation in Namibia are between 25 000 and 27 000 years old. The art tradition ended in the mid-19th century when the last of the San artists was killed.

THE ARMED SOLDIERS *represent aggression. Medicine men believed that simply by pointing or clicking a finger at another person, the person would be harmed.*

THE CROSS-LEGGED POSE *copies that of a dying eland. Because the San language does not contain a word for 'trance', dying has become a metaphor for it.*

THIS PHOTOGRAPH *(far left) was taken in the 1930s during a study tour of South Africa by a delegation from the University of Denver (Colorado, USA). With the purpose of their visit being to study the San, the group travelled throughout the Cape and Namibia to speak to members of this community.*
TRAVELLING *through the Kalahari Desert by ox-wagon (left) and with her camera always at the ready, during the 1920s Dorothea Bleek compiled an extensive collection of photographs of life in San communities. The people pictured here were her travelling companions.*

Similarities between Khoikhoi and San

The process of assimilation of San by Khoikhoi groups was facilitated by the fact that they both belonged essentially to the same group, and shared the same primal hunter-gatherer heritage. Even their languages were possibly related. Although it was often noted by early commentators that the Khoikhoi were generally taller than the San, it is thought that this denoted not so much a genetic characteristic as a difference in diet, the Khoikhoi having access to a fairly regular supply of meat and milk from their herds. (In modern times, where the San of the Kalahari have taken employment on farms and received a regular, balanced diet, their children grow taller than when they are living the life of the hunter-gatherer.)

When the first Dutch settlers arrived in the 17th century there existed a clear social distinction between the Khoikhoi and San. The term 'San' was one which was used by the Khoikhoi in a derogatory manner, although its original meaning is not known. Some used it to connote others of their kind who had no stock and were thus obliged to go into the service of the richer Khoikhoi.

The Dutch settlers, in turn, introduced their own terminology when referring to these two groups. Collectively, the small yellow-skinned people encountered at the Cape – no matter what their social or stock-owning status – were referred to as 'Hottentots' by the colonists. Later, the people whom the Khoikhoi referred to as 'Souqa', and other variants, were given the derogatory name 'Bosjesmans' (Bushmen) by the Dutch.

By the time the first whites had arrived at the Cape in the 16th and 17th centuries, the Khoikhoi had long since emerged as the dominant society of the Cape. Roughly nine major Khoikhoi groupings had evolved in the Cape, these being situated mainly along the coastal area from the Orange River on the west coast to the Great Fish River in the eastern Cape.

These groups were all made up of smaller clans, whose members were related to one another patrilineally. Individuals were normally loyal to the clan rather than the overall grouping, and clans often broke away from larger units to form new groupings with other clans. In fact, a marked feature of Cape Khoikhoi society was its relative fluidity, with clans and the overall groupings being in a more or less constant state of flux. What doubtlessly contributed towards this constant fission and fusion was the essentially mobile nature of the Khoikhoi clans, these always being on the move within a circumscribed area as they sought new pastures for their stock.

Khoikhoi leadership

The large Khoikhoi groups usually had an overall chief called a *khoeque* ('rich man') who was often assisted by a second-in-command. Leadership shared equally between two men was also common, although it sometimes led to the splitting of groups – some following one chief, some the other. Chieftainship normally passed from father to son, with the son's responsibilities increasing as his father grew older. Where a chief died young, without a male heir, his brother could assume this position.

Khoikhoi chiefs were seldom surrounded by any ostentatious signs of their position. However, their superior social standing was generally indicated by subtle material externals, such as a bigger hut or the wearing of a rare or prized animal skin. Although polygamy was rarely practised among the Khoikhoi – signifying as it did exceptional wealth – it was often indulged in by chiefs.

Although the term 'chief' often implies an autocratic rulership, this was seldom the case in Khoikhoi society. The chief was assisted by a council of clan heads in dealing with matters such as interclan disputes and relations with other groups. (Individual justice was normally dealt with at a gathering of all the males of a particular clan.)

Apparently the Khoikhoi were quick to react if a chief overstepped his mark in any way, and he was often subjected to social ridicule if he was despotic, or abused his authority.

Although they had no standing armies or military commanders, there were often skirmishes between Khoikhoi groups, as there were between Khoikhoi and San. Conflicts usually resulted from disputes over grazing, cattle raiding and blood feuds – many of the latter being passed down through generations. It has been said that although the Khoikhoi often changed their allies, they tended to keep the same enemies for decades. Another cause of disputes was the abduction of women – normally the wives of chiefs or important people in the group.

When conflict did break out, it usually consisted of one major battle, seldom lasting more than a day. Spears, bows, stones and short sticks, used as darts, were the most common weapons. Women and children usually watched the spectacle from a safe distance. Although poisoned arrows were standard equipment during a hunt, they were seldom used in battle since the poison took hours, sometimes days, before it finally brought the victim down. An interesting tactical manoeuvre in many Khoikhoi battles was the use of oxen, which were used to hide behind to escape enemy spears and arrows, or commanded to stampede the ranks of the enemy, trampling and goring those standing in their path. Prisoners of war were usually executed, though ransoming of prisoners and prisoner-exchanges were probably practised.

Apart from these battlefield confrontations – after which enemy huts were usually plundered and livestock driven off – the Khoikhoi were also well-versed in their own particular brand of guerrilla tactics, this consisting

IN A BOOK ENTITLED '*Sketches of Some of the Various Classes and Tribes Inhabiting the Colony of the Cape of Good Hope and the Interior of Southern Africa*' this illustration was simply called 'Hottentot'.

mainly of hit-and-run raids on enemy herds. These sudden, surprise attacks – usually under cover of darkness – were eventually used to good effect against the Dutch, whom the Khoikhoi preferred not to engage in open combat due to the former's superior weaponry.

Trading with other people

Although their frugal needs made them basically self-sufficient for all the essentials of life, the Khoikhoi nevertheless placed a very high value on particular items that were not – at least initially – readily available in the Cape, namely metals and dagga. These items were willingly bartered for their sheep and cattle.

Compared with the traditional fire-hardened wooden tips of arrows and spears, iron provided the Khoikhoi with the means to produce vastly superior and more durable weapons. Copper, which was referred to as 'red iron', was prized as a material from which a wide variety of ornaments – such as beads, bangles, bracelets and chains – were fashioned. The source of some of the iron was the Xhosa in the east while copper was obtained from Little Namaqua, Damara and the Tswana to the north.

Dagga (*Cannabis sativa*) was not indigenous to southern Africa, having probably been introduced into the Mozambique area by Arab traders, from where its use and cultivation spread southwards. It is unknown exactly when this euphoriant was adopted by the Khoikhoi, but it appears to have become a much-valued intoxicant, as well as being used as a herbal remedy for a variety of ailments.

Although dagga required little attention when sown in areas of summer rainfall (such as the country's eastern coastal belt), in the Cape it required constant watering during the dry summer months. Since the Cape Khoikhoi were constantly on the move in search of new pastures, the adequate watering and maintenance of dagga plantations was not practical, though it was apparently cultivated by the more settled Khoikhoi communities – such as those residing on the banks of the Orange River. Consequently, the drug was eagerly bartered from the Xhosa to the east beyond the Great Fish River – they being well-versed in agricultural techniques as well as having a climate more suitable for dagga cultivation. The actual smoking of dagga by the Khoikhoi and black people of southern Africa only began after the introduction of the smoking pipe by whites. Prior to this, dagga was chewed, or boiled in an infusion and drunk.

The arrival of European seafarers at the Cape in the 16th and 17th centuries introduced a whole range of additional commodities for which the Khoikhoi eagerly bartered their stock – such as tobacco, beads, knives, alcohol and salt. However, it was not long before the Khoikhoi realised that the periodic visits of the Europeans, and their eventual permanent presence, was a very mixed blessing – and finally, a definite curse. Within a mere 60 years of Jan van Riebeeck's arrival in 1652, the centuries-old social and economic order of the Peninsular Khoikhoi had been irrevocably shattered. And as a grim finale, the Khoikhoi population of the western Cape was decimated by a smallpox epidemic in 1713 – a disease against which this indigenous people had very little resistance.

Reading the past in pottery

Generations of South Africans have been taught that the Sotho and Nguni people moved
south and west at roughly the same time as early colonists moved east and north,
until the two groups met on the eastern frontier around present-day Ciskei.
Recent research proves otherwise, indicating that Iron Age societies were established
in the northern Transvaal as early as 300 AD, and that the eastern frontier separated the
Khoikhoi and San (Khoisan) from the Nguni for hundreds of years.

WHEN IRON REACHES the frighteningly high temperature of 1 535 deg C it melts, turning to a white-hot liquid that can be moulded into the tools of civilisation . . . a metal plough that will slice through unyielding soil, a decorative bangle to entice a mate, or an arrow head that will drive deep into an enemy's flesh.

It follows, therefore, that men who know how to smelt and work iron must triumph over those who do not.

But just exactly where or when the secret of iron was unlocked remains a mystery, although Iron Age man was emerging in various parts of the world, including north Africa, around 1 000 years before the birth of Christ. It was a great leap forward, replacing the Stone Ages that had marked man's progress from the earliest times, and staying with us until well into the last century.

Iron-working probably came to sub-Saharan Africa in about the year 500 BC, through trans-Saharan trade between Phoenicians settled on the coast and the people of west Africa. The same knowledge may also have filtered south from the Sudan, as iron-workings around Lake Victoria are thought to date from the same period. Tools made from iron led to improved techniques in agriculture, creating a need for more land and resulting in fairly rapid increases in populations that can be traced, in part, through similarities in the languages spoken among the people throughout the eastern half of Africa. Crop production, rather than foraging, led to the establishment of the first settled communities – settled for at least as long as it took for the crops to be harvested, or until the land became too impoverished.

Archaeologists refer to this period as South Africa's Early Iron Age, which lasted roughly from 250 AD until 1100 AD. At this time pottery and other evidence found by archaeologists began to change, and the Later Iron Age began, lasting until the end of the last century. This change is more marked in some areas than in others; while for some communities the transition from Early to Later Iron Ages was very smooth.

Those who brought this first Iron Age to South Africa belonged to the group described as 'Bantu-speaking people', although there is no way of knowing just what language they spoke. At first they were not numerous, and examination of skeletal material found at Early Iron Age sites indicates that they intermarried with Khoisan people. Evidence for relationships between the Iron Age people and Khoisan comes not only from human remains, but also from San paintings dating from the time of the Later Iron Age. Some of these portray little ochre-coloured men with bows and arrows, driving off cattle and being pursued by tall, black men. Other paintings show the two groups apparently at peace with each other.

The economy of Iron Age communities was geared to the production of food and the rearing of livestock such as cattle, sheep and goats. This contrasted starkly with the way of life of the Stone Age people, whose existence depended entirely on hunting and foraging. In areas where cultivation was practised, the land could support greater numbers of people, but increasingly concentrated populations dictated fairly frequent cycles of movement in search of more fertile land or fresh grazing.

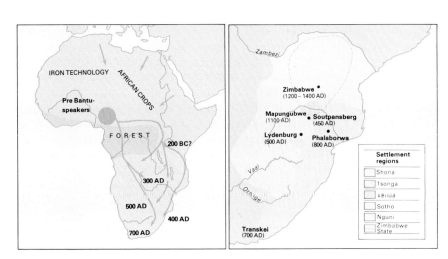

MOST LINGUISTS AGREE *that the Bantu family of languages originated in the Cameroon region of west Africa, and that from there dispersal (see map far left) occurred in two main streams – eastwards towards Lake Victoria and southwards into north-western Angola. Further divisions brought the Iron Age to most of the savanna lands of southern Africa.*

The economies of the important Iron Age settlements, Mapungubwe and Zimbabwe (left), revolved around stock-farming and trade.

THE INCISED DESIGN *on the jar (above) identifies it as an example of Lydenburg pottery, while the ceramic sculpture (right) is one of seven 'Lydenburg Heads', thought to have been used by Early Iron Age people on ritual occasions.*

Locating the pottery

The longer any site was occupied, the more evidence was left for the modern archaeologist and, in the case of the Iron Age, the characteristic relics are fragments of pottery and other items such as bones. Like the clues of language, pottery enables the routes of migration to be traced, and links to be made between groups of people. Thus pottery found in the Soutpansberg, described as Matokomo, is related to pottery that is found over large areas of Botswana. Typically, this pottery consists of large, thick-walled vessels with heavy rims, and is characterised by stamped and incised decorations. The pottery found along the Soutpansberg has been radio-carbon dated to around 450 AD. A little further south near Tzaneen, on the farm Silver Leaves, road-building uncovered a storage pit that held pottery vessels, some decorated with parallel furrows around the rim. The impressions left by grains of millet in the vessels suggest that Iron Age people practised some farming. Similar pottery, called Silver Leaves from the farm where it was first identified, occurs at other lowveld sites, and is more widely distributed in Mozambique, suggesting that the people who made it came to the Transvaal from there. It has also been found at St Lucia Bay, where it has been dated to about 300 AD.

Another style known as Lydenburg, somewhat resembling the Matokomo style, has been found at several sites in the Transvaal and also in Natal. The Natal sites have been radio-carbon dated to 500 AD. Lydenburg pottery has also been recovered from a shell midden on the Transkeian coast, dated at 700 AD.

A development of Early Iron Age pottery is represented by the 'Lydenburg Heads' found by a schoolboy on a farm near Lydenburg. These curious pottery fragments painstakingly assembled at the University of Cape Town, proved to be a number of bizarre human-like heads made in about 500 AD, one of which has an animal-like snout. The heads were found grouped together and it is thought that they may have formed part of a storage area. The forms of incised decoration on the heads match those of the Lydenburg pottery vessels.

Although the people of the Early Iron Age kept numbers of domestic animals, they also hunted to supplement their crop production. They settled in small communities, building huts that were probably little different from those still to be seen in some rural areas. No complete iron tools have been recovered from the very earliest sites, because of the rapidity with which iron rusts. However, the slag or cinder that remains proves that iron was smelted. By concentrating on crop production, they acquired new skills as well as new implements such as the hoe which, so superior to the stone-weighted digging stick, made feasible the working of fields. Again, because of a salt-deficient diet, they needed to obtain salt from an outside source, unlike the hunter-gatherer, whose salt intake was provided by the meat he consumed. Early Iron Age man made wide, shallow bowls in which he evaporated brackish water to obtain the salt. At a brackish spring close to Silver Leaves, salt was obtained by this method as early as 250 AD. Salt Flats, such as those of the Soutpansberg, became important meeting places and trading centres. Other natural trading centres were at the rich outcrops of ore that were worked by the mining methods of the time.

Crops and tools

MILLET   SORGHUM

Stone Age people in South Africa are not known to have planted food crops, but depended for their nourishment on grubbing for 'veldkos' in the form of roots or berries, and on hunting. The search for food was an almost unending occupation. Deliberate food production in Africa began in the far north, in what is now the Sudan and the Sahara Desert, several thousand years BC. This was preceded by an increase in the population of hunter-gatherers, which reduced the carrying capacity of some areas, and may have led to the development of trading relationships between groups, with resultant interdependence. Reduction of natural plant resources prompted the deliberate scattering of seed, especially of the sorghums and millets. Furthermore, the intensified exploitation of game and of vegetable foods sparked a process that led eventually to the domestication of both.

Grain sorghum probably evolved in the highlands of Ethiopia some 6 000 years ago, and was brought south by people of the Iron Age or, possibly, even before that period. A major grain crop, it is still widely grown in South Africa, where it was formerly known as 'Kaffir-corn'. Babala, or bulrush millet, is indigenous to many parts of Africa, and is the most widely grown crop on the continent, being resistant to insect attack when stored. Ground into powder, babala is used in the making of porridge and, like sorghum, in the brewing of beer. Maize was introduced through contact with Portuguese, who originally brought seed from the Americas and West Indies; but it suffered badly from parasitism by witch-weed until modern farming methods were introduced.

Agricultural technique was based on the principle of 'slash and burn'. Trees were felled and bushes were cut down or uprooted and laid in piles which, when dry, were set alight. Later, seeds were planted below the ash layer, and the same field would be used for several years, until its yield became poor. No sickles or scythes are known to have been made, and the implement used for reaping might have been a form of axe. Then it was time for the clan to move away to repeat the process. Although the areas required for planting were relatively small, uncontrolled burning must have caused tremendous damage to the forests. They cultivated millet, which they ground by crushing it on a flat stone known as a quern, using another stone with a rubbing and rocking motion.

It is likely that, in the Early Iron Age, stone tools were used in mining. Such implements have been found in Castle Cavern in Swaziland, which has been mined for specularite – an iron ore much in demand as a cosmetic – for 28 000 years. Copper was being mined in the 8th century at Phalaborwa, to which man was probably first drawn because of the tremendous iron reserves. At around the same period, iron was being mined in the Soutpansberg. Although they were relieved of the necessity to be continually on the lookout for food, as were the hunter-gatherers, the Early Iron Age people were very poor in material terms. Of ornaments, only a few copper items have been recovered, with ostrich eggshell beads and some imported beads possibly acquired on their southward movement. About 100 sites surviving from the Early Iron Age are known in the Transvaal.

The Later Iron Age

A gradual change in pottery occurred in the 11th century, ushering in the Later Iron Age that lasted until the 19th century. Where the pottery had had thick, in-folded and decorated rims, pottery at the start of the Later Iron Age tended to have tapered rims. Vessels were frequently left undecorated and, where decoration was applied, it tended now to cover the entire surface rather than be concentrated on the neck and rim. It is thought that these stylistic changes, and the origins of the Later Iron Age may lie with the arrival of a significant new group of Bantu-speaking immigrants, including Nguni and Sotho-Tswana, around 1200 AD.

For the hundreds of Early Iron Age sites, there are thousands from the Later Iron Age, mainly spread over the interior highlands and the lowlands east of the Drakensberg. These new settlers, arriving about 1500 AD, built in stone, obtained locally and usually used untrimmed and, often, without mortar. The pattern of settlement was probably based on the extended family system, with round huts linked by walls that served as stock enclosures. It is thought that the surrounding walls were intended to keep stock inside and to exclude predatory animals, rather than to act as a line of defence. The huts open into the enclosed area, and may be corbelled – that is, built entirely of stone in a beehive shape – or have had thatched roofs. Some huts had raised stone platforms next to the hearth, and many had shallow depressions in the hut floor, which probably served as pot-stands.

Early white travellers and missionaries found that some of the stone-walled sites in eastern Botswana and the southern Transvaal were still occupied in the first two decades of the 19th century, long before the arrival of the Voortrekkers. In 1815, in his book 'Travels through South Africa', the missionary John Campbell described the Bahurutse-occupied stone-walled town of Kurreechane – present-day Kaditshwene near Zeerust – and mentioned metalworking and cattle-keeping. He wrote that 'every house was surrounded . . . by a good circular stone wall'. Following the northward movement of Mzilikazi's army in the 1820s and 1830s, many settlements were abandoned, although the veld was by no means deserted, as is frequently claimed.

THE MASORINI *Iron Age site near the Kruger Park was painstakingly transformed into an Iron Age homestead by archaeologists.*

Discovery at Mapungubwe

Close to the confluence of the Shashi and Limpopo rivers in the Messina district are two hills'separated by a valley on the farm Greefswald – the one named Bambandyanalo and the other Mapungubwe. On the last day of 1932, a farmer, E S van Graan, with his son and three friends, climbed the steep-sided sandstone hill of Mapungubwe, which was held in awe by local Africans. On the flat summit they found remains of dry-stone walls, iron tools, fragments of pottery, and intact pots half-buried in the sand. They also found fragments of beaten gold, copper wire and bangles, glass beads and evidence of human burials. The find was reported at Pretoria University and, after professional archaeological investigation, the farm was bought by the government of the day for the nation.

With the advent of radio-carbon dating, it was discovered in the 1950s that nearby Bambandyanalo had been settled some three centuries before Mapungubwe, in about 1055 AD, and that its people had been in continuous occupation for 200 years. Bambandyanalo yielded some 74 human burials. Animal burials were probably the result of some periodic ritual slaughter to ensure that livestock flourished. Many of the human burials contained glass beads and copper bracelets, and flat, highly burnished dishes, and a variety of profusely decorated pottery bowls, pots and beakers, some with pierced lugs through which a cord could be passed for carrying. The animal burials, which consisted of skulls or jawbones, contained copper ornaments, seashells and pottery fragments.

Later Iron Age people came to Mapungubwe from Bambandyanalo in about 1250 AD, as Bambandyanalo was in the final stages of decline. Settlement flourished on the easily defended hilltop and the surrounding ground. Eleven human burials were excavated, with the same interpretation and re-evaluation as at Bambandyanalo. Gold objects found at Mapungubwe included a bowl, a small rhinoceros, lengths of gold wire and hundreds of small ornamental beads and rods. There were also large glass beads, made by melting together in a clay mould smaller beads probably obtained from trade with the east coast. Mapungubwe was probably an important trade centre but, like Bambandyanalo, it too, declined after about 50 years and was abandoned.

Gold was mined, haematite at Ngwenya, and iron and copper at Phalaborwa. Virtually all of the copper and tin deposits of the northern Transvaal were worked, and hundreds of workings remain.

The main pottery types of the Later Iron Age are the Moloko and Phalaborwa. The Moloko pottery has banded and stamped decoration, with tapered or out-turned rims, and occurs mainly at sites between the Witwatersrand and the Magaliesberg. Phalaborwa pottery shows little change in 400 years, and bears simple, cut designs originally produced by Venda speakers and still produced by the present, Sotho-speaking, inhabitants of the district.

An age of stability

For almost 800 years the Later Iron Age was one of stability in South Africa. People learnt to spin and weave fibres into cloth, to twist and plait ropes, and there was a greater reliance than before on domestic livestock as a source of meat. It is estimated that about 50 percent of the meat intake was supplied by cattle, sheep or goats, and the remainder obtained by hunting. Millets and sorghum were the staple crops, supplemented by maize after contact had been made with Portuguese traders. Trade with the Mozambique coast increased dramatically during the Later Iron Age, and the demand for ivory reflected confidence in weapons with iron tips – although Stone Age man, too, had occasionally tackled elephant.

There is no doubt that Iron Age people encountered the people of the Stone Age – sometimes peacefully, sometimes violently. It has been demonstrated that, in all the south-eastern Bantu languages, excepting Venda and Lobedu, the words for cattle, sheep and milk are derived from the Khoisan, which is taken as evidence of prolonged and probably peaceful contact. It is possible that cattle-keeping Khoikhoi made their way north to the grazing-lands of the highveld and were absorbed into the growing communities of Bantu-speaking farmers. Examples of such absorption are known from the Gona/Gonaqua clans on the eastern Cape frontier. Among Iron Age artefacts recovered from Olifantspoort in the Transvaal are many stone implements, although there is no evidence of an earlier Stone Age settlement on the site. It appears, rather, that elements of both cultures lived here together.

Although the repetition of certain architectural features implies a common culture, the settlements themselves, varying enormously in size, were scattered over a large area. Lack of political integration led to a failure to unite when the southern communities were successively attacked and overwhelmed by Mzilikazi's initially small army of 300 Ndebele warriors in 1824. Five years later, when Robert Moffat, the missionary, travelled through the Magaliesberg, he described 'the ruins of innumerable towns, some of amazing extent . . . every fence being composed of stones . . . averaging five or six feet high. Some of the houses which escaped the flames of marauders were large and showed a far superior style and taste to anything I had before witnessed . . . now since the invasion . . . and the terror of the Matabele it had become the habitation of wild beasts . . . .'

The settlements in the northern Transvaal survived a while longer, mainly because they were out of reach of Mzilikazi and, later, of white Voortrekkers. Eventually, the trek caught up with hundreds of Ndebele, who were smashed by a commando led by M W Pretorius and Piet Potgieter in 1854 at Makapansgat. But by then, they had themselves acquired items of the whites' 'iron age', including firearms, and Potgieter was among those shot dead. The last Later Iron Age stone building was probably the fort at Mapochstad, near Roos Senekal in the eastern Transvaal. Here, tradition was embodied with European influence in the use, in some places, of mud bricks and mortar, and the loop-holing of the perimeter wall. But not even the acquisition of firearms by the Ndebele defenders withstood the final assault in 1883. Still further north, the Venda were 'subdued' in the 1890s but rose again during the South African War of 1899-1902, forcing the abandonment of the town of Louis Trichardt.

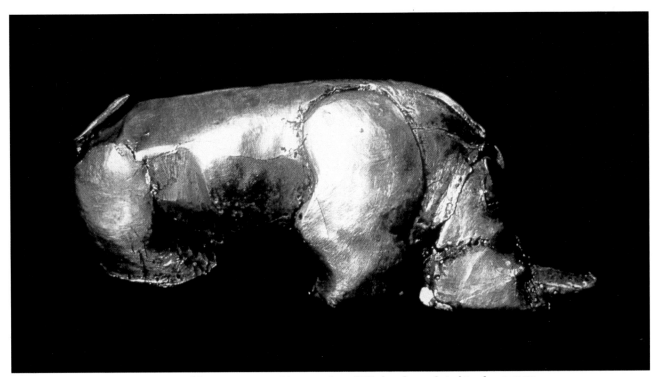

THIS GOLDEN RHINOCEROS, *excavated from a grave on Mapungubwe Hill, has been dated to about 1200 AD.*

Secrets of Iron Age metal-workers

The working of metals was attended by much ritual and secrecy and, in the case of iron smelting, no women were allowed near the smelters. Haematite outcrops were the source of the purest iron ore, and were broken by blows from lumps of almost pure ore bound with thongs to form a hammer. Iron products included spear points, axes and hoes, and ornamental items such as bangles. Malachite, a copper oxide, was the preferred source of copper, because it could be smelted very easily. Veins of ore were followed by digging shafts and drives, some of them running for hundreds of metres at depths of around 15 metres. The ore was dug with iron picks and short, iron chisels and, where it occurred in very hard rock, this would be split by building a fire next to it and then dashing it with water. Copper-smelting furnaces occur near Messina, at Phalaborwa, and at Rooiberg, where tin was also smelted for adding to the copper to produce bronze. Apart from alluvial gold, which was found in stream beds, the metal was obtained from quartz outcrops and also by open-cast mining. Many of the old sites were destroyed by prospectors in historic times, before any archaeological survey or dating could be carried out, an example being the tin mines of Rooiberg, near Warmbad in the Transvaal.

Smelting took place at sites where there was water, clay suitable for constructing a furnace, and a source of fuel. The simplest smelter consisted of a hollow in the ground, over which was built a dome-like structure of clay. Around the bottom, a number of furnace-pipes made of reed penetrated the smelter. The reed would burn away, but the hole in the smelter wall would remain, through which a heat-induced draught would enter once the smelter was fired. Smelters obtained their draught through the action of skin bellows. Smelters for copper were often fairly crudely constructed, as a lower temperature was used than that required for smelting iron ore.

When the iron ore had been reduced to crude metal, it was immediately worked into the desired pattern as a weapon or implement. This is deduced from the fact that no iron ingots have ever been found, whereas ingots of tin and copper are known. At Rooiberg, where some thousands of tons of high-grade tin ore were mined, only a few tin ingots and a small amount of bronze pellets have been found.

One of the 'standard' products of the iron industry was the Phalaborwa hoe, with its distinctive diamond-shaped blade and long tang for attaching it to the handle. Late in the 19th century, Phalaborwa pattern hoes were manufactured in Portugal and imported as trade goods via Delagoa Bay. Although of inferior quality, they eventually pushed the locally made item off the market. In mid-century, the British army in Natal considered using local iron for wagon-fittings, and found it superior to that imported from Britain. The direct-reduction smelting method of iron ore as practised in the Iron Age actually produced steel, albeit of variable quality, because of the admixture of carbon particles.

A RECONSTRUCTION *of a typical Iron Age smelting furnace.*

AN IRON AGE MINE SHAFT *at Thabazimbi in the Transvaal.*

IRON IMPLEMENTS made by Sotho-Tswana-speaking people in the late 18th century.

Strangers from beyond the sea

For hundreds of years, adaptation and innovation had been the key weapons
in the successful response of the Khoisan and Bantu-speaking people to the challenges
of man, beast and nature. But from the second half of the 15th century,
the stable societies of the sub-continent came under threat from new and
powerful enemies: groups of European explorers, searching for a sea route to India.

SINCE THE BEGINNING OF TIME, in the eyes of men, the sea had been 'empty'; the playground of wheeling birds, great schools of leaping dolphins and, occasionally, the massive, spouting presence of whales. It was the end of the earth, where men could never survive. It had always been so – and it always would.

For the Khoikhoi people who inhabited the southern coast of Africa the sea was both a benefactor and a mystery: along its shores the land was rich, with plentiful rainfall and good grazing. But what lay beyond that line where the waters and sky collide remained forever unknown. The sea was the limit of the only world they knew.

And into this world, on a balmy summer's day over 500 years ago, came the future – and it came from the sea.

A group of Khoikhoi herdsmen watching over their cattle near the present town of Mossel Bay saw it first: two white specks, tiny at first, looming ever closer as they approached the shore. The Khoikhoi could see that the specks of white were like large sheets of cloth suspended above a wooden tower that incredibly rose above the water. Eventually these apparitions stopped in a small bay below the herdsmen, and it was easy to see human figures as the cloth was folded around strange wooden poles that grew from the tower. Initial fear turned to curiosity as the figures climbed down from their towers into small boats that started towards the shore – and the waiting Khoikhoi.

The men who landed from the boats were unlike anything the Khoikhoi had seen before; taller, and wearing strange clothes that covered most of their pale bodies. The two groups eyed each other nervously, and then the strangers made towards a nearby stream, obviously in need of fresh water. At this the Khoikhoi reacted, and one of their number picked up a stone and hurled it at the invaders. Others joined in as the strangers shouted at them in a language that was utterly incomprehensible. There was a sudden hissing sound, and one of the herders lay dying with a crossbow bolt protruding from his body.

The Khoikhoi fled, leaving the strangers to fill their water casks in peace. But the incident became legend as the tale of the strangers from the sea was told and retold around the cooking fires of the southern Cape Khoikhoi. The first meeting of two very different worlds was over and, sadly, it had ended in tragedy.

For the men from the sea, the landfall at Mossel Bay had come after months of terrible hardship as they had edged their frail ships ever southwards in an effort to find the end of Africa, and perhaps a way beyond it to the spice islands of the East. Their captain, Bartolomeu Dias, named the landfall *Baia dos Vaqueiros* (Bay of the Cowherds). He and his men had left Portugal in August 1487 with two caravels of about 100 tons each – the *São Cristovão* and the *São Pantaleão* – and a small supply ship. Apart from their crew, the ships carried some black men and women, captured in Guinea, who were put ashore at strategic points to demonstrate the grandeur of the Portuguese nation.

Dias is believed to have left his supply ship in the *Baia dos Tigres* (Bay of the Tigers) in southern Angola, before continuing down the Namibian coast. Battling against strong southerly winds, he courageously tacked out to sea and took a southerly, then easterly course, rounding the Cape unseen. Turning his ships north he sighted land, and the first contact was made between the local inhabitants and the Europeans in February 1488.

Sailing east, Dias reached Algoa Bay and set up a wooden cross on the island of St Croix. But tired, and frightened by high seas, the crew were all for heading back to their supply ship and home. Unable to persuade them to continue, and bound by his king to abide by a majority decision of his senior men, Dias reluctantly turned back.

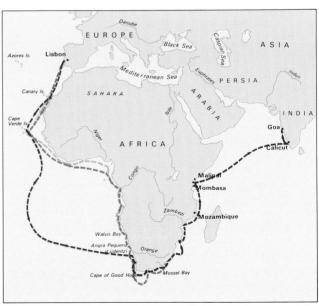

IN JUST OVER 12 years, three Portuguese sailors unlocked the secret of a sea route to India via the Cape: In 1486 Diego Cão reached a point just north of the present Namibian town of Swakopmund; two years later Bartolomeu Dias rounded the Cape of Good Hope; and finally, in 1498 Vasco da Gama reached India after a voyage lasting almost a year.

n the return voyage, Dias erected a cross at Kwaaihoek, t of the mouth of the Bushman's River. Seeing the Cape he first time, he named it *Cabo da Boa Esperança* – but as off this Cape of Good Hope that he was to die in a m at sea on a subsequent voyage in 1500. He probably not see Table Bay, but put into Hout Bay, which he ed *Porto Fragoso* (Craggy Port), and raised a cross near- A third cross was erected at Lüderitz.

lthough he did not realise it at the time, Dias' epic age had, indeed, solved the problem that had been tax- the merchant minds of Europe for half a century: how nd a sea route to India that would end European depen- ce on Arab middlemen who controlled the land routes he East. It was the Portuguese especially who were de- ined to open up these routes, led by Infante Dom Hen- e, 'Prince Henry the Navigator'.

quering the 'sea of darkness'

cting tales that the southern 'sea of darkness' was boil- hot, and that the sun turned all men to negroes, Prince ry, assisted by shipbuilders, instrument makers, car- aphers and astronomers, sent expeditions ever further n the west coast of Africa, reaching the region of nea by the time of his death in 1460, and establishing ofitable trade in tropical products and slaves.

ANCE MEETING *between Vasco da Gama (above) and an* o *pilot named Ibn Majid helped Portugal to become the* European *nation to discover a sea route to the East. Majid,* xpert *in celestial navigation, guided Da Gama from* ndi *on the east African coast to Calicut in India.*

The wreck of the *São Tomé*

On its way from India to Portugal in 1589, the *São Tomé* ran into strong March winds, heavy seas and rainstorms near Mauritius and sprang a fatal leak. When the only boat was launched, the crew had to be forcibly restrained from swamping her.

Among the 104 passengers who were lowered into the boat was a recently widowed young woman named Dona Joana de Mendoça, who intended join- ing a convent and was travelling with a baby daugh- ter. Despite the frantic mother's pleas, Dona Joana's child was held on the ship by her nurse who refused to release her unless she was also taken on board.

As the overloaded boat drifted out to sea, the officers decreed that six of the passengers had to be thrown overboard to save the rest – and this was ruthlessly ex- ecuted. At midnight, after drifting around for sever- al hours, they rowed towards the foundering *São Tomé* to discover that its decks were under water, but candles were burning and women slaves were 'wail- ing piteously' around a picture of the Virgin Mary. Some sailors swam from the boat and collected kegs of water and biscuit. Then suddenly the *São Tomé* lurched and disappeared from sight.

Landing north of St Lucia Bay, the 98 castaways burnt their boat to retrieve nails for barter, and with water in skin bags and a ration of two or three hand- fuls of biscuit each, set off north. Dona Joana dressed in a habit, but the other women wore doublets and breeches. Winding their way slowly up the coast, they sheltered in the dunes at night. Soon they ran out of food and water.

Their chances of survival seemed grim, when after five days of marching, they were followed and then attacked by about 300 Africans. Their attackers, however, unaccustomed to the sound of discharging matchlocks, fled after the order to fire was given.

Later on the same day the fortunes of the wretched group took a turn for the better: a band of friendly in- habitants escorted them to their village beside a lake, and offered them food and shelter.

Further north, the castaways were befriended by the hospitable king of Inhaca and learnt from a man who spoke Portuguese that a ship carrying ivory had left the Lourenço Marques river a few days earlier for Mozam- bique. It was decided that some of the party would stay in some huts on a nearby island, while others took two small boats to seek help.

The larger boat, manned by *São Tomé* crew, ran aground but after a bitter overland journey the sur- vivors, decimated by fever, reached Sofala on the Mozambican coast. The smaller boat's party got to the Nkomati River where they found some Portuguese, who had been stranded when their ivory ship was wrecked and had been persuaded to remain in a friendly village until another trading vessel was able to pick them up.

On the island, life was hard and many died of the dreaded fever. Those who survived eventually re- joined the Nkomati River group, but it was a year be- fore a ship reached them from Mozambique. All three women survived their ordeal, and Dona Joana spent the rest of her days in a convent in the city of Goa.

After Prince Henry's death, the Portuguese voyages of exploration and the scientific research into navigation he had inspired continued. In 1483, Diego Cão reached the mouth of the Zaire (also known as the Congo River) and three years later sailed as far as Cape Cross, just north of Swakopmund, where he died. It had been thought possible to sail eastwards from Guinea around what was assumed to be a flat south coast to India, but Cão's expedition brought news of a bleak coastline that stretched to the south with apparently no end to the continent. Dias' voyage proved that this was wrong, but that Africa was bigger than anyone could have imagined.

The way to India

When Manuel I of Portugal ascended to the throne in 1495 he was determined to continue the exploration begun by Dias, and preparations were put in hand for a new expedition to round the Cape. This time the ships, the *São Rafael* and *São Gabriel*, were nearly three times the size of Dias' caravels, and carried 20 cannon each. They were accompanied by a lookout ship, the *Berrio*, and a cargo vessel.

Command of the expedition was given to the 38-year-old son of a magistrate, Vasco da Gama. Unlike the gentle Dias, he was a ruthless disciplinarian who solemnly swore to his king he would discover the oceans and countries of the East. Although he was unskilled in navigation, he made up for this by having the latest in navigational aids and experienced pilots (Dias among them) on board.

When the expedition set sail in July 1497, it took a calculated risk, sailing out boldly across the Atlantic in a wide arc to avoid the doldrums, then south to the Cape with the west wind. After this remarkable voyage – more than 90 days out of sight of land – Da Gama's ships anchored in St Helena Bay, where he stayed a few days, cleaning ships and taking on firewood and water.

Contact was made with local inhabitants who had 'many dogs like those of Portugal, which bark as do those', and one man was captured while collecting honey and brought on board the Commander's ship. Having clothed and fed him and given him some 'little bells and glass beads', they set him ashore again and later bartered with several Khoikhoi for 'shells that they wore in their ears, that looked silvered over, and foxtails, that they carry fastened to sticks'. Later a misunderstanding arose, and some Khoikhoi threw spears at the Europeans, wounding three or four.

Sailing around the Cape directly into a stiff south-easter, Da Gama landed at Mossel Bay where gifts were exchanged with friendly Khoikhoi, before continuing up the east coast, where he named the lush land (off the Pondoland coast) *Terra do Natal* on Christmas Day.

North of the Limpopo, the expedition encountered a Nguni group and was favourably received at the 'land of good people' as the Portuguese called it. Then after an eternity of desolate African coast with its wild beasts and unfamiliar inhabitants, Da Gama at last sailed into the bustling commerce of Islamic east Africa, and then on to India. With a cargo of pepper and cinnamon, he returned to Portugal. Although he had opened the way to India, so many men were lost to scurvy that the *São Rafael* was burnt and its crew transferred to the other ships.

On African shores

Conditions were harsh and punishment severe on board those early ships. The crew lived in continual dampness, there was no sleeping accommodation (except for senior officers) and the food consisted of salt meat, ship's biscuit and chickpeas. Water soon became undrinkable and thirst was a constant hazard. Even the promise of remission of sins by the Pope (an exploration enthusiast) did not compensate for the prospect of death.

Yet fleets from Portugal made the perilous voyage around the Cape in ever-increasing numbers, intent on reaching India more than on exploring an unknown land – they touched on the African coast here and there simply to draw water, barter and name some of the landmarks.

In 1503, an error of navigation sent Antonio de Saldanha into Table Bay, where he climbed Table Mountain. He was later injured in a skirmish during trading.

It was at Table Bay too that in March 1510 the Viceroy of Portuguese India, Francisco de Almeida (on his way home to a hero's welcome after ensuring Portuguese superiority in the East), was inadvisedly persuaded to 'punish' the local inhabitants for some insult to his trading party at a kraal. Before dawn the following day, he led a force of 150 soldiers to attack the kraal. But the Khoikhoi whistled up their oxen ('trained to this warlike device') to present a menacing, defensive wall, and counterattacked fiercely with spears and stones. The Portuguese, weighed down by their heavy armour, crossbows, swords and pikes, were chased to the beach by their nimble, almost naked attackers. The men could not reach the landing-boats which stood at a distance to keep out of the battering surf, and 58 of their number – including De Almeida with a lance through his throat – were killed near the mouth of the Salt River. In the evening, after the Khoikhoi had withdrawn, the dead were buried where they had fallen.

One of the greatest fears of the early explorers was shipwreck, and many vessels were indeed lost in the stormy seas and gales, especially off the east coast. It is from castaways' accounts of their journeys inland that we get glimpses of the Nguni – survivors from the wreck of the

THIS WOODCUTTING (*with the Virgin Mary comforting an already drowned seaman) dramatically depicts the panic on board the Portuguese galleon the São João shortly before it was wrecked off the Pondoland coast on 3 February 1552.*

São João in 1552 off Pondoland, were sheltered by a chief 'Inhaca' (probably the Tsonga chief Nyaka) at the Lourenço Marques River and helped him defeat 'a rebellious kaffir'. Two years later, *São Bento* survivors (wrecked somewhere between the Kasuka and Mthatha rivers) told of a village: 'about 20 huts built with poles and thatched with dry grass ... they move them from place to place with the seasons, according to the abundance or barrenness of the ground'. The country was 'thickly populated and provided with cattle'. They also reported meeting survivors from previous wrecks who were living with the natives and who refused to leave.

Pitifully few of the *São Bento* company survived their terrible journey – hunger made friends fight over a beetle or lizard, and they sometimes 'supped upon the sandals' they wore. Even after centuries, the accounts of castaways tell vividly of human drama and tragedy. . . .

The Portuguese blazed a trail around Africa and established a monopoly on Eastern trade, but towards the end of the 15th century the power of Portugal, now united with Spain under Philip II, began to decline.

During the closing years of the century, sailors from many nations sailed round southern Africa and walked its shores. But it was the Dutch in the next century who were to break the Portuguese monopoly of Eastern trade and eventually set their seal on the Cape – the first ripple of the waves of European settlers who in time to come would follow the African dream.

Science lends a hand in the fight to tame the oceans

Fifteenth century seamen had no way of finding out their position when out of sight of land – and so hugged the shoreline. When the simple charts of the day proved inadequate for African exploration, a single meridian (usually Cape St Vincent) was added, marked with degrees of latitude.

Latitude could be calculated only by observing the stars, and in 1462 the first calculation of latitude from a European ship using the Pole Star was recorded. But as mariners explored further south, the Pole Star fell below the horizon. In 1484 a group of astronomers in Portugal found they could use the sun's position at midday for their calculations. (The longitude problem, however, was not to be solved until the 18th century.)

Mariners took their celestial sights with a simple astrolabe (an instrument consisting of a graduated circular disc with a movable sighting device) – usually from a nearby shore – until a primitive quadrant was developed for taking sights at sea. A compass with the 32 points we know today was in use by the 1400s – but the speed of a vessel was still guessed by watching flotsam floating past.

It was the era when the oared galley ruled the Mediterranean, and the clumsy square-rigged ship with raised fo'c'sle and poop used for deep-sea work was more suited to transport than exploration. The Portuguese turned to an Arab design for the lateen caravel, with its rakish, triangular lateen sail. Later when bigger ships were needed, the Portuguese and Spanish found a combination of square and lateen sails proved most practical.

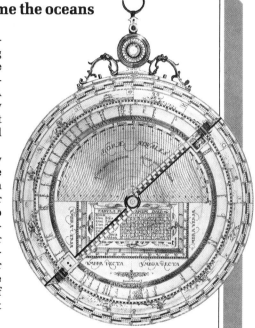

UNTIL THE SEXTANT *was invented in 1730, navigators calculated latitude by using the astrolabe (above) to measure the altitude of stars and planets.*

THE INFORMATION *which became available as a result of the voyages of 'discovery' in the 15th century led to major improvements in the art of cartography. Despite the fact that this world map (left), created in 1489 by the German cartographer Henricus Martellus, has a rather squarish southern Africa, it was the first to incorporate data based on Bartolomeu Dias' journey round the Cape of Good Hope in 1488.*

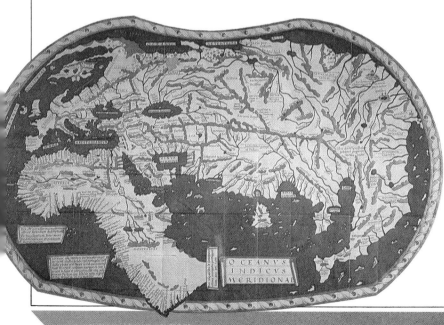

Settlement built from a fort of sand

By the middle of the 17th century the Peninsular Khoikhoi had become quite used to the comings and goings of European sailors and the ships that carried them to and from the East. Some, usually shipwrecked crews, had even stayed for a while on the shores of Table Bay until the next passing fleet could rescue them.

On 25 March 1647 just such an incident occurred when the Dutch East Indiaman *Haerlem* went ashore near Rietvlei, where today a lighthouse sends its warning beam across the waters of Table Bay. Rather than abandon the ship and its valuable cargo altogether, the Commander of the accompanying fleet ordered an assistant merchant, Leendert Jansz, to remain ashore with some of the crew, salvage what they could, and await the arrival of the following year's return fleet.

It led to the establishment of a permanent European settlement on land belonging to the Khoikhoi.

Jansz and his 58 reluctant settlers built a fort of sand, propped up by timbers from the wreck, between present-day Milnerton and Bloubergstrand, and named it Fort Zandenburgh. They went hunting, explored Robben Island, and traded for cattle from the Khoikhoi before boarding ship for Holland over a year later. Also returning with this fleet were Matthys Proot, an army officer, and Jan van Riebeeck, a merchant who was under a cloud for having indulged in what the Dutch East India Company regarded as the reprehensible practice of private trading.

It was a time of considerable concern among the directors of the Company for the safety of their ships and, indirectly, for the health of their sailors, of whom at least one sailor in six was likely to die on the voyage between Europe and the East. The cause of illness and death was a vitamin deficiency – notably Vitamin C or ascorbic acid – leading to a condition known as scurvy, with symptoms that included swollen gums with loose teeth, spontaneous bleeding and general malaise. It could be prevented and, frequently, cured by the consumption of fresh fruit and vegetables. Somewhere along the route an outpost would have to be established, that could grow enough food for its own use as well as an excess to feed the scurvy-ridden sailors. Jansz was ordered to write a report on the suitability or otherwise of Table Bay as a possible site.

THIS PLATE *is an example of the porcelain brought to the Cape by the Dutch East India Company (Vereenigde Oost-Indische Compagnie).*

Together with Proot, he drew up a memorandum or *Remonstrantie* dated 26 July 1649 but, as he was only a junior merchant, he was not considered for the command of the settlement. It was Van Riebeeck who, in December 1651, was appointed on a five-year contract as 'merchant and head of the Company proceeding to the Cape of Good Hope in the ship *Drommedaris*' and, with his wife and son, sailed the same month from Texel in company with the ships *Reijger* and *De Goede Hoop*. Two more ships, *Olifant* and *Walvis*, were found to be overloaded and so sailed later. Miraculously, when the little fleet of three ships sighted Table Mountain on 5 April 1652, there had been only two deaths at sea. By contrast, when the *Olifant* and *Walvis* arrived the following month, they had lost 85 and 45 men respectively.

Within a week of his landing on 6 April, Van Riebeeck had begun work on the Fort of Good Hope and, a week later, he was writing to the directors of the Company reminding them that he wished to proceed to India when he had finished his work at the Cape. He had strict instructions to preserve peace with the indigenous people, as well as with foreigners who might also establish their own outposts at the bay. From this it appears that the intention was not to lay claim to the land, but merely to utilise it for the provision of fresh food. Very soon, however, Van Riebeeck was lamenting that he did not have the labour of 'hard-working Chinese' to assist with the building and with the agriculture – the kernel, perhaps, of the later decision to import slaves when it was found that the local people had no interest in labouring for the newcomers.

Despite his anxiety to be returned to the East, Van Riebeeck proved to be an able and conscientious commander, paying particular attention to his instructions to keep the peace with the Khoikhoi, with whom the first serious quarrel arose only in 1659. The settlement, although it was able to supply a homeward-bound fleet, in March 1653, with cattle, sheep and some vegetables, was not self-supporting, and relied on imports of rice and wheat. This did not please the directors, who wanted the settlement to pay for itself – and, if possible, show a decent profit.

One way of cutting costs was to save on salaries and so, early in 1657, nine men were released from Company service, and each was granted 11,5 hectares of land along the Liesbeek River. They were exempt from tax for a period of 12 years, and they were allowed to trade with the Khoikhoi for sheep and cattle, so long as they did not pay more than the Company did. They were supplied with the necessary implements at cost price, with the Company holding a mortgage over their lands. They were permitted to grow only those crops not already grown in the Company's own garden, the cultivation of cereals being encouraged. Since they were now landowners, these first 'free burghers' naturally required labour; and with strict instructions from the Company not to enslave the local Khoikhoi, they had to look elsewhere.

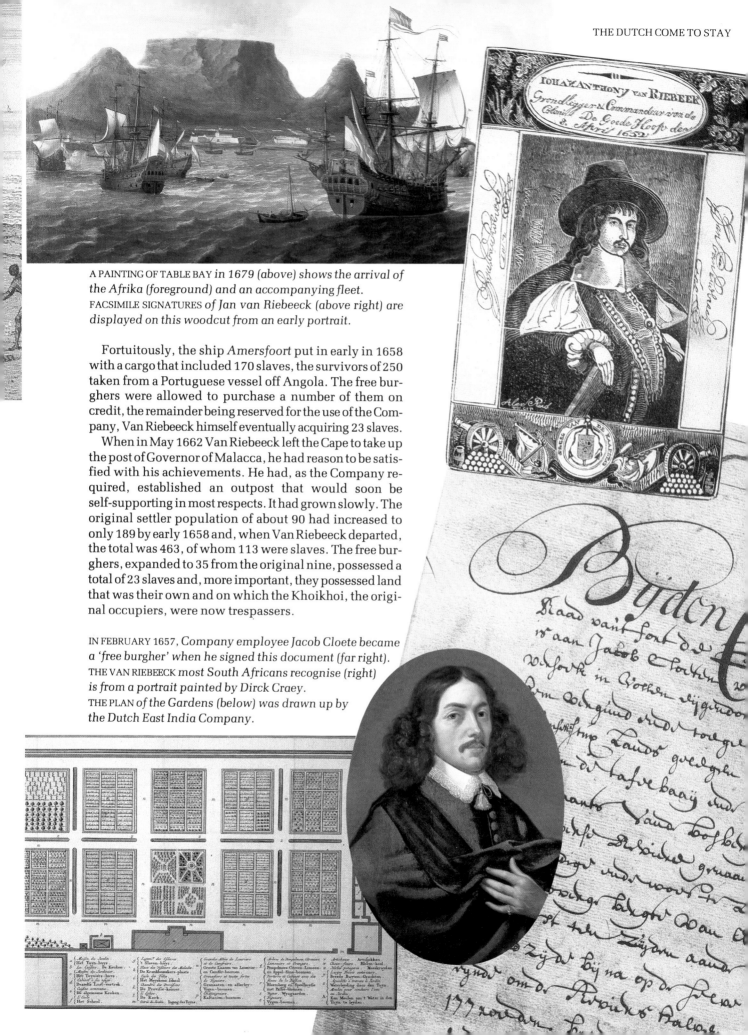

A PAINTING OF TABLE BAY in 1679 (above) shows the arrival of the Afrika (foreground) and an accompanying fleet.
FACSIMILE SIGNATURES of Jan van Riebeeck (above right) are displayed on this woodcut from an early portrait.

Fortuitously, the ship Amersfoort put in early in 1658 with a cargo that included 170 slaves, the survivors of 250 taken from a Portuguese vessel off Angola. The free burghers were allowed to purchase a number of them on credit, the remainder being reserved for the use of the Company, Van Riebeeck himself eventually acquiring 23 slaves.

When in May 1662 Van Riebeeck left the Cape to take up the post of Governor of Malacca, he had reason to be satisfied with his achievements. He had, as the Company required, established an outpost that would soon be self-supporting in most respects. It had grown slowly. The original settler population of about 90 had increased to only 189 by early 1658 and, when Van Riebeeck departed, the total was 463, of whom 113 were slaves. The free burghers, expanded to 35 from the original nine, possessed a total of 23 slaves and, more important, they possessed land that was their own and on which the Khoikhoi, the original occupiers, were now trespassers.

IN FEBRUARY 1657, Company employee Jacob Cloete became a 'free burgher' when he signed this document (far right).
THE VAN RIEBEECK most South Africans recognise (right) is from a portrait painted by Dirck Craey.
THE PLAN of the Gardens (below) was drawn up by the Dutch East India Company.

TO BE SOLD & LE
BY PUBLIC AUCTION,
On MONDAY the 18th of MAY, 1
UNDER THE TREES.
FOR SALE,
THE THREE FOLLOWING
SLAVE

VIZ.

HANNIBAL, about 30 Years old, an excellent House Servant, of Good Ch

WILLIAM, about 35 Years old, a Labourer.

NANCY, an excellent House Servant and Nurse.

The MEN Belonging to "LEECH'S" Estate, and the WOMAN to Mrs. D. SMIT

The fatal impact 1652-1800

'We... will not leave the Dutch in peace.'
Unnamed Khoisan after a party of trekboers had raided his settlement.

On a cold, drizzling day in May 1659 a Goringhaiqua Khoikhoi named Doman decided that the time had come to put into action a plan that had been forming in his mind for months... nothing less than an attempt to force the Dutch to quit their seven-year-old settlement at De Kaap.

Doman and his followers had chosen the day carefully, knowing that the wet weather would make the Dutch muskets, unreliable at the best of times, useless. He chose his targets with equal care – the farms that had recently been started by the so-called free burghers, men who had been allowed to quit the service of the Dutch East India Company to work for themselves. He was also careful not to kill any of the farmers, but confined his attacks to the destruction of crops and stealing of cattle.

Doman, by all accounts, was nobody's fool; having worked for the Dutch as an interpreter. He had even been selected to visit Java for further training, a visit that had strengthened his determination that the Dutch should not subjugate the Khoikhoi in the way they had subjugated the indigenous people of Batavia. The Dutch, he decided soon after his return, had to be forced to leave the Cape before the new settlement had a chance to consolidate and expand.

It was nearly a year before peace was restored... and it was the Dutch who emerged as the eventual victors. Not only had Doman and his small group of helpers failed to expel the colonists, but they were now faced with an ever-increasing number of free burghers and settlers, including Huguenots from France, who set about taking the Khoikhoi land in an ever-widening arc, spreading outwards from the shores of Table Bay. The Company did at least listen to complaints against settler excesses and expansionism; the free burghers, however, became less and less amenable to reason as they moved further and further inland away from Company control.

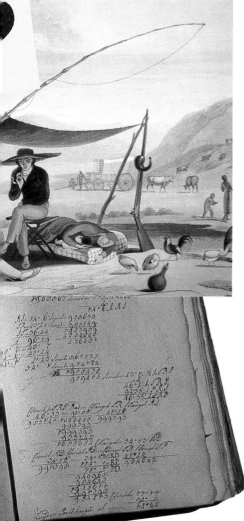

Up until the 1680s the Khoikhoi were still vitally important to the Dutch as the main suppliers of livestock, traded for iron and copper. The Company protected this trade vigorously, and no free burgher was allowed to deal with the Khoikhoi. However, once it was in a position to raise its own cattle, this prohibition was lifted, giving the burghers a free hand to denude the Khoikhoi of their source of livelihood. Although this ban was reimposed, and then lifted again, it was the death knell of the Khoikhoi. Their demise was hastened with the emergence of the trekboers, wandering white farmers who were always ready to increase their herds and their lands at the expense of the indigenous people.

Resistance flared again and again as desperate efforts were made by both Khoikhoi and San to halt the trekboer advance; but the superior technology and mobility of the mounted and armed trekboers led remorselessly to the defeat of the herders and hunters. Inevitably, too, Khoikhoi warred against Khoikhoi as desperate attempts were made to replace cattle lost to the Dutch by stealing from neighbouring clans. With their land and livelihood lost, the Khoikhoi had no option but to work for the victors, often in positions of dreadful servitude. By the end of the 18th century those Khoikhoi who were not working for a white master were liable to be shot on sight, called disparagingly by the trekboers 'bosjesmans' (bushmen), which described them as living wild 'in the bush'. In the very last year of the century many of those living on white farms took one last gamble on freedom in the 'servants' revolt' in the Zuurveld of the eastern Cape.

For the trekboers, South Africa's first white 'Africans', the destruction of Khoikhoi societies was the necessary outcome of their own thirst for land. But from the late 1770s they were to come up against new resistance in the east on a frontier that had existed for hundreds of years: the frontier between the Khoikhoi and the Bantu-speaking people of southern Africa. Although Bantu-speakers and Khoikhoi mixed fairly freely (the 'clicks' in the Xhosa language are borrowed from the Khoikhoi), the Xhosa shared greater similarities with other Bantu-speakers to the east and north. (These were Iron Age people who, hundreds of years earlier, had settled the area which was to become known as the eastern Cape.)

The Xhosa frontier, although to be whittled away in successive 'frontier wars', was to hold firm against the trekboers. Further white expansion, when it came, was forced northwards in a migration that has become known as the 'Great Trek'.

But by then the people who had once lived and herded their cattle over vast areas of southern Africa – the men who had vainly called themselves Khoikhoi (men of men) – had all but ceased to exist.

Their place, to some extent at least, was taken by slaves – imported from various parts of Africa and the East to the Cape after the Dutch East India Company had forbidden the first Governor of the Cape, Jan van Riebeeck, to enslave the local Khoikhoi. Slavery flourished throughout the 18th century, providing workers for a wide range of duties, from household servants to farm labourers. As the Cape frontier moved inexorably east and north, so the slaves and their descendants moved with it.

Impact of the Europeans

1652	Jan van Riebeeck, first command permanent Cape settlement, arri to acknowledge Khoikhoi title to fosters good trading relations. Van Riebeeck's request for slaves
1656	First slave freed in order to marry Dutchman.
1657	Goringhaiqua Doman sent to Bat become interpreter; his experien engender opposition to the Comp he returns to Cape. First nine free burghers released Company service to farm on Kho
1658	Slaves from Angola and West Af Cape.
1659	Van Riebeeck owns 18 slaves. First serious quarrel between Du Khoikhoi when Doman leads 'W Liberation' against Dutch, raidir the free burghers, who seek safet Khoikhoi disunity causes rebelli
1660	Peace restored, end of independe Peninsular Khoikhoi. Dutch erect fortified posts and a against Khoikhoi. First Dutch exploratory parties t east seeking land and trade.
1660s	First horses arrive at Cape, from Dutch further superiority over K
1663	Doman dies, his power shattered Autshumao (Harry) dies. Dutch settlement expands; outp Saldanha Bay and Hottentots Ho
1673	Jeronimus Cruse's expedition ra Cochoqua for livestock; second Khoikhoi war.
1677	With peace restored, white expa proceeds.
1685	Commissioner Hendrik van Ree Cape, decrees that male slaves ca freedom at age of 25, females at 2
1688	French Huguenot refugees arrive settler numbers.
c1690s	Trekboer class emerges.
1690	Abortive slave uprising at Stelle
1699-1707	Wilhem Adriaan van der Stel is Governor.
1710-20	Surplus wheat and wine causes
1713	Smallpox epidemic brought ash visitors decimates Khoikhoi, kil whites.
1724	Short-lived Company slave stati Delagoa Bay.
1730s	Company again trades for slaves Mozambique and Zanzibar.
1750s	Dutch world influence wanes.
1751-71	Ryk Tulbagh appointed Cape Go
1765	Meermin sails from Cape to purc in Madagascar; slave rebellion o journey fails.
1789	Merino sheep imported from Ho
1795	First British Occupation begins.
1798	Tuan Guru founds Dorp Street m in southern Africa.

African societies

1700s	Dlamini chiefdom moves south from Delagoa Bay to settle north of Phongolo River.
1730-75	Phalo rules Xhosa; warring sons cause rift in Xhosa.
Until 1750s	Northern Nguni territory occupied by small chiefdoms.
c1778	Xhosa chief Gcaleka dies, succeeded by Khawuta, then Ngqika (under Regent Ndlambe). Chief Rharhabe and heir, Mlawu, die in battle against Thembu: unsettled times.
c1785	Shaka born.
c1786	Moshoeshoe born.
c1795	Ngqika defeats Ndlambe, contends for Xhosa paramountcy but opposed by rival chieftains.
c1798	Mpande settles in Babanango.
1800	Ndlambe moves west of Fish River.

Struggle for land/expansion of eastern frontier

1700-1800	Increasing contact between Khoikhoi and Xhosa.
1655	First of many Peninsular Khoikhoi protests against land seizure by Dutch.
1657	First free burghers settle on Khoikhoi land.
1659	Armed Khoikhoi resistance to land seizure.
1672	Dutch attempt to transact formal transfer of land seized from Khoikhoi.
1673	Further armed Khoikhoi resistance to land seizure.
1679	Simon van der Stel becomes Cape Governor, with orders to expand Colony; founds Stellenbosch. First farmers settle along Eerste River.
1687	Stellenbosch district fully settled by Dutch colonists.
1688	Huguenot refugees granted land at Franschhoek. Dutch farming beyond original Cape boundary.
1700	Open trading between free burghers and Khoikhoi permitted, leads to Khoikhoi impoverishment.
1701	First Khoisan cattle raid against Dutch farmers.
1702	Early cattle-gathering expedition ends in clash with Xhosa; illicit trade commences.
1702-4	Company temporarily reimposes ban on trading with Khoikhoi.
1705	Stellenbosch *landdrost* Starrenberg sets out to barter cattle with Khoikhoi north of Saldanha.
1710-20	Trekboer ranks swell as a result of wheat and wine surpluses.
1715	Trekboer cattle-raid against farmers at Saldanha Bay.
1717	System of freehold title to land ends, by which time some 400 farms granted.
1725	Company temporarily reimposes ban on free trading with Khoikhoi.
1726	Company sets up administrative post in east at Ziekenhuys to enforce control.
1728	Clash between Khoisan and trekboers.
1730	First trekboers reach forests around George, travel inland into Langkloof.
1731	Khoisan women and children kidnapped after armed confrontation.
1732	Annual rental of a *leningplaats* doubled to 24 rix-dollars. Quitrent system of land tenure introduced.
1734	Company sets up administrative post in east at Rietvlei, proclaims Great Brak River the eastern boundary of Cape.
1739	Last armed resistance by Khoisan in south-western Cape.
1740	Remaining western Cape Khoikhoi reduced to labourer status. Shipwreck of *Visch* in Table Bay.
1743	Governor-General Baron van Imhoff inspects Cape, establishes new district of Swellendam, orders establishment of churches at Malmesbury and Tulbagh, changes land tenure system to discourage trekking.
1754	Khoisan raid farms in Roggeveld.
1770	Northern and southern trekker parties meet at Camdeboo.
1771	Cape boundary crosses Gamtoos River; trekker and Xhosa clashes begin.
1774-6	Khoisan resistance to trekboers reaches climax.
1778	Great Fish River becomes eastern boundary.
1785	New district of Graaff Reinet proclaimed.
1799-1802	Unsuccessful revolt by eastern Cape Khoikhoi (third frontier war).

Sold – for a load of old iron

As the 17th century dawned, the shore of Table Bay became increasingly busy as more and more
European ships called for provisions while travelling to and from the East.
Although some sailors bartered with the Khoikhoi for their needs, many simply took
what they wanted. The most devastating blow of all for the local inhabitants, however,
came when the Dutch decided to set up their own provisioning station.

ADMIRAL CORNELIS MATELIEF took pride in the fact that, as a founding member of the Dutch East India Company (VOC), he knew how to trade with the natives of Holland's far-flung commercial empire. And when in 1608 he went ashore in Table Bay to barter for sheep he took no chances. In one hand he held on firmly to a copper bracelet, while with the other he grasped the leg of a sheep. His trading partner, a Peninsular Khoikhoi, was no less careful. Only when he had a firm grasp of the bracelet did he let go of the sheep – and the barter was warily concluded.

Fourteen years earlier, the English navigator James Lancaster also stopped at the Cape to trade with the local Khoikhoi, bartering iron for 1 000 sheep and 42 oxen. On a subsequent visit in 1601 he bartered again – with a number of pikemen and musketeers kept within hailing distance in case of a dispute.

The contacts between the indigenous people of the Cape and European adventurers followed a similar pattern for over a century: fear, distrust and, of course, some mutual benefit. The Europeans had iron, something which the Khoikhoi badly needed to perfect their ornaments and weapons. The Khoikhoi had sheep and cattle, which the Europeans needed to replenish their badly depleted supplies after the long haul from the Indies. In 1591 the going rate for an ox was two knives, with smaller stock and calves costing proportionately less. And as the local Khoikhoi's superior weaponry became more vital to their dominance over other clans, so their demand for iron increased, and the price of animals dropped still further until an ox could be bought for just a handful of old scrap iron and nails. Within a few years, 200 old barrel-hoops fetched 450 sheep and 66 cattle.

Inevitably the market became over-supplied and iron ceased to be as important as copper, from which the Khoikhoi usually made ornaments. Previously the Peninsular Khoikhoi had obtained copper from the Nama living far to the north in present-day Namaqualand. Now they found a cheaper and easier source right on their doorstep – the European sailors; and the Khoikhoi in turn used the copper to trade with other clans for cattle, sheep or dagga. However, this shift in demand forced the price of cattle up, and by 1610 the Europeans were reporting that the days of cheap barter at the Cape were over. A further shock followed when the Khoikhoi began demanding even more expensive brass, an alloy made from copper, zinc and other metals.

This hardening of the cattle price was largely due to a Khoikhoi named Gorachouqua (or Goree as he was known to the Dutch), who in 1613 was kidnapped and taken to

TRADE BETWEEN *Khoikhoi inhabitants of the western Cape and European sailors was seldom as peaceful a process as this 17th-century Dutch engraving indicates. In most cases the visitors simply stormed ashore, chased off or killed the unprepared Khoikhoi herders and took what they wanted.*

London where he soon learned the art of trade. Uprooted from the warm country of the Cape and thrust into the cold, crowded city, he begged to return home – and was appointed to act as a kind of local trading agent on behalf of his former captors. For the Europeans it was perhaps not such a wise move: Goree insisted that they pay a proper price for their livestock.

Despite their rather arbitrary treatment of him, Goree preferred the English to the Dutch, whom he accused of 'ill and evil usage of the blacks'. And when a group of English convicts was 'transported' to Table Bay in order to establish a colony at the Cape, Goree suggested that the convicts be given firearms so that he and his people could be protected from neighbouring clans. At first the British refused, but in 1617, after the convicts had been repatriated, a new group of Englishmen tentatively agreed to assist him against his inland enemy, the Cochoqua. On finding the odds against them, however, the English hastily withdrew. Goree had more luck with the Dutch, and later that same year a group of Dutch sailors and soldiers attacked the Cochoqua on his behalf, netting a rich booty of cattle and sheep. Once the Dutch had departed, however, Goree returned to his old alliance with the English, and in 1626 he was killed by Dutch sailors for refusing to allow his people to trade with them, although trading freely with the British ships that called at the Cape.

Taking by force

By this time relations between the rough and ready sailors who called at the Cape and the Khoikhoi had reached an all-time low. The men who manned the Dutch, English and Portuguese ships were usually the dregs of European society. Discipline was rigorously enforced, and punishment for the slightest misdemeanour was brutal. Given the fact, then, that most sailors, the sweepings of seedy wharfsides, had little consideration for one another, it is not surprising that they had even less feeling for 'heathen blacks' at remote calling places such as Table Bay. Instead of bartering for cattle, many sailors found it easier simply to storm ashore and to help themselves, killing anyone foolish enough to oppose them.

A further problem for the Khoikhoi was the fact that the callers at the Cape came from several different European countries, many of which were often at war with one another. Thus a uniform policy by the Europeans towards the Khoikhoi was impossible to formulate, and they were never able to understand that what they described as the Khoikhoi's 'erratic' behaviour – now friendly, now aggressive – was merely a reflection of how they themselves had dealt with the indigenous inhabitants.

In March 1647 a Dutch ship, the *Haerlem*, was wrecked in Table Bay and the stranded crew built a fortress on the beach for protection. Khoikhoi leader Harry (Autshumao), suspecting that the encampment would be permanent (in fact it lasted only a year), asked whether he and his followers could live under Dutch protection. This gave each side the opportunity to study the other and draw conclusions. Leendert Jansz, who was in charge of the temporary settlement, held the view that the Khoikhoi killed Europeans only because they had been provoked – and that Europe-

Harry's *Strandlopers*

When European ships stopped in at the Cape during the more than 160 years prior to the establishment of a permanent colony at the Cape in 1652, they encountered not only the stock-owning Khoikhoi, but also a small beach community in Table Bay which one Dutch commander disdainfully referred to as 'rabble out of the interior'.

The *Strandlopers* – as they came to be called – were the outcasts of Khoikhoi society. They had very little in the way of possessions and were bound together not by kinship, but rather by common misfortune. They called themselves the 'Goringhaicona' (children of the Goringhaiqua), and they scraped a living wherever they could find it.

Never numbering more than a few dozen, they acknowledged as their leader a man named Autshumao – whom the whites came to know as Herry or Harry. He had been taken to Java by the English captain John Hall in about 1631, and by the time he was returned to the Cape, had acquired enough knowledge of English to act as interpreter on bartering expeditions. He was also appointed as 'postmaster' for the English, who left him letters to be handed on to the captains of passing ships. At Harry's request, he and his people were taken to Robben Island, where they were safe from their enemies and lived happily for a while among the penguins and seals. When a French ship called at the island, Harry, claiming to be employed by both Dutch and English, succeeded in persuading the Frenchmen to make use of Saldanha Bay instead.

By 1640, the *Strandlopers* were back on the mainland, having almost exterminated the seal and penguin colonies on the island. With the rewards they received from the Europeans, Harry's people were able to trade with other groups, acquiring livestock, mostly for immediate consumption.

After 1652, Harry's intimate knowledge of local Khoikhoi politics proved invaluable to Dutch officials of the newly formed refreshment station at the Cape. He died in 1663.

VISITING CAPTAINS *left messages for one another on rocks.*

DUTCH *surgeon-turned-author Abraham Bogaert drew this picture of a Khoikhoi village near Table Bay in 1706.*

ans would do the same in a similar situation. He expressed the hope that the Khoikhoi would learn the Dutch language and accept Christianity.

In this he differed from the first commander of a permanent European settlement at the Cape, Jan van Riebeeck, who recorded that the Khoikhoi were an untrustworthy 'savage set, living without conscience', against whom it would be necessary to build an impregnable fort. When he landed at the Cape in 1652, he treated the Khoikhoi fairly, as required by his superiors, but did not acknowledge their title to the land. The first Khoikhoi whom the new settlers encountered were the Goringhaicona – the *Strandlopers*. Also living on or near the Cape Peninsula were the Gorachouqua and the Goringhaiqua. Apart from occasional clashes, they lived at peace with one another, warring at times with the powerful Cochoqua further inland. But mistrust of the Europeans still remained.

White settlement becomes permanent

Even while the fort was being built, it is doubtful whether any of the Khoikhoi realised that this time the settlement would be permanent. Gogosoa, the paramount chief of the Gorachouqua and Goringhaicona, known to the Dutch as 'the fat captain', was old and fast losing his influence. These two Peninsular groups, numbering about 6 000 people, claimed the Cape Peninsula and adjacent land for themselves, believing that they had a priority claim to grazing rights. At first, the Dutch hardly infringed on this; their fort was small and enclosed, and the garden lands were neither extensive nor prized as grazing. But a settled white community, with a set policy and continuity of command, was a different story from bands of looting sailors from passing ships.

Van Riebeeck needed to regain the trust of the Khoikhoi – the success of the settlement depended on cattle-

bartering, from which the Company's own flocks a herds would eventually be built. Despite his earlier favourable attitude towards the Khoikhoi, Van Riebee managed to develop and maintain good relations w them, even raising a young Khoikhoi girl in his home in fort. Her name was Krotoa, but the Europeans called Eva – a girl from the Cochoqua group and apparent niece of Harry. She was instructed in Dutch, in which became fluent, and was taught the Christian religion

The Khoikhoi groups, living in the shadow of the set ment and on good terms with the foreigners, were quic seize the opportunity to prosper. Sheep and cattle wer constant demand by settlers and sailors, who were n calling more often at the Cape. Trade with the Peninsu groups led to the reopening of inland trade; and the Per sular groups exchanged their copper or tobacco for ca from the interior. And to make sure that their grip on tr with the Europeans remained secure, the Peninsu Khoikhoi told horrific tales about the Dutch settl designed to put the interior clans off visiting the fort. H ing no interpreters of their own, they were easily couraged, and often sold their cattle to the Peninsu Khoikhoi, who kept the best animals and sold the mainder, at a profit, to the Dutch. When up-country Kl khoi did visit the fort to barter cattle they usually did s the company of a Peninsular Khoikhoi who could sp some Dutch, and who would claim a percentage of the chase price for services as interpreter. In turn, the Per sular Khoikhoi tried to prevent the Dutch from mak contact with the inland groups.

This virtual monopoly on trade with the Europeans eventually broken by Eva, who was descended from major inland group, the powerful Cochoqua. As she g older she encouraged contact between her clan and Dutch, and before long the Cochoqua were arriving at

The great smallpox epidemic of 1713

In the summer of 1713, a parcel of dirty linen from a fleet of visiting Dutch ships unleashed a devastating trail of death and suffering that engulfed the tiny white settlement at the Cape before spreading like brushfire into the interior.

The tragedy began on 13 February when a convoy under the command of Commissioner Joannes van Steeland limped into Table Bay, after a voyage in which several crew and passengers (including his own children) had gone down with smallpox. The fact that all had recovered from this normally fatal disease was to have tragic consequences for the inhabitants of the south-western Cape. For, certainly, had those who contracted the disease died, their clothing would not have been included in the laundry that Van Steeland sent to the slave lodge for washing.

On 9 April, authorities at the Cape were told that their slaves were beginning to die like flies. By 19 April, up to eight slaves a day were being buried and the first whites began to display symptoms of the pox.

In the first few days of May the death toll for white inhabitants of the settlement stood at between two and five a day, and coffins were dispensed with as wood could not be brought into town fast enough. On 9 May, when two pigeons toppled from the roof of the Governor's home, and died for no apparent reason, observers fearfully declared their deaths to be an omen of catastrophe.

They were correct.

By the end of May, 110 whites had died, and panic-stricken authorities were offering slaves a rix-dollar a day and food to watch over the sick and the dying. By June the worst was over in Cape Town and it became the turn of the countryside to be devastated. Towards the end of that month it was reported that there were only 20 healthy whites in the whole of the Drakenstein district. Farmers could neither plant nor harvest their crops and emergency supplies had to be imported from Batavia.

By December, however, the crisis had passed for white society and reconstruction could begin. But the local Khoikhoi population was not as fortunate.

When the first Khoikhoi began to die late in April, it soon became evident that they had far less resistance to the disease than the settlers and the slaves. With no medical lore to resist what was to them a totally foreign illness, scores of Khoikhoi simply died where they fell ill.

Said a Dutch official, Francois Valentyn: 'The Hottentots died in their hundreds. They lay everywhere on the roads. Cursing at the Dutchmen, who they said had bewitched them, they fled inland with their kraals, huts, and cattle in hopes there to be freed from the malign disease.'

Even as the Dutch were burying as many of the Khoikhoi corpses as they could to prevent more of the 'bad air' which they believed prolonged the plague, other sufferers of the pox who fled inland were being killed by fearful local groups.

In February 1714 the survivors of four kraals, in reporting to the Governor that their captains were all dead, announced that scarcely one in 10 of their number had survived.

Although smallpox continued to afflict the indigenous people of southern Africa for the next century, the plague of 1713 effectively decimated the Khoikhoi population of the south-western Cape. Those who survived lost their old clan names and became known collectively as 'Hottentots'.

AN 18TH-CENTURY *painting of whites and Khoikhoi trading (left).*
A KHOIKHOI *woman in Western dress (below) holds a baby.*

fort regularly and fearlessly to trade. Once contact had been made with the Dutch, the Cochoqua began moving nearer to the source of their wealth – the fort – and began grazing their herds on pastures which the Peninsular Khoikhoi claimed as their own.

This pressure on available land was increased still further in 1657, when nine men were released from the service of the Company in order to farm on land previously grazed by herds belonging to the Peninsular Khoikhoi. Within a year, still more 'free burghers' were 'granted' land, and the Goringhaiqua now found themselves under pressure from both the Cochoqua and the new white farmers.

The first Khoikhoi-Dutch war

Into this increasingly volatile situation stepped a Goringhaiqua named Doman, who in about 1657 was sent to Batavia to learn to become an interpreter. But having witnessed first hand the capacity of the Dutch to reduce indigenous people to positions of servitude, he became a staunch opponent of European colonisation.

In a ploy to ensure his safe return to the Cape, he told Commissioner Joan Cunaeus of his wish to become a Christian and of the fact that he had become so devoted to the Dutch that he doubted whether he could live with his fellow Khoikhoi again. But almost as soon as he landed, he emerged as the staunchest Khoikhoi critic of Van Riebeeck's policies. When Van Riebeeck seized several Khoikhoi leaders as hostages in 1658, Doman was the lone protester (the Khoikhoi chiefs themselves welcomed imprisonment as an opportunity to enjoy Dutch hospitality).

He was particularly scathing in his criticism of Eva, tauntingly calling out whenever she passed by: 'See, there comes the advocate of the Dutch; she will tell her people some stories and lies and will finally betray them all.' Whenever Eva tried to pass on information to the Dutch, Doman tried to stop her. When the Dutch planned trips into the hinterland, he tried to stop them. From his hut near the fort, he tried to intercept all inland visitors.

Unfortunately for Doman, his earlier attempts to make Khoikhoi trade with the Dutch the exclusive preserve of the Peninsular groups left him dangerously short of allies. Thus his attempts to persuade local chief Gogosoa to attack the Dutch was bluntly refused. Without the help of the inland Cochoqua, the old chief replied, an attack on the fort was doomed to fail. Doman, however, was able to persuade some of the younger leaders to join him in what he regarded as a war of liberation.

On a cold and drizzling day in May 1659 a series of raids started on the free burghers' herds. Doman had waited for rainy weather, knowing that the Dutch matchlock muskets (unreliable at the best of times) could not be fired in the rain with damp powder. The Khoikhoi were careful not to kill the farmers, fearing retaliation, but hoped to persuade the Dutch to quit the Cape by burning their crops and stealing their cattle. The Dutch, however, had no such scruples, and revenge was swift and savage – freemen were ordered to shoot Khoikhoi on sight. In the end there were few deaths on either side during the year that the war lasted, but it did force the free burghers off the land and back into defensive positions in and around the fort.

The war ended in a stalemate: the Khoikhoi were unwilling to attack the fort, and Dutch forays against the Khoikhoi were usually unsuccessful due to the wildness of the terrain and lack of guides. And all hopes of rallying the Cochoqua to the Khoikhoi cause were dashed when their leader, Oedesoa, refused to become involved, instead moving with his people away from the fighting into the interior. Eventually, with their lucrative trade at an end and often forced to take refuge in the hills, Goringhaiqua resolve began to falter, and peace negotiations were opened with the Dutch – despite protests from Doman.

Strandlopers were allowed to return to the vicinity of the fort and representatives of the Goringhaiqua, and after them the Gorachouqua, settled in the area. Peace was finally restored in April 1660 after months of negotiations, during which the Khoikhoi complained bitterly about the usurpation of their pastures and the abusive behaviour of the free burghers who, once freed from the discipline of the fort and its commander, had exploited their situation. The Dutch did not demand that looted property or stock be restored – which may have been a tacit acknowledgement of misbehaviour on the part of the freemen.

It appeared that the Khoikhoi had won the war and also the peace. But if it was a victory, then it was a hollow one, for the war had failed to achieve its prime objective – the departure of the Dutch, who were now firmly entrenched in their position of power. Fortified posts were erected and almond hedges (some of which still survive) were planted to prevent cattle being driven off again. Khoikhoi were obliged to use specified routes and paths, and to enter the settlement only at certain guarded gaps in the hedge. Horses which arrived from Batavia gave the colonists the mobility they had lacked in the war, and expeditions from the fort became longer and more frequent. As trading contacts were established with more Khoikhoi groups, the settlement gradually became independent of the Peninsular Khoikhoi, whose wealth and importance waned rapidly.

THE MATCHLOCK gun used at the Cape by the Dutch in the 17th century fired one shot every two minutes.

A RECENT *photograph of the almond hedge which Van Riebeeck planted to separate Dutch from Khoikhoi.*

The failure of the Khoikhoi to drive out the Dutch shattered Doman's position as a leader, and he was tolerated only because his people needed him as an interpreter. When he died in December 1663, the Company diarist recorded: 'For [his] death none of us will have cause to grieve, as he has been, in many respects, a mischievous and malicious man towards the Company.'

The second Khoikhoi-Dutch war

Following the conclusion of peace, exploratory parties of Dutch moved out north and east. Beyond the Hottentots Holland Mountains (to the east) lay fertile plains grazed by the extensive herds of the Chainoqua, while still further east were the Hessequa and Gouriqua, who displayed a willingness to trade. In the north were many small, independent chiefdoms, all of which owned livestock and were also eager to barter with the settlers.

But all too often the Khoikhoi discovered too late that copper trinkets and the memory of tobacco or brandy were no substitute for healthy herds of cattle. The inevitable result was a dramatic increase in inter-group hostility, as clans raided one another to replace cattle traded with the Dutch. Wars and raids between the Chainoqua and a section of the Cochoqua under the co-chief Gonnema, continued for some 10 years from the early 1660s.

The settlement, meanwhile, was expanding within Table Valley, and outposts were built at Saldanha Bay and in the Hottentots Holland where, for the first time, land was actually purchased or bartered from the Khoikhoi chieftain Dhouw. Inevitably, as European explorers, hunters and traders (legally or illegally) criss-crossed the countryside there were incidents of cattle-stealing and a hunter killed or wounded. Incidents and casualties mounted. Encouraged by the many enemies of the Cochoqua, the Dutch blamed Gonnema for this uneasy truce, and determined to break the Cochoqua.

On 18 July 1673, an expedition under the command of Jeronimus Cruse launched a highly successful campaign against Gonnema. Pursued by Dutch horsemen, dozens of terrified Cochoqua fled into the mountains, leaving behind their livestock. By the end of the day the raiders had seized 800 cattle and 900 sheep.

With most other Khoikhoi groups siding with the Dutch, there was little Gonnema could do beyond trying to defend what few possessions his people still retained.

The Company, however, was far from finished – and in 1674 launched another attack on the Cochoqua. This time the booty included 800 cattle, 4 000 sheep and a large number of weapons. The war dragged on inconclusively until June 1677 when Governor Isjbrand Goske's successor, Joan Bax, accepted a pledge from Gonnema that he would live at peace with the settlers and pay a tribute of 30 cattle annually. Despite their submission to the Dutch, the Cochoqua were not totally impoverished by the war. In fact, Gonnema continued to be regarded as one of the richest chiefs in the region. From a Dutch viewpoint, he also became a model leader, pursuing escaped slaves whenever officials at the fort requested him to do so, and allowing his people to aid white hunters.

Once peace was restored, white expansion proceeded at a rapid pace. The number of settlers increased with the arrival of French Huguenot refugees in 1688 and a new class arose, that of the trekboer. These were whites who, released from Company service, elected to live a nomadic life, always on the move with their livestock in search of better grazing and water. They had slaves or Khoikhoi servants and were, for the most part, outside the Company's control. On the wide plains, they lived a life remarkably like the one which the Khoikhoi themselves had led a few decades earlier. For the Khoikhoi, most of whom were either impoverished or 'in service', such a life of independence was now just a memory.

Cheaper than servants

Slaves were the labour force which transformed the small refreshment station
into a significant agricultural colony – and in some ways, agriculture in the western Cape
still reflects its slave origins. They were a class who could not enter into any legal contract,
or own property. In civil law they simply did not exist – but criminal law was a savage reality.

JAN VAN RIEBEECK'S INSTRUCTIONS from the Dutch East India Company were perfectly clear: he was forbidden to enslave the indigenous people of the Cape – an order which he was careful to obey.

However, slaves from elsewhere were another matter, and in May 1652, only weeks after arriving in Table Bay, he asked for slaves to be sent to help erect the fort and till the land. The Company replied that slaves could not be spared, and for the first five years of the fledgling colony's existence the only slaves at the Cape were stowaways or gifts from the captains of passing ships.

By 1658 there were 11 slaves, eight women and three men. One of these, Abraham, was a stowaway who, in 1653, arrived from the East aboard the ship *Malacca*, claiming to have run away from his master, Cornelis Lichthart of Batavia. Abraham was set to work, and Van Riebeeck wrote to Lichthart reporting Abraham's arrival. For three years he heard nothing, until a letter arrived from Adriaan van den Burgh of Batavia, claiming that Abraham belonged to him and demanding compensation for the loss of Abraham's labour. Van Riebeeck replied that, because of illness, Abraham had done little work, and that it would be more appropriate if his owner paid the Company for the costs of Abraham's food and accommodation.

Van Riebeeck frequently repeated his request for more slaves, suggesting that slaves could work the nearby salt-pans so that salt could be profitably exported, or hunt seals, or assist with agricultural tasks. He argued that they would be cheaper than Company servants, as they did not have to be paid a salary. However, although the Company was reluctant to agree, fate was more obliging . . . .

On 28 March 1658, the ship *Amersfoort*, which two months earlier had intercepted a Portuguese slaver bound from Angola to Brazil, arrived in Table Bay with a shipment of slaves. The Portuguese ship had surrendered 250 of a cargo of 500 slaves to the *Amersfoort*. Many slaves died before reaching the Cape, and a few were sent to Batavia. Of the 38 men and 37 women who remained, 21 men and 22 women were set to work in the fields and gardens. The rest were assigned to various Company officials.

A second group of slaves was purchased at Popo on the West African coast, and arrived at the Cape in May 1658 aboard the ship *Hasselt*. Van Riebeeck described the 228 newly enslaved people as 'exceptionally handsome, sturdy and cheery'. About 80 were shipped to Batavia, the remainder being sold to free burghers and Company officials. As with the Angolans, many of these slaves from Guinea were soon to die of disease, and their numbers diminished rapidly.

Rijckloff van Goens, a Company commissioner, instructed Van Riebeeck to treat slaves well. They were to be taught the basic principles of agriculture and a trade, as the Com-

ADVERTISEMENTS like this one (left) lured prospective customers to slave auctions in the 1820s.

THE CHILDREN of slaves born in captivity were registered with the Cape of Good Hope Slave Registry Office in order to prove ownership. This certificate (below), issued in 1816, confirms the birth of a male infant named Joseph.

pany hoped there would be no need to send more free men to the Cape – a considerable financial saving. The slaves were not to speak or be spoken to in Portuguese – Dutch was the official language spoken between owner and slave. According to some observers, the patois which ensued eventually evolved into the Afrikaans language. (Language was indeed a barrier even among the slaves, as they came from many different parts of the world.)

Almost from the start, slaves began to run away, because of ill-treatment, overwork and the natural desire to live as a free person. The perils of the unknown were preferable to the humiliation and degradation of slavery – something which the whites could not acknowledge. 'These ignorant people,' wrote a disgruntled owner, 'still believe that they will be able to reach some country where they will be relieved of their bondage,' and he ended with the prediction that 'they may expect nothing else than to be destroyed in a most miserable manner by hunger, the beasts of prey, or brutal natives'. Indeed, many of the runaways did come to a miserable end. But few returned voluntarily to the misery of enslavement. Soldiers and burghers were sent in pursuit, and Khoikhoi were offered tobacco or brandy to track down runaways, though without much success. It was only when Khoikhoi hostages were taken and kept at the fort against their will that the Khoikhoi showed any interest in co-operating.

Runaways sometimes formed their own 'colonies' – two which lasted the longest were high on Simonsberg above Stellenbosch and at Cape Hangklip on the eastern rim of False Bay. The 'colonies' grew gradually from a group of people who, intent on escaping, equipped themselves with plundered firearms or implements and stole a few cattle or sheep. Secure on the remote mountain tops, they grew crops and grazed their flocks and herds. Eventually, however, a commando arrived on the scene which brought an end to the settlements. Those who survived the onslaught were severely punished for running away.

Most slaves carried names given by slave-dealers or their owners. Slaves owned by the Company often retained versions of their real names, usually misspelt by the Company's clerks, such as Sao Balla, Revotes Kehang or Indebet Chemehaijre. Privately owned slaves were generally called Anthony, Jan, Pieter, Anna or Catrijn. They also received classical and biblical names, such as Titus or Rachel. Others were named after the months of the year, especially April, September and October. Their 'surname' usually referred to their place of origin, as in Paulus van Malabar (Paul of Malabar) or Lisbeth van Bengalen (Lisbeth of Bengal), while those born at the Cape were known as 'Van de Kaap' (of the Cape).

It is difficult to assess precisely what the effects of slavery were on slaves themselves. Fear and insecurity, at the very least, were their lot. But of their lives and feelings – and those of successive generations – we know little, just incidental information gleaned from an examination of the records of the Council of Justice.

From the corners of the earth

By 1659 Van Riebeeck possessed a total of 18 slaves, two of whom came from Guinea, one from Madagascar, three from Bengal, and the remainder from Angola, Van Riebeeck's personal preference. He was particularly prejudiced against slaves from Guinea and Madagascar, believing them to be 'unreliable' and likely to desert.

Slave trade with the West African coast did not last long, however: another private Dutch empire, the West India Company, had sole rights to trade – including slave trade – as far south as Angola and did not hesitate to remind its rival, the East India Company, of the fact. (For a brief spell, the West India Company actually laid claim to the Cape settlement.) So Van Riebeeck and his successors were obliged to look to the East, and many slaves were despatched from the coast of India, from such places as Coromandel, Malabar and Nagapatam.

THE FIRST SLAVES *at the Cape came mainly from West Africa – particularly Guinea and Angola. Later, expeditions were despatched to bring slaves from Mozambique and Madagascar. The most highly prized, however, were those from the East – such as present-day Java, Bali, Timor, the Malayan Peninsula and China. Slaves were also imported from India, particularly Coromandel, Malabar and Nagapatam.*

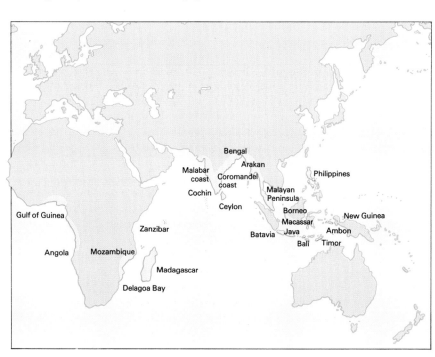

With extensive interests in the East Indian islands, and a trade centred on Batavia (Java), the Dutch rounded up slaves from Bali, Batavia itself, Macassar, Timor and, on the mainland, from Burma, the Malayan Peninsula and China. Ships' officers returning from the East often invested in a few slaves which they resold at a profit at the Cape. Slavers bound for North or South America and the West Indies were also induced to part with a portion of their cargo at the Cape.

'Casual' trade by Company officials became so rampant that, in 1713, return tickets for slaves were booked and paid for in advance. A few years later, however, this was stopped altogether, when it was discovered that private people were making enormous profits at the cost of the Company's cargo revenue.

For a few years from 1724 a slave station was maintained at Delagoa Bay, but the high mortality rate among Company servants led to its closure. The Company turned its attention again to Mozambique and later to Zanzibar.

Coming from different continents and cultures, the slaves had little in common except their bondage. They rarely formed a strongly united group with common aims. The mortality rate was extremely high, and their numbers increased not through procreation but due to the continued importation of slaves. Groups, and even families, were broken up and scattered at auction sales – there being no obligation on a buyer, for instance, to purchase a mother as well as her children. Although slaves formed a large part of the population of the Cape, they were never accepted as being true members of the community.

Slaves from Madagascar and the African coast were the least valuable, although when Guinea slaves were first introduced they fetched 100 rix-dollars apiece, as opposed to the 50 paid for a Malagasy. Generally they were set to the hardest work, such as collecting firewood, for which they might have to search all day in order to collect just enough for a household's needs for the next day.

At the other extreme was the Malay, described as the 'king of slaves'. More quickly than any other group, the Malays learnt the skills of almost all the trades practised at the Cape. When freed, many prospered commercially. Against this, however, they were regarded as temperamental and dangerous. 'Running amok' was something to be feared. On one occasion an Eastern slave, in utter desperation and beyond caring, rushed through the streets, dagger in hand, slashing at everyone in sight and eventually stabbing himself to death.

Most valued of all slaves was a Cape-born child of a slave mother and white father. In the early years of the colony, several marriages took place between white men and slave women, due to the shortage of white women at the colony. Later, sexual intercourse between whites and slaves took place without a formal union. During most of its existence, the Company's slave lodge was renowned as the town's leading brothel. Although forbidden, action was seldom taken against transgressors – except in the early years . . . .

In one incident, Van Riebeeck noticed that Maria van Bengalen, one of his slaves, was often seen with Constable Willem Cornelis. His suspicions led him, with three others as witnesses, to burst into Cornelis' bedroom one Sunday at around midnight. The two were found 'in one another's arms'. The next day, Cornelis was sentenced to pay a fine of 100 reals of eight (a Portuguese currency) and 'labour for 50 years on public works'. The second part of the sentence was commuted to a fine of a further 50 reals. There is no record of a punishment imposed on Maria.

When Commissioner Hendrik van Reede visited the Cape in 1685 he noted that among the Company's slaves there were no fewer than 57 children who obviously had white fathers. Van Reede decided that males could buy their freedom for 100 guilders on reaching the age of 25 years, provided that they had been confirmed in the Dutch Reformed Church and could speak Dutch. The same applied to women, but their age of freedom was 22 years.

Societies in fear

Slavery – the imposition of enforced servitude by a powerful group on another group – inevitably breeds fear in both groups, and resentment in the oppressed. Van Riebeeck recognised this, and more than once alerted the free burghers to the risk of being murdered by their slaves. Yet during his period as Commander, he abolished the use of chains (except for escaped slaves) and allowed slaves to be armed with clubs and pikes during the war with the Khoikhoi. Slaves, however, were not allowed to carry firearms and, if they did so with the knowledge of the owner, the owner was severely fined and had his slave confiscated by the Company.

That there was no large-scale slave uprising is not an indication that slaves were content with their lot, but rather it pointed to their fragmented status as a community. The greatest concentration of slaves was in Cape Town, of which the largest group was owned by the Company and housed in the Company's slave lodge at the foot of the Gardens. Also in Cape Town was the largest concentration of soldiers, so an uprising was out of the question. On farms, the slaves were too few in number and too accustomed to ill-treatment to even think about staging a revolt against their masters.

One attempt at an uprising took place on a farm in Stellenbosch in 1690. Four slaves attacked a farmhouse, killed one burgher, wounded another and fled with stolen firearms. Burghers, soldiers and Khoikhoi auxiliaries were despatched in pursuit and, in a gun-fight, three of the slaves were killed and the fourth wounded and taken prisoner. Interrogated, the prisoner said it had been their intention to murder a number of farmers and set fire to their fields, hoping this would attract other slaves to their side. Then they planned to seize some white women and make their way to Madagascar. But after their first attack they had panicked and taken to the hills.

Among the slave population, men outnumbered women by four to one. The lack of any form of 'family life' contributed to the fragmentary nature of the slave society. It also led to homosexuality, which was a capital offence in the Cape but was condoned by many owners as it gave them additional control over slaves who practised it. Rivalry and jealousy frequently led to fights, and most slaves lived in an atmosphere of continuous tension.

There was also tension among the whites, who constantly feared a mass rebellion and death at the hands of a slave. There was always the fear that slaves who had run away might return to rob or kill, and so large rewards were offered for their recapture. Public warnings of an escaped slave included the tolling of bells and flying a large blue flag at the Castle and other signal-posts.

Control and punishment

Slave ownership and all matters relating to slaves were controlled by the Statutes of India, promulgated in 1642. But, in practice, slave-owners themselves were the immediate instrument of control and punishment. The Statutes permitted a slave-owner to punish his slaves for a mild offence with extra duties, but beating and flogging were forbidden. When the free burghers were allowed to buy slaves, Van Riebeeck made it a condition that they keep a whip or lash in the house for chastising their slaves. But when, almost immediately, slaves began to escape, he allowed owners to keep escaped slaves in chains. Where owners thought that slaves deserved severe punishment, they were to report to the Council of Justice. Slaves, in turn, were to report ill-treatment, although it is debatable whether slaves fully understood this.

The whites' fear of an uprising is reflected in a law which forbade more than two slaves belonging to different owners, to meet at any time. There was also a curfew which required any slaves out of doors after 10 pm to carry a lantern, unless accompanying a member of the owner's family. In practice, slaves often disregarded these restrictions and pursued their amusements such as gambling with dice, cockfighting, fishing, drinking coffee or brandy, and even smoking opium.

Under criminal law – and there were many offences which, when carried out by a slave, were crimes – slaves received harsh punishment. Exceptions were made in the case of bigamy and adultery, for which whites were severely punished and not the slaves.

A law forbidding sexual intercourse between white men and slave women was broken with impunity. In one case, however, a soldier named Jan Rutter and a slave named Catrijn van de Kaap were found guilty of this offence. Rutter was sentenced to be deprived of one month's salary, while his partner was sentenced to be flogged and to work for six months in chains.

It was considered more reprehensible if a white woman committed adultery with a slave than if a white man did. Hester Jansz, found guilty at the Cape of committing this offence on the island of Mauritius, was sentenced to be flogged and to work for five years in chains. The slave's fate was not recorded at the Cape.

In the case of gambling, which was forbidden, the court ordered two young officials to repay a slave, Catrijn van Bengalen, 50 of the 80 rix-dollars which they won from her in an evening of card-playing. In addition, the officials were fined, but there appears to have been no charge against Catrijn.

TWO SLAVES *were depicted in this 'view of Cape Town from Amsterdam Fort' by H R Cook. The buying and selling of slaves continued in the colony until 1834.*

A privately owned slave, Paul van Malabar, was found guilty of keeping a female Company slave named Calafora in his room for three days and nights. He was sentenced to be flogged and branded – not for the sexual offence, but for depriving the Company of the labour of one of its slaves. Calafora was pregnant and sentence was postponed until after she gave birth.

Slaves sent by their owners beyond a certain distance were obliged to carry a pass, signed by the owner, stating the particulars of the mission. Owners who could not write had to buy a lead token from the Company, engraved with the names of owner and slave, which served as a pass. Anyone who arrested a slave without a pass received a reward from the slave's owner.

Farm slaves often worked under the immediate supervision of a *mandoor* (overseer), who was himself a slave, usually Cape-born and chosen for this senior position by his owner. A *mandoor* received benefits, such as permis-

---

A failed bid for freedom on the *Meermin*

Under the command of Captain Gerrit Muller, a two-masted coaster, the *Meermin*, was despatched from the Cape in 1765 to purchase slaves in Madagascar. There the merchant Johan Crause bought 140 slaves, while members of the crew traded for spears and other African weapons.

Instead of following the usual practice of keeping them in chains, Captain Muller decided to put the male slaves to work on board his ship. All went well until the *Meermin* was just a day or two off Table Bay, when the merchant Crause decided to use some of the slaves to clean his stock of firearms and spears. Seizing this opportunity for freedom, the slaves turned on the deck crew, killing some of them and driving the rest up the rigging, while about 30 sailors barricaded themselves below deck. The men in the rigging were coaxed down but once on deck were thrown overboard.

The *Meermin* drifted for two days, with the slaves unable to navigate and the sailors refusing to come up. Later, negotiations were started through a female slave after the sailors threatened to destroy the ship with gunpowder. It was agreed that the sailors would not be harmed, provided they agreed to return the slaves to Madagascar.

The sailors, realising they would probably be killed on arrival at Madagascar, duly sailed east under reduced sail during the day. But at night they crowded on more sail and headed west, somehow maintaining this deception for several days until they came in sight of Cape Agulhas, where they anchored several kilometres from the shore, telling the slaves that this was Madagascar. About 60 slaves, in two boats, set off to investigate, having agreed to light three fires as a signal that this was indeed their home.

Puzzled by the presence of the ship, a number of farmers gathered ashore and when they saw, through a telescope, that the approaching boats were crowded with well-armed blacks, they set off to collect reinforcements. Once ashore, the slaves moved inland but were caught in an ambush and surrendered after a number were killed.

The 80 or so slaves still aboard the *Meermin* waited impatiently for the three signal fires, while the crew nervously wondered what to do next. One of them wrote two messages, asking that three fires be lit, sealed them in bottles, and dropped them overboard. By a stroke of good fortune both messages (one of which is preserved in the Cape Archives) were found and the fires were lit.

The slaves on the *Meermin*, believing they had indeed returned home, cut the anchor ropes, and the ship began to drift toward the shore. The pace was too slow for some, who launched the last small boat and rowed for the beach, where they were promptly surrounded by the farmers and one of their number shot. This was seen by those aboard the *Meermin* and the slaves, realising they had been tricked, turned on the crew.

A battle raged on board for three hours. With both sides exhausted, the ship's mate, Olof Leij, persuaded the slaves that, if they consented to be rechained, they would not be punished. By the time this was completed, there was no hope of saving the ship, which ran ashore. But all aboard were saved.

Of the original cargo of 140 slaves, 112 reached Cape Town. It is not known whether or not they were punished, but Captain Muller was deprived of his rank and salary and dismissed from the service of the Company. Crause, who had carried Muller's casual attitude to ridiculous lengths, had been killed in the initial attack.

THIS LOGBOOK *of the Meermin is kept in the South African Library in Cape Town.*

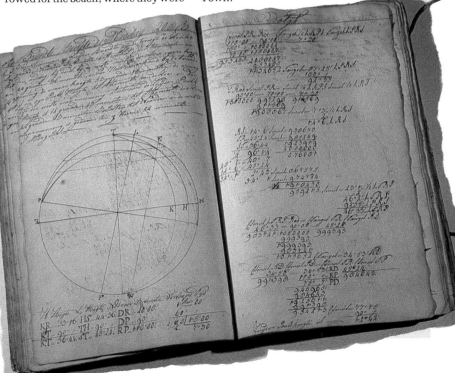

sion to sleep in the women's section of the slave quarters. Other supervisors were the *knechte*, unskilled European labourers or soldiers of the lowest rank, who were not far above the slaves in the social hierarchy. The *knechte* had to keep the balance between a high rate of production and the welfare of the slaves who, in turn, felt they were overworked and retaliated with violence – fights between *knechte* and slaves were frequent.

An owner who felt that his slave deserved a beating could take him to special assistants of the Fiscal (prosecutor), known as 'kaffirs', in order to be flogged. The kaffirs were Asians who had committed criminal offences in other Dutch colonies and been banished to the Cape, where they now served as an elementary police force.

Justice was rigorously administered – and sentences were barbaric in the extreme. Runaway slaves who were recaptured were flogged, branded with a red-hot iron on the back or cheek and sentenced to a lifetime in chains. A second attempt to run away would result in the slave having his ears, the tip of his nose and, possibly, his right hand cut off. This practice of mutilation was later discontinued, not for humanitarian reasons, but out of consideration for those who might take offence on seeing the disfigurements. Runaways were often hanged, which was also the sentence meted out to slaves found guilty of theft.

A slave woman found guilty of murdering her baby (on dubious evidence, although she 'confessed' under torture) was sentenced to have both breasts torn from her body with red-hot pincers, after which she was to be burnt. But the Council of Justice reduced the sentence – it felt it would be more merciful for Susanna to be sewn into a sack and dropped from a ship, far out in Table Bay.

For a slave to raise his hand, whether armed or not, against his owner, or against almost any other European, meant slow and painful torture on the wheel – an instrument that disjointed and broke bones, but did not actually kill. A slave woman who set fire to her owner's house was chained to a stake and burnt to death. The remains of executed criminals were usually left on display, until devoured by scavengers, at the place of execution or at the scene where the crime was committed, as a 'warning' to other slaves.

The most severe sentence imposed on a white for the murder of a slave during the Dutch period is thought have been that against burgher Godfried Meyhuijsen who, after beating one of his slaves to death, was taken to the place of execution, blindfolded and made to kneel while the executioner swung a sword above his head to signify that he deserved to die. After that, he was banished for life to Robben Island and all his possessions were confiscated by the Company.

The British took a different view, however. In 1822, Wilhelm Gebhart, 22-year-old son of the Dutch Reformed Church minister in Paarl, appeared before Chief Justice Sir John Truter, charged with the murder of a slave, Joris of Mozambique, whom Gebhart had allegedly beaten to death. A plea of manslaughter was rejected, and Gebhart was found guilty of wilful murder and hanged. Some legends have grown around the Gebhart case, presenting the young man as a victim of a slave conspiracy.

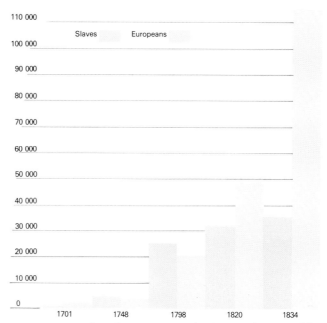

SLAVES *outnumbered Europeans at the Cape at the time of the first British occupation – as this table shows. The number grew throughout the 18th century, overtaking the number of Europeans by 1748.*

Freedom

A free black or *vrijgelaten swarte* was a former slave who had been released from slavery, or 'manumitted'. The first slave to gain freedom was Catharina Anthonis, who was born in Bengal, and liberated because Jan Woutersz from Middelburg wished to marry her – this was in 1656. Soon after the wedding, Woutersz was promoted to the position of supervisor on Robben Island. This was not due to merit, but was rather a way of putting the couple out of sight, for he was later found 'unsatisfactory' and sent to Batavia. A few years later, Jan Stael from Amsterdam married Maria van Bengalen, a union found more acceptable as Maria could speak Dutch and had some knowledge of Christianity.

When a Company official, Abraham Gabbema, was promoted to Batavia, he freed Angela van Bengalen and her three children. She requested, and was granted, a plot of land in what is now Cape Town's Adderley Street and she married the free burgher Arnoldus Basson, by whom she had three sons. Left widowed in 1689 with an inheritance of 6 495 guilders, Angela managed her affairs well – when she died in 1720, her own estate was valued at 14 808 guilders, and she also owned a small farm.

In 1807, shortly after Britain occupied the Cape for the second time, the slave trade was banned. Slaves could still be sold within the colony, but no more slaves were to be imported. Slaves removed from visiting ships were landed at Simon's Town and housed in an area which came to be known as 'Black Town' – before being 'apprenticed' for a number of years to approved employers. The British settlers of 1820 were not permitted to own slaves, and slavery at the Cape was formally abolished on 1 December 1834, although the former slaves were obliged to work for their ex-owners for a further period of four years.

'They lost everything they had'

In a sense the trekboers were southern Africa's first white Africans; poor, nomadic men
whose tenacity and lust for individualism was to take European control
far beyond the confines of Jan van Riebeeck's fledgling colony into the vast hinterland of the Cape.
Khoisan resistance, tough at first, soon crumbled into sporadic outbursts of rebellion,
leaving them as virtual slaves on the land they had once called their own.

IN 1705 THE *landdrost* of Stellenbosch, Johannes Starrenburg, set out for Verlore Vlei (north of Saldanha) hoping to barter trek-oxen from the local Khoikhoi. He had every reason to feel confident: his employers, the Dutch East India Company, had never dealt with these particular Khoikhoi before, which would surely mean that they would have plenty of oxen to spare. In the event, however, he found very few oxen, although he did find something else that disturbed him deeply....

Someone had been there before him.

Writing about his trip, Starrenburg recorded: 'I asked [the Khoikhoi] how it happened that they had so little cattle, seeing that the Honourable Company had never bartered with them, whereat they informed me that a certain freeman, generally called Dronke Gerrit, was come to their kraal a few years previously, accompanied by others, and without any parley fixed on it from all sides, chased out the Hottentots, set fire to their huts, and took away all their cattle, without their knowing for what reason since they had never harmed any of the Dutch. By this they lost everything they had.'

The 'freeman' referred to by Starrenburg was one of a new and increasing band of colonists whose quickest road to fortune lay in simply stealing cattle from the easiest available source – the Khoikhoi. It was, perhaps, an inevitable conclusion to the loosening of the reins of control that the Company had traditionally tried to enforce over its servants. The problem was that, by now, most Europeans at the Cape were no longer servants of the Company. The first of these so-called free burghers had been released from Company service in Van Riebeeck's time, both as an economy measure and in the hope that they would be able to establish themselves as farmers. However, intensive farming, as practised in the Netherlands, did not succeed at the Cape in the early years – because of a shortage of money to establish the farms, and labour to work them. Disillusioned, some of the free burghers returned to Company service. Others hung on to their lands, but turned their attention to livestock that they could graze on the surrounding veld. But because of sparse ground-cover, each animal required a large grazing area, and the wide-ranging grazing pattern made it impractical to collect the animals' droppings for use as manure – an essential part of the intensive farming system.

Meanwhile the Company was growing increasingly impatient: the wheatfields it had hoped to see established around the new settlement could still not even supply the colony's needs, never mind a surplus for its ships. In fact,
it became clear that if it was to stop being a financial burden to the Company, the settlement would have to expand. Most of the intended wheatlands, in any case, were soon given over to grazing.

Opening up the land

When a new Commander, Simon van der Stel, arrived in 1679, he carried with him the Company's orders to extend the colony. He threw open for agricultural settlement an area along the Eerste River, and the first farmers moved in before the year was out. In 1687, when 60 freehold grants, averaging 50 hectares, had been made, the area – known

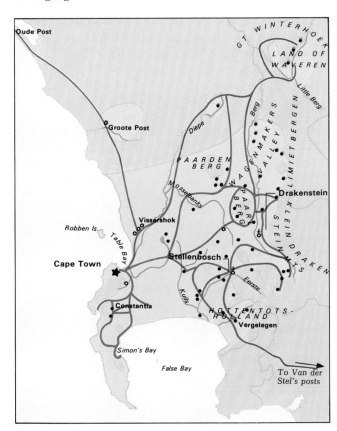

	Extent of the Cape Colony	•	Farms
	Land known to Europeans	○	Company posts
	Wagon tracks	⚲	Church

BY THE END *of the 17th century, Dutch settlers were farming far beyond the original boundaries of the Cape.*

IN OCTOBER 1679, *two weeks after becoming Governor of the Cape, Simon van der Stel founded Van-der-Stel's Bosch (later* Stellenbosch) about 60 kilometres from De Kaap. This is how cartographer E van Stade saw the village in 1710.

as Stellenbosch – was reckoned to be fully occupied, with a fair degree of successful intensive farming taking place. No further grants were made, however, even though only about 20 percent of the available land had been granted. The unallotted area was used by the Company for grazing. The next year, land was granted at Franschhoek to Huguenot refugees from France, and more grants were made at Drakenstein, Paarl, Wagenmakers Valley (later Wellington) and in the 'Land of Waveren' (later Tulbagh). Some 400 farms had been granted in freehold by 1717, when this system of title came to an end.

This continuing seizure of land which the Khoikhoi claimed as their own was not undertaken without considerable resistance. As early as 1655 the Peninsular Khoikhoi had objected to white expansionism, and were to do so again and again over the next half century; and on at least two occasions, in 1659 and 1673, their resistance flared into open warfare. Only in 1672 was an effort made to formalise the land seizures, when purchase transactions were drawn up and signed by two Peninsular chiefs friendly to the Dutch. However, whether they understood exactly what the transactions meant is doubtful: the concept of individual land ownership was unknown to the Khoikhoi. For them, land belonged to the community.

Unfair though this parcelling out of land may have seemed to the Khoikhoi, worse was to follow. The problem was that good agricultural land was at a premium at the Cape, which forced many of the colonists to seek pastoral land further from the Company's immediate area of control; the trekboer was born of necessity. While the Khoikhoi had never been tillers of soil, they were very much pastoral farmers, tending large herds of cattle and sheep. Thus, tragically, the course was set for a collision between white colonist and indigenous Khoikhoi, both of whom were now competing for land, grazing, water and, of course, the cattle themselves.

And as Starrenburg had discovered, for many colonists the quickest way to acquire cattle was to take them from the countless herds belonging to the Khoikhoi. Gradually they were to lose their livestock, their grazing-land, their water rights – in fact everything that had made Khoikhoi soci-

ety unique. By 1740, less than half a century and many skirmishes later, the only Khoikhoi left in the western Cape were working as labourers for the colonists, many of them in conditions of dreadful servitude.

The 'vagabonds'

While publicly making some effort to control the depredations of the trekboers, the Company was, perhaps unintentionally, taking decisions that made control even more difficult. Such a decision was made in 1700 when it opened trading with the Khoikhoi to free burghers, which immediately led to a sharp decline in Khoikhoi cattle ownership and a rapid rise in free burgher cattle ownership. Whether these cattle were bartered or stolen was impossible to detect; after all, how could the Company know, and if it did, what could it do about it? To quote Starrenburg once more, after a 12-day trip between the Berg River and the site of present-day Klawer: 'I have realised with regret how the whole country has been spoilt by the recent freedom of bartering, and the atrocities committed by the vagabonds.' He found two kraals containing 12 captains (chiefs), but few cattle. Deprived of their livelihood, many Khoikhoi were forced to become 'vagabonds' themselves: 'Men who sustained themselves quietly by cattle-breeding, living in peace and contentment divided under their chiefs and kraals, they have nearly all become Bushmen, hunters and brigands, dispersed everywhere between and in the mountains.'

In an effort to control the brigandage, the Company temporarily reimposed its ban on free trading with the Khoikhoi in 1702, while it conducted an investigation into the number of trading expeditions that had taken place. But two years later it lifted the embargo. (The ban was again imposed in 1725, but by that time the damage had largely been done.) A further nail in the Khoikhoi coffin followed when the Company decided to grant the colonists land on loan, known as *leningplaatsen* (loan farms), each with an area of 2 420 hectares and made available for specific periods of time. This was ideal for a stock-farmer, who could lease two such farms, allowing one to lie fallow while grazing his animals on the other. This way, the vegetation would have an opportunity to recover between 'seasons' of usage. This system of loan farms encouraged the way of life of the trekboer, and from legal occupation of registered land, it was a short step to the occupation of land beyond the boundary and what was considered the irksome control of the Company.

Initial outlay on implements, slaves and animals discouraged many burghers from the pursuit of settled agriculture. It was simpler and cheaper to acquire a wagon and the nucleus of a herd, trek beyond the 'mountains of Africa', find a suitable area of watered grazing, and apply to occupy it as a loan farm. Inland, men of the disintegrating Khoikhoi clans were often prepared to work as herders for little more than food and shelter. Unlike the costly slaves, they were accustomed to stock-keeping under local conditions, and soon learnt new skills such as hunting with firearms, at which they became adept. The area of the loan farm was determined only roughly, by walking for 30 minutes from the *opstal* (homestead), first in one direction and then in the opposite direction. Theoretically, such a farm would have a circular boundary but, in practice, it was enough that one man's territory did not trespass on what another burgher regarded as his own.

For a poor man – and most of the burghers were poor – the alternative would be to enter or re-enter the Company's service, or set up business as an artisan. For those who had no skills, however, the only work available at the Cape was that of a labourer. But this would be to reduce oneself almost to the level of the slave. Against this, the glamour of the trek was irresistible. In addition, the decision to open more land to intensive agricultural production had, by the second decade of the 18th century, proved so successful that the local market could not absorb the amount of food being produced, especially wine and wheat. While wheat could be exported to Batavia, there was little demand for Cape wine, which at this time was of very poor quality. Prices slumped accordingly, forcing even more settlers to opt for the life of the trekboer.

By 1717 the Company decided that there were too many farmers at the Cape, and put a halt to further immigration, while continuing to allow the importation of slaves.

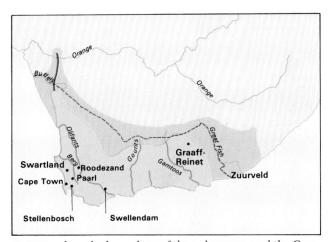

IN 1771, *when the boundary of the colony crossed the Gamtoos River, trekboer colonists and Xhosa began clashing with each other with greater frequency.*

Almost all commercial activity was regulated by monopolies leased from the Company, which also fixed the prices at which it would purchase the burghers' produce. Thus, without the right connections with the men at the top, life on a farm could be very difficult. These difficulties were compounded by the fact that Governor Wilhem van der Stel, his brother Frans and other senior Company officials, were also farmers – and they first made certain that they supplied many of the Company's wants before considering any of the other farmers.

The colony expands

The alternative to trying to beat the system was to leave it. At this time official and unofficial trading and hunting expeditions were probing further and further from De Kaap (Cape Town), reporting on the condition of water and grazing in the interior. In their wake, the Company set up posts in an attempt to administer the new areas: in 1726 at Ziekenhuys on the River Zonder End to the east, and still further east at Rietvlei on the Buffeljachts River in 1734.

Typically, each post consisted of six men under the command of a corporal, and they were intended as way-stops for official expeditions, and also as checks on the activities of wandering burghers, many of whom had adopted the life of the trekboer – moving with their livestock from place to place in search of grazing. Northwards, graziers were probing beyond the Cedarberg towards the present districts of Vanrhynsdorp and Calvinia. The thick forests of the present district of George checked the trekboers' expansion along the coastal plateau in about 1730. They then moved inland, crossing the Outeniqua Mountains at the Attaquas Kloof near Mossel Bay, where the farm Hagel Kraal was described as the most easterly 'outpost of Christianity in Africa'. Once in the Langkloof, the trekboers continued eastwards, on through the Little Karoo.

Those who had trekked north from De Kaap reached the fringes of arid Namaqualand, and turned east through the Bokkeveld, skirted the Great Karoo and joined those who had travelled along the southern coast at Camdeboo, near the site of the present town of Graaff-Reinet on the Sundays River. This union took place in about 1770, after which the advance to the east continued, with a small number of trekboers gradually making their way northwards to reach the Orange River by 1778.

Attempts at control

Attempts by the authorities to control the trekboers were hampered by the enormous distances, lack of roads and a shortage of officials. Even when the settlement was still relatively small, it was difficult for the authorities at De Kaap to enforce border control. No formal border had actually been defined, and farmers regularly sent their flocks and herds, often under the care of Khoikhoi labourers, far beyond the settled areas in search of grazing. They were not scientific graziers, and treated the land harshly. In the Swellendam district, overgrazing led to the proliferation of short, bushy plants that the animals would not eat and, after the Camdeboo had been occupied for fewer than 10 years, the grazing had so deteriorated that it was thought the area would have to be abandoned.

BARON GUSTAV VAN IMHOFF *(above) inspected the Cape in 1743.*
THE ONLY PORTRAIT *positively identified as being that of Simon van der Stel disappeared in 1934. However, this one (left) is thought to be of him.*

The trekboer rarely bothered to apply for the right to occupy a *leningplaats*, causing a loss in Company revenue that was compounded by his neglect to pay tax on his livestock. Where the trekboer was within the reach of the Company's law, misleading figures would be filled in on the annual returns on which taxes were calculated. In 1732 a *placaat* (proclamation) was published to express the Company's concern at this deceit, and also to announce that the annual sum payable for a *leningplaats* would henceforth be doubled, and fixed at 24 rix-dollars. The quitrent system was introduced, which guaranteed the farmer occupation of land for at least 15 years, after which, if the land reverted to the Company, he would be paid the value of all fixed improvements, such as dwellings or stables. Although this gave the burgher greater security than before, it still failed to discourage trekking, which was rapidly becoming a way of life.

The trekboer forced the pace of white expansion at the Cape in the 18th century by obliging the Company to set up new administrative posts ever further from De Kaap, in an attempt to ensure that its laws were adhered to, and its taxes paid. Thus, in 1743 a new district was established at Swellendam, with its eastern border vaguely defined as 'where the power of the Honourable Company ends'. This was done at the instigation of Baron Gustav van Imhoff, Governor-General of the Dutch East Indies, who also ordered that churches for the remote and itinerant burghers be built at Swartland (Malmesbury) and Roodezand (Tulbagh). He was greatly concerned at what he regarded as the moral deterioration of the trekboers, and by the fact that they were able to wander beyond the border without check. (In 1734 the Great Brak River, east of Mossel Bay, had been proclaimed as the eastern boundary, but by then, trekkers were already in the vicinity of the Gamtoos River.)

Another of Van Imhoff's bids to end the inclination to trek was to change the land laws. To tempt families to settle permanently, he proposed that, for a maximum payment of 200 rix-dollars, a burgher might convert 50 hectares of his *leningplaats* to freehold property, paying only a proportion of the former rental on the remainder. On those

who had succumbed to the *trekgees* (wanderlust), this new offer had no effect.

As the trekboers moved east, so the boundary of the colony followed them until, by 1778, it was placed at the Great Fish River. In the process, land occupied by another people – the Xhosa – was annexed. As early as 1702 a cattle-gathering expedition had entered Xhosa territory and the resultant clash had left one Dutchman and an unknown number of Xhosa dead. Since then, illicit trade between colonists and Xhosa had been almost continuous. In 1785, with many trekboers already living side by side with Xhosa stock-owners in the Zuurveld, a new district, Graaff-Reinet, was proclaimed in order to place the frontier under closer Company supervision.

The Khoisan fight back
As the trekboers fanned out ever deeper into the interior, so the Khoikhoi and San fell back before them; if not fighting every bit of the way, then at least putting up considerable resistance. In the end, however, the superior mobility, weaponry and sheer ruthlessness of the invaders ensured the defeat of the Khoikhoi and the virtual extermination of the San. As the trekboers' livestock destroyed the grazing, so the game animals – the San's source of meat – moved away, and the San took to raiding the invading herds. There were killings on both sides but, mounted and possessing firearms, the trekboer had a great advantage, although in some areas it was the San who triumphed, albeit temporarily. Adult San of both sexes were shot, and captured children were reared as servants. The Khoikhoi adapted more easily, although no less happily. Their experience of pastoral farming made them useful as servants – and many went on to take up service with the whites, sometimes keeping herds of their own, while others were absorbed into trekboer households.

It became more and more difficult to differentiate between Khoikhoi and San due to the fact that, in many ways, the difference lay not so much in appearance as in lifestyle. The Khoikhoi regarded themselves as superior to the San because they owned and reared cattle. Once the

White pastoralists: the trekboer way of life

In the early 1700s, with a heavily over-traded Cape offering diminishing employment and farming opportunities for its growing white population, dozens of disillusioned colonists began seeking a living beyond the arable lands of the south-western Cape.

These trekboers, as they called themselves, were the surplus people of a Cape economy which revolved almost entirely around the maize and wine industries (controlled by a rich and influential clique of farmers).

Poor and landless, and therefore unable to compete with this landed 'gentry', the majority of early trekboers were men who were convinced that their only hope of survival lay in moving far beyond the jurisdiction of what they perceived to be an uncaring Cape bureaucracy.

Yet once the trek had gathered momentum, the majority of participants quickly demonstrated that their ambitions were not confined to subsistence farming: by bartering with – but more often stealing from – the indigenous people whose paths they crossed, many trekboers built up extensive herds of livestock. Certainly, by the middle of the 18th century, the trekboer, despite a reputation for 'independence' and 'defiance of authority', was significantly integrated into the Cape economy, satisfying much of the colony's meat needs in return for increasing amounts of essentials.

And yet, for all this, the trekboer lived a simple life: on his grazing-land – whether it was an official *leningplaats* or not – his home was a simple hut with walls of mud, roofed with reeds. Some did not bother to create even this flimsy symbol of permanence, but lived in their wagons, and under canvas awnings alongside. With Khoisan servants to tend their flocks and herds, the men were free to go hunting, an occupation that provided them with ivory and skins for barter on rare visits to town. Wives and servants tended small gardens that produced vegetables just sufficient for the household's needs.

Perhaps once a year the trekboer and his family would make the journey to De Kaap – to trade, sell animals, have children baptised and to stock up on essentials. These included lead and gunpowder, coffee, tea and sugar.

This isolated and monotonous existence presented few opportunities for intellectual advancement or even basic education. If he could afford it, a trekboer might hire an itinerant *meester* (schoolmaster) to teach his children. The *meester* would almost certainly be unqualified, and probably a deserter from a ship or from the Company's service. The trekboer developed, in general, as a highly individual personality, to whom any matter that did not concern him directly was of little importance,

although most were extremely hospitable to white travellers.

Although his capital outlay and operating costs were low, the trekboer's prosperity in relation to the fixed-domicile cultivator declined steadily throughout the 18th century. In the 1730s the average value of a trekboer's estate had been 40 percent that of an average cultivator's estate, but by 1780 it had dropped to less than 12 percent. The cultivator's economy differed from that of the trekboer, in that they were close to their markets (De Kaap and the shipping) and also, because a major source of opposition – farming by the Company – came to an end in 1705. They were able, too, to profit from the trading that resulted from the appearance of an unusually large fleet, or major increases in the garrison – circumstances from which the trekboer was becoming increasingly far removed. For the trekboers, conditions had changed for the worse in that, whereas at the start of the century their numbers were relatively low and the grazing area apparently limitless, as the numbers of trekboers and livestock increased, so pressure on the land increased as grazing was over-utilised. Putting nothing back into the land, the trekboer took ever-smaller rewards, while his voluntary withdrawal from society developed him into a person vastly different from the burgher of De Kaap.

THE INTERIOR *of a trekboer tent (below) was drawn by artist Charles Bell in 1835, more than a century after the emergence of the first wandering white families. The spartan existence that life in the southern African veld imposed was also the theme of the painting (right) by Samuel Daniell.*

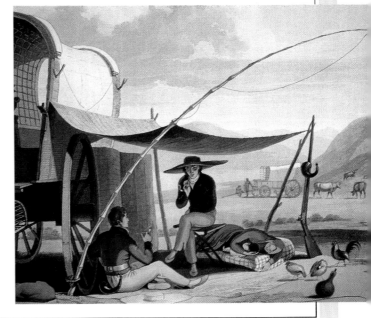

white man had stolen their cattle, however, they were often forced into living like the San – by hunting and gathering food. For this reason the two are often referred to simply as 'Khoisan'. In any case, it had always been difficult to separate the two geographically; perhaps because the Khoikhoi had never been strong enough to expel the San from their grazing areas.

Signs of rebellion came in 1701 when a group of 'Ubikwase Hottentots' stole 40 cattle belonging to a Riebeeck Kasteel farmer, Gerrit Cloete, wounding a herder in the process, and going on to attack the Company's post in the nearby Land of Waveren. This was followed by an attack on the Berg River post which netted the raiders a further 137 cattle. In spite of punitive raids against the Khoisan by both individual farmers and Company officers, sporadic raids against white farmers continued until 1715.

It was in this year that trouble broke out at Saldanha Bay when Pieter Willemsj lost 32 cattle and 700 sheep which he and a party of free burghers had just taken from a Khoisan kraal. Immediately a commando set off in pursuit, following the Khoisan for two-and-a-half days before finding six dead cattle, 200 dead sheep and two dead men, a Khoisan and a slave. That same year two other farmers in the Witzenberg lost 136 cattle and 500 sheep; while in a raid on another farm, the Khoisan were said to have killed two slaves. By now thoroughly alarmed, the farmers took to sleeping with guns in their hands.

Conflict escalates

Into this extraordinary mix of Khoikhoi, San and colonist there now stepped a new force: bands of freebooters made up of Company deserters, escaped slaves and rough adventurers who roamed the south-western Cape raiding the herds of the Khoisan or colonist as the opportunity arose. Many of these groups found refuge in the camps of the Khoisan, and helped strengthen the resistance of these indigenous people to the trekboers.

A major clash between the colonists and the Khoisan took place in 1728 after cattle had been stolen from Jan Volck's farm at Lange Valley. A commando made up of local farmers finally caught up with the cattle – and a force of 300 'Bushmen', who answered a demand for their return with arrows and spears. One farmer was wounded by an arrow in the foot, while 12 Khoisan were killed as the commandos opened fire. The rest fled, leaving the farmers to seize both the 23 stolen cattle and 62 belonging to the Khoisan. Appeals to the Company for the return of these cattle failed through lack of evidence.

Three years later a trekboer commando tracked down a group of Khoisan suspected of having stolen 33 cattle from a farmer named Hans Jürgen Potgieter. Once again, the Khoisan let fly their arrows – and six of them died as the trekboers returned the fire with lead. Ten cattle were recovered, and a woman and three children captured – the first recorded instance of a practice that was later to become widespread: the taking of women and children into forced labour. As the trekboers withdrew with their cattle and captives, a defiant voice rang out from the safety of a krans: 'We Bushmen have still more people, and will not leave the Dutch in peace.'

A tale of broken promises

The 'Bushmen' were as good as their word, and sporadic resistance continued, with various alliances being struck and broken between Khoisan and trekboers. Often those who attacked the trekboers had previously worked for them as servants – frequently because of broken promises.

It was just such a broken promise that led in 1739 to the most serious outbreak of violence to date when a party of trekboers and their Khoisan servants raided a Nama settlement in the north-west of the colony. The trekboers had promised the Khoisan a share of the spoils, but when the day came for sharing out the cattle, the trekboers reneged on their promise, and handed out the looted cattle to their neighbours around Piketberg. The Khoisan, led by a man named Swartebooij, complained to the Company's Council of Policy, which was both alarmed at the news of the expedition against the Nama and sympathetic to Swartebooij's complaint. However, when the council attempted to confiscate the stolen cattle, they were quickly forced to back down: open rebellion was prevented only by the restoration to the trekboers of cattle that had already been recovered and handed to Swartebooij and his followers.

The result was an immediate attack on farms in the Olifants River and Bokkeveld areas. Badly frightened, the council took the cynical step of offering a pardon to the trekboers who had taken part in the Nama raid, provided they joined a commando against the disaffected Khoisan – their wronged servants. All pretence of justice was forgotten as the commando went into action, cornering a group of Khoisan in a cave in the Bokkeveld. This time resistance was fierce, and a hail of poisoned arrows sent the trekboers scuttling for cover before they retreated with several captured cattle. More raids followed, farms were burnt and hundreds of cattle and sheep stolen, and the council realised that it would have to commit regular troops to the field in support of the commandos.

In August commandos set out northwards and westwards while regular troops guarded the Olifants River. Within a few weeks they had taken a terrible revenge: several kraals had been attacked, more than 100 Khoisan killed and hundreds of cattle taken. By the end of September the council felt confident enough to recall its troops. Swartebooij was shot dead together with 30 or 40 of his followers during a skirmish on 2 October. His son Titus was cornered and shot shortly afterwards, and the last flicker of resistance in the south-west Cape was snuffed out.

As the trekboers moved ever further from the Cape, conflict flared again and again. In 1754 bosjesmans hottentoten were reported to have raided farms in the Voorste and Agterste Roggeveld; while resistance reached a fever pitch in the mid-1770s along the northern frontier, north of the Sneeuberge. In many ways this was almost the last stand of the Khoisan; squeezed between colonists to the west and the Xhosa in the east, they resisted desperately. Not only were cattle stolen, but those that could not be driven off were killed, and farmhouses burnt to the ground. Settler reprisals were swift and brutal, as the entire frontier area took up arms. Despite appalling losses, some Khoisan fought on for years, and raids against white farms continued until the end of the century.

The tavern of the seas

The 17th century had been the golden age of the Netherlands, with the thrusting fingers of expansionism prying loose the treasures of far-flung lands. Thus the Cape – the ideal halfway station on the rich East trade route – had been settled under the Dutch East India Company.

By the mid-18th century, however, Dutch world influence was on the wane, buffeted by other rising European powers. Established as it had been by commercial enterprise, the Cape Town of shopkeepers and innkeepers, too, felt the chill of economic recession, but by then the settlement had begun to assert an independent identity.

The basis of Cape Town's economy was its situation between two 'trade routes': that is, agricultural produce was bought from the rural interior and sold to ships in port; and ship freight was in turn sold to the rural community. The location of the Company's administration here meant an additional circulation of money in the economy.

This ruling and mercantile class could be said to represent 'respectable' society, underpinned of necessity by a working class – generally slave – sub-culture. Broadly, slave occupations could be classified into household, productive (notably fishing and craftsmanship) and retail (mainly hawking) activities. At best, these classes rubbed along together, but always with the dictates of the upper class handed down to the lower.

For the upper class, a major unifying factor was the predominant Dutch Reformed Church, under Company protection. Not only was Calvinism the only religion tolerated, but it also formed the basis of all education, limited until the end of the century to primary level.

So Cape Town was something of an intellectual backwater. There was no newspaper – not even a government printing press – and even the better educated inhabitants seemed to visitors rather insular. A shining exception proved to be Governor Ryk Tulbagh, and aptly, during his term of office (1751-71), the first library was founded.

Tulbagh did much to promote scientific curiosity, establishing a plant and animal collection in the Company's gardens. As visitor William Hickey enthused: 'In the mornings and evenings we walked in the Company's gardens, which are well stocked with curious plants, the choicest fruits and vegetables. There is also the finest menagerie in the world, in which are collected . . . animals and birds of every quarter of the globe.'

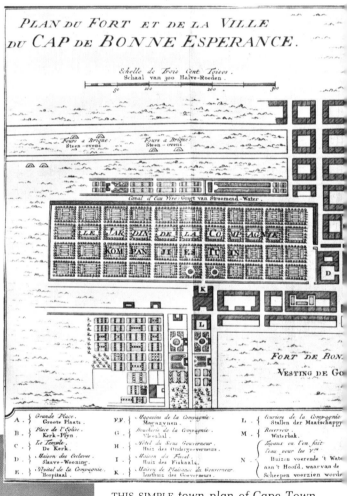

THIS SIMPLE *town plan of Cape Town (above) features the Castle on the far right and the Company's gardens on the left, as well as the Slave Lodge (D) (the town's most renowned brothel) and Greenmarket Square (A).*
A WATERCOLOUR *of Parade Plein (left) in 1779 by Samuel Davis shows the entrance to the Castle on the right.*

This was, in fact, one of the few public entertainments to be had. Most burghers contented themselves with exchanging visits for their amusement. In one another's homes they would pass their time in idle conversation or cardplaying, or perhaps indulge in musical evenings.

Music was a great leveller, for it was universally loved and among the most highly valued of the slave skills. Not only did the slave orchestras excel at instruments such as the violin, flute, trumpet and harp, but they and the local Khoikhoi introduced new instruments and sounds to traditional European music: the four-stringed plucked *ramkie* was brought to the Cape by Malabar slaves, while the Khoikhoi created a 'seaweed trumpet' of kelp.

The thread of music ran alike through society balls, slave quarter feasts, and numerous taverns to which large numbers of burghers would repair for a musical interlude.

Taverns were the setting for more riotous entertainment, too. Besides the respectable inns were those where rough-and-ready sailors and soldiers would gather to celebrate their safe arrival at the Cape after a long and arduous voyage or to prepare themselves for the moment the kettledrums would signal their departure.

Completing an altogether livelier picture of Cape Town were the pleasures of prostitution and of gambling, either at gaming houses or anywhere men met with something to bet on a couple of fighting cocks.

JOHANNES RACH *painted this lively watercolour (above) of Greenmarket Square in 1764, showing the Old Town House and other local architecture, vegetable sellers, a chained prisoner under escort and a sedan chair carried by uniformed servants.*
'THE WRECK OF THE VISCH' *(below) in 1740 depicts Cape Town inhabitants gathering to witness one of the many shipwrecks off the treacherous Cape coast.*

A settled people

The pattern of settlement of those Africans who spoke Bantu languages familiar to us today was already fairly well established by the beginning of the 17th century, with Nguni people occupying Natal, Transkei and Ciskei, and Sotho groups spread widely across the Transvaal, Orange Free State and Lesotho. These societies were never static, however, as chiefdoms formed, coalesced, fell apart, and finally joined again in ever larger and stronger alliances to meet new threats or to share dwindling resources.

THE WORD 'Bantu' has an unhappy history in South Africa, being linked for generations to official harassment of 'Bantu' people by departments such as 'Bantu Affairs' and documents to control 'Bantu labour'. As a result the word has taken on a nasty political connotation that has all but removed it from daily circulation. However, there is one area where the word 'Bantu' simply cannot be replaced by any other, and that is in the area of language. 'Bantu', which means 'people', is the scientific name for the language group to which all South African Africans, except the Khoisan, belong, and is the simplest way for historians to distinguish between those indigenous inhabitants who spoke the Khoisan languages and those who did not.

The Bantu-speakers share a common heritage with nearly 100-million Africans speaking some 300 languages over a wide area of southern and central Africa. No one is exactly certain where this group originated, but it is thought to

have been between the Niger and the Congo deltas. What is known is that the language spread rapidly and had established itself in the Transvaal and Natal by 300 AD, and in the Transkei area by 700 AD.

By the time the first Portuguese navigators were calling at our shores, two main language groups had emerged – the Nguni and the Sotho – as had two smaller groups – the Venda and the Tsonga. Among the Nguni were Xhosa, Thembu, Mpondo, Mpondomise, Mfengu, Ndebele, Bomvana and the people living in what became Natal and Zululand. The Sotho group may be divided into southern Sotho (Basotho), northern Sotho (Pedi and Lobedu) and western Sotho (Tswana).

Land was freely available up until the end of the 18th century, although the Khoisan still hunted over vast areas of the interior. Tensions created by overcrowding and overgrazing were largely unknown, and the fierce wars of conquest that would dominate events in the region lay in

---

Just how different?

If there is one thing upon which South African historians agree, it is that they cannot agree on the origins or the naming of the Bantu-speaking inhabitants of southern Africa.

At the root of the problem is, of course, the fact that no written records were kept until the arrival of the Europeans, and it was not to be until late in the 19th century that any serious attempt was made at collecting evidence about African settlement and movements before the arrival of the white man.

Archaeological evidence has put paid to the long-cherished view that the Bantu-speakers arrived in southern Africa at more or less the same time as the white man, but that still leaves the problem of how to describe the different groups and the use of names such as 'Nguni' and 'Sotho'. And are their sub-groups really so different as to justify the 'nation' status urged on them by the

'retribalisation' policies of recent South African governments?

Many historians – and the people themselves – generally think not. The term 'Nguni', for example, which is generally used to describe Zulu- and Xhosa-speaking people, became fashionable in academic circles only after the publication in 1929 of a book entitled 'Olden Times in Zululand and Natal' by A T Bryant, a missionary who had collected oral traditions in the area.

However, the terms are useful when indicating language differences. The Nguni languages, Zulu and Xhosa, show marked similarities, although Xhosa is especially noted for its 'clicks', probably acquired from the Khoisan; while the Sotho languages, northern Sotho, southern Sotho and western Sotho, can also be grouped together. There are also some differences in the way Sotho and Nguni settlements evolved.

Nguni people tended to be widely scattered in homesteads and villages, while the Sotho lived in more concentrated settlements.

Complicating the situation is the obsession by successive governments with ethnic identity, which has tended to seek out and magnify differences in pursuit of the 'homelands' policy. This has led at least one angry historian to conclude that the 'Nguni' label serves to 'impose a spurious primordial ethnic unity on the African people of the eastern seaboard of South Africa'.

Despite these misgivings, most historians have continued to use the names simply because it is difficult to trace the movements and settlement patterns of the Bantu-language speakers without them, and we have done the same. It is important to remember, however, that similarities between the groups far outweigh differences.

the future. But with white colonists moving eastwards into Xhosa territory in the Cape, and population pressures building up in the area known today as Natal, this situation could not last.

These African societies were, in the main, fairly similar. Whether they existed by gathering, hunting, the keeping of stock or by planting, all flourished or declined at the whim of nature, over whose forces they had little control. They were subsistence farmers, producing just enough to meet their own needs, as opposed to commercial farmers who produce primarily to sell. Grains were stored in pits, baskets, or in woven structures raised above the ground. Storage techniques were imperfect, however, and there was usually a period of hardship before the next harvest. Cultivation was essentially the work of the women, although men assisted with the heavy work, and a system of mutual assistance – along the lines of a co-operative – often applied, especially where there were ties of kinship.

Some were specialists, such as the miners who toiled for iron ore or for ochre, or the smiths who smelted the ore and worked it to produce the blade of a hoe or the razor-

sharp point of a spear. Others tanned skins for clothing and night covering, achieving a softness and durability that eluded the woven fibres of Europe.

Almost all engaged in trade. Those who had no surplus to offer also took part, as middlemen or relay stations along the extended trade routes. It was the chief's responsibility to ensure that goods were distributed or acquired for the maximum benefit of his community. Successful distribution within the community, as well as external trade, were likely to attract new members, thereby strengthening both the chiefdom and the personal authority of the chief.

The extended family was the basic social unit in African life, but around this relatively calm and constant centre whirled forces of change and realignment. Kinship was important, although its authority applied only to members of the particular family. Nguni lineages, people claiming a common ancestor, formed clans that were socially ranked according to the directness of the senior member's kinship with the ancestor. Marriage between relatives was not allowed among the Nguni, but marriages within the clan – especially between first cousins – were the

TOWARDS THE END *of the 18th century, African chiefdoms were undisputed masters of the central and eastern parts of southern Africa. But soon a series of wars among different groups would break down and scatter many established societies, leaving them totally unprepared for a foe advancing from the south: the white man.*

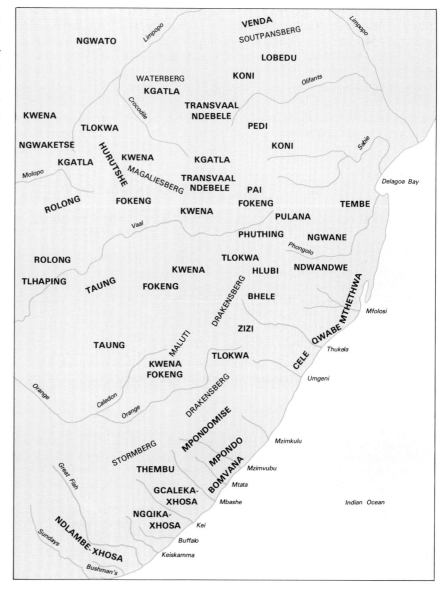

SOME THINGS *never change, as this contemporary picture (right) of a Xhosa woman grinding maize shows. Two centuries ago, women prepared grain the same way (above).*

favoured union among the Sotho. Marriage was a contract between families, rather than individuals, and was sealed by the transfer of bride-wealth from the groom's family to that of the bride. Bride-wealth was paid in cattle but, especially among the Tsonga and Venda, iron hoes were sometimes given instead. Only after payment of the bride-wealth did children of the marriage legally belong to their father's lineage. Bride-wealth had to be paid for each wife, so polygamy, although allowed, was the privilege of the wealthy only. Marriage was sometimes used to create or maintain a political alliance.

Southern Nguni

For hundreds of years the broad coastal strip south of what is now Natal, Transkei and Ciskei was the home of the southern Nguni, of whom the Xhosa, Mpondo, Mpondomise, Bomvana and Thembu were the most prominent groups. In the early 19th century they were joined by the Bhaca and Mfengu, who had fled the rampaging Zulu armies of Shaka in Natal.

Nguni economy was based on the keeping of herds, hunting and cultivation of the 'slash-and-burn' type. The staple crop was sorghum, although maize was observed growing in Transkei by shipwrecked Europeans in 1635. Added to these were melons, beans, bananas, sugar cane, tobacco and dagga. Some clans, in addition to cattle, also kept sheep, goats and poultry. Hunting produced not only food, but also materials for clothing and trade articles, such as ivory. They made pottery and knew how to mine and work iron.

Trade with other areas was important, especially for iron and copper (used for implements and decoration), and beads. All of these had entered the region from the northeast, but after the establishment of the white settlement at the Cape the colony eventually became the major supplier. Khoikhoi, especially members of the Chainouqua chiefdom, played an important part as middlemen in the Xhosa-Cape trade, while by the mid-17th century the Xhosa dominated most of the Khoikhoi groups in the eastern Cape. The word 'Xhosa' is derived from the Khoikhoi word meaning

'to destroy', and Xhosa is the only Bantu language to contain a significant number of the clicks which are so characteristic of the Khoisan languages. This suggests a long association with the Khoikhoi, some groups of whom were absorbed into Xhosa society. Other Khoikhoi associated with the Xhosa as clients, offering their hunting skills or labour in return for food and Xhosa protection.

In the 17th century there were many small chiefdoms, made up of clans, most of whose males could claim descent from a common ancestor. In Xhosa society, however, there was always a tendency for chiefdoms to divide along the lines of the descendants of the Great Wife, and those of the wife of the right-hand house. The Great Wife, who often married the chief late in his life, produced the heir, whose oldest half-brother, by the first-married wife of the right-hand house, sometimes resented this line of succession. Often, though, a son of the right-hand house acted as regent during the minority of the heir, exercising authority as though he were chief.

The basis of authority was the household, of which a number together formed the chiefdom. Land rights were vested in the chief, who allocated land to the homesteads for cultivation. Among the Xhosa the highest level of authority was the paramount chief, though for long his position was of ritual significance only. While there was abundant fertile and well-watered land, an extended family or lineage could move away when pressures of population or politics built up. Rather than consolidation, there was a tendency towards decentralisation.

Strife among the Xhosa

However, a degree of Xhosa political unity was achieved in the first half of the 17th century by Tshawe who, with the aid of the Mpondomise, overthrew his half-brother, Cira, to seize the paramountcy. The next distinguished chief was Phalo, who ruled from about 1730 until his death in 1775. Two of his sons, Rharhabe and Gcaleka, each claimed during their father's lifetime to be his successor. The dispute led to war, to the defeat of Rharhabe who moved west of the Kei River, and to a rift in the Xhosa.

IN 1803, *respected Dutch official Ludwig Alberti dropped out of public life in order to make a study of the Zuurveld Xhosa. The knowledge he gained formed the basis of a book, as well as a series of aquatints that depicted African life. The picture (left) is entitled 'View of a Kaffir homestead, on the south coast of Africa'.*

Gcaleka, who died in 1778, was succeeded by the ineffectual Khawuta who, although in theory the paramount chief of all the Xhosa, ruled only the Gcaleka section. He married the daughter of a minor Thembu chieftain and generally lowered esteem for royalty by appointing commoners to positions of great authority. Rharhabe, meanwhile, was consolidating his power across the Kei preparatory to attacking Khawuta, which he did without achieving a decisive result. He died later in a clash with the Thembu. With his heir, Mlawu, having being killed in the same battle, the succession fell to Mlawu's son, Ngqika. But because Ngqika was only a minor, his uncle, Ndlambe, acted as regent and greatly built up Rharhabe power by creating tensions and even open hostility between other chiefdoms and the frontier Dutch. It appears that Ndlambe was reluctant to relinquish his position of power when Ngqika attained his majority, and the two clashed in 1795. Although Ndlambe obtained help from the Gcaleka, he was defeated and taken prisoner. Stripped of his former power, he was allowed to live on at Ngqika's Great Place on the Tyhume River.

By the end of the 18th century Ngqika was strongly placed to contend for the paramountcy, but in 1800 Ndlambe escaped into the Cape Colony with many adherents. To the east, the Gcaleka were gathering strength and, under Hintsa, were to pose a threat to Ngqika who, pressed on the west by Ndlambe, was obliged to seek an alliance with the white colonists (see page 72).

Northern Nguni
Like that of the southern Nguni, the territory occupied by the northern Nguni was settled by small chiefdoms until about midway through the 18th century, when the pattern began to change and four dominant groups emerged.

The first of these were the Dlamini, the royal line of the Ngwane, who had lived around Delagoa Bay for several centuries until, in the 18th century, they moved south under pressure from the Tembe. The Dlamini settled among other chiefdoms, which they conquered and incorporated, north of the Phongola River.

The second group were the powerful Ndwandwe, who lived between the Phongola and Black Mfolosi rivers, straddling the trade route from the coast to the interior, and subjugated the surrounding chiefdoms.

The third were the Mthethwa, who were settled between the Mfolosi and Mhlatuze rivers and were ruled over by Jobe, whose eldest son, Dingiswayo – according to legend – was forced into exile after plotting with his brothers to kill their father. The place of exile is unknown, but he is said to have returned, after his father's death at the end of the 18th century, on horseback and carrying a firearm. The Mthethwa dominated their area even before the return of Dingiswayo, which was to signal their rise to even greater prominence.

The fourth and most southerly dominant northern Nguni group were the Qwabe, who had settled in the Ngoye hills between the Mhlatuze and Thukela rivers in the 16th century, rising to power in the next century under the leadership of Kuzwayo.

Although tensions developed between the Qwabe and the Mthethwa and, in the north, the Ngwane and the Ndwandwe, an uneasy peace prevailed for the remainder of the 18th century. Consolidation as well as conflict were influenced by the importance of trade through Delagoa Bay, which had probably been conducted between the Portuguese and the northern Nguni since the 16th century. The principal export was ivory, exchanged, in the main, for beads and metals, especially brass. As representatives of other European countries competed in the ivory trade, increased demand pushed up the price, thus making control of the trade even more important to the African suppliers. It is thought that, to protect their interests, smaller chiefdoms consolidated to form larger, more powerful groups, among the earliest of which were the Ngwane and Ndwandwe. The need to control elephant hunting led to the calling up of active men in a system called *amabutho*, a process that Shaka was able to draw on to form the basis of the later Zulu army.

Severe droughts towards the end of the 18th century led to increased competition for available water sources, especially those close to suitable grazing. This heightened inter-group tensions and made it unlikely that dissident factions would split from the main groups. Around the same time, European demand for ivory dropped sharply. To maintain consolidation, and their own positions as distributors of foreign wealth – which was what attracted their supporters in the first place – chiefs were forced to substitute cattle as the article of trade. Since cattle were the visible source of wealth and respect, a chief could not take away those of his own people, so the *amabutho*, already conveniently called into service as hunters, were diverted to cattle-raiding. The stage was being set for alliances and enmities from which, in the new century, would emerge the Zulu kingdom.

The northern Sotho (Pedi and Lobedu)

The principal group among the northern Sotho were the Pedi, a branch of the iron-working Kgatla people who, in the mid-17th century, moved east from the vicinity of present-day Pretoria and settled below the Leolu Mountains in the Steelpoort River valley. By judicious marriage, as well as by conquest they absorbed those clans already living in the vicinity. Their cattle wealth and control of the important iron industry attracted clients who, in time, were brought within the evolving Pedi statehood. Another reason for the rise to prominence of the Pedi was their position astride the trade route from Delagoa Bay to their former homeland and even further west. At the coast, the Tsonga traded with the Portuguese, and then retraded with the Pedi, who acted as brokers for the clans to the west and at Phalaborwa.

To maintain control of this commercial enterprise, it was necessary for the Pedi to have strong, centralised control, a practice at variance with the more usual Sotho tendency to split up and establish numerous minor chiefdoms. The need for centralisation grew even stronger as the ivory trade declined and cattle raiding took its place – to ensure that the wealth lost through the trading recession was regained elsewhere. By the end of the 18th century,

although full Pedi statehood had not yet been achieved, control was vested in the Maroteng chiefdom at the head of a loose confederation of subordinate chiefdoms.

Each chiefdom consisted of a village that might have a population of between 50 and 5 000 people, but the Maroteng paramount was the one who controlled land access and usage. By giving close female relatives as brides to the subordinate chiefs and by assisting struggling chiefdoms – through the loan of cattle, for instance – the paramount formed bonds through family connection as well as the gratitude that could be expected to express itself as loyalty. The Pedi, because of this movement towards unification, would be better able than most to withstand the assaults that lay ahead.

A much smaller group, in the north-eastern Transvaal, were the Lobedu, whose hereditary leaders had come from Zimbabwe when a powerful ruler fled south with some supporters, bringing with her the secrets of rain-making. This power attracted adherents from a number of chiefdoms, mainly Sotho, and, despite disagreements over succession, the new group did not split up but lived in fairly inaccessible country near the present town of Duiwelskloof.

Southern Sotho (Basotho)

The country now known as Lesotho has probably been occupied by southern Sotho people, called the Basotho, since the 16th century. Many chiefdoms descended from the Fokeng lineage occupied land to the south-east of the Caledon River, while Kwena descendants – also split into numerous chiefdoms – were scattered around the upper reaches of the Caledon River. In the south-east of what is now the Orange Free State were yet more scattered chiefdoms, those of the Phuthing and Tlokwa.

The southern Sotho social and political structure was characterised by a tendency for groups to split up, with branches moving away to establish new villages, usually of between 50 and 100 inhabitants. Some of the new chiefdoms were independent, refusing to recognise the overlordship of the group from which they had separated. The

THIS IS HOW *the first white visitors saw the Tlhaping village of Dithakong (left) in 1801.*

MANY OF THE EARLY *contacts between Africans and whites were made at trading posts (such as below), where ivory was eagerly sought by Europeans.*

SEPARATING *the grain from the chaff – Basotho style.*

A FAMILIAR *beehive-shaped Basotho house.*

tendency to split and scatter may have been influenced by factors such as poor grazing, which would necessitate moving part of the herds to some other place where, in due course, a new chiefdom arose. This was feasible only so long as unclaimed land was available, which was still the situation by the end of the 18th century; by that time there was also some inclination towards a reversal of the tendency to separate. The reasons for this probably lie in control of the trade with Delagoa Bay to the east, and with the Tswana to the west: a chief who was able to control this trade attracted more followers. Also, as the population grew, there were fewer suitable areas in which newly detached groups could settle, and so they often attached themselves to a different leadership.

The western Sotho (Tswana)

Archaeological evidence shows that people built with stone along the Witwatersrand centuries ago, and oral tradition says that among them, in the 15th century, were the people of the chief Masilo. About this time his lineage split, to produce the Hurutshe and Kwena chiefdoms. Later divisions produced the Ngwaketse, Ngwato, Kgatla, Tlokwa, Rolong and Tlhaping.

The basis of western Sotho society was the family, of which several went to make up a ward, under the authority of a hereditary headman, within the settlement. The headmen formed an advisory council under the chief, whose power was great, although not absolute. The chief regulated trade and agricultural activities and administered the law. The ward was rarely a single topographical unit (except when on its own it comprised the village), as farmland and grazing areas were separated – sometimes by long distances – from the residential area, which was often surrounded by a stone wall. Unlike other Sotho settlements, the average Tswana settlement was large and densely populated. The likeliest reason for this is the relative aridity of the area, which includes part of the Kalahari semi-desert where sources of permanent water are scarce.

Apart from trade, the economy depended on the keeping of cattle, sheep and goats and on the production of crops such as tobacco, dagga, sorghum and melons. The food supply was supplemented by hunting and the setting of traps, and it is known that the Tlhaping mined and worked iron.

Despite their common ancestry, Tswana chiefdoms were frequently at war with one another and, overall, failed to achieve any sort of political unity. The Hurutshe, based near present-day Rustenburg, were constantly at war with the Kwena and their offshoot, the Ngwaketse, late in the 18th century. Warfare was so widespread, and probably aggravated by the two decades of drought that began in 1790, that it is thought that most chiefdoms lost their leaders in battle.

The Venda and Tsonga

In the far northern Transvaal were the Venda, relatively recently arrived from north of the Limpopo. Although their original settlement was cohesive under a single chieftain, disagreements over succession had led to members of the royal house breaking away with their respective followers and establishing themselves elsewhere. The southward advance of the Venda was halted by contact with the Sotho and Tsonga, and they retreated to the security of the Soutpansberg range.

The Tsonga, who occupied the coastal strip from Kosi Bay to the Sabi River, were probably one of the first southern African communities to make contact with European traders at the end of the 15th century. Ideally situated – they controlled one route from the middle Limpopo River to the old trading port of Sofala in Mozambique as well as all the approaches to Lourenço Marques – they enjoyed a lucrative trade with Portuguese merchants, swopping copper and ivory for linen cloth.

In the 19th century, the upheaval among African chiefdoms drove many Tsonga westwards – and into much closer contact with Sotho and Venda groups.

Ferment on the frontier

By the end of the 18th century the trekboers had migrated as far east as their guns and horses could take them, decimating the indigenous Khoikhoi as they went. Those Khoikhoi who survived were forced into the service of the whites, following the trekboers east to the Bushmans and Fish rivers – the new boundaries of the Cape – where further expansion was checked by the Xhosa and the regulations of the Dutch East India Company. The trekboers responded by rebelling against Company authority and launching commandos against the Xhosa. More violence flared when the Khoikhoi servants turned on their masters.

FOR HUNDREDS OF YEARS the area of the eastern Cape we still call 'Border' was the meeting ground between the Bantu-speaking southern Nguni people and the Khoisan of the Cape. Although friction between the two occasionally flared, it seems that by and large contact was friendly and mutually compatible – so much so that the 'clicks' which still form part of Xhosa speech were learned from the Khoisan.

The Khoikhoi were hunters and herders, while the Nguni were a more developed agricultural society, growing crops and working with iron. Inevitably, the Nguni, with their more stable political and economic systems, came to be the dominant force – and many Khoisan found themselves ruled by Xhosa chiefs, intermarrying with Xhosa and to a large extent losing their identity.

Sometime in the 1770s a new group of people began to arrive in the 'Border' region – the first of many trekboers seeking new pastures and lands.

Initially, there was no sudden clash of opposing fronts but rather a gradual intermingling of trekboer and Xhosa. Boers went into Xhosa territory to trade iron, copper and trinkets for cattle and ivory, while Xhosa sometimes worked for the whites – the men as herders, the women doing gardening and domestic work. Over the years, these economic links between Xhosa and trekboer were strengthened and operated to their mutual advantage.

However, even at the outset, there were sources of friction between white and black.

Accustomed to dealing with the more submissive Khoisan the whites were inclined to cheat or bully Xhosa traders, and to intimidate Xhosa servants. However, any household that ill-treated its servants or refused to pay the agreed wage would find that the Xhosa were quick to avenge the insult or claim their due – for example, by driving off some of the household's livestock.

A Xhosa practice that at first amused, but then annoyed the trekboers, was that of begging. In Xhosa society, it was acceptable that a stranger arriving at a homestead would be fed, the principle being that one never knew when one might require the same charity oneself. The trekboers, although hospitable themselves, became resentful at what they regarded as an unreasonable demand, and it is probable that some Xhosa may have looked on them as a permanent source of hand-outs.

Certainly, the Xhosa were not in awe of the settlers, although guns and horses were regarded with some respect until – under actual bush-warfare conditions – it was seen that the spear was not greatly at a disadvantage. They did not envy the pale skin or the features of the whites, and presumed they covered their bodies with so many articles of clothing because they were unwell. To some extent, Xhosa had mixed with the Khoisan and they

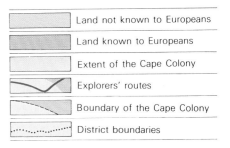

IN THE SECOND HALF of the 18th century, the pioneering work of explorers such as Robert Gordon paved the way for later trekboer expansion. By 1795 the Cape boundary stretched from the Buffels River to the Great Fish River.

	Land not known to Europeans
	Land known to Europeans
	Extent of the Cape Colony
	Explorers' routes
	Boundary of the Cape Colony
	District boundaries

probably anticipated they would mix with the whites and share in a single economy with them. After all, their stock-keeping economies were similar. But it was this very factor that was to lead to trouble, since both were invariably competing for the same grazing-land.

Another factor which created a rift between the two groups was that the trekboers regarded themselves as superior – possibly due to their white skins and 'Christian' upbringing – and tended to look down on African, non-Christian people as being 'heathen'. As Governor J W Janssens noted after visiting the eastern border region in 1803: 'They (the whites) call themselves people and Christians, and the Kaffirs and Hottentots heathens, and on the strength of this they consider themselves entitled to anything.' In the same year *Landdrost* Alberti of Uitenhage complained that it was impossible to persuade the colonists that the Khoikhoi were equally entitled to the protection of the law because the colonists believed that the 'heathens' were not really human, although they could not be classified as animals either.

Consequently, it was perhaps inevitable from the start that the conflict between black and white could only escalate. The first major division occurred over the fixing of a new eastern boundary for the Cape.

A new eastern border

In response to a petition from frontier trekboers, the Governor of the Cape, Baron Joachim van Plettenberg, toured the territory in 1778 and affixed beacons to mark its boundaries. At a farm on the Upper (Great) Fish River, the Governor met some Gwali chiefs whom he claimed agreed to fix the colony's eastern border as the line of the Upper Fish River and the Bushman's River.

As Van Plettenberg understood the arrangement, all Xhosa would remain to the east of this line. In Xhosa law, however, the agreement was binding only on those who had made it – namely the whites and the adherents of those Gwali chiefs who had acquiesced. But then, in addition to this contentious arrangement, Van Plettenberg announced two years later, in 1780, that the border was in fact to be the Great Fish River throughout its length, thereby adding to the colony the heart of the Zuurveld which was then unoccupied by whites.

Although the Zuurveld literally means 'sour pasture', it was in fact ideal grazing land. It consisted of an area extending west from the Great Fish River to around present-day Humansdorp. Governor Lord Charles Somerset was later to describe the Zuurveld as 'a succession of parks from the Bushman's River to the Great Fish River in which upon the most verdant carpet Nature has planted in endless variety; the soil, well adapted to cultivation, is peculiarly fitted for cattle and pasturage'.

The Xhosa protested that the Gwali chiefs had no mandate to speak for others and objected to the peremptory extension of the colony and their consequent exclusion from the Zuurveld. Furthermore, the Gonaqua people claimed that they owned the land by right of occupation, while the Gqunukhwebe claimed they had bought a portion of it from the Khoikhoi. Other Xhosa laid claim to the land as far west as the Sundays River.

THIS BEACON, *planted at the Seekoei River by Joachim van Plettenberg, marked the Cape's boundary in 1778.*

Forced removals

By 1780, despite the proclamation of the new border, the people of at least five Xhosa chiefdoms were still living to the west of the Fish River and in December of that year the 'Commandant of the Eastern Country' – Adriaan van Jaarsveld – received instructions to remove them. He was to attempt to persuade them to leave peaceably but, if they refused to go, he was empowered to raise a commando and 'forcibly compel them to go to the further side of the Fish River and remain there'.

Van Jaarsveld and his commando set out on their eviction expedition in May 1781. The first Xhosa they encountered were the Gwali, under the chieftain Koba, one of those with whom Van Plettenberg had arranged the original boundary, in terms of which the Gwali were not trespassing at all. Nevertheless, they were warned to depart, as were the Dange of chief Jalamba. Jalamba stated that he intended to stay where he was and, as the commando rode on, was warned to be gone within two days. When Van Jaarsveld returned some days later, the Dange still had not gone, so he requested a conference with the elders – with a particularly treacherous plan in mind. As they gathered, Van Jaarsveld, whom the Xhosa referred to as the 'Red Captain' because of the colour of his beard, scattered a goodwill gift of tobacco on the ground. As the Dange men scrambled for their individual share, specially picked men among the commando opened fire on them. Van Jaarsveld's report does not state how many were killed, but these included the 'Captains and all their fencible men'.

Others to be attacked were the Gwali, another group of Dange under Mahote, the Ntinde of Tshatshu, and Langa's Mbalu. Those Xhosa who survived soon left, and the commando was disbanded. However, a few weeks later, on

A CONTEMPORARY *photograph of the old Graaff-Reinet drostdy (and its coat-of-arms), where more than two centuries ago, a succession of landdrosts battled unsuccessfully to contain the first popular rebellion by burghers against Dutch Company regulations.*

hearing that not all the Xhosa had crossed the river, Van Jaarsveld reassembled the commando and, with '92 Christians and 40 Hottentots, with guns', attacked the Ntinde, killing large numbers of them. He then attacked the Gwali but afterwards bemoaned the fact that 'from the number of forests [we] could kill very few'. Van Jaarsveld's blitz netted the colonists 5 330 cattle and led to the deaths of an unrecorded number of Xhosa. This came to be known as the First Frontier War.

About this time, there were developments in Xhosa politics which were to have an important bearing on what was to follow. Khawuta succeeded to the chieftainship of the Gcaleka; and Rharhabe and his heir, Mlawu, were killed in battle against the Thembu. Because the chieftainship of the Rharhabe now devolved on the 11-year-old Ngqika (Gaika). Another of Rharhabe's sons, Ndlambe, was appointed as regent until the boy was old enough to rule directly. The Rharhabe at this time occupied the approximate area of the present Ciskei, and the ambitious Ndlambe sought the aid of Langa, the chief of the Mbalu, against the Gqunukhwebe.

Establishment of Graaff-Reinet

On the frontier, the situation quickly reverted to what it had been before Van Jaarsveld's raids. Many Xhosa again shifted across to the west of the Fish River while the trekboers pressed for more farmland to be granted to them to the east of the river. Concerned at the failure of the border to keep the trekboers and Xhosa apart, the Council of Policy advised the new Governor, Cornelis van de Graaff, to establish a new district where officials would be present to enforce the administration of Company policy.

In 1786 this district was formally established and named Graaff-Reinet, with Moritz Woeke appointed as *landdrost*. It consisted of the Zuurveld, the Sneeuwberge and Bruintjieshoogte to the north, and the Nieuweveld and Camdeboo in the west.

Right from the outset, Woeke's task proved to be a very difficult one. Although assisted by a team of officials, almost all he was able to achieve was a vigorous programme of rent collection, which was greatly resented by the burghers and served only to estrange them further.

Matters finally came to a head when the Gqunukhwebe, attacked by Ndlambe and Langa, crossed the Fish River in great numbers in 1789 and occupied land as far west as the Kowie River. Woeke allowed them to remain, but the consequences of doing so made relations between him and the burghers even worse.

Burgher dissatisfaction increases

Because the Gqunukhwebe herds had been greatly depleted in the clash with Ndlambe, many of these clansmen were forced to seek work with the local trekboers. However, these farmers soon complained that their cattle were being stolen by their new workers. They also objected to the fact that many of their servants and slaves were joining the Gqunukhwebe who – still harried by Ndlambe – were pushing further west into the Zuurveld. Yet another Boer complaint was that their farms were being overrun by the remaining Gqunukhwebe herds.

Eventually the somewhat ineffectual Woeke was replaced by his secretary, Honoratus Maynier, who was given written instructions from De Kaap (Cape Town) that differences with the Xhosa were to be solved peacefully. The frontier burghers, meanwhile, led by the undisciplined Adriaan van Jaarsveld, were incensed at officialdom's inability to 'control' the Xhosa. Ironically, from the Company's point of view, these rough and ready Boers were equally out of control.

But just as the burghers were demanding action against the Xhosa, so the Xhosa in turn were angry at the conduct of the burghers, who they complained were pillaging their stock east of the Fish River. They were especially galled by the arrogance of many of these burghers, pointing in particular to a trekboer called Coenraad de Buys (see box) who, with his wife, moved through their lands at will, abducting the wives of minor chiefs with impunity.

De Buys was in fact to play a decisive political role in the situation. He had befriended Ndlambe and helped to establish a pact between this Xhosa leader and one of the more militant Boers, Barend Lindeque. The latter wrote to Maynier saying that since the authorities refused to assist the burghers in controlling the Gqunukhwebe, the frontier farmers were going to do so with Ndlambe's help.

A XHOSA CHIEF, *possibly Ndlambe, depicted in the 1820s.*

Attack and retaliation

The advantage of this liaison for Ndlambe was that he would have trekboer guns on his side when he finally went to deal with the Gqunukhwebe and, at the same time, the Mbalu. Although he forbade it, Maynier was powerless to prevent this alliance, which proceeded to advance west from the Fish River against the two unsuspecting groups. After two days of running battles, the combined forces of Lindeque's and Ndlambe's men made off with almost 2 000 of their opponents' cattle.

The Gqunukhwebe and Mbalu lost no time in retaliating and went on the rampage through the countryside. Right across the Zuurveld, homesteads were burnt down and livestock taken in unprecedented numbers – an estimated 50 000 cattle, 11 000 sheep and 200 horses. Faced with this onslaught, many farmers chose to abandon their farms and trekked westwards.

Appalled at this turn of events, Maynier immediately entered the field, hoping to bring peace by reasoning with Tshaka of the Gqunukhwebe and Langa of the Mbalu. However, he was unable to establish contact with either of them, probably because they deliberately kept out of his way until their vengeance was complete. After a few months, Maynier gave up and returned to Graaff-Reinet intent on raising a commando to deal with the situation.

Meanwhile, at De Kaap the Council of Policy had been monitoring the worsening situation with growing dismay. It finally ordered the burgher force of Swellendam to go to the aid of the Graaff-Reinet burghers, drive the Xhosa across the Fish River and – in compensation for burgher losses – take as many cattle as possible.

WANTED

Coenraad de Buys, outlaw

The descendants of this turbulent frontier character, known as the '*Buysvolk*' (Buys-people), still occupy land near Mara, in the far northern Transvaal, where Buys trekked many years before the Voortrekkers. Buys, a huge and powerful man, was an adventurer who engaged in illegal cattle-trading with the Xhosa and, by his treatment of them, contributed to the outbreak of the Second Frontier War. Despite this, he had a certain amount of influence with the Xhosa and was passionately opposed to the British, who banished him from the colony and later declared him an outlaw with a reward on his head.

During the rebellion of 1799 De Buys tried, but failed, to persuade the Xhosa to side with the Graaff-Reinet burghers in an uprising against the British. For many years he lived among the Ngqika people and had a powerful influence over the young Ngqika, with whose mother he developed an amorous relationship. During the period of Batavian rule he was ordered to return to the colony and was granted a farm in the Langkloof where, for many years, he lived with his extensive household consisting of a Thembu wife and numerous children of this and an earlier liaison with a Bastard-Khoikhoi woman named Maria van der Horst.

With his family and a number of Khoikhoi adherents, De Buys moved, first to the vicinity of the present Beaufort West, and later to the northern Cape, where he disrupted mission work and raided the cattle of the local clans. By 1815 he had reached the western Transvaal, living at peace with the various chieftains whose territories he passed through. His wife died while the family party was trekking eastwards along the Limpopo River and it is said that the grief-stricken Buys, after telling the rest of his family to remain in the Soutpansberg area, wandered off alone and disappeared. His sons were of great assistance to the Voortrekkers Louis Trichardt and Hendrik Potgieter and, in recognition of this, the '*Buysvolk*' were granted their land in perpetuity by the Transvaal Government.

Prior to the arrival of the Swellendam burgher force, Maynier's Graaff-Reinet commando set out, pursuing the Gqunukhwebe and Mbalu across the Fish River and beyond. Tshaka, with most of the Gqunukhwebe and the Mbalu, hoped to cross the Kei and seek refuge with the Gcaleka, but they were intercepted by Ndlambe's forces – who had re-entered the fray – and were cut to pieces. Tshaka was killed and Langa taken prisoner.

Still in pursuit, Maynier's force attacked the remainder of the Gqunukhwebe along the Buffalo River. After killing 'a large number' of them, his force withdrew with 8 000 cattle, as well as women and children as prisoners. On his return, Maynier met the Swellendam commando, who reported seeing a large number of Gqunukhwebe and Mbalu in the Zuurveld – the only place that offered them relative safety.

Ngqika and his relations with the Cape Colony

Heir to the chiefdom of the Rharhabe section of the Xhosa – those who lived west of the Kei River – Ngqika was born in about 1775. His grandfather and father died in battle when he was very young, and he became the ward of his uncle, Ndlambe. The two were destined to become bitter rivals and, ultimately, sworn enemies. Both sought to maintain their respective positions of power by enlisting the help of the colonists, with their guns and horses.

It was Ndlambe who built up the Rharhabe into the dominant Xhosa group in the region by cleverly pushing rival chiefdoms into disastrous wars against the Dutch settlers. But precisely when he was at the height of his power, Ngqika, now at the end of his minority, turned against him. In the inevitable showdown that followed, Ngqika came off best.

Ngqika, however, proved to be an unpopular leader. Although his subjects respected his bravery on the battlefield, they were less impressed by his greed. During his reign he thought up many different schemes to deprive people of their cattle, such as arbitrarily changing the laws of inheritance. When Ndlambe escaped from his custody, he drew considerable support away from the young king who, in a bid to stem the exodus, claimed that the colonial forces had promised to support him in any struggle between the chiefdoms.

Ngqika committed a grave error in abducting one of his uncle's wives, the beautiful Thuthula, an act that provoked a rebellion among his own supporters and gave Ndlambe an ideal opportunity to attack. Ndlambe gained a marginal victory but, nevertheless, agreed to recognise Ngqika as senior to himself. Supported by a bevy of relatively minor chiefs, Ngqika had declared himself king of all the Xhosa, and it was to be his misfortune that the colonial authorities cynically accepted him as such while knowing that he was not. Thus, he was held responsible for the return of cattle stolen by his supporters, whom he could not afford to alienate, yet, at the same time, he was obliged to placate the colonial government.

After a Boer commando seized cattle belonging to the minor chiefs – believing that they belonged to Ndlambe's supporters – Ngqika was placed in the awkward position of being urged to attack his 'protector', the white colonists, to recover the herds. Resort to negotiation weakened his support, while Ndlambe's strength continued to grow, until his forces defeated those of Ngqika at the Battle of Amalinde in 1818. The colonial government, in the belief that Ngqika had been attacked for his attempts to suppress cattle-raiding, sent their forces against Ndlambe, resulting in the latter's defeat after an attack on Grahamstown.

In 1819 Cape Governor Lord Charles Somerset knocked another nail in Ngqika's coffin when he forced him to give up the land between the Kei and Keiskamma rivers as 'neutral

A COMBINATION of greed and liquor proved to be the undoing of Ngqika, chief of the Rharhabe Xhosa.

territory', to be occupied by neither the settlers nor the Xhosa. This failed to stabilise the frontier, and lost Ngqika the support of many of his people. From this period he spent much of his time in hiding from colonial forces that held him responsible for continued cattle thefts, and he could call on few allies to support him. Ravaged by alcoholism, he died practically an outcast among his own people in 1829, and was buried near Burnshill on the Keiskamma River.

An uneasy truce

After a few months spent vainly trying to hunt down and evict the remnants of the two chiefdoms, Maynier decided to make peace. Chungwa, who had succeeded his father as chief of the Gqunukhwebe, agreed to a truce, but refused to return any of the cattle or to move from the land he occupied between the Fish and Kowie rivers. Chungwa claimed that this land belonged to the Gqunukhwebe since they had bought it from the Khoikhoi. Langa's sons also agreed to peace, but under the same conditions as those of Chungwa. Consequently, this Second Frontier War ended in an uneasy truce that failed to satisfy the demands of the land-hungry burghers.

Ndlambe, in the meantime, had benefited considerably from the hostilities, with his Rharhabe people now by far the most powerful chiefdom west of the Kei River. However, he personally was not to enjoy the benefits for long. His ward, Ngqika, although only 15 years old, had fought with distinction against the Gqunukhwebe. Ngqika began to fear that Ndlambe – in his position as regent – might actually attain the chieftainship that was rightly his. Caught in a surprise attack organised by Ngqika, Ndlambe fled. Appeals for help made to his former allies, the burghers, went unheeded, so he turned to the Xhosa paramount chief's regent, Bhurhu. A combined army marched against Ngqika but was decisively beaten, with Ndlambe and the paramount chief designate, Hintsa, being taken prisoner. Ngqika shrewdly kept Ndlambe captive, but released Hintsa.

Maynier under fire

Meanwhile, discontent among burghers over Maynier's failure to deal effectively with the 'kaffir' problem continued. In the northern part of the district, San raiders were meeting with success as farm after farm was abandoned along the Tarka and Nieuweveld mountains and the Sneeuwberge. In savage counter-attacks by the burghers, 2 504 'Bushmen' were reported killed between 1786 and 1795, 669 were captured, and 276 'colonists' – most of them Khoikhoi herders – perished.

Burgher hostility towards Maynier was exacerbated by a number of other factors, such as the new system of rent-collection and Maynier's new defence policy which was primarily directed against the San of the northern Sneeuwberg areas, thus leaving the other colonists exposed to renewed Xhosa raids. This 'preferential' defence policy caused a major rift among the burgher population: the Sneeuwberg settlers favoured it, and the others, of the Zuurveld and Bruintjieshoogte, opposed it. Burghers of the last two areas refused to do duty against the San in the Sneeuwberge, insisting rather that action should be directed against those Xhosa still present in the Zuurveld.

Yet another bone of contention was Maynier's 'interference' in the relationship between the burghers and their Khoikhoi servants. Any burgher who was accused by his servant of unfair treatment would be summoned to Maynier's drostdy (official residence) to answer to the charge. In doing this, Maynier was merely acting on orders, but his high-handed manner often gave offence, and caused added resentment amongst the burghers.

Matters finally came to a head when Maynier refused to confirm Adriaan van Jaarsveld as a member of the court of heemraden, even though the fiery trekboer leader had been properly nominated. At the time, Van Jaarsveld was having financial problems and Maynier estranged him even further by sending him a letter demanding that he produce two guarantors for a loan that Van Jaarsveld had requested from the Orphan Chamber, failing which 'unpleasant proceedings will be instituted'.

The burghers expel Maynier
As a result, a number of burghers who sympathised with Van Jaarsveld's predicament gathered at the village of Graaff-Reinet and demanded that Maynier call a meeting of heemraden and all former officials. Surprisingly, Maynier did so. At the meeting – held on 6 February 1795 – the burghers referred to themselves as Patriots. By doing so they were aligning themselves with the ideals of the Cape Patriots whose central tenet was that it was the duty of a people to replace a government that did not have the common interest as its principal doctrine. Marthinus Prinsloo was chosen as their interim leader. Maynier was ordered to leave the Graaff-Reinet district and officials who had supported his policies towards the Xhosa were expelled from their posts.

Maynier was left with no choice: he left Graaff-Reinet and reported back to the authorities at De Kaap, who cut off all supplies of lead and gunpowder to the rebels. The President of the Council of Justice, Olof de Wet, was sent to Graaff-Reinet as the head of a commission of enquiry. After refusing to take action against the Zuurveld Xhosa – who refused to cross the Fish River, fearing they would be slaughtered by the Rharhabe – the commission was summarily expelled from the village by a force of some 200 armed burghers. What was more, these burghers made it clear that they no longer recognised the administration of the Dutch East India Company.

The rebels made new appointments – C D Gerotz became provisional landdrost, with Jan Booysen as president of the heemraden. Adriaan van Jaarsveld was named as 'President of Military Affairs'. At this point, the British took over power at De Kaap and the rebels requested that the British appoint formal magistrates, adding, however, that their own chosen representaten would continue to participate actively in the administration of local government. Frans Bresler was sent as the new landdrost but, as a former employee of the Company, he was unacceptable to the rebels, and soon returned to De Kaap (which the British would later refer to as Cape Town).

However, the burghers' independent stand was short-lived. Owing to the embargo on gunpowder and lead, the fight against the San in the Sneeuwberge was going badly and a meat boycott of Cape Town instigated by the burghers had failed to induce the government to resupply the much-needed ammunition. Finally, in August 1796, the burghers of the western and northern areas decided to accept British authority. Only the Bruintjieshoogte and Zuurveld burghers held out, but promised loyalty on condition they could retake cattle from the Xhosa and occupy

BY THE 1800s, *Khoikhoi soldiers were an important part of the colonial military force at the Cape. This painting is entitled 'A Hottentot Sergeant of the Cape Mounted Rifles'.*

farms to the east of the Fish River. But General Craig, who was in charge of the government, demanded unconditional surrender – which came early in 1797.

It was not, however, the end of frontier discontent. Bresler – once rejected by the rebels – was sent as their new *landdrost* and practised the despised policy of reconciliation toward the Xhosa. He also saw to it that taxes and land rents were collected effectively and ordered whites who had fled from their farms in the Zuurveld to return to them or risk confiscation. With large areas of the Zuurveld abandoned, the Gqunukhwebe probably thought that the tide of white expansion had ebbed, and they continued their westward movement until parties of Xhosa were seen for the first time in the vicinity of Swellendam. The conciliatory policy of persuading the Xhosa to leave by means of 'friendly exertions' infuriated the burghers, and it needed only a small spark to set off another rebellion.

That spark was the arrest of Adriaan van Jaarsveld, in January 1799, on a charge of forgery in connection with his Orphan Chamber loan. He was soon set free by fellow burghers, who proclaimed a state of revolution and besieged Bresler in his *drostdy*. Leaders of the new rebellion were Marthinus Prinsloo, Coenraad de Buys and Van Jaarsveld. They were unable to persuade the burghers of the Sneeuwberge to join them, despite proclaiming the slogans of liberty, equality and fraternity – applicable, however, only to the whites.

Quelling the burgher rebellion

In March, a force of infantry and dragoons, as well as men of the 'Hottentot' Cape Corps, landed at Algoa Bay under the command of General Thomas Vandeleur and marched on Graaff-Reinet. At Prinsloo's farm, Boschberg, the rebels surrendered and Vandeleur despatched 18 of their leaders by sea to Cape Town, where Van Jaarsveld and Prinsloo were condemned to death for high treason. They were pardoned after a few years, but Van Jaarsveld died while still imprisoned in the Castle. De Buys and other rebels found refuge with Ngqika.

Vandeleur's instructions did not stop at ending the colonists' rebellion. He was also commanded to clear the Zuurveld of Xhosa. Before he could start this, however,

he was confronted by a large group of Khoikhoi formerly employed by the Zuurveld trekboers. Their leader, Klaas Stuurman, claimed they had been ill-treated and underpaid and consequently had raided their employers' homes in order to take clothing and firearms as compensation. Now they sought the protection of the British.

Vandeleur persuaded them to lay down their arms and proceed to Algoa Bay where, in the meantime, some 150 trekboer families from the Zuurveld had arrived to ask for protection against their former servants. While Vandeleur trailed off after the Xhosa, the Governor's secretary, John Barrow, kept the two factions apart at Algoa Bay.

Battles in the Zuurveld

On the Sundays River, Vandeleur found Chungwa, but failed to persuade him to leave the Zuurveld. Fighting erupted, the British repelling the Gqunukhwebe with artillery and rifle fire, but nonetheless losing 16 soldiers to the 'darts' of the Xhosa. Vandeleur withdrew to Algoa Bay and prepared to re-embark his troops. The Khoikhoi, concerned that they were to be left to the mercy of the trekboers, fled into the bush. Many allied themselves to Chungwa, who welcomed this reinforcement of some 700 Khoikhoi, of whom about 150 were mounted and in possession of firearms. Mixed bands of Khoikhoi and Xhosa now ranged across the Zuurveld, looting as they went. With most of his troops departed for Cape Town, Vandeleur could take no effective action against them, but ordered a commando to take the field. In a fierce clash with Khoikhoi and Xhosa the commando was defeated and the raiders moved westwards into the Swellendam district, along the Langkloof, to a point on the coast midway between Plettenberg Bay and Knysna.

Reinforcements for Vandeleur, along with a prefabricated wooden fort, were sent by sea from Cape Town. Meanwhile, the acting Governor, General Francis Dundas, marched overland with 500 soldiers, ordering Maynier to meet him at Swellendam. Dundas, feeling that Maynier's experience of the frontier would be invaluable, was guided entirely by the advice of this ex-*landdrost*. Eventually it was decided to 'remedy the evils of the country by making peace with the Caffres and at the same time to pacify and

THE LUSH *Kat River valley was the venue of a meeting between Batavian Governor Jan Janssens and Ngqika in 1803.*

regain the confidence of the Hottentots'. Maynier was reappointed as *landdrost* of Graaff-Reinet and, to maintain the peace, a small force of dragoons and men of the Cape Corps was stationed at Graaff-Reinet, along with 350 regular soldiers at the newly erected wooden fort – named Fort Frederick – at Algoa Bay. In January 1800 Dundas returned to Cape Town. Another significant move in that year was made by Ndlambe who, with a few followers, eluded his guards and slipped across the Fish River into the Zuurveld, where he began to re-establish his influence.

Although some Khoikhoi returned to their former employers after promises of better protection against exploitation and ill-treatment, others stayed in the bush or remained allied to Chungwa. Many encamped in the vicinity of Graaff-Reinet village in order to be close to Maynier, whom they regarded as their protector. Early in 1801 the Reverend Theodorus van der Kemp, a missionary of the London Missionary Society, arrived at Graaff-Reinet to preach to those Khoikhoi still gathered there. There were objections to Maynier allowing Khoikhoi converts to use the church and to their being taught to read and write. In an atmosphere of extreme mistrust, rumours of war again began to flourish.

Uncertainty and panic

Many Khoikhoi, fearing that they were to be killed, converged on Graaff-Reinet. The trekboers, uneasily eyeing this growing congregation, feared this was a prelude to attacks on their farms. Armed burghers from all over the district appeared at the *drostdy* in July 1801 to demand that the Khoikhoi soldiers of the Cape Corps be sent away, but Maynier managed to placate them. The mere appearance of so many armed burghers increased the panic, and more Khoikhoi streamed into Graaff-Reinet as burghers abandoned their farms once again and trekked to the north. Khoikhoi adventurers, under their leaders Boesak, Stuurman and Trompetter, took advantage of the situation and plundered far and wide.

Eventually law and order collapsed. After skirmishes with Maynier's troops, a large force of burghers laid siege to the village. Dundas, meanwhile, was bombarded by letters demanding that Maynier be recalled and accusing him of harbouring Khoikhoi known to have committed serious crimes. A force of 300 soldiers, under Major Francis Sherlock, sent to restore order, arrived at Graaff-Reinet in November. Within a few days Sherlock had persuaded the burghers to return to their farms and he himself stayed on as the new Resident Commissioner in place of Maynier, who was recalled to Cape Town.

Commandos organised to subdue the Khoikhoi failed, and in the second half of 1802 Swellendam district was invaded. To compound the insecurity of the colonists, British troops were withdrawn to Cape Town in preparation for the return of the Cape to Dutch control. This Third Frontier War dragged on into 1803, when the new Dutch Governor, General J W Janssens, concluded a peace by granting the Khoikhoi leaders their own lands.

The matter of the Xhosa evacuating the Zuurveld was allowed to stand over, and a condition of the peace was that neither side would be obliged to return looted cattle. This created much resentment among the trekboers, who reckoned that they had lost a total of 50 000 cattle, 50 000 sheep and 1 000 horses. Almost 500 of the 1 400 farms in the Swellendam and Graaff-Reinet districts lay in ruins and large areas of the country had been abandoned by whites, whose expansion had thus received a severe check. The problems of the frontier, despite the heavy costs suffered by all parties, remained unsolved.

£5
No. 0144
No. 0144
We Promise to pay the Bearer on Demand
CAPE TOWN.
at our Office here the Sum of FIVE POUNDS,
Five Pounds.

Muy

A Wohnungen an den Muysenberg B das Holländische Camp. C Retizade der Hä

THE CAPE OF GOOD HOPE

Government Gazette.

Published by Authority.

FRIDAY, JULY 25, 1828.

Numb. 1176.

No. 50.
(Signed) RICH. BOURKE.

ORDINANCE

Of His Honor the Lieutenant-Governor in Council.

For improving the Condition of Hottentots and other free Persons of colour at the Cape of Good Hope, and for consolidating and amending the Laws affecting those Persons.

No. 50.
(Getekend) RICH. BOURKE.

ORDONNANTIE

Van Zyne Edelheid den Luit.-Gouverneur in Rade.

Tot verbetering van den stand der Hottentotten en andere vrye Personen van kleur aan de Kaap, de Goede Hoop, en tot vereeniging en verbetering der Wetten betrekkelyk deze Personen.

GRAHAM'S TOWN JOURNAL.

Conquest & dispossession 1800-68

'Make them [the Zulu kings] out as blood-thirsty as you can. . . .'
Letter from Nathaniel Isaacs to Henry Fynn

In the early 1800s, Nathaniel Isaacs, Henry Fynn and Francis Farewell earned themselves a prominent place in South African colonial folklore by becoming the first whites to penetrate the Zulu kingdom of Shaka.

For more than 150 years the diaries they later published were the main source of information about the Zulu leader. But, as the extract from the letter quoted above (and on page 87) shows, their reliability as witnesses is deeply suspect.

It is probably true that Shaka was a powerful and despotic ruler; but that he was also a blood-thirsty tyrant is, in all likelihood, historical fiction – a lie deliberately spread by Isaacs and Fynn to try to persuade the British to annex Natal (which would have made the land they had been given by the Zulu leader extremely valuable).

White fortune-seekers arrived in Natal at a time of great change in south-east Africa: increased demand for grazing-land, over-use of resources and a period of bone-bleaching drought had unsettled the old order of small chiefdoms living in relative harmony. Responding to the changed environment and the need for self-protection, many of these chiefdoms formed alliances that eventually led to the creation of larger chiefdoms. This, in turn, resulted in a greater emphasis on militarism – with leaders such as Shaka proving themselves masters at developing new and more aggressive battle tactics. The effects of these alliances, conquests and assimilation of other groups spread throughout southern Africa – from present-day Swaziland, across the highveld to the mountain kingdom now known as Lesotho, and to the fertile plains beyond.

Into this melee stepped a new force – with a new technology of gun, wagon and horse: the Voortrekkers. Their forays beyond the Orange River created yet another historical myth – that the highveld in which they trekked was empty – depopulated as a result of the disorder among African chiefdoms. The reality, however, was different: the Boers, in fact, had to fight for most of the territory they eventually settled.

The Great Trek, as the Voortrekker migration to the interior has become known, began in the eastern Cape in response to much the same pressures as were experienced by the African societies – but overlaid with pride, racism and religion.

Behind all the lofty phrases that have turned the trek into an Afrikaner Exodus lay the same story of dwindling, over-used resources and mounting population. The endless horizons that had lured their forefathers ever eastwards were blocked by the powerful Xhosa and threatened by British laws and settlement. No longer could every son of a Boer household count on setting

up his own farm on unused grazing-land – unless it could be found in the interior far from British control.

The Boers were also fleeing – perhaps without realising it – a profound change in the way men created wealth; a change that demanded social and economic adjustments that many Boers simply could not accept. This was mercantile capitalism, the product of a long period of evolutionary adjustment in Europe – and which was entrenched in South Africa with the British occupation of the Cape following the outbreak of the Napoleonic Wars. Capitalism worked because it harnessed the most basic human instincts – survival and greed – to productivity, demanding capital and labour to produce a surplus of goods that could be sold for cash in an ever-widening circle of trade and economic activity. An intriguing spin-off was that it made most people freer than they had ever been, simply because it could not work effectively in autocratic and feudal societies; which is why slavery – an expensive anachronism in the new world of free, cheap labour – had to go, to be followed in the Cape by the removal of other restrictions on labour.

All this was a far cry from the almost feudal world of the Dutch-speaking subsistence farmer, who ruled like a medieval lord over his handful of slaves. Rather than adapt to the new order, some Boers – initially less than 10 percent of the population – attempted to cling to the past by quitting the new capitalist world of the British for the unknown interior.

But while the Boers fled the new order, many Africans adapted to it successfully, growing and selling surplus crops to the new towns and settlements that were springing up, particularly in the eastern Cape. Their relationship with the British, however, was far from harmonious, particularly along the frontier with the Xhosa, where violence flared repeatedly as settlers moved on to grazing territory belonging to the various chiefdoms.

Once the Cape officially became a part of the British Empire it became subject to the three 'laws' that London applied to all its colonies – that they should be able to support themselves, supply raw materials for British industry and buy British exports. A prime example was wool, which the Cape Colony exported to Britain in increasing quantities during the 1830s and '40s. As a result, sheep – and the land on which to graze them – became vital to the Cape economy, and the wealthy settler farmers who built their fortunes on wool, became a vociferous and influential lobby behind British expansionist policy in the eastern Cape.

Events in the Cape

1805	Napoleonic Wars commence in Europe.
1806	Britain re-occupies the Cape.
1807	Britain bans slave trading; importation of slaves ends.
1809	Severe drought unsettles eastern frontier.
1811	Cape Governor Caledon resigns, replaced by John Cradock.
	John Graham appointed Commissioner for eastern frontier.
	Outbreak of hostilities on frontier.
	Regular circuit courts introduced.
1812	Cape Regimental headquarters renamed Graham's Town (later Grahamstown).
	Apprenticeship law promulgated.
1813	Government tries to regulate landownership.
	Court proceedings opened to the public.
1814	Charles Somerset becomes Cape Governor.
1815	Slagtersnek rebellion.
1816	Xhosa diviner Ntsikana Gaba embraces Christianity.
1818	Ndlambe's forces thrash Ngqika's Xhosa at Amalinde.
1819	Start of fifth frontier war.
	Ndlambe's Xhosa defeated at Battle of Grahamstown.
1820	British settlers arrive in Algoa Bay.
c1822	Arrival of Mfengu in eastern Cape.
1828	Ordinance 50 repeals Pass laws.
1829	Khoikhoi and other 'coloureds' settle in Kat River valley after expulsion of Xhosa chief Maqoma.
	Rharhabe and Gcaleka Xhosa bury differences in face of British military threat.
1834	Slaves officially freed, but apprenticed for four years.
1834-5	Sixth frontier war.
1835	Gcaleka chief Hintsa killed by British.
	16 000 Mfengu settle around Fort Peddie.
1835-6	Xhosa land annexed as Province of Queen Adelaide; Cape Governor told to hand it back.
1836	Andries Stockenström appointed Lieutenant-Governor of Eastern Districts. Implements treaty system.
1840s	Merino sheep farming begins to transform colonial economy.
	Pedi (Transvaal) migrate to work on Cape farms.
1841	Masters and Servants ordinance supersedes Ordinance 50.
c1842-4	Treaty system collapses.
1844	New Governor Peregrine Maitland scraps treaty system.
1846-8	War of the Axe (seventh frontier war).
1846	Tiyo Soga sent to Scotland for missionary training.
1847	Henry Pottinger becomes Cape Governor, but is later replaced by Harry Smith.
1847-8	Victoria East and British Kaffraria set up on Xhosa land.
1849	Convict crisis in Cape Town.
1850	Eighth frontier war; Kat River rebels side with Xhosa; Chief Sandile joined by the Thembu.
1852	George Cathcart becomes Cape Governor.
1854	Cape Colony granted representative government.
1856	Tiyo Soga ordained as Presbyterian minister.
	Masters and Servants Act passed.
1856-7	Xhosa cattle-killing, thousands die.
1858	Xhosa finally broken after series of wars against British and decision to kill their own cattle.
1862	Philip Wodehouse becomes Cape Governor.
1862-3	Griquas from Philippolis settle in No Man's land between Cape and Natal, regard themselves as independent.
1865	Ostriches first domesticated.
1867	Pebble found near Hopetown verified as 21,25 carat diamond.

The Voortrekkers and Transorangia/Transvaal

c1804	Griqua settle north of Orange River at Klaarwater, merge into one group under Adam Kok II.
c1820	Moshoeshoe moves Basotho capital to Butha Buthe Mountain.
1824	Sotho besieged by Tlokwa, flee to new capital, Thaba Bosiu.
1828	Sotho repulse Ngwane attack.
1831	Sotho defeat Ndebele.
1834	*Kommissie* treks from Cape begin.
1834-5	Boers suffer heavy losses in sixth frontier war.
1835-6	Louis Trichardt, Hans van Rensburg and Andries Potgieter trek north.
1836	Cape of Good Hope Punishment Act passed.
	Potgieter's trekkers defeat Ndebele at the Battle of Vegkop.
1837	Piet Retief publishes his 'Manifesto', then treks into Transorangia.
	Potgieter and Piet Uys, helped by Rolong and Griqua forces, defeat Ndebele at Mosega and drive them across Limpopo.
	Louis Trichardt arrives in Lourenço Marques.
1838	Trichardt dies of malaria.
Late 1830s	Griqua settle at Philippolis under Adam Kok III.
1841	Trekker council established at Potchefstroom, A H Potgieter as Chief-Commandant.
1842	Boers declare a republic at Alleman's drift on the Orange River.
1843	Republic of Natalia annexed to the Crown.
	Cape Governor Napier and Moshoeshoe sign treaty defining Basotho territory.
1845	A H Potgieter founds Andries-Ohrigstad; treaty with Pedi.
	Trekkers invade Adam Kok III's territory; British intervene, defeat Boers at Zwartkoppies.
1846	Swazi chief (Mswati) grants trekkers land in eastern Transvaal.
1848	Boers declare Winburg republic; defeated by Smith at Boomplaats.
	Potgieter founds Soutpansberg (later Schoemansdal).
	Governor Harry Smith proclaims Orange River Sovereignty.
1849	Treaty of Derdepoort signed by three Boer statelets in Transvaal to formalise unity talks; fruitless.
	Warden Line between Basotho kingdom and Orange River Sovereignty fixed.
1850	Lydenburg replaces Ohrigstad as adminstrative centre of Boer statelet.
1851	Basotho defeat Warden's forces at Viervoet.
1852	Transvaal Boers granted independence in terms of Sand River Convention.
	Battle of Berea Mountain between British and Basotho.
1854	More than 1 000 Ndebele die in a cave besieged by Boers.
	Bloemfontein Convention leads to the establishment of Orange Free State republic.
	Piet Potgieter dies in battle against Ndebele.
1856	*Grondwet* (constitution) accepted by Lydenburg and Potchefstroom Voortrekkers.
1858	Soutpansbergers agree to be incorporated into a united South African Republic (SAR).
1860	Boer republics north of Vaal unite in the SAR.
1865	Orange Free State at war with Basotho.
1867	Schoemansdal sacked by Venda warriors.
1868	British annex Basutoland.

Upheaval in African societies

1800-20	Stone-walled sites in eastern Botswana and southern Transvaal settled but many abandoned after 1820 as a result of Ndebele and Griqua raiding.
c1802	Drought and famine in Natal lead to upheaval among chiefdoms.
c1804	Dingiswayo exiled after a bungled plot to assassinate his father, Mthethwa Chief Jobe.
c1809	Jobe dies; Dingiswayo returns from exile to assume chieftainship of the Mthethwa.
c1810	Shaka becomes supreme commander of the Mthethwa army.
c1815	Shaka succeeds Senzangakona as chief of the Zulu.
c1817-22	Ngwane people attacked by Dingiswayo and later Shaka; they in turn attack the Hlubi, who flee to the Transvaal. Mzilikazi flees to eastern Transvaal.
c1818	Ngwane chief Zwide has Dingiswayo assassinated. Shaka defeats Ndwandwe.
1820s	Bhaca and Mfengu enter eastern Cape.
c1822-4	Hlubi and Ngwane wage war against Tlokwa.
c1824	Tlokwa led by MaNthatisi settle near Caledon River. Taung attack on Rolong repulsed.
1825	Ngwane defeat Hlubi.
1827	Ndebele set up base in Magaliesberg.
1828	Matiwane's Ngwane defeated by Thembu/colonial force at Mbholompo in eastern Cape. Shaka assassinated, succeeded by Dingane. Mpondo withstand a series of attacks by Zulu.
1829	Moletsane's Taung defeated by both Ndebele and Griqua. Kololo (Fokeng) cross Zambezi River after being beaten by Ndebele.
1830-3	Zwangendaba and Nxaba flee across the Zambezi to form Nguni Kingdom in east Africa.
1830s	Kololo found Lozi state in Zambia. Sekonyela becomes chief of Tlokwa.
1832	Ndebele attack Tswana and Rolong from Marico valley base. Dingane's army repulsed by Ndebele. Ndebele drive Tswana from land between Crocodile and Marico rivers.
1834	Port Natal renamed Durban.
1827	Ndebele attacked by Zulu army.
1838	Voortrekkers arrive in Dingane's kingdom. Battle of Blood River.
1838-9	Mpande and 17 000 followers flee Dingane.
1839-40	Mpande and allies (including trekkers) plan overthrow of Dingane, who flees into Swazi territory. Pretorius proclaims Mpande king of Zulu.
1838-43	Trekkers administer their own republic of Natalia. Tsonga from Mozambique become migrant labourers in Natal.
1843	Britain annexes Natal.
1845	Natal becomes autonomous district of the Cape Colony.
1846	Locations commission set up to divide Natal between Africans and whites.
1847-8	Boers trek from Natal to the Highveld.
1848	Hlubi refugees pour into Natal; British settle them in Drakensberg.
1847-9	British immigrants arrive in Natal.
1850	Benjamin Pine becomes Lieutenant-Governor of Natal.
1851	Sugar first produced from cane in Natal. Zulu unwilling to work for plantation owners, who demand Indian labour.
1854	Boers crush Ndebele group at Makapansgat.
1855	Vain bid by Natal to 'requisition 300 coolies' from Calcutta.
1856	Natal granted representative government; Shepstone appointed Secretary for Native Affairs.
1856	Natal legislature formulates regulations for employing indentured Indians.
1859	Natal labour shortage severe; laws passed to speed up importation of labourers.
1860	First indentured Indian labourers arrive in Natal. (Between now and 1911 about 152 000 Indians arrive, 50 percent opting to stay.)

Shaka's conquering armies

Land was the key to Nguni societies of south-east Africa in the 18th century:
as chiefdoms became too large, new settlements sprang up. But as the new century dawned,
a land shortage forced many of the smaller chiefdoms into defensive alliances against
land-hungry foes. This led to larger groupings, greater competition for trade with the Portuguese
at Delagoa Bay, the growth of militarism, and the emergence of the Zulu kingdom.

IN THE LATE 18TH CENTURY, before the battle-cries of conquering armies echoed through the countryside, the land now known as Natal was green and fertile – but deceptively peaceful.

For 40 years, the rains which blew in from the Indian Ocean had been extraordinarily good, and on time. And from the lowlands of the south to the highlands of the west – at thousands of scattered homesteads – stocked-up foodstores and large herds of cattle provided vivid testimony of the prosperity being enjoyed by the majority of the region's inhabitants.

Between the Thukela River in the south, the Phongolo in the north and the valley of the Mzinyathi (Buffalo) in the west lay a region of fertile soil, good rainfall and variable temperatures – perfect for people whose fortunes had been tied to the land for hundreds of years.

Population explosions

In many ways, the impetus which led to the destruction of the old way of life in this little corner of south-east Africa was provided by the principal unit of wealth: the cow.

For hundreds of years, cattle had bought men their brides and chiefs their prestige. And although there had seldom been shortages of these animals, prospective husbands often had to wait several years before acquiring enough to secure their wives.

But the situation changed as an increase in the numbers of cattle not only enabled marriages to take place sooner and with greater frequency, but also allowed husbands to take more than one bride. The offshoot of this was a population explosion which put intense new pressures on both human relationships and the environment.

The first people to feel the effects of the devaluation of cattle were those in authority – and it was with growing alarm that chiefs and homestead heads watched a tried-and-tested system (whereby the extent of their power was determined by the sizes of their herds) fall apart at the seams. Now, even relatively minor homesteads were in a position to accumulate as much stock as their superiors. And when they did, they often broke away to form their own independent settlements.

In the beginning, while land, water and grazing remained plentiful, the proliferation of new communities did not have too serious an effect on relations between rival groups. But when clans which had previously controlled large tracts of land began rubbing uncomfortable shoul-

THE PEACEFUL SETTING *of south-east Africa before the upheaval that followed the rise of Shaka is captured in this painting entitled 'On the Umnonoti River' by George French Angas. Rapid population growth in the area helped set in motion a devastating competition for resources.*

ders with one another, and when erosion compounded the problem by turning previously arable areas into arid wasteland, northern Nguni society underwent a bewildering transformation.

For generations, members of different clans had seldom found it necessary to fight one another over living-space or grazing-lands. But now, as the land shortage bit deeper, increasingly bitter dogfights raged for control of the few remaining pockets of unclaimed territory.

The first casualties of this era of insecurity were the small, independent homesteads. The fact that bigger clans always came off best in the now-regular disputes, left smaller settlements with little choice but to enter into defensive alliances with stronger neighbours. It was a process which, once started, became impossible to stop: for as resources dwindled even further, so chiefdoms became bigger – and their intentions towards others more menacing. Indeed, the dominant features of the new social order which evolved during this period of flux were the formation of centralised systems of authority and, ominously, the rapid build-up of armies.

In this respect, the abandonment of circumcision ceremonies and the reorganisation of armies into an *amabutho* system (an age-grade basis) were developments of crucial significance. It meant that young men – who would normally have been initiated – could now be assembled by chiefs and formed into regiments with names of their own. It was a system which not only provided a more efficient fighting force but also increased coherence by uniting men from different territorial segments in a common regimental bond.

Previously, a newly incorporated group formed a separate contingent in the army, thereby preserving its identity and capacity for independent military action. In the *amabutho* system, however, young men were categorised according to age. And when they fought be-

The importance of the homestead in Shaka's kingdom

The homestead was the centre of the social structure, lifestyle and traditions of the northern Nguni people. For centuries, the production of food, clothing, implements and virtually everything else was concentrated in and around tens of thousands of *imizi* (homesteads) scattered over the hills and ridges of the country that was later to become Zululand.

These were the homes of the ordinary clans, consisting of a circle of *izindlu* (huts) situated around a cattle kraal. Each hut was occupied by the *umnumzana* (head of the homestead) and perhaps two or three wives and their children.

To a large extent, the homestead was self-sufficient, its occupants subsisting almost entirely on the products of their own labour. Work was divided strictly according to sex: the men took charge of the livestock, while the women were responsible for domestic chores and the production of cereals and other staples. The manufacture of tools, implements and handicrafts was also determined by gender, though this might depend on an individual's particular talents and such variables as the availability of raw materials.

It was the products and the surplus created by day-to-day labour within these units, and in the lands that surrounded them, that supported and strengthened the Zulu kingdom.

Although an estimated 90 percent of the region's population lived in such homesteads, the kingdom was

A ZULU HOMESTEAD *of Shaka's day consisted of a circle of huts around a central enclosure for housing the very valuable livestock.*

nevertheless highly stratified. As a result, the king exercised authority over all the homesteads, demanding tribute and uniting them politically.

The homesteads occupied by men of rank were generally far larger and more populous than those of their subordinates, but they operated on essentially the same principles.

The *amakhanda* (royal homesteads) functioned both as production communities – supported by the labour of the king's relatives and retainers – and as barracks for the Zulu army while serving the king.

Under the Zulu military system, all men and women, on reaching the age of puberty, were gathered into *amabutho* (age-sets). Females in these sets did not give direct service to the king, instead remaining at their fathers' homesteads. They could marry only with the king's permission. However, members of the king's regiments served him directly, raiding beyond the kingdom's borders, acting as a coercive force within the kingdom and – while they were living in the royal homesteads – providing a labour force.

In this case, the division of labour according to sex did not apply, and the soldiers' duties would include crop production.

Whereas the army received some of its food from the king while in service, it depended mostly on the fruits of its own labour. The soldiers also depended heavily on supplies brought in from their fathers' homesteads.

EVERY YEAR *many of the northern Nguni chiefdoms took part in a ceremony known as incwala: a unifying event held during the rainy season. During the ceremony, the chief reviewed* his army, *which danced his praises. The incwala was introduced to the northern Nguni people by Zwide of the Ndwandwe, who adopted it from the southern Tsonga.*

side their peers from other sections, the results were astounding: in fact, by the early years of the 19th century the changes in military strategy had led to the emergence of three major groupings in what later became known as Zululand: the Ndwandwe under Zwide in the north; the Ngwane under Sobhuza in the far north; and the Mthethwa under Dingiswayo in the south.

Famine – and the rise of Dingiswayo

In 1802 an event occurred which pushed long-simmering tensions between rival chiefdoms to breaking point: the rains dried up, and a devastating famine began to take hold of the country.

As foodstores emptied, wandering bands of marauders, desperate with hunger, fought pitched battles for dwindling leftovers with members of already starving clans – and panic-stricken refugees fled to the camps of the Ndwandwe, the Ngwane and the Mthethwa.

It was against this backdrop, in 1804, that Godongwana, an ambitious but impatient son of the Mthethwa chief Jobe, sparked a minor crisis in the chiefdom by plotting to kill his father. Jobe, though ageing and ailing, was no fool – and when details of the assassination plan reached his ears he decided to strike first. The upshot of this bungled plot was that instead of a triumphant rise to power, the young pretender was sent into an unplanned and ignominious exile – with a spear protruding from his back.

Nothing was heard from Godongwana for the next five years. But in 1809, shortly after Jobe had died, he returned with a new name – Dingiswayo (The Outcast) – and after removing a brother who had assumed control of the chiefdom, he declared himself chief.

Despite the violent manner of his rise to power, Dingiswayo proved to be an astute and innovative ruler who, by adapting faster than his rivals to the changes in Nguni society, was able to gain a head start in the scramble for power and influence.

One of the reasons for the Mthethwa chiefdom's success in broadening its sphere of influence was the implementation by Dingiswayo of a deliberately generous policy towards vanquished foes. Certainly, by allowing defeated opponents to retain their leaders and most of their cattle, he was able to make loyal allies out of long-time enemies which, in the long run, meant additional men to draft into his regiments.

A cleverly planned campaign to win control of the lucrative trade route to the Portuguese port of Delagoa Bay also increased his popularity. Well aware of how political power could be expanded by the accumulation of rare goods, Dingiswayo's decisive move in securing the route to Delagoa Bay probably made him the most influential figure in the region and greatly increased his chances of realising an even greater ambition: to unite the different northern Nguni chiefdoms under a single ruler (himself). Although he was aware that in order to achieve this goal he first needed to settle with two equally ambitious opponents – Zwide of the Ndwandwe and Sobhuza, chief of the Dlamini branch of the Ngwane – he was prepared to let them make the first move. For with a bigger, better-trained fighting force at his command, he had no cause to be fearful about the outcome of any confrontation....

The first clash, however, was between Zwide and Sobhuza, whose territories adjoined on the upper Phongolo River. A quarrel over the ownership of land led to a war, which although won by Zwide, also benefited Sobhuza. Forced to flee inland to what later became Swaziland, the Ngwane found themselves in the neighbourhood of many small Sotho and Nguni groups whom they defeated one by one and amalgamated into a composite group which later became the Swazi nation.

To the south, meanwhile, the murder of a relative of Dingiswayo on the instructions of Zwide cleared the way for the long-awaited confrontation between the Ndwandwe and the Mthethwa: challenged by an angry Dingiswayo to produce the body of the murdered man, Zwide, realising that his forces stood little chance in a full-on confrontation with the Mthethwa, extended an invitation to his arch-enemy for peace talks.

It was a trap which surprisingly snared Dingiswayo: when he reached the location agreed on for the talks, he found only assassins waiting for him. . . .

Over the next few months, the Mthethwa whom Dingiswayo had built into such a cohesive unit were driven by the rampant Ndwandwe across the Mfolozi River almost as far as the Thukela.

Zwide's supremacy in the region, however, was to be of short duration – for in murdering Dingiswayo he had merely set the stage for the emergence of a far more formidable enemy – the man destined to become the most powerful military ruler in all Africa: Shaka.

The rise of Shaka

Shaka, so the legend goes, was the product of a casual sexual encounter between Senzangakona, heir to the throne of the insignificant Zulu chiefdom, and Nandi, a member of the even tinier Langeni clan.

One day in 1785, Senzangakona observed Nandi bathing in a stream and, overcome with lust, proposed *uku-hlobonga*, a custom which allowed the young a whole range of sexual love play – everything, in fact, except actual penetration. However, things got out of hand that day – and three months after the encounter a Langeni messenger arrived at the Zulu court with the news that Nandi was pregnant and Senzangakona was the father.

Highly amused, the Zulu elders at first dismissed the claim, suggesting that Nandi had caught *ushaka*, a bug which delayed menstruation. But after she had given birth to a son whom she fondly named Shaka, Senzangakona grudgingly admitted that he was the father.

To the elation of the Langeni and the embarrassment of the Zulu, Nandi became a chief's wife. But although the marriage produced a second child (a daughter), the relationship was not a happy one – and after the young Shaka had been blamed for causing the death of a sheep, mother, son and daughter were sent packing.

Unwanted, the unhappy family wandered round the countryside – first returning to the Langeni, then proceeding to the Qwabe and finally, in 1809, ending up with the Mthethwa, where Shaka came under the influence of another outcast – the recently installed chief, Dingiswayo.

The Mthethwa leader, obviously impressed with what he saw, quickly made his tall, brooding recruit a regimental commander. Shaka, in turn, repaid the confidence shown in him by playing a leading role in reorganising the fighting methods of the Mthethwa army.

From the start of his military career with the Mthethwa, Shaka was openly critical of the old way of fighting, believ-ing that it was highly inefficient for two armies to line up about 50 paces apart and to throw spears and abuse at each other until one of them lost heart. Just how inefficient, the 24-year-old commander demonstrated with dramatic effect in 1810, in a war with the Buthelezi chiefdom: the conflict started in the usual way, with the trading of insults. However, matters took an ominous turn when the champion fighter of the Buthelezi stepped forward and challenged anyone to fight him. It was a moment for which Shaka had been waiting: armed only with a shield and what looked like a cut-off spear, he advanced on his opponent who was armed with three traditional long-handled spears. As Shaka advanced, the confused Buthelezi hurled one of them, then another. Both were easily deflected. Before he could hurl the third missile, Shaka had sprinted up to him, hooked his shield around the man (thereby exposing his armpit) and plunged his curious-looking spear in with such force that it emerged on the other side. The Buthelezi was dead before he touched the ground – and Shaka became a national hero.

The revolution in military tactics that followed the invention of the stabbing spear had grave consequences for the other chiefdoms in the region: it made for bloodier, more decisive wars – and, after the death of Dingiswayo, it was the prime reason for Shaka's success in conquering an area the size of Portugal.

Shaka's reward for routing the Buthelezi – the post of supreme commander of the army – presented him with the opportunity to introduce even more changes: for instance, after banning the use of sandals in battle, he took his men on gruelling cross-country runs until their feet were as hard as leather. Shaka himself accompanied his troops on these exercises, and it was said that he was the best runner in the country.

Chief of the Zulu

In 1815, the Zulu leader Senzangakona died and Shaka, backed by his powerful patron, had little difficulty in seizing the chieftaincy from his half-brother Sigujana.

Among his first actions were the installation of his mother as the Great She-elephant of the Zulu and the execution of all who had tormented her and her family during their years of struggle. To commemorate the occasion, he built a new capital which he named Bulawayo (the Place of Killing) overlooking the valley of the Mhlatuze.

With old scores settled, the new Zulu leader turned his attention to building up his little army into an efficient fighting force. It was no easy task: when Shaka took over the reins of power, the Zulu army consisted of no more than 500 men of whom the majority had never fought in a war. Within a few months, however, the tiny army had grown to 2 000 highly trained men.

Although careful to demonstrate his continuing allegiance to Dingiswayo, Shaka also embarked on a low-key, but highly successful campaign to subjugate weaker neighbours and assimilate them into his chiefdom. Certainly, when Dingiswayo was murdered at Zwide's behest in 1818, he had built up such a highly skilled following that he emerged as the only real candidate to take over the leadership of the Mthethwa confederacy.

VERY FEW PICTURES *exist of Shaka – due to the fact that few Europeans penetrated his kingdom before his death. The accuracy of this striking portrait, entitled 'Chaka, King of the Zooloe', is therefore impossible to judge.*

With thousands of soldiers now at his calling, Shaka began organising his armies into the deadliest fighting force in Africa: to ensure that recruits concentrated only on war, he ordered that all conscripts be celibate; the stabbing spear became the standard killing weapon, and he developed brutally efficient new tactics for attack. In this respect, the bull-and-horns formation – whereby the main army advanced on the enemy at the same time as units of the fastest runners created diversions down the opposition's flanks – became a hallmark of a series of bloody wars of conquest.

Shaka's military manoeuvres both united and divided the northern Nguni population of Natal. On the one hand they were responsible for the drawing of clan after clan into the fledgling Zulu state. On the other hand they forced thousands who refused to accept the authority of the Zulu to flee to other regions of southern Africa.

Shaka's new kingdom was built on a strict discipline which united hundreds of diverse communities behind the central authority of the king. Although he ruled like a despot, an inner circle of chiefs advised him on matters of national importance and acted as a check on possible abuses of power. A second tier of *indunas* ensured that the orders of the king and his 'cabinet' were carried out. They also assisted in matters such as the allotment of land, the settling of minor disputes and the distribution of cattle.

Trials for 'capital' crimes such as murder, robbery, rape, adultery, treason, cowardice and spying were conducted only by Shaka and his most trusted advisers. The penalty for these crimes was usually death by clubbing, in a special killing field.

No one owned property in Shaka's Zululand. Land belonged to everyone, and was there to be exploited for the mutual benefit of all. Ivory, however, which was exchanged for beads at the Portuguese port of Delagoa Bay, was the exclusive property of the king. But the trade in elephant tusks proved to be a two-edged sword for the Zulu – for it was the lure of unlimited amounts of this commodity and other riches which drew a far more formidable enemy into Shaka's realm: the white man.

The coming of the white man

In the spring of 1823, a young Xhosa named Jakot Msimbithi walked into the camp of a minor Zulu chief and claimed that he had a message of great importance for the Zulu chief.

Msimbithi knew that he was taking a calculated risk. The northern Nguni people and the Xhosa had been enemies for many years – and under normal circumstances his hosts would have had few qualms about plunging a spear into him. But, as he suspected, the name Shaka opened doors . . . .

Messengers were rapidly despatched to the king, and shortly afterwards he was summoned to the Zulu royal house for an audience which lasted several days. A party of white traders had been marooned near the present-day port of Durban and were on their way to see him, Msimbithi told Shaka.

Always eager to learn more about these strange people and their guns, Shaka could not have asked for a better informant: Msimbithi's whole outlook on life, almost from the time he was born on the eastern Cape frontier, had been shaped by his relationship with Europeans. The son of a minor chief, he had spent some time as an 'apprentice' to a Boer farmer who had seized him during a commando raid on his father's homestead. After a brief spell as an interpreter for the British, he and the legendary wardoctor Nxele had been sentenced to life imprisonment on Robben Island for their part in the disastrous daylight attack by the Xhosa on Grahamstown (see page 105). Following an abortive attempt to escape (in which Nxele drowned), he had been taken from Robben Island to the HMS *Leven*, one of a group of vessels commissioned to chart the east coast of Africa. He was to serve as an interpreter.

At Algoa Bay, on the way back to Robben Island, Msimbithi again changed ships: this time his linguistic skills were required by Lieutenant Francis Farewell, who was on his way to Zululand to open up trade links with Shaka.

After the chartered vessel, the *Salisbury*, had dropped anchor at the mouth of the Mfolozi River, Farewell set off with an advance party which included Msimbithi to look

Woman's role in a marriage by royal concession

The inferior status of women was impressed upon members of the Zulu chiefdom from a very early age.

When they were between five and eight years old, children of both sexes underwent a ceremony in which their ears were pierced. From this time on, the girls were drawn increasingly into 'women's' duties, working long hours in the fields and carrying out a variety of domestic chores while the boys were taught to herd livestock.

As they grew up, the children learned to eat, drink, dance, sit and sleep apart from the opposite sex. And there began the pattern of behaviour and taboo that would remain with them for the rest of their lives.

Females were avoided by boys undergoing puberty rituals, and by herbalists, male diviners and any male who intended to go on a hunt or hold a ritual sacrifice. A woman who had just given birth was shunned because she was regarded as a potential source of harm.

The nuptials in the Zulu state were more complicated than a simple agreement between a man and a woman to marry and set up home together.

Instead, they were subject to the absolute authority of the king, who was unlikely to grant permission to men of his regiments to marry before they were well into their thirties, and the women of their *amabutho* (age-sets) around 10 years younger.

Until a few decades ago, the majority of historians ascribed the restrictions on marriage to reasons associated with Shaka's own personality, suggesting they were prompted by the belief that an accumulation of sexual energy could somehow be transmuted into military vigour. In fact, sexual relations within Zulu society were likely to occur long before marriage.

There was another crucial factor: when a Zulu man married, he left his father's homestead and established a new production community of his own, usually augmenting his family by more wives and their children. Thus by controlling marriage in his kingdom, the king in effect controlled the rate and direction of production and reproduction.

When a woman left her father's household to join that of her new husband, she was immediately subject to the authority of her husband and her in-laws; this continued until after she had given birth to her first child. The new bride also encountered a whole set of taboos, including rules regarding her style of dress and even her hair. Like the other women of the household, she was excluded from the decision-making process, which remained the preserve of married men.

And while it was the husband's duty to provide each of his wives with an area of agricultural land large enough to support her and her children, with a private granary and perhaps a few milch cows, this placed the husband in the position of provider and superior.

As befitted his status as a 'superior being', the husband functioned as an arbiter of disputes and dispenser of favours in the household, where his control of the relative ranking of wives allowed him to discriminate in favour of an obedient wife.

On the other hand, Zulu women had certain undeniable rights and expectations. Fathers were obliged to support their unmarried daughters, husbands were expected to look after their wives and sons were responsible for the well-being of their widowed mothers.

Within the bounds of the *status quo*, women were able to acquire considerable prestige in their communities. Older women are known to have wielded great influence in their sons' households, and in the case of chiefs and royal households, wives and close female relatives were sometimes appointed to influential positions as heads of homesteads.

TRADITIONAL DRESS *remains popular at Zulu festivals, providing a link with the past – and a reminder of former greatness. The leopard skin cape and headband worn by the man above indicate his position as a chief. The unmarried girls (right) dance alone – without married men or women.*

LIEUTENANT *Francis Farewell (left) of the Royal Navy was anxious to open trade links with Shaka's kingdom, landing near present-day Durban in 1823.*
HENRY FYNN *(right), a determined adventurer who joined Farewell in his expedition to Shaka's capital of Bulawayo. Both men later tried to discredit Shaka in an attempt to persuade Britain to annex the region.*

for signs of people. While they were away a storm blew the *Salisbury* out to sea. During their long wait to be rescued, and after a row with one of the white traders, Msimbithi stormed off to seek an audience with the Zulu king.

Shaka, grateful for the information he supplied, appointed Msimbithi a chief – and then settled down to wait for the arrival of the traders.

When the Europeans finally arrived at Bulawayo, a full 12 months later, Farewell had been joined by another adventurer, Henry Fynn. In many ways, Zululand would never be the same again.

Natal – bought for a handful of beads

Farewell, Fynn and the ruthlessly ambitious teenager, Nathaniel Isaacs, have been described as the first white pioneers of Natal. In a sense they were – and certainly, the diaries of Fynn (rewritten from memory 20 years after he had lost his original copy) and Isaacs constitute the main source on the Zulu people during the rule of Shaka and Dingane. Yet, brave though they were in venturing into a world unknown to whites, their writings indicate that they were motivated above all by greed. And in their bid to get rich quickly, they were prepared to lie, cheat and even kill. In their very first meeting with Shaka, they claimed to be envoys of the British monarch King George – and the Zulu king, because he had no way of knowing any better, took them at their word and lavished them with gifts.

Fynn particularly became a favourite at the Zulu royal house after he had 'saved' Shaka's life by washing with camomile tea a stab wound inflicted by a Ndwandwe attacker. The grateful king presented his saviour with a huge portion of what later became Natal, for a few shillings' worth of glass beads.

Fynn declared himself king of Natal, took a harem of Zulu wives and fathered dozens of children. It was an example which the equally unscrupulous Isaacs quickly followed. Both men were absolute masters of their white fiefdom – and, like true despots, regularly ordered the exe-

cution (by clubbing) of Zulu who had been virtually given to them by Shaka. Yet, when they published their diaries years later, they described this method of execution as particularly barbaric.

Of course, it did not take too much for Shaka to order the killing of a man. But these white traders were well acquainted with gory methods of execution long before they came to Zululand. In England in the 1800s there were no fewer than 200 offences for which people could be sentenced to death by hanging. These included the theft of five shillings from a shop; a sailor caught begging; stealing from a rabbit warren; or cutting down a tree. It was an age when women could be burnt alive at the stake for treason, while their male counterparts were hanged until half alive, made to watch as their entrails were removed, and finally put out of their misery by being cut into quarters. And England was the most civilised country on earth.

Although Fynn, Isaacs, Farewell and their companions broke Zulu laws dozens of times, Shaka always treated them with the utmost respect, even under the most extreme provocation. In their greed for ivory, they had no qualms about bribing minor chiefs to supply them with tusks, even though they were well aware that only the king handled this commodity and that anyone else who did so faced certain death. Although Shaka acted ruthlessly against these chiefs, he took no action against the real culprits and, in fact, supplied them with even more ivory. Yet these ungrateful visitors could never get enough – and in the end, their greed led to a substantial reduction of the elephant population in Zululand.

Lying, scheming and cheating, they abused the hospitality of the Zulu chiefs and their king – and when the Cape Government finally got wind of what they were doing, they tried to justify their actions by claiming to be the victims of Zulu savagery.

Of course, Fynn and Isaacs in particular had good reason for wanting to portray Shaka and his people as a 'race of barbarians': should Britain have decided to annex the

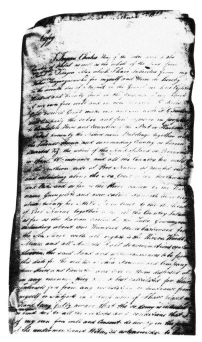
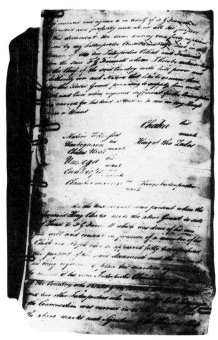
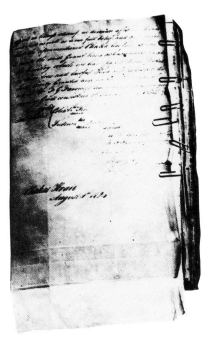

ACCORDING to this document, Shaka granted to Francis Fare-well and company 9 065 square kilometres of land in the vicinity of Port Natal. The white adventurers made use of Shaka's hospitality to line their pockets.

territory, their landholdings would have netted them a very handsome fortune.

Although they tried to cover up their indiscretions, they were not entirely successful: in 1941 a letter written by Isaacs while on his way to London to publish his memoirs was discovered. In it he urged Fynn to do the same: 'Make them (the Zulu kings) out as blood-thirsty as you can and endeavour to give an estimate of the number of people they murdered during their reign, and also describe the frivolous crimes people lose their lives for. It all tends to swell up the work and make it interesting,' he said.

In his book, 'Travels and Adventures in Eastern Africa' (published in 1836), Isaacs described Shaka as an unpredictable tyrant who killed many of his own subjects for pleasure. But despite Isaacs' efforts, the British, at first, showed no interest in wanting to fly the Union Jack over Natal. It was only in 1843, five years after the Voortrekkers had declared their Republic of Natalia, that the British decided to annex the territory; Zululand itself was only annexed in the 1880s, following the capture of Shaka's nephew, Cetshwayo.

Misjudging these white visitors was not the only error made by Shaka during his short, bloody reign. In an era where succession by assassination had become virtually a northern Nguni custom, he failed to recognise the danger posed by his half-brother Dingane.

When Shaka first came to power, he had executed everyone he thought capable of challenging him for the throne. However, for some inexplicable reason he had overlooked his half-brother, Dingane who, realising his precarious position, had kept as low a profile as possible.

But in 1828, Dingane (who was then about 31 years old) was ready to make a bid for power: with another brother, Mhlangane, he entered into a conspiracy with Shaka's chief induna, Mbhopa. They made their move on 22 Sep-

tember 1828, at a small village outside the Zulu capital, while Shaka was speaking to a group of Sotho emissaries who had brought him a tribute of cranes' feathers. To distract the king, Mbhopa intervened and drove off the visitors, berating them on the grounds that they had come too late. Then Mhlangane crept up behind Shaka and stabbed him in the back. Dingane darted forward and stabbed him a second time. According to some accounts, the Zulu king shouted out in anguish as he died: 'O children of my father, what have I done to you?'

A STEEL ENGRAVING depicting the death of Shaka. In reality, he was stabbed in the back by his brother Mhlangane. The final blow was struck by another brother, Dingane.

A time of troubles

In the early 1800s African societies of southern Africa were rocked by a series of upheavals that altered the political structure of much of the region. For the many members of long-established chiefdoms, change often came at breakneck speed: in the battle for influence and power, old allies became sworn enemies, new alliances were forged, previously independent chiefdoms were assimilated into other groups and fierce wars scattered refugees over a wide area.

THE TERROR STARTED WITH a chorus of shouts and a volley of shots. Then, as the screams of the panic-stricken echoed across the dusty countryside, teams of horsemen came charging – blocking off all avenues of escape for the fleeing villagers....

It was 1824, and in what is today known as the far northern Cape a small band of Griqua mountain men were waging a vicious battle for control of the region with Tlharo and Tlhaping members of the ailing confederation of southern Tswana chiefdoms.

Although the Bergenaars (as they were known to local missionaries) planned and executed their campaign brilliantly – with a series of morale-sapping hit-and-run raids – their opponents had already been weakened by the defection of key members of the confederation. Long before the first shots were fired, the influential Rolong community had trekked north to the greener pastures of Heuningvlei and Morokweng. And even though the Tlharo and Tlhaping had stayed – and, for their troubles, had borne the brunt of the Bergenaar attacks – it had soon become clear that they had little stomach for a fight.

By 1828 the confederation (as then constituted) was on the verge of collapse.

The end of the old order
The Bergenaar Griqua and the southern Tswana were not the only communities to be caught in a crisis: all over southern Africa, old orders were disintegrating – peacefully in some instances, in a spate of bloodletting in others. Although reasons for the fighting (and the immense social changes that stemmed from it) varied from area to area and from chiefdom to chiefdom, there were common strands....

In the early 19th century, for instance, most of the land now known as Natal was struck by a crippling drought (followed by a famine). As competition intensified for limited resources, many smaller chiefdoms sought protection from more powerful rivals by forging alliances with other groups. But in an era of growing militarism, large groupings of chiefdoms meant bigger armies and fiercer wars. While the majority of conquered peoples were assimilated into the structures of the victors, some chose to flee to territories controlled by other groups – and this invariably sparked new bouts of fighting.

Increased contact between white and black traders was another cause of strife in African communities. In less complicated times, when the bead and the cow were the chief monetary units, the economies of African societies were strictly controlled by the chiefs. But when white traders began offering firearms in exchange for ivory and slaves, it was not only royal families who started scrambling to oblige: in a dangerous land, a gun, whether in the hands of a commoner or a king, often meant the difference between survival and death or between power and serfdom. It was not surprising, therefore, that in the early years of the century, many commoners were prepared to do the unthinkable: to break away from their chiefs and build their own armouries (and armies).

A dangerous subcontinent
It was the prospect of controlling the trade route to the far north-east to Delagoa Bay and southwards to the Cape Colony that prompted the Bergenaar Griqua to declare war on the southern Tswana confederation.

Yet, just a few months before their first attack on the Tlharo and Tlhaping, the Bergenaar were regarded by members of the confederation as both trusted allies and valuable trading partners. In fact, in 1823, when Phuthing and Hlakwana raiders stormed the southern Tswana capital of Dithakong, it had been the Bergenaars who had driven them off.

At the same time as the Bergenaars were bidding for power and influence at the expense of the Tlhaping and Tlhora, other Tswana chiefdoms were under attack by the Kololo (remnants of a Fokeng group led by Sebetwane) and the Taung (who had been driven from the eastern highveld by Hlubi and Ngwane forces). Under Moletsane's leadership, the Taung made increasingly ambitious

TWO BOYS *who killed a lioness preying on their cattle, receive Mzilikazi's thanks in this 1835 watercolour.*

THE TLOKWA CHIEF *Sekonyela was described by a missionary source as sturdy, with dull eyes and a deep voice. His surly manner, it was claimed, earned him the fear, rather than the love, of his subjects.*

The *Mfecane* – fact or fable?

For generations, South African schoolchildren were taught how a tyrannical Zulu king named Shaka was responsible for one of the worst periods of black-on-black violence in the history of the sub-continent: the *Mfecane* (the 'crushing').

According to the majority of early historians, Shaka ordered his men to attack every rival – both big and small – after he had built the most powerful army in Africa. The effect was devastating: tens of thousands of people were killed, dozens of chiefdoms were destroyed or assimilated into new, predatory states and wide areas of the highveld were depopulated. This suited the Afrikaner view of history which claimed that the Voortrekkers entered undisputed territory.

Even historians sympathetic to the struggle of southern Africa's indigenous black people tried to provide the *Mfecane* with legitimacy. It was, claimed one prominent historiographer, a time of state-building in African societies.

By the 1990s, however, many prominent historians had come to the conclusion that the *Mfecane* did not, in fact, exist. While they agreed that there was indeed disorder among African societies in Natal and on the highveld, they were adamant that Shaka could not be held solely responsible for this.

The least controversial of the reasons offered for the upheaval was the drought of the early 1800s, which sparked fierce competition for resources. The availability of guns from white traders also led to the rise of warlords, it was claimed. Another, far more controversial theory, was that the disorder which plagued the sub-continent was caused by 'converging imperialistic thrusts' – from the British in the Cape, to acquire labour after the reorganisation of the colony's labour procurement system and from the Portuguese at Delagoa Bay, to supply slaves for their plantations in Brazil.

raids to the north and west of their headquarters. After an unsuccessful attack on a Rolong community near the Molopo River, Moletsane began eyeing the pickings north of the Molopo. It was to prove to be his downfall....

In 1829, after a devastating defeat at the hands of the Ndebele, the Taung ceased to exist as a military force. The Kololo, seeing what had happened to their allies, decided to settle north of the Zambezi.

The rise of the Ndebele

The Ndebele influenced events in the area north of the Vaal more than any other group. Their leader, Mzilikazi, had first risen to prominence during the Zulu-Ndwandwe conflict, when he had switched his allegiance from Zwide to Shaka. But after a successful campaign as a military commander, he had flouted Shaka's authority by keeping plundered cattle for himself. When messengers of the Zulu king enquired about the booty, he had contemptuously cut the plumes off their headdresses, knowing this action would provoke Shaka. To escape his inevitable

punishment, he had fled with about 300 followers across the Drakensberg into the eastern Transvaal.

In 1822, the tiny group moved north-west across the northern Drakensberg onto the highveld, and it was while he was in this region that Mzilikazi transformed his band of fugitives into a powerful and cohesive unit.

Ndebele ranks were swelled significantly by Nguni refugees from the Zulu army, by conquered Sotho clans and by hundreds of others who joined voluntarily. By the mid-1820s, Mzilikazi and his army controlled an area of almost 80 000 square kilometres between the Limpopo, Vaal, Crocodile and Molopo rivers.

In 1827, the Ndebele abandoned their Vaal River base and set up new headquarters in the Magaliesberg, from where they conquered Tswana chiefdoms to the west and gradually expanded their control over surrounding territories. By 1829, the Ndebele had an army of between 6 000 and 8 000 men.

This pattern of migration and settlement was repeated in 1832, when they left the Magaliesberg and moved into

AN ENGRAVING *of a Sotho armed with club, spear and shield. In fact, warriors preferred more than one spear.*

the Marico valley in the western Transvaal. From here they continued to attack the Tswana and Rolong.

Although the Ndebele army was relatively small (compared with the Zulu forces), their members more than made up for this in fighting skill. They seldom killed young men whom they encountered in raids or battle, preferring instead to draft them into their regiments.

Although Mzilikazi accommodated his regiments in barracks close to his capital, he also maintained outposts throughout his vast area of influence. Young soldiers, who made up the bulk of the permanent army, were not allowed to marry. Older men formed the military reserve.

Sotho refugees were subjected to forced labour, although some were allowed to remain in their own villages within Mzilikazi's territory.

Discipline was strict and punishment harsh in the Ndebele state. Strict rules governed every aspect of life, from agriculture to warfare, from matrimony to taxation. Despite his reputation as a warlord, Mzilikazi brought order to the area he controlled by welding diverse elements into a single, apparently stable state. Whites who visited him went away impressed by the effectiveness of his rule. In 1836, an American missionary wrote: 'The people, as individuals, are restricted from some crimes which are prevalent among other tribes. Although these people are accustomed to plundering on a large scale, stealing from a stranger in the community is unheard of.'

In July 1832, Dingane, chief of the Zulu, sent out a massive force in search of the Ndebele. In their sweep through the countryside, the Zulu soldiers attacked outlying homesteads and confiscated cattle, but when they came face-to-face with the main Ndebele army, they were soundly beaten.

Besides having to be on constant alert against attack by the Zulu, Mzilikazi also had to contend with Griqua and Korana raiders based in the south-west. After first trying to eliminate this threat by refusing to allow anyone to cross the Vaal River without his permission, he later changed this strategy: in 1832 he drove Tswana chiefdoms from their homes in the vicinity of the Crocodile and Marico rivers and settled his own people in their place. In a bid to acquire firearms, he tried to build up contacts with traders and missionaries.

When the first groups of Voortrekkers arrived in the area in the 1830s, Mzilikazi's enemies found a ready ally in the whites. It quickly became apparent that Mzilikazi and the newcomers were not going to live together in peace....

The crunch came in October 1836, when the Ndebele attacked a Voortrekker laager at Vegkop. The trekkers stood firm, but lost all their horses. Three months later, a combined Voortrekker, Griqua and Rolong force defeated the Ndebele at Mosega. Soon afterwards, the Ndebele were attacked by the Zulu army. In 1837, after yet another attack by the joint forces of Voortrekker leaders Piet Uys and Andries Pretorius, Mzilikazi and his followers crossed the Limpopo to settle in the Matopo Hills.

Upheaval in Natal

Warfare among chiefdoms in Natal started a few years before the rise of Shaka. First to be uprooted were Matiwane's Ngwane people, who were driven from their homes in north-western Natal by one of the most ambitious of the Nguni leaders – Dingiswayo of the Mthethwa.

Rather than submit to Dingiswayo's superior fighting force, Matiwane fled westwards into the foothills of the Drakensberg, where he attacked and defeated the Hlubi (of which one group fled southwards and joined other refugee bands known as Mfengu). Another group that remained in the vicinity of the Drakensberg was incorporated for a short period into the Zulu state that Shaka had started building. A third remnant – led by Mpangazita – fled across the Drakensberg to settle on the highveld. These refugees were followed a year later (in 1822) by the Ngwane, who, after having occupied the territory of the defeated Hlubi, had themselves been forced to flee the Zulu army.

The Ngwane and the Hlubi were not the only Nguni people to have been forced to move to other areas of southern Africa. A third group (who became known as the Ndebele) led by Mzilikazi broke away from Shaka and migrated across the Drakensberg.

Towards the end of 1818, when the Ndwandwe were defeated by Shaka, three chiefs who were previously subordinate to Zwide took fright and led their people into southern Mozambique, where they disrupted the lives of both the Portuguese and local Tsonga people. Clashes among the refugees led to the rise of a leader named Soshangane, a confident and capable man who emerged from the fighting with sufficient power to found the Gaza state in southern Mozambique.

Zwangendaba and Nxaba, the two other refugee leaders, moved even further north in the early 1830s, making their way across the Zambezi. From there they spread out into present-day Zambia, Malawi and Tanzania, where they formed a number of chiefdoms known as the Ngoni kingdom.

Disorder among the Sotho people

Meanwhile, in southern Africa, Sotho communities on the highveld came under increasing pressure from the three bands of Nguni refugees: first to bear the brunt of this pressure were the Tlokwa, ruled by a woman called MaNthatisi. While acting as regent for her minor son, Sekonyela, MaNthatisi acquired a formidable reputation, her enemies spreading grotesque rumours that she was a giantess with a single eye in the middle of her forehead who fed her warriors with her own milk before sending them into battle behind large swarms of bees. But among her own people she was known affectionately as Mosadinyana (Little Woman). She was an efficient and intelligent ruler, whereas Sekonyela, according to missionary sources, was a bad-tempered person who inspired fear rather than love among his people.

As the invading Hlubi, led by Mpangazita, drove the Tlokwa from their villages, MaNthatisi and her followers fled westward. For two years, the Tlokwa and Hlubi fought pitched battles that destroyed Sotho communities along the upper Caledon River.

It was not long before the Hlubi were followed across the Drakensberg by Matiwane's Ngwane – and again the unfortunate Tlokwa became victims. In 1825, a five-day battle between the Ngwane and the Hlubi ended with the defeat of the Hlubi and the death of Mpangazita. Again the Hlubi disintegrated and dispersed – some attaching themselves to their Ngwane conquerors, others to the Ndebele, and yet others to the tough and resourceful Sotho leader, Moshoeshoe.

Matiwane maintained his dominance over other communities in the Caledon River region until 1827, when he was attacked by the Zulu and driven south. Soon afterwards, his people fought two unsuccessful battles against Moshoeshoe's Sotho and against the Ndebele. Finally, in 1828, Matiwane led his war-weary people into southern Nguni territory. It was the beginning of the end for him. Well aware of the nature of the threat, the Thembu in the region appealed to the Cape colonial authorities for aid. A force under Henry Somerset was rushed to the area – and with the help of local Africans inflicted a disastrous defeat on the Ngwane at the Battle of Mbholompo.

Again a group had been shattered beyond recognition. Some Ngwane remnants joined the Sotho, while others returned to Zululand, where Matiwane was later killed by Dingane.

The fighting also brought unprecedented turmoil and dislocation to the southern highveld, where the small size and social structure of the southern Sotho communities made them particularly vulnerable to individual attack.

During this period, many independent Sotho communities broke up under endless pressure from marauding bands. The survivors either fled from the conflict or entered into protective alliances with other clans. While

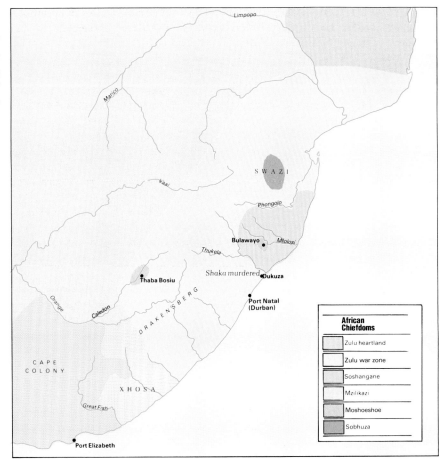

WARS, CONQUEST *and a process of assimilation in the early 1800s sent a shock wave of fleeing chiefdoms and clans across a wide area of south-east Africa, extending over the Drakensberg into the interior, north-west beyond present-day Swaziland and north into the highveld.*

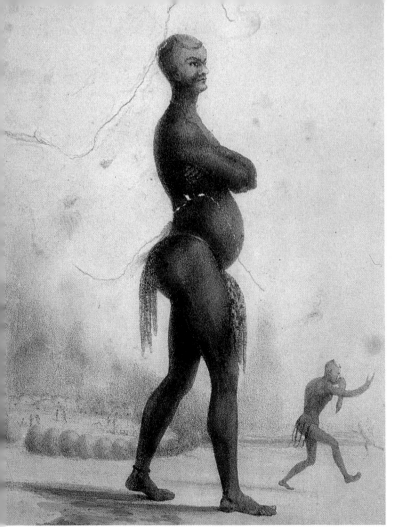

MZILIKAZI *insulted the Zulu king by chasing plundered cattle into his own kraal. It was to escape the inevitable punishment that he led his people over the Drakensberg into the highveld.*

groups such as the Kololo remained reasonably cohesive during their flight, others degenerated into motley bands of refugees. At the same time many Sotho refugees fled to the Cape Colony, where they took up employment with white colonists.

While some clans disintegrated, others consolidated. This happened to two groups in particular – the Tlokwa and the Sotho of Moshoeshoe. The Tlokwa had been the first victims of the Nguni invasions across the Drakensberg. Abandoning their territorial base in the face of the Hlubi onslaught, they adopted a semi-nomadic existence. Despite this, they remained a cohesive group under MaNthatisi. Around 1824, however, their life style changed when they established themselves in two mountain fortresses at Joalaboholo and Marabeng, near the Caledon River. Refugees from broken communities – attracted by the apparent security of the Tlokwa stronghold – flocked to join them, and the chiefdom expanded rapidly. By the mid-1830s, the Tlokwa comprised about 14 000 Sotho and 2 000-3 000 Nguni. By the time Sekonyela came of age and assumed the chieftainship in the 1830s, his sphere of power extended to the north and east as far as the Caledon River. Similarly, Moshoeshoe managed to build up the Sotho state by skilfully exploiting the turmoil in the area. (see box).

The Pedi and southward migrations

The wars on the highveld also disrupted and dislocated northern Sotho society. During the late 1700s and early 1800s, the Pedi had formed themselves into a powerful group under the leadership of Thulare, chief of the Maroteng section of the group. Owing mainly to a series of successful military campaigns over a wide area of what later became known as the Transvaal, he had managed to expand Pedi influence. Yet the Pedi state did not emerge intact from the disorder.

One of the major contributory factors for its decline was the death of Thulare in about 1820 and the bitter succession disputes among his sons. The clashes left the Pedi ill-equipped to deal with the growing threat from outside. In 1822, the Ndebele defeated them, remaining in their territory long enough to deplete stock and food supplies. Raids by the Ndwandwe provided other serious setbacks and the theft of cattle and grain effectively wrecked the Pedi economy. Chiefdoms began to compete among themselves for the few resources that remained.

The process of degeneration, however, began to slow down under the growing influence of the new Pedi leader, Sekwati. In two years, he enlarged his following by attacking neighbouring settlements and forging new alliances. He restocked his cattle herds through raids and managed to ensure the subordination and loyalty of newly incorporated groups by giving them a share of the spoils. Like Moshoeshoe, Sekwati saw no point in military confrontation without gain or specific purpose. In 1828 he returned to the Pedi homeland in the Steelpoort River area, where he steadily gained recognition as the dominant power in the region.

East of the Drakensberg the Mpondo were attacked by the Zulu twice during this time, and in a raid in 1828 settlements were razed. But they soon recovered under the leadership of Faku, who replenished his people's herds by raiding. The chief also enlarged his following by incorporating captives and refugees, subsequently emerging as a significant power south of the Zulu state.

The best-known of the northern Nguni refugees to migrate southwards were those later known as the Mfengu, a heterogeneous group of diverse origins. They had first travelled to Gcalekaland, where they had approached minor chiefs and headmen for food and shelter. They attached themselves to the Xhosa in several ways, some paying tribute in return for the loan of Xhosa cattle and the use of Xhosa land. But their inferior status rankled, and many began to look to Cape colonial society as a means of improving their lot. Many settled on the newly formed mission stations.

In 1835 about 20 000 Mfengu were encouraged by Methodist missionaries and Governor Benjamin D'Urban to move from Gcalekaland into the eastern part of the Cape Colony. These adaptable people were able to survive by using their individual wits and skills. In fact, many became prominent in the ranks of peasant proprietors and urban landholders at the Cape. Later, members of their educated elite played a prominent role as scholars, voters and as 'modernisers' – they were also in the forefront of early African political organisations.

From village headman to founder of a nation

Like most leaders of his time, Moshoeshoe rose to prominence from humble beginnings. Starting off as a simple village headman, he expanded his power to become the founder and first paramount chief of the Sotho. His first big chance came in about 1820 when he moved his people to the slopes of the Butha Buthe Mountain, from where he stood firm against the first raids from the edge of the Drakensberg . . . .

Born in 1786, he received the name Moshoeshoe from a song of praise dedicated to him after he had captured a large number of cattle during a daring raid on a neighbouring chiefdom. In the song, he was likened to a barber, thus his name that supposedly imitated the sound made by a knife shaving off a beard or hair.

Moshoeshoe was a fine strategist and (when he needed to be) an unashamed opportunist. For instance, when his Ngwane neighbours became a threat, he threw his energies into developing good relations with the Zulu people by sending gifts to their king, Shaka. Then, when the gifts stopped arriving, Shaka was told that the Ngwane were hindering Moshoeshoe from sending them. Shaka immediately attacked the Ngwane, defeating Moshoeshoe's greatest enemy.

To avoid confrontation and war, Moshoeshoe would attempt to buy off raiders with offerings of cattle. In 1822, when he was attacked by an Ngwane raiding party he retreated and persuaded their leader, Matiwane, to accept a gift of cattle. Moshoeshoe's deferential attitude caused Matiwane to refer to him scornfully as 'little Sotho'.

Despite his caution, Moshoeshoe and his followers could not escape the conflict. In the winter of 1824, they were besieged at Butha Buthe by MaNthatisi's Tlokwa, and fled to the more secure mountain base of Thaba Bosiu ('mountain of the night'). There was plenty of water in this lofty stronghold, and the sheer cliffs were a deterrent against attack. But Thaba Bosiu was also perilously close to Matiwane's headquarters, with the result that Moshoeshoe thought it expedient to maintain diplomatic ties with the Ngwane chief.

Came 1827, and a Zulu force swept across the Drakensberg capturing large quantities of Ngwane cattle. Intent on rebuilding his herds, Matiwane attacked his Sotho neighbours the following year. But this time he met with spirited resistance, and the Ngwane were forced to retreat southwards. As a result, Moshoeshoe gained control of a large area of Ngwane territory.

When Matiwane was finally defeated by a Cape colonial force led by Henry Somerset, many refugees from his forces returned to the southern highveld to seek the protection of their former enemy.

After eliminating the Ngwane threat, Moshoeshoe maintained a tentative peace with the Tlokwa, his main rivals, but was repeatedly attacked by marauding bands of Kora and, in 1831, by the Ndebele, whom he defeated in battle.

Throughout this period of attack and counter-attack, Moshoeshoe continued to consolidate and expand his chiefdom. He offered protection and a place to live for displaced leaders and their followers (and in return expected their protection). This way he also created a buffer state against outside invaders. By 1840 his followers numbered 40 000 – a remarkable achievement in the time of upheaval that was the *Difaqane*.

Inevitably, the expansion of white society into the interior led to clashes between Moshoeshoe and both the Voortrekkers and the British, who annexed his territory in 1868 (see page 161). He died in 1870 aged 84.

AN EARLY PORTRAIT *of Moshoeshoe (left) dated 1833. By this time he had managed to enlarge his Sotho kingdom in the face of repeated attacks, attracting an increasing number of refugees to his impregnable mountain fortress of Thaba Bosiu (above), shown here in an 1834 engraving entitled 'Thaba Bosiu (Mountain of darkness) stronghold of Moscheshwe'.*

Enter the British…

At the end of the 18th century, and again at the beginning of the 19th,
a new element was added to an already complex mix of people at the Cape: the British.
Motivated by imperialism, deceit, greed, prejudice and humanitarianism, the colony's new rulers
would play a leading role in constructing one of the world's most troubled societies.

IN 1795, WHILE THE COUNTRIES of Europe were toppling to the troops of a French military genius called Napoleon Bonaparte, a squadron of British warships was racing 10 000 kilometres across the broad swells of the Atlantic Ocean on a mission that would redirect the course of South African history . . . .

Its destination was the Dutch-owned Cape of Good Hope. Its orders were to seize it. At stake was Britain's lucrative trade link with the East, now at grave risk following the overthrow of the Dutch monarchy and its replacement by a French-satellite administration calling itself the Batavian Republic.

On 9 July, four sloops-of-war sailed into Simon's Bay and five days later soldiers were set ashore at nearby Simon's Town. On 7 August, after almost a month of abortive talks, British troops, supported by gunfire from their ships, began a sweep along the coast towards Muizenberg. By 15 September, the tiny Dutch garrison had been crushed – and the settlement, their possession for almost 150 years, captured.

Although many inhabitants were opposed to the occupation, the British, masters at placating conquered people, moved quickly to win the confidence of their new subjects: language rights and religious freedom were guaranteed; the monetary and legal systems were retained; and some key Dutch officials were absorbed into the new administrative structure. But the masterstroke of this public relations exercise was a decision to abolish some of the worst aspects of the trading monopoly previously enjoyed by the Dutch East India Company. Welcomed by even their most outspoken opponents, it led to more open trade, even though the continued existence of monopolies and restrictions on international trade meant that the economy still fell far short of operating on a free trade basis.

But in 1802, while the British were still transforming the tiny settlement from a position of near-bankruptcy into a viable concern, the politicians of Europe were engaged in another round of wheeling-and-dealing . . . .

In terms of the Treaty of Amiens, which brought peace to Europe for the first time in 10 years, the Cape was returned to the Batavian Republic. But the truce between Britain and France was a fragile one – and it lasted just three years. In 1805, the first shots in what became known as the Napoleonic Wars were fired and the British again moved quickly to reoccupy the Cape. This time, however, they had come to stay – and over the next century would make the settlement the nucleus of a huge area under British rule, spanning most of southern Africa.

Yet initially, the Home Government regarded its new possession essentially in terms of its strategic geographic position – a land fortress protecting its trade links with India. It therefore showed little interest in implementing fundamental changes – until the end of the Napoleonic Wars forced a drastic rethink. Certainly, victory over the French could not have come at a worse time for an already struggling British economy: the discontinuation of war industries – such as the making of uniforms – and the return to civilian life of thousands of soldiers swelled the already long queues of unemployed. It led to growing dissatisfaction and violent protest . . . .

ON 7 AUGUST 1795, *British warships opened fire on the Dutch before sweeping northwards from Simon's Town towards Muizenberg, while land-based troops began an advance that would end 150 years of Dutch rule at the Cape.*

MUYZENBERG den VII AUGUST anno MDCCXCV.

THE WINE INDUSTRY *flourished under the British, as the letter (above) authorising the purchase of wine for the King of France shows. The wine was brought to Cape Town by cart (right).*

As economic and political strains increased, the government began looking to its overseas possessions not only as a means to bail it out of its financial difficulties, but also to serve as labour recruitment centres for British unemployed. In both respects, the Cape of Good Hope played an important role.

Ironically, it was during the Napoleonic Wars (which proved so costly to Britain) that the Cape's economic potential was first recognised. An increase in the shipping traffic at Cape Town harbour – and later, the exile of Napoleon to the south Atlantic island of St Helena – opened up new opportunities for local traders. This, coupled with legislation reducing import duties on certain goods bound for the British market, ushered in a period of unprecedented settler prosperity. Exporters, particularly of meat, hides, skins, ivory and aloes (for medicinal purposes), thrived. But none could compete with the wine industry, which generated more income than all other exports put together. A British decision to reduce customs duties on Cape wines to a third of that of its continental rivals had a lot to do with the success story of this industry. In 1822, its best year, more than 10 percent of the wine consumed in Britain was exported from Cape Town. But three years later full customs duties were imposed and the wine industry – and indeed the Cape economy – tottered.

Nevertheless, partnership with Britain again proved advantageous in the 1830s when a preferential trade agreement with the Home Government led to rapid growth for the eastern Cape wool industry.

The population of the Cape

At the time of the Second British Occupation, the population of the Cape consisted of some 22 000 settlers, about 25 000 slaves, an indeterminate number of indigenous hunter-gathering and pastoralist Khoisan inhabitants who had been pushed out of the area defined by whites as the colony and those Xhosa chiefdoms in the Zuurveld region.

When the first large contingent of British settlers arrived in 1820, the white population had increased to about 47 000 – of which 43 000 were of Dutch extraction. And yet it was the smaller English community that made the biggest impact. For, unlike the Dutch, the new settlers were eager to participate in the economic system which was introduced at the Cape by the Crown.

Within a few years of the start of the British Government's settler scheme, part of the colonial landscape had been overlaid with social and physical features of English life, such as newspapers, debating societies, horse-racing and village-green cricket matches. Even the buildings began to change, with the distinctive square-built architecture of Georgian Britain moving into the towns.

British predominance was based in part on education. In 1812 the Governor, Sir John Cradock, unveiled plans to establish white English-medium schools throughout the colony. In 1795, at the time of the first occupation, a number of primary-level schools, catering mainly for the better-off white population, had been started in Cape Town – while in the countryside, education was left largely to the devices of wandering tutors, mainly former soldiers. Illiteracy was common among whites and the norm among slaves and servants. Cradock's proclamation, therefore, aimed to put education within reach of both the poor and those living in rural areas.

In 1813, the Cape Town Free School for the needy was founded – and by 1814 was educating more than 200 students of both sexes. Over the next decade, the success of a government scheme which offered bonuses to competent English-speaking teachers who moved to rural areas led to the establishment of free public schools at Graaff-Reinet, Uitenhage, George, Stellenbosch, Tulbagh and Caledon.

Yet, because it was in the interests of those who ruled to see to it that the law was understood by all, proclamations, ordinances, and Acts of parliament were gazetted in Dutch as well as English throughout the century.

The power behind Britain's Industrial Revolution

In 1769, one of the world's greatest peacetime revolutions was started by a young Scottish engineer demonstrating a curious-looking machine.

Within a few decades, James Watt's steam engine would push Britain into a new era – of mechanisation, industrialisation, mass production and, most of all, social upheaval.

The basis of what became known as the Industrial Revolution was the application of steam power to machinery for use in production and transport. Watt's invention created a new demand for iron, and for coal to make the steam – and because Britain was rich in both these commodities, it had a natural advantage over France, its closest rival.

But although the steam engine, coupled with other inventions such as John Kay's 'Flying Shuttle' (1733), James Hargreaves' 'Spinning Jenny' (patented in 1770) and Richard Arkwright's 'Water Frame' (1769), meant that for the first time commodities could be produced cheaply and in large quantities, it also created a demand for new markets and sources of raw materials. It was to its colonies that Britain looked to meet both these needs. Having lost the American colonies, it began to attach increased significance to the markets of the East

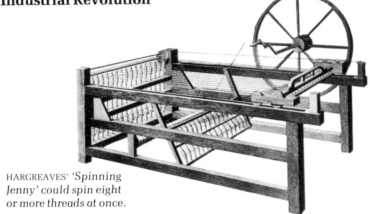

HARGREAVES' '*Spinning Jenny*' *could spin eight or more threads at once.*

– and in this respect the strategically situated Cape of Good Hope played an important part in helping to maintain British dominance in India.

In many ways, however, the Industrial Revolution demanded a heavy price of British society. Uncontrolled expansion of factories and the collapse of the domestic system (where workers worked in their own homes) and of small workshops, led to an influx of displaced people into the towns in search of new jobs. In most cases, unskilled labour was sufficient to operate the new machines. Not only did skilled workers find themselves less in demand, but they were often replaced by women and children, at lower wages. Bosses forced conditions of work and wages down to the breadline, and the whole character of the labour market underwent a fundamental change. It was an age of workhouses, drab factory towns and child labour. Unemployment and poverty soared and depression and dissatisfaction were rife. Certainly, while British nationalism may have triumphed abroad, at home working class militancy reached a peak of unrest.

And although thousands of dissatisfied workers expressed their dissatisfaction through protests, strikes and riots, others packed their bags and set off for the colonies – including the Cape of Good Hope.

Black-white tensions

The colony's growth as a commercial centre was overshadowed in many respects by rising tensions – and sometimes brutal warfare (see page 102) – between settlers and the indigenous black population on the eastern frontier of the colony.

At the centre of the conflict was the ownership of land and the recruitment and control of (black) labour. Acknowledging this – and the fact that economic prosperity depended on a plentiful labour supply – a succession of British governors gave priority to the formulation of policies defining the relationship between white master and black servant.

In 1799, during their first occupation, the British had been given a demonstration of the extent of escalating black-white strife when Khoisan servants, in alliance with the Xhosa of the Zuurveld, tried to drive more than 8 000 whites from land between the Fish and Gamtoos rivers. By 1802 more than a third of the white population had fled the area – and when the British arrived for the second time, tensions were still running high. A major problem for eastern Cape stock-farmers – the settlement's major meat suppliers – was the mass desertion of Khoisan servants.

The labour shortage was compounded in 1807 when Britain abolished the slave trade. It led to heated calls for action, which came a few months later when the first Governor in the Second British Occupation, the Earl of Caledon, instructed his trusted military advisor, Colonel Richard Collins, to investigate white complaints.

Collins' report confirmed white fears. Not only did it provide evidence of Khoisan-Xhosa unity, but it also drew the attention of the Governor to the growth of mixed-race communities of white men, Khoisan women and runaway slaves. Collins recommended, and Caledon agreed, that these developments had to be stopped if whites were to maintain their privileged position in the colony. To bring this about, Caledon launched a two-pronged initiative, which involved pushing the Xhosa beyond the Fish River, and setting up a mechanism to create and control a Khoisan labour force.

Dealing with the labour question, Caledon issued a 'Hottentot Proclamation' in 1809 which compelled every Khoisan to have a fixed and 'registered place of abode' and to be in possession of a 'certificate' (issued by a *landdrost*) in order to travel from one district to another, forcing the Khoisan to live (and thus work) on white farms.

THE FIRST GOVERNOR *under the second occupation was the Earl of Caledon (above), followed by Sir John Cradock (left), who introduced English-language schools to the Cape. Acting Governor Sir Rufane Donkin (right) welcomed the 1820 settlers to Algoa Bay, naming Port Elizabeth after his late wife.*

Although other provisions in the legislation were designed to protect servants against gross ill-treatment, the withholding of wages or detention after the expiry of contracts, white farmers and, indeed, *landdrosts* simply ignored the parts which they did not like. Furthermore, in 1812, Caledon's successor, Sir John Cradock, opened the way for the permanent 'apprenticeship' of adult servants when he issued another proclamation – which allowed farmers to apprentice children over the age of eight for 10 years. It meant that parents had to continue to work whatever the terms of their contract.

Despite this, the labour shortage became so critical after the arrival of the 1820 settlers that Cradock's successor, Lord Charles Somerset, predicted to the Colonial Secretary, the Earl of Bathurst, that the shortage of labourers in the Albany district would threaten the success of the whole settlement. In a bid to solve the problem, Somerset enclosed a proposal for the apprenticeship of 600 English youths, aged between 11 and 16 years, and 250 girls between the ages of 10 and 14.

By then the Khoisan had acquired an important ally in the missionary Dr John Philip, who as a director of the London Missionary Society wielded great influence among prominent British politicians. It was partly as a result of his prompting that the Cape authorities published Ordinance 50 of 1828 which guaranteed to all 'Hottentots and other free persons of colour' residing in the Cape the same freedom and protection as enjoyed by whites. It meant, among other things, that the Khoisan could now legally own land and were no longer required by law to carry Passes. Even though the abolition of the Pass laws created conditions for a far more mobile labour market, farmers reacted angrily to a development which, in theory, allowed the Khoisan

GOVERNOR *Lord Charles Somerset was given the task of trying to solve the chronic labour shortage in the eastern Cape. However, his proposal for the apprenticeship of children from England was not acted upon.*

Settlers flock for a place in the sun

On 9 April 1820, the sailing ship the *Chapman* dropped anchor in Algoa Bay – and dozens of eager passengers swarmed on deck for their first glimpse at what they had been promised would be a land of opportunity.

Lured by offers of a free passage and a piece of ground, hundreds of families from economically depressed areas such as London, Bristol and parts of East Anglia had jumped at the chance of starting a new life in a colony 10 000 kilometres from home.

But before long the majority of the 4 000 people who had been approved by the government would be sadly disillusioned . . . .

A little more than four years after finally crushing Napoleon at Waterloo, Britain found its welfare was again under threat – from a post-war economic depression punctuated by rising taxes, long unemployment queues, mass meetings, protest marches and violent demonstrations. There was trouble brewing in the colonies, too, with dispatches from the eastern frontier of the Cape of Good Hope telling a story of an increasingly grave security problem.

In July 1819, the Home Government devised a single plan to counter both the threat of unrest at home and black insurrection at the Cape: it involved moving some of the disaffected unemployed more than halfway across the world.

The first part of the scheme was made public: a £50 000 donation to help relocate approximately 1 000 mostly unemployed families in the Cape. But the second part – that applicants would also be expected to act as part-time soldiers on the volatile eastern frontier – was kept a well-guarded secret.

Although a 16-page booklet savagely attacked the proposal, and a flood of cartoons ridiculed it, the response was overwhelming. Up to 90 000 applications flooded the Colonial Office, because information about conditions at the Cape was deliberately kept to a minimum.

To ensure that settlers would have sufficient capital and labour of their own, free sea passages, provisions and land grants were offered only to those who could afford to maintain at least 10 workers over the age of 18, with or without families. The director of each party had to be able to pay £10 for each single man or family group after arrival to ensure a temporary means of subsistence. In return each group leader was promised approximately 100 acres for each adult male in his party. However, full title to the land would be handed over only after the land had been lived on and worked for three years.

Of the approximately 60 parties selected, only about 12 were made up of a master and his indentured servants. The rest were people who had come together on a joint-stock basis, each paying his own deposit and selecting a nominal leader to satisfy the Colonial Office's requirements. The provisions of the scheme were altered to accommodate another more affluent group of settler individuals who could afford to pay their own passage and required from the government only a grant of land. Thus, even before they left, the continuation of the class divisions of British society was ensured.

The prospect of a free piece of farmland was one of the drawcards of the scheme. Yet artisans and tradesmen made up the bulk of the emigrants who set sail in 21 ships from December 1819. Ministers of religion, merchants, school-teachers, bookbinders, blacksmiths, discharged sailors and soldiers, professional men and candlestick makers were also well represented. A few were farmers – but even they would quickly discover that tilling a piece of ground in the African bush was vastly different from a patch of green in Britain.

Early shocks

John Barrow, who travelled to the Cape Colony in the 1790s, had provided the first English account of the area of settlement, praising the Zuurveld as representing a 'gentlemen's park in England'. Yet in the same breath he had cautioned against extravagant hopes. Further than these vague reports, the settlers had to rely on the information given by the Governor, Lord Charles Somerset, and his officials at the Cape. And this information, they soon found out, was often exaggerated.

'When you go out to plough, never leave your guns at home,' Colonel Jacob Cuyler, the resident *landdrost* of Uitenhage, warned the settlers while escorting them to their land not far from the Great Fish River. It was only then that settlers became aware that they were also expected to form a civil defence force and to supplement the military might of the imperial forces against the indigenous population of the area.

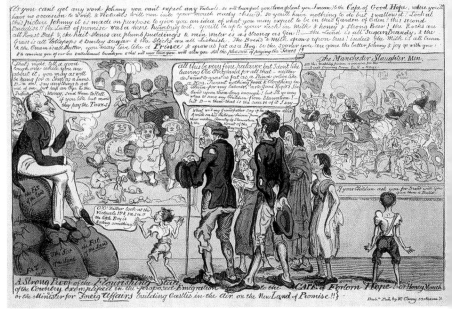

AN UNEMPLOYED *artisan is tempted by a Cape farmer in this 19th-century cartoon, which labelled the settlement scheme as 'castles in the air'. Despite this, thousands of Britons applied to come to the Cape.*

This was not the only shock: because officials at the Cape were afraid that slave-raiding might get out of hand and threaten a precarious peace between Xhosa and European, settlers were forbidden to own slaves. Neither could they travel freely to more populous sections of the colony to further their commercial interests. Movement between Bathurst (founded by acting Governor Sir Rufane Donkin as the administrative centre for the settler community) and Grahamstown required written permission from local authorities – while travel beyond the Albany district was even more strictly regulated, and could be undertaken only on receipt of a 'District Pass' countersigned by Donkin himself.

All this might have been accepted had the settlers been able to reap benefits from the land they farmed. But the area – described as the 'Zuurveld' (literally, sour country) by Boer stock-farmers – was not suitable for agriculture. The soil was unyielding, the rainfall irregular, and the lack of experience of many of the newcomers made their task an arduous one.

After three unsuccessful harvests and a disastrous flood, a large section of the community was up in arms. Most of them had run short of both capital and labour, and they were forced to mortgage land, stock and buildings in order to get further government rations. Increasingly frustrated by these curbs and controls, many aspirant farmers began to show their displeasure. In 1823, two separate petitions were sent to the Home Government. In one, containing 171 signatures, a group described by Somerset as the 'Albany Radicals' protested at inadequate land grants, the lack of markets and a free port, the removal of the seat of magistracy from Bathurst to Grahamstown, and the loss of cattle to the Xhosa.

But long-simmering tensions among settlers burst into the open two months later when another group sent a counter-petition to the Secretary of State in support of Somerset. However, a Commission of Enquiry found against the Governor and forced him to reverse many of his hard-line policies.

Within four years of their arrival at the Cape, more than 60 percent of the settlers had moved on to other parts of the country (in defiance of Donkin's 'District Pass'). Nevertheless, as others moved in to take their places, the settlement at Albany thrived and Grahamstown became the hub of commercial activity. But by far the biggest contribution of the region to the Cape Colony's economy was the introduction by settlers of merino sheep farming, which led to wool becoming the Cape's biggest export money-spinner by the 1830s.

A SURVEY DIAGRAM *and deed of grant for land in the Grahamstown district signed in 1825 by Governor Lord Charles Somerset.*

A GROUP *of 1820 settlers land at Algoa Bay in the eastern Cape. The excitement soon turned sour as the harshness of the new environment became known.*

ORDINANCE 50 *of 1828 (left) freed the Khoisan and 'other free persons of colour' from the harsh shackles of successive labour laws – mainly thanks to the efforts of missionary John Philip (above centre). The Khoisan, who in theory had the same rights as whites, could now negotiate better working contracts (above right).*

to sell their labour to the highest bidder. Another blow to the settler community – and a triumph for the missionaries – was a British Government decision in 1834 to disallow the passage of a vagrancy law designed to neutralise Ordinance 50.

Although measures to prevent excessive abuse of black servants were often half-hearted and seldom understood or appreciated by the people they were meant to help, they were angrily criticised by farmers: Dutch frontiersmen had long considered it a fundamental right to punish errant labourers – and they believed they knew better than any magistrate how to handle workers. To them a thrashing swiftly delivered seemed much more certain to bring the offender into line than a trial, a jail sentence or a fine. On the other hand, the strong community spirit and sense of familiarity which existed among white inhabitants often forced magistrates to identify with the interests of employers anyway. In one instance a woman was said to have called out from the gallery in court to a magistrate trying a servant of hers for desertion: 'Punish her Percy.'

Revamping the legal system

Notwithstanding this, under British influence the legal system at the colony was injected with a new vigour and a more professional character.

Courts increasingly began to be used in administrative capacities, as well as to 'bind diverse peoples to a common political authority'. Moreover, when London-based Commissioners of Enquiry recommended, among other things, an overhaul of the judicial system, the introduction of British judges, the application of British court procedures, and the gradual assimilation of the local Roman-Dutch law into the British system, the authorities quickly concurred.

This led to a new system for the administration of justice, one which was seemingly impartial and with outlets for the airing of grievances. A host of new judges – some with colourful pasts – played leading roles as representatives of the Cape Governor. Typical of these was the first Chief Justice, Cape Town-born Johannes (later Sir John) Andries Truter, who after being suspected of having helped to loot the Cape treasury shortly before the Second British Occupation, went on to become an expert on land tenure, tax law and criminal procedure.

Until 1860, judges travelled on circuit in ox-wagons twice a year, often covering thousands of kilometres. Escorted by cavalcades of police and horse-driven carriages, they were greeted in small rural towns with triumphal arches, fireworks and speeches. *Nagmaal*, the Dutch Reformed Church's Communion Feast, was usually timed to coincide with their arrival.

In 1827, the legal system was further transformed when resident magistrates replaced *landdrosts* and *heemraden* who had been left over from the Dutch era. But practice lagged behind policy – and at first anyone could become a magistrate on payment of a fee. Consequently, legal procedure, especially in the rural areas, was often casual and slipshod. In one instance, a policeman-turned-magistrate, who conducted simple, impromptu trials from a wagon, described how he had tried a Boer farmer charged with assaulting an African: the farmer, the magistrate recalled, had ridden up to the wagon with the witnesses. It was breakfast time and they all sat down to eat. 'The table cleared, the accused stood up for trial just where he had sat. I, sitting in my chair, the same. A £5 note protruding from his pocket was the penalty imposed. Afterwards he shod my horse gratis . . . .'

THE FIRST *Chief Justice of the Cape, Sir John Andries Truter, brought sweeping changes to the legal system, helping to secure colour-blind justice for all the colony's citizens – in theory at least.*

However, proceedings in the larger centres were never as casual as this – and when trial by jury was introduced under the first Charter of Justice in 1827, the courts, for the first time, could hear complaints from servants and receive evidence from Christian slaves. Because the Charter made no reference to the colour or class of litigants or witnesses, technically there was no discrimination. But, in practice, with the exception of a handful of law agents and court interpreters, the administration of justice was exclusively white. Most civil disputes involved white litigants, whereas most criminal prosecutions were against accused who were black. The 'local public' referred to in proclamations and ordinances meant the local white public. Slaves and Khoisan servants had little access to the law, and juries, in practice, consisted of white men only.

Nevertheless, many missionaries took advantage of the new court system to forward complaints on behalf of servants (see page 150). But they did so by manipulating the machinery of white power rather than by helping to organise black resistance. Yet, to the extent that they created new communities apart from the workplace, the missionaries represented a threat to Cape employers that their labourers would desert them for mission stations where they would find champions for their grievances. Many farmers were indignant about the presence of missionaries, and about the changed laws which seemed to put servants in a stronger bargaining position.

With punishment such as mutilation banned in Britain since 1796, flogging, hanging and imprisonment became the major weapons of criminal law – and until as late as the 1830s, the death sentence was still being imposed for cattle-killing, theft, arson, incest and rape, attempted murder and serious cases of house-breaking.

The fight for Press freedom

Cape Governor Lord Charles Somerset reacted with undisguised hostility towards a request by Thomas Pringle, a Scottish poet, and Abraham Faure, a Dutch minister of religion, to start a monthly magazine.

It was February 1823 – and it was not until almost 10 months later that he reluctantly gave permission. On 5 March 1824, the first privately owned publication, the 'South African Journal' ('*Het Nederduitsch Zuid Afrikaansche Tijdschrift*'), rolled off the presses.

But it lasted just one edition. An article by Pringle on the 'present state and prospects of the English emigrants in Albany, South Africa', pitched him into a headlong battle with the autocratic Cape Governor. Cease publishing such stories or face the consequences, Pringle was bluntly warned. Rather than be dictated to, he shut down the magazine. Somerset had won the first round of what would be a bitter five-year battle for Press freedom.

Unbowed, however, Pringle needed little persuasion to accept the joint editorship, with John Fairbairn, of the 'South African Commercial Advertiser', a newspaper started in the same year by a printer called George Greig. In the fifth edition, reports on a libel action involving the Governor led to another clash, and voluntary closure. But Somerset was not prepared to leave it at that. After sealing the presses, he instructed Greig to leave the colony within a month, despite angry protests.

In 1825, the 'Advertiser' resumed publication, with Fairbairn as sole editor (Pringle had rejoined his family in the eastern Cape). But when the newspaper was again suppressed in 1827, Fairbairn went to London to seek redress and was allowed to publish again in 1828. A year later the Press was freed from the control of the Governor and his council, but publishers still had to provide substantial security in case of libel actions being brought against them. It was not until 1859 that the Cape Parliament passed an Act to abolish the need for providing these securities.

SCOTTISH *poet and newspaper editor Thomas Pringle paved the way for a free Press in the Cape Colony with his 'South African Journal'.*

Terror tactics...

From the late 1700s, Boer and Xhosa were locked in an intense but inconclusive struggle
for control of the rich grazing-lands of the eastern Cape.
But in 1811, five years after they had occupied the Cape for the second time,
the British introduced a new factor into the frontier struggle: military intervention on the
side of the settlers. It was the beginning of the end of Xhosa independence.

IN THE SPRING OF 1811, a career soldier with a reputation for needlessly spilling blood launched the first in a series of military strikes to expel the Xhosa from land they had held for generations.

His name was John Francis Cradock, knight of the most honourable Order of Bath and Crescent, Colonel of His Majesty's 43rd regiment of foot and, from 6 September 1811, Governor and Commander-in-Chief of the Cape of Good Hope.

Good judgment was not one of the 49-year-old Governor's strengths. And, judging by his record, neither was he a particularly talented military strategist: in the five years prior to his Cape posting, he had been replaced as Commander of a British garrison in Portugal; had been seriously injured in a clash with anti-British rebels in Ireland; and had sparked a bloody mutiny in India when he insisted that Sepoy soldiers appear on parade without, among other things, the marks on their faces which proclaimed their caste.

Nevertheless, when he was sworn in less than 24 hours after arriving at the Cape, he remained as determined as ever to resurrect his military career.

It did not take him long to find a target on which to hang his ambitions: the Xhosa of the Zuurveld, extending to the Great Fish River.

Frontier friction
The seeds of what became a long, bitter and often brutal black-white contest for supremacy in a region which had been ruled by the Xhosa for at least 200 years, were sown more than 30 years earlier – in 1778 – when the Cape Governor, Baron Joachim van Plettenberg, made the Great Fish River the colony's eastern boundary.

In many ways, the weather-beaten Dutch farmers, traders and bootleggers who flocked into the area were not the type of people to foster good relations with the Xhosa: the majority of them were hard, unscrupulous misfits who, having cheated and bullied the Khoisan of the western Cape out of land and cattle, tried to do the same to their new rivals in the east.

The Xhosa, however, were far more formidable opponents – and even though they lacked the modern weaponry of the settlers, their numerical strength helped not only to slow down the pace of white expansion, but (on occasion) even forced the 'invaders' back towards the west (see page 68).

Before the beginning of the 19th century, a clear pattern had evolved: Xhosa resistance highlighted by sporadic murders and widespread cattle theft; and settler retaliation in the form of commando raids.

When Britain occupied the Cape for the second time in 1806, the spiral of violence had widened so much that the new Governor, the Earl of Caledon, in one of several measures aimed specifically at the eastern Cape (see page 96), banned raids on Xhosa homesteads – in return for a promise by selected chiefs to accept a system of voluntary racial segregation.

The plan, however, had one crucial weakness: it was based on the assumption that the Xhosa were a united people. That they were not was quickly demonstrated by the failure of those chiefs the Cape administration negotiated with to persuade others to remain within the 'black sector' of the frontier.

The onset of drought in 1809 finally killed the scheme: as hundreds of Xhosa trekked into what colonial authorities saw as the 'white sector' in search of grazing for their cattle, dozens of very scared colonists trekked out. Cattle theft became endemic and many deserted settler homesteads were burnt to the ground as the triumphant Xhosa moved west to reclaim land they had always regarded as their own.

A series of written and personal appeals found its way to the Governor's office. All were couched in hysterical language and all contained a similar appeal: use force to drive the 'trespassers' back to 'their own areas'.

Caledon, however, was filled with self-doubt. Never entirely convinced that the Zuurveld legally belonged to the colonists, he adopted an anti-war stance, which was bit-

GOVERNOR CRADOCK
*responded to
appeals for
protection by
frontier settlers by
sending colonial
troops against
the Xhosa.*

A KHOIKHOI *member of the Cape Mounted Rifles (left). These troops were widely used in the colonial wars against the Xhosa.* LIEUTENANT-COLONEL *John Graham (right) earned his Governor's gratitude for subduing the frontier Xhosa – and lent his name to the headquarters of the colonial forces, Grahamstown. The memorial (far right) can be seen in Grahamstown cathedral.*

terly criticised by fellow officials: in July 1811, when it became clear that he no longer enjoyed their support, he resigned and returned to England.

To the relief of the frontier authorities, the new Governor, Sir John Cradock, had no qualms about taking up arms against the Xhosa. Indeed, within a few days of his arrival, he was already looking for a person to oversee an eastern Cape military sortie. By the end of September 1811 he had found his new Commissioner for the frontier – 34-year-old Lieutenant-Colonel John Graham, the founder and instructor of the all-Khoikhoi Cape Regiment.

Preparations for war

Graham, whose military career had been curtailed by recurring attacks of gout, accepted Cradock's invitation with mixed feelings. Although flattered by the Governor's apparent faith in him, he was not overly impressed by the commission. In a letter to his father, he wrote: 'Tell my mother and the ladies that they have no cause to be alarmed at the idea of my going to fight with the blacks. There will be much running and riding, but no danger . . . .'

It was mid-October – the rainy season in the eastern Cape – when he arrived at the frontier to an ecstatic welcome from a settler community eager for a quick, decisive strike against their hated rivals.

Graham, however, determined to wait for the right moment to launch his campaign, was in no hurry.

In the weeks of waiting, he had to cope not only with a mountain of paperwork, but also with an outbreak of venereal disease which put his bored troops at risk. After an 'inspection' of the Bethelsdorp Khoikhoi had revealed 19 cases of the disease, a hurried examination of the soldiers brought to light three new cases, and a stern warning to the men to avoid a woman named Rosina.

Finally, in mid-December, as the Xhosa prepared for their 'first fruits ceremony' – in which chiefs were offered the first taste of newly harvested pumpkin, sorghum and green mealies – troops were ordered to take up positions along the frontier.

On Christmas Day 1811, the colonial forces began marching into the Zuurveld.

'Stay . . . so long as a kaffir remains alive'

Lieutenant-Colonel Graham was determined that his war against the Xhosa would teach them a lesson they would never forget – and he set about his task with a ruthless efficiency that Cradock could only admire.

On 1 January 1812, troops reached the hideout of Xhosa chiefs Chungwa and Ndlambe, and Graham declared: 'My intention is now to attack the savages in a way which I confidently hope will leave a lasting impression on their memories, and show them our vast superiority in all situations. I have ordered 500 men to enter the wood on foot . . . with orders to stay there so long as a kaffir remains alive . . . .'

While some of the troops were instructed to root out the Xhosa, others were sent to the vegetable gardens of the enemy where they confiscated and destroyed vast quantities of corn and other crops.

It was a short, brutal war, in which the colonial troops showed no mercy. Graham's adjutant Robert Hart wrote later that Xhosa women and men were shot indiscriminately, wherever they were found, and whether or not they offered resistance.

Many of the women, he added, were killed unintentionally because, in the bushes, Boer commandos could not distinguish them from men.

It was a bewildering experience for the Xhosa. Before the arrival of Graham, frontier wars were essentially running skirmishes – not this bloody onslaught that laid to waste the only world they knew.

Cradock, however, was delighted with the success of the operation, and on 14 August 1812, he ensured that Graham's name would long be remembered in the region: a proclamation issued by Henry Alexander, the Colonial Secretary for the Cape, stated that the Governor had 'thought it proper to make known, and to direct, that the present headquarters of the Cape Regiment situated in the Zuureveldt . . . shall in future be called . . . by the name of Graham's Town . . . in respect for the services of Lieutenant-Colonel Graham, through whose spirited exertions the kaffir hordes have been driven from that valuable district'.

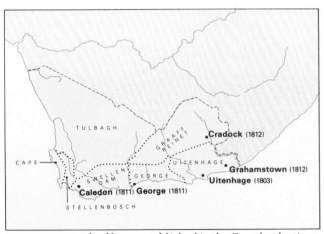

SEVEN DISTRICTS *had been established in the Cape by the time the 1820 settlers arrived.*

The struggle over land continues

In the deceptive calm which followed the Fourth Frontier War Cradock resigned and was replaced as Governor by Lord Charles Somerset.

In 1815, following a new outbreak of drought, colonists again began accusing the Xhosa of stealing cattle. But Somerset, mindful of the expense involved in assembling a commando every time a cow was stolen, decided to make the Xhosa leaders responsible for keeping their countrymen in line with a scheme which involved offering Ngqika the monopoly on trade with the colony – on condition he stamped out cattle raiding.

Less-than-keen at first, Ngqika had to be virtually frogmarched to the Governor's tent to hear the offer. But after he had been offered a bribe of a grey horse, clothes, handkerchiefs, knives and a tinder-box, he promised not only to return all stolen property and runaway slaves, but also

The era of the diviner as the Xhosa fought back

In Grahamstown he was known as Makanna or Links the left-handed.

But his real name was Nxele – and in the turbulent years which followed the death and destruction wreaked by John Graham, he and a rival diviner named Ntsikana played a key role in formulating new Xhosa attitudes towards the white settlers.

To his followers, Nxele was a prophet – a link between long dead ancestors and the present. Yet, as a young man he had been fascinated by the Christian religion.

The son of a commoner who worked for a Dutch farmer, Nxele and his mother went to live among the followers of Ndlambe after his father had died. By then he was already showing signs of being a most unusual person.

After his circumcision, Nxele returned to Grahamstown where he spent a lot of his time in the company of the chaplain of the Cape Regiment, Aart van der Lingen. Inspired by his mentor, he returned to 'Xhosaland', claiming that God had sent him to punish the sins of the people.

Although he recklessly attacked Ndlambe for practising polygamy, the Rharhabe chief still appointed him official diviner of his chiefdom.

By 1816, Nxele was identifying himself closely with the missionaries, seeing himself as their colleague in pursuit of a common goal. But Nxele was soon calling himself the younger brother of Christ, and after an attempt to raise the dead in a public ceremony at Gompo Rock (near what is today East London), he began to move away

from Christianity. Daubing his body with red ochre and dancing in the manner of the traditional diviners, he also dropped his earlier opposition to certain Xhosa customs, and he began to demand *ruma* – the diviner's fee, paid in cattle.

While Nxele became an uncompromising wardoctor who saw life only in terms of war between the forces of good and evil, another leading diviner, Ntsikana, was an ordinary head of a homestead in Ndlambe's territory. Having experienced visions, and convinced of divine intervention, he went to Ndlambe with his story and offered his services as a diviner. But Ndlambe declined in favour of Nxele, who was by then already well established. The chastened Ntsikana then turned to Ngqika, establishing himself as Nxele's rival.

Ntsikana believed people would find the peace and protection they sought by submitting completely to the will of God. His pacifist views were strongly shaped by the political vulnerability of Ngqika, his sponsor. On the other hand, Nxele's nationalist fervour expressed not only his own sense of rejection by colonial society, but also Ndlambe's posture of military resistance.

But although very different, Nxele and Ntsikana owed their prominence and influence to one common factor: they could interpret a world thrown into confusion by the coming of the whites. Even then, their success was dependent largely upon their respec-

NXELE *turned his back on missionary teachings in favour of war.*

tive messages: they lived differently and died in characteristic fashion – Nxele was defiant to the last, Ntsikana was serene in the face of death. Legend has it that in 1821, when he felt death was near, Ntsikana asked his family to bury him in the manner of Christians. And when they hesitated, he picked up a spade and turned the first sods himself.

ON 22 APRIL 1819, *the newly established frontier settlement of Grahamstown was attacked by 6 000 Xhosa warriors, who believed that their leader, Nxele, would turn the British bullets into water. The attack was a disaster, and scores died as the British opened fire with cannons and muskets. This picture of the town was painted four years later in 1823.*

to put to death any of his followers who were caught stealing from the colonists.

Rival chiefs angrily denounced this agreement, and in 1818, after his forces had been routed by his old enemy Ndlambe at the Battle of Amalinde, Ngqika convinced Somerset that he had been attacked because he had tried to stop cattle thieving. Already deeply involved in internal Xhosa politics, the Governor instructed his troops to punish the errant Ndlambe. And this they did – by seizing 23 000 of his cattle.

The attack on Grahamstown

Infuriated by what they considered an unprovoked act, Ndlambe's Xhosa made frequent and damaging attacks on any colonial targets they perceived as vulnerable.

But the campaign came to a bloody end when a diviner named Nxele led a daytime attack on Grahamstown.

Initially, the plan had been to take the town under cover of darkness – and with this in mind, Nxele had even created a diversion to take part of the garrison out of town. But things went awry when the Xhosa army was spotted by British scouts and the time of the attack had to be brought forward. Just before noon on 22 April 1819, 6 000 warriors, convinced that Nxele would turn British bullets into water, charged the town.

The attack was a disaster. Unprotected against the muskets and cannons of the enemy, scores of Xhosa were killed (compared with the colonial army's losses of just two men and two horses).

Three months after this devastating setback, Nxele surrendered and was imprisoned on Robben Island. He drowned in 1820 while attempting to escape.

The war of 1834-5

In 1819, shortly after the Battle of Grahamstown, the uneasy alliance between the Cape Government and Ngqika was shattered when Somerset confiscated land between the Fish and Keiskamma rivers in order to create a buffer zone between the Xhosa and the colony.

The horrified Ngqika had good reason to feel hard done by. He had played no part in recent hostilities and, in fact, had openly backed government troops in the campaign

against Ndlambe. Somerset, however, was unimpressed, claiming that the appropriation was a result of Ngqika's failure to control his people.

Although discontent over this and other actions of the Cape Government simmered away for many years, the authorities saw little reason for alarm: mindful of long-standing divisions within Xhosa society, they were able to reduce the threat of a major uprising by cleverly playing off the different groups against one another.

But in 1829 they overplayed their hand: with the region in the grip of a severe drought, they expelled Maqoma, the brother of Sandile, Ngqika's successor, from a fertile area in the Kat River valley and set it aside for Khoikhoi and 'Bastards'.

Stung by what they considered an act of aggression, and angry over the regular commando raids into their territories, the Rharhabe and Gcaleka Xhosa buried their differences and resolved to resist further acts of dispossession. In December 1834, after five more years of rising tensions, the sixth and most violent yet of the frontier wars between British and Xhosa began.

In their formal declaration of war, the Xhosa stressed that the last thing they wanted was a fight to the death.

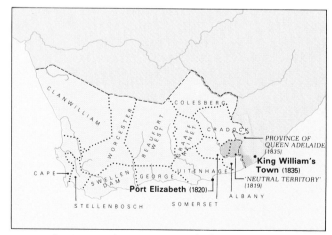

IN 1835 *the Cape authorities annexed Xhosa land between the Keiskamma and Kei rivers as the Province of Queen Adelaide. Later, they were forced to hand it back.*

COLONEL HARRY SMITH *chases the Xhosa chief Hintsa in this contemporary print. In fact, Hintsa was seized after he entered the British camp for talks in 1835 – and was then threatened with hanging if he did not call upon his fellow Xhosa to surrender. He refused – and was shot and killed while trying to escape. Later his ears were cut off by souvenir-hunting British officers.*

Their primary aim, they said, was a negotiated settlement of grievances – especially the return of all confiscated land east of the Fish River.

Having said that, they swept into the colony, forcing the settlers to abandon their homes and most of the territory east of Algoa Bay (with the exception of Grahamstown and Fort Beaufort).

It was not an easy campaign for the British – and initial attempts by Colonel Harry Smith to force Xhosa under the command of Tyhali and Maqoma out of their Amatola Mountain hideout met with little success.

The turning point of the war came when Smith, realising the futility of taking on the Amatola Mountain fighters, threw his resources into a sweep across the Kei River. It immediately netted him Hintsa, the Gcaleka chief.

The Xhosa king's 'neutrality' had not fooled the British, and they demanded that he hand over Rharhabe chiefs (whom he had taken under his protection) as well as 'compensation' of 50 000 cattle and 1 000 horses. On 29 April 1835, Hintsa, having been assured of safe passage, entered the British camp for talks . . . .

It was a trap. He was taken prisoner and subjected to several days of threats and interrogation by both Smith and the Cape Governor Benjamin D'Urban. While Smith tried to win the monarch's trust by pulling funny faces, D'Urban threatened to hang Hintsa from the nearest tree if he persisted in refusing to call on the other Xhosa leaders to surrender. Hintsa, however, was not prepared to betray his countrymen, even though his life was at risk. Finally, in trying to escape, he was shot and killed. Later, souvenir hunters cut off his ears to show around the military camps, although attempts to dig out his teeth with bayonets were less successful.

Meanwhile, Smith, flushed with the success of his sweep across the Kei, struck into territory west of the river

– declared by D'Urban to be the Province of Queen Adelaide (until 1836). But even this failed to cow the chiefs, who, in September 1835, eventually made peace without actually surrendering.

The cessation of hostilities notwithstanding, the search for a formula for a lasting peace remained the region's most vexing problem.

The treaty system

Shortly after the end of the war, Andries Stockenström, a former *landdrost* of Graaff-Reinet and Commissioner-General for the Eastern Districts, proposed a system which set him on a collision course with D'Urban.

Based on a system of treaties, Stockenström's plan contained two fundamental propositions: that the Xhosa chiefs were sovereign rulers who could be dealt with through signed treaties overseen by Diplomatic Agents; and that the problem of cattle theft had to be solved not in 'Xhosaland', but in the Cape Colony itself.

Giving evidence before the Aborigines Commission in London, he blamed the commando system (whereby farmers could raid the homesteads of suspected cattle thieves and take whatever compensation they thought necessary) as the prime cause of the Sixth Frontier War.

Impressed by his knowledge of frontier life, the British Government appointed him Lieutenant-Governor for the Eastern Districts in 1836. But in attempting to implement his scheme, Stockenström soon ran into problems.

For a start, D'Urban, angry that the British Government had not consulted him on the matter, tried his utmost to wreck the plan. Furthermore, a suggestion that Khoikhoi herders be armed was greeted with undisguised horror by farmers. Armed herdsman would increase the temptation for the Xhosa to murder them, the settler community argued in unison.

The arrival of the Mfengu in the eastern Cape

In 1823 the first African refugees from disorder in the interior of southern Africa arrived impoverished at the Cape Colony's eastern frontier, where they went about repeating a simple request: *'siyamfenguze'* ('We seek work'). Although they were mainly members of the Bhaca, Bhele, Zizi and Hlubi chiefdoms, they (together with others who had been forcibly brought to the area to work for labour-starved white farmers) became known as Mfengu.

Most settled in Gcalekaland where, from an initial client-patron relationship – the Gcaleka called them their 'dogs' – the Mfengu were able to rebuild their morale as well as, to some extent, their herds. They traded successfully and aroused the envy of their Gcaleka patrons, almost to the point of estrangement.

The presence of the Mfengu in the frontier region proved a godsend for the British authorities – because they introduced a natural 'buffer' between Xhosa and settlers.

In 1834 several hundred Mfengu arrived at a camp near Butterworth – where Governor Sir Benjamin D'Urban was directing operations against the Xhosa chief Maqoma – brandishing spears and shields, and waving strips of white cloth. Through an interpreter they explained that they were Mfengu and that their missionary, John Ayliff, had sent them to ask for the Governor's protection. To D'Urban, the 'Fingoes' – 'a fine athletic set of fellows' – were welcome allies whom he could use to advantage; and when the war was over, some 16 000 Mfengu were escorted by D'Urban's army westward across the Kei River, to be settled in Ciskei in the vicinity of the recently established Fort Peddie.

The new community, 'well skilled in the tasks of herding and agriculture', would act as a buffer between colony and Xhosa, providing military assistance as well as labour. However, the Gcaleka regarded the move by the Mfengu as treachery, and an act of ingratitude.

Many of the Mfengu worked for white farmers, adding to their skills, and were soon farming for their own account. After a few years they were selling grain, tobacco, cattle, milk and firewood, and had acquired a reputation for hard work and shrewd trading. The Mfengu did not take part in the great cattle-killing of 1857, but took the opportunity of buying up Xhosa cattle at low prices, to resell profitably in the subsequent famine. Ayliff recorded that the Mfengu living in the Fort Beaufort district raised twice as much grain as they needed and sold the surplus to government agents 'to supply the wants of the starving multitudes'.

Their initial misfortune actually formed the basis of their later progress in that, bereft of traditional leadership, they were in a state of social flux and receptive to new ideas and techniques. They were prepared to observe the techniques of farmers and missionaries and to adapt them to their own use, whereas most Xhosa were suspicious of the motives of the whites and, therefore, resisted these changes. Through their adoption of peasant agriculture, the Mfengu became integrated with the colonial mercantile economy and, in addition, became involved in general trade as well as transport.

Mfengu warriors went to war on the side of the colony in the three frontier wars that were fought after their arrival in their new location. In return, they received extensive grants of land, particularly in former Gcaleka territory. From their former status as 'dogs', the Mfengu rapidly moved to a position of prominence, illustrated by the request of Kona, Maqoma's son, to live among them so that 'he and they [might] become one people'.

THE MFENGU *rewarded the British for their protection by taking their side in three frontier wars.*

THIS PAINTING *of Mfengu villagers was described by 19th-century artist Thomas Baines as a Fingo village in the Fort Beaufort district.*

ANDRIES STOCKENSTRÖM *was appointed Lieutenant-Governor for the Eastern Districts by the British after giving evidence before the Aborigines Commission in London. His 'treaty system' for dealing with the Xhosa put him on a collision course with Governor D'Urban.*

But it was a farmer named Thomas Robson who probably gave the real reason for settler objections. The sympathies of the herdsmen, he observed, lay with the Xhosa – and since the herdsmen earned only two pence or three pence a day, they could probably earn more by stealing the cattle and selling the gun themselves 'than by a whole year's work for a farmer'.

Simply put, the settlers were not interested in anything which offered blacks security or protection. As far as they were concerned, the land which the Xhosa occupied could be put to far better use by white farmers.

Yet despite white antipathy, Stockenström's treaty system worked reasonably well until 1842, when a severe drought struck the region. It set the scene for more cattle theft – and the Seventh Frontier War.

The War of the Axe

Even by frontier standards, the theft of an axe, followed by a murder and a jailbreak, hardly seemed good enough reasons to start a full-scale war.

But trouble had been brewing for a long time.

In 1844, when Sir Peregrine Maitland took over as Governor of the Cape, Stockenström's treaty system was on the brink of collapse, the Xhosa chief Sandile was struggling to assert proper authority over his subjects and the 'Grahams Town Journal' was campaigning energetically for the return of the Province of Queen Adelaide to the settlers.

To the dismay of the Xhosa, the new Governor's first action was to scrap Stockenström's treaty system and to replace it with one of his own. In many ways, Maitland's new set of rules was a recipe for conflict: it paved the way for forts to be built and troops to be stationed in the ceded territory; it gave farmers not only the right to follow stolen cattle at any time, but also permission to demand equivalent compensation if they could not find their animals; it made provision for tribunals to be set up to hear the appeals of farmers against chiefs and Diplomatic Agents; and it placed black Christian converts beyond the jurisdiction of the Xhosa chiefs.

As tension mounted, many Xhosa began to move into the mountains in preparation for war.

It was in this hostile atmosphere that Tsili, a member of Sandile's chiefdom, was caught stealing an axe from a Fort Beaufort shopkeeper. Tsili's stay in the town jail, however, was of short duration. A group of friends staged a daring break-in into his cell and, finding him handcuffed to a Khoikhoi fellow prisoner, cut off the luckless Khoikhoi's hand. The man subsequently died.

The escape caused an uproar which turned to fury when Sandile refused to return the prisoner.

The War of the Axe which followed was a vicious conflict in which Maitland's troops were at first unpleasantly surprised. The first British column to enter the Xhosa's Amatola Mountain stronghold was attacked and all the supplies captured.

The Xhosa carried all before them. Port Elizabeth was threatened by the Gqunukhwebe as they thrust into territory captured long before from their ancestor, Chungwa. A wagon train was attacked and captured on the road to Peddie, and for a while it seemed as if the Xhosa might well hold off the might of the Empire.

At the end of May, however, the Xhosa received their first major setback when a Ndlambe regiment was decimated at the Battle of Gwangqa. Some 500 warriors were killed when they were caught on an open plain by charging colonial cavalry.

In an ironic twist, the Xhosa turned the tables on the British with a scorched earth tactic of their own: they burnt all the grass in the battle-zone, causing hundreds of horses and cattle to die of starvation. Finding it impossible to fight a war under these conditions, the British withdrew in September 1846.

But remarkably, with victory seemingly within their grasp, the Xhosa offered to discuss peace. Told that the British would accept only an unconditional surrender and that the government intended to annex all the land west of the Kei, they persisted in their efforts to end hostilities. Maqoma gave himself up on 26 October and Sandile – after an extended truce – two months later. In their eyes, however, the decision represented a unilateral peace

MUSTER OF THE MALAY VOLUNTEERS IN THE MAIN BARRACKS, CAPE TOWN, MAY 6, 1846.

DURING *the War of the Axe, the British launched a campaign for volunteers among Malays in Cape Town – as this 1846 cartoon shows.*

FIVE HUNDRED XHOSA *died when British cavalry, including Khoikhoi of the Cape Mounted Rifles, charged into their unprotected ranks at the Battle of Gwangqa in May 1846. It was, however, a hollow victory for the British – who were forced to withdraw in the face of a Xhosa decision to burn all the grass in the battle-zone.*

rather than capitulation. They had simply taken a decision to stop fighting.

It did not take long for the real reason for their peace initiative to become apparent: the Xhosa soldiers and their families were starving to death. Left without cattle, and with their grain stores having been destroyed, they had been reduced to raiding rubbish heaps and to eating their shields and sandals to stay alive. Maitland informed the Colonial Secretary that 'the sowing season has been passing by unemployed owing to the scouring of the country by the troops'. Many Xhosa were 'much wasted', particularly the women. Clearly the scorched earth policy had affected both sides in the conflict.

Nevertheless, in the first few months of the peace, the Xhosa chiefs embarked on a highly effective policy of 'passive resistance'. Said a perplexed Maitland: 'They will not go from the country which we require them to evacuate, nor will they fight for it.'

It was the Ngqika Xhosa especially who refused to admit they had ever been defeated. And when Maitland was replaced by Sir Henry Pottinger, Sandile refused to reopen discussions with the new Governor, claiming he had already made peace and that there was nothing more to speak about.

Pottinger at first bided his time. But once he had received all the reinforcements and supplies he needed, he seized on the theft of a few goats to make an example of Sandile. With the Xhosa still refusing to fight, colonial troops made straight for their houses, their cattle and their grain pits. In supporting this tactic, the 'Grahams Town Journal' thundered: 'Let the war be made against kaffir huts and gardens. Let these be burnt down and destroyed. Tell them [the Xhosa] that the time has come for the white man to show his mastery over them.'

With starvation again staring the Xhosa in the face, their resistance collapsed in October 1847 (see page 133).

KHOIKHOI *and Mfengu volunteers fought on the side of the British regulars during the War of the Axe. The black soldiers were hated by the Xhosa.*

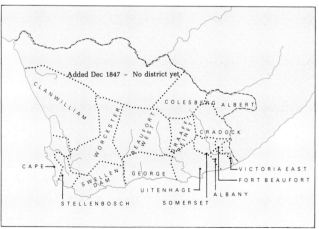

FOLLOWING *the collapse of Xhosa resistance in 1847, the colonial administration of Sir Harry Smith annexed more territory, calling it Victoria East.*

'Contrary to the laws of God'

In the first half of the 19th century the eastern Cape no longer offered the endless horizons
that the Boer settlers had become used to – and competition for good grazing-land was fierce.
Imported British justice threatened the independent life style of the Boers, while the new
imperialism stripped them of the right to defend themselves and attack their African neighbours,
as they had done in the past. While most accepted the new order, a minority did not –
and their response was to have a profound effect on South African history.

IN 1843 A 46-YEAR-OLD VOORTREKKER living in Natal sat down to write a letter to relatives in the Cape Colony setting out the reasons for the Great Trek. In that letter Anna Steenkamp blamed 'the continued depredations and robberies of the Kafirs' for making life on the eastern frontier unbearable; and the emancipation of slaves – 'not so much their freedom … but their being placed on an equal footing with Christians, contrary to the laws of God and the natural distinction of race and religion'. Her sentiments were closely shared by fellow emigrants such as her uncle, Piet Retief. During the previous decade they had left the eastern part of the Colony to embark on the greatest move of their lives.

Over the years the Great Trek has taken on the appearance of an exodus of biblical proportions – when, in fact, only a fraction of the Dutch-speaking settlers living at the Cape joined the trek inland. Nevertheless, the political, cultural and spiritual implications of the trek make this for many Afrikaners the most important event in their history; it would be hard to define Afrikaner nationalism without considering it.

And yet the causes of the trek were both varied and complex – far more so than Anna Steenkamp's famous letter would indicate. Few eastern Cape Boers owned any slaves, slavery being the preserve of the wealthier farmers in the south-western Cape – and they did not trek.

It is in the eastern Cape that the roots of the trek began to grow; not so much from fiery patriotism as from pure economic necessity.

Not enough land

With both Xhosa and Boer dependent for their survival on sufficient grazing, it had become clear by the 1830s that the eastern frontier region was becoming over-populated – not only by Xhosa and British demands for land but also by the Boers themselves. The farmers married young and spawned large families, the sons expecting to become their own bosses on a workable share of good grazing land. The result was a rapid increase in the white population of the region with little or no increase in the amount of land available for settlement.

The ownership of land had been a vexed question for years; many white farmers held large tracts, with tenuous proof of ownership. This complicated the task of the administrators and weakened the frontier itself. In 1813, in an attempt to regulate the holdings, the Colonial Government offered to lease restricted parcels of land within the colony at low rentals. But this move was rejected by the farmers (many of whom did not own the land they were occupying anyway).

The Colonial Government tried a second time to control land on the frontier by creating a barrier of British immigrant farmers (on smallholdings) between the Xhosa and the other white farmers. These immigrants were also to act as an unofficial garrison. But when about 4 000 British settlers arrived in 1820, it was discovered that the smallholdings were unable to support the immigrant families in any sort of comfort. The arrival of the British settlers, however, did create an increased demand for land – as did the introduction of merino sheep farming in the 1820s and '30s – and land prices rose sharply.

The shortage of labour was another major problem for the frontier farmers, one aggravated by Ordinance 50 of 1828 that not only allowed the Khoikhoi greater freedom in choosing their employers but also gave them the right to own land. The abolition of slavery also played a part – although it affected only wealthier men such as Gert Maritz. The result was, according to one Voortrekker leader, that the Boers 'together with their children, had to do all the work and tend to the livestock, so that it was no longer possible to farm in the Cape Colony'.

ANNA STEENKAMP *cited British attempts to place ex-slaves 'on an equal footing with Christians' as the main reason for the trek. The underlying cause, however, was economic.*

Yet another economic reason for the trek was the increasing role of cash in the economy – which struck at the roots of the barter system preferred by the Boers. Mobile traders in the region were used to conducting much of their business on the basis of non-monetary exchange. The position of labourers on white farms was also based on a form of exchange rather than a contract of employment – the worker was given goods and perhaps a small piece of land in lieu of wages. What emerged was a patriarchal community headed by a patron and his family. The introduction of money required farmers to produce a surplus which they could sell for cash – completely out of line with the traditional subsistence farming methods of the Boers.

This left an increasingly unhappy population with four choices: fight the British and Xhosa for more land; work for someone else; switch from subsistence farming to intensive, surplus farming; or fill a wagon with a few bare necessities and look for something better.

The first choice was hardly viable: the British hold on the region was simply too powerful; the second was unthinkable – working for someone else was simply not part of the Boer culture; the third would have been a lengthy process requiring advanced technology and favourable climatic conditions; which left, for many, the fourth: leaving familiar terrain and migrating to the interior to look for new land and new grazing.

Enough of the British

Overlying these economic pressures were political problems arising from British administration of the eastern Cape – and it is these causes for the trek that have found their way into Afrikaner nationalist folklore. The Boers strongly believed that the British did not have their interests at heart. A fiercely independent people, they objected not only to the way they were governed but also to the fact that the British were governing them at all.

One of their major grievances was that disputes which had once been settled by informal discussion and negotiation were now debated in court. Regular circuit courts were introduced in 1811 and two years later court proceedings began to be thrown open to the public. Boers could not entertain the possibility that their black employees might not only take them to court but might actually win a suit against them.

The number of whites charged with ill-treating their Khoikhoi servants increased significantly from 1812 onwards, during sittings of the so-called 'Black Circuit' court. In fact, with the missionary James Read an energetic ally, some servants even had the satisfaction of seeing their masters convicted.

In 1815, however, the 'Black Circuit' indirectly sparked a revolt among a group of eastern Cape settlers....

The Slagtersnek rebellion began when Frederik Bezuidenhout, a farmer accused of maltreating one of his servants, was shot dead while resisting arrest by Khoikhoi soldiers. Although Bezuidenhout's hot-headed brother, Johannes, promised retribution – just 60 volunteers answered his call for help to overthrow the Colonial Government. In the short series of skirmishes that followed,

GERT MARITZ *was one of the few wealthy Boers who trekked. This statue of him stands outside the Voortrekker Museum in Pietermaritzburg.*

Bezuidenhout was killed and six other ringleaders captured, tried and sentenced to death by hanging. Five rebels eventually ascended the gallows, with four having to make a second trip after the ropes on their scaffolds snapped.

Regarded at the time as a fairly minor frontier episode, the Slagtersnek rebellion was elevated to almost heroic proportions by a host of Afrikaner nationalist historians of the 20th century.

Another source of outrage was Ordinance 50 of 1828, which, in theory, granted 'Hottentots and other free persons of colour' equality before the law. Wealthier farmers were further incensed by the abolition of slavery. Although they relied more on cheap or 'free' labour than on slaves, farmers nevertheless felt that this was yet another form of interference in the way they treated their workers. The Emancipation Act provided compensation for slave owners, but the sum was at most a third of the slave's market value. Worse still, compensation was payable in England, which meant that farmers had to deal with agents (who in turn charged a fee for their services).

Another cause of tension between the British authorities and the white settlers was the attempt to anglicise the local white population. English was encouraged in schools and made compulsory in the courts. An attempt to introduce the language in church congregations was made by recruiting Scottish ministers, but it had little effect since many of them married local women and quickly learned to speak Dutch. The result of anglicisation in schools was also minimal as few Dutch-speaking children attended school anyway. Yet the government's rather timid policy of anglicisation, coupled with the assisted immigration of British settlers, caused the farmers to grow suspicious of the authorities.

So when the great majority of the Voortrekkers migrated from the eastern frontier districts such as Uitenhage, Albany, Somerset, Cradock and Graaff-Reinet, hardly any British settlers left with them. Along the northern border, it was only from Beaufort West that an appreciable number of Boers joined the trek, while relatively few left the western districts (of these, most came from Swellendam).

A troubled frontier

In 1834 the Xhosa invaded the colony in an attempt to recover territory that they had lost in the earlier frontier wars. The Governor, Lieutenant-General Sir Benjamin D'Urban, prepared a devastating response, moving against the Xhosa with British regulars, the Cape Regiment, Boer commandos and African allies. After his troops had burned crops and destroyed villages, D'Urban issued a proclamation annexing even more Xhosa territory. He intended settling Mfengu (see page 107) and white settlers in their place; but this was too much for his superiors in Britain, who had been convinced by missionaries that the Xhosa were justified in fighting for the recovery of their land. D'Urban was reprimanded and ordered to hand back the land he had annexed.

For the farmers, this was the last straw. Having been promised a share of the newly conquered land, this was now being snatched from under their noses. Already bitter over the emancipation of the slaves and what they regarded as manipulative legislation, the farmers decided that the Cape Colony was no longer tolerable as a home.

In these areas there had been mounting conflicts with the Xhosa, made worse by the fact that many refugees of wars among African chiefdoms had wandered into the frontier region hungry, homeless and adding to an already intense feeling of insecurity. The Boers had developed their own methods of dealing with these problems – dispensing justice according to their own dictates of fair play. However, as a stronger British Government made its military and political authority felt in the region, the role of the Boer commando – a military system developed by the farmers – was drastically curtailed.

It seemed to the Boers that the British were not capable of dealing with the Xhosa, as evidenced by the frontier wars of 1812 and 1834-5. To them, the actions of the British bordered on the imbecilic: although they seemed intent on taking away what the Boers regarded as their traditional freedom of self-defence, they could not offer any guarantee of security in its place. The only explanation seemed to be that the British did not care.

The British frontier policy (or apparent lack of it) resulted in general dissatisfaction and a feeling of insecurity among the Afrikaner farmers, who suffered heavy losses in the Sixth Frontier War. In addition to these setbacks, they were required to use their own horses and equipment while engaged in punitive expeditions. Although they expected to be compensated by the British Government for their losses, no money was forthcoming. They were also expected to pay their normal taxes to the authorities even while they faced ruin.

The decision to migrate northwards was further prompted by the farmers' fear that they were losing their already tenuous identity. As growing numbers of black families absorbed the culture, customs and Christian religion of the white community, the distinctions between the groups became increasingly blurred. This caused the farmers great concern, for they were inordinately proud of their own language and their status as authentic *boere* (farmers). The Afrikaner farmer also regarded himself as a Christian while dismissing the blacks as heathen. He simply could not come to terms with the official policy of equality in State and Church.

Which way to go?

Precisely when (and with whom) the idea of the Great Trek originated cannot be ascertained. It is clear, however, that among the prime organisers were Louis Trichardt and Hans van Rensburg (both of whom left in 1835), Hendrik

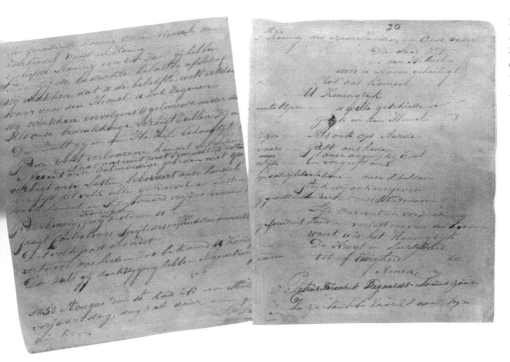

PAGES FROM *the diary kept by Boer leader Louis Trichardt. Although nothing is known of Trichardt's youth and education, his knowledge of Dutch was far better than the average among Boers of his day.*

Potgieter (1835 or 1836) and Gert Maritz (1836). Although at first they managed to keep their activities secret – at least from the British – their aims seem fairly clear. The trekkers reasoned that, once across the colonial borders, they would be beyond British control and able to establish their own independent state where they could look after their own interests. They believed that vast expanses of territory north of the Orange River and east of the Drakensberg had been depopulated by recent wars among African chiefdoms, and they expected to be welcomed by the remaining populace as guardians and allies. Adequate labour resources and good soil would be there in abundance. Vital to this theory was the importance attached to opening up trade links with Europe without having to deal through imperial middlemen. Relying on their own initiative, their swift horses and their effective firearms, they would also take it upon themselves to ensure the safety they lacked under colonial rule....

Preparations for the trek had already begun in 1834 when *kommissie* treks (scouting parties) were secretly dispatched into the interior. The trekkers also acquired valuable information about their destination from traders, hunters, missionaries and trekboers. (It is important to note that many of the trekboers, who ventured northwards only to search for new grazing and game, considered themselves loyal colonial subjects and even welcomed the authority of the Colonial Government. The Voortrekkers, on the other hand, were intent on freeing themselves from British rule and on establishing their own republic.)

At first the early trek leaders had to surmount some major obstacles. For example, most of them lacked experience in public administration and the art of governing. Furthermore, a sufficient supply of arms and ammunition could not be taken across the colonial border without breaking the law.

There were also many practical considerations that had to be tackled before the trekkers could set out for their Promised Land, and once they arrived there they experienced further problems in adapting to the new environment. One of these was how to cater for a divergence of needs: some of the frontier men were cattle ranchers (most of them living along the banks of the lower Bushman's River), while others were sheep farmers (from just south of the Orange River).

The Voortrekkers had a choice of two routes: one which would take them into the interior to north and south side of the Vaal River and the other into Natal. The northern areas were closer and more accessible across the open plains, but the north-eastern region needed to be explored – either via the more dangerous territory of Kaffraria or by crossing the Drakensberg range. The passes on the latter route were unknown at this time, but Natal – offering a safe harbour and ready access to trade with Europe and the outside world – nevertheless beckoned invitingly.

At first, the British were unsure of how to react to the trek. Governor D'Urban thought the trek was unnecessary and made an effort to improve the lot of the farmers. Lieutenant-Governor Andries Stockenström, on the other hand, was convinced that the trek was inevitable and

could not be stopped. The colonial authorities were thrown into confusion and almost nothing was done to counter the exodus. It was unlawful for British subjects to leave the Cape without permission and to move arms and ammunition across the border. Since practically all trekkers crossed the Orange River at one of the six or seven drifts (near the present town of Aliwal North) they could have been stopped, but were not.

Not all the trekkers were poor or landless; many gave up their farms to join the adventure northwards – although the loss of their farms was an emotional rather than a financial loss (since many had been free grants). In other cases, however, the farms fetched pitifully low prices, or were simply abandoned out of despair. Whatever the obstacles, the Great Trek was on.

Retief on the eve of the trek

In February 1837 Piet Retief announced on behalf of all Voortrekkers: 'We quit this Colony under the full assurance that the English Government has nothing more to require of us, and will allow us to govern ourselves without interference in future' – and with these words took on the responsibility of leading his people into a Promised Land ....

Piet Retief was descended from the Huguenots. As a young man, he spent several years in Cape Town where he acquired business experience. After a spell on a farm near present-day Riebeek East, he moved to the frontier capital of Grahamstown. Here he became a wealthy man, thanks to his substantial share in the contract for conveying rations to the newly arrived 1820 settlers. He was also appointed commandant of the district burghers.

But then came a major setback: for reasons which remain unclear, he became bankrupt after winning a contract to build the new magistrate's offices in Grahamstown in 1824. Moving to the Winterberg, Retief watched from the sidelines for 10 years as his people grew increasingly bitter. Then at the age of 54 he became restless again as he saw how the Afrikaners were unable to follow an unhindered lifestyle under British rule. In March 1837, a month after his 'Manifesto' had appeared in the 'Grahams Town Journal', Retief was ready to trek.

RETIEF'S MANIFESTO *called on the British to allow the Boers to govern themselves.*

Search for a 'Promised Land'

The Great Trek was a landmark in an era of expansionism and bloodshed, of land seizure and labour coercion. Taking the form of a mass migration into the interior of southern Africa, this was a search by dissatisfied Dutch-speaking colonists for a promised land where they would be 'free and independent people' in a 'free and independent state'.

IT WAS NOT the first time the Africans had seen wagons crossing the Orange River; small parties of trekboers, missionaries and adventurers had been venturing into the interior for at least half a century. But this time the reports that reached the chiefs of the Sotho clans on the northern bank were more alarming: the white men were coming in their hundreds.

The men, women and children who set out from the eastern frontier towns of Grahamstown, Uitenhage and Graaff-Reinet represented only a fraction of the Dutch-speaking inhabitants of the colony, and yet their determination and courage has become the single most important element in the folk memory of Afrikaner nationalism. However, far from being the peaceful and God-fearing process which many would like to believe it was, the Great Trek caused a tremendous social upheaval in the interior of southern Africa, rupturing the lives of hundreds of thousands of indigenous people.

Threatened by the 'liberalism' of the new colonial administration, insecure about conflict on the eastern frontier and 'squeezed out' by their own burgeoning population, the Voortrekkers hoped to restore economic, cultural and political unity independent of British power. The only way they saw open to them was to leave the colony. In the decade following 1835, thousands migrated into the interior, organised in a number of trek parties under various leaders. Many of the Voortrekkers were trekboers (semi-nomadic pastoral farmers) and their mode of life made it relatively easy for them to pack their worldly possessions in ox-wagons and leave the colony forever.

After crossing the Orange River the trekkers were still not totally out of reach of the Cape judiciary – in terms of the Cape of Good Hope Punishment Act (1836), they were liable for all crimes committed south of 25 deg latitude (which falls just below the present-day Warmbaths in northern Transvaal).

The trekkers had a strong Calvinist faith. But when the time came for them to leave they found that no Dutch Reformed Church minister from the Cape was prepared to accompany the expedition, for the church synod opposed the emigration, saying it would lead to 'godlessness and a decline of civilisation'. So the trekkers were forced to rely on the ministrations of the American Daniel Lindley, the Wesleyan missionary James Archbell, and a non-ordained minister, Erasmus Smit.

The trekkers, dressed in traditional *dopper* coats (short coats buttoned from top to bottom), *kappies* (bonnets) and hand-made *riempieskoene* (leather thong shoes), set out in wagons which they called *kakebeenwaens* (literally, jawbone wagons, because the shape and sides of a typical trek wagon resembled the jawbone of an animal).

These wagons could carry a startling weight of household goods, clothes, bedding, furniture, agricultural implements, fruit trees and weapons. They were ingeniously designed and surprisingly light, so as not to strain the oxen, and to make it easier to negotiate the veld, narrow ravines and steep precipices which lay ahead. Travelling down the 3 500 metre slope of the Drakensberg, no brake shoe or changing of wheels could have saved a wagon from hurtling down the mountain were it not for a simple and creative solution: the hindwheels of wagons were removed and heavy branches were tied securely underneath. So the axles were protected, and a new form of brake was invented.

The interior represented for the trekkers a foreboding enigma. The barren Kalahari Desert to the west of the highveld, and the tsetse fly belt which stretched from the Limpopo River south-eastwards, could not have been a very inviting prospect. Little did they realise that neither man nor

THE REVEREND JAMES ARCHBELL, *an English Wesleyan missionary who established himself at Thaba Nchu in 1833, was ideally placed to minister to the religious needs of the trekkers.*

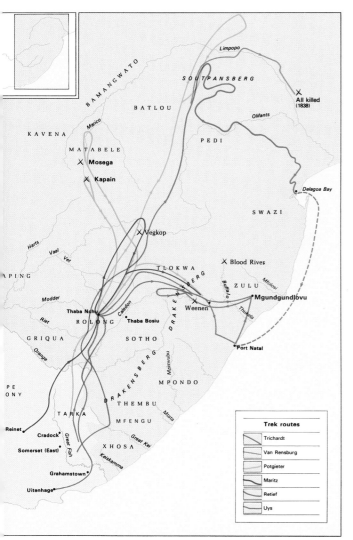

Trek routes

Trek routes	
	Trichardt
	Van Rensburg
	Potgieter
	Maritz
	Retief
	Uys

Trek parties and routes

Though united in a common endeavour, the Voortrekkers hailed from different districts and held allegiance to various leaders . . . . First there was Louis Trichardt, a natural rebel (the Cape Colony had, in fact, put a price on his head for having allegedly incited the Xhosa to continue with the Sixth Frontier War of 1834-5) and the only leader to keep a diary on his travels. With a handful of neighbours, including nine weapon-bearing men, he set out northwards from the eastern Cape in May 1835. On the south bank of the Orange River, he joined up with Hans van Rensburg and his party. Travelling at an average speed of 12 kilometres a day, the two pioneers opened the way to the Transvaal lowveld and Portuguese East Africa.

Constant friction between them, however, culminated in a split at a place later named Strydpoort (literally, quarrel pass). The Van Rensburg party headed for the fever-ridden port of Delagoa Bay and was never heard of again (they were annihilated by the Tsonga), while Trichardt and an exhausted group of 52 trekkers and seven servants arrived in Lourenco Marques in April 1838. In the Portuguese settlement, with its unhealthy climate and marshy surroundings, 20 trekkers were to die of tropical diseases over the next few weeks. In October Trichardt himself died of malaria.

Other parties followed, and soon what began as a trickle became a torrent. Towards the end of 1835, Andries Hendrik Potgieter, a man of imposing height and few words (and later the leader of the first trekker group to settle in the Transvaal), with a group of 40 armed men and their families, headed north, hoping to make use of Portuguese ports for trading.

But most leaders, including Gert Maritz, favoured Port Natal. A legal adviser, wagon-maker and farmer in Graaff-Reinet, he left the eastern Cape in September 1836, linking up first with the Potgieter trek and later with Piet Retief in Natal. Retief himself had trekked into Transorangia in February 1837 with 120 armed men and 100 wagons. From there he swung eastwards, reaching Port Natal in October. Elected as chief leader and supreme military commander, his undemocratic ways often conflicted with those of fellow trekkers.

More trek parties were to join the migration, which already comprised about 2 000 people. In April 1837, Piet Uys, the youngest of the Voortrekker leaders and later the only one to be killed in battle, trekked from Grahamstown into Transorangia. That year Andries Pretorius led an exploratory trek to Natal, meeting up with Maritz and Retief – but it was only the following year that he too left the Cape never to return.

IN THE EXODUS *which started from the eastern Cape, the Voortrekkers set off in several groups, each under its own leader. Although they followed much the same route through Transorangia, they then split, some heading for Natal and others continuing north.*

animal would escape the fatal malarial mosquito. Yet the Voortrekkers ploughed on through treacherous terrain, eliminating all obstacles in their path, and intent on gaining access to ports beyond the sphere of British control, such as Delagoa Bay, Inhambane and Sofala. In order for their new settlement to be viable, it was crucial that they make independent links with the economies of Europe.

Trek and the 'empty lands'

Reconnaissance expeditions in 1834 and 1835 reported that Natal south of the Thukela and the central highveld north and south of the Vaal River, were fertile and largely uninhabited, much of the interior having been unsettled by a series of wars among African chiefdoms in the region. The truth of these reports – many of them from missionaries – has been argued at length by historians. Recent research indicates that the so-called 'depopulation theory' (see page 80) is unreliable – the devastation and carnage by African warriors is exaggerated with every account, the

number of casualties of wars among chiefdoms ranging between half a million and 5-million.

This kind of historical inaccuracy strengthens the trekkers' claim that the land which they occupied was 'uninhabited and belonged to no-one', that the survivors of the disorder were conveniently spread out in a horseshoe shape around empty land. Probably in an attempt to justify their land seizure, the trekkers also claimed to have

VOORTREKKER WAGONS *were ideally suited to the rough terrain they were forced to cross, being light and strong. They were called* kakebeenwaens *(jawbone wagons) because they were similar in shape to the jawbone of an animal. Despite their manoeuvrability, they could carry a surprising amount of household and other goods. This picture shows a wagon crossing a particularly difficult drift.*

actually saved the smaller clans in the interior from annihilation, and defeated the 'barbarous' Ndebele and Zulu warriors.

Africans did indeed move temporarily into other areas, but were soon to reoccupy their land, only to find themselves ousted by Boer intruders. For example, in Natal the African population, estimated at 11 000 in 1838, was increased by 'several thousand refugees' after Dingane's defeat at the hands of his half-brother Mpande two years later. In 1843, when the Republic of Natalia was annexed by the British, the official African population was put at 'between 80 000 and 100 000 people'. But even this may have been an underestimation.

Trekker communities and technology

Military prowess was of paramount importance to the trekker expedition. It had to be, for they were invading and conquering lands to which African societies themselves lay claim. Bound by a common purpose, the trekkers were a people's army in the true sense of the word, with the whole family being drawn into military defence and attack. For instance, the loading of the *sanna* (the name they gave to the muzzle-loading rifles they used) was a complicated procedure and so the Boers used more than one gun at a time – while aiming and firing at the enemy with one, their wives and children would be loading another.

Armed with rifles on their backs and a *kruithoring* (powder horn) and *bandolier* (a bullet container made of hartebeest, kudu or ox-hide) strapped to their belts, formidable groups of trekkers would ride into battle. Bullets were often sawn nearly through to make them split and fly in different directions, and buckshot was prepared by casting lead into reeds and then chopping it up. Part of every man's gear was his knife, with a blade about 20 centimetres in length. When approaching the battlefield, the wagons would be drawn into a circle and the openings between the wheels filled with branches to fire through and hide behind. When they eventually settled down, the structure of many of the houses they built – square, with thick walls and tiny windows – resembled small fortresses.

The distinction between hunting and raiding parties was often blurred in trekker society. Killing and looting were their business, land and labour their spoils. When the trekkers arrived in the Transvaal they experienced an acute labour shortage. They did not work their own fields themselves and instead used Pedi who sold their labour mainly to buy arms and ammunition.

During commando onslaughts, particularly in the eastern Transvaal, thousands of children were captured to become *inboekselings* (see page 146). These children were indentured to their masters until adulthood (the age of 21 in the case of women and 25 in the case of men), but many remained bound to their owners for a much longer period. This system was similar to child slavery, and a more vicious application of the apprenticeship laws promulgated at the Cape in 1775 and 1812.

Child slavery was even more prevalent in the northern Soutpansberg area of the Transvaal. It has been suggested that when these northern Boers could no longer secure white ivory for trade at Delagoa Bay, 'black ivory' (a euphemism widely used for African children) began to replace it as a lucrative item of trade. Children were more amenable to new ways of life, and it was hoped that the *inboekselings* would assimilate Boer cultural patterns and create a 'buffer class' against increasing African resistance.

Dispossession and land seizure

The trekkers' first major confrontation was with Mzilikazi, founder and king of the Ndebele. After leaving the Cape, the trekkers made their first base near Thaba Nchu, the great place of Moroka, the Rolong chief. In 1836 the Ndebele were in the path of a trekker expedition heading northwards and led by Andries Hendrik Potgieter. The Ndebele were attacked by a Boer commando led by Potgieter, but Mzilikazi retaliated and the Boers retreated to their main laager at Vegkop. There in October, in a short and fierce battle which lasted half an hour, 40 trekkers succeeded in beating off an attack by 6 000 Ndebele warriors. Both sides suffered heavy losses – 430 Ndebele were killed, and the trekkers lost thousands of sheep and cattle as well as their

WOMEN LOAD *the rifles while their men-folk fire at advancing Ndebele during the battle of Vegkop in October 1836. After a short and bloody battle, the Boers succeeded in beating off 6 000 warriors, killing 430. However, the trek-kers lost thousands of sheep and cattle as well as their oxen.*

VOORTREKKER LEADER *Andries Pretorius (below) nurses a wounded arm in this painting by an unknown artist. He helped pioneer the route to Natal.*

trek oxen. But a few days later, Moroka and the missionary Archbell rescued them with food and oxen.

Gert Maritz and his party joined these trekkers in Transorangia (later the Orange Free State) and in January 1837, with the help of a small force of Griqua, Kora, Rolong and Tlokwa, they captured Mzilikazi's stronghold at Mosega and drove the Ndebele further north. The trekkers then concluded treaties of friendship with Moroka and Sekonyela (chief of the Tlokwa).

When Piet Retief and his followers split away and moved eastwards to Natal, both Potgieter and Piet Uys remained

determined to break the Ndebele. At the end of 1837, 135 trekkers besieged Mzilikazi's forces in the Marico valley, and Mzilikazi fled across the Limpopo River to present-day Zimbabwe. He died there, to be succeeded by Lobengula, who led a rather precarious life in the area until he was eventually defeated by the forces of the British South Africa Company in the 1890s (see page 218).

Meanwhile, Retief and his followers continued marching towards Port Natal (later Durban). After Retief's fateful encounter with Dingane, chief of the Zulu, and the ensuing Battle of Blood River (see following page), the trekkers declared the short-lived Republic of Natalia (1838). They formed a simple system of governing, with Pretorius as President, assisted by a *volksraad* (people's assembly) of 24 members, and local government officials based on the traditional *landdrost* and *heemraden* system. In 1841, an adjunct council was established at Potchefstroom, with Potgieter as Chief-Commandant. The trekkers believed that at last they had found a place in the sun....

But the British would not recognise their independence. In December 1838, the Governor, Sir George Napier, a determined military man who had not allowed the loss of his right arm in battle to ruin his career, sent his military secretary, Major Samuel Charters, to occupy Port Natal, which effectively controlled Voortrekker use of the harbour. Three years later, when the Natal *Volksraad* resolved to drive all Africans not working for the whites southwards beyond the Mtamvuna River (later the border between Natal and the Transkei), Napier again intervened. He was concerned that this would threaten the eastern frontier of the Cape, and so instructed Captain Thomas Charlton Smith to march to Port Natal with 250 men. Smith, who had joined the Royal Navy at the age of nine and was a veteran of the Battle of Waterloo, tried to negotiate with Pretorius, but to no avail.

On the moonlit night of 23 May 1842, Smith attacked the Boer camp at Congella but Pretorius, who had been alerted, fought back. The trekkers proceeded to besiege the British camp. One of their number, Dick King, who became known as the 'saviour of Natal', evaded the siege and rode

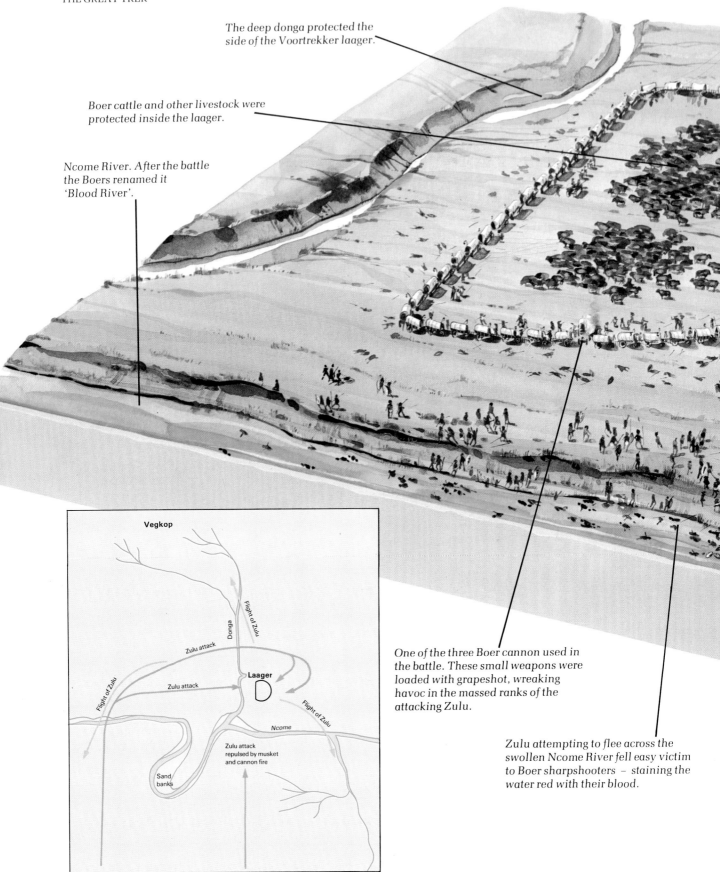

The deep donga protected the side of the Voortrekker laager.

Boer cattle and other livestock were protected inside the laager.

Ncome River. After the battle the Boers renamed it 'Blood River'.

One of the three Boer cannon used in the battle. These small weapons were loaded with grapeshot, wreaking havoc in the massed ranks of the attacking Zulu.

Zulu attempting to flee across the swollen Ncome River fell easy victim to Boer sharpshooters – staining the water red with their blood.

Vegkop

Flight of Zulu

Donga

Zulu attack

Flight of Zulu

Zulu attack

Laager

Flight of Zulu

Ncome

Zulu attack repulsed by musket and cannon fire

Sand banks

THE ZULU crossed the Ncome River at a nearby drift and swung in a wide arc towards the Voortrekker laager, attacking from the open plain between the river and the donga. They were beaten back by the Boers' superior firepower.

Blood River

'This man,' declared the widow of slain Voortrekker leader Piet Retief, 'has been sent by God. He will help us take revenge.' The man was Andries Pretorius, a dynamic, pistol-packing farmer from Graaff-Reinet who had made a name for himself among the Boers as a natural leader.

It was November 1838 – a bleak month for the pioneering Voortrekkers, whose bid to settle Zulu land had ended in death, disaster and dissension. Unable to choose a leader after the death of Retief, they had finally and desperately called on Pretorius to lead them to victory.

He arrived on 22 November, a tall, imposing figure in a well-cut suit with a pistol and cutlass at his belt, and 60 volunteers at his back. Within a week he had organised a commando of 468 trekkers – and set off for a final reckoning with the Zulu king, Dingane. On 9 December he reportedly climbed onto a gun carriage, asking his men to join him in a vow that, if God gave them victory, 'we would note the date of the victory . . . to make it known even to our latest posterity in order that it might be celebrated to the honour of God'.

On 15 December, Pretorius' scouts reported a heavy Zulu presence near the Voortrekker column – and he ordered his commandos to form a laager not far from present-day Dundee, choosing a site between the Ncome River and a deep donga; with the unprotected flank facing an open, treeless plain. The wagons were securely tied together and cannon placed in the only three openings.

As the thick mist of early morning on 16 December cleared, the Zulu charged – but the short Zulu spears were no match for musket balls and grapeshot. The first attack was repulsed – and then a second and a third. 'Nothing remains in my memory except shouting and tumult and lamentations,' wrote one Boer later. 'We had scarcely time to throw a handful of powder in the gun and slip a bullet down the barrel, without a moment even to drive it home with the ramrod.'

Finally, with hundreds of their comrades dead, the Zulu faltered – and Pretorius ordered a party of Boers out of the laager on horseback to cut them down. Defeated and desperate, many tried to hide in a deep ravine – where the Boers shot them in droves. Boer chaplain Sarel Cilliers later recalled that the 'word of the Lord was fulfilled: ''By one way shall your enemies come, but by the blessing of the Lord they shall fly before your face.'' ' When it was all over, he said, the 'Kaffirs lay on the ground like pumpkins on a rich soil that has borne a large crop'.

Scores more died trying to flee across the river – staining the water red with their blood. No prisoners were taken. When it was all over, the Boers counted 3 000 Zulu bodies – against three injured Boers, including Pretorius, who had been speared in the hand.

The Boers had taken a terrible revenge.

Zulu flee from the advancing Boers. More than 400 were systematically shot after they were discovered hiding in a small ravine.

Mounted Boers leave the laager in pursuit of the shattered Zulu. Anyone who came within range of the Boer guns was immediately shot without quarter. No prisoners were taken.

A VIEW *of the reconstructed battlesite today, showing one of the three cannon used in the battle, in position.*

some 1 000 kilometres on horseback to seek reinforcements in Grahamstown. In June a British relief force under Lieutenant-Colonel Abraham Cloete arrived on the scene and Boer resistance was crushed. On 15 July the *volksraad* at Pietermaritzburg signed the conditions of submission.

Although most trekkers had travelled into Natal or into the far north with the main expeditions, some had remained on the fertile land above the junction of the Caledon and Orange rivers, and gradually began to move north-eastward.

The trekkers' pioneer in this area was Jan de Winnaar, who settled in the Matlakeng area in May-June 1838. As more farmers were moving into the area they tried to colonise the land between the two rivers, even north of the Caledon, claiming that it had been abandoned by the Sotho people. But although some of the independent communities who had lived there had been scattered, others remained in the kloofs and on the hillsides. Moshoeshoe, paramount chief of the Sotho, when hearing of the trekker settlement above the junction, stated that '...the ground on which they were belonged to me, but I had no objections to their flocks grazing there until such time as they were able to proceed further; on condition, however, that they remained in peace with my people and recognised my authority' (see page 139).

The trekkers proceeded to build huts of clay (instead of reed), and began planting their own food crops (no longer trading with the Sotho). This indicated their resolve to settle down permanently. A French missionary, Eugene Casalis, later remarked that the trekkers had humbly asked for temporary rights while they were still few in number, but that when they felt 'strong enough to throw off the mask' they went back on their initial intention.

In October 1842 Jan Mocke, a fiery republican, and his followers erected a beacon at Alleman's drift on the banks of the Orange River and proclaimed a republic. Officials were appointed to preside over the whole area between the Caledon and Vaal rivers. Riding back from the drift, they informed Chief Lephoi, an independent chief at Bethulie, that the land was now Boer property and that he and his people were subject to Boer laws. They further decided that the crops which had been sown for the season would be reaped by the Boers, and they even uprooted one of the peach trees in the garden of a mission station as indication of their ownership. In the north-east, they began to drive Moshoeshoe's people away from the springs, their only source of water. Moshoeshoe appealed for protection to the Queen of England, but he soon discovered that he would have to organise his own resistance.

Land seizure and dispossession were also prevalent in the eastern Transvaal where Potgieter had founded the towns of Andries-Ohrigstad in 1845 and Soutpansberg (which was later renamed Schoemansdal) in 1848. A power struggle erupted between Potgieter and Pretorius, who had arrived with a new trekker party from Natal and seemed to have a better understanding of the political dynamics of southern Africa. Potgieter, still anxious to legitimise his settlement, concluded a *vredenstraktaat* (peace treaty) in 1845 with Sekwati, chief of the Pedi, who he claimed had ceded all rights to an undefined stretch of land. The precise terms of the treaty are unknown, but it seems certain that Sekwati never actually sold land to the Boers.

Often in order to ensure their own safety, chiefs would sign arbitrary treaties giving away sections of land to which they in fact had no right. Such was the case with Mswati, chief of the Swazi, who, intent on seeking support against the Zulu, in July 1846 granted all the land bounded by the Oliphants, Crocodile and Elands rivers to the Boers. This angered the Pedi, who pointed out that the land had not even been his to hand over.

There was no uniform legal system or concept of ownership to which all parties interested in the land subscribed. Private land ownership did not exist in these African societies, and for the most part the land which chiefs ceded to the Boers was communally owned. Any document 'signed' by the chiefs, and its implications, could not have been fully understood by them. Misunderstandings worked in the favour of the Boers.

Large tracts of land were purchased for next to nothing. For example, the northern half of Transorangia went to Andries Potgieter in early 1836 for a few cattle and a promise to protect the Taung chief, Makwana, from the Ndebele. The area between the Vet and Vaal rivers extended about 60 000 square kilometres. This means that Potgieter got 2 000 square kilometres per head of livestock! Also the 'right of conquest' was extended over areas much larger than those that chiefs actually had authority over. After Mzilikazi's flight north in November 1837, the trekkers immediately took over all the land between the Vet and Limpopo rivers – although Mzilikazi's area of control covered only the western Transvaal.

But it was only after the Sand River Convention (1852) and the Bloemfontein Convention (1854) that independent Boer republics were formally established north of the Vaal and Orange rivers respectively.

Retief and Blood River

Voortrekker leader Piet Retief had been exactly one year on the move when he visited Dingane, chief of the Zulu, on 6 February 1838 at his capital Mgundgundlovu ('the place of the great elephant'). At this meeting, the chief, who 10 years previously had murdered his half-brother, Shaka, to assume the chieftainship, reportedly agreed to cede to the trekkers the territory between the Thukela and Mzimvubu rivers as well as the Drakensberg – in exchange for 63 cattle which Sekonyela, the Tlokwa chief, had stolen from the Zulu. Along with the cattle, he also requested 11 rifles. The trekkers, who had been in alliance with the Tlokwa (against Mzilikazi), speedily returned the cattle to Dingane, but Retief failed to deliver the guns.

When Retief and his men dismounted at Dingane's cattle kraal, they found Dingane sitting with two of his chiefs and warriors dancing before them. The trekkers were instructed to leave their guns outside and invited to share a drink with Dingane. Suddenly he commanded his men to catch the 'witchdoctors', tie them up and drag them to a hill to be stoned. This was witnessed from a distance by Francis Owen, the missionary at Dingane's kraal, who later described the scene in his diary. The mutilated corpses of the Retief party were discovered by a search party of trekkers who reported that a land deed, signed by Dingane, was found among the possessions of the dead men (many historians doubt that this ever, in fact, existed – certainly none exists today, although reports claim that it disappeared in 1900 during the South African War).

Distraught and temporarily immobilised without their leader, the trekker community in Natal argued over a new course of action . . . .

In the early hours of 17 February the unsuspecting trekker laagers on the Bloukrans and Bushmans rivers suddenly awoke to find themselves surrounded by Zulu warriors. At the place which later would be called Weenen ('weeping'), approximately 500 people (mainly servants) were killed, and the Zulu seized 25 000 head of cattle and thousands of sheep and horses.

Two months later, on 6 April, the Boers launched a counter-attack. A commando led by two rival leaders, Piet Uys and Andries Potgieter, marched towards Mgundgundlovu in a scissors formation (a two-pronged attack). But just across the Buffalo River, at Italeni, they were ambushed by the Zulu. A British Port Natal expedition rushed to assist the trekkers, but to no avail. Most of the trekkers escaped but Uys was among the 10 who died.

It was only with the arrival towards the end of that year of Andries Pretorius, who had been roaming as a scout in the Transvaal, Transorangia and Natal, that the trekkers could

consolidate against the Zulu. On 25 November 1838, ignoring accusations of cowardice which had followed him after Italeni, Pretorius, who was an experienced commando leader, took over leadership as Commandant-General in Natal and immediately started preparing a retaliatory attack on the Zulu. On Sunday, 9 December, Pretorius and his followers reportedly took a vow that if God granted them victory over the Zulu the trekkers and all their descendants would observe an annual day of thanksgiving. (Recent research has put a question mark over the vow, indicating that it may never have existed. Certainly it was not commemorated in the years immediately following the battle.)

After scouts had warned that a Zulu army was in the vicinity, the trekkers drew their 57 wagons into a laager on the banks of the Ncome River (a tributary of the Thukela). At dawn on 16 December 1838, 10 000 Zulu warriors swept towards the laager. The trekkers responded with musket and cannon fire, and when the warriors showed signs of weakening, mounted trekkers charged from the laager and dispersed the last of the warriors – 3 000 Zulu were killed, while of the 468 trekkers only three suffered casualties, none fatal. Flooded with the blood of the victims, the Ncome River was afterwards referred to ominously as 'Blood River'.

After the Battle of Blood River, the Zulu kingdom was thrown into a civil war and Dingane was overthrown by Mpande, his half-brother. Mpande, who was more amenable to the demands of the trekkers, was installed by Pretorius as king of the Zulu, and the southern part of his territory was annexed by the Natal Republic.

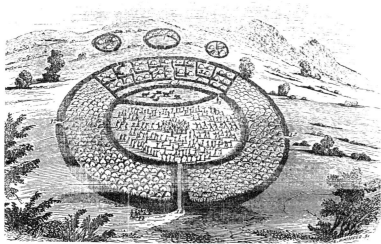

DINGANE'S KRAAL *at Mgundgundlovu (Place of the great elephant), where Piet Retief and some of his followers were killed by the Zulu chief in 1838 after he had reportedly ceded land to the Voortrekkers.*

With 'courage in their breasts...'

Africa 'was suggestive of little but waterless wilds, burning suns, the death-wind of the desert, and the slave trade . . . . But despite the appalling, which is so often associated with the unknown, and despite the gloomy pictures drawn by those who would fain have detained them, there was courage enough in the breasts of those pioneers . . . to brave the dangers, real or imaginary . . . .'

So wrote Henry Hare Dugmore of the British men and women – among them his parents – who came to distant southern Africa in 1820 to start a new life. As they voyaged into the unknown, so too, not quite a score of years later, the Voortrekkers pushed the frontiers of white expansionism ever deeper into the sub-continent.

On a shared stage against the same backdrop of hardship and often heartbreak, they pursued their separate dreams of the future.

The British settlers

They were left, among their boxes and bundles, on the alien land that had been allocated to them, miles from 'civilisation' as they knew it. Some settlers had come prepared, bringing their essential tools and implements from home; others had stocked up with what they could at the government depot at Algoa Bay – axes, hammers, spades, harrows, ploughs, and, of course, the seed from which their wheatfields would spring.

The first task of the British settlers was to set up home – initially the government tents they had on loan until they could build more permanent homes. The sites they chose reflected their hopes and fears in a new country: an easily defensible spot, one where the soil seemed rich, or one in a picturesque setting.

As soon as they were able to, they erected primitive wattle-and-daub shacks, whose simple framework of saplings was plastered with clay – and which were to prove hopelessly inadequate for the extreme climate.

TWO SETTLER FAMILIES *(left and below left) pose for the camera, in typically English dress.*

Then, they tended their lands . . . again, as best they could. Some early accounts tell of these pioneer 'farmers' sowing carrots in trenches, planting corn still on the cob or onions roots up. But even their best efforts seemed doomed, with floods following hard on the heels of three harvestless seasons.

Life was lean and the drift to towns – more suited to a mercantile people – soon began. But their spirit remained unquenched. They resisted government restrictions on trade with the Xhosa, on freedom of movement and of speech, and a reluctant government was forced to give way or at least look the other way.

Thus it was that the British settlers began to make their real – and lasting – contribution to a new society.

Perhaps most significant was their determination to establish a free Press, and the implications this had for a literate, even literary, future. But hand in hand with this went other advances.

Where education had initially been dictated by the often limited time and ability of parents to teach their children, it began to be channelled, first through tutors, then Sunday schools, then the formal classroom situation that laid the foundation of the eastern Cape's reputable educational institutions.

In the same way the early, fairly primitive style of worship – at any convenient clearing or under a shady tree – developed into more organised religion, and within a quarter of a century more than 35 churches had been erected. This frontier religion inspired mission work, leading not only to the spreading of the Word among non-Christians, but also – assisted by the settlers' publishing skills – to the printing of a Xhosa gospel before 1840.

THE SOUTHWELL SCHOOL (above) near Port Alfred, one of the earliest settler schools and still in use today.
A RECONSTRUCTION (left) by Frederick T I'Ons of 1820 settlers camped on the banks of the Great Fish River. It is believed to depict the Bowker family, with the principal figures being Miles Bowker, his wife and daughter Mary.

GRAHAMSTOWN (above) in the Albany district became the focus of British settlement at the Cape. Today its origins are commemorated in numerous monuments and buildings and a memorial to the 1820 settlers. This picture, showing the early layout of the town, dates back to 1833.

Those that stayed on the land began at last to prosper, and their new sense of permanence was reflected in the sturdier homes they now built: high-ceilinged, double-storeyed houses designed along late Georgian lines, with larger, glass windows replacing the old oiled paper, shuttered affairs. Although at one time it was popular to construct the living quarters between two solidly built towers, where families could take shelter from the violence of the frontier wars, with increased military presence, elegant Regency residences – complete with attractive wrought ironwork and ornamental ceilings – as befitted this new class of gentleman farmers soon became the vogue.

The 1820 settlers had come to stay . . . but, ironically, their presence was one of the factors that led to the departure of the Voortrekkers.

The Voortrekkers

Pressure for land and resistance to British 'liberalism' and imperialism contributed to the Voortrekkers' decision to quit the Cape. This Boer migration was not the unified affair that the British settlement scheme had been, but the way of life on any of the individual treks probably differed only slightly.

Central to the trekker was his wagon. A family might have more than one of these light, narrow wagons, loaded with bedding, fabric and clothes; groceries and supplies; what furniture could be accommodated, including a table and stools; implements and seeds; and – of course – gunpowder and firearms. This world in miniature represented the trekker's sole security during the trek years, and his livestock his sole wealth.

Life on the move was painstakingly slow, perhaps covering only 10 kilometres a day, or even less in the face of such obstacles as rivers and mountains. Descending the Drakensberg was the most arduous, with the Voortrekkers removing the back wheels and using only two oxen to brake the wagon, and in some cases unpacking the contents of the wagon to carry themselves.

Wherever the Voortrekkers struck camp, life would fall into a more settled pattern, beginning before dawn with

A TYPICAL *Voortrekker scene (below) with the man of the family repairing a wagon wheel and his wife – in distinctive 'kappie' (poke bonnet) – hanging out the washing.*

THE BIBLE
(above) was the mainstay of many of the Voortrekkers and often their only book.

THE 'SANNA' *(left) was an unwieldy, muzzle-loading rifle, about twice the weight of a modern rifle. Because loading was complicated, many Boers had more than one gun so that wives and children could load one while they fired the other.*

GUNPOWDER *was poured from 'kruithorings' (powderhorns) like this one (below) into the muzzle of the rifle. Today this symbolic horn appears in the emblem of the National Party.*

prayers. Before the boys departed to herd the livestock, they would be taught their lessons – a rudimentary education aimed at being able to read the Bible. Between their 'household' chores – washing, cooking and sewing – the women might find time to instruct the younger children playing about the camp. The men would spend their day hunting for the pot or doing any necessary repairs to the wagons, while some would ride out ahead to reconnoitre the territory.

In the evenings, the all-important livestock would be herded into a temporary kraal at the laager (the circular formation of wagons) and people would gather and chat around the campfire to while away the evening. Trader John Montgomery gave a glimpse of some trekker leisure activities: ' . . . We had resort to many amusements such as target-shooting, putting the stone, racing and leaping . . . . The evenings were spent by the old people in reading their bibles and singing psalms, whilst the young folks went in for music and dancing – a place being scuffed level in front of a tent for a ball-room floor. It was fine fun in the moonlight skipping about with the Boers' wives and daughters. Thus time passed pleasantly enough . . . .'

Where settlements became more permanent, homes began to be built, initially tentlike structures of wood covered with grass and with untanned hides for doors. Voortrekker architecture as such followed an austere plan, generally one room wide with a veranda in front.

The house walls consisted of sun-dried mud reinforced with grass clods and bagged with a mud and dung mixture before being whitewashed. Under the thatched roof would be a reed ceiling, bound with *riempies* (leather thongs) – also used to hinge the doors and shutters. The mud floors, covered with oxblood and dung for a polished finish, were embedded with peach stones to strengthen the spots that took the most wear.

Into these homes went the sturdy wooden furniture that had been carted from the Cape, with pride of place in the bedroom going to the *wakis* (wagon-chest) – mounted in front of the wagon to serve as a seat for the driver, and now used to store linen and clothes. What few ornaments the trekkers had been able to bring with them from their original homes – a cherished porcelain plate or a copper candlestick – completed the simple furnishings.

Like the 1820 settlers before them, the Voortrekkers were now prepared to 'colonise' a new land.

VOORTREKKER *wagons like the one below were known as 'kakebeenwaens' because their shape resembled the jawbone of an animal.*

The rocky road to reform

The Second British Occupation of the Cape in the early 19th century brought with it
a change in the way white rulers viewed their responsibilities towards
the local population. Within half a century these new rulers had abolished slavery,
granted blacks the right to own land and, eventually, given the colonists
a large measure of self-government.

BRITAIN AFTER THE END of the Napoleonic Wars in 1815 was flushed with victory and a sense of its own power – a strength that burgeoned over the next half century as the imperial writ spread ever further – searching for raw materials and markets to feed the Industrial Revolution. Capitalism, a way of harnessing greed to production, was transforming the world from Birmingham in England to Botany Bay in Australia. But capitalism without conscience made for a brutal age: children hauled coal in blackened pits; women laboured for 14 hours a day to make cloth; cholera stalked decaying inner cities; while the streets of London teemed with prostitutes.

Inevitably, these excesses led to a plea for reform and a belief that perhaps the rewards were not always worth the candle; that poverty need not have to be the unavoidable consequence of capitalism; that if poor people had a say in how they were governed, their lot would improve.

It was this liberalism, a movement that began by seeking to abolish slavery and went on to seek a more representative form of government, that found its way to the Cape in the early years of the 19th century, brought by immigrants, some missionaries and British justice, which gave teeth to the theory – shared but seldom practised by Roman-Dutch law – that all men were equal before the law, whatever their skin colour. Its two most notable early achievements were the abolition of slavery and the proclamation in 1828 of Ordinance 50, which repealed Pass laws and discriminatory legislation, and extended to 'Hottentots and free persons of colour' the right to own land. It also prohibited employers from making contracts with their servants for longer than one year, or from 'apprenticing' children without the consent of their parents.

The end of slavery

Although the importation of slaves was banned in 1807, it was not until 1834 that slaves were officially granted their freedom, and even then they were obliged to work as 'apprentices' for their former owners – unpaid – for a period of four years.

Even at the end of this period there was little change in economic relationships, as most of the former slaves had no assets other than their labour. Those who had become artisans could practise their trades as freemen and, for a number of years, maintained control over their crafts such as building, wagon-making, tailoring, and as wheelwrights and coopers.

Not all former slaves left their masters at the end of the period of apprenticeship. Some were not confident of being able to make a living on the open market, while others were detained through having been advanced goods or money, for which they had to give value by labour. This was a process that could be repeated indefinitely.

The majority of former slaves, although technically free, quickly found that their positions had hardly changed at all. Legally the equal of the white man, they were still, socially, inferior and expected to show respect. Nevertheless, it was a step forward, and the Masters and Servants Ordinance of 1841, which superseded Ordinance 50, made no distinction of race in the case of servants.

Land for the Khoikhoi

Inevitably, perhaps, liberalism mixed philanthropy and self-interest, particularly in the decision to award so-called 'neutral' ground (that, in fact, belonged to the Xhosa) to the dispossessed Khoikhoi of the eastern Cape.

EX-SLAVES *celebrate their freedom with a march through the streets of Cape Town. The abolition of slavery was one of the most important achievements of early Cape liberalism – although economic reasons also played a part.*

After their final unsuccessful revolt against white domination in 1799 (see page 74), the Khoikhoi were finally reduced to servants on the land they had once owned. With the coming of the missionaries, notably Dr John Philip (see page 97), their lot gradually improved. At last they had a voice, and one that could be heard in London. It was largely because of Philip's campaign that Ordinance 50 of 1828 – providing for landownership by certain qualified 'non-whites' – was passed by the Cape Government. Although Philip played no part in drawing up the ordinance, among those who did was Andries Stockenström, Commissioner-General for the Eastern Districts.

It was this ordinance which paved the way for setting up in the Kat River valley of the frontier region a buffer state of Khoikhoi and descendants of slaves – called 'coloured' people – to be, in the words of Stockenström, 'a breastwork against an exasperated, powerful enemy in the most vulnerable and dangerous part of our frontier' (see page 134). But the most significant step forward for the liberal cause came with the new constitution in 1853, the granting of which followed an attempt by the British Government to land deported convicts at the Cape in the same way as it had done in Australia.

The convict crisis
Capetonians who opened their copy of the 'South African Commercial Advertiser' of 30 June 1849 had their attention drawn to a large advertisement headed 'Immediate. Convicted felons'. The leader of the newly formed Anti-Convict Association was John Fairbairn, the newspaper's proprietor and editor, who went on to urge 'all men' to sign a 'pledge . . . not to employ and to drop all intercourse with' any person who employed 'convicted felons under sentence of transportation'.

The real reason why slavery had to go

If you've always assumed that the abolition of slavery was motivated by philanthropy, a simple revulsion at the concept of one man owning another for his labour, think again: the truth is far more complex and, like so much in history, has its origins in economic forces rather than humanitarian ones.

The abolitionist movement grew in Britain and the United States at the same time as capitalism; and it is not hard to see why: slavery belongs to a more feudal age of landed wealth, of simple divisions between the haves and the have-nots; it has no place in a capitalist economy, which demands a vast pool of labour from which industry can draw in accordance with the laws of supply and demand.

Slaves in themselves represented capital – and as every capitalist knows, capital should be looked after as carefully as possible in order to maximise the return on investment. Free market labour as it existed in Britain during the Industrial Revolution heyday of capitalism was patently cheaper than slaves as it required no capital outlay – the purchase price of a slave – and could be worked to a standstill before being replaced from the labour pool at no extra capital outlay.

This is why the hard life of a plantation slave in the American south often paled into insignificance when compared with the horrors of working class life in Dickensian Britain or the immigrant-fed sweat shops of New York.

In South Africa the situation was made more complex by the fact that, although slavery was abolished, there was no labour pool from which to draw workers, except for scattered Khoisan and those Bantu-speaking people who could be persuaded to work for the white man. It was this crucial labour shortage that was to bedevil 19th-century economics in South Africa – at a time when the region was being transformed from a monopolistic outpost of the Dutch East India Company into a free market, capitalist economy.

It is easy, with the hindsight of history, to see the trend. To the authorities of the day, dealing with grumbling, influential employers, reaction was often contradictory. At first the new British occupiers of the Cape, while outlawing the slave trade, passed restrictive codes aimed at forcing the Khoisan to work for the white farmers. It was only in 1828 that an understanding of the capitalist labour requirement emerges; Ordinance 50 freed the Khoisan from their restrictions and even allowed them 'equality before the law'. Although viewed by most historians as a triumph of humanitarianism, which by the standards of the day it was, it was also the first attempt to encourage more labour by freeing it.

Ordinance 50 was just one of a number of measures taken by the British to try to create in the Cape a self-supporting colonial economy that could both produce raw materials to feed the factories of Britain and provide a market for its manufactured goods – an ideal of trade following the flag. Why else expend so much money and energy on containing the Xhosa on the eastern frontier; or on importing 4 000 British settlers to Algoa Bay in 1820? These and other measures, including the granting of a colour-blind franchise in mid-century, achieved some success – the Cape rivalled Australia as the main source of wool in the 1830s and '40s, but output continued to be seriously curtailed by the lack of labour.

Naturally Ordinance 50 produced a howl of protest from the Boer subsistence farmers – whose labourers could now drift away to seek better conditions elsewhere – but they belonged to a feudal age rather than a capitalist one; and during the 19th century many were in retreat before the advancing tide of capitalism, first attempting to escape it by trekking inland, and then, finally cornered at the end of the century, turning to fight it and the British imperialism on which so much of it was based.

The capitalism that established itself at the Cape up until 1868 was mercantile and agricultural, an economy in which many Africans could share by providing foodstuffs for the expanding markets opened up by white settlement. The new form of capitalism that was about to be ushered in through the discovery of diamonds and gold was to be very different – demanding enormous capital and labour that only a radical shift in society could provide.

Transportation to the colonies had been a favourite sentence of British courts for many years, with most convicts being sent to Australia. By the 1840s, the growing 'respectable' population of Australia was protesting strongly against receiving any more convicts, and in 1842 it was proposed that criminals be sent to the Cape, where the proposal raised an outcry. Despite these protests, in 1848 Earl Grey, the British Colonial Secretary, raised the spectre of convict settlement again, and the transport ship *Neptune*, with 282 convicts on board, sailed for the Cape from Bermuda.

Outside the Commercial Exchange on the Grand Parade in the centre of Cape Town some 5 000 people listened to fiery speeches by Fairbairn, John Ebden and Saul Solomon, all prominent liberals. Insurance companies announced that they would not provide cover to people who employed convicts, and almost every trading establishment published similar statements. A number of field-cornets resigned, as did four members of the nominated Legislative Council. When three new nominated members took their seats in the Legislative Chamber, they were assaulted by a large crowd and resigned within a week.

With the arrival of the *Neptune* in Simon's Bay on 19 September 1849, all business transactions with the Colonial Government were suspended until the order to land convicts was rescinded and the ship sent away. The Governor, Sir Harry Smith, although personally opposed to the establishment of a penal colony, was advised by the Chief Justice, Sir John Wylde, that he could not, legally, order the ship to sail. Smith did, however, order that no convict was to land, and wrote a letter of protest to the Colonial Office. Public petitions were sent to Queen Victoria, to both Houses of the British Parliament and even to the British public by colonists who, among other objections, 'reasonably dreaded the evils which might ensue if felons and bush-rangers once got intermixed with the uncivilised natives along the borders'.

In the British Parliament, the colonists' cause was taken up vigorously by Charles Adderley, and the government finally reversed its decision. The *Neptune* sailed for Tasmania on 21 February 1850, and the delighted colonists voted Adderley the sum of £100 and renamed the main street of Cape Town in his honour.

A vote for all who qualified

It was the first time that a British colony, governed from London, had successfully defied the central government since the American Revolution, and the result suggested that the Cape might be ready to govern itself. Fairbairn and Sir Andries Stockenström drafted a proposed constitution and took it to London where the Colonial Secretary, still Earl Grey, refused to recognise them as official representatives. Grey did, however, appoint a committee that drafted a constitution for the Cape in 1851, and the colonists secured representative government in 1854. The vote was granted to all adult males, regardless of race, provided they occupied property worth at least £25.

A BRITISH GOVERNMENT *attempt to land 282 convicts at the Cape was opposed by John Fairbairn (left), who used his newspaper, the 'South African Commercial Advertiser' (far left), to call his fellow Capetonians to a meeting on 4 July 1849 to protest against the plan (below). After a war of words between the authorities in Cape Town and London, the convicts were diverted to Tasmania. This defiance of British authority led indirectly to limited self-government for the fledgling colony.*

Portrait of a liberal – the story of Saul Solomon

Saul Solomon

One of the leading advocates of the liberal policy of the Cape was Saul Solomon, who was born into a Jewish family on the island of St Helena in 1817. He attended the South African College for a few years before family circumstances obliged him to find work as a printer's apprentice under George Greig, whose business he later acquired. His firm of Saul Solomon & Company eventually became the largest printing works in the country, and he had many other business interests, including a directorship of the South African Mutual, of which he was a founder.

As there was no Hebrew congregation at the Cape, he joined Dr John Philip's Union Chapel – his brother Edward was, like Philip, a missionary of the London Missionary Society. Saul Solomon, who married late in life, desired that his wife should not have to take the vow to 'obey' him, but was advised that this might render the marriage invalid. He became one of the MP's for Cape Town in the first parliament in 1854, and was returned regularly until he retired through ill health in 1883.

Saul Solomon was so small that, in order to be seen, he had to stand on a special stool when addressing parliament. But the childhood disease that stunted his growth in no way limited his intellect and his very real concern for justice for all. Throughout his long parliamentary career he strictly adhered to his original election manifesto, 'to give my decided opposition to all legislation tending to introduce distinctions either of class, colour or creed'.

He repeatedly 'demanded that natives should be allowed to sell their labour as they desired, and that no semblance of coercion should be employed to provide labour for the farmer'. This attitude frequently made him unpopular, especially in the eastern Cape, whose 'separatist' doctrines he opposed. He consistently refused ministerial appointments, in order to be free to follow his own conscience rather than have to adhere to a party policy with which he might have to disagree.

His insistence on equality also extended to religion, and he presented his Voluntary Bill (for the abolition of state aid to certain churches) in parliament for more than 20 years before it was passed. Although he was an early advocate of confederation, visualising a 'United States of South Africa', he had misgivings about the 'native policies' of the republics and of Natal, and never pressed for it, opposing Carnarvon's proposals for confederation.

He died in Scotland in 1892.

The vote was a matter of principle to the liberals, not a matter of convenience, despite the flippant remark by Attorney-General William Porter that he 'would rather meet the Hottentot at the hustings voting for his representative, than meet the Hottentot in the wilds with his gun in his hand'.

This contrasted markedly with the Transvaal, where an absolute colour bar was written into the constitution of 1858, stating that 'the people desire to permit no equality between coloured people and the white inhabitants, either in Church or State'. A similar colour bar operated in the Orange Free State, and in Natal the qualification for black voters was so rigorous that fewer than 200 had obtained the vote by 1905 – only two of them Africans. By these standards, the Cape was indeed liberal.

At the Cape some missionaries played a part, albeit a small one, in both the registration of voters, through a local Civil Commissioner, and swaying the voters in favour of a particular candidate. Frequently, this would not be the candidate favoured by the local farmers, who sometimes ill-treated employees who did not vote for their masters' choice. Candidates likely to be approved by the missionary and his flock were in most cases town-based merchants with trading interests in the area that they sought to represent.

Losing the vote

In the eastern Cape many liberals were in favour of individual land tenure in place of the traditional system of collective ownership. By 1887, the 'Kaffir vote' made up around 40 percent of some constituencies. The Registration Act of that year made it clear that communal land tenure did not count as a qualification towards the franchise, which effectively excluded many blacks.

With the annexation of the Transkeian territories raising the spectre of a massive black vote, the qualification was raised in 1892. Voters were now required to occupy premises valued at at least £75 or to earn at least £50 a year. In addition, each voter had to be able to write his name, address and occupation.

Despite the raising of qualifications, the vote in the Cape remained colour-blind. In 1875 Saul Solomon, the diminutive Cape Town Member of Parliament, said that he could never believe 'that this colony will ever degrade itself to prevent by law any coloured man from having a right to vote for members of the legislature....'

The black vote in the Cape survived Union, despite pressure from the three other colonies to have it abolished, lasting in a limited form for coloured people until 1956, when it was finally abolished by the National Party Government of Johannes Strijdom (see page 392).

Wolves in sheep's clothing

For more than 50 years the border region of the eastern Cape had been a virtual battleground as four main groups – Khoisan, Xhosa, trekboer and British settlers – fought for land on which to build their homes and graze their cattle. Towards the middle of the 19th century two more groups were added to this volatile mixture: first, the mixed descendants of Khoikhoi, slaves and whites (the so-called 'coloured' people); and second, sheep, the unwitting root of much of the upheaval that was about to be unleashed on this troubled frontier.

IN 1789 A VERY PRECIOUS CARGO arrived at De Kaap from the *Maatschappij tot Nut van't Algemeen* in Holland for the military commander, Colonel Robert Gordon. There was nothing particularly unusual about the cargo, but its impact on the future development of the Cape Colony was to be enormous.

It consisted of six sheep – four ewes and two rams – that had been bred in Holland from sheep presented to the House of Orange by Spain. Sheep were not new at the Cape – the Khoikhoi had large herds of the fat-tailed variety long before Jan van Riebeeck founded the first white settlement in southern Africa. These sheep, however, were different. For a start, they did not look like the fat-tailed type: their coats were thicker and curlier and the rams had long, curled horns. But more important, these sheep were bred not so much for eating, but for the clothing their coats could produce.

Before Colonel Gordon sent his precious cargo to a farm at Groenkloof near Darling – where the present town of Mamre stands – he was able to explain to curious onlookers that his sheep were Spanish merinos of the Escoril type, the best-known wool-bearing sheep in Europe. These new arrivals at the Cape took to the sunlit fields of Groenkloof as if they had been born there; and even though the Colonel was forced to return the originals – after the Spanish had

protested to the Dutch that the sheep should not have been sent out of Europe – before long the hillsides were covered in these small, hardy animals. Soon other farmers, envious of Gordon's success, started buying his sheep to breed herds of their own; 20 of his sheep even found their way to Australia, forerunners of that country's giant wool industry. The Cape's wool boom had to wait a little longer, though – until the 1830s, when London wool merchants woke up to the fact that the Cape was only half the distance to Australia, which made Cape wool cheaper to import than its counterpart from down under.

The real boost to Cape wool, however, came when Britain's own wool crop failed to keep pace with the insatiable appetite for raw material to fuel the 'dark satanic mills' of the Industrial Revolution – brought about by enormous technical advances in wool spinning, carding and weaving. As the 1840s dawned the price of wool began a climb that it was to sustain for over a decade. Soon it became clear to colonists at the Cape that the quickest way to make money was to breed as many wool-bearing sheep as possible in the shortest possible time. For this, three things were needed: good stock, good grazing-land and good labour. The first was easy enough to obtain; apart from local purchases emanating from Gordon's original stock, prime Saxon merinos were imported on a large scale from

TWO ADVERTS *from the 'Eastern Province Herald' dated 10 August 1852 give notice of auctions for merino rams. The 'golden fleece' revitalised the Cape's sagging economy in the 1840s and 1850s, as wealthy merchants fanned out across the eastern Cape, selling bloodstock and buying the wool clip for shipment to the insatiable textile mills of northern England.*

Germany. However, the second and third, land and labour, provided a far greater challenge; and in their scramble for both, the new barons of what a Cape newspaper editor was to call the 'golden fleece' were to become, for the indigenous people of the eastern districts, wolves in sheep's clothing, motivated by one enduring guiding light: greed. Much of the best grazing-land was in the north-east of the colony, along the uneasy border of broken promises that separated the Cape Colony from the Xhosa. It did not take a genius to realise that the best way to solve both the land and labour problems was to take land from the Xhosa and the so-called 'coloured' people, descendants of Khoikhoi and slaves, who lived in the Kat River area of the frontier, leaving the now landless people with no alternative but to work on the white sheep farms.

The wool boom takes off

Wool soon replaced wine as the Cape's staple product and its most important export – and in 1840 London wool brokers began to speak of 'a large and valuable export' from the Cape. The value of the wool depended on such variables as quality and the ruling price at the quarterly sales on the London market but, apart from occasional setbacks, prices generally rose each year until 1860, earning an impressive £286 000 by 1851 – 59 percent of the revenue from all Cape exports.

Predictably, the boom attracted a new type of immigrant from England (and elsewhere in the British Empire) after 1840. He had plenty of money, and was keen to invest it in sheep farms. In an effort to lure this wealth to their districts, towns and villages in the colony competed with one another in order to attract investment, and soon pamphlets and newspapers were trumpeting the appeal of one area over another while shamelessly decrying others.

The settler population in the eastern districts had originally been made up mostly of Boers, but many left during the Great Trek. The British settlers in Albany, many of whom had arrived with the original 1820 settlers, took advantage of the exodus to establish themselves in place of the Boers. Not surprisingly, many of the British settlers tried to acquire land in areas where sheep farming was the most profitable occupation. They were joined later by new immigrants from Britain who further consolidated the British character of the area. Settlers were also able to move into Xhosa sheep country when Victoria East was annexed by the colony after the Seventh Frontier War – the War of the Axe (see page 108).

Land worth its weight in gold

It was inevitable that land speculation should become rife during this period. In the densest areas of British settlement, many farms were left unoccupied or held on lease by tenants. As a result, many colonists equated 'land speculators' with absentee landlords – an assumption which was often far from the truth. This exchange of land for no purpose other than monetary gain caused the Boers to value their land more highly as British buyers began to penetrate Boer territory. The result was the creation of an artificial scarcity of land in the eastern Cape. As the frontier advanced, a circle of wealthy men bought farms and

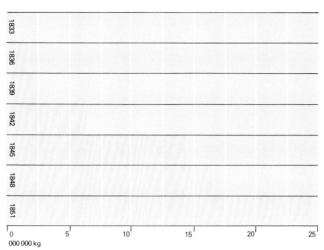

THE DRAMATIC RISE in wool exports is illustrated in this table.

held on to them until the prices rose to a level they found acceptable in terms of profit. Historians regard even the annexation of Victoria East as being for the purposes of land speculation – albeit on a larger scale. By the mid-1840s, the government had granted practically all the productive farming land in the Cape to private individuals. The remaining land, excluding unusable areas such as mountainous terrain and arid plains, was made up of loan-tenure farms, missionary institutions, town commons, outspan places and land for which title deeds had not yet been issued by the authorities.

Although Crown Land was almost fully occupied, some pamphleteers tried to conceal this, luring new immigrants to the Cape with stories of huge tracts of vacant land (in fact, some land across the Cape's eastern and northern borders was occupied by Boers, while Africans accounted for the rest). The strategy was prompted by deep fears among wealthy British settlers that the Imperial Government would grant some form of limited self-government to the colony – a step which became a distinct possibility after the publication of a report in Britain on self-government for Canada in the 1830s. It was reasoned that since the Boers outnumbered the British settlers in the Cape, they would inevitably gain the upper hand – and the financial interests of the British community would suffer (it seems the typical British settler had little regard for the business acumen of the Boers). British settlers began to see themselves as the only people capable of 'opening up' the country through the promotion of commercial farming. With smug self-assurance, they predicted a time when Boers, Africans and 'coloured' people would all have to relinquish their land through their inability to compete with the economic enterprise of the British.

Finding the money

The established landowners made the successful conversion to wool against heavy competition from the moneyed immigrants. In the process they surmounted some daunting obstacles, not the least of which was lack of money with which to start their flocks. There was another money-related problem, too: once having acquired sheep, they had to find the money to transport them to the markets. But

LEADING WOOL MERCHANTS, *the Mosenthal Brothers, issued banknotes (above) and signalled ships from their Port Elizabeth office when cargo was ready for shipment (right).*

thanks to the intervention of the Cape Town merchants, who provided a variety of essential services during the formative years of the industry, these obstacles were overcome. Among the most important of these merchants were German immigrants Maximilian Thalwitzer and the two Mosenthal brothers – Adolph and Joseph. Thalwitzer provided an indirect spur to wool production in the early 1830s by acting as an itinerant wool buyer in the western Cape's sheep country. He became more directly involved after 1840, when he hired a ship to import merino sheep. He also brought in men from Holstein to teach farmers how to tend and shear their flocks. In his capacity as Consul for the Hanseatic cities of Hamburg, Lubeck and Bremen, Thalwitzer was admirably placed to encourage German investment in Cape wool, and it was through him that the Hamburg firm of Lippert and Co built up a lucrative connection as wool importers.

Mosenthal Bros opened a branch at Port Elizabeth in 1842 as part of a rapidly spreading network designed to eliminate the collection problems resulting from poor communications. They established a chain of stores and agencies throughout the eastern districts to which farmers could bring their wool (and where they would be paid) without incurring the expense and inconvenience of a long journey. When a sufficient quantity of wool had accumulated, it would be transported in bulk, and therefore more cheaply, to the nearest port or market. Not all the merchants confined themselves to the role of middlemen: they also became financiers and bankers to the first generation of eastern Cape wool farmers. When times were tough, they provided the credit without which their clients would have gone under. So secure were they that their notes began to circulate (these were drawn on their Cape Town offices). When this practice was abandoned, the merchants joined the boards of banks. There was a mutually beneficial relationship between farmer and merchant that had a major impact on the area's economy.

Looking for labour

As money poured in from the London wool markets, sheep fever reached boiling point in the eastern Cape, where the twin problems of land and labour still bedevilled efforts to increase the local clip. For many, however, the answer to

both problems lay close at hand – in an area north of Fort Beaufort on the Upper Kat River. Here, in 1829 a burgher force under Captain Andries Stockenström had driven out the Xhosa chieftain Maqoma and his people. In an effort to prevent the Xhosa returning, Stockenström decided to grant the land to the Khoikhoi and so-called 'coloured' people consisting of Khoisan remnants and freed slaves. Known since then as the 'Kat River Settlement', it formed a buffer between white farmers and the Xhosa chiefdoms on the eastern Cape frontier. Inevitably the Cape Government used it as a sort of dumping ground for dispossessed people from all over the colony. The standard of living declined in proportion to the population increase, inspiring an enduring belief among white colonists in the Cape that the settlement had become a refuge for 'vagrants' and 'idlers' (see box).

However, a far more sinister motive lay behind these accusations. To the white farmers, desperate for workers, the Kat River area seemed an obvious place to recruit the people needed to work the sheep farms. Thus the issue of the Kat River Settlement became an integral feature in a wider debate on labour resources – a crucial issue after 1840. While Cape businessmen and farmers agreed on the need for labour, they had different ideas on the best manner of procuring it. One influential group, which included journalist, publisher and businessman Robert Godlonton, was emphatic that labour should be sought outside the colony. This group regarded the local 'coloured' people as 'too independent', claiming they were too indolent to submit to continuous employment. On the other hand, imported labour was discovered to have serious drawbacks: apart from being expensive, it was unreliable. Those who did arrive to work were quick to discover that they could earn enough to survive without entering service. As a result, Godlonton and his friends changed their minds and echoed the general cry for measures to find a way to force the 'coloured' people and Khoisan living in the Kat River Settlement to work.

Most Cape farmers and businessmen had never agreed with Godlonton's ideas about the inadequacy of 'coloured' labour, anyway. In fact, one leading Boer politician and landowner told the Cape Legislative Council in 1849 that the 'coloured' people provided the labour most sought af-

ROBERT GODLONTON, *journalist and businessman, argued that labour must be cheap to make investment worthwhile.*

ter by the Boers. What appeared to upset the colonists most was the geographical mobility of 'coloured' labourers, who tended to work only so long as it suited their own purposes before going off to 'squat' on the most convenient vacant land. There was one aspect of the 'coloured' people's reluctance to enter service on which few, if any, colonists bothered to comment – the low wages they offered prospective workers. Godlonton argued that labour must be cheap to make investment worthwhile. He believed that wages should be no more than 'adequate'. At the time, the highest wage for unskilled labour on sheep farms in the Albany district was one shilling and sixpence a day. This rate did not alter between 1842 and 1858 (the pay in surrounding districts was even lower).

Do it our way – or else
As a rule, employers provided food and lodging for their workforce as well as money, but 'lodging' often consisted of no more than the farmer's go-ahead to build on his land. With such little incentive to work, it is hardly surprising that the 'coloured' labourers were often unwilling to exert themselves to the extent their employers expected. The response was an outbreak of self-righteous fervour among the colonists. They demanded the repeal of laws protecting the interests of labour and the provision of new and stricter measures to regulate the relationship between master and servant.

While agitating for action to make it easier to 'control' labour already employed on white farms, the moneyed settlers were also seeking ways of getting the 'idlers' out of the Kat River Settlement and onto their farms. An added incentive to clear the settlement of its inhabitants was the fact that it occupied some of the best sheep country in the eastern Cape.

But by this time the suspicions of the Kat River people had been thoroughly aroused, and they began to fear for their land and their freedom, claiming that they would be 'enslaved' by the settlers. And when the Eighth Frontier War broke out in 1850, many people sided with the Xhosa, rebelling against a government that they no longer trusted to leave them in peace. The short-lived rebellion was quickly suppressed and all rebel-owned land confiscated and given to white farmers, who began to buy up other arable areas of the settlement. The presence of the white farmers caused prices of land to rocket: a property which sold for £20 in 1850 later fetched up to £1 400. The Kat River district was duly integrated into the colonial economy on the terms desired by Godlonton and his supporters, while many of its former inhabitants were dispersed or forced into the service of the colonists.

The end of the line for the Xhosa
Covetous eyes were also glancing further east, at land still occupied by Xhosa – one wealthy British wool farmer declared quite openly that Xhosa land should be 'taken, sold and settled' and its former occupants taught to earn their living 'in an honest, industrious way, which might eventually lead to their Christianisation'. The arrival of Colonel (later Sir) Harry Smith at the Cape as Governor was a heaven-sent opportunity for men like Godlonton and his fellow colonists, some of whom were appointed to key posts in the colonial administration. It was a development that caused great concern among Boer leaders and citizens of Cape Town who still hoped for a loosening of imperial reins at the Cape and a local, 'representative' government. Smith, supported only by the business community of the eastern districts and a few Cape Town merchants, resisted and the colony was ruled by a virtual oligarchy – of which Godlonton and another leading settler, Richard Southey, were influential members.

Meanwhile, the Xhosa were succumbing to the relentless colonial advance. The Seventh Frontier War, the costly War of the Axe (1846-8) had left the Ngqika, or western Xhosa, an almost broken people. The Cape Colony was extended to the Keiskamma River, incorporating Victoria East; and a new British colony, British Kaffraria, was established on Xhosa territory between the Keiskamma River and the Kei, where the Xhosa would be allowed to live under British rule. Smith enjoyed himself immensely as he met the leaders of what he saw as an imperial vassal people, ordering them to kiss his feet under the bayonets of British soldiers. When the chief Maqoma, who had tried his hardest to prevent war in 1846, offered Smith his hand, he was ordered to the floor. But even with the Governor's boot in his neck, he was able to show some resistance: 'You are a dog, so you act like a dog,' he told Smith. 'This thing [Smith] was not sent by Victoria [Queen Victoria], who knows I am of royal blood as she is.'

Smith's plans for the incorporation into the colony of British Kaffraria were very much in line with the contemporary thinking of early Victorian imperialism. He told the chieftains that their land would be 'divided into counties, towns and villages bearing English names. You shall all learn to speak English at the schools which I shall

The Kat River Settlement –

One hundred and fifty years ago the valley of the Kat River north of Fort Beaufort in present-day Ciskei was reckoned by settlers and the local Xhosa to be one of the most fertile areas of the eastern Cape.

Back in the 1820s this well-watered basin was strategic to the defence of the frontier and was occupied by Maqoma, son of Ngqika, and his followers, who had sought refuge from the *Mfecane* unleashed by Shaka. Formerly, it had been the home of his father. It was here, after ordering Maqoma to leave, that the Commissioner General for the Eastern Districts, Andries Stockenström, decided to establish settlements of Khoikhoi and freed slaves – so-called 'coloured' people – not merely to give them a home, but in order that they could be 'a breastwork against an exasperated, powerful enemy in the most vulnerable and dangerous part of our frontier'. Maqoma, who had been told that the Kat River land was 'neutral', had to live on land uncoveted by other clans because it was so poor.

The first of the new settlers moved in mid-1829, consisting of the remains of the Gonaqua Khoikhoi under their headman, Andries Botha, 'Bastards' from Graaff-Reinet under Christian Groepe, and others from the Bethelsdorp and Theopolis mission stations. About 4 000 people settled during the first year, in locations that developed into villages with such names as Philipton, Buxton and Readsdale, honouring missionaries and others interested in the new settlement. In time, the smallholdings produced a variety of crops, orchards were laid out, and an efficient irrigation system was operated. Some 10 years after it was established, the Governor, Sir George Napier, visited the settlement. That he was favourably impressed is apparent from his remark to Stockenström that if he had been 'the creator of this settlement, I would fancy I had done enough for one man's life'.

In the frontier wars that began in 1834 and 1846, men of the Kat River Settlement joined the various 'Hottentot Levies' and fought alongside the British and colonial forces against the Xhosa, acquitting themselves well, but suffering Xhosa reprisals as a result. Andries Botha, in particular, distinguished himself, as recorded in a dispatch by Stockenström: 'Her Majesty has not in her dominions a more loyal subject, nor braver soldier.' However, apart from this, there was little recognition of his service. Rather, there was envy of the fine land, and the continuous publication of insulting allegations by Robert Godlonton, editor of the widely read 'Grahams Town Journal'.

With a covetous eye on the rich grazing-land of the settlement, Godlonton and his fellow settlers also lashed out at the London Missionary Society at the settlement, claiming that the land made available to 'coloured' people allowed them to live self-sufficient lives (in other words, they were not forced to work for the white farmers); and the missionaries in turn were accused of 'abominable false philanthropy' in perpetuating this system. The settlers went on to claim that the isolation of the 'coloured' people worked to their disadvantage because it inspired different and perhaps even opposing interests to those of the rest of the community. The colonists also argued that it was a grave error to separate labour from capital.

The appointment of T J Biddulph as magistrate of the settlement in 1847 was a boost to the settler cause and a blow to the residents, whom he had described as 'a large assemblage of able-bodied paupers living partly on the credulity of the public' and their home as 'the abode of idleness and imposture . . . .' Early in 1847, during the War of the Axe, Governor Sir Henry Pottinger, in the mistaken belief that they held tenure only in exchange for the performance of military service, ordered 400 men of the settlement to report for duty. However, of the some 1 000 able-bodied men, close to 900 were already under arms at the front and so, clear-

THE KAT RIVER SETTLEMENT *in 1838, shortly before a visit by Governor George Napier, who commented that if he had created the settlement 'I would fancy I had done enough for one man's life'.*

ANDRIES BOTHA *was among men of the settlement who fought on the side of colonial forces against the Xhosa.*

'breastwork' on a dangerous frontier

ELANDS POST *in the Kat River Settlement later became known as Seymour – the name of the present town.*

ly, another 400 could not be raised. Without checking the true facts, Sir Henry stopped the settlement's wartime rations, calling the place 'worse than useless'.

Later in the year he was succeeded as Governor by Sir Harry Smith who, on a visit to the settlement, dismissed Biddulph and appointed Thomas Holden Bowker in his place.

The arrogant Smith was completely in tune with the settlers' motives, and government pressure on the Kat River Settlement intensified. In 1848, in an effort to force 'idlers' out of the settlement, he suggested to his Legislative Council that they consider the introduction of 'vagrancy' legislation. When news of this proposal reached the settlement, the 'coloured' leaders reacted with such hostility that there was panic among whites in parts of the colony and the proposal was quickly abandoned.

But in June 1850, the openly hostile Bowker allowed his Xhosa police to destroy a great deal of property during a campaign to expel 'squatters' from the area. Houses were burned and their occupants turned out into the cold of winter. Andries Botha wrote a restrained letter to Smith, in which he reminded the Governor that he was 'an old servant of Government', adding: 'I never feared to face the enemy – and that with the very men who have now so shamefully been expelled from the settlement.'

Within six months, on Christmas Day 1850, the Eighth Frontier War erupted, and Smith appealed in vain to the 'old servant of Government' and his men, whose marksmanship and tracking skills were sorely need-

ed by the army. But this time the men of Kat River chose to stay home and defend their own property – except for those who had decided that their real enemy was not the Xhosa, but the white government that reviled them and then demanded their service. Hermanus Matroos, Smith's former interpreter, threatened with eviction, led a band of men from the settlement on raids through the Fort Beaufort district, and was finally killed in an attack on the town itself.

Leadership of the rebels was taken over by Willem Uithaalder, who occupied Fort Armstrong near the present village of Seymour, allowing the whites who had taken refuge there to leave. The fort remained his stronghold for several weeks, until it was retaken by a vastly superior government force armed with artillery. Afterwards, 47 men of Kat River captured at the fort were tried and found guilty of high treason. Death sentences were passed on all, but were commuted to life imprisonment with labour on the colony's roads. After the war, all were pardoned. Andries Botha, who had taken no part in the uprising and had, at some risk to himself, helped to escort a white official from Philipton to Fort Beaufort, was taken to Cape Town to be tried for the same offence of high treason.

SIR HARRY SMITH *backed colonialist demands against the settlement.*

The first trial was abandoned for lack of evidence, but at a second trial the old man, who was kept in chains throughout the hearing, was found guilty and sentenced to death. This was commuted to life imprisonment with hard labour.

With the rebellion over, the Kat River Settlement went into a steady economic decline. Rebel land was given to whites, who gradually began to buy up arable land from the remaining people in the valley.

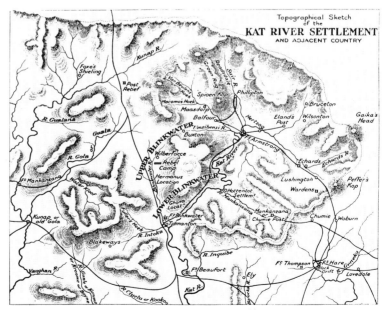

THIS MAP *of the Kat River Settlement was compiled by a government surveyor in 1852, a year after the rebellion against colonial authority had been suppressed. Rebel-held land was given to white farmers.*

THE LEADER of the Kat River rebels, Willem Uithaalder, made his head-quarters at Fort Armstrong (left) near the present-day town of Seymour. After occupying the fort for several weeks, he was attacked by colonial troops of the Royal Artillery and Cape Mounted Rifles, supported by a burgher force from Fort Beaufort and Mfengu levies. The rebels were forced to surrender – and tried for high treason.

THE NGQIKA chief Sandile (below) struck against British rule when he led his forces against a colonial patrol at Boomah Pass, sparking the Eighth Frontier War.

establish for you . . . . You may no longer be naked and wicked barbarians, which you will ever be unless you labour and become industrious . . . . You must learn that it is money that makes people rich by work.'

Smith was as good as his word, and chief Sandile found himself ruling from York, Phato from Bedford and Mhala from Cambridge. The unfortunate Xhosa in the region did not even have the protection of British law, as Smith used annexation as an excuse to impose military rule. In an effort to make the area pay for itself, fines were imposed for petty offences, and those who could or would not pay were flogged with up to 100 lashes.

Smith's actions prompted sympathy of sorts – from a missionary turned government official, Henry Calderwood, who offered a solution to the suffering of the Xhosa in Kaffraria that was music to the ears of the eastern settlers: 'The opportunity should not be lost of scattering the people far into the colony where they can find food and be useful.'

Soon the first batch of 170 Xhosa were on their way, of whom only 58 were men, a situation for which Calderwood apologised saying that the 'women will be as useful as the men . . . and many of the children will soon be useful'. Soon many more were on their way to the colony under a scheme whereby 'kaffir youths' were indentured for three years' service to white farmers.

Smith's high-handed actions in Kaffraria came to a head in October 1850 when the principal Ngqika chief, Sandile, refused to attend a meeting called by the Governor. With support from the Thembu, some Gcaleka and even some rebellious 'kaffir police', the Ngqika attacked a colonial patrol at Boomah Pass, and the Eighth Frontier War was on in earnest. Numerous attacks followed, including one on Fort Beaufort in January 1851. The outbreak of renewed hostility between the colony and the Xhosa gave some of the 'coloured' people of the Kat River Settlement what they saw as a last chance to rid themselves of the constant threat of settler erosion – and they sided with the Xhosa rebelling against the Colonial Government.

With the 'coloured' people on their side, the Xhosa now had access to more modern fighting techniques, and firearms were extensively used on both sides. The colonial forces first concentrated on quelling the so-called Kat River Rebellion, which they did by the end of February 1851, before turning their attention to the Xhosa. Smith was replaced as Governor in January 1852 by Sir George Cathcart, who vigorously pursued the war to a finish by the end of the same year.

Once again the best interests of the settlers had been served to the full. Not only had they gained access to the rich grazing-lands of the Kat River Settlement, but now new land previously settled by Xhosa in the Amatola Mountains became available for white farmers and the all-important sheep. The cherry on top was the thousands of displaced 'coloured' and Xhosa people who now had no alternative but to seek work on white farms; and to ensure that these new workers behaved themselves, the moneyed settlers, now in control of the Cape Government, in 1856 passed a 'Masters and Servants Act', which greatly favoured the white employers. Painstakingly drafted, it covered virtually every conceivable circumstance and imposed harsh penalties on the offending servant. In fact, the Act seemed so determinedly penal to one observer that (with the characteristic racism of his age) he expressed the hope that no British-born labourer would fall foul of it.

The last gasp of a desperate people

Following their defeat in the Eighth Frontier War, a period of unmitigated hardship set in for the Xhosa. Their political structures had been fragmented by partial incorporation into the Crown Colony of British Kaffraria, their beliefs were being eroded by a mixture of missionary teachings and European technology, and their remaining economic resources were devastated by the onslaught of lung sickness among their cattle from 1855. Inevitably, they looked elsewhere, anywhere, for some hope. In April 1856, an adolescent girl named Nongqawuse, who lived near the Kei River in a part of the country still ruled by the independent Xhosa paramount, Sarhili, was reputedly addressed by her ancestors. Their message spelled disaster and death for the Xhosa: 'Tell that all the community is to rise again from the dead! Tell that all cattle must be slaughtered, for they are herded by hands defiled with witchcraft! Tell that there should be no cultivation, but that the people should dig new granaries, build new houses, erect great and strong cattle-folds . . . .'

Tragically, Sarhili became a firm convert of Nongqawuse and her guardian, Mhlakaza. He ordered all his subordinate chiefs, including those living under colonial rule in British Kaffraria, to obey the injunctions of the prophets. The date of the first resurrection was set for 11 August 1856. The failure of this prediction was blamed on those who had refused to kill their cattle. And as disappointment followed disappointment, similar rationalisations brought the Xhosa to the brink of civil war. They also prolonged the life of the cattle-killing movement to such an extent that when Sarhili finally renounced all belief in July 1857, some 15 months after it all began, the Xhosa had been effectively decimated.

The colonial authorities were understandably puzzled by this sequence of events, and obviously concerned about its implications for the peace of the Cape frontier. But while freely recognising the sincerity of the ordinary believers, they insisted that at the root of the belief was a sinister plot to destroy colonial power in southern Africa. The primary movers behind this alleged plot were said to be Sarhili and the Sotho king, Moshoeshoe. However, evidence indicates that there was no such plot at all, and that the cattle killing was no more than a tragic delusion. It soon

NONGQAWUSE'S *prophecy spelt disaster for the Xhosa.*

became apparent that the ordinary believers had no intention of waging war on anyone. Indeed, many of them were soon incapable of walking, let alone fighting, hoping for a time when their ancestors would return and new, healthy cattle (free of the dreaded lung sickness) would appear in the place of those they had killed. One observer wrote after a visit to the Xhosa: 'I never saw such a deplorable sight as the neglected fields in Mhala's location. Everywhere, I found the people cheerful although the neglected fields spoke of future starvation and death. I spoke to several but they merely smiled.'

A final twist to the plot theory was the belief held by many Xhosa that the true plotters were the land-hungry colonial authorities, and the victims the Xhosa people.

XHOSA PARAMOUNT *Sarhili – it was 15 months before he renounced the prophecy of Nongqawuse.*

Turmoil on a troubled frontier

In the middle of the last century the land beyond the Orange River was in a constant state of turmoil as Voortrekkers, Griqua and British sought to farm their sheep on land claimed by the Sotho, Tlokwa and other indigenous people. In an attempt to regulate this troubled region, the British first annexed it and then, tired of policing fights between black and Boer, they withdrew, paving the way for the establishment of the republican Orange Free State.

THE KHOIKHOI CALLED IT *Gariep* (Great River), a wide slash of muddy water meandering across the seemingly endless plains of central southern Africa on its journey from the mountain fastness of what is now Lesotho to the Atlantic. The first white men to settle across the river, trekboers seeking new pastures far from the Cape, translated the name into their own language and called it *Grootrivier*. But the name that has come down to us is the one given to it by Colonel Robert Jacob Gordon, Commander of the garrison at the Cape, who in 1777 named the river after the royal Dutch House of Orange, calling the land beyond it Transorangia. Later this land became the Orange River Sovereignty, and then split between the Orange Free State and the Cape.

For centuries this dry but relatively fertile region had been the home of the scattered settlements of people we now know as the southern Sotho, but like so much of southern Africa in the last fateful years of the 18th century, change was coming – in the form of four new arrivals.

The first were, perhaps, the most unusual. They called themselves the Griqua, and they prided themselves on being descendants of both Europeans and Khoikhoi, and in some cases Malay or African slaves. They could trace their forefathers to two clans, the Koks and the Barendses, the first made up mainly of Khoikhoi and the second of mixed European descent – which led to the name by which they were more commonly known in the 18th century, the Bastards.

These two groups, under their respective leaders, Cornelius Kok and the brothers Barend and Nicolaas Barends, roamed the area around the Orange River until 1804 when they were persuaded by two missionaries from the London Missionary Society to settle down with their followers north of the Orange River in an area between the present towns of Prieska and Danielskuil, with their capital at Klaarwater. Within 10 years they had merged into a single group calling themselves the Griqua, choosing as their leader Cornelius Kok's son, Adam Kok II (the first Adam Kok, his grandfather, had founded the clan in the middle of the previous century), and changing the name of their headquarters to Griquatown.

Not all Griqua, however, accepted Kok's leadership, and after months of squabbling – in which the missionaries played a major part – a new leader, Andries Waterboer, emerged. This led to a further split as some continued to recognise Kok and the older chiefs as their leaders. By the late 1830s two distinct factions had emerged: a group at Griquatown led by Waterboer, and another at Philippolis (on the middle Orange River) under the leadership of Adam Kok II's son, Adam Kok III.

ADAM KOK III, *leader of the Griqua people of Philippolis, found himself playing a difficult diplomatic role in the ongoing struggle between Boer and British across the Orange River.*

MOSHOESHOE'S *mountain fortress of Thaba Bosiu was approached up the steep incline on the right.*

The second group of newcomers to cross the Orange were the trekboers, first a trickle, and then, by the time of the Great Trek in the 1830s, a comparative flood. Even before the trek, in the first quarter of the 19th century, there were several hundred trekboer families, most professing allegiance to Britain, wandering beyond the Orange River with their herds of cattle and flocks of fat-tailed Cape sheep. Once the trek was under way, thousands of Boers began to settle the fertile plains, often moving in on land traditionally claimed by the southern Sotho.

The third group of newcomers were the British, led initially by missionaries, but soon to be augmented and stiffened by the administrators of Queen Victoria's far-flung empire who strove to impose the imperial writ across the Orange on both Griqua and Voortrekkers.

The fourth, and final, group to cross the Orange River were sheep; not the traditional fat-tailed creatures farmed by trekboer and Khoikhoi, but the thick-woolled merinos that were already transforming the economy of the eastern Cape region (see page 130) and were about to do the same to Transorangia. In 1838, for instance, there were fewer than 20 000 merinos in the colony as against almost 800 000 Cape sheep. But by 1855 the woolled (merino) sheep outnumbered the Cape sheep by 555 000 to 387 000. Wool had become a major export, most of it being routed through Port Elizabeth. In Transorangia, merino wool was described as the 'staple article of commerce', with 85 percent of the sheep in the region being at least partially woolled.

The wool revolution affected everybody – both trekboers and Griqua changed to running woolled sheep. Indeed, in the 1850s the Griqua leader Adam Kok claimed that his people possessed about 200 000 merinos. But, as the flocks and herds grew, so did the competition for grazing become more intense.

Keeping the Boers at bay

The arrival of Boer, British and Griqua posed a new threat to the indigenous southern Sotho people under the leadership of their paramount, Moshoeshoe. This skilled diplomat and warrior was above all a survivor – and it was with survival in mind that he decided in 1824 to occupy a great flat-topped mountain called Thaba Bosiu. From this natural fortress he was able to control the plains around him, retreating to his mountain when the *Difaqane* threatened to engulf him and his people.

Inevitably the stability he offered attracted thousands of refugees, resulting in a new and powerful nation emerging in the central area of southern Africa – the Basotho. Their territorial claims were reinforced in 1843 in a treaty agreed with the Cape Governor Sir George Napier, which defined Moshoeshoe's territory as including all the land between the Orange and Caledon rivers, as well as a strip varying from between 40 to 48 kilometres wide on the north-western side of the Caledon River, except near its source and its confluence with the Orange.

Although no stranger to warfare, Moshoeshoe built a reputation as a man of peace who was able to keep his people more or less intact despite the ravages of the *Difaqane*. Now he faced the armed raiding parties of the Griqua and the land-hungry Boers, who were venturing further and with growing confidence into his territory. From Thaba Bosiu, the 'mountain of the night', Moshoeshoe looked down with concern. By 1845 there were as many as 300 white farmers in his territory, many of whom regarded themselves as owners of the land they occupied and, in some instances, even 'sold' it to other Boers.

Unable to read or write, Moshoeshoe used a missionary from the Paris Evangelical Missionary Society, Eugene Casalis, to write to the Cape Governor, Sir Peregrine Maitland, that he 'had never ceased to warn' the whites that he

CAPE GOVERNOR *Sir Peregrine Maitland proposed that Boers pay rent for their land to Adam Kok and Moshoeshoe.*

'viewed them as mere passers-by' to whom he had shown temporary hospitality. He was adamant that he could never allow them 'any right of property . . . .'

The Boers, many of them forced out of Natal after it was taken over by the British, were also acquiring land from the Griqua – this time legally, buying land in exchange for horses, liquor, firearms and ammunition. Inevitably trouble followed – and when Kok arrested a Boer accused of ill-treating his people, the trekker community tried to take over his entire territory. A British force stationed at Colesberg, however, crossed the Orange River and defeated the settlers at Zwartkoppies.

Maitland's answer to the territorial ambitions of the Boers was to invent a complicated system of land tenure whereby each chief's lands would be divided into two parts: one to be occupied by the chief and his people, and one by Boers who would pay rental to the chief. This rental would be divided equally between the chiefs and the Cape Government, which would use it to pay the salaries of a proposed magistrate and his staff.

Kok readily agreed to this plan, which also ensured that the region south of the Riet River would remain an inalienable Griqua property; while the area north of the river, although remaining under his control, could be leased by Boers who were British subjects.

Moshoeshoe also agreed, but only in part, to allow whites to lease land within the triangle formed by the confluence of the Orange and Caledon rivers. The only snag, however, was that some of this land was occupied by lesser chiefs who claimed it as their own, a claim that Moshoeshoe dismissed by saying that these chiefs were, in fact, his subjects and subordinates.

Despite the problems, Maitland decided to go ahead, and in 1845 he appointed a British Resident to Transorangia to oversee the implementation of his system. Although the first Resident resigned shortly after he was appointed, the second, Major Henry Douglas Warden, an officer in the largely Khoikhoi Cape Corps, had more staying power. He was given a force of 70 men from his own corps with which to keep the peace, and told not to interfere in quarrels between the indigenous inhabitants.

Warden had scarcely taken office when, in 1846, the Seventh Frontier War broke out in the eastern Cape, diverting attention and material assistance from Transorangia. Moshoeshoe, taking advantage of the situation, strengthened his claims to the territories of the minor chiefs by sending many of his relatives and their followers to live among them. However, realising that once the British army had defeated the Xhosa it would be free to intervene in Transorangia, he made it known that he was on the side of the British. As good as his word, he refused a plea of help from the trekkers who wanted to set up a republic around Winburg, paving the way for their defeat by Warden. Moshoeshoe also offered to help the British against the Xhosa, but Maitland tactfully declined.

Moshoeshoe's skill as a diplomat, however, failed to impress the Governor, especially after Basotho warriors helped Warden mount a commando to investigate reports that large herds of stolen cattle were being concealed in the Witteberg. Unhappily, the commando clashed with a group of Thembu who counter-attacked and took back most of the cattle. Maitland accused Warden of having been bluffed by 'the duplicity and perfidy of Moshesh . . .' to which Warden replied that 'Chief Moshesh I have ever found honest and straightforward, and most willing to meet the wishes of Government'.

Sir Harry takes over

Maitland's days as Governor, however, were coming to an end, and in 1847 he was replaced by Sir Henry Pottinger who within a year gave way to the irrepressible and irresponsible Sir Henry George Wakelyn Smith, a vigorous soldier known to his men as 'Hurry Charge Whackalong Smite', a nickname that admirably summed up his temperament. Sir Harry, as he liked to be known, had served at the Cape before, and had lately returned from India, where a victory over the Sikhs had earned him the sobriquet of 'the hero of Aliwal' and his knighthood.

Sir Harry had a nose for trouble, and in 1847 trouble meant the eastern frontier where the War of the Axe was all but over. Hardly pausing at Cape Town, he hurried east to proclaim the new Colony of British Kaffraria between the Kei and Keiskamma rivers (see page 133). He then turned his attention to Transorangia, for which he had a similar plan in mind. He met first with Kok, who had been carefully putting into practice Maitland's system of renting land to whites. Smith bluntly told the Griqua leader that in future all the rent from white tenant farmers on Griqua land north of the Riet River would divert to the Crown, in-

MOSHOESHOE *and his advisors were determined to retain some degree of independence over their land – fighting both Boer and British. Finally, however, he won British protection against further encroachment.*

BOER LEADER *Andries Pretorius was furious at Moshoeshoe's alliance with the British.*

stead of only half as agreed with Maitland, and that whites would be allowed to obtain farms to the south of the river, in an area which, in terms of Maitland's system, could never be settled by whites.

With Adam Kok suitably humbled, Sir Harry then turned his attention to Moshoeshoe, summoning the paramount and his chiefs to meet him at the village of Winburg. Moshoeshoe was lucky that he had earned the respect of the British, and instead of the usual Smith welcome of a foot in the neck, he was given saddles, a gold watch and a large tent. The two leaders then got down to the real reason for Smith's visit – to proclaim the sovereignty of Queen Victoria over the land between the Orange and Vaal rivers. According to Sir Harry's plan, whites could remain on the land they occupied, but could not make new acquisitions, except in Adam Kok's Griqualand. When Moshoeshoe claimed territory also claimed by the rival chiefs Moroka and Sekonyela, Smith announced that, if necessary, a commission could be appointed to investigate the respective claims, adding: 'Trust to me, and no-one will dare to raise his hand against the Great Chief of the Basutos.'

Moshoeshoe agreed – and Smith issued a proclamation protecting and preserving 'the just and hereditary rights of all the Native Chiefs' in the area. Thus Moshoeshoe effectively gained British protection against trekkers' claims to his lands, and British acquiescence in his plans to unite the scattered minor chiefdoms in the region under his single authority.

Bad news for the Boers

There was one serious problem with Smith's proclamation: no one had bothered to test Boer opinion, despite an assurance by Smith to Commandant-General Andries Pretorius that he would not proclaim British sovereignty over the land between the Orange and Vaal rivers until Pretorius had assessed the views of the majority of Voortrekkers. If fewer than four out of five were in favour of British sovereignty, Smith had indicated, he would not proceed with the proclamation. Impetuous as usual, Smith went ahead with his plan while Pretorius was still canvassing the trekkers.

Angry at the proclamation, the Voortrekkers, many of whom were still smarting from British interference in their attempts to establish a republic around Winburg, now headed north beyond the Vet River – not far enough, however, to escape Sir Harry's net, which now extended all the way to the Vaal River. In an effort to undo the proclamation, Pretorius rode to Moshoeshoe to ask why the chief had allied himself to the British, especially after the Voortrekkers had relieved Moshoeshoe of the threats posed by Mzilikazi and Dingane. Moshoeshoe refused to see Pretorius, but sent him a message to the effect that the very first Boers he had encountered, in 1831, had stated that they were British subjects. In many instances this was still true, as the trekboers, with no particular political aspirations, did indeed regard themselves as British subjects, and did not necessarily ally themselves with the republican-minded Voortrekkers.

MAJOR HENRY WARDEN *had a force of 70 Khoikhoi – and orders to keep the peace across the Orange River.*

The Voortrekkers now decided to take matters into their own hands and the British magistrate at Winburg, Thomas Biddulph, was run out of town and a new republic proclaimed. Pretorius then headed for Bloemfontein – where Warden still held sway as British Resident – with a force of 700 commandos. Warden, still with his 70 men of the Cape Corps, first appealed to Moshoeshoe for help, and then decided to make a run for the safety of the Orange River, telling Moshoeshoe to remain neutral.

Sir Harry Smith now took command of a combined force of British regulars and Cape Corps, and in a sharp engagement at Boomplaats, between present-day Trompsburg and Jagersfontein, soundly defeated Pretorius' Voortrekkers. Pretorius took refuge beyond the Vaal, with a price of £1 000 (later doubled) on his head, and Warden was reinstalled at Bloemfontein. In his report on the campaign to the British Colonial Secretary, Smith stated that 'the chief Moshesh has been staunch in his allegiance....'

The end of the alliance

The alliance between the British and Moshoeshoe was, however, about to come to an end. The first crack appeared when Smith's private secretary, Richard Southey, whom he had left at Bloemfontein with a force of 250 soldiers, asked Moshoeshoe to hand over the land on which white farmers had been allowed to settle, writing that 'no farmer is to be moved against his will, to make way for natives, on farms owned and occupied by him on 3rd February, 1848'. Against the advice of his councillors, Moshoeshoe decided to accede.

More trouble with the British soon followed when Warden, on Smith's orders, decided to annex land north of the Caledon River, over which Moshoeshoe claimed paramountcy. The British warned Moshoeshoe that unless he agreed they would side with his old adversary, the Tlokwa leader, Sekonyela. This land was then to be further subdivided and recognised as belonging to the chiefs Sekonyela and Moroka, with an intervening strip for 'coloured' occupation. With the land now in dispute, tensions rose between Basotho who had been sent by Moshoeshoe to live in the area and the Tlokwa, ending in a cattle-stealing raid by the Basotho on Sekonyela's people, despite a threat by missionaries at Thaba Bosiu that those who took part would not receive Holy Communion (which simply led to a large-scale rejection of Christianity and a return to the old traditions and rituals).

Warden held Moshoeshoe liable for the return of the stolen cattle, and informed Smith that 'the time I imagine is not distant when it will be necessary to place the Basuto people under some restraint'. Meanwhile he set about enforcing the new boundary by sending a force of Mfengu, commanded by an Englishman named Bailie, to drive groups of resident Basotho back across the boundary lines, going back on his promise to guarantee them permanent right of occupation. The Mfengu were defeated, Bailie fleeing across the border into the Cape Colony; and Warden himself took the field in June 1851, with an ultimatum to Moshoeshoe to pay more than 6 000 cattle and 300 horses as compensation for damages inflicted by the king or his allies. Long before the ultimatum period had expired, Warden attacked, and his ragged army was roundly defeated at Viervoet. His personal prestige, and that of Britain in general, was in tatters, and Moshoeshoe, through the French missionary Casalis, wrote a letter of complaint to the Secretary of State.

The British Government intervenes

Alarmed by the turn of events in this far-flung corner of its empire, the British Government decided to send two special Commissioners, W S Hogge and C M Owen, to southern Africa to reassess Smith's expansionist policies. It did not take Hogge long to discover that Smith had been deluded in thinking that the majority of whites in the sovereignty welcomed British authority, and castigated Warden for his interference in the quarrels of the 'native tribes'. They then summoned Pretorius and representatives of the Voortrekkers north of the Vaal to a convention at Sand River in January 1852, where it was acknowledged that the Transvaal Voortrekkers were no longer British subjects and had the right to rule themselves as they saw fit, so long as they kept out of affairs south of the Vaal.

There was good news, too, for Moshoeshoe, who was assured that the south-west boundary would be altered back in his favour, a decision that promptly led his warriors to attack those farmers still in occupation, driving off their cattle. There was also a reckoning with Sekonyela, who lost most of his livestock.

These disturbances led Commissioner Owen to warn Sir George Cathcart (who had replaced Smith as Governor) that the sovereignty 'could neither be retained nor aban-

GOVERNOR SIR GEORGE CATHCART *rode with 2 000 men against Moshoeshoe – but failed to dislodge the wily old king. In the* lull that followed the attack, Moshoeshoe successfully sued for peace, and Cathcart withdrew.*

doned with honour in the present unsatisfactory state of things'. Stung by this report, Cathcart, fresh from the latest war with the Xhosa, entered the sovereignty with some 2 000 soldiers and artillery. An ultimatum was sent to Moshoeshoe, demanding compensation of 10 000 cattle and 1 000 horses within three days. It was clearly impossible for Moshoeshoe to comply within so short a time, yet Cathcart refused an extension and an attack was launched on 20 December 1852 on the Berea mountain and plateau – despite the fact that Moshoeshoe managed to hand over 3 500 cattle before the deadline expired. The British lost 38 men killed in the attack, more than those suffered by the Basotho warriors, although many Basotho women and children were killed. They did, however, manage to capture several thousand cattle before retiring to lick their wounds.

In the lull that followed, Moshoeshoe, after debating with his councillors, realised that to continue the fight might well lead to the destruction of his kingdom and the scattering of his people. To save both, he dictated a letter to Cathcart in which he diplomatically said 'you have shown your power, you have chastised, let it be enough I pray you; and let me no longer be considered an enemy of the Queen . . . .' With honour satisfied, Cathcart and his soldiers withdrew, reporting victory over 'the enlightened and powerful chief Moshesh'.

The chief's councillors, however, were eager to settle old scores with Sekonyela, and a successful attack was carried out. Although Sekonyela escaped, many of his subjects who survived submitted to Moshoeshoe.

Withdrawal of the British

Moshoeshoe's letter gave the British the chance they were looking for to 'abandon' the sovereignty with 'honour' and in April 1853 Sir George Clerk, British Under-Secretary of State, arrived in Bloemfontein to preside over the British withdrawal. On 23 February 1854, after months of delicate negotiations during which he had to placate loyalist whites who feared trekker domination, Clerk signed the Bloemfontein Convention with Voortrekker and British leaders, paving the way for the establishment of the republican Orange Free State. No blacks signed the convention, and by no means all whites were in favour of it. But Britain was determined to be rid of this troublesome and expensive property that yielded no profit.

Among other things, the convention declared that there existed no alliance with 'native chiefs or tribes', except Adam Kok, north of the Orange River, nor would any treaties be made that might injure or prejudice the government of the new state. On the subject of that new state's boundary with Lesotho, the convention was silent. Appalled by this omission, Moshoeshoe rode to Bloemfontein to confer with Clerk, only to be told that everything was 'settled' and if any dispute should arise it should be settled by arbitration. Satisfied that he had done well, Clerk withdrew. And Moshoeshoe, then about 68 years old, rode sadly back to his Mountain of the Night.

Without Moshoeshoe's approval, however, the Boers had no alternative except to try to police the 'Warden Line' by force. The fight against the Basotho was still a long way from over (see pages 160, 193).

The making of an Afrikaner republic

The British takeover of the short-lived Republic of Natalia convinced the majority of Voortrekkers
of the futility of trying to establish an independent state near the sea.
Their best bet was to find a place inland – and the land north of the Vaal River, where the town
of Potchefstroom had already been founded, seemed ideal. But squabbles broke out continually,
and within a decade two more statelets – Ohrigstad and Soutpansberg – had been formed.
At the same time, African chiefdoms began to regroup.

ABOUT 12 KILOMETRES west of the northern Transvaal town of Louis Trichardt, near a sleepy railway siding, stands an old disused cemetery where Voortrekker leader Hendrik Potgieter lies buried.

An unremarkable place, today most of the handful of visitors to its cluster of nameless headstones are those who remain committed to the ideals of trekker forefathers who settled these parts more than a century ago.

How times have changed....

In the 1850s, the cemetery served Soutpansberg, a Boer colony that, by most accounts, was both the Sodom and the Gomorrah of the Voortrekker world. And like the biblical villages, it also came to grief.

In March 1872, five years after Schoemansdal, its bustling administrative centre, had been sacked by a rampaging force of Venda warriors, Berlin Society missionary Bernhard Beyer passed through the burnt-out ruins, and remarked: 'The *dorp* [village] ... makes a gloomy impression on the visitor. No wonder too, for wickedness formerly had its residence here in the highest degree. Here drunkenness and gluttony were the order of the day, with the buyers and sellers of many valuable African products among which slaves too were numbered. The market and site of the town hall were manured by the thousands of tears and the blood of poor blacks who were lashed unmercifully, and of these doubtless a good many gave up the ghost under the beating. The Lord scented this offence; to that the ruins of the formerly prosperous spot now testify.'

Because Beyer had never travelled this way before, due allowance for exaggeration has to be made for much (but not all) of what he said. For instance, while he was correct in stating that the trade in African workers was a lucrative pastime, as indeed it was in all other Boer settlements in the Transvaal, he overstated the importance of slavery in this trekker stronghold. In many ways, Soutpansberg *had been* a prosperous place – but it owed its affluence to another African commodity: ivory.

The village of Schoemansdal was situated in the middle of elephant country – and elephant-hunting was the easiest get-rich-quick scheme imaginable. All that was required was a gun, a supply of superior quality gunpowder, a good eye and a steady hand. Unfortunately, the lure of lucrative returns for minimal outlay drew to the region a type of settler whose morals seldom rose higher than the gutter. Some were English, Irish and German adventurers, but many were Voortrekkers who only a few years earlier had set off, Bible in hand, in search of a land free of Brit-

ish interference. So godless were they, that later commentators were to claim that the far northern settlers generally were unrepresentative of Voortrekker colonisation.

A republic through the barrel of a gun

The first Voortrekker parties crossed the Vaal in the late 1830s – and contrary to what was once popular belief, they did not find a deserted country. Although it is true that internecine warfare caused havoc among many African chiefdoms in the Transvaal, the innovative among them found ways not only to survive, but also to thrive.

But they had no answer to the power of the Boers....

Moving in compact groups, and mowing down all who disputed their authority, the new settlers quickly established their superiority in the region. With their guns making them masters over all, chiefdom after chiefdom wisely but reluctantly put away their spears for another day. It was, for the trekkers, a dream come true: at last they had their own country – free of the British, and with enough subjugated African people on call to satisfy all their labour requirements.

And yet, mainly through their own deficiencies, their visions of a milk-and-honey existence in a land they believed had been given to them by God were quickly shattered. Thanks to their guns, conquest of African rivals had been easy; it was holding onto what they had taken that taxed them to the limit.

In many respects, the Boers were totally unsuited to running a country. A far from united people, they spent much of their time bickering over matters as diverse as how to split the spoils of raids on African homesteads, or who was the most important of many self-styled leaders. To make matters worse, flare-ups between opposing warlords were seldom amicably settled: the losers often packed their wagons, gathered their followers and set off to start a new colony in territory belonging to some other African chiefdom.

In 1838, Potchefstroom was the only Boer settlement in the Transvaal. A decade later, two new colonies had come into being: Ohrigstad in 1845 and Soutpansberg in 1848.

New alliances with African neighbours

When the compact, highly mobile trekker parties first entered the Transvaal, the scattered African groups were unable to withstand them. But once the white emigrants themselves began to spread out, the situation was largely reversed: now it was the African chiefdoms that formed the concentrated blocs.

The Boer counter to this new danger made nonsense of later claims that their isolation and insecurity gave rise to a heightened sense of group solidarity and separateness from other racial groups. On the contrary, the evidence suggests that when the chips were down, they had few qualms about entering into relations of mutual interest with black neighbours. Thus, from the late 1840s, a series of friendship treaties that led to increasing settler involvement in African politics was concluded ....

Perhaps the most important white-black agreement in the Transvaal was sealed on 27 June 1846, between the *volksraad* of the Ohrigstad statelet and Mswati, the young Swazi king. At first glance the terms of the treaty seemed ridiculous: in return for 110 cattle (to be paid in two instalments over six months), Mswati ceded to Ohrigstad a vast piece of land, situated between the Crocodile and Olifants rivers.

The real purpose of the deal, however, had little to do with land, and even less with cattle. In Mswati's case, the motivation was a promise of Boer support in the event of a Zulu invasion, or a challenge to his kingship by his elder brother, Malambule. From the *volksraad*'s point of view, the treaty had been concluded to counter an earlier agreement between the Pedi chief, Sekwati, and the followers of Hendrik Potgieter.

For a time, the alliance worked reasonably well: in 1847 when the Swazi were attacked by the Zulu, Mswati, having put his cattle under Boer protection, had the added satisfaction of seeing the raiders being put to flight by a commando of Ohrigstad burghers.

The community that died in a cave

On 25 October 1854, an entire Ndebele community fled into a network of caves near the present-day town of Potgietersrus – and waited to die.

They could not escape – for outside waited several hundred Boer commandos and 300 of their Kgatla allies. The leader of the Ndebele was a chief called Mokopane (or Makapan as he was known to the Boers), who was killed in the siege. Later, the caves were named Makapansgat.

Mokopane's people had been living in relative peace in the northern Transvaal since the 1600s. But when the first Boers began arriving in the area during the 1850s, tension between the two groups over land and labour built up rapidly. Conflict also arose over the control of the lucrative ivory trade – and settler demands for child 'apprentices'.

When Britain recognised the independence of the South African Republic in 1852, it did so on condition that slavery was not practised. Although the Boer authorities readily agreed to this and, in fact, passed laws outlawing slavery, Africans were not fooled. When farmers could not get voluntary cheap labour, they simply assembled a commando and raided African homesteads for workers. A special target was children (see page 146).

The most notorious of these slave raiders was Hermanus Potgieter, a cold-blooded killer, who was feared throughout the region for his violent methods. Few Ndebele communities could claim not to have lost children as a result of Potgieter's frequent swoops: 'The Boers have for a long time been robbing and oppressing

him,' said a follower of a chief named Mankopane, a neighbour of Mokopane. 'Ask him how many of his children ... have been taken and made slaves, and how many of his people have been murdered?

'The Boers went ... to demand tribute and to take what they liked. His heart was full of anguish for the loss of his eight children. His heart was full of anguish for his people who came mourning their losses.'

Although most of the clans in the area were affected by commando slave raids, it was the groups led by Mokopane and Mankopane that bore the brunt of these attacks. The Ndebele retaliated by mutilating settler animals and attacking their servants.

As anger began to mount on both sides, the Ndebele launched simultaneous attacks in four different places, killing 42 Boers (including Potgieter). Furious, the settlers assembled a commando and marched on to Mokopane's stronghold – but he and his people were no longer there. They had fled to the caves.

It did not take long for the commando to track down Mokopane's clan, but because the entrances were too narrow, the angry Boers soon gave up the idea of storming the Ndebele hideout. After attempts to smoke them out proved as unsuccessful, the Boers sat back and waited.

Inside the caves, the Ndebele had enough food to last them several days, but water was a problem. As the water supply diminished, about 900 of the fugitives tried to rush outside to a nearby stream. They were shot and killed. With the situation inside becoming even more critical, some of

The Makapansgat complex – a place of tragic memories.

the warriors tried to give themselves up. By 12 November, the Boers had taken 400 women and children who had surrendered. Five days later, another 300 surrendered and the commandos felt comfortable enough now to enter the caves. Inside, they found 34 guns, two chests of clothing and a quantity of lead and gunpowder. The siege had lasted 25 days and had resulted in the deaths of more than 1 000 Ndebele.

They called their slaves *Inboekselings*

In those stormy years between the 1830s and 1850s the majority of Voortrekkers in the Transvaal were involved in a reprehensible though highly profitable occupation: the kidnapping of African children.

It was a practice that sparked waves of terror in African homesteads . . . .

Cheap, captive labour formed the basis of the patriarchal economies of the Boer statelets between 1838-48. And when negotiation failed to draw sufficient African workers into the workforce, instructions went out to bring them in by force.

As a long-term investment, the acquisition of children was a highly enticing prospect – and Boer commandos conducted a series of raids on African homesteads in search of 'black ivory'. These raids netted them thousands of children. According to the captors, most were orphans, but if this was so, it was because the trekkers had killed their parents.

In acting the way they did, the Boers were walking a tight-rope: in 1852, when Britain recognised their independence, they agreed not to practise slavery. The Boers, however, refused to believe that they had reneged on this agreement. To them, a slave was someone who was sold into permanent bondage at a public auction for cash. By contrast, their captives were required to work only until the age of 25 (in the case of men). And while they could be bartered for goods such as iron or cattle, they could not be sold. Furthermore, claimed the Boers, the system whereby children were registered (or booked in) by a *landdrost* had been devised to ensure that only respectable families would require servants in this way.

Inboekselings (as captured African juveniles became known) were mostly well-fed, but, as Walter Inglis of the London Missionary Society remarked: 'Many horses and dogs are well fed. This good feeding has ever been a favourite dodge with slave holders, and its abettors. I do not say that they are driven like the slaves in the West Indies and America, but I say their masters have complete power over them.'

Rich householders and state officials such as *landdrosts* were the chief beneficiaries of the *inboekseling* system: Andries Pretorius was known to have acquired eight children after the defeat of Dingane in 1838, while, after another raid, Hendrik Potgieter returned with 15 *inboekselings*. Even Marthinus Wessel Pretorius, who has been described as an ardent anti-slaver, regularly acquired African children. On one occasion Hendrik Bührman, the *landdrost* of Lydenburg, recorded in his diary: 'I, the undersigned, declare hereby that the kaffir upper chief Umwaas has sent three kaffir orphan children for the Honourable President M W Pretorius, his ally.' The wealthy Bührman himself dabbled extensively in the trade, having 16 children registered under his name.

Inboekselings were welcome additions to the Boer household, performing a variety of activities. Some were used as herdsmen, *voorleiers* (ox-wagon leaders), diggers of irrigation canals and constructors of dam and kraal walls, and the builders of Boer houses. *Inboekseling* labour was even responsible for the construction of the first church at Rustenburg.

In gratitude for services rendered, Swaziland opened its borders to Ohrigstad hunters and traders; supplied the Boers with more 'apprentices', and gave the go-ahead for the republic to build a road through Swazi territory to Delagoa Bay.

Within two years, however, the trekkers were drawn into a dispute between Mswati and another older brother, Somcuba, and the agreement fell apart amid a torrent of threats and counter-threats.

In an era when ambition was synonymous with death, it was no secret that Somcuba badly wanted to rule Swaziland. It was, however, a grave mistake for him to have been so open about it. He quickly found that Mswati, despite a myriad of external and internal security problems, was as determined as ever to hold onto his rickety chieftaincy. A swoop on Somcuba's northern stronghold failed to snare the ambitious pretender who, forewarned, slipped away just in time to seek sanctuary in Ohrigstad.

Given the benefits they had accrued as a result of their alliance with Mswati, the logical thing would have been for the Boers to deliver the fugitive to his pursuers. But in the tempestuous highveld, logic was sometimes made to stand on its head – and so, much to the disgust of the young Swazi ruler, they refused.

In reaching this decision the trekkers were deeply conscious of the fact that survival in what they perceived as a hostile world depended on their always having the backing of the most powerful African leader in the region. In this respect, Mswati's precarious position hardly filled them with confidence. Somcuba, on the other hand, despite his present predicament, was regarded as the rising star of the Swazi kingdom. Even if they handed him back, and he was put to death, what was there to stop another of his followers from usurping the throne? And if this happened, how would it affect them?

Nevertheless, the decision to buck Mswati was a far from unanimous one – and when the Swazi chief hit back by cancelling the agreement on the building of a road through his territory to Delagoa Bay, by stopping the supply of slaves and, finally, by attacking the new administrative centre of Lydenburg, the trekkers argued long and hard about the wisdom of their decision.

In the end the Boers were rescued from their predicament when Somcuba was killed during a sneak Swazi attack on his hideout. Thereafter the relationship between the Boers and Mswati improved immeasurably.

A vain search for unity

Ohrigstad was not the only Boer colony to be caught up in the disputes of African neighbours: Potchefstroom and Soutpansberg had similar problems, decreasing even further the already slim prospects of a united Boer republic.

Certainly, amalgamation had been discussed before – and at some length. In 1849, the three statelets put their signatures to the Treaty of Derdepoort, which formalised previous unity talks. However, the agreement was hardly worth the paper it was written on. And in a way, this was not surprising: the different trekker leaders still disliked one another intensely; Boer involvement in the affairs of their African neighbours was increasing, and the enormous distances between the various white communities hardly made things any easier.

Despite these difficulties, attempts were made in the 1850s to find solutions – one being an instruction to the *volksraad* to rotate its meetings between Potchefstroom and Ohrigstad (Soutpansberg was ignored). It was a good try – but it did not work: representatives of the statelet that was not the host usually stayed away. This was especially so between 1852-4 when all three Boer communities were involved in disputes with Africans.

The upshot was that none of the statelets was in a position to offer military assistance to any of the others: Potchefstroom could not help Lydenburg; nor could Lydenburg help Potchefstroom, while Soutpansberg was far away and little concerned.

Potgieter country

In many ways, Soutpansberg belonged to Andries Hendrik Potgieter, a person with a remarkable ability to make enemies faster than any of his fellow countrymen.

Unable to adjust to life in Potchefstroom and Ohrigstad, Potgieter had loaded his wagons and had trekked north to found the colony that remained a Potgieter possession from its inception in 1848, to its incorporation in a united South African Republic in 1860. When he died in 1852, his son, Piet, took over the reins until he was killed in a battle with the Ndebele in 1854. His successor, Stephanus Schoeman, secured the right to the Potgieter fiefdom by marrying Piet's widow and naming the main town in the colony after himself.

In a sense, Soutpansberg had a personality of its own. It asked no favours of its counterparts in the south and east, and it offered none. Here too, 'kaffirs' were under no illusion about their station in life: their job was to work for the white man and to pay their taxes on time.

Certainly, events in nearby Mozambique guaranteed many white Soutpansbergers an abundance of African

THIS MEMORIAL *to Voortrekker leader Andries Hendrik Potgieter stands in the western Transvaal town of Zeerust.*

workers and taxpayers. In 1858, for instance, when civil war broke out among the Gaza people, hundreds of Tsonga-speaking followers of a chief named Umzila fled into the Soutpansberg where they were given a warm welcome by Joao Albasini, an unscrupulous Portuguese hunter-trader (and 'kaffir farmer').

In 1857 Albasini had moved out of Schoemansdal in order to throw all his energies into creating his own African chiefdom. Despite stiff competition from local chiefs, he did quite well for himself, attracting not only Gaza refugees to his 'kingdom' on the Delagoa Bay trade route, but also numbers of Venda-speakers from chiefdoms living in the mountains north of the Levubu River.

The secret of Albasini's success was the fact that he allowed his followers to retain their clan-names, culture and chiefs. Recruits were also offered the possibility of rapid advancement as hunters, traders and tax-collectors.

Of course, there were advantages in it for Albasini too. As self-proclaimed 'chief' he claimed the lion's share of the not inconsiderable tribute collected and stolen by his henchmen. On the other hand, there were risks involved in running a patchwork chiefdom: for a start, he was never able to win the total loyalty of his followers. At the height of his power, after the fall of Schoemansdal in 1867, he won over thousands of Tsonga-speaking followers. But in the 1870s, when his power began to wane, many of these people began to desert him for wealthier masters.

Inevitably the huge influx of Africans into the area forced the white colonists to re-examine their attitudes towards their black neighbours – and the Soutpansbergers, despite a reputation for brutality, did introduce one change that was to have a far-reaching effect on black-white relations: they taught Africans to use firearms.

In a way, they were forced to – for, having decimated the elephant population in their immediate vicinity, they were obliged to expand their activities over a wider field. In this case, however, it meant moving eastwards into the much-feared malaria zone. Although few trekkers were prepared to risk contracting the disease, there was no question of abandoning the search for ivory. Hunting, after all, was the lifeblood of the colony. A solution was quickly arrived at: it involved teaching African servants to shoot, and thereafter sending them into malaria country. At first, the *swartskut* (black shot) experiment proved a great success, allowing Boers the luxury of simply waiting for the ivory to come pouring in.

Few things, however, were ever simple in the Transvaal – and the Soutpansbergers soon faced a major problem when many of the *swartskuts* absconded, taking their newly acquired firearms with them. This, coupled with the fact that other Africans – labour migrants – were using part of their wages to add to the growing armoury being assembled in the chiefdoms, began to pose a major threat to white superiority. With the odds now greatly evened out, those chiefdoms with weapons to match those of the Boers openly refused to honour labour and tax obligations. It was with great concern that the Boers realised there was nothing they could do about this defiance. Significantly, African access to firearms led to a marked decrease in settler attempts at labour coercion.

M W PRETORIUS, *a tireless worker for Boer unity, became the first President of the South African Republic in 1860.*

PIET JOUBERT *shrugged aside childhood poverty to become one of the most successful businessmen in the Transvaal.*

The search for unity continues

With the future of his people becoming increasingly insecure, trekker leader Marthinus Wessel Pretorius began a new initiative to unite the three statelets. In 1856, a new *grondwet* (constitution) was accepted by Potchefstroom and Lydenburg (formerly Ohrigstad) but rejected by the Soutpansbergers, who for the next two years remained outside mainstream Boer politics. In 1858, however, a promise of high office in the proposed united state persuaded Stephanus Schoeman to bring his people back into the fold, and by 1860 the three communities were finally amalgamated. All that was left to be sorted out was the composition of the new government – and it took four years and a near civil war before Pretorius was installed as the first President.

From the start, the new administration showed itself incapable of running a country. The problem was that the burghers proved to be totally ungovernable, especially when it came to contributing towards the state's welfare: while most trekkers were in favour of stiff taxes on the African population, they were openly hostile to any suggestions that they too had to pay. To make matters worse for the government, the little revenue that found its way to the coffers was often misappropriated. Some members of the government were decidedly long-fingered.

As far back as 1850 the white rulers of the Transvaal had shown themselves totally incapable of devising a system that would bring in sufficient revenue to finance both military expenditure and civil administration. And unity, if anything, served only to compound their difficulties.

Because the cost of acquiring and defending land was far more than the treasury could afford, payment was made by securing land against debts. At best it was a short-term holding operation – for it meant having to find new land with the further expenditure again secured by the provision of land against republican currency.

When large areas of the country became unavailable for burgher occupation, the authorities tried to solve the problem with a two-pronged initiative: the first involved using land rather than currency to pay officials; the second revolved around the issuing of exchequer bills (known as *Mandaaten*) for services rendered to the State.

But without capital, labour or markets, the land acquired by many of the less well-off proved almost worthless. Indeed, the only way they could profit by its acquisition was to sell it – at first to richer members of the Boer community, and later to speculators outside the republic.

At a time when large tracts could change hands for as little as £25, an array of Boer notables – usually top-ranking government officials – acquired 'little countries'. In the Lydenburg district, *volksraad* member Hendrik Bührman owned 18 farms by 1869. But even this paled into insignificance when compared with the landholdings of Johannes Vos, the *landdrost* clerk of Marthinus Wesselstroom: taking advantage of yet another badly thought-out government scheme (that offered burghers one or more quitrent farms in addition to their freehold farms), Vos had acquired 120 such holdings by 1866.

Other prominent Boers such as Paul Kruger and Piet Joubert, both of whom had access to privileged information, made small fortunes buying and selling off land. Kruger, in fact, went as far as quitting his favourite pastime – hunting – to concentrate on land speculation.

But while the rich got richer, the country got poorer. In 1865, in a new bid to bail the republic out of its financial difficulties, the government decided to print paper money,

IN 1850, *Lydenburg was founded to replace unhealthy Ohrigstad as the administrative centre for the Boer statelet in the north-eastern Transvaal. In 1867, when this engraving was made, the town consisted of a church (centre), a rectory (left), the landdrost's office (right), a school and a few houses.*

again using land as security. But the currency was so worthless that it was rejected even by state officials, who together with clergymen, traders and other private individuals chose rather to pay with credit notes called 'good-fors'. In 1868, 1 000 farms totalling 3-million morgen were used to guarantee the issue of paper money. When the bubble burst and creditors started presenting their chits, vast chunks of the republic passed into the hands of British absentee landlords such as Parker Wood and Company, the Harmony Company and A L Devenish, who between them acquired 77 farms. Smaller companies and private individuals acquired dozens more – usually at public sales in the bustling, diamond-rich northern Cape town of Kimberley.

The passing of large chunks of their 'country' into the hands of foreigners was criticised by many burghers – and in 1873 a group of Boers from Lydenburg felt sufficiently incensed to compile a petition in which they complained that 'some of the most eligible and beautiful lands in the Republic are owned by non-residents, people residing in the neighbouring colonies and in Europe who have no interest in the development of the country further than in the enhanced value it gives to their land'.

They would have been even angrier had they known that Africans had also benefited from the treasury's problems: using missionaries as frontmen, the original inhabitants of the area had bought back large areas that the Boers had earlier taken from them.

In its desperation to ward off bankruptcy, the government became fair game for a host of smooth-talking, usually British, confidence tricksters. One of them, Alexander McCorkindale, proposed, among other schemes, the establishment of a commercial bank; the institution of an immigration scheme; the setting up of a commercial, farming and mining company; the construction of a harbour at Delagoa Bay, and making the Maputa and Phongolo rivers navigable. To undertake these schemes he asked the government for 100 farms as security for raising an overseas loan of £250 000, while at the same time setting his own fee at 200 farms. Fortunately for the republic, these schemes quickly fell through, enabling it to cut its losses.

It was only after British annexation in 1877 (see page 181), when its chaotic financial situation was put on a sounder footing and its major security problems eased by the crushing of the Zulu and the Pedi, that the Afrikaners in the Transvaal became really united. After the discovery of the Witwatersrand goldfields in 1886, it began to emerge as the most important region in southern Africa. But this, in itself, led to even bigger problems (see page 232).

ALEXANDER MCCORKINDALE *offered to raise an overseas loan for the Transvaal Boer republic – for a fee of 200 farms.*

Mixed blessings

Determined to maintain their human dignity in ways laid down by their ancestors,
a majority of Xhosa chiefs rejected the approaches of missionaries who in the early years
of the 19th century tried to convince them of the combined joys of the gospel and manual labour.
Towards the end of the century, however, a massive loss of territory,
following a series of disastrous frontier wars, pushed thousands of devastated Africans
into previously almost empty mission stations.

IN 1816, JUST FOUR YEARS after John Graham's soldiers had cut a path of death and destruction through the lands of the indigenous people of the eastern Cape (see page 103), a 56-year-old Xhosa diviner named Ntsikana Gaba made what must have been the most difficult decision of his life: he decided to embrace Christianity.

Missionary endeavour had little to do with his surprise pronouncement: it was a vision – a light shining on an ox with which he enjoyed a decidedly unchristian relationship – that moved him to seek conversion.

The 'defection' of a 'witchdoctor' into the ranks of the 'civilised' was regarded by the guardians of the gospel as a crucial breakthrough – a prelude to thousands of Africans rejecting their old life of 'sin and sloth' for the industry and guidance offered by officials of mission stations. But it proved to be wishful thinking. For other than the captive congregations of misfits and fugitives from African justice who were given refuge at mission headquarters, Ntsikana's move did not spark a rush of Xhosa to Sunday church services.

THIS ILLUSTRATION *of Ntsikana, the first Xhosa prophet, is based on a sketch by Elizabeth Williams, the wife of eastern Cape missionary Joseph Williams.*

To add to missionary disappointment, Ntsikana also showed himself to be a less than ideal addition to the fold. Although he was able to persuade a group of devotees to follow his path, his interpretation of Christianity often differed radically from that of the missionaries. Indeed, the main reason for his success in recruiting a core of faithful followers to his brand of religion was his ability to adapt Christianity to suit particular African needs.

It was an approach many missionaries would have done well to emulate – for their biggest problem in those early years of evangelisation was a refusal even to try to understand the people they were so eager to save.

But fortunately for them, time was on their side – and although many years of hard work (not to mention widespread complicity in the land-grabbing and forced-labour schemes of the white government) still lay ahead, by the end of the century many of their ambitions for the Xhosa would come to fruition.

Why the Xhosa rejected Christianity

In a sense, the early problems of missionaries were understandable: because they were accustomed to a society that had been conditioned to accept, without question, their interpretation of the gospel, eastern Cape evangelists were often bewildered by the sceptical Xhosa reaction to their teachings: 'How did these words get into the book [the Bible] you tell us about?' asked one chief. 'How did the first man who wrote them, know them? If God was so powerful, and the Devil was the author of sin, why didn't God just convert the Devil and save everyone a lot of trouble?'

While the Xhosa reacted with a mixture of amusement and mild indifference to the bumbling attempts to explain to them the mysteries of the Bible, they were horrified by missionary rejection of some of their most treasured institutions, of which polygamy, bride-wealth (*lobola*) and 'witchcraft' were considered irreplaceable. This was not surprising: in Xhosa society, polygamy and bride-wealth cemented all social relationships, while 'witchcraft' and 'witch hunting' were proof of the existence of diseases.

And yet, despite their rejection of Christianity, many chiefs were canny enough to realise that missionaries, if kept on a carefully mapped out path, could prove very helpful indeed: accepting that they would need to acquire new skills to compete successfully with white traders and farmers, some of the indigenous people who, through trading contacts with whites had acquired a taste for profits, were especially keen to learn the latest farming methods.

Tiyo Soga . . . sowing the seeds of African nationalism

Christian compassion was in short supply in 1846 when Tiyo Soga, a 17-year-old Xhosa youth, left for Scotland to learn to become a missionary.

The War of the Axe (see page 108), the seventh frontier conflict between Xhosa and settler in under 50 years, was in full swing. As representative of a society that regularly claimed to be the standard-bearers of Christianity, the colonial army showed a remarkably unchristian talent for devising new ways of brutality – and when Soga returned in 1848, the war

TIYO SOGA, *regarded as the first African 'nationalist'.*

was over, thousands of his people had been starved to death and more land had been confiscated by the victors.

Ironically, the devastating nature of their defeat made many previously stubborn Xhosa much more susceptible to the teachings of the gospel. Having qualified as a catechist during his stay overseas, Soga proved to be a highly persuasive teacher.

Unlike the other 'modernist' Africans of that period, Soga did not try to copy the white man at every turn. Nor did he reject the majority of Xhosa customs. Africans, he believed, had achieved many things of which they could be proud – and given the proper opportunities would probably be able to hold their own quite comfortably with the settler societies.

'Be proud of what you are' was a recurring theme in talks with his children, his congregants and, indeed, anyone who would listen. The encroachment of 'civilisation', he stressed, did not mean subservience to whites. 'Raise your hats to chiefs and respectable people,' he advised on one occasion. 'To White gentlemen bow your heads gently even though you do not utter a word. Do that to White people who deserve this. This is pleasing. But we do not advise this even to poor Whites of no repute who are no better than yourselves. This "Morning Sir" of the Xhosa people whenever they see a white face is very annoying.'

In 1851 he returned to Scotland to continue his studies – and in 1856 was formally ordained as a minister of the Presbyterian Church. In 1857 he married a Scot, Janet Burnside, and shortly afterwards returned to southern Africa. His marriage to Burnside produced four sons and three daughters – all of whom studied in Scotland. That Soga believed in a form of black consciousness was aptly highlighted in the advice he gave each of his children before they left for overseas: 'You will ever cherish the memory of your mother as that of an upright, conscientious, thrifty, Christian Scotch woman. You will ever be thankful for your connection by this tie to the white race. But if you wish to gain credit for yourselves – if you do not wish to feel the taunt of men, which you sometimes may well feel – take your place in the world as coloured, not as white men; as Kafirs, not as Englishmen . . . . For your own sakes never appear ashamed that your father was a Kafir, and that you inherited some African blood. It is every whit as good and as pure as that which flows in the veins of my fairer breathren.'

An accomplished writer and composer, Soga's best known works are translations into Xhosa of John Bunyan's 'The Pilgrim's Progress' and the four Gospels of the Bible. He also penned several hymns.

He died in 1871 at the age of 42.

For their part, the missionaries, always on the lookout for opportunities to broaden their influence among Africans, were only too eager to be of assistance.

But while permission for schools to be started in the vicinity of chieftaincies was usually granted, the go-ahead was qualified by a ban on the teaching of the Christian religion. This, commented one missionary, provided 'quaint' proof of the 'backwardness' of the 'native mind'.

It was an observation clouded by arrogance and prejudice: for what were often held to be examples of Xhosa 'backwardness', were, in fact, conscious efforts by the indigenous people to take advantage of new economic opportunities – but on terms other than those laid down by whites. Thus, while it was true that the first plough to turn up soil north of the Kei River was guided by Wesleyan hands, and the first store to sell clothing in 'Kaffirland', the first cotton to be grown, the first wagon, the first European-type house . . . were all products of missionary endeavour, these innovations would not have come about without the active participation of Africans. In retrospect then, what

have generally been claimed to be missionary successes, might well have been African successes.

Missionaries and economic change

But success, the Xhosa hierarchy soon discovered, came at a price. In the early years of black-white interaction, when land and resources were plentiful, chiefs had little difficulty in dictating the pace and nature of change in their societies. The story, however, changed appreciably after a succession of defeats in frontier wars resulted in a massive loss of land to the white colonists, and an influx of destitute Xhosa into the mission stations.

For reasons that quickly became abundantly clear, most missionaries welcomed military intervention against the Xhosa: in the frontier equation, defeat equalled landlessness . . . landlessness equalled shattered morale . . . shattered morale equalled loss of confidence in chiefs . . . which equalled missionary joy as it became easier to wean ordinary clan members away from what was considered an indolent way of life.

A MISSIONARY *tries to spread the gospel at an African kraal. Early efforts to convert Africans met with little success.*

Work, as far as the majority of missionaries were concerned, excluded anything to do with cattle, the prime reason, they believed, for the Xhosa's 'idle' lifestyle. Real work involved ploughing fields – and in a bid to encourage greater numbers of Xhosa men to participate actively in crop production, missionaries often paid the workers out of their own pockets.

Because ploughing was traditionally a woman's chore, those who joined mission stations and began to work the fields cut themselves off permanently from the world of cattle and homage to chiefs. In their new world, material affluence became the main indicator of social prestige.

Once the break was made, integration into the European economy proceeded at a rapid pace. And when missionaries on their stations and white colonists in the towns insisted that Xhosa be 'decently' attired, the purchase of clothes became a priority of some of the more eager participants in this new way of life. A spinoff of this was the development of a fashion consciousness which, by 1845, had white settlers complaining that the Xhosa were wearing 'coats, knee-breeches, and silk-stockings, umbrellas and parasols'.

The purchase of clothing, as well as other goods such as iron pots, axes and ploughs, all formed part of a greater plan that the doyen of South African missionaries, John Philip, succinctly outlined in a letter to the Cape authorities in 1820. 'Tribes in a savage state are generally without houses, gardens, and fixed property,' he wrote. 'By locating them on a particular place, getting them to build houses, enclose gardens, cultivate corn land, accumulate property, and by increasing their artificial wants, you increase their dependency on the colony, and multiply the bonds of union and the number of securities for the preservation of peace.'

He added that by 'scattering the seeds of Civilisation', missionaries could appreciably extend British trade and influence. 'Wherever the missionary places his standard among a savage tribe, their prejudices against the colonial government give way; their dependence upon the colony is increased . . . confidence is restored; intercourse with the colony is established; industry, trade and agriculture spring up; and every genuine convert . . . becomes the friend and ally of the colonial government.'

Square houses

Efforts to turn 'savage tribes' into 'friends and allies' sometimes bordered on the ludicrous. For instance, one of the great missionary campaigns involved encouraging Africans to live in square houses: 'Why . . . square houses?' asked the missionary mouthpiece, the 'Kaffir Express', in 1875. The answer, it explained, was simple: 'With a proper house, then comes a table, then chairs, a clean table-cloth, paper or white-wash for the walls, wife and daughters dressed in clean calico prints, and so forth . . . . The church-going Kaffirs purchase three times as much clothing, groceries, and other articles in the shops as the red [traditional] Kaffirs; but with a change in their habitations the existing native trade would soon be doubled.'

The frequency of references in missionary correspondence and publications to the superiority of square over round dwellings is, in fact, quite astounding: in a 'Kaffir Express' article entitled 'Social Reform among the Kaffir People', an earnest appeal was made for an intermediate stage between round and square buildings – 'a new form of hut, oblong but rounded at the ends'. In a sense, missionary misgivings over 'round' houses were understandable. Given the fact that the traditional house did not have separate rooms for different members of the family, many preachers cringed at the thought of what children might see at bedtime. It was, after all, the Victorian era.

Red is best

Despite their enthusiasm, an abundance of funds, the chaos wrought by the frontier wars and government backing for their schemes, the success rate of missionaries remained low for much of the 19th century. Certainly, by 1850 only about 16 000 Africans out of 400 000 had moved into the 32 mission stations dotted around the eastern Cape. Of this number, only a small minority had genuinely succumbed to the call of 'Christianity' and 'civilisation'.

For a long time many of the early converts were women who had rejected the oppression of unwanted husbands, accused witches, blind people, albinos, lepers and cripples. Because most of them lived on the fringes of Xhosa communities anyway, they were not considered a loss. Reaction, however, was markedly different in the cases of higher placed members of African society – especially chiefs – who leaned towards Christianity. Great pressure was put on them, usually by rank-and-file members of their chiefdoms. Even in cases where individuals were able to withstand community pressures – Khama and Dyani Tshatshu were notable examples – their Christianity had hardly any effect on their own families, let alone on the people over whom they ruled.

Furthermore, the conversion of some often led to a hardening of attitudes in others. The result was that chiefs

A DELEGATION *of missionaries and 'Christian' Africans led by Dr John Philip (standing, second from left) gave evidence before a Select Committee on Aborigines that sat in London in 1835-6. Philip campaigned tirelessly for the integration of Africans into the white economic and social system, claiming this was the only way to guarantee peace in southern Africa. Others in the picture are (from left to right) Dyani Tshatshu, Andries Stoffles, James Read (junior) and James Read (senior).*

who previously tolerated the presence of missionaries in their territories now became openly hostile towards them. Initially many Xhosa leaders had accepted that their people could benefit by the acquisition of certain of the secular skills offered by missionaries. Subsequent events, however, quickly made them change their minds. With a large number of evangelists supplementing their incomes by acting as either government spies or land agents, chiefs quite justifiably began to regard them as grave threats to the chosen way of life of the Xhosa. 'When my people become Christians, they cease to become my people,' commented a chief to the missionary Henry Calderwood. Another ruler told a parliamentary select committee in 1851: 'I like very much to live with the missionaries if they would not take my people and give them to the government.'

Simple economics also played a crucial role in persuading many Xhosa that being 'red' (those choosing the traditional way of life) as opposed to 'school' (those opting for a European lifestyle) was, perhaps, a better option in the long run: certainly, the institution of new obligations, such as the paying of rent and taxes, which were imposed on those who were drawn into the European economy was a turn-off to many Africans who watched developments from the sidelines.

Towards the end of the century, a group of disillusioned peasants complained bitterly of the new Christian order: 'We are taught two things – the word of the Lord, and the payment of rent . . . .'

The amazing J T van der Kemp

Notwithstanding stubborn Xhosa opposition to the spreading of the gospel, some missionaries were, in fact, well-liked by local African people. And the most popular of them all was Johannes Theodorus van der Kemp.

If anyone knew sin, it was this gangling Dutchman. As a young adult, he had spent much of his spare time in

drinking houses and bedrooms of available women. But after his wife and daughter were drowned in a boating accident, he threw himself into religion – and when he arrived at the Cape in 1797, it was as a representative of the London Missionary Society.

Working from Bethelsdorp in the eastern Cape, he quickly proved himself to be no ordinary 'man of God'. For a start, he rejected the favourite theory of his contemporaries that manual labour and religion were inextricably linked. This made him less than popular among both the colonial authorities and fellow missionaries.

Inevitably, his outright dismissal of many white values drew him closer to local Africans. When Dyani Tshatshu, the Xhosa Christian chief, first saw him, he had been 'on foot, without a hat, shoes or stockings'. He ate Xhosa food, lived in a Xhosa hut (and married a Khoikhoi woman). It was this type of unorthodoxy – on one occasion he successfully prayed for rain, Xhosa-style – that won him the respect and friendship even of those who had no intention of converting to Christianity.

Xhosa reaction to other missionaries varied: the 'liberal' James Read, for instance, was 'loved' by Africans, while William Thompson, who was also a government agent, was disliked. In most cases, however, the popularity of individual missionaries depended on the political situation in their spheres of influence. Thus, the conservative William Shaw who worked in a relatively trouble-free area had more success than the liberal John Ross, whose station in the Kat River valley was a target of frequent raids by the colonial army. When troops arrived to expel the Xhosa chief Maqoma from the valley in 1829, all Ross could do was ask them not to burn huts on the Sabbath – and even this request was disregarded when he turned his back.

The army's attitude prompted the disillusioned Tshatshu to ask: 'Why do not the missionaries first go to their own countrymen and convert them first?'

Today Natalia, tomorrow Natal

With 3 000 of his warriors dead at Blood River, Dingane was finally in retreat –
and Natal lay open before the conquering Voortrekkers. Taking advantage of a split in Zulu ranks,
they established the Republic of Natalia – helping Dingane's half-brother Mpande
to the leadership of a vassal Zulu state. The new republic, however, was short-lived –
in 1843 Britain annexed Natal, giving Mpande a smaller, independent Zululand north of the Thukela.
Two years later Natal was incorporated into the Cape Colony –
and a new system of land division between settler and African was instituted.

AS A YOUNG ADULT, the man who would later rule the Zulu kingdom for 32 years was dismissed as a weakling, more interested in looking after his numerous wives and children than following in the military footsteps of his half-brothers, Shaka and Dingane. It was an under-estimation that was to cost Dingane dearly.

Mpande was born in the Babanango district of what is now Natal in 1798, the beginning of a period of immense change in the Nguni settlements of south-east Africa that was to culminate in the emergence of his half-brother Shaka as king of the Zulu, a position he held until murdered by Dingane in 1828.

With Shaka dead, Dingane next turned his attention to removing any possible threat to his chieftainship from Mpande – who hurriedly moved his kraal from Mlambonqwenya, near present-day Eshowe, further west to Gqikazi. Then, lured by his half-brother's apparent harmlessness, Dingane backed down – and left Mpande to enjoy his wives in peace.

The arrival of the Voortrekkers

Peace, however, was rare in a region still settling down from the effects of Shaka's militarism – and it became rarer after the Voortrekkers had invaded Dingane's territory in 1838. After initial successes against the Boers – including the killing of Boer leader Piet Retief – Dingane lost 3 000 of his warriors in a wild attack on a Voortrekker laager at Blood River (see page 118). With his army shattered, the Zulu leader fled northwards, calling on Mpande to send a force to help him attack the Swazi.

Mpande duly sent one of his regiments – the inexperienced uKhokhothi – towards Dingane's new headquarters in the vicinity of Nongoma, but it was unable to locate the Zulu king, who was forced to attack the Swazi unaided – and was driven back. Angry and bitter, he decided that Mpande could no longer be trusted – and had to be killed.

It was the signal for a split in Zulu ranks that worked to the advantage of the Boers and their new Republic of Natalia. Mpande fled south across the Thukela with about 17 000 followers, who pronounced him king of the Zulu at Shaka's grave near present-day Stanger.

In October 1839 Mpande asked for Boer assistance to invade Zululand and defeat Dingane – a request that met with enthusiasm from the trekkers who, realising the importance of splitting the Zulu, proclaimed him 'governing prince of the emigrant Zulus'. Meanwhile, men were recruited from the Cape Colony for a white commando, and support for Mpande was promised by two chiefs, Matiwane and Jobe, and the queen-regent of Swaziland.

By January 1840 the invasion force was ready, and Mpande advanced into Zululand, his army stiffened by 350 mounted commandos. Dingane fled northwards across the Phongolo River to Swaziland and an uncertain fate (probably murder at the hands of the Swazi), while

THE ZULU LEADER *Mpande sided with Boers against Dingane, and then with the British against the Boers.*

IN 1845 *Natal became a district of the Cape, with Theophilus Shepstone (left) as 'Diplomatic Agent to the Native Tribes',* *Martin West (centre) as Lieutenant-Governor, and Hendrik Cloete (right) as Chief Justice.*

Mpande was proclaimed king of the Zulu by Andries Pretorius, leader of the Natalia *Volksraad* (parliament) on 10 February. In fact, the Boers installed Mpande as the ruler of a vassal state stretching from the Thukela to the Black Mfolozi.

With Dingane out of the picture, many Zulu who had earlier fled his reign now returned to a land occupied by Boers. At first they were welcomed by the labour-hungry white farmers, and 'allocated' to the trekkers at a rate of up to five families a farm. However, as more and more Zulu flooded back to their old homeland, the *volksraad* decided to relocate them along the Mzimvubu River, which they regarded as Natalia's southern boundary.

Here come the British

Their plan, however, was forestalled by the British annexation of Natal in 1843, following military intervention a year earlier – a decision prompted by a fear that another European power might occupy Durban, and so deny Britain a potential harbour on the eastern trade route.

The man chosen to explain the annexation to the indignant Boers was Hendrik (Henry) Cloete, a leading Cape advocate, who assured them that land claims would be registered in favour of those who could prove they had occupied the land for the past 12 months. Further, with the exception of military costs, the British Government could offer no financial support to Natal. There was also, by law, to be no 'distinction of colour, origin, race or creed', nor would slavery be permitted.

After attempting to soothe the Boers, Cloete visited Mpande who, still insecure upon his new throne, agreed to cede St Lucia Bay to the British and signed a treaty whereby the Zulu undertook to remain north of the Thukela River and east of its tributary, the Buffalo. Mpande initiated no hostility against Natal, although there were occasional floods of refugees into the territory as a result of internal upheavals. One of the worst of these occurred

when Mpande murdered his only surviving brother, Gqugqu, and his family. Only Mpande's aunt, Mawa, escaped, fleeing to seek British protection.

A new administration

Late in 1845 Natal became a district of the Cape, with Martin West as Lieutenant-Governor, Cloete as Recorder or Chief Justice, and Theophilus Shepstone as 'Diplomatic Agent to the Native Tribes'. Shepstone had arrived at the Cape as a young child with his 1820 settler parents, learnt to speak fluent Xhosa and acquired a reputation as a 'native administrator' on the eastern Cape frontier. However, after an attempt on his life that resulted in the death of a missionary, Shepstone was transferred to Natal.

One of the most pressing problems facing the new administration was how to divide the new territory between black and white – and in 1846 a so-called Locations Commission was set up to explore a proposal by Cloete to establish 'six or more locations, keeping them, if possible, a little way removed from the contaminating influence of the chief town and the port'. The commission recommended the establishment of 10 locations, each to be under a government-appointed superintendent who would act as magistrate, and to have a black police force with white officers. Funds were to be raised by a hut tax, which soon produced £10 000 annually, although, as it turned out, little of it was spent on the locations. Agricultural and industrial training was to be provided, and the superintendent was to have the power to punish minor offenders and to 'decide upon civil disputes to a certain amount, after which there would be a right of appeal to the diplomatic agent'. Shepstone, as Diplomatic Agent, would then decide according to 'British law, at the same time adapting his decisions to the usages and customs of the native law...' with local 'chiefs and councillors... as a sort of jury'.

In practice, the system of 'native magistrates' did not succeed, because a shortage of funds did not permit any of the appointed superintendents to have adequate staff, and only one of them had a reliable interpreter. Seven of the proposed locations were actually established (the number later reaching 42, with 21 mission reserves), and Shepstone was able to persuade the people to enter them peacefully. A general complaint from the white settlers was that the locations were too large. If a location was large enough to support its population, they argued, the 'natives' would remain in their 'superstitious and warlike' state, the power of their chiefs would be reasserted, and there would be a shortage of labour on white farms. Apart from proposing himself as a sort of judge of appeals, Shepstone envisaged the recognition of hereditary chiefs and the perpetuation, on his terms, of a modified form of clan existence. Chiefs were to be responsible for the maintenance of law and order in a system of indirect rule in which the Lieutenant-Governor was supreme chief, although Shepstone apparently believed that he himself was looked up to as a 'great chief' or 'father'.

When a minor chief, Fodo, threatened to attack another in 1847, Shepstone, at the head of a force of white and black soldiers, formally deposed Fodo and appointed his successor. He also imposed a fine of 500 cattle and 200 goats, thereby assuming the authority of both the Lieutenant-Governor and the Recorder in an action that he said 'produced a very great effect upon the minds of the Native population', and showed them 'that the Government intended to be supreme in its own territory, and that all independent action on the part of Chiefs and Tribes would be prohibited and punished'. To emphasise this, chiefs had 'to do homage to the Lieutenant-Governor'.

The following year a new flood of refugees, the Hlubi, poured into Natal under their leader Langalibalele after being attacked by Mpande for plundering royal cattle. The British established them in the Drakensberg foothills as a convenient buffer against troublesome San incursions.

The Boers trek north
Bitter and unhappy, the Afrikaners trekked back over the Drakensberg, resentful that their own land claims appeared to be subordinate to those of blacks and that the despised British principle of 'equality' was to be applied.

Colenso and the religious revolt

On Sunday, 5 June 1853, Theophilus Shepstone recorded in his diary 'a sensation'. Two rival clergymen named Fearne and Green had apparently preached what he called 'counter sermons'.

It is clear from this entry in Shepstone's diary that unity in the Anglican Church in Natal was in tatters even before the arrival of its first Bishop, controversial John William Colenso. The divide was between those who followed the new 'Anglo-Catholic' movement described by its opponents as 'leaning towards Rome', and the adherents to the doctrinal basis of the Church of England, as laid down in the 16th century. Bishop Robert Gray, known irreverently as 'the Pope of Cape Town', was senior Bishop and a pronounced Anglo-Catholic, while Colenso, whom Gray chose as first Bishop of Natal, held somewhat unorthodox and liberal theological views. He was, however, a brilliant academic and mathematician.

Colenso, after a preliminary 10-week visit to his new diocese, arrived in Natal to take up his position in 1855. From the first, he regarded himself as, primarily, a missionary Bishop, and learnt the Zulu language, producing his first 'elementary grammar' in the year of his arrival. He went on to translate the entire New Testament into Zulu, as well as parts of the Old Testament. His theological views, when published, alienated him from both camps within the church. One of his Zulu converts, William Ngide, while assisting in the translating of the Book of Genesis, queried whether it was literally true that Noah had been able to gather a pair of every living animal, from all over the world, and accommodate and feed them in his ark. 'My heart answered,' wrote Colenso, 'in the words of the prophet, "Shall a man speak lies in the name of the Lord?"'

Colenso's reply implied that much of the Old Testament was mythology, but illustrated certain truths. The first of seven volumes re-examining the first six Books of the Bible and published in 1862, it shocked orthodox believers and inspired the taunt that he had gone to Natal to convert the Zulu, but that they had converted him. Colenso was duly deposed by Bishop Gray, and locked out of his church by his own Dean – the same Green whom Shepstone recorded as preaching the 'counter sermon'. The colonial Supreme Court, however, ruled in favour of Colenso, and in the end it was Green who was obliged to leave. Gray sought to solve the problem by consecrating a new 'Bishop of Maritzburg', but Colenso retained many adherents.

His popularity among the Zulu, whose cause he championed incessantly, earned him the nickname of Sobantu, or 'father of the people', and the village of Commando Drift on the Thukela River was renamed in his honour. He continued to champion the Zulu cause until his death in 1883.

THIS CONTEMPORARY *cartoon accused Colenso of denying the Creation.*

THE BISHOP WHO GAVE UP MOSES, BUT STUCK TO THE PRO[...]

I
Mathematical Doctor Colenso
Read the Pentateuch quite in extenso
When he found up(Oh rare!) a non-ruminant Hare
The sensation produced was immense oh!

II
A Bishop there was of Zulu
Who quite longed to have nothing to do
So with fractions and figures – he puzzled the Niggers
And demolished the Faith of Zulu.

III
A Bishop there was of Natal
Who denied both Creation and Fall,
Cried the truthful? Zulus – when he told them the Ne[...]
"Well now believe nothing at all"!

A Supplementary Page to "the BOOK of NONSENSE."

IN THE LATE 1840s a considerable number of settlers arrived in Natal from Britain – filling the vacuum left by departing Boers who were unhappy at British rule. The newcomers arrived on ships such as the Lady Bruce (far right) and brought with them books like the 'Emigrant's Guide to Port Natal' (left).

It was to try to check this exodus that Governor Sir Harry Smith arrived in Natal early in 1848.

Smith dissolved the Locations Commission and appointed a Lands Commission (which included Afrikaners, but not Shepstone or any missionaries) to ensure that each trekker claimant received a farm, and that 'a distinct line' be drawn between black and white areas. The Lands Commission also made provision for excising portions of the existing locations for 'mission reserves' and unsuccessfully proposed a number of reductions in size.

A new wave of colonists

Despite these measures, few trekkers remained in Natal – and their place was taken by new settlers from England.

Between 1845-9, during West's tenure as Lieutenant-Governor, land allotment was chaotic. In the first place, Cloete had provisionally given out large tracts to Voortrekkers, most of whom left the colony after selling their holdings to absentee speculators, most of them Cape-based. Yet other land had been set aside as 'native locations' or assigned to white settlers. On the orders of the British Colonial Secretary, no title deeds could be issued until land had been correctly surveyed, but the Surveyor-General and his staff were occupied with the survey of plots in the urban areas of Pietermaritzburg, Durban and Weenen. In 1843, some 65 percent of Natal was claimed by Voortrekkers; a few years later almost 90 percent of this had been abandoned and was owned by Cape speculators, and 80 percent of 'landowners' had left Natal.

West died in 1849 and was succeeded in 1850 by Benjamin Pine who, while agreeing with Shepstone that absolute chieftainship was a 'tyranny', felt that the 'enormous and unwieldy' locations should be reduced in size. Pine also favoured a form of individual land tenure, and the introduction of a single legal and administrative system for all races. (Unlike at the Cape, customary law in Natal had the same status as Roman-Dutch law.) But many of Pine's ideas were opposed by Shepstone – and when Natal became a separate colony with limited representative government in 1856, it was Shepstone who became Secretary for Native Affairs.

The Natal constitution effectively denied the franchise to blacks, although, theoretically, a black man could obtain a vote. First, he had to be literate and the owner of fixed property. He could then petition the Lieutenant-Governor to be exempted from customary law, which was granted or denied at the Governor's discretion. If granted exemption, the man was placed under the restraints and penalties of Roman-Dutch law and, seven years later – provided he had resided in the colony for at least 12 years – he could apply to be registered as a voter. The application had to be accompanied by a certificate of recommendation endorsed by three white voters and signed by a Justice of the Peace. Again, the final arbiter was the Governor's discretion. In all, only three blacks were granted the vote during the existence of the Colony of Natal.

The change to wage labour

Although Natal had become a separate colony, its capitalist economy was still in its infancy. Edmund Morewood had produced the first Natal sugar in 1851, although survivors of a Portuguese shipwreck near the Mzimkulu in 1635 reported that blacks nearby were cultivating a type of sugar cane. Commercial farmers and planters complained incessantly about the shortage of (black) labour, blaming the Shepstonian system of large 'locations', which managed to retain intact the traditional African homestead system. This was the system in which the family, or extended family, lived in one settlement unit, maintaining close contact with other units, in order to regulate production and the barter of surplus.

An essential factor in the success of the homestead system was unrestricted access to land for grazing, cultivation and hunting. To re-establish themselves in Natal after the defeat of Dingane, Africans took part in hunting expeditions, especially for ivory. White traders supplied firearms and ammunition, and the hunters were entitled to a share in the ivory obtained, and usually took payment in cattle. Homesteads close to white towns or villages were successful in producing surplus crops for barter.

But while the homestead system remained viable, there was no reason for Africans to seek work on white farms – although attempts to force Africans onto the labour market included the imposition of a hut tax, a marriage tax and even a decree that no male was allowed to appear in Pietermaritzburg unless wearing trousers.

157

Gun law on a dozen frontiers

Much had changed in the 60-odd years that Britain had occupied the Cape Colony:
from a small outpost of a colonial monopoly, the Cape had grown into a regional power base,
surrounded by strong independent chiefdoms vying for land with the new Boer republics
of the Orange Free State and the Transvaal, and the fledgling British colony of Natal.
These chiefdoms soon learned that the only way to hold the colonists in check
was to fight fire with fire; and the gun became the most important currency on a dozen
troubled frontiers from the Soutspansberg to the Caledon valley.

IN THE MIDDLE of the last century a 19-year-old youth named Jonas Podumo said goodbye to his family in the Transvaal, wrapped a few essentials in his blanket and headed south towards the Cape Colony. He left the comparative security of his clan to walk hundreds of kilometres through difficult country in search of the most important thing a man could own in a dangerous and unpredictable world: a gun.

First, however, he had to get a job in order to earn the money with which to buy the gun; and he was hired by a farmer in the Colesberg district, staying for eight months. As was nearly always the case at the time, Podumo was not paid in cash, but with livestock: three calves and six sheep. He sold one calf, using the money to buy an 'old English soldier's gun'. Then, herding his sheep and remaining two calves ahead of him, he set off back to the Transvaal where he settled among the Pedi people.

Guns were vital in the shifting frontiers of southern Africa on the eve of diamond discoveries in the 1860s. Although the Cape Colony maintained a fair degree of law and order, the scattered African chiefdoms and Boer settlements generally did not, and the borders between the two were constantly in flux. In the north, towards the very limit of Boer penetration, the gun was vital for hunting and raiding – particularly for child labour; and later, when Africans learned that there was only one way effectively to counter the Boer threat to their land and children, thousands like Jonas Podumo made the long journey south to earn enough money to bring home a gun.

In addition to giving Africans a counter to Boer power, guns introduced many to migrant labour, forerunner of a system that remains with us to this day. Guns helped rebuild the Pedi power base in the Transvaal in the 1860s and '70s, leading Sir Garnet Wolseley to note in his diary during a visit to the north-eastern Transvaal that they had even persuaded Boers to 'recognise a master in the black man. This is shown in the number of Boers who in recent years have been paying taxes to Native Chiefs in consideration of being protected by them.'

His diary also sheds light on the transient nature of power in the northern Transvaal – where the Boers found themselves increasingly up against strongly developed chiefdoms. Trade links between these societies, particularly the Pedi, and the Portuguese at Delagoa Bay were already strongly established by the time the Boers began scouting and hunting in the northern and eastern Transvaal. Having survived a long period of disorder in the region, these chiefdoms were still strong enough to resist

A GROUP *of South Africa's first migrant workers make their way home after working on the farms of the Cape Colony. Like most migrant labourers, they were not usually paid in cash, but in kind – cattle and other livestock. The real object of making the long trip to the Cape and working for the white man, however, was the purchase of a firearm. The original title of this picture by Thomas Baines was 'Kaffirs leaving the Colony for their native seat, with all their acquired property'.*

UP UNTIL 1860 *there were no fewer than three Boer republics in the Transvaal, each run by independent-minded Voortrekkers. Frans Joubert (left) ruled in the eastern Transvaal around the town of Lydenburg; M W Pretorius (centre) ran the South* *African Republic in the south-west from Potchefstroom; and Stephanus Schoeman (right) and his followers fought against the Venda in the north in order to retain their tiny republic in the Soutpansberg.*

Boer incursions, and some made allies of the well-armed white men to settle old scores.

Africans also found themselves taking sides in Boer squabbles – where personal ambitions added to the divisions caused by distance. Until 1860 three distinct Boer quasi-republics existed in the Transvaal, and personal hostilities for a few years longer. M W Pretorius settled in the south-west, around Potchefstroom, and called his particular enclave the South African Republic. Another group of trekkers was concentrated around Lydenburg, under Frans Joubert, in the eastern Transvaal; while in the far north, the followers of Stephanus Schoeman battled against the Venda in the Soutspansberg. Although the Boers successfully won control of the southern and central Transvaal, by the late 1860s they were on the retreat against armed African resistance in the north. Thus it was that Boers who wished to remain in the area – mainly for hunting – were forced to pay tribute to the local chiefs.

Guns for bread
Other Africans were also acquiring guns – bought with the money they made from selling food to white traders, something many of them proved very good at. In the troubled eastern Cape region, for example, the Mfengu and others profited from selling agricultural produce to traders and settlers, adapting to the markets opened up by capitalism with ease. It was a trend which the authorities made some effort to foster, encouraging so-called peasant farming in areas such as the Kat River (see page 134) and elsewhere in the frontier region. But their efforts – and those of the African farmers – were to be undone, at first by land-hungry eastern Cape sheep farmers, and later by the attempts to force Africans to work for whites rather than produce a surplus on their own land.

It was the same in the Orange Free State (OFS) in the 1850s and '60s, where the Sotho farmers were the main suppliers of foodstuffs – going on to feed the rapidly increasing population of diggers who arrived in Griqualand West following the discovery of diamonds. In the 1870s and '80s it was the Tswana who fed the immigrant prospectors rather than the Boers, who were still mainly subsistence farmers. However, the capitalist economy, which first stimulated the growth of small African farmers by providing a market for food and cash crops, began to undermine them after the discovery of gold. Faced with new demands for a cheap workforce, the authorities began forcing African farmers off their land, leaving them with no alternative but to sell all they had left: their labour.

The centre of power
In 1870, when the Cape Colony could boast 200 000 white inhabitants, the two Afrikaner republics of the OFS and the Transvaal had a total of around 45 000, widely spread out and, especially in the recently unified Transvaal, only loosely governed. Although by far the strongest of the sub-continent's territories, the Cape Colony was beset by strife between western and eastern (Border) factions. The easterners favoured annexation of British Kaffraria to the Cape, as this would give them an additional four seats in parliament as well as the prospects of more land and labour, while the more conservative westerners, who controlled most of the capital, were opposed to any expansion that would lead to increased expenses. At the beginning of 1862 the Cape received a new Governor and High Commissioner, Philip Wodehouse, who favoured the expansionist policy of his predecessor, Sir George Grey, but was to find himself in almost continuous conflict with parliament, which he referred to as 'an infernal machine'.

159

The clash with Moshoeshoe

The Pedi trek south to seek guns brought a welcome windfall to the southern Sotho – through whose land they had to pass in order to reach the Cape. Travelling bags had to be refilled – and the Sotho were well placed to replenish the migrant workers' needs, at a price. This, and their sale of food to the scattered settlements of the OFS, ensured that plenty of guns found their way into the hands of Moshoeshoe, who saw to it that his men were armed with the best weapons he could obtain. Most of his 10 000 mounted men were armed with smooth-bore muskets, and some had the more modern and accurate Enfield rifles.

As a result he was able to provide stiff resistance to both Boer and British incursions into his territory. The boundary between Basutoland, an independent kingdom, and the former Orange River Sovereignty had been fixed by the so-called Warden Line of 1849, giving to the OFS a large tract of arable country that had been proclaimed as belonging to Moshoeshoe by Governor Napier in 1843 (see page 139). The British found, to their cost, that the only way to enforce the line was by force – and British troops had twice been defeated by Moshoeshoe. The OFS Boers, although more unified than the Transvaal trekkers, were no more successful, and were defeated by Moshoeshoe among his mountain strongholds in 1858.

The Treaty of Aliwal North that followed the war restored some of the land to Moshoeshoe, though many Basotho continued to live and to plant their crops on the 'wrong' side of the boundary and Boer incursions continued into his territory.

An appeal for protection

Once again threatened by the OFS, Moshoeshoe saw his salvation in appealing to the British for protection for Basutoland. For the time being, however, nothing was done, except to warn the OFS that hostile action against the Basotho might lead to Britain revoking the Bloemfontein Convention which had granted independence to the OFS Boers. However, when asked in 1862 to arbitrate in the border dispute, Governor Wodehouse declared himself in favour of the Warden Line, once again depriving the Basotho of territory. Basotho who were settled and farming north of the line were to be given time to reap their crops before moving but, in some cases, crops were burnt, cattle were driven off and huts destroyed.

Border troubles continued, and in June 1865 the OFS President J H Brand called out his commandos against Moshoeshoe. Wodehouse declared the Cape Colony to be neutral but, in practice, many men from the Cape as well as Natal went north to join the commandos, lured by the prospects of loot, or the grant of a free farm in conquered territory. The disillusioned High Commissioner wrote that 'Englishmen all along composed the main fighting element of the OFS Commandos'.

Natal's bid for land

The hostilities between the OFS and Basutoland gave Natal – then suffering from an acute labour shortage – an opportunity to obtain more territory and, with it, control over a potentially large labour force.

CAPE GOVERNOR *Sir Philip Edmond Wodehouse annexed Basutoland to the Crown in March 1868, in the face of strong competition from the Natal authorities.*

Early in the war, OFS burghers and some cattle were pursued by Basotho across the border and into Natal, where a Zulu was killed. This minor affair gave Natal the excuse to proclaim that it had been invaded, and to devise plans for the invasion of Basutoland (with a force composed mainly of African levies). Wodehouse, however, quickly forbade this action and, instead, imposed a fine of 10 000 cattle on Moshoeshoe.

PRESIDENT *of the Orange Free State, Johannes Henricus Brand, called out his commandos against Moshoeshoe in 1865 – and many Englishmen from the Cape, hungry for loot, joined in, despite their government's decision to adopt a neutral stand.*

Covetous eyes were also watching from the Transvaal – and the death of a Transvaal volunteer serving with the OFS commandos gave the Transvaal an excuse to enter the war, and Paul Kruger arrived at the head of 300 men.

The initial popularity of the war among the colonists soon gave way to resentment against the OFS as trade, already in the doldrums, suffered a serious decline, especially in the eastern Cape and Natal. In Grahamstown the 'Anglo-African', while expressing sympathy for the OFS, nevertheless criticised it for not taking into account even the basic needs of the Basotho. 'The OFS people seem never to have thought of this – never to have thought of anything in fact, beyond extermination of the black races, or their perpetual subjugation to their dominion.' The 'Natal Witness' expressed dismay at the loss of life and property, and condemned the Boers' wanton destruction of Basotho crops, which had led to thousands of Basotho entering Natal to barter livestock for cereals.

Having received no response to his appeal for British protection from Wodehouse, Moshoeshoe despairingly proposed in July 1866 that his country be annexed to Natal. Eager to accept, Natal Native Affairs Secretary Theophilus Shepstone wrote that, if annexation were effected, 'we should be in a position to dictate measures to all the neighbouring tribes'. To him, this was an important step in the expansion of British influence, as well as his personal authority. To Wodehouse, Shepstone's attitude represented an attempt to usurp his own authority as High Commissioner, and he was reluctant to proceed any further with the matter.

Undefeated in the field, despite artillery bombardment to which they were unable to reply, the Basotho were desperately short of supplies and munitions, and Moshoeshoe was obliged to sue for peace, which was established by the Treaty of Thaba Bosiu early in 1866. In terms of the treaty, the OFS claimed a large slice of Basotho land, which became known as the Conquered Territory, in which several hundred farms were granted in January 1867. The farms were not occupied, however, and Basotho returned to the territory and planted there as they had done in the past. Within a few months, OFS commandos were riding about destroying the growing crops, and war broke out again. The Basotho concentrated on defending the high ground and mountains, while the commandos tried to force a victory by destroying their food supplies. Moshoeshoe appealed again to Natal for aid.

Protection at last

The petition from Moshoeshoe, together with supporting memoranda from Shepstone, Natal traders and businessmen, and Lieutenant-Governor Robert Keate, was forwarded to London, with careful emphasis that the proposed annexation was for the sake of security, and not merely to acquire more territory. But the Natal Government felt that, once annexed, Basutoland should not 'remain purely a native Colony, but that certain portions of the land be made available for white settlers'. Natal was eager to expand by annexation, despite the warning that Britain would provide neither financial nor military support. Wodehouse, warned by his agents and missionaries that most of their arable land had already been taken from the Basotho by the OFS, and suspicious of Shepstone's ambitions, was vigorously opposed to the Natal scheme. Although instructed by the Secretary of State for the Colonies to enter into negotiations with Natal, he disregarded this, and announced in March 1868 that Basutoland had been annexed to the Crown.

When commandos continued to destroy crops and wage sporadic warfare, Wodehouse impounded all arms and ammunition bound for the OFS through ports in the Cape or Natal and sent a detachment of the Frontier Armed and Mounted Police to occupy the Conquered Territory. The Secretary of State reluctantly agreed to accept the annexation, but warned that Wodehouse should not risk a war with the OFS. Consequently, at a series of meetings in Aliwal North in which the Basotho themselves were neither present nor directly represented, Wodehouse and Brand came to terms, which included the retention by the OFS of most of the Conquered Territory. Deprived of much of their agricultural and grazing-lands, many Basotho were obliged to enter the labour markets of the white territories that bordered on their country. The founder of the nation, Moshoeshoe, died in 1870 and was buried on the heights of Thaba Bosiu, his home and his fortress that had never been conquered.

MOSHOESHOE, *the man who had kept Basotho independence intact for 40 years, died in his mountain home in 1870.*

Colenso

Diamonds, gold and war 1868-1902

*'This diamond is the rock upon which
the future success of South Africa will be built.'*
Richard Southey, Colonial Secretary of the Cape

After months of curiosity and doubt, the matter was finally settled. The pebble picked up on a farm on the banks of the Orange River near Hopetown was the real thing – a diamond.

And southern Africa would never be the same again.

The discovery of diamonds, and then gold, brought immense changes to the sub-continent, turning it from a forgotten corner of the British Empire into a fount of wealth to rival that ultimate jewel in the imperial crown: India.

Yet at first no one believed that southern Africa held the key to such immense wealth. The glittering bauble that so excited Richard Southey eventually found its way to England and a wall of scepticism. Southern Africa, said the experts, did not look like diamond country.

This time, however, the experts were wrong – and a stampede of adventurers was soon scratching over the dark red earth of what is now the northern Cape as more and more glittering prizes tumbled into the sorting trays. The biggest find of all was on a hillside just outside the present-day town of Kimberley.

But the days of the small prospector rapidly drew to a close. As diamonds became harder to find, the thousands of small claim-owners were forced into alliances and partnerships in order to pool resources in an effort to mine more inaccessible areas of the earth. Out of these alliances grew the corporate giants who were to become household names in the new South Africa – ruthless, powerful men such as Cecil Rhodes, Barney Barnato, Alfred Beit and many others.

When gold was discovered – first in patchy seams in the eastern Transvaal and then in an apparently endless, slanting reef under the Witwatersrand – these were the men who already had access to the money, skills and resources needed to exploit the new Eldorado.

The Witwatersrand gold had to be extracted from very low grade ore mined from increasingly awkward depths as the reef slanted into the earth. This required two vital ingredients: capital to purchase or develop the complex technology required for deep-level mining; and labour – not hundreds, not thousands, but hundreds of thousands of workers prepared to face the hardships and danger of life underground at pitifully low wages.

Migrant labour was not new to southern Africa. For two decades before the discovery of diamonds, Pedi from the eastern Transvaal had walked to the Cape Colony to earn money to buy firearms. Diamonds paid better than farming – and soon tens of thousands of Pedi and other Africans were heading for the diamond fields, where Rhodes and his colleagues introduced closed compounds to house them – to ensure that they did not desert or steal diamonds.

But the labour requirements of the diamond fields were chicken feed compared with deep-level gold mining. Only a radical change in the Transvaal's still largely rural – and in most cases subsistence – economy could hope to provide the gold barons with the workers they needed. And, with a view to long-term investment, it became apparent that Paul Kruger's South African Republic, although willing to introduce changes, would not allow itself to be dictated to by the imperialists.

At the same time, Britain's position as the centre of world commerce – which it desperately needed to maintain to ward off the rise of German and US industries – was being threatened by a severe drop in the Bank of England's gold reserves. Britain had easily secured the diamond fields of Griqualand West, brushing aside the Orange Free State's claim, but the Witwatersrand was clearly slap bang in the middle of the Boer republic in the Transvaal.

An attempt at intervention by a swashbuckling sidekick of Rhodes called Leander Jameson ended ignominiously for the British. But in the last years of the 1890s, with a golden light beckoning at the end of the tunnel, Britain threw the weight of the empire behind the interventionists, using the grievances of British mineworkers living in the Transvaal to whip up public feeling at home.

In the end the British Government got what it wanted – a society better tuned to the requirements of the capitalist future than an agrarian past, over which the Union Jack could fly unhindered.

Labour – and the difficulties of getting it – dominated southern Africa during the second half of the 19th century; and yet very little credence was given to the golden rule of capitalism: that workers will sell their labour only if the reward is adequate. Instead, the bosses – farmers and mine-owners – preferred coercion to get Africans to work for them. The favourite strategy was to strip the African of his livelihood – the land on which he farmed – so leaving him no alternative but to sell all he had left: the labour of his hands. (From a white point of view, an added bonus was that the land he had been forced to quit became available for settlement.) Other methods included taxation – forcing Africans to earn money to pay the taxes – and employing worker/tenants, African families allowed to 'squat' on white-owned farms in return for their labour.

There was very little of non-colonial Africa left by this time – and with the annexation of South West Africa by Germany, and with Bechuanaland, Rhodesia and Pondoland coming under the British flag, at the end of the century no part of southern Africa was ruled by the people to whom it had once belonged.

Diamonds and gold

1867	Pebble found near Hopetown verified as 21,2 carat diamond; sparks diamond rush.
1870-1	Short-lived Diggers Republic on Vaal River.
1870	At least 10 000 diggers at 'river diggings' alo Vaal; discoveries on farms Bultfontein and Dorstfontein lead to abandonment of many alluvial diggings.
1871	New diamond diggings at De Beer brothers' farm Vooruitzicht; then at Colesburg Kopje (Beers New Rush).
	First gold strike in eastern Transvaal by Edward Button.
	Strikes at Eersteling and Murchison Range.
	Griqua claim to Griqualand West recognised after tussle with SAR and Orange Free State (c
1872	First elementary hospital opened in Kimber
1873	Richard Southey appointed Lieutenant-Governor of Griqualand West. Population at diamond diggings over 50 000.
	International diamond price slump.
	Railway link between Cape and diamond fie mooted.
	Cape Government buys Cape Town-Welling railway.
1875	Combined Diggers' Association called to arr Black Flag Rebellion, white miners refuse to disarm.
1880	Twelve joint-stock diamond mining companies formed; Rhodes and Rudd buy small claims, form De Beers Mining Compa
1881	59 more joint-stock companies formed.
	Banks withdraw credit; crash in share price
1883	Reverend Gwayi Tyamzashe, the last black t hold claim at Dutoitspan, loses claim.
1885	Cape to Kimberley line completed.
1886	George Harrison discovers part of Main Reef farm Langlaagte.
1887	Chamber of Mines formed to promote intere of mine-owners.
1888	Rhodes acquires control of all Kimberley m

Land and labour

1870s	Diamond mining stimulates migrant labour.
1870s and 1880s	African crop and sheep farmers in eastern Cape and elsewhere; very successful.
1871	India halts emigration to Natal after adverse reports; Natal commission of enquiry leads to protective laws.
c1872	Kokstad founded in Griqualand East.
1874	Orpen declared British Resident in charge of government of Griqualand East.
	India once again permits emigration to Natal.
1875	Adam Kok III dies and Griqua community in No Man's Land begins to disintegrate.
1879	Griqualand East annexed to Cape.
1877-8	Gcaleka-Mfengu conflict over land leads to war.
1878	Western Pondoland chief Nqwiliso sells land to Cape Government under pressure.
1879	War to subdue Pedi and dispossess them of land.
1879-97	Zululand partitioned and dismembered, then annexed.
1880	Former indentured indians hold 30 out of 37 retail trading licences held by Durban Indians.
1883	Kruger opens Lewis and Marks' distillery on Rand – adverse affects on African labour soon felt.
1884	Basutoland made British High Commission territory.
1885	Eastern Pondoland chief Mdlangaso grants land concession to Emil Nagel.
	Phylloxera lays waste Cape winelands, labourers leave land; wine farmers increase wages to entice back labour.
1886	Migrant labour stimulated by discovery of gold on Rand.
	Carl von Brandis proclaims 'public diggings' on Rand; Johannesburg born.
	'The Diggers' News and 'Witwatersrand Advertiser' first published.
1888	Party of Germans in eastern Pondoland arouses Cape fears; British Resident sent to monitor activities.
1889	Rinderpest appears in far North Africa.
c1890	Depression sets in when conventional gold recovery process becomes unproductive.
1892	African peasantry in Transkeian territories openly defy headmen.
	Cape first warned about rinderpest epidemic.
1893	Mohandas Gandhi arrives in Natal.
	Ndebele raid against Rhodesian 'pioneers'; attempts to cut off labour supply to mines.
1893-96	Ndebele forced to give up more than 100 000 head of cattle to Rhodes' British South Africa Company.
1894	Capital of Ndebele, Bulawayo, sacked by British South Africa Company forces and becomes 'white' settlement. Death of Ndebele chief Lobengula.
	Glen Grey Act passed in Cape to control African labour and land; extended to four districts of Transkei.
1895	South African Republic (SAR) volksraad (parliament) limits to five the number of African squatter families allowed on white farms.
1896	Ndebele rebellion against mining settlements in Rhodesia; Shona rebellion put down by 1897.
1897	Rinderpest reaches southern Africa.
1897-1902	African miners' earnings drop by 40 percent.

Politics, imperialism, nationalism

1868	Rhenish missionaries in German South West Africa (SWA) appeal to Prussia for protection against Africans.
1870	Moshoeshoe dies.
1871	Tiyo Soga dies.
1872	Cape Colony granted responsible government.
	Cape begins extending control over Transkeian territories.
	Mpande dies; succeeded by Cetshwayo.
1875	Genootskap van Regte Afrikaners (Association of True Afrikaners) formed.
1876	'Die [Afrikaanse] Patriot' newspaper established.
1877	SAR annexed by Britain.
1877-8	Cape-Xhosa war.
1877-80	Afrikaner political consciousness and resistance movement spurred by SAR annexation.
1878	Walvis Bay proclaimed British territory.
	Bartle Frere delivers ultimatum to Zulu as pretext for annexation.
1879	Start of Anglo-Zulu war.
	Afrikaner Bond formed in the Cape.
	Combined British-Swazi force crushes Pedi.
1880	Cetshwayo captured and imprisoned in Cape Town.
	Cape annexes Griqualand West.
	'Gun War' in Basutoland leads to fall of Sprigg Government.
	Transvaal Afrikaners declare their independence; war breaks out with Britain.
1881	British force defeated by Boers at Majuba.
	J T Jabavu becomes editor of mission newspaper 'Isigidimi Sama-Xhosa' ('Xhosa Express')
	Transvaal Boers win back large measure of independence in terms of Pretoria Convention.
	Pedi king Sekhukhune murdered by Mampuru.
1882	Boers proclaim republics of Stellaland and Goshen in Tswana territory.
1883	Cetshwayo returns to a partitioned Zululand.
	Kruger becomes president of SAR.
	J T Jabavu opens own newspaper, 'Imvo Zabantsundu' ('Native Opinion').
1884	Cetshwayo dies; New Republic declared on Zulu land.
	German flag raised at Angra Pequena in SWA.
1885	Warren expeditionary force into Bechuanaland ends Boer republics of Stellaland and Goshen; southern Bechuanaland becomes British colony, northern part remains a protectorate.
1887	Britain annexes Zululand; Dinuzulu exiled to St Helena.
	Cape Parliament passes Parliamentary Voters' Registration Act to limit African voting rights.
	First uitlander protest associations formed in SAR.
1888	'Rudd concession' signed by Lobengula.
1889	German force lands at Walvis Bay.
1890	Kruger establishes second volksraad for uitlanders.
	Rhodes forms British South Africa Company to exploit 'Rudd concession'.
	Rhodes becomes Cape Prime Minister.
1891	German headquarters set up at Windhoek.
1891-2	Railways from Cape and Natal reach SAR.
1892	Cape Franchise and Ballot Act triples property qualifications for the vote, excluding many Africans.
1894	Pondoland annexed to the Cape.
	Uitlander question hots up; Cape Governor Loch tests opinions on armed uprising against Kruger Government.
	Joseph Chamberlain becomes British Colonial Secretary.
1895-6	Dr L S Jameson, Administrator of Mashonaland, moves to Pitsani for raid on SAR; raid ends in failure.
1896-7	Rinderpest in SWA leads to Herero rebellion.
1897	'Nkosi Sikilel' iAfrica' composed by Enoch Sontonga.
	Alfred Milner becomes Governor of the Cape and High Commissioner for southern Africa.
	Natal annexes Zululand.
1898	A K Soga starts 'Izwi Labantu' newspaper.
1899	South African War breaks out.
	Kgatla take up arms against Boers; Louis Trichardt razed by Venda.
1900	Roberts, Kitchener and British reinforcements arrive.
	OFS annexed to Crown as Orange River Colony.
	British enter Johannesburg, then Pretoria; guerrilla war begins.
	Louis Botha becomes Commandant-General of SAR forces.
	Kruger goes into exile.
	SAR becomes British colony of Transvaal.
	First 'refugee camps', then 'concentration camps' set up.
1902	31 May, peace signed at Pretoria.

The bauble that built a boom

In 1868 a distinguished British geologist was asked to investigate a number of reported diamond finds in the Orange River region of southern Africa. 'The geological character of that part of the county renders it impossible . . . that any could have been discovered,' he reported. But for once the experts were wrong – and the prospectors right; and within a few years the arid plains of Griqualand West were bursting with diamond-hungry diggers. The impact on southern Africa was immense – turning the region from a poor, agricultural and colonial backwater into a promised fount of still-untapped riches.

FOR THE TWO JACOBS CHILDREN, Erasmus and Louisa, it was just a toy: a shiny pebble picked up on their neighbour's farm, De Kalk, near the south bank of the Orange River not far from Hopetown. To John O'Reilly, a passing trader and transport rider who was given the bauble by farmer Schalk van Niekerk, it looked quite different.

He first took it to Hopetown, where local storekeepers dismissed the pebble as worthless – although one ventured that it might be topaz – and O'Reilly took it on south to Colesberg, where the acting Civil Commissioner, thinking it might be a diamond, tested it on a pane of glass.

The test proved positive – but failed to impress the sceptics; so the pebble was sent in an unsealed envelope to a Grahamstown doctor who asked a local jeweller for an opinion. Definitely a diamond, was the reply, and a handsome 21,25 carats at that. From Grahamstown the stone found its way to Richard Southey, the Colonial Secretary of the Cape, who forecast somewhat pompously: 'This diamond is the rock upon which the future success of South Africa will be built.'

It was 1867 – and although it was to be a few more years before the scramble for diamonds became a stampede, it marked a turning point in southern Africa's development from a rural, forgotten corner dominated by the British Empire to a depository of riches that in time would touch the lives of nearly everyone in the sub-continent.

More discoveries quickly followed, mainly in the flat and arid territory that was to become Griqualand West – which extends north from the Orange River to the Botswana border – particularly at the so-called 'river diggings' along the Vaal River – and by 1870 it was estimated that there were at least 10 000 diggers, most of them spread along the banks of the Vaal River, from its confluence with the Orange to Klipdrift (later Barkly West), a distance of about 160 kilometres. Besides prospectors from southern Africa, others, mainly from the United States of America, brought to bear on the new industry valuable experience gained in California and Australia.

In the latter part of 1870, discoveries between the Vaal and Modder rivers led to many of the river diggings being abandoned, as diggers 'rushed' the new areas on the farms Bultfontein and Dorstfontein. The heat and drought, with difficulties of obtaining water, made conditions unpleasant, and news of large finds at the river drew many back again. Early in 1871 a new digging was established on the farm Vooruitzicht, owned by Johannes and Diederik

de Beer, and this was followed within a few months by a fabulously rich find at Colesberg Kopje – the top of an ancient pipe of diamondiferous lava which grew into the deepest man-made hole in the world: De Beers New Rush – later the Kimberley Mine.

The territory of Griqualand West was claimed, not only by the Griqua, who had lived there for close to 70 years, but also by the Orange Free State (OFS) and the South African Republic (SAR)(see page 168). A court of arbitration, presided over by Robert Keate, Lieutenant-Governor of Natal, found in favour of the Griqua, whose chief, Nicolaas Waterboer, was persuaded to ask the British Government for protection. Griqualand West became a separate Crown Colony in 1871 and was formally annexed to the Cape in 1880. (For a short while the diggers had actually proclaimed their own republic under their 'president', Stafford Parker, a former seaman.) With the acquisition of colonial status, the rapidly growing mining village took the name of Kimberley, after the British Colonial Secretary.

Living conditions for the fortune-seekers on the dry diggings were uncomfortable and unhealthy. Many lived in tents, or in shacks constructed of wood and canvas, with

THE FLAG *of the short-lived Vaal River Diggers Republic flies over a trading store, canteen and diamond buyer's office at Klipdrift in* 1870.

THE MEN *who first uncovered the fabulous wealth of the Colesberg Kopje called themselves the 'Red Cap' Company – with matching headgear to prove it. Their leader was Fleetwood Rawstorne, the son of a Colesberg magistrate (left), who named the small hill – later to become famous as the largest man-made hole in the world – after his home town. The first three diamonds at the Kopje were, in fact, found by Rawstorne's African cook, Damon.*

practically no furniture. There were no sanitary services, and deaths from fever were frequent, even after the opening of an elementary hospital in 1872. In some areas it cost 10 cents a month for two buckets of muddy water daily, in others a single bucketful might cost two-and-a-half cents. Supplies came by ox wagon from Cape Town (six weeks) or Port Elizabeth (four weeks). Coaching companies flourished, such as the Gibson brothers' Red Star Line, which operated from the railhead at Wellington and reached Kimberley via Beaufort West in about seven days.

By 1873 the population of the workings exceeded 50 000, of whom about half were white. Not all had the cash to purchase a claim, and there evolved the system of share-working. A practical digger would be approached by the claim-owner with a view to his working the claim. Once agreement was reached, the digger hired labourers, for whose pay he was responsible, and, in return for a percentage of the value of the diamonds found, set to work.

The digger faced a number of problems once the sterile overburden was removed to reveal the diamond-bearing gravel. His absence from the claim invited theft, or his labourers might be persuaded by buyers – both licensed and illegal – to conceal diamonds for secret sale. Even as share-workers, two men often formed a loose partnership in which one man would supervise work in the claim, while the other would attend to the sorting of the gravel. There was always the fear that the claim-owner might sell his claim to an active miner, or employ blacks, at a much lower rate, in place of whites.

Blacks on the mines

Colonial Africans and 'other persons of colour' were entitled to buy digger's licences, although most of them were allotted claims in the relatively poor Bultfontein and Dutoitspan mines. The African and coloured miners, as opposed to labourers or servants, were always resented by the whites. It was argued that blacks who had digger's licences could legally sell diamonds that they had stolen

from the claims of whites, although no statistics for such thefts were ever produced. It was also asserted that, since black miners could employ servants, a large number of undesirable 'vagrants' would obtain Passes entitling them to be on the diggings. All servants were supposed to be registered, but in practice this applied only to blacks, who had to carry Passes at all times.

After the annexation of Griqualand West in 1871, equal rights were supposed to be extended to all British citizens, but (white) diggers' committees petitioned the local government to permit the diggings to be controlled by the diggers themselves. The Government Commissioners, after white miners had rioted and burnt tents and a number of liquor stores following allegations of diamond theft, met

BEFORE *the railway reached Kimberley, the fastest way to travel was by the Gibson brothers' mail coach.*

The struggle to control the diamond fields

The discovery of diamonds in Griqualand West brought to a head a wrangle over the ownership of the wealthy land – disputed between the Cape Colony, the two Boer territories of the OFS and the South African Republic (SAR), and the Griqua leader Nicolaas Waterboer.

Waterboer was fortunate to have as his agent David Arnot, the shrewd son of a Scottish artisan and his Khoikhoi wife, who claimed that the southern boundary of Griqua territory was the course of the Orange River between Kheis and Ramah, and that the eastern boundary (with the OFS) was a line from Ramah to Platberg, passing through the marked grave known as Davidsgraf at the confluence of the Modder and Riet rivers. This was based on a supposed treaty between Andries Waterboer and Adam Kok that pre-dated the Bloemfontein Convention of 1854, whereby the OFS' boundary had been defined as further west. Arnot also claimed a northern and western boundary that would give the Griqua land claimed by the SAR.

The Cape and British governments took no action, but in 1863 the OFS authorities asked the Cape Governor, Sir Philip Wodehouse, to mediate in the matter. By a series of delaying tactics, Arnot had the matter postponed indefinitely but, a few years later, when diamonds were found, he persuaded the Cape Colonial Secretary, Richard Southey, to his views. By then, a new Governor, Sir Henry Barkly, had taken office, and he allowed himself to be convinced by Arnot's arguments. The Cape Parliament, not realising the extent and wealth of the diamond deposits, was against annexation of the troublesome territory. Barkly, however, managed to persuade all claimants to submit to the decision of an arbitrator, who was to be Robert Keate, the Lieutenant-Governor of Natal. Arnot was able to manipulate the proceedings, with the result that the Keate Award favoured Waterboer, and Griqualand West was proclaimed to be British territory.

After a meeting with Waterboer, who was represented by Arnot, the Presidents of the OFS and SAR remained unconvinced, and issued proclamations asserting their claims to sections of the territory, including – in the case of the OFS – the 'dry diggings'. From a study of the map, it was clear that the diggings lay east of the Ramah-Davidsgraf-Platberg line in OFS territory, and President Johannes Brand wrote a note of protest to the British Colonial Secretary, the Earl of Kimberley, to point this out. Kimberley immediately contacted Barkly who, alarmed now at having accepted Arnot's claims at face value, ordered a new survey.

A hasty survey by G Gilfillan, a land surveyor working on the diggings, 'bent' the boundary slightly from Davidsgraf to Platberg, but failed to place the diggings within Griqualand West. The newly appointed Surveyor-General of Griqualand West, Francis Orpen, was instructed to resurvey the disputed boundary line and to report 'officially, and in confidence' whether the 'dry diggings' lay to the east or west of it. In earlier correspondence with Brand, Barkly had referred to 'Platberg, on the Vaal River', yet, in fixing his beacons, Orpen ignored the real Davidsgraf and placed it several kilometres east, and used, not Platberg, but Paardeberg, which is not 'on the Vaal River' and is also east of Platberg. Paardeberg thereby became Platberg. The annexation was not repealed.

GRIQUA LEADER *Nicolaas Waterboer defied Boer claims to his territory.*

Brand made a last effort, by going to London to plead his case. In this he was unsuccessful, but the British Government paid the OFS £90 000 on the condition that it dropped its claims. Embittered, Brand was obliged to concede. As his reward, Arnot received some 37 farms with river frontage, as well as payment of £4 000 for 'services rendered' and a pension of £500 a year.

WATERBOER'S *agent David Arnot was a shrewd negotiator.*

CAPE GOVERNOR *Sir Henry Barkly annexed the diamond diggings for Britain.*

representatives of the diggers. An outcome of the meeting was the suspension of all licences held by blacks, who might then reapply for a licence, in writing and supported by the signatures of five 'respectable' white diggers. The Cape Governor, Sir Henry Barkly, however, declared that this was against 'reason and justice', and invalidated the Commissioners' decision. Barkly also appointed a Lieutenant-Governor of the new colony – Richard Southey, formerly the Colonial Secretary of the Cape.

One of Southey's ordinances was to limit to 10 the number of claims that could be owned by a single individual or company. This protected the smaller worker against the growth of companies, but Southey also supported the right of claim-ownership for blacks. Blacks were also permitted to take part, for their own account, in a new form of diamond recovery, the sorting of 'debris' or soil dumps discarded as sterile. Because debris-sorting required virtually no capital, it became a particularly attractive proposition.

But blacks nevertheless soon lost their claims: the last black to hold a claim at Dutoitspan was the Reverend Gwayi Tyamzashe in 1883. At the river diggings, however, blacks continued to work their own claims until well into the 20th century.

The rise of migrant labour

For more than two decades before the discovery of diamonds, Pedi from the north-eastern Transvaal had made the long journey southwards – a walk of some two weeks or longer – to find work on farms in the Cape Colony or on government works such as road-building. By the 1850s, Tsonga ('Shangaan') from Mozambique sought work in Natal and by 1870 south Sotho were at work on farms in the OFS. The discovery of diamonds made huge new demands for labour – with an enormous increase in the number of migrant Africans travelling to and from the diamond workings. In the early years, the only regulating factors were the control of chiefs, and 'tribal' policy and strategy; such as in 1876 when, in response to an attack by the Transvaal Boers under President Burgers, the paramount chief of the Pedi, Sekhukhune, called his subjects back from the diamond fields, and more than 6 000 returned home.

Between 1871 and 1875 an estimated 50 000 Africans arrived every year at the mine workings, with the same number leaving each year. Generally, the main reasons behind the desire to work for cash wages were to acquire firearms or basic farming implements, or to raise the traditional bride-price. The Pedi, in particular, required firearms to counter the potential threats of Zulu, Boer and Swazi militarism and, having no surplus cattle, were obliged to obtain firearms by labour. The south Sotho (Basotho), however, sometimes traded cattle or grain for colonial and imported products, and firearms. The weapons most commonly obtained were Tower Enfield muzzle-loaders at £4, and the breech-loading Snider modification at £12.

Rates of pay for a black labourer were between 10 and 30 shillings a week, including a daily ration of mealie-meal and some 500 grams of meat a week. Vegetables were generally in short supply – for whites as well as blacks. Wages in Kimberley were higher than anywhere else in southern Africa, including the alluvial goldfields of the eastern Transvaal, and there was also the chance of receiving a bonus on the finding of an especially valuable diamond, or by theft and illicit sale. Whites also worked as labourers, and were paid more than blacks, not merely because of the assumed inherent superiority of the white, but because, in many cases, of their practical superiority based on a lifetime of work as labourers or 'navvies'. In the artisan class, whites received a daily wage of around £2 while 'persons of colour' were paid from £2 to £4 a week, with food and lodging.

ONE YEAR *after the discovery of diamonds, Colesberg Kopje was already on its way to becoming the 'Big Hole'.*

ACCOMMODATION *in the early days of the diamond diggings was anything but luxurious – even for the Lieutenant-Governor of the new colony of Griqualand West, Richard Southey, whose first 'camp' consisted of a prefabricated hut and a wagon.*

Black labourers were contracted to work for the same employer – usually for a period of between three and six months. The south Sotho, known as 'Moshesh's people', generally worked for three months, while Natal Africans, coming from much further afield, stayed for six, and were regarded as the best workers.

In the early years, the labourers lived on the small patch of land occupied by their employer, close to his claim. As an air of permanence and confidence grew in the late 1870s, whites began to build in brick, at some distance from the claims, and, as the average work-crew grew, their black labourers congregated in a different place that eventually became an open compound. In the Kimberley Mine, prior to the introduction of mechanisation, the usual work-crew consisted of 15 labourers, of whom five were involved in sorting the soil that the others had dug, loaded into buckets, and hoisted to the surface. Labourers were expected to be on site at sunrise and to work until sunset.

Once registered as a labourer to a particular employer, a black labourer was obliged to work for the period of his contract. Although desertion was a crime, relatively few deserters were caught. The commonest reasons for desertion were poor wages, non-payment of wages, the brutality of employers, the dangers (especially the collapse of side walls) of working a particular claim, and the shortage of food. To most employers, however, desertion signified only one thing – theft. The laid-down punishment for diamond theft was one year's hard labour and 50 lashes. In law, too, diggers were allowed to search the property of their employees with the presumption that any diamond so found was stolen. Physical punishment was undoubtedly and illegally meted out by employers for a variety of annoyances such as working too slowly or for carelessness.

The Black Flag Rebellion

As the more easily recoverable diamonds grew scarcer, so recovery costs increased. Finance houses did not, in general, care to advance the large sums required to individual diggers. World-wide depression and the flooding of the European market with Brazilian diamonds added to the insecurity of diggers. Diamond prices fell, yet the diggers were obliged to sell at the lower prices rather than wait for better times, as they needed the constant injection of work-

ing capital. Many diggers left for the new goldfields of Mac-Mac and Pilgrim's Rest in the eastern Transvaal, while those who remained grew increasingly insecure as it was realised that profitability could be maintained only by the consolidation of claims. Owners of land on which the diggings lay charged ever-increasing rentals.

Diggers were plagued, too, by increasing taxes and by what they regarded as diminishing control over their African labourers, who they said had forced up wages and lived where they chose. Southey refused to proclaim separate areas for occupation by the various races. And then, in March 1875, following torrential rains, only about half the claims in the Kimberley Mine could be worked. The others were flooded or covered by collapsed, unproductive walling. It was in this month that the Combined Diggers' Association called out its members under arms.

Southey's police force was hopelessly inadequate, and the armed diggers claimed to be assuming the functions of the police. Black and white diggers, under the same pressures, failed to form a united front, but split along racial lines, with armed whites attacking blacks in the streets. Southey sent to Cape Town for British troops. When his police managed to arrest a wrong-doer, the diggers prevented his imprisonment by barring the entrance to the

AS THE DIGGINGS *at Kimberley went deeper, each claimant set up his own pulley to extract the diamond-bearing ore.*

jail with several hundred armed men. At the same time, a black flag, 'a signal of mourning, desolation and unity', was raised on a debris dump known as Mount Ararat.

A deputation of the Diggers' Association travelled to Cape Town to see Governor Barkly, who demanded that they disband and surrender their weapons in return for a general amnesty for all except the ringleaders. The deputation returned to Kimberley, where a full meeting insisted that all rebels should be pardoned, and refused to give up their arms 'in the presence of so many armed niggers'. It was agreed, though, that the association would disband.

When the 1st Battalion of the 24th Regiment marched into Kimberley, one of its officers recorded, 'to our disgust, the rebellion had subsided, and the force was received with great enthusiasm by the inhabitants'. Southey was retired on a fairly handsome pension, blacks soon lost their right to own claims and, five years later, Griqualand West, where the era of the small miner had passed, was annexed to the Cape Colony.

The concentration of power

For the pioneer diggers of Kimberley, wealth depended on producing as many diamonds as possible within the shortest possible time. For the dealer, however, this raised the danger of over-production and a consequent fall in diamond prices. During a period of international financial instability in 1873, prices did fall, exposing the hazards that threatened to overwhelm the diamond industry. Individu-

---

Getting at the diamonds

The fantastic riches discovered underneath the Colesberg Kopje just outside present-day Kimberley were split into hundreds of small claims – at first organised among the diggers themselves, and then laid out according to a grid devised by the Orange Free State's Government Surveyor, Albert Ortlepp, who insisted that they should be broken up by 14 strips, or roadways, each some 4,5 metres wide, running along a north-south axis. The roadways were to provide access as well as sites for lifting-equipment, but the diggers resented the loss of workable ground and frequently came to blows over the moving of claim pegs. Nominally, each claim was 31 feet (9,5 metres) by 31 feet, but on one side of each claim

a strip of 2,25 metres went to form half of the width of the roadway, and was not to be worked.

The roadway system might have worked well had not the mine extended to a depth greater than expected, when the sides of the roadways collapsed into the workings. Although only 500 claims were allotted, diggers sold halves, quarters or even sixteenths of their claims so that, soon, there were about 1 600 owner-diggers at work. Working space was desperately crowded, a problem partially solved by the employment of fewer labourers and the removal of sorting tables and sieves to a position outside the mine. A digger who originally pegged a claim was required to pay only a licence fee of 10 shillings (R1)

per month, but could sell his rights to the claim for whatever he could get – and some got as much as £15 000.

On the surface lay a 2-metre thickness of reddish soil that sometimes contained diamonds, followed, in some places, by a thin layer of limestone. Below this a layer of yellow, diamond-bearing soil extended for some 20 metres, gradually darkening to a blueish colour. At variable levels was the so-called 'floating reef' of extremely hard rock that often collapsed into workings as it was undermined. A 'reef tariff' was imposed to cover the costs of its removal. The 'blue ground', or kimberlite, which was worked on the open-cast system to a depth of 365 metres below the surface before underground mining took over, also proved diamondiferous, although many diggers sold out when they reached it, thinking it to be completely sterile.

After the complete collapse of the roadways, which occurred after about one year, pulleys and ropes were rigged for the removal of earth. There were so many individual claims that the entire circumference of the mine did not provide enough frontage for the erection of a windlass for each claim, so massive six-storey timber stagings were built. The upper level was linked to the claims nearest the centre of the mine, and the lowest to those nearest the perimeter. In 1874 horse-operated 'whims' were introduced, to be followed a few years later by steam-powered winding-engines, the introduction of which had been delayed by the high cost of transport from the coast – up to £40 per ton – until the extent of the diamond deposits became apparent.

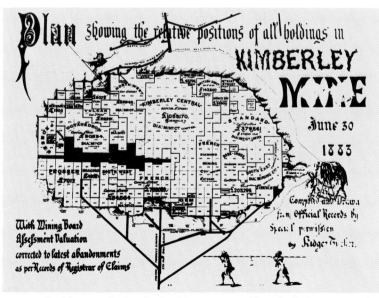

A PLAN of holdings at the Kimberley Mine in 1883. Already the big companies owned most of the claims.

Kimberley

It began as a hill – and it ended as the world's largest man-made hole in the ground. Around it grew a boom town of imported corrugated iron houses, tents and shacks that by July 1873 had mushroomed into Kimberley, named after the Earl of Kimberley, Secretary of State for the Colonies in the British Government.

As news of the strike at Colesberg Kopje in 1871 spread around South Africa and the world, prospectors poured into this dusty area of Griqualand West – followed by the prostitutes, bar flies and diamond dealers whose living depended on the sweat of the diggers.

As more and more claims were staked in and around the hillock, so the diggers drove deeper and deeper in a scramble for riches. Claims could be highly profitable right up to the outer edge of the diamond 'pipe', and then stop so abruptly that the next claim would be worthless. At the

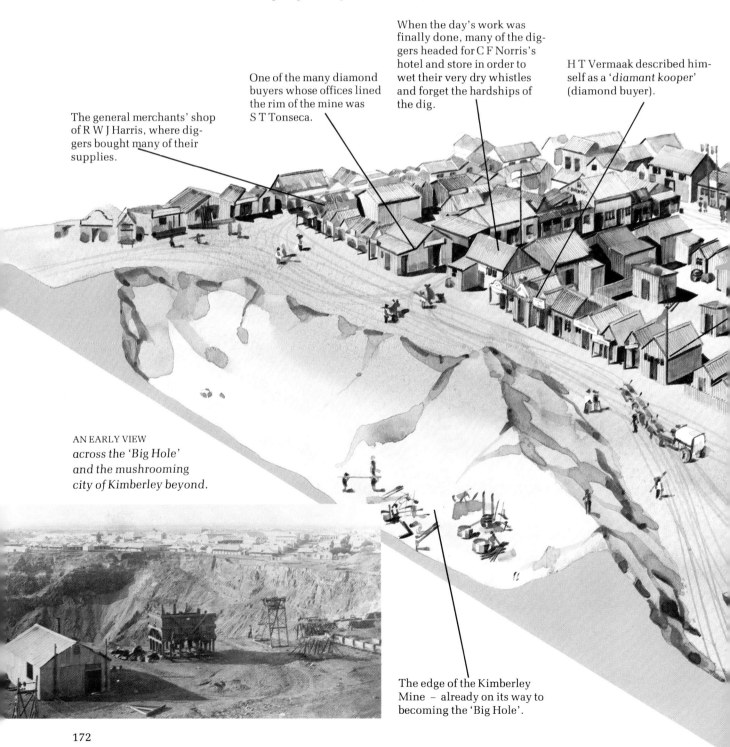

The general merchants' shop of R W J Harris, where diggers bought many of their supplies.

One of the many diamond buyers whose offices lined the rim of the mine was S T Tonseca.

When the day's work was finally done, many of the diggers headed for C F Norris's hotel and store in order to wet their very dry whistles and forget the hardships of the dig.

H T Vermaak described himself as a '*diamant kooper*' (diamond buyer).

AN EARLY VIEW
across the 'Big Hole'
and the mushrooming
city of Kimberley beyond.

The edge of the Kimberley Mine – already on its way to becoming the 'Big Hole'.

peak of operations up to 30 000 men worked all day and most of the night clearing the choked-up throat of the Kimberley Mine. At night the town echoed to the carousing yelps of miners and the women who lived off them.

Once a strike had been made, the diggers headed for one of the many diamond merchants whose offices sprang up along the edge of the mine, selling their diamonds before going on mammoth sprees, lighting cigars with bank notes while their women bathed in champagne. A favourite pastime for the newly rich was to ride a wooden horse on one of the merry-go-rounds that were imported to the town, drinking and shouting ribald comments to the envious spectators.

In those early days there seemed no end to the riches that came pouring out of the mines – no one could have dreamt that the fabulous pipe would go on and on delivering its hidden treasure. However, the deeper the workings went, the more complicated the mining became, and fights over rights of way to claims – and even over the claims themselves – became common. Eventually a cat's cradle of cables and ropeways linked the central claims to the rim. With no safety regulations or control, there were many accidents when loads of rubble being hauled over the heads of workers suddenly collapsed. As working became more difficult, the smaller claims amalgamated – and the age of the mining giants began.

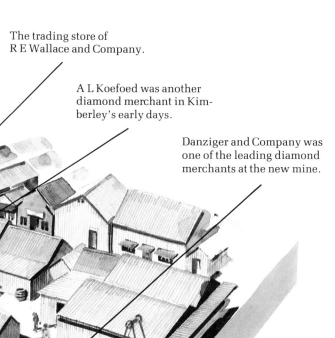

The trading store of R E Wallace and Company.

A L Koefoed was another diamond merchant in Kimberley's early days.

Danziger and Company was one of the leading diamond merchants at the new mine.

THE 'BIG HOLE' *and Kimberley today. Digging at the mine was finally abandoned in 1914 when the First World War brought about a slump in the international diamond market.*

WORKERS *in search of the elusive diamonds sift through gravel dug from the Kimberley Mine.*

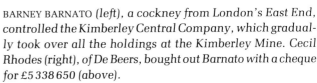

BARNEY BARNATO (left), a cockney from London's East End, controlled the Kimberley Central Company, which gradually took over all the holdings at the Kimberley Mine. Cecil Rhodes (right), of De Beers, bought out Barnato with a cheque for £5 338 650 (above).

al diggers, few with any substantial backing, and all in competition with one another, financed their operations by selling diamonds as they found them. Similarly, few of the many buyers could afford to hold on to their diamond stocks at times of low prices in order to force prices to rise. It was the nature of the diamond deposits themselves that helped to effect part of the solution.

As digging proceeded ever deeper, there seemed every reason to believe that diamond-mining in South Africa had a long and viable life ahead of it. Increasing depths, however, raised practical problems – such as flooding and rockfalls – that the average digger simply lacked the cash to overcome. The solution, as a number of entrepreneurs such as Cecil Rhodes and C D Rudd saw early on, lay in amalgamation, and these two, in 1880, formed the original De Beers Mining Company after buying up a number of small claims. Soon, other joint-stock companies were formed and, at about the same time, a similar consolidation took place among dealers, the combination of their capital placing the diamond market on a slightly more secure footing.

By the end of 1880, some 12 joint-stock companies had been formed, and the following six months saw the formation of another 59, with the total share capital of all the companies being in the region of £8-million. Speculative buying caused share prices to fluctuate wildly and, eventually, to crash when banks withdrew credit facilities in 1881, having previously advanced large sums against the securities of shareholdings. Many were ruined, and survivors faced increasing working costs at depth, coupled with sagging prices caused by over-production.

The De Beers Mining Company was among the survivors, as were the Kimberley Central Company and the so-called 'French Company' (Compagnie Française des Mines de Diamants du Cap). Unable to persuade competing mine-owners to limit their output until the market stabilised, Rhodes used his easy access to European capital to achieve large-scale amalgamation. By 1888, when Rhodes had acquired full ownership of the De Beers Mine, his De Beers Company had a share capital of around £2,5-million, compared with £200 000 in 1880. The Kimberley Central Company of rags-to-riches Barney Barnato (real name Barnett Isaacs) steadily bought up the shares of other companies working the Kimberley Mine, including the 'French Company', to achieve complete ownership of the mine by 1888. Backed by the Rothschild family of European financiers, Rhodes had bought a one-fifth share in Kimberley Central and, soon after, was set to buy out Barnato himself. A cheque for the sum of £5 338 650 changed hands, and the Kimberley Mine was absorbed into the new De Beers Consolidated Mines Ltd. In addition, Barnato also received a 'life governorship' of the new company and, almost as important, membership of the exclusive Kimberley Club.

But Rhodes had not finished. Backed by still more foreign capital, he bought up the nearby mines of Bultfontein and Dutoitspan, thereby acquiring control of all the 'dry diggings' in the Kimberley area. Rhodes and a handful of other capitalists, most of them resident in the Cape for only a few years, now controlled the colony's greatest producer of revenue, a portion of which Rhodes was determined to devote to the advance of British imperialism in Africa.

Their control was not merely over production – their monopoly assured them a prominent place in directing the economic and political future of the country.

Closed compounds

From the early days, Kimberley whites feared that they would be swamped by African workers – and began demanding that Africans be 'localised' in their own area of the diggings. Then, as mining developed, management demanded the same thing, but under ever-increasing control. A strike in which whites, Africans and coloured workers joined forces, raised the horrors of an alliance between black and white workers, and its potentially disruptive effect on production. Management advocated a plan to separate black and white completely above ground, which might also have the additional merit of restricting the flourishing practice of illicit diamond-buying (IDB). Engineered by Rhodes, a parliamentary enquiry concluded that African 'canteens', the social centres of their off-duty hours, were at the heart of IDB.

The 'solution' they hit upon was to house Africans in barracks, or closed compounds, from which they moved solely to go down the mine or to return home at the end of their contract. Many shopkeepers objected, saying that this deprived them of legitimate custom. Rhodes, the chief spokesman of those who supported the closed compound system, pressed on, placating the Chamber of Commerce with assurances that the mining companies would buy all that they required for the compounded Africans from Griqualand West dealers only.

In addition to being a purely racial division, the closed compound effectively divided unskilled labour from skilled labour and lessened the likelihood of an alliance between the two groups being formed.

A closed compound was exactly that: enclosed by high walls, usually of corrugated iron, that shut out the view of the world outside. Indentured Africans passed through a guarded gate, along a fenced walkway to the pit-head, and returned the same way – with the difference that they were searched on their return. There was no significant difference between the closed compounds erected for so-called 'free' labourers, and the barracks built for convict labourers, except that if a convict escaped he could be shot. The compounds increased the spread of disease – and even in the open compounds, on average, one in 15 occupants was ill at any time. This contrasted tellingly with the sick rate among the night-soil removers, whose illness ratio was 1:100, in what was supposedly the most unhealthy occupation in town.

The great railway boom

The discovery of diamonds brought about dramatic changes in the Cape economy, in which agriculture and stock-farming had occupied some 90 percent of the workforce – and prompted the building of a railway line between Cape Town and Kimberley. When railway expansion was first proposed in 1873, it was not entirely as a result of the discovery of diamonds but, rather, to link the agricultural hinterland with the ports. Wool was still the major export and, at the time, it was not realised for how long the diamond mines would be productive. Successive ministries disagreed on the routes to be taken and towns to be served, but the Cape Government purchased the privately owned Cape Town-Wellington railway line as early as 1873. The first problem to extension was formidable – taking the line over the Hex River Mountains. The track gauge was the standard 4 feet eight-and-a-half inches (approximately 1,5 metres) which was considered too wide for the many tight bends that it would be necessary to construct, so the narrow gauge of 3 feet 6 inches (1 065 millimetres) was employed.

There were political problems, too. The construction of a line to the north was seen by the SAR and the OFS as a threat to their independence, but certain Cape parliamentarians, notably John X Merriman and Saul Solomon, were determined to press ahead. A line was also started from Port Elizabeth, to link with the Cape route at De Aar junction, and a third line led from East London to Aliwal North, to be linked at some future time to Kimberley.

The most dramatic effect of the arrival of the railway service in Kimberley in November 1885 was the drop in the prices of just about everything – coal, for instance, fell from £24 per ton to just over a quarter of that price. Although an American visitor complained that the standard of the coach accommodation compared poorly with that in his home country, Kimberley was delighted with the new service.

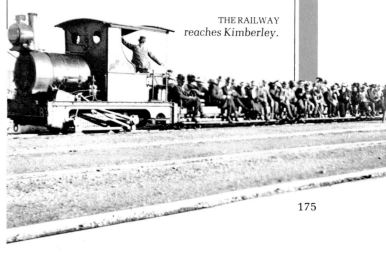

THE RAILWAY *reaches Kimberley.*

BY 1900, *African workers were housed in 'closed compounds', with strict security to prevent diamond smuggling.*

The sweet taste of empire

It started with the wealthy rulers and sugar barons of Natal – pressure to open the colony
to the potential labour pool of Mozambique and the eastern Transvaal
by uniting the republics, colonies and black states of southern Africa in a confederation.
The idea received enthusiastic support from Britain's Colonial Office – which, after the
discovery of diamonds, wanted to pave the way to a capitalist future in southern Africa.
It led to the disastrous annexation of the Transvaal in April 1877.

OUTRAGE WAS IN THE AIR as the white farmers, riding in from their holdings that were spread over a wide arc around the Bushman's River in Natal, filed into the meeting at Estcourt to listen to one of their colleagues, J B Wilkes, talk about the very emotive subject of labour – or, to be more precise, the lack of it.

'You are aware,' he told his audience, 'as employers of labour of the great difficulty in obtaining it.'

Indeed they were – Natal in 1871 had attracted a great many European settlers whose farms now dotted the rolling hillsides, from the sugar plantations of the coast to the sheep farms of the northern districts. The local Africans, however, could not be induced in any numbers to work for the immigrants – as Wilkes was about to explain:

'... In the locations, and in various other places – Crown lands – these natives have plenty of land and large flocks, and they are independent of labour.'

His words no doubt brought loud applause from his audience, and sharpened their resolve to persuade the Natal authorities to reverse what Wilkes described as 'a native policy opposed to labour'. Adding insult to injury was the fact that the Africans were proving more successful at selling their produce to local markets – and the booming diamond workings in Griqualand West – than the white farmers. In the words of the 'Natal Witness': 'the Kafirs ... are coming into competition with the white man and are fairly beating them in the markets.'

Their immediate source of anger was land occupied by the Hlubi who, after being settled years earlier by the Natal Government on the Upper Bloukrans and Little Bushman's rivers, had proved themselves to be successful farmers – much to the chagrin of the whites (see box). As one Estcourt farmer thundered in an 1873 letter to the 'Natal Witness': 'There is a green and fertile country above us ... but this is reserved for the favoured black children of Cain.'

Jealousy of the Hlubi, however, was also linked to the wider problem of labour shortage – an issue that was so vital to colonial interests in the 1870s that it prompted the virtual ruler of Natal, the ambitious and impetuous Secretary for Native Affairs, Theophilus Shepstone, to try to solve it by attempting to unite white South Africa in a unitary confederation.

The sugar planters

Hardest hit by the labour shortage were the coastal sugar planters, whose plantations required a large and reliable workforce. These planters – never numbering more than a few hundred – had become the new aristocracy of the young colony; hard, powerful men whose lust for accumulating money soon began to echo down the corridors of colonial government all the way to the very heart of the empire itself – the distant corridors of the Colonial Office in faraway Whitehall in London.

As early as 1852 Shepstone had tried to 'persuade' Africans to work for the planters by offering to remit a portion of their taxes, including an annual hut tax and payment of £5 on registration of a marriage, if they agreed to work for whites. But there were few takers. And in 1873, in order to promote the 'natural and desirable relations of master and servant', he made it compulsory for Africans who stayed for more than five consecutive days in Pietermaritzburg to accept any offer of employment at a prescribed rate, adding an ominous warning that conditions would inevitably 'force the civilised man, when he inhabits the same country with the savage, to encroach upon the unoccupied lands claimed by the latter'.

Despite these measures and threats, the labour shortage continued, forcing the planters to look further north for their labour, particularly in Mozambique. However, between Mozambique and Natal lay the kingdom of Zululand, whose people did not take kindly to streams of strangers passing through their territory on their way to seek work in Natal, something which the Zulu themselves were disinclined to do. An arrangement had been made with the Portuguese Commandant at Delagoa Bay for the temporary accommodation of labour recruits until they could be removed, by sea, to Durban. But this was unsatisfactory as it involved a cash outlay. Also, ownership of Delagoa Bay was contested by Britain and Portugal, and was the subject of international arbitration that might easily go against Britain, giving the South African Republic (SAR) an unrestricted outlet to the sea and, additionally, depriving the port of Durban of a large slice of trade.

The solution, then, was to develop and maintain an overland route along which trade could proceed northwards, and along which labourers could walk, economically, southwards. This route Shepstone saw as being through the disputed territory lying between Zululand and the SAR, which had supposedly been 'ceded' by Zululand some years earlier. A stronger and independent SAR, in which gold had recently been discovered and which had an alternative outlet to the sea might easily encourage the Boer leaders to close its borders to Natal, thereby ruining both trade and labour supply.

IN ORDER *to reach Natal and the diamond fields of Griqualand West, Africans had to travel either through the Boer republics of the* OFS *or* SAR, *or through Zululand.*

Heading for the glitter

To make matters even more complex, a further critical labour shortage was building up at the diamond diggings in Griqualand West. The main source of supply was the Pedi of the eastern Transvaal who had engaged in migratory labour for decades, encouraged by their chiefs who welcomed the firearms such labour brought to the chiefdom, and who also claimed their own tribute. The opening of the 'dry diggings' at Kimberley, and the relatively high wages paid there, changed the pattern of Pedi labour distribution from agriculture, including work in the Transvaal, to mining. It was a change that did not find favour in the SAR *Volksraad* – already smarting from the loss of a portion of the diamond country – which rigorously enforced a Pass system for migrant labourers, especially those moving in the direction of Griqualand West. By 1875, Lieutenant-Governor Richard Southey was complaining that the implementation of the Pass laws caused harassment to the labourers en route, and disrupted the mines.

It was clear to Shepstone and the wealthy planters that the political fragmentation of southern Africa was undesirable and a hindrance to British commercial and industrialising expansion. What was needed was some form of federation; not a new idea, but one that was to be given a sympathetic hearing by the new Colonial Secretary in London, Lord Carnarvon.

How much more of Africa?

Britain's position as the imperial power at the Cape was fairly clear: the Cape Peninsula was to be held at all costs in order to protect the sea route to India. However, how much more of southern Africa Britain should administer was not so clear; some politicians, particularly the Treasury, with an eye on taxpayers' money, believed that the

Peninsula was enough. Others – the majority – felt that the Peninsula could be held only by annexing a certain amount of inland territory. Adding to this view was the newer argument that Britain had a duty to protect the colonies of the Cape and Natal from the Africans – and the Africans against British and Afrikaner depredations.

A further impetus to the arguments of the federalists was the hoary favourite about trade following the flag. In South Africa, the 'spread of civilisation' or the 'advance of imperialism', amounted to little more than the expansion of a capitalist economy and, almost inevitably, the destruction of traditional structures in the face of increasing demands for cheap labour. Imperialism has been defined as not merely the gaining of new colonies, but as the pursuit of a vigorous foreign policy for economic gain. If profit could be made without annexation or the proclamation of another colony, so much the better – it was far cheaper.

For much of the 19th century, Britain was clearly the dominant power in southern Africa, despite the series of messily conducted wars that plagued the eastern Cape frontier. There was little need for formal proclamation – indeed, when Sir Benjamin D'Urban created the Province of Queen Adelaide, it was briskly repudiated by the British Government. No such restraint, however, greeted the assertion of British interests at Port Natal and the annexation of the short-lived Boer Republic of Natalia. The British regarded the coastal areas as their own domain, leaving the Boers to conduct their own affairs in the in-

THE COLONIAL SECRETARY *in London, Henry Howard Molyneux Herbert, Earl of Carnarvon, backed plans for confederation in southern Africa.*

terior – but only until they posed a threat to the economies of Natal and the newly annexed diamond fields.

The favourite counter to this threat was some sort of federal union of British, Afrikaner and African states stretching from the Cape to the Limpopo and perhaps beyond. Such a union, it was felt, could become a dominion along the lines of Canada, which had been federated in 1867, and would be strong enough without British assistance to keep law and order – although the Royal Navy would protect it and British entrepreneurs would control its trade.

It was one thing to dream of federation – and quite another to implement it. The Treasury was prepared to go along, provided the funds could be generated locally – and not at the expense of the British taxpayer. Thus the earliest attempts at federation were really aimed at decreasing British involvement rather than increasing it. Lord Kimberley, Carnarvon's predecessor, had considered that some form of confederation might be desirable if it could cut costs and bring about a reduction of the military establishment at the Cape. The newly elected responsible government of the Cape, however, had declined to incorporate even Griqualand West, which had to be proclaimed as a separate colony and so the matter had died away.

Now, with the imperialist Lord Carnarvon running affairs at the Colonial Office, it was brought forward again, with the powerful new argument that, without some form of confederation, British interests would suffer irreparable damage, particularly if the SAR moved beyond the sphere of British economic influence and drew the Orange Free State (OFS) along with it.

Leading the lobbying was Shepstone, beaten but unbowed over his handling of Langalibalele (see box). Summoned to London for an imperial rap over the knuckles, he nevertheless found plenty of time to punt his view that the real answer to the labour troubles of Natal and the diamond fields lay in confederation – opening up 'migratory' labour routes across a unified country.

Testing the water
Pondering his arguments in Whitehall, Carnarvon decided to send to South Africa a historian who had written a series of articles in support of imperial unity. James Froude was asked to report on the state of southern Africa and the possibilities for federation. His report was generally favourable, although damning the annexation of the diamond fields (see page 168) as 'a crime and a blunder' which had alienated to some extent the loyalty of Cape Boers who felt a strong sympathy for the Boers of the republics. He proposed that, as long as the Boers were conciliated and allowed to deal with Africans in their own way, the republics could join the colonies in a self-governing dominion – except for the Cape Peninsula, which should fall under direct British rule.

Suitably heartened, Carnarvon's next act was to appoint Britain's most popular soldier, Major-General Sir Garnet Wolseley, as Commander-in-Chief and Special Commissioner for Natal, with a secret instruction to gain control of native policy and, if necessary, to ensure a pliable legislative council by amending the constitution and loading the legislature with federalists.

Shattered by the warriors of Shaka, and attacked again in 1847 by Mpande, the Hlubi people of hereditary chief Langalibalele obtained permission to settle in Natal. Rich in cattle, they were settled for some 18 months along the Klip River and then ordered to move to an ill-defined location along the Little Bushman's and Bloukrans rivers. Here, they were to act as a buffer between San raiders and the holdings of white colonists. Those settled within the location were obliged to pay the standard hut tax, but those who found themselves on occupied white farms were obliged to offer their labour in lieu of cash rental. The need to raise the cash for tax or rent caused many Hlubi to find employment outside the location, thereby weakening the authority of the chief, who was nevertheless held responsible for their actions by the white authorities. After the discovery of diamonds, many Hlubi went to work at the diggings, usually returning with a firearm and plough as part of their remuneration.

From the 1850s many white farmers left their lands because of the difficulty of obtaining labour and the smallness of the local market. Land was frequently leased by Africans who, with family labour, found that supplying the domestic market was fairly profitable. The establishment of the diamond diggings created an enormous market for the northern and midlands agriculturalists, but the white farmers, impeded by lack of labour, found little advantage. This led to a great deal of resentment towards African crop-producers, especially in the Weenen district adjacent to the Hlubi location. Absentee (white) landowners profited, but active white farmers, in general, were less successful than Africans, who had changed from hoe cultivation to the extensive use of the plough.

As the Hlubi prospered, so Langalibalele's prestige increased, although without strengthening his authority over his more distant subjects, whose small chiefdom, in 1873, reaped a record harvest and owned more than 15 000 cattle. To the whites, it seemed that the better the Hlubi fared, the more 'arrogant' they became. 'They would not have answered so some years ago,' complained a farmer

CHIEF LANGALIBALELE *was sent to Robben Island after his lands were seized.*

The Langalibalele affair

COLONIAL FORCES *under Major Anthony Durnford attempted to prevent the Hlubi reaching the safety of the Drakensberg by blocking the Bushman's River Pass.*

who, on demanding to see the Pass of a Hlubi cattle-herd, was told that he did not need one, as he was herding his chief's cattle. As resentment built up, an unproven charge of illegal entry against an African servant in Estcourt raised white fears of rape and plunder.

John Macfarlane, resident magistrate of Estcourt, chose this time to enforce the Gun Law on the Hlubi, and demanded that Langalibalele send in all unregistered guns for registration. Langalibalele did not reply, although it was later claimed that he did not know which of his subjects possessed firearms, and had not the means of forcing them to comply with Macfarlane's order. There was also a suspicion that the weapons might be confiscated.

In April 1873, messengers from Macfarlane ordered Langalibalele to appear in Pietermaritzburg to explain why he had ignored the order. The chief went to Estcourt to explain that he was suffering pain from an old leg wound and that, on earlier occasions when he had reported this, no less a person than Shepstone had rescinded a summons to the capital and had himself travelled to see him. Unfortunately, as the magistrate was away, he had to explain this to the interpreter, Gert Rudolph, and the visit ended in an argument that heightened the tensions. In reality, Langalibalele probably feared that, in the present atmosphere, if he did go to Pietermaritzburg, he might be arrested and his people dispersed.

Macfarlane again ordered Langalibalele, in May, to go to Pietermaritzburg, and it seems that the chief agreed to go, but later in the month, Rudolph reported that the 'old ruffian' appeared to have no intention of leaving. Then, early the following month, the Weenen and Karkloof Volunteers set up their camp close to the Hlubi location. It was, in reality, a routine training camp, but to the Hlubi it appeared that the whites were gathering for an attack. Even after the camp broke up the tension did not ease. Although Macfarlane's attitude hardened, he awaited Shepstone's return from a long visit to Zululand before taking action. The action he visualised as appropriate is evident from a letter he wrote to Shepstone, stating 'signal punishment it must be'.

As the unease and restlessness grew, many Hlubi returned to their location – a movement that panicky whites saw as preparatory to a raid on their properties and, worse, a general uprising of all blacks. In the location, control was slipping from Langalibalele and his elders to the young men, who demanded that their chief refuse to go to Pietermaritzburg. By October, they had replaced the elders as the chief's advisors, and some of the elders, fearing for the fate of their people, asked missionaries to intervene with the government on behalf of Langalibalele. The missionaries, however, did nothing. A final summons was sent in the name of the Lieutenant-Governor, Sir Benjamin Pine. Fearful and suspicious, the Hlubi searched the messengers, and this 'insult' provided the final excuse for military action.

The force sent against the Hlubi outnumbered the entire chiefdom, and consisted of two companies of the Gordon Highlanders, 8 000 Natal Native Levies, the Richmond Mounted Rifles and the Karkloof Troop of the Natal Carbineers, all under the command of Lieutenant-Colonel Milles with Major Anthony Durnford as second-in-command. Against all this, the Hlubi had a total of 111

firearms, of which 48 had been correctly registered. The 'signal punishment' was on its way. The Hlubi, meanwhile, drove their cattle before them as they made for the safety of the Drakensberg passes and Basutoland (Lesotho). Farmers sent their cattle and families to safety in the vicinity of the towns.

A part of the field force under Durnford moved to block the Bushman's River Pass, through which Langalibalele had travelled two days earlier. Confronted there by the Hlubi, volunteers and Native Levies fled down the road and regrouped out of range, although not a shot had been fired. The Highlanders, who were Regular Army soldiers, were not present. Durnford stood his ground with the pathetic appeal: 'Will no-one stand by me?' Three white troopers and a few of the levies came forward, and the firing of a single shot – it was never discovered by whom – unleashed a general action. Of the forward party, Durnford alone escaped, with two assegai wounds. The three whites and two of the levies were killed.

Vengeance was now taken on those Hlubi who still remained on the location. All cattle were confiscated and, under the pretext that they were hiding Hlubi cattle, the nearby Ngwe lost their cattle as well. Hlubi prisoners, as well as the women and children, were given out as servants, and their land was offered to, and rapidly occupied by, white farmers. In Basutoland, Langalibalele surrendered and was returned to Natal, where he was tried for high treason by an illegally constituted court that sentenced him to banishment for life. To oblige Natal, the Cape Parliament passed the Natal Criminals Act, and Langalibalele and one of his sons were transported to Robben Island, where they 'would be more comfortable and might be allowed greater liberty than on the mainland'.

When word of the affair reached England, it caused a public outcry. The Natal Criminals Act was disallowed, which was a humiliation for the Cape Government. Langalibalele's sentence was repealed, but he was held for several years on the government farm of Uitvlugt (now the 'garden city' of Pinelands), then returned to Natal in 1887, where he died two years later. The granting of self-government to Natal was set back, and Sir Benjamin Pine was recalled to England, and retired from the colonial service. Little attention was paid to the instructions that the Hlubi were to have their lands and cattle returned. Shepstone survived, but the Zulu, over whom he claimed such influence, lost a great deal of their faith in him. They could not have known that the destruction of Langalibalele was, in a way, a dress rehearsal for the fate that awaited them.

BRITISH HISTORIAN *James Froude (left) was sent to southern Africa by the Colonial Office in London to test opinions regarding possible confederation. His report was favourable – and he was ordered back to the Cape to try to sell the concept in particular to the Cape Government of Prime Minister John Molteno (right), who turned the proposal down flat, saying that only the Cape could make such a proposal.*

Fresh from his latest triumph of crushing the Ashanti of West Africa, Wolseley and his staff embarked on a campaign of 'champagne and sherry' politics, lavishly entertaining the more influential colonists and sowing the seeds of a southern African confederation. As persuasive socially as he was successful on the battlefield, Wolseley followed Carnarvon's instructions to the letter, persuading the legislative council to agree to an increase in the number of nominated members from five to 13, as against 15 elected members. The members to be nominated, of course, would be those who agreed with the policies of Shepstone and Carnarvon. In exchange, Wolseley held out the bait of a loan from the British Government for a railway line between Durban and Pietermaritzburg.

While Wolseley was lionised in Natal, Carnarvon plotted the next stage of his plan – a despatch to the Cape Government, stating that because of 'recent occurrences in Natal' it had become desirable that the indigenous population of southern Africa should be treated according to a common policy in all territories. 'Her Majesty's Government is desirous that a conference of delegates, representing the Colony of Natal, the Province of Griqualand West, the Orange Free State, the South African Republic, and the Eastern and Western Provinces of the Cape . . . should meet at the earliest practicable time at some convenient place within the Cape Colony for the discussion of Native Policy and of such other questions as it may be agreed to bring before the conference.' Carnarvon did not, directly, demand that confederation be discussed, but stated that if the question of confederation should arise at the conference, 'Her Majesty's Government would be willing to render any assistance needful'.

This enthusiastic message from Whitehall landed in the Cape with all the verve of a lead balloon. The government of Prime Minister John Molteno spurned the proposal and refused to take part in any conference whatever, saying it was felt improper that the suggestion of confederation, however delicately worded, should come from the British

Government. The Cape had been entrusted with responsible government, and it was from the Cape that such a proposal should come, when it was adjudged that the time was favourable.

Carnarvon's mistake had been to mention the 'Eastern Province of the Cape' as a separate province – and to rub salt in the wound by suggesting as candidate for the region an arch separatist, John Paterson.

Into this prickly atmosphere now stepped Froude, the historian whose support for federation had made him Carnarvon's choice to represent him at the proposed conference at the Cape – except that, thanks to Molteno's opposition, there now was not going to be one. Unperturbed, Froude set out instead on a tour of the country, trying to whip up enthusiasm for the proposed confederation, but failed. Finally a conference was held in London in August 1876, but Molteno, although he was in London at the time, refused to attend. Only Shepstone, President Brand of the OFS, Froude representing Griqualand West, and Carnarvon debated a few aspects of 'the native problem'.

Time for action

While Carnarvon was wheeler-dealing in London, Shepstone was becoming more and more insistent that the time for talking was fast coming to an end and the time for action approaching. In a private meeting after the London conference he and Carnarvon agreed that their fears of a few years earlier had been only too well founded: Delagoa Bay had been awarded to Portugal, and President Thomas Burgers of the SAR was scouting about Europe trying to raise money to build a railway to Delagoa Bay. It was a situation that needed nipping in the bud before an unthinkable flower had time to blossom – a SAR beyond the reach of British commercial interests which could block the route from the Cape to central Africa.

The solution was daring, if somewhat rash: Shepstone was to annex the SAR to the British Crown. On the surface, there were reasons that could be presented as perfectly

SIR THEOPHILUS SHEPSTONE *and his staff strike a suitable pose during the annexation of the SAR in 1877. Seated on the ground is Shepstone's private secretary, Rider Haggard, later to earn fame as the author of books such as 'King Solomon's Mines' and 'She'.*

valid: continuing friction between the SAR and Zululand, the restlessness of the Pedi after their defeat of a commando led by Burgers and the fact that the state coffers were almost empty. Shepstone was to go through the motions of obtaining popular assent, but the SAR was to be annexed regardless of its citizens' will.

Shepstone sailed for South Africa on the *Windsor Castle* which, within sight of Table Mountain, ran onto a reef near Dassen Island. For a while, the fate of the SAR was at the mercy of wind and wave, but both were calm, and all passengers and crew were brought safely by lifeboats to the island. When he was asked what he did when he realised that the ship had been wrecked, Shepstone replied: 'I thought that I should like to die decent, and spent the time in hunting for my trousers.' It was important to keep up appearances.

SAR PRESIDENT *Thomas Burgers found himself without a country to run after British annexation.*

Into the SAR

In January 1877, accompanied by a small escort of mounted police, Shepstone (newly knighted and therefore Sir Theophilus) entered the SAR and established himself at Pretoria. Over the next few months he conducted interviews with selected people of prominence, playing on the disunity and insecurity that arose from the unpopularity of Burgers, hinting that his own influence over the Zulu could avert armed confrontation. Bemused and dispirited, the *volksraad* ended its session and its members dispersed to their homes and farms. On 12 April 1877, Shepstone proclaimed the SAR to be a British colony and, the next month, former President Burgers left the country to return to his old occupation as a church minister in the Cape. Although at first Shepstone encountered no serious resistance, it did not take long for the Boers to express their opposition (see page 194).

In the Cape, however, there was an uproar – that even the newly appointed Governor, Sir Henry Bartle Frere, could not quell. He had taken over from Sir Henry Barkly only weeks before the annexation with the understanding that, if a new dominion was created as the result of confederation, he would be the first Governor-General. But unfortunately the annexation alienated a great number of Cape parliamentarians, and he merely inherited the hostility that the republics had felt towards Barkly.

As one of the final steps towards confederation, the British Parliament passed the South Africa Act of 1877, which provided for the unification of the various southern African colonies and the OFS in a single political unit loyal to the Crown. Fate, however, was not ready for a united South Africa – and the British annexation of the SAR was destined to end within a few years in humiliation after the colonial forces were to suffer a series of crushing defeats at the hands of Boer commandos.

As for the sugar barons of Natal – they satisfied their labour needs with cheap 'coolie' workers from India, while the confederationists eyed a new target: Zululand.

Confederation from the barrel of a gun

The discovery of diamonds at Griqualand West in 1867 brought more than just fortune-hunters to southern Africa – it also changed the way it was perceived by the Colonial Office in London: a fount of riches that could be fully exploited only if the dozen or so different colonies, republics and independent African states could be 'confederated' into a single unit of government under the Union Jack. War followed: against the Gcaleka of the eastern Cape, the Pedi state in the Transvaal, the Griqua south of Natal, the Basotho of the interior and the toughest nut of all, the Zulu.

IN MARCH 1881 the exiled Zulu King Cetshwayo ka-Mpande dictated a letter to the Governor of the Cape Colony, Sir Hercules Robinson: 'I have done you no wrong, therefore you must have some other object in view in invading my land.'

Languishing at Cape Town Castle, the once-mighty leader of the Zulu was a broken, beaten and baffled man, who still did not know why the British Empire had found it necessary to send armed troops into his small independent state in south-eastern Africa, despite the fact that he had taken every conceivable step he could think of to persuade them not to. And now, with 10 000 of his people dead and his nation dismembered into 13 chiefdoms, he was still none the wiser.

What made it even more puzzling was the fact that out of all of Mpande's considerable offspring, Cetshwayo was favoured by the British to succeed his father as king of the Zulu – despite the fact that Mpande had originally preferred his second eldest son, Mbuyazi. Rivalry for the succession between Cetshwayo and Mbuyazi escalated into civil war in 1856 – when Cetshwayo and his followers defeated and killed his brother at the Battle of Ndondakusuka. Cetshwayo then vied for power with his own father – leading the British, in the person of Natal Native Affairs Commissioner Theophilus Shepstone, to mediate between the two, ceremonially proclaiming Cetshwayo as Mpande's successor in return for an expression of loyalty by Cetshwayo to Mpande as king.

Although Cetshwayo adhered to this loyalty throughout his father's life, he nevertheless became immensely powerful, bolstering his power by accumulating firearms with the help of a wealthy white trader named John Dunn who had married into a leading Zulu family, and who was to play an important role in the breaking up of the Zulu kingdom after the war with Britain.

When Mpande died in 1872 after 32 years of rule, Cetshwayo was unchallenged as his successor – and was even given Shepstone's formal blessing. No wonder Cetshwayo wrote in his letter to the Cape Governor: 'How is it that they [the English] crown me in the morning and dethrone me in the afternoon?'

The answer lay in the discovery of diamonds, which had changed South Africa from a half-forgotten backwater of the British Empire into the promised source of untold wealth. Suddenly southern Africa was very much on the colonial map in distant Whitehall – the only problem, however, was that not enough of the map was the right colour – red for the British Empire. Instead Colonial Secretary Lord Carnarvon was confronted with a patchwork of two British colonies, two independent Boer republics and a scattering of African states – such as the Gcaleka Xhosa, the Pedi and the Zulu.

Such an arrangement was, to Carnarvon's mind, not only untidy, but it held back the development of the area into a modern, capitalist state – tuned to the needs of capitalist production and the infrastructure of communications and transport that it needed.

THE NEWLY APPOINTED *High Commissioner for southern Africa, Sir Henry Bartle Frere, was an ardent confederationist.*

TO HIS DYING DAY, *Cetshwayo never really knew why the British had decided to invade his Zulu kingdom.*

The answer, Carnarvon assured his Tory Prime Minister Benjamin Disraeli, was 'confederation', with one overall authority of a single system of government replacing the various existing political structures. And he made sure that there were plenty in South Africa who agreed with him, appointing a 'confederationist' High Commissioner, Sir Henry Bartle Frere, and giving his backing to Natal supremo Theophilus Shepstone, who had proved his support for confederation by leading the annexation of the Transvaal in 1877, taking over as Administrator until 1879 (see page 181).

Shepstone's annexation had been motivated by Carnarvon's imperial ambitions – and a persistent lobby from influential sugar farmers and diamond diggers who wanted easier access to the Pedi labour of the eastern Transvaal.

Both these lobbyists were only too well aware that just across the Natal border in the independent kingdom of Zululand lay a vast reserve of land, and potential labour still engaged in the traditional homestead system of farming; and showing no desire to swop it for work on white-owned farms or mines – apart from occasional short forays to earn money for firearms. Almost unique among African communities that had encountered white expansionism, the Zulu still preserved their independence through systematic discouragement, and even ejection, of missionaries, traders and speculators.

Shepstone, however, they trusted, inviting him to the coronation in 1873 of King Cetshwayo, to formally recognise, on behalf of the Colony of Natal, his right of succession to his father, the late King Mpande. At this time, Shepstone sided with the Zulu in a long-standing north-western border dispute with the Transvaal Boers, but very quickly changed his tune when he became Administrator of the Transvaal and it suited his own and imperial ambitions to placate the Boers. Accordingly, he switched loyalties, supporting the Boers' claim to the disputed land, and wrote of his former friends: 'Had Cetywayo's thirty thousand warriors been in time changed to labourers working for wages, Zululand could have been a prosperous, peaceful country instead of what it now is, a source of perpetual danger to itself and its neighbours.'

Creating a cause

One of the neighbours was Natal, nervous but not in danger, choosing to disregard Cetshwayo's message 'that he has no intention or wish to quarrel with the English'. And the 'thirty thousand warriors' whom Shepstone conjured up were not, as he wanted Frere and the Colonial Office to believe, a standing army. The division of men and women into age-grades was the basis of the Zulu national system. Men performed duties according to their age-group, such as looking after the royal herds or cultivating the lands, maintaining the royal and military homesteads and acting as a police force. They were the executors of the king's will and the administrators of his rule, as Frere and Shepstone knew full well.

By the end of the 1870s, Shepstone and Frere were determined to scrub an independent Zululand off the southern African map in a premeditated, unprovoked attack, as is clearly evident from remarks made in April of 1878 by Commodore Sullivan of the Royal Navy, who was ordered by Frere to patrol off the Natal and Zululand coast. Sullivan wrote that it appeared 'almost certain that serious complications must shortly arise with the Zulus which will necessitate active operations'.

General Frederic Thesiger, having 'dealt with' the Xhosa in the eastern Cape and due, on his father's death in October 1878, to become the second Baron Chelmsford, recorded early in June that 'it is still, however, more than probable that active steps will have to be taken to check the arrogance of Cetywayo'. Cetshwayo's 'arrogance' is not defined, but what is clear is that preparations were under way to invade his kingdom and, by the beginning of October, British troops were stationed at three places along the Zululand border. Appeals were made to white volunteers who had fought against the Xhosa, and many responded, eager for another 'glorious go in'.

With his troops in position, Frere delivered an ultimatum to Cetshwayo on 11 December 1878, magnifying a number of minor border incidents into threats that Natal was about to be invaded. The one given most prominence occurred when the sons of Sihayo kaXongo pursued their father's two adulterous wives across the Buffalo River into Natal, seized them, and dragged them back into Zululand where, according to law, they were put to death. The ultimatum demanded that the sons of Sihayo be handed over

'We're here because we're here'

On a windswept hillside near a towering fortress of rock known to the Zulu as Isandlwana, a proletariat army from the world's foremost capitalist nation was defeated by a part-time force of peasant farmers in a short, bloody and eventually inconclusive battle that rocked the British Empire to its core.

The Zulus attacked the red-coated British because they feared for their land and their independence. The British soldiers, drawn from the very poorest level of the working classes, fought back because they had been lured, like Private Moss from Wales, to 'take the Queen's shilling'.

Neither side had a clue as to why they were desperately hacking each other to a bloody standstill, not even the officers – on either side. In the words of an old soldier's song: 'We're here because we're here.'

With the hindsight of history, it is perhaps simplest to say that the African peasants were fighting to stop themselves becoming the same as their red-coated adversaries: the working class of a new capitalist South Africa modelled on Britain.

Most of the British dearly wished they were somewhere else, like the private who wrote to his family: 'I repent the day I took the shilling. I have not had a bed since I left England. We have only one blanket, and are out every night in the rain – no shelter.'

For the British officers, most of them from the landed classes and raised at dehumanising boarding schools such as Tom Brown's Rugby, the war in the far-flung corners of the empire was more of a game than a serious instrument of imperial policy, as one recorded: 'We had a glorious go in, old boy, pig-sticking was a fool to it . . . . With a tremendous shout of "death, death!" we were on to them. They tried to escape, but it was no use, we had them any how, no mercy or quarter . . . . '

For the Zulu, it was a war fought to defend their land, homes and families against unprovoked aggression by the most powerful military force in the world. As Kumbeka Gwabe, a member of the u*Mcijo* regiment, later surveyed the battlefield on which some 1 500 of the enemy, and even more of his own comrades, lay dead, he recalled: 'I myself only killed one man. Dum! Dum! went his revolver as he was firing from right to left, and I came beside him and stuck my assegai under his right arm, pushing it through his body until it came out between his ribs on the left side. As soon as he fell I pulled the assegai out and slit his stomach so I knew he should not shoot any more of my people.'

A British Army sergeant who arrived at the battlefield later 'could not help crying to see so many of our poor comrades lying dead on the ground, when only a few hours before that we left them all well and hearty. You could not move a foot either way without treading on dead bodies. Oh, father, such a sight I never witnessed in my life before. I could not help crying to see how the poor fellows were massacred'.

His use of the word 'massacre' gives another insight into the colonial view of the war – in which Zulu victories were usually referred to as 'massacres'; while the British won 'victories' over their enemies – destroying homesteads, shooting down thousands with volley fire or blowing them to bloody rags with artillery.

Nevertheless, the British authorities were hard put to explain how an an army of 'savages' had inflicted such a shattering defeat on their forces, and the myth was created that, because of a lack of screwdrivers, soldiers were unable to open reserve ammunition boxes – whose lids were secured by as many as nine screws, some 'rusted into the wood'. In truth, the lids of the Mark V and VI ammunition boxes used in the campaign were each secured by only a single (brass) screw.

The British Commander during the war, Lord Chelmsford, came in for a particular drubbing – and was defended as recently as 1939 by an apologist who wrote in all seriousness: 'He was a cricketer, and long before his first experience of war had learnt to accept defeat with a good grace and to make no excuses. His critics on the other hand, can hardly have been cricketers.'

It is unlikely many of the working class soldiers who died at Isandlwana would have agreed. A better tribute to them and the Zulu dead was paid by Bishop Colenso in a sermon after the battle: 'We ourselves have lost very many precious lives, and widows and orphans, parents, brothers, sisters, friends are mourning bitterly their sad bereavements. But are there no griefs – no relatives that mourn their dead – in Zululand? Have we not heard how the wail has gone up in all parts of the country for those who have bravely . . . and nobly died in repelling the invader and fighting for the King and fatherland? And shall we kill 10 000 more to avenge. . .that dreadful day?'

COLONIAL FORCES *check their horses and equipment during a break in the Anglo-Zulu War of 1879. Army life was hard and unrewarding.*

THE MISSION STATION *at Rorke's Drift blazes after British forces had beaten back an ill-conceived attack by Zulu warriors –* *who had been warned by Cetshwayo not to throw themselves against entrenched British positions.*

for trial in Natal; 500 cattle be paid as compensation; that Mbilini, a Swazi nobleman living in Zululand after having led an attack on the SAR, be handed over to the Natal authorities; that the army be disbanded, and that the age-group system be abandoned.

Cetshwayo was given a maximum of 20 days in which to comply with the demands – impossible to meet if the Zulu people were to continue to exist; yet he replied, just two weeks before his country was invaded, that 'the king has, however, declared and still declares that he will not commence war but will wait till he is actually attacked before he enters on a defensive campaign'.

The British invade

In January 1879 three columns of British infantry, cavalry, artillery and long lines of supply wagons crossed into Zululand. Cetshwayo sent an army against each column, and collected a large reserve force at oNdini, fearing that invasion might also come from St Lucia Bay. On 21 January, after several days' march, a Zulu army occupied a valley about 6 kilometres east of Isandlwana Hill, where the British centre column, accompanied by Chelmsford himself, was encamped. A soldier named Nzuzi recalled 'the officers of the different regiments assembled in order to come to an agreement as to which chiefs they should send to confer with the English . . . to settle matters by words and not by arms'. Early next morning Chelmsford led a large force out of camp to reinforce temporarily another

detachment, unaware that the Zulu army was resting nearby. At the camp, no entrenchments had been dug, and the wagons had not been formed into defensive laagers when, quite by accident, a mounted British patrol stumbled across the uMcijo regiment, fired a volley at it, and retired. It was the signal for a general attack by the Zulu, who quickly overwhelmed the British (see following page).

In their next engagement, against the hastily fortified mission buildings at Rorke's Drift, the Zulu disobeyed the instructions of their king, who had told them not to enter Natal and warned 'if you come near to the white man and find that he has made trenches and built forts that are full of holes, do not attack him, for it will be of no use'. In an attack lasting some 12 hours, about 500 men were lost, to the defenders' death toll of 17.

More horrific losses were sustained by the Zulu – on the very day of Isandlwana – in a battle fought on the Nyezane River between an army under Godide kaNdlela and the right-hand column under Colonel Charles Pearson, a battle 'so fierce that we had to wipe the blood and brains of the killed and wounded from our heads, faces, arms, legs and shields after the fighting'. Here, and at other engagements, concentrated rifle and cannon fire prevented the Zulu from being able to close with the invaders. At Khambula 'our hearts were full, and we intended to do the same as at Isandlwana', but 'the bullets from the white men were like hail falling about us. Not one of our force doubted our being beaten, and openly said that they had had enough and

Isandlwana

On the afternoon of 17 January 1879 the Zulu king Cetshwayo addressed 20 000 of his warriors at the great military kraal of Nodwengu: 'I am sending you out against the whites, who have invaded Zululand and driven away our cattle. You are to go against the column at Rorke's Drift and drive it back into Natal.'

The march to confront the invading British forces began almost at once – and by 22 January the Zulu army had reached a valley about 6 kilometres from a pinnacle of rock named Isandlwana, south of the present-day town of Nqutu. There, according to a Zulu eyewitness named Nzuzi, they settled down to rest. 'There was no intention of making any attack, on account of a superstition regarding the state of the moon,' he said.

Their rest, however, was to be short-lived. At midday a small troop of British cavalry spotted some cattle being driven by a party of Zulu scouts – and gave chase. Within

THE BATTLE SITE *today – now part of KwaZulu. The white structure in the foreground commemorates those who were killed during the short, fierce battle.*

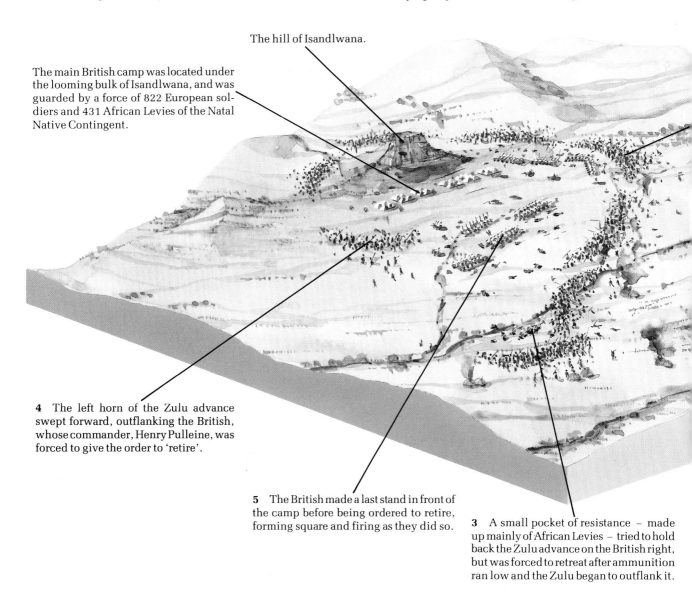

The hill of Isandlwana.

The main British camp was located under the looming bulk of Isandlwana, and was guarded by a force of 822 European soldiers and 431 African Levies of the Natal Native Contingent.

4 The left horn of the Zulu advance swept forward, outflanking the British, whose commander, Henry Pulleine, was forced to give the order to 'retire'.

5 The British made a last stand in front of the camp before being ordered to retire, forming square and firing as they did so.

3 A small pocket of resistance – made up mainly of African Levies – tried to hold back the Zulu advance on the British right, but was forced to retreat after ammunition ran low and the Zulu began to outflank it.

moments they reached the lip of the valley, pulling up with astonishment as the entire Zulu column came into sight – a packed mass of 20 000 men sitting in complete silence.

It was a sobering moment for the British – at last they had located the Zulu force they had been seeking since crossing the Buffalo River into Zululand 11 days previously, a search that had split the British invasion into two – the main body under Lord Chelmsford and a smaller force of 822 British and colonial troops and 431 African Levies guarding the British camp in the lee of Isandlwana.

The discovery also meant that the Zulu force could no longer sit out the rest of the day. According to Nzuzi, 'The *uMcijo* (regiment) at once jumped up and charged, an example which was taken up by the *Nokenke* and *Nodwengu* on their right and the *inGobamakosi* and *uMbonambi* on their left.' Two other regiments, the *Undi* and the *uDkloko*, together with the two commanders, Mavumingwani and Tyingwayo, headed north-west, staying on the northern side of the hill and then turning right without meeting any opposition.

The British, who had not bothered to construct proper defensive positions around the camp, were in terrible danger. As the Zulu came forward at a steady trot, the British attempted to hold a line facing north and east – banging away with shrapnel and rifle fire. For a moment the Zulu advance was checked – and then the left 'horn' of the Zulu attack overran the British right. A second stand was made – the British 'making every round tell' – before that, too, crumbled, reportedly through lack of ammunition, imperilling the entire British position.

The British commander, Henry Pulleine, ordered the 'retire' to be sounded – and as the stunned redcoats fell back, the Zulu surged forward into the main camp and engaged the enemy in a bloody welter of hand-to-hand fighting. A few pockets of resistance continued on the western slopes – and as their ammunition ran out, the surviving British desperately tried to defend themselves with bayonets. Nothing, however, could stop the Zulu advance. In the words of one warrior, Uguku: '...We...killed a great many of them by throwing our assegais at short distance. We eventually overcame them this way.'

By early afternoon it was all over – of the 1 200 British and colonial forces who had been left in camp, only a lucky handful had managed to escape.

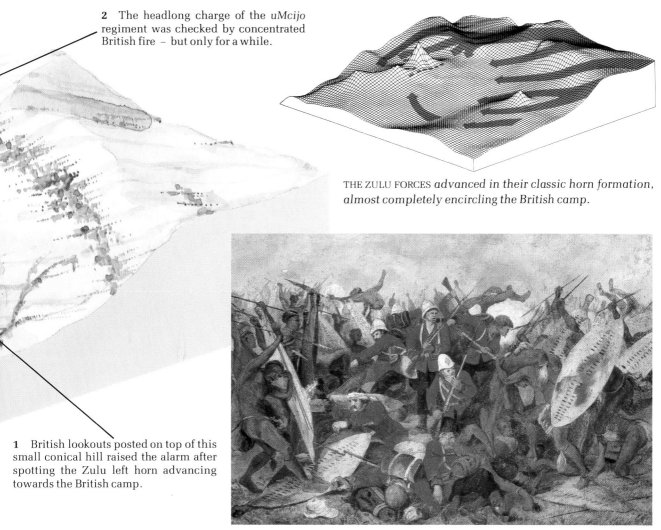

2 The headlong charge of the *uMcijo* regiment was checked by concentrated British fire – but only for a while.

THE ZULU FORCES *advanced in their classic horn formation, almost completely encircling the British camp.*

1 British lookouts posted on top of this small conical hill raised the alarm after spotting the Zulu left horn advancing towards the British camp.

A VICTORIAN VIEW *of the battle was captioned: 'The last order we heard given was, "Fix bayonets and die like British soldiers do", and so they did.' This picture first appeared in the 'Graphic' magazine in March 1879.*

'Get away-o for Cetshwayo'

With his army decimated, King Cetshwayo was hunted down by the British and shipped to Cape Town, where he was detained, under guard, first at the Castle and then at nearby Oude Molen. Determined not to accept his exile, the king had letters written to Queen Victoria and other prominent people in England, pleading that he be allowed to return to Zululand. He also asked for permission to visit England to plead his own case – and this was granted, despite vigorous objections from Natal.

He was supported by Bishop Colenso and other 'liberals', including the Cape parliamentarian, Saul Solomon, to whom the king wrote a touching letter of sympathy on hearing of the death of Solomon's young daughter – 'I feel so sorry to hear that one of your branches has withered and left you'. The king was a guest at a Highland sports gathering at Rondebosch when a heavy wooden caber, tossed by a brawny competitor, narrowly missed him. The new Cape Governor, Sir Hercules Robinson, was heard to observe: 'Had it fallen on the king's head a great problem would have been settled.'

England's Conservative Government fell in April 1880, and was replaced by the Liberals under Gladstone, who started undoing the expansionist policy in southern Africa. Greatly aided by Robert Samuelson, whose father had founded St Paul's Mission in Zululand in 1865, Cetshwayo continued his correspondence with governments and officials, and also with his people in Zululand. In 1882 the king travelled to England and, in London, was installed in a house in Kensington and taken on tours of the capital, drawing admiring crowds wherever he was recognised. Strikingly good-looking in tailored European clothing, he was dubbed 'The Ladies' Man' and inspired some very bad verse:

'White young dandies, get away-o!
Clear the field for CETEWAYO . . . .'

He lunched with Queen Victoria, who found the occasion 'enjoyable', and it was decided that the king should be allowed to return to rule over at least a portion of Zululand, where he was to be formally 'enthroned' by, of all people, Theophilus Shepstone.

A DEFEATED *Cetshwayo embarks for exile at the Cape.*

would go home . . . . We lost far more men at Khambula than at Isandlwana.'

After battles at Khambula and Gingindlovu the morale of the army was broken. Cetshwayo sent messengers with tusks, emblems of peace, to ask that the British force withdraw from his country, but Chelmsford was determined to salvage what remained of his reputation by defeating the Zulu on the open field rather than, as he had done, from entrenched positions. In the Battle of Ulundi, on the Mahlabatini plain a few kilometres west of oNdini, the Zulu made little more than a token attack on the hollow square formation of heavily armed infantry and cavalry, bristling with artillery and machine guns.

Cetshwayo went into hiding and was finally captured in the Ngome forest, and sent as a prisoner to Cape Town.

Dismembering the carcass

Isandlwana put paid to any British hopes that the war would be quick and inexpensive. Shepstone's plan to use Zulu land and labour as a bridgehead from Natal into the African interior also failed – simply due to the fact that Zulu resistance had proved much stronger than Britain could happily stomach. The imperial tide now turned against confederation in southern Africa – at least for the time being – and the annexationists could no longer count on British backing for their plans, as Shepstone was later to find out in the SAR.

By achieving this, at least, the Zulu had emerged from the war as victors, although their victory was most certainly a Pyrrhic one. The war severely disrupted their social and economic life, and the arbitrary settlement at the end proved ruinous. On the principle of 'divide and rule', Cetshwayo was exiled, and the Zulu kingdom was carved into 13 chiefdoms, supposedly to restore the land to what it had been before the rise of Shaka. In practice, it was a recipe for continuing destruction and civil war. The largest chiefdom – about one-third of Zululand – went to John Dunn, who had ingratiated himself with Cetshwayo and, after a friendship of some 20 years, turned against him in the war. Other wartime collaborators who were rewarded with chiefdoms were Hlubi (who also was not a Zulu) and Hamu (who was a Zulu). Another appointed chief was a distant relative of the king, Zibhebhu, who had fought bravely in the war but was, nevertheless, opposed to Cetshwayo and his *Usuthu* faction.

The new British Commander in Natal, Sir Garnet Wolseley, commanded the appointed chiefs to collect all firearms, as well as the royal cattle, an order carried out with enthusiasm, especially by Dunn, Zibhebhu and Hamu, who were quick to grasp the chance to enrich themselves. Resentment and tensions led to an *Usuthu* deputation travelling to Natal to complain of the roughshod methods of Hamu and Zibhebhu, and to enlist the support of Bishop Colenso in obtaining the restoration of Cetshwayo. The king returned to Zululand in January 1883, after accepting restrictions on his authority, as well as a reduction in the size of his 'official' kingdom. Zululand was partitioned again, with Zibhebhu being given a large tract in the north, and the southernmost area set aside for occupation by *Usuthu* opponents but to be administered by whites.

DINUZULU *(above), Cetshwayo's eldest son, was tried by the British and exiled to the island of St Helena.*
THE RESIDENT MAGISTRATE *at Ladysmith and his staff (right) collect hut tax from the Zulu in 1879.*

Violence was inevitable, and the British authorities merely looked on as Zibhebhu's *Mandlakazi* faction, aided by Hamu, rampaged through Cetshwayo's territory. The king escaped from his residence shortly before it was razed to the ground and was obliged to find safety with the British Resident Commissioner at Eshowe, where he died in 1884, just over a year after his return to Zululand. In desperation, the *Usuthu* turned for aid to the Boers in the SAR, promising to give them land in exchange for their help. The combined force smashed the *Mandlakazi* at the Mkhuze River, but the cost was high. The Boers demanded, and received, a grant of land equivalent to one-third of

the former kingdom, in which they formed yet another independent state, the New Republic.

Having presided over the disintegration of Zululand, Britain annexed the shattered state in 1887. Zibhebhu, who had fled to the southern Reserve, was allowed to return to his former territory in the north, where he was attacked by the *Usuthu* under Dinuzulu, eldest son of Cetshwayo. Determined not to sanction anything that looked like continuing the royal succession, the British turned on Dinuzulu, who was tried and exiled to the island of St Helena. When he returned, in 1898, it was to a very different Zululand, administered no longer by a king, nor even a British Crown, but directly by the Colony of Natal, which had annexed it in 1897.

The demands of the new hut tax obliged many to sell what cattle they still possessed, or to enter the labour market in order to raise the money. Young men travelled far to find work, on railway construction and, in increasing numbers, on the Witwatersrand. Drought, locust invasion and the rinderpest plague joined in completing the disruption of traditional Zulu society.

The end of Pedi independence

With his annexation of the Transvaal complete (see page 181), the new Administrator, Theophilus Shepstone, found that his most pressing need was to raise revenue for the empty state coffers. Based on his Natal experience, he considered that the best way to go about this would be to apply 'judicious taxation of the Native population'. Commissioners and magistrates were instructed to inform the chiefs not just of the tax, but also that the tax had to be paid in cash. They were also advised that 'in order to enable their people to go to work for wages either in this country or elsewhere, payment for Passes on their way to seek labour will be abolished, and arrangements made for their

THE LARGEST SLICE *of Cetshwayo's dismembered kingdom went to 'white' Zulu John Dunn (on the left of this picture).*

The end of Griqua independence

Independence was a fragile commodity in the heydey of colonialism – and as the 1870s drew to a close the threat of annexation loomed ever closer for one of the most unusual independent states of all: a small pocket of land between Natal and Transkei occupied by the Griqua.

Under Adam Kok III, the Griqua had trekked from the vicinity of Philippolis, where they had lost their lands to the emigrant Boers, to find a new home. Granted a safe passage by Moshoeshoe, they crossed Basutoland, using gunpowder on occasion to blast their pathway through the Drakensberg, and descended, after two years, to the territory known as No Man's Land, between the Cape and Natal, in 1862. Insecure and distrustful, they lived in laager for some 10 years, before founding their own town of Kokstad.

Despite its name, No Man's Land was not an empty territory when the Griqua arrived, but was peopled by, among others, Mpondo and Sotho over whom they were expected to establish some sort of authority, thereby saving the colonial governments the trouble and expense. The Griqua regarded themselves as independent, but reluctantly accepted as British Resident J M Orpen, who had formerly been active in negotiations between Moshoeshoe and the British authorities. So far as Orpen was concerned, the Griqua were not independent, but were British subjects. Kok must have realised that his territory might, one day, come under British or colonial authority, but he had been assured that he would be consulted first. His position in this respect was insecure, because the land he occupied had been ceded by the Mpondo to the British, at whose pleasure the Griqua were in occupation. Kok was unaware that Orpen was lobbying for annexation.

Escorted by Orpen, Governor Sir Henry Barkly arrived at Kokstad in October 1874, to announce that government of Griqualand East 'will for the future be carried out under instructions by the British Resident, Joseph Millerd Orpen, Esq'. Kok was to be president of a council with vague, undefined authority, and would receive £1 000 a year.

It was not so much the take-over the Griqua resented, but the fact that they had not been consulted, and had been 'taken over like so many cattle or sheep'. They possessed great pride in their identity which, in the face of advancing white colonisation, they had so far preserved. One of the factors that secured this preservation was the political astuteness of Adam Kok, but the Griqua were deprived of this when, in December 1875, he was killed in a cart accident. Kok had banned the sale of land to foreigners, and had also enacted strict regulations over the sale of liquor. Orpen lifted these restrictions, and many Griqua sold their land at relatively high prices. With the community on the verge of breaking up, and still resentful of the high-handed treatment it had received, many individuals turned for solace to the liquor shops that now flourished in various parts of their territory.

Public discussions by the Griqua were regarded by Barkly as a threat to law and order, so he despatched Captain William Blyth, a tough disciplinarian, as additional Resident to Kokstad. Blyth showed little respect for the leaders of the community, antagonising not only them but also the younger people. He raided houses, including Adam Kok's house, which was still occupied by his widow, and imprisoned one of Kok's relatives, in 1878, on a charge of using 'treasonable' language. Adam 'Muis' Kok per-

suaded a number of Mpondo to join him in rebellion, and was strengthened by an alliance with Smith Pommer, a former 'Kat River rebel'.

About 500 rebels gathered near the old laager on the slopes of Mount Currie, where they were attacked by a combined force of Frontier Police and Cape Mounted Riflemen. After a four-hour battle in which 12 Griqua were killed, the remainder fled towards Pondoland, but were caught on the slopes of Ingeli Mountain, where another 20, including Pommer, were killed. The survivors were taken to Cape Town and imprisoned until, after a long period of argument, their detention was ruled illegal. Their country was formally annexed to the Cape in 1879, thereby ending their cherished independence.

Demoralised and dispossessed, some of the surviving Griqua once more trekked in 1917 – this time by rail – to a site near Touws River in the Karoo. This attempt to found a new community failed, and most returned to Kokstad. The last trek was made in 1928 by donkey cart, wagon, on horseback and on foot to a site at Kranshoek, near Plettenberg Bay, where the Griqua spirit still survives.

THE DEATH *of former Kat River 'rebel' Smith Pommer, who had allied himself to the Griqua cause.*

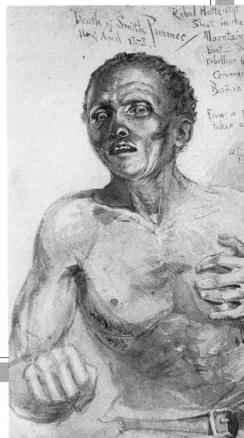

JOSEPH ORPEN, *British Resident in Adam Kok's Griqualand.*

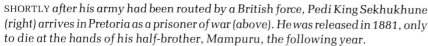

SHORTLY *after his army had been routed by a British force, Pedi King Sekhukhune (right) arrives in Pretoria as a prisoner of war (above). He was released in 1881, only to die at the hands of his half-brother, Mampuru, the following year.*

safe journey back to their homes'. Under republican government, the flow of labour to the diamond workings and railway projects had been seriously affected, and this had provided one of the justifications for Britain's annexation of the territory (see page 177).

Another was Shepstone's argument that the republic's failure to defeat Sekhukhune had seriously undermined the authority of the 'white man' in southern Africa. The truth was that, in legitimising land grants made by the bankrupt SAR Government to its burghers, Shepstone was expanding the state's boundaries into land claimed and occupied by the Pedi. The war between the SAR and the Pedi had reached stalemate at the time of annexation, but Shepstone was determined that Pedi independence should be brought to an end, and the chiefdom made subject to the new state.

Sekhukhune was duly sent an official message advising him that if he wished to enjoy British 'protection and also other benefits', he would have to 'render due obedience to the Government and to pay such tax as may be found necessary'. He was also instructed to hand over 2 000 cattle as compensation arising from the war with the republican authorities. Sekhukhune's options were to accept these terms, or leave the territory. Having previously denied the former republic's right to authority over the Pedi, Shepstone was now claiming the authority for himself.

On the subject of cattle, Sekhukhune stated that he could not understand 'why the English who have taken the land should enforce a penalty exacted by the Boers'. Shepstone, however, refused to allow his representative in Lydenburg to accept anything but the full tribute and, in an interview with Sekhukhune's messengers, implied that failure to pay in full would be taken as an act of war. He ignored the very real plea that as a result of war and droughts, the Pedi were unable to afford to part with 2 000 cattle, as they needed these to barter for grain. A number of minor incidents were magnified into full-scale threats of war on the part of the Pedi, which Shepstone interpreted as 'a common

desire in the native mind' to get rid of the whites. He added that for so long as the clans failed to co-operate to this end, they would be dealt with one by one. He would start with Sekhukhune.

War began in 1878, with some inconclusive skirmishing and, on the part of the whites, a spate of fort building. To Shepstone's considerable surprise, the Pedi did not collapse overnight, but resorted to hit-and-run attacks and continual harassment. Whites were peering nervously over the fortress walls when news came that the British had invaded Zululand. This resulted in a further reduction of troops and volunteers in the Transvaal, and the subjugation of Sekhukhune was postponed until the Zulu had been dealt with. From Natal, Sir Garnet Wolseley ordered all Transvaal operations to be halted until he arrived to take charge. In September 1879, having dismembered Zululand and seen to the capture of Cetshwayo, Wolseley duly arrived in Pretoria.

Wolseley and Shepstone expected that the defeat of the Zulu army would have demonstrated to Sekhukhune the futility of armed resistance, and he was presented with 'conditions' for avoiding conflict. These were subjection to British rule, payment of taxes and a fine of 2 500 cattle, and an undertaking to maintain law and order in his territory and not to interfere with the construction and maintenance of police posts in that territory. Rejection of any of these terms, in Wolseley's view, meant that 'it will be necessary to destroy Sekhukhune's power by force'. Shepstone argued that this was desirable in any case, to prevent 'a general rising among the numerous native tribes'.

These outside pressures emphasised the tensions that already existed among the Pedi, between the paramount and his nephew, Phokwane, and also his own half-brother, Mampuru, who claimed the paramountcy for himself. At a meeting called to discuss Wolseley's conditions, Sekhukhune said he was tired of war and that all who could afford it should bring cattle so that the fine could be paid. A petty chief who expressed himself in favour of peace was chased from the meeting, and another, Putlakle, was applauded when he said: 'Let the white people fight for the cattle if they want them . . . . ' To this, Sekhukhune replied: 'Your words are my words, but I wished to hear what you thought . . . .'

An overwhelming defeat of the Pedi would not only illustrate imperial strength to the African population but would also cause the burghers to think seriously before attempting a military confrontation with the British. When Wolseley finally went to war, it was at the head of an army composed of 3 500 British soldiers and white volunteers, 3 000 Transvaal Africans – including Mampuru and his followers – and 8 000 Swazi soldiers who had been invited to join in. Against this force, Sekhukhune's capital, Tsate, was defended by no more than 4 000 Pedi, as many of the subsidiary chiefs were obliged to hold back some of their forces to defend their villages against Swazi raids.

Wolseley's attack was halted by heavy rifle fire from concealed positions, and only when the Pedi were attacked in the rear by the massed Swazi forces was he able to continue his advance. Those Pedi who escaped the slaughter were able to retreat to the hill known as Ntswaneng, which was riddled with caves and tunnels into which the attackers were reluctant to venture. During a heavy shower of rain, most of the survivors were able to slip away, leaving more than 1 000 of their comrades dead. Of the attackers, 13 whites and some 600 Swazi were killed.

Wolseley then turned the Swazi loose on the countryside, and recorded that 'my object is to strike terror into the hearts of the surrounding tribes by the utter destruction of Sikukuni, so the more that Swazis raid and destroy, the better my purpose is effected'.

While the British were militarily successful against the Pedi, once again the dream of confederation was not to be

The wedding that led to war

In 1877 the troubled border region of the eastern Cape was a war waiting to happen – all it needed was a spark to set the whole frontier ablaze.

Behind the smouldering unrest was the annexation by the Cape Colony of land belonging to the Gcaleka Xhosa – and granted to the Mfengu, a group of farmers whom many regarded as allies of the colonial authorities. The spark that led to war came at the marriage of a Mfengu chieftain called Mgenga. The wedding was open to all, even the Mfengu's traditional enemies, the Gcaleka. During the celebrations, old enmities surfaced, there was an argument, and a Gcaleka chief was struck by a Mfengu. The Gcaleka returned home, but next day they were back and fighting soon spread along the border.

As the Mfengu were, technically, British subjects and entitled to protection, the Governor, Sir Henry Bartle Frere – who happened to be visiting the frontier – sent instructions to Sarhili, paramount chief of the Gcaleka, to cease fighting and to return all Mfengu cattle. Sarhili, whose father, Hintsa, had been murdered while supposedly in the care of an earlier Governor, Sir Harry Smith, refused to attend a meeting with Frere.

Much land that had formerly been occupied by the Gcaleka had been given to the Mfengu, and it was this that lay at the root of Sarhili's decision to risk war with the whites. 'The country is too small,' he said, 'and I may as well die as be pushed into a corner.' Not realising the extent of hostilities, Frere sent a detachment of police to support the Mfengu. The police and their Mfengu allies were routed at the Battle of Gwadana, but repulsed an attack at Ibeka.

Later, reinforced by volunteers – colonists as well as Mfengu – the police invaded Gcalekaland, only to find it deserted, all the people and their stock having moved to the east. Sarhili's homestead was destroyed, and the Gcaleka were pursued as far as the Mbashe River, where it was decided that the danger of war was over. Grants of land were offered in the newly vacated territory, and 51 applications were received within the first 10 days.

The Gcaleka, however, had not run away. They had merely taken their families and livestock to a place of safety. Now, the warriors returned, and soon they were joined by the Ngqika of Sandile. Short of food and ammunition, they decided to attack the military camp at Centane Mountain, although it was defended by almost 1 000 men, including British regular soldiers. In a head-on charge at the entrenched position, the Gcaleka were shattered by fire from rockets, cannons and rifles. The Ngqika, however, knew better than to attack such a position, and remained in sight of the defenders, but out of their range, hoping to lure them into the open. In this they were successful and, after a sharp fight, were obliged to withdraw when the arrival of another group of police threatened to take them in the rear.

After Centane, the Gcaleka were broken as a fighting force, and the Ngqika army, led by Sandile himself, made their way to their old home among the Amatola Mountains, from where they had been driven almost 30 years earlier. They occupied the rugged area known as the Pirie Bush, and there waited to be attacked. In the end, they were defeated by cold and starvation rather than by force of arms, although Sandile was fatally wounded in a skirmish. Afraid to surrender, hundreds of Nqgika soldiers remained hiding in the bush, from which they were flushed and killed – 'cruelly shot, some of them in the act of begging for mercy'.

In parliament, Saul Solomon, the member for Cape Town, demanded to know how much longer the government was to allow the 'slaughter' to continue. Two weeks later, on 2 July 1878, an amnesty was proclaimed.

Close on 4 000 Xhosa had died in battle, compared to only 171 taken prisoner, figures that suggest that the taking of prisoners was not a high priority. More than 45 000 Xhosa cattle were taken, and many women and children were sent by sea from East London to exile near Cape Town. John Gordon Sprigg, the new Prime Minister of the Cape, determined that the Xhosa were to be 'effectually conquered' and shown that whites were the true 'masters of the land'. To do this, he decided, it would be necessary to disarm all Africans, even the Mfengu allies. No black person was to be permitted to possess a firearm.

CAPE TROOPS *march into Basutoland in a bid to disarm Basotho during the so-called 'Gun War' of 1880-1 (above). The war cost the Cape Government £3-million and led to the fall of Prime Minister John Sprigg (right).*

realised. Changing sentiment in Britain – and a change in government – was to lay the confederation dream to rest, at least for the time being. Within a few years, the SAR had regained its independence – and the Pedi found themselves ruled by their old enemies, the Boers.

The right to carry a gun

The Zulu victory at Isandlwana led whites in the Cape to demand that all Africans should be disarmed. Possession of firearms was to be a right reserved for whites only.

But when Cape Prime Minister John Sprigg announced this to the Sotho in October 1879, the news was received with dismay and indignation. Possession of a rifle was a sign of manhood, and to be deprived of the rifle was to be reduced to the status of a child.

Apart from the symbolic, there were also practical considerations. In most instances, the firearms had been bought with wages earned on the diamond fields, and so represented weeks of their owners' labour. There was also the possibility that firearms might be required for the defence of their kingdom and, finally, the intention to disarm them clearly showed the Sotho that they were not trusted. It was, in fact, just another move in the systematic undermining of the authority of the chiefs.

Moshoeshoe's successor, Letsie, was old and unwell, and he advocated obedience to Sprigg's decree, but this was the minority view. A younger son of Moshoeshoe, Masupha, espoused defiance, and attracted Letsie's son and heir, Lerotholi, to his side. Where magistrates were successful in persuading people to hand over their firearms, these people were attacked and their property confiscated. Law and order broke down, and Sprigg travelled to Basutoland in an attempt to avert full-scale war. He offered a revised policy of arms control at a meeting that Masupha did not bother to attend. Lerotholi, who did attend, refused to surrender any firearms. Sprigg returned, unsuccessful, to the Cape.

In Basutoland, whites were besieged in the various magistracies and in stores across the country. In the Cape, Mhlontlo, chief of the Mpondomise, rebelled against the government, and a few whites were killed at Sulenkama, near Qumbu, while others were besieged at Maclear and Ugie. Mhlontlo and some of his followers fled into Basutoland, eluding the troops and volunteers who pursued them. Troops were sent also to Basutoland, where the main fighting took place at Mafeteng in the west of the country before a truce was declared in April 1881. The next month, Sprigg's ministry fell as a direct result of his Basutoland policy, the war having cost the colony the enormous sum of £3-million.

The peace terms provided for the surrender of firearms, but there was no practical way of enforcing this and it became watered down to mere registration of weapons. Masupha refused to accept even this, and openly broke with Letsie and Lerotholi, who were now regarded as 'loyal'. This did not act in their favour, as they were responsible for collecting 5 000 cattle demanded as a fine, as well for compensation to whites. Once again chaos ensued, with the Cape Government powerless to restore order.

The best it could do was to propose that the people of Basutoland be ruled directly by the Crown rather than the Cape Colony, and this took place in 1884. Masupha's feud and intermittent warfare with Lerotholi were to continue until 1898. Had Basutoland remained a territory administered by the Cape Colony, it would have become a part of the later Republic of South Africa, subject to all its laws, rather than the independent kingdom that it is today.

'With God on their side...'

At 11 o'clock on the morning of 12 April 1877 the first South African Republic (SAR) ceased to exist. A proclamation read out in Church Square, Pretoria, informed the outraged burghers that their countr had been officially annexed by Britain. Anger and resentment were soon to give way to an organised movement of resistance, fostered by a new nationalism.

THE WINDS OF WAR were already puffing gently across the Transvaal in the spring of 1880 – and by the time the first highveld storms were ushering in another summer, the former Boer republic was seething and fermenting.

For many weeks small groups of Boers – future mainstays of a guerrilla army – had been hoarding arms and ammunition in preparation for a showdown with the soldiers of the strongest nation on earth. At the same time, skilful behind-the-scenes prompting by an alliance of Boer political leaders and Calvinist ministers was pulling every man, woman and child into an increasingly strident anti-British protest movement.

By December Afrikaner leaders, buoyed by a new-found unity, consumed by hatred for their colonial masters and convinced that they had the backing of their God, were ready to lead a revolt to reclaim the republic they had surrendered with hardly a whimper to the British three years earlier. On 16 December, 42 years after the guns of their forebears had triumphed over Zulu spears at Blood River, Transvaal Afrikaners hoisted the flag of their republic at Paardekraal, near present-day Krugersdorp, and declared themselves independent once more. That same afternoon the first shots in a war of independence were fired.

The countdown to war
At first glance, the SAR hardly seemed a worthwhile addition to Britain's southern African empire. Since 1852,

when the Sand River Convention had guaranteed the region's trekker communities their independence, problems had rolled in thick and fast.

In fact, shortly before the British Special Commissioner Theophilus Shepstone issued the proclamation which brought 25 years of self-rule to an end, a combination of an unpopular President, looming bankruptcy, hostile African neighbours and never-ending bickering among Boer warlords had pushed the republic to the brink of collapse.

Yet when Britain finally claimed the SAR as part of its southern African confederation scheme (see page 181), self-interest was not among the reasons mentioned for its actions. A far more noble coloration had to be given to what was after all a blatant violation of the Sand River Convention: thus, the official reason given for intervention was the desire to save the Boers – not only from themselves, but also from African neighbours such as the Pedi led by the doughty Sekhukhune, who only a few months earlier had inflicted a sharp defeat on a commando led by President Thomas Burgers.

And so, convinced that Boer protest against the takeover was no more than a face-saving gesture by disaffected former leaders, Shepstone immediately set about trying to win the trust of the rank-and-file by crushing the Pedi after a 20-month campaign (see page 188).

But it was to prove a Pyrrhic victory: the defeat of the Pedi and the Zulu within a few months of each other removed the Boers' most pressing security problems and al-

SHEPSTONE *hoped to win Boer approval for his annexation of the Transvaal by crushing the Pedi under the leadership of Sekhukhune. After a 20-month campaign in the Steelpoort area of the eastern Transvaal, a combined force of British regulars and Swazi soldiers stormed Sekhukhune's stronghold in the Leolu Mountains on 28 November 1879 and burned it to the ground.*

lowed republican leaders to apply all their energies to an anti-British campaign that was highlighted by calls for consumer boycotts and civil disobedience.

The republican struggle continues

For a community which over the years had leaned towards settling disputes with guns rather than diplomacy, the Boers quickly showed themselves to be adroit political strategists. Although their leaders never ditched the option of an armed uprising, much of the early part of their plan to regain independence was spent trying to unite their divided *volk*.

At the same time, they also launched a diplomatic initiative, with Paul Kruger leading two delegations to London – in 1877 and 1878 – to argue for the reinstatement of the SAR. When both missions returned home empty-handed, republican leaders reacted with renewed calls for the moulding of the *volk* into a powerful, cohesive force that could eventually oppose foreign rule. At numerous church services, at rally after rally, Boers were reminded of their special calling: God had given them their language; God had given them their land; God had chosen them to rule southern Africa and to civilise its savages . . . .

Initial British response to the growing unrest was to blame it on the work of a small group of agitators. Later they tried to arrest some of the Boer leaders – but faced with rising hostility they were quickly made to backtrack. Finally, they tried to ban the by now regular Boer mass rallies. But again, their instructions were simply ignored.

PAUL KRUGER *led two delegations to London to plead for the reinstatement of the South African Republic.*

The beginnings of a new nationalism?

In many ways, the growing petulance of the authorities towards these displays of civil disobedience played right into the hands of the Boer leaders: each arrest, and every attempt to ban a meeting, was skilfully used to whip up emotions and to draw together people who shared a common grievance.

Before annexation, even the President would have struggled to get together 1 000 men for a punitive commando. But now, up to six times that number needed little prompting to travel hundreds of kilometres to attend protest rallies. In a sense, these mass meetings (or people's meetings, as Boer leaders dubbed them) were more than just occasions for the venting of collective anger. Of far more importance was the fact that they were used to expand the new political message of shared interests, Boer unity and obedience to 'real' leaders.

As political consciousness increased, so did the organisational structure of what was rapidly evolving into an 'underground' resistance movement. For instance, 'people's committees', whose tasks involved the compilation of reports as well as the gathering of information, were established throughout the Transvaal and, in effect, formed a type of state within a state.

All burghers – men, women and children – were expected to join the budding resistance movement. Those who did not were regarded as 'traitors' – 'despicable creatures [who displayed] disloyalty [to their] blood relationship'. Thus, Adriaan Stander, a Shepstone supporter, was banned by church leaders from attending *Nagmaal* (communion) and other 'traitors' were executed after hostilities had broken out on 16 December 1880.

The extensive coverage given to the events surrounding annexation, by Afrikaans newspapers such as '*Die Afrikaanse Patriot*' and '*De Zuid Afrikaan*', sparked a wave of sympathy among 'Africanders' in the Cape Colony and the Orange Free State (OFS) for their 'blood-brothers' in the Transvaal. In 1877, '*De Zuid Afrikaan*' reported that 'throughout the entire length and breadth of the [Cape] Colony, thousands of families were disgusted at the deed of annexation'; and in 1878, '*Die Patriot*', in a special message to the Transvalers, wrote: 'The hearts of all true Afrikaners throughout the whole country are with you.' In the OFS, where feelings of solidarity with the Transvalers were even more pronounced, the *volksraad* came under great pressure from many burghers to abandon its official policy of neutrality and to assist its former sister republic to regain its independence.

Naturally, the Transvalers welcomed these displays of public sympathy – which were further cemented when activists such as Paul Kruger and Piet Joubert undertook extensive speaking and fundraising tours of the Cape and the OFS. To the increasingly jittery colonial authorities, the growth of Cape Afrikaner support for the cause of the Transvaal republicans raised the unwelcome prospect of a general Boer uprising. Confederation, clearly, was not turning out to be such a good idea after all. But even though officials now realised this, abandonment of the policy did not come into their reckoning: the humiliation would be too great . . . .

COLONEL SIR OWEN LANYON, *who took over as Administrator of the Transvaal from Sir Theophilus Shepstone, was a hardnosed career soldier whose tough line against tax evaders led directly to confrontation with the Boers.*

The spark that led to war

By 1880 Boer frustrations had reached breaking point. All that was needed to set off the explosion was a spark – and it was provided early in November, in the western Transvaal town of Potchefstroom.

The principal actors of this drama were Piet Bezuidenhout, an obscure farmer, and Sir Owen Lanyon, an army colonel whose appointment as Administrator of the Transvaal in place of Shepstone signalled a tough new approach towards the Boer population.

From the British point of view, the key to the prosperity and smooth administration of the region was the implementation of an effective tax-collection system. The problem, of course, was that the Boers, even when they ruled themselves, were not noted for their willingness to contribute towards state coffers. Thus, it stood to reason that they would be even less inclined to give freely to people whom they considered to be 'foreign invaders'.

Lanyon's dogged determination to root out tax evaders was a direct cause of the fracas involving a wagon belonging to Bezuidenhout: it started with a tax demand for £27 5s – roughly £14 more than Bezuidenhout believed he owed. After a long wrangle he offered to pay £13 5s on condition that it be put aside for the coffers of a future Boer republic. Lanyon would have none of this and, eager to make an example of the stubborn farmer, ordered that his wagon be confiscated and auctioned.

But by now news of the row had spread, and on the day of the auction, Piet Cronje, a well-known activist, marched into town with several dozen armed companions, commandeered the wagon and returned it to its owner.

Lanyon was furious but, convinced he was dealing with just an isolated case of Boer mischief-making, merely issued instructions for the ringleaders of the Potchefstroom mutiny to be arrested. But his attempt to bring the Boers to book had to be abandoned for there were simply not enough troops. Lanyon's manpower shortage had not gone unnoticed by the Boers.

Building Afrikaner nationalism –

His name was Stephanus Johannes du Toit – the 13th son of a Paarl wine farmer – a Dutch Reformed Church minister, a journalist, an author, a champion of the Afrikaans language and finally, a traitor.

In many ways, he was a man ahead of his time: for, quick to recognise how the frustrations of individual Afrikaners could be channelled into group grievances against the common British enemy, he soon emerged as one of the most enthusiastic proponents of Afrikaner nationalism in the Cape.

Taking advantage of Britain's intervention in the 1870s in the affairs of the Boer states in the north, and the feeling of insecurity which this brought about among Boers throughout southern Africa, Du Toit, his brother Daniel and a small group of friends, including Arnoldus Pannevis and Casper Hoogenhout, formed *Die Genootskap van Regte Afrikaners* (The Fellowship of True Afrikaners) in August 1875. It was an organisation dedicated, as they put it, 'to stand for our nation, our language and our country'.

Arguing passionately that the Afrikaners, made up of a blend of Dutch, German and French, were a culturally distinct group with their own language and history, *Die Genootskap* intensified the nationalistic feelings already stirring in many Dutch-speakers.

The formation of the organisation, however, was only a first step in a grander Du Toit plan. By now his vision of a single Afrikaner nation cutting across all boundaries had become an obsession. So to broaden his base he started a newspaper called '*Die Afrikaanse Patriot*'. To it he contributed a number of editorials encouraging Afrikaners to

'DIE AFRIKAANSE PATRIOT', *founded by Stephanus du Toit, enjoyed enormous popular support after annexation.*

through the power of print

register as voters and to keep an eye open for potential parliamentary candidates.

Pushing a strong nationalist line, '*Die Patriot*' struggled along on a small circulation until the British annexed the South African Republic (SAR) in 1877. While other newspapers at first adopted a cautious approach to the annexation, '*Die Patriot*' condemned it strongly – at one stage urging the Boers to take up arms to drive out the British. It became the only newspaper the Boers trusted – and for a brief period after the SAR had regained its independence, it enjoyed a boom among 'Africanders'.

In 1877, Du Toit published a history book entitled '*Die Geskiedenis van Ons Land in die Taal van Ons Volk*' ('The History of Our Country in the Language of Our People'). No more than a crude attempt to rewrite history from the Afrikaner viewpoint, it hammered away at the concept that Afrikaners were a distinct people, occupying a distinct fatherland and speaking a God-given language. The British were viewed as the enemy, and the Slagtersnek incident of 1815, which had been regarded as a matter of little importance at the time, became a major example of British perfidy.

Weaknesses of the new nationalism

Within a decade of the Transvaal War of Independence, the 'nationalism' which had blossomed among Dutch-speakers had run out of steam.

In a way, it was inevitable that it would flounder: for Boer togetherness during the hostilities had been built on the flimsy foundation of emotionalism. In the less heated atmosphere which prevailed after the Transvalers had won back their independence, many of the divisions which had long plagued Boer society began to reappear.

The growth of true nationalism is dependent on several factors – the chief among which are the domination of a country by a ruling ethnic elite; uneven industrial development, and the forging of an alliance of classes by 'professionals' eager to overcome the economic oppression of the ruling elite.

But in southern Africa in the second half of the 19th century there was little industrial development and even less sign of an emerging Boer professional class.

In the main, Dutch-speakers held education in low esteem. In the Cape Colony, which was considered the most developed part of the region, only 43 percent of white children between the ages of five and 15 were literate. And most of them were English-speaking. To further complicate matters, of the few Dutch parents who recognised the advantages offered by an education, most preferred to send their children to English-language schools.

Politics was another field which held little interest for the Dutch – and often, those who voted simply did so for an English shopkeeper, an agent, or for someone recommended by them. There were no secret ballots in those days, and those who wielded power in the towns and villages, made certain that all who were indebted to them voted according to their instructions.

Things were no different in the SAR and OFS, where class cleavages between large landowners and poor *bywoners* (tenants) continued to plague Boer society. In many ways, the *bywoners* were kept in perpetual poverty by their powerful kinsmen: while theoretically they were

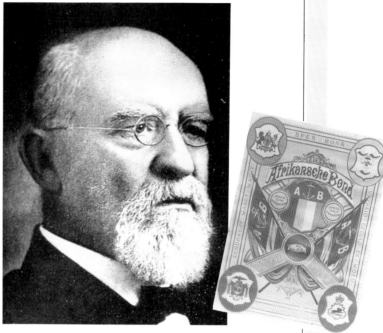

IN 1883 *Jan Hendrik Hofmeyr took over as leader of the Afrikaner Bond (Afrikaner League), which had been formed to encourage Afrikaner commercialism.*

free to participate in the political process as equals, the reality was that they stood no chance of being elected to top political offices. These positions were the exclusive preserve of the landowners, who also allocated land to newcomers, distributed African labour, settled disputes and decided who should be called up for commando duty. Often it was the poor whites who were sent out to fight African neighbours. The anger and divisions which arose from this tended to stunt the growth of nationalism.

Struggling on regardless

Insurmountable though these problems might have seemed, Du Toit refused to be cowed. In 1879, he formed the *Afrikaner Bond* (Afrikaner League), a political organisation which quickly became established in the central and eastern districts of the Cape Colony. Its aim was, first of all, to consolidate the various existing groups such as *Die Genootskap* and the various farmers' protection associations into one body. Secondly, it was to mobilise Afrikaners into a force capable of winning concessions in the commercial field dominated by the British: thus, Afrikaners were encouraged to establish their own trade cooperatives and open their own banks.

After the war (1881), the *Bond* branched out into the two Boer republics. But in 1883, when it merged with the *Boeren Beschermings Vereniging* (Farmers' Protection Society), and its leadership was taken over by Jan Hendrik Hofmeyr, it was transformed into a Cape political party closely allied to the interests of rich Cape farmers.

Impressed by his loyalty to their cause, the Transvalers appointed Du Toit to the post of Superintendent-General of Education in their reinstated republic. But ironically, after a series of clashes with Paul Kruger, he became a supporter of Cecil John Rhodes, perhaps the greatest British imperialist of them all.

Paul Kruger – super-Afrikaner?

On the evening of 10 September 1900 a frail old man dressed in a shabby black coat, a clumsy-looking pair of black boots and a black top hat stood on a bridge over the Crocodile River on the eastern Transvaal's border with Mozambique and said a last, tearful farewell to three companions.

Then, on the first stage of a journey which would take him into exile in Europe, he turned and walked slowly into Portuguese territory. The Paul Kruger era – the remarkable story of the lowly Cape cowherd who rose to President of the South African Republic (SAR) – had come to an end.

But his British pursuers had created a hero. Over the next few years, as Afrikaner nationalism began to grow in the aftermath of the South African War (see page 299), a special place would be reserved in the Afrikaner roll-of-honour for the bearded man with the swollen eyelids, some of it fact, some fiction.

By modern standards, Stephanus Johannes Paulus ('Oom Paul') Kruger was a religious fanatic and a crusty old racist. But in 19th century Transvaal, where a white man's political clout depended on the extent of his commitment to God and ability to fight off the Africans whose land he had taken, Kruger had few peers. Bible, gun and single-minded belief in Boer self-determination swept him from cowherd to cattle farmer; from commando leader to President of a Boer republic.

Kruger's religious and political philosophy – which he stubbornly clung to throughout his life – was shaped and nurtured in the Colesburg district of the Cape Colony where he had been born on 10 October 1825.

He was born into a landless, but well-to-do farming family in Cradock in October 1825, and soon became adept at watching over his father's stock as they moved about the eastern Cape in search of grazing.

Even as a boy he disliked the British. The abolition of slavery, coupled with the fact that former slave-owners (like his parents) were expected to travel to London to claim their promised compensation, had a lot to do with this.

In 1835 the Kruger family joined hundreds of other eastern Cape Boers in trekking across the Orange River in search of better grazing along the banks of the Caledon River. The following year, 11-year-old Paul received his baptism of fire against the Ndebele at the Battle of Vegkop.

On a religious level, he became a strong supporter of the *Doppers*, a conservative section of the Dutch Reformed Church, who refused to sing hymns because the words were not contained in the Scriptures.

By 1850 he had become firmly established in the Transvaal, where his knowledge of the Bible and prowess as a hunter of both animals and troublesome African neighbours had thrust him into a prominent position in burgher politics.

But it was immediately after Shepstone's annexation of the SAR in 1877 that Kruger's political star shone brightest. Leaderless and confused, the Boers looked to him to step into the breach, and in a few months he was able to channel the rising anger into a cohesive, unified movement for republican freedom.

Two trips to London, in 1877 and 1878, failed to win back independence for the Boers, but it established him as a skilled negotiator. (Even the British were forced to admit this.)

When the Boers unilaterally declared themselves independent in 1880, Kruger was the key figure in the triumvirate (which included Piet Joubert and Marthinus Wessel Pretorius) elected to govern the country. He became President of the Boer republic in 1883 and remained at the head of affairs until his exile in 1900.

Yet Kruger the politician was an enigma – an intriguing mixture of stubbornness, ruthlessness, compassion, conservatism and pragmatism all rolled into one.

As a Transvaal nationalist, he was loath to enter into any agreements which might compromise the state. For instance, after the Jameson Raid in 1895, it took him eight months to respond to an OFS proposal for much closer unity.

He used the Scriptures ruthlessly – often shamelessly – to score political points. 'He seems to believe that the more he quotes from the Bible, the more likely he is to win,' a frustrated opponent once said of him. And although his narrow brand of conservatism frequently frustrated more liberal thinkers in the Transvaal *Volksraad* (parliament), he could also

PAUL KRUGER, *the cowherd who became president of a Boer republic.*

also be pragmatic. All said, Kruger was a shrewd politician – the way he turned the Jameson Raid to the Boer state's advantage was hailed as a masterstroke that swept him to an overwhelming victory over Joubert in the poll for the presidency later that year.

A DEFEATED *Kruger sets sail for Europe and exile in October 1900.*

Between 13 and 16 December, at an emotion-charged rally at Paardekraal, 5 000 burghers reaffirmed their faith in God as they declared themselves and their country independent of Britain. Kruger, Piet Joubert and Marthinus Wessel Pretorius were entrusted with the running of the reborn South African Republic. There was now no turning back – and on 16 December the opening shots of the rebellion were exchanged at Potchefstroom.

The Boer leaders wasted little time in contacting Lanyon. In a letter couched in diplomatic language, they outlined the reasons for their actions. And while they stressed they had no desire for war, they warned that they would be forced to fight if the reins of government were not handed over to them within 24 hours.

Lanyon's reaction was to try to bolster British troop strength in the main Transvaal towns. But he received a devastating setback on 20 December when a column led by Colonel Philip Anstruther was decisively defeated by a Boer commando at Bronkhorstspruit, less than 50 kilometres from the British stronghold of Pretoria.

That night a shocked Lanyon sent a call for help to Natal. Sir George Pomeroy Colley, Governor of Natal and south-east Africa, was composing a poem when the message arrived. Sandhurst-trained from the age of 13, 45-year-old Colley's claim to fame was his compilation of a chapter of British military history in the 'Encyclopaedia Britannica'. Now the Boers were giving him a chance to carve his own name in military history. Although his wish would be granted – it would not quite be in the way he imagined.

Colley's mission to reconquer the Transvaal began on 24 January 1881, with a march from Newcastle on the northern Natal border. By 28 January he was ready to make his first move: to capture the strategic Boer position of Laing's Nek, a mountainous area from which troop movements out of Natal could easily be observed.

But his attack was a disaster – and of the 480 men who were sent into the fray, 150 were killed by Boer sharpshooters. Worse was to follow for the luckless general – and on 8 February he lost another 150 men in a shootout with the Boers on a small plateau called Schuinshoogte. The defeats at Laing's Nek and Schuinshoogte caused panic in Whitehall. Britain had no desire to be involved in a drawnout, expensive war. Some politicians also feared that the conflict in the Transvaal could escalate into a Boer uprising in the rest of southern Africa. It would be far better to grant the Transvaal self-government, they argued. A message was sent to Colley instructing him to inform Boer leaders that the British Government would be prepared to discuss self-government if they agreed to cease hostilities.

Colley was furious. He saw the offer as capitulation. But he passed on the message – with one important addition: he gave the Boers 48 hours to react to the offer – an impossible condition considering that their leadership was spread throughout the territory.

Meanwhile, the ambitious general had already planned his next move. It involved scaling the Hill of Doves, Majuba. From the top he reckoned he could pick the enemy off at his leisure. On the night of 26 February, about 400 British troops scaled the summit. The next day, a Sunday, Boer

ON SUNDAY, *27 February 1881, 150 Boer volunteers stormed Majuba (the Hill of Doves) in a successful bid to winkle out 400 British troops.*

hymns and prayers were interrupted when a sea of Redcoats was spotted high above them. After the initial panic had subsided, 150 men volunteered to scale the steep walls of the hill to flush out the enemy.

Colley, meanwhile, believing his position to be impregnable, omitted to order his men to dig trenches and to set up barricades. When the Boers made their surprise appearance at the top of Majuba they exacted a terrible toll. Colley himself was killed in the skirmish. It was a pointless waste of lives. On 3 August 1881, in terms of the Pretoria Convention, the Transvaal became a self-governing state subject to certain conditions. The burgher community, so deeply divided when the country had been annexed four years earlier, was now united as never before.

A GROUP *of British and Boer leaders gather for a photograph outside O'Neil's farmhouse, Majuba, during armistice talks in March 1881. Among those present were Marthinus Wessel Pretorius and Paul Kruger.*

Lucky for some...

For centuries the Africans of the eastern Transvaal had worked and traded in gold –
recovering it from the beds of streams and rivers, totally unaware of the value of the metal
that lay beneath their feet. It was only with the coming of the white man that these riches
were to be rediscovered and exploited: first deep in the valleys of the eastern escarpment,
and then along an unbelievably rich Main Reef in the central Transvaal.
Africans, however, were denied a share in this newly discovered bounty. They were looked
on as the labour reservoir that complex mining so desperately needed. As the mines went deeper
so the costs of mining rose – and the wages paid to increasingly impoverished workers fell.

FROM ALMOST THE VERY BEGINNING blacks were denied any share in the gold that lay waiting to be
discovered under the Transvaal – except as labourers. The first South African Republic (SAR) mining law,
passed soon after the initial strikes had been made, ensured that 'no coloured person may be a licence holder, or
in any way be connected with the working of the gold
mines, except as a working man in the service of whites'.
In addition, Africans were refused permission to trade in
minerals. Neither could they live (except as servants) or
establish shops on proclaimed ground.

The goldfields of the Witwatersrand did not offer the
easy pickings of the diamond fields at Kimberley: the ore
was very low in gold and became increasingly difficult to
get at – which meant that only enormously wealthy companies could mobilise the capital, the machinery and the
expertise required to extract the yellow metal.

The first strikes

An English immigrant named Edward Button made the
first strike on the slopes of Spitskop near the present town
of Sabie in a picturesque valley in the eastern Transvaal
Drakensberg in 1871. A combination of good luck – and
some rough-and-ready geological knowledge – later led
him to more strikes at the nearby farm of Eersteling, and
then further north, in the Murchison range.

Soon, gold was being found throughout the eastern
Transvaal, most of it alluvial – that is, free lumps in sizes
ranging from the Peacock Nugget of 178 ounces (about 5,5
kilograms) to tiny grains found in the 'tail' of prospectors'
pans after washing river gravel. A section of the Blyde River
valley was proclaimed 'public diggings' by the SAR's President Thomas Burgers, centring on what was to become the
town of Pilgrim's Rest. New finds followed around Barberton, but most of the gold was soon worked out.

In its alluvial phase, the gold industry was little more
than a nuisance to Africans, whose lands were tramped
over and occupied by a rough and more-or-less lawless influx of white adventurers. Digger communities, however,
provided a market for the sale of food, an opportunity
which many African farmers grasped rapidly.

At this early stage, relatively few African men hired themselves out as labourers, and the method of production did
not, in fact, require a great number of workers. Those who
did seek work, often sought the higher rewards available at
Kimberley, despite the long journey made hazardous by
harassment from officials, farmers and robbers.

The Witwatersrand strike

The eastern Transvaal strikes made a few men wealthy and
a lot of men bitter – the biggest strike of all had to wait until
March 1886 when an immigrant, George Harrison, dis-

EARLY MINING *was alluvial – something
that a few men with picks and shovels,
and lots of luck, could easily manage
without enormous capital or labour requirements. As the mines went deeper,
however, new technology – and a vast
labour force – were needed to extract
the precious metal.*

BY 1899 *gold had been found in various parts (right) of the eastern and southern Transvaal. The biggest strike of all was along the Witwatersrand – the 'ridge of white waters'.*

THE SOUTH AFRICAN REPUBLIC *entered a traumatic period of political and economic change after English immigrant Edward Button (below) discovered gold in the eastern Transvaal in 1871.*

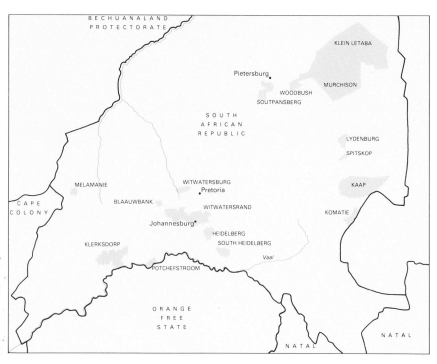

covered the first signs of the fabulous riches of the Main Reef at an outcrop on the farm Langlaagte, situated on the Witwatersrand, extending in an arc for over 500 kilometres. A few months later, having received a free 'discoverer's claim' which he sold for £10, Harrison turned his back on the Witwatersrand and set out for Barberton and oblivion.

Behind him, he left on the Rand hundreds of diggers – small-scale operators of restricted means and with no more than the few basic tools of pick, shovel, hammer and pan. These scratched away at the surface, excavating long trenches along the line of the exposed reef. The ore that they recovered they broke themselves or took to one of the few steam-powered stamp-batteries that were in operation nearby. The crushed material was swirled with water in their pans, until the glittering 'tail' of gold appeared.

They soon discovered, however, that although the gold-bearing reef was remarkably regular, it was also of a very low grade. Even worse, as work progressed, it was found that the reef dipped ever more deeply underground. Obviously further exploitation of the reef would need a massive investment of capital and an enormous supply of cheap labour. As at Kimberley, the days of the digger had passed and the era of the Randlord was about to dawn. Thanks to the wealth generated at Kimberley, capital proved less of a problem than labour – but from now on the African would have to be made to 'work for his living'.

Following the reef

The rulers of the SAR, under whose jurisdiction the Witwatersrand fell, were Paul Kruger and his *volksraad* (parliament). They regarded the discovery of gold as something of a mixed blessing. Their Boer state, chronically close to bankruptcy, now seemed assured of at least a temporary economic reprieve, but the price was high – an invasion of fortune-seekers and capitalists, *uitlanders* (foreigners) whose morals and way of life were not in line

with those of the Boers. Principally, they were concerned about the English, whose ungodly liberalism had played no small part in creating the Great Trek.

A two-man deputation consisting of the head of the Mines Department, C J Joubert (a farmer who, so far as is known, knew nothing about mining), and Johann Rissik, the acting Surveyor-General was sent to the Witwatersrand from Pretoria. Among their instructions was one 'to decide on a place for a village'. After several meetings – opened with prayers for heaven's blessing and guidance and attended by several hundred diggers and Kimberley notables – they submitted their report: 'The need for costly machinery calls for a large amount of capital. We do not recommend that the fields should be thrown open to individuals. There is a danger that men who have staked off good claims will be unable to work them, but be forced to leave and, through necessity, take to lawless ways.'

Although somewhat naively worded, the report was essentially accurate. From the start it was clear that mining of the low-grade ore at increasingly deeper levels would require, in addition to vast sums of money, considerable administrative and technical ability – many of the skills that had already been learned by the big mining houses formed out of the diamond boom at Kimberley.

Among the most powerful of the groups now investing on the Witwatersrand were Cecil John Rhodes' Consolidated Gold Fields and the Corner House of H Eckstein & Company, both of which drew capital from Kimberley and overseas. There was one important difference between the diamonds of Kimberley and the gold of the Witwatersrand: the price. The diamond price was fixed by supply and demand, while the world price of gold was fixed and likely to remain constant. Consequently, in order for the low-grade ore of the Witwatersrand to remain profitable it was necessary to mine it at reduced cost – and the only area where this could be done was in labour.

A MIGRANT WORKER *on his long trek to the goldfields. New mining methods were highly labour-intensive.*

CONDITIONS *for African labourers in the new mining compounds were harsh. The sleeping quarters for workers at Crown Mines, near Johannesburg, were lined with concrete bunks.*

The key to labour

Although Africans were not allowed to own land in the SAR, thousands of them were welcomed as worker/tenants by the richer Boer farmers. It was a lucrative partnership for both employer and employee: for after the white owners of the land had taken their share of the harvest, enough remained for African tenants to feed not only their families but also many of the early prospectors. This did not please the less well-off Boer farmers, who regularly complained of the 'insolence' of Africans in the market-place (which, in a sense, was an admission that Africans were the better farmers). Nevertheless, the *volksraad* of the SAR reacted sympathetically to the complaints of the less affluent farmers – and in a bid to push more African labour their way, passed a law limiting to five the number of tenants permitted to stay on a white farm.

In this they found common cause with the mine-owners, who wanted the Africans off the land and down their mines. Distrust and opposition among mine-owners were unaffordable luxuries in this new intensive-production, low-profit industry, and the realisation of the need to cooperate led to the founding of the Chamber of Mines in 1887, which acted in the interests of the mine-owners. Once off the land – that is, deprived of the means to exist by subsistence farming – Africans would have to seek wage-labour, conveniently slotting in to the capitalist economy generated by the mines. By stressing that gold-mining was the economic life-support of the country, the chamber could persuade the *volksraad* that damage to the industry might easily mean disaster for the republic, and so a degree of collaboration was achieved, with mutual interest marginally easing out mutual distrust.

The migrant system

The first problem in obtaining labour was recruitment, and mines sent their recruiting agents, or touts, who received a fee for each man they sent to the mine. To boost their income, they lied shamelessly about conditions under which Africans lived on the mines, and greatly inflated the salaries that could be expected. In addition to cheating Africans, touts also cheated the mines – which led the Chamber of Mines to take over labour recruitment itself.

Once recruited, the labourer had to find his way to the mines – and that was never easy. To quote the chamber itself: 'The supply of native labour would be much improved if the difficulties met with by the kaffirs in the course of their long overland journeys, could be done away with.' The African journeying to the mines was prey to a host of swindlers, robbers and even killers, from the white down-and-out who demanded a shilling for a bogus inoculation to the policeman who exacted a fine (for no particular offence) before allowing him to proceed.

Having got the labourer to the mine, it was necessary to keep him there, at least for as long as the period of his contract and, if possible, even longer. Whereas white workers eventually sent for their families and lived in houses in the developing suburbs of Johannesburg, Africans were housed in compounds similar to those at Kimberley, although they were not closed due to the fact that gold could not be smuggled out as diamonds could (see page 175). A Pass system prevented the labourer's family from visiting him; and even if they had been able to reach him, they would have found no 'legal' accommodation.

So far as whites were concerned, Africans worked on the mines because it was an attractive way of providing for

AMONG *the fortune-hunters who flocked to the Witwatersrand was Cecil John Rhodes, who was convinced that only Britain possessed the know-how to exploit the region's riches.*

Randlords, workers and capitalism

It is easy to be critical of the Randlords and their ruthless manipulation and exploitation of workers. But it is important to remember that the appalling scenes of deprivation and brutality that shocked liberal observers were in many ways similar to those which had shocked liberals in Britain years before – when that country was undergoing a social revolution from an agrarian economy to an industrial one.

There were differences, of course – the most important being that migrant labour as it developed in South Africa never took hold in Britain, which made it all the easier to employ women and children in very low-paid, demeaning jobs. And, of course, migrations did occur – such as the mass movement of Europeans, particularly impoverished Irish agricultural workers, from Europe to North America.

What all these riches, hardships and migrations had in common was industrial capitalism – a revolution in the way human beings created wealth. In Britain, where the revolution happened first, it took more than a century – but in southern Africa it was telescoped into a few years following the discovery of diamonds and gold, as the small but wealthy elite grappled to impose industrial capitalism on a largely peasant society consisting mainly of subsistence farmers – Boer and African.

The Randlords had masters, too – markets that demanded gold at an internationally fixed price, which made profit margins on the Main Reef's low-grade ore thinner and thinner as the miners were forced deeper into the earth's crust to get at the gold. Their response was to cut costs in the only variable they had – the cost of buying labour.

The discovery of diamonds and gold – particularly gold – has had a profound effect on South Africa: contributing both to its regional power base and the rise of apartheid, persuading the Randlords to ally themselves with many of the worst racial excesses of the republican and, later, the South African governments. In some cases, they even set the pace, favouring any legislation that forced Africans into a cheap, pliant labour pool – in order to ensure that they were able to keep profit margins largely intact on the sale of gold in the international market.

their families' wants. The reality was different. The wages were just sufficient to enable the worker to maintain himself in town, with a little left over, if he was lucky, to take back to his family. The families of men who had left their holdings on white-owned farms, bereft of their strongest menfolk, struggled to exist – and the land gradually became impoverished to the point where it could no longer support them. Thus many women were also forced to work for wages in order to buy food at trading stores.

Life on the mines at least offered some an opportunity to desert and return sadder, wiser and poorer. In most cases, poverty dictated a return, if not to the mine, then to the outer edges of the 'white' towns that grew up around the mines, where African 'townships' swiftly evolved.

Conditions, far from improving, got worse as owners struggled to maintain the profitability of the mines. From an already low average of 50 shillings a month of 30 shifts in 1897, an African miner's earnings dropped, by 1902, to 30 shillings. Even desertion was ruled out as a remedy, by a new series of laws that made breach of contract a criminal offence; and a modification to the Pass laws made it an offence for a worker to move from one mine to another offering better wages. Furthermore, a ban on African trade unions effectively undermined their bargaining power, especially for better wages.

Workers from overseas

Africans were not the only workers on the mines. From Europe, and especially from the English counties of Cornwall, Cumberland and Lancashire, came skilled miners and machine-operators. Low on the class-riddled social scale of England, in South Africa they became 'masters'.

The new class structure into which they entered was divided along the lines of colour. That 'white' was superior was held as obvious and propagated as one of the laws of nature. The skilled white worker, free from racial suppression, was in short supply and was able to defend his wage through the formation of trade unions that negotiated improved conditions with employers. Once the Witwatersrand had settled down to permanence, the white worker brought in his wife and family and lived a 'normal' life, something that was denied the African worker. Nevertheless, working at the increasing depths demanded by the steeply inclining reef was a difficult, dangerous and extremely unhealthy job and for many years the death-rate on the mines was appalling.

RECRUITING OFFICES *for African workers opened in many rural areas of the country (above), the first step in a traumatic transformation from peasant farmer to the hardships and dangers of life underground (right).*

Workers and alcohol

One of the ways in which the government of the SAR raised money was to award concessions or monopolies, such as for the manufacture of liquor. An enterprising Hungarian immigrant, Alois Nellmapius, in return for a handsome payment, was granted 'the sole right to manufacture [alcoholic beverages] from grain, potatoes, and other products growable in the Transvaal'.

Nellmapius promptly formed a syndicate with Isaac and Barnett Lewis, and Sammy Marks, and erected a distillery that they optimistically called *De Eerste Fabrieken in de Zuid-Afrikaansche Republiek* (the first factory in the South African Republic). In 1883 President Kruger personally declared it open, and gave it the curious name of *Volkshoop* (people's hope).

The discovery of gold on the Witwatersrand ensured that the distillery grew enormously, occupying a large site on Marks' farm, Hatherley, and even being listed on the London Stock Exchange. For a while, Hatherley was the sole legal supplier of cheap liquor to the growing and conveniently centralised African market. A trade treaty with Portugal, however, enabled 'produce of Portugal' to enter the republic duty free, and a large rum distillery was built close to the Mozambique border (then a Portuguese colony) – and another source of cheap spirits flooded the market. In addition, German potato-spirit was exported to Portugal, where it officially became produce of that country and entered the SAR by the already established rum route. The SAR, needing the outlet to the sea at Delagoa Bay, could do nothing to turn the tide.

Very early, liquor became an instrument used for the control of the African workforce. Workers from Mozambique had been exposed to cheap Portuguese liquor for years and, to varying degrees, many were addicted. For others, liquor – however bad – provided almost the only form of escape from the squalor and misery of the mine compound. Paradoxically, use of liquor helped to provide a more stable labour force, as employers quickly noted. Free spending on liquor reduced the amount a worker could save for taking home at the end of his contract and, accordingly, the less he saved the longer he worked. A Mining Commissioner stated in court that 'nearly everyone is agreed that total prohibition would be disastrous to the native labour position'. It was also argued, in defence of a form of 'tot system', that 'the "boy" so humoured and so refreshed is the better labourer'.

After some years, however, even the Chamber of Mines was obliged to concede that 'drunkenness was on the increase at the mines, and that, in consequence, the scarcity of labour was intensified . . . .' It was becoming clear that increased expansion of the liquor industry might well disable the mining industry. President Kruger, however, was extremely proud of Hatherley, and was also among the many farmers who supplied it with raw ingredients – in the President's case, with citrus for orange wine.

Nevertheless, persistent lobbying by the chamber paid off, and it became a crime to sell liquor to an African who did not possess a permit signed by his white 'master'. In addition, the president of the chamber was granted a seat on the Johannesburg Liquor Licensing Board. After deliberately using liquor to manipulate the labour force, the chamber finally realised that it had gone too far and, allying itself to 'public outrage', succeeded in having a 'total prohibition clause' introduced into new legislation. Ways would be found of circumventing its provisions, but it seemed at the time to be a moral victory.

Morals, in general, were not of the highest during the early days, nor were any conspicuous attempts made to improve them. In the male-dominated mining society, the

City of 'unbridled squander' on a golden reef

On the day Johannesburg was born a group of mostly English-speaking diggers listened to a speech in Dutch that most of them did not understand.

The year was 1886 and the speaker was Carl von Brandis, first Commissioner of Mines, who declared a 'public diggings' on the Witwatersrand, as well as the setting aside of land for 'cultivated areas, gardens, arable land and water furrows . . . .'

A successful tender for the survey of the new town was made by Joseph de Villiers, who claimed to 'have had much experience on the Diamond Fields and [to] know the requirements of a digger population very well'. Through bitter experience of other boom towns that folded when the gold ran out – and expecting the same of Johannesburg – the government was determined to make as much out of it as possible in the short time it was expected to last. Accordingly, it stipulated small plots and many narrow streets to create corner stands, for which higher rates were payable.

Some of the stands, at the first auction, sold for 25 cents each, although T W Beckett, a wealthy Pretoria merchant and landowner, paid £1 065 for five adjoining stands on Market Square. Even as De Villiers did his survey work, the population grew at such a rate that, when he finished, he had surveyed close to 1 000 stands instead of his projected 600. The *volksraad*'s original scheme, to lease the stands at 10 shillings a month, received such opposition from the diggers that it was abandoned. Control was vested in a Diggers' Committee, although Von Brandis did duty as magistrate in a stuffy, corrugated-iron courthouse. A hospital and jail were built of mud and poles.

The 'Barberton Herald' slightingly continued to refer to the new town as

CARL VON BRANDIS, *first Commissioner of Mines in the Transvaal Government, declared a 'public diggings' in 1886 – paving the way for Johannesburg's first newspaper.*

Ferreira's Camp, after one of the earliest diggers, but Johannesburg soon received its own newspaper, 'The Diggers' News and Witwatersrand Advertiser'. In Cape Town, the 'Mercantile Advertiser' commented of Johannesburg in October 1886 that 'there are now 28 canteens, and the rest of the tents and huts are occupied by land sharks'. (Within a year there were to be more then 200 canteens, many of them run by 'businessmen' from Eastern Europe.) Grahamstown's 'Eastern Star' disappeared from the streets of the Settler City in 1887, to reappear a few weeks later as a Johannesburg newspaper, changing its name after a few years to 'The Star'.

Water supply and sanitation lagged sadly behind development, and the *volksraad*, characteristically, sold a

concession for the supply of water, which sometimes fetched 25 cents a bucket. Flush sanitation was introduced only in 1905, when the population was about 150 000.

Depression set in around 1890 when it was found that ores recovered by deep-level mining did not yield their gold by the recovery techniques then practised. However, the MacArthur-Forrest cyanide and zinc precipitation process proved to be the solution, and the town continued to grow, developing a distinct character that a visiting Australian journalist attempted to describe in 1910: 'Ancient Nineveh and Babylon have been revived. Johannesburg is their twentieth-century prototype. It is a city of unbridled squander and unfathomable squalor.'

canteen-keeper who could boast a barmaid – preferably a reasonably attractive one – had a distinct advantage over his rivals. The Johannesburg Sanitary Board, empowered to act against vice, did nothing, as more and more prostitutes arrived. A move against prostitutes would affect the bars where they worked, and an attack on the liquor trade would, by inference, also be an attack on the Hatherley Distillery, of which the President and *volksraad* were proud. This would also be seen as a threat to the Boer agriculturalists who supplied the raw materials to Hatherley.

Mine-owners could exert authority not only over the government of the Transvaal, but also over the other southern African states which benefited from the industry. Cape and Natal harbour revenues and customs duties increased dramatically, as a constant stream of machinery was imported. Transport systems that had begun to develop after the great diamond discoveries expanded with renewed vigour. Gold was vital to the sub-continent and really cheap labour was vital to gold, so there were no loud or sustained protests at that system of labour.

'Is not this country ours...?'

In the second half of the 19th century, African societies in both countryside and town were undergoing rapid change. In some rural areas, a thriving peasantry, living mainly on 'white' land, emerged, while in the urban areas of the eastern Cape a small but rapidly growing group of 'educated people' began to play an increasing political role in several constituencies.

At first white authorities accepted these new developments; but after the discovery of diamonds in 1867, and new deposits of gold in 1886, they began enacting a series of new laws to force more Africans into the wage-labour market.

IT WAS A TYPICAL Cecil John Rhodes speech – full of arrogance, optimism and outrageous exaggeration. But for more than 100 minutes the millionaire Prime Minister (and Minister for Native Affairs) held fellow members of the all-white Cape Legislative Assembly spellbound as he opened the debate on the Second Reading of a 'Native' Bill he had been working on for two years . . . .

The date was 27 July 1894, and the 'liberal' parliamentarians of the Cape Colony were preparing for a new bid to exert greater control over the lives of their African subjects.

Rhodes never worked in half measures – so it should not have come as a surprise to his fellow legislators that he had elevated a routine chore to bring administrative order to an overcrowded eastern Cape district called Glen Grey into something far bigger: the formulation of what he described as a 'Native Bill for Africa'.

Much of his marathon address was concentrated on spelling out, in brutally unambiguous terms, the chief purpose of the Act: to force more 'kaffirs' into the wage-labour market – by first limiting their access to land, and then, by imposing a 10-shilling labour tax on all those who could not prove they had been in 'bona fide' wage employment for at least three months in a year.

The crucial element in the Glen Grey formula was the creation of a land shortage – and this, Rhodes told the Assembly, could be brought about in two ways: by limiting the head of each family to just four morgen; and by making the eldest son in a household the sole heir to the family property. A drastically reduced land-holding, he explained, would reduce uncontrolled squatting, while a change to the rules of inheritance would ensure that in future generations all but one member of an African family would be made landless, or as he so succinctly put it, would 'remove these poor children out of their state of sloth and laziness, and give them some gentle stimulants to go forth and find out something of the dignity of labour'.

Music to the ears of white farmers and mining magnates, the Glen Grey Act was written into the Cape statutes, becoming law in August 1894.

The sugar-coating on a bitter pill
Although the Act was essentially a racist and coercive piece of legislation, it was composed so that it appeared to accord with the best traditions of Cape 'liberalism'. Certainly, during a tour of Transkei prior to the debate in the legislative assembly, Rhodes, wearing his liberal face, went to great lengths to convince African communities of the new opportunities the Bill would usher in for them: more schools; improved roads; the development of districts; and, as an alternative to the common voters' roll for most Africans, the implementation of a council system which would give indigenous people a bigger say in matters of local interest. (In any case, land title granted under the Act fell outside the ambit of the property qualifications needed for the franchise.)

Clearly, Rhodes regarded the implementation of the Glen Grey proposals as a matter of extreme urgency – and for good reason: in several eastern Cape constituencies, the numbers of registered African voters had reached a point where they held the balance of power; and, at a time when mine-owners and farmers were calling increasingly stridently for cheap labour, far too few rural Africans were being 'persuaded' to enter into the service of the white man.

The rise of the Cape peasantry
In many ways, white attitudes towards their African neighbours were shaped by a belief that rural Africans were 'lazy savages', a myth which served to push those Africans who had no need to enter wage-labour into a no-win situation: the harder they worked to remain self-sufficient, the lazier they became in the eyes of the colonists.

Yet throughout Transkei and the north-eastern Cape, evidence of African industry abounded . . . .

In 1870, for instance, a state-appointed statistician noted that 'taking everything into consideration, the native district of Peddie surpasses the European district of Albany in its productive powers' – and that the Wittenberg reserve raised so much wheat, maize and millet that it served as 'the granary of both the Northern Districts and the Free State too'.

And in 1880, after a trip through Glen Grey, politician and lawyer Victor Sampson commented that 'man for man the Kafirs of these parts are better farmers than the Europeans, more careful of their stock, cultivating a larger area of land, and working themselves more assiduously'.

It was not only as crop-growers that peasants in places such as Peddie, Bedford, Glen Grey, Stutterheim, Victoria East and Queenstown excelled: many of them also became successful wool farmers. Initially, the Peddie district set the pace, selling 17 000 pounds of wool in 1864. Other areas soon followed – and by the 1870s increasing numbers of Africans were selling cattle in order to buy sheep.

THIS PHOTOGRAPH *of a rural homestead reflects all the trappings of prosperity. Many African farmers showed themselves to be very adept at producing a food surplus for profitable sale to the newly created white settlements. In 1870 a state-appointed statistician said that the 'native district of Peddie surpasses the European district of Albany in its productive powers'.*

Rural class divisions

Of course, not all Africans reaped the financial rewards that came with participation in the Cape economy – and the growing affluence of some tended to hide the fact that thousands of others were landless, desperately poor, and barely able to eke out a living. In the pre-colonial era of pooled resources, a situation such as this would never have arisen – chiefdoms either grew fat together or starved together. But those days were gone. In the new order, the better-off, having acquired a taste for profits, rejected not only the concept of traditional responsibility towards kinship groups, but also the authority of their chiefs.

The rejection of old values by a section of the peasantry caused great bitterness in the ranks of the 'traditionalists'. Yet it was a split which had long been inevitable – for quite simply, the majority of the more successful cultivators were no longer peasants. In both deed and attitude they had become capitalist farmers: like their white counterparts, they sought tenants and wage-labourers to work their lands – and, like the whites, they exploited these workers wherever they could.

At first the colonial authorities welcomed, and even encouraged, class divisions in African societies – especially since those who opted for the 'civilising influence of the white way of life', as opposed to the 'barbarism' of those who did not, tended to be ardent supporters of the government. But as increasing numbers of this 'new elite' began qualifying for and using their vote, worried Cape administrators began looking for new ways that could be used to protect white privileges.

When diamonds were discovered in Kimberley in 1867, followed by strikes of rich new veins of gold on the Witwatersrand in 1886, the authorities began looking at the entire African population in a totally different light.

With the creation of a cheap labour reservoir for the mines, and with white farmers, roadworks and railways becoming the chief priority of government, it no longer made sense to encourage Africans to adopt colonial values: after all, digging for gold hundreds of metres underground was hardly likely to be a favourite career choice among the growing corps of 'educated' Africans. And so it was to the tens of thousands of Africans who remained committed to a life on the land that the authorities looked to meet their labour demands. Although most peasants were far from keen to work for wages, their opposition to white pressure was severely weakened by the fact that the majority of them lived on white-held land. It was therefore a simple matter for the authorities to pass legislation, such as anti-squatting laws, in an attempt to cut them off from their livelihood by forcing them off the land that supported them – and which also gave some a surplus income in order to pay government-imposed taxes. But although evictions drew thousands into the migrant labour net, by the final decade of the 19th century demand for workers still by far outstripped supply.

Getting ready for battle

In a sense then, Rhodes' Glen Grey Act was meant to be the ultimate solution to the vexing labour shortage. But it had one crucial weakness: it tried to solve all the white man's 'kaffir' problems in one sweep.

To 'educated' Africans, the majority of whom valued the franchise more than anything else, the council system as envisaged in the Bill seemed suspiciously like a first step towards relieving them of their 'national' vote.

African voters had good reason to be wary of white motives: protected (or so they thought) by a constitution which, in theory, granted them equality with their white counterparts, many had eagerly adopted the colonial way of life, only to discover that whites – even professed liberals – were prepared to tolerate them only while they were a political minority. The moment they became an electoral danger (as was rapidly happening in some eastern Cape constituencies), new plans to counter them were quickly formulated . . . .

One such scheme was the Cape's 1887 Parliamentary Voters' Registration Act, passed when the franchise was being extended over the newly acquired Transkeian territories, which departed from previous practice by nullifying 'tribal' tenure as a basis for property qualification. This was followed in 1892 by the Franchise and Ballot Act which tripled property qualification for the vote from £25

Days of hope and despair

John Tengo Jabavu was a perfect example of what many white colonists disparagingly referred to as a 'kaffir with too much education . . . .'

But to a small but growing community of eastern Cape urban Africans he was for many years a hero – the flag-bearer of a concerted campaign to bring about equality between educated blacks and whites.

Born in 1859, in Healdtown in the eastern Cape, to a 'modernist' Mfengu couple, Jabavu qualified as a teacher at the age of 17. But his career in the classroom did not last long: his real love was politics and journalism.

Already as a teenager he had started making a name for himself among the 'educated' communities of the eastern Cape, by becoming a regular contributor to the letters pages of the 'Cape Argus' newspaper. His popularity rose even further when a powerful white political lobby led by liberal parliamentarian James Rose-Innes began to take a lively interest in his writings.

In 1881, Dr James Stewart, principal of Lovedale College (run by the United Free Church of Scotland), invited Jabavu to edit the mission newspaper, 'Isigidimi Sama-Xosa' ('Xhosa Express'). But in 1883, after running an article criticising the 'anti-native' utterances in parliament of the 'very members sent thither amidst election acclamations by unsuspecting native voters', his angry employers presented him with an ultimatum: tone down on political content – or get out. Jabavu got out.

In 1884, however, he opened his own newspaper, 'Imvo Zabantsundu' ('Native Opinion'), thanks to the financial backing of businessmen whom Jabavu described as 'friends of the native cause'.

The aim of 'Imvo', according to Jabavu, was to give 'untrammelled' expression to African views and to bring about closer bonds between Africans, and between Africans and whites. True to his word, his newspaper carried African grievances on a wide range of subjects – including the hated Pass laws, liquor laws, the inequality of justice in the courts and racist legislation emanating from the supposedly liberal Cape Legislative Assembly.

As a high-profile newspaper editor, Jabavu was ideally placed to assume a position of leadership among the eastern Cape's urban African communities. Indeed, he was often the sole strategist of the political actions waged by 'modernists' in the late 1800s: for instance, he was the kingpin of a campaign to get Africans to register as voters; and in 1887, when the Parliamentary Voters' Registration Act was placed before the Cape Legislative Assembly, it was he who led widespread African protests against its implementation.

It was also through his efforts that the *Imbumba Eliliso Lomso Ontsundu* (Union of Native Vigilance Associations) was formed in 1887 to protect African interests.

Yet, even though the contribution he made to the African struggle was immense, by the 1890s Jabavu began to display an arrogance which increasingly cut him off from a significant section of the population. In 1898, the split between him and a group led by Alan Kirkland Soga became final when he offered electoral support to the *Afrikaner Bond*, regarded by many blacks as the chief stumbling block in the way of more African rights. One of the results of the rift was the emergence of another African newspaper – '*Izwi Labantu*' ('Voice of the People') in direct opposition to Jabavu's '*Imvo*'.

Cricketers and teetotallers

One of the big mistakes of 'modernists' such as Jabavu was a misguided faith in what they referred to as a 'white sense of fair play'. They believed, naively as it turned out, that if they showed how easily Africans could adapt to 'white civilisation', the racists of the Orange Free State, Natal and the South African Republic would look at their indigenous populations in a new light.

That they failed was not for want of trying. In many respects they were model European-type citizens: a typical member of their group wore formal Victorian attire; had a portrait of Queen Victoria in the sitting room of his brick house; was a regular church-goer; and was a teetotaller who advocated disenfranchisement for anyone abusing alcohol.

Their adoption of colonial values and culture affected many areas of their lives: cricket, for instance, was a favourite leisure pursuit because it was held to be the 'most gentlemanly and Victorian of sporting activities'. By the 1880s the St Marks, the Fear Not, the Komani (still in existence to-

J T JABAVU'S *real love was journalism – and in 1881 he became editor of a mission newspaper called 'Isigidimi Sama-Xosa'*

MANY AFRICANS *became model European-type citizens, complete with the latest in Victorian fashions.*

day) and the Ethiopian cricket clubs had become household names in local sporting circles – often beating white opposition.

But all this brought them no nearer to being accepted as equals by eastern Cape whites, let alone by whites in other parts of the country.

The new urban Africans

While the tightly knit communities of 'educated people' in the eastern Cape (and to a lesser extent, in Natal) were waging their gentle campaigns for equality, other, very different groups of urban Africans were mushrooming around the diamond fields of Kimberley and the gold mines of the Witwatersrand.

Uneducated, unskilled and therefore cheap and highly exploitable, they had been brought (and often forced) into the towns and cities as migrant labour. But having made the move from the countryside, many quickly lost any inclination to return to their rural homes.

The God-fearing teetotallers of the eastern Cape who, by virtue of their relative affluence, perceived themselves as leaders of the African people, were horrified by the lifestyle of these new urban dwellers: in Kimberley, for instance, thousands of African women flocked to the diamond fields, providing home-brewed beer, liquor, and sexual and house-keeping services to men of all races.

Recalling a visit to the diamond camps in 1874, evangelist Gwayi Tyamzashe said: 'On my first arrival at the New Rush [Kimberley] I observed that nearly every evening was devoted to private and public amusements . . . . The evenings resounded with the noise of the concert, the circus, and all sorts of dances from one end of the camp to the other. The life then of both Coloured and Whites was so rough that I thought the place only good for those who were resolved to sell their souls for silver, gold, and precious stones, or for those who were determined to barter their lives for the pleasures of a time.'

In Johannesburg, the degradation, squalor and disease were even worse.

The black population on the Witwatersrand included a significant percentage of mission-educated Africans, whose expectations of better treatment were quickly shattered: whites condemned them for dressing 'foolishly'; they were denied skilled jobs; mission churches scoffed at their ambitions of playing a greater role in the direction of church affairs; and migrant workers accused them of being traitors and 'tools of the Europeans . . . .'

The suffering of Africans in the cities is reflected in the moving strains of 'Nkosi Sikelel' iAfrica' ('God Bless Africa'), composed by a Xhosa teacher named Enoch Sontonga at Johannesburg's Nancefield hostel in

1897. First performed in 1899, it made a strong impression at the inaugural meeting of the South African Native National Congress in 1912, and in 1925 was adopted as the anthem of the African National Congress (ANC).

In the absence of organised African pressure groups, political activity in the northern provinces during this period was provided mainly by independent black churches – breakaways from increasingly discredited mission churches (see page 285).

By preaching a message of black self-reliance, the Ethiopian movement (as they became known) drew thousands of disaffected members of the European missionary churches into their ranks. As the movement grew, so did its increasingly popular battle-cry of 'Africa for the Africans' grow in intensity.

But despite their success in mobilising the masses, the belief of Ethiopians in a form of 'black consciousness', was widely criticised by middle-class African leaders. Jabavu led the criticism of the Ethiopians, claiming that their philosophy ran counter to 'loyalty and peace'. In fact, it was only with the formation of the South African Native National Congress that efforts were made to include them in existing political networks.

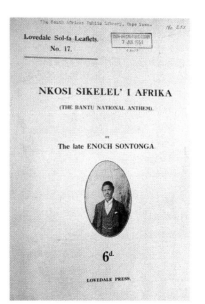

'NKOSI SIKELEL' IAFRIKA', *composed by Xhosa teacher Enoch Sontonga in 1897, became the anthem of the African National Congress.*

to £75. Hundreds of educated Africans were drawn into the (very respectful) protests against what they described as *tung'umolomo* (the 'shutting of mouth'). Although opposition proved to be unsuccessful in terms of getting these laws scrapped, the protest campaigns – highlighted by newspaper editorials, petitions and delegations to government authorities – were crucially important for another reason: they afforded literate Mfengu voters, as well as other politically aware figures in the African community, first-hand experience of political issues and techniques.

Before these lessons could be put to practical use, however, a far more important task confronted opponents of the Glen Grey measures: somehow, they had to unite the urban and rural opponents of the Bill.

'Educated' people had never really been forgiven by the peasant community for seemingly siding with the white man. And, in many respects, the relationship between 'modernists' and the peasantry had deteriorated even further after the Cape had started a process of gradual annexation of the Transkeian territories in 1872.

Almost from the beginning, the Cape Government's obsession with 'order' had become a source of irritation to the inhabitants of the region: inflexible new administrative techniques were promulgated – followed by a series of decrees which touched on everything affecting the African, from the power of chiefs to the collection of taxes, to access to fields and forests.

In most cases, the responsibility for the implementation of what were essentially unpopular regulations was put in the hands of a group of African bureaucrats called headmen who, not surprisingly, were regarded with open hostility by the inhabitants of rural villages.

By 1892, peasant anger towards headmen had been replaced by open defiance – and nervous white magistrates began calling with ever-greater urgency for increased powers for their African officials.

And the headmen themselves, seeing their power being rapidly whittled away, also approached the Cape Government. 'We headmen cannot control our people or carry out the laws of the Government as we should do, because our people won't listen to us,' said a group from the Tsomo district in a petition to the authorities. 'They [the people] say: "You have no authority." When we call them to attend a public meeting ... they won't come. When we warn them to attend ... they refuse to come. We can do nothing .... Then, again they won't pay school fees and Road Rate which we headmen consider necessary to the advancement of our country and we want laws made giving us authority to make our people do these things and we want to be able to bring them before the magistrate and get them punished if they will not do as we tell them.'

Within two years, however, the stance of many headmen had undergone a dramatic change.

The fight begins

In September 1894, the Glen Grey Act was extended by proclamation to four districts of Transkei – and as its aims became clearer, 'modernists' and 'traditionalists' throughout the eastern Cape were forced into a drastic re-examination of their attitudes towards each other.

Realising the danger the Act posed to their chosen way of life, rural and urban Africans pooled their resources to wage what was at times a highly effective campaign against the Glen Grey proposals. Certainly, the expertise offered by urban 'political communicators' (educated individuals with experience of negotiating with colonial administrators on behalf of themselves and the wider community) became a cause of concern to magistrates.

And in this respect, John Tengo Jabavu, the editor of *'Imvo Zabantsundu'* ('Native Opinion')(see box) was singled out for special attention by white officialdom: in February 1895, J M Morris, the magistrate of Elliotdale spoke of 'a great undercurrent of agitation' that was sweeping through the district as a result of the Glen Grey Act; and of the rise of 'educated men like Jabavu' into 'important authorities' among ordinary Transkeians. To Morris, the implications of these developments were ominous: the next step, he warned, would be the formation of a Native Bond, 'which will prove a far greater difficulty than the Africander Bond, and with growing advancement the Native Tribes will discover their power'.

Jabavu was not the only 'educated man' to cause consternation among government officials: Campbell Kupe, whom the magistrate of Nqamakwe described as being 'just sufficiently educated to be mischievous', not only ran a committee representing three districts, but also found the time to draft and dispatch several telling petitions to the government. Other prominent 'modernists' such as Reuben Damane, Caleb Jafta and Charles Tonjeni also joined the clamour against the Act.

Further problems for the authorities came in the form of regular 'defections' by headmen into the ranks of the 'opposition'. In Tsomo, an annoyed magistrate described how a headman called Matthew had evaded a new decree about

A LOCAL MAGISTRATE *in the Thembuland district poses with his headmen, chief and interpreter.*

the cutting of firewood: 'Instead of carrying out my instructions Matthew at once convened a meeting of the people at which he discussed my instructions and sought their advice and counsel with the result that he decided not to do as I had told him,' the magistrate reported.

The masses too, played an important part in keeping the pressure on officialdom – by refusing to have their lands surveyed and by ignoring tax demands – even in the face of threats to confiscate their cattle.

Largely as a result of the widespread opposition to the new legislation, which for a brief period even transcended long-held ethnic enmities, the Glen Grey legislation could not be implemented in the way the government intended. In 1905, for instance, the labour tax was simply dropped, as were the principles of individual land tenure and inheritance by the first-born son.

Judged in terms of what it set out to achieve, the Act was a failure. But that does not diminish its importance: for, although it did not become, as Rhodes envisaged, a 'Native Bill for Africa', it provided one of the foundations on which National Party ideologues of the 1950s were able to build a 'native policy' for (white) South Africa.

The rise and fall of headman Mamba

ENOCH MAMBA, *government man of the people.*

In March 1885, a Gcaleka chief named Sigidi and his Ndlambe counterpart, Zenzile, presented a forceful and detailed complaint to the Secretary for Native Affairs about a group of village headmen who, they claimed, were 'setting their authority at defiance'.

'Many of these people,' said the two chiefs, 'are Fingoes [Mfengu], and we feel that they are trying to usurp our authority, and to push us aside to make room for their friends.'

Sigidi and Zenzile had good reason to be concerned: among the African (mainly Mfengu) 'modernisers' ranged against them was one particularly talented man: an ambitious and, at times, unscrupulous former schoolteacher, Enoch Mamba.

The rise of Mamba
Born in Fort Beaufort in 1861 or 1862, Mamba attended the Healdtown mission school, qualifying as a trainee teacher in 1880. In 1883 – after a three-year teaching stint – he joined the office of Idutya Regional Magistrate Charles Bell as an interpreter and assistant clerk.

Although Mamba enjoyed a rapid rise to prominence, his career in the village politics of what is now Transkei was dogged by a series of controversies.

The partnership between Bell and Mamba blossomed almost immediately: Mamba's network of location informers kept Bell in touch with developments in the locations – and the magistrate, in turn, showed his appreciation by appointing Mamba to the post of headman.

Mamba proved to be as diligent a headman as he had been a clerk: in 1895, in a well-presented motivation for a pay increase, he pointed out his success in combating crime and collecting taxes without having resort to 'seizure' in his Lota location.

He also started a school and built a schoolhouse in his area of jurisdiction – which drew fresh criticism on his head from diehard 'traditionalists' such as Sigidi.

Yet despite the widespread, and often perfectly well justified hostility of the people towards headmen who had been appointed by the British, Mamba was able to build up a strong following. And the reason for this was his talent for fence-sitting: although the aims of the government and the wishes of the people were often at variance with each other, few headmen were able to create the image of being both a man of the masses and a faithful state employee as well as Mamba did.

Decline
But inevitably, as his powerbase broadened, so did the number of his opponents – and in the early 1890s he was involved in bitter disputes with, among others, a powerful commoner in his location, a missionary and a trader. Mamba emerged victorious in all three instances – amid accusations that he had threatened important witnesses.

In 1895, however, he badly overplayed his hand when he tried to take on T W Brownlee, Bell's successor as magistrate of Idutya.

The relationship between the two men, strained from the very beginning, deteriorated even further when two of Sigidi's sons were appointed to positions in the police force and the local jail.

Taking advantage of the magistrate's unpopularity among many of Idutya's white population, Mamba launched a vicious campaign that came close to getting Brownlee bundled off to another district. But in the end, it was Mamba who lost his job – after Brownlee had been given the opportunity to defend himself at a public hearing.

'I can . . . show,' the hard-pressed magistrate told the hearing, 'that this whole matter is got up by Enoch Mamba, who has gone about the district cajoling and intimidating, and would be delighted to see me away from this [district], as I have been trying to curtail the almost unlimited power he has until recently assumed to himself.'

W C Scully, the chairman of the hearing (and himself a magistrate who later became well-known for his short stories on life in Transkei) was as sympathetic to Brownlee as he was hostile to Mamba. Describing Mamba as 'a man who by his own admission leads an evil life', Scully recommended that he 'be sacked forthwith'.

Mamba's fall from grace was a steep one. Repeated requests for reinstatement were dismissed without discussion – and by 1901, he was still being referred to by officials of the Native Affairs Offices as 'the discredited and notorious Enoch Mamba'.

Pimps, prostitutes and white slavers

The tiny village of Vilna Krevo in what is now the Republic of Belarus is about as far removed from the dusty highveld of southern Africa as it is possible to imagine. And yet in the middle of 1898 a woman arrived at the village after a long and difficult journey from the gold-mining centre named Johannesburg.

Her name was Bessie Levin – and she had come to eastern Europe on a pressing mission: to find young girls to fill the burgeoning number of brothels that were opening their doors in the boom town of Johannesburg. In Vilna Krevo she spotted a likely candidate in 15-year-old Fanny Kreslo who, with the blessing of her parents, accepted Levin's offer of employment as a shop assistant in London for a salary of 100 roubles a year.

After a tearful farewell, Levin and Kreslo left for London – where Levin told the girl that her would-be employer had suddenly departed for South Africa, leaving instructions that the two women should follow. Penniless and speaking only Russian, the girl agreed to accompany Levin to Johannesburg, where the awful truth finally, and very forcibly, dawned.

She was lodged in a brothel in Anderson Street and told that if she wanted to return home she would have to earn her passage by becoming a prostitute. Her first 'customer' was a Pole who could speak Russian and with whom the young Kreslo could at least converse. Thereafter, however, she was forced to have sex with a variety of black and white men.

Fanny Kreslo's experience was similar to that of many other young women caught up in the darkest days of Johannesburg's 'white slave trade'. But her story came to light only because she was arrested by police in mid-1899 for being under age.

Her recruitment was made necessary by the simple fact that by the mid-1890s the demand for prostitutes on the Rand far outstripped supply – in tune with the increasing male population of the town. When the first census was conducted in Johannesburg in July 1896 there were 25 282 white men and 14 172 white women living within 5 kilometres of the Market Square. Among Africans, men outnumbered women by more than 1 000 percent – and this figure did not include the 28 000 African men living in the compounds.

All of which made Johannesburg a prostitute's 'paradise'. During the same census, 114 'continental women' openly professed to being prostitutes, the hard core of an estimated 1 000 'ladies of the night' – one for every 50 white inhabitants of the town, or 10 percent of all white women over the age of 15.

The prostitutes were the visible tip of an iceberg of vice that flourished in the boom town in the 1890s. An estimated 200-300 pimps, 'white slavers' and gun-toting gangsters controlled the brothels, while the police, in spite of an 1887 order providing for the 'punishment of prostitutes' and the suppression of 'houses of ill-fame', could do noth-

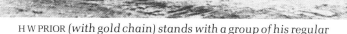

THE BARS *that flourished around Johannesburg attracted the 'ladies of the night' in droves. Among them was the 'Alexandra Restaurant & Bar' run by Joseph Barnett (left), the 'Star Beerhall' (below) and the 'Bodega', photographed with some of its customers and staff (bottom of the page).*

H W PRIOR *(with gold chain) stands with a group of his regular customers in front of the 'Criterion Bar'.*

ing. The best the authorities of the South African Republic could hope for was to 'regulate' and 'control' commercial sex in the metropolis.

Prostitution began almost as soon as the first nuggets came out of the Reef in the 1880s – spurred by the proclamation in the Cape of the Contagious Diseases Act, which required all prostitutes to register and undergo compulsory medical examinations. The Act forced many prostitutes to seek their living beyond the long arm of the Cape law – and where better than the new goldfields of the Witwatersrand, where they rented rooms in the growing number of canteens and bars frequented by miners. Quick to spot a likely new source of profit, the bar owners formed the powerful Licensed Victuallers' Association, which overtly supported prostitution.

The locals, however, were about to be challenged by a new, and far more ruthless, supporter of prostitution – organised gangsters of mainly Russian and Polish descent who had been driven from the seamier side of New York by sweeping anti-vice laws. Their arrival coincided with an economic slump in Europe that brought many unemployed women to the goldfields in search of domestic service – or anything else. By October 1895, 36 of the 97 brothels in central Johannesburg were 'staffed' by French prostitutes, while another 20 were German and five were filled with Russian prostitutes.

By 1898 the American pimps had virtually cornered the vice trade, as the 'Standard and Diggers News' reported: ' . . . there is a large and thriving colony of Americanised Russian women engaged in the immoral traffic, who are controlled by an association of *macquereaus* [the local name for pimps] of pronounced Russian pedigree embellished by a twangy flashy embroidery of style and speech acquired in the Bowery of New York City, where most of them . . . have graduated in the noble profession.' As the 60 or 70 New Yorkers rose to the top seam, so an army of minor pimps jockeyed beneath them – led by Frenchmen and Germans. Africans also found a good living – both as pimps and as translators in the brothels.

The hottest part of town was the square formed by Bree, Anderson, Kruis and Sauer streets – popularly known as Frenchfontein – where women advertised their wares in various stages of undress. Printed cards bearing the names of brothels such as the 'Monte Cristo', 'Phoenix' and 'Spire House' also made the rounds. One of the ritziest was 'Sylvio Villa' on the corner of De Villiers and Rissik streets, where the nine resident prostitutes – who readily produced certificates in order to prove they were free of disease – charged £1 a time or £5 'all night'. The 'working' girls, however, had to pass some of this to the 'madam' – £4 a week for board and lodging plus a percentage of the takings, probably about 25 percent. On a busy Saturday night in December 1897 detectives watching the brothel counted 96 customers entering 'Sylvio Villa'. On Sunday, however, the number dwindled to only seven.

Kruger acts

That such a den of iniquity should operate less than 60 kilometres from Paul Kruger's deeply religious following in the capital, Pretoria, did not go unnoticed – and after many false starts, prostitution was outlawed in 1897, with a 'Morality Squad' appointed to ensure compliance. Despite an initial exodus of prostitutes, however, the law was largely ineffective – because most of the poorly paid members of the 'Morality Squad' were on the payroll of the 'Bowery Boys'.

Now more powerful than ever, the flashy ex-New Yorkers in late 1898 formed the 'American Club', which soon became known simply, and more accurately, as the 'Pimps Club', with the Polish-born Joe Silver as president and Salus Budner ('Joe Gold' to his associates) as secretary. It was this club that initiated the 'white slave trade' of young girls from Europe in order to keep the pleasure palaces filled with new 'talent'. One of their favourite hunting grounds was the east end of London – and in 1897 they began operating from a hotel in Waterloo, enticing young immigrant Jewish girls from their dreary jobs in the London clothing trade with promises of marriage or, if that didn't work, by

brute force before the innocents were 'escorted' to Johannesburg. At the same time French pimps lured young servant girls from Brussels and Paris to the Rand with lucrative offers of employment.

As the vice sank to new levels, Kruger once again decided on action – and in 1898 asked State Attorney Jan Smuts to investigate police corruption in Johannesburg. His solution was to appoint a new public prosecutor, Mostyn Cleaver, with instructions to give teeth to Kruger's earlier law against prostitution. Playing on a split in the ranks of the 'American Club' and armed with warrants signed by Smuts, Cleaver raided several brothels in the city – and by the end of January 1899 Silver and many of his henchmen were in jail. Fearing that local jurors would be bribed, the authorities set the trial for Pretoria – and despite attempts to threaten and bribe witnesses, Silver was jailed for two years. However, when the South African War broke out later that year – and prison warders were needed for military service – Silver was freed in a general amnesty. Over the next five years he operated vice rings in Kimberley, Cape Town and Windhoek.

When peace returned to the Transvaal in 1902, so did the pimps and prostitutes – most of whom had fled south during the war – and the 'white slavers' were back in busi-

GROWING UP *in the mushrooming metropolis of Johannesburg – a group of street urchins photographed in the 1890s.*

ness, this time also importing immigrant girls from the USA. Responsibility for cleaning up the vice now fell on the disinterested shoulders of the new High Commissioner to South Africa, Alfred Milner, who preferred to turn a blind eye to the brothels, believing that they were necessary as an inducement for attracting English-speaking immigrants to the Rand. However, he was far less happy at the prospect of white whores entertaining increasing numbers of African customers – and to this extent, at least, he took action, forcing many brothels that regularly entertained Africans to institute an elaborate system of alarms to warn of approaching police raids.

Finally, official prodding from Whitehall forced Milner to act against all brothels and pimps – a move, however, that was only selectively enforced. It was left to his successors to act more firmly, forcing many of the pimps and their women out of business, and in many cases out of the country. By this time, however, a new class of prostitute was beginning to emerge – local black and white women whose social background had been seared by the transformation from a rural to an industrial society. From then on, prostitution became a home-grown industry rather than an imported one. Never again, however, would it reach the shoddy depths of the 'naughty nineties'.

AN UNUSUAL PHOTOGRAPH – *of a woman crossing Joubert Street in 1898. Women hardly ever appear in street scenes from this period.*

WROUGHT-IRON *lacework so beloved by Victorian architects dominated Rissik Street (above) in the 1890s. The picture on the left shows Jack Cohen's betting shop on race day, with the inevitable bar right next door – ideally placed for a lucky winner to buy his fellow punters a celebratory drink.*

215

And then there were none...

Towards the end of the 19th century the last areas of southern Africa not yet under the control of the white man fell to the colonialists. A relative newcomer to the colonial scene, Germany, established a military presence in South West Africa (Namibia) in 1884, while Britain, fearing that the new German colony might link up with Paul Kruger's SAR, established a protectorate in Bechuanaland (Botswana) the following year. Further east, Cecil Rhodes declared Rhodesia (Zimbabwe) for the British Empire in 1890, while on the southern coast, Pondoland nominally independent, was taken over by the Cape in 1894.

IT IS HARD TO IMAGINE a drier, harsher, more inhospitable landscape than the southern plains of Namibia. Stretching endlessly to a shimmering horizon, they bake under a merciless sun that saps the willpower and numbs the mind.

And yet here, and in the cooler and better-watered lands around the present-day city of Windhoek, lived the Nama – while from the south in the early 19th century came the Oorlams and the Basters, driving their sheep before them from waterhole to waterhole.

At the same time, other inhabitants of the high country, the Herero, began to spread south, seeking new pastures for their increasing herds – and by 1840 the scene was set for a long period of intermittent warfare between themselves and the Nama-Oorlams, a group of whom used firearms to establish themselves under their leader Jonker Afrikaner around Windhoek.

It was into this dangerous mix that the first Germans stepped: Rhenish missionaries who established stations in various parts of the country. They were followed by more whites, a sprinkling of German settlers and a fair number of trekboers from the Cape Colony to the south – and by the 1870s the nuclei of a number of towns had been established, as well as a rudimentary transport system. The warfare, however, continued, with alliances being struck and broken, and the Nama first being defeated before emerging more powerful than ever under Afrikaner's successor, Jan Jonker Afrikaner.

Unhappy about the security situation, the missionaries in 1868 asked the King of Prussia for his 'protection'. Prussia, about to embark on a war with France – which broke out in 1870 – did nothing. The privations of warfare also led both Jan Jonker Afrikaner and the Herero chief, Maherero, to appeal for protection – to the Governor of the Cape, Sir Philip Wodehouse. The Cape Government, however, was not in an expansionist mood, and nothing was done except to proclaim Walvis Bay and certain guano islands British territory in 1878 in the interests of securing a monopoly of any future trade in the region (Walvis Bay still remains part of the Cape Province of South Africa).

In 1882 a German tobacco trader, Franz Lüderitz, aided by the missionaries, succeeded in 'purchasing' large sec-

MAJOR THEODOR LEUTWEIN (left) arrived in German South West Africa in 1894 to face a guerrilla attack by Nama leader Hendrik Witbooi (right). After a tricky period of negotiations, Leutwein persuaded Witbooi to stop fighting and even to assist the Germans assert the new colonial policy of trying to make the territory a province of Germany rather than a colony. But in 1905 Witbooi took up arms against the Germans again and fought until his death in 1907.

tions of the coast – including the bay of Angra Pequena – from the Nama, who were once again at war with the Herero. Lüderitz expanded his private empire with further purchases, until it became too large and expensive for him to exploit alone. A request to Otto von Bismarck, the German Chancellor, for protection of his enterprises was passed on to Britain and, after considerable dithering on the part of these two powers, as well as the Cape Colony, the German flag was raised at Angra Pequena (later Lüderitzbucht) in August 1884.

The first administration consisted of a Commissioner, his secretary, and a police sergeant, loosely based at Lüderitzbucht. The Commissioner, Heinrich Göring (father of Nazi Herman Göring), succeeded in making treaties with the Herero, the Basters and a number of other groups. Göring withdrew to the safety of British-owned Walvis Bay, where 23 German soldiers under Captain Curt von Francois landed in 1889. Two years later, and reinforced by 43 more soldiers, Von Francois made his headquarters at Windhoek, being appointed Commissioner in 1891.

German authority was to be implemented by military action, if necessary, and when Nama leader Hendrik Witbooi declined to accept German 'protection', Von Francois, further reinforced, promptly attacked him in 1892. Thanks to a long-standing trade in firearms with Cape Town merchants and others, Witbooi's men, armed with modern breech-loaders, were able to make a successful fighting retreat, although some 70 of their women and children were killed. Von Francois, to his great surprise, found himself with a guerrilla war on his hands. He was only too happy to pass on the problem to his successor, Major Theodor Leutwein, who arrived in 1894. Witbooi was persuaded to surrender, and even to lend his fighting men to assist the Germans as they tried to assert the new colonial policy, making South West Africa a province of Germany rather than a colony in distant Africa.

The authority of chiefs was undermined by proclamations stating that no chief might arbitrate in any matter between different chiefdoms, or between indigenous people and Germans, who were now starting to arrive as settlers in significant numbers. The chief's authority was restricted to the internal affairs of his own group.

The threat was quickly recognised by the chiefdoms, Leutwein himself writing that they had 'correctly sensed that they are threatened by us with the loss of their free state', and that 'it will prove to be no easy matter to settle it all without a clash of swords'. Leutwein, although he attempted to govern as 'humanely' as possible in the circumstances, conceded that colonial policy 'can, after all, result only in the restriction of the right of the native population in favour of the newcomers'.

It was the newcomers themselves, German farmers and traders, with their arrogant treatment of the 'native population', who fired the greatest resentment. Large tracts of land were occupied without permission from the chiefdoms that claimed them as their own. Goods were sold on credit and defaulters were taken to court, where they were often sentenced to work for their creditors. An outbreak of rinderpest in 1896 killed many Herero cattle, which had more than mere economic value, oxen being important in the ancestor-worship cult. Cattle were shot by the German authorities to try to contain the epidemic. This was seen as an overt act of aggression against the Herero, who, displaced on the land and despised as inferiors, with their institutions threatened or in tatters, rebelled violently in 1904. The war cost 2 000 German lives and brought the Herero close to extinction (see page 462).

Bechuanaland – the land between

From a tiny mission station at the northern Cape settlement of Kuruman, where Robert Moffat was to serve for almost 50 years, the London Missionary Society gradually spread its workers among the surrounding Tswana. Although Moffat was concerned only with the 'saving of souls', some of his colleagues took an active part in more secular affairs, until missionaries came to hold influential and even powerful positions, advising particularly on contacts with whites, whether traders, hunters, prospectors or trekboers.

When gold was found in the Tati district of the Tswana country, President Marthinus Wessel Pretorius issued a proclamation 'annexing' it to the South African Republic (SAR). Nothing was done, however, to put the proclamation into effect. The threat was renewed with the discovery of diamonds along the Vaal and Harts rivers. This time Britain acted, annexing the diamond area as Griqualand West (see page 168). Boer pressure on the Tswana was reduced by the British annexation of the SAR in 1877, but after the British withdrew in 1881 an even more confused situation resulted.

In the southern part of Tswana country, Boer mercenaries allied themselves to various chiefs of the Rolong, Tlhaping and Korana. In return for conducting raids, they were rewarded with cattle and grants of land that they promptly set up as the independent republics of Stellaland and Goshen – conveniently based for further incursions into Tswana country. It was now that a missionary, John Mackenzie, who had worked among the Tswana for many years as missionary and unofficial administrator, and who realised that these republics would inevitably be incorporated into the Transvaal, took time off from his ministrations to campaign in England for the Tswana.

In England, Mackenzie was able to form a South African Committee of men who supported his view that some form of British protectorate should be proclaimed over Bechuanaland – with the result that a protectorate was established over southern Bechuanaland as far north as the Molopo River, with Mackenzie as the first Deputy Commissioner. He returned to his new territory in 1884, but was recalled after a few months at the insistence of Cecil Rhodes, who manipulated his own appointment as Mackenzie's successor. Trouble in Goshen, where an English adventurer, Christopher Bethell, agent of chief Montsiwa of the Rolong, was apparently murdered by Boers, led to the dispatch of an expeditionary force under General Charles Warren.

Warren's orders were to 'remove the filibusters from Bechuanaland' – that is, to deproclaim the republics of Stellaland and Goshen, and 'reinstate the natives on their lands'. He was also to prevent further inroads by the Boers, and to occupy Bechuanaland until some final decision was

Cecil Rhodes gives his name to a country

It is not often that an entire country is named after one man, but it happens. Bolivia in South America, for example, was named after the liberator Simon Bolivar; while North and South America were named after just one man – the Italian explorer Amerigo Vespucci.

Thus, Cecil John Rhodes joined a fairly exclusive club when the colony his money had helped to fund was named Rhodesia in his honour. And it all began because an American mining engineer had assured him that the Witwatersrand gold strike was literally just a flash in the pan. 'If I were to ride over those reefs in America, I would not get off my horse to look at them.'

As a result, Rhodes held back while other Kimberley capitalists hastened to the Transvaal and staked the best claims. When finally he did act, his company, Gold Fields of South Africa, produced such poor results that much of its remaining capital was used to buy diamond shares as a hedge against what Rhodes viewed as the coming crash on the Rand. Rather than risk even more money by buying additional properties there, Rhodes – encouraged by his partner, Charles Rudd – decided to exploit the land between the Limpopo and the Zambezi rivers, believed by many people

LOBENGULA, *son of Mzilikazi, tried in vain to stop Rhodes' advance.*

to be the biblical Land of Ophir, an ancient source of gold.

That it had been a source of gold was obvious from the many ancient workings that dotted the countryside, some penetrating the ground to a depth of as much as 50 metres. Here, Rhodes decided, lay a 'second Witwatersrand' and perhaps even 'two or three Johannesburgs'.

In a letter to a London newspaper editor, Rhodes acknowledged there would be difficulties, but expressed the hope that 'Providence' would furnish 'a few paying gold reefs. Please understand that it is no personal avarice which desires this, but... gold hastens the development of a country more than anything.'

The south-west of the country was ruled by Lobengula, son of the founder of the Ndebele state, Mzilikazi. Some of the Shona occupying the north-east were vassals of Lobengula. Armed with the Rudd concession granting exclusive rights to minerals in Lobengula's section of the country, Rhodes formed the British South Africa Company, obtaining from Queen Victoria a royal charter whereby the company was given the right to rule the territory in which it operated.

In 1890 a heavily armed 'pioneer column', consisting of 192 prospective miners and settlers guarded by 500 troopers of the newly formed British South Africa Company Police, established a camp at the site of the present city of Harare, and then scattered to find their fortunes. However, they found little. Mining experts who were called in gave dismal reports and, by the end of 1891, the company was close to bankruptcy, being propped up by investments from Rhodes' other interests.

An Ndebele raid, which attempted to cut off labour to mines in the Victoria district in 1893, was easily beaten off, and suggested a way out of the trouble. In the first place, Rhodes' confidant, Dr Leander Jameson (later to achieve notoriety for attempting to invade the Transvaal), reasoned that 'getting Matebeleland open would give us a tremendous lift in shares and everything else'. Second, Ndebeleland could be 'opened' on the cheap, by using volunteers from among the settlers, backed by guns of the Royal Artillery and a sprinkling of

imperial units, as well as imperial regulars who were given time off from duties in Bechuanaland to form a 'Special Service Mounted Infantry'.

Lobengula, who had long since repudiated the Rudd concession, sent messages begging for peace, but these were ignored, and the well-armed invaders soon fought their way through to his Great Place, Bulawayo, which they burnt to the ground. Lobengula died on a retreat towards the Zambezi. This 'removal of uncertainty' resulted in a two-year period of prosperity that was a reflection of the current boom on the Witwatersrand, from where a portion of capital was diverted to the supposed goldfields of Ndebeleland. On a wave of speculation, mainly in land, a new Bulawayo soon grew to a population of more than 2 000 whites.

Cattle 'levies' demanded that the Ndebele give up more than 100 000 head between 1893 and 1896, and a hut tax was enforced by armed groups of the company's police. In one instance, a headman who refused to sanction mine recuitment in his village was fined and publicly flogged. A system of forced labour was introduced, as there was great reluctance among the Africans to work in the mines. 'If a boy will not work, or tries to run away, the usual thing is to take him to the native commissioner, and have him given 25 lashes.'

An opportunity for retaliation arose when many of the troopers of the company's private army were posted away to take part in Jameson's ill-fated Transvaal adventure. Soon af-

CHARLES RUDD *encouraged Rhodes to try his luck in the north.*

A STATUE *of Rhodes in Cape Town's Botanic Gardens.*

terwards, rinderpest broke out, and company officials shot many cattle in an attempt to limit the spread of the disease. In 1896 the Ndebele rebelled but, although they achieved success in the outlying areas, they were unable to make headway against the larger settlements. Volunteers and imperial troops were rushed to the territory and inflicted heavy losses on the Ndebele. When it seemed that the 'troubles' were all but over, the Shona staged a number of local uprisings which, like the revolt of the Ndebele, achieved initial successes. Only in October 1897 was armed resistance by Africans overcome, but the war had cost the company millions of pounds. By now, however, Rhodes' Witwatersrand mines were paying off at deep levels, so the loss was cushioned.

Mining development in the country now called Rhodesia, halted during the war, was resumed as a serious undertaking for large capital, rather than as a speculation for wandering prospectors. The rapid development of railway links to the coast enabled the necessary machinery and plant to be brought in, and white optimism revived. It also meant that foodstuffs could be railed into the country, and

this spelt the ruin of many African cultivators, who had adapted from subsistence level to the principal suppliers. Labour recruitment, in the hands of the Labour Board and the Native Department, thus drew in workers who had no other means of raising the money that government levies demanded. As the gold output rose, so African wages fell, from around 40 shillings a month in 1897 to 22 shillings in 1900, when the South African War cut rail traffic with the south.

As grain prices rose due to interrupted communications, so more and more Africans left the wage-labour market and returned to the lands. An official commented that 'the natives are agriculturists, and do not view the prospect of becoming miners with any enthusiasm'. A missionary, observing that the Africans regarded the white man's lust for gold as the prime reason for the loss of their country, added that 'they are unwilling to cooperate in the development of what they consider their great misfortune'. It would have been small compensation for them to know that, throughout the years that it administered Rhodesia, the British South Africa Company never once paid a dividend on its shares.

A GROUP *of Ndebele warriors await execution after being accused of 'murder'.*

LOOTING *from an Ndebele kraal.*

CHIEF KGAMA 'the good', ruler of the Ngwato, agreed to accept British protection over his territory.

taken. He accomplished all this peaceably, apart from arguments with Rhodes, who had insisted on accompanying him. When it was decided to extend the protectorate northwards, Warren found that chief Kgama of the Ngwato was willing to accept, although he pointed out that latitude 22 deg, the northern boundary, left half of his country outside the protectorate. The chiefs Setshele and Gaseitsiwe also accepted British protection, and offered large tracts of their lands for settlement by English immigrants.

In 1885 southern Bechuanaland was proclaimed a British colony, known as British Bechuanaland, while the country between the Molopo and latitude 22 deg was placed 'under Her Majesty's Protection'. Here, it was expected that the Africans would manage their own internal affairs, with Britain responsible for protection against foreign aggression. Sidney Shippard, a judge of the Eastern Cape Supreme Court, was appointed Administrator of the colony and Deputy Commissioner for the protectorate.

Shippard was an ardent supporter of Rhodes, whom he kept informed of affairs in the northern, independent Ndebele state. His assistant, John Smith Moffat, a missionary and son of Robert Moffat, secured from Lobengula, king of the Ndebele, an undertaking that Lobengula would not cede any part of his country to any power other than Britain. In effect, the Moffat treaty of 1888 virtually placed Ndebele foreign policy in the hands of the High Commissioner for South Africa. Just a few months later, Shippard was at the court of the Ndebele king, successfully urging him to sign the 'Rudd concession', which assigned the mineral rights of Lobengula's territories to a group of adventurers and financiers backed by Rhodes. It was to exploit the Rudd concession that the British South Africa Company was formed, and from a base in Bechuanaland that it launched its invasion of Shona country (see box).

The fall of Pondoland

Bordered by a covetous Natal to the north, and lying between the Mtamvuna and Mtata rivers, Pondoland managed to retain its independence long after most African states had been occupied by whites and annexed. It

was divided by the Mzimvubu River into the two chiefdoms of eastern and western Pondoland, in both of which a number of whites – most of them of dubious character – established themselves as 'advisers' and traders. The move to end independence by annexation to the Cape gained momentum in the late 1880s, when a co-ordinated and uniform 'African policy' was required to ensure a smooth response to the ever-increasing demand for labour.

Nqwiliso, chief of western Pondoland, provided the toehold in 1878 for subsequent annexation by 'selling' to the Cape Government, when threatened with annexation, some 4 000 hectares of land at the mouth of the Mzimvubu River, where Port St Johns was subsequently developed. Nqwiliso also granted permission for the construction of a road through his territory, from Port St Johns towards Umtata. In return, he received £1 000. Another road from Port St Johns was to be built to Kokstad, having to pass through eastern Pondoland, ruled by Mqikela, paramount chief of the Mpondo. Mqikela, however, was little more than a figurehead by this time, being seriously debilitated, it is believed, by alcoholism, and real control was in the hands of his nephew, Mdlangaso.

In 1885 Mdlangaso granted a concession to Emil Nagel, a German, over a large tract of land on the east bank of the Mzimvubu, and three years later a party of Germans, representing the 'Berlin Pondo Society', arrived to investigate the region. This immediately raised fears at the Cape of a German protectorate, and a British Resident, J H Scott, was foisted onto the Mpondo in order to keep an eye on subsequent developments. By this time Mqikela had died, and the succession had passed to his son, Sigcawu, bypassing a resentful Mdlangaso. Sigcawu refused to acknowledge the status of Scott, or even grant him a place to establish himself, knowing that the imposition of a Resident was a direct move to undermine his own authority. He was quite content, he said, to conduct any business

CHIEF SIGCAWU rightly feared that acceptance of a British Resident in Pondoland would lead to annexation.

MISSION ACCOMPLISHED, *the British expeditionary force celebrates with a cheer and the raising of the Union Jack at O'Connell's Fort after the annexation of Pondoland to the crown.*

with the Cape Government through Walter Stanford, Chief Magistrate at Kokstad. Clashes between the supporters of Mdlangaso and Sigcawu, and occasional crossings of the Natal border, kept Scott in a state of anxiety and led to demands that Pondoland should be annexed to Natal.

Across the Mzimvubu, in western Pondoland, Nqwiliso's authority was being severely tested. White agents, including members of the police force, deliberately subverted Nqwiliso's authority by encouraging wrong-doers who had been summoned to the Great Place of Nqwiliso to report instead to the office of the magistrate in Umtata, Major Henry Elliot. As a result, although only nominally British Resident in western Pondoland, Elliot gradually came to be seen as an authority superior to the chief. To add to the troubles, Gwadiso of the Khonjwayo clan rebelled

SIR WALTER STANFORD, *Chief Magistrate at Kokstad, gave Chief Sigcawu 10 days to accept British demands.*

against Nqwiliso, and this led to what Elliot eagerly described as 'inter-tribal quarrels and barbarous atrocities'. For 'humanitarian' reasons, it was said, Pondoland should be annexed, although to Bishop Bransby Key of St John's, Umtata, it was clear that 'the white man is thirsting for the possession of Pondoland'.

Cecil Rhodes, one of the thirstiest, and Prime Minister of the Cape since 1890, added 'Native Affairs' to his portfolio in 1894. He ordered 600 Cape Mounted Riflemen to be moved to Umtata. 'The time has come,' he declared, 'to bring that country [Pondoland] under Cape Colony rule.' Elliot was instructed to despatch letters to Nqwiliso and Sigcawu, advising them that their countries were to be annexed, and demanding their immediate reply. Elliot and Stanford met Sigcawu a few weeks later and threatened that unless he accede to their demands, the Cape Mounted Riflemen would enter his country within 10 days. Elliot then confronted Nqwiliso with the same ultimatum.

Sigcawu demanded to know whether other chiefs were similarly treated, by being required to surrender their country and then have troops move against them even before they had made their reply. He was not aware, he said, of any quarrel between himself and the (Cape) government. His council of chiefs, while realising that they could make no effective resistance, was nevertheless reluctant to yield. There was no alternative, however, and after a few days the oldest counsellor, Ndunga, gave their decision. 'His voice quavered and he showed considerable emotion' recorded the missionary Peter Hargreaves, 'whilst he told them that they had decided to surrender.' Stanford sent a telegram to Rhodes, advising him that Sigcawu had 'cheerfully submitted'.

Nqwiliso also yielded, demanding to know 'why this government should bring an army, as the whole business might be settled without bringing troops into the country'. Within a month, Rhodes was in his newest domain, formally receiving surrenders. Pondoland, object of greed and desire for more than 20 years, passed the way of Mashonaland and Ndebeleland, albeit less bloodily.

No more than units of labour

When sugar was first produced from cane in Natal in 1851, the colony seemed set for a major economic boom. But there was just one snag: the plantation owners lacked a source of cheap labour. At first they hoped that the indigenous people would be able to supply their needs.
But once it became obvious that toiling in the fields for the white capitalist held no attraction for most Zulu, planters began to turn their attentions elsewhere.
And they looked – as planters throughout the empire had looked – to India.

DAVARUM WAS 30 YEARS OLD when he put his thumbprint to a document he could not even read: 'We the adult male emigrants,' it said, 'do hereby agree to serve the employer to whom we may respectively be allotted by the Natal Government under the Natal Act No. 14 of 1859 and we all understand the terms under which we are engaged . . . . '

Davarum – or Coolie No. 1, as the recruiting officer named him, had no idea where Natal was, let alone the implications of Act No. 14 – but for 10 shillings a month he, and hundreds of thousands of his countrymen, were prepared to travel anywhere to escape the poverty and starvation of India . . . .

On 12 October 1860, he and his wife (Coolie No. 2), and their two children (Coolies 3 and 4), joined 338 others aboard the *Truro* at Madras harbour. A few hours later, the dangerously overloaded vessel began its long journey to south-east Africa.

The fight for 'coolie' labour

The go-ahead for Natal to recruit 'coolies' in Madras (and Calcutta) followed protracted and often bitter negotiation between the governments of the colony, Britain and a far-from-keen India. As far back as 1851, plantation owners had been demanding the importation of workers from India. In 1855, Cape Governor Sir George Grey, acting on behalf of a group of Natal farmers, tried to 'requisition' 300 'coolies' from Calcutta. Although the Indian Government turned down this request, it promised to reconsider once the colony had stipulated the terms of indenture.

In 1856 the Natal legislature passed an ordinance empowering the Lieutenant-Governor 'to make rules and regulations for Coolies introduced into this District from the East Indies'. But in the next year, much of India erupted in rebellion against the rule of the English East India Company that, for decades, had systematically plundered, taxed and exploited the country and its people. By the time the last mutineer had been blown from the muzzle of a cannon, rule in India had passed to the British Crown and, as memory of the horrors of war faded, Indians were given a greater say in the new system of government which developed. Mindful of the racist attitudes of white colonists in southern Africa, and therefore unconvinced that workers would be properly treated, the new Indian administration again turned down a Natal request for 'coolie' labour.

By 1859 the labour shortage in Natal had reached crisis proportions – and the 'Natal Mercury' proclaimed that 'the fate of the Colony hangs on a thread, and that thread is labour'. Legislation was rushed through to enable colonists to bring in labour from India at their own expense, and also to allow the colonial government to introduce Indian labourers 'at the public expense'. Although the government bore the major share of the expenses, planters to whom the labourers were assigned had to pay three-fifths of their passage money of some £8 per head, as well as certain other costs.

INDENTURED INDIAN *labourers arrive at the quayside in Durban after being unloaded from ships carrying them from India. Between 1860 and 1911 – when indentures ceased – about 152 000 Indians landed in Natal, with roughly 52 percent deciding to remain in southern Africa after serving out their contracts.*

INDIAN LABOURERS *at work in the sugar plantations. They were paid 10 shillings a month in the first year of service, rising annually by one shilling a month for the remainder of their contracts. Cutting the tall cane was back-breaking work – after a breakfast of cold porridge, the labourers marched to the fields, where they began work before dawn.*

The contract, or indenture, provided that a labourer would be assigned to a particular planter for a period of three years (later amended to five years) and then be reindentured, perhaps to the same planter, for another two years. After a residence in Natal of a further five years as a 'free' worker, the labourer had the choice of accepting a free return passage to India or of remaining in Natal on a small grant of Crown land. While they were indentured, their welfare was the responsibility of a 'Coolie Immigration Agent', who also assigned them to plantations.

Once on the plantation, treatment of the indentured labourer was not subject to the ordinary master and servant ordinance. Special regulations demanded that the employer provide food and lodging, clothing and any necessary medical attention. He was also obliged to pay wages of 10 shillings a month for the first year, followed by an annual increase of a shilling a month thereafter in each successive year. His workers' welfare would be guarded by the Coolie Immigration Agent, who would visit each plantation at least twice a year. On the other hand, if a labourer missed work for what his employer regarded as an inadequate reason, a portion of his already meagre wages could be deducted as a fine. If he left his employer's plantation without a signed Pass, he was liable to imprisonment. Once his five years of indentured service were over, the immigrant Indian was subject to the ordinary law of the colony. It was scarcely an attractive package, but ever-increasing pressure on the land in India led to growing impoverishment of a rural class that owned no land and was scarcely able to survive. Emigration, whether to Natal or any other part of the empire, was an act of desperation in an attempt to secure survival.

The pioneers

On 16 November 1860 the *Truro* dropped anchor in Natal Bay under the curious gaze of a crowd of white spectators who had come to see the arrival of the Indians. The Coolie Immigration Agent was not at the dockside because, to save money, the Natal Government had not yet formalised his appointment (they did not do so until two days later). Once ashore, the immigrants were herded by armed police into an uncompleted barracks with no toilet, washing or cooking facilities, set amid pools of stagnant water. Here they remained under guard for eight days (during which time four of them died), waiting for their new masters to collect them.

The planters wanted only strong, healthy young men – and as rumours began circulating that families would be split up, some of the workers tried to abscond in a bid for freedom. The reaction of the authorities was to build high walls around the barracks.

Although the terms of the agreement between the governments of India and Natal stipulated that families were not to be separated, this did, in fact, occur: a 34-year-old woman, Choureamah Arokuim (Coolie No. 99), arrived with her daughters, eight-year-old Megaleamah (Coolie No. 100) and three-year-old Susanah (Coolie No. 101). Although the family was originally assigned to Grey's Hospital, just over six months later Magaleamah was apprenticed to A Brewer, and Susanah – perhaps aged four by this time – to Isabella O'Hara. Once assigned, the immigrants walked to their plantations, clutching a few pathetic possessions and their rations for the road.

At first, the plantation workers erected their own shacks and were able to cultivate small patches of the surrounding ground for their own account – if they were not exhausted by the day's work. Later, however, planters were obliged to provide accommodation, building barracks, known as 'coolie lines', of corrugated iron, mud, or stone, in which the workers led a cramped and uncomfortable existence devoid of any privacy. A lean-to shed, generally without a chimney, was used for cooking the rations of rice, mealie-meal and ghee, a clarified form of butter.

About 250 grams of dried fish each week was their only luxury. Few barracks were provided with toilets, and analysis of samples of water used for drinking revealed them to be 'quite unsafe for use'.

Before dawn every day, the *sirdar* (foreman) rang a bell or, more commonly, struck a bar of iron suspended from a tree, to wake the workers who, after an unappetising breakfast of cold 'porridge', marched to the fields so as to begin work as the sun rose. And they worked, planting, digging, breaking new soil, cutting, harvesting, carrying, building, until the sun set. There was a brief break for lunch, which was a repeat of breakfast. It was dark by the time they reached their homes, where they managed another brief meal before falling into exhausted sleep. Sundays were supposed to be free, but few planters observed this.

Also unobserved was the condition that employers of more than 20 Indians should provide elementary hospitals. The 'hospital' at the receiving depot lumped all patients together – men, women and children – regardless of whether or not any were suffering from infectious diseases. Latrines were four holes in the ground, and there were neither water basins nor baths. Corpses were laid out in the open. By 1885 only three plantations had set up sick rooms, and these were worse than that at the depot.

Despite the appalling conditions, few complaints reached the courts. Principally, this was because the worker could not leave the estate without his employer's permission, and because the over-worked Coolie Immigration Agent was unable to visit the estates as he was supposed to. When he did, he was rarely able to speak to the workers in private and, in the presence of employers and *sirdars*, the workers were afraid to complain, knowing that they could expect even worse treatment if they were found out.

If some part of the worker found peace in death, it was not his body. Cremation, customary in India, was not permitted. In Durban, some ground near a butchery was allocated as an Indian and African cemetery. Workers, anxious to return to work to forestall pay stoppages, sometimes did not bury the corpses deep enough, and they were rooted out and eaten by pigs that had acquired a taste for flesh from offal thrown out by the butchery. Not even in death was there dignity.

Tales of horror

The fact that 'coolies' were regarded as units of labour rather than people left them open to widespread abuse. In an editorial which aptly summed up the attitude of white colonists, the 'Natal Witness' commented: 'The ordinary Coolie . . . and his family cannot be admitted into close fellowship and union with us and our families. He is introduced for the same reason as mules might be introduced from Montevideo, oxen from Madagascar or sugar machinery from Glasgow. The object for which he is brought is to supply labour and that alone. He is not one of us, he is in every respect an alien; he only comes to perform a certain amount of work, and return to India . . . .'

Many did, in fact, return to India, carrying with them horrific tales of life on the sugar plantations of Natal.

Illegal punishments meted out by employers included flogging. A 10-year-old Indian shepherd, afraid to return to his employer because a sheep had strayed from the flock, was suspended from a rafter for two hours and thrashed with a hunting crop. When released, he ran away and was not seen again. His parents, who worked for the same planter, were beaten on suspicion of taking food to the boy at night. This was an extreme case, but the prevailing callousness is summed up in the case of a man called Narayanan, who returned to his hut one evening to find that his ill wife and child had gone. He walked the plantations for months, vainly searching for his family – until he eventually discovered that the authorities had decided, because of his wife's illness, to return her and the child to India.

In 1871, confronted by reports and filed statements of abuses, India halted emigration to southern Africa – and the Governor-General of India explained: 'We cannot permit emigration [to Natal] to be resumed until we are satisfied that the colonial authorities are aware of their duties towards Indian emigrants and that effectual measures have been taken to ensure that class of Her Majesty's subjects full protection in Natal.' A commission hastily set up in Natal recommended that flogging be abolished, medical services be improved, and that the Coolie Immigration Agent be given wider powers and the new title of Protector of Indian Immigrants. Once these recommendations had passed into Natal law, together with another that safeguarded the immigrants' wages, the Indian Govern-

THE IMPORTATION *of Indian labourers into Natal was bitterly opposed by many whites, who demanded that they be repatriated at the end of their contract periods. One of the main agitators was Harry Escombe, seen addressing a protest meeting in Durban in the 1890s.*

ment allowed recruiting to resume, and the next group arrived in 1874.

Improvements, however, turned out to be mainly cosmetic and, although the Protector claimed that their fair treatment of immigrants 'was a credit to the Natal Planters', the Indian Government raised further objections, claiming that wages were far too low, and that unfairly large deductions were made when a labourer was unable to work because of illness. Living conditions were unsatisfactory, and many labourers were obliged to use water supplies that were dangerously contaminated.

By that time bigotry and discrimination were being increasingly written into the law. In Pietermaritzburg and Durban local legislation provided for the arrest of 'all persons of Colour, if found in the streets after 9 o'clock [at night] without a Pass'. A law of the Natal Parliament restricted Indian rights by classifying them as 'an uncivilised race'. Natal then unsuccessfully approached the Indian Government with its proposal that labourers should be indentured for the full 10-year period, which provoked indignant reaction. A Bengali newspaper declared: 'The only difference between Negro slavery and coolie emigration is that the former was open slavery and the latter is slavery in disguise.' Natal's reaction was to cease issuing grants of land in lieu of passage money to Indians who had been resident for 10 years and who wished to remain.

Despite their many hardships, Indians, after serving their period of indenture, filled many positions in the colony, some of them to the great indignation and resentment of whites. They were active in agriculture, and by 1885 were virtually the sole producers of fruit and vegetables for Durban and Pietermaritzburg. Others established a fishing and fish-curing industry based on Salisbury Island, while yet others were occupied in coal mining and on the Natal Government Railways. Some went into domestic service or practised a variety of trades. In reply to demands that time-expired workers be repatriated, the Protector was able to say that 'with but very few exceptions every industry in existence at the present time [1894] would collapse . . . if the Indian population should be withdrawn'. Their numbers were considerable, sometimes exceeding the total white population, and between 1860 and 1911, when the practice of indentured immigration ceased, some 152 000 Indians had entered Natal.

The coming of 'Passenger' Indians

Not all Indians came to Natal to sell their labour: there were others who came at their own expense, most of them as traders.

Known as Arabs or 'Passengers', and most of them Muslims from the state of Gujarat, they began to arrive in the 1870s and constituted the upper stratum of Indians in southern Africa. They associated with the indentured or ex-indentured Indians only so far as trade and labour required it. Yet, racial discrimination did not distinguish one from the other.

The 'Passenger' merchants arrived in Natal with considerable capital, and soon set themselves up as storekeepers selling not only to Africans and Indians but, increasingly, to whites. With their shops staffed by members of their families, 'Passenger' merchants were able to keep prices below the level the white trader regarded as the minimum on which he could make a profit.

When the first 'Passenger' merchants arrived, there were already 10 stores owned by ex-indentured labourers, whose customers were their still-indentured compatriots. By 1880, ex-labourers held 30 of the 37 retail trading licences issued to Indians in Durban – but, from then on, the assertion of the 'Passengers' was rapid: within five years, they owned 60 of the 66 Indian stores in Natal.

THE FIRST *Indian-owned shop in Natal opened in West Street, Durban, in 1874.*

Wealthier, more confident and ambitious, they formed an elite group, members of which submitted the first petition of grievances to the Colonial Secretary in London. They complained, among other things, of the 9 o'clock curfew, of the lack of interpreters in many courts, of the absence of Indians from juries, and of police brutality and harassment. They also requested permission to open their shops on Sundays, the only time when indentured Indians could do their shopping.

Faced by white hostility and rejection, groups of 'Passengers' who in India would never have associated with one another, were drawn together in the fight for political and civil rights. Their situation grew more serious from 1893 when Natal was granted responsible government. It meant that appeals to England or to India were much less likely to succeed.

But in the same year of 1893 a young, London-trained lawyer named Mohandas Gandhi left India to act in a matter concerning two Indian merchants in southern Africa. In Durban, he bought a first-class railway ticket and took his seat in a coach where, during the journey, a white traveller objected to sharing with an Indian. Ejected after refusing to move to a third-class compartment, Gandhi spent a thoughtful night on Pietermaritzburg station, pondering over what he was to call the 'most important factor' in directing his future political life (see page 272).

More work for less money

Despite the gold and diamond discoveries of the 1880s and '90s,
most of southern Africa remained dependent on farming – whether by Boers
of the Transvaal, sugar cane growers in Natal, sheep farmers of the interior, wealthy wine farmers
of the western Cape, or the pioneers of the ostrich feather industry in the Little Karoo.
All had one important need in common: labour to work the land – and yet virtually none
was prepared to pay a fair wage in order to attract more workers,
clinging to the extraordinary belief that labourers who were paid more would work less.

WHEREVER THE ENGLISH NOVELIST Anthony Trollope went during his visit to southern Africa in the 1870s, the story was the same: 'Every farmer, every merchant, every politician . . . swore that the country was wretched simply because labour could not be had.'

Trollope, who had a keen grasp of economic reality, was not slow to see why: the employers were simply not prepared to pay workers a fair wage, preferring to induce them to work by force – first slavery, and then a complex web of legislation, ranging from draconian labour laws to measures that made Africans landless, leaving them no alternative but to become wage-labourers.

With a few exceptions, farmers expressed opposition to increased wages by arguing that labourers would work less if they were paid more. The chairman of a select committee looking into labour problems in the Cape in 1879 asked a farmer whether workers would work more days if they got higher wages. The answer was unequivocal: 'On the contrary, if you pay them more they will work less.'

How this extraordinary belief arose is hard to explain, especially when most of the evidence collected by a plethora of special committees inquiring into labour shortages on farms in the Cape suggested otherwise. In 1891, for example, a sergeant from Fort Jackson in the eastern Cape wrote: 'How a man can expect to have labourers decently dressed, honest and generally living like other civilised people, for his food and 10 shillings a month to feed his family is beyond my comprehension. I am convinced that were more liberal wages offered the labour market would

not be in its present state.' And in 1892 a Cape parliamentary select committee was told by a labour recruiter recently back from a trip to Transkei that 'the natives would not think of accepting the terms offered, 15 shillings a month with board and lodging'.

The main reason, of course, was a reluctance to pay more – and a reliance on coercion, including the notorious 'tot' system, to obtain labour; a reliance that continued in many areas of the country until very recent times.

Keeping wages low

Wages for agricultural labourers in the western Cape were generally higher than in the rest of the country – about one shilling a day with rations, plus wine five or six times a day; with an increase to two shillings or more during harvest time. Wages were higher for more skilled men, such as wagon drivers; and on some farms, labourers were also given a place to live and land to cultivate.

The eastern Cape was much worse – 10 shillings was the average monthly wage, plus a food ration; and Natal worse still – seven shillings a month with a ration of maize. In the Transvaal most of the labourers were tenant farmers – leasing their land by working on the landowner's farm. Where cash wages were paid for day labourers, they ranged up to one shilling a day plus mealies, while long-term workers could expect a daily allowance of maize and sometimes a heifer a year.

Despite the relatively high wages being paid by public works, such as the railways and the docks, farm wages

A GROUP of Zulu women working in a mealie field during the closing years of the last century. Many Africans were able to avoid working for white farmers by producing just enough surplus to pay the government-imposed taxes.

Making a fortune from feathers

The thousands of tourists who flock annually to the Little Karoo town of Oudtshoorn near the Olifants River are lured by two major attractions: the Kango Caves north of the town, and one of the most unusual agricultural industries in the world – the farming of ostriches. No tour is complete without a visit to one of the so-called 'ostrich palaces', built during the height of the ostrich feather boom – when Victorian women appeared in all their feathered finery.

These large and elaborate homesteads of sandstone and wrought ironwork contrasted radically with the stick and reed huts of the labourers, whose earnings averaged between 10 shillings and £1 monthly.

It was the passion for ostrich feathers that created the ostrich industry, established from Riversdale in the west to Albany in the east, with the greatest concentration of wealth in the valley of the Olifants River around Oudtshoorn. Here, mixed edible grasses and bushes, as well as irrigated lucerne lands, provided an ideal environment for ostrich rearing.

The domestication of these great flightless birds dates from 1865, when 8 000 kilograms of feathers from wild ostriches were exported for a total of £65 736. The potential for domesticated ostriches was immediately realised – and by 1882 some 115 193 kilograms of feathers, all clipped from domesticated ostriches, brought in £1 093 989.

The new industry inevitably attracted great numbers of commercial operators, most of them reasonably honest, but some, especially among the itinerant feather-buyers, decidedly crooked. But ignorant and isolated farmers were not the only ones to be sold short. Labourers, mostly mixed descendants of early white trekboers and the Outeniqua and Attaqua Khoikhoi, as well as some Xhosa, did not share in the general bonanza. A number of labourers working on the ostrich farms also came from the mission stations of Amalienstein, Zoar and Dysselsdorp.

In addition to a meagre wage, they received rations of milk (as most ostrich farmers also ran dairy herds), mealie-meal and, occasionally, meat. Tobacco, wine and brandy were issued in lieu of a portion of the wages, all being produced locally, although the less profitable vineyards were gradually uprooted to make way for lucerne fields to feed the ostriches.

Ostrich feathers retained their popularity, and farmers their prosperity and labour, until 1914 when, with the outbreak of the First World War, feathers went out of fashion. And out into the veld went excess labourers and their families, to make their way on foot or, if they were unusually prosperous, by donkey cart, back to the already overcrowded agricultural allotments on the mission stations, or to try their luck in the surrounding villages.

THE HOMESTEAD *of the Welgeluk farm was built in 1910 during the boom.*

IN 1904, *actress Mary van Buren was at the pinnacle of fashion in her ostrich feather hat and boa.*

---

barely increased during the last three decades of the 19th century – with the exception of wages paid to migrant labourers who were in a better position to demand money for their services, particularly as wages varied widely from area to area.

Most Africans, particularly in Transkei and Zululand, did not need money – being able to subsist on their own smallholdings, producing just enough surplus to pay the required taxes without having to accept the very low wages offered to most migrant farm labourers. At the beginning of the 1890s, for example, most areas of Transkei were producing a fair food surplus – with considerable exports of wool, grain, hides and cattle to the diamond workings at Kimberley. In addition, some African farmers sold vegetables, fruit and dairy produce in the local towns and villages. Nevertheless, migrant labour was already fairly well established – with about 20 000 young men seeking work on the diamond diggings, on the railways or on farms during sheep-shearing or harvesting.

But it was not enough for the labour-hungry farmers, one of whom told an 1893 commission: 'The natives are independent. They have land and grow what they choose, and their wants are extremely small.' The commission concluded that 'these people do not, therefore, feel impelled to work'. The president of the Chamber of Mines – whose labour needs were just as acute – had much the same thing to say: 'The native . . . cares nothing if industries pine for want of labour when his crops and home-brewed drink are plentiful.'

The truth was that many Africans were proving able agriculturalists themselves, particularly the hard-working Mfengu of the frontier region who organised the building of schools and roads from money raised by the sale of surplus agricultural produce. Farmers near the Mbashe River turned their hand to coffee farming, others in Tembuland planted fruit trees, while in Xalanga 4 000 bags of wheat threshed by machinery were judged to be equal to the 'best grown in the colony'. Only in the late 1890s, with the coming of the fearful rinderpest cattle epidemic, did this period of prosperity come to an end (see box).

For the non-migrant labourer, escape from the dreary drudge of farm life was virtually impossible – unless he was lucky enough to secure employment in the towns, particularly on the ever-spreading network of the western Cape railways or at the Cape Town docks, where much higher rates of pay could be obtained.

Wine and workers

The wine farmers of the Stellenbosch district had once constituted the biggest group of slave-owners in the colony and, some 50 years after emancipation, many longed for a return to what they must have regarded as 'the good old days'. First, the diamond fields had enticed labour away, and then, as the economy expanded, still more workers had left to find work on the railways, at the ports, or in pri-

A trail of bleaching bones

Like some belated biblical plague of Egypt, rinderpest, a highly contagious and fatal cattle disease, showed itself in far north Africa in 1889. Leaving a trail of bleaching bones and poverty, it made its relentless way south – and by November 1897 game on the estate of Cecil Rhodes at Groote Schuur showed the classic symptoms of bloody diarrhoea and fever. Although they had been warned as early as 1892, the Cape authorities had done almost nothing and, north of the Cape Peninsula, the vultures gorged over a dying landscape.

There were political repercussions to this virus-spread sickness. Cattle deaths, and the deliberate killing of cattle to contain the disease, played their part in rebellion against white authority in Rhodesia, Bechuanaland and East Griqualand. Africans believed that rinderpest was spread deliberately by whites to deprive them not only of one the most important forms of their wealth, but of the status that went with ownership of cattle. On the other side, there were whites who were convinced that the disease was spread by Africans. Of the two theories, the Africans' was nearer the truth. Whites tended to be more mobile, and their trading and social activities required frequent journeying, with little regard or understanding of the risks. Despite this, it was to Africans that the tardy preventive measures were more vigorously applied.

Travellers were obliged to use disinfectants at certain strategic places along the roads, supervised by government officials. But only Africans had to be completely dipped, like cattle, a distinction that they resented, especially the more 'Europeanised' Africans. To convince local Africans of the devastating effects of an uncontrolled spread of rinder-

GUARDS man a roadblock at the height of the rinderpest epidemic.

pest, the Cape Government arranged for a number of them to visit Bechuanaland to see the destruction and, if they wished, to prove the inefficacy of their traditional medicines. Unfortunately, the timing was bad, and the visit took place when the worst of the infestation was over, and only when the full force of the disease struck their home territories did the Africans appreciate its severity.

Meat was imported, expensively, from as far away as Madagascar. With draught oxen dying by the thousands, transport costs rocketed, pushing up the prices of almost all commodities, often to an unjustifiably high level. It was not only the shopkeeper who was able to reflect that rinderpest was not all disaster; missionaries, too, noted that great numbers of Africans who had stayed beyond their influence were now seeking refuge and solace at their stations. And, most important of all for the white entrepreneur, Africans in large numbers were forced onto the labour market in an effort to obtain cash to rebuild their cattle holdings. Many migrated temporarily – some

permanently – to the towns, leaving their lands to an uncertain future.

For Transkei, the disease was an unmitigated disaster, impoverishing thousands of peasant farmers and forcing them onto the labour market, proving not 'altogether an unmixed evil' to white farmers. Commented a missionary: '. . . With the natives, the possession of great numbers of cattle is as a rule conducive to idleness. After the fields are planted, they have little to do until harvest time if they have plenty of milk and a supply of grain on hand from the previous season's crops. Now, however, we have them going off in all directions to earn money to provide for their family.'

The magistrate of Kentani observed that the loss of security caused by the rinderpest had 'left the native less independent, more inclined to work, less impudent, and generally better in every way than he was before.'

In a way, nature had achieved what the white farmers could not – by killing off their livelihood, it had forced Africans onto the labour market.

vate employment in the towns. The truth was, almost any other job was more attractive, and certainly better paid.

For the 'permanent' farm labourer, the farm was the entire world, with the master or mistress as the supreme authority. The Masters and Servants Acts made it illegal for them to beat him, but they beat him nevertheless. He could, of course, complain to the magistrate, as did a domestic worker of a farmer named Prol. The 'master', called to answer the charge of assault, said his servant had been cheeky. The case was dismissed. Then there were the hours – sunrise to sunset on the farm, eight or nine hours a day in most other jobs.

A wine farm labourer, in addition to accommodation and basic rations, received around two shillings a day. However, about half of this was not in cash, but in wine, and the labourer was not given the option of choosing between cash or wine. This tot system, whereby the labourer consumed more than a litre of wine daily, had the dual advantages of disposing of surplus stocks (possibly of unsaleable quality) and of ensuring continuity of employment through addiction.

Distinct from the permanent labourer who, if he did not move off the farm, was likely to remain a mere chattel for the rest of his short working life, was the labourer who moved, according to seasons, between the wine farms and the grain farms. At the end of the threshing season, many grain farmers paid their temporary labourers an advance to ensure that they would return in the next season. Thus financed, many saw no need to find immediate work on the wine farms, which were fast approaching the harvest and pressing time, when all hands were required. Desperate though they were, wine farmers steadfastly refused to acknowledge that they were under-paying.

From 1885 the wine industry was struck another blow, as phylloxera, a vine-root disease caused by aphids, laid waste almost all of the Cape's winelands. By the time the problem was solved by grafting onto imported American resistant rootstock, still more labourers had left the land.

Big money now joined the ranks of farm-owners. The ravaged vineyards were sold relatively cheaply, and many were planted with other fruits to take advantage of a new export market opened by the introduction of refrigerated holds. Among the new land barons were parliamentarians John X Merriman, James Sivewright and Cecil Rhodes, who purchased no fewer than 29 farms. These newcomers, at least, recognised that under-payment was a major part of the problem, Merriman stating to a labour commission that 'complaints arise because people say they can't get their work done so cheaply as they used to'. At the same time, a labour agent supported this by saying that 'if wages rose, there would be no difficulty getting labour'.

Another source of complaint was that labourers were accumulating a small amount of capital and actually hiring and working land for their own account – not that the white farmer considered this to be 'work'. A regular complainant, J P Louw, bemoaned the fact that 'they will not work, but live from the small gardens they have under cultivation'. Attempts to compensate for this loss by importing African labour from Transkei and even from as far afield as Mozambique proved unsuccessful because of

THIS CARTOON, *published in the 1890s, foreshadowed the effect of the rinderpest epidemic on the price of meat. In fact, the price of nearly everything went up after transport oxen died in their thousands.*

large-scale desertions. Eventually, wine farmers agreed to pay an extra shilling a day in lieu of the 'wine wage', but in many cases they had waited too long.

And there was one lesson that went unlearnt, especially concerning the experiment with recruited African labour. A Burgersdorp farmer named Vermaak pointed it out as early as 1879. 'Single Kafirs will never stay . . . I advise the government if they get Kafir labour, to bring the families.' It was an acknowledgement of the human status of the labourer and was to fail, for generations, to receive serious recognition.

Lodgers on the land

Having taken possession of the land, by conquest or dubious purchase, the white farmer sometimes allowed Africans to return, but always on conditions favourable to himself. The white farmer was the landlord, the African the tenant, so naturally, there was a rental to be paid. In the Boer republics, it included the condition that the landlord 'retained the right to the Kaffers living there' – in other words, to their labour.

By the 1880s many Boers were themselves land tenants or *bywoners*, although not in such numbers as the Africans. In general, Africans preferred to be tenants of the larger landowners, especially if these were local officebearers since this meant that they would be less likely to be harassed by other officials. The smaller landlord, needing to exploit his land to the full, tended to be a much harsher taskmaster, and endured frequent desertions that, in many cases, led directly to his bankruptcy and to an increase in the land-holding of a larger neighbour.

The large landowners often required tenants to pay a cash or kind rental, in addition to supplying labour. Tenants were assigned a portion of ground to work on their own account, and permitted to graze their own cattle with those of the landlord. In return, 'the native must then give three or four of his children to the farmer to work for him and perhaps one or two of the other men to look after the cattle'. As a rule, tenant families supplied the farmer only with their adolescent sons, so that the stronger and more experienced men were available to work their own section.

Land, labour and uitlanders

The South African Republic (SAR) before the outbreak of the South African War was a land of contrasts: the new wealth of the mining magnates contrasting with the increasing poverty of the rural poor – where the key to survival was the ownership of land with which to attract African tenants who paid for their land with labour. Determined to remain in control of this explosive mixture was an emerging class of rich Boer leaders – their wealth often based on land speculation – whose refusal to allow political rights to *uitlanders* (foreigners) was exploited by some of the mine-owners in a desperate bid to topple the government of Paul Kruger.

EVERY WINTER DURING THE LAST two decades of the 19th century the South African Republic's Native Commissioner for the Lydenburg district, a prosperous landowner named Abel Erasmus, set out with a force of armed men to collect taxes from Africans in the area.

It was an impressive, if somewhat undisciplined, sight: in front rode a handful of local *veldkornets*, followed by a force of African constables led by a Pai chief from the lowveld, Tobys Malambo. Erasmus himself was surrounded by a small coterie of white staff – local burghers who were quick to seize on the opportunity of lining their own pockets while helping the state to swell its own.

And by all accounts they did very nicely: David Wilson, a Barberton mining official who watched Erasmus in action, later wrote that the Commissioner 'would arrive unexpectedly in a Kaffir kraal, and demand payment of hut tax, 10 shillings for each hut'. The homestead head would be extremely wary about letting them see where he kept his money . . . 'to which he goes only at night', according to Wilson. 'So when suddenly called upon to produce his half sovereign he would ask time to obtain it.'

This, of course, was playing into the hands of the tax collectors; there was no profit in 10 shillings – all of which would have to be sent to Pretoria, and pleas by the unfortunate victims to be given an hour's grace to find the money were refused. Instead, the escort was 'ordered to seize an ox or a cow . . . . The ox, worth £5 on average, would be driven to the Commissioner's farm, with perhaps 50 others similarly escorted, and 10 shillings per head may have been remitted to Pretoria.'

Taxation had been forced upon the African people of the Transvaal from the earliest days of Boer settlement – but seldom successfully. Only in 1870 did the *volksraad* (parliament) decide that all Africans must pay a hut tax – the structure of which gives a revealing insight into the way in which land and labour were inexorably linked in the young republic: 2s 6d for those living on a white-owned farm and providing labour for the Boer household; 5 shillings for those not living on the farm but providing labour; and 10 shillings for those not providing labour at all. This was amended in 1876 to distinguish between those Africans living on land held by absentee white landlords (10 shillings) and those living on land not held by white landlords (5 shillings, plus one shilling for every male over 20). Anyone working for a white farmer, however, was exempt from tax.

But the authorities found a vast difference between the promulgation of a law and its actual implementation. While Africans had access to land many were able to evade the wage-labour net. Even when faced with higher tax bills as a penalty for being independent, large numbers of Transvaal Africans simply grew more crops to cover their additional expenses. As a result the mines were forced to import thousands of workers from places such as Transkei.

Work for rent

As the descendants of the Voortrekkers roamed further out across the highveld in the search of land, so Africans found themselves increasingly living on land that was not theirs. Although some were forced to pay rent by way of labour for the white farmer, others preferred to pay cash to an increasing number of absentee landlords.

The farmer, in turn, was usually dependent on travelling traders both for selling his produce and for supplying him with items needed to run his farm. Often they had no choice but to accept low prices for their commodities – while having to pay high prices for purchases, leaving a mounting debt that forced many to sell their lands.

The key to survival in this vicious circle was to control enough land – either rented or owned – with a 'live-in' African population whose rent was paid in part-time labour which in turn could be used to create enough surplus produce to keep the debt collector from the door. By the last two decades of the 19th century, this new landlord/boss-tenant/worker relationship had largely replaced the earlier methods favoured by the Voortrekkers of obtaining labour by raiding African homesteads and taking children as 'apprentices'.

Not all farmers survived; and land speculation became rife during the 1880s and 1890s. For example, Commissioner Abel Erasmus used his position to build up a considerable fortune by the time of his death in 1912, in spite of the privations of the South African War. And there were many others who did likewise. Ironically, land speculation allowed many Africans to buy back land lost by their forefathers to the first Boer settlers – although, because Transvaal law forbade Africans to own property, they had to buy through an intermediary, usually a missionary.

Inevitably, competition for African tenants – and therefore labour – was fierce; and white farmers were careful to stipulate when renting or buying farms that the Africans already in residence stay put. However, for the African

Divided loyalties among the Randlords

The Randlords, many of them Jewish and most of them veterans of Kimberley, were a mixed bunch, some of them siding with the *uitlanders* and others openly supporting Kruger.

There was the socially charming Edward Lippert, who had not made a success of Kimberley, despite being a cousin of Alfred Beit. Flinty in business, Lippert purchased from the *volksraad* the sole concession to manufacture dynamite, and then openly violated the terms of the deal by importing the commodity, and selling it to his fellow Randlords, including cousin Alfred, at a profit of 200 percent.

Samuel Marks had interests not only in gold, but also in coal, forestry, land, manufacturing and the production of outstandingly low-quality liquor for the African trade. The son of an impoverished and itinerant tailor from Lithuania, Marks' first foray into business was hawking cheap goods around the western Cape. The diamond fields of Kimberley beckoned, and he arrived with his distant cousin, Isaac Lewis, and a wagonload of diggers' requisites. They made their first fortune there, supplying the diamond diggings with coal from farms they owned on the Vaal River. Marks did not acquire a great stake in Witwatersrand gold mining, a blunder he later regretted, but he acquired other businesses: a distillery, glassworks, tannery, food-processing plants, a brewery and brickworks, and shares in a number of other concessions. He could speak the version of Dutch/Afrikaans spoken in the Transvaal and gained the ear and affection of Kruger.

Though his formal involvement in politics remained limited, he attempted to mediate between Kruger and Rhodes, and forecast to Chamberlain that any war with the republics would be longer and far costlier than could be imagined.

Utterly uninterested in politics or in obtaining a vote in the SAR was Barnett Isaacs, whose only academic education was received at the Spitalfields Jews' Free School in London, until he was 14 years old. He then became a prize fighter and conjurer, giving himself the stage name of Signor Barnato.

Aggressive and uncouth, but at the same time public-spirited and generous, Barney Barnato soon made his mark in southern Africa, and was Rhodes' main rival for control of the diamond fields. Although deciding rather late to buy into the Witwatersrand, he nevertheless acquired large holdings, as well as interests in many other mines. He founded the Johannesburg Consolidated Investment Company, and was a major shareholder in the company controlling the stock exchange.

Although his nephew, Solly Joel, was involved with the Reform Committee, Barnato stayed aloof, preferring his British citizenship to a SAR franchise. Kruger appreciated his forthright approach – and Barnato took advantage of this to help the Cape railway bosses get permission to extend their operations to the Witwatersrand. Barnato publicly denounced the Jameson raid and, after the dust had begun to settle, presented Kruger with the fine pair of marble lions still to be seen at Kruger's dwelling in Pretoria. Sensitive beneath the sometimes coarse exterior, Barnato committed suicide the year after the raid.

JOSEPH ROBINSON *was a difficult and argumentative man.*

Not suffering unduly from sensitivity was the quarrelsome Joseph (JB) Robinson, a Cradock farm-boy who served in a store at Dordrecht before reaching the diamond fields. By then he had also fought in a Free State commando against the Basotho, and appeared to regard the world at large as his enemy. Solitary and argumentative, he was bailed out from near bankruptcy in Kimberley by Alfred Beit, who generously formed a company with him to develop a portion of the Witwatersrand. Robinson, however, disliked almost everyone, especially those who were associated with De Beers, and soon added his own partner to the list. After an argument with Beit, he successfully pressed for a separation of their holdings. But having done that he unwisely decided to sell his share to the Wernher-Beit company for a giveaway price of a quarter of a million pounds.

He had an advantage over the *uitlanders* in that he had been born in a *platteland* (country) town and worked in another, and knew the Boer temperament and language well – something that Kruger appreciated. Robinson allied himself unreservedly with Kruger and founded a newspaper published from Cape Town that, even during the South African War, championed the Boer cause. But despite these 'indiscretions' he was awarded a knighthood after the war.

SAMUEL MARKS *arrived with a distant cousin and a wagon at the Kimberley diamond diggings.*

there was often a more attractive alternative – to rent land from one of the larger, absentee landowners; in which case, although he would have to pay rent, he would not have to work for the white farmer. In many cases this preference was shared by the large landowner – who could make more money from a larger number of African families on his land than a smaller number of large Boer households. An added advantage was that the Africans improved the land more quickly than the Boers – which meant it could eventually be sold at greater profit.

Many of the larger landowners were missionary societies – controlling land they had either purchased themselves or as intermediaries for Africans. However, Africans living on mission land had to pay not just a hut tax – but also a 'tythe' to the mission for the construction of church buildings, schools and so on, the money for these often being earned from working for the mines on short contracts.

Inevitably, many white farmers found that their tenant/workers were drifting away to become tenants on land owned by absentee landlords or missionaries – despite the higher hut tax they had to pay. In a bid to stop this drift, the *volksraad* in 1895 re-enacted an anti-squatter law which forbade any landowner to have more than five African households a farm, unless he could show that they were necessary for his own labour requirements. He could claim labour for up to five farms, unless he had white tenant farmers – *bywoners* – in which case each tenant could claim five families.

Although the law was passed to ensure that the smaller farmer also received a piece of the labour cake, it did not work, mainly because the district officials who administered it were large landowners with a lot to lose if they lost their African tenants. A further problem was the fear that many Africans – forced to become wage-labourers – would simply decamp to those areas still conceded by the state as being African owned. In an attempt to nip this pos-

sibility in the bud, the *volksraad* instructed the executive to deny tenant/worker Africans access to these areas – an impossible order to carry out.

Gold and foreigners

The divisions created in Boer society by the economic gulf that had opened between small farmer and large landowner were also felt in the political arena; even the Dutch churches, after an attempt at unification, split into three factions, President Paul Kruger himself adhering to the Gereformeerde Kerk, which was the most conservative and whose members were referred to as 'Doppers'.

The rule of Kruger – himself a large landowner – was almost ended in the 1893 presidential election by his longstanding rival, the equally well-off Commandant-General Piet Joubert. Kruger's salary, duly approved by the *volksraad* which he dominated with alternating pleas and threats, was the large sum of £8 000 a year, most of which he invested in land.

However, if there was one thing on which the Boers did unite – it was their fear and distrust of the *uitlanders*, who had arrived in the SAR in increasing numbers since the discovery of gold, first in the eastern part of the country and then only a few miles south of Pretoria itself – on the Witwatersrand. After only a short time, massive investment, most of it from Europe, was concentrated in the hands of a few mining companies whose proprietors – the so-called Randlords – were to play an increasing role in the economic and political future of the republic, despite the fact that they were denied citizenship and voting rights in their adopted land.

There was another foreign invasion, but this time by invitation, and not so great, by Hollanders who were appointed to senior positions in the administration, the *volksraad* remaining the preserve of Transvaal Boers of whom most were uneducated and suspicious of ways not their own. One of the first was Dr Willem Leyds, appointed in 1884 to the post of State Attorney and later, as State Secretary, Kruger's principal adviser. Although he served the state well, he chose not to mix socially with its citizens who, aware of his contempt, returned the dislike not only for him, but for most of the other Hollanders in senior positions.

Apart from the Hollanders, the civil service was staffed largely by relatives of *volksraad* members and of other officials. Appointments were also made in return for favours received, which further contributed to a grossly inefficient administration. No specific qualification was required, and a proposal that a civil service examination be introduced was firmly rejected by *volksraad* members who might otherwise have found themselves lumbered with a host of unemployable cousins and in-laws. The majority of officials were not merely incompetent, they were also corrupt, and bribery was a standard way of transacting business with them.

One example involved the cyanide extraction process that had to be used on ores from the deeper levels. The *volksraad*, ever eager to claim what revenue it could, favoured selling a monopoly on the use of the process, something to which the Chamber of Mines strongly object-

DUTCH-BORN *Willem Leyds became State Secretary in Kruger's government, earning the dislike of many of the locally born Boers.*

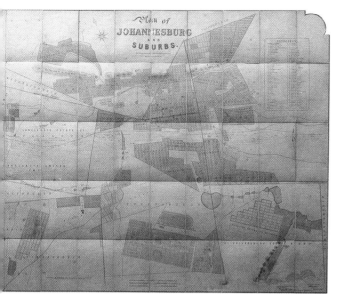

THIS 1902 PLAN *of Johannesburg clearly shows many of the suburbs familiar to us today – including Turffontein, Braamfontein, Fordsburg and Yeoville.*

ed. To persuade the *volksraad* otherwise, wrote Lionel Phillips of the firm of Wernher & Beit and president of the chamber, would involve 'spending lots of money in bribes and we shall probably have to spend more next year than this . . . .' SAR officials took money not only from the *uitlanders*, but also from the state itself. Thus, in 1898 it was revealed that, since 1883, the sum of £2,4-million which had been 'advanced' to various officials was unaccounted for. It was later recalled that half a million pounds had been deposited with a bank in the Netherlands, but the remainder, £1,9-million, had simply vanished.

Votes for *uitlanders*

But if the administration was somewhat casually run, there was at least one matter about which there was clarity, and that was the matter of votes for *uitlanders*. It was a simple question of numbers, as shown by the only proper census ever conducted in the SAR. The Johannesburg Sanitary Board found that, in 1896, within three miles (4,8 kilometres) of the centre of town, there lived 50 907 whites, of whom only 6 205 were citizens of the SAR. The rest were *uitlanders*. Within the same radius there were also 42 533 Africans, 4 807 Asiatics and much smaller numbers of 'Cape Malays', and 'Cape coloureds'. The proportion of *uitlanders* to Afrikaners was frequently exaggerated by both sides. Cecil Rhodes, now Prime Minister of the Cape Colony, Milner and Colonial Secretary Joseph Chamberlain inflated the numbers of *uitlanders* to illustrate the unreasonableness of not giving them a say in government, while Kruger happily used the same figures to point out that 'if we give them the franchise tomorrow, we may as well give up the republic'.

Instead of giving up his republic, however, Kruger in 1890 established a second *volksraad* with limited powers to deal with certain prescribed matters such as mining affairs. It could only make recommendations to the first *volksraad* which, if it approved, might pass them into law.

Uitlanders could vote for a member in the second *volksraad* after two years' residence in the Transvaal and on payment of a registration fee of £5; and stand for election after four years' residence. However, as the only constituencies likely to return an *uitlander* to the second *volksraad* were Barberton and Johannesburg, with one representative each out of a house of about 26, the gesture was largely cosmetic. For an *uitlander* to qualify to vote for the 'real' *volksraad*, a residence of 14 years was required, in addition to the stipulation that the full franchise – which included voting for the State President and Commandant-General, and actually standing as a candidate – would not be granted to any 'new burgher' under the age of 40 years. At one stage Kruger also tinkered with a vague proposal to grant the franchise to 'trustworthy' *uitlanders*, but nothing came of this.

Apart from the lack of the franchise, *uitlanders* (and Africans) complained that Dutch, the language of the minority, was the only official language of the state, the railways, and the sole medium of instruction in schools.

Controlling the railways

The railways were another source of grievance. In the pre-gold era, the colonial ports had mulcted the republics for duty on items from abroad, and had effectively kept them financially unsound. Now that he had gold, Kruger could look about for other seaports, and by the end of 1887 a rail route had been surveyed from Pretoria as far as the border of Mozambique. A concession or monopoly was granted to a Dutch consortium, which called itself the *Nederlandsche Zuid-Afrikaansche Spoorweg-Maatschappij* (NZASM) to construct and operate the republic's railways, with priority going to the Pretoria-Delagoa Bay line in order to be independent of the routes through the British colonies. Railways from both the Cape and Natal reached the SAR border in 1891-2, the Cape line being connected almost at once with the Witwatersrand by a section operated by the NZASM, which charged exorbitant rates for carriage over this section. Since much of the freight consisted of mining machinery, this manipulation of freight rates added to the frustrations of the Randlords, especially when, in a desperate bid to win back trade after the opening of the Delagoa Bay line in 1894, the Cape Railway slashed its tariffs to the bone. The NZASM countered by raising its freight charges between the border and the Witwatersrand still higher.

In a bid to outflank the NZASM, the Cape unloaded its trucks just before the border and transferred the goods to ox-wagons in order to complete the journey. Since there were only a few points at which wagons could cross the Vaal River, Kruger in October 1895 promptly closed the drifts to all vehicles carrying imported goods, only reopening them after receiving threats from Britain and protests from the Cape.

'Insist and insist'

Uitlander disenchantment with the Kruger Government began early. Rallies were held, and associations, all more or less toothless, were formed from 1887 with a view to improving the lot of the *uitlanders*, most of whom managed

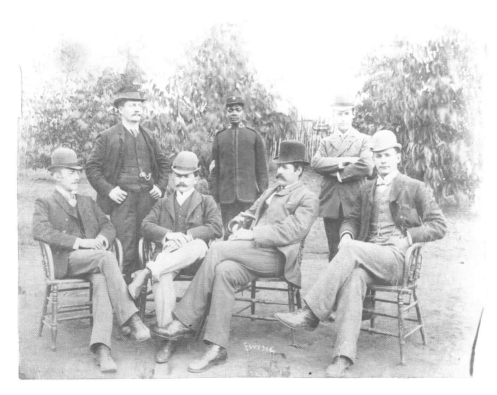

THE SELF-MADE *directors of the Consolidated Goldfields Company posed for this photograph in 1895. They are (seated from left to right) Alfred Beit, Lionel Phillips, Frances (Frank) Rhodes and Abe Bailey. Standing behind them (from left to right) are John Hays Hammond, an unidentified African and George Herbert Farrar.*

to live like kings compared to the Africans on the mines. Little was achieved until Charles Leonard, an ardently imperialistic attorney, moved his practice from Cape Town, where he had played a large part in forming the Empire League, to Johannesburg, where he joined in establishing the Transvaal National Union, in 1892, to campaign on behalf of *uitlanders*, and 'to insist, and insist, and insist, by every means that civilised people can adopt, to have rights granted to them'. Accordingly, a petition was presented to Kruger, who replied that, to protect 'the rights of the old burghers in the country . . . admission of the newcomers to full burger rights must be regulated with great care'.

A YOUNG ATTORNEY, *Charles Leonard, was one of the founders of the pro-uitlander Transvaal National Union in 1902.*

He also hinted that the residence qualification might be reduced from 14 years to 10.

Since this was considerably less than they had demanded, it failed to satisfy the National Union or its controlling body, the Reform Committee. To add insult to injury, British *uitlanders* were called up for commando duty against the Tswana chief, Malaboch. Those who refused were arrested and sent to the front – which prompted an appeal for intervention to Sir Henry Loch, Cape Governor and High Commissioner for South Africa, who travelled to Pretoria, where he succeeded in having the names of British citizens removed from the list of military reservists.

While in the SAR, Loch sounded out the possibilities of some kind of armed uprising against the Kruger Government, asking the Chamber of Mines president, Lionel Phillips, some 'very pointed questions, such as what arms were already in Johannesburg, whether the population could hold the place for six days until help could arrive, etc'. Loch later pursued these thoughts in England with the Colonial Secretary, Lord Ripon, whom he horrified by asking for authorisation to mobilise the Bechuanaland Protectorate Police to intervene should a rising in Johannesburg be in need of propping up, and asking that the British Army presence in South Africa be increased by 5 000 men. Both requests were refused. However, Kruger was invited to London to attend a conference to discuss the enfranchisement of British subjects in the SAR – but he declined.

Enter Joseph Chamberlain

With tensions rising on both sides, the Colonial Office now fell under the monocled eye of Joseph Chamberlain, who was soon exchanging friendly letters with Rhodes, whom he had previously disliked, and with the new Cape Governor and High Commissioner, Sir Hercules Robinson.

JOSEPH CHAMBERLAIN, *Britain's Colonial Secretary, played an uncertain and murky role in the Jameson Raid.*

LEADING THE RAID *into the South African Republic was Leander Starr Jameson, Administrator of Mashonaland.*

Rhodes was asking for a slice of territory from the eastern side of the Bechuanaland Protectorate to be transferred to his Chartered Company, and Sir Hercules was advising on how he thought it best to cope with an uprising in Johannesburg. That there would, in fact, be an uprising, was still far from certain, and only a few men were fully 'in the know'. Among them was Alfred Beit, who visited the SAR in 1895, staying with Rhodes en route. Lionel Phillips wrote that Beit 'thoroughly shared my opinion that a revolution was coming . . . and thought we should take a hand to ensure success if possible'.

The purpose of the revolt was not necessarily to raise the flag of England over Pretoria, but rather to re-establish the republic along more liberal lines better suited to big business. Coded telegrams flashed to and fro, and Rhodes diverted vast sums of money to a new account named New Concessions, on which his brother, Colonel Frank Rhodes, drew sums to pay for the purchase of rifles, ammunition and other supplies. A secret base camp was established at Pitsani in the Bechuanaland Protectorate, where Rhodes had obtained his grant of land, supposedly for railway extensions. Smuggled rifles and ammunition – concealed in oil drums, were distributed about the mines, and the Administrator of Mashonaland, Dr Leander Starr Jameson, moved to Pitsani. The British Press was fed lurid stories of ill-treatment of *uitlanders* to prepare them for coming

events on which, however, the conspirators were unable to agree. Tension ran high in Johannesburg, and a sudden collapse of the over-manipulated stock market fuelled a panicky exodus of *uitlanders* from the SAR. Equally panicky and undecided, the would-be revolutionaries decided not to revolt – at any rate, not just yet.

All these supposedly secret preparations had not escaped the notice of Kruger's intelligence service, and on 26 December 1895, in a speech at Bronkhorstspruit, he warned: 'I am often asked about a threatened rising, and I say "Wait until the time comes." Take the tortoise; if you want to kill it you must wait until it puts out its head; then you can cut it off.'

Kruger did not have long to wait before cutting off the tortoise's head.

The Jameson Raid

Dr Jameson, by all accounts a competent doctor but a poor military tactician, had met Rhodes during the early days of Kimberley, and been drawn more and more into his service – which was why the last days of December 1895 found him fretting in the dust of Pitsani, along with 400 well-armed men and an invitation in his pocket from the *uitlanders'* Reform Committee, asking him to 'come to the rescue . . . .' The letter painted a picture of a proud but cowed English majority, cruelly oppressed and in immi-

MEMBERS *of the uitlander Reform Committee ended up in Kruger's jail after the raid ended in ignominious defeat for Jameson and his backers.*

A LUKEWARM *effort was made by the uitlander Reform Committee to rally support for the raiders – and these armed volunteers turned out to guard the Pretoria Road.*

nent danger from the Boers – 'thousands of unarmed men, women and children of our race will be at the mercy of well-armed Boers, while property of enormous value will be in great peril'.

Thoughtfully, the Reform Committee had left the letter undated; the theory being that when they were ready to stage their uprising in Johannesburg, Jameson would be advised of the precise hour, and could date the letter to make it look like a frantic last-minute appeal. The threatened rising, however, was a long time in coming, and Jameson and his backers became impatient. Colonial Secretary Chamberlain wrote that the raid 'should either come at once or be postponed for a year or two at least'. Postponement seemed the best policy to the Reform Committee, but Rhodes, encouraged by Chamberlain's remarks, promptly wired them in code: 'Our foreign supporters urge immediate flotation.' Rhodes' brother, Frank, quickly sent another coded telegram, to an anguished Jameson: 'The polo tournament here postponed for one week or it would clash with race week.' To complete the circle, Jameson directed a somewhat ungrammatical telegram to Cecil Rhodes: 'Do you consider races is of supreme importance?' Back came the reply: 'Delay dangerous'.

On 26 December, Jameson received a telegram that stated: 'Absolutely necessary to postpone flotation.' To make matters clearer, it continued, 'You must not move.' Jameson replied, again by telegram, 'Unless I hear to the contrary I shall leave tomorrow evening.' As good as his word, on 29 December, Jameson assembled his men and read them the 'women and children letter', told them they were invading in the name of the Queen (which was a lie), called for three cheers, and rode towards the SAR border. Rhodes,

with a final burst of code, informed the Reform Committee: 'The Veterinary Surgeon has left for Johannesburg with some very good horse-flesh.' He also wired the 'women and children letter' to 'The Times' in London.

The raid was a fiasco. Troopers told to cut the telegraph wires severed the wrong ones, so that loyal SAR postmasters along the route were able to inform their government of Jameson's progress; and in Johannesburg, 64 *uitlanders* declared themselves to be a provisional government – to which Kruger responded by withdrawing his police from the city to avoid unnecessary confrontation.

Confrontation with Jameson and his men, however, was swift, and the raiders were surrounded near Krugersdorp and forced to surrender. Within a few days both the raid-

THE JAMESON *raiders left Pitsani and Mafeking for the ride to Johannesburg – but surrendered at Vlakfontein farmhouse.*

A LARGE CROWD *gathered to give an enthusiastic send-off to volunteer members of 'Bettington's Horse' as they set off to meet Jameson on the road to Johannesburg.*

ers and the Reform Committee ended up in Pretoria Jail. Jameson and four of his leading military advisers were shipped to England for trial, and four members of the Reform Committee were sentenced to death. Others were sentenced to terms of imprisonment and fines of up to £2 000. Shortly afterwards, however, the shrewd Kruger commuted the death sentences, substituting instead a fine of £25 000 each. Two refused to pay up – but were released after a year in honour of Queen Victoria's Diamond Jubilee.

Chamberlain ensured that he escaped the ensuing witch-hunt by getting himself elected to the committee established to determine the extent of his involvement. Known cynically as 'the committee of no enquiry', it found

THE TRIAL *of uitlander Reform Committee members in the Market Hall, Pretoria, following the raid.*

that he was blameless. Rhodes did not even try to brazen out the crisis, but resigned at once as Prime Minister of the Cape and travelled to England. He had enough evidence, by way of letters (and telegrams) to ruin Chamberlain who, on the other hand, had sufficient evidence to destroy Rhodes' Charter Company. In the end, both thought it wiser to remain silent, although Rhodes did modestly say: 'I do not like to say anything.'

It was a sentiment shared by most of the key mining figures involved in the conspiracy – especially with Kruger's threat to cut off the tortoise's head still very much in their thoughts. This understandable silence, however, has made it difficult for historians to pinpoint the true cause of the raid: a move by certain mining magnates to swing things their way. There were two types of mining men in Johannesburg at the end of the century: those who made their money mainly from short-term market manipulation, and those who wanted to invest in long-term development of deeper and more difficult mines designed to get at the low-grade ore found at increasingly greater depths, particularly Rhodes and the German-born Alfred Beit – owner of Phillips' Rand Mines.

The evidence is overwhelming that Beit supported and Rhodes masterminded the conspiracy to topple Kruger, thereby hoping to remove at a stroke his frequently obstructive policies, such as the controversial dynamite monopoly, which both hindered their plans and scared off badly needed development capital from overseas.

The raid intensified the power-struggle in the SAR between Boer and British, with the Boers, not unreasonably, convinced that Britain was aiming at nothing less than the destruction of their republics. To Alfred Milner, Robinson's successor as High Commissioner, it seemed that policy should be directed towards 'working up a crisis'. In due course, the crisis was to arrive.

The glittering prize

At the end of the 19th century Britain's economic power was being challenged by the rise of the USA and Germany. The empire, however, had given Britain an enormous advantage as the historical centr of world finance and banking, a dominance it could retain only if more gold could be found to replenish the dwindling reserves held by the Bank of England to underpin sterling. The obvious source of supply was in the Transvaal – but only if the Afrikaner republic led by Paul Kruger could be brought into the empire and transformed into the type of capitalist society required to mine the gold from increasingly difficult depths.

IN 1897 THE STATE ENGINEER for California, William Hall, was called upon to give evidence before the Transvaal Industries Commission in Johannesburg on the vexing problem of deep-level mining. The solution to the problem, as he saw it, was not just one of pure engineering – it also needed social engineering to create a society geared to the requirements of the capitalist economy that such massive and complex mining demanded.

Hall was one of a new breed of men who, in the latter part of the 19th century, were to use their skills and experience to transform the economic landscapes of nations from Latin America to South-east Asia. Sweeping aside the traditional values of carefully structured societies, they worshipped instead the gods of efficiency and maximisation of resources. A contemporary observer very accurately described them as the 'new industrial intelligentsia, standing between capital and labour'. They could equally be described as the shock troops of capitalism.

The gold-rich Witwatersrand of the 1890s was full of such men – mainly American mining engineers such as Hall, with experience that ranged from the goldfields of the American West to the new mining opportunities that were opening up in Latin America, Australia and Asia. Hall had been specially brought out from California by the major mines on the Central Rand to advise them on water supply problems. Like his fellow-countrymen, he could not abide 'partisan', 'corrupt' and 'inefficient' government; and in the South African Republic (SAR) led by President Paul Kruger, he found all three. Particularly irksome were controversial dynamite and railway monopolies that forced costs up, the need for bribery and, above all, what they believed to be the 'general inability of the Boers to understand capitalism, industrialisation and progress'.

The problem that had brought Hall to South Africa was perhaps an obvious one: all the easily mined gold had already been shipped to the bank vaults of Britain and Continental Europe. There was plenty more where that came from – but deep and difficult to get at, and often to be extracted from ore of a much lower grade. His proposed solution went far beyond the complexities of engineering – nothing less than the restructuring of government and society in the SAR to create the labour and attract the capital that such a complex operation required.

The root of his argument to the Transvaal Industries Commission was the need to create a large, inexpensive labour force to develop the new, deeper mines – and this,

he said, required increasing immigration, improved farming to reduce food costs, better water and sewerage, and proper transport and police services. More white workers, he said, should marry and have children, something which could be achieved only by lowering produce prices through better farming methods.

Naturally, the mineworkers would need an efficient administration and infrastructure to ensure that all these things worked, particularly in one vexing area: the control of African labour. Despite having to carry or wear Passes or badges, and other devices, African labourers, rather than face the appalling conditions underground and the soul-destroying compound life above, deserted by the thousand, and Kruger's police were incapable of retrieving them. The answer to the problem, according to Hall, was a more effective police force, although 'the administration of kaffir labour and of all mine labour matters . . . will have to be left to mine managements under some government law, which would make all of them come in and stay in it for their own good'.

The estimated labour force of 250 000 Africans and more than 50 000 whites who were needed for the mines would require an administration that Kruger's rickety administration was neither equipped to handle nor showed any inclination for. By comparison with such a headache as this, the issue of high dynamite prices and rail tariffs was, quite frankly, small beer.

Filling the needs of empire

While Hall was dealing with the practical problems of deep-level mining, the situation in London was no less urgent but overlaid by other, more pressing concerns: for one, the rising industrial challenge of Germany and the USA in the face of falling productivity at home, and the dwindling gold reserves at the Bank of England.

There was a way to tackle the first problem; Britain, after all, had the empire, and all the advantages in trade, communications and international money management that this meant. However, London could remain preeminent as the centre of the world's money market only for as long as sterling was underpinned by gold; which is what made the second problem exceptionally worrying.

The importance of a currency underpinned by gold was not lost on the USA and the other emerging industrialised states of Europe: increased world trade had led inevitably to an increased money supply, which meant an ever-

BRITAIN *was concerned that southern Africa might unite under the flag of the Boer republics, rather than under the Union Jack, posing a serious threat to Britain's naval base at Simon's Town (right), which guarded the vital sea route to India.*

increasing demand for gold. The more yellow stuff you had in your bank vault, the better, particularly at a time when the international monetary system was being transferred to a gold exchange standard (see page 333), paper money backed by gold. Among the countries moving to the gold standard was, significantly, India, the jewel in the imperial crown, which was also clamouring for its own gold currency. Gold was also vital as a weapon: in time of war it could be used to secure provisions or armaments.

By the end of the 1890s gold was proving a major headache to the men who governed from London, and the position of the gold reserves – a mere £30-million in 1896 – was the nub of the problem. These men were only too aware that the major source of gold was in the Transvaal – tantalisingly just out of reach in a seemingly archaic, squabbling republic run by a bunch of wealthy landown-

ers who called themselves farmers (Boers) but were not even capable of producing a satisfactory food surplus. To make matters worse, further development of these gold fields – if men like Hall were to be believed – was being blocked by an administration that could not, or would not, come to terms with the requirements of modern industrial capitalism.

More and more the solution seemed clear to members of the British Cabinet: Kruger and his whole obstructionist administration had to go. The only question was: how? The best answer from Britain's point of view was the union of the SAR with the Orange Free State (OFS), the Cape and Natal under the Union Jack. To the men at the Colonial Office, a union seemed possible, but they feared it would not necessarily come about under the Union Jack: the SAR, now the dominant state in the region thanks to gold, was fairly closely tied by treaties to its sister Boer republic of the OFS and, spiritually, these states had a claim on the loyalties of thousands of Afrikaners, nominally British subjects, living in the Cape and Natal. This raised the spectre of a possible confederation under the *vierkleur* flag of the SAR, which would pose a threat to the Royal Navy's base at Simon's Town, required by Britain more than ever now that rival nations such as the USA, Germany and France were asserting themselves militarily and economically beyond their traditional spheres of influence.

Enter Lord Milner

The man chosen to unravel the Transvaal knot was no stranger to problems at the British Treasury; for five years Alfred, Lord Milner had been chairman of the Board of Inland Revenue in Britain following a spell as Private Secretary to Lord Goschen – later to become Chancellor of the Exchequer in Lord Salisbury's Tory Government – and three years as financial adviser to the British administration of Egypt.

He also typified a quality in many Englishmen of his day that can best be described as social imperialism, advocat-

ALFRED MILNER *in stereo – a Victorian view of a late-Victorian administrator, who believed in the continuing virility of British imperialism.*

ing a need for benevolent state responsibility, national efficiency and planning in a growing empire. Hand-in-hand with this belief went another, more dangerous one, which had more to do with the continuing virility and vitality of the British as imperialists – and the need to guard against any dimming of that vitality. He would have agreed with a remark by a contemporary, Lord Asquith, who asked: 'What is the use of empire if it does not breed and maintain in the fullest sense of the word an imperial race?'

Milner was just the man to stoke up the fires of imperial indignation and misinformation in what became a bumbling, but ultimately successful attempt to remove Kruger in order to ensure that as much gold as possible was got out of the Witwatersrand and into the Bank of England.

There was plenty of trouble a-brewing when he took over in 1897 as Governor of the Cape Colony and British High Commissioner with responsibility for the whole of southern Africa. The British people living in the SAR – called *uitlanders* (foreigners) by the Boers – were largely voteless. Here was a cause that could be used to rally support for whatever action became necessary to drag the region into the 20th century; not that there would have been any joy in the corridors of Whitehall if the Kruger Government were to have changed its mind and granted the uitlanders the vote. Such an action, imperialists in the British Government argued, would incline the newly enfranchised away from Britain. At best, uitlander participation in the SAR electoral process would bring about a more enlightened government – but the country would continue to remain beyond formal British influence.

To make matters even more worrying, it became apparent that many of the Randlords – particularly those with shorter-term interests – now seemed content with the limited reforms Kruger introduced after the Jameson Raid (see page 235). Support for British intervention remained strong only among a few mine-owners with longer-term commitments – particularly to deep-level mining, which required major administrative reforms to make such capital- and labour-intensive work possible.

Reforms were one thing, allegiance to the Union Jack another – and it was obvious to Chamberlain and his Tory Prime Minister, the Marquess of Salisbury, that agitation against Kruger must not only press for reform, it must also press for union with the Cape under the aegis of the empire. Such a movement existed in the Transvaal under the name of the South African League, an *uitlander* organisation formed in Johannesburg after the Jameson Raid in 1896 for the ultimate union of the white races in southern Africa.

Groping towards war

With an election looming in the SAR in 1898, Chamberlain and Milner pinned their hopes on the young leader of the progressive element in the *volksraad* (parliament), Schalk Burger. As chairman of the Industrial Commission of the year before, Burger had tabled a report that tended to favour the capitalists and mining magnates. Their hopes were dashed, however, when Kruger was elected by an overwhelming majority, and Milner wrote to Chamberlain that he saw 'no way out of the political troubles of South Africa except reform in the Transvaal or war'.

BRITAIN'S HOPES *that the more progressive-minded Schalk Burger would beat Kruger at the elections were ill-founded.*

At the end of February 1899, the *volksraad* proposed that, in exchange for the ending of 'agitation' against it and repudiation of the South African League, it was prepared to remedy certain grievances, including granting the franchise to all who 'sought it' and an 'equitable' solution to the dynamite concession.

This offer was welcomed by Milner and Chamberlain, who authorised Percy FitzPatrick to negotiate with the *volksraad*. He soon discovered that the franchise proposal was not quite as generous as it had first appeared: enfranchisement would be granted to an *uitlander* only five years after becoming a naturalised burgher. This was rejected, with a counter-demand of immediate enfranchisement following the naturalisation of all who had already lived in the SAR for five years.

With that, negotiations ended and the *uitlanders* appealed to the British Government to intervene, Milner urging Chamberlain to keep the issue prominently before the British public so that, should war become a reality, they would be prepared for it. In a telegram to Chamberlain he thundered: 'The spectacle of thousands of British subjects kept permanently in the position of helots . . . calling vainly to Her Majesty's Government for redress, does steadily undermine the influence and reputation of Great Britain . . . .' For good measure, he added that 'the case for intervention is overwhelming'.

Chamberlain prepared for the republican government a message which, while stiffly worded, fell far short of an ultimatum, pinning his hopes on a proposal by President Johannes Brand of the OFS for a conference between Milner and Kruger at the end of May, with Bloemfontein as a venue. Milner told Chamberlain that, at the conference, he would harp on *uitlander* grievances in an attempt to goad Kruger into terminating proceedings, saying that although they were scarcely a good enough case for going to war, it was at least a popular and well-understood cause.

Squaring up to the biggest empire in the world

The price of Britain's struggle to gain control of the Transvaal gold was to be higher than anyone could have imagined when the first Boer commandos rode down from the SAR into Natal in October 1899. Before it was all over, Britain was to put 448 000 men in the field.

Although the 20th century was about to dawn, British military thinking had advanced little since Napoleon's defeat at the Battle of Waterloo in 1815. Military maps had not been prepared for many areas, and field officers consulted an ordinary school atlas. Not only maps were absent. There was, also, no overall plan of campaign.

The Boers were little better. The technique they favoured as the least wasteful of men and energy was to lay siege to the enemy and wait for him to surrender. This worked against African chiefdoms, but was not appropriate against an empire that could ship limitless reinforcements from all parts of the world. The Boer was not a professional soldier; if things went badly, it was not dishonourable to gallop away and resume the contest under more favourable circumstances. Unlike the parade-ground soldier, the Boer was not wedded to the idea of set formations and manoeuvres, nor did he act only when given a command. On balance, the disadvantages of every Boer being his own general probably outweighed the advantages.

At the start of the war, the British infantry advanced across the open

THE BRITISH, *besieged in Mafeking, made their own howitzer.*

veld in fairly close formations, ideal targets for the Boers who, unsportingly, fired on them from concealed positions. At many engagements, notably those at Colenso and Modder River at which the British sustained high losses, many soldiers failed to see even a single Boer.

Contrary to widespread belief, not every Boer grew up with firearms. At the time of the Jameson Raid it was feared that there were not enough rifles to arm the commandos called up to resist the invasion. After the raid, Commandant-General Piet Joubert was instructed to buy rifles as soon as possible to remedy a situation that showed that some 41 percent of SAR burghers liable for military service possessed no firearms at all, while the

remainder owned old and obsolete weapons. Joubert purchased some 20 000 Martini Henry rifles from the British firm of Westley Richards, but these were single-shot weapons, firing (with a debilitating recoil) a soft, lead bullet with a diameter of 11,4 millimetres.

The British were armed with the Lee Metford and marginally different Lee Enfield rifles, which held a reserve of 10 rounds in a box-shaped magazine. The design, which was to remain basically unchanged for more than 50 years, was far in advance of the Martini Henry. Fortunately for the republics, the Johannesburg agent of the German firm of Fried Krupp Grusonwerk was able to persuade Joubert to test the Mauser magazine rifle. This, together with the proverbial Bible, was what the majority of Boers eventually carried into battle.

The republics, particularly the SAR, also invested in artillery, some of it of fairly dated design, but nevertheless effective. This was especially true of the four Schneider siege guns, nicknamed Long Toms, that threw a 43 kilogram shell over a range of up to 10 kilometres. To counter these, the British were obliged to dismount guns from some of their warships at Cape Town and Durban. Mounted on improvised carriages hauled by oxen, they became known as 'cow guns'. It was Britain's navy which, by blockading southern African ports, ensured that the republics did not receive significant amounts of replacement ammunition.

THE BOERS *relied heavily on their four Schneider siege guns – nicknamed 'Long Toms'.*

PRESIDENT KRUGER *at the head of the* SAR *volksraad in 1895. It was difficult for foreigners either to vote or sit in the volksraad – one of the grievances used by the British to foment public opinion against the Boer state.*

At the conference, Kruger offered the franchise after seven years' residence but, in return, made a number of demands that included the incorporation of Swaziland into the SAR, arbitration over the London Convention – an ongoing squabble concerning British suzerainty over the republic's foreign relations – and compensation for the Jameson Raid. Demanding that the franchise be granted after five years' residence, which Kruger refused, Milner brought the conference to an end. He did not, however, regard the talking as over for good, but wrote to a nervous Chamberlain that 'if the President is sufficiently pushed there is still a chance, though a small one, of his adopting my minimum'. He impressed on the South African League the need to keep 'cool and moderate', and not to exceed its previous demands, as this might alienate public opinion, which was 'steadily settling on our side'.

Adding fuel to an already dangerous fire, Chamberlain warned in a speech at Birmingham on the South African situation that a time might come when 'patience' might be construed as 'weakness', and that other methods would be called for. In the SAR, the speech was seen not as an appeal for reform, since no specific grievances were mentioned, but rather as a justification for going to war.

In an attempt to counter this – and to appease increasing *uitlander* unrest – the *volksraad* proposed a seven years' qualification for the franchise. This was rejected by an emboldened *uitlander* council already preparing itself to demand an enfranchisement qualification of three years' residence, as in the OFS.

It was beginning to look as if the situation that Milner had feared might come true: the *uitlanders* would obtain their rights on their own, rather than through British Government intervention, and he urged Chamberlain for intervention now, asking for 'the practical assertion of British supremacy . . . .'

The British Government responded by asking for a commission of enquiry to examine the latest SAR offer, to be followed by another conference between Kruger and Milner in Cape Town. Further, the British Agent in Pretoria, W Conyngham Greene, was instructed to repropose the

five-year franchise which Kruger had rejected at the Bloemfontein Conference, and to inform the *volksraad* that Britain would under no circumstances waive its right to suzerainty. Further, Greene was to advise Kruger that unless he issued a formal statement of the precise reforms he proposed to implement, apart from the franchise, Britain would be obliged to make its 'own demands for a settlement not only of the *uitlander* question, but also of the future relations between Great Britain and the Transvaal'.

Even at this late stage, Milner believed that war was not inevitable. A strong show of force was needed, he cabled Chamberlain, so that 'with an army actually on their borders, they will submit to anything and everything . . . .' But having whipped up the *uitlander* storm, Milner was now reaping the whirlwind: they rejected the five-year

THE BRITISH *Agent in Pretoria, W Conyngham Greene, asked Kruger for a precise statement of reforms he proposed to implement in the Transvaal.*

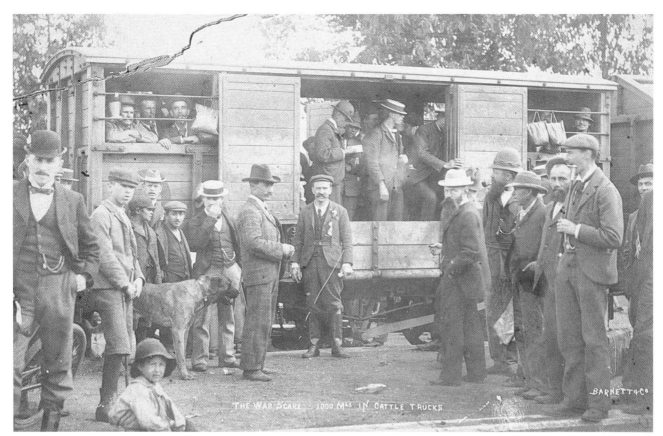

AS BRITISH TROOPS *concentrated on the borders of the two Boer republics, panic gripped the uitlander community in Johannesburg. There was a rush for seats on trains leaving the* Transvaal – *and many foreigners had to settle for all that was available – cattle trucks. African mineworkers also joined the rush to leave the republics.*

franchise offer as too late, adding that the Boer attitude demonstrated 'how futile it is to expect the government and the *volksraad* to have any friendly regard for our just claims'. So far as they were concerned, Britain need not 'waste time' in discussing the franchise any further.

The ultimatum

The time had come for Chamberlain to draw up some sort of ultimatum, which he did with regret, not out of consideration for the tiny republic he planned to teach a lesson it would never forget, but because its publication would make Britain seem to be the aggressor. And while he dithered, wondering whether it should be delayed until more troops were actually in position, the SAR salved his public conscience by presenting its own ultimatum: the decision to move troops to the borders of the republic had indeed goaded Kruger into action – not to grant concessions, however, but to demand that they be withdrawn. On 11 October 1899, the SAR and OFS were at war with the British Empire.

The red herring of *uitlander* grievances had worked only too well for Milner and Chamberlain – so well in fact that it had made a peaceful transition of power to Britain impossible. The irony of the situation was not lost on the international 'Bankers' Magazine' for November, which noted the 'exceptional circumstance' of 'the leading monetary power in the world' being at war with 'a country producing the greater proportion of the world's supply of gold'

A WAVE *of patriotism swept across the two Boer republics as thousands of commandos began arming themselves for the coming war against the British.*

A people's army challenges the empire

The talking was over – and in the South African Republic (SAR) and Britain the politicians called in their generals to try to achieve by force of arms the objectives they had failed to reach after months of wrangling. British Colonial Secretary Joseph Chamberlain and his South African High Commissioner, Alfred Milner, had finally pushed Paul Kruger too far in their bid to hoist the Union Jack over the Witwatersrand.
A final ultimatum from the SAR leader calling on British troops to withdraw from his frontiers expired at 5 pm on 11 October – and the war was on.

ON THE MORNING of 12 October 1899, Jacob van Deventer, a gunner of the SAR's State Artillery, sent the first shot of the South African War screaming towards a British armoured troop train near the rail siding of Kraaipan, between Mafeking and Kimberley.

The attack that followed was an unqualified success for the Boers: the armoured train, although bulletproof, was not shellproof and, with the tracks torn up to north and south, the British troops inside were forced to surrender to General Koos de la Rey. As De la Rey's men began a tentative advance into the northern Cape towards Kimberley, Commandant-General Piet Joubert launched his 16 500-man force against the British in Natal.

It was less than 24 hours since the expiry of an ultimatum by Kruger threatening war unless British forces were removed from the borders of the SAR. Martial law was proclaimed in the republic, and in the Orange Free State (OFS) President Marthinus Steyn honoured a mutual defence treaty between the two countries by mobilising his commandos.

Panic hit the Witwatersrand as the *uitlanders* (foreigners), whose agitation for votes in the SAR had been used by Milner as an excuse for proposing annexation, scrambled for the last available trains leaving for the Cape and Natal. The mines were closed and African workers ordered out of the country.

By the time the war started most of the commandos had been called up – already moving towards the four battle fronts that were to open on their borders: northern Natal; the southern front from the Basutoland border along the Orange River; the western front extending from the Vaal River to Derdepoort centring on Mafeking; and the western border of the OFS pivoting on Kimberley. Young Deneys Reitz, son of the SAR State Secretary, was close to the Natal border at dawn on 12 October, and recorded: 'As far as the eye could see the plain was alive with horsemen, guns, and cattle, all steadily going forward to the frontier.'

The commando system
Apart from a few well-trained members of the OFS and SAR artillery, and scattered units of the SAR police, it was a people's army wearing civilian clothes and based on the traditional commando system: the able-bodied men of each district called up under an elected Commandant assisted by field-cornets, one from each ward of the district. All told, the SAR was able to muster about 30 000 armed men aged between 18 and 60, and the OFS about 20 000, plus about 2 000 volunteers from Boer communities in the Cape and Natal. In October 1899 only about 35 000 men had reported for duty, but by the end of the war the desperate shortage of soldiers led to boys of eight

A GROUP OF *commandos rides through Johannesburg on its way to the front. The republican forces consisted mainly of men who were called up from each district under the command of an elected field-cornet. Nearly all wore civilian clothes – although towards the end of the war, many were forced to use captured British uniforms.*

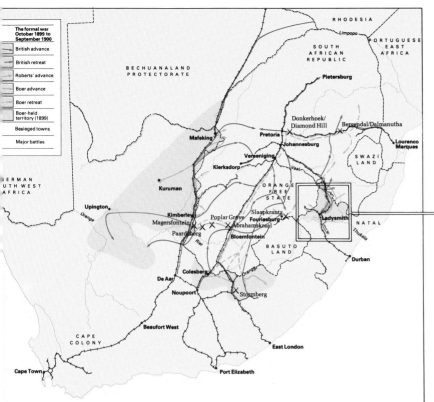

BOER ADVANCES *in the Cape and Natal were quickly halted, but not easily repulsed. In Natal, Redvers Buller toiled to lift the siege of Ladysmith, after reverses at Colenso, Spioenkop and Vaalkrans. In the Cape the thrust to relieve Kimberley and Mafeking began after Boer victories at Stormberg and Magersfontein – and the arrival of British reinforcements under a new Commander-in-Chief, Lord Roberts.*

and men of 70 being called up. This dependence on part-time soldiers extended all the way to the top – and only the SAR had a full-time professional soldier, an elected Commandant-General; while in the OFS the Chief Commandant was elected only in wartime. As a result, the direction of operations in the field was fairly haphazard, traditionally being decided by a *krygsraad* (council of war) of senior officers. Strategy was directed by the two republican governments who were kept informed of developments at the front by telegraph.

Despite their 'amateur' status, the Boers had a distinct advantage over the regular British troops: familiarity with the country and its climate, and superb horsemanship and marksmanship. It is a testament to Boer skill and courage that before the war was over the British would commit a total of 448 715 troops in South Africa – outnumbering the Boers by nearly five to one.

Oddly, perhaps, in a region where whites constituted only one-fifth of the total population, neither side officially sanctioned the use of black troops; this was supposed to be a white man's war in which, according to Jan Smuts, blacks must not 'become the arbiters in disputes between whites and in the long run the predominating political factor or "casting vote" in South Africa. This,' he warned 'would soon cause South Africa to relapse into barbarism.' Despite his fears, both sides did use blacks in a variety of armed and support roles (see box).

It was a war that no one in Britain expected the Boers to win; a point of view that must have been shared by many SAR Boers, at least in private if not in public. How could their tiny republic, with support from the OFS,

hope to overwhelm the inexhaustible army of Britain's far-flung empire? It was with this haunting question in mind that the Boer forces threw nearly everything they had into Natal in a bid to reach Durban before the British had time to ship in reinforcements.

At the outset of the war in October 1899, British troops in South Africa more or less matched the Boers in number – and their first task was to try to stop the Boer advance into Natal and the Cape until more soldiers could arrive from Britain and the colonies for a general advance on Pretoria. Garrisons were stiffened in Natal and the northern Cape, particularly at Kimberley and Mafeking near the Bechuanaland border, while more troops fanned out along the western border with the SAR, for fear that a Boer advance in the Cape could spark a general uprising among sympathetic Afrikaners in the northern and north-eastern districts of the Cape.

In Natal, at least, it was touch and go. Within a few days of the Boer invasion, Joubert's army had occupied Newcastle with hardly any resistance from the two British armies in Natal: the main force of 16 000 under Lieutenant-General Sir George White, who had arrived at Ladysmith just two weeks earlier as Natal Commander-in-Chief; and a smaller, 4 000-man force under Major-General Sir William Penn Symons in Dundee. The first battle of the war, however, was not long in coming, and on 20 October Joubert's left flank, made up of commandos from Utrecht and Vryheid under General Lucas Meyer, clashed with the Dundee garrison at Talana Hill just outside the town. Penn Symons, scorning cover, was fatally wounded by rifle fire and his second-in-command, General James Yule, who had been in South Africa for

245

Black people under arms

The South African War was fought by whites in a region where four-fifths of the population were black. Although for the most part Africans were spectators of the conflict fought over land which had once belonged to them, they were often used in a variety of roles by both sides.

Despite an informal agreement between Boers and Britons to keep armed Africans out of the conflict, many were pressed into service in support roles, and some were even allowed to carry arms.

The Kgatla who lived in the western region of the SAR, for example, took up arms against the Boer forces as early as November 1899 – egged on by the British. The British also supplied arms and ammunition to the Ngwato of the chief Kgama, to be used in protecting the frontier of the Bechuanaland Protectorate and, with it, the Mafeking-Bulawayo railway line. In the south, some 4000 Mfengu and Thembu were organised into armed levies to stave off any Boer attempt at invasion, and to suppress a possible Afrikaner – or, indeed, African – rising. In the Herschel district of the north-eastern Cape, African special constables were hastily enlisted and instructed to patrol the border with the OFS.

The Zululand Native Police, already in existence at the outbreak of the war, were armed with rifles, and a number of them were mounted. Also armed were the Edendale Horse. They, like other Africans who served as scouts or fighting men, were denied the campaign medals to which they were entitled: Sir George Leuchars, Natal Minister of Native Affairs after the war, succeeded in blocking the awards on the grounds that he feared 'these men would parade their medals before the Boers and irritate them'.

Both sides denied that armed Africans served with them, each accusing the other of doing so. Thus, General Jan Kemp complained of the war being fought 'contrary to civilised warfare on account of it being carried on in a great measure with Kaffirs'. Earlier, in Natal, word went round the British lines that 'there are armed natives fighting with the Boers' – probably because of the Boer practice of going to war accompanied by a coloured or African *agterryer* (bat-man) who tended the horses, collected firewood, cooked and generally saw to the chores that needed doing about the camp. In the field, the *agterryer* carried spare ammunition belts and, if his employer had one, an extra rifle. At least 10000 coloured or African men went along with the commandos, not only as *agterryers*, but also as drivers and herders. It is known that the Boers armed Africans at the three major sieges of the war, especially for outpost duty at night.

Although the republics' law held that all males between the ages of 16 and 60 years were eligible for war service, in general only whites were affected, although provision was made for *kleurlingen* (coloureds) to be called up. In most cases this merely meant going along with the employer, but refusal to serve could be punished by a fine of £5, imprisonment or 25 lashes. As a general rule, labour conscripted by the Boer forces received no pay.

On the British side, African poverty was the major spur to enlistment, a fact soon recognised by recruiting agents, who concentrated their activities in areas that had suffered poor crop yields. Recruitment was usually on the basis of a three-month contract, with monthly wages averaging between 40 and 50 shillings. Rations were usually provided and, in some cases, clothing and blankets. Apart from scouting and military duties, Africans were used for bringing in the cattle of displaced Boers, and received a percentage of what they collected. About 100000 blacks (African and coloured men) were employed by the army and, although Kitchener gave the official number that actually received arms as 10053, the real figure must have been much higher because of the issue of weapons to subordinates under pressing local circumstances.

The arming of Africans was cited by the Boer peace delegates as one of their major reasons for discontinuing the war, as 'the Kaffir tribes, within and without the frontiers of the territory of the two republics, are mostly armed and are taking part in the war against us, and through the committing of murders and all sorts of cruelties have caused an unbearable condition of affairs in many districts of both republics'.

ARMED AFRICANS *were used fairly extensively by the British – as this photograph of a British regular with a group of bandolier-slung men shows.*

GENERAL PIET JOUBERT *and his staff posed for this photograph at Newcastle after Boer forces under his command had taken the town from the British in October 1899. Further victories followed as his men captured Dundee and then went on to besiege Ladysmith – which proved a much tougher nut altogether.*

less than a month, withdrew into Dundee after losing about 100 of his cavalrymen as prisoners.

Boer elation, however, turned sour the next day when a commando aided by Dutch and German volunteers was routed by British forces at Elandslaagte Station near Ladysmith and 336 men out of a force of 800 were killed, wounded or captured.

Dundee, however, was now almost surrounded by Boer forces and, with rail communication to headquarters at Ladysmith disrupted, Yule was ordered by White to withdraw. Accordingly, during the rainy night of 23 October, Yule and his force straggled quietly out of Dundee, leaving behind mounds of supplies and their dying Commander. It took four days and nights to cover the soaking 100 kilometres to Ladysmith, unhindered by the Boers, who had been ordered not to interfere.

With Dundee taken, Joubert next turned his attention to Ladysmith, where a desperate British army made an ill-conceived attempt to break the advancing Boers on 30 October at Modderspruit, losing 1 764 men, 1 284 of whom surrendered. As the survivors fled back towards Ladysmith, Joubert refused to pursue them, allegedly citing a homely maxim to the effect that 'when God holds out a little finger, do not take the whole hand'. If ever the Boers had a chance of forcing an honourable peace, this was it: with four-fifths of the Natal army locked up in Ladysmith, the road to Durban lay virtually open. But apart from attacks on Weenen, Estcourt and Mooi River, a cautious Joubert stayed put.

War of sieges

The war quickly developed into a state of siege and defend. First was Mafeking, a town of no military importance whatever, but one of the starting points of the Jameson Raid. Further south, and just across the border fence from the OFS, another Boer army invested Kimberley, which was defended by about 4 000 men, including a scratch Town Guard. One of the attractions of

taking Kimberley was that Cecil Rhodes, whom the Boers regarded as arch-imperialist and arch-enemy, was in residence. Other towns in the northern Cape were scarcely garrisoned at all, beyond the presence of a few police troopers. So towns such as Aliwal North, Colesberg and Dordrecht were occupied by commandos and annexed to the OFS, generally to the approval of the majority of white inhabitants. Many Cape Afrikaners tagged along with the commandos, but nothing like the hoped-for mass rising occurred.

For the battered British, help was already on the water; and the new Commander-in-Chief for South Africa and his headquarters staff stepped ashore from the *Dunottar Castle* at Cape Town on 31 October with an army corps at his back. General Sir Redvers Buller, who was soon to earn the nickname of Sir 'Reverse' Buller, planned to

A FATHER AND SON *pose with their rifles and womenfolk before leaving for the front in 1899. As war losses mounted, boys of eight and men of 70 were called up.*

A Victorian hero

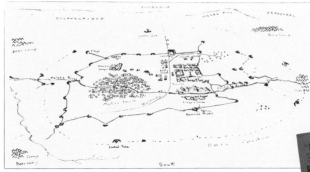

On a sweltering Christmas Day in 1899 the leading white citizens of Mafeking, a dusty town in the far northern Cape, sat down to a sumptuous dinner at Reisle's Hotel with the town's Commander, Colonel Robert Baden-Powell. Starting with anchovy croutons and soup, they went on to oyster patties, calves' tongue, poultry, nine varieties of joint for the main course, Christmas pudding and mince pies, Sandringham jellies and Victoria sandwich.

On the same day, magistrate Charles Bell, whose powers had been taken over by Baden-Powell with the declaration of martial law, wrote: 'I am considerably worried during all hours of the day by hungry Natives, who lean against the garden wall and stare at me, exclaiming at intervals – ''Baaije hongore Baas . . . .'' These people will soon be a source of anxiety to us . . . .'

Meanwhile, the Boers outside the town continued a siege that Victorian Britain lauded as the finest example of British courage at its best. Baden-Powell, whose flippant, jolly messages to the outside world were taken to be masterpieces of understatement and fine examples of British pluck, was loving every minute of it; and in later years progressively exaggerated the number of Boers involved, from 5 000 in 1899, to 12 000 in 1937.

Baden-Powell had been selected to raise two irregular regiments for the protection of the Rhodesian and British Bechuanaland borders, and the railway lines, in what was rightly anticipated would be an unimportant sector of the war. He succeeded in scraping together enough men, and divided his force, with one half – the Rhodesia Regiment, based in Bulawayo, and the other, known as the Protectorate Regiment, first based in Ramathlabama within the Bechuanaland Protectorate and then at Mafeking, a small town of some 2 000 whites, reduced to about 1 200 in the weeks before the war. The town took its name from the nearby, and much larger, African town of Mafikeng – the place of stones – and was generally referred to as the 'stad', where the population was swollen by refugees to about 6 000.

AFRICANS *at Mafeking wait their turn for a share in the soup kitchen.*

Throughout the siege, there was a marked distinction, in all matters, between white and African. The healthy rations, which were relatively plentiful throughout, were for whites only, and were denied to Africans, even those who could afford to buy them. When it was suggested to Baden-Powell that Africans be allowed to share these rations, he recommended that 'the toe of the boot' be applied to such 'grousers'. Africans enrolled for service fared much better, although also denied access to 'white' rations.

As the siege dragged on, Africans became more active than the whites in pugnacious defence of the town and procurement of supplies. Sol Plaatje, a Rolong who, although he had reached only the fourth standard at school, passed the entrance examination for the Cape civil service after just seven months' study, recorded some of their activities in his diary. During and for some time after the war, Plaatje served as court interpreter and magistrate's clerk at Mafeking. He gave accounts of raids conducted by Rolong – known to the defenders as the Black Watch (after a Scots regiment) – on the Boer lines, in which cattle were lifted and driven back to

BADEN-POWELL *himself drew this sketch of the siege of Mafeking (above), showing the railway line dividing the 'white' town from the 'native town'.* THE 'NATAL MERCURY' *(right) records the end of the sieges.*

Mafeking, to supply meat for the tables of the whites.

In an attempt to alleviate African suffering – and raise money – soup kitchens were set up, with a charge of threepence for about two cups. Those who could not pay were theoretically free to seek food at the town of Kanye – if they could cover the 100 kilometres in their debilitated state, and if they could evade Boer patrols which might shoot them as spies, or drive them back.

The pitiable condition of the Africans was confirmed by journalist Emerson Neilly, who 'saw them fall down on the veldt and lie where they had fallen, too weak to go on their way . . .'.

advance along the rail route to Pretoria via Bloemfontein, but on learning of the dire situation in Natal and the northern Cape, he split his force, taking charge himself of operations in Natal, where he had served in the Anglo-Zulu War of 1879, and sending General Lord Methuen to relieve Kimberley. To defend the Cape Midlands, Major-General Sir William Gatacre established himself, for the time being, in Joplin's Hotel at Queenstown, while General Sir John French advanced from Noupoort to try to prevent the advancing Boers from sparking off a general uprising of Afrikaners in the area.

Methuen's force of 9000 began its advance along the rail line towards Kimberley on 21 November. After sharp engagements at Belmont, Graspan and Modder River, he was pushing the Boers steadily northwards, ever closer to Kimberley. At Modder River the British had been caught cruelly unawares by Boer riflemen who fired at them from the cover of the river bank, a position selected for them by General de la Rey. It was De la Rey also who selected their next position, at the line of hills at Magersfontein. Here, working at night, while Methuen rested his own troops at the Modder River, the Boers under the supervision of General Piet Cronjé dug trenches and built low stone parapets at the foot of the hills, facing south across a flat, bare plain.

Methuen's response was a frontal attack on Magersfontein Hill, preceded by a heavy but ineffective artillery bombardment on the afternoon of 10 December. Methuen planned a night march to be followed by a dawn attack, and selected for the task the Highland Brigade, commanded by Major-General Andrew Wauchope, known to his men as 'Red Mick'. Half an hour after midnight, on the morning of 11 December, Wauchope led his 3400 men through the dark, in a compact mass of humanity towards Magersfontein Hill. There was a delay as they passed through a dense clump of thorn bush and, at about 4 am, the brigade began to change formation, so as to make the final advance in line abreast. Just then, a shattering volley of rifle fire, totally unexpected, was let loose at them from a range of just a few hundred metres. Some fixed bayonets and attempted to charge, some lay down or tried to go back against a tide of men still surging forward. Many died in subsequent volleys and during the long, searingly hot day as they lay in the open, the slightest movement immediately drawing accurate fire. Wauchope and his second-in-command were among the first to be killed. Next day there was a truce to allow the dead and wounded to be brought in and then, rather than renew the attack, Methuen retreated to his base at Modder River.

Black Week

Methuen's reversal was the second the British had suffered in a string of disasters to become known as 'Black Week'.

The first came on 10 December in the midlands, where Gatacre – an energetic soldier known to his men as 'General Back-acher' – was concerned that the Boers, occupying the Cape as far eastward as Molteno and beyond, might combine to attack a significant target and

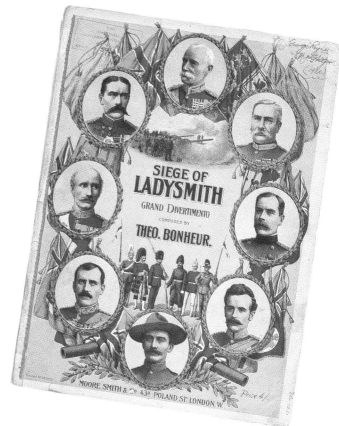

THE MAIN *British commanders during the South African War were pictured on the cover page of this contemporary song, the 'Siege of Ladysmith'. Topping the bill is British Commander-in-Chief Lord Roberts, flanked by Redvers Buller and Herbert Kitchener.*

thus attract large numbers of Cape Afrikaners to their cause. The solution, he decided, was to dislodge them from the important railway junction of Stormberg; and it might have worked but for a last-minute change of route that Gatacre failed to communicate to his intelligence officer. In the event, after a night march from Molteno, instead of surprising the Boers at Stormberg, Gatacre's force of 3000 men ended up some 5 kilometres away, and were themselves surprised in a dawn attack by OFS Boers and rebel sympathisers commanded by J H Olivier. After three hours, Gatacre gave the order to withdraw, but the order failed to reach more than 600 men who had found shelter in a large rocky overhang and, exhausted by their march, had fallen asleep. They emerged to surrender, and the venture, with killed and wounded, cost Gatacre a third of his force and achieved nothing.

Disaster struck again for the British on 15 December in Natal when Buller launched 18000 troops in a frontal attack across the Thukela at Colenso in a bid to relieve Ladysmith. The Boers, 6000-strong under Louis Botha, had established themselves in well-fortified positions which British reconnaissance had failed fully to reveal. After a series of disasters, which cost the British 10 guns (see page 250), Buller gave the order to withdraw, telegraphing White in Ladysmith to fire as much of his ammunition as possible and then to make the best terms he could with the Boers. *(Continued on page 252.)*

Colenso

With Boer forces dug in south of Ladysmith, the war had reached virtual stalemate by December 1899: the British could not advance northwards, while the Boers were unable to penetrate further south into Natal. It was a situation that the British Commander-in-Chief, Redvers Buller, was determined to end – by an advance across the Thukela in an attempt to lift the siege of Ladysmith.

After first informing the British Government that the Boers were too strong for a frontal attack across the river at Colenso, Buller changed his mind – and on 15 December delivered what he hoped would be a knockout blow: a 'demonstration' would be made in front of the only Boer position south of the Thukela – the heights of Hlangwane Hill – while his Second Brigade, under General Henry Hildyard, pushed across the railway bridge just north of the town. At the same time the Irish Fifth Brigade under Fitzroy Hart would attempt to force its way across the river to the west of Colenso.

After a bombardment by naval guns, Hart's Irishmen moved forward in a dense mass towards a loop in the river, where an African guide had assured them a ford existed. Instead of a ford, however, they found the river bed strewn with barbed wire, laid by the Boers, who decimated the trapped troops, forcing the survivors to retreat.

Meanwhile, the attack on the railway bridge (see main illustration) got off to a disastrous start when batteries of British field guns, ordered to pave the way for the advance, unlimbered too close to the Boer positions – and the gunners were cut to pieces before running out of ammunition and abandoning most of the guns, despite near-suicidal attempts to recover them. Hildyard, who had managed to reach Colenso in a bid to reach the railway bridge, was ordered to retire – and the attack was called off.

Forced to retreat, Buller was given the nickname 'Reverse' Buller by the angry British Press.

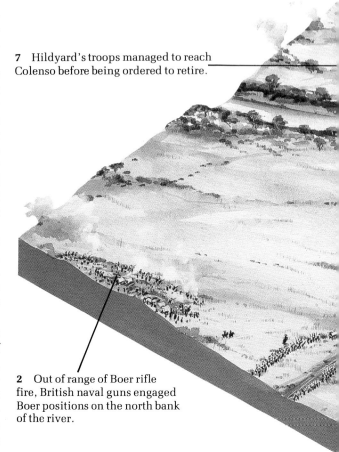

8 This wagon bridge over the Thukela was the furthest point reached by British troops before they were ordered to retire.

7 Hildyard's troops managed to reach Colenso before being ordered to retire.

2 Out of range of Boer rifle fire, British naval guns engaged Boer positions on the north bank of the river.

BOER SHARPSHOOTERS *in action on the heights above the Thukela halted the British advance.*

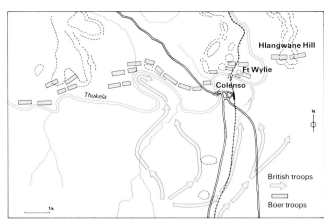

THE LEFT WING *of the British attack – General Fitzroy Hart's Irish Fifth Brigade – was the first to go on the offensive, hoping to ford the Thukela at the top of a loop in the river. Meanwhile the Second Brigade under General Henry Hildyard began an advance towards the railway bridge north of Colenso. The first attack was beaten back, while the second was called off.*

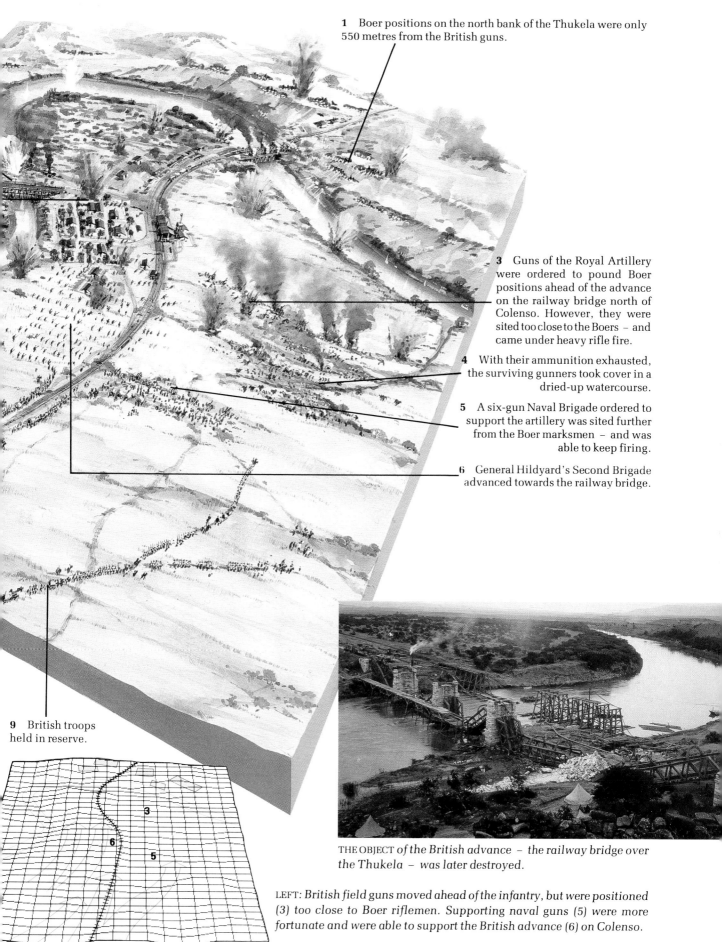

1 Boer positions on the north bank of the Thukela were only 550 metres from the British guns.

3 Guns of the Royal Artillery were ordered to pound Boer positions ahead of the advance on the railway bridge north of Colenso. However, they were sited too close to the Boers – and came under heavy rifle fire.

4 With their ammunition exhausted, the surviving gunners took cover in a dried-up watercourse.

5 A six-gun Naval Brigade ordered to support the artillery was sited further from the Boer marksmen – and was able to keep firing.

6 General Hildyard's Second Brigade advanced towards the railway bridge.

9 British troops held in reserve.

THE OBJECT *of the British advance – the railway bridge over the Thukela – was later destroyed.*

LEFT: *British field guns moved ahead of the infantry, but were positioned (3) too close to Boer riflemen. Supporting naval guns (5) were more fortunate and were able to support the British advance (6) on Colenso.*

251

FIELD-MARSHAL *Lord Roberts of Kanda-har (left) was 67 when he offered his services to the War Office in London – and within a month had set sail for South Africa as the new British Commander-in-Chief. Under his command, the imperial forces advanced swiftly to Bloemfontein and Pretoria.*
HERBERT KITCHENER *(right) was Chief-of-Staff to the new Commander-in-Chief, a career soldier who took charge of British forces in South Africa after Roberts had occupied Pretoria and left for home. His 'scorched earth' policy finally broke the Boers.*

Roberts to the rescue

Among the British killed at Colenso was young Lieutenant Freddie Roberts, only son of 67-year-old Field-Marshal Lord Roberts of Kandahar who, on the next day, 16 December, offered his services to the War Office in London. Less than a week later the *Dunottar Castle* was bearing him towards South Africa as the new Commander-in-Chief, with the floridly whiskered Horatio Herbert Kitchener as his Chief-of-Staff. Telegrams were despatched by Roberts to Buller urging him to remain on the defensive.

Roberts arrived in Cape Town on 10 January to find stalemate on all fronts. The Boers, flushed by their triumphs of Black Week, once again failed to advance on Durban, hoping that Britain would have a change of heart, or of government. They could not have been more wrong: stung by the reverses of Black Week, the British were more determined than ever to see the war through to a victorious end, and the Australian, New Zealand and Canadian colonies raised volunteer forces to fight alongside those of the 'Mother Country'. The three besieged towns of Kimberley, Ladysmith and Mafeking became a symbol of British prestige. It was unthinkable that any one of them should fall.

Roberts planned to use the western railway system to relieve Kimberley and then launch a flank advance on Bloemfontein. In the meantime, despite Roberts' explicit instructions, 'poor blundering Buller' decided on a flanking movement of his own, setting out from Chieveley with 23 000 men on the very day that Roberts arrived in Cape Town, and crossing the Thukela some 30 kilometres west of Colenso. After failing to capture the Boer-held heights of Tabanyama Hill, it was decided to occupy another hill of the range, named Spioenkop. On the night of 23 January, 1900 men led by General Sir Edward Woodgate, whose knighthood had been announced just two weeks earlier, climbed to the summit of Spioenkop, much as the ill-fated Sir George Colley had done at Majuba in 1881. The results were similar. Woodgate was killed, and the battered remnant of his troops, torn to pieces all day by artillery fire and by rifle fire from two enfilading heights, made their way down the hill under cover of darkness. The Boers, believing the British would reinforce their hold and bring up their own artillery, prepared to abandon the position. Dawn, however, found the British army streaming back over the Thukela. Once again, Buller had changed his mind. His next attempt came on 7 February, at Vaalkrans, midway between Spioenkop and Colenso. Like his previous efforts, it failed utterly.

More successful were Roberts and Kitchener who, with great secrecy, managed to move some 60 000 men to the vicinity of Ramdam in the OFS. From there the cavalry division, led by Sir John French, exploited a gap in the Boer siege lines and galloped into Kimberley on 15 February. The besiegers, and the defenders of Magersfontein, promptly withdrew in the direction of Bloemfontein, their wagon trains fatally delaying them. After just a few hours' rest, the cavalry division set out in pursuit, trapping 4000 burghers under Cronjé at Paardeberg Drift on the Modder River. Ignoring entreaties from OFS Commander, Christiaan de Wet, to break out, Cronjé surrendered on 27 February – a catastrophe for the Boers. Next day there came surprising news from Natal: Buller, after fighting a series of fairly minor consolidating battles, had at last relieved Ladysmith.

'We are marching to Pretoria'

The main British army, brushing aside only slight resistance, entered Bloemfontein on 13 March, forcing President Steyn to move his government to Kroonstad, where he and Kruger met for a council of war on 17 March and decided to continue the war, but on a more informal scale, avoiding frontal clashes with the invaders in favour of highly mobile units, raiding the British lines of communication. It was the first stamp of approval on the guerrilla tactics which had already been used with considerable success by De Wet and which within weeks were completely to change the nature of the war – and keep the fire of republicanism burning for another two

THE STRUGGLE *for possession of Spioen-kop, a small hill overlooking the Thukela River about 30 kilometres from Colenso, was one of the most viciously fought battles of the war. The British crossed the river on the night of 23 January 1900 and made their way up to the summit (above) – almost under the noses of Boer forces (above right), who poured rifle and artillery fire into the British trenches. After being torn to pieces all day, the British survivors withdrew under cover of darkness, leaving hundreds of their comrades dead (right).*

years. Twelve days later Joubert died, to be replaced as Commandant-General of the SAR forces by 38-year-old Louis Botha.

After six weeks of waiting for transport and supplies, the British resumed their advance, with Roberts leading the main force of 43 000 men along the main rail route to Johannesburg and Pretoria, while Buller, with 45 000 troops, was ordered to move north from his position in Natal to meet him.

The eyes of empire now turned to the military farce being enacted at Mafeking, although the proceedings were elevated to the status of an epic of endurance which, for the Africans of Mafeking, it was. The sole importance of the half-hearted siege was that it tied up an unknown number of burghers who could have been more usefully employed elsewhere. The relieving force rode into the town on 16 May, and the empire indulged in an orgy of rejoicing.

Eight days later, on Queen Victoria's birthday, the OFS was annexed to the crown as the Orange River Colony. President Steyn and his now outlawed government took to the veld, becoming a government on the run with De Wet and his guerrilla forces.

Meanwhile the main British army was fast approaching Johannesburg, with the Boers alternately attacking and falling back in front of them – and on 31 May, two days before Roberts entered Johannesburg at the head of his victorious army, Kruger left Pretoria to set up the seat of government in Machadodorp on the eastern highveld. Pretoria was abandoned to the British – and while Roberts occupied the SAR capital, Buller at last was able to move over the Drakensberg to join him. On 1 September 1900 the SAR became the British colony of Transvaal and Roberts, convinced the war was as good as over, went home to a hero's welcome and a handsome purse of gold from a grateful parliament.

Command of the British army now devolved on Kitchener, but although the war of set battles and major troop movements was over, the war did not end. The Boer forces now split up, continuing the fight in smaller, more mobile guerrilla bands. The formal war was over; the guerrilla war was just beginning.

To the bitter end

The British Commander-in-Chief in South Africa, Lord Roberts, was convinced that once
Pretoria was in British hands, the republicans would surrender. He was wrong.
After Pretoria had fallen, the Boers began a guerrilla war that prompted vicious counter-measures
by the British, including the burning of farmhouses and the establishment of concentration camps.
With the country ravaged, many Boers sought surrender, some even joining
the ranks of the British forces – earning the undying scorn of those determined to carry on.

'WE ARE MARCHING to Pretoria . . . .' For months
the long khaki lines of British troops had been
singing as they slogged northwards, plagued by
dust, disease and sniping Boers. But at last the capital of
the South African Republic (SAR) lay open before them; the
war was surely almost over.

But when Field-Marshal Lord Roberts' columns entered
the city there was no government left to surrender: Kruger
had moved the seat of SAR power east to Machadodorp,
leaving Louis Botha to hand over Pretoria to the occupying forces. Even the Treasury was empty – Attorney-
General Jan Smuts thoughtfully cleared £500 000 out of the
state vaults before decamping ahead of the British troops.
The nearest the Boers came to surrendering was a secret
communication between Roberts and Botha – which soon
came to nothing.

Not that the republicans were taking the British occupation of their capital with equanimity; at a meeting outside
the city following its surrender, the Boer leaders argued
long and hard on whether or not to continue the fight. The
clincher was the success of the Orange Free State (OFS)
commando leader Christiaan de Wet in disrupting British
supply lines to the Cape. With plenty of military stores and
Smuts' £500 000 in their hands, they decided to carry on
until either a foreign power could be persuaded to inter-

vene or in the hope that a more sympathetic Liberal Party
would unseat the Marquess of Salisbury's Tory Government in Britain's forthcoming general election.

The immediate need was to stop the British consolidating their hold on the SAR – and Botha, who as
Commandant-General was now virtual ruler of the republic threw his remaining forces across the Delagoa Bay railway just east of Pretoria on 12 June 1900 in a vain bid to
hold the British advance. He tried again near Belfast in a
vicious six-day battle at Berg-en-dal, and once again was
forced to fall back, the SAR Government moving first to
Waterval-Onder, where Kruger had been living for some
time, and then to Nelspruit. Finally Kruger, too old and infirm to stay on the run with his commandos, left Delagoa
Bay to try to whip up support for his cause in France.

Berg-en-dal was the last set battle of the war. From now
the British would have authority only over what ex-OFS
President Marthinus Steyn described as 'the range of their
guns'. In dwindling numbers and with a diminishing faith
in a victory that had once seemed so close, the Boers
snapped at the heels of the British army. It was no longer
a war that professional soldiers relished, but a series of
raids on supply dumps, of attacks on troop columns, and
of some enterprising long-range strikes deep into the Cape
Colony, where the commandos found plenty of sym-

BRITISH TROOPS *march past the Rissik
Street Post Office in Johannesburg after
the city was surrendered by the Boers on
31 May 1900. However, the occupation
of Johannesburg and the SAR capital,
Pretoria, did not signal the end of the
war; the Boer forces quickly switched
to a guerrilla war that dragged on for
nearly two more years.*

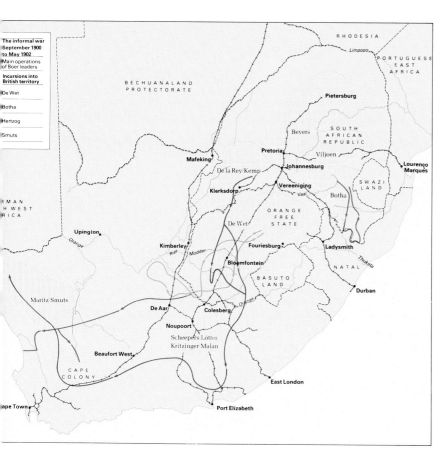

The informal war
September 1900
to May 1902
Main operations
of Boer leaders
Incursions into
British territory

De Wet

Botha

Hertzog

Smuts

BOER COMMANDOS were active in many parts of southern Africa, penetrating deep into the Cape Colony and the borders of Natal. The most determined of the guerrilla leaders was General Christiaan de Wet, who harassed British forces in the OFS and the Cape. Equally courageous was General Jan Smuts, whose commando operated in the north-western Cape, crossing the path of General Barry Hertzog who raided as far as the west coast. General Louis Botha operated in the eastern Transvaal, fighting south to the Natal border.

pathisers. Then, following the replacement of William Schreiner's Cape Government with a more subservient administration under Sir John Sprigg, parliament passed a Bill making collaboration a treasonable offence. Martial law was declared throughout the Cape, and parliament did not meet again for two years, until the war was over.

Burn them out

Although it had garrisons in most towns throughout South Africa, the British army was heavily dependent on the railway system for its continued supply. But Boer sabotage of the railway lines seriously threatened the entire campaign. As a counter-threat, Roberts issued proclamations in June 1900, to the effect that houses nearest to any break in the railway would be burnt, the inhabitants imprisoned, and their property destroyed or confiscated. There had been complaints of farm-burning since as early as January, but from June, the rate of destruction was stepped up. It was expected that the people rendered homeless would attach themselves to a commando, and so impair its mobility.

The first 'refugee camps' were established in September 1900, not for those deliberately turned out and displaced, but for the families of burghers who had surrendered voluntarily, to protect them against the anticipated vengeance of those still in the field. However, there were soon strong protests, even in England, against the practice of turning women and children adrift on the veld, so they were concentrated at points close both to the railway line and to sources of water. From this development, the name of the camps gradually changed to concentration camps.

Under Lord Kitchener, who took over command from Roberts at the end of 1900, the policy of farm-burning developed rapidly, and soon included the destruction or confiscation of crops and livestock, on the grounds that burghers still in the field were able to replenish their supplies from this source. It was a method of waging war that had been employed in the American Civil War and, more recently, by Roberts in Afghanistan. The British army, however, was neither prepared for, nor able to deal with, the enormous numbers of displaced people. These factors, coupled with a general degree of incompetence (rather than a deliberate policy of extermination), were the main reasons for the appalling death rates.

Fencing in the Boers

Gradually the Boers' mobility was restricted by long lines of barbed wire fences that divided the country into massive 'paddocks'. Blockhouses, built of stone near strategic features such as railway bridges, and of earth and corrugated iron in other places, sprang up along rail lines and the barbed wire until, by war's end, there were 8 000 of them.

The commandos took to living off the English, even replacing their ragged civilian clothes with captured uniforms, although some were forced to wear grain bags, with holes cut for arms and head. Most were now armed with Lee Metford or Enfield rifles, as bullets for their Mausers became unavailable. Horses became a problem, many Boers being forced to walk, carrying their saddles as they trailed after their mounted comrades, until they found a horse to replace one that had died.

255

Life and death in a concentration camp

Boers were not the only inhabitants of the concentration camps established by the British to house the victims of farm burnings; also rounded up were their African workers, usually tenant farmers who paid their rent in labour.

At first these African families were lodged on sites adjoining the Boer concentration camps. Populations of entire locations, and even mission stations, were also uprooted and transferred to camps, so that by the end of the war there were some 115 000 Africans in 66 camps, compared with 136 000 Afrikaners in 50 camps. The camps claimed the lives of about 28 000 whites, while more than 14 000 black deaths were actually recorded on lists known to be incomplete. Although numerous organisations, including churches, took part in compiling lists of those who died in the white camps, no such interest was shown in those for Africans. Emily Hobhouse, who brought to the attention of Britain the conditions in the white camps, never, so far as is known, visited an African concentration camp.

A Native Refugee Department was created in June 1901 to administer the African camps, although its first priority was 'the supply of native labour to the Army'. Prior to this, Africans in the camp at Heidelberg in the SAR had kept themselves alive only by eating the carcasses of cattle that had died of disease. At least one person died each day in that camp, and the records, approximate though they are, show that the worst month for fatalities was December 1901, when the death rate per annum for Africans rose to 436 per 1 000 in the camps of the OFS and 320 per 1 000 in the SAR camps. The worst month for deaths in white camps was October 1901, with 401 per 1 000 in the OFS and 326 per 1 000 in SAR.

In the case of Africans, causes of death of individuals were not recorded, although it is known that certainly among the whites, pneumonia, measles, chicken pox and dysentery predominated. All of these were aggravated by poor living conditions and inadequate diet, particularly for the Africans, who received almost no medical care. Early in 1902, in the OFS, the average daily rations of a white camp inmate cost 8,5 pence, while the equivalent cost for an African was only 4,5 pence. Of the Africans, less than a third of those interned received free rations, as those who had employment were obliged to pay for their meals. In the SAR, the daily cost of feeding an African concentration camp inmate was less than a penny.

Towards the end of the war, shops were opened in the camps, at which Africans might buy 'luxury items' such as tinned milk, cereals, blankets and clothing. Since these were almost vital to survival, the shops had the effect of encouraging inmates to seek labour. In the SAR, Africans spent thousands of pounds on 'luxuries'. Camps were made smaller and more widespread, and surrounding land was cultivated by the inmates, in order to feed themselves, and to provide for the military. Since cultivation was carried out by the aged and women and children, the Native Refugee Department's labour recruitment drive was not affected.

For protection of the African camps against raids by Boer commandos, it was necessary to organise armed groups to patrol the crops and livestock enclosure. Despite this, raids were carried out on the camp at Potchefstroom in the western part of the SAR, in which 258 cattle and 400 sheep were stolen, and another commando raided the Taaibosch camp in the OFS, robbing Africans of money and clothing. The system of arming Africans to protect their camps was eventually discontinued by the British, as it was claimed that this seemed to 'only invite attack'.

According to the official reports of the Native Refugee Department, Africans in the camps were as contented as could be under the circumstances, and thankful for the protection that the camps afforded against starvation and the Boers. Missionaries who visited the camps were unable to come to the same happy conclusion. At Krugersdorp, the Reverend Mr Farmer was told that 'cattle, gardens, houses have gone – that families are separated, that there is no knowing if fathers or mothers, sisters and even wives, certainly many husbands, are alive or safe'. The Reverend Mr Brown visited the African camp at Dryharts in the northern Cape and reported that 'between the Dutch and the English they have lost everything . . . .'

A memorial to the dead of the white concentration camps, a 'national shrine of the Afrikaner people', was erected at Bloemfontein in 1913. There is no memorial to the Africans who died.

THE INMATES *of a Boer concentration camp gathered in front of their tents for this photograph, which was later used as a postcard.*

A LONE *British trooper watches a Boer farmhouse burn during Kitchener's campaign to deny food to guerrillas.*

The most successful of the commando leaders was De Wet, who earned the grudging admiration of the British for his guerrilla prowess. A British officer who was involved in the so-called 'De Wet hunt' recalled later that the OFS Commandant had 'an immense reputation. The rapidity of his movements is extraordinary.' The guerrilla war tied down thousands of British troops who were, at the same time, tempting targets because they had to be spread so thinly on the ground. De Wet humiliated the British time and again, capturing trains and troops seemingly at will. He also had a wry sense of humour, as the officer remembered: 'After one of his many train captures, he sent a message to the base to say that "he was sufficiently supplied with stores now, and would they [the British] kindly send up some remounts".' De Wet's whereabouts were far more than a military headache – he was usually accompanied by ex-President Steyn, forming a government on the run.

Kitchener was keen to end the war, not least because his next appointment was to the coveted post of Commander-in-Chief, India. Although it had been announced earlier that only 'unconditional surrender' would be acceptable to Britain, he arranged a conference with Botha at Middelburg in February 1901. The terms were that the republics surrender their independence in exchange for a promise of a form of self-government 'as soon as possible'. Enfranchisement of Africans would not be considered until this stage had been reached, and financial assistance would be provided for rebuilding the shattered republics. The Boers, however, were not prepared to surrender their independence, and demanded an assurance that colonial rebels would be pardoned. Milner, however, insisted that rebels be prosecuted, causing an exasperated Kitchener to remark that 'we are now carrying on a war to be able to put 2-3 000 Dutchmen in prison at the end of it. It seems to me absurd, and I wonder the Chancellor of the Exchequer did not have a fit.'

A split in Boer ranks

The war dragged on and, if the Chancellor of the Exchequer did not have a fit, at least a powerful 'stop the war' movement began to grow in England. In South Africa, too, there were those who no longer believed the war could be won

by the republics, and a number of burgher peace committees were formed. At about the time of the Middelburg conference, some Boers who had surrendered went out to find the commandos to put the view that honour had been satisfied, and that it was time to come to terms with the British. Known contemptuously as 'joiners' or *hensoppers* (hands-uppers), they received scant sympathy from the Boers still in the field – the *bittereinders* (bitter-enders). At least two of these emissaries were executed by their former comrades-in-arms, and others were fined or imprisoned. Nevertheless, the number of surrenders did increase at that time and, by the end of the war, more than 5 000 burghers were on active service with the British army – against a total commando force of no more than 17 000.

Most of the *hensoppers* were from the poorer Afrikaans families, particularly *bywoners* (tenant farmers), although one of them was De Wet's younger brother Piet who, deeply troubled by the cost of the war to his country, surrendered to the British together with some of his men at Kroonstad in the OFS on 26 July. Later he wrote to his outraged brother that he (Christiaan) was being deceived by the 'SAR burghers and generals. May God not allow you to shed more innocent blood.' Furious, De Wet flogged the man who had brought him the letter and sent a warning to his brother that he would shoot him 'like a dog' if he ever caught him.

This serious split in the ranks of the Boers led Kitchener to write that 'if the Boers could be induced to hate each other more than they hate the British, the British objective would be obtained'. Such an outcome, he felt, would lead to 'a [political] party among the Boers themselves depending entirely on British continuity of rule out here'. Although Kitchener's vision did not fully materialise, disunity added to the despair felt by many of the *bittereinders* as the struggle became increasingly difficult to continue.

Drives were organised, whereby thousands of British soldiers would form ranks that stretched from one barbed wire fence to another, and march steadily forward, 'sweep-

GUERRILLA LEADER *General Jan Smuts poses with his commando while operating against the British in the Cape Colony. Smuts later became Prime Minister of unified South Africa.*

Death for defending the Union Jack

Boer fighters who rode across the Cape frontier, some of them penetrating as deep as 100 kilometres from Cape Town, found widespread enthusiasm for their cause among whites in the country districts. One of the commando leaders was the young Gideon Scheepers, who was captured, tried, condemned and somewhat shabbily executed outside Graaff-Reinet early in 1902. He has passed into history as an Afrikaner martyr. Another martyr, Abraham Esau of Calvinia, carpenter, blacksmith and market gardener, who was tortured and murdered, has only recently been rescued from oblivion.

Esau was born at Kenhardt in Bushmanland, the eldest child of Adam Esau and his wife, Martha April, in about 1855. Deeply influenced by Wesleyan missionaries, the family frequently spoke English at home, which was (and is) unusual in the rural labourer context. Some education at an English church school in Prieska impressed both English as a language and a creed, and the Bible, into the being of Abraham Esau. In 1880 he settled in Calvinia, where he practised successfully as a blacksmith, had his own smithy, and also grew and sold vegetables.

African and coloured communities in the Cape were acutely aware of Boer incursions into the colony, and of the consequences. In occupied districts, the laws of the SAR or OFS, with their 'traditional native policies', were held to be effective, and were administered by local rebels. The new 'magistrates' could be relied upon to give swift judgment against any African, and illegally enacted provisions whereby they were drafted to serve the invaders or to work, to their own disadvantage, on white-owned farms. Peasant produce and stock were often seized without the issue of a requisition slip whereby compensation might have been claimed. Yet when coloured people or Africans, many of whom held the franchise, asked the government for weapons with which to protect their lives and property, many rural Cape Afrikaners threatened to go into rebellion.

That Esau was a man of some prominence in Calvinia became apparent on 19 May 1900, when he organised the celebrations on the market square to commemorate the relief of Mafeking. There were speeches by the magistrate and by Esau, who also raised the Union Jack, establishing himself publicly as the leader of the coloured community. It was as such that, when news reached the town that republican Boers were about to attack, he went to the magistrate to demand that his people be given arms. The magistrate, however, seemed confident that the small Town Guard would be able to cope with the threat, and issued only a few swords. With these, and improvised weapons, Esau formed a militia company that drilled and manned outposts with a system of warning signals whereby the town could be alerted. The coloured community was solidly behind Esau, and remained so when the danger of invasion passed.

As raiding continued in the Cape, Esau did not abandon his idea of forming a home defence force. He wrote to the magistrate at Clanwilliam, and also to the British intelligence agent there, suggesting the formal establishment of a Calvinia Native Levy. The magistrate, concerned about threats of Afrikaner mutiny, refused to grant permission. The intelligence agent, Lieutenant Preston, replied that 'the forming of a natives' guard such as you so sensibly

propose would set an excellent example'. Unfortunately, he was not in a position to sanction it, but Esau went ahead and organised, not a private army, but a highly effective intelligence network covering a large area of the northern Cape. Word of it soon reached the Boer commandos, by whom Esau was described as 'the most poisonous Hottentot in Calvinia', and who were determined to take vengeance on him.

Early on the morning of 10 January 1901 an OFS commando, reinforced by Cape rebels, galloped into the little town, headed by Commandant Charles Niewoudt, who may have been related to one of the many local families of that name. Unarmed, but inspired by Esau's energy, the coloured people of Calvinia put up a spirited resistance

THE CALVINIA MARTYR.

A PHOTOGRAPH of Abraham Esau was published in the 'Cape Times' in March 1901, together with a report of his death at the hands of 'inhuman brutes' who should be 'arraigned for murder'.

with sticks and stones, but were savagely lashed, and a number were shot. Esau and local officials were thrown into the jail, while Niewoudt ordered the population to assemble in the market square to hear him proclaim himself as the new magistrate.

He also proclaimed new laws in the style of those of the republics, especially with regard to 'Hottentots and Kaffirs'. They were to pay tax or to present themselves for labour and, under threat of severe punishment, were forbidden to speak English in public. There were other punishments for being outdoors after curfew, 'unlawful assembly', not having a pass, or disturbing the peace, by which was meant, principally, the singing of British patriotic songs. Messages were sent to local farmers to bring in their 'insubordinate' or 'troublesome' labourers for correction and, a few weeks later, the 'Diamond Fields Advertiser' reported that 'every Dutchman in the district who had a grudge against his employees brought them before the Landdrost'. More than 100 labourers were brought in to be beaten, subjected to hard labour, or have their children taken away to serve the commando as 'apprentices'.

For every supposed 'crime' or misdeed, Esau was held to be the real culprit. Local farmers, resenting his influence, presented the new *landdrost* with a petition accusing Esau of inciting labourers to commit arson, and of maiming stock belonging to republican supporters. This came on top of what was regarded as Esau's arrogance in refusing to name the members of his organisation, refusing to disclose an alleged arms cache, and refusing to renounce in public his allegiance to Britain.

Esau's supporters were far from cowed, and marched through the streets at night in defiance of the curfew, chanting his name and singing hymns. Goaded, Niewoudt had three people, chosen arbitrarily, publicly flogged. Esau was dragged from the jail, beaten, smeared with dung and offal, and left chained to a pole in the searing heat of midday. Children brought him water, and an ugly confrontation between the commando and some 80 of his supporters was narrowly averted. The next day Esau was hauled before Niewoudt, who sentenced him to 25 lashes 'for having spoken against the Boers and for having attempted to arm the natives'.

Abraham Esau was tied to a tree, and the lashes were administered by Niewoudt himself. When Esau was untied, and collapsed to the ground, he was kicked. Throughout the next two weeks he was lashed and beaten again and, on one occasion, stoned by the men of Niewoudt's commando. Finally, on 5 February, he was placed in leg irons, tied between two horses and dragged for about a kilometre out of town, where he was shot.

Some 3 000 mourners attended his funeral, at which oral tradition tells of a sudden and violent thunderstorm, and a rushing wind that tore to pieces the Union Jack draping his coffin. A few weeks later, the commando that had spread so much terror among Africans withdrew.

News of the atrocity soon reached the outside world, and violent indignation was expressed, although Cape pro-Boer newspapers tried to find justification by saying that Esau had been shot in 'self defence'. A British newspaper summed up by saying of Esau that 'he has suffered cruel martyrdom for no worse crime than loyalty to the British'.

GENERAL *Christiaan de Wet earned the grudging admiration of the British for his prowess as a guerrilla leader.*

ing' the countryside as they went. For the Boers, escape became more difficult. There was little shelter, and obtaining food became a serious problem. When supplies could not be lifted from the British, they were obtained from the Africans, often without payment.

In many parts of the country, the Africans themselves constituted yet another threat, taking advantage of the unsettled state to avenge themselves on individuals, as well as to disregard white-imposed obligations, such as the provision of labour or payment of tribute. As early as December 1899 three Kgatla regiments led a British unit in an attack on a commando encampment in the western part of the SAR, and were hard put to extricate themselves when the British broke off. Many farms in this area were abandoned for fear of Kgatla attack and, in the north, the newly established town of Louis Trichardt was likewise abandoned, being later razed to the ground by the Venda. In the west, the Pedi also rebelled against their former masters.

The clash that most upset the *bittereinders* came early in May 1902, in what had been a part of Zululand, then the so-called New Republic and, finally, had been annexed to the SAR. A commando under Field-Cornet J Pretorius raided the cattle of a Zulu clan at Holkrans, near Vryheid, and challenged the Zulu to come and retake them. Armed with spears and some firearms, the Zulu did just that, killing 56 Boers for the loss of 52 of their own killed and 48 wounded.

BOER LEADER *General Louis Botha meets British Commander-in-Chief Lord Kitchener at Klerksdorp on 9 April 1902 to begin discussions on a truce. The war, however, dragged on until the end of May, when the final peace treaty was signed at Pretoria.*

Suing for peace

In January 1902 an offer by the Dutch Government to mediate between Boers and British was turned down by the British, but Kitchener nevertheless sent a copy of the offer to the SAR leaders. They, in turn, asked for permission to contact and confer with the former government of the OFS which, like themselves, was 'somewhere in the field'. This was granted by Kitchener, and the governments met on 9 April at Klerksdorp. Although they conceded a great many points, such as equality of franchise for whites and equal language rights for English and Dutch, they insisted that they were not empowered to 'sign away' their countries' independence. Kitchener promptly arranged for a more representative gathering to be held, and sent out messengers under a flag of truce, offering Boer commanders safe conduct to a meeting at Vereeniging, south of Johannesburg, to be held on 15 April.

Sixty representatives were elected by the men still in the field – and a total of 72 representatives of the two erstwhile republics finally assembled in order to formulate their proposals. During the days of debate, it became clear that while some districts could still support commandos in terms of food and shelter, others were desolate and on the point of collapse. The conditions presented to Kitchener and Milner at Pretoria on 19 May stated that the former republics were prepared to surrender their independence 'as regards our foreign relations'. They wished to 'retain self-government in our country, under British supervision', and were prepared to cede a part of their territory. During the first discussions, some delegates had been in favour of ceding the Witwatersrand, but most had agreed that its wealth would be necessary to assist in reconstruction. The 'territory' alluded to, although not named, was Swaziland which, since the British annexation of Tongaland, no longer offered a route to the sea, and was of little value to the SAR in any case. Milner and Kitchener had instructions to accept only unconditional surrender.

At the Pretoria conference, the Boer delegates were Botha, De la Rey, Smuts, De Wet and Barry Hertzog, and on 29 May they duly reported back to their colleagues at Vereeniging. Some, like De Wet, were in favour of continuing the war, while Smuts made the point that to do so would be to 'sacrifice the Afrikaner nation itself upon the altar of independence'. Shortly before midnight on 31 May 1902, peace was signed at Pretoria.

Terms of the peace

The terms of the treaty provided for an amnesty for most rebels, and a guarantee that none of those to be tried would be sentenced to death. The Dutch language was guaranteed a degree of protection in the law courts, and all prisoners of war would be returned from places as distant as Ceylon and Bermuda as swiftly as possible, subject to their signing an oath of allegiance to the British Crown. Britain guaranteed a sum of £3-million to repay the republics' war debts, and also considerable relief aid, and recognition of property rights.

For their part, the republics gave up their independence and recognised King Edward VII as their sovereign. The decision to accept the British conditions was carried by a vote of 54 to six. Of this, Acting President Schalk Burger of the SAR said: 'Here we stand at the grave-side of the two republics.'

One of the thorny issues at the conference was the rights of Africans, described by the Boer delegates as becoming 'out of hand'. From the British side, it was later to be a source of regret to Milner that he was unable to extend the franchise to Africans before the new colonies were granted self-government. At the time, however, he was anxious to press for a settlement as soon as possible, and knew perfectly well that the enfranchisement of the black communities would antagonise not only the Boers, but also the English-speaking community whose help he would need to implement his reforms.

Cashing in on the crisis

Manufacturers of everything from playing cards to pottery were quick to spot a chance for profit in the craze for South African War mementoes that swept Britain and the Cape.

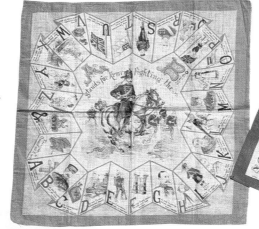

THIS GERMAN-MADE *set of playing cards shows Boer leaders, members of various African groups and several scenes in the Transvaal.*

THESE LINEN *handkerchiefs helped whip up public support for the British army 'fighting the Boers' and for the colonies rallying 'round the old flag of England'.*

THE OBJECT *of this simple game was to get Paul Kruger's teeth back into place inside his mouth.*

THIS 210 *millimetre-high bronze statuette shows the 'Absent-minded soldier' made famous in a poem by Rudyard Kipling and based on a painting of the 'Gentleman in Kharki', which was reproduced on items such as the cup and jug (right), and helped raised £250 000 in royalty fees.*

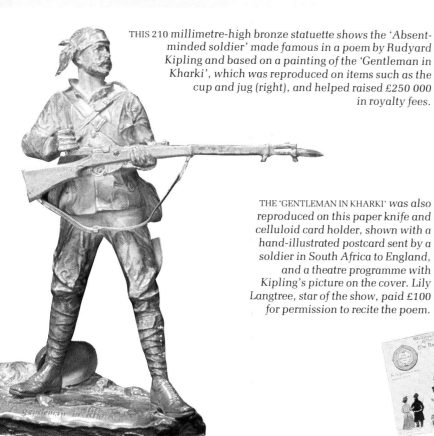

THE 'GENTLEMAN IN KHARKI' *was also reproduced on this paper knife and celluloid card holder, shown with a hand-illustrated postcard sent by a soldier in South Africa to England, and a theatre programme with Kipling's picture on the cover. Lily Langtree, star of the show, paid £100 for permission to recite the poem.*

Christiaan de Wet.   Gen. Louis

NATIVE LABOUR PASSPORT.   (To be held

VACCINATED Labour District of JOHANNESBURG.

Union and disunion 1902-48

'.... When I consider the political future of the natives in SA... I look into shadows and darkness....'
Letter from J C Smuts to John X Merriman,
13 March 1906.

With thousands of their comrades dead or wounded, their farms devastated by the 'scorched earth' tactics of the British and their families languishing in concentration camps, the Afrikaners' cause in May 1902 seemed lost forever. Independence from British imperialism had never seemed so unattainable.

And yet the next half century would see the cause of Afrikaner nationalism emerge triumphant. Having lost the war, the Afrikaner set about winning the peace with a political will born of hardship and a sense of historical injustice.

The South African War ended at the conference table in Vereeniging, but the final surrender document contained a key clause assuring the Boers that the vote would not be given to blacks in the ex-republics before the restoration of self-government. This effectively ensured that when elections were finally held in the Transvaal and Orange Free State, Afrikaners would dominate, despite attempts by the British High Commissioner Alfred, Lord Milner to flood the north with English immigrants.

Thus, when representatives of the parliaments of the four colonies met to discuss the possibility of unification, the strong hand of the Transvaal and Free State, allied with Natal, was able to keep blacks effectively off the common voters' roll; although the Cape representatives not only secured the continuance of their existing 'colour-blind' franchise, but also had it entrenched in the new constitution.

The Act of Union that followed brought the four colonies under one flag, but it failed to unite the country. By excluding blacks it sowed the seeds of discontent that another generation, and another epoch in South Africa's history, would have to reap.

Bitter and betrayed, educated Africans reacted to the Act of Union by forming – in 1912, two years after Union – the South African Native National Congress (SANNC), forerunner of the African National Congress (ANC). This was followed in 1919 by the Industrial and Commercial Workers' Union (ICU) and in the 1930s by the All-African Convention.

But by the middle of the century, African efforts had not only failed to win them more political rights, they were not even able to retain what few rights they had enjoyed at the beginning of the century. The architects of Union had agreed that the thorny question of a common 'native policy' would be left to the first Union parliament – and it was not long in coming: the 1913 Natives' Land Act divided South Africa into 'white' and 'black' areas – and led to the ejection of African 'squatters' from their homes.

263

This Act, one of the cornerstones of segregation, was followed in 1923 by the Natives (Urban Areas) Act, making possible the setting up of 'native locations' that still dot the periphery of white cities. Africans were allowed to be in the cities only on a temporary basis 'to minister to the white man's need' and should leave when 'they ceased so to minister'.

Worse was to follow. In 1936, Barry Hertzog finally persuaded Jan Smuts to support a package that stripped Africans of the vote, setting up a Natives' Representative Council and consolidating the land proposals made in 1913. Africans were left with 13 percent of the land.

As African rights dwindled, so the political power of the Afrikaner, often with English-speaking support, grew. Throughout the 1920s and 1930s the newly formed National Party went from strength to strength, despite occasional setbacks. Formed in 1914 to serve Afrikaner farming interests, the party soon found support among the increasing number of urban Afrikaners who resented the mine-owners' policy of giving jobs previously done by whites to lower-paid blacks.

This resentment culminated in the 1922 Rand revolt, when armed white strikers were savagely repressed by government forces. The white backlash came two years' later at the 1924 elections – allowing the nationalist leader, Hertzog, to form a government in alliance with the Labour Party. His share of the vote increased in 1929 in a 'black peril' election, but the depression of the 1930s forced him into coalition with Smuts, leading in 1934 to the formation of the United Party and to the breakaway of 'purified' Nationalists under Daniel Malan, who formed the Party that would win power at last in 1948.

War with Germany in 1939 renewed the old animosity between English- and Afrikaans-speakers – and Hertzog broke with Smuts, refusing to support South Africa's entry into the war on Britain's side. The war brought hundreds of thousands of Africans into the cities – as influx control was relaxed in order to allow industrial production to grow – and it was largely white reaction to this that secured the National Party victory in 1948.

At long last, nearly 50 years after the humbling treaty of Vereeniging, the peace that the victorious British had forced the Afrikaners to accept had been won . . . .

Labour

1902	Mining magnates lobby Milner for the importation of Chinese labour.
1903	Commission appointed to study labour shortage on mines.
1903-7	South Africa's gold output rises from £12,6-million to £27,4-million (32,3 percent of world output).
1904	Louis Botha and 14 others protest to British Government about plan to import Chinese labour.
1904-7	Chamber of Mines imports 63 695 Chinese workers.
1905	Olive Schreiner calls for unionisation of all workers.
1907	White miners strike in protest against the importation of Chinese workers.
1910	Last of Chinese workers repatriated. Labour Party adopts 'segregation' as policy platform. White trade union membership stands at paltry 10 000.
1911	Mines, Works and Machinery Ordinance amended to preclude African workers from more skilled categories of work. Natives' Labour Regulation Act makes it offence for Africans to break labour contracts.
1913	Strike by 19 000 white miners. About 9 000 African miners strike for three days.
1914	Smuts mobilises 70 000 troops to crush strikes called by railwaymen and South African Federation of Trades.
1916	White miners negotiate shorter working hours.
1917	Mining magnates threaten to shut down mines that are not paying their way.
1918	African railwaymen win 3 pence increase after strike. African 'bucket boys' arrested after strike for a pence increase. Flu epidemic hospitalises more than a third of the Reef's 157 000 African miners.
1919	Industrial and Commercial Workers' Union (ICU) founded by Clements Kadalie.
1920	More than 70 000 African miners strike for more pay.
1921	Chamber of Mines threatens to shut down 21 mines.
1922	The Rand revolt begins at Witbank coal mines. Thousands of striking miners march through streets of Johannesburg; seize control of most of the city; Smuts orders 20 000 troops into the fray; strike crushed at cost of 214 lives. Police and white vigilantes fire on 3 000 ICU supporters in Port Elizabeth.
1924	Industrial Conciliation Act lays down strict procedures for dealing with collective bargaining; Mines and Works Act amended to give Minister of Mines power to extend job reservation.
1925	About 25 000 ICU supporters stage work stayaway in Bloemfontein.
1927	ICU membership reaches 100 000. African union leaders cut ties with Trades and Labour Council.
1929	Kadalie quits ICU to form Independent ICU.
1938	Council for Non-European Trade Unions formed.
1941	Formation of African Mineworkers' Union.
1943	Lansdowne commission investigates working conditions and wages of African miners.
1946	Strike by African mineworkers crushed by police.

White politics

1903 Inaugural conference of the South African Customs Union.
South African Native Affairs Commission (SANAC) set up.
1905 *Het Volk* Party established.
1906 SANAC backs a policy of segregation.
Transvaal law makes it compulsory for Indians to carry Passes.
1907 Transvaal and Orange River Colony granted self-government.
Het Volk wins Transvaal elections, *Oranje Unie* in Orange River Colony.
Selborne Memorandum backs single 'native policy' for a future united South Africa.
1908 Conflicting economic interests of the four colonies lead to calls for unification; National Convention sittings begin.
1909 Draft South Africa Act published.
W P Schreiner travels to London to campaign for removal of racist provisions in draft South Africa Act, but unsuccessful;
South Africa Bill passed by House of Commons.
1910 Union of South Africa comes into being, Botha as Prime Minister.
The new government wins first general election.
Parliamentary select committee suggests limits on African landownership and on squatting.
1911 South African (National) Party (SAP) launched.
1912 Botha resigns after clash with Barry Hertzog; drops Hertzog from cabinet when asked to form new government.
1912 Land Bank established to help struggling farmers.
1913 Natives' Land Act passed.
Beaumont commission asked to investigate ways of expanding African Reserves.
Hertzog and supporters quit SAP.
1914 National Party (NP) formed in Bloemfontein.
First World War breaks out.
Leading Boer generals plan coup; Botha crushes Boer rebellion.
Amendment to Riotous Assemblies Act.
Union Defence Force invades German SWA; Germans surrender.
1915 D F Malan heads new Cape branch of NP.
1916 Beaumont commission reports that it is too late to expand African Reserves.
Native Affairs Administration Bill confirms segregation.
Battle of Delville Wood.
1918 Formation of *Afrikaner Broederbond* (Brotherhood).
SANLAM insurance company established.
1919 Botha dies; Smuts becomes Prime Minister.
1920 Native Affairs Act creates separate administrative structures for Reserve inhabitants.
South Africa granted League of Nations mandate over SWA.
1922 Bondelswarts rebellion crushed in SWA.
1923 Natives (Urban Areas) Act extends segregation to towns.
1924 National/Labour Party alliance wins general election.
1925 Afrikaans becomes an official language.
Hertzog offers to increase size of Reserves in return for removal of voting rights of Cape Africans.
1926 Hertzog places three 'native' Bills before parliament.
SWA granted partial self-government (adult white suffrage).
1927 Compulsory segregation proclaimed in 26 urban areas; 64 locations established in terms of Natives (Urban Areas) Act.
Carnegie Foundation funds commission into 'poor whites'.
Native Administration Act gives Governor-General wide powers of control over Africans.
1929 Wall Street crash.
Hertzog's NP wins overall majority in general election.
1932 South Africa goes off gold standard.
1934 Hertzog and Smuts form the United South African National Party; Malan breaks away to form the 'Purified' National Party; disgruntled former SAP MPs form the Dominion Party.
Volkskas bank established.
1937 Department of Social Welfare set up.
1938 Centenary celebrations of Great Trek.
1939 Start of Second World War.
Hertzog resigns as Prime Minister; new Premier Smuts leads South Africa into Second World War.
Hertzog returns to a *Herenigde* (Reunited) National Party.
Launch of the *Ossewabrandwag* (Ox-wagon Sentinel).
1940 Hertzog forced out of the NP.
1943 United Party wins general election.
Post-1945 United Nations refuses to allow South Africa to incorporate SWA.
1946 Asiatic Land Tenure Act.
Fagan commission deliberates on 'native policy'.

Resistance politics

1902 Rent boycott in Ndabeni location, Cape Town, costs Department of Native Affairs £12 000 in lost revenue.
African Political (later People's) Organisation (APO) founded.
1903 South African Native Congress establishes its 25th branch.
M K Gandhi starts 'Indian Opinion' newspaper.
1904 Gandhi establishes Phoenix self-help scheme.
1905 Natal authorities introduce £1 poll tax aimed at forcing more Africans into wage labour market.
Abdullah Abdurahman becomes president of APO.
1906 Two Natal policemen murdered by African opponents of poll tax; 12 men charged with complicity in killings are executed.
African chief Bambatha leads rebellion that ends in a hail of bullets in a forest in central Natal.
1907 South African Native Congress meets in Queenstown to plan African response to Union; APO prominently represented.
1908 Zulu chief Dinuzulu convicted of high treason and jailed for four years.
Indians launch massive anti-Pass campaign.
1909 Orange River Colony Native Congress calls for a 'convention' for Africans.
South African Native Convention held in Bloemfontein.
Open letter on behalf of blacks sent to British MPs.
Eight-man delegation of African and coloured politicians travels to London to protest at the draft South Africa Act.
1910 Gandhi purchases Tolstoy Farm to maintain families of jailed resisters.
1911 Lawyers Pixley Seme, Alfred Mangena and George Montsioa plan a national congress for Africans.
1912 South African Native National Congress (SANNC, later ANC) founded.
SANNC delegation meets government ministers to discuss issue of Passes for women.
1913 Natives' Land Act passed.
African women in Orange Free State (OFS) choose jail rather than carry Passes.
Split between Gandhi and Natal Indian Congress.
Start of another Indian passive resistance campaign.
1914 SANNC delegation goes to London to protest Natives' Land Act.
First World War break outs.
Gandhi returns to India.
1916 South African Native College (later Fort Hare University) opened.
1919 SANNC sends delegation to signing of Treaty of Versailles.
1920 Transvaal Native Congress launches anti-Pass law campaign.
1921 Dozens of members of African religious sect, the Israelites, gunned down by police at Bulhoek in the eastern Cape.
1922 Rural Africans in Herschel, eastern Cape, boycott shops.
1923 SANNC changes name to African National Congress (ANC).
Wellington Buthelezi becomes leading opponent of Transkei administration.
1928 Communist Party adopts plan for a 'native republic'.
ANC begins organising workers in western Cape rural areas.
1929 Communists form African League of Rights; contest two seats in general election and lose badly.
1930 ANC executive resigns in protest at president Josiah Gumede's close ties with communists; Pixley Seme replaces Gumede as president; ANC 'radicals' in western Cape form Independent ANC.
Communists launch Pass-burning campaign; communist leader Johannes Nkosi killed during protest in Durban.
1935 All-African Convention founded.
1936 Cape African franchise abolished.
1940-5 Series of bus boycotts in Johannesburg's townships.
1940 Alfred Xuma becomes president of the ANC.
1942 Government relaxes influx control measures.
1943 Leading middle-class Africans outline black political demands in a document entitled 'African Claims in South Africa'.
Communist Party of South Africa draws 7 000 votes in the general election.
Formation of the ANC Youth League (CYL).
Communists launch anti-Pass campaign.
Coloured Advisory Council (CAC) established; anti-CAC group allies with All-African Convention to form Non-European Unity Movement.
1944 James Mpanza starts the *Sofasonke* squatter movement.
1946 Indian Representation Act offers Indians limited representation (by whites) in parliament and Natal Provincial Council.
1947 Lembede dies; Peter Mda becomes new president of the CYL.
1948 Mda proposes a militant Programme of Action at the 1948 ANC conference.
M K Gandhi assassinated in India.

'A white man's country'

Just eight years after being defeated in the South African War, a new breed of Afrikaner was about to assume a leadership mantle in a Union of South Africa – and this despite concerted efforts by arch-imperialist Alfred Milner to anglicise the Transvaal.
The drive for Afrikaner power started in the Transvaal where the *Het Volk* party, employing a mixture of emotionalism and skilful negotiation, led the way.
Soon Afrikaners elsewhere were ready to follow suit.

IT HAD TAKEN THREE YEARS of savage fighting and had cost the lives of more than 22 000 British soldiers, but in May 1902, the British Government had finally conquered the two Boer republics and gained control of a state which was already providing more than a quarter of the world's gold.

The outcome of the South African War had been shaped by Britain's overwhelming military strength; now the victors would shape peace into the foundation of a modern capitalist state supported by the power of the mining magnates and identified with the interests of British imperialism. This reconstruction was the task of Alfred, Lord Milner, High Commissioner in South Africa and Governor of the conquered Boer colonies. He embarked on a programme of 'social engineering', often held to have been a failure but which may, in fact, have laid the base for a political economy equal to the vision of British imperialism.

Milner had arrived in South Africa in 1897 imbued with the mission of empire, and strongly convinced of the need for greater state intervention in shaping social and economic development. He also believed firmly in the political superiority of whites: non-British whites in the colonies should be accorded the same political rights as British settlers, but blacks were another matter altogether! In a speech in 1903 he told his audience: 'A political equality of white and black is impossible. The white man must rule, because he is elevated by many, many steps above the black man; steps which it will take the latter centuries to climb, and which it is quite possible that the vast bulk of the black population may never be able to climb at all.'

This belief obviously permeated his thinking when, to make the Treaty of Vereeniging more palatable to the Boer generals, he persuaded Britain's Colonial Secretary, Joseph Chamberlain, to postpone the issue of black franchise until after the granting of reponsible government under the Crown. With the proviso that they be 'justly treated', blacks were necessary only to supply cheap labour without threatening economically the natural superiority of whites. Milner later regretted this manoeuvre when, according to him, he realised the 'extravagance of the prejudice on the part of almost all the whites, not only the Boers....'

Nevertheless, his vision was of 'a white man's country' in which a largely increased white population could live 'in decency and comfort'. It was a development which required capital, and a large amount of 'rough labour'. It was essential, Milner believed, to increase the British element of the population into a permanent majority of about 60 percent, with the rest 'Dutch', and the economy itself should ideally be 60 percent industrial and 40 percent agricultural. Boer children were also to be inculcated with the values of imperialist Britain and of a wider world, to divert them from their narrow, insular nationalism. Only when the Boers had been drawn out of cultural isolationism would it be safe, he believed, to shift from direct rule of the colonies towards a united self-governing dominion in South Africa.

Milner also intended to speed up the development of gold mining and to promote more scientific agricultural methods, in the hope that economic growth would assist efforts to eliminate Afrikaner nationalism. But behind it all was the need to transform social and economic relationships in the two colonies, particularly the Transvaal, in order to create systems and stability which would permit the region to be shaped in the interests of the mining industry and imperial Britain. If Milnerism was a failure, it was a short-term one. Certainly, within five years of Milner's departure in 1905, a united dominion under the leadership of the former Boer generals had come into being. But much of his vision was to be realised in the long term: a government dominated by whites, an economy expanding rapidly on the foundations of gold and the industrial power of the Reef, and blacks in the political cold.

Following the peace treaty, Milner and his coterie of Oxford-trained young administrators – dubbed the 'kindergarten' – moved swiftly to rehabilitate the defeated Boers: 31 000 had been exiled, 110 000 imprisoned in concentration camps, and their land, stock and homes had been ravaged by British soldiers. By March 1903, most had been re-established on their farms and nearly £19-million had been paid out in war damages, grants and resettlement loans. State departments were established with the special task of modernising agriculture, pursuing policies of soil preparation and stock control which bore fruit by 1908 in the first maize and beef stock surpluses since the early 1890s. The administration attempted to solve the problem of a growing number of poor whites by settling them as tenants on state land but failed in this because it did not provide capital or labour assistance to this ill-equipped yeomanry.

Milner also pushed ahead with efforts to create a majority of Britons in the colonies, but was able to attract only 1 200 settler families to the land – an eighth of what he wanted. This policy was also destined to fail.

WITH PEACE *in prospect, the British High Commissioner in South Africa, Alfred Milner (left), was installed as Governor of the conquered Boer colonies; and, with his team of Oxford-educated young administrators – dubbed the 'kindergarten'* (right) *– set about rebuilding what he hoped would be a British-controlled Dominion of South Africa. His anglicisation policy failed through a lack of British settler interest in South Africa and a change of government in Britain.*

Chinese labour

The issue which gave Afrikanerdom a platform from which to relaunch its bid for political power in the Transvaal was the importation of Chinese workers to deal with the mine labour crisis that had arisen during the 1890s and been exacerbated by the war. By the 1890s, gold mining on the Reef was becoming ever more expensive: the ore was low grade and at ever-greater depths, which forced the mining houses to look for even cheaper labour. By 1896, the wage bill for African labour represented 28,6 percent of working costs, and white labour was even more expensive. The mining houses tried to cut costs by reducing African wages and maintaining a high ratio of unskilled to skilled workers.

When war broke out in October 1899, mining on the Reef came almost to a standstill until the end of 1901, by which time the viability of the mines had been seriously affected. Post-war revitalisation of the industry was therefore accorded priority by Milner. But African mineworkers in 1902 numbered only about 45 000 – half as many as before the war: Africans had begun to resist mine labour because of the wage cuts. The Chamber of Mines was determined not to use more unskilled white labour because of its high cost, nor did it wish to create too large an urban African pool of labour and thereby lose the benefit of low wages offered by the migrant labour system. But efforts to recruit elsewhere in Africa were failing.

By 1902, some mining magnates were quietly lobbying with the Milner administration on the need for Chinese labour and, at the end of the year, the chamber despatched an engineer to China to investigate the possibility. Milner was supportive; in 1903 he hand-picked a commission to study the labour shortage and it did not disappoint him. It reported that the mines were short of at least 129 000 unskilled labourers and would need 196 000 more within five years. At the inaugural conference of the South African Customs Union in March 1903, the chamber resolved that Chinese labour would be required.

White labour and Boer leaders reacted sharply. White miners feared the Chinese would take over skilled jobs from them or undercut them in wages; white farmers were anxious to avoid competition from the Chinese in agriculture. A referendum on the issue was demanded and white labour organisations held a series of rowdy meetings on the Reef, which the chamber ensured were well attended by its own supporters who were not averse to strong-arm disruption tactics. The Boers, too, began to hold public meetings to mobilise opposition to the plan. Meanwhile, the British Government had already made it known to the mining magnates that the importation of Chinese labour would have to be approved by the public.

The president of the chamber, Sir George Farrar, therefore adopted two strategies. Firstly, to allay the fears of white labour, he promised that Chinese workers' rights would be severely restricted to prevent them from competing with whites for labour, land or trade, and that they would be sent home when their three-year contracts expired. Farrar told miners in Boksburg: 'You are agitating against [Asians] coming into the country, and against them trading and holding land. I am absolutely with you . . . . If Asian labourers unfortunately have to be brought into this country, they can only be brought in under government control, and only as unskilled labourers, prohibited to trade, prohibited to hold land or compete with any white man . . . .' He also made it clear to white miners that, without Chinese labour, the very existence of the mines – and therefore their jobs – would be at risk.

Secondly, to give the appearance of gaining consensus for the implementation of the policy, he placed a proposal before the Transvaal Legislative Council, whose members were favourably disposed to the mining industry. The council approved the proposal in two ordinances and by

Chinese migrants find a place underground

Natural disaster, land shortages, overpopulation and other economic pressures made emigration to South Africa appear as a possible escape for many Chinese at the turn of the century.

Thus the Chamber of Mines found a ready supply of cost-efficient labour for the Reef gold mines, importing 63 695 Chinese labourers between June 1904 and November 1906.

The restrictions to which they were subjected on arrival were shaped largely by the Chamber of Mines' desire to win the support of white workers for its Chinese labour policy: they would be repatriated when their three-year contracts expired; their contracts would limit them to unskilled work, and they would not be allowed to own or lease land, take up trades or cultivate any agricultural produce.

The conditions they encountered were extremely harsh – they were treated as little more than paid slaves, confined to cramped and poorly equipped mine compounds, and were given Passes for a maximum of 48 hours. The Chinese also faced stiff penalties for offences which affected their rate of productive output. Desertion, laziness and inefficiency were both criminal and civil offences, and the employers were able to punish such offences through floggings, fines and imprisonment. Magisterial powers were given to mine inspectors to punish offenders, and rewards were offered for the capture of Chinese deserters.

The cost of Chinese labour, including recruitment, transport, wages, food and housing, was actually higher than that of African labour. But the singular advantage of using Chinese was that they were under three-year contracts, during which time they acquired greater skill than their African counterparts, and were therefore more efficient in mining lower-grade ore at ever-deeper levels. Also, the work was back-breaking: for Africans the option to desert was far easier; for Chinese it was almost impossible.

Chinese labour broke the supply logjam and Africans began to flow back to the mines. By 1906, the mines were in full production with 163 000 workers – 18 000 whites, 51 000 Chinese, and 94 000 Africans. The value of gold output had risen from £12,6-million in 1903 to £27,4-million in 1907, by which time South Africa's share of world output had risen to 32,3 percent. But continued Afrikaner opposition to the policy, although it had become more pragmatic, spelled the end of the chamber's scheme. By 1910 the last contracts for indentured Chinese labour had expired and the men had been repatriated; without them the revitalisation of the South African gold-mining industry might have taken much longer.

But their conditions of work left a legacy of job reservation on the mines; the Mines, Works and Machinery Ordinance which had set out the restrictions on Chinese doing skilled work in up to 56 categories, was amended after most of the Chinese had left South Africa in 1911 to preclude African labour from these categories, thus perpetuating the widely criticised system of racial bars on wage and job rights.

A BOATLOAD *of Chinese labourers arrives in Durban – watched by a group of Africans on the quayside.*

CHINESE *labour made it possible to mine to deeper and at previously uneconomic levels.*

'GREETINGS FROM CHOWBURG' *reads this garish postcard depicting Chinese working and gambling in Johannesburg.*

early 1904 the chamber was gearing itself for the massive logistical effort of recruiting and transporting Chinese labour almost 20 000 kilometres.

White workers, intimidated by chamber threats and tactics, came gradually to accept the Chinese labour plan but the Boers remained decidedly unhappy. In February 1904, Louis Botha and 14 others sent a telegram to the Colonial Secretary, Lord Lyttelton, protesting against the plan on behalf of the Transvaal Boers, but were rebuffed on the grounds that they did not represent Boer opinion.

There were three parts to Milner's strategy for the pacification of the Boer populations of the Transvaal and Orange River Colony: the first, which failed, was to alter the ratios of Boer to British in the colonies by importing sufficient numbers of the latter to ensure their majority; the second, which caused more bitterness, was to 'denationalise' the Boers by suppressing their own cultural development and re-educating their children through a deliberate policy of 'anglicisation'; and the third was to rule both colonies directly until the first two parts of the strategy were complete – a policy decision which was reversed in 1906 by Britain's new political masters, the Liberals.

'Anglicisation' produced an effect exactly opposite to that for which it had been designed. In 1900, Milner had set out in a memorandum his views on the need for 'anglicisation': 'Next to the composition of the population, the thing which matters most is its education... Dutch should only be used to teach English, and English to teach everything else.'

Thus, even before the war had ended, schools with British teachers had been set up in the concentration camps. After the war a network of government schools was set up in which English was the principal language of instruction and Dutch was taught for only five hours a week. But the Boers resisted: first they argued that Article 5 of the Treaty of Vereeniging implied that Dutch could be used as a medium of instruction, and when that failed they opened private schools at which Afrikaner values were promoted.

The movement for the development of Afrikaans also flourished in the atmosphere of intense resentment fostered by Milnerism. Organisations were formed to promote the newly emerging language of Afrikaans, although

CHAMBER OF MINES *president Sir George Farrar tried to persuade white mineworkers to accept Chinese labour by threatening that, without the importation of Chinese, their own jobs would be at risk.*

Afrikaners generally remained divided for some years on whether to promote the new language or foster the old.

On the political front, the Boers had been finding their way back to self-government much faster than Milner had envisaged, but political forces beyond his control were at work in Britain. Since the war, the colonies had been administered by legislative and executive councils whose members were nominated by the British administration. In May 1903, Milner had offered seats to Botha, Jan Smuts and Koos de la Rey in an enlarged Transvaal legislature, but they had turned the offer down. In 1904, when the generals' claim to represent Boer opinion on the Chinese labour issue had been snubbed by Lord Lyttelton, Botha

THE THREAT *to white jobs posed by the importation of Chinese mineworkers was the spur that Louis Botha used to establish Het Volk in January 1905 – the first popular political grouping of Afrikaners since their defeat in the South African War. In February 1907 party supporters posed for this photograph outside the Masonic Hotel in Standerton. Het Volk went on to win 37 of the 69 seats in the Transvaal Legislative Assembly.*

had decided to put the issue beyond doubt by organising a political movement. This movement held its first *volkskongres* (people's congress) in May, demanding full self-government, and was formally established as *Het Volk* in January 1905.

At the same time, the support of the Transvaal's British political component was being canvassed by three other new parties: the Transvaal Progressive Association, dominated by the mining industry and calling for representative government; the Transvaal Responsible Government Association, and several labour groups which banded together as the Independent Labour Party.

Boer hopes for a restoration of self-government had centred for some years on the opposition Liberal Party in the British Parliament, who believed the Boers had been the victims of an unjust war fought at vast expense to the British taxpayer.

Since the war, leadership of the Boers had passed to the generals who had signed the peace, and they had set out to counter Milner's Briton-Boer numbers strategy by promoting Boer unity. Furthermore, by the time Botha and Smuts had established *Het Volk* as a political association in January 1905, they had begun to formulate a policy of reconciliation with Britain, which they knew would win favour with the Liberals.

The Boers were anxious that any moves towards self-government for the colony should be based on terms which would effectively restore them to political power and in January 1906 they were presented with the opportunity they had been waiting for when the Liberals, led by Sir Henry Campbell-Bannerman, came to power and immediately began to reshape British colonial policy towards the former Boer republics. Smuts went to London and succeeded in persuading the new government to accept a formula which guaranteed *Het Volk* the majority over their Progressive Party rivals in the new legislative assembly.

The election, scheduled for 20 February 1907, was fought on two issues: Chinese labour and British 'domination'. On the first, *Het Volk* had moderated its earlier demands for immediate repatriation but insisted that an alternative source of workers for the mines be found at the first opportunity. On the second issue, *Het Volk* – hoping to attract English labour votes – branded the Progressives as the party of the mining capitalists and stressed its policy of conciliation with Britain. On election day, *Het Volk* won 37 of the 69 seats.

Afrikaner political mobilisation was also under way in the Orange River Colony, which received its own Letters Patent for self-government in June 1907. Here, the large majority of the population were Afrikaners, and the victory of their party, the *Oranje Unie* (Orange Union), was assured: in the election of November that year, the *Unie* won 30 of the 38 seats in the legislature. In the Cape, Afrikaner rebels had been re-enfranchised and the South African Party, led by John X Merriman and supported by the powerful *Afrikaner Bond*, won elections for the legislative assembly by a large majority.

By 1908, Afrikaners had returned to power in three of Britain's four South African colonies but their ties with the empire remained assured: the scene was set for Union.

DELEGATES TO *the National Convention posed for this official photograph before agreeing to bury the bitterness between British and Boer in a new constitution.*

THE UNION *of South Africa became official on 31 May 1910 – and to celebrate the occasion, Cape Town's railway station (above) was lavishly done up, while the city's morning newspaper, the 'Cape Times', published an impressive commemorative supplement (below).*

Union: a triumph for the Boers

On 31 May 1910, eight years to the day after the Boer generals had signed the surrender of their republics to the British Empire, General Louis Botha became the first Prime Minister of a united South Africa.

It was a stunning triumph for the Boer negotiators of 1908-9. For it was a unity built on their terms: except in the Cape, blacks would not have the right to vote; and in the delimitation of constituencies, loading procedures would give greater weight to the rural vote to ensure future Afrikaner political control.

By 1908, pressures for unification were mounting in the face of continuing clashes of economic interests among the four colonies. The Customs Union which had been set up by Milner after the war had already been split by serious disputes over customs rates and rail tariffs. Natal and the Cape were feeling the effects of economic recession and needed to boost revenue by increasing rates and tariffs. Moreover, they were finding that the Transvaal and Orange River Colony were diverting an increasing proportion of their rail traffic away from the colonial ports to Lourenço Marques. The Transvaal, now economically dominant among the four colonies, had given the Portuguese preferential rates and tariffs in exchange for labour for the mines. Because it was a relationship too important to sacrifice, the Transvaal – knowing its economy could survive alone – threatened to leave the Customs Union.

In Natal, meanwhile, the Bambatha rebellion (see page 286) had raised fears among white colonists about their ability to control the Zulu people

'MAY WE BE *a united people*', *wrote Louis Botha on the eve of Union, 'hearts united as well as lands.'*

without the co-operation of Britain or the other colonies. This led to broad agreement among imperialists that only unification and a consistent 'native' policy would secure white control in South Africa.

In May 1908, Transvaal Colonial Secretary Jan Smuts proposed that the colonies seek a political solution to their economic disputes by establishing a National Convention. Widely welcomed, the convention began its deliberations in Durban in October 1908, under the chairmanship of the Chief Justice of the Cape, Sir Henry de Villiers. The 30 delegates with voting rights included 12 from the Cape, eight from the Transvaal, and five each from Natal and the Orange River Colony. Of the total, 16 were of British stock and 14 were Afrikaners. Their task was to find a political balance of power between the different economic and racial interests of Boer and Briton, and this involved three critical decisions: a choice between unitary and federal government; who would vote, and how voting power would be distributed between town and country, the power bases of English-speaking and Afrikaner leaders respectively.

By the time the convention sat, John X Merriman, Prime Minister of the Cape and an early proponent of a unitary constitution, had already gained the support of Smuts and together they quickly disposed of long-held assumptions that unification would follow the American, Australian or Canadian federal models. Natal, seeking looser ties with a united South Africa, had its own federal proposal quashed in favour of Smuts' predisposition to the British model. 'What we want,' said Smuts, 'is a supreme national authority to give expression to the national will of South Africa, and the rest is really subordinate.' Thus the convention opted for a sovereign central parliament with control over the powers of new provincial authorities (the former colonies), but it yielded to Natal's demand for an upper house – the Senate – with limited powers. The result was a cabinet executive which was accountable to the legislature. Parliament itself would have the right to amend the constitution by a simple majority vote, but a two-thirds majority was stipulated for amend-

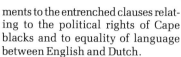

AS HEAD OF STATE, *King George V decorated this stamp commemorating Union in 1910.*

ments to the entrenched clauses relating to the political rights of Cape blacks and to equality of language between English and Dutch.

The matter of black voting rights was settled relatively easily. Smuts and Merriman were well aware that the Boer delegates of the Transvaal and Orange River Colony, supported by the British from Natal, would not accept any enfranchisement of blacks. The Cape delegates, on the other hand, would not consent to the removal of the existing limited voting rights of their own colony's black people. Smuts and Merriman therefore proposed a compromise: each colony would retain its existing franchise arrangements. After a tough debate, the issue was referred to a committee under Sir Henry de Villiers. Lord Selborne (who had replaced Milner as High Commissioner in 1905) told De Villiers that Britain preferred that 'civilised' men of colour be given the vote but that, if the convention could not agree, then Britain would accept the Merriman-Smuts proposal. Despite widespread criticism from coloured and African organisations, as well as Cape liberals such as former Prime Minister of the Cape, William Schreiner, the convention adopted the Smuts-Merriman compromise proposal.

The delegates placed more emphasis on the weighting of constituencies than on the question of black rights. In the heated exchange which followed, it was decided that rural seats would have 15 percent fewer voters than the norm, and urban seats 15 percent more.

Thus the additional weight of the rural vote became entrenched in South Africa's political system and was able to ensure future Afrikaner domination of national politics.

A draft constitution was completed in February 1909, debated by the four colonial parliaments, and finally accepted with amendments by the convention. It was then sent to London for approval and enacted by the British Parliament without alteration.

271

Trapped in the middle

In the early 1900s, South Africa's Indian and coloured people were jolted out of many years of political apathy by two remarkable men: one was Mohandas Gandhi, a lawyer who helped shape Indian protest movements on two continents; the other was Abdullah Abdurahman, who articulated the grievances and aspirations of coloured people for more than three decades. Guided by these two leaders, the Indian and coloured communities were pushed on slow, tortuous and, for a long time, separate journeys towards greater political awareness.

TINY, SKELETON-THIN, timid and painfully shy, Mohandas Karamchand Gandhi could hardly be described as an imposing figure. Yet for almost four decades his name was synonymous with a political philosophy that blossomed briefly in South Africa, emerged triumphant in India and took root in dozens of other countries. Called passive resistance, it offered millions of rightless (and usually weaponless) people around the globe a non-violent option in the universal fight for political rights.

When a Hindu fanatic who thought him too tolerant of Muslims assassinated Gandhi in 1948, millions of people around the globe shared in India's sorrow – and helped to create a myth. For in their eagerness to keep alive his ideas, some of his followers grotesquely romanticised his achievements, glossed over his failures and elevated him to near-sainthood.

That he *was* a remarkable man is beyond dispute. But he was neither a saint nor a particularly astute politician: indeed, in southern Africa, his political stamping ground for more than two decades, his efforts were marked by bewildering policy switches, flashes of opportunism and frequent displays of naivety.

The rise of a hero

In a country where poverty, illiteracy, disease and starvation were a way of life for millions of people, Gandhi was more fortunate than most: born in 1869 at Porbander in the Indian state of Gujarat to a 'merchant caste' couple, he went to school in India and to university in London, where he qualified as a lawyer in 1891.

Unlike many other British-educated Indians who returned home to throw their energies into the fight against imperial rule, he showed little interest in politics and tried instead to establish himself in the legal profession. But in Bombay, where he opened an office, he proved to be a dismal failure: having waited several months for his first client, his nerve failed him so badly that he was unable to utter a word when he rose to argue his case in court. Not surprisingly, his practice crashed, and he returned to Porbander a totally disillusioned young man.

It was here, while gloomily contemplating his future, that a representative of an Indian business firm based in the Transvaal threw him a lifeline: an offer of 12 months' work in southern Africa for a large fee of £105. In 1893 he arrived in Durban, little dreaming how dramatically his decision would affect his life.

After a stay of a week in Natal, in which time he was involved in an altercation with a magistrate who insisted he remove his turban in court, he left by train for Pretoria to begin work on his lawsuit. When the train reached Pietermaritzburg, a white passenger complained about the presence of a 'coolie' in a first-class compartment. Two officials asked Gandhi to move to a third-class carriage – and when he refused, he was ejected from the train. Later, Gandhi described the incident as the 'most important factor' in directing his future political life.

WITHIN A FEW YEARS *of his arrival in southern Africa Mohandas Gandhi (seated in the middle) had become a successful lawyer and an influential political leader.*

Indians under pressure

Since 1860, when they first began arriving in Natal to supplement the colony's cheap labour reservoir, discrimination and oppression had become part of the daily lives of tens of thousands of Indians (see page 222). 'Coolie' labour, at the time, was eagerly sought after in a number of far-flung colonies of Britain and France. And it was easy to see why: to plantation bosses, whether in Natal, Fiji, Mauritius or Guiana, 'coolie' labour was ultra-cheap, and made possible massive profits....

It took the Natal authorities almost 10 years of hard slog to earn a stake in the lucrative 'coolie' market. But once they got the go-ahead they more than made up for lost time by shuttling tens of thousands of 'coolies' into their sugar-based economy.

From a white perspective, the new arrivals from the slums of Madras and Calcutta were ideal immigrants: illiterate, frightened, cheap and exploitable, and therefore hardly a threat to white political superiority.

No society remains static, however – and, despite overwhelming odds, 'coolies' were occasionally able to chip away at their chains. But because their acts of resistance – mainly desertion, the mutilation of livestock and other minor acts of sabotage – were usually sporadic, unplanned and largely ineffective, the authorities were given little cause to take them seriously. Of far more concern to the governments of the four southern African states was the growth of two new classes of Indians: ex-indentured workers (those who had served out their contracts and had decided to stay) and a group known to whites as 'Passengers' or 'Arabs'.

Unlike the indentured workers who had been driven to Natal by poverty in India, the 'Passengers' – primarily businessmen from the state of Gujarat – had come out of choice. Their arrival had a profound effect, not only on the white business community who soon began to resent them intensely, but also on the enterprises of ex-indentured workers. For, with greater financial resources at their disposal, they were able to buy out (or drive into bankruptcy) many of the businesses of their ex-indentured rivals until by the turn of the century almost all the wealth of the Indian communities of Natal and Transvaal was concentrated in their hands.

The emergence of 'Passenger' and ex-indentured communities came as a shock to the authorities, most of whom were incapable of seeing Indians as anything else but indentured labourers. But now a fear began to grow among them that growing affluence would encourage these groups of 'aliens' to demand greater political rights. It was a threat that the law-makers of the region were determined to nip in the bud.

In many ways, the capacity of Indians to resist oppression was severely weakened by traditional caste divisions. Thus, while 'Passengers' tended to lead opposition to discriminatory laws, their protests were often made with feet firmly on the necks of their indentured and ex-indentured countrymen. Indeed, many of them treated 'coolies' as badly as did whites. Considering the intensity of the assault being made on their rights, class division was a luxury Indian society could ill afford.

INDIAN *street vendors were a familiar sight in turn-of-the-century Johannesburg.*

The noose begins to tighten

In the final two decades of the 19th century, the objections of 'merchant caste' Indians to discrimination almost always took the form of petitions.

But although these were usually well set out and articulately argued, they were invariably rejected, mainly because middle-class Indians had nothing to bargain with: no votes; no labour to withhold; and, most of all, no inclination to rebel. All they could do then was to appeal to the British sense of justice because they came from a British colony. The problem with this approach, however, was that fair play and racial prejudice never go hand-in-hand....

Perhaps inevitably, the most far-reaching of the early anti-Indian legislation was devised by the Boer republics, the Orange Free State (OFS) and the South African Republic (SAR). The innocuously named Law 3, passed by the SAR in 1885, was a particularly vicious 'Indian-bashing' exercise: working on the premise that personal hygiene did not feature high on the list of Indian priorities, it cited sanitary considerations as a reason for wanting to move a group of Indian traders from lucrative stands in the centre of Johannesburg to a deserted spot in the veld, about 7 kilometres outside the city boundaries. Fortunately for the merchants, however, the republican government was seldom able to back up its words with deeds, and the *status quo* remained until after the South African War, when the new British administration (which the majority of Indians had looked to for protection against the excesses of southern African legislators) launched a vigorous campaign to implement Law 3.

Merchants in the OFS also felt the chill of official disapproval – and, in fact, a year before the SAR's Law 3, the Free State *Volksraad* had pushed through legislation that classified Indians as 'coloureds' (Africans). Only too aware what this would mean, the merchant community had reacted with justifiable alarm. In a petition addressed to the *volksraad*, 13 Gujarati Muslims pointed out that 'even in Natal where the coloureds are restricted, they [Indians] are not treated equally with the coloureds ...[but] are treated like Europeans; they have the right to vote and the right to become landowners'.

It was, however, hardly the type of argument to impress the law-makers of the OFS.

Gandhi's mission

When Gandhi arrived in southern Africa, the anti-Indian outcry had shifted to Natal where, following the granting of self-government in 1893, politicians were coming under increasing pressure to introduce legislation to contain the 'merchant menace'. In 1894 they obliged with an Immigration Law Amendment Bill that stipulated that at the end of a five-year term of indenture an Indian had to return to India or be re-indentured for a further two years. If he refused, he would be required to pay a £3 annual tax. Despite strong objections, the Bill became law in 1895.

A Franchise Amendment Bill, designed to limit the franchise to those Indians who already had the vote, also made its appearance in 1894. That only 300 of them had registered as voters (as opposed to 10000 whites) was a clear indication that whites were not about to be swamped at the polling booths by an Asian tide. All the same, the new Bill outraged the merchant leadership, who threw everything into the fight against the measure.

Gandhi was a key figure in their carefully conceived campaign: a letter-writer of considerable talent and a meticulous planner, it was he who compiled petitions, arranged meetings with politicians, addressed letters to newspapers, campaigned in India and made a direct (and, at first, successful) appeal to the Secretary of State for the Colonies, Lord Ripon.

A crucial event – and one that reflected the growing political maturity among 'free' Indians – was the formation on 22 August 1894 of the Natal Indian Congress, the first 'permanent' political organisation to strive for the rights of Indians. Although open to all, its £3 annual membership fee meant that only the very wealthy could afford to become members. Nevertheless, in a significant development, many western-educated children of ex-indentured workers – their commercial interests also threatened by government hints of a reduction in the number of Indian civil servants – joined the congress.

In 1896 Gandhi, now firmly established as a political leader, returned to India to launch a crusade on behalf of the merchants. It took the form of letters to newspapers, interviews with top nationalist leaders and a series of public meetings. Whereas in southern Africa he had shown little interest in indentured workers, and, in fact, was remarkably ignorant of their plight, in India he tried to use them as a lever to win concessions for the merchants. Thus, in interviews with Indian officials he suggested that the continued availability of 'coolie' labour be made dependent on the scrapping of laws that affected the commercial interests of the elite group.

Gandhi's mission sparked an uproar in India and consternation among the authorities in Britain and Natal: cer-

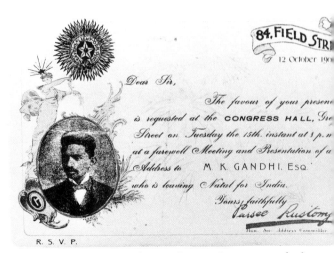

SELECTED GUESTS *received printed invitations to attend a farewell function for Gandhi in 1901.*

tainly, he embarrassed the British Government enough to persuade it to take the unprecedented step of blocking the passage of the Franchise Bill, that in turn pushed anti-Indian feelings in Natal to dangerous new levels. By the time Gandhi returned to the colony, white hostility threatened to spill over into open violence. Daily dockside demonstrations, coupled with government quarantine regulations, kept him and 800 other passengers on board ship for almost a month. When they were finally allowed to disembark, Gandhi was confronted by a crowd of protesters and assaulted. Only the intervention of the Durban police commissioner's wife, who took him into her home, saved him from serious injury. Later, as demonstrators outside the house chanted, 'We'll hang old Gandhi from the sour apple tree,' officials disguised him as a policeman and smuggled him out through a back entrance.

The British Government, meanwhile, alarmed at the uproar, offered the Natal authorities a cynical compromise whereby it would agree to the passing of Franchise Bill provided that Indians were not specifically mentioned in the provisions. Subtly reworded to deny the vote to anyone whose home country did not have its own parliamentary representation (as was the case in India), the Bill was rushed through parliament in 1896.

Two more laws aimed specifically at 'Passenger' Indians – the Immigration Restriction Bill and the Dealers' Licences Bill – quickly followed. The terms of the Immigration Bill – prospective immigrants had to possess £25 and, most importantly, had to be able to speak and write English – effectively put an end to voluntary Indian immigration, while the Dealers' Licences Bill, that empowered municipal authorities to refuse trading licences on the grounds of 'insanitation', contained even graver implications for the merchants. As municipal officials began turning down applications for licences simply because the applicants were Indians, many merchants blamed Gandhi for pushing the authorities too far. In 1901 when Gandhi returned to India after a stint as the leader of a corps of Indian stretcher-bearers for the British in the South African War, he was convinced that merchants in Natal had lost the fight to conduct their businesses unhindered.

Gandhi in the Transvaal

In 1902, after an unsuccessful attempt to win a leadership position in the Indian nationalist movement, Gandhi returned to southern Africa. In 1903 he founded the 'Indian Opinion' newspaper and less than a year later started the Phoenix self-help settlement scheme near Durban. The 'Indian Opinion' especially played an important part in spreading the philosophy that gave rise to passive resistance. But it was in the Transvaal that he launched his next major political campaign.

Under British administration, Indian merchants in the former Boer republic looked forward to greater freedom. But due to the efforts of Alfred Milner and Godfrey Lagden, the question of separate trading areas, as envisaged in Law 3 of 1885, was tackled with even greater urgency.

In a confidential despatch to Milner, Arthur Lawley, the newly appointed Lieutenant-Governor, argued that whites had to be protected against Indians because, as he put it, he saw in the presence of Asians a 'struggle between East and West for the inheritance of the semi-vacant territories of South Africa'. Supporting him, Milner stated that to allow 'coloured' people equality with whites was 'wholly impracticable' and 'in principle wrong'.

Under the Boer Government many merchants had escaped being moved to locations. But now the British set about closing all the loopholes ....

Gandhi's response to the new threat was to launch a British Indian Association (BIA) to fight the proposed evictions. The by now familiar letter-writing and petitioning followed. Locations were for 'kaffirs', not useful citizens, he argued in one of the letters. Lagden's cynical response was to rename the locations bazaars.

Ironically, the need to import 10000 indentured labourers to reconstruct the Transvaal railway system bought the merchants some time when the Indian Government stated that it would allow labour recruitment only if merchants were allowed to trade in their pre-war sites.

But more trouble was on the way – and it started in 1906 when the Transvaal authorities passed a law making it compulsory for Indians over the age of eight to carry a Pass bearing their thumbprint. Indians reacted angrily – and at a mass meeting attended by more than 3 000 representatives (including a Chinese delegation), the famous *satyagraha* ('truth force' – see box) oath was taken whereby no one would apply for registration, and attempts to enforce the Act would be passively resisted.

The meaning of *satyagraha*

'None of us knew what name to give to our movement. I then used the term "passive resistance" in describing it. I did not quite understand the implications of "passive resistance" as I called it. I only knew that some new principle had come into being.'

This is how Mohandas Gandhi began explaining the motives behind the political tactic that was first used in South Africa, and later perfected in India....

'As the struggle advanced,' he continued, 'the phrase "passive resistance" gave rise to confusion and it appeared shameful to permit this great struggle to be known only by an English name. A small prize was therefore announced in "Indian Opinion" to be awarded to the reader who invented the best designation for our struggle.'

Because the nature of the struggle had been fully discussed in the newspaper and competitors for the prize had sufficient information with which to work, a number of suggestions were received.

Said Gandhi: 'Shri Maganlal Gandhi was one of the competitors and he suggested the word *sadragraha*, meaning "firmness in a good cause". I liked the word, but it did not fully represent the whole idea I wished it to connote. I therefore corrected it to *satyagraha*. Truth (*satya*) implies love, and firmness (*agraha*) engenders and therefore serves as a synonym for force. I thus began to call the Indian movement *satyagraha*, that is to say, the Force which is born of Truth and Love or non-violence, and gave up the use of the phrase "passive resistance" in connection with it....'

Taking the fight to London, Gandhi won a promise from the Colonial Secretary, Lord Elgin, that the Act would be withdrawn. But Asian jubilation was shortlived. In January 1907, when the Transvaal was granted self-government, the new administration reintroduced the Pass law (Act 2 of 1907). This time Lord Elgin said: 'Everyone has the right to go to hell in his own way.'

Disregarding government threats, barely 500 out of a possible 7000 Asians registered by the deadline of 30 November. On 28 December the first arrests were made. By the end of January more than 2000 Asians had been jailed or deported. Gandhi himself went to jail several times. But the campaign ran into trouble when some of the leading

NINE OF THE MEN *who, between 1906-9 led the passive resistance movement against Pass laws for Asians, pose outside Gandhi's Johannesburg offices. They were (from left to right) C M Pillay, Nawah Khan, Gandhi, Thambi Naidoo, P K Naidoo, M Eastun, J Foteon, M E Karwa and Leung Quin.*

Abdullah Abdurahman and the African Political Organisation

A hum of expectancy swept through the crowd at the International Winter Gardens in Hanover Street, Cape Town, as Abdullah Abdurahman rose to deliver a speech that was destined to thrust him into the forefront of national protest politics.

'We are here,' he told the largely coloured audience, 'to protest against the disabilities that have been placed on our fellow-kinsmen in the Transvaal and Orange River Colony . . . .'

It was 22 March 1904 and a hushed silence fell over the crowd as the young, Scottish-trained doctor, described the next day by the 'South African News' as being 'possessed by a thoroughness and thoughtfulness wanting in many members of Parliament', continued his address.

Two years had passed since the Peace of Vereeniging had shattered black hopes of 'equal rights for all civilised men south of the Zambezi'. For the demoralised, leaderless middle-class coloured communities of southern Africa, they had been wasted years – years of waiting in vain for British Government intervention.

Now a grandson of a slave couple was trying to kick them out of their political stupor. Abdurahman's speech was forceful, prophetic and tinged with just enough bitterness to prick the consciences of his audience. Long before he finished speaking, he had convinced them that at last they had found a spokesman who could articulate their political aspirations. In the coming years they would be proved correct.

Reserving most of his anger for the British Government, Abdurahman lashed out at it for turning a blind eye to the continued denial of coloured rights in the northern colonies. And although he praised the political system of the Cape, where a 'colour-blind' qualified franchise existed, he warned, prophetically: 'We may even expect that the evil effects and pernicious influences of the barbarism practised in the north may extend to this Colony, and undo much that we gained in the past.'

Yet in spelling out the grievances of his northern countrymen, Abdurahman also demonstrated a racist streak. At Brandfort in the Orange River Colony the term 'native' included 'all coloured subjects of his Majesty', he complained. In the same vein, he hit out at the regulation that forced coloured people to live in locations and to ride in cabs marked 'natives'. Certainly, at the start of his political career, Abdurahman shared with the majority of coloured people a contemptuous dislike of Africans and on at least one occasion referred to them as 'barbarous natives'. But as the assault on black rights gathered momentum in the early years of the 20th century, he would be forced into a drastic change of tactics.

Into the APO hotseat

Within a year of his Winter Gardens address Abdurahman became president of the fast-growing but, in many ways, ineffective African Political Organisation (APO).

Founded on 30 September 1902 to demonstrate to the Cape government that there existed 'an educated class of Coloured people in Cape Town, who could no longer be treated as part of an undifferentiated mass of uneducated barbarians', the APO boasted 300 members in five branches after just two months of existence. A year later it had 15 branches and more than 1 000 paid-up followers. In 1904, when its membership had risen to 2 000, the APO had felt confident enough to appoint a full-time secretary, Matthew Fredericks.

And yet, this rapid growth failed to hide the fact that the organisation under the leadership of commercial traveller and lay preacher W Collins and his deputy, cafe owner John Tobin, could show very little for their gentle protests, deputations and petitions to the white authorities. A major problem was that the APO catered exclusively for a coloured middle-class eager to be integrated into white society. Campaigns, therefore, had to be conducted in a way befitting 'civilised' men. The result was that far too much effort went into schemes designed to break down white stereotypes of coloured inferiority. Certainly, by 1904 the main preoccupation of the many APO branches appeared to revolve around tea parties, bazaars, poetry readings and musical evenings.

This state of affairs might well have continued for a long time had not Collins and Tobin fallen out in 1904 over support for the Cape's two white political parties – the Progressives

ABDULLAH ABDURAHMAN *built up the* APO *into the strongest black political organisation in the country.*

and the Afrikaner Bond-South African Party alliance. Disregarding an APO resolution to back candidates rather than parties in Cape elections. Tobin openly called for blanket support for the Bond in the 1904 poll. An angry Collins retaliated by announcing his support for the Progressives.

Both men were expelled at the 1905 conference of the APO when Abdurahman became president.

It took Abdurahman less than five years to rebuild the APO into the most powerful black political grouping in the country, with a membership of more than 20 000 concentrated in 111 branches throughout southern Africa. As it flourished, so rose Abdurahman's stature. Already a city councillor, he later became a provincial councillor and a confidant of many white politicians. And many who knew him claimed repeatedly that had he been white, he would have gone on to become one of South Africa's greatest parliamentarians.

And yet many of the APO's activities under Abdurahman continued to focus on the political plight of coloured people in the Orange River Colony and the Transvaal. But although a string of fiery anti-Afrikaner speeches further enhanced his standing among his followers, it had little effect on the politicians of the former Boer republics. Indeed, what emerged quite clearly was that every time Abdurahman criticised white-power proponents he was merely highlighting the fundamental weakness of black protest politics: a commitment to working within the law left its activists with few options once their criticisms, compromises, pleas and petitions had been rejected.

An added weakness of early 20th-century black politics was the reluctance of many organisations to forge any sort of unity with groups outside clearly defined 'tribal' lines. Thus, while Abdurahman proved to be a doughty fighter for coloured rights in the Cape and the northern colonies, he was quite prepared (at first, anyway) to see Africans denied those same rights. To further complicate matters, Africans were deeply suspicious of any moves towards cooperation with coloured people.

By 1907, however, Abdurahman had begun an initiative to cut through the barriers that divided the two groups. He was forced to. Moves to grant self-government to the former Boer republics on the same segregationist terms as the Peace of Vereeniging were greeted with alarm by black

A JOINT MEETING *of the APO and the ANC in 1931. Meetings between African and coloured groups were rare in the pre-war years.*

political groups. Abdurahman, acknowledging the need for a massive show of black opposition to these measures, started tentative moves towards cooperation with Africans. When an APO delegation consisting of Abdurahman, Matt Fredericks and Peter Daniels went to London in 1906 to protest against the proposals, they did so on behalf of all black people (that is, all coloureds, Africans and Indians). Although the mission was a failure, the APO's new stance helped to break down many long-standing barriers between coloured people and Africans.

In 1907, when the South African Native Congress met at Queenstown in the eastern Cape to discuss the impending unification of South Africa, the APO was prominently represented.

In 1909, after African leaders called a meeting of the South African Native Congress in Bloemfontein to discuss the implications of the draft South Africa Act, Abdurahman wrote to the 'Izwi Labantu' ('Voice of the People') newspaper stating that he had advised all APO branches to send observers, 'for it matters not who initiates the movement so long as we attain our object'. With several APO delegates present, the meeting unanimously rejected the racist provisions in the draft Act and called on the British Government to intervene to secure 'equal rights for all civilised men'.

On 13 April 1909, the APO held its seventh annual conference in Cape Town at the same time that the Cape parliament debated the draft South Africa Act. In an atmosphere of high tension, delegates from throughout the country gave Abdurahman a standing ovation when he dealt with the question of black unity: by the term 'coloured', he declared, he meant 'everyone who was a British subject in South Africa, and who was not a European'.

Abdurahman's tenure as president of the APO lasted 35 years – until his death in 1940 – and through most of this period he was its sole policy-maker. Looking back, his decision to seek closer ties with Africans was a watershed in coloured politics. It meant that for the first time coloured people had to choose between a less-than-equal alliance with white South Africans or unity with the African majority. This sparked a long debate that continued into the 1990s.

THESE WERE *the delegates who attended the 10th anniversary conference of the APO in 1912. More than 100 branches were represented at this meeting.*

ON 29 AUGUST 1908 *more than 2 000 In-dians gathered at the Mosque market in Grey Street Durban to protest against the Dealers' Licences Act. Their protests were ignored, however.*

figures in the protest movement left the colony rather than court repeated arrest. Amid rumours that opposition was about to collapse, Gandhi and the Chinese leader, Leung Quin, reached agreement with Transvaal Colonial Secretary Jan Smuts, whereby (according to Gandhi) the Act would be repealed if everyone registered voluntarily. Although harshly criticised for agreeing to this compromise, Gandhi offered to be first to register. But on his way to the registration offices he was attacked and beaten up. Smuts, who denied promising Gandhi anything, did not repeal the Act and the *satyagraha* movement degenerated into chaos with members engaging each other in verbal slanging matches.

The Pathan community was particularly opposed to giving fingerprints and Gandhi again came under fire when it was discovered that he had accepted an offer from Smuts that wealthy Indians need not give their prints. Although Gandhi publicly forgave the people who assaulted him, privately he tried to stop the radicalisation of his movement. Thus after two other prominent members had been attacked, he wrote to Smuts, naming the culprit and suggesting that he be deported in terms of the Immigration Restriction Bill (that Indians strongly opposed).

On 16 August 1908, in a massive demonstration of defiance, more than 3 000 Asians burnt their registration certificates. But even then, conflict within the movement, bad organisation and a lack of funds were taking a heavy toll. By the middle of 1909 most of the Transvaal Asian community had registered for fingerprinting.

In June 1909, having fought off a challenge for his position as leader of the Transvaal merchant community, Gandhi travelled to London.

A man of the masses?
When he returned in December to find the number of active *satyagraha* supporters had dropped to about 100, he began to look increasingly towards indentured and ex-indentured workers to recoup lost support.

In a sense, Gandhi was fighting for his political life: the gentle murmurs of dissatisfaction that had followed many of his decisions during the campaign against the Pass laws had become a roar, with former colleagues in the Natal Indian Congress openly plotting against him.

What Gandhi needed was to create enough time for himself to ride out the storm and to build up a new constituency. By now he had become an expert at walking political tightropes – and in 1911, after a period of inactivity at Tolstoy, the farm he had purchased in 1910 to maintain families of jailed resisters, he approached Union Interior Minister Smuts with what appeared to be a generous offer: the suspension of passive resistance pending the formulation of an immigration Bill to replace the immigration laws of the four former colonies. There was a decided element of bluff in this gesture: his movement appeared to be in its death throes – and the wily Smuts must have been aware of this. But with nothing to lose, he played along.

A visit to South Africa in 1912 by Indian statesman Gopal Krishna Gokhale put Gandhi back in the public eye, but also drew more criticism from his detractors, who accused him of preventing opponents of his policies from conferring with the important visitor.

On 26 April 1913, after almost four years of bickering and mudslinging, Gandhi and his rivals in the Natal Indian Congress finally went their separate ways. On 12 October, his leadership was again called into question when, at a stormy public meeting in Durban, angry critics blamed him for the deterioration of merchant rights over the past 20 years and slated him for refusing to adopt alternative policies and for choosing white 'lieutenants' above educated Natal-born Indians.

At the same time, his battle of wits with Smuts continued, with gentle reminders of the dire consequences of a racist immigration Bill. A new condition – that the £3 tax imposed on ex-indentured men, women and children be removed, was made specifically to gain the support of the working-classes.

This policy switch won him everlasting fame. And yet, to start off with, he had little to do with the first major strike by Natal's Indian workers – at Newcastle in northern Natal. The spadework was done by one of his chief lieutenants, Thambi Naidoo, a veteran *satyagrahi* and a popular president of the Johannesburg-based Tamil Benefit Society. Beginning his campaign on 13 October 1913 with a successful mobilisation of Newcastle merchants, Naidoo next turned his attention to railway workers and miners whose support he secured two days later.

ON 29 OCTOBER 1913 *Gandhi became 'a champion of the masses' when he led a protest march of mainly working class Indians from Newcastle in Natal to the Transvaal.*

On 16 October, 78 workers at the Farleigh Colliery struck, were quickly arrested and were hauled before a magistrate who warned them they would be jailed if they were not at work within 24 hours. The next day, however, 2 000 workers downed tools – and two weeks later, the number had risen to between 4 000 and 5 000.

In order to demonstrate his new-found political clout, Gandhi desperately needed the strike to spread. But a low-key government response to the stoppage made this extremely difficult. Finally, in desperation, he decided to court arrest by threatening to lead striking workers out of their compounds and over the Transvaal border. On 29 October, he led 200 strikers and their dependants out of New-

castle towards the border. Twenty-four hours later, he was followed by a second party of 300 led by Naidoo. A day later, a third party of 250 set off.

So eager was Gandhi for the workers to be arrested that he appealed to the government to act against them before they crossed into the Transvaal. But Smuts, confident that the strike would collapse of its own accord, preferred to wait. It was a wise move: by November many strikers were ready to throw in the towel.

But then, a spontaneous strike by workers in the more populous southern Natal changed the situation completely. Here, the reaction of employers and officials differed radically from the low-key approach of their counterparts in the northern districts – and when suspected ringleaders were detained in police swoops, to which workers retaliated by starting cane fires and riots, the scene was set for violent confrontation.

After several strikers were shot dead and many injured in clashes with police, increasing numbers of workers were persuaded to join the protests. By the end of November, the Durban and Pietermaritzburg produce markets had come to a standstill, sugar mills had been closed down and many hotels, restaurants and private homes were without domestic workers.

Reports of police brutality, and the arrest of Gandhi, led to an uproar in India. Under pressure from the British Government, the union authorities agreed to try to reach a settlement with the strike leaders. Gandhi was released from prison to negotiate with Smuts – and soon after, an 'Indian Relief Bill' that scrapped the £3 tax on ex-indentured workers came into being.

When Gandhi returned to India on 18 July 1914, he was already being hailed as a *Mahatma* (literally, a great soul).

INDIAN *protests in 1913 were aimed at a new £3 tax on ex-indentured workers, a racist immigration policy and a Cape Supreme court judgment that nullified Indian marriages. Although opposition was meant to be peaceful, violence often broke out – as this picture of a clash between mounted police and protesters in Ladysmith shows.*

Clutching at straws...

In the first decade of the 20th century, a series of political upheavals – war, rebellion and racist legislation – shattered the hopes of thousands of mission-educated Cape Africans. Members of this new elite – active participants in Cape politics – had long believed that Cape-type voting rights would be extended to Africans in the other colonies. But in 1910 the general policy of newly 'united' South Africa was racial segregation . . . .

MAY 1902 – AND THE FINAL SHOT in a bitter war between Englishman and Afrikaner had been fired. As the bedraggled Afrikaner commando leaders wandered into Vereeniging to talk peace, a wave of jubilation – and expectancy – began sweeping through thousands of African households.

For three years many blacks had applauded the victories and mourned the defeats of troops carrying the Union Jack. Many had died for the British cause. Now, as the diplomats sat down to plan a new order, a new factor had to be considered – a rapidly growing and organised African elite expecting maximum political reward for wartime loyalty.

But they were too optimistic. The British quickly showed they had no intention of keeping the vague promises of reform they had made at the height of hostilities. Indeed, the denial of rights to Africans was the carrot used to effect a quick reconciliation with the vanquished Afrikaners. The Peace of Vereeniging offered little to blacks in the Orange River Colony and the Transvaal, and later, in a move which sent shivers of apprehension through the ranks of African voters in the Cape, the British High Commissioner, Alfred, Lord Milner, convened a South African Customs Conference in Bloemfontein, where one of the matters discussed was the need to arrive at a 'common understanding on questions of native policy'.

This led to the formation of the South African Native Affairs Commission under the chairmanship of Sir Godfrey Lagden (see page 312) who, in April 1905, after 16 months of collecting evidence, released a report that rejected political equality between the races, recommended separate voters' rolls for Africans and whites (with Africans voting only for a limited number of representatives) and advocated territorial separation between the races.

The 'new elite'

The report came as a blow to mission-educated Africans who from the late 19th century had eagerly embraced the colonial lifestyle (and politics) alongside Christianity. During this period, John Tengo Jabavu (see page 208) probably did most to push Africans from being passive onlookers to active participants in the Cape Political system.

In the early years of black mobilisation, no one reflected the new militancy of educated Africans more than he.

IN 1884, *top eastern Cape political leader John Tengo Jabavu (far left, seated) launched 'Imvo Zabantsundu' (left), a weekly newspaper which quickly established itself as the mouthpiece of 'modernist' African political thinking in the eastern Cape. When Jabavu died in 1921, his son, Davidson Don (standing), continued the family involvement in politics.*

Indeed, so profound was his influence that no new organisation could hope to flourish without his approval. More than anyone else he articulated the aspirations and plotted the strategies of the growing new elite. And for many years it was an arrangement that worked well . . . .

Ironically, the Jameson Raid in 1895, which led to a realignment of white Cape politics, also resulted in a split between Jabavu and a rival group calling for the formation of a national, and far more radical, black political organisation. In 1898, when Jabavu threw his weight behind a group of English-speaking 'Independents' who had joined the *Afrikaner Bond*, his opponents responded by launching the South African Native Congress (the forerunner to the African National Congress.

Jabavu's attempts to steer a neutral course during the South African War increased the strains among members of this new elite, leading to a newspaper war between the congress' *Izwi Labantu* ('Voice of the People'), edited by Alan Kirkland Soga, and Jabavu's *Imvo Zabantsundu* ('Native Opinion').

After the war, the congress leaders – clergymen, teachers, law agents and the like – moved quickly to build their organisation into a vociferous political machine. By 1903 it had established 25 branches, mainly in the Cape. The thrust of its campaigns, highlighted by pressure groups, petitions and newspaper editorials, was aimed at

ALAN SOGA, *a member of a well-known missionary family, became a staunch opponent of J T Jabavu.*

the British. Despite a succession of 'betrayals', many congress members continued to believe that salvation would come in the form of British intervention on their behalf.

Jabavu, on the other hand, rejected the formation of an Africanist organisation. Claiming that a blacks-only body would highlight the racial distinctions he wanted to see removed, he pinned his hopes of more rights for Africans on closer co-operation with liberal Cape politicians.

A new assault on the African vote

On 7 January 1907, the report of the South African Native Affairs Commission was taken a step further in the Selborne Memorandum (see page 271), a document that examined the desirability of the formation of a united South Africa. It caused consternation in African ranks. Pandering to Afrikaner sentiments especially, the report described the 'native question' as one of the most difficult problems facing white South Africa. Five or six different 'native policies' would make the problem even more difficult to solve, it argued. The report offered no solutions, but to many Africans the signs were ominous: a single 'African' policy in a Union of South Africa would almost certainly mean the continuation of statutory segregation in the northern provinces and the eventual loss of the franchise in the Cape.

On 27 November, more than 80 delegates from 29 centres throughout the Cape met at Queenstown to plan a response to the question of union. Jabavu did not attend – the meeting had been organised by the congress – but in a move that ushered in the start of coloured-African co-operation, a delegation from the coloured African Political Organisation was prominent. The meeting lasted two days and among the resolutions passed were that federation would be preferable to union, and that the Cape franchise should serve as a basis for a federal franchise.

Jabavu, meanwhile, having dismissed the Queenstown proceedings as a 'pantomime', called his own conference on 17-18 January 1908. Addressing about 350 people, he welcomed possible union or federation, claiming it would encourage the other colonies to adopt the enlightened native policies of the Cape.

But he was wrong. On 12 October 1908 a National Convention, consisting of white representatives from the Cape, Natal, Orange River Colony, Transvaal and Rhodesia, met in Durban to discuss the formation of a 'united' country (see page 271). On 9 February 1909 the draft South Africa Act was released to the Press – and among its provisions were that parliament would be an all-white institution, and that there would be no franchise for blacks in the then Natal, Transvaal and Orange River colonies. Cape Africans, however, were guaranteed their voting rights after delegates had eventually agreed that changes to the Cape franchise would require a two-thirds majority in a joint sitting of the upper and lower houses of parliament.

As far as Africans were concerned the proposed Act was a sell-out to the northern colonies. 'This is treachery,' said Soga in a typically forthright response. 'It is worse. It is a successful betrayal, for the Act has virtually disenfranchised the black man, even before the meeting of the Union Parliament . . . .'

. . . KEEPING HIM QUIET. . . .

The proceedings of the South African Convention are being conducted in profound secrecy.

DR. DE VILLIERS. "He's got run down; been suffering badly from depression; we can only patch up his Constitution by keeping him quiet and forbidding him to talk."

THIS IS HOW 'The Pictorial' magazine viewed National Convention chairman Henry de Villiers' ruling that unity talks between the Cape, Natal, Transvaal and Orange River colonies be conducted behind closed doors.

And Jabavu, while expressing his gratitude to the Cape delegates for preserving African voting rights, added: 'The colour bar in parliament has taken away the prized guarantee of political freedom and political contentment, and has made the African franchise illusory.'

A black convention

The publication of the draft Act sparked a period of hectic political activity among both Africans and whites. The Orange River Colony Native Congress, having anticipated the decisions of the National Convention, called for a convention, with Bloemfontein as the venue, for Africans throughout the four colonies and the protectorates. Both the 'Imvo' and the 'Izwi' backed the plan. In agreeing on the necessity for Africans to voice their opinion before the constitution was enacted, Jabavu offered to print the names of delegates in his newspaper and to make any other preparations to ensure the success of the meeting.

At the same time the organising committee headed by Thomas Mapikela started contacting associations 'guarding the rights of the people' to ask them to prepare for a convention where African opinion would be expressed. The meeting, they stressed, would be as crucial to enfranchised Cape Africans as to the rightless masses in the Orange River Colony, Natal and the Transvaal. Although Africans in the Cape had retained the franchise, they predicted that the 'anti-native' majority in the northern provinces was likely to agitate for the removal of this right.

Hopes of overturning the provisions of the draft Act were boosted by the passionate denunciation of the measures by whites such as William Philip Schreiner. However, expectations of a united African response were dashed after a decision was taken to elect delegates to the convention. Realising he had no broad organisational base, Jabavu withdrew his support.

Nevertheless, in what was a major step towards the formation of a permanent African national political organisation, the South African Native Convention met in a schoolroom in Bloemfontein's Waaihoek township from 24 to 26 March 1909.

Despite the emotive issues at stake, the mood of the conference reflected the mild approach of that generation of African politicians. Opposition to the draft Act was calmly – even respectfully – set out. For, even in the middle of the African population's greatest crisis, its leaders still found it necessary to try to prove their loyalty and suitability to participate in politics. Thus, in typically 'respectable' tones, the Prime Minister of the Orange River Colony was thanked for 'giving the delegates the opportunity to hold the meeting and to exercise free speech' and expressions of loyalty were conveyed to the Governor, the High Commissioner and King Edward VII.

A call to the British Government

The convention itself was modelled on the white National Convention, with most of the proceedings of the first two days – discussion of the draft Act – held behind closed doors. By Friday 26 March, two sets of resolutions that summed up feelings towards the Act were released. The first dealt with the opinion of Africans in the colonies and the second with the future relationship between the protectorates and the Union.

Dealing with the future of Africans in the colonies, the convention agreed that union was 'essential, necessary and inevitable'. But it also pointed out that the draft Act had failed in its most fundamental purpose – to promote the progress and welfare of all British subjects in South Africa. The colour bar constituted an injustice and it was up to the British Government, to which blacks owed their loyalty, to ensure that a constitution that allowed all South

Africans 'full and equal rights' was drafted. Failure to do this would leave blacks at the mercy of a white government in which northern Afrikaners would be well represented.

As far as the protectorates were concerned, delegates felt that the record of the northern colonies in their dealings with Africans did not inspire confidence. It would therefore be preferable, they suggested, for the protectorates to remain under direct British control.

Jabavu's Cape Native Convention met in King William's Town on 7 and 8 April 1909 – and although its main purpose was to discuss the protection of the Cape African franchise, opposition to the terms of union differed little from that expressed at the South African Native Convention. Agreeing that attempts to deprive Africans of their rights would be fought 'to the end', the conference decided as a first step to send petitions to both the Cape Parliament and the National Convention, even though it was well aware that Cape politicians, almost to a man, had swung their weight behind the proposals of the National Convention. And so, with the pleas and protests of both congress and convention falling on deaf ears in southern Africa, preparations were made to take the fight abroad . . . .

A mission to London

In July 1909 an 'open letter' from southern Africa found its way to the desks of more than 1 000 British politicians.

Its author was William Schreiner, a Cape lawyer and brother of novelist Olive Schreiner, and its contents echoed the fears of the region's growing African middle-class communities. With their protests against the racist provisions of the draft South Africa Act having being rejected – even by politicians whom they thought they could trust – representatives of the African and coloured communities had given up the fight at home. Only the British Government they now believed, could help them secure a brighter political future . . . .

Schreiner's document, entitled 'An Appeal to the Parliament and Government of Great Britain and Ireland', was both eloquent and prophetic – and among the concerns it voiced were:

● the 'evil effect' the denial of human rights would eventually have on white South Africans;
● the fact that the 22 000 black voters – more than all the voters in Natal – had not been counted in allotting the proportion of Cape members in the proposed South African Parliament;
● that the interests of blacks in the native territories and the protectorates might not be properly safeguarded under a Union Parliament.

The contents of the appeal had been leaked on 14 May, and this, coupled with the news that Schreiner intended leading an African and coloured delegation to London, caused great concern in Cape political circles. It led to a high-level campaign – orchestrated by Prime Minister John Xavier Merriman himself – to scuttle the mission. Merriman's crusade involved the discrediting of delegates, the elevation of minor black opponents of the delegation into figures of national importance and spying on Schreiner. Indeed, so seriously did Merriman regard the threat posed by the man who had once been Prime

Jabavu's college

Its official name was the South African Native College but to many Africans in the eastern Cape it was simply: *i koliji ka Jabavu* (Jabavu's college). And in many ways it was . . . .

For 10 years John Tengo Jabavu put as much into the scheme for the establishment of a black institute of higher education as he had contributed to the development of early African politics. He travelled thousands of kilometres, addressed countless meetings and wrote hundreds of letters of appeal. He was the chief publicist, assembler of funds and treasurer of what became the Inter-State Native College Scheme. Indeed, the college earmarked for Alice in the eastern Cape quickly became his obsession.

Yet the idea for the project was stolen from his political rivals, the South African Native Congress. And not even the grave political crises in which African society found itself in the first two decades of the 20th century could heal the bitterness this 'hijacking' engendered. In 1902 the congress had made the first significant move into the field of higher education when it unveiled ambitious plans to establish a 'native college' in memory of Queen Victoria who had died the previous year. But because its fundraising appeals were aimed at blacks only, the Memorial Scheme struggled to get off the ground.

At the end of 1905, however, Godfrey Lagden's South African Native Affairs Commission, having called for tougher segregation measures between blacks and whites, tried to soften the blow by announcing its own scheme for a 'native college'. Jabavu was invited to serve on the organising committee – and backed by the Cape Government and many influential whites as well as Africans, the Inter-State Native College Scheme surged ahead of its rivals.

In 1916 the South African Native College was officially opened – a triumph for the political 'moderates' of that era. Ironically, in later decades, as the University of Fort Hare, it provided the academic training for some of Africa's most famous nationalists – men such as Robert Mugabe, Nelson Mandela and Robert Sobukwe . . . .

THE EXECUTIVE *board of the Inter-State Native College Scheme. Jabavu, its most active member, is standing fifth from left in the back row.*

IN 1909 *William Schreiner, seated in the centre, a former Prime Minister of the Cape Colony, led a delegation of African and coloured representatives to London to protest the racist provisions of the draft South Africa Act. Others in the picture are, seated left to right: John Tengo Jabavu; Abdullah Abdurahman; Walter Rubusana; Matt Fredericks. Back row left to right: Thomas Makipela; J Gerrans; Daniel Dwanya; D J Lenders.*

Minister of the colony that he instructed Sir Henry de Villiers, the president of the National Convention, to spy on him when he left for London on 16 June 1909.

African and coloured leaders, meanwhile, found the planning of the trip more difficult than they imagined it would be. It quickly became obvious that a lack of funds would force them drastically to reduce the size of their delegations. Bickering over matters of minor importance also marred preparations. The South African Native Convention, for instance, which had hoped to send a delegation of 12, ended up with a three-man team – and a row between Walter Rubusana, who was chosen to go, and his long-time friend Alan Kirkland Soga, who was not.

Even Abdullah Abdurahman's well-organised African Political Organisation (APO) encountered problems. A group of dissidents led by a former chairman, John Tobin, and Francis Peregrino, a newspaper editor and leader of the Coloured People's Vigilance Association, hit out at their decision to go to London. Equal rights would come about only through the intervention of sympathetic local whites, they argued. Although both men represented minority viewpoints, their claims were readily used by the government delegation to discredit the APO.

But despite these setbacks, the last of an eight-man deputation arrived in Britain on 17 July 1909 to assist Schreiner in the fight against the constitution. They were: Abdurahman, Matt Fredericks, D J Lenders, Rubusana, Thomas Mapikela, Daniel Dwanya, John Tengo Jabavu and J Gerrans. Ranged against them was a delegation including political heavyweights such as Sir Henry de Villiers, Merriman, Jacobus Sauer, Leander Jameson, Louis Botha and Jan Smuts.

Schreiner, who arrived first, quickly cemented contacts with sympathisers inside and outside parliament. By the time the others joined him he had already won the support of parliamentarians Sir Charles Dilke, Keir Hardie, Ramsay MacDonald, Frederick MacKarness and G P Gooch – and of pressure groups such as the London Missionary Society. But this was not enough. Despite strenuous lobbying they could not stir up the massive public outrage they had hoped for.

Without wide-scale opposition, the British Government saw no need to wreck what it regarded as a remarkable reconciliation between English and Afrikaners. This was borne out on 22 July when the Colonial Secretary, Lord Crewe, heard representations from Rubusana, Mapikela, Abdurahman, Lenders and Fredericks. Although he received them courteously, he refused to give any assurance that the colour-restrictions would be removed from the draft Act.

Only seven peers took part in the debate in the House of Lords on 27 July. The Archbishop of Canterbury was by far the most outspoken of the six who supported the Bill. It was justifiable, he said, to impose on the black people in South Africa restrictions and limitations that 'correspond with those which we impose on our children', because the overwhelming majority of the South African population would for generations to come be quite unfit to share equal citizenship with whites.

Said Abdurahman later: 'It was the most hypocritical piece of humbug I have ever listened to.'

Although by then it had become apparent that there was little hope of major amendments to the Act, Schreiner and his deputation struggled on. In the run-in to the debate in the Commons, they addressed many meetings and wrote numerous letters to the Press. Finally, on 5 August, the Labour Party indicated that it would move amendments to the racial provisions in the constitution.

But it was a small consolation – on 19 August the South Africa Bill was enacted in the House of Commons – and in a final twist, Schreiner later became the South African High Commissioner in Britain.

'Africa for the Africans . . .'

Their battle-cry was 'Africa for the Africans', their message was a popular mixture of politics and gospel – and for more than two decades they articulated the aspirations of thousands of Africans.

They were a group of 'independent' church ministers, thrust into political leadership in the 1890s as a result of white missionary attitudes, economic developments (especially the discovery of gold on the Rand) and the over-cautious approach of African pressure groups in the eastern Cape.

Their adherents numbered among them the first Africans to have received formal (missionary) education – and this, coupled with religious training and everyday contact with whites, led them to expect that once they had acquired a suitable level of 'civilisation' they would be assimilated as equals into white society. But this did not happen. Instead, they found that the Church simply mirrored the racism in other areas of white society. For although missionary churches preached equality, African ministers were regarded as inferiors with no immediate prospects of attaining full equality. The backlash to paternalistic white control of the Church gave rise to independent African churches.

The first breakaway occurred in 1884 in Tembuland in the eastern Cape soon after Nehemiah Tile, a young Methodist preacher, had been accused by his white superiors of participating in politics, encouraging hostility towards magistrates, holding a public meeting on a Sunday and donating an ox at the circumcision of the heir to the Tembu paramountcy. Tile resigned and set up his own church, the Tembu National Church, with its headquarters at the Tembu royal kraal. Despite efforts to expand, Tile's congregation made little impact beyond its tribal base.

The next, and far more significant walkout came eight years later – and it was led by Mangena Mokone, a former sugar-cane labourer and domestic worker, who became a preacher after being baptised by the Wesleyans in 1874. Mokone made his move in 1892 after strenuously opposing a segregated Wesleyan Congress in Pretoria. With 20 followers he founded the Ethiopian Church – so called because he interpreted the biblical prophecy, 'that Ethiopia shall soon stretch out her hands unto God', as referring Africans.

Although operating from Pretoria initially, the Ethiopian Church quickly spread to other areas. But by far its biggest achievement was its unification in 1896 with the American-based African Methodist Episcopal (AME) Church. Ironically, unity with the Americans led to a split between Mokone and James Dwane, an outstanding eastern Cape religious leader whose defection to the separatists came as a blow to the Wesleyans. Sent to America to consolidate the union, Dwane had returned as superintendent of the South African branch of the AME Church.

The formation of other independent churches led to concern in missionary circles and fear among the white public that these developments were a prelude to their being driven into the sea. In the northern colonies especially, American missionaries were criticised for instilling false hopes in the masses.

Although the cradle of modern African politics was the eastern Cape, it was among the squalid compounds of the Transvaal gold mines that the movement made the biggest impact. Preaching a mixture of Gospel and, significantly, Africanist politics, separatist ministers found a willing flock among a workforce disillusioned with a political system that offered them not even the long-term prospect of equal rights. It was inevitable that they would be drawn to the movement.

Although the notion of a country for blacks, run by blacks – 'Africa for the Africans' – had wide appeal, especially among menial workers, it was not until the formation of the South African Native Congress in 1898 that the separatists were able to make major inroads in the more sedate eastern Cape. J T Jabavu was scathing in his reaction to the movement. Describing it as a 'dangerous delusion' that would backfire on blacks, his opposition was based on the grounds that it was 'incompatible with loyalty and peace' and that it preached that Africans should have nothing to do with white institutions.

Animosity between groups often erupted into violence. Said eastern Cape modernist Elijah Makiwane after his house had been burnt down by separatists: 'Those who refuse to join this movement are now called white men or Britons.'

But after the Jameson Raid in 1895 had hastened the split in black eastern Cape politics, separatists were readily welcomed into the ranks of the group which in 1898 would become the South African Native Congress. Certainly they played an important part in the formation in 1912 of the South African Native National Congress – the first national African political organisation.

JAMES DWANE (second from right) meets officials of the AME church in the USA. He later headed the South African branch of the church.

Bambatha's rebellion

'Shoot to kill', the army sharpshooters had been told – and throughout the morning the staccato sound of machine-guns, mixed with screams of dying men, echoed across a narrow valley in central Natal.

It was 10 June 1906 – and the whispered hopes of freedom of an embittered peasant population were being crushed by a white army's know-how – and its bullets.

For six weeks, an African chief called Bambatha had waged a 'war of liberation' from a forest hideout in the Natal midlands. Although his military manoeuvres were confined mostly to evading pursuing troops, his resistance led to a mixture of panic among whites and extravagant expectation among Africans. But a mass uprising did not materialise. On the night of 9 June the guerrillas, watched by army scouts, pitched camp at the entrance to the valley. By the early hours they were surrounded, and at dawn the air began to sing with bullets . . . .

More than 500 warriors died in the massacre at Mome Gorge, and later, in an ominous warning to other would-be rebels, the victors marched through the countryside with a bizarre trophy – the head of Bambatha.

The first rumblings of discontent started at the end of 1905 when the authorities introduced a new £1 poll tax on top of existing hut and dog taxes. Although, in theory, the tax affected all males over the age of 18, it was aimed primarily at the African peasantry. The authorities were well aware that the only way Africans could accumulate enough to pay this new obligation was by working in the labour-hungry white farming and mining sectors. The tax became payable for the first time on 1 January 1906, and although there were many rumours of African discontent over the new measures, Natal newspapers stilled white fears with reports that the black population was paying up well. But panic set in on 20 January when a white farmer in the Camperdown district was murdered shortly after he had taken his labourers to Pietermaritzburg to pay their taxes. Despite renewed assurances from the media and the Secretary of Native Affairs, reports of black 'insolence' began filtering in from all around the country. Furthermore, when Afri-

cans began killing off their white-coloured animals and destroying European-made tools, whites needed no further proof that an uprising was imminent. Dozens of farmers began abandoning their holdings for the safety of the towns.

By the end of January 1906, opposition to the measures reached breaking point. And on 10 February two policemen were killed in a fracas which followed the refusal of 27 followers of a chief called Mveli to pay the tax. The ringleaders of the alleged killers were prominent members of the small but highly vocal Ethiopian church movement. Convinced that 'agitators' were behind the flare-up, the angry white community found a ready scapegoat in this separatist religious movement and called repeatedly for its banning.

Faced with growing hysteria in settler ranks, the government declared martial law and instructed the colony's most respected soldier, Colonel Duncan McKenzie, to restore order. McKenzie, a known hard-liner, tackled this task with relish. Indemnified by the martial law provisions, he marched through the territory, administering corporal punishment to Africans reported to be insolent or restless, sacking chiefs, burning crops and kraals and confiscating cattle. In April, 12 men accused of complicity in the killings of the policemen were captured, tried by court martial and executed. But more trouble was brewing . . . .

And it flared when Bambatha, the head of the small Zondi clan, returned to his homestead from a visit to Zululand to find that he had been sacked and replaced as chief by his uncle, Magwababa. Furious, he kidnapped the usurper and then fled into the nearby Nkandla Forest, where he was granted refuge by a clan of ironworkers and assegai-makers led by the 96-year-old Sigananda. Called upon by the government to arrest Bambatha and hand him over to the authorities, the old chief replied by throwing in his lot with the rebels. Aware that the majority of his compatriots regarded the Zulu royal house as the head of African society, Bambatha claimed the support of Dinuzulu, the son of Cetshwayo, the last Zulu king. Although Dinuzulu denied involvement, several promi-

UMVOTI MAGISTRATE *J W Cross explains the implications of a hut tax to African chiefs. Anger over taxes sparked a Zulu revolt in 1906.*

nent chiefs and hundreds of young warriors, convinced of an imminent wide-scale uprising, took to the bush in support of Bambatha. However, their crushing defeat on 10 June and the quick suppression of another rebel group in the Mapumulo district brought resistance to an end. More than 3 000 Africans and about 30 whites died in the fighting.

Dinuzulu was arrested and brought to trial in 1908 on charges of high treason, public violence, sedition and rebellion. Although defended by William Philip Schreiner, one of the Cape Colony's top lawyers, he was found guilty and sentenced to four years' imprisonment and a fine of £100. He was released in 1910 and exiled to the Transvaal.

Bambatha's rebellion was the last time – at least until the 1960s – that Africans resorted to armed insurrection. In the coming decades a new type of freedom-fighter – one who carried no weapons – would increasingly define the pace and tone of the black man's struggle for political and social fulfilment. In many ways, white supremacy was about to be tackled by a far more enduring opponent.

INSTEAD OF *arresting Bambatha – as instructed by the Natal authorities – 96-year-old Sigananda (above) threw in his lot with the rebels. This photograph was taken shortly after his arrest on 10 June 1906.*
AFTER KILLING *Bambatha, colonial troops hacked off the head (below right) of the dissident chief.*

AFTER MARTIAL LAW *had been declared in Natal, colonial troops burnt huts (above) and destroyed crops of suspected rebels.*

BAMBATA'S HEAD.

Original negative broken by order of the authorities.
Parts found and reproduced.

Fighting the 'demon of racialism'

With 'white union' in 1910 having shattered their hopes of equal rights,
African leaders began working feverishly to start an organisation that could 'peacefully' articulate
their political aspirations. The result was the South African Native National Congress.
But within seven years of its triumphant launch it was battling for survival – a victim of
its own naivity and the Union Government's increasingly hard-line segregationist policies.

ON A SWELTERING DAY in January 1912, more than 60 prominent African community leaders, watched by several hundred observers, gathered in Bloemfontein to take a decision that would change the course of South African history – to found the South African Native National Congress (SANNC), which became the African National Congress in 1923.

Although they were dressed conventionally in suits, frock-coats and top hats, their mission represented a sharp break with the past. Impatient with the notion that their best interests could be served by sympathetic whites, and mostly ineligible to take part in formal politics – only in the Cape did qualified Africans have the vote – they came together to start a united political organisation dedicated to creating national unity and defending the rights and privileges of Africans.

They were the products of mission school education and therefore mostly members of a small middle class who believed in equality of opportunity for all. But having hoped that the relatively liberal traditions of the Cape would be extended to the other three provinces, they discovered that the more repressive conditions of the Transvaal, the Orange Free State (OFS) and Natal were to be the norm. Before Union Africans had, in theory, been eligible for election to the Cape Parliament. But the South Africa Act of 1910 had removed this right, although 'qualified' Africans there were still entitled to the vote. Developments during the first two years of Union had confirmed the misgivings of those who had opposed the terms of Union – and there were fears that worse was to come.

The role of Pixley Seme

The conference was called by Pixley Ka Isaka Seme, a young attorney who, despite severe financial strains, had been educated at Columbia University in the USA and at Jesus College, Oxford. Seme was young and impatient, and believed by some of his older colleagues to be arrogant and impulsive. Soon after he returned to South Africa he was arrested for drawing a loaded revolver on a group of whites who had objected to his travelling in a first class train carriage. After being convicted of using a firearm in a threatening manner, he explained: 'Like all solicitors, I, of course, travel first class.' The incident was in sharp contrast to the behaviour of the more experienced African political leaders, such as the newspaper editor and author Sol T Plaatje, who often went to great lengths not to alienate their white sympathisers.

In 1911 Seme and three other foreign-educated lawyers, Alfred Mangena, Richard Msimang, and George Montsioa, held an inaugural conference to launch a national congress. It was called at a time of increased government attention to the demands of the right-wing *plattelanders* (literally, rural-dwellers) and the apparent eclipse of Cape liberals in Louis Botha's cabinet. Pandering to right-wing demands, the Botha Government had passed, in quick succession, the Natives' Labour Regulation Act (which made it an offence for Africans to break a labour contract), the

PIXLEY SEME, *an outspoken young lawyer, played a major role in the formation of the South African Native National Congress, the forerunner of the African National Congress.*

Mines and Works Act (the forerunner of job reservation) and the Dutch Reformed Church Act (which barred Africans from full membership).

All this meant that anxious African leaders were responsive to Seme's call to set up a 'native union'. Writing in 'Imvo Zabantsundu' ('Native Opinion') in October 1911, he made an impassioned plea for unity. Rejecting intertribal conflicts, he said: 'The demon of racialism must be buried and forgotten; it has shed among us sufficient blood. We are one people. These divisions, these jealousies, are the cause of all our woes and of all our backwardness and ignorance today.'

After three more months of intense planning the majority of the country's educated African elite were ready for unity. On 8 January 1912, in Bloemfontein, a crowd of several hundred – made up of delegates and observers – opened what was to become a landmark conference with a moving rendition of Tiyo Soga's hymn 'Lizalise Dinga Dingalako tixo We Nyaniso' ('Fulfil Thy Promise God of Truth'). Then Seme rose to speak: it was the first time, he said, 'so many elements representing different tongues and tribes ever attempted to cooperate under one umbrella'. And, tracing recent developments, he lashed out at a political system that he claimed was designed to make Africans hewers of wood and drawers of water. White people, he said, had formed a Union of South Africa. But it was a Union in which Africans had no voice in the making of laws and no part in their administration.

By any standards it was a stirring speech – and the proposal that 'delegates and representatives of the great native houses from every part of South Africa should establish the South African Native National Congress' received a standing ovation and was passed unanimously by the cheering delegates.

NATAL EDUCATIONIST *John Dube was a popular choice to head the SANNC. His political philosophy – African advancement through education – was shaped by the murder of his father by the Zulu king, Mpande.*

Dube becomes president

The election of office-bearers was a delicate matter. The future success of the organisation depended on the different regions and interests agreeing that they were satisfactorily represented. So although Dr Walter Rubusana, 54, of East London – a Congregational church minister, the only African ever to be elected to the Cape Provincial Council, and former president of the South African Native Convention (the first nationwide example of black political action) – was expected to win the presidency, the post was offered instead to another minister and schoolmaster, the Reverend John Dube, who although not present at the conference, had sent a message of support. Dube, who received part of his education in the USA where he became influenced by the ideas of black American educationist Booker T Washington, was felt to be more widely acceptable; the election of Rubusana would have made it impossible to attract supporters of his long-time opponent, John Tengo Jabavu, to congress. The fact that most delegates wanted to emphasise that future African political activity would not only be focused on the Cape – Dube was based in Durban – also counted in his favour. Rubusana was elected an honorary president, along with 22 chiefs; Plaatje secretary-general; Seme treasurer; Thomas Mapikela Speaker; and Montsioa recording secretary.

The conference then appointed a committee to draw up a constitution to provide an umbrella federation for all the scattered and weak African organisations, to serve as a fo-

WALTER RUBUSANA, *a member of the Cape Provincial Council, was overlooked for the presidency of the SANNC to placate supporters of his arch-foe, John Tengo Jabavu.*

Sol Plaatje – a South African giant

He was an author, an intellectual and a lobbyist who counted cabinet ministers among his friends. He spoke eight languages, edited three newspapers and wrote several books, including the classic 'Native Life in South Africa'. Yet Solomon Tshekisho Plaatje's formal education did not go beyond primary school.

He was born near Boshof in the Orange Free State in 1876 – a place he referred to bitterly as the 'Free' State throughout 'Native Life in South Africa' – and after attending school at a Berlin Mission near Barkly West in the northern Cape, went to Kimberley to be a letter carrier for the Post Office. Already able to speak Dutch, English and German, he studied several African languages and in 1898 became an interpreter and a clerk in the magistrate's court in Mafeking. During the siege he worked for several war correspondents, experience which stood him in good stead when he became editor of the English-Tswana newspaper 'Koranta ea Becoana' ('Bechuana Gazette'). In Mafeking he came to know Henry Burton, a lawyer willing to defend Africans in court, who later became Minister of Native Affairs. By 1910 he was also on good terms with John X Merriman, the last Prime Minister of the Cape Colony, and W P Schreiner, one of the four newly appointed 'native senators'.

But his greatest coup in the field of personal contact came in 1919 when he secured an interview with British Prime Minister, David Lloyd George. This came as a result of his involvement with the South African Native National Congress (SANNC). Plaatje played an important behind-the-scenes role in the establishment of the SANNC, and with his access to the leaders of the government, his concern for the rights of his fellow Africans, his fluency in the country's major languages and his capacity for hard work, he was an ideal choice for the post of the organisation's first general secretary.

After the passing of the Natives' Land Act in 1913 he travelled the country by bicycle to research the law's effects on the people and in 1914 was part of the SANNC deputation to England to appeal against the Act. He began writing 'Native Life in South Africa' while on board ship.

In 1917 Plaatje, who had spent the previous three years campaigning against the Land Act in Britain, returned to South Africa. But two years later he headed a second (unsuccessful) SANNC delegation to Britain. He also visited the USA and Canada. In Britain his contacts made a meeting with Lloyd George possible. Plaatje told Lloyd George that blacks were helpless in their own country because they were voteless. 'Great Britain has thrown us away', he said. Britain had intervened when blacks in the Belgian Congo were oppressed but if ever there was a case which called for protection, it was the case of natives in South Africa who had been told they had no right to buy or lease land in their own country, he said.

Lloyd George replied that he had listened with 'some distress', but reminded Plaatje that Britain was unable to intervene in the internal affairs of a self-governing dominion. However, he said he had been convinced it was a case which ought to be carefully considered by the South African Government.

He wrote to General Jan Smuts, referring to the 'deep sense of injustice' felt by the deputation: They . . . asked what was the use of calling upon them to obey the law and observe constitutional methods . . . if they were given no adequate means for doing so?' Lloyd George concluded this correspondence with a strong hint that Smuts should see the deputation. 'I am sure that you will be impressed by them, and I am equally sure that you will be able to remove the impression which seems to rest there at present, that they cannot get people in authority to listen to them with sympathy.'

But apart from his letters there was little Lloyd George could do, and while the meeting and the Prime Minister's sympathetic response represented a triumph for Plaatje, the deputation returned home empty-handed.

Plaatje died in Johannesburg in 1932, spending the last nine years of his life campaigning for African rights in South Africa and doing a great deal of writing in Tswana, including translating two Shakespeare plays, 'Julius Caesar' and 'The Comedy of Errors'.

IN 1920, *pamphlets such as the one below urged Americans to 'come and hear' South African lobbyist Sol Plaatje (above) deliver 'thrilling' accounts of the plight of Africans in his home country.*

COME AND HEAR
Mr. SOL
PLAATJE
Of Kimberley, South Africa

Gives thrilling account of the condition of the Colored Folk in British South Africa.

The story has gripped nearly a thousand audiences in England, Scotland, Canada & USA

IT WILL THRILL YOU

Bethel A. M. E. Church
West 132nd Street, bet. Lenox and 5th Aves.

Sunday, March 13, 11 a. m.
THE BLACK MAN'S BURDEN IN SOUTH AFRICA

Friday, March 18th, 8 p. m.
THE BLACK WOMAN'S BURDEN IN SO. AFRICA

Interspersed with Quaint African Music sung in his own native tongue

Free Will Offering for Brotherhood Work among the South African Tribes

ADMISSION FREE
COME EARLY AND AVOID THE CRUSH !!
Dr. MONTROSE W. THORNTON, Pastor

rum for all African viewpoints to present grievances to the Union Parliament, to mobilise sympathetic white public opinion and to rally political pressure on behalf of all the African people in South Africa.

In accepting the presidency, Dube said there was a pressing need for political vigilance in the pursuit of emancipation and African rights. But, naively, he also came out in favour of a policy of 'hopeful reliance on the sense of common justice and love of freedom so innate in the British character'. He added that 'perseverance, patience, reasonableness, the gentlemanly tendencies of Africans, and the justice of their demands' would eventually break down colour prejudice and 'even force our enemies to be our admirers and our friends'.

After papers were read on topics as diverse as marriage and divorce, schools and churches, current issues of labour, segregation and the land issue, delegates sang John Knox Bokwe's 'Give a Thought to Africa' and dispersed to carry news of the congress across the country.

Not a single white newspaper reported the event.

Dube, especially to white audiences, stressed the moderation, gradualism and 'responsibility' of the new body, and justified its existence in terms of Christian morality. 'We feel,' he said in a speech reported in the 'Cape Times', 'that the time has come when we should have some measure of legislative representation, some way of making our influence felt in the law-making powers. Our progress in the Gospel life and its accompanying civilisation demands it; our liberties and rights are taxed and governed bodies are not safe without it.' Both the Dutch and the British, he said, had fought and died for freedom. Surely they would not deny Africans comparable privileges, the right to improve themselves and to labour in freedom and peace in their native land?

The constitution

These objectives were formalised in the constitution of 1919. Among its aims were:

● to express the opinions of Africans and to formulate a standard policy on 'Native Affairs' for the benefit of the Union Parliament;

● to inform white legislative bodies and the white public generally of African needs and aspirations;

● to educate Africans on their rights, duties and obligations and to promote mutual help and a feeling of brotherhood between them;

● to discourage racialism and tribal feuds;

● to propose laws for the benefit of Africans and to lay these before the government for adoption;

● to agitate 'by just means' for the removal of the colour bar in politics, education and industry, and for equitable representation of Africans in 'those public bodies vested with legislative powers';

● to record African grievances and to seek their redress by constitutional means, obtaining legal and financial aid when necessary.

The constitution made it clear congress would try to achieve its goals by constitutional means, including resolutions, protests, deputations, pamphlets, petitions, passive resistance and propaganda.

The land issue

Immediately after the founding conference, congress became preoccupied with the issue of land, and the government's determination to fix the terms on which blacks and whites would live in South Africa. Only three years after the end of the South African War, the South African Native Affairs Commission recommended in 1905 that certain areas be reserved only for Africans 'with a view to finality'. After Union in 1910 a parliamentary select committee proposed legislation that included limits on African landownership and on the number of Africans allowed to squat on white-owned land as sharecroppers.

The result was a 'Squatters Bill', which was bitterly opposed by Africans as well as a few influential whites. A paper on the Bill had been read at the Bloemfontein conference, in which it was stated that, if passed, its effect 'could only be to turn the native population of South Africa into wanderers and pariahs in the land of their birth'.

In March 1912, at a protest meeting called by the Cape Peninsula Natives' Association, speaker after speaker concluded that the Bill would benefit only the white mine-owners and farmers, because it would force Africans off the land into white hands on terms that would be the equivalent of slavery. It would be opposed to the last, said the president of the association, Thomas Zini, because it was a gigantic invasion of African liberties. It would adversely affect hundreds of thousands of African families who, until then, had lived on landed estates and farms, paid rents to the owners, and tilled the soil for a subsistence, happy and contented in their way of life. Zini said that if the 'mischievous proposition' became law, thousands of families would 'be driven into locations with the sole object of forcing them to work in the mines or on the farms'.

In the same month, congress secretary Plaatje, who had excellent contacts among government ministers, arranged for a delegation to meet Minister of Native Affairs Henry Burton and his secretary, Edward Dower, to discuss the issue of Passes for women and the Squatters Bill. Burton said that while the last thing the government wanted was injustice to Africans, it had to be realised that 'those who battle for their rights must exercise patience'. He promised, however, to adopt 'a most reasonable attitude' when these matters were discussed in parliament.

In the end the Bill was dropped, mainly because of pressure from certain white interests, particularly the influential large absentee landlords, who stood to lose most from it. But Plaatje and Dube believed their own representations had counted as well, and being keen to establish the congress among the people, told them so.

But in April 1913 a far more draconian Bill was rushed through parliament by J W Sauer, the new Minister of Native Affairs – and this time no representations could stop it. In less than two months the Natives' Land Act was law – it was signed by the Governor-General on 16 June – and its provisions laid some of the foundations of the bitterness that still bedevils South Africa's future prospects.

Essentially, the Land Act established the principle of territorial segregation under which Africans and whites were to acquire and occupy land in separate, designated areas. But it was also an attempt to suppress squatting and other unauthorised occupation by Africans of Crown and private lands, and to outlaw certain forms of tenancy on white-owned farms.

The law restricted African landownership to the so-called 'scheduled areas', about 10,5-million morgen or 7,5 percent of the total land area of South Africa of 142-million morgen. Africans were to be barred from buying land except from other Africans or in existing tribal Reserves. And although provision was made for more land to be added after a commission under the chairmanship of Judge William Beaumont had reported, nothing was done until Barry Hertzog's Natives' Trust and Land Act of 1936 increased the maximum African areas to just over 13 percent.

The census of 1911 had shown the total population of the Union was 5 973 394 people, of which 4 019 006 were Africans, 1 276 242 whites, 525 943 coloureds and 152 203 Indians. The Act therefore apportioned 7,5 percent of the land to 67,3 percent of the population. Most of the area set aside for Africans was in overcrowded 'Reserves'. Africans were excluded from the areas demarcated as white, and could stay there only as labourers even though nearly a million people lived on white-owned land as tenants, sharecroppers and labour tenants. The Act had its most drastic consequences in the OFS, where the system of 'sowing on the halves' – the practice of African sharecroppers giving half their produce to the farmer in return for land – was made illegal. It left the tenant with an unpalatable choice of either changing his status from that of reasonably self-sufficient peasant to labourer, or taking his family and his stock and leaving.

The government's determination to deprive Africans of any status other than that of labourer in white areas was made clear by the Act's definition of labourer: it excluded everyone, such as the squatters, who did not give at least 90 days' service a year. People who paid rent or any other 'valuable consideration' for the land were also excluded from the definition.

The fight against the Land Act

The SANNC reacted to the passage of the Bill with shock. It struck at the heart of its belief in both a common society and the innate decency of the legislators. Said a deeply upset Plaatje: 'If anyone had told us at the beginning of 1913 that a majority of members of the Union parliament was capable of passing a law like the Natives' Land Act, whose object is to prevent natives from ever rising above the position of servants to whites, we would have regarded that person as a fit subject for the lunatic asylum.' However, congress leaders also realised that it was an issue that affected almost every section of the African population and therefore could be used to attract support for their organisation. In May, shortly before the Bill became law, a delegation went to Cape Town and had four interviews with Sauer who, ironically, until the passing of the Act, had been regarded by both whites and Africans as a 'friend of the African'. But protests were ignored and the Bill was gazetted on 20 June 1913.

The effects were immediate. Delegates to the July conference of the congress complained bitterly that farmers were using the new law to rid themselves of unwanted

'FRIEND OF THE NATIVE', *Jacobus Sauer, was the mastermind behind the Natives' Land Act that set aside 7,5 percent of the total land area of South Africa for the exclusive occupation of the African majority.*

tenants. At first many OFS Africans did not realise the new provisions applied throughout the country and thought they would be able to find new homes for their families and stock in the Transvaal. But as they trekked off in the middle of a bitter winter, slowly the realisation dawned that there was nowhere to go.

On a journey from Kimberley to Johannesburg by bicycle, Plaatje spoke to bands of refugees and saw scenes that he remembered for the rest of his life. He recounted the experiences of a man called Kgobadi, whom he met in the OFS. The farmer on whose land Kgobadi had worked wanted him and his wife and oxen to work on the farm for 30 shillings a month. When Kgobadi, who had been making more than £100 a year, refused, he was ordered to leave. His baby had been ill at the time he was evicted and, two days after being transferred from house to draughty ox-wagon, had died. The child, Kgobadi told Plaatje, had to be buried on stolen land in the dark 'lest the proprietor of the spot should surprise them in the act'. Plaatje observed: 'Even criminals dropping straight from the gallows have an undisputed claim to six feet of ground in which to rest their criminal remains. But under the cruel operation of the Land Act little children, whose only crime is that God did not make them white, are sometimes denied that right in their ancestral home.'

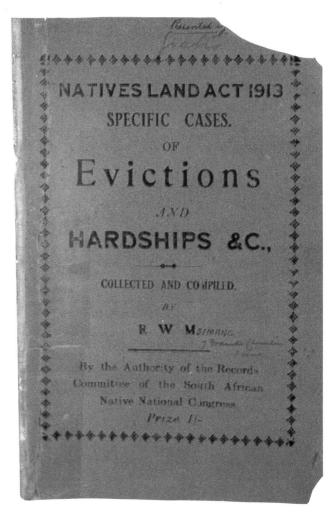

THE MOVEMENT *of Africans to 'white' urban areas was strictly regulated. Those without a 'Native Labour Passport' (left) were quickly sent back to their designated Reserves or white farms.*

LAWYER *Richard Msimang compiled a weighty document (below) of evictions and hardships suffered by Africans as a result of the Natives' Land Act.*

Acting on behalf of the congress, Richard Msimang drew up a list of evictions, including the details of livestock owned by those who had been uprooted. He found that in the OFS evictions occurred at 10 days' notice. Hundreds of people were trekking into Bechuanaland. The evictions were designed solely to obtain forced labour, said Msimang. Not only unable to acquire land, African communities, he added, also lost homes, schools and churches without compensation, and were reduced to a state of 'vagabondage' with no prospect of permanent settlement.

Having studied the effects of the Land Act, the congress decided to organise a protest against the legislation within South Africa and, if necessary, to appeal directly to the King and the British Parliament. In terms of the Act of Union, legislation passed in South Africa was still subject to the Royal Assent. In practice this was regarded as a formality, and the congress would have realised this. But an appeal to Britain was the only constitutional option open, and congress decided to take it.

In a petition to Botha, Dube said congress did not protest against the principle of separation 'so far as it can be fairly and practically carried out'. But clearly the aim of the law, he said, 'was to compel service by taking away the means of independence and self-employment. This compulsory service at reduced wages and high rents will not be separation, but an intermingling of the most injurious character of both races.' And he added: 'We have seen our people driven away from the places dear to them as the inheritance of generations, to become wanderers on the face of the earth. We have seen our rents raised to the point of desperation. We have seen many of our people, who by their frugality, have laid by a little money in the hope of buying a small piece of land where they might make a home for their families and leave something for their children now told their hopes are in vain – that no European is now permitted to sell or lease land to a native.' Dube asked that the Act be amended to allow land to be sold to Africans until after the Beaumont commission had reported, that sharecropping be allowed, and that an African nominated by the congress sit on the commission. His appeal, however, was ignored.

Congress made a series of appeals to Botha, to Francois Malan (Sauer's successor) and to parliament. Dube described the new law as 'class legislation, pure and simple', and added that he did not expect parliament to add a single acre to African areas while Africans lacked political representation. And Plaatje, summing up the government's lack of response to congress petitions, said: 'The lengthy official arguments, so far from promising relief to the native sufferers under the Land Act, may be summed up in five short words – give up going to England.' So, not very optimistically, the delegation sailed in the middle of May 1914.

They were right to restrain their hopes. The meeting with the Colonial Secretary, Lewis Harcourt, was not a success. He was determined to respect the precedents of self-government within the empire, asked no questions, took no notes and when told about the Act's severe impact, said he had the assurance of Botha to the contrary.

A 'whites-only' war
The 1914 conference of the SANNC was in session when the First World War broke out. Responding with a sustained show of loyalty and patriotism, delegates immediately decided to suspend all public criticism of the government,

and assured Pretoria of African support during the crisis. Rubusana was instructed to convey to the Minister of Defence, Jan Smuts, a congress offer to raise 5000 troops to serve in German South West Africa. But a less-than-keen Smuts replied that the war had originated among the white people of Europe, and that the government did not want to use citizens 'not of European descent' in combat. Nevertheless the congress supported a national relief fund for the war effort, and assisted the Department of Native Affairs to recruit Africans as a labour force for the South West African campaign. Despite their determination to be loyal, however, the Africans were hurt deeply by the attitude of the Defence Ministry, and they saw their loyalty in sharp contrast to the Boer rebellion in the Transvaal.

The Beaumont commission, meanwhile, was touring the country, hearing evidence from Africans and whites and trying to find areas that could be added to the Reserves without unduly upsetting the whites. In their evidence, members of the congress emphasised the importance of racial harmony, discussing with the commission the principle of segregation, of which there was a wide range of opinion, even within the congress itself. While one faction of the SANNC objected strongly to laws that established discrimination among British subjects, others indicated a preparedness to accept defined rural areas for Africans – provided they had political representation. This led to a great deal of soul-searching within the organisation – the chief problem being that, although the majority of members instinctively disliked the Land Act, they were forced to accept its political reality.

In 1916 the saga of broken promises continued when the Beaumont commission, amid congress accusations of having failed to fulfil official promises, reported that it was too late to define large compact areas for Africans. This was

'There is winter in the Natives' Land Act...'

Shortly after the Land Act of 1913 was gazetted, the Beaumont commission toured the Union to hear evidence from Africans and whites – and to try to establish how African Reserves could be enlarged. But the suffering caused by the provisions of the Act – reflected starkly in the testimony of Africans – became a dominant theme of its sittings....

● In a statement to the commission on behalf of the Heidelberg District of the South African Native National Congress, T M Dambuzu said: 'The Natives' Land Act breaks our people and puts them back in the rearing of their stock and ruins what they term their bank. It causes our people to be derelicts and helpless. We beg the Commission to approach the government and make our grievance clear and find a haven of refuge for our oppressed. There is winter in the Natives' Land Act. In winter the trees are stripped and leafless....'

● The Reverend J D Goronyane of Thaba Nchu in the OFS said: 'Whenever the government is determined to do away with the native people or to destroy them, they generally adopt a plan of removing them from their original homes.'

● Pastor M K Mancobo of Knysna told the commission: 'Owing to our vagrant condition year after year and the absence of any security of tenure, we are unable to erect substantial dwellings capable of sheltering us and our little ones from rain, wind and cold. The occupation of the tumble-down dwellings to which we are condemned has had a marked effect on our health. Also, it has never been practicable to make provision for education. Requests to landlords for permission to erect schools are met with refusal, notwithstanding that in some cases we lease land and in others sow on half shares. On top of this, when the landlord wishes to get rid of a tenant he has to go, however unwilling, and leave behind him, without compensation, any improvements he may have effected in the way of dwellings....'

● Headman Silas Mankuroane said: 'People who are getting married now can get no land to plough in the Reserve owing to its scarcity.'

● 'This law has caused us to shed tears,' said an angry Chief Kristian Lutayi of Empangeni. 'The government makes us pay 14 shillings per hut per annum as a tax, but the farmers make us pay even up to £6 per annum and that happens in the case of natives who earn no more than £1 per month as wages. Is the government merely a government in name? Is it not a Government to whom we can appeal for protection?'

● And on the same theme, Chief Sandanezwe of Dundee added: 'This Act seems to us like a one-edged knife – its cuts a big piece off the native and is very gentle with the European....'

White farmers, MPs and magistrates also had strong views on the Land Act and did not hesitate to tell the commission of them.

● Said J G Keyter MP: 'There are certain natives who have come here and who absolutely refuse to be servants. They are fairly well-to-do and they want a part of a farm to sow on shares. They have their youngsters to look after their stock and they themselves are free to go about and do what they like. They will be affected in so far they will have to become servants. They will be no loss at all.'

● And farmer J M Buijs added: 'On some farms there are too many natives and on some, I am sorry to say, the farmers allow the natives to farm.... In our district we have no room for a native Reserve – our land would be too valuable to put natives on.'

● Winburg magistrate R N Harley told the commission: 'With increasing stocks and herds, the native has become less... inclined to be a servant and more... inclined to be the semi-independent nomad, working only when his crops demand it and loafing the rest of the time, while the farmer has... difficulty in obtaining servants. This system, encouraged by the whites and tolerated by the government, has instilled into the native the belief that he has an equal right with the whites to the hire and purchase of land. This doctrine is openly taught by the native papers.'

quickly followed by the introduction of the Native Administration Bill, designed to confirm the principle of territorial segregation and to establish a uniform 'Native policy' throughout South Africa. It gave the Governor-General the right to legislate by proclamation in the African areas, offered residents in the Reserves a voice in their own affairs through Native Councils and made provision for the establishment of special courts for Africans. Another section of the Bill took into account Africans living outside the Reserves. Eight categories could do so – provided they served white interests.

African reaction was antagonistic. Giving evidence before a parliamentary select committee, members of the Natal Native Congress, a branch of the SANNC, stressed their dislike of the provision allowing the Governor-General to govern by proclamation and instead urged that the Cape franchise be extended throughout the country. Finally, in a call that would be echoed throughout the ensuing decades, they asked for a national convention of representatives of all races to decide the country's future.

The Native Administration Bill was eventually dropped, partly because white interests had argued it should be postponed until after the war, and partly because it was thought it might be difficult to apply in the Cape because of the qualified franchise. But the tensions it raised among Africans were exacerbated by a speech made by the influential Smuts at the Savoy Hotel in London in May 1917. It was useless, he said, to try to govern blacks and whites the same way. Native policy was designed to keep white and African apart as much as possible 'in our institutions, land ownership, in forms of government, and in many other ways. As far as possible the forms of political government will be such that each will be satisfied and developed according to his own proper lines.'

The end of the war brought little relief to Africans. Wartime expansion, which had drawn many into the workforce for the first time, had fallen off. And while well-organised and skilled white workers were able to exert pressure, including strikes, to obtain their demands, low-paid African workers, tied by the Pass laws and their labour contracts, had no legal means of putting pressure on their employers.

IN 1913, Natal Supreme Court judge Sir William Beaumont headed a commission that sought ways of expanding existing African Reserves. But it was a wasted exercise: whites, generally, were unwilling to allow more land to be set aside for African occupation.

But despite the dangers, a wave of protests swept through the African community (see page 320)

The SANNC too was feeling restless. Thwarted on the land issue, convinced the country's African policy was a reflection of a racially prejudiced parliament, its leaders increasingly began to demand representation in parliament. Various factors – including the democratic speeches made by Britain's Lloyd George and President Woodrow Wilson of the USA, the loyalty of Africans during the war, and a letter of support from Lloyd George's secretary to Plaatje in 1917 – had led to new optimism that Britain would intervene on behalf of the African population.

When demands that an African be included in the South African peace delegation to Versailles in 1919 were ignored by the government, congress decided to send its own mission, which on arrival called for a royal commission to adjust land allocations, asked for the establishment of free institutions for all, and for the extension of the vote to all Africans in South Africa. But although Lloyd George received the delegation sympathetically, the mission was a failure and a watershed in congress history. It was the last time the organisation tried to get British intervention in South African affairs. It also ended a period in which congress was regarded as the champion of the black masses. It was seven years after the triumph of Bloemfontein, and the SANNC was set to slip into a long, desolate period of stagnation.

IN 1914, A SANNC delegation consisting of (left to right) Walter Rubusana, Thomas Makipela, John Dube, Sol Plaatje and Saul Msane travelled to Britain to convey to the British Government the strong African objections to the Natives' Land Act. However, Colonial Secretary Lewis Harcourt claimed there was nothing he could do: 'The day the deputation saw me the period of 12 months during which that Act could be disallowed on my recommendation had already expired,' he told the House of Commons.

Strife between brothers...

The early years of Union were marked by disunity and distrust within Afrikaner ranks.
The rebellion of 1914 when brother fought brother, the problem of poor whites and the dispute
over participation in the First World War resulted in Afrikaners becoming alienated from one another.
But in these turbulent times came a growing awareness of Afrikanerdom, expressed in a
Second Language Movement which boosted nationalism.

I N A HALL in the shadow of Cape Town's Groote Kerk, two Boer generals were preparing for a bitter show-down after many years of close friendship . . . .

One was former Boer leader Louis Botha – Prime Minister of the Union of South Africa, a tireless campaigner for reconciliation between English and Afrikaner and a master of political compromise. The other was the Orange Free Stater, Barry Hertzog, a fearless, outspoken watchdog of Afrikaner rights.

In a sense, both men were engaged in a fight for their political lives.

It was 20 November 1913 – summer in the western Cape – and a day of high tension as delegates of the governing South African Party (SAP) filed into the Hofmeyr Hall for a make-or-break congress. Three years after the triumph of Union, Afrikanerdom was locked in one of its periodic bouts of *broedertwis* (strife between brothers). And worse was to come . . . .

Yet on 21 May 1910 the future of the *volk* (people) could not have been brighter: after weeks of speculation, Herbert Gladstone, the Governor-General of soon-to-be-united South Africa, had invited their man, Botha, to form the new country's first government.

It was an inspired decision – guaranteed to win over to the cause of union at least some of the remaining pockets of uncommitted Afrikaners. Botha's credentials were impeccable. In both war and peace – as a soldier fighting British imperialism and as a politician preaching reconciliation – he had served Afrikanerdom with distinction. In addition, he shared with many of his white countrymen a passionate conviction that blacks should never be granted equality with whites. In a sub-continent undergoing rapid political change, this was a comforting thought to those whites.

So, on 31 May 1910, to a countrywide fanfare of flags, posters and thanksgiving services, Boer and Briton offi-

LOUIS BOTHA *during the First World War. His government's decision to declare war on Germany led to a rebellion by Afrikaner opponents of his administration.*

BARRY HERTZOG, *the founder of the National Party, attacked English 'fortune-hunters' (mine owners) who, he said, had no interest in South Africa apart from getting rich.*

cially shut the door on more than a century of bitter political rivalry to concentrate their efforts on building a new order – on a foundation of white dominance.

Blacks were in no position to challenge the might of the new state – and in pandering to the racial prejudices of their constituents, white politicians were ignoring – at their peril – the real threats to the stability of their Union: a poor white problem, aggravated by drought, unemployment and economic depression; growing labour militancy, and a small but vocal group of militant Afrikaners who had never lost sight of the ideal of a Boer-dominated republic. This error of judgment would cost the government dearly. For soon the poor and the disaffected, roused by the oratory of the republicans, would combine to spark a series of explosions which would shatter the fragile unity between English and Afrikaner and split Afrikanerdom down the middle . . . .

Hertzog quits

Two days after Union, Botha, whose administration consisted of a loose alliance of the dominant parties in pre-union Transvaal, Orange Free State (OFS), and the Cape, as well as some Natal Independents, called his first general election. Ranged against him were the predominantly English Unionist Party led by Leander Jameson, and Colonel Frederic Creswell's Labour Party. In September white South Africans went to the polls and returned 68 government-supporting MPs against 37 Unionists and five Labourites. But in a stunning setback to his reconciliation policies, Botha, standing in a mainly English-speaking constituency, was soundly beaten by the Unionist, Sir Percy FitzPatrick, author of 'Jock of the Bushveld'.

The storm clouds were already gathering when, 14 months after their election triumph, Botha supporters formally united to become the South African Party (SAP). With Botha, reconciliation had become an obsession – and it was not long before a distinct chill began to set in in relations between him and Hertzog. The crusty Free Stater's political views since Union had not changed – but to many Afrikaners Botha's stance had. Hertzog continued to attack English 'fortune-hunters' (an obvious reference to mine-owners) whom he claimed had no interest in South Africa save getting rich. And he still demanded 'absolute' equality between the English and Dutch languages. Although it boosted his stocks among Afrikaners, English-speakers regarded him as an ogre who wanted to grab total political control for the Boers.

And so it was left to Botha to reassure them. But the more he tried to quell English fears, the wider became the rift that opened between him and a significant section of the Afrikaner community.

Finally, in December 1912, just two days after another Hertzog broadside, the SAP lost an important by-election in Grahamstown and Botha lost his cool with the man he had once regarded as one of his most trusted lieutenants.

Conform or resign, the angry Prime Minister demanded. An unrepentant Hertzog refused. So, in order to dissolve the cabinet, Botha himself resigned – and when asked to form a new government, left out Hertzog. Support for Botha within the SAP caucus was overwhelming. Only

Sowing the seeds of apartheid

A former mine manager and his partner – a man fondly referred to by his supporters as 'Mr Segregation' – were among the architects of a political policy which after 1948 became apartheid.

At the time of Union in 1910 F H P Creswell and Wilfred Wybergh, the leading lights of the Labour Party, were already pushing for the type of segregationist policies which (to some extent) Daniel Malan would claim as his own after 1948.

Creswell, the Labour Party leader, had once managed a mine run almost entirely on white labour. This, he believed, was the only way to reduce growing white unemployment. But although his views were welcomed by white labour organisations, bosses were not enthusiastic. They preferred the cheap, passive black migrants.

Wybergh's contribution to the political debate around the Union's first general election was the advocacy of a geographical, political and social separation of white and black South Africans. However, his party's support for free education to university level, equal rights for women, generous old-age pensions, and for industrial diseases such as miner's phthisis to be brought into the ambit of Workmen's Compensation were policies ahead of their time.

The election manifesto of Botha and his allies was built around a promise of cementing the new-found unity between the two language groups. This, said Botha, meant placing 'the native question' above party politics; encouraging white and discouraging Asian immigration; language equality and mother-tongue instruction in schools; the development of the country's mineral resources; stable conditions for the mining industry and the promotion of agricultural expansion and land settlement.

Botha's most powerful backer in the Cape was John Xavier Merriman, the last Prime Minister of the colony and a man who had dearly hoped to be the first Prime Minister of the Union of South Africa. Although Merriman differed with the men from the north on the approach to 'the native problem', he nevertheless offered the government his support – as long as the country was run with clean government, economical financial administration and party traditions.

The main opposition for the new government was provided by the unashamedly pro-imperialist Unionist Party led by Dr Leander Starr Jameson, leader of the ill-fated Jameson Raid (see page 235).

Nevertheless, except for a more liberal 'native policy' – they believed that political rights had to be tied to the degree of 'civilisation' reached by Africans – the Unionists pushed policies which differed little from that of the government. Indeed, Jameson stressed that he was not opposed to Botha's policies – but rather that they were not being implemented. And the reason for this, he claimed, was that Botha, instead of leading, was being led by 'reactionaries' in the cabinet – an obvious reference to Hertzog.

Although the Unionists were comfortably beaten in the elections, the fact that they were able to draw most of the English vote was a shattering blow to Botha's dream of reconciliation.

the Free Staters supported Hertzog. However, it was not in the nature of the general to bow meekly to setbacks. After several months of testing the political climate, he resolved to take his fight to the highest level of SAP decision-making – its National Congress, scheduled for Cape Town on 20 and 21 November 1913.

The Free State delegation leapt straight into the attack after the congress had been opened. Christiaan de Wet, another Boer general, offered a brutally blunt solution to the impasse: he moved that Botha resign, and that Marthinus Steyn, a former Prime Minister of the Orange River Colony, be appointed leader of the party outside parliament with the power to nominate a new Premier.

Botha objected. His resignation, he said, would be a confession of guilt and weakness on his part. He added, however, that he had no personal quarrel with Hertzog and expressed the belief that even at that late stage a solution could still be found.

Hertzog replied immediately. On personal grounds, he said, he could give Botha his hand – but on political grounds he would have to withdraw it. It was deadlock. Finally, an amendment to De Wet's motion, 'that the meeting requests the government to proceed with the administration of the country', was easily carried.

Hertzog was out, but the real fight was only about to begin. On 7-9 January 1914, at the Ramblers Hall in Bloemfontein, 450 delegates decided to form a new party. But because some Hertzog supporters in the Transvaal believed that the split with the Botha supporters could still be healed, the Free State and Transvaal branches, led by Hertzog and Tielman Roos respectively, were officially launched only on 1 July.

The new party was called the National Party of South Africa, and it promised to represent the 'national convictions and aspirations of the South African people, under the guidance of God'; called on the two white races to form one nation, adding, however, that there should be mutual respect for language, morals and customs; and offered a 'native policy' which would strictly avoid any attempts at racial mixing. In September 1915, a Cape Branch was formed under the leadership of former dominee Daniel

Francois Malan, who was also chosen to edit the party's official newspaper, 'De Burger' ('The Citizen').

Roos and Malan were even more ardent nationalists than Hertzog. Roos was a strong supporter of republicanism and secession from the empire, while Malan, in contrast to Hertzog's desire for equal rights for English and Dutch, wanted Dutch dominance.

Although scorned intially by the powerful Afrikaner middle-class, the National Party found willing listeners among the unemployed and unskilled section of the community. Soon the Labour Party, which until then had regarded itself as the champion of the white worker, would have a powerful new rival . . . .

Labour pains

In 1913, the reconstituted Labour Party under the leadership of Creswell and Wilfred Wybergh was on the verge of an important political breakthrough as hundreds of Afrikaner workers, disillusioned with the policies of the Botha Government, began flocking into their ranks.

But within a year they would be flocking out again – lured by a fresh call to nationalism by new, 'purified' leaders of the *volk*. Thus ended another chapter in the story of South Africa's labour movement.

In many ways the tale of the South African worker in the early years of the 20th century is one of opportunities made – then betrayed. By 1910, countrywide trade union membership numbered little more than 10000, with the Transvaal Chamber of Mines, the largest employer of both black and white labour in the country, having to contend with barely a thousand unionised miners. Noted for their union-bashing and their relentless drive for profits, mine bosses tolerated no militancy among their workforce, and even though fatality rates were enormous they made little effort to improve the working conditions of their employees.

Yet the key to worker bargaining power – the massive army of unskilled African workers – was deliberately ignored. For as far as labour leaders were concerned the drawing of blacks into the bargaining process was an option too ghastly to contemplate. Because they constituted a cheap and passive workforce, whites regarded them as

A new nationalism: the 'discovery' of Afrikaans

In April 1905, when Gustav Preller, the assistant editor of *'De Volkstem'* ('The People's Voice') newspaper, published the first in a series of articles pleading for the 'professionalisation' of the Afrikaans language, few took him seriously: it was, after all, a call which had been made – and rejected – before.

In the 1870s, a similar appeal from Stephanus du Toit, a Paarl dominee who headed *Die Genootskap van Regte Afrikaners* (see page 196), had found little support outside the organisation's Paarl stronghold.

That the Du Toit campaign had failed was not surprising: to the majority of Boers, Afrikaans was a mish-mash of bastardised Dutch, English, Xhosa and Malayan words – *'Hotnotstaal'* (Hottentots' language) – and was therefore fit to be spoken only by coloured servants and very poor whites.

It was an attitude which remained unchanged for 30 years – until Preller began drawing thousands of Boers into a massive, organised crusade for the official recognition of the Afrikaans language.

Whether it was through astute reasoning, or just sheer luck is hard to ascertain – but Preller could not possibly have chosen a better time to launch his campaign.

In 1905 Boer society was in a crisis. The discovery of gold in 1886 (and the scramble for land which accompa-

nied it), war (particularly the effects of the 'scorched earth' tactics of the British) and drought had forced thousands of tenant farmers and small landowners off ground they had been working for decades. It led to a mass migration of Afrikaner have-nots from rural areas to towns. Illiterate, unskilled and therefore unwanted, this new class of urban poor began to pose a grave social and moral dilemma for municipal authorities, politicians and ministers of the Dutch Reformed Church.

The awesome effects of ghetto life were highlighted in many ways – by the rebellion of children against parental control; the exodus of hundreds of families from Dutch Reformed Churches to hand-clapping, foot-stomping Apostolic congregations; the abuse of liquor, and, worst of all, by increased social contact between white families and members of black communities.

Faced with a deepening crisis, leaders of the *volk* began searching for a new cause to entice their wayward compatriots back into the laager. What was needed was something with which both rich and poor could identify – and it was the perceptive Preller who provided the answer: the reinvention of Afrikaans as a white man's language.

The 30-year-old journalist's first step was to start infusing the Afrikaans of Du Toit, the 'poor whites' and the coloured servants with more Dutch words (to rid it of its 'coloured' taint). His next move was to launch an intensive newspaper campaign to sell the new, improved *volkstaal* (people's language).

It was not an easy task. Besides their old prejudices towards the language, many upper-class Afrikaners wanted nothing to do with a venture in which Preller, a man from a low-class background, was involved.

Nevertheless, he soldiered on – and in 1910 his attempts at rebuilding Afrikaner pride were taken a step further with the publication of a magazine called *'Die Brandwag'* ('The Sentinel'). Written in a style almost childlike in its simplicity – the poorer, less-educated members of the community had not been forgotten – articles amounted to no more than appeals to the emotions. Just as Du Toit had done almost 40 years earlier, *'Die Brandwag'* embarked on a campaign to rewrite history: new heroes (always Afrikaners) were created, while the 'deviousness' of the British and the 'barbarity' of the Africans were stressed. Inevitably, this led to a new surge of nationalism.

The Second Language Movement, as it became known, spawned a whole new generation of writers and poets. Although many of the published works were gloomy accounts of Afrikaner suffering, book sales soared and new magazines modelled on the lines of *'Die Brandwag'* flourished. The most significant of these was *'Die Huisgenoot'* ('The Home Companion'), which in 1922 was regarded as the most popular Afrikaans magazine in South Africa.

Despite splits in Afrikanerdom, the movement for recognition of the Afrikaans language continued to gain support, until it triumphed in 1925 when Afrikaans replaced Dutch as an official language of the Union.

GUSTAV PRELLER, *assistant editor of 'De Volkstem', pleaded for official recognition of Afrikaans, and in 1910 launched 'Die Brandwag' ('The Sentinel') magazine in Afrikaans, with articles retracing the great days of the Boer republics.*

a threat to their livelihood. Yet they were cheap and passive only because they had no rights. And they had no rights because white voters did not want them to have any. For Africans, it was a no-win situation.

To make matters worse, there were divisions among white workers themselves. Afrikaners, who streamed into the cities in the aftermath of the South African War, struggled for a long time to gain membership of unions long dominated by British immigrants.

Labour leaders were not unaware of the need for worker solidarity and had been warned about the dangers of division often enough. In 1905, for example, novelist Olive Schreiner, speaking at the launch of the Johannesburg Shop Assistants' Union, said: ' . . . There must be organised union of all workers . . . for as long as there is an Italian girl willing to take the work for five shillings which a French girl did for ten, or a Chinaman who will take the miners' work for half of what the Englishman or Kaffir demanded, there is always a hole in the bottom of the boat through which the water will creep in.'

And the 'Rand Daily Mail' newspaper, attacking the 'white socialism' of the Transvaal Labour Party, commented: 'In every country the Independent Labour Party represents, or professes to represent, the workers. Here it represents those who are desirous of watching other people work . . . .'

But the warnings and advice went unheeded and, indeed, trade unionists, if anything, stepped up their efforts to win white job security – even if by doing so they increased black unemployment.

Yet white worker hostility towards Africans was polite compared with their attitude towards Indians. By 1907 Asian adroitness at accumulating wealth, even during times of acute economic depression, led white politicians, commerce and workers to combine to form what almost became an anti-Indian industry: the Transvaal Government enacted a Pass law for Indians; white businessmen called for a boycott of their traders; and a 'White Hawkers Association' was formed to counter Indian hawkers.

The attitude of white workers was summed up by trade unionist Tom Mathews, who said: 'I would not do an injustice to any man. But I would not work with a "Sammy" who lived on rice . . . .'

And Thomas Kennerly, another union man, lashed out at the 'Coolieland' colony that Natal had become, where, he said, free Indians lived 'on the smell of their socks'.

Many of the more extreme measures proposed to see off the 'threat' of the black worker came from the Labour Party. Pushing policies that would be copied in later years by Daniel Malan's Nationalists, the party began to grow steadily and was a leading supporter of workers during the miners' strike of 1913.

But in 1914, at the outbreak of the First World War, Labour leaders decided to support the war effort. This signalled the end of a brief Afrikaner flirtation with the idea of (white) worker power.

Five shillings a day for rebel Free Staters

Five shillings a day to overthrow a government they firmly believed had betrayed them was an offer many Orange Free State Afrikaners found hard to resist.

So, within weeks of a promise by Boer generals to turn back the clock on 15 years of poverty, more than 7 000 burghers dusted off the guns they had used against the British more than a decade earlier, in readiness for a new fight – this time against fellow Afrikaners.

It was four years after union and the initial optimism of many Afrikaners that the country's Afrikaner-dominated government would begin to embark on an urgent programme of reconstruction had long disappeared; for the region had not yet recovered from the devastation of war.

Free Staters felt their plight deserved attention. In the South African War, few had fought harder for the Boer cause than they. And few were made to suffer more. Vast tracts of their farmland had been destroyed by the British and towns such as Lind-

ley and Frankfort had almost been wiped off the face of the earth. Then, after the war, more disaster in the form of drought and stock disease had swept through vast areas. Although the formation of a Land Bank in 1912 had raised hopes, these had just as quickly been dashed: only the rich were allowed to borrow – small farmers were considered a high risk. Desperate, they turned to borrowing from better-off relatives, shopkeepers and moneylenders – at exorbitant rates of interest. Unable to repay the loans, and acknowledging the hopelessness of their task, they left their farms for one of the many squatter camps which had sprung up all over the province.

The northern Free State was the hardest hit area. And it was from there that the majority of the rebels came. In the south-west, only Brandfort and Dewetsdorp rose to rebellion, while in the fertile, settled and relatively well-off eastern part of the province the rebellion was confined to two districts: Ficksburg, an area influenced

by nearby Bethlehem, the centre of discontent in the province, and Smithfield, the constituency of General Barry Hertzog. Of the approximately 11 000 men who took up arms against the government, 3 000 came from the western Transvaal and a little more than a thousand from the Cape. The rest were Free Staters.

Yet the rebellion which broke out shortly after South Africa's entry into the First World War was not a spontaneous uprising of the downtrodden masses. Indeed, some of the rebels agreed to fight only because they had been promised payment. In many respects, though, the aims of the leaders of the uprising – men such as Boer General Christiaan de Wet – were quite clear: convinced that Afrikaner politicians such as Louis Botha and Jan Smuts had sold out Afrikanerdom to protect the interests of the British-controlled gold-mining corporations, they wanted to take back their country – even if it meant fighting against men they had once regarded as brothers.

War and rebellion

On 4 August 1914 Britain declared war on Germany – and for the next 35 days South Africans waited, debated and wondered whether the Union would choose neutrality or follow suit and declare war itself.

On 8 September Botha finally gave his answer: It was going to be war.

As South Africans celebrated on a wave of patriotism and propaganda, a group of Afrikaner nationalists, supported by remnants of the army and an assortment of western Transvaal and Free State 'poor whites', were preparing for a dramatic bid to seize the country . . . .

A month previously, immediately after the outbreak of the First World War, Koos de la Rey, another Boer war hero, had called a mass meeting of burghers at Treurfontein, near Lichtenburg in the Transvaal. Disenchanted with the Botha Government, the Boers had resolved to set off for Pretoria on horseback, take control of the government and declare an Afrikaner republic.

Botha, however, had heard of the plan, had summoned De la Rey to his office and had talked him out of it. For the time being, at least, the threat of rebellion seemed to have been averted.

Botha's next step was to call in his top Transvaal officers to discuss their wartime commitments. They included General Christiaan Beyers, Major Jan Kemp, Lieutenant-Colonel Manie Maritz, Major J J Pienaar and General C H Muller. Although all of them were openly hostile towards the idea of a war with Germany, Botha left them in charge of their garrisons. This proved to be a major blunder, for as two Commissions of Enquiry uncovered later, within a few days of their meeting with Botha the officers began piecing together the plans for a mid-September takeover of the government.

According to the plan, Kemp would summon the army to Potchefstroom in readiness for the arrival of De la Rey, who together with Beyers would raise the old Transvaal Republic flag, the *vierkleur* (literally, the four-colour). Kemp and De la Rey would then spread the revolt to the western Transvaal while Beyers and Pienaar were to seal off the railway line and occupy Krugersdorp before march-ing on to Roberts Heights (known today as Voortrekkerhoogte), where they would release German prisoners. General Christiaan de Wet, meanwhile, would take control of the OFS while Maritz, from his base in Upington, was to liaise with the Germans.

The government's decision to accede to a British request to invade German South West Africa was the signal for Beyers to resign, and late on the night of 15 September he and De la Rey set off for Potchefstroom from Pretoria in preparation for the first phase of the takeover operation.

But then fate took a bizarre hand. At Langlaagte railway station police had set up a roadblock to intercept a notori-

SOUTH AFRICAN WAR *heroes (above) Christiaan de Wet, Koos de la Rey and Louis Botha photographed together in 1910. Botha and his ex-colleagues were to fall out over the issue of South African involvement on the side of Britain in the First World War, with De Wet and De la Rey joining the rebels.*

FOUR *of these Union Defence Force officers (left) defected to the rebels (each marked with a letter of the alphabet): General Christiaan Beyers (A), Major J J Pienaar (B), Major Jan Kemp (C) and Lieutenant-Colonel Manie Maritz (D).*

ous band of robbers known as the Foster gang, and had been ordered to shoot at any cars that failed to stop. Spotting the roadblock ahead and believing they were being sought, the two generals ordered their driver to crash the police barrier. A ricocheting bullet pierced the car and hit De la Rey in the heart. He cried out *'Dit is raak'* (literally, 'it is a hit') and died in Beyers' arms.

With the death of De la Rey the 16 September coup plan was dropped, but Boer resentment smouldered on. On the same day as De la Rey's death, a small group of German-supporting Afrikaners, living in South West Africa and calling themselves the *Vrij Korps* (the Free Corps), seized Nakob, a small village on the South African side of the border. Asked by Smuts to repel the invasion, Maritz refused, claiming that his men had been called up for peacetime training and were not all volunteers.

On 9 October, Maritz and about 500 men crossed over to the German side. On 13 October, a gathering of burghers at Koppies in the OFS called on the government to withdraw its troops from South West Africa. Botha refused and on 22 October De Wet was instructed to call up the OFS commandos as the first step of an armed rebellion.

But Botha, for the first time, took decisive action. Taking personal command of government forces and using, as far as possible, only Afrikaner troops to avoid reopening old South African War antagonisms, he set out to crush the rebellion.

By 16 November most of the rebels were scattered. And in the next few weeks De Wet was captured on the Bechuanaland border and Beyers, in trying to escape from government troops, had drowned in the Vaal River after becoming entangled in his army coat. Kemp, after helping Maritz to capture Upington on 25 January, surrendered a week later, while Maritz fled to Angola.

After the rebellion had been crushed, the government treated the rebels leniently. There was just one execution, that of Captain Jopie Fourie who, besides having failed to resign his commission when he joined the rebels, had also fired at government troops during a brief truce. Other ringleaders escaped with fines and jail sentences.

The First World War fuels a boom for South Africa

The outbreak of the First World War had a major impact on the country's fledgling economy, boosting some segments and depressing others.

Shipping services were curtailed and state regulation of prices and rationing increased. Yet by the end of the war the South African economy was healthier than it had been at the start, with gains in agricultural production, new export markets opened up, and an increase in local manufacturing.

In 1916 a government commission appointed to enquire into living costs found that the price of a man's suit had increased by 36 percent since before the war, a hat by 19 percent and boots by between 20 and 40 percent. An important reason for these price rises was the increase in the cost of importing raw materials such as fabrics, due to higher freight rates (partly because a great number of ships had been requisitioned for the war effort), customs duties, war insurance and shipping delays.

Food prices also increased considerably during the four years of war, with the average cost of living for a family of five rising by about 40 percent in Durban, 39 percent in Cape Town, 30 percent in Johannesburg and Bloemfontein, or an average countrywide of about 33 percent.

Exports, however, received a major boost. Meat was exported for the first time and cotton received a lucrative boost because of the high prices in Britain. South Africa also increased its exports of jam, dried fruit, liquor, dairy products and some minerals.

By November 1917 trade returns were showing a marked decline in the value of imported goods, while a newspaper observed that export prices for food especially had rocketed.

After the war South Africa experienced an economic boom, but as in many countries it was short-lived and was followed by a sharp recession. The country's two major economic supports, gold-mining and agriculture, were both hard hit.

South Africans in the First World War

At sunset on 20 July 1916 an eerie silence descended over a wood near the French village of Longueval – and the acrid stench of death and suffering wafted through the broken trees . . . .

For five days South African and German forces bombarded each other with guns and heavy artillery in one of the most vicious battles of the First World War – the nightmare of Delville Wood.

At the beginning of July, after bombarding the German lines, the South Africans started their advance. By the middle of the month they had captured Longueval and were on the fringes of Delville Wood.

'Take that wood, and hold it at all costs,' commanding officer Brigadier-General Henry Timson Lukin had been ordered. And, fighting with a tenacity which would earn them a place in military history, the 3 153 South Africans did just that. But the cost in human life was horrific. When the guns finally grew silent, all but 755 men had been either killed or wounded.

Almost two years earlier, on 8 September 1914, South Africa had entered the 'war to end all wars', to a response which again highlighted the divisions in white society. The decision, welcomed by the vast majority of English-speakers, was bitterly criticised by many Afrikaners, who had never forgiven the excesses of the British during the South African War. A promise of German assistance prompted some of them to start a rebellion which was easily put down – ironically by fellow Afrikaners.

But opposition notwithstanding, 146 000 whites volunteered for service. And although Jan Smuts had declined African and coloured offers to fight because it was a 'white

POSTCARDS sent home by Union Defence Force volunteers serving at the front were heavily censored.

man's war', 83 000 Africans and 2 000 coloured men did service in a non-combatant capacity. Indeed, in one of the seldom-remembered tragedies of the conflict, 615 Africans died when the troopship, the *Mendi*, sank after a collision with another ship in the English Channel.

The first operation of the war for South Africa was the invasion of German South West Africa. The brief was to seize control of a long-range radio station at Windhoek and to deny the Germans the use of the territory's harbours. Within six days of parliament's decision to enter the war, 1 800 members of the Active Citizen Force had landed at Lüderitz and raised the Union Jack. On 9 July 1915, after a 10-month cat-and-mouse chase across the territory, the heavily outnumbered Germans surrendered. Later, South Africans fought – and died – in the campaigns of central and north Africa, and in Europe.

A HAUNTING *painting of Delville Wood (above) where nearly 2 400 South African troops were killed or wounded.* MORE THAN 80 000 *Africans volunteered for duty in the South African forces, serving in various non-combatant roles. This group (below) was photographed in France.*

GENERAL LOUIS BOTHA, *Commander-in-Chief of the South African forces invading German South West Africa, accepts the surrender of Windhoek from the town's mayor. It was the culmination of a 10-month campaign in which outnumbered German forces fought a losing battle.*

Revolt in the cities

Between 1907 and 1922, South Africa was racked by conflict between mineowners and mineworkers. Strikes were endemic – placing enormous pressure on the state as white miners resisted efforts by mining corporations to reduce labour costs by opening up to black miners jobs which had previously been done by whites.

AT 4.30 IN THE MORNING of 10 March 1922 bloody street battles between heavily armed white mineworkers and hard-pressed units of police and soldiers were raging throughout the Witwatersrand.

By 5.20 am, the eastern Transvaal town of Brakpan had been captured by strikers. By 10.30, nearby Benoni was under siege and enveloped in a pall of smoke as fighter aircraft, summoned from the military base at Roberts Heights, bombed and machine-gunned strikers' positions.

In Johannesburg, dozens of policemen were taken prisoner as armed strikers took control of the working-class suburbs of Fordsburg, Newlands, Brixton and Vrededorp.

That same morning, Prime Minister Jan Smuts declared martial law and ordered more than 20 000 troops into the fray. For what had begun as just another miners' strike 10 weeks earlier had escalated into a campaign to overthrow the state and to replace it with a 'White Workers' Republic'. Over the next few days the sounds of tanks, machine-guns, aeroplanes, bombs and charging soldiers would echo across the Reef . . . .

To the socialists, who hoped to dominate the white labour movement, the revolt of 1922 was a protest by 20 000 white workers against more than a decade of union-bashing and cuts in living standards. To the Afrikaner miners, the rebellion was a forerunner to the restoration of the defunct Boer republics. Although the politics of socialists and nationalists differed fundamentally – both agreed on one crucial issue: that the massive African labour force constituted a major threat to their relatively privileged positions in the workplace.

Their fears were not unfounded. Over the years, job segregation had served white workers well, reserving the skilled work for them and guaranteeing earnings of up to 10 times more than Africans, who did all the hard work anyway. But now, with the expansion of the mining industry, mine-owners were increasingly agitating against the job colour bar – not because they found it morally wrong, but because it whittled away profits. Soon, attempts by the bosses to push more (cheap) blacks into skilled positions would spark a series of confrontations with white workers . . . .

Earlier strikes

The first of these clashes occurred before Union – in 1907 – when workers downed tools over plans by the mining houses to reduce their wages and to allow Chinese and African labourers to take more skilled jobs. The Transvaal Government – and indeed the Union Government later – viewed worker opposition to cost-cutting with a mixture of irritation and concern: mining revenue was vital to the

economy and had to be protected at all costs. Prime Minister Louis Botha therefore had few qualms about calling in the help of imperial troops. But although the strike was quickly put down, two trends emerged which in later years would have a profound effect on labour relations on the mines: in the first, in a process offering the government at least a partial solution to a growing poor white problem, sacked British miners were replaced with Afrikaners, whom mine-owners believed would be cheaper, less militant and less inclined towards trade unionism. But what both the government and the mining bosses failed to take into account was the fact that the majority of Afrikaner miners were ardent supporters of a restoration of the Boer republics. It was an oversight that would cost the government dearly over the next decade.

The second trend was the mine-owners' continued attempts to move Africans into semi-skilled jobs under the supervision of white foremen. The erosion of the colour bar was an ongoing source of grievance to the white miners and much symbolic significance was attached to it. But there were other grievances, too – for example the generally poor working conditions underground, the deadly health threat posed by phthisis (a consumptive disease of the lungs that afflicted thousands of miners), and the outright refusal by mine-owners to recognise trade unions for collective bargaining.

In May 1913, a dispute over the working hours of five men at the New Kleinfontein mine near Boksburg led to sackings – and a strike that quickly spread to other mines. The Transvaal Chamber of Mines, confident of government backing, and eager to force a showdown with the unions, refused to back down. The attitude of mining bosses was summed up by Lionel Phillips, the chief executive of the powerful Wernher-Beit group of mines, who wrote to his principals in London: 'A general strike would of course be a serious matter from a dividend-paying standpoint. I do not think, however, that it could last very long and, if it does happen, we must make up our minds once and for all to break the unions here . . . .'

Defence Minister Smuts, the government's strongman, seemingly resigned to confrontation but, fearing that violent insurrection might prove too much for the year-old Union Defence Force to handle, sought, and was granted permission to use, imperial troops to protect vulnerable mine property. On 2 July, 5 000 of the 22 000 white miners downed tools, and on 4 July, calls by union leaders for a general strike were answered by 18 000 white miners on 63 of the 69 Reef mines. As tensions rose, rioting broke out in central Johannesburg, Park Station was set on fire and

THE JULY 5th, MASSACRE.

MONTY DUNMORE.
The little 13 year old boy who was shot through the back while selling "Strike-Heralds" to the crowd at the Rand Club.

IN JULY 1913 *Union troops were ordered to quell the violence that erupted during a strike over working hours by 19 000 white mine-workers. While mounted police waded into angry strikers (above right), several innocent bystanders were shot – including a 13-year-old newspaper seller who was hit in the back (above). On 4 July, as workers at 63 of the 69 Reef mines stopped work, the offices of 'The Star' newspaper were torched by angry strikers (right).*

the offices of 'The Star' newspaper attacked. On 5 July, every mine was affected and the number of men on strike had risen to 19 000.

Fierce fighting broke out between government troops and workers – and in the first two days of the stayaway more than 100 strikers and onlookers were killed, and public opinion swung behind the miners. Prime Minister Botha and Smuts were persuaded by the mining corporations to try to negotiate a settlement. This they did – by agreeing at a meeting in the Carlton Hotel in Johannesburg that sacked New Kleinfontein miners would be reinstated.

Apart from scattered incidents of violence, the strike was over by 12 July – and although the government had been deeply humiliated, it had actually conceded very little. By contrast, the strikers had missed a golden opportunity – Smuts and Botha, determined to prevent a repetition of the New Kleinfontein debacle, began developing legislation to reduce the threat to state security posed by industrial

disputes. Two Bills on industrial conciliation and the recognition of trade unions went to parliament later that year but did not pass into law and did not resurface until 1922. However, an amendment to the Riotous Assemblies Act in 1914 gave the government the power to ban meetings which threatened public order.

Smuts acted decisively in January 1914 to crush a strike, over retrenchments, by Pretoria and Reef railwaymen. By 9 January, he had mobilised the Active Citizen Force – at the same time ordering the arrest of union leaders. When the South African Federation of Trades retaliated by calling a general strike, Smuts did not dally: by 14 January 70 000 troops had been put on a countrywide alert – with more than 10 000 of them stationed on the Witwatersrand.

The strike was quickly smashed and its leaders – including two Labour Members of Parliament, Frederic Creswell and Tommy Boydell – arrested. Later, ignoring protests, the government deported nine union leaders.

The cost of living spirals

In August the First World War broke out, putting new economic pressures on the mines and adding impetus to the mine-owners' own ceaseless war on costs. The price of gold had remained fixed at about 85 shillings a fine ounce between 1910 and 1918, but under the pressure of wartime inflation production costs began to soar.

At the same time, an index of prices showed a 50 percent increase in the cost of living. By 1920 prices had climbed a further 50 percent and inflation touched 20 percent. While mine production costs did not rise quite as steeply, the profitability of the deep-level 'low-grade' mines was in serious jeopardy under economic conditions that saw a drastic increase in production cuts without a commensurate rise in the gold price. Labour productivity had begun to decline in 1916 after white miners had successfully negotiated shorter working hours – a concession they had wrung from the chamber as a result of the improved bargaining position afforded them by the war. In 1917, gold production slackened and the Transvaal Chamber of Mines claimed that 14 low-grade mines producing 25 percent of gold output were 'barely paying their way'.

With the price fixed and with costs rising, profits began to plunge. By the end of the year the chamber, aware that many 'white jobs' could easily be done by Africans, started a renewed but oblique offensive on the colour bar. But mindful that direct approaches to the issue would evoke a sharp response from white workers, they opted to tackle the broader issue of mining costs in general.

The chamber suggested to the government that either the four most marginal mines be subsidised by the state or be closed. Already, sentiment was growing among whites that the importance of mining to the economy might justify some level of support for marginal mines. The government responded by appointing a commission to investigate the situation, which, when it reported in 1920, recommended that the legal colour bar be abolished. It was only in the following year that the possibility of state aid – by way of compensation to the mines for losses attributable to higher white wages – was seriously mooted. But by late 1921, with the government clearly unable to subsidise the mining industry, Smuts, who had taken over as Prime Minister after Botha's death in 1919, again bowed to the inevitability of a clash between workers and the mining corporations.

Prelude to revolt

A widespread strike by black mineworkers in 1920 encouraged mine-owners to resist white miners' demands that the colour bar be reinforced. Now even more determined that job segregation had to go, they decided to ignore demands by white miners for the extension of the *status quo* agreement (see box), arguing that the colour bar was morally and economically unjustifiable. The clouds were gathering for a stormy clash.

The events leading up to the 1922 revolt left no doubt that the mining houses and government were both determined to crush the power of the white unions: the mines were faced with a gold price crisis which severely endan-

---

The job colour bar wrangle

A difference in the working costs of gold mines of only a shilling a ton meant a difference in profits to the vitally important gold-mining industry of about £1,5-million.

This was the crucial motivation behind a concerted campaign by mine-owners in the years between 1910 and 1922 to dismantle the job colour bar, which guaranteed white workers a privileged position in the workplace. But efforts to open a variety of semi-skilled jobs to African miners served only to pitch mining bosses into a series of headlong confrontations with their 20 000-strong white workforce.

By 1919, the Transvaal Chamber of Mines was in the middle of a major crisis: profits were dwindling as working costs rose to 24 shillings a ton, compared to 17s 5d just four years earlier. Although most of this increase was due to wage increases for white workers – 40 percent over seven years – it was to the African compounds that the bosses turned for a way out of the financial mire.

The solution was arrived at through a popular South African social equation: blackness equals rightlessness equals powerlessness equals cheapness. Thus, while the chamber agreed that the colour bar had to go, it was adamant that the wage bar had to remain. In other words, although it wanted to push Africans into higher job brackets, it was not prepared to change significantly the size of their pay packets, which between 1912 and 1919 had grown by less than a penny.

The colour bar itself operated on three tiers. The first was the legal tier established by the Mines and Works Act of 1911; the second, the customary tier which informally maintained certain jobs as white or black because they had always been so. The last, and probably the most significant one as far as the chamber was concerned, was the *status quo* tier, which offered to the mine-owners some leeway in what would be a process of hard bargaining with the white unions.

During the war years, a whole new range of job categories not covered by legislation had been created by industry rationalisations, and the mines had rapidly begun introducing cheaper African and coloured labour into these areas.

In 1916, the chamber, under pressure from the unions to reimpose strict job segregation, proposed a *status quo* agreement, which would allow blacks who had been pushed into semi-skilled jobs to keep their positions, but guaranteed that there would be no further encroachments upon 'white' jobs. Although the miners were unhappy over this development – they wanted the trend of the war years completely reversed – they eventually ratified the proposal two years later.

Both sides now had a stick with which to beat the other: mine-owners could threaten to dismantle the agreement if white workers refused to back cost-cutting measures, while the miners could threaten to resist cost-cutting if the colour bar was lifted.

gered the viability of the low-grade mining operations. This in turn threatened state revenues that had been under increasing pressure since 1914 as a result of drought and growing white unemployment.

On the political front, Smuts' handling of the 1914 strike, as well as the rebellion of militant Afrikaner nationalists over South Africa's entry into the war, had lost the South African Party (SAP) significant support among white workers and Nationalists in the 1915 election. Although the National Party made further gains in the election of 1920, a rise in the gold price bought Smuts time to deal with the miners. In February 1920, the price stood at 127s 4d a fine ounce – a level at which the public would not have supported action against the white miners. But by the end of the year the price had fallen to 97s 7d, and by March 1921, the cost of living started to follow the gold price down. Public opinion began to swing against the miners' wage demands.

The Chamber of Mines, impressed with the results achieved by the US Government in suppressing a damaging coal strike in 1919, was meanwhile hard at work on a strategy to convince the government of the need to support strong action. It had also established a reserve fund to tide it over a prolonged strike. In February 1921, the chamber told miners that, with three mines already closed, 21 more might also have to be shut if they did not abide by the wage agreements of 1919 which allowed for cuts in the event of a fall in the cost of living. At a meeting in London, Lionel Phillips (who was now chairman of the Central Mining and Investment Corporation, into which the Wernher-Beit group had been absorbed) told Smuts that the mining industry would need the government's help to bring white labour to heel. Smuts replied that he was concerned over which way public opinion on the Witwatersrand would go in the event of a clash. As a result, the chamber began to campaign for public support through a series of newspaper advertisements. In August, the chamber and the South African Industrial Federation agreed on cost-of-living adjustments, starting with a cut in October. The Federation, however, refused to accept a cut for coal miners and opted instead for arbitration of the dispute. But the chamber disagreed.

On 24 October, workers were pushed closer to a strike when mining executives announced a series of stern cost-cutting measures – including the scrapping of the *status quo* agreement (see box) and renewed pressure for a lifting of the statutory colour bar. In December, as the crisis intensified, the cabinet decided to keep the mines operating – even if this meant placing them under police protection. At the same time the government offered to be mediators when the unions rejected a chamber proposal to scrap the *status quo* agreement and the customary colour bar, and to retrench 2 000 semi- and unskilled white workers.

The revolt begins

The strike began in Witbank on 2 January 1922, when coal miners downed tools over the proposed pay cuts. On 10 January the South African Industrial Federation's 24 000 members joined the colliers. Smuts, acting on police information that the National Party was in contact with the unions and stirring the pot to secure political advantage,

CENTRAL MINING *and Investment Corporation chairman Lionel Phillips asked for government help in bringing white mineworkers to heel.*

postponed the opening of parliament until late February. On 28 January, after two rounds of negotiation with the unions, the chamber announced proposals calculated to inflame the crisis: an increase in the ratio of black to white workers from 8,2:1 to 10,5:1, which would have entailed the loss of up to 2 000 more white jobs; and the abolition of paid holidays on May Day and Dingane's Day – days of symbolic significance to English and Afrikaans workers respectively.

By early February, several political forces were at work in the strike: the Nationalists were seeking Afrikaner worker support, as was the Labour Party – both pledging to support the interests of white workers against black encroachment; and the communists were urging workers to strike, not over the colour bar, but rather for higher wages. Smuts, on the other hand, adopted a neutral stance, promising that the government would 'draw a ring around both parties, do its best to maintain law and order, and let the two parties fight it out'. But the strike was being increasingly taken over and driven by militant Afrikaner nationalists organised on 'commando' lines – and on 7 February, Johannesburg was greeted by the sight of striking miners marching through the streets under a banner proclaiming: 'Workers of the World Fight and Unite for a White South Africa.'

On 12 February, Smuts called on the miners to return to work, promising police protection to those who did. By then the strike leadership had passed from the South African Industrial Federation to a militant Action Committee, including members of the Communist Party who repeatedly urged the Afrikaner mining commandos not to attack Africans. But their cries fell on deaf ears and several Africans were murdered in racially motivated attacks. On 21 February, the chamber asked the Prime Minister to declare martial law. Smuts was obviously torn: on the one hand, he recognised the state's need for stability in the mining industry; on the other hand, he was incapable of completely repudiating the rights of white workers. Moreover, he would have to justify whatever actions he took to the electorate....

TROUBLE *was already simmering in February 1922 when several union leaders appeared in the Johannesburg Magistrate's Court. In the streets outside the court, mineworkers demonstrated their support.*

ON 10 MARCH *the strikers, backed by Afrikaner commandos, unleashed an orgy of violence in Johannesburg – leading to the formation of hastily recruited 'loyal' commandos, like this group manning a roadblock.*

PERMITS *(left) were needed to move from one part of Johannesburg to another, and the unions organised meal tickets (below) for strikers.*

MOVE PERMIT UNDER MARTIAL LAW.

STRIKE DISTRESS FUND.
MEAL TICKET.

Meanwhile, the strike leaders had lost control to the Afrikaner commandos, who by 10 March had seized virtually the whole of Johannesburg and were calling for armed insurrection and the overthrow of the state. It was then that Smuts made his move: the same day, he declared martial law, went to the Rand, and personally took control of more than 20 000 troops backed by aeroplanes, tanks and field artillery.

Fifteen hundred strikers were arrested at the Johannesburg showgrounds and the strike leaders, who had been trapped in their headquarters in the Trades Hall, were picked up and jailed in The Fort. The commandos retaliated by raiding police stations for arms but after five days of skirmishes with trained government troops – during which the Johannesburg suburb of Fordsburg was rocked by thunderous artillery fire – the strike was broken and it was called off a day later. It had cost 214 lives – of which 76 were strikers. Seventy-eight troops, 30 Africans (murdered by strikers) and 62 bystanders were also killed. Troops and police arrested 4 748 strikers, of whom 46 were charged with murder. Of these, 18 were sentenced to death but only four were hanged. They went to the gallows singing the communist anthem, 'The Red Flag'.

The mining houses had won, but the government knew that only its increasing intervention in future industrial disputes would ensure a lasting peace between the bosses and the workers.

African revolt

Since 1914, the government, preoccupied with white labour, had failed to recognise that Africans, too, were under economic and political pressures of a severity beyond the comprehension of most whites.

Segregation and the demands made by a developing mining and agricultural economy – as well as drought, crop failures, floods and cattle disease – had forced hundreds of thousands of Africans off the land into vast urban slums on the outskirts of 'white' towns and cities. Equally subject to inflation, they also had to contend with a battery of regulations controlling almost every aspect of their lives in the cities.

In May 1918, frustration over low wages, poor housing and the hated Pass laws boiled over into strike action: when white municipal workers won a pay increase after a five-day strike, African railway workers followed suit and managed to gain a 3d increase. Encouraged by this, 50 municipal sanitary workers – the 'bucket boys' – refused to work until they had been given a 10d increase. When they were arrested, sanitary workers at other compounds came out in support. More arrests followed, and in June, 152 'bucket boys' appeared before Johannesburg's chief magistrate, T G Macfie.

Their sentences were tough: they would not be paid for three months; they would be shot if they deserted and flogged if they refused to work.

Their treatment was roundly condemned by Johannesburg Africans – and a campaign for their release, tied to a demand for a 1s-a-day increase, was initiated by the Transvaal Native Congress, the provincial branch of the South African Native National Congress (the SANNC, later

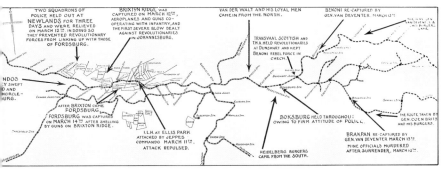

A PLAN showing where most of the violence occurred during the 1922 miners' strike. Worst hit was Fordsburg, which was shelled by loyalist troops.

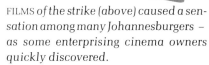

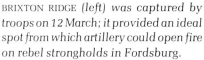

FILMS of the strike (above) caused a sensation among many Johannesburgers – as some enterprising cinema owners quickly discovered.

BRIXTON RIDGE (left) was captured by troops on 12 March; it provided an ideal spot from which artillery could open fire on rebel strongholds in Fordsburg.

BEFORE the first shots were fired, the government dropped leaflets on Fordsburg urging people to leave. Some, however, like this family photographed outside their home (left), chose to remain.

AS GOVERNMENT troops (below) swept into Fordsburg on 14 March, strike leaders Fisher and Spendiff apparently shot themselves. The surviving members of the strike Action Committee were arrested, and four eventually hanged.

STRIKERS captured during government action (left) against Brixton Ridge and Vrededorp on 12 March were interned at the Wanderers Cricket Ground.

the ANC). Warnings by national leaders of the congress that strike action might be dangerous were ignored – and after more work stoppages, the sentences of the 'bucket boys' were overturned.

Despite the fact that the Transvaal Native Congress had called off the strike, 15 000 African miners on three mines went on strike on 1 July and were given short shrift by the police, who drove them underground at bayonet point. Some fought back with axes, pickhandles and iron bars, but to no avail. Later, two delegations of Africans presented Prime Minister Botha with a list of grievances over Passes, wages, housing, the colour bar, health hazards and poor educational facilities. Although some concessions were made, most Africans remained dissatisfied.

On 30 March, after an unsuccessful meeting with government, municipal and mine officials in Johannesburg, Transvaal Native Congress officials informed the chief Pass officer that because wage demands of Africans had not been met, they would refuse to carry Passes. Then, at an impromptu rally at Von Brandis Square, the congress delegation addressed a growing throng of Africans. A report in 'The Star' quoted one speaker as saying: 'Our voice . . . will never be heard as long as the present conditions exist. We count for nothing in parliament, although we are the majority of the population of the country.'

By the afternoon, more than 2 000 Passes had been collected from Africans in Johannesburg. But the following day, after plans had been discussed to spread the anti-Pass campaign to other parts of the Witwatersrand, police charged a 3 000-strong crowd, injuring many. And

AN ORGANISER *makes his way through the crowd with a sack in order to collect Passes during the 1919 anti-Pass campaign spearheaded by the* SANNC.

although some of the movement's leaders were singled out, arrested and taken to Marshall Square, the campaign took off like brushfire. Several times, black and white civilians clashed violently – and in one incident a crowd of Africans attacked police taking Pass offenders from court to jail. However, by the end of April, the arrest of about 700 people and fears by congress leaders that the situation was getting out of control, brought the campaign among workers on the Reef to a halt.

But by now, the struggle was set to continue in the Orange Free State, where African women had long been waging a grim battle against the Pass laws. In 1913, after a campaign involving thousands of women, who chose jail rather than carry Passes, the Provincial Council had been forced to abandon temporarily a regulation forcing women to carry the document, a requirement which had previously only applied to men.

In 1920, the struggle was again highlighted when 62 women Pass offenders refused to pay fines, electing instead to march under escort to Senekal 40 kilometres away to serve their jail sentences.

Africans on the mines

In many ways, the struggle of African mineworkers was overshadowed in the years between 1907 and 1922 by the vicious battles between white workers and mine-owners. But by no means did Africans meekly accept their harsh working and living conditions . . . .

In 1913, following the example of white miners, some 9 000 Africans had gone on strike for three days. By early 1916, three strikes had been provoked by poor wages – while in 1917, a solid boycott by African mineworkers of mine stores had taken hold across the Reef. In 1918, three Johannesburg mines had been hit by sympathy strikes over the 'bucket boys', although the 'flu epidemic later in the year offered the mines a temporary respite from black industrial strife – a third of the Reef's black mine force of 157 000 was hospitalised and more than 1 000 miners died.

But by mid-1919, as the anti-Pass campaign spearheaded by the South African Native National Congress gathered momentum, the Chamber of Mines announced a 3d pay increase to 2s 3d plus bonuses, to take effect on 1 January, 1920. But it was not enough. Strikes and boycotts continued to plague the Reef mines, climaxing in the 1920 strike (see box) and leading on some occasions to the intervention of government troops.

However, the movement which rocked white South Africa in the 1920s had its roots in Cape Town. It was called the Industrial and Commercial Workers' Union of Africa (ICU), and from small beginnings as a union of dockers it quickly spread through town and country across the Union, provoking a serious backlash by the white government, amid fears of national uprising. Throughout this period, the ANC – dominated by conservatives who were unwilling to make the transition from protest to action – was eclipsed by the ICU which, by 1927, claimed a membership of 100 000 and an even broader base of popular support. Numbers such as these persuaded the government and white politicians to proceed carefully in their relations with the ICU. Indeed, before the 1924 elections, even Barry Hertzog courted the union's support, particularly in the Cape where a significant number of Africans had the vote. And later in the decade, the Pact Government – anxious not to provoke African retaliation against violent attacks by white farmers on ICU members – dragged its feet over demands for strong action against the union.

The ICU was founded on 7 January 1919 when 24 members were signed up. By mid-1919 it had absorbed a rival union and went over to strike action in December, demanding higher pay and protesting at the export of foodstuffs when domestic prices were so high. Although the strike collapsed in early January 1920, when white workers failed to give it their support, the union continued to organise, establishing itself first in Port Elizabeth and East London then moving inland to include the Orange Free State and Transvaal.

On 23 October 1920, bloodshed overtook the union for the first time when Port Elizabeth police and white vigilantes opened fire on a crowd of 3 000 Africans who had converged on the police station to demand the release of Samuel Masabalala, president of the local ICU branch. Twenty-four were shot dead and another 126 injured.

Conditions for the 11 500 Africans living in the city's two townships of New Brighton and Korsten at that time were typical of those in South Africa's urban areas: the cost of living had doubled in six years, wages had risen only 60 percent, accommodation was 'strained to the limit', and living conditions were generally 'dreadfully overcrowded and unsanitary'.

In January, 4 000 Africans met in New Brighton and appointed Masabalala, a 43-year-old clerk for a pharmaceutical company, to place a wage demand for 10 shillings a day before the employers. As the year wore on, the employers conceded two increases of 6 pence, but the union's 4 000 members were still not satisfied. At a meeting on 17 October, Masabalala called for a general strike from 3 November. When Dr Walter Rubusana, a founder member of the SANNC, attempted to dissuade the members from their course, he was attacked by protesters. Masabalala rescued him, but was accused of having incited the attack and was arrested the following Saturday.

Immediately, a 300-strong crowd gathered outside the police station, bent on freeing Masabalala. Union leaders tried to bail him out, but the police refused. By now, 3 000 Africans had flocked to the scene, and whites had also begun to gather. The police tried to disperse the demonstrators with mounted charges and a firehose. Then two shots were fired. The police and vigilantes followed with a volley of fire as the crowd retreated and fled back to their townships. During the next 24 hours, there were several attempts at arson and sabotage, but police reinforcements were rushed to the city and calm was restored.

By 1923, the ICU was mobilising support in the eastern Cape, gradually turning its attention to the northern provinces and poising itself for a leap into militant nationalism. Its leaders were switching the emphasis of union rhetoric and protest action away from specific labour issues towards broad political demands for African freedom. Herein lay the true measure of the ICU's mass appeal, as well as of its threat as perceived by the established order.

The 1920 African miners' strike

On 16 February 1920, two African miners named Mobu and Vilikati were arrested at the East Rand Proprietary Mines for trying to organise a strike.

The next day, 2 500 of the 2 900 workers refused to work until their colleagues were released, working conditions were improved and they were given pay increases of 3 shillings a day to keep up with the rising cost of living.

By 19 February, 12 compounds housing about 30 000 workers had been drawn into the dispute. During the intervening weekend, the mining authorities watched anxiously for signs of a petering out of the strike. But it was a vain hope. By Monday, 23 February, 46 000 workers were out – and later in the week, the number rose to 71 000, more than half the entire black labour force on the Reef.

In many respects, the strike had its roots in the same factors – low wages, poor housing, poverty and mounting inflation – which triggered African resistance in other major urban areas. But the miners also had other specific grievances – for example, being forced to replace their working clothes and boots at their own expense several times a year. Moreover, they had become increasingly hostile to the colour bar which retarded their ability to progress and consequently be able to earn better wages.

The Chamber of Mines reacted to the growing crisis by stressing to concerned whites that 'this is not, as all previous native troubles have been, a riot; it is a regular strike organised on the European model'.

But then, having given this assurance, they proceeded to deal with the matter as if it were indeed a riot: troops and police were called in, compounds surrounded, 'ringleaders' identified and arrested and miners forced back to work at bayonet point. Inevitably, clashes occurred, and in violence at two shafts 11 miners were killed and another 120 injured. But the chamber had achieved what it set out to do: by 28 February, the strike was over.

GOVERNMENT TROOPS *were sent into compounds with orders to force workers back down the mines. Eleven miners died in the violence that followed.*

'Every native must have a warren too ...'

Few words in South African history are as emotionally charged as 'apartheid'.
But just when and how did apartheid begin? Although total separation on every level
between black and white became official policy only after the National Party election victory
in 1948, its foundation had been laid nearly half a century previously in a policy
then known as segregation – not by Afrikaners but by British Government officials.

I N A CAMPAIGN of bluff and bluster, a hardnosed British High Commissioner named Alfred Milner and an assortment of Boer generals led by Jan Smuts began the task of shaping a new society in a region that had been shattered by war ....

The year was 1903; the killing fields of the Transvaal, Orange Free State (OFS), Natal and the northern Cape had been quiet for more than 12 months; and the search was on for a political system best suited to the needs of a 'reconstructed' southern Africa.

Milner felt nothing but contempt for the defeated Afrikaner communities, while they hated him – perhaps more than they did any other Englishman. Yet despite their bitter enmity, Boer and Briton were united on one critically important issue: white domination had to be maintained at all costs.

Soon a nightmare destined to haunt generations of South Africans would begin ....

The revival of Afrikanerdom

Milner had mapped out the future of the region long before a combination of superior military forces and weaponry had bludgeoned the outnumbered Boers into defeat. Sensible in parts, typically arrogant in others, his scheme involved uniting the four colonies, anglicising the Afrikaner population and using African labour to build a modern economy around the lucrative goldmining industry.

But the Boer generals, still clinging to the notion of regaining Afrikaner independence, had other ideas.

Twelve months of spirited negotiation had won them two crucial concessions in the Peace Treaty of Vereeniging: a promise of future self-government for the conquered territories; and an agreement that the question of the 'native franchise' would be decided only after the attainment of self-government. Taken together these concessions offered Afrikaners a strong – even winning – hand in any discussions on the future of the territory.

And so, as the political debate was stepped up, Boer opinion-makers began to realise with growing excitement that the formation of a united country did not necessarily mean that Afrikanerdom would be swamped by English-speakers. On the contrary, with their superior numbers, it would not be impossible for the *volk* to end up running the new country on largely Afrikaner terms. But crucial to the realisation of these whispered ambitions was the need for unity, the support of at least some English-speakers and the neutralisation of the more liberal 'native policy' of the Cape Colony.

These problems were tackled in three ways: by adopting what appeared to be a conciliatory attitude towards Milner's attempts to rebuild the country; by elevating the bogey of *die swartgevaar* (the black threat) into a major political issue; and by appearing to champion the cause of white workers in their fight against exploitative bosses.

Of course, the canny Boer leaders were well aware that there was little danger of whites being 'swamped' by the African masses. Many English-speakers in Natal, the OFS, the Transvaal and the Cape were equally racist – while Milner himself had stressed often enough that the 'ultimate end' of the reconstruction process was a 'self-governing white community supported by a well-treated and justly governed black labour [force] from Cape Town to the Zambezi'. But the Boers, in acting as they did, were in effect ensuring that their viewpoints were placed near the top of the political agenda.

Thus, in the face of the anti-African (and later, the anti-Chinese) onslaught, even those Cape-based politicians who were known as 'friends of the natives' were forced into a rethink. For the sake of a broader (white) South Africanism – and as a result of an influx of Africans into the colony – they began to change their cautious calls for voting rights for 'civilised' Africans in the four colonies to one of 'fair treatment for all natives'.

Their change of heart cleared the way for a single 'native policy' for the whole region ....

Moves towards a common 'native policy'

Milner quickly found his man to tackle this task: Sir Godfrey Yeatman Lagden, the 52-year-old Native Commissioner for the Transvaal.

Lagden became a humble post office clerk upon his arrival in South Africa in 1878. But after holding down various clerical and secretarial jobs, he had moved into the remote areas of Swaziland and Basutoland where he built up a glowing reputation as a specialist in 'native affairs'. In 1897, he had used his deft negotiating skills to prevent an armed uprising by a Sotho chief named Moiketsi, and the grateful British Government had rewarded him with a knighthood.

But Milner had other plans for conscientious Sir Godfrey: chairmanship of a prestigious new body, the South African Native Affairs Commission (SANAC), along with a brief to draw up a 'native policy' which would be supported by all four colonies.

The SANAC commissioners met for the first time in October 1903, and thereafter travelled extensively to gather evidence from a wide range of opinion. Finally, in 1905, Lagden presented Milner with a report which ran to five volumes and which confirmed the worst fears of the small but growing group of Western-educated Africans . . . .

Land and labour

Based on the premise that whites were of 'superior intellect', the bulk of the commission's recommendations revolved around ways of creating separate, different worlds for the black and white communities of the country.

Pointing to what they referred to as the 'traditional homelands' of the Zulu in Natal, the Xhosa in the eastern Cape and the Sotho in Basutoland, the commissioners argued that a basis for a great deal of 'natural separation' already existed – and that a good starting point would be for these areas to be surveyed, gazetted and protected by legislation against further white encroachment.

But in looking at the question of African Reserves, the commissioners were also deeply aware that they could not give Africans too much land. A key part of Milner's reconstruction plans – a united anglicised country – depended on drawing thousands of British immigrants into an expanding economy. But the economy could expand only if there was a cheap labour force – and although Milner had earmarked blacks for this task, not enough Africans were prepared to leave the Reserves and white farms (where they subsisted as peasant producers) to work for a pittance in 'white' towns.

The answer to the problem was cynical but simple – it involved creating a land shortage in the Reserves in order to force more and more rural Africans into the service of white industry and agriculture. In proposing this the commission stressed that labour secured by these means should always be male, single, based in the Reserves, regarded as temporarily employed in 'white' areas and

SIR GODFREY LAGDEN *and his South African Native Affairs Commission were charged by Milner to draw up a 'native policy' that would be acceptable to all four colonies. His report called for land occupied by Africans to be strictly limited, to force out labour.*

paid at rates which mining, agriculture or 'the country' could afford. Furthermore, they suggested that the Pass laws be strictly applied to ensure that 'surplus' or 'idle' Africans were promptly returned to the Reserves.

Arguing for the implementation of this policy, Lagden said: 'A man cannot go with his wife and children and his goods . . . on to the labour market. He must have a dumping ground. Every rabbit must have a warren where he can live and burrow and breed, and every native must have a warren too.'

Education and political rights

The commission's recommendations on education came as a particular blow to those Africans who had adopted a Western style of life.

Black tuition, the commissioners recommended, had to be tailored to 'fit [the African] for his position in life'. And while they acknowledged that compulsory education for blacks would benefit the country in the long term, they felt that Africans were not yet ready for such a step. And even if they were, it would cost too much to implement.

These arguments merely camouflaged the real reason for their opposition to the creation of more educational opportunities for blacks: fear.

Ndabeni – and the fight against segregation

In 1899, a fearful white community called on the government to act against what it claimed to be a 'kaffir invasion' of Cape Town.

The fact that the African population had increased from its 1891 figure of 800 to several thousands had led to the build-up of anti-black feeling. Within a year, Africans were being blamed for almost every misfortune striking the city; and within two years the Cape Government was sufficiently moved by both the editorials of the 'Cape Times' and the opinions of prominent 'native experts' to embark on a policy of racial segregation every bit as brutal as that being practised by its northern neighbours.

Yet the majority of Africans who flocked to the Peninsula at the turn of the century were simply looking for work. And they had chosen Cape Town because it was generally agreed that working conditions and wages there were far better than those in other industrial centres.

Many, however, had quickly become disillusioned.

For a start, accommodation was a major problem. Few whites were prepared to rent out houses or rooms to blacks. Except in the most run-down areas of District Six and Woodstock (Papendorp) where a few fortunate families were able to find lodgings, the majority of the new work-seekers were forced either to build their own shacks on vacant pieces of ground or to live in caves or under bushes on the slopes of Table Mountain.

This created a health problem which provided welcome ammunition for the supporters of segregation.

Francis 'Matabele' Thompson, a well-known 'native expert' (and friend of Cecil John Rhodes), offered a blunt solution to the 'native problem': the government, he said, should 'enclose five and fifty or sixty acres of its land near Maitland with a fence 10 feet high, barbed wire, and, forcing all natives within that area, sound the curfew bell at eight o'clock, arresting under a Pass law every native out and abroad after the bell . . . .'

He was supported by Cape Town's Medical Officer of Health, who added that the living conditions of Africans were 'very undesirable, both from the point of view of sanitation and socially, by bringing uncleanly, half-civilised units into intimate contact with the more cleanly and civilised portion of the community'.

He suggested that instead of Africans being allowed to house themselves 'indiscriminately over the city', they should be placed in government-run locations.

Few white officials disagreed with this proposal. But the problem was where to build a location.

A suggestion by Native Affairs Department official Walter Stanford that a site in Maitland be chosen was angrily opposed by local residents who objected to Cape Town 'shunting its kaffirs' in their direction. But their protests were ignored: in 1900, a government commission headed by Stanford recommended that an African area be established on Uitvlugt, a state farm near Maitland.

Work on the location began on 19 February 1901, immediately after an outbreak of bubonic plague in Cape Town. Within three weeks, the first group of 500 Africans was moved under existing health regulations to Uitvlugt from District Six. By 19 March more than 5 000 people had been rehoused under the same regulations, and by the middle of the year the only Africans who remained in the centre of Cape Town were those who were there illegally or who had been granted special permission to stay.

Accommodation at Uitvlugt consisted of five large dormitories, each housing 500 men; 615 corrugated iron lean-tos, measuring approximately 6 m by 4 m and housing seven or more people; and a smaller number of tents.

From the start the authorities exercised tight control over the location: no strangers were allowed to stay longer than 24 hours; liquor was banned; women visitors were not allowed to stay overnight; and new arrivals had to

THOUSANDS *of Africans were forced to move out of Cape Town to a 'native contact camp' at present-day Ndabeni.*

ASPIRANT LAWYER Alfred Mangena led a highly successful rent boycott by Africans at Ndabeni.

present themselves to the superintendent, who would provide them with an identity card and a place to live.

Although not all whites supported the principle of separate locations for Africans, many of those who criticised the practice seldom did so on moral grounds. Cape Town merchants, for instance, complained that it was inconvenient to have their workers living out of town. But it was half-hearted opposition which received little support. In fact, the 'Cape Register' probably summed up the feelings of most whites when it commented in March 1901 that 'the protection of the metropolis from the insanitary disease-spreading nigger is a much more vital matter than the convenience of a few St George's Street merchants'.

Although some Africans had supported the idea of a location, mainly because they believed it would lead to cheaper rentals and the opportunity to buy their own ground, many had resisted the move to Uitvlugt (soon to be renamed Ndabeni) from the outset. It was mainly these people who from June 1901 began organising strong resistance to conditions in the camp.

Led by Alfred Mangena, an aspirant lawyer and later a founder member of the South African Native National Congress, residents embarked on a highly successful rent boycott. By January 1902, worried Department of Native Affairs officials estimated that tenants owed more than £12 000 in unpaid rents. In an attempt to break the boycott the authorities reduced the rent from 10 to 8 shillings a month. But when this did not work they introduced a system whereby those who paid were given metal tokens. Those without the tokens were ordered to be arrested.

Among those hauled before the courts was Arthur Radas, described by the authorities as a 'well-known agitator'. When Radas took the matter to the Appeal Court and explained that he had refused to pay because he had been forced against his will to live in the location, he won his appeal on a technicality.

In July 1902, the government issued Act 40 (of 1902) which was aimed at putting the administration of the location on a proper legal footing. In terms of the new law, Uitvlugt was recognised as a duly established 'native reserve location' and its name changed to Ndabeni.

Nothing, it now seemed, could prevent the government from establishing more such exclusively African residential areas . . . .

To the SANAC and other leading proponents of segregation, a 'native' in the classroom was a step away from a 'native' demanding 'white' jobs, the vote or a say in the running of the country.

Wilfred Wybergh, a leading member of the South African League, summed up the fears of the majority of his countrymen when he said: 'Those who say that in the long run the natives are or will be fit to share our civilisation are saying in so many words that they will dominate it, for in numbers they exceed ourselves.'

Turning to the question of political rights, the SANAC noted the growing influence of the African vote in the Cape but expressed doubts as to whether Cape liberals would allow the growth of a black majority. In any event, the commissioners were quick to point out that the other three colonies would never allow the implementation of a Cape-style franchise in a united South Africa.

On the other hand, the commission was not against Africans having a forum where they could discuss matters which specifically affected them. And in this respect, the commissioners suggested that existing tribal structures be strengthened in order to give Africans an 'authentic' voice to make representations to the white government – provided, of course, that this was done 'without conferring on them political power in any aggressive sense, or weakening in any way the unchallenged supremacy and power of the ruling race . . . .'

The possibility of whites representing blacks in a future union parliament was also discussed at some length, but the majority view was that white and black political institutions be kept separate.

In retrospect, although the SANAC's recommendations had a profoundly paternalist and conservative cast, these flowed naturally from colonial (and British) assumptions and intentions.

In many ways, the authors of the report, as well as those who took part in the debate which followed its publication, found it convenient to rely in varying degrees on claims that the 'noble savage' had to be 'protected' and that the ruling white race bore a responsibility to preserve tribal ways and institutions by minimising the exposure of Africans to the 'corrupting' influence of European culture.

Developments after Union

The doctrine of segregation – which wove together strands of existing white colonist racism with the interests of administrators and employers – was critical to the achievement of Union. By common consent, the 'native question' was raised beyond other serious political and economic divisions that existed within the white community, providing much-needed common ground between English- and Afrikaans-speakers in the uneasy years immediately after Union.

By 1910, the term 'segregation' was in common use, with the Labour Party being the first to adopt it as a policy platform in the election campaign of that year.

But the man who did most to build on – and to tie up the loose ends of – the SANAC report was Jan Smuts, the deputy leader of and arguably the most gifted ideologue in the governing South African Party (SAP). Recognising the advantages offered by a cheap, docile and therefore highly exploitable labour force, Smuts masterminded a series of laws which sought to control the movement, settlement and economic status of blacks.

Thus the Mines and Works Act of 1911 effectively barred blacks from skilled jobs on the mines and confirmed them as suppliers of cheap labour. The Natives' Land Act of 1913 (see page 291), which established the principle of territorial separation, soon followed. In 1920, the Native Affairs Act was passed, creating separate administrative structures for Reserve inhabitants. This was followed in 1923 by the Natives (Urban Areas) Act which extended the principle of segregation to urban areas, laid the groundwork for locations to house black workers in white urban areas, and amended the Pass laws to restrict African access to these areas.

The building blocks of segregation

In the early 1900s, South African legislators, motivated by insecurity and greed, set out to devise a defensive bastion against black advancement and to ensure that African labour remained cheap and easy to control. The result was the so-called 'Bedrock' legislation – in which the basic principles of segregation were enshrined in statutes.

The 1911 Mines and Works Act
The Mines and Works Act forced blacks into the category of cheap labour. It became the cornerstone of job reservation – racial discrimination in the allocation of jobs – by putting a wide range of skilled jobs beyond the 'competency' of blacks on the mines and the railways. It had its origins in a similar ordinance passed by the British administration in the Transvaal seven years earlier when, to allay fears of white workers that they would be undercut by imported Chinese labour, severe restrictions were placed on the Chinese, limiting them to unskilled labour only. The provisions of this ordinance were later extended to blacks, and then transferred to the Mines and Works Act of the first Union Government. Certificates were issued for skilled jobs; a regulation was passed in terms of the Act to the effect that 'coloured persons' in the Transvaal and Orange Free State would not be granted these certificates and that certificates issued to such persons in the Cape or Natal would not be recognised.

The 1913 Natives' Land Act
The Natives' Land Act provided the base for territorial separation of white and African in the rural areas, and was derived from the recommendations of the South African Native Affairs Commission. It effectively froze existing 'tribal' areas, scheduling about 10,5-million morgen of land as areas for exclusive African occupation – primarily in Zululand, Ciskei and Transkei, but it also stopped Africans from acquiring additional land outside these areas. Court action to prevent the government from extending these provisions to the Cape was subsequently upheld. But the Cape was included in 1936 legislation which gave added weight to the 1913 statute by finalising the apportioning of land to the Reserves. The Act also undermined the rights of African sharecroppers on white farms, but preserved labour tenancy. In this Act was the source of one of the chief black grievances against the white government: Africans were given ownership rights in just over 7 percent of the land area of South Africa (extended to 13 percent in 1936).

The 1920 Native Affairs Act
The Native Affairs Act was yet another spinoff of the South African Native Affairs Commission report of 1905. It paved the way for the creation of a countrywide system of tribally based, but government appointed, district councils modelled on the lines of the Glen Grey Act of 1894. The principle of separate, communally-based political representation for Africans was extended by the 1936 Representation of Natives Act.

The 1923 Natives (Urban Areas) Act
The Natives (Urban Areas) Act legislated on a broad front to regulate the presence of Africans in the urban areas. It gave local authorities the power to demarcate and establish African locations on the outskirts of white urban and industrial areas, and to determine access to, and the funding of, these areas. Local authorities were expected to provide housing for Africans, or to require employers to provide housing for those of their workers who did not live in the locations. Africans living in white areas could be forced to move to the locations. Local authorities were empowered to administer the registration of African service contracts, and to determine the extent of African beer-brewing or trading rights in the locations. Municipalities were also instructed to establish separate African revenue accounts based on the income from fines, fees and rents exacted from 'natives' in the locations; this money was to be used for the upkeep and improvement of the locations. The critical function entrusted to the local authorities was, however, the administration of tougher Pass laws: Africans deemed surplus to the labour needs of white households, commerce and industry, or those leading 'an idle, dissolute or disorderly life', could be deported to the Reserves. In implementing the Act, local authorities were careful to consider the needs of industry. In Johannesburg, for instance, where industrialists made no bones about wanting a large pool of permanent standby labour, it was only intermittently applied until the end of the 1940s. The Act was amended in later years.

On this foundation, and based on the assumption that the 'native' was – as Lagden put it – the 'unit of work' in South Africa, segregation developed primarily as a complex and delicately balanced part of labour control.

But if segregation was the foundation, the Reserves, the workers' compounds and the 'native' locations situated in the 'white' urban areas provided the building bricks of the evolving labour system.

And it was here that the government began exercising more and more control.

The Stallard report

Although industrial compounds were built and run on the assumption that the worker was not entitled to any of the comforts of a normal family life, the Parks and Estates Committee of the Johannesburg municipality reported in 1912 that it had issued almost 10 000 permits for the building of compounds.

Yet the massive trek from countryside to town did not keep the Reserves intact. As overcrowding increased and as more labour was drawn away, so the Reserves became increasingly run down, forcing even greater numbers of Africans to seek permanent employment in urban areas.

At first the government appeared to be sympathetic to the plight of the new urban dwellers (most of whom technically had 'no right' to be in the towns). Indeed, during discussions with members of the Native Conference, a body of state-nominated African leaders, government spokesmen promised to relax the Pass laws and to enact legislation to allow Africans living lawfully in towns to have proper security of tenure.

But in 1922, a report on urban Africans by a Transvaal Local Government Commission led by a hardline segrega-tionist named Frederick Stallard persuaded the state drastically to change its stance: 'It should be a recognised principle,' declared the commission, 'that natives – men, women and children – should only be permitted within municipal areas in so far and for as long as their presence is demanded by the wants of the white population . . . . The masterless native in urban areas is a source of danger and a cause of degradation of both black and white . . . . If the native is to be regarded as a permanent element in municipal areas . . . there can be no justification for basing his exclusion from the franchise on the simple ground of colour.' By 1923, Smuts' attitude had changed. Swayed by Stallard's arguments, the government he now led (since the death of Louis Botha in 1919) pushed through the Natives (Urban Areas) Act which reaffirmed that blacks would be allowed into white towns only to work.

Although bitterly attacked by African leaders for what was seen as a breach of promise, an unrepentant Smuts defended his government's actions in parliament: 'The whole idea of a proclaimed area is to keep a watchful eye on the population as a whole . . . . Where [you have] thousands and thousands of natives from all parts of South Africa together, unless [you take] special precautions and [exert] special control, the situation must get out of hand . . . . [You need] practically every man to be identifiable so that you may know where you are . . . .'

Smuts' decision to bow to pressures for greater control over Africans presaged a new harshness in the laws

PROVINCE OF TRANSVAAL

REPORT

OF THE

LOCAL GOVERNMENT COMMISSION

(1921)

T.P. 1–1922.   GOVERNMENT PRINTING AND STATIONERY OFFICE PRETORIA 1922

FREDERICK STALLARD'S 1922 *Transvaal Local Government Commission recommended that 'natives' be permitted in municipal areas only 'for as long as their presence is demanded by the wants of the white population'.*

governing black township life. Over the next two decades, 'native policy' was closely modelled on the recommendations of the Stallard report. By 1927, 64 locations had been formally established in terms of the Natives (Urban Areas) Act – most of which had been in existence prior to the legislation, and compulsory residential segregation had been proclaimed in 26 urban areas.

But worse was to come for Africans – in the form of a new government which was even more right wing than the administration headed by Smuts . . . .

Pact and segregation

In 1924, after the ruling SAP had suffered a series of by-election defeats – including a shattering setback in the 'safe' Transvaal constituency of Wakkerstroom – Smuts called a general election.

It was a decision which surprised no one – least of all the leader of the Opposition, Barry Hertzog, whose inspired decision to sign an election pact with the Labour Party in 1923 made it almost a foregone conclusion that the Pact would be swept into power.

In terms of the agreement, the parties entered the election fray on a 'White South Africa First' platform. Not only would there be more segregation, party leaders Hertzog and Frederic Creswell explained, but legislation would also be enacted to protect white workers against cheaper black competition. Furthermore, to stimulate local industry (and thus create more jobs for whites) heavy taxes would be imposed on overseas goods.

It was a winning formula.

With Nationalists triumphing in 63 seats and with the Labour Party coasting home in 18 – against the 53 of the SAP – Hertzog was able to form a new government with a comfortable majority of 28 seats. It was an important step forward for Afrikaners. Daniel Malan used his new cabinet position to campaign for bilingualism in the Public Service, and in 1925 the meaning of 'Dutch' in the constitution was extended to include Afrikaans, which became recognised as an official language for the first time.

The Pact Government pursued segregation with vigour, firing the opening shots in the legislative process which, by 1936, would finally remove Cape Africans from the common voters' roll.

It started in 1925, when Hertzog offered to increase the size of African Reserves in exchange for the voting rights of Cape Africans. In July 1926, he placed three Bills before parliament: the Native Lands Further Release Bill, designed to make additional land available for inclusion in the Reserves; the Union Native Council Bill, intended to establish a 50-man African Council to replace the Native Conference established by the Native Affairs Act of 1920; and the Representation of Natives in Parliament Bill, which sought to remove Cape Africans from the common roll and appoint seven white MPs to represent Africans throughout South Africa.

Although it took him another 10 years to get his way (see page 342), Hertzog did succeed in 1927 in pushing through the Native Administration Act, which conferred wide-ranging powers on the government. The Governor-General was made Paramount Chief of all Africans, with the power to appoint chiefs and headmen, move 'tribes' from one area to another, define 'tribal' boundaries, rule by proclamation in any African area, impose censorship, prescribe the wearing of clothes, control the registration of land, determine judicial procedures, and – the most controversial clause of all – proscribe any utterance or action made 'with the intent to promote any feelings of hostility between natives and Europeans'.

A 1924 ELECTION POSTER *urges voters not to vote for the new Pact combination of Barry Hertzog's National and Frederic Creswell's Labour parties. The 'White South Africa First' election platform of the Pact lured thousands of disillusioned voters away from Smuts' South African Party – and Hertzog formed a new government with a comfortable majority of 28 seats in parliament. The new administration wasted little time in trying to put its segregationist policies into effect.*

THE NATIONAL-LABOUR GOVERNMENT *after the election victory in 1924. Among those in the cabinet were (front row, left to right) P G W Grobler, F H P Creswell, J B M Hertzog, the Earl of Athlone (Governor-General), T J de V Roos, D F Malan and T Boydell. Back row (left to right): N C Havenga (third from left), C W Malan and J C G Kemp.*

Pact and the white worker

Although these segregationist measures were welcomed by those who had voted it into power, the Pact Government did not receive such support in the field of white labour relations, despite the introduction in 1924, following the 1922 white miners' strike, of the first Industrial Conciliation Act, which laid down strict procedures for dealing with collective bargaining in an effort to minimise the disruption to industry caused by industrial unrest.

In some respects, its white labour programme was similar to that of the previous government, while in other ways it was worse. Creswell, the Minister of Labour, tried hard, but he was unable to persuade the cabinet to impose a 'civilised labour' policy on the mines or to pursue his radical and economically unfeasible dream of completely replacing African mine labour with white. Neither did the wages of white miners – which had dropped sharply after the 1922 strike and were also a major determinant of general industrial wages – improve markedly during the Pact's tenure, despite public pressure and threats from Creswell. Nor was there any dramatic increase in the number of white mining jobs, despite amendments to the Mines and Works Act which gave the Minister of Mines the power to extend job reservation.

While the Chamber of Mines had indirectly supported the SAP in the election of 1924, and viewed the Pact victory with a degree of alarm, its fears were largely unfounded. In the cabinet, Creswell alone showed serious antipathy towards the mining industry; the other Ministers were increasingly aware of the need for co-operation between the interests of mining and the State. And so, instead of forcing the mines into implementing its policy of 'civilised labour', the Pact Government placed the burden of providing jobs for the growing white urban population on the Public Service by expanding white employment in the central administration, on the taxpayer through public works programmes such as railways or irrigation schemes, and on the manufacturing sector.

All told, white labour had traded its strike weapon for a promise of government protection, and mining had sacrificed its autonomy in dealing with labour disputes in return for industrial peace, reduced costs and increased control over its employment policies. Government, which was steadily increasing its reach over the process of modern economic development, was also inclined to preserve its accommodation with the mining houses. The result was growing white prosperity and a dramatic drop in lost production time, illustrated by the fact that, between 1919-22, 2,8-million man hours were lost by South African industry as a whole, compared to only 114 000 man hours between 1924-32.

In sum, the years between Reconstruction and the 1929 election saw the development of segregationist ideology and its translation into a legislative programme aimed at ensuring a supply of cheap African labour to industry and agriculture. During the same period, the growing confrontation between white labour and the mining industry over efforts to derive the maximum advantage from African labour at the expense of white workers was defused: firstly, by the intervention of government troops, and then by the passing of legislation aimed at the settlement of labour disputes with the minimum of disruption to industry.

Revolt in the countryside

Few people – least of all the government – were prepared for the political upheaval
that swept through the South African countryside during the 1920s.
But driven by anger over poverty, low wages and increasingly tough government laws –
and supported by trade unionists, communists, political activists
and independent church leaders – thousands of rural Africans began a revolt
that was both frantic and unplanned – and that in the end ran out of steam . . . .

IT WAS A SERIES OF CAMPAIGNS designed to win hearts
and minds, waged by an assortment of white communists, trade unionists, 'independent church' leaders, bogus doctors – and a young Nyasalander named Clements Kadalie . . . . It involved the mobilisation of a massive, but largely illiterate and politically unsophisticated
African rural population.

It was an awesome task – certainly the most ambitious
ever undertaken by opponents of white racism – and
progress, at first, was painfully slow. By 1925 scornful
government spokesmen, who from the start had predicted that 'these pseudo-enlightened natives . . . will get very
little sympathy or encouragement from kraal natives',
were pronouncing the campaign a failure.

But they had misread the situation. Within a year they
would be using every law at their disposal to contain what
quickly became a tide of rural African protest. In so smugly
dismissing the build-up of political activity in the countryside, state authorities had failed to take into account two
crucial factors: the tenacity and, in some cases, the charisma of the activists, and, more significantly, the extent of
African dissatisfaction.

By the early 1920s, drought, cattle fever and crop failure
had led to rampant poverty in already overcrowded
Reserves – forcing many young men to trek to the towns
to seek work as migrant labourers. Conditions were also
deteriorating on white farms where the expansion of plantations and grazing areas resulted in the eviction of many
African tenant labourers. As economic depression bit
deeper, already low wages were lowered even further. By
1926, increasingly desperate rural Africans in their tens of
thousands began responding to appeals for mobilisation.

Enter the Industrial and Commerical Workers' Union
In this respect, no one made a bigger impact than Clements
Kadalie, a young Nyasalander who spoke no black South
African language but used English to spread the universal
message of worker unity.

Filled with a burning ambition to lead a mass movement
of workers to political and economic freedom, Kadalie had
founded the Industrial and Commercial Workers' Union
(ICU) among Cape Town dock workers in 1919 (see page
310). Urban-based at first, the ICU had flourished after its
formation – but by the mid-1920s, fights over money, mis-
appropriation of funds and autocratic decisions by top officials had pitched it into rapid decline. As disillusioned
members began drifting away, the ICU, rather than mend

its fences with disappointed supporters, decided to seek
its salvation in a drive for rural membership in the Orange
Free State (OFS), Transvaal and Natal.

Between October 1926 and July 1927, 43 branches were
opened in these three provinces. By the end of 1927 there
were more than 100 ICU branches with a claimed membership of more than 100 000 throughout the country.

CLEMENTS KADALIE (seated), the young Nyasalander who
organised workers in the Industrial and Commercial Workers'
Union. With him is George Champion.

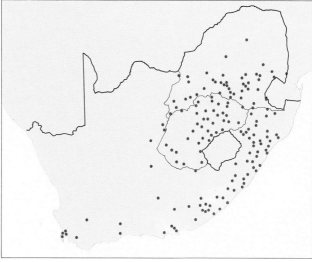

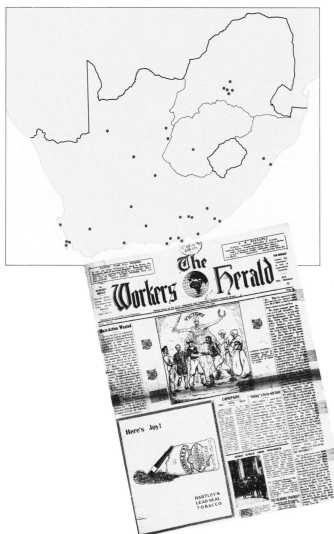

THE ICU QUICKLY SPREAD *throughout South Africa, publishing its own newspaper, 'The Workers' Herald' (left). An indication of the union's enormous popularity can be gained from the two maps (above). The left map shows the location of* ICU *branches between 1919 and 1925, while the right map shows the* ICU*'s enormous penetration of the Transvaal, Orange Free State and Natal between 1926 and 1930. By the end of the 1920s, however, the union had begun a decline that soon saw it fade into oblivion.*

As it started shifting from town to country, so its emphasis switched from trade unionism to militant nationalism. In doing so, it ignited a powder-keg of seething African disaffection and protest, which exploded into violence when 23 000 ICU supporters staged a work stayaway in Bloemfontein in 1925. Angry over low wages and police raids on backyard breweries, the protesters marched through the streets, waving the union's red flags and attacking police property. In the confrontation with the police, five marchers were shot dead. Over the next few months this scenario would be repeated several times ....

Into the Transvaal

By 1926 the ICU bandwagon had reached the Transvaal rural districts where most African workers were tenant labourers who had earned their slender land rights through work under often brutal conditions: 'You people,' a Piet Retief farmer was reported to have told his tenants, 'you ... shit on my farm, you rear stock on my farm, and you till my land, so you are not going to be paid, you bloody fools!' At first, many African workers accepted this state of affairs. Given the choice of working for nothing to retain a house on a farm – or being forced to return to an overcrowded Reserve, many opted to forgo wages – until Kadalie told them otherwise ....

'What is good enough for the white man is good enough for you,' he said at a rally in Middelburg in 1926. In Lydenburg, another ICU speaker told his audience: 'Our aim is to be one with the white race.'

Swept along on a tide of nationalism and emotionalism, workers opened and closed meetings by singing the 'Red Flag' (the communist anthem), delivered fiery speeches, and sometimes fought pitched battles with local police. At the same time pressure was put on the undecided to join. In an editorial, the union's official newspaper, 'The Workers' Herald', said: 'We say farewell to you who do not want to join the ICU, for we are marching forward to meet Africa ... *Vuka Afrika! Mayibuye iAfrika!*' ('Africa arise! Let Africa return!').

Inspired by these demonstrations of opposition, many rural Africans left white churches and stopped carrying Passes. Others refused to renew dog licences or pay taxes and cattle-dipping fees. In another development, ICU provincial leader Thomas Mbeki toured eastern Transvaal towns, directing blacks to walk, not in the streets (where they were supposed to), but on the pavements with whites. A rash of strikes started on farms, and workers defied their employers by attending meetings, discussing the ICU, seeking the union's intervention in disputes, and occasionally maiming cattle.

July 1924

THE FIERY RHETORIC of ICU speakers such as George Champion (left) spearheaded the ICU's growing popularity in Natal, where supporters proudly posed for group photographs – such as the one above, which includes uniformed union members who described themselves as ICU 'soldiers'.

Yet, looking back, resistance by the ICU was neither well-organised nor comprehensive. Its biggest failing was its inability to mobilise large-scale support for action on specific issues. The reason for this was that rural Africans were too isolated by poverty and distance to come together in massive displays of strength. Others believed that the union would liberate them without their active support. In addition, tensions began to rise between the 'moderate' and 'radical' wings of the ICU: whereas the majority of the union's hierarchy favoured a policy of *hamba kahle* (proceeding carefully) and were strongly opposed to actions that broke laws, the 'radicals' wanted more direct methods to be used to challenge the state.

In 1928, the ICU, by now badly over-extended in the rural areas, discarded 'militant nationalism' for formal trade unionism. This change followed talks in London between Kadalie and British trade union leaders. Convinced that British-style unionism was the answer to the problems of African workers, ICU leaders began urging members away from broad political protest towards wage demands and increased cooperation with landowners. Promises such as 'liberation before Christmas 1927' were quietly forgotten and the strident threats of land repossession gave way to schemes where people were urged to bring money so that they could buy their own land.

Meanwhile, farmers, still furious that 'cheeky kaffirs' had dared to make demands and had even dragged them to the courts, took advantage of the new situation to hit back strongly. In a systematic campaign of harassment, they evicted ICU members from their farms, threatened organisers, and persuaded local magistrates to ban meetings and prosecute union leaders.

Membership fell off, new branches became harder to form and isolated ICU court victories did nothing to improve labour conditions. By 1930 the old fire was gone – the ICU was a spent force in the Transvaal.

The fight for Natal

The ICU had also found a willing audience in rural Natal, where Africans were fighting a losing battle to hold onto their land and cattle.

At the turn of the century, especially in the Umvoti area, African homesteads had often run to 90 acres. Now they had been reduced to between one and two acres, and cattle restricted to 10 a household. Many Africans found themselves unwelcome guests on land which they had once owned. So in desperation they turned to the ICU.

In Greytown, more than 5 000 workers attended the union's first meeting – and the Umvoti district as a whole claimed 16 000 members by 1928.

However, many recruits were under the impression that the ICU would give them farms and cattle – and the union, initially, did little to correct this impression. Certainly, when Kadalie remarked at a meeting in Estcourt that it would not be long before 'natives take over the farms of the white man', a surge of optimism swept through African ranks. And in a show of bravado, the Greytown organiser Zabuloni Gwaza destroyed wreaths on the graves of white policemen killed in the Bambatha rebellion. Then he drove to a wedding reception where he proclaimed: 'You white farmers' servants better tell your masters . . . I have broken the glass on the European's grave.' A second rampage through the cemetery earned him a jail sentence.

The ICU's campaign in Natal, however, was spearheaded by its dynamic 32-year-old provincial secretary, George Champion, who between 1925 and 1927 built his power-base into the mainstay of the national ICU. But there was little he could do when the destitute began crowding local offices, pleading for the farms and cattle they claimed they had been promised.

When strikes occurred in 1927, farmers hit back with evictions, hut-burning and the confiscation of cattle. Soon midlands towns thronged with homeless Africans.

MARCUS GARVEY

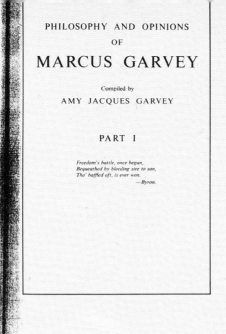

PHILOSOPHY AND OPINIONS
OF

MARCUS GARVEY

Compiled by
AMY JACQUES GARVEY

PART I

Freedom's battle, once begun,
Bequeathed by bleeding sire to son,
Tho' baffled oft, is ever won.
—Byron.

IN THE 'Philosophy and Opinions of Marcus Garvey', the West Indian-born American claimed that negroes would achieve liberty only if they returned to their ancestral homes. His teachings had a profound effect on the opponents of white rule in South Africa, many of whom adopted his belief that land must be returned to its ancestral owners.

Nevertheless, the ICU, masterminded by Champion, successfully challenged many evictions in the Natal Supreme Court, forcing the police in some areas to stop implementing magisterial eviction orders for fear of prosecution themselves. In some cases, those who had been evicted simply returned to the farms, believing their red membership cards would shield them from the wrath of the farmers and the law.

Soon angry farmers began calling for the banning of the union. Surprisingly, Prime Minister Barry Hertzog, anxious to avoid a head-on confrontation with the ICU, refused. On the other hand, the new and sweeping powers of the Native Administration Act meant jail for union organisers who promoted hostility between black and white. Union meetings were also banned in the Reserves.

Farmers, however, were not impressed. Furious at the government's apparent unwillingness to crush the ICU and its 'Bolsheviks', they decided to take the law into their own hands. In Greytown, a crowd of armed farmers tried twice to storm the local prison to get at Gwaza, who had been re-imprisoned for a further attack on headstones in the cemetery. Later they smashed up the local ICU office and set fire to union papers before chasing several thousand union members into the hills. White vigilantes took similar action in other midlands towns and an 'Anti-ICU' organisation was formed.

By the middle of 1928, the ICU's grip on Natal's rural Africans was fading fast: renewed drought, violence and unkept promises had broken their resolve and shattered their faith in the union. Moreover, Champion and Kadalie had fallen out – and the Natal strongman seceded from the ICU, taking his local followers with him into a competing regional body.

With this, the ICU began its slide into oblivion. Riddled with dissension, unable to meet the militant expectations of its rural supporters, and internally confused by its leadership's drift towards the British trade union model, it began once more to fall apart, the glory of its mass appeal now only a fading dream.

The teachings of Marcus Garvey

The majority of the political activists of the 1920s – including members of the ICU, the Communist Party and the African National Congress (ANC) – were influenced to varying degrees by the teachings of Marcus Garvey, a West Indian who had moved to the United States during the First World War. Preaching the unity of all blacks, he claimed that liberty would come about only through the return of all Afro-Americans to their ancestral homes – and to this end he had founded the Universal Negro Improvement Association in 1914.

By 1925 opponents of white racism, in cities and rural districts – but especially in the eastern Cape – had adapted the teachings of Garvey to fit in with the black South African experience. Thus the return of land to its ancestral owners became one of the central themes around which opposition to white settler rule was mobilised.

Not surprisingly, it was in Transkei that Garveyism had most appeal. Here, a devastating series of crop failures, cattle disease, drought and locust plagues put intense pressure on people already struggling to eke out an existence on ever-diminishing land.

At the same time, political and administrative changes served to compound grievances: chiefs were stripped of most of their traditional powers; cattle-dipping and restrictions on the movement of herds, that Transkeians had opposed since their introduction in 1906, were enforced more strictly; new taxes were demanded, and the government wanted them to give up their limited Cape voting rights in return for more land.

A newspaper commented: 'These are the general conditions of life; poverty growing into hunger, debt with no hope of escape. No people under the sun who have not been tamed and weakened by centuries of low diet and despotism can fail, in such conditions, to get into a state of unrest.'

The broad mass of Reserve-based Africans were still deeply rural, clinging tenaciously to a way of life now under serious threat. And so they adopted Garveyism, which

The bizarre 'Dr' Wellington Buthelezi

Wellington Buthelezi was a charlatan and a liar. But in the turbulent 1920s, he was able to capture the mood of Transkei at a time when its people sought leadership, and bind them into a mass movement.

He was born around 1895 near Melmoth, Natal, and educated at a Lutheran mission school. Aged about 23, he began to travel in southern Africa although little is known about his life from 1918-21. Then he registered at the Lovedale College in the eastern Cape, where he was remembered more for the fancy clothes he wore than for his academic achievements.

In 1923 he was fined for practising medicine with only a herbalist's licence. By 1925 he was running a thriving business, peddling medical concoctions in Transkei and diagnosing all types of illness with a stethoscope and a battery (he ran electrical currents through his patients).

Then, claiming to represent Marcus Garvey's Universal Negro Improvement Association and the African Communities League, he joined a separatist church. By now he had changed his name to Dr Butler Hansford Wellington and had concocted for himself a new history: born in Chicago, qualified as a doctor, travelled from New York to Portuguese East Africa. Later he claimed to have been born in Liberia (the African state founded by freed slaves in the 19th century) and to have studied at Oxford and Cambridge. In 1925 Buthelezi fell briefly under the influence of Ernest Wallace, a West Indian Garveyist clergyman who preached divine intervention; Buthelezi changed it to the coming of the Americans.

Short and stout, he sported mutton-chop whiskers and a large moustache. He is said to have worn glasses and to have had six suits into which he would change at different times of the day. At meetings, he preached in the flowing robes of a minister.

Buthelezi treated history with cavalier disregard for facts, claiming on one occasion that King George V had given South Africa to the Americans as payment for their war services.

At one stage the authorities tried to deport him to the USA, but he appealed to the Natal ICU boss George Champion, who confirmed that he had been born in Natal. He was not heard of after 1937.

quickly developed into a strong anti-white sentiment, with 'Africa for the Africans' becoming their new slogan.

Nowhere was agitation against government attempts to introduce administrative change more marked than in the eastern Cape area of Herschel, settled many years before by refugees fleeing the forces of the Zulu king, Shaka. Two changes in particular raised traditionalist tempers in the region – a proposal to to establish local councils, with an accompanying increase in taxation, and a demand that landownership be registered, which was seen as upsetting existing communal ownership patterns and inserting the thin edge of a wedge that would end with the imposition of the feared councils.

The opposition that followed was a classic example of organised political resistance by rural Africans – led by an organisation called *Iliso Lomzi* (Vigilance Association) with particular support among women. The first clashes with the authorities were sparked by a more bread-and-butter issue than land tenure – a spate of high prices at local stores following poor rainfall in the summer of 1921-2. In March 1922 the Aliwal North newspaper reported a 'general boycott' of shops in Herschel, mainly by women who 'organise pickets near the shops and molest all natives coming away with purchases and take the goods from them'. The women demanded that people stop buying from the white shopkeepers until prices were cut – and the purchase price paid for wheat bought from local Africans increased. The boycott was halted after six months of sporadic action.

In the years that followed, further attempts were made to step up land registration, which prompted two kinds of protest – a renewed swing away from established mission churches to newly established independent churches, and in 1925 a serious boycott of schools, which worsened in early 1926 when, according to a teacher, groups of angry women 'drove . . . the children out of school and told them not to go to school again'.

The protest movement became organised under the name *Amafelandawonye* (the Diehards) or *Amafela*, with a plea for a political system based on a popular chieftancy with protection for customary rights (differing from the ANC, which sought to protect African rights in a common society). These differences in approach led to considerable tensions within the protest movement, with the mainly rural-based 'Africanists' attracting the attention of Wellington Buthelezi (see box), a long-time critic of the ANC, who had preached the gospel of Garvey in the region for up to 10 years winning a following that ran to many thousands, particularly in Transkei. A day of judgment was drawing near, Buthelezi claimed, in which American blacks would arrive in aeroplanes from which they would bomb all white and African non-believers with burning lumps of charcoal.

Buthelezi's supporters cheered lustily when he told them to stop paying taxes and to stop dipping their cattle. In fact, his strongholds in Transkei were precisely those areas in which people had protested so vigorously against cattle-dipping in 1914.

Transkei magistrates and the missionaries did not take kindly to the Wellingtonites, who were subverting their

KENNON THAELE (above left), brother of Western Province ANC leader James Thaele, speaking at Worcester in March 1930 during the ANC's struggle in support of rural workers – which in May erupted in violence that left five dead. The man next to him is an interpreter, while a boy holds the ANC flag. In December of the same year, Kennon was expelled from the ANC for 'communist tendencies'.

THE ICU executive (left) in 1925. Standing (left to right) are Thomas Mbeki, Jimmy la Guma and John Gomas. Seated are Clements Kadalie and George Champion.

authority, and Buthelezi was jailed and fined several times. By 1927 he had become such a menace to the state's ability to collect taxes and enforce dipping that he was permanently banned from Transkei. Although he continued his work elsewhere in the eastern Cape, his results were never as spectacular. By 1937, his following had dwindled to a few thousand. However, the ideas he had propagated held sway among eastern Cape Africans for many years, and at least one major separatist church still flies a flag of Garvey's colours.

The programme for a 'native republic'

The Communist Party of South Africa (CPSA), meanwhile, was pushing ahead with its plans for a new South Africa – adopting, in 1928, a plan for a 'native republic' based on a programme of mobilising rural Africans.

Two years earlier, when the party's policy had included merely the rejection of discriminatory legislation, the extension of the Cape franchise and the scrapping of Pass laws, its African membership had jumped from 200 to 1 600 out of a total of 1 750 members. Now as it set out to shift its focus from white workers to mass rural mobilisation it looked forward to even greater growth.

Early in 1927, the CPSA had sent James la Guma, the secretary of the ANC's Cape Town branch, to a League Against Imperialism conference in Brussels and from there on to Moscow. La Guma returned with a proposed programme based upon African majority rule – with one man, one vote. The CPSA's task, it was said, was to dismantle British and Afrikaner rule and to establish a 'democratic, independent native republic' run by black workers and peasants as a first step towards the overthrow of capitalism.

Many South African communists, including party leader Sydney Bunting, opposed the proposal. Arguing against it, Bunting said that although rural Africans were by far in the majority, they could not be the mainstay of a successful revolution because of their 'extreme backwardness and widespread apathy'.

Bunting's biggest fear was that the policy would destroy hopes of black and white worker unity, alienate white workers and drive them towards Afrikaner nationalism. It was his firm belief that socialism would be achieved only through worker unity under white leadership.

La Guma took a different view: white workers, he said, were 'saturated with imperialist ideology'. The key was national liberation through the mass of rural Africans.

In August 1928, Bunting argued – and lost – his case before the sixth international conference of the Communist International (Comintern) in Moscow. However, he accepted defeat with grace and returned to South Africa to throw all his energies into promoting La Guma and the Comintern's policy: an Independent South African Native Republic as a stage towards a Workers and Peasants Republic, which would guarantee protection and complete equality to all national minorities.

Although most white and many African communists were dissatisfied with the new policy, the party nevertheless took it to the electorate, contesting two seats during the 1929 parliamentary elections. It lost both heavily, partly because of poor organisation and police harassment. Thereafter the CPSA fell into decline, following a series of ideological shifts, wrangles and expulsions of some of the most talented members of the party.

The ANC in the western Cape

Although the western Cape branch of the ANC had forged close links with the CPSA and supported the 'native republic' policy, its work among rural Africans at first focused on local issues rather than broad political aims.

But as turmoil spread through the rural areas, and as Garveyism asserted itself in the branch through the strident rhetoric of its USA-educated president James Thaele, it could not remain aloof from internal conflict.

Yet few members of the ANC outside the Cape were prepared to support Thaele and 'radicals' such as Elliot Tonjeni and Bransby Ndobe even though Cape African and coloured farm workers, like their counterparts in the north, also faced problems of overcrowding, poverty and unemployment. Another grievance was the tot system – where workers received at least half a litre of wine each day in part-payment for their labour.

The Bulhoek massacre

On 24 May 1921, a detachment of police gunned down and killed 183 members of an African religious sect called the Israelites near Queenstown in the eastern Cape.

Led by the 'prophet' Enoch Mgijima, the group had built 'a refuge from oppression' at Ntabelanga, near Bulhoek. It was a society, that gave substance to a dream cherished by many rural Africans: land for the landless, an escape from taxes and self-rule without white oppression.

Converts were taught the virtues of cleanliness and purity and were ordered to abstain from fornication, adultery, riotous living, drinking and smoking. When the Day of Judgment came, accompanied by blood, fire and destruction, the Israelites would be transported to Heaven in wagons, Mgijima predicted.

By 1921, membership of the sect numbered more than 3 000.

But their quest for 'independence' put them on a collision course with both government officials and neighbouring Africans who feared Israelite encroachment on their valuable lands. As their numbers grew, converts took to squatting – illegally, according to government officials. 'Shorn of all absurdities,' commented the Secretary for Native Affairs, Edward Barrett, 'it simply amounts to a Bolshevik seizure of land .... The Israelite cult has spread, and other natives from elsewhere, attracted by the charms of a workless life, have joined the insurgents.'

In December 1920, when the government sent its new Native Affairs Commission to persuade the sect to leave, Mgijima's son Charles replied: 'God has sent us to this place. We shall let you know when it is necessary that we go.'

Converts, meanwhile, were continuing to stream in, attracted by the imminent confrontation, and fearful of the coming of Mgijima's 'judgment day'. Rumours that the Israelites were making swords and had obtained guns and ammunition increased fears among officials that the sect was planning an armed uprising.

In April 1921, the commission offered free rail tickets and rations to Israelites – on condition that they leave. But there were no takers – and when a similar offer was turned down a few weeks later, 800 policemen were assembled in Queenstown ....

On 21 May, the police commander, Colonel Theo Truter, sent an ultimatum to Mgijima: his men would arrest Israelites who had refused to obey subpoenas, would deport illegal residents, and would tear down illegally built houses.

But the determined Mgijima replied: 'I understand that you, Sir, intend to come out to Ntabelanga with an adequate force. May it therefore be known by one and all that the arms and forces shall be ruled by blood. As for myself, I am the messenger before the blood. The whole world is going to sink in ... blood. I am not the causer of it, but God is going to cause it. If you then, Sir, Mr Truter, are coming out to make war, please inform me. I shall then write or say my last word before you destroy me.'

On 24 May, while the Israelites were at their morning prayers, police armed with machine guns and artillery took up positions on the surrounding hills. The Israelites responded by assembling 500 men to defend the settlement.

There was a final parley at which Colonel Ernest Woon told an Israelite delegation: 'Go back to your people and tell them to surrender. If they fail to do so and oppose my advance, force will be used.'

But the Israelites were defiant: 'If it is to be a fight ... Jehovah will fight with us and for us,' they said. Police claimed later that they heard Mgijima order his men to charge, even though the two sides were several hundred metres apart. Other police said they heard shots and returned fire, but only two guns were found afterwards, both of them in Mgijima's house.

Dressed in white tunics and brown khaki shirts, and armed with knobkieries (a type of stick used as a club) and assegais, the Israelites surged forward. The police fired two volleys over their heads, but still they continued their advance.

Then the police lowered their aim and their bullets scythed through the Israelite ranks. Only a few warriors reached the police lines; behind them 183 of their fellows lay dead, and a further 100 injured.

Later Mgijima, his sons and more than 100 followers were jailed, despite widespread protest from Africans and many sympathetic whites over the government's bloody handling of the affair.

It was under these circumstances that the ANC began organising in Worcester – and from there in smaller towns such as Carnarvon, George and Ladismith – in 1929. But it was not easy. Farmers, enraged by Ndobe's 'agitation' among their workers, kicked him out of both Swellendam and Robertson. Realising the success of their campaign depended on resisting this kind of opposition, Ndobe and Tonjeni scheduled another meeting for Robertson – and set the scene for a violent clash between ANC supporters and their white opponents. Trouble started when a group of more than a thousand whites attacked a 200-strong crowd returning home from the ANC meeting. Several people were injured in the fight.

But by now the dominant conservative faction of the ANC, perturbed by the violence, decided to expel the 'radicals' of the western Cape branch, including Thaele's own brother, Kennon.

A MONTAGE of pictures shows the 'Israelites' being rounded up by police and the 'prophet' Enoch Mgijima (centre).

In justifying the expulsions, Thaele said: 'Having noticed the spread of bolshevistic tendencies among the non-Europeans in the Western Province, Congress is of the opinion that leaders and propagandists with communistic doctrines should not be allowed to address meetings organised by Congress.' Angry clashes broke out between supporters of Thaele and those who sympathised with the rebels. The purge of 'radicals' in the Cape ANC was in line with the conservatism which dominated African politics in the 1930s. In this instance, the shift to the right led to the replacement of national president Josiah Gumede by Pixley Seme and a decision by expelled western Cape members to form the Independent ANC. The frequent demand by the 'Independents' and their communist allies for 'universal' free education, full franchise rights for South Africa's people and the return of land to the African people pushed them into the forefront of the fight against 'white' racism.

But after further clashes with white vigilantes – in Carnarvon, Rawsonville, Barrydale and Worcester – both farmers and police moved to root out the Independent ANC. And in further developments, the Minister of Justice, Oswald Pirow, using new powers under the Riotous Assemblies Act, banned Sunday meetings and stopped ANC leaders from entering the Boland.

With the law effectively denying them a counter-strategy, the movement never fully recovered from these blows, and resistance, for the time being, came to an end.

But for nearly five years, whites throughout the country had witnessed African resistance – fearing all the time that it would spill over into general insurrection. Indeed, whether it was Garveyite or communist calls for an African republic; or the millennial expectations of religious groups in rural areas; or whether it was the organisational expansion of the ICU – there was much to alarm whites.

The initial response of the state to African unrest had been the Native Administration Act of 1927 which gave the Governor-General broad powers of control by making him a paramount chief. This had been followed up in 1929 with amendments to the Riotous Assemblies Act – which made it an offence to incite race hatred. In the same year Hertzog called what subsequently became known as the 'black peril' elections. Campaigning on the issue of colour, he tried to rally support for four Bills, which parliament had already rejected twice but which were aimed at curbing African and coloured voting rights.

Jan Smuts and his South African Party, Hertzog charged, stood for racial equality and integration, whereas the National Party was the only true champion of South African whites. In the Nationalists' 'black manifesto', Smuts was labelled as the 'apostle of a black kaffir state'. The result was that Hertzog and the National Party won their first outright majority – 78 seats to the 70 of the combined opposition of the South African and Labour parties. But he was denied the two-thirds majority he required to pass the Bills. Although Afrikaner nationalists now had sole power, the time was not yet ripe for them to rid parliament of black participation.

Nevertheless, legislative action had achieved at least one end: black resistance was on the retreat.

'Like spectres from the tombs'

From the 1860s onward, more and more whites in the Cape and the Transvaal were forced off the land to join a burgeoning working class while the landed entrepreneur became wealthier at the expense of less efficient farmers. Reacting to the poverty which resulted, the mainly Afrikaans-speaking poor whites nurtured a nationalism that sought to unite wealthy and impoverished Afrikaners – first under organisations such as the *Afrikaner Broederbond* (Afrikaner Brotherhood), and then in financial establishments to rival those of English-speaking capitalism – such as Volkskas Bank and the SANLAM Insurance giant.

THE MAGISTRATE OF THE tiny eastern Cape town of Alice had seen such cases before, and would do so again. Standing before him in the dock was George Gibson – who described himself as a carpenter from Dordrecht – charged with begging while drunk. After the briefest of hearings, he was fined and sent on his way.

Reporting the case, the 'Alice Times' referred to Gibson as a 'European loafer', a description that crops up time and time again in *dorp* (village) newspapers of the period. The year was 1876 – and the magistrate was seeing for himself the evidence of an increasing number of poverty-stricken Europeans who by the early 1890s were being described for the first time as poor whites.

Although pockets of white poverty had existed since the earliest days of colonialism, it was only after the 1860s that it began to occupy newspaper and official reports – suggesting a growing class of landless poor forced to scratch a living any way they could.

For example, reports from the Albany district in 1866 speak of 'so much distress' that 'unfortunate men' were 'wandering about the colony almost naked and completely penniless'. Reports from Fort Beaufort told a similar tale of 'unfortunate Europeans . . . in a state of destitution', as did harrowing accounts of 'skin and bones specimens of

humanity' and 'emaciated forms . . . seen to move about like spectres from the tombs'.

This seemingly sudden cycle of poverty had its roots in the greater concentration and commercialisation of farming, as well as a series of disastrous slumps that afflicted the Cape in the 1860s, '70s and '80s. A report from the district of Stockenstrom spoke of small farmers 'driven to eat roots and other edible wild productions' after their crops had failed. Pinpointing the increasing number of insolvencies as a result of trade depressions, the report noted that because little leniency was shown by 'the merchant with his letters of demand . . . the poor man has to part with land, wagons, oxen or sheep, to pay a debt which nature would not pay for him'.

Most of the smaller farmers who were driven off the land in this way ended up as carriers or transport riders in an economy increasingly dominated by rail.

The chief beneficiaries of the string of insolvencies were the wealthy sheep and ostrich farmers, who snapped up the vacant smaller farms for bargain prices. Their access to capital allowed them to build dams and buy pumps – and thus escape the worst effects of drought.

The installation of fencing on sheep and ostrich ranches was another blow to those living on the breadline: because

THIS POOR WHITE *family photographed at home in the Christiana district of the western Transvaal is typical of hundreds of impoverished, landless Afrikaners in the closing years of the last century. 'Home' was a wagon and a roughly made shelter as the family trekked around the country, staying for a year or two at a stretch as a bywoner (tenant farmer) on land owned by wealthier farmers before moving on, often accompanied by their livestock.*

it reduced labour costs, it meant that the landholder no longer needed to rent out land to white or black *bywoners* (literally a 'by-dweller', a tenant or squatter on another man's land). Inevitably, as the bigger farmers got richer, so the smaller producers went to the wall – being forced to join the growing ranks of men who could earn a living only by selling their labour – a system of proletarianisation that favoured the spread of agricultural capitalism.

Whites who ended up as farm labourers lived much the same as their African counterparts, as a traveller in the late 1870s noted when he visited a wealthy farmer in the Middelburg (Cape) district: 'All the servants, black as well as white, are provided with little, square built rooms which are furnished with table, chair, box, etc, grouped together like a small hamlet.'

The growth of the sheep industry even touched the lives of those poor whites who scratched a living gathering thatch. In 1875 the 'Alice Times and Seymour Gazette' reported that 'the only reason why a poor family can't get a living at thatch cutting is because the rich sheep farmer wants green pasture for his sheep, and to get this he saddles up his horse, and rides along the veldt with a box of favourite Tandstickors [matches], and drops them lighted into the grass'

Most of those forced off the land went to the nearest village or town, trying to eke a living from a combination of market gardening, transport riding, selling firewood, driving cabs or hawking prickly pears. Nearly all of them tried as long as possible to resist the almost inevitable slide into becoming wage-labourers.

The rising numbers of poor whites were boosted by immigrants – about 10000 arrived at the Cape between 1857 and 1863, and nearly 23000 between 1873 and 1883. The expanding rail network was a favourite source of work for, among others, Belgian navvies who were described by John Merriman, the Commissioner of the Public Works Department, as 'the scum and refuse of large towns'.

Navvies also found work digging dams for the more successful farmers – but this occupation was regarded as the bottom of the social scale and seemed to be reserved for immigrants who lacked the support and assistance of family and society. Other Europeans drifted into the police force, although the magistrate at Cradock complained in 1879 that 'such Europeans as join the force are, with two or three exceptions, a very low, drunken and disreputable class of men who give us a great deal of trouble'.

By 1875 the census reported that the Cape had more than 2000 white domestic workers, 2000 casual (undefined) labourers, 4000 in the transport sector (drivers, porters, stevedores and storemen) and more than 5000 in 'mechanical production' (rail and road navvies and builders).

In the cities, areas occupied by poor whites were known as 'low' or 'rough' quarters. In Port Elizabeth the poor quarter was situated between Main Street and the sea. There black and white children grew up 'inhaling the reeking atmosphere of dung-heaps, slaughter houses and tanneries'. The slum area of Grahamstown was known as 'bog-o'-me-finn', and was tenanted by a 'miscellaneous herd of whites and blacks who lived together in the most promiscuous manner imaginable'.

THE DWELLING *of a rural bywoner (tenant farmer) and his family, photographed by the Carnegie commission.*

Inter-racial marriages and casual sex among the urban poor took place on a large scale – and in 1893, a labour commission reported that whites were increasingly 'mixing with coloureds', marrying coloured women and 'assimilating more to the black race'. When an ex-*bywoner*, who had found work as a post-cart driver, was asked if there were 'many poor whites like yourself', he replied: 'I am a coloured man. My father was a Scotchman and my mother a black woman.' During this period, it was reported by a Uitenhage Divisional Council member, J S Grewer, that poor white men were happy enough to work among coloured men.

But while white and black workers appeared to be moving closer together, the gulf between wealthy and poorer whites was widening – and little sympathy was shown by the authorities for the poor, whose 'indolence' was often blamed for their misery. For example, the editor of the 'Graaff-Reinet Advertiser' welcomed the Vagrancy Act of 1879 because, as he put it, 'the town had hardly ever been free of . . . brandy-stinking whites who went about begging for a sixpence or a shilling'.

As the problems of the white destitute increased, abandoned children – some as young as five – were made available for indenture. In one case in 1876, an advertisement offering three sisters for indenture elicited a letter from a Mr Montague who said he 'should much like to get one of the Girls, the one of 12 years would be most useful, but if I can't get her the one of 8 would do'.

By the 1890s, however, this apparent callousness had softened – to be replaced by a view, imported mainly from England, that economic circumstances had more to do with poverty than the lack of a moral backbone – a standpoint that arose from the increasing groundswell of socialism in reaction to the growth of unbridled capitalism. This new point of view also helped to foster Afrikaner nationalism, particularly as the number of poor whites began to grow in the Transvaal.

Poor whites in the Transvaal

After the Great Trek, the Boers in the Transvaal settled down to a rural existence, living as much as possible off the land by hunting and a little farming. As land and game became scarcer, the search for more territory prompted explorations further afield.

The Boers were fiercely independent and family-bound. The wealthier farmers were always willing to lodge a needy person on their property in exchange for odd jobs and commando service. This *bywoner* often arrived with his family and two or three cows, and settled down more or less permanently on the farm. He tilled the soil and paid a minimal rent to the farmer from the crops he grew. The farmer never considered him a labourer – he kept Africans for that kind of work (see page 144).

But by the end of the 19th century the best land had run out – and when many farms were burnt by British soldiers in the South African War, in an attempt to stop guerrilla warfare, thousands of families were left destitute.

During the post-war years severe droughts scorched crops and there were sporadic locust plagues. Cattle and sheep began dying of stock diseases such as gall sickness and scab disease, and in 1896-7 a rinderpest epidemic wiped out the entire wealth of many farmers. As one catas-

'Once again, we lost nearly everything'

As the 1920s drew to a close a travel-worn Ford rattled over the corrugated dirt road into the northern Cape town of Kakamas on the Orange River. Inside the car sat the Reverend Johannes Albertyn, a Kimberley minister, who had come to see for himself how the people of this South African *dorp* (village) were coping with drought, economic depression and a changing society.

The stories that Albertyn meticulously recorded form a unique account of Afrikaners in crisis – what was later described as the lowest ebb that they had ever reached during two centuries of expansion into southern Africa. This is how one impoverished farmer described a life of disaster: 'I grew up in Prieska. After I was married I trekked about with my stock, even as far as German [South] West Africa. I got on, bit by bit, until I owned 700 head of small stock and 96 head of cattle. Then came the drought of 1896 and I was left with only 16 head of cattle and 11 goats. For the second time I improved my position, but it took years. For a long time I went about digging wells and making dams. At last I again owned 300 stock and 30 cattle. Then came the drought of 1915 and I lost absolutely everything. So I threw up the sponge and settled here [at Kakamas].'

Albertyn was one of five men appointed to gather evidence for a unique and unusual enquiry. At a time when the world was teetering on the edge of an economic slump, the Carnegie Corporation of New York agreed to grant money towards an 'investigation on the poor white question in South Africa' (see page 336).

Albertyn and his colleagues drove around South Africa listening to tale after tale of broken dreams and dashed hopes: 'I used to own a good farm in Hopetown, but it was too small. After my stock had accumulat-

CLERGYMAN *Andrew Murray helped highlight the plight of South Africa's poor white families long before the Carnegie Commission released its report (above).*

ed I sold the farm and bought a large one in Bechuanaland. Most of my cattle died there of a pernicious cattle disease. I dug 13 wells in a fruitless quest for water. After endless trekking I eventually lost all I possessed, and came to live in this town.'

Or the farmer who lived for 20 years in a wagon: 'My father was a landowner in Vanrhynsdorp, but he lost all his stock owing to drought. For a time he took to transport riding. When I grew up, he and I took out a licence in Bushmanland and after a while we owned 1 000 small cattle and 91 donkeys and cattle. But once more lost nearly everything. I made one more attempt but the drought of 1913 ruined me completely. So I sold my wagon etc and bought an erf here at Kakamas. For 20 years I had had no fixed abode – the wagon was my

home. My nine children were born while we were on trek.'

With monotonous regularity the same pathetic tale was told by countless rural Afrikaners who, in the 1920s and '30s, constituted the class known as the poor whites. Eyewitness accounts of the pitiful living conditions at the time add to the heart-rending picture: 'A hovel was seen in the corner made by two corrugated iron fences. The room was 6 feet by 4 feet in area, and 5 feet high. The two fences served as the two sides of the room; the other two sides were of iron sheets. The roof was the framework of a bed covered with bags. Here a mother and five children lived.' The 'kitchen' would be outside in the open, where there would be a pot of mealie-meal porridge for breakfast, lunch and supper.

trophe followed closely on the heels of another, the once proud spirit of many a farmer began to break – and a sense of fatalistic resignation took over.

Adding to the problem was the inability of most Boers to adapt to the new era of surplus production – and it was the Africans of the Transvaal, many of them on white-owned land, who were proving more successful. In the 1890s a Pretoria merchant told the 'Standard and Diggers News' that Africans were outselling the Boers by nearly two to one. 'Kafirs take away £47 000 from the local market for every £26 000 taken away by Boers.' A contemporary reported that Africans were growing immense quantities of maize 'for their own consumption and for sale to the mines to feed their brothers at work there'.

Ironically, one of the reasons for this stiff competition from African farmers was the very system that had been imposed by the authorities to try to force more Africans to work for white farmers – taxation. Instead of seeking work in order to pay the taxman, however, many African farmers increased their production – and would have increased it still further had more markets been open to them, as an observer remarked just after the South African War: 'The native grew a very large proportion of the mealie crop and would grow much more if they had better facilities for marketing it.'

On the other hand, many Boers were still subsistence farmers, producing only enough surplus crops to secure an income for a few necessities that could be bought only with cash or barter. The Johannesburg 'Star' commented: 'The average Dutch farmer grows a certain amount with the object of making a certain profit. If prices decline, he tries to produce a little more and still obtain his fixed minimum. If prices appreciate, he takes a little less trouble, and grows a little less, still pocketing the same profit.'

Many farmers were unable to adjust to new farming methods and soil was overworked, resulting in extensive soil erosion. Farmers who were too far away from main markets sold their products locally at a loss. And with the introduction of commercial farming, *bywoners* became a financial burden to farmers and found themselves evicted. (In fact, the popular Afrikaans song, '*Vat jou goed en trek, Ferreira*', literally 'Take your goods and move, Ferreira', refers to the fate of many *bywoners* from that era.)

In addition, farms were also not as large as they used to be. Under the Roman-Dutch law of inheritance, property was customarily divided between the sons upon the death of their father – and after several generations, a once productive farm had been split up into small, unproductive plots. Smallholdings were often mortgaged but, as debts increased, despondent farmers, who had never learnt a trade, were forced off the land to drift towards the towns to join the ranks of the unemployed or, if they were lucky, the unskilled workers.

At first they received a reluctant welcome – despite the fact that the mines, the main source of employment, desperately needed unskilled labour. The problem was that, being landless, poor whites and their families were totally dependent on the wages they could earn – as opposed to migrant African labourers whose families were left largely to support themselves, either at distant homesteads or as worker/tenants on white-owned land. As far as mine-owners were concerned, white unskilled labour would force wages up.

When government pressure after the South African War paved the way to greater use of whites on the mines, those employed were paid higher wages than Africans.

The mines, too, had another serious spin-off effect on poor Afrikaner farmers: some of the wealthier landlords, many of them also Afrikaners, found it far more profitable to rent their land to Africans than to whites. It enabled them (the farmers) to create reservoirs of black labour (for which mine recruiting agencies were prepared to pay handsome commissions), while at the same time it enabled them to draw far more in rent from their African tenants. In the

GOVERNMENT SCHEMES *to help poor whites concentrated on self-help and job creation rather than on hand-outs, which the Carnegie commission believed would weaken the Afrikaner's sense of initiative and encourage dependency. Instead, they were given jobs as labourers such as building roads, digging ditches and the like.*

AS THE *Great Depression tightened its grip on South Africa, more and more whites were forced to queue at hastily organised soup kitchens – filling mugs, pitchers and even buckets.*

past, landholders had leased land to blacks in return for labour. But now the demands of the mines for workers provided a highly profitable alternative to white *bywoners*. This so-called 'kaffir farming' was outlawed in the 1913 Natives' Land Act, which forbade more than five African families from living on each 'white' farm as peasant squatters. However, the practice became so profitable that many ways were found of evading the law: for example, one extensive landowner south of Middelburg (Transvaal) still had 70 African families living on his land in 1920. Indeed, it was only in the 1930s, when intensive maize cultivation became more profitable, that 'kaffir farming' began to die out.

Carnegie commission

By 1927 the number of destitute whites had increased so rapidly that the Carnegie Corporation of New York, on the recommendation of its president and secretary who had recently visited South Africa, decided to fund a commission of investigation into the problem of poor whites. The Union Government and the Dutch Reformed Church each matched the Carnegie Corporation's grant, and five commissioners were appointed: two lecturers from the University of Stellenbosch, Dr Johannes Grosskopf and Dr Raymond Wilcocks; a lecturer from the University of Cape Town and member of the Department of Education, Dr Ernie Malherbe; a member of the Department of Health, Dr W A Murray; and a minister of the Dutch Reformed parish at Kimberley, the Reverend Johannes Albertyn. A sixth contributor was the Afrikaans author Maria Rothmann, better known as MER.

Between 1929-32 the five travelled around the country, interviewing a cross-section of poor white society: these included nomadic trek farmers in the Cape; *bywoners* and labourers in the Karoo; pioneering bushveld farmers in the Transvaal; woodcutters in the Knysna and George areas; diamond diggers, Reef miners and others. They concluded their investigatory work with a five-volume report on economic conditions, the psychology of the poor whites, education, health and sociological aspects.

The commission calculated that out of a white population of 1,8-million in 1931 (a million being Afrikaners), more than 300 000 were extremely poor, living as paupers. A poor white was defined as 'a person who had become dependent to such an extent, whether from mental, moral, economic or physical causes, that he is unfit, without help from others, to find proper means of livelihood for himself or to procure it directly or indirectly for his children'.

The report stressed that 'laziness' was not to blame (as had been suggested by the Transvaal Indigency Commission in 1906-8) but that poverty was in itself a demoralising influence which often caused loss of self-respect and a feeling of inferiority. The commission felt that the *bywoner*, who roamed the country making a precarious existence as a fencer, transport rider or woodseller, seemed to embody the poor white problem.

The commission reported on the high birthrate – the white population more than doubled between 1904 and 1936 – and on overcrowding and insanitary conditions which led to disease and death. In the schools, thousands of children were classified as retarded. Most children did not even complete primary school.

The report also contained a study of urban Afrikaners who were finding it hard to adjust to life in the city. They had to compete for employment with the more skilled *uitlanders* (foreigners) and could not compete with the cheap African labour favoured by the mainly English-speaking mine-owners and industrialists. Afrikaners also suffered psychologically because of their inbred prejudice against doing a job traditionally reserved for Africans. Even the most poverty-striken *bywoner* considered himself a master and would not stoop to do 'kaffir work'.

The commission reported that attempts by the Dutch Reformed Church and the *Arme Blanke Verbond* (Poor White Alliance) of 1917 to help poor whites seek jobs and obtain suitable training had been insufficient. For example, the indignation expressed by Daniel Malan, a future South African Prime Minister, that 'the children of Afrikaner families were running around as naked as kaffirs in Congoland' was never followed up.

The commission did not favour state hand-outs, relief work and charity which, it said, weakened the Afrikaner's sense of initiative and encouraged dependency. Instead, it suggested that the government concentrate on setting up a department of social welfare (which it did in 1937). Later the state tried to protect white workers by introducing what it termed a 'civilised labour' policy – in other words, a system that guaranteed work for whites at the expense of blacks. Thus, between 1924 and 1933 the percentage of unskilled white workers on the railways rose from 9,5 to 39,3 percent while it dropped for blacks from 75 to 48,9 percent. In effect, it meant the creation of 13 023 more jobs for whites against a loss of 15 556 jobs usually done by blacks.

On grounds of a white skin, unskilled Afrikaners were employed as overseers at a salary of £10 a week, while unskilled Africans received 12 shillings, with free food and compound housing. There was not much more that the government could do for poor whites because an event which adversely affected the economy of the entire capitalist world was just round the corner.

Worldwide economic crisis

The Wall Street crash of October 1929 ushered in a severe economic crisis for the entire Western world. At first South Africa was not affected; few South Africans had investments in the USA and in December the National Party (NP) Prime Minister, Barry Hertzog, confidently announced that there was 'no reason to anticipate a slump'.

But soon, the price of wool fell sharply, from 14 pence a pound in 1929 to 4 pence in 1932; over the same period, the price of maize fell from 15s 4d a bag of yellow mielies to 9s 4d. Wages dropped rapidly – and bankruptcies and unemployment soared. To make matters worse, during 1932-3 the country experienced one of the longest and severest droughts of the century. Whites joined the queues at soup kitchens and openly begged in the streets. In 1932, of the 188 000 whites registered at labour bureaus, only a handful were able to get subsidised work – mainly on the railways. By 1937 as many as 25 000 were still on the dole. Perhaps one reason for the government's inability to deal with unemployment was the fact that another, more biting problem had arisen . . . .

Gold standard

On 20 September 1931 Britain announced that it was going off the gold standard – the system that obliged a government to exchange its paper money for gold if called upon to do so (see box). Jan Smuts of the South African Party (SAP) and then leader of the Opposition, encouraged South Africa to follow suit. Prime Minister Hertzog, however, advised by his Minister of Finance, Nicolaas Havenga, decided that the country should remain linked to gold, hoping that South Africa, the world's leading producer of the metal, would benefit. Doing so would also stress the country's independence of Britain.

But fears that South Africa would abandon the gold standard caused many investors to send large sums of money out of the country. This steady outflow of capital, plus a marked decline in exports from the country, led the Union to experience for the first time the full impact of the depres-

On and off the gold standard

Have you ever read what is written on the face of a R10 note – or any other paper money?

If not, take a look now. It says: 'South African Reserve Bank. I promise to pay the bearer on demand at Pretoria ten rand,' and is signed by the Governor of the Reserve Bank.

Once upon a time the bearer could, indeed, demand R10 from the Governor, who, in theory at least, would be able to give him R10 in real money: gold. Today it merely means that you'll get R10 – which you've got anyway.

This backing of paper money by gold was known as the gold standard, and the wealth of nations was measured by the amount of gold they had in their vaults – and for which they could issue paper notes. The reason gold stayed in the vaults instead of people's pockets was that paper is easier and lighter to carry around.

Although the use of gold as currency is as old as recorded history, the modern gold standard began in 1816 when Britain passed the Gold Standards Act, which ensured that gold coins became the only real measure of value. Five years later Britain adopted the gold bullion standard, making it possible for Britons to convert their money into gold on demand. It was very much a measure of the wealth of Britain and its growing dominance at the centre of world trade. The United States, for example, did not join the growing number of nations on the gold standard until 1879.

The gold standard remained more or less intact throughout the first quarter of the 20th century, except for a few years during the First World War when the normal flow of international trade was interrupted by warfare. South Africa, however, did not re-adopt the gold standard – this time based on gold coin rather than bullion – until 1925.

During the days of the gold standard, the price of gold was generally fixed by international agreement – so that gold could be used as an international currency for the settling of debts. Consequently the gold standard among major trading countries until after the First World War provided an automatic mechanism for adjusting a nation's balance of payments (the difference between the amount of goods imported and exported, either surplus or deficit) and regulating its internal economy. A balance of payments surplus naturally led to an inflow of gold, which allowed interest rates to fall and economic activity to accelerate, including employment. However, in time, more money led to increased prices and imports from other countries – and so the opposite began to happen and the balance of payments deteriorated. Once a deficit appeared, the outflow of gold slowed down the economy and unemployment rose.

The gold standard, however, was particularly harsh on nations – and people – with a continuing balance of payments deficit, being more concerned with the debits between nations than the internal economy. The terrible unemployment that flowed from the Wall Street crash in the 1930s made governments realise that sticking to the gold standard was too costly when measured against the misery of unemployment it caused at home.

AFTER EX-JUSTICE MINISTER *Tielman Roos* (pictured right) called for a coalition government to help the country through the crisis caused by the depression, Barry Hertzog of the National Party (on the left in the photograph left) and Jan Smuts of the South African Party (centre), pictured with Minister of Finance Nicolaas Havenga, agreed to merge their two parties in March 1933. The 'Fusion' of the two became known as the United South African National Party (later the United Party).

sion. At a hurriedly called emergency session of parliament in November, Smuts, now supported by many of Hertzog's NP colleagues, again urged that South Africa abandon the gold standard.

Then, on 16 December 1932, at a ceremony at Haakboslaagte, Tielman Roos, an ex-Minister of Justice, announced his return to politics by demanding that South Africa leave the gold standard and that a coalition government be formed to help the country through the depression (see page 348).

The response to his speech was astounding. Convinced that government would heed Roos' advice, and fearful of the devaluation of the South African currency which would surely follow, investors sent more than £2-million out of the country in three days.

As rumours abounded that Roos and Smuts were working together in order to threaten Hertzog's shaky majority, the government finally acted: on 27 December Havenga announced South Africa's departure from the gold standard. The price of gold rose and money began flowing back into the country.

Smuts and Roos did start negotiating the possibility of a coalition, but when it became clear that the ambitious Roos wanted the premiership for himself, Smuts instead turned to Hertzog . . . .

Talks between the two began in January 1933 – and by March they had formed a coalition government, with Hertzog as Prime Minister and Smuts as his deputy. As expected, the new alliance won an overwhelming majority at the general election in May.

By the end of the year the NP and SAP were ready for much closer ties, and on 5 December 1934 the United South African National Party was formed. In disgust, staunchly Afrikaner nationalists under the leadership of Daniel Malan broke away from the Hertzog Government to form the *Gesuiwerde* (Purified) National Party, while dissatisfied SAP supporters founded the Dominion Party.

The Smuts/Hertzog alliance, however, lasted only until the eve of the Second World War when differences over whether South Africa should participate in the war led to a split in September 1939.

Rise of the *Broederbond*

The Purified NP, meanwhile, began to receive considerable support from an underground movement that had been started in April 1918, immediately after a public meeting addressed by Malan in Johannesburg had been broken up by English-speaking demonstrators.

The brawl had left a severe impression on one member of the audience, Henning Klopper, a former inmate of a South African War concentration camp, who believed that the Afrikaner still held a secondary position in the country of his birth. Within 24 hours of the fracas at the NP meeting, Klopper, together with two friends, Danie du Plessis and H W van der Merwe, formed an organisation called *Jong Suid-Afrika* (Young South Africa). By July, more clerks, teachers and dominees had joined – and the young organisation had decided to change its name to the *Afrikaner Broederbond* (Afrikaner Brotherhood).

In 1921, the *Broederbond* became a covert organisation, acting with such secrecy that members were forbidden to speak of their membership even to their wives.

Potential *Broeders* were, and still are, carefully screened before they are accepted into the ranks of the organisation. A member has to be a regular church-goer, his children have to attend an Afrikaans-medium school – and a divorce could result in expulsion.

New members are sworn in at initiation ceremonies. (In the early days this ritual would culminate with the ominous threat that 'he who betrays the *Bond*, will be destroyed by the *Bond*. The *Bond* never forgets. Its vengeance is swift and sure.')

In its heyday, the *Broederbond* derived its strength from a system of administration based on branches. This ensured effective infiltration into a community by a headmaster or doctor or lawyer. Each branch had between five and 20 members who appointed a delegate to the General Council. Every member was directly answerable to the Executive Council which controlled the whole organisation.

In the 1930s this elitist, semi-religious organisation managed to secure a firm foothold in almost all of the country's cultural, economic and political activities – becoming a policy-making co-ordinating body. It promoted the

Afrikaans language in schools and pushed for the formation of single-medium schools. Apart from education, the *Broederbond's* other great concern was with the plight of the poor whites. It supported, for instance, the *Helpmekaar* (Mutual Aid) movement which helped needy Afrikaners to buy land and set up businesses.

In 1929 the *Broederbond* established the *Federasie van Afrikaanse Kultuurverenigings* (FAK) (Federation of Afrikaans Cultural Organisations), which co-ordinated a wide range of national cultural activities and which soon became the *Broederbond's* most important public front organisation.

Another exclusively Afrikaner club founded by the *Broederbond* was the *Afrikaanse Taal en Kultuurvereniging* (ATKV) (Afrikaans Language and Cultural Society) of the South African Railways, which employed most of the country's white labour.

The *Broederbond* also sought to infiltrate parliament. It sided with Malan and the Purified Nationalists so strongly that the two groups became practically synonymous. By 1933 Malan had become a *Broeder*, making him the country's first *Broederbond* Prime Minister (as were all the subsequent Prime Ministers) when his party won the white general election in 1948. Many Afrikaners – including Barry Hertzog – were shocked at the way the *Broederbond* unashamedly propagated its neo-fascist nationalist ideology. In a warning letter to his son, Albert, Hertzog wrote that he foresaw only national destruction ahead.

Economic movement

The *Broederbond's* intervention in politics was closely linked to its concern with Afrikaner poverty. And in this respect, it saw as its duty the mobilisation of capital to ensure that money flowed into the pockets of white Afrikaners. Its ultimate aim, however, was to strengthen unity among all Afrikaners.

Class divisions, it firmly believed, could not be allowed to stand in the way of unity. For in the eyes of its members such divisions were the products of imperialism and exploitation by foreign, particularly English, capitalists. In the *Broederbond* scheme of things, the Afrikaner capitalists and workers, rich or poor, all belonged to one *volk* (nation) and, as such, all were entitled to an equal share in their *volkskapitalisme*.

In 1934 a people's bank – which proved an instant success – was secretly started from a first floor office in Pretoria. Today, Volkskas (literally, the people's chest), still in Afrikaner hands, is the third largest banking group in the country.

One up-and-coming *Broederbond* economist, the young Albert Hertzog, felt that a financial empire could not be built on an ideology of *volkskapitalisme* alone. He saw a need for trade unions to protect the Afrikaner worker. Christian-national trade unions were immediately formed to draw Afrikaner workers out of other less sympathetic organisations and bring them back into the fold. One particularly successful union was Klopper's *Spoorbond* of 1934, a union of railwaymen, which rivalled the National Union of Railways and Harbours Servants. The union mobilised the savings of its members and established a bank three years later which, even though it went bankrupt, nevertheless promoted the first Afrikaans building society, Saambou ('building together').

The rise of SANLAM

Possibly the greatest achievement of the economic movement was the SANLAM-*Broederbond* collaboration which began in 1937. SANLAM (South African National Life As-

FOUNDER MEMBERS *of the Afrikaner Broederbond (Afrikaner Brotherhood) pose for a group photograph soon after the launch of the organisation in 1918. The leading force behind the Broederbond was a young former concentration camp inmate, Henning Klopper (seated, second from left). Only in 1921 did the organisation's activities become secret.*

THE OPENING CEREMONY *at the first branch of the exclusively Afrikaner-controlled South African National Life Assurance Company (SANLAM) and the letterhead of an early policy.*

surance Company) had been formed in June 1918 by an ex-chairman of the Peninsular *Helpmekaar* movement, William Hofmeyr. Capital had been provided by western Cape farmers for the creation of a South African National Trust Company, SANTAM, which offered both short- and long-term assurance. Shortly afterwards these two operations were split and SANLAM, a subsidiary life assurance company, came into being. SANTAM and SANLAM served as credit institutions which successfully pooled the money resources of Afrikaners into a central fund to be converted into productive capital. Between 1918 and 1937 they concentrated capital in Cape agriculture – their most important source of funds being Afrikaans farmers.

SANLAM expanded, but perhaps not fast enough for the eager financial strategist, Marthinus Louw. In 1937 he decided that SANLAM could do with help from the *Broederbond*, especially as that organisation had such a vast cultural influence. The *Broederbond* in turn would benefit from SANLAM's economic expertise and its capital investments. Louw approached the *Broederbond* at a time when the *Broeders* were planning a *volkskongres* (people's congress) to discuss the issue of the poor whites. Louw could not have chosen a better moment, for the *Broederbond* also found itself in the throes of preparations for the *Eeufees* (Centenary) of the Great Trek (see box). Louw made plans for the formation of a financial company that would strengthen the position of the Afrikaner in commerce, and the *volkskongres* was receptive to the idea. By cleverly using the capitalist methods of the English-speaking moneyed class, Afrikaners were seeking new solutions to the problem of the poor whites.

Recreating the Great Trek –

'The whole feeling of the trek was the working not of man, not of any living being. It was the will and work of the Almighty God. It was a pilgrimage, a sacred happening.'

There has perhaps never been a more ardent, visible expression of Afrikaner solidarity and patriotism than in the symbolic ox-wagon trek of 1938, the main event of the centenary celebrations commemorating the Great Trek.

To retrace the steps of his Voortrekker forefathers had always been the dream of Henning Klopper, Port Superintendent at Mossel Bay and founder member of the *Afrikaner Broederbond*. When Klopper heard of the government's plan to build a memorial to the Voortrekkers outside Pretoria, and to inaugurate it on 16 December 1938 – 100 years after the Battle of Blood River – he could think of no better occasion to make his dream come true.

Klopper's idea – a symbolic trek from Cape Town to Pretoria – was enthusiastically taken up by the *Broederbond* which in turn undertook to co-ordinate this event. It was to be sponsored by the Federation of Afrikaans Cultural Organisations (FAK), organised by the Afrikaans Language and Cultural Society (ATKV) of the South African Railways and Harbours, and chaired by Klopper.

On 8 August 1938 two stinkwood ox-wagons, the 'Piet Retief' and the 'Andries Pretorius', stood before Jan van Riebeeck's statue on the Foreshore in Cape Town surrounded by a jostling, cheering crowd of some 100 000 people. Klopper was astounded by this overwhelming response. He spoke to the crowd, reminded them of the Covenant and then prayed that the trek would unite Afrikaners everywhere.

The slow trek pulled out of Cape Town and headed north on a carefully charted course, the work once again of Klopper. At every town where they stayed overnight,

A MASSIVE CROWD *lined Adderley Street, Cape Town, in 1938 as the wagons set off to relive the Great Trek.*

'the will and work of God'

the trekker pilgrims were assured of a friendly reception organised by the town's dominee and someone from the *Broederbond*. They were further inspired by the news that six more wagons from different points were winding their way to the capital.

With undiminished fervour, the pilgrims visited places where Afrikaners had fought and often died. Streets were renamed after Voortrekker heroes – Seventh Street in Boksburg became 'Sarel Cilliers Street' and so on. Thousands of men grew bushy Voortrekker beards and donned corduroy breeches, waistcoat and knotted scarf. Women were seen in traditional Voortrekker dresses.

In Bloemfontein a team of torchbearers from the Cape caught up with the trek. The burning torch was immediately seen as a symbol of nationhood, and the *Broederbond* was inspired to collect money for the poor urban Afrikaner in what became a *Reddingsdaad* (Act of Rescue).

The ox-wagons eventually entered Pretoria amid more speeches, sermons, the singing of the new Afrikaner anthem, *'Die Stem'*, as well as rumours that Klopper was about to proclaim a republic.

An enormous bonfire was lit at the foot of the Voortrekker Monument and the torches flung into the flames. The wagons were drawn up the hill by teams of people and three women laid the foundation stone of the monument. The following day a minister of the church, Paul Nel, was asked to lay another foundation stone, that of a marble replica of a wagon erected on the battlefield of Blood River.

In a rousing speech, Daniel Malan, the leader of the Purified National Party, told the masses that just as 'the muzzleload [had] clashed with assegai' at Blood River to preserve the interests of whites, now too it was the duty of Afrikaners to strive 'to make South Africa a white man's land'.

THE MAN BEHIND *the centenary celebrations, Broederbond founder Henning Klopper (centre), sets out on his 'sacred happening'.*

LIKE THEIR FOREFATHERS *a century before, the enthusiastic 'trekkers' approach the Natal capital of Pietermaritzburg in a spirited recreation of the Great Trek. The centenary was a startling success for Afrikaner nationalists.*

Fall of the 'last bastion'

On 6 April 1936, Barry Hertzog finally convinced parliament to endorse legislation to abolish the Cape African franchise. But the decision, loudly cheered by white MPs, came as a cruel blow to an African community already devastated by the effects of the Great Depression and political splits that had led to the virtual collapse of even its most radical protest movements.

SUMMING UP THE FEELINGS of thousands of his compatriots, Dr James Moroka, an executive member of a newly formed political alliance calling itself the All-African Convention (AAC), turned to South African Prime Minister Barry Hertzog and very simply and very bluntly said: 'I want the [black] vote to be extended from the Cape to the Orange Free State and the Transvaal – to the whole country.'

It was a dramatic moment in a predictably fruitless meeting between a self-confessed white supremacist who was determined to remove the last vestiges of an African vote from a common voters' roll shared with whites and a delegation wanting the opposite: equal rights for blacks.

But if Hertzog was horrified by Moroka's proposal, he did not show it. Instead, displaying all the charm of a man who knew he could not lose, he repeated his standpoint: the Cape African franchise had to go (in the interests of a uniform 'native policy'). This, his guests had to understand, was non-negotiable. But he was prepared to be reasonable: as a special compromise Cape Africans could have, if they wished, a separate voters' roll in order to enable them to choose three extra whites to represent them in parliament.

The year was 1936 – and the Union's black middle-class communities were united in a last-ditch effort to protect the voting rights Cape Africans had enjoyed for more than 80 years. It did not matter to them that, except for a few rural eastern Cape constituencies, where they held the balance of power, black influence in formal post-Union parliamentary politics had been minimal. What was important was the symbolic importance of the Cape vote: while they had it, the hope remained that one day it would be extended to the whole of South Africa. It was something worth fighting for . . . .

But it was a fight they were doomed to lose – and the men of the AAC must have realised this. For, the Prime Minister, to whom they had come to express their concern, was the driving force behind the assault on their rights. Indeed, to James Barry Munnik Hertzog, the Cape franchise was a corn on the foot inside the white supremacist boot. It opened the way, he believed, to eventual black domination in South Africa. It had to go – and for 10 years he had worked towards this end.

The Hertzog Bills

In 1925, within a year of assuming control of a Pact government (an alliance of the National and Labour parties), Hertzog had turned his attention to the African vote – an issue which in the coming years would become his obsession.

He was prepared, he announced, to make more Reserve land available for Africans to purchase – but in return the Cape African franchise had to go.

In 1926, he took the matter further by tabling four Bills in parliament: the first to abolish the African vote and replace it with white parliamentary representation; the second to establish an expanded African advisory council; the third to set aside additional land for the Reserves; and the fourth to redefine coloured voting rights.

It led to widescale protest, with the African National Congress (ANC) leading the way. At its national conference in 1927, congress delegates rejected the land allocation as completely inadequate, reaffirmed the 'inalienable right of Africans to unlimited land ownership', and pointed to the increasing poverty in the existing Reserves.

Delegates were equally firm on the question of the Cape franchise: it was, they argued, the 'last bastion against injustice and exploitation' – and, in any case, Africans were an 'integral and inseparable element in the population' and therefore should not be denied a say in the government of the nation. With many other African, coloured and Indian organisations adding their voices to ANC protests, black rejection of Hertzog's proposed legislation was virtually unanimous.

But with single-minded determination the old Free Stater soldiered on. In 1927, he saw his Bills spurned by parliament and damned by a variety of black organisations who gave evidence before a parliamentary select committee. The outright rejection of the franchise proposals by the South African Party (SAP) was another setback. But Hertzog was a patient man. A swartgevaar (black threat) election, called in 1929, returned him to power with a clear majority, but it was not enough to muster the required two-thirds majority at a joint sitting of the two houses. The gathering depression and the government's increasing unpopularity deferred the Bills until 1935, by which time the Nationalists had joined with the SAP to form the United Party. Ironically, it was the unity with his old political enemies that gave him the backing he so badly needed.

In May 1935, the Bills, reduced from four to two after several revisions over the previous eight years, were again tabled in parliament. The Natives' Trust and Land Bill made provision for the extension of Reserves from 7,5 percent to 13 percent of the area of the Union. However, it also barred rural Africans from acquiring land outside their stipulated areas. The Representation of Natives Bill dealt with the question of the African vote. Foremost among its provisions were the election of four Senators to represent Africans throughout the Union, the gradual elimination

IN A BID *to stop the disenfranchisement of Africans in the Cape, 400 delegates from all over the country gathered in Bloemfontein on 16 December 1935 – the day on which Afrikaners celebrated their Blood River victory over the Zulu – to form the All-African Convention, electing Professor Davidson Jabavu (right) president, and Dr Alfred Xuma (far right) vice-president.*

of the Cape African vote by refusing any further applications for registration and the establishment of a Natives' Representative Council. Both Bills, Hertzog announced, would be considered at a special sitting of parliament to be held in 1936.

Black reaction
The newspaper 'Bantu World', echoing widespread concern among middle-class Africans, called for a national convention of Africans to fight the attack on their rights. Backing the proposal, the ANC's Reverend Z R Mahabane described the Bills as 'a direct challenge to the African community'.

The threat to the Cape vote provoked a broad revival of African political activity, and on 16 December 1935, more than 400 delegates from every corner of South Africa – from the major political groups, local organisations, trade unions, the churches, student movements and study groups in the protectorates – gathered in Bloemfontein for the founding conference of the All-African Convention.

The leading lights of the AAC were Professor Davidson Jabavu and Dr Alfred Xuma, who were elected president and vice-president respectively. In his address, 45-year-old Jabavu, one of the country's leading intellectuals, described the Cape vote as a 'key experiment in the world-wide problem of race relations'. And the 38-year-old, widely travelled Xuma called on white South Africa to 'invite and welcome to its institutions all those who are capable of rising to its standards and are able to make it richer by their different cultural and temperamental origin'.

Although the convention condemned not only the proposed Bills but also the whole thrust of government policy towards Africans since 1910, delegates were at pains to stress their loyalty to South Africa and the British Crown, and, in fact, called on the British Parliament to intervene on their behalf.

In a further demonstration of what were basically moderate views, delegates also expressed a willingness to concede to a qualified franchise and 'civilisation tests' for Africans. And while they admitted that they sought a common political identity between whites and blacks, they accepted that the two groups might 'develop on their own lines, socially and culturally'.

Calls by communist and other radical delegates for militant action to reinforce opposition to the Bills were firmly rejected by the main African leaders – and so, except for agreeing to arrange protest meetings throughout the country, the AAC's plan of action was based mainly on the failed ANC model of prayer meetings, appeals, petitions and meetings with government authorities.

It was at one of these meetings – in Cape Town – that an AAC delegation came agonisingly close to agreeing to Hertzog's 'compromise' proposal on the Cape franchise. Only the intervention of Moroka and Xuma prevented this.

But by then, time had run out for opponents of the Hertzog Bills and on 6 April 1936, parliament approved the measures by an overwhelming 168 votes to 11.

It was an angry and disillusioned AAC that met in June that year to decide on its next step. There were two choices open to delegates: they could boycott the new Natives' Representative Council (NRC) and their white MPs – or they could use the new system to win more concessions. Jabavu, arguing that a boycott would probably fail, urged delegates to accept participation – under protest. It was a view which won overwhelming support, despite the contradiction involved in accepting institutions that a short time earlier had been rejected.

But although elections for the NRC, the Senate and the three parliamentary seats were held in 1937, a new bitterness was creeping into the African leaders, and attitudes were hardening . . . .

Poverty in the countryside
Parliament's successful assault on the African franchise came at a time when the struggle by Africans to resist the political and economic dominance by whites was at its lowest ebb: the Industrial and Commercial Workers' Union (ICU), which Hertzog once feared, had collapsed; the ANC remained dominated by leaders who preferred moral argument to open confrontation; and the Com-

munist Party, suffering from long-distance interference by Moscow, had become increasingly isolated from the main arena of African political debate.

Apart from the factionalism that weakened them, African nationalists' inability to resist government measures was also due to other factors: chief among these were the granting to police of new powers to subdue protest and militant action – and the depression years which eroded what little economic security blacks still had.

Certainly, if whites had been hard hit by the Great Depression of 1929-32, Africans were affected even more. Yet the government insisted on focusing only on white poverty, overlooking the extent to which blacks had been integrated into 'white' industry and agriculture and had come to rely on it.

As far as the authorities were concerned, redundant Africans could be easily reincorporated into the Reserves. White workers, on the other hand, unaccustomed to the poverty which blacks 'took for granted', had to be protected – and this was done by means of a 'civilised' labour policy, designed to push whites into jobs from which Africans had been pushed out.

The Pass laws were applied with greater zeal in a bid to control the number of Africans streaming into white towns and cities. But they did not help. Faced with overcrowding in the Reserves and, consequently, an increase in poverty, thousands of Africans, guided by their stomachs, were fully prepared to take their chances against government red tape. But in many cases, they found that evading the guardians of the Pass laws was less of a problem than that of actually finding work.

ANC publicist, Selby Msimang, summed up the feelings of many disillusioned members of the organisation when he wrote: 'My friends and countrymen, let us now admit . . . that parliament and the white people of South Africa have disowned us, flirted and trifled with our loyalty . . . have treated us as rebels . . . have declared we are not part of the South African community.'

And, cautioning that the stage was approaching where moral argument would no longer be considered sufficient to counter government repression, he added: 'If we refuse to be made slaves and outcasts in our fatherland . . . we should seek emancipation by such means as the dictates of self-preservation may lead us to.'

But it was a warning that went unheeded. And, indeed, even when the economy began to expand after South Africa had abandoned the gold standard in 1932, the ready availability of cheap, unskilled labour and the Pass laws that regulated this workforce ensured that wages remained low.

In the urban areas, employers refused to grant increases to their workers for fear of disturbing the economic balance that kept the African with one foot in the city and the other in a Reserve. For the same reason they refused to support rent increases needed by local authorities to upgrade rundown, disease-ridden townships on the outskirts of 'white' towns and cities.

The collapse of radical protest

On the face of it, African society was ripe for rebellion. But the reality was that, except for the gentle protest campaigns of the ANC, black opposition had all but collapsed.

Since its formation in 1912, the ANC had shied away from radical protest to concentrate on matters that would enhance its members' hard-won middle-class status. Vehemently opposed to communism – or anything that in their opinion smacked of it, the congress had offered little contribution to the passionate political debates that raged during the 1920s.

It was left to the ICU to mobilise the masses. But after a highly successful campaign of urban and rural mobilisation, it had discovered, by the late 1920s, that numerical strength alone was insufficient to counter the forces ranged against it. And the union began a slide that was hastened by bitter strife between its founder, Clements Kadalie, and Natal strongman George Champion. By 1929, barely 18 months after membership had peaked at 100 000, the ICU was lacking in credibility, swamped by financial scandal, the object of recrimination by embittered members, and rent by splits in its leadership.

Yet the decline of the union had begun even prior to its successes of 1927. In 1925, after Kadalie had moved his headquarters from Cape Town to Johannesburg, the Cape branch ceased contributing to union funds and was virtually defunct. In 1928, after another argument with Kadalie, Champion stormed out and formed his own ICU yase Natal (The ICU of Natal), thus depriving the parent union of its main source of finance. (Within months the Natal ICU found itself involved in a boycott of municipal beer canteens, which erupted in violent clashes between white vigilantes and Africans that left seven dead.)

By the time British trade unionist William Ballinger arrived in 1928 to try to sort out the union's affairs, there was little he could do to stop its disintegration. Ballinger openly criticised the way in which the ICU leadership had allowed the financial chaos to develop, and he and Kadalie were soon at loggerheads.

A COMMUNIST PARTY *meeting addressed by John Gomas on the steps of the Johannesburg City Hall in 1932. The party's ideological base failed to attract wide support.*

For Kadalie things were now about to turn full circle: in 1926, having been advised by British trade unionists that it would be in the interest of the ICU's relations with the authorities to get rid of the militant 'reds', he had expelled some communist members. But now these same advisors had grabbed control of the union, and were pushing it into a more radical direction.

In February 1929 Kadalie quit to form the Independent ICU – and based himself and his wing of the union in East London. By the early 1930s, eight separate ICU organisations were operating in the main centres of South Africa. Of these, the ICU yase Natal, backed by the Communist Party, was probably the most radical. For three years, it carried the increasingly drooping flag of militant African nationalism, until a temporary lull fell over the black struggle for liberation (partly due to the compliance of the ANC and partly through government repression).

The Communist Party

The Communist Party, meanwhile, was also undergoing radical change. In 1928 it departed from fruitless efforts to promote solidarity between black and white workers – to concentrate on the concept of black liberation and the formation of a 'black republic'. This followed a successful campaign to expand its African membership. But although the party was predominantly black by 1929, few of their recruits – many of whom were young and ill-educated – were well versed in doctrine. In fact, Eddie Roux, a prominent member of the party at that time, wrote: 'It began to seem that the Party might be swamped by members who had little knowledge of Marxist principles and theory.'

CLEMENTS KADALIE, *the young Nyasalander who led the Industrial and Commercial Workers' Union to become the most potent force in African politics between the wars.*

THE CONTINUING LINKS *between* ANC *president Josiah Gumede (far left) and the Communist Party led to a split in* ANC *ranks, culminating in a showdown at the congress' April 1930 conference at which Gumede and his fellow 'radicals' were ousted by incoming president Pixley Seme and his 'moderates'. The communists responded by calling for a massive Pass-burning protest on 16 December – which led to the death of a young Natal communist, Johannes Nkosi (left), in a confrontation between protesters and police.*

But then, in a move aimed at preserving the 'purity' of their doctrine, Moscow suggested that the party should remain a small and select body of trained revolutionaries who could give a clear lead to the masses on all questions.

The idea of a popular front for black liberation led to the establishment of the African League of Rights (ALR) in 1929. Drawing on the memberships of existing black political and labour organisations, the league succeeded in persuading ANC president Josiah Gumede to become its first president. It was a major coup for the communists – especially when the new movement seemed set to grab the imagination of Africans – in particular those who had been left without a political home after the virtual collapse of the ICU.

League activities began on a high note – with the launch of a major anti-discrimination petition aimed at taking a million signatures to parliament. But just as the campaign began to get off the ground, Moscow did an about-turn: convinced that the capitalist system was about to collapse – as a result of the Great Depression – Communist Parties everywhere were ordered to terminate alliances with non-Marxist organisations. A telegram ordered the immediate dissolution of the ALR.

As the petitions rolled in, they were thrown into the wastepaper basket.

The existence of the league, however, was viewed with consternation by a section of the ANC's membership. Amid fears that it would undermine the ANC's claims to the leadership of the African nationalist movement, and also dissatisfaction by congress' conservative faction over Gumede's continued romance with the communists, the ANC executive resigned in January 1930 in protest at Gumede's role as president of the ALR.

Gumede was challenged for the leadership by Pixley Seme and, at a conference in April, the inevitable showdown came. Gumede – backed by the Transvaal communists, Champion of the ICU *yase* Natal and Bransby

Ndobe and Elliot Tonjeni of the western Cape branch of the congress – reaffirmed his support for the communists, adding that the ANC's demands were too mild and that its appeals for justice to Britain were in vain. 'Let us go back from this conference,' he urged, 'resolved to adopt militant policy which will bring us liberation. This is the quickest, effective, most logical and least expensive road to emancipation.'

Seme, in turn, cautioned the delegates against 'the humbug of communism'. He and his supporters felt that only the ANC should be permitted to articulate African political demands, and that equality of opportunity and participation in the system was what they sought. Their weapons were persuasion, moral force and consultation; they were not prepared to go over to mass confrontation. Seme won by 39 votes to 14.

The victory of the 'moderates' led within eight months to the expulsion of Ndobe and Tonjeni and the formation in the western Cape of the Independent ANC to continue the spirited, although losing battle against Boland farmers and police who regularly harassed their organisers and members (see page 325).

The communists, meanwhile, were in the process of launching another campaign. During 1930, together with what remained of the ICU, the Communist Party began to canvass support for a new Pass-burning campaign scheduled to begin in the main centres on 16 December – a day on which Afrikaners commemorated their victory over Dingane, but which was now also becoming a regular occasion for black political activities.

In Bloemfontein, hundreds of Africans had joined the party and had pledged their support. At a conference in Johannesburg, the ANC, the local ICU and other unions all endorsed the Pass-burning campaign and called for strikes. And in Durban, the young African communist, Johannes Nkosi, helped by the ICU *yase* Natal, was drumming up widespread support.

On 7 December, in Bloemfontein, Kadalie, in a controversial return to the public spotlight, warned ICU followers not to take part in the Pass-burning.

The campaign in Natal was poorly supported, with only Durban giving any real backing. But despite this, police and white vigilantes moved in on a protest meeting at Cartwright's Flats, and in the ensuing fracas Nkosi and three others were killed.

Said an eyewitness: 'Towards 4pm the crowd was tremendous. As they were putting their Passes into bags, the native police charged, making towards the table on which the speakers were standing. I saw Nkosi struck from the table. The police used knobkieries, while the crowd picked up stones. When the crowd was dispersed I saw them pack the wounded on a lorry . . . . There was a trail of blood dripping from the lorry.'

Nkosi died in hospital the following day, his skull fractured and his body covered in deep gashes. Reports that he had been carried from Cartwright's Flats with only a single bullet wound led to claims that he had been murdered while in police custody.

In February 1931, isolated incidents of Pass-burning were still being reported, although by then the campaign had been effectively smashed by the police. More than 200 communists were deported from Natal in the aftermath of the battle of Cartwright's Flats. Thereafter, the Communist Party began to drift. Internal dissension resulted in the dismissal of Sydney Bunting and other leading members who had done much to promote the party among Africans.

Adopting a more rigid Moscow line, the new bosses, Douglas Wolton and Lazar Bach, tried to restructure the party into small, supposedly highly disciplined revolutionary cells. But this did little for the need to mobilise the African masses and Wolton gave up in 1933 and returned to England. By 1935, the Communist Party had been pushed into the background as Africans prepared to defend the African vote on a common voters' roll in the Cape by flocking into the ranks of the ANC-dominated All-African Convention. Although, in the end, the convention could not prevent the abolition of the Cape franchise, it played a crucial role in recreating the possibility of a nationwide black political organisation.

Closing the 'door' on African 'domination'

To South African Prime Minister Barry Hertzog, the Cape African franchise ran counter to a fierce and long-held view that blacks could never be equal to whites.

It was, he believed, a simple matter of 'civilisation'. Whites were the standard-bearers of civilisation in South Africa while blacks had not yet progressed beyond the stage of 'semi-barbarism'.

It was inconceivable, then, that Cape Africans should be allowed an equal vote with whites. So, on 6 April 1936, three days after his 70th birthday, Hertzog stood up in parliament to launch his final assault on an African right he had been campaigning against for 10 years.

There were two things which caused anxiety to whites, he thundered: the danger of 'intermingling of blood' and the danger of being 'dominated' by Africans. The Cape franchise had left open a door through which Africans could eventually come to dominate whites.

Arguing that the Bill would 'enable us to obtain conditions in which we really feel we can assist the Natives', he added that the removal of the franchise would free whites of their fears, and free them to do 'justice' to the black man.

Supporting the Bill, Daniel Malan, leader of the 'purified' Nationalists, declared that it would finally 'put an end to 80 years of struggle between whites in the North and South', and added somewhat graphically, 'We would build a bridge over the Orange River, and over the Vaal River, and make a road through the Drakensberg. The whole of the Union would have one Native policy.'

United Party 'native expert' Heaton Nicholls unwittingly exposed the real motives of white South Africans: 'This Cape vote is a sham and a fraud . . . it has held back the progress of the native people in this country,' he said. Urging parliament to accept the Bill, he called for the immediate purchase of land for the Reserves, adding: 'If we do not find it we shall expose ourselves to the criticism that [the Bill] is merely a cloak designed to hide our repressive instincts.'

Only Jan Hofmeyr (a relative of 'Onze Jan') disagreed: 'The central feature [of the Bill] is to give the natives an inferior citizenship, a citizenship which has the marks of inferiority and which bears the added stigma that whatever may be the advance of the Native in civilization, to all intents and purposes he is limited for all time to three members in a House of 153. . . . Once franchise rights have been given and exercised by a section of the community, then no action save at the cost of honour and ultimate security should take away those rights.'

But Hofmeyr's voice was not heard: parliament accepted the Bill by 168 votes to 11 – and afterwards Hertzog was given a standing ovation.

Only the 'purified' Nationalists opposed the Natives' Trust and Land Bill, which increased the land area of the Reserves from 7,5 percent of the Union to about 13 percent, and laid the foundations of the 'homelands' policy of the National Party under H F Verwoerd some 30 years later – by adding to land set aside for African occupation under the 1913 Natives' Land Act.

'Purified' Nationalist Johannes Strijdom said it would cost a great deal of money which would be better spent on South Africa's poor whites. Another Nationalist claimed the Africans were getting too much productive land, while another claimed that, since the Cape African vote had not been scrapped, but merely placed on a separate roll, parliament was under no obligation to fulfil the terms of the trade-off. But United Party speakers, claiming now to be faced with the moral responsibility of 'keeping our word', were adamant that the Bill be passed, or else 'the whole of our Native policy will fall to pieces'. The Bill was passed with ease. Coloured franchise rights would, 20 years later, be similarly despatched after a protracted battle between parliament and the courts (see page 392).

'Fusion' splintered by war

Not all white South Africans welcomed the decision of the South African and National parties to form the United South African National Party in 1934: in Natal, an unashamedly jingoist wing of the old SAP quit the new alliance to form the pro-British Dominion Party – while a staunchly republican bloc in the old NP launched a *Gesuiwerde Nasionale Party* (Purified National Party). Opposition to Fusion, however, was largely eclipsed by a spectacular economic recovery, led by the goldmining industry. In the end, however, the optimism which greeted South Africa's recovery from the Great Depression was shattered by another World War.

IN FEBRUARY 1933, South African Prime Minister Barry Hertzog and his old political foe, Opposition leader Jan Smuts, shook hands again – after two decades of bitter enmity.

It was a reconciliation which led, by December 1934, to the 'fusion' of the National and South African parties – and to another split in Afrikanerdom.

Hertzog's motivation in turning to the party from which he had stormed out 20 years earlier (see page 296) was based on the harsh reality that the country was in the grip of a devastating depression with which his National Party (NP) could not cope: it had tried, but failed to provide relief for farmers battling against drought and falling prices; it had been unable to solve the growing problem of unemployed urban 'poor whites'; and its austerity measures – further taxes and salary cuts – had sparked widespread discontent, leading to defeats in parliamentary by-elections in 1930 and 1932.

By the second half of 1932 it had become clear that the South African Government's determination to remain on the gold standard (see page 337) was costing both the state and industry dearly.

At the time it had seemed a good decision: even the powerful mining corporations, always on the lookout to boost their profits, had backed Prime Minister Hertzog. But once they saw the extra revenue from cheaper imports and lower internal price structures being raked off in taxes and diverted into agriculture, they too joined the growing ranks of the disenchanted.

To compound the government's problems, opinion-makers in the influential rural areas of the Transvaal were calling increasingly stridently for Hertzog to do the un-thinkable: to hold 'reunion' talks with Smuts and his South African Party (SAP). The stubborn old Free Stater, however, held firm – until 16 December 1932, when Tielman Roos, a former leader of the NP in the Transvaal, made a dramatic return to politics by calling on the government to abandon the gold standard. As 15 Transvaal MPs and a senator rallied behind their former leader, a furious Hertzog had no choice but to change his stance. And so, on 27 December 1932, South Africa abandoned the gold standard. But the NP's troubles were far from over.

The re-entry of Roos into the political arena – after an absence of three years – plunged the NP into complete disarray. With the party having a mere 14-seat majority in

THE 20-YEAR *political enmity of Jan Smuts (left) and Barry Hertzog (right) was buried with Fusion – a coalition of the National and South African parties in response to the crisis sparked by the Great Depression.*

parliament, Roos, in the happy position of holding the balance of power, demanded the formation of a new government headed by himself.

Although Hertzog rejected this proposal out of hand, his options were rapidly diminishing – until he decided to try one of the few avenues remaining which had not yet been fully explored: an approach to Smuts to form an alliance of their two parties.

If anything, however, the SAP was in even deeper trouble than the NP: the party's rural supporters in the Transvaal, whose support was crucial for any future election success, were virtually demanding 'reunion' with the NP. But equally adamant that there should be no accommodation with the NP were the SAP's 16 Natal MPs, who argued that such a move would jeopardise the preferential tariffs enjoyed by the province's sugar manufacturers.

TRANSVAAL NATIONAL PARTY leader Tielman Roos sparked a political crisis by calling on South Africa to leave the gold standard – and then demanding the formation of a new government headed by himself.

To fight or not to fight – the battle of the generals

In the early hours of Friday, 1 September 1939, German troops stormed across the Polish frontier. Britain and France, bound to the defence of Poland, immediately demanded a German withdrawal. By Saturday, it was clear to the South African Government that another world war was imminent.

By a fateful coincidence, parliament, normally in recess, had been summoned for a special sitting to prolong the life of the Senate that was due to expire on 5 September. The government was aware that at this session it would have to decide finally on South Africa's position in the war, an issue of critical importance to national unity.

With this in mind, Hertzog summoned the 12 members of his cabinet to a meeting at his Groote Schuur residence on the Saturday afternoon to discuss the crisis. At stake were the Fusion Government and five years of work by Smuts and Hertzog to bring about unity between English- and Afrikaans-speakers.

Smuts, supported by six ministers, was adamant that while South Africa could refuse to fight, it would be in the country's interest to enter the war as Britain's ally. Hertzog, backed by the remaining five ministers, was equally determined that the country should remain neutral. The meeting ended with Hertzog quietly confident that he would command a majority in the house the following Monday.

A grim atmosphere of crisis hung over the house of Assembly as it opened its proceedings on the morning of 4 September. Hertzog moved

that the house accept that 'existing relations between the Union of South Africa and the various belligerent countries [would], in so far as the Union is concerned, persist unchanged and continue as if no war is being waged'. Smuts moved an amendment to the statement in terms of which the Union would declare war on Germany.

As the debate swung back and forth, there seemed reason for Hertzog to feel confident – but then, unintentionally, he overplayed his hand by moving from a defence of neutrality to an apparent defence of Adolf Hitler. His opponents were incensed. And it was enough to persuade those who were wavering to

throw their support behind Smuts. The debate finally ended at 9 pm when a division was called. By the time the tally was complete, Smuts' amendment had been carried by 80 votes to 67.

The next day, Hertzog resigned the premiership and requested the Governor-General, Sir Patrick Duncan, to dissolve parliament and call a general election. But Duncan refused, it being clear that Smuts could form a government from what remained of the United Party and with the support of the Labour and Dominion parties. On Wednesday, 6 September, he asked Smuts to form a new government.

South Africa was at war....

HOW THE 'Star' newspaper saw the split in government ranks over the war.

THE FORMATION *of the United South African National Party (later the United Party) coincided with the opening up of new economic opportunities for the Union, which helped establish* ISCOR, *founded in 1927, as the country's own supplier of iron and steel. From the official opening of the new foundry (right),* ISCOR *began publishing its own magazine (far right).*

It was the mine-owners, fearful of the formation of a new rural-based party, who forced the issue. By January 1933, it was no secret that the corporations were ready to throw their weight behind an SAP-Roos alliance – even if it meant having to dump Smuts.

Smuts, however, was well aware of his precarious position, and on 24 January (a week before the SAP caucus was due to vote on the alliance with Roos) he effectively killed Roos' political aspirations by proposing a coalition of the National and South African parties.

In December 1934, after long debate and acrimonious splits in both the NP and the SAP, the United South African National Party (later the United Party) came into being. White South African politics was about to enter a new era.

Certainly, the birth of the new party coincided with a period of economic growth – boosted by the goldmining industry – which in 30 years brought the white standard of living on a par with the world's most affluent.

A boom for the yellow metal

South Africa's departure from the gold standard, and the subsequent devaluation of the US dollar, opened up lucrative new opportunities for both the mines and the state: the devaluation of the dollar raised the international price, while the South African pound's devaluation opened the way for a surge in local earnings. By the end of 1933, the gold price had climbed from about £4 a fine ounce to more than £6; it shot beyond £7 during 1934, and continued to nose up towards £8 for the rest of the decade – a bonanza for mine-owners.

The increase in price unlocked vast reserves of previously unprofitable ore in the existing mines, allowing the mining of these reserves without additional capital expenditure. It also financed the opening of vast new mines. Between 1931-40, mine earnings almost tripled – rising from £46,2-million in 1931 to £118-million in 1940.

For the state, the price rise meant rocketing revenue receipts – which rose even further when it imposed a surplus profits tax on the mining houses. And so, as the money poured into the coffers, the government was able to report record budget surpluses between 1933-7 and was able substantially to reduce its foreign debt (replacing it with local borrowing).

Although there was some resistance to the imposition of surplus profits taxes, in reality the mining houses had little cause for complaint: their profits were still huge and they knew that if the industry were threatened, they could call on the government for protection.

Secondary industry took off – and although new industries were at first closely allied to the needs of the mining sector, some of the profits found their way into the importation of the increasingly sophisticated technology required by related industries.

Thus, ISCOR (the Iron and Steel Corporation), which had been established by the Pact Government in 1927, finally came on stream, producing iron and steel for the fast-growing engineering sector. As the boom took hold, more than £100-million in foreign capital flowed into the country between 1933-9, of which about 60 percent went into the goldfields themselves.

In 1932, the gross national product stood at only £217-million; within five years, it had increased 70 percent to £370-million. With inflation being relatively low, this enormous growth led to a significant rise in the standard of living, particularly for the white population.

Sector by sector, employment shot up between 1932-9. On the mines, it increased from 308 000 to 475 000 – an increase of 167 000 workers; in the manufacturing and construction industries it grew from 161 000 to 331 000, while on the railways, the number of jobs expanded from 86 000 to 123 000.

In the seven years between the abandonment of the gold standard and South Africa's entry into the Second World War, the 'poor white' problem, which had occupied the attentions of successive governments, eased considerably as the economy absorbed another 100 000 white workers. But while the country was flush for whites, the boom was not enough to enable blacks to shake off poverty. Although an estimated 400 000 Africans, coloureds and Asians were drawn into the economy, real wages of farm labourers and black mineworkers remained static, or actually declined, for the entire period between 1911 and 1970.

During the Second World War, when German attacks on the shipping lanes of the Atlantic led to a sharp decrease in imports, the government pumped millions of pounds into the development of the local steel, chemical and textile industries. From ISCOR came steel for armoured cars, shells and bombs, guns and tanks; South African Railways' workshops turned out munitions and heavy armament; mine workshops produced shells, howitzers and mortars. With thousands of whites joining the army, the blossoming wartime industries created employment opportunities for thousands of blacks. But the war was fought by South Africa at the price of Fusion . . . .

Division over war

In September 1939, parliament voted to declare war on Nazi Germany (see box), and the bulk of the Afrikaners who rejected the decision (including Hertzog) regrouped under the banner of Dr Daniel Malan's *Gesuiwerde* (Purified) National Party.

It was a major breakthrough for the man who had rejected Fusion, and who, with the help of 19 other 'purified' Nationalists and the *Afrikaner Broederbond* (Afrikaner Brotherhood), had started an all-out battle to win the support of the Afrikaner community.

In their first test of strength – the 1938 general election – Malan and his followers had issued an election manifesto that called for separate residential areas, separate trade unions and places of work, the abolition of all forms of African representation in parliament and a halt to further land purchases for Africans.

Against this, however, the UP could point to an enormous improvement in the economy, as well as its own segregationist measures, such as proposals for the extension of job reservation and separate parliamentary representation for coloured people.

Not surprisingly, the Nationalists did not fare as well as they had hoped, gaining only seven seats to increase the party's representation to 27 (against the 111 seats of the UP). In terms of popular support, the Nationalists had attracted the votes of only 60 percent of Afrikaners and it became apparent that Malan's only hope of seizing power now depended on a split in the UP....

It did not take long for this to happen.

In September 1938, after the British and French had negotiated away half of Czechoslovakia in a fruitless attempt to appease the territorial appetite of Adolf Hitler, the South African Cabinet met to discuss a proposal by Hertzog that the country remain neutral in the event of a major European war.

It was already clear by then that Hertzog and Smuts saw developments in Germany quite differently. To Hertzog, the rise of Nazism was the understandable reaction of an oppressed nation; to Smuts, who had participated in the 1919 deliberations at Versailles, it was a terrifying aberration in the national life of Germany. Although Smuts had initially leaned towards neutrality, the division of the Czech state had prompted him to change his views.

South Africa, he now argued in speeches around the country, could not stand alone; it needed to retain the friendship of its British and Commonwealth allies.

Off to war . . .

It was a time of posters, patriotism, propaganda and long queues outside hastily erected recruiting depots. The date was September 1939, and every day hundreds of South Africans were taking the first steps of a journey which would eventually take them to the battle fields of North Africa and Europe.

'Don't miss the greatest adventure of all time,' urged posters tagged to lampposts and walls in every major town and city. 'The only dress for non-key men is a Union Defence Force uniform,' suggested others. A dozen variations of the same theme whipped up such a frenzy of anti-German feeling that government officials were soon claiming that response to their call for volunteers had surpassed their wildest expectations . . . .

When South Africa declared war on Germany, the Permanent Force was made up of 3 350 officers and men. There were 14 600 part-time soldiers in the Active Citizen Force, while the Seaward Defence Force had a meagre 70 officers and 900 men. But by the end of 1939, 137 000 men were under arms and volunteers were still pouring in.

The first task of South Africa's largely volunteer army was to help drive Italy (which had sided with Germany) out of Africa. Within hours of South Africa having formally declared war on the Italians on 11 June 1940, South African Air Force bombers began strafing Italian positions in Abyssinia (present-day Ethiopia) and Italian Somaliland.

By 10 January 1941, Italian losses were estimated at 139 aircraft, 98 officers, 186 pilots and 67 non-commissioned officers. Sir Archibald Sinclair, Britain's Secretary of State for Air, later said: 'When the Italians come to draw up a list of factors which caused them to lose their East African Empire, they will place the SAAF bombers somewhere near the top of the list.'

But on 21 June 1942, South African morale was delivered a devastating blow when General H B Klopper surrendered Tobruk to the Germans.

News of the surrender stunned the British Empire – 35 000 men, including more than 10 000 South Africans, were taken prisoner.

But other victories helped to soften the blow: in 1942, a South African contingent seized the island of Madagascar, which had joined the collaborators of Vichy France in supporting the Axis powers. Later, South African troops made up for the setback at Tobruk when they helped Bernard Montgomery's reconstituted 8th Army to sweep the Axis forces out of Africa. Thereafter, the South African 6th Armoured Division joined the American Fifth Army in its drive to overthrow Mussolini and to push the Germans out of the Italian peninsula.

FASHION NOTE FOR THE DURATION

THE ONLY DRESS FOR NON KEY MEN

MEN ARE WANTED *for all units of the* UNION DEFENCE FORCE JOIN UP NOW!

POSTERS *called on men to volunteer for the Union forces.*

LOCAL PRODUCTION *(above) was stepped up during the war: the Pretoria Mint, for example, was used for the manufacture of 'doppies' – small shells and percussion caps.*
FIELD-MARSHAL SMUTS *(centre, in cap) visits the graves of South African troops killed at Castiglione in Italy after fierce fighting against German infantry.*

That the two generals would clash was a foregone conclusion. The crucial question was: who would the other United Party MPs follow? The answer came on 4 September 1939. By a margin of 13, members decided to support a declaration of war on Germany – and two days later Smuts was Prime Minister.

On 8 September Hertzog returned to a *Herenigde* (Reunited) National Party (HNP): at an emotional anti-war rally at Monumentkoppie near Pretoria, Hertzog and Malan shook hands and walked arm in arm to the podium to tumultuous applause from a crowd of 70 000.

Welcoming them, a former *Broederbond* chairman, J C van Rooy, said: 'Such unity as we are experiencing today is unique in the history of our people. This happening stands out above all past happenings. We thank you for this, but above all we thank God.'

The massive crowd raised their hands and vowed never again to break away from one another.

In his speech Malan called for the 'blessings of the sacred past' on this new-found unity. 'In spirit,' he said, 'I see the figures of Piet Retief, Andries Pretorius, Sarel Cilliers, Hendrik Potgieter and . . . it is as though I hear them saying: ''Even when you were divided we loved you, but now that you are one, our love for you is doubled.'' '

But Hertzog's return to the fold was to prove very temporary indeed . . . .

Spurred on by Hitler's early successes, Free State Nationalists set the scene for a head-on clash with their former leader by demanding that Afrikaans be the only medium of educational instruction (Hertzog believed in equal language rights). They also indirectly tarred Hertzog by describing Fusion as the creation of British-Jewish capitalism. Finally, in October 1940, the Free State congress of the party, backed by the Transvaal, rejected the principle of equal language rights.

Hertzog left the congress with this parting shot: 'We remain Afrikaners. Let us do nothing which is unworthy of the *volk* [nation] or which will lead to its downfall.' Shaken by the apparent disintegration of his life's work in the pursuit of a broader white South African loyalty, he retired from public life and died early in 1942. His ideals were briefly kept alive by Nicolaas Havenga, who established the Afrikaner Party which played a junior role in the Nationalist election victory of 1948.

Despite being leader of the Opposition, Malan's major battle during the early years of the war was outside parliament where Afrikaners, although united in their political objectives, differed significantly on how to achieve them. Malan and his party came under considerable pressure from organisations such as the *Ossewabrandwag* (OB – Ox-wagon sentinel)(see box) which, influenced by the stream of propaganda that poured out from a German station, Radio Zeesen, hoped for a victory by the Axis forces and expressed militant opposition to Smuts' war effort.

Malan was confronted with a serious challenge to his party's leadership of Afrikanerdom by the OB, the *Handhawersbond* (Defence League) of Gert Yssel, and by former Defence Minister Oswald Pirow, who led a separate parliamentary group which propagated a Nazi-influenced 'New Order'. A fragile truce took hold in mid-1941 when a People's Unity Committee was created to co-ordinate activities of these disparate organisations.

Malan was elected *volksleier* (national leader) by this committee. But while his efforts to pacify the rebellious groups failed and he eventually disowned the OB, other groups were forced by the results of a series of by-elections in 1942 to give their support to the Nationalists in the general election of 1943. It was a typical 'khaki election', held in the shadow of war, in which the UP won 89 seats, the Nationalists 43, the Labour Party nine, the Dominion Party seven, and independents two.

Encouraged by the results, the HNP began planning for a 1953 election triumph. Little did they realise that success would come sooner than they expected . . . .

Following the 'way to greatness' – the rise of the *Ossewabrandwag*

With his hand on the Bible, with a loaded revolver pointing at his chest and another at his back, the grim-faced young man slowly recited: 'If I advance, follow me. If I retreat, shoot me. If I die, avenge me. So help me God . . . .'

He was taking the oath of the *Stormjaers* (Stormtroopers), the military wing of the pro-Nazi *Ossewabrandwag* (OB) – and in the coming months hundreds more would follow him. For, encouraged by the early successes of Nazi Germany, thousands of Afrikaners were now openly backing the cause of Adolf Hitler.

One of them, the Reverend Koot Vorster, a Dutch Reformed Church minister (and a brother of future Prime Minister John Vorster), summed up the feelings of the pro-Hitler group during an address to a student group on 15 September 1940: 'Hitler's ''Mein Kampf'' shows the way to greatness – the path of South Africa,' he said. 'Hitler gave the Germans a calling. He gave them a fanaticism which causes them to stand back for no one. We must follow this example because only by such holy fanaticism can the Afrikaner nation achieve its calling.'

Vorster was later jailed for three years for contravening the Official Secrets Act. Activists such as Vorster, future government minister Ben Schoeman, future Speaker of parliament Henning Klopper and OB chairman Hans van Rensburg found willing audiences among the Afrikaner masses. Among these were men who were prepared to demonstrate their support for Hitler's ideals in more concrete ways than by simply making speeches.

By 1942, the *Stormjaers* had started a campaign of violence, which included blowing up pylons, powerlines, post offices, shops and banks as well as beating up Jews and soldiers.

At the height of the campaign, two *Stormjaers*, sentenced to death in July 1942 for blowing up the Benoni Post Office, escaped the hangman only because of the last-minute intervention of Prime Minister Jan Smuts. In the same period, security forces uncovered a plot to sink a ship in Durban harbour and 58 men were subsequently brought to trial. Then, when military intelligence disclosed that the OB had infiltrated the police, more than 370 policemen were suspended from duty and arrested.

Soldiers who had volunteered for service outside the country's borders and who were easily distinguishable by the red flashes they wore on their uniforms were singled out for special attention. In fact, running street battles between nationalists and these '*Rooi Luisies*' (Red Lice) became a regular occurrence in many South African towns.

Backing the Nazi cause

For every Afrikaner male who enlisted, probably as many joined the *Ossewabrandwag*, which by the 1940s began to eclipse even the *Herenigde* National Party (HNP) as the focus of anti-war activity.

Officially launched in Bloemfontein in February 1939 to give cultural expression to the growing Afrikaner nationalism that had been boosted by the centenary celebrations of the Great Trek, the OB had enjoyed a remarkable rise to prominence: in 1940, when Smuts had 137 000 men under arms, the OB claimed a membership of twice that number. Later it would claim 400 000 followers. The first OB 'commandant-general' was a farmer and part-time soldier, Colonel J C Laas, who was replaced in 1941 by Dr J F J 'Hans' van Rensburg, a former Secretary for Justice and Administrator of the Orange Free State.

Although it was founded to promote 'cultural activities' and ideals, and its stated aim was to transcend the constant political wrangles which seemed to sow division among the *volk* (nation) the OB quickly took on a distinctly military flavour. As wartime tension rose, members began building up an arsenal of hand grenades and guns for acts of sabotage – and murdering at least two 'treacherous comrades'.

So great was the movement's appeal, and so dangerous did the UP government consider it, that officers of the Union Defence Force were banned from becoming members. At the outbreak of the war, Prime Minister Smuts extended the ban to all civil servants.

And in a later crackdown on the organisation, up to 2 000 OB members – including John Vorster and many others who in later years would become prominent members of National Party Governments – were detained for the remainder of the war at Koffiefontein in the OFS.

As prospects for a German victory receded, the movement lost much of its appeal and members began streaming back into the fold of the *Herenigde* National Party.

OSSEWABRANDWAG *leader Dr J F J 'Hans' van Rensburg (centre) flanked by torch-bearing members during a rally at Stellenbosch in the Cape Province. At the height of its popularity, the movement claimed that it had 400 000 followers.*

The home front

'The Union of South Africa ... takes its stand for the defence of freedom, and the destruction of Hitlerism and all that it implies.'

With these impassioned words, General Jan Smuts, the newly appointed Prime Minister of South Africa, committed the nation to joining Britain and the Commonwealth in the war against Germany. It was 6 September 1939. The war of words that had split the United Party over whether or not to fight was over. But the campaign to win the people to the Allied cause had only just begun.

The political row between Smuts and the anti-war faction of Barry Hertzog over whether or not to declare war ensured that coercion would not be used in the raising of troops: the Union Defence Force was for volunteers only. So in an effort to encourage men to sign up, the government launched a vigorous recruiting drive. 'Don't be left out of the greatest adventure of all time', blazoned one poster, while another appealed: 'Was there ever a girl who didn't prefer a man in uniform?'

More posters warned the public about spies and informers: 'Careless talk costs lives' and 'Don't talk about ships and shipping'. Yet others called on South Africans to help fund the war effort, particularly the National War Fund, which was to receive a massive £11,2-million before hostilities ended.

Urged to save more than just money, South Africans learned to keep everything from old motorcar tyres to used light bulbs and pots and pans. Staples such as razor blades became rarer as steel was needed for war production – people even wrote to newspapers boasting of how long they could make one last.

Suddenly all sorts of things seemed to be in short supply – the Post Office saved paper by printing smaller

stamps, men's suits appeared without pocket flaps or turnups, and frills, pleats and buttons disappeared from women's dresses and frocks.

As enemy plane losses mounted, factory and office workers were asked to contribute one penny each a day for every aircraft reported shot down. As losses among Italian aircraft in North Africa increased, poorer contributors asked for this to be reduced to a halfpenny.

Knitting needles suddenly became vogue as thousands of women began knitting furiously for the 'boys at the front', eagerly following magazine patterns for pullovers, mittens, balaclavas and socks. Wrote one woman: 'There must be many of us who have knitted a million and more stitches for the troops in the present war.'

VARIOUS WAYS of raising money for the war effort included horseracing contests, sweepstakes and even budgerigar shows (below). In addition, War Loan bonds were sold at local post offices for five shillings each (opposite page). The National War Fund received a massive £11,2-million from patriotic investors before hostilities against Germany ended in 1945.

RATIONING became a hard fact of South African life during and just after the war, particularly following the issue of rationing books (right) and petrol coupons (below).

Music, too, took on a more jingoistic tone as 'forces' sweetheart' Vera Lynn sang 'The white cliffs of Dover', 'There'll always be an England' and 'We'll meet again', while old favourites from the First World War such as 'Tipperary' and 'Pack up your troubles in your old kitbag' were rediscovered. Leading the local songsters was Perla Gibson, who sang to departing troops through a megaphone from the quayside in Durban. Always dressed in white and wearing a characteristic wide-brimmed hat, the trained opera singer – known as the 'Lady in white' – sang up to 250 songs a day. On one occasion her rendition of 'Waltzing Matilda' brought so many visiting Australian troops to the wharf side of their ship, that it listed and the masts crashed into a grain elevator.

Increased German naval activity off the southern African coast prompted the government to order nightly blackouts of ports and coastal towns – while Civilian Protective Service wardens made nightly rounds to ensure that these instructions were carried out.

Petrol rationing was introduced in November 1941 when weekend sales were forbidden. But the screws were really put on in February the following year when coupons were issued allowing each car to travel only 400 miles (640 kilometres) a month. Night-time driving became a particularly hazardous exercise after regulations required masked headlights, allowing only a thin sliver of light to penetrate the darkness.

THE WAR *produced a plethora of posters and stamps that reminded South Africans about the war and urged them to play their part – either by contributing towards the war effort, avoiding the overuse of strategic resources or guarding against unwittingly giving information to the enemy. Harold Hart's song 'On the Road to Victory' (below) aided Red Cross Funds; while scaled-down stamps (below, left) saved paper. A poster warning against the excessive use of petrol and clothes also asked South Africans not to 'keep more servants' than they really needed.*

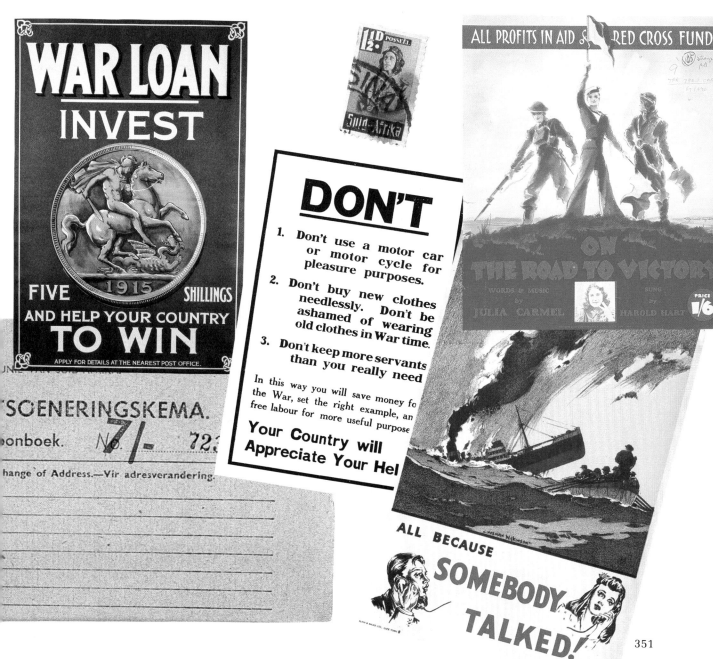

These hardships, however, were pinpricks when compared with the air raids on Britain and other European nations – and in August 1940 a 'guest children' scheme was announced for the placing of young evacuees from Britain in the safe care of local foster parents. However, fears of German U-boat attacks on ships bringing them to Cape Town kept the numbers low. Only when Japan entered the war did the numbers increase after a substantial flow of children from India and Singapore.

Blacks and the war

In general, the wave of patriotism that swept South Africa was supported by blacks, who were quick to grasp the ideological dangers of nazism and were only too well aware that supporters of the German cause – led by many members of the Opposition National Party – were also the most vociferous advocates of segregation in South Africa. The African National Congress (ANC) declared that the government was correct in going to war, and that it was time to 'consider the expediency' of admitting African 'and other non-European' races into full citizenship, with the duties that went with it – including taking part in the defence system on equal terms with whites.

Africans were certainly welcome in the Defence Force – but not as armed fighting troops; instead they were used in a variety of non-combatant roles such as driving, digging trenches, cooking and carrying the wounded. During severe fighting at Sidi Rezegh in North Africa, a number of African stretcher-bearers were killed and buried in a common grave with whites. According to subsequent reports, South African Army Headquarters ordered that the bodies be disinterred and buried in separate black and white graves.

Africans from Bechuanaland and Basutoland were promised arms, but when they arrived at the front in North Africa they were handed knobkerries and assegais so as not to upset South African blacks.

Many black servicemen earned the respect of their white colleagues-in-arms – and earned distinctions for bravery under fire while rescuing wounded troops. The better relations between black and white, however, did not always extend to the home front. In one instance, a dance in the Pietermaritzburg City Hall organised by the Coloured Welfare League in November 1943 was broken up by white soldiers – and two white and three black civilians were injured. The military authorities blamed the City Council which, it said, should not have permitted a dance for coloured people in the City Hall. The Mayor, Mrs Russel, replied bravely that she was 'not impressed by, or interested in, what the military thought'.

When the war in Europe ended in May 1945, 20 000 Africans joined a 'People's Day of Victory' celebration march in Johannesburg organised by the Council of non-European Trade Unions, the ANC and the Communist Party. In contrast, the government published cash and clothing allowances for discharged servicemen: while whites received £5 in cash and a £25 clothing allowance, coloured men received £3 and £15 respectively, and Africans only £2 and a khaki suit worth £2.

DURBAN'S *famous 'Lady in white', Perla Gibson (left), welcomes South African troops returning from Italy in* HMTS *Fanconia in 1945. She and thousands of other women, like these collecting clothing for the men at the front (right), took up the challenge to do their bit in the fight against nazism.*

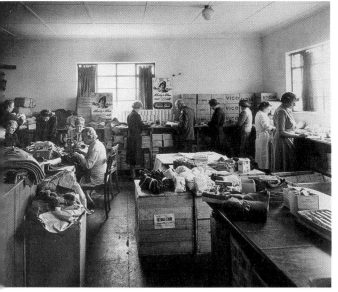

THE WAR changed the face of South Africa in many ways –
from this strange, charcoal-driven car (above, left), to the curls
of barbed wire erected at Durban's South Beach in case of a
Japanese invasion (above). It also brought a sense of purpose
to volunteer members of the Imperial Troops Comfort Fund
(left), who laboured in their Johannesburg offices, and encouraged blacks to volunteer in droves to fight nazism. Thousands of Africans served in the Union Defence Force as
stretcher-bearers (below).

Johannesburg... or starve

Evicted from white farms and driven out of overcrowded, drought-stricken Reserves, thousands of Africans had poured into the cities by the time the Second World War broke out in 1939. But those hoping for a better life were soon disappointed: for the majority, conditions in the urban slumyards were as wretched as they had been in the countryside. Yet out of this seemingly hopeless situation rose a spirit of resistance which helped to push the political organisations of the African middle class in a far more militant direction.

THE LETTERS ON THE BANNER which hung at the entrance to their squatter camp were crudely designed – but the message they spelt out echoed the feelings and aspirations of thousands of Johannesburg's African urban dwellers: 'Alexandra Tenants' Association – we want land.'

Homeless and desperate, the small group of squatters under the leadership of a man called Schreiner Baduza had first tried to set up home at Lombardy East, near Alexandra. But the police had moved in, demolished their shacks and arrested Baduza and his lieutenants. A second attempt to squat at Alexandra was discontinued on the advice of the Native Commissioner, who suggested they try Orlando (the municipal location which later became part of the giant African township complex of Soweto). On 29 November 1946, Baduza, accompanied by between 600 and 800 families, arrived at an Orlando already teeming with squatters. James Mpanza and his *Sofasonke* community numbering more than 20 000 (see box) had claimed

land between the communal hall and the railway line. Another group under the leadership of Oriel Monongoaha had set itself up on open ground in the south-west corner of the location. Next to this, at a place named Tobruk, were about 300 ex-servicemen and their families. Baduza and his group put up their hessian homes near Tobruk – and prayed that the police would stay away.

Meanwhile, at dozens of rural railway sidings and bus depots, long queues of Africans waited outside booking offices to buy their one-way tickets to the City of Gold....

From rural poverty to an urban slum

In 1930, the noted historian W M Macmillan wrote that rural Africans were 'dragging along at the very lowest level of bare subsistence'; they lived in 'poverty, congestion and chaos'; they were blighted by 'ill-health and starvation, endemic typhus and almost chronic scurvy'; they suffered 'an often appalling mortality rate among infants'; they lived in 'heavily over-populated' and 'grossly neglected'

DRIVEN BY *grinding poverty at home, thousands of Africans arrived in Johannesburg in the 1930s and early '40s, boosting the black population by 100 percent. Housing, however, was minimal – forcing Africans to resort to squatter communities on vacant land at Orlando (now part of Soweto) and Alexandra. As the squatter towns mushroomed, makeshift buildings were erected with corrugated iron (left) and hessian (below). Rentals for more permanent accommodation, such as this room to let in Alexandra (right), rocketed.*

areas where they were 'utterly dependent on wage-earning outside' to relieve 'a dead level of poverty' inside.

Two years later, the government-appointed Native Economic Commission ran out of adjectives to describe the poverty it had encountered in the Reserves. Yet in 1936, when the flight to the cities began in earnest, conditions had deteriorated even further and the choice for the majority of rural Africans had become brutally simple: either trek – or starve to death. Once the exodus started, it continued week after week, month after month, year after year, until, by 1946, Johannesburg's African population stood at 400 000 – a rise of almost 100 percent in just one decade.

Although the Natives (Urban Areas) Act of 1923 made provision for the construction of African housing, the Johannesburg municipality reacted to calls for more accommodation by claiming that it did not have the cash to cope with the needs of the spiralling black population. Local industry, on the other hand, had the money but not the will to assist African employees. And so a belt of slums sprang up from east to west across central Johannesburg.

For the majority, life in these urban ghettos was tough – and as degrading as it had been in the Reserves. And yet, in many ways, the slumyards bred more than merely squalor, prostitution, drunkenness, disease and an infant mortality rate between five and 10 times higher than that for whites. For out of the mire of these teeming, reeking, violent and tumble-down acres of apparently hopeless misery rose a spirit of proud survival. Africans called it *Marabi* (see box) – and although it did not develop into a coherent expression of political resistance, it represented, nevertheless, a way of life that enabled residents of the slumyards to pull together in the face of adversity.

The strong sense of unity which was forged in these urban ghettos occasionally encouraged African working-class communities to embark on determined, innovative – and sometimes successful – political campaigns to protect their precarious interests.

Their two most important struggles involved the Alexandra bus boycotts (between 1940 and 1945) and the squatters' movement (from 1944 to 1947).

Because Alexandra, a black freehold suburb situated about 15 kilometres to the north of Johannesburg, did not have a rail link, a cheap bus service to the centre of town was of vital importance to thousands of its commuters. But in 1940, shortly after the price of mealie-meal – a staple food – had shot up by 20 percent, bus operators decided to increase their fares from 4 to 5 pence. It led to nine months of unsuccessful negotiation, a bus boycott and, finally, a reduction of fares to the old level.

But the fight was far from over. In 1942, fares were again raised to 5 pence, and again passengers refused to pay the extra penny. When the bus owners retaliated by moving the terminus to the edge of the township, clashes broke out between employees of the companies and protesters. Later, following more negotiations, the old fare was restored and an official investigation promised.

In August 1943, the investigation ruled in favour of the bus companies and 20 000 people decided to walk to work and back. The protest lasted 10 days, and in that time communists, white left-wingers and liberals, led by Senator Hyman Basner, organised lift-clubs to help some of the people to get to work on time. Police and traffic department officials also assisted, and the Department of Native Affairs appealed to companies not to sack latecomers. On 10 August, the government appointed a commission of enquiry and, for the time being, the 4 pence fare was restored.

In November 1944, the government gave the go-ahead for the fare increase – and this time the protest which followed was marked by increasingly tough action by police and Transportation Board officials: lift-givers were harassed, workers were arrested in Pass raids and meetings of more than 20 people were banned. Finally, after seven weeks of deadlock, a compromise was reached when a coupon scheme, which allowed passengers to buy tickets in advance at the old price and companies to claim the deficit from the city council, was started.

But by then the focus of African discontent had already shifted to a new area: housing.

The rise of squatter communities

In Johannesburg during the war years, the construction of new houses for Africans had ground almost to a halt, with only 750 units being built in 1941 and 1942 (the year the government relaxed the application of the Pass laws in the main industrial areas of the Transvaal and Natal) – and none in 1943 and 1944. Faced with a major housing crisis, Johannesburg City Council began to issue more and more permits to allow householders to take in sub-tenants.

But it was a short-term solution which succeeded only in pushing more people into locations such as Pimville (today a suburb of Soweto), which had only 63 water taps for more than 15 000 people – and where much of the accom-

A BACK STREET *in Pimville (now part of Soweto) in the 1940s, when the infant mortality rate meant one in five children died before their fifth birthday.*

modation had been condemned again and again as being unfit for human habitation.

In March 1944, the long-ticking time bomb exploded when thousands of Africans, tired of waiting for dwellings they now believed they would not get, moved out of their overcrowded hovels and began setting up homes on any vacant piece of land.

It was the era of the urban squatter.

Municipal authorities were appalled by this new development – more so when they discovered that the new communities were determined to live by their own rules. Frantic appeals were made to the central authorities – and among the solutions suggested was the use of force to break up the camps. But for once the government wavered, giving the squatter leaders time to consolidate. James Mpanza's *Sofasonke* settlement in particular became a no-go area for white officialdom. Even when shacks of smaller parties were demolished, squatters simply moved to other pieces of ground. Not even the belated implementation of a low-cost housing programme could at first curb the phenomenon. Squatting, quite simply, had become a means of survival: it was cheaper than council-built dwellings; camps could be set up nearer to places of employment, thus cutting down on transport costs; and it offered

Sofasonke – and the birth of the squatter movement

All he had promised was to lead them to a piece of ground where they could erect their hessian shelters . . . .

Yet, when James Mpanza started the short walk from the Orlando location to the veld between the railway line and the communal hall, hundreds followed him. It was March 1944 – and a new social phenomenon, which would further complicate an already complex South African political set up, and which in the coming decades would defy all government efforts to crush it completely, was to be unleashed: squatting.

By the first week of April, 8 000 people had streamed into the hessian township. At the end of 1946, its population had risen to 20 000 – and Mpanza, who had once languished in a prison death cell for killing an Indian trader, had proclaimed himself king of Orlando. A man of great charisma, he had escaped the noose by converting to Christianity, which he then took up so seriously that he became convinced that he had much in common with Jesus Christ. This claim would draw hundreds of slum-yard dwellers into his *Sofasonke* ('we shall all die together') Party.

'You are soldiers now. You have joined forces with me and you will die

where I die,' Mpanza told recruits. 'We are your soldiers,' they were instructed to reply. 'We have joined with you – we shall die where you die.'

Families had to pay 6 shillings to join his squatter group. Thereafter a fee of 2s 6d entitled them to a site – while an additional 2s 6d a week contributed to the day-to-day administration of the camp.

To the thousands of Africans who flocked into the ranks of the party it was money well spent. The main attraction of the *Sofasonke* camp was the protection it offered its vulnerable inhabitants. Indeed, in many respects, it was a state within a state, where laws regulating entry, administration and discipline were drawn up by Mpanza himself, and enforced by 'police' recruited from the ranks of the squatters.

Although he was also an unscrupulous character who took advantage of the black housing shortage to amass a vast personal fortune (including a string of racehorses), Mpanza nevertheless proved to be more than a match for the council officials who tried to persuade him to dismantle the community he had built up.

In January 1946, the authorities, unable to master him at the negotiat-

THE 'KING' *of Orlando, James Mpanza, whose Sofasonke squatter movement housed 20 000 people.*

ing table, tried to crush his movement by seeking his expulsion to Natal. But Mpanza took his fight all the way to the Appeal Court – and won.

Although his power began to wane after 1948 when the authorities embarked on a massive rehousing programme, Mpanza – the man whom doting followers described as the 'Peeler' (because he had 'sliced' land from the white municipality) – is remembered even today.

inhabitants – especially those in the bigger communities – some protection against the myriad laws aimed at African urban-dwellers.

In 1947, Pimville squatter leader Oriel Monongoaha summed up the growing determination of these new communities – and the magnitude of the state's task – when he said: 'The government is beaten, because even the government of England could not stop the people from squatting. The government was like a man who has a cornfield which is invaded by birds. He chases the birds from one part of the field and they alight in another part . . . we squatters are the birds. The government sends its policemen to chase us away and we move off and occupy another spot. We shall see whether it is the farmer or the birds who get tired first . . . .'

The state, however, was far from beaten – and by the end of the decade it had virtually crushed the squatter movements and had pushed them into the massive housing estates which would later become known as Soweto. Future government policy on urban Africans was now set to take the form of greater control over both housing – and the new threat to political order – labour.

African trade unionism

After almost a decade of inactivity, concrete signs of a new spirit of defiance among African workers had begun to emerge in 1936 when black labour leaders, tired of the constant rebuffs from representatives of white unions, decided to sever ties with the Trades and Labour Council (TLC) and to form their own organisation. On 7 August 1938, the strongly pro-Africanist Council for Non-European Trade Unions (CNETU) was formed amid accusations of racism (followed by a walkout) by Max Gordon, a white Trotskyite socialist who was secretary of four African trade unions. But Gana Makabeni, the organisation's first chairman (and himself a former communist), was unrepentant: 'White men govern the country, supervise all establishments, own the factories and commercial enterprises. Must we have European leaders even in our own establishments?' he asked.

It was a popular move – by 1941 all the important African trade unions had linked up with the CNETU, transforming it into one of the most powerful black union groupings ever to exist in South Africa.

In the same year, two prominent communists, Edwin Mofutsanyana and Gaur Radebe, persuaded the Transvaal African National Congress (ANC) to call a conference to discuss the formation of an African mineworkers' union. In August 1941, 80 delegates from 41 organisations unanimously decided to organise workers both at the mines and before their recruitment in the Reserves into an African Mineworkers' Union (AMWU). But the proposed membership drive immediately ran into problems when union officials were banned by the Chamber of Mines from entering African housing compounds.

Nevertheless, by making use of contacts inside the compounds, the union was still able to reach the workers – and by 1944 would claim a membership of 25 000.

In 1943, after a series of work stoppages on the mines, the union boosted its image when it played a key role in persuading the government to appoint the Lansdowne commission of enquiry to investigate the wages and working conditions of African miners.

During its evidence to the Lansdowne commission, the AMWU called for regular wage increases; payment of a cost-of-living allowance; statutory minimum wage levels to be determined by Wage Board enquiries; the 'total abolition' of the compound system, the tribal division of the work force and restrictions on freedom of movement, and finally, recognition of the AMWU.

Against this, representatives of the Chamber of Mines stressed the industry's dependence on cheap migrant

J B MARKS, *first president of the African Mineworkers' Union. Founded in 1941, the union's membership mushroomed.*

A GROUP *of African migrant workers attend a trade union meeting in the 1940s after the formation of the African Mineworkers' Union. By 1944 membership of the union stood at 25 000.*

Marabi – the beat of the slums

It was the culture of the slumyard – and it thrived on music, shebeen queens, beer-brewing, 'exquisite ladies of the night', unsophisticated migrant workers and smooth-talkers with oiled hair, pencil-moustaches and two-tone shoes . . . .

Some referred to it as *Marabi*. To others it was *I-Tswari* or *Mabokwe*. But whatever it was called, to its followers it was black and beautiful and slick and vibrant – and in the 1920s, '30s and part of the '40s, it put smiles on the scarred faces of Johannesburg's sprawling ghettos.

The heart of *Marabi* was its music – a throbbing blend of Christian spirituals, Negro rags, Boer *vastrap* (up-tempo music composed for a popular Boer folk-dance) and traditional rural rhythms and harmonies. It was a new, distinctively African sound – and the men and women who sang and played it at shebeens and smoke-filled 'joints' such as the E-Sidikidikini in Johannesburg's Newclare township, the African Hall in Doornfontein and the Ebenezer in Ferreirastown, were different too. Most of them had no music training, but they taught themselves – by a process of trial and error. And when 'songbirds' such as Snowy Radebe, piano 'maestros' such as Meekly 'Fingertips' Matshikiza, and trombonists such as Vy Nkosi began creating their own sounds, they drew massive followings.

No shebeen could hope to thrive without a resident *Marabi* musician. And it did not matter if sometimes the 'artiste's' instrument was a humble tin can with a few stones inside. What was important to the customers was the sound he created.

But *Marabi* was not only about music. Other vital components were home beer-brewing, weekend shebeen parties and drinking *skokiaan* and *isiqataviku* ('kill me quick') in order to forget the drabness of life in urban ghettos. Run mainly by women, called shebeen queens, these unique and sometimes profitable township enterprises were often the only avenue of recreation for thousands of slum-dwellers. It was a multipurpose convenience – a drinking hole, an all-night restaurant, a dance hall and a brothel. And for an entrance fee of about 6 pence, it was good value for money.

Although brewing was a high-risk occupation – frequent police raids put many operators out of business and into jail – the innovative survived by constantly developing new methods of keeping their valuable merchandise out of the reach of prying policemen. These included

POLICE *empty cans of illicit liquor after a raid on a shebeen. The drinking of illegally brewed beer and isiqataviku ('kill me quick') helped thousands of urban slum-dwellers to forget their drab existence.*

elaborate hiding places, as well as a system of child-guards who gave the familiar warning cry of 'Araraai', whenever the police arrived.

Looking back now, perhaps the biggest contribution of the *Marabi* culture to the new urban societies was the fact that it made living in a ghetto just a little more tolerable.

But when the slumyards began to be cleared in the 1930s *Marabi* started to lose its sparkle. And, by the mid-1940s, when the illegal beer trade was being strangled by the colourless municipal beerhalls, it was breathing its last . . . .

AFRICAN MUSIC *boomed in the 1930s and '40s – from the raw beat of township jazz to the more sophisticated sound of the Harmony Kings.*

BREWERS *pour beer into individual bottles ready for sale.*

labour. The wages paid to African miners, it argued, were 'perfectly adequate', considering that workers were housed and fed in the compounds and that Reserve production was another source of income. In fact, representatives claimed that the average wage of between 2s 1d and 2s 3d a shift for a six-day week was sufficient to support a miner's family for his 14-month contract – as well as for another year of 'idleness'.

However, after an investigation of conditions in the rural homelands, the commission reported that 'Reserve production is but a myth' and that poverty, landlessness and severe malnutrition were a 'cause for grave concern'.

Yet it refused to support AMWU calls for an end to the migrant labour system: mindful of the 'profitability constraints' of the mining industry, the commission backed the retention of the system at wages that provided 'a proper livelihood'. It recommended a cost of living allowance of 3 pence a shift; a boot allowance (with a free or cost price repair service); a minimum wage of 2s 2d a shift for surface workers and 2s 5d for underground workers; payment of an overtime rate, and leave pay for long service employees.

On the question of recognition for the AMWU, the commission stated that while it was in favour of some sort of system of collective bargaining for Africans, black miners had not yet reached the stage of development which would enable them safely and usefully to employ trade unionism as a means of promoting their advancement.

At an AMWU conference in August 1944, delegates described the recommendations as 'hopelessly inadequate and unsatisfactory', but nevertheless urged their implementation 'as a step in the right direction'.

The Chamber of Mines and the government adopted a two-pronged response to the Lansdowne report: overtime and Sunday pay was granted and wages were raised by a maximum of 5 pence a shift (the costs were carried by the taxpayer). But at the same time the chamber banned all union activity in the compounds. This was followed in August 1944 by a government War Measure which banned gatherings of more than 20 people on mine property.

It was the start of a rapidly deteriorating relationship between the workers on the one side and the government-Chamber of Mines alliance on the other. Within two years more than 60 000 workers would down tools in one of the biggest strikes in South African history (see page 365).

In the meantime, African workers in other industrial sectors had also been flexing their muscle: in September 1942 a rash of work stoppages swept across the Witwatersrand, despite an attempt by the government to ban strikes by Africans.

It was the perfect time to demand wage increases – for, the government, already deeply concerned over the divisions the war had created in white society, was prepared to go to great lengths to secure the loyalty of Africans. In 1942, for instance, the Minister of Native Affairs, Deneys Reitz, ordered a relaxation of influx control measures in the main industrial centres of Transvaal and Natal, the Orange Free State and the northern Cape. And in the same year, Minister of Labour Walter Madeley promised the CNETU that legal recognition of African trade unions was imminent.

But, with a major victory within its grasp, the CNETU waited instead of pressing the minister to carry out his promise. By the time it again took up the matter in 1946 (at the time of the miners' strike), the war was over, white workers were streaming back into the factories – and Madeley had changed his mind.

WORKERS LISTEN *to trade union organisers during a meeting in the 1940s. Note that many of the workers are inside the factory behind the barbed wire fence – listening to the organisers* on the outside of the factory premises. In a bid to curb trade union activity, the government forbade gatherings of more than 20 people on mine property.

The road to resistance ...

By the 1940s, a new generation of black activists was growing to maturity. Determined, and much more militant than the stodgy conservatives who had dominated African politics for more than three decades, they began to reject old perceptions and to form new ones. In the coming years African political campaigns would be closely tied to the aspirations of the working classes.

I N THE END it was only an interlude, an interruption which the guardians of segregation did not want but were forced to accept ....

Yet for six drama-packed months in 1942, South Africa's ever-optimistic black middle-class communities seemed perfectly justified in believing that racial discrimination had at last come off the rails.

Even Prime Minister Jan Christiaan Smuts appeared to admit as much when he savagely attacked white political attitudes at an Institute of Race Relations meeting in Cape Town on 21 February. South Africa appeared to be under a serious threat of invasion by Japan when Smuts told the large crowd that he saw 'white and black as fellow South Africans, standing together in the hour of danger'. Later, he declared that if Japan's aggression made it necessary, 'every native and coloured man who can be armed, will be armed'.

Somehow it seemed inconceivable that a man who had supported racial separation all his life, could, at the age of 72, now argue so forcefully that segregation 'had fallen on evil days'. But Smuts was a canny politician....

The beginnings of an African revival

The labour needs of thriving wartime industries had opened the way for a massive influx of Africans to the cities. This in turn had created ideal conditions for the growth of trade unionism. And Smuts was only too aware that an organised workforce would inevitably lead to demands for higher wages, strikes and calls for political reform.

Like Louis Botha and J B M Hertzog (the other Prime Ministers since Union), Smuts was committed to a policy of segregation. But, unlike the other two, he was prepared to bend the rules and concede on certain issues – if the need arose, and if it would benefit the white state.

It was the need for black-white unity in the face of the Japanese threat which prompted his 'retreat from segregation' speech – and the dramatic but short-lived relaxation of influx control measures in May 1942.

Few would have guessed that one of the pillars of segregation would be examined – and be found wanting – when the government appointed a commission early in 1942 to investigate the socio-economic, educational and health conditions of urban Africans.

The report, tabled by the Secretary of Native Affairs, Douglas Smit, was a damning indictment of state policies. In calling for the scrapping of the Pass laws, it spoke of the 'tremendous price' the country was paying in respect of these laws; it pointed out the vast loss of labour due to detention during arrest and imprisonment; and it noted that fines paid constituted a drain on income that Africans could ill-afford. Apart from this, it added that 'the harassing and constant interference with the freedom of movement of Natives gives rise to a burning

IN 1942 *Minister of Native Affairs Deneys Reitz suspended influx control in the country's main industrial areas.* AT THE AGE *of 72, Prime Minister Jan Smuts called for a retreat from segregation in order to prepare the country for a possible invasion by Japan.*

A charter for human rights

In August 1941, at the height of the Second World War, British Prime Minister Winston Churchill slipped out of his beleaguered country for a round of secret talks with his US counterpart Franklin Roosevelt.

A few days later, from a battleship stationed off the coast of Newfoundland, the two leaders offered the world 'a blueprint for future peace and security'.

It was called the Atlantic Charter – and its initial purpose was to pave the way for the entry of the USA into the war. It therefore placed heavy emphasis on the maintenance of human rights, with one of the major clauses being an undertaking that 'the great nations of the world would do what they could to afford assurance that all men in all lands may live out their lives in freedom from fear and want'.

Thousands of kilometres away, on the other side of the world, black South African nationalists adopted the charter as a symbol of the freedom for which they had been striving since before Union.

As an ally of Britain and the USA, South Africa was morally obliged to abide by the terms of the document, they argued. Claims by the state that the charter was aimed primarily at Hitler-style oppression, were countered with the argument that there was little difference between the German dictator's brand of Nazism and the Union Government's policy of racial segregation.

In a quandary, the government decided to keep quiet and offered as few comments as possible. But ever-hopeful African spokesmen refused to let the matter rest, and when it was raised again in 1942 during a sitting of the Natives' Representative Council, a government spokesman told councillors: 'The freedoms vouchsafed to the people of the world in the Atlantic Charter were indicated for the African people as well.' Significantly, he failed to say how and when the terms of the charter would be implemented.

In 1943, leading African professionals and politicians, including members of the ANC and the CPSA, outlined the full extent of black claims in a document entitled 'African Claims in South Africa' (which was in effect an interpretation of the Atlantic Charter from an African point of view). Among the demands put forward were the abolition of racial discrimination, the granting of full franchise rights, freedom of movement and residential rights, equal education, equal pay, equality of ownership and property and full social services for Africans.

Although Prime Minister Smuts rejected this interpretation of the charter, the African claims were later well received at Pan-Africanist congresses, in the United Nations and, after 1947, in newly independent India.

---

sense of grievance and injustice which has an unsettling effect on the Native population as a whole. The application of these laws also has the undesirable feature of introducing large numbers of Natives to the machinery of criminal law and makes many become familiar at an early age with prison.'

To the government, total abolition of influx control measures was out of the question. But in what amounted to a major policy shift, the Minister of Native Affairs, Deneys Reitz, instructed the departments of Justice and Native Affairs to suspend their activities under influx control legislation. The new dispensation, he announced, would be effective in Pretoria, the Witwatersrand and the main urban areas of Natal, the Orange Free State (OFS) and the northern Cape.

The relaxation of the Pass laws was accompanied by limited attempts to improve the living and employment conditions of Africans. Notable in this regard was the extension of certain welfare services to Africans. Although only modest amounts were set aside for this, the principle of government responsiblity for such services was established.

Other advances were the inclusion of African workers in determinations by the Wage Board (which trade unionists used skilfully to win wage increases) and government sanction of the unionisation of workers in secondary industry. This was followed by an announcement by the Minister of Labour, Walter Madeley, of the imminent inclusion of African workers into the system of collective bargaining (which white workers already enjoyed under the Industrial Conciliation Act). These developments were seen as positive signs that segregation was about to be reversed. But it was not to be.

Within a few months of their relaxation, the Pass laws had been reimposed in Johannesburg – and in 1946, when it became clear that Daniel Malan's *Herenigde* National Party was making fresh inroads into traditional government support, the countrywide prosecution of 'offenders' was pursued with even greater vigour.

The stage was now set for increasingly bitter confrontation between the state and its black opposition, led by the Communist Party of South Africa (CPSA) and the African National Congress (ANC).

The revival of the Communist Party

In 1939, at the outbreak of the Second World War, the CPSA existed only in name. Ravaged by internal fights and rejected by both black and white activists, its membership had dwindled to about 300 supporters.

But on 22 June 1941, when the Soviet Union was drawn into the conflict, and white South Africans began singing the praises of a 'glorious and respected' new ally, communism began to thrive as never before.

Within a year, Moscow had established a diplomatic presence in the Union; fringe groups such as the Friends of the Soviet Union (FSU) and Medical Aid for Russia packed out halls at nation-wide meetings; and prominent public figures, such as the Minister of Justice Dr Colin Steyn, agreed to become patrons of pro-Soviet clubs such as the FSU.

It opened up limitless new possibilities which the CPSA faithful were determined not to let slip. Choosing patriotism as their battle-cry, they expertly manipulated the new situation. A countrywide series of 'Defend South Africa' rallies won over hundreds to their cause. And speakers who only a few months earlier had been calling on South Africans not to support an 'imperialist' war now urged their followers to 'avenge Tobruk', and the government to 'arm the people'.

Even the most hard-bitten Marxists were caught up in the emotions of the moment: noted Cape Town trade unionist Jimmy la Guma, who had been fiercely anti-war at the outbreak of hostilities, enlisted – while Edwin Mofutsanyana, editor of the Party newspaper, 'Inkululeko' ('Freedom'), donned an air-raid warden's uniform and patrolled the dusty lanes of the Orlando location in the Transvaal.

The South African Broadcasting Corporation (SABC) played its part too. First, it allowed a choir from the Jewish Workers' Club to sing the communist anthem, the 'Internationale', over the radio. Then, in 1942, it broadcast CPSA leader Bill Andrews' May Day speech.

One effect of the party's new-found respectability was a rapid growth in membership – with a low of 300 in 1939 rising to several thousand by 1943. And although most of the recruits were Africans, whites also joined in sufficient numbers to encourage the CPSA to contest elections for the first time since the 1920s.

In many ways the party's foray into white electoral politics was tinged with opportunism: only too aware of the extent of white fears and prejudices, it adopted a deliberately vague and ambiguous approach to African aspirations – especially during its campaign in the 1943 general election. In this respect, African opinion-makers in the party collaborated fully in the compilation of pamphlets such as one entitled, 'We South Africans', in which it was suggested that 'Africans may prefer a policy of total segregation under a socialist state'.

The CPSA, which fielded nine candidates in the election, failed to capture a seat, but drew a satisfactory 7 000 votes. During the next year, it was given further encouragement when communist candidates won a total of four seats in municipal elections in Cape Town, East London and Johannesburg.

Blacks and the Communist Party

But the moderation the CPSA projected to white voters was tempered with the knowledge that it could not afford to alienate its black supporters. Thus the party also regularly called for black soldiers to be armed; for African trade unions to be recognised; for the extension of voting rights to Africans; and for the scrapping of the Pass laws.

Indeed, in 1943, when the government revoked its moratorium on the Pass laws, it was the CPSA which arranged an anti-Pass conference where more than 150 delegates representing 80 000 people, resolved to set up a countrywide network of anti-Pass committees and 'to undertake every form of activity which will bring pressure on the government to abolish the Pass laws'.

FEARS OF *Japanese invasion sparked a wave of patriotism around the country, with calls to arm Africans.*

On 20 May, the nation-wide campaign was officially inaugurated when 540 delegates, representing organisations as diverse as trade unions, churches, vigilance associations, food clubs, the CPSA, the ANC, student groups and Advisory Boards, met in Johannesburg's Gandhi Hall to plan strategy. After rejecting calls for militant action by Trotskyite groups, delegates voted to embark on a million signature petition – to be presented to the government in August that year.

But after a promising start, the campaign became bogged down – and in June 1945, when the petition was finally delivered to deputy Prime Minister Jan Hofmeyr, only 100 000 signatures (which the government ignored anyway) had been collected.

Compared to previous forms of protest, a signature campaign seemed rather tame. But by then it had long been apparent that the CPSA had lost its nerve ....

In a sense, the party was caught between two stools. While a policy of avoiding open confrontation with the state had won some white support, it had also resulted in the communists missing out on several golden opportunities to mobilise the African masses.

In 1944, for instance, when African squatter camps near Johannesburg began to mushroom, the CPSA kept its distance despite a call for cooperation by James Mpanza, the main squatter leader. And in the same year, when thousands of residents of the African township of Alexandra started a seven-week bus boycott, the CPSA, together with the ANC, advised caution. As a result, the

The life and times of Anton Lembede

For three years the destiny of the African National Congress Youth League (CYL) was tied to the ambitions of one man – a young lawyer named Anton Muziwakhe Lembede.

Between assuming the leadership of the CYL in 1944 and his death in 1947, he injected a new spirit of militancy into the ANC and helped propel it towards programmes of mass action.

Overcoming the obstacles of his poverty-stricken background, Lembede's courage, intelligence and ambition drove him into a daunting programme of self-education which saw him develop into one of the foremost ideologues of his generation. He was born into a family of poor sharecroppers near Durban in 1914, and his parents, anxious to spare him the arduous labour of the fields, managed to place him in a mission school.

In 1933, aged 19, he had enrolled at Adams College to train as a teacher and by 1937 had matriculated with a distinction in Latin. During the next six years, while holding down a series of teaching posts in Natal and the Orange Free State yet driven still by his zest for learning, he gained a law degree from the University of South Africa. In 1943 he moved to Johannesburg to do his articles in the law firm of the former ANC president, Pixley Seme.

From his earliest contact with the ANC, Lembede had immediately become convinced that what Africans needed most of all was an ideology that would restore to them an aggressive sense of self-worth, a new pride in their essential blackness, a deep love of Africa and a confidence in its future. 'Africa is a black man's country,' he wrote in 1946, 'Africans are the natives of Africa and they have inhabited Africa, their Motherland, from times immemorial; Africa belongs to them. Africans are one.... The basis of national unity is the nationalistic feeling of the Africans, the feeling of being Africans irrespective of tribal connection, social status, educational attainment, or economic class.'

Writing in 1945, he argued that African society was fundamentally socialistic in structure, and that this would have to be developed by the infusion of modern socialist ideas. Nevertheless, the immediate task of the Africanists was national liberation rather than socialism. In addition, the struggle for liberation was inherently racial, and not based on class lines – a distinction which automatically put him at odds with Marxism and the Communist Party.

NATAL-BORN *Anton Muziwakhe Lembede, the theorist of Africanism, studied for a degree in law through the University of South Africa.*

It also meant the rejection of co-operation with whites, however like-minded they might be, certainly until such time as Africans had secured sufficient political cohesion and self-confidence. This attitude was central to the early philosophy of the CYL, and drove the league initially to reject any links between the ANC and the Communist Party.

Lembede died before much of his thinking on the need for militancy prevailed. But it was largely due to his spadework that the ANC accepted a new strategy of militant resistance in 1949.

---

party's role was reduced for a long time to running soup kitchens in the squatter camps, and protesting about the lack of drains and the risk of smallpox in Alexandra.

Communist caution also extended into trade unionism. Because of its support for the war effort, the thrust of the CPSA's union activities was increasingly aimed at the resolution of industrial disputes without having to resort to strike action. This trend had started in 1942 when communist union leaders stepped in to stop a strike by gas and power workers because they felt it was their 'duty to prevent trouble when the country was in the midst of a serious war crisis'.

It was an approach which did not always find favour with members of the workforce and other union officials. In September 1942, for instance, during the Council for Non-European Trade Unions' (CNETU) campaign for a weekly minimum wage of 40 shillings, thousands of workers in a variety of industries ignored communist calls for restraint and went on strike. And in 1945, a 'progressive' Trotskyist group in the 150 000-strong CNETU was expelled for accusing the dominant 'Stalinist' faction of, among other things, not supporting strikes.

Changes in the ANC

In the ANC meanwhile, a growing number of rank-and-file members were becoming more and more convinced that if the organisation was to play any part in the struggles that lay ahead, new leaders would have to be found.

For more than 30 years the movement's 'Old Guard' had spent their lives trying to win the acceptance of their white countrymen. They had been openly contemptuous of the 'lower classes' and had shied away from attempts to mobilise the masses, fearing that this would antagonise the government and the white public.

But there was a group – young, ambitious and determined – who did not suffer from pangs of political squeamishness. It would be left to them to grasp the nettle and push the organisation on a new road.

The call of youth was answered in 1943 – with the founding of the Congress Youth League (CYL).

The election of Dr Alfred Xuma to the presidency of the ANC in 1940 had paved the way for gradual transformation. A capable and energetic organiser, Xuma had reorganised the ANC by centralising control in the presidency and an executive of five who lived within

DR JAMES MOROKA (*left*) *gained the presidency of the ANC thanks to the support of the* CYL, *led by men such as Walter Sisulu (right).*

80 kilometres of the president. The House of Chiefs was abolished, women were given equal rights within the organisation, and steps were taken to secure the financial base of the movement through paid membership. Xuma had also recognised that younger men in the movement were restless and had therefore started pressing for more thorough-going reforms. Thus, during 1943, he permitted himself to be drawn into consultation by younger activists who needed his support for the proposed establishment of a youth wing.

The formation of the Congress Youth League
The most prominent among the youth group were Peter Mda, Jordan Ngubane, William Nkomo, Nelson Mandela and Walter Sisulu; later they were joined and led by Anton Lembede, a 33-year-old lawyer and political strategist who gave new shape to the development of radical African nationalism (see box).

In December 1943, the annual conference of the ANC accepted the proposal for the formation of the CYL, despite a prophetic warning by the old Natal warhorse, George Champion, that it would prove to be Xuma's eventual undoing.

Xuma first clashed with the CYL early in 1944 when the league made it clear that it would be critical of ANC leadership and its passivity. Although Xuma countered that the ANC was not yet sufficiently well organised for mass action, the CYL pressed on. In March 1944, it published a manifesto in which it castigated the ANC for its elitism and for 'giving way in the face of oppression'. The following month, on Easter Sunday, the CYL held its inaugural conference, proclaiming: 'The hour of youth has struck! As the forces of National Liberation gather momentum, the call to youth to close ranks in order to consolidate the national Unity Front, becomes more

urgent and imperative.' Membership was open to all Africans between the ages of 12 and 40, and all those older than 17 would automatically become members of the ANC. Lembede was elected its first president.

To Mandela and Sisulu especially, the CYL was no more than a vehicle through which to gain control of the parent body. But in the meantime, they bided their time, directing attacks at communist members of the ANC.

The plot to overthrow the 'Old Guard'
It took five years of intense preparation and consolidation before the CYL felt confident enough to challenge the leadership of Xuma and the 'Old Guard'.

On Lembede's death in 1947, Mda took over the presidency and, as a first step towards a grab for power, members began to look for new ways to expand the group's base within congress. This entailed the circulation of a new policy document which represented a shift away from Lembede's 'radical' position. The 'Basic Policy', as they termed it, recognised the need for limited co-operation between Africans, coloureds and Indians, and characterised African nationalism as 'the militant outlook of an oppressed people seeking a solid basis for waging a long, bitter and unrelenting struggle for its national freedom'. This expression of policy was accompanied by efforts to increase their voting power within congress: by the end of the year, CYL branches had been formed in Natal, the eastern Cape and the Orange Free State. Simultaneously, and against the backdrop of a newly installed Nationalist Government in 1948, Mda took to the ANC national conference a 'Programme of Action' which proposed the use of boycotts, strikes, stay-at-homes, civil disobedience and non-collaboration, aimed at the abolition of all 'differential institutions'. It also called for the establishment of a national 'fighting fund'.

The programme became the object of a year-long, tough-minded battle between the 'Old Guard' and the CYL, as the former did its best to avoid the issue. Behind it all, however, were the deeper motivations of both factions. The 'Old Guard', while sympathetic to the nationalist goals of the CYL, had warned the youth not to overestimate the ability of the masses to 'march barefoot' to liberation. And they were also anxious to protect their positions of power within the movement. The Youth Leaguers, on the other hand, had vowed to crush the 'Old Guard', and their numbers in congress were beginning to tell.

In July 1949, Xuma, sensing the new wind blowing through the organisation, backed the programme at the Cape congress of the ANC. In December, shortly before the ANC was due to hold elections in Bloemfontein for the national leadership, Mandela and a fellow member of the Youth League named Oliver Tambo approached Xuma and offered him the CYL's voting support – now vital to any aspirant president – in exchange for his endorsement of the programme and a boycott of the virtually defunct Natives' Representative Council (NRC). To Xuma this seemed suspiciously like blackmail. Refusing to accept a boycott of the NRC, he also warned that he would not be dictated to. When the conference met and debated the programme, delegates accepted it unanimously. Outside the hall, the CYL met to discuss their options: Xuma still appeared to be the best possible candidate and he was also facing a challenge from J B Marks, whose communist links were strongly opposed by the CYL. Then, at the eleventh hour, Dr James Moroka declared his support for a boycott, and the CYL decided to adopt him as its man. Its votes won Moroka the presidency, and Walter Sisulu was elected secretary-general. The CYL had won the day: on the eve of the 1950s, the ANC had at last fallen in behind a programme of militant resistance.

NATAL *Indian Congress leader Dr G M Naicker criticised plans to stop Indians buying land from whites – the so-called 'Ghetto Act' (see page 384). Relations between the ANC and Indian political organisations improved during this period.*

The 1946 miners' strike

For several weeks, thousands of African mineworkers had been bracing themselves for a showdown with the country's mine-owners and their staunch ally, the government of Jan Smuts.

And on Monday morning, 12 August 1946, the crunch came when more than 60 000 workers downed tools in support of demands that included improved working conditions and a minimum wage of 10 shillings a day.

Smuts acted quickly to reassure both the white electorate and the mine bosses. Claiming that the strike was the result of agitation and not legitimate grievances, he promised that 'appropriate action' would be taken.

He quickly showed what he had in mind: on 13 August, police arrested J B Marks, the president of the African Mineworkers' Union, and raided union offices. On the same day, during unrest at the Sub-Nigel mine, six strikers were shot dead and another six trampled to death in the ensuing panic.

The following day, attempts by strikers to stage an underground sit-down protest were met by a police baton charge. Stope by stope, level by level, the miners were driven up to the entrance – and into their compound.

And in other developments, dozens of miners were injured when police dispersed a crowd of several hundred who had attempted to march to the Native Commissioner's offices in Johannesburg; a Council for Non-European Trade Unions meeting – called to discuss a general strike – was banned by the chief magistrate; and several prominent trade unionists and 'radicals' were detained.

By Saturday, 17 August, the strike had been crushed – at a cost of 12 lives and more than 1 000 injured. In terms of what it set out to achieve, it was a dismal failure – it took another three years before mine-owners were moved to grant their African workers an extra 3 pence a shift.

Yet, ironically, the action by the 60 000 migrant workers ushered in the beginning of a new era for both black and white political organisations. Particularly alarming for the government (hence its violent response) was the fact that the strike had threatened the very foundation of the country's segregation policies – the cheap labour system.

POLICE *act against striking miners in 1946.*

365

5th OCTOBER

VOTE YES

Issued and Published by D. S. Martin, Burton Street, Cape Town and printed by Railway Commercial Printers Ltd, Birds Street, Rosen River.

back to school

John Orrs
JOHANNESBURG

Daily RAN

JOHANNESBURG, SATURDAY, JULY

BOMB HORRO

MINUTES LATER: THE DAMAGE

Victim
flame
concou

BOMB EXPLODED HERE

A TIME-BOMB explo
giant concour

Apartheid and defiance 1948-76

'Today South Africa belongs to us once more.'
National Party leader Daniel Malan after the 1948 election.

Forty-six years after its defeat in the South African War, Afrikaner nationalism finally triumphed on 28 May 1948, when the *Herenigde* (Reunited) National Party (HNP) dislodged Jan Smuts's United Party with a promise to preserve white power in general – and Afrikaner power in particular. The instrument used to put this policy into practice was apartheid (literally separateness), designed to ensure that the interests of Afrikaans-speaking voters remained dominant in a parliament representing a white minority, giving the impression, if not the substance, of a Western-style democracy.

The HNP, renamed the National Party (NP) in 1951, needed a battery of legislation to prop up its policy, which aimed to regulate every aspect of private, social and economic life. This period saw the introduction of laws such as the Prohibition of Mixed Marriages Act and the Immorality Act, which outlawed sexual and marriage unions between people of different races; the Population Registration Act, which allowed for the classification of people according to race; the Group Areas Act and the Reservation of Separate Amenities Act, which reserved residential suburbs and public areas for the exclusive use of designated race groups; the Pass laws, which required Africans to carry 'reference books' at all times; and the Bantu Education Act, which introduced a system of vastly inferior teaching for Africans. Within the first few years of assuming power, the new government had also scrapped parliamentary representation for Indian and coloured voters.

Black resistance failed to halt or even retard the implementation of apartheid – despite a rapid revival of the African National Congress (ANC) in the 1950s. The 'new-look' ANC sought alliances with Indian and coloured activists in organising a 'Defiance Campaign' that ended in a wave of arrests by the government under a number of new security laws intended to stifle resistance to apartheid. In 1955, the ANC-inspired Congress of the People adopted the Freedom Charter, designed to give expression to black political aspirations. Although it was a moderate document, emphasising non-racialism, liberty and individual rights, it was the proverbial red rag to a bull and sparked a massive government crackdown on extra-parliamentary opposition.

In 1960, a turning point in liberation politics was reached. The Pan-Africanist Congress (PAC) – which had broken away under Robert Sobukwe from the ANC in the late 1950s – organised a protest against the Pass laws that culminated in the police shooting 69 people at Sharpeville, south of Johannesburg, on 21 March 1960.

Faced with increasingly tough state action and then banned altogether, the liberation movements turned from non-violent protest and civil disobedience to armed insurgency. The ANC organised a series of sabotage attacks on strategic targets through its military wing, *Umkhonto we Sizwe*, while the more radical *Poqo* members of the PAC struck at random. The police retaliated with greater repression – and most of the black leaders either fled the country or – like Nelson Mandela and many others – ended up in jail.

Having doused the fires of internal revolt, the Afrikaner nationalists seemed to have realised their dream: they had created their Republic outside of British colonial influence and their people (indeed, all white South Africans) were experiencing unprecedented economic prosperity. The Afrikaner government pursued its ideal of total racial segregation – now called 'separate development' – with new determination under the 1960s regime of Hendrik Verwoerd. The patchwork of 'homelands' that had been consolidated by the Natives' Land Acts became the basis of separate 'nation states', each offering pseudo-citizenship rights to Africans – which would have left South Africa with no African citizens at all.

This plan, along with the concept of separate 'group areas' for different races, required social engineering on a massive scale – and over the next two decades an estimated 3,5-million people were uprooted from their homes.

At the height of the NP's power, in the mid-1970s, the government was rocked by the liberation of the Portuguese colonies of Mozambique and Angola, which brought the threat of cross-border raids by guerrillas of the South African liberation movements to the Republic's doorstep. South Africa over-hastily became involved in the civil war for supremacy in Angola, further damaging the NP Government's credibility in Africa and the rest of the world. Having faced growing international attempts to shake its system of apartheid through boycotts and sanctions, the government now found itself with few friends beyond its borders ....

White politics

1948	Fagan Commission tables report.
	Herenigde (Reunited) National Party (HN election.
1949	Prohibition of Mixed Marriages Act.
1950	Population Registration, Immorality an Areas Acts.
	Suppression of Communism Act.
	Indian Representation Act scrapped.
1951	Malan's first assault on coloured franch Separate Representation of Voters Bill e tested in court.
	High Court of Parliament Act.
	Prevention of Illegal Squatting Act; labo bureaus created.
	HNP renamed National Party (NP).
1952	Native Laws Amendment Act; Abolitio Passes Act introduces reference book fo Africans.
1953	Government wins general election with mandate to remove coloured people fro common voters' roll in Cape.
	Reservation of Separate Amenities Act.
	Bantu Education Act.
	Bantu Authorities Act creates separate authorities for blacks.
1954	Strijdom succeeds Malan as Prime Min expands Appellate Division to include government sympathisers.
	Tomlinson report on Reserves tabled.
1955	Moves to expel Africans from western C
1956	Sophiatown subjected to forced remova Senate Act enables government to pack with supporters and remove coloured p from voters' roll.
	Right of appeal of Africans against influ control denied.
	Riotous Assemblies Act amended.
1958	NP wins general election.
	Verwoerd becomes Prime Minister afte Strijdom's death.
1959	Extension of University Education Act way for 'non-white' universities.
	Bantustans become 'self-governing'.
1960	Police kill 69 marchers at Sharpeville.
	State of emergency declared; later lifted in Pondoland.
	White referendum on establishment of republic.
1961	South Africa leaves Commonwealth.
1962	Sabotage Act.
1966	Cape Town's District Six declared a wh Verwoerd assassinated; B J Vorster becc Prime Minister.
1967	Terrorism Act.
1968	Prohibition of Political Interference Ac
1971	Homeland Citizenship Act.

Economic changes; foreign affairs — Resistance politics

1951	International Court of Justice confirms original SWA mandate.
1957	In Angola, MPLA formed by Agostinho Neto, FNLA by Holden Roberto.
1958	Andimba (Herman) Toivo ja Toivo founds Ovamboland People's Organisation.
1960-1	Sharpeville precipitates economic crisis.
1960	Harold Macmillan's 'wind of change' speech.
	South West African People's Organisation (SWAPO) formed.
	South Africa's alleged contravention of SWA mandate taken to International Court: no decision (1966).
1960-73	Defence budget increases 1 200 percent though spending declines against Gross Domestic Product in 1970s.
1962-72	West Germany and France supplant traditional importers such as Britain.
1962	UN urges members to isolate South Africa.
1963	Organisation of African Unity founded, supports SWAPO in SWA; guerrilla thrust begins.
1964	Kuwait bans oil exports to South Africa; the Organisation of Petroleum Exporting Countries follows suit in 1973.
1965	Rhodesian Government of Ian Smith declares UDI.
1966	Jonas Savimbi's UNITA formed in Angola.
	United Nations (UN) General Assembly terminates South African mandate in SWA; calls for South Africa's withdrawal ignored.
After 1966	Local arms manufacturing industry promoted through Armscor.
1968	England XI's tour cancelled over D'Oliviera affair.
1969	South West Africa Act increases South Africa's control over SWA.
1970	South Africa formally expelled from Olympic movement, although it had not taken part in Games since 1960.
1971	International Court and UN Security Council back General Assembly's decision to revoke mandate; SWA renamed Namibia by UN.
1974	Caetano toppled in Portugal, African colonies affected.
	Rhodesian settlement talks between Smith and Mugabe fail.
	Giscard d'Estaing elected President of France, sale of submarines to South Africa announced; USA offers aircraft and uranium.
	UN denies South Africa participation; invites ANC and PAC as observers.
1975	Turnhalle Conference in Namibia; blueprint for interim government; Democratic Turnhalle Alliance set up under Dirk Mudge; rejected by UN, which sends 'contact group' to Namibia.
	Independence for Mozambique and Angola.
1975-6	South African forces invade Angola, then withdraw.

1949	James Moroka ousts Alfred Xuma as African National Congress (ANC) president.
	Militant Congress Youth League-inspired Programme of Action adopted at ANC congress.
1950s	Bus boycotts on Reef after fare increases.
1950	CPSA disbanded ahead of Suppression of Communism Act; later goes underground as SACP.
	J B Marks, a communist, elected president of Transvaal ANC.
1951	Franchise Action Committee formed; War Veterans Torch Commando stages marches in support of coloured voters.
	Bantu Authorities Act abolishes Natives' Representative Council and introduces system of tiered authorities.
1952	ANC launches Defiance Campaign.
	Riots lead to passage of Public Safety Act and Criminal Law Amendment Act.
	ANC membership rises from 7 000 to 100 000.
	Congress of Democrats and Coloured People's Organisation formed.
	Albert Luthuli elected ANC president.
1953	Torch Commando cooperates with United Party against NP in general election.
1954	Trade unionist Ray Alexander elected to parliament, but prevented from entering House of Assembly.
1955	Federation of South African Women formed.
	South African Congress of Trade Unions formed.
	Freedom Charter presented to Congress of the People.
1956	About 20 000 women march on Union Buildings.
	Crackdown on extra-parliamentary organisations by Security Police leads to Treason Trial.
1956-61	Treason Trial of 156 activists.
1959	Anti-Coloured Affairs Department group withdraws from Non-European Unity Movement; African group under I B Tabata forms All African People's Democratic Union.
	Pan-Africanist Congress (PAC) formed under Robert Sobukwe.
	PAC's 'status campaign' falters.
1960	Anti-Pass law campaign.
	Sobukwe arrested; sentenced to three years, but held for six more.
	Sharpeville shootings; march on Cape Town led by Philip Kgosana of PAC who later flees into exile.
	ANC and PAC banned; leaders flee into exile; both set up military wings; attempt to reunite ANC and PAC unsuccessful.
	Oliver Tambo leaves South Africa to establish the ANC's mission in exile.
1961	Nelson Mandela proposes to ANC executive the adoption of armed struggle to achieve African aims; Lilliesleaf farm, Rivonia, acquired for armed wing's operations; sabotage begins.
	Albert Luthuli awarded Nobel Peace Prize.
1962	Mandela gets guerrilla training in Algeria; arrested on his return.
	Potlako Leballo moves to Lesotho to reorganise PAC, but Security Police break the organisation.
1963	'Ninety-day Act' to crush *Poqo* and *Umkhonto we Sizwe*.
	Police swoop on Rivonia base of *Umkhonto*: Rivonia trial.
1969	South African Students' Organisation founded under Steve Biko.
1972	Black People's Convention set up to co-ordinate black consciousness adherents.
1972-3	Wave of strikes against low wages in face of spiralling inflation.
1975	Bantu Education Minister M C Botha maintains Afrikaans as teaching medium.

A triumph for Afrikaner nationalism

In 1948, in a development which Afrikaner nationalists described as a 'miracle' and clear proof
that God was 'watching over his *volk*', the white South African electorate voted into power
a political party that stood for Afrikaner domination and total racial segregation.
It ushered in the era of apartheid . . . .

'TODAY,' THE 74-YEAR-OLD former Dutch Reformed Church dominee solemnly declared, 'South Africa belongs to us once more. For the first time since Union, South Africa is our own. May God grant that it will always remain so.'

During the coming years, few South Africans would forget the date on which these words were uttered: it was Friday, 28 May 1948 – and after spending most of his political career as an Opposition Member of Parliament, Daniel Francois Malan was about to form the country's first exclusively Afrikaner government.

Before the poll on 26 May, the ruling United Party (UP) held 89 seats to the 48 of Malan's *Herenigde* (Reunited) National Party (IINP) in the 153 seat House of Assembly. With 15 more seats held between potential UP allies – the Labour Party (6), the South African Party (3), the Natives' Representatives (3) and Independents (3) – an HNP victory seemed beyond the bounds of possibility: to gain a majority, the Nationalists had to gain 28 seats, a swing unparalleled in South Africa's history.

But the uninspired leadership of 78-year-old Jan Smuts gave the HNP a free hand to exploit the bread-and-butter issues of the day. And although it took almost 36 hours to determine the final result, once in, it demonstrated a dramatic reversal of fortunes for both the now-victorious HNP and the defeated UP: the HNP pushed its seats up to 70; its ally, the Afrikaner Party (AP), won 9; the UP's share dropped to 65; and Labour still held 6.

Although it won more seats, the HNP/AP alliance did not, however, win a majority of the votes cast: its share of the vote amounted to 443 719 – nearly 181 000 fewer than the 624 500 garnered by the UP, Labour and the parties which had failed to win representation.

But this was small comfort for Smuts, who had had to endure the added humiliation of being beaten by 224 votes in the Standerton constituency by Wentzel du Plessis, who three years earlier had been kicked out of the Public Service for refusing to resign from the *Afrikaner Broederbond*.

Smuts' defeat – and that of other top UP office-bearers – surprised even the most optimistic of HNP supporters. Indeed, on the morning the final results came in, future Cabinet Minister Ben Schoeman told the Johannesburg 'Star' newspaper: 'We expected to gain several seats, but nobody thought there would be such a landslide.'

And yet, Schoeman and fellow Nationalists should not really have been surprised: at a time when many African communities were openly defying laws which defined them as implements of labour rather than as human beings, the HNP had offered increasingly disillusioned members of the *volk* a vision of a future genuine white baasskap (supremacy) of a country in which a 'kaffir' would always be a 'kaffir'.

It was a concept that won the HNP crucial support in the election – especially in the powerful, labour-hungry farming sector . . . .

The tide turns against the UP
In the relatively uncomplicated years between the demise of the Industrial and Commercial Workers' Union (see page 344) and the start of the Second World War, the secret of good 'native management' lay in striking a balance between the labour needs of urban industrialist and rural

THE UNSMILING FACE *of Daniel Malan belies the fact that his party had just won the 1948 white general election. His supporters, however, showed no such restraint when the results were announced.*

agriculturalist. In this respect architects of 'native policy' had good reason to be pleased with their efforts: on the one hand, regular adjustments to influx control regulations kept the migrant conveyer-belt between African Reserves and 'white' cities working smoothly, while on the other, a Natives Trust and Land Act, promulgated in 1936, ensured that the agricultural sector also received a reasonable share of the cheap labour cake. In terms of this legislation, farmers in 'proclaimed' areas could transform squatters into labour-tenants and extend compulsory labour service from 90 to 180 days. At the same time, the Masters and Servants Act was revised to provide for the whipping of African juveniles who broke their labour contracts.

By the 1940s, however, thousands of rural Africans, driven to desperation by poverty in the Reserves and ill-treatment and poor wages on white farms, began drifting into the cities of the Witwatersrand – in open defiance of influx control and Masters and Servants regulations.

The knock-on effect of this great black trek was to have a direct bearing on the outcome of the 1948 white elections . . . .

A new militancy

The new urban workers proved to be far more resolute opponents of oppression than their easily exploitable migrant counterparts: they demanded decent housing – and when they did not get it, they squatted as near as possible to their places of work; they flocked into trade unions, and they backed up calls for 'living wages' and cheap transport with strikes and boycotts.

Although the UP Government reacted to these developments with suitable expressions of alarm and promises of swift action, in reality there was not much it could do to reverse what was happening. It was caught between too many stools: to 'repatriate' the tens of thousands of 'illegals' would have sparked an outcry from the labour-hungry captains of secondary industry; but to allow them to stay would have given rise to further conflict with white blue-collar workers, long fearful of cheaper black competition, and the already angry farming bloc; if it ignored protests from these quarters and acknowledged the 'permanence' of urban Africans, the logical next step (given the conditions in the Reserves) would have been to scrap the migrant labour system; but if it did this, it would incur the wrath of the powerful mining industry whose continued profitable existence depended on the retention of the system.

As thoughts turned towards the 1948 elections, the apparent collapse of 'native policy' became a political hot potato for the governing UP – and a potentially powerful vote-catcher for the HNP.

Fagan versus Sauer

The first shots in what promised to be a heated campaign were fired immediately after the war when the HNP appointed a team of top ideologues headed by Paul Sauer to investigate and formulate a new 'native policy' – to which the UP replied, in August 1946, with the appointment of a Native Laws Commission under the chairmanship of Judge Henry Fagan.

African reaction to the 1948 elections

'For most of us Africans, bandied about on the field while the game was in progress and then kicked to one side when the game was won, the election seemed largely irrelevant. We had endured Botha, Hertzog and Smuts. It did not seem of much importance whether the whites gave us more Smuts or switched to Malan. Our lot had grown steadily worse, and no election seemed likely to alter the direction in which we were being forced.'

This was how Albert Luthuli described the reaction of black South Africans to the 1948 elections in his autobiography 'Let My People Go'.

Luthuli, who later became president of the African National Congress (ANC), added: 'The Nationalist win did not either surprise nor extremely interest us, though we did realise that there would probably be an intensification of the hardships and indignities which had always come our way. Nevertheless, I think it is true that very few (if any) of us understood how swift the deterioration was to be.'

His colleague, Z K Matthews, a member of the Natives' Representative Council (NRC) at the time, recalled in his autobiography 'Freedom For My People' that the Council was summoned to decide how it should respond to the unexpected election victory of the Nationalists: 'The victory of the Nationalists had come as a great disappointment because the Councillors knew that a period of reactionary measures would follow,' he wrote.

He added that he had told the NRC: 'Our plain duty is to fight not for the retention of the present system of representation which we all condemn, but to fight against the entrenchment in South Africa of the idea that the African people are not entitled to a say in the government of the country. That fight we must wage with every weapon at our disposal. The claims of the African people will, however, not be heeded until we are organised into a fighting unit instead of the disgruntled rabble which we tend to be today.'

FOR NRC MEMBER *Z K Matthews the election result was a 'great disappointment'.*

MEMBERS *of the Native Laws Commission under the chairmanship of Judge Henry Fagan were given the task of reporting on the future 'native policy' of the United Party Government. Their report, issued in 1948, rejected complete segregation as 'totally impracticable'. African urbanisation, they said, was a natural and inevitable economic phenomenon, and migrant labour could not endure forever. Malan's victory at the polls, however, ensured that the report would never be put into practice.*

In many ways, the perceptions of the members of both enquiries – as well as those of the Africans being investigated – were shaped by an event which occurred on 12 August 1946, shortly after the Fagan commission began its deliberations: a strike by more than 60 000 African mineworkers (see page 365).

The state's response to the stoppage was swift and brutal: in a display of force which shocked and angered Africans, armed police marched into compounds, rounded up the striking workers, and frogmarched them down the shafts. Those who resisted were shot or bayonetted, and by 17 August, when the last of the strikers had returned to work, the casualty toll stood at 12 miners dead and more than a thousand injured.

Judged in terms of what it set out to achieve – higher wages, better working conditions, union recognition and an end to the migrant labour system – the strike was a failure. Yet it is regarded by historians as the event which forced the previously fractured and ineffectual black political organisations into a radical change of tactics. For, united in their revulsion over the way the state had put down the strike, migrants, communists, unionists and members of the middle-class African National Congress (ANC) began thinking in terms of a more broadly based movement to oppose segregation.

Even the toothless Natives' Representative Council (NRC) was persuaded by Alfred Xuma, the president of a revitalised ANC, to suspend its sittings until oppressive legislation such as the Pass laws was scrapped.

The new militancy caused consternation among whites – and in parliament, Natives' Representative Edgar Brookes urged Deputy Prime Minister Jan Hofmeyr to consider instituting a meaningful programme of reform. The Pass laws, African education, the status of the NRC and the recognition of trade unions needed attention, he warned. But in passing the message on to Smuts at a United Nations conference in Paris, Hofmeyr suggested that whites would see 'improvements' in these areas as 'surrender'. Smuts' reply was a masterpiece of ambiguity: while agreeing that 'native policy would have to be liberalised at a modest pace', he also pointed out that '[white] public opinion has to be carried with us . . . .'

In November 1946, Hofmeyr, who had acquired the reputation of being a liberal in matters of race relations, was chosen by the UP to spell out to the NRC the administration's reform plans. But his address, a rambling rehash of the government's past record, served only to deepen the crisis. It led to a walkout by the long-suffering councillors, a scathing attack on Hofmeyr, and a hard-line demand for direct African representation at all levels – from municipal councils to parliament.

Smuts, when he returned from making his contribution towards world unity, was unimpressed. Accusing the NRC of wanting nothing less than effective political power, he added that this would amount to an 'unthinkable concession'. It was a statement that pulled the rug from under the feet of African 'moderates' and strengthened others' calls for mass action against unjust laws. Gentle protest, argued the new activists, had failed dismally. It was time for direct challenge . . . .

Fagan's recommendations

Ironically, when the Fagan commission finally reported in February 1948, it recommended much that would have pleased members of the NRC. For example, although rejecting integration, it nevertheless described complete segregation as 'totally impracticable' in view of the decline of the African Reserves. It also dismissed the notion that the flow of Africans to the cities could be reversed, although it accepted that this could be regulated and possibly limited. African urbanisation was a natural and inevitable economic phenomenon, and migrant labour on a mass basis could not endure forever. On the contrary, the commission argued, the permanent settlement of an increasing number of urban Africans would actually be to the advantage of industrial demands for labour. Its recommendations effectively confirmed a growing trend in government thinking: that Africans in the cities were there to stay.

The commission further suggested that the practice of ejecting Africans surplus to urban labour requirements be abandoned in favour of stabilising labour in the cities. This meant the establishment of a large pool of African labour in the urban areas, which would favour industrial and commercial demands for labour over those of agriculture.

THE HERENIGDE NATIONAL PARTY (HNP) *feared that post-war English immigration would weaken its power base – while its wartime Nazi sympathies prompted this cartoon.*

Sauer's recommendations

The Sauer report took an opposite tack. It maintained that the country could either progress towards equality between black and white communities or to complete separation, which would protect the whites and ensure the development of Africans in their own areas.

Refusing to acknowledge either the disintegration of the Reserves or the degree of permanent settlement among urban Africans, it declared that the process of 'detribalisation' had to be stopped. Africans, it recommended, should be permitted to enter the cities only as temporary workers who would have to return to their homes once their labour contracts had expired. This, clearly, would favour the strong farming constituency.

Much of the difference between the two reports lay in degree rather than in substance; while the Fagan commission implied a degree of economic integration in the cities, it certainly did not propose the dismantling of social and political segregation. But Nationalists described it as opening the door to 'integration'. The Sauer report, however, left nothing to chance; it offered a definite solution to both 'race' and labour issues.

Not surprisingly, therefore, it proved eminently attractive to the electoral coalition which the HNP had been building among white workers, the farmers of the Cape, Transvaal and Orange Free State, and the emerging Afrikaner capitalists and middle class. For this coalition, the notion of *oorstroming* (being inundated or overrun) by urban Africans raised the spectre of competition in the urban labour market, the loss of workers to the farmers, the heightened risk of African trade unionism, and growing African demands for political equality.

A plan for white supremacy

Malan took to the voters a vision, based on the Sauer report, of the entrenchment of white supremacy and racial purity. Africans, he argued, would have to 'develop along their own lines in their true fatherland, the Reserves'. The HNP, he said, 'realises the danger of the flood of Africans mov-ing to the cities and undertakes to protect the white character of our cities and to provide a forceful and effective way for the safety of individuals and property and the peaceful life of the inhabitants'. Furthermore, he promised that mixed marriages would be stopped, African parliamentary representation scrapped, black trade unions banned, job reservation tightened, and Indian immigration halted and Indians preferably repatriated. This was the promise of 'apartheid', a phrase the Sauer report introduced into the political language of South Africa, and the world.

The UP's platform included the government's acceptance of the Fagan report, the creation of African urban local authorities, and a commitment to the maintenance of white civilisation and 'Western Democracy'. The NRC would be given further powers and coloured people would be drawn closer to the white community.

With Smuts rapidly approaching the end of his political career, the HNP made Deputy Prime Minister Hofmeyr, known for his relatively 'liberal' views on black political rights, a special target for attack: a vote for Smuts was a vote for Hofmeyr, the HNP claimed, appealing to voters to 'vote against Hofmeyr and save South Africa from ruin'.

While the dominant issue in the 1948 election was race, the HNP was also able to harp on housing and food shortages, rationing and rising prices. The government was also attacked for encouraging white immigration, ostensibly because it was reducing the numbers of jobs available to Afrikaners at a time when unemployment was rising quite sharply. But behind this attack lay the HNP's fear that, if current rates of immigration continued, Afrikaners would within a decade become a minority of the white population, which would rob the Nationalists of their chance for political power.

Smuts himself was painted as a leader who had achieved international prestige at the expense of his own people, one who was more familiar with world affairs than the crisis in his own backyard. The HNP's electoral attack was an indictment of the UP's shortsightedness on the future of 'native policy' and its failure to address domestic issues.

All told, the new concept of apartheid as well as the shortcomings of the Smuts Government brought into sharp relief the choice before the electorate in 1948. However, the policy foundations on which apartheid rested were not altogether new to voters: the HNP had been preaching total segregation since 1934. It was clear, therefore, that underlying the immediate appeal of the 'new' policy and the pressures of bread-and-butter politics, the shift away from Smuts represented a realignment of Afrikaner support.

Fusion (see page 344) had temporarily persuaded many Afrikaners that the political control of South Africa need not necessarily be based on Afrikaner domination in order to secure a government which put 'South Africa first'. The war vote had changed many of those minds, and the election of 1943 had been dominated by the war. By 1948, however, those Afrikaner nationalists who had remained with Hertzog through Fusion, then supported Smuts, had mostly returned to the 'purified' fold. That, in concert with the decisions of the Ninth Delimitation Commission which made it easier to win a rural seat, was sufficient to cause a significant swing to the HNP.

Creating the apartheid society

With the reins of power at last in its hands, South Africa's first exclusively Afrikaner government
set about creating a society in which Afrikaner control would become permanent.
The road to salvation, it was convinced, lay in its own exclusive form of *baasskap* (supremacy).
Political separation from English fellow citizens, strict segregation between black and white
and the suppression of its enemies were to become the main features of its policies.
In many ways, South Africa would never be the same again....

IN JULY 1948, just 43 days after its stunning sweep to power, Daniel Malan's new Nationalist administration produced its first major shock when it demoted the country's most celebrated soldier – Deputy Chief of Staff, Major-General Evered Poole – and sent him to run an insignificant Military Mission in West Germany.

A terse Press release issued by Defence Minister Frans Erasmus informed the South African public of the fate of the man who had been widely tipped to become the next head of the army. Two lines long, it simply stated that 'the position of Deputy Chief of the General Staff now held by Major-General Poole was created during the war. The Government does not intend to fill the post of Deputy Chief of the General Staff now vacated by Major-General Poole.'

A few days later, Erasmus paid an unannounced visit to army intelligence chief Charles Powell, gave him 24 hours to vacate his post, and ordered aides to seize what were later described as 'two lorry-loads' of wartime files filled with *Afrikaner Broederbond* secrets and uncomfortable reminders of the time only a few years earlier when Afrikaner activists had planted bombs and beaten up soldiers to demonstrate their solidarity with the Nazi cause.

Nationalists had a special reason for disliking Powell: during the war he had been a key member of a crack army spy team that had done much to expose the activities of the *Broederbond* and other dissident Afrikaner groups.

Now, the very men on whom he had spied were in a position not only to take revenge, but also to destroy the evidence of the wartime activities of many of their supporters. Certainly, on the eve of the launch of one of the most concerted law and (especially) order campaigns in South Africa's history, the dossiers of treason and terror that Powell and his helpers had so carefully compiled were hardly the type of skeletons the new rulers would have wanted to hear rattling in their cupboards . . . .

The new order flexes its muscle

The shunting aside of Poole and Powell – mere pinpricks when weighed against later social upheaval – nevertheless signalled the beginning of a concerted *Herenigde* (Reunited) National Party (HNP) drive to reduce the white Opposition to that of permanent political also-rans.

Until the removal of the two army officers, the consensus among English-speakers was that the thrust of the new government's policies would be directed at Africans, leaving them relatively untouched.

Convinced, also, that the election victory of the Nationalists was one of those inexplicable quirks that crops up

MAJOR-GENERAL EVERED POOLE, *Deputy Chief of Staff in the South African Army, was the first casualty in the National Party's campaign to oust its wartime opponents from senior office. Poole, who had earned fame as Commanding Officer of the Sixth South African Armoured Division, is photographed (centre) with his wife examining plans for a subsidised housing scheme for ex-servicemen in 1945.*

MINISTER OF DEFENCE *Frans Erasmus ordered the seizure of army intelligence files detailing Broederbond activities.*

from time to time, they resolved to accept whatever minor irritations came their way – until the next poll, when the United Party (UP) would surely be returned to power.

It did not quite work out that way. For what they failed to appreciate was the lengths to which the new government was prepared to go to perpetuate Afrikaner rule. To the Nationalists, the concept of total control meant exactly what it implied: a political system in which Nationalists – preferably *Broederbonders* – ran the government, the Civil Service, and anything else that was worth running. In the new order, government spokesmen repeatedly stressed in those heady days following their ascent to power, the interests of the Afrikaner would take precedence over everything else.

And so, determined to back up these words with deeds, they chose the Public Service – where four years earlier the UP had initiated a purge of *Broederbond* employees – as a first target of their programme of 'Afrikanerisation'.

A seemingly innocent directive making bilingualism compulsory for all government employees signalled the start of their campaign. Although it appeared to be a perfectly reasonable instruction, the motivation behind it had little to do with promoting efficiency. On the contrary, its prime aim was punitive – to force out English-speakers who had not bothered to learn Afrikaans and replace them with Afrikaners who could speak English.

As the campaign gathered momentum, summary sackings and early retirements were followed by one of the most intensive jobs-for-pals schemes ever launched in South Africa. In the new white order, where talent counted for nothing if it was not coupled with a sworn allegiance to the *volk*, dozens of *Broederbonders* – many of them of dubious ability – were slotted into strategic positions in the Public Service.

And yet, frightening though these developments might have seemed to many people, they represented only the opening shots in the Nationalist master plan . . . .

Consolidation

Although HNP (NP from 1951) leader Malan had attributed his party's victory in the 1948 election to Divine Providence, he was realistic enough to accept that, with its slender majority, the party would require more than just faith in God for it to hold on to power.

Work towards entrenching its position began almost immediately – and within two years, Malan was able to offer his followers a legislative programme for perpetual domination: a *Broederbond* creation based on rigid separation of the races, the reformulation of 'native' policies and the neutralising of political opponents.

It was, in many ways, a remarkably creative period for the high disciples of Afrikaner nationalism – but also a time of great trauma for those who ran foul of their legislative creations.

Although the laws aimed specifically at Africans were the most vicious, the upheaval they caused went largely unreported. Instead, it was the plight of the white casualties of a government attempt to regulate the two most basic of human impulses – falling in love and sexual intercourse – that attracted the most publicity.

Mixed marriages and immorality

An average figure of only 100 'mixed' marriages a year from within a population of several million seemed to indicate quite clearly that the 'white race' was not on the verge of 'dilution'.

The Nationalists, however, were determined to stamp out marriages between white and black altogether – and in 1949, the Prohibition of Mixed Marriages Act became their first major piece of apartheid legislation.

The most vehement parliamentary opposition to the measure came not from the official UP Opposition (many of whose members were opposed to 'mixed' marriages), but from a lone communist – Natives' Representative Sam Kahn: to angry interjections from the Nationalist benches, he described the Bill as 'the immoral offspring of an illicit union between racial superstition and biological ignorance'. And he added that there was nothing biologically disharmonious, inferior or evil about the offspring of 'mixed' marriages – but that the evil lay in the social pattern that doomed them to an inferior status and deprived them of privileges that should be the inherent right of every citizen. It did not help: the Nationalist juggernaut was on an unstoppable course.

In 1950, the ban on 'mixed' marriages was followed by an amendment to the Immorality Act, passed in 1927 by Barry Hertzog's Pact Government to ban extra-marital sexual relations between Africans and whites. The amendment had the effect of outlawing sexual relations between all blacks and whites.

Ironically, one of the first people to be charged under the tightened-up version of the law was a northern Cape Dutch Reformed Church minister, caught red-handed with a domestic worker in a garage his parishioners had erected

JUSTICE MINISTER *Charles Swart's declaration that reasonable amenities would be provided according to people's aptitude and standard of civilisation meant virtually nothing in practice.*

next to his house. The errant churchman was given a suspended sentence, but his irate parishioners bulldozed the offending garage to the ground.

Before it was scrapped (together with the Mixed Marriages Act) in 1985, Section 16 of the Immorality Act was slated by all, except its architects and some of their followers, as one of the most immoral pieces of legislation ever to be devised anywhere. Certainly, its implementation during its heyday in the 1960s was frequently marked by policemen, binoculars at the ready, hiding in trees to observe offending couples; late night raids; the checking of bedsheets and underclothes for signs of sexual intercourse; not to mention numerous shattered lives and frequent suicides.

When black-white sex became risky in South Africa, white males consumed with the urge for black flesh had only to cross the border into neighbouring Swaziland, Lesotho or Botswana to satisfy their needs. Many of them were Afrikaners.

The Population Registration Act

The next piece of the apartheid jigsaw puzzle – in terms of Nationalist logic, it should have come first – was a law that sought to define who was of what 'race'.

Passed in 1950, and amended several times to close loopholes, the Population Registration Act was designed to provide definitions of 'race' based on physical appearance as well as general acceptance and 'repute'. And once this had been established, it made provision for the carrying of identity cards in which the 'race' of a person would be clearly marked.

Some of the early classification procedures were crude in the extreme. For instance, white officials were occasionally known to have resolved doubtful cases by using what became known as the 'pencil in the hair' test. If a pencil pushed in the hair stayed there, it signified *kroes* (frizzy) hair – and the classification of the subject as coloured or African. If it fell out, it signified straight hair – which usually meant classification as coloured or white.

In a country with as many shades of skin colour as South Africa, it is almost impossible to categorise people into racial compartments. Yet it took just a stroke of a bureaucrat's pen to change thousands of coloureds into whites, whites into coloureds, Indians into 'Malays', Cape coloureds into 'other' coloureds, 'Malays' into Chinese, Chinese into whites, and so on.

Inevitably, many 'wrong' decisions were made – resulting in families being split, people being evicted from their homes, (for suddenly living in the wrong 'group area'), and children driven from their schools.

Even solid, upright Afrikaners were occasionally caught in its web: in the 1960s, in the eastern Transvaal town of Piet Retief, parents of pupils at an Afrikaans school complained that one of the children, Sandra Laing, 'looked coloured'. Although her parents were staunch members of the community, the law had to take its course. And so, much to their shame, she was reclassified and kicked out of school. After much protest, she was 'made white' again – but no school would take her. No longer accepted by the community in which she had been raised, she later eloped with an African vegetable seller.

Group areas and separate amenities

The next pillar of apartheid was the Group Areas Act, which was passed in the same year as the Population Registration Act. While residential segregation of Africans and Indians had a long history, with increasingly rigid measures having been passed for Africans from the 1920s, and for Indians from the mid-'40s, the principle was now greatly extended. This entailed – in countless city suburbs throughout the Union – the unscrambling of the multiracial omelette, at enormous cost to those affected, in particular the coloured and Indian communities. Through an array of detailed racial definitions and regulations, the Act's intention was to restrict each group to its own residential and trading sections of cities and towns by controlling the purchase or occupation of land or dwellings in specified areas under the Act.

Lashing out at 'mixed' suburbs as 'the deathbeds of the European race', Nationalists justified the measure as 'the price we have to pay … to achieve certainty as to the future environment of our homes and places of business'. Naturally, they got their way.

In 1953, after the government had been challenged in the courts on several occasions over the reservation of separate and unequal public facilities – post offices, trains and the like – it introduced the Reservation of Separate Amenities Act, which covered public premises and transport, and permitted owners or operators to establish separate (but not necessarily equal) facilities for whites and 'nonwhites'. Later provincial ordinances extended the definition to cover places such as offices, beaches, parks, bus stops, benches, service counters and lifts.

THE RESERVATION *of Separate Amenities Act allowed owners or operators of public transport to reserve separate facilities for blacks and whites. Some buses, like these in Cape Town, were split into black and white seating areas, while others were reserved for one group only.*

In explaining the purpose of the Act, Justice Minister Charles Swart declared: 'We will always find that reasonable amenities are provided for all classes according to their aptitude, according to their standard of civilisation and according to their need.' He was supported by P W Botha (later Prime Minister and first executive State President), who argued that in order 'to gain a clear view regarding fair treatment and the rights of non-Europeans, we should first answer another question and that is: do we stand for the domination and supremacy of the European or not? For if you stand for the domination and supremacy of the European, then everything you do must be in the first place calculated to ensure that domination.'

There was a loophole, however: the Act did not compel people in charge of public facilities to segregate them, and a number of local authorities refused to toe the Nationalist line. This made it necessary for the government to pass provincial ordinances to force 'liberal' municipalities such as the one in Cape Town to segregate public areas when ordered to do so.

'Native policy'

In many ways, the upheaval caused by laws enforcing statutory separation paled almost into insignificance when measured against the effects of legislation aimed specifically at the African population.

Under the baton of Hendrik Verwoerd – Minister of Native Affairs from October 1951 – 'native policy' sought to extend migrant labour and shore up the Pass laws; refurbish the Reserves as well as the rickety system of 'tribal' authorities, and impose complete government control over African education in order to shape it as an instrument of apartheid.

Verwoerd was a brilliant ideologue – and when he argued for the implementation of one or other piece of legislation, he did so in a way that often suggested (to many whites, at least) that Africans affected ought to be grateful for his foresight.

The reality, of course, was different . . . .

The intentions of many 'native' laws placed in Government Gazettes, or carried in newspapers, seldom indicated how profoundly they would affect the lives of the people at whom they were aimed.

Thus, while the purpose of Verwoerd's Native Laws Amendment Act of 1952 was clear enough – it extended government control over the movement of Africans to all urban areas throughout the Union; made provision for African women to carry Passes; ruled that 'disqualified' persons could not remain in an urban area for longer than 72 hours without a Pass, and gave local authorities the power to remove 'idle or undesirable natives' – it was composed with little regard as to how it would break up families, increase poverty and criminalise a large section of the African population.

The passage, also in 1952, of the bizarrely named Abolition of Passes Act, also caused Africans great trauma. To make the policing of the new Pass restrictions easier, Verwoerd, in terms of this measure, 'abolished' the Pass in favour of a consolidated document called a reference book.

The very survival of Africans depended on the possession of this book, 96 pages thick, and standard green or brown issue. It had to be carried at all times by all Africans – from university professors to railway labourers – with failure to produce it on the demand of a policeman a punishable offence. It provided the authorities with an instant guide to any African's life history and rights of movement. Identification was backed up by taking the finger-prints of the holder – a process normally reserved for criminal suspects – and these were stored in a central bureau in Pretoria.

At the height of the law's implementation, few Africans could claim not to have made a trip (usually lasting a few seconds) to the dock of a Bantu Commissioner's court to answer charges of either being in an urban area without a reference book or for not producing one on demand.

In 1956, the government took influx control even further when it removed the right of Africans to appeal to the courts against removal from an urban area, and included the provision that such removals might also be authorised to secure 'the maintenance of peace and order'. Two years later, police and local authorities were empowered to raid, without a search warrant, any dwelling in search of illegal African residents.

Eliminating 'black spots'

Although the African squatter camps that had mush-roomed near Johannesburg as a result of wartime industrial expansion, evictions from white farms, and land hunger in the Reserves, had largely been disbanded and their oc-cupants rehoused by 1950, squatting continued to pose major headaches for authorities in Cape Town and Durban – until the government stepped in with the Prevention of Illegal Squatting Act in 1951.

Its purpose was to prevent Africans from occupying any private or public land without the permission of the authorities or if their shelters constituted a health hazard. Its effect was to 'endorse' thousands of Africans out of ur-ban areas (see page 424).

This was followed by moves to eliminate black land-ownership in white farming areas, and to put an end to

PROTEST MEETINGS *against apartheid – like this one in Cape Town's Gardens – prompted security legislation.*

African squatting on white farms. New restrictions were also placed on the mobility of African farm workers through the creation in 1951 of a network of labour bureaus to stabilise and improve the distribution of labour on white farms. Any African who wished to leave a given rural area would have to apply to the local bureau for permission – and this was granted only if officials were satisfied that there was sufficient farm labour in the district.

Beginnings of the 'homeland' system

Another of the government's priorities was to strip Afri-cans of the last vestiges of their access to the white politi-cal system and to substitute these with political rights in the Reserves. 'The fundamental idea throughout,' Ver-woerd told parliament in 1951, 'is Bantu control over Bantu areas as and when it becomes possible for them to exercise that control efficiently and properly for the benefit of their own people.'

The first plank of the policy was the Bantu Authorities Act of 1951, in terms of which the moribund Natives' Representatives Council was formally abolished and a tiered system of local, regional and territorial 'tribal' authorities with limited executive functions was estab-lished. These 'tribal' authorities would, in time, provide the basis for local African self-government in the Reserves – the 'restoration of the natural Native democracy', as Ver-woerd described it. In this legislation were embodied the founding principles of what later came to be known as 'separate development'. All Africans would, in future legislation, be categorised according to their various 'tribal' antecedents and forced to accept citizenship of the appropriate designated 'homelands', where they would exercise their political rights.

Verwoerd's 'native policy' involved a stick-and-carrot strategy. His stick was the restriction of African mobility between the rural and urban areas; his carrot involved the agricultural and economic rehabilitation of the Reserves, and the siting of decentralised industry near them to ab-sorb their supply of labour.

In 1951, Governor-General E G Jansen appointed a com-mission under Professor Frederik Tomlinson 'to conduct an exhaustive enquiry into and report on a comprehen-sive scheme for the rehabilitation of the Native Areas with a view to developing within them a social structure in keeping with the culture of the Native and based on effec-tive socio-economic planning'.

When the Tomlinson Commission tabled its final report in 1954, its primary assumption was that South Africa would not evolve into a common, unitary society, chiefly because whites would never abandon their position of dominance. The task it set itself, therefore, was to examine how best the Reserves might be developed to support the 'Bantu' population.

Noting that the Reserves were already seriously run down and would require a massive cash injection simply to stabilise them, the commission found that there was sufficient land in the Reserves to meet the needs of 51 per-cent of their population as of 1951. With the purchase of at least the 7,25-million morgen still to be incorporated in terms of the 1936 Land Act, the Reserves would be able to

The birth of 'Bantu' education

A CHILDREN'S *protest march against 'Bantu' education.*

By 1949, the country's 4 500 African mission schools were increasingly falling under the hostile gaze of the National Party Government.

The concern of the state had little to do with the fact that the facilities at these institutions were often woefully inadequate to cope with the influx of children wanting an education.

To NP ideologues, the 'native' was different from his white counterpart – and, therefore, had to be taught differently. But at these schools, they claimed, 'dangerous, liberal ideas were being fed by outsiders into untrained minds'. A commission set up by Malan in 1949 echoed these sentiments when it tabled its report in 1951: missions, it said, had 'achieved nothing but the destruction of Bantu culture . . . nothing beyond succeeding in making the native an imitation Westerner'.

Clearly, mission school education had to be shelved – and replaced with a system that would teach Africans to accept their 'proper place'.

Enter Hendrik Verwoerd

It was a task that Hendrik Verwoerd, the newly appointed Minister of Native Affairs, obviously relished . . . .

The first step of his Bantu Education Bill was to remove control of African education from the provinces to his own department. Then, by reducing government aid to the mission schools (and later stopping it altogether), he forced most of them into the state system.

His department also assumed reponsibility for the employment and training of African teachers. Said Verwoerd: 'The Bantu teacher serves the Bantu community and his salary must be fixed accordingly.' Thus, a black teacher in 1953 earned just over £2 a week and a university graduate just over £4, rising to £7 after 13 years. The result was a dramatic drop in the number of trainee teachers.

Verwoerd explained that Africans had to be measured by different standards: 'The school,' he said, 'must equip the Bantu to meet the demands which the economic life . . . will impose on him . . . . What is the use of teaching a Bantu child mathematics when it cannot use it in practice? . . . Education must train and teach people in accordance with their opportunities in life . . . .'

Alternative education

Black political organisations, led by the African National Congress (ANC), reacted with anger to the new law. Since its formation in 1912, the ANC had argued that education was the key to African political advancement. Now, to its horror, the government was trying to place even that out of the reach of Africans.

As opposition mounted, numbers of parents vowed that they would sooner see their children roaming the streets than have them subjected to Bantu Education.

The ANC, however, while backing a boycott of the new state-run schools, suggested that 'alternative' schools be set up to give African children a proper education.

But Verwoerd was prepared for such an eventuality: in terms of the law, no private schools could be set up without being registered by the Native Affairs Department. Those who transgressed faced prosecution for the 'illicit selling of education'.

The ANC's response was to set up 'cultural clubs' for boycotting children. Run throughout the Witwatersrand from disused buildings, shebeens and open plots of ground, these clubs catered, in the beginning, for up to 8 000 children. But a lack of funds, teaching equipment and expertise, as well as the constant risk of police raids, led to their programme being confined mainly to playing games, physical training exercises, counting stones and singing freedom songs. By 1956 the majority of the children had been forced into Bantu Education schools.

Africans and universities

Apartheid education was extended to university level in the late 1950s, despite strong protests from the English-language universities that they wished to continue admitting black students. The government's intentions, published in a Bill in 1957, were regarded as a serious inroad into academic freedom. The legislation was held over for two years while a parliamentary commission investigated the matter.

In 1959, the Extension of University Education Act provided for the establishment of 'non-white' universities, and empowered the Minister of Bantu Education to admit only members of specified 'Bantu' ethnic groups to particular colleges. Africans who were already enrolled at 'white' universities were to leave by the beginning of 1961. The political activities of students at Fort Hare and the newly created Turfloop, Ngoye, Durban and Bellville campuses were subjected to strict control. The measure enraged African and white liberal opinion, and was passed amid widespread protests.

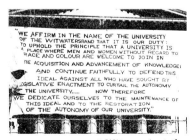

A GIANT PROTEST *at Wits against the exclusion of blacks.*

PROFESSOR *Frederik Tomlinson recommended the acquisition of further land before the Reserves could be made viable.*

support about 2,2-million African commercial farmers. Nearly 300 000 other pastoralists and mixed farmers would have to be accommodated elsewhere in the economy; to meet their needs and cater for future growth, industrialists would have to be encouraged to invest capital in developments in or near the Reserves.

Based on optimum projections for industrial and agricultural growth, the commission estimated that by the turn of the century the Reserves would be able to support about two-thirds of South Africa's African population of 21-million. Seven 'Bantu' territories were proposed, but the commission concluded that the system of 'tribal' authorities was not compatible with modern industrial development. Overall, the government would have to sink nearly £105-million into the development of the Reserves over the next 10 years.

But the Cabinet – not willing to force this level of expenditure on the white public – looked for a cheaper way to implement this policy. In rejecting the basic recommendations of the Tomlinson commission, Verwoerd claimed that its estimates of necessary expenditure were four times too high. Furthermore, he added that white capitalists would not be permitted to invest in the Reserves, only near their borders; that the government would not buy more land for the Reserves than was stipulated by the Land Act, and that it would not depart from its intention to establish 'tribal' authorities as the basis of African political power and rights in the Reserves.

Coercion

To Verwoerd and the other designers of apartheid, the fact that the majority of Africans were probably bitterly opposed to their schemes was of little consequence.

In this respect, their attitude was chillingly candid: those who disagreed with their policies had to be forced to agree. And if they persisted in their opposition, they had to be crushed . . . .

At the top of the government's list of political bogeys was the Communist Party of South Africa (CPSA).

The CPSA, despite a series of internal upheavals, policy reversals and frequent rejection by the major African political and industrial organisations since its inception in 1921, was by 1948 dug into the political landscape and was exercising a strong influence in the black trade union movement. The party's membership had grown – and it was also gradually developing a new rapprochement with the African National Congress (ANC) and the South African Indian Congress. It had even won representation in parliament through the election in 1948 of Sam Kahn as one of the three Natives' Representatives.

The Smuts Government had not ignored the CPSA's union activities; its offices, and those of its newspaper, the 'Guardian', were frequently the target of police raids, and in 1946, following the African Mineworkers' Union strike, the state had tried to press charges of sedition against the whole national executive.

The NP fired its first shots at the communists almost immediately on assuming power; a committee was set up to investigate communism in the Union – and when it reported early in 1949, Justice Minister Charles Swart informed parliament that it had uncovered evidence that communists had infiltrated trade unions and universities and that the party posed a danger to 'our national life, our democratic institutions, and our Western philosophy'. He called on the Opposition to support whatever measures were necessary, although he did not suggest what these might be. But the UP replied that it believed the best safeguard against communism was the maintenance of the traditions of political freedom, an atmosphere in which the doctrine could not flourish, rather than simply to brand all dissent as communism and to stamp it out.

The Nationalists, however, were unimpressed – and towards the end of the parliamentary session Swart banned Kahn from addressing meetings on the Witwatersrand for a year. In December 1949, when another communist, Fred Carneson, secured election to the Cape Provincial Council as a Natives' Representative, Afrikaans newspapers began urging that strong measures be taken to counter the 'communist threat'. In May 1950, the government referred the Unlawful Organisations Bill to a parliamentary select committee in the hope of gaining UP support for it. When it was passed on 24 June 1950, it was with a new name and several amendments: now known as the Suppression of Communism Act, it provided for the outlawing of the CPSA and any other organisation the government might deem fit; the seizure and liquidation of their assets; the compilation of a list of the names of all their members; the banning of meetings considered likely to promote communism, and the barring of 'listed' persons from attending gatherings or from being members of certain specified public bodies, offices or organisations.

A crucial feature of Minister Swart's Act was its sweeping definition of communism: Marxist Socialism as expounded by Lenin, Trotsky, the Comintern or the Communist Information Bureau, 'or any related form . . . expounded or advocated in the Union for the promotion of the fundamental principles of that doctrine, including any . . . scheme' that was geared towards:

- the establishment of a despotic government based on

THE LONE COMMUNIST PARTY *member in the House of Assembly was Natives' Representative, Sam Kahn. Kahn's parliamentary opposition to the new apartheid measures was short-lived, however: his party was outlawed in 1950, and he was forced out of parliament in 1952.*

the dictatorship of the proletariat, in which only one political party was recognised and all others suppressed;

● bringing about any political, industrial, social or economic change in South Africa through the promotion of disorder, or through actions that could be deemed by the authorities as having the possible consequence of disorder;

● bringing about such change under the guidance of any foreign government or organisation committed to the dictatorship of the proletariat;

● encouraging hostility between black and white in order to further any of the above objectives.

On 20 June 1950 – four days before this became law – Kahn informed the House of Assembly that the CPSA had disbanded to protect its members from the penalties of a 10-year jail sentence and to save its assets from being liquidated. But the government reacted by introducing further amendments to make the law retroactive and to redefine a communist as anyone who had ever been a member of the party, or could be deemed to have been a communist by his or her actions. Kahn and Carneson clung to their seats in the Assembly and the Cape Provincial Council until 1952 when they were forced out.

Communist Brian Bunting stood immediately for the seat vacated by Kahn, won a resounding victory, and took his seat in January 1953. He was ousted by August. In 1954, trade unionist Ray Alexander stood for parliament as a Natives' Representative. Although she, too, won her seat with a solid majority, police prevented her from entering the House of Assembly.

In another development, the CPSA went underground and changed its name to the South African Communist Party (SACP). Its newspaper, the 'Guardian', had been banned in May 1952, but continued to be published under a variety of titles – 'Clarion', 'People's World', 'Advance', 'New Age', 'The Spark' – for the next 10 years, switching to a new title as the old one was outlawed.

'A reign of terror'

The Communist Party was not the only target of the security legislation. Other measures followed: the Native Adminstration Act was used to banish Africans to specified districts; the Criminal Law Amendment Act of 1953

made it an offence to protest against any law, or to incite others to campaign or protest; the Riotous Assemblies Act (as amended in 1956) made it an offence to intimidate or harass people for going to work during a strike. This battery of measures was used to conduct what was described in parliament as 'a reign of terror' against members of the ANC, trade unionists, and the leaders of the Defiance Campaign, which began in 1952 (see page 382).

This, ultimately, was the meaning of apartheid: a policy that allowed the Nationalists to pursue their goals and their opponents with equal vigour, regardless of the human cost. Their first decade of power had been marked by the determined imposition of divisions between people of different colours. And they were only just beginning . . . .

TRADE UNIONIST *Ray Alexander was prevented from entering parliament to take up her seat as a Natives' Representative.*

A united front against apartheid

Backed by anti-apartheid groups in the coloured, Indian and white communities, the African National Congress (ANC) demonstrated its growing militancy in 1952, staging a Defiance Campaign that pushed it into a head-on confrontation with the government. When defiance petered out, a new campaign was initiated by the anti-apartheid allies: in June 1955, the 'Freedom Charter', a blueprint for a new, non-racial South Africa, was adopted. The government, however, reacted to these developments with an ever-widening battery of laws.

ON A COLD June day in 1951, in the middle of a hard, dry Highveld winter, a group of sombre men stood clustered around a grave, watching in silence as the coffin of their former leader was lowered into the red Transvaal earth. They had come to pay their last respects to the old warhorse of African politics, Pixley Seme, one of the founders of the African National Congress (ANC) in 1912, and an ex-president of the organisation. As the earth thudded onto the coffin lid, it buried not just a veteran fighter for African political rights, but also a belief in political moderation that the younger members of the organisation felt had achieved precisely nothing.

Among them were men who would soon become household names in South Africa: Nelson Mandela, Walter Sisulu and future ANC leader Oliver Tambo. Under Seme's successor, Alfred Xuma, the congress had been accused of elitism and excessive moderation, and of resisting calls

JAMES MOROKA *was elected president of the ANC with the backing of members of the Congress Youth League.*

by its newly formed Congress Youth League (CYL) – of which Mandela, Sisulu and Tambo were members – for organised resistance. Xuma, ironically, had done much to improve the administration of the ANC during his tenure as president. It was he, too, who gave the go-ahead for the formation of the CYL (against the advice of members of the old guard).

But, having done that, he had immediately crossed swords with younger members by refusing to back a CYL-inspired 'Programme of Action'. Until the masses were properly organised, he had argued, action would only lead to exposure.

But for many young African activists the time for talking was over . . . .

A Programme of Action

When Daniel Malan's National Party (NP) Government followed up its 1948 election triumph with the promulgation of new apartheid laws such as the Group Areas Act and the Stock Limitation Act – as well as the stricter application of existing discriminatory legislation such as the Pass laws – more and more young Africans began to reject the notion that change would come about through the process of negotiation alone.

African opposition to such legislation had to be demonstrated in a much more direct way, they now argued. And if the present leadership of the the ANC refused to show the way, a new leadership had to be found . . . .

The first stirrings of change surfaced in 1949 at the annual conference of the ANC: Xuma was ruthlessly manoeuvred out of the presidency and replaced by James Moroka, who clinched election by promising Youth Leaguers places on the national executive. At the same time, the Programme of Action was adopted which, while mild compared to the ANC's programme today, was the most militant in the history of the congress. The aims of the programme were to achieve political independence and to reject white leadership and racial segregation through civil disobedience and work stoppages.

It was Moroka who chaired the first meeting of a Joint Planning Council (made up of representatives of all the main anti-apartheid groups), fittingly, on the day Seme was buried. Joint planning with non-African organisations was an important new development in the emerging new style of opposition to apartheid: earlier measures called for by the ANC Council of Action, the executive body for the

Programme of Action, had been organised separately by the different groups involved. The stay-at-home strikes of May and July 1951 had been only partially successful owing to the disjointed cooperation between the ANC, the South African Indian Congress (SAIC), the Communist Party of South Africa (CPSA) and coloured organisations. At first, the majority of CYL members were openly hostile to the participation of coloureds, Indians and whites in the Programme of Action. And they were even more opposed to forging closer ties with the CPSA. But events had rapidly overtaken them: on 20 June 1950, the CPSA had disbanded ahead of the enactment by the government of the Suppression of Communism Act, and some 1 500 African communists had sought entrance into the ANC. This had been followed in November that year by the election of J B Marks, a communist, as president of the Transvaal branch of the ANC.

Although these developments had led to much soul-searching, pragmatism had won the day in the end. In this respect, an about-turn by Sisulu, the leader of the Africanist bloc in the Congress, had proved decisive. Realising that a mass co-ordinated effort of all groups opposed to apartheid would provide the only effective resistance to increasingly repressive government action, Sisulu had persuaded his supporters to put aside their misgivings over communists and other organisations.

It had turned out to be a perfectly timed tactical manoeuvre: Indian and coloured people were increasingly feeling the effects of apartheid that had, up to then, largely been restricted to Africans. Coloured people in the Cape were particularly incensed at Nationalist attempts to deprive them of a vote on a common roll with whites (see page 392), while politically active Indians were beginning to wonder whether they even had a future in South Africa. Furthermore, when clashes between Zulus and Indians in January 1949 left 142 people dead (see box), many politically active Indians had become even more convinced of the necessity of forging closer ties with the ANC.

And so, as the new Joint Planning Council, consisting of two ANC men (Sisulu and J B Marks) and two members of the South African Indian Congress (Yusuf Dadoo and Yusuf Cachalia), began its deliberations, Moroka declared: 'The old exclusive Congress has been buried with Seme.' And Albert Luthuli, the soon-to-be-elected national president of the ANC, was equally enthusiastic: 'The very fact that it [the council] was able to be formed and to function is a sign that all but the white races in South Africa are starting to think and act across barriers of race,' he said.

Two months after Seme's funeral, the newly formed council delivered a report on what was to become known as the Defiance Campaign.

Chief among its recommendations was that an 'ultimatum' calling for the scrapping of 'unjust laws' by February 1952 be delivered to the government. Failure to comply would result in a 'Defiance Campaign' which would start on 6 April – the date set aside by the government for countrywide celebrations to mark the tercentenary of Jan van Riebeeck's arrival at the Cape in 1652. This would be followed by large-scale strikes on 26 June – a date soon to become known as the 'National Day of Freedom'.

The plan included recruiting volunteer corps to contravene selected laws and regulations around the country and thus overburden the state's law-enforcement machinery. Mass rallies, marches and demonstrations also formed part of the proposed campaign.

The letter, or 'ultimatum', signed by Moroka and Sisulu, reached Prime Minister Malan in January 1952: speaking of 'democracy, liberty and harmony' it declared that the African people were 'fully resolved to achieve this in our lifetime'. But it also made clear that what was being opposed was a system, and not a 'race'. 'The struggle which the national organisations of the non-European people are conducting,' declared the signatories, 'is not directed against any race or national group, but against unjust laws which keep in perpetual subjection and misery vast sections of the population.'

Action from both sides

Malan's government did not repeal the laws. In an unequivocal but measured reply, the Prime Minister reiterated the Nationalist ideology that 'Bantu differ in many ways from the Europeans' and that the 'government had no intention of repealing . . . the laws'. Malan warned of the extreme gravity of the ultimatum's threat and that his government would 'use the full machinery at its disposal to quell any disturbances'. He urged the writers to reconsider their strategy and to 'help the government carry out its programme of goodwill'.

Thus the die was cast: for the black resistance movements the road of peaceful supplication had come to an end; for the white nationalists, 'patience' with black 'troublemakers' had run out. A pamphlet distributed by the ANC, in both English and Afrikaans, proclaimed: 'We stand on the eve of a great national crisis. We call on every true South African to support us.'

The campaign begins

As white South Africans prepared for a massive climax to the Van Riebeeck celebrations on 6 April, the ANC and SAIC appealed to blacks to observe the day as a 'National Day of Pledge and Prayer'. Mass rallies were held in all the main centres – and hard and bitter words were exchanged on both sides. Moroka told 50 000 people gathered in Freedom Square, Fordsburg, outside Johannesburg that 'whites . . . cannot escape the fact that whatever page they turn in the history of South Africa they find it red with the blood of the fallen, with ill-will and insecurity written across its pages'. In Port Elizabeth, another ANC leader, Professor Z K Matthews, spoke of 'economic exploitation and social degradation'.

Opposing slogans and pamphlets highlighted the divisions: 'Freedom or Serfdom', 'South Africa for the Whites', 'A Kaffir is a Kaffir' and 'Afrika Must Triumph'.

Adjudging their mass rallies an overwhelming success, the leaders of the Joint Planning Council then turned their attention to the next step: the setting of 26 June as the start of the Defiance Campaign.

The government, however, now thoroughly alerted to the potential support of its opponents, started taking its own steps to crush the defiance movement. Within six

Indians feel the apartheid lash

Even before the Nationalists came to power, the Smuts Government had attacked the position of the Indian population with the introduction of the Asiatic Land Tenure Act in 1946, which placed tough restrictions on where Indians might live and trade, although they were offered the sop – ultimately rejected, and then withdrawn – of limited representation by whites in parliament.

After the NP victory, however, the position of Indians became even more perilous. The Sauer report, which had provided the electoral platform for the policy of apartheid early in 1948, had made clear the NP's attitude to the 500 000-strong Indian population: they were regarded as 'a strange and foreign element which is not assimilable', to be treated as 'an immigrant community'. Immigration was to be halted and as many Indians as possible repatriated. While the former was achieved, repatriation was not. The Sauer report had gone on to promise whites that the Indian Representation Act would be reviewed immediately, that Indians would not be given any representation in the legislative and executive processes of government, and that they would be forced to live and trade in separate areas.

The machinery of the Group Areas Act had its origins in the Asiatic Land Tenure Act; the Land Tenure Advisory Board created by that Act now became the Group Areas Board, whose task it now became to restructure completely the pattern of residential settlement and trading areas which had developed throughout South Africa to that point. Africans were more or less untouched by the provisions of the new legislation; segregationist legislation had been attacking the settlement of Africans in towns and cities with increasing vigour for almost 30 years.

The government introduced the new law with the claim that it had received petitions from whites objecting to the presence of coloured and Indian people in so-called white areas, that this had led to an erosion of white property values, and that coloured and Indian businesses were unfairly competing with those of neighbouring white traders. The first to feel the impact of the new law were the Indians who, throughout the Transvaal and Natal, were subjected to demands by white municipalities that their homes and businesses be moved out of town. And the limited representation in parliament and the Natal Provincial Council that had been granted to Indians in terms of the Indian Representation Act of 1946, was quickly scrapped by the Nationalists.

In 1949, in Durban, tensions between Zulu and Indian erupted when armed Africans stormed into the Indian business districts in a bloody clash which left 142 people dead and more than 1 000 injured. Arguments still continue as to the cause of the riots, which seems to have been rooted in the bitterness felt by many Africans towards Indian traders. Natal's leading African newspaper '*Ilanga Lase Natal*' ('The Sun of Natal') commented at the time that the 'whole grim business was logical, simply inevitable' because of what it called Indian 'blackmarketeering', opposition to African economic expansion and 'shaketeering' (letting of shacks to Africans) by Indian landlords. It also blamed the favoured treatment of Indians by whites which, it said, gave the Indians 'not only better rights, but a sense of snobbishness and superiority over the Africans'.

The Natal Indian Congress, however, took a more sober view, blaming the Urban Areas Act which had forced Africans to live in shocking conditions in and around Durban. One of Natal's Indian newspapers, the 'Leader', commented that African workers were forced to live in compounds where there were no social or civic responsibilities, no future for their children and no outlet for 'energies and emotions'. 'He [the African] has nothing worthwhile enjoying or living for, and when somebody set off the spark the Indian, more or less a fellow-sufferer, caught the brunt of his fury, hate and pent-up frustrations.' An all-white commission of enquiry into the killings blamed the disturbances on the 'bad precepts' of the Indians and the 'racial characteristics' of the Africans.

The tragedy sparked renewed attempts to co-ordinate black resistance against apartheid. Alfred Xuma, then the president of the ANC, realised that the racial divisions which separated the liberation struggle should be buried – and had, in fact, already lent his moral support to a two-year disobedience campaign organised by the Natal and Transvaal Indian Congresses in defiance of the Asiatic Land Tenure Act, despite the reservations of the ANC's Africanist bloc.

Unity moves were fostered by communists in the leadership core of all three organisations, who pointed out that cooperation was both necessary and desirable. The riots, they argued, underscored the point that polarisation fragmented the liberation struggle.

Their efforts led to the signing of the so-called 'Doctors' Pact' by Xuma, G M Naicker of the Natal Indian Congress and Yusuf Dadoo of the Transvaal Indian Congress. This joint declaration of cooperation dedicated the three congresses to action against the race policies of the Union Government and was to lead to the formation of the Joint Planning Council for the Defiance Campaign. However, in the campaign that followed, acts of defiance in Natal were mild compared with those in the rest of the country.

YUSUF DADOO *of the Transvaal Indian Congress signed the so-called 'Doctors' Pact' with the Natal Indian Congress and the* ANC.

A CROWD OF 50000 *packed Freedom Square in Fordsburg, just outside Johannesburg, on 6 April 1952 to hear* ANC *leader James Moroka declare the start of the Defiance Campaign. 'I am glad to see you here in such numbers,' he told the cheering throng.*

weeks of the demonstrations on 6 April, the state, acting under the Suppression of Communism Act, started banning known communists. Among those caught in the security net – and thus forced to resign their executive positions on the Planning Council – were J B Marks, Moses Kotane, David Bopape and J N Ngwevela of the ANC and Dadoo of the SAIC.

Also banned was the left-wing 'Guardian' newspaper – which reappeared immediately as the 'Clarion'. However, most of the banned persons refused to be muzzled, and in the following weeks were arrested for speaking in public and attending political meetings. But far from crushing protest, the government clampdown served only to increase enthusiasm for the coming Day of Defiance.

The big day – 26 June 1952 – dawned bright and clear and demonstrations took off throughout the Witwatersrand, eastern Cape and Natal. Watched by cheering, chanting crowds, groups of protesters in all the major centres deliberately broke 'unjust laws'. They walked through 'forbidden' areas without Passes, they broke curfews, they walked through 'Europeans only' entrances and stood at 'Europeans only' counters and waiting rooms. As the campaign took hold among the people, a mood of almost religious fervour gripped the resistance. Days of prayer, fasting, hymn-singing and church services took place throughout the country.

And as police began arresting protesters by the hundreds, white South Africans were forced to sit up and take notice. 'They were forced at last,' noted Albert Luthuli, 'to register our presence . . . the white rulers were left in no doubt about what we intended.'

The white rulers were indeed in no doubt and acted swiftly. Legislation was rushed through parliament imposing dire penalties on those taking part in the campaign, and the police began a wave of raids on the homes and offices of campaign organisers. Vast quantities of papers and documents were seized and 35 key resistance people in the Cape and Transvaal were arrested and charged with promoting communism. As the campaign gathered momentum, the number of arrests increased daily. By October 1952 nearly 6000 people had been arrested. But during the same period, paid-up membership of the ANC increased from 7000 to more than 100000 – almost 17 new members for each arrest.

Many of the court decisions involving the resisters were surprisingly lenient and based on the fact that equality of treatment was considered an essential feature of segregation if it was to have the force of law. In one case, the Appellate Division of the Supreme Court in Bloemfontein upheld the acquittal of a coloured man, George Lush, on a charge of refusing to leave a 'Europeans only' waiting room in Cape Town because the facilities for 'non-Europeans' were inferior.

Needless to say, the government was not amused at these findings and hastened to close any loopholes in the apartheid laws. (By the following year, 1953, parliament would pass the Reservation of Separate Amenities Act which held that separate amenities need not be 'substantially similar to or of the same character, standard, extent or quality as those set aside for the other race'.)

Meanwhile arrests continued, reaching some 8400 (with 7986 convictions) by December. The breakdown for arrests was: eastern Cape, 5941; Transvaal 1578; western Cape 490; Orange Free State 125 and Natal 192. Although the majority were charged under the Suppression of Communism Act, Z K Matthews observed that 'the campaign was strongest and best organised precisely in those areas where so-called communist influence was weakest'. In Cape Town, he pointed out, where the communist influence was strongest, there was a negligible number of ar-

AFRICANS *defying train apartheid give the* ANC *'thumbs up' salute as they board a 'whites only' carriage in Mowbray for the ride to Cape Town, where they were arrested.*

rests. In the eastern Cape, on the other hand, where the 'communist influence was practically nil', the largest number had been arrested.

A noteworthy aspect of the Defiance Campaign in its initial stages was the almost total lack of violence. As Mr Justice Rumpff commented in a trial judgment towards the end of 1952: ' . . . You have consistently advised your followers to follow a peaceful course of action and to avoid violence in any shape or form.'

Violence breaks out

But as the demonstrations continued with more deliberate law-breaking and more arrests, tensions within the police and the resistance groups mounted daily. Riots – in which both blacks and whites were killed – first broke out in Port Elizabeth in October 1952, and from there spread rapidly to Johannesburg, Kimberley and East London.

The East London riots were particularly horrifying: although a countrywide ban on public meetings had been imposed following the unrest in Port Elizabeth, ANC officials in East London managed to obtain police permission to hold a prayer meeting on the evening of Sunday, 10 November. During the meeting, while hymns were being sung, armed police burst into the hall and charged the crowd with bayonets. In the ensuing melee, shots were fired. For several hours thereafter the African area of the town was rocked by arson, stone-throwing and police gunfire. Among the many people killed was a Dominican nun, whose body was mutilated by the enraged rioters.

The government's immediate reaction was to blame the riots on the Defiance Campaign. The campaign leaders blamed the police and the government for 'deliberately provoking' the situation. East London city councillors blamed the government, saying the town was peaceful before the ban on meetings. The police blamed troublemakers at the meeting. The majority of whites blamed the ANC. Most of the Afrikaans Press blamed the barbarism of 'primitive Africa', while some of the English Press placed the blame on irresponsible juveniles. Albert Luthuli, however, had his own views: 'The Defiance Campaign was far too orderly and successful for the government's liking,' he said, adding that 'the prospect before the white

supremacists, if they were going to react to our challenge in a civilized way, was that arrests would continue indefinitely. Behind the thousands already arrested were more, many more. The challenge of non-violence was more than they could meet. It robbed them of their initiative. On the other hand, violence by Africans would restore this initiative to them – they would then be able to bring out the guns and the other techniques of intimidation and present themselves as restorers of order . . . .'

In turning down demands for a judicial enquiry into the riots, Minister of Justice Charles Swart declared that the only thing law-breakers understood was for the police to 'hit hard'. 'If I cannot suppress violence with violence,' he added, 'then I do not want to be Minister of Justice.'

A new round of laws

Wherever the blame lay, the campaign achieved certain results for both sides. From the government side it presented the opportunity to introduce a battery of laws designed to silence dissenters and protest. These were contained in the Criminal Law Amendment Act and the Public Safety Act, which made protest virtually illegal and gave the authorities the power to declare a state of emergency. An additional spinoff was a surge of new white voters to the National Party, which helped it to consolidate its power in the 1953 general election.

All this meant that organised extra-parliamentary opposition to the government would now be fraught with difficulty – and from this perspective some participants believed that the Defiance Campaign had backfired. The majority, however, regarded it as a great success.

After all, they argued, it was the biggest organised demonstration of resistance ever shown by the black people of South Africa; it had sent a message to white voters that something was wrong in the country; it had demonstrated that cooperation between black groups could work; it had put the question of institutionalised racism under the international spotlight at the United Nations, and not only had it boosted ANC membership, but it had also given the organisation greater popular credibility.

The campaign itself was dead by the end of 1952. The last whimper was heard at a meeting in Alexandra in De-

CURIOUS ONLOOKERS *peer through the windows of the Johannesburg Magistrate's Court while the leaders of the Defiance Campaign are brought to trial in 1952 on charges under the Suppression of Communism Act.*

THE DECISION by ANC leader James Moroka (left) to enter a plea of mitigation at his trial led to his replacement as president by Albert Luthuli (right).

cember of that year in a surreal atmosphere of almost melodramatic pathos.

The ANC leadership was in tatters. Twenty of its leaders, including the president, James Moroka, were on trial under the Suppression of Communism Act. Moroka had elected to have his own lawyer, who subsequently entered a separate plea of mitigation, basically asking whites to shield him from white laws. As a result, Moroka was removed from his office and Albert Luthuli was voted in as president. Shortly after this the CYL asked Luthuli to address a meeting in Alexandra in a bid to feed the dying fires of the campaign and recruit new volunteers for acts of defiance. But the moment had passed. Luthuli undoubtedly sensed this, but out of politeness agreed to address the meeting in any case.

The hall was almost empty. Less than 100 supporters turned up. Luthuli spoke and the people cheered as best they could. Then one of the Youth League members stood up and made a rambling speech calling for volunteers. As he spoke the people in the audience began to drift out. Eventually only a handful were left. When the speaker called for volunteers, only one old man put up his hand. But he could not stand. He was drunk.

A new direction
Nevertheless, as far as Luthuli was concerned, the complexion of South African extra-parliamentary opposition had been changed for good. 'On both sides, 1952 was the turning point . . . ,' he said.

Indeed, cooperation among all groups had reached a high point. After the demise of the Communist Party a new white left-wing organisation calling itself the Congress of Democrats emerged. And in Cape Town a Coloured People's Organisation (which later became the Coloured People's Congress) was formed. Together with the ANC and the SAIC these two bodies formed a co-ordinating committee known as the Congress Alliance.

Even so, the two years following the Defiance Campaign saw a lull in overt black political action; the government had put mass campaigns beyond the law and was doing its utmost to immobilise major organisations such as the ANC and the SAIC by banning their leaders and confining them to their home districts. Luthuli was restricted to his home at Groutville in Zululand; most of the SAIC executive had

been banned by the end of 1954, and 42 ANC leaders were under restrictions by the end of 1955.

Nevertheless, this period was a vital one for the black liberation movement, anxious to retain what it could of the momentum gained by the Defiance Campaign. Of crucial importance now was to seek ways of moving beyond protest – and to articulate a vision of a new order.

Congress of the People
In August 1953, Cape ANC leader Z K Matthews proposed that a national conference, representing all groups, be called 'to draw up a freedom charter for the democratic South Africa of the future'. Its main objective, said Matthews later, was to instil political consciousness in the people and encourage their political activity.

In March of the following year, executives of the ANC, SAIC, the South African Congress of Trade Unions (SACTU), and the Coloured People's Congress met in Tongaat under the eyes of a contingent of now-ubiquitous security police. The newly established Liberal Party also sent observers, but subsequently decided to withdraw its support in protest at the prominent role played by communists in the Congress of Democrats. Despite similar reservations by Africanists in the ANC, a National Action Council, which later became known as the Congress Alliance – was given the go-ahead by the participating movements to plan a Congress of the People for 25-26 June 1955.

The goal of the council was to draw up a document which truly represented the political aspirations of all South Africans. With this in mind, it sought an input from people in cities, towns, villages, factories and farms throughout the country.

Although organisational inadequacies, a lack of resources and police harassment prevented the council from executing its brief fully, it managed to attract a fairly broad mass response at grassroots level, in the form of thousands of written or dictated submissions.

The Freedom Charter was drafted in the weeks prior to the congress by a committee of the National Action Council, and reviewed by the ANC's national executive committee on the opening day of the congress. However, neither Luthuli nor Matthews saw the final draft before it was put to congress delegates: restriction orders prevented Luthuli from travelling, while Matthews was caught in the middle of a student crisis at Fort Hare University.

In many ways, the Congress of the People, held in a field at Kliptown near Soweto, was an extraordinary gathering. It had been organised against the odds, hampered by government interference, strapped by a shortage of finance and burdened by the complex logistics of transporting, housing and feeding 2 884 delegates from every corner of South Africa. Yet, wrote Luthuli, 'nothing in the history of the liberatory movement in South Africa quite caught the popular imagination as this did, not even the Defiance Campaign. Even remote rural areas were aware of the significance of what was going on.'

Simply getting there was a matter of high adventure, particularly for those travelling by road; hundreds of delegates were stopped along the route by police who used every possible means to obstruct them. In Beaufort West,

The Freedom Charter

Describing the Freedom Charter, Chief Albert Luthuli wrote: 'The Charter produced at Kliptown is, line by line, the direct outcome of conditions which obtain – harsh, oppressive and unjust conditions. It is thus a practical and relevant document. It attempted to give a flesh and blood meaning, in the South African setting, to such words as democracy, freedom, liberty.'

The charter is regarded by liberal and Marxist political analysts as essentially a moderate document emphasising a non-racial society, liberty and individual rights, while its inclusion of socialist elements such as nationalisation is said not necessarily to imply the abolition of private ownership.

It comprises 10 clauses, headed by a preamble which commits its adherents to strive for the achievement of a government based on the will of all people, black and white:
● *Clause 1, The People Shall Govern*, affirms the right of all, regardless of race, colour or sex, to vote;
● *Clause 2, All National Groups Shall Have Equal Rights*, affords equality before the law, in the instruments of government, and in schools, and forbids racial insults;
● *Clause 3, The People Shall Share in the Country's Wealth*, calls for the nationalisation of the mines, banks and industrial monopolies, for trade and industry to be controlled for the benefit of the people, and for all people to have equal economic and job rights;
● *Clause 4, The Land Shall Be Shared among Those Who Work It*, demands a redistribution of the land and state assistance for the peasantry, as well as the abolition of any restrictions on movements of people, access to land, and stock holdings;
● *Clause 5, All Shall Be Equal before the Law*, promises the abolition of detentions or bannings without trial, as well as all discriminatory laws;
● *Clause 6, All Shall Enjoy Human Rights*, guarantees freedom of speech, worship, and association, and unfettered freedom of movement;
● *Clause 7, There Shall Be Work and Security*, recognises the right of all to work and to equal pay for equal work, lays down minimum working conditions, and promises the abolition of child labour, compound labour, contract labour, and the tot system;
● *Clause 8, The Doors of Learning and Culture Shall Be Opened*, sets out principles of free, universal, compulsory and equal education, promises to wipe out illiteracy, and undertakes to remove all cultural, sporting and educational colour bars;
● *Clause 9, There Shall Be Houses, Security and Comfort*, promises decent housing for all and the rationalisation of accommodation, the demolition of slums and fenced townships, the provision of proper suburban amenities, proper medical care for all as well as care of the aged, the disabled and orphans;
● *Clause 10, There Shall Be Peace and Friendship*, says South Africa will respect the rights of other states and will strive for world peace.

The Freedom Charter concludes: '*Let all who love their people and their country now say, as we say here: these freedoms we will fight for, side by side, throughout our lives until we have won our liberty.*'

for instance, a group of delegates from Cape Town, forced to miss the congress because they did not have transport permits, spent the weekend organising in the local townships. In another instance, a group of Indian delegates without permits to enter the Transvaal bluffed their way out of police custody in Heidelberg by pretending they were going to a wedding and singing and playing musical instruments so loudly that police hurried them out of town without asking for their permits.

The weather was perfect as thousands of delegates, and thousands more observers, began to swarm across the site, a private athletics track, for this historic 'national convention'. The scene was thus described in a British newspaper: 'Large African grandmothers, wearing Congress skirts, Congress blouses or Congress *doeks* (scarves) on their heads traipsed around with bagging suitcases; [there were] young Indian wives, with glistening saris and shawls embroidered in Congress colours; grey old African men, with walking sticks and Congress arm-bands; young city workers from Johannesburg, with broad hats, bright American ties and narrow trousers; smooth Indian lawyers and businessmen, moving confidently among the crowds in well-cut suits; and a backcloth of anonymous African faces, listening impassively to the hours of speeches that are the staple of every Congress meeting.' The security police were also well represented, taking photographs of every white face on the platform or in the crowd, and scribbling notes on every speech.

The Freedom Charter

The congress opened with the presentation of awards to Luthuli and Dadoo (who were both absent), and Father Trevor Huddleston, the Anglican priest of Sophiatown and a fierce critic of apartheid. Once this was over, attention was turned to the task in hand – the approval of the Freedom Charter.

At about 3.30 pm on the 26 June, with two sections of the charter remaining to be discussed, the police – who up to then had been content to watch the proceedings – arrived in force. Armed with sten guns, they formed a cordon around the field as 15 security policemen mounted the platform and announced to the crowd that they suspect-

BLACK POLITICAL *meetings were often attended by plainclothes policemen, like these at Alexandra.*

ed that treason was being committed. After announcing that the names and addresses of all the delegates would be recorded, they began confiscating documents, posters – even the catering signs – and film.

Everybody was under arrest – and as tension mounted congress officials had their work cut out to placate the angry crowd. After the ANC anthem, *Nkosi Sikelel' iAfrika* ('God Bless Africa'), had been sung, discussion of the charter was continued. At 8 pm police were still busy taking down names and addresses as people slowly filed out, taking with them whatever documents and film they could hide. Later, the Congress Alliance proceeded to gain the charter's ratification by individual member organisations, and launched a campaign to get a million signatures endorsing the document.

The 'Treason Trial'

In September 1955, police conducted a co-ordinated raid on the homes of at least 500 activists, seizing documents relating to the charter and searching for any possible evidence of high treason or sedition; it was the prelude to an unprecedented crackdown on extra-parliamentary opponents of the government. Bannings and restrictions were served thick and fast as the state stepped up the pressure on the black liberation movement. The charter became the chief object of the government's attentions, and would later serve as the focus of the so-called 'Treason Trial', which was initiated with the arrest of 156 leading activists in December 1956.

The swoop came in the early hours of 5 December and was executed with the precision of a military manoeuvre: surrounded by elaborate security precautions, those arrested – a veritable Who's Who of the liberation movement – were driven, or flown in military aircraft, to Johannesburg, where they were incarcerated in The Fort prison. One unintended consequence of the mass detentions was the chance they offered to resistance leaders – quartered in two large adjacent cells – to meet openly and unhindered, a circumstance which the government had been at pains to prevent for several years. 'What distance, other occupations, lack of funds, and police interference had made difficult – frequent meetings – the government had now insisted on,' Luthuli recalled.

POLICE CHECK DOCUMENTS *at the offices of the ANC during a massive crackdown following the Congress of the People – which led directly to the 'Treason Trial'.*

The trial, which opened in 1957 in the Johannesburg Drill Hall with a preparatory examination that lasted nearly two years, was a long and arduous affair which dragged on until 1961. But it proved to be a rallying cry to the supporters of those charged. Funds poured in from around the world to sustain the accused and their families, and to pay their legal costs. International observers flocked to the trial. Teams of women worked ceaselessly to provide food for the accused each day. Most of those charged were subsequently freed without going to trial, and it ended in March 1961 when Mr Justice Rumpff acquitted the remaining 30 of the charges of treason. As Johannesburg's townships celebrated, police marked the occasion by raiding a party at the home of Joe Slovo and his wife, Ruth, both members of the Communist Party. They searched the house for alcohol, in terms of regulations that forbade the serving of wine and brandy to Africans.

Boycotts on the buses

Throughout the 1950s, there was little material advance in the economic position of urban Africans. Bus boycotts in the southern Transvaal township of Evaton in 1955 and in Alexandra (near Johannesburg) two years later, were triggered by proposed fare increases. These boycotts were lengthy and frequently violent as thousands of commuters

IN THE EARLY HOURS *of December 1956, police swooped on* ANC *and other activists all over the country, arresting 156 leading figures. The following year they were charged with treason – in a trial that was to last for more than four years. Among the defendants was veteran campaigner Helen Joseph (above centre), pictured with a group of fellow accused. Emotions outside the Pretoria Supreme Court – where the trial was held – ran high (top right) as police arrested photographers. In October 1958 defendants cheered outside the court (right) when some of the indictments against several of the accused were withdrawn. However, only in March 1961 were the remaining accused finally acquitted by Mr Justice Rumpff.*

demonstrated a remarkable solidarity, despite frequent infighting among different factions. Although the bus boycotts exacted only short-term concessions, they became important weapons in the African struggle for quite another reason: they drew communities together. Walking was protest, requiring positive action in a way that other boycotts did not.

Boycotts were not new – Evaton, in particular, had a history of boycotts throughout the early 1950s, but on 24 July 1955 a public meeting called by the Evaton People's Transport Council resolved to boycott the Evaton Transport Company unless newly imposed fare increases were scrapped. The following morning buses were stopped by pickets, mainly women, who ordered passengers off – one woman threw herself in front of a moving bus in order to force it to stop. For the next seven weeks there were violent clashes between the boycotters and an anti-boycott

group which began to gather around Evaton's desperately poor Basotho group – called the 'Russians'.

The violence came to a head on 7 September 1955 when a bus was burnt out – and the company withdrew its buses from the township. Normal service was resumed on 24 October, but the returning buses were greeted by angry crowds, stone-throwers and roadblocks. Two boycotters were killed in clashes between boycotters and anti-boycotters – a situation that worsened after the bus company employed the Basotho leader, Ralekeke Rantube, and several of his followers to protect their buses, and in December five more boycotters died.

More trouble flared in May 1956 when a bus conductor died after being beaten up, and on 11 May – the day of his funeral – Basotho rode into Evaton on the buses in order to launch a surprise attack on picketers at the township terminus. The worst fighting between the two groups took

PEDAL POWER *takes over from engine power in January 1957 as thousands of bus boycotters take to the streets of Alexandra to begin the 15-kilometre trek to the Johannesburg city centre after an increase of one penny in the fare sparked a massive boycott of* PUTCO *buses. Within a few days 60 000 commuters were boycotting the buses on the Reef and in Pretoria.*

place between 24-29 June, during which time nine people were killed and several houses destroyed, before 100 police armed with sten guns were able to restore order. Thousands of people sought refuge by camping out around the town's police station, while thousands more fled the township altogether. In August, after meetings between boycotters and the bus company, the fares were reduced to pre-boycott levels – and the boycott was called off.

The Alexandra boycott, which began the following year, was sparked when the Public Utility Transport Company (PUTCO), increased the fare between Alexandra and the city centre of Johannesburg by one penny in response to rising operating costs. On Monday, 3 January 1957, 15 000 people walked the nearly 15 kilometres to the city centre in a highly visual protest at the fare rise. At the same time, boycotts began in Sophiatown and the Pretoria townships – and by the end of the week 60 000 people had stopped using PUTCO buses.

The boycott lasted three months – during which most Alexandra commuters walked 30 kilometres every day, despite efforts by white sympathisers, particularly members of the Liberal Party, to organise lift clubs. As they walked they sang and chanted slogans such as 'asinimali' ('we have no money') and 'azikwelwa' ('we will not ride').

The boycott ended at the urging of the ANC (although Africanist ANC members urged that it continue) after a subsidised coupon scheme had been confusingly hammered out between PUTCO, the Johannesburg Chamber of Commerce and the Alexandra Transport Committee. However, the ANC involvement in the boycotts was never particularly strong – and it was later accused of a 'marked failure... to give positive leadership to the people of Alexandra'.

In contrast to the boycotters' solidarity, their leaders were seriously split: ANC Africanists were determined to maintain the action until all demands had been met, while others favoured calling it off when it began to show signs of faltering. The Alexandra boycott ended in early April, but continued for several more weeks in parts of Soweto where the Africanists were strongest. In Pretoria, the bus boycott lasted into 1958.

POLICE DEMAND *the Passes of workers who were carried by a sympathiser during the 1955 bus boycott.*

Fight for the right to vote

For nearly 40 years, while the thrust of segregation under the governments of Barry Hertzog and Jan Smuts was being directed at the African population, coloured people and Indians were able to maintain a relatively higher degree of privilege. But the new policy of apartheid introduced after Daniel Malan's National Party victory in 1948 drove both groups into a closer relationship with African nationalists, particularly after the National Party introduced legislation which removed the coloured franchise from the single voters' roll in the Cape.

A BRICKLAYER, a van driver, a trade unionist and a merchant. Four ordinary men who in the early 1950s suddenly found themselves in the front line of the battle to stop the newly elected National Party Government from ending the 100-year-old Cape tradition of a common voters' roll for white and coloured people. But for an extraordinary piece of constitutional gerrymandering, they would have succeeded.

When Daniel Malan's *Herenigde* (Reunited) National Party (HNP; NP after 1951) won the 1948 general election, about 48 000 coloured voters still retained a qualified franchise on the Cape electoral roll, despite attempts by the Nationalists to have them removed in the same way that qualified African voters had been disenfranchised in 1936.

Prior to 1948, however, the ruling United Party (UP) was firmly committed to the coloured franchise – knowing only too well that nearly all the 'coloured' votes were for their own candidates. Nevertheless, in 1943, the UP sanctioned the establishment of a so-called Coloured Advisory Council (CAC), ostensibly to alleviate poverty among coloured people as their reward for military service during the Second World War. Whether or not the council was philanthropically inspired, it divided coloured political leaders at the Cape – on the one hand, those prepared to collaborate, and on the other, those who, believing it was an instrument of segregation, formed the Anti-CAC (later Anti-CAD) committee, which then united with the All-African Convention to form the Non-European Unity Movement (see box).

Apartheid tightens its grip

Once in power, the Nationalists wasted little time in bringing the full force of apartheid to bear on both coloured and Indian people. The Prohibition of Mixed Marriages Act of 1949, the Population Registration and the Immorality Acts of 1950, followed by the Group Areas Act later that year, now began effectively to classify people by race and to determine their rights according to that classification. The prohibition of sex and marriage across the colour line erected humiliating and grievously painful barriers in communities where, in particular, coloured and white people had lived in harmony. In some cases, these barriers ran straight through families and extended kin.

Apartheid legislation, however, was not enough to satisfy the HNP diehards, who were determined to break once and for all the remnants of a Cape common voters' roll that had existed in one form or another since 1853. Nationalist Minister Ben Schoeman summed up the government's feeling in June 1949 when he said: 'We will take the Hottentots off the white man's voters' roll.'

And yet, despite these threats, the HNP was slow to take action owing to a difference of opinion between Malan and his parliamentary ally, Nicolaas Havenga, leader of the Afrikaner Party on whose six seats the HNP relied for its majority in parliament. Any action against the coloured franchise would require, as had been the case with the African franchise, that parliament obey the provisions of the South Africa Act which had set up the Union in the early

THE 1948 *white general election brought Daniel Malan to power with a burning determination to remove coloured people from a common voters' roll in the Cape. The full 1948 Cabinet was, back row from left: B J Schoeman, F C Erasmus, T E Dönges, A J Stals, E H Louw, S P le Roux. Front row from left: C R Swart, E G Jansen, D F Malan, G Brand van Zyl, N C Havenga, J G Strijdom and P O Sauer.*

Coloured voters in the Cape

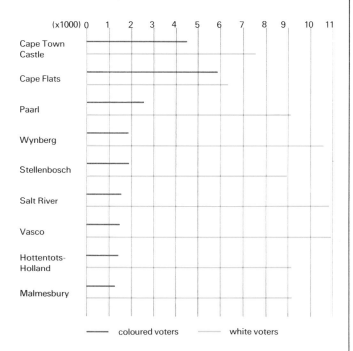

IN 1953 – *the last election before coloured people were removed from the common voters' roll – there were nine constituencies with significant numbers of coloured voters.*

years of the century. The constitution required that any change to its entrenched clauses be passed by a minimum two-thirds majority in a joint sitting of both Houses of Parliament.

Malan took the view that, since the enactment in 1931 of the Statute of Westminster by the British Parliament, the South African Parliament was sovereign over its own affairs and could therefore decide for itself the manner in which it would legislate in terms of the entrenched clauses. Havenga, however, disagreed. While the coloured franchise was of no particular importance to him, he nevertheless believed that parliament was bound by the special legislative provisions incorporated in the entrenched clauses. Malan, unwilling to compromise his party's majority in the House of Assembly through a feud with Havenga, let the matter lie for two years.

By October 1950, however, Malan felt strong enough to make an assault on the coloured franchise; he and Havenga had reached an accommodation on the basis of which coloured voters would be placed on a separate voters' roll and given the right to elect four white MPs, one senator and two members of the Provincial Council. The Separate Representation of Voters Bill was placed before parliament in March 1951. Despite UP objections that the procedures followed were unconstitutional, the Bill cleared both houses at separate sittings and by simple majorities, and was duly signed by the Governor-General in June.

The political struggle

The government's action sparked two reactions among coloured voters: a protracted legal battle against the legislation, and the creation of a new movement to protest their

Coloured, white or black?

One of the enduring myths in South Africa is the existence of a so-called 'coloured community', a separate group of people with a common heritage and culture that can somehow be lumped together in a convenient political grouping known as 'Coloured' (with a capital 'C').

Unlike Africans or Indians, with their different language and, in some cases, cultural backgrounds, there was no real difference between coloured and white people; they shared languages (Afrikaans and English), religions (mainly Christian Protestant) and aspirations (towards Western cultural and intellectual values). Therefore the only thing that made a coloured person different to a white person was the status that apartheid and its racial cornerstone, the Population Registration Act, gave him.

For example, a 'coloured' man in Britain or America is any person whose skin is darker than obviously white. When explaining to visitors from overseas who and what 'coloured' people are, South Africans are forced to add a quick explanation along the lines of: 'they are people of mixed descent'. Which is true, to a point, but even the Population Registration Act is unclear, sub-dividing 'Coloured' into no less than seven sub-groups: Cape Coloured; Cape Malay; Griqua; Indian; Chinese; Other Asiatic; and Other Coloured.

In a step towards unscrambling the difficulties, the NP 'think tank' on racial affairs, the South African Bureau of Racial Affairs (SABRA) argued that coloured people formed a *volksgemeenskap* (people's community) which possessed certain undefined characteristics 'which are inherently spiritual and traditional by nature, and find expression in attitudes, mental constructs, lifestyles and community forms'.

These rather imprecise words, however, did nothing to help the administrators of apartheid to unscramble the differences between white and coloured people – and they were forced back on the Population Registration Act, which used appearance and general acceptance as a member of particular group to determine whether a person was 'Coloured' or 'White'.

In a further bid to clarify the vital dividing line between the two, the Act even set up a special racial classification board to hear appeals from people who claimed they had been wrongly classified either as 'Coloured' or 'White' – using both genealogy and appearance in reaching its decision. Children of white and African (or coloured) parents automatically became 'Coloured', while the child of a coloured and African marriage took the classification of the father – which led to the intriguing possibility of a person being 'African' (according to the Population Registration Act) and 'Coloured' under the Group Areas Act. A person claiming to be white had to prove that both parents were white, or that he or she was white in appearance and accepted by other whites as such.

In order to ensure continued racial separation between coloureds and whites, in 1950 the government extended a 1927 law prohibiting sexual intercourse between whites and Africans also to cover sexual relations between whites and members of any other group. This Act was repealed in 1986.

threatened disenfranchisement, which quickly became allied to the national effort to mobilise for the Defiance Campaign of 1952 (see page 382). The new organisation was called the Franchise Action Committee and was first mooted at a meeting in February 1951, a month prior to the introduction of the legislation to parliament. The meeting

Apartheid and a colour-blind law

The basis of law in South Africa is called Roman-Dutch law, which means exactly what it says: a law based on ancient Rome modified by Dutch law introduced to the country by Jan van Riebeeck in 1652. Overlaying this are certain aspects of English law introduced following the British occupation of the Cape during the Napoleonic Wars.

This legal base is known as common law – and it is utterly colour-blind, treating all people as equals before the law. However, the South Africa Act of 1909, which set up the Union of South Africa, decreed that parliament would be the supreme law-giver, with the provision that certain entrenched clauses in the constitution – such as the coloured vote in the Cape and equal language rights – would require a two-thirds majority before they could be changed.

Because the law is colour-blind, every aspect of apartheid had to pass through parliament before it could become law – which is why it requires such a plethora of legislation. In the event of a dispute arising from a clumsily worded Act, judges tend to rule against apartheid, falling back on the basis of our law: common law.

An example of this was train apartheid, introduced after the 1948 election on suburban trains in the Cape (main line trains had been separated for years). A mass protest meeting was called in September 1948 on the Grand Parade under the auspices of a newly convened Train Apartheid Resistance Committee, which had managed to bring together the Communist Party and the Non-European Unity Movement (NEUM). The meeting was addressed by Abdullah Abdurahman, who urged those attending to break the new regulation by getting into any (railway) coach – for which he was prosecuted on a charge of incitement and fined £5. On appeal, however, this was set aside with the comment that the regulations were wrong because they resulted in unequal treatment between different races – whites could ride anywhere on the train, while blacks could only ride in the coaches reserved for them. This loophole was quickly closed by reserving certain coaches for whites only.

Supreme Court judges commented that it was 'the duty of the courts to hold the scales evenly between the different classes of the community and to declare invalid any practice which, in the absence of the authority of an Act of Parliament, resulted in partial or unequal treatment between different sections of the community'. The government responded by passing the Reservation of Separate Amenities Act in 1953, which not only gave it the power to segregate public facilities, but also stopped the courts from challenging it on the grounds that the different services provided were not equal.

included representatives from the major national organisations – the African National Congress (ANC), the South African Indian Council (SAIC), the African People's Organisation (APO) and various trade unionists. Only the left-wing Non-European Unity Movement (NEUM) rejected the committee, claiming that it focused only on the issue of the coloured franchise and did not adhere to its (the NEUM's) broader principles.

The Franchise Action Committee's appeal for support was in curious contradiction to the nature of the alliance which it represented; while, on the one hand, it was supported by the most pre-eminent African political movement (the ANC), its message to coloured voters was that the loss of the vote would reduce their status to the level of Africans, robbing them of that tenuous socio-economic status which placed them between white and African. While the Franchise Action Committee was able to organise a fairly effective strike in Port Elizabeth and Cape Town, it was the activities of the War Veterans' Torch Commando – with its massed torchlight rallies – that grabbed the headlines in 1951. This offshoot of the largely white Civil Rights League – which had collected 100000 signatures opposing the Bill – was made up mainly of white ex-servicemen opposed to the HNP. In May 1951, more than 50000 protesters took part in a march on parliament in Cape Town, clashing fiercely with police who tried to stop them (see box).

For its part, the Franchise Action Committee helped launch the Defiance Campaign in the western Cape. However, it attracted little support in the Peninsula, and the organisation began to fizzle out – until rejuvenated as the South African Coloured People's Organisation, which went on to organise boycotts against bus apartheid and protests against Group Areas removals.

Struggle in the courts

The Separate Registration of Voters Act set the scene for a major confrontation between the government and the courts. The Nationalists were fairly certain that the Bill could be passed by a simple majority of both Houses of Parliament, despite the provisions of the South Africa Act, which had entrenched the coloured franchise in the constitution – and which required a two-thirds majority of parliament in order to repeal the relevant clause.

But when the Bill was placed before parliament in March 1951, the UP immediately opposed it on the grounds that it violated the entrenched clauses of the constitution. The government's answer to this was that no parliament could bind its successor to special legislative procedures. Nor, it added, was morality an issue; in fact, it claimed, the Bill represented the higher morality of the people's will.

The Act was duly passed, but the battle now moved to the Cape Provincial Division of the Supreme Court after four coloured voters applied for an order restraining the electoral officer from removing their names from the common roll on the grounds that the Act was invalid. They were W D Franklin, a Woodstock van driver; W D Collins, a Cape Town businessman; Edgar Deane, a trade union worker; and Ganief Harris, a Woodstock bricklayer. The

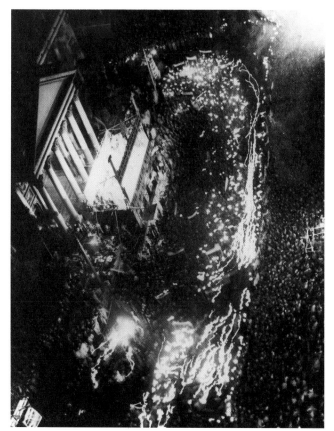

THE TORCH COMMANDO *organised huge protests around the country in an effort to halt coloured disenfranchisement.*

judge dismissed the application for the law to be set aside on the grounds that the court could not question the way the Act had been passed. The four appealed to the Appellate Division of the Supreme Court, which in February 1951 declared the Act null and void on the grounds that that it had not received the two-thirds majority assent of both Houses of Parliament.

Furious, the Nationalists hit back; Malan declared that the 'legislative sovereignty of the lawfully and democratically elected representatives of the people' had been denied. Just over a month after the Appellate Division judgment, the government introduced the High Court of Parliament Bill, making parliament the highest court in the land, with the power to overturn any judgment by a lower court. This, said the government, would save the courts from 'the invidious necessity of becoming involved in constitutional issues which have a party political bias or which impinge on the legislative sphere'. Again, the UP would have none of it; the Leader of the Opposition, J G N Strauss, described the measure as 'a bogus court set up to express the will of the caucus of the Nationalist Party'. Although there were waverers inside the Opposition, the UP vowed to fight the legislation in court. The Act came into force in June 1951, and was almost immediately taken to the Cape Provincial Division of the Supreme Court.

Parliament nevertheless constituted itself as the High Court during August and threw out the Appellate Division's judgment on the Separate Representation of Voters Act, thereby declaring the legislation valid. The Cape

Lighting the fire of protest

While many whites supported government assaults on the coloured franchise, a group of white ex-servicemen calling themselves the Torch Commando took to the streets to voice their opposition to the Nationalists, although their main objection was based not so much on coloured franchise rights, as on the legislative methods which the government intended to employ to achieve its ends.

The War Veterans' Torch Commando – whose membership (much of it based on UP supporters) peaked at 250 000 in 1952 – began its activities in May 1951, organising massed torchlight rallies of ex-servicemen in Cape Town, Port Elizabeth and Johannesburg. It called for the defence of the constitution and condemned the proposed legislation as a bitter blow to the hopes of coloured people. The Torch Commando generally sought to avoid taking a stand on the issue of African rights, and lost credibility with the coloured community – those it was sworn to defend – when it decided against admitting coloured ex-servicemen to its ranks.

As the constitutional battle developed, so the Torch Commando's membership grew, deciding to co-operate with the United and Labour parties in an effort to topple the government at the 1953 elections. The strategy failed because the Torch was unable to gain sufficient support in the rural areas. It had also become bogged down in an internal row over the vexed question of Natal secession. Its light began to fade soon after the elections, in which the Nationalists were returned with an increased majority.

EX-BATTLE OF BRITAIN *fighter ace 'Sailor' Malan was one of the main organisers of the Torch Commando.*

Provincial Division now temporarily suspended coloured voters from the common roll, in anticipation of a judgment on the High Court Act. But when the Cape Provincial Division turned its attention to that Act, in an application by the same four coloured voters, it overturned the new legislation. This decision was upheld by the Appellate Division in November on the grounds that MPs had no judicial training, nor could they sit in judgment on their own case.

Once more, the government had been defeated. Its remedy was to seek a mandate for the removal of the coloureds from the roll in the general election of 1953, and Malan called on Opposition voters to defect in sufficient numbers to give the Nationalists the two-thirds majority they required. He was to be disappointed; while the Nationalists were returned with 94 seats, the combined Opposition in the House of Assembly was 61.

Undeterred, Malan called a joint sitting of the two houses soon after the election in a bid to repeal Section 35 of the South Africa Act, which provided for coloured voting rights, and to validate the Separate Representation of Voters and High Court of Parliament Acts. He hoped to drive a wedge into the UP and win enough support for the Bills to get them through parliament and, in the process, destroy the unity of the Opposition. But he overplayed his hand, declaring in September 1953 – shortly before the third reading of the new Bill – that he would divide the Appellate Division into three divisions which would separately deliberate on civil, criminal and constitutional matters. That was enough to send the UP dissidents back to the fold and when the measure – after returning from a select committee – finally came before the joint session of parliament for its final reading in June 1954, it failed to get the two-thirds majority by nine votes.

Malan, now 80, had given the coloured vote his best shot; now the issue would fall to his successor. He had hoped that Eben Dönges would succeed him and had resigned the Cape leadership of the NP a year before in order to improve Dönges' status in the party. His immediate strategy was to keep out the ailing Strijdom by trying to secure Havenga's election as a caretaker Premier, who

---

Coloured politics and the

NEUM *ideologue and president of the Anti-CAD group, Dr Goolam Gool.*

In the heyday of apartheid coloured political leaders were split into three main groups: those who believed in the concept of a coloured ethnicity in order to improve their lot, those who insisted that the struggle by coloured people to attain equality with whites was no different to that of Africans and Indians; and those who believed that all working-class people – white and black – faced the same predicament under the heel of the white (and possibly the black) capitalist.

Which does not mean that those in the first group were necessarily compliant. On the contrary, many of them were the most vocal in political agitation to improve the living standards and political rights of coloured people. However, they urged their followers to take pride in their status as 'coloureds' in order to seek and attain equality with whites.

Coloured political leaders were drawn from the upper and middle class – mainly teachers, with a sprinkling of professional people, artisans and small businessmen. They formed a small cadre of leadership at the top of a very large pyramid of urban and rural poor, whom they treated with a distinctly patronising attitude – such as the call by the grand old man of coloured politics, Abdullah Abdurahman, for a ban on liquor sales to coloured people.

Inevitably, this upper echelon enjoyed privileges that set it apart from both its poorer brothers and the Africans; an elite status that rested on income, occupation, religion and position in society – and, in some instances, on a lighter skin colour. Not surprisingly, many coloured politicians became even more concerned with retaining and advancing these privileges than with creating a totally equal society, regardless of skin colour. Those who remained true to the latter, however, displayed another characteristic: a preoccupation with theory and ideology that often left their followers – and African allies – confused and sometimes bewilderingly angry. This was particularly so among the far left.

The formation of the Coloured Advisory Council (CAC) by the Smuts government in 1943 brought this split clearly into the open, with the almost immediate formation of an Anti-CAC (later Anti-CAD) organisation. While the pro-CAD members achieved some reform of purely 'coloured' grievances through co-operating with the government, the Anti-CAD faction concentrated on theoretical ideals of class conflict – which held little appeal for the working-class coloured man, who often found the promise of protection from the cheaper competition of African labour more compelling than the theoretical arguments of the Anti-CAD group.

Nevertheless, the Anti-CAD group, with its broader view of the liberation struggle, did attain greater unity with African freedom groups. This was particularly so in 1943 when it allied with the All-African Convention (AAC), which had been formed in 1935 to oppose the 1936 Natives' Land Act and the disenfranchisement of Cape Africans, to form the Non-European Unity Movement (NEUM).

The NEUM declared as its aim the 'liquidation of the National Oppression of the Non-Europeans in South Africa' and the 'acquisition of all those rights which are at present enjoyed by the European population'. The founding congress adopted a 10-point programme calling for, among other things, equal franchise, free and equal education, civil liberties, redivision of land, and equal labour laws.

would soon give way to Dönges. But Strijdom's supporters were stronger, and secured his nomination.

Strijdom resolved the crisis in just over a year. His first step was to alter the structure of the Appellate Division, increasing its membership from five to 11 and requiring a Full Bench to deliberate on constitutional matters. The new Appellate Division judges were carefully selected for their adherence to the Nationalist view of parliamentary sovereignty. Then Strijdom pushed through the Senate Act of 1956, which increased the number of elected senators from 48 to 89 – and ensured that they would be elected by MPs and Members of Provincial Councils (MPCs) on a simple majority basis from each province. This meant that instead of the old system, under which the number of NP senators had to be proportionately the same as the number of seats it held in a particular province, the NP could now appoint all the senators from a particular province, provided it controlled more than 50 percent of the MPs and MPCs in that province. As the party controlled all the provinces except Natal, it was a simple step to pack the Senate with

government supporters, changing its composition from 29 Nationalists and 19 Opposition senators to 77 Nationalists and only 12 Opposition senators (eight from Natal and four 'native' representatives). The rest was a formality; during the 1956 session of parliament the two houses sat together again – and this time the government easily gained its constitutionally required two-thirds majority, by 173 votes to 68.

Once again the law was challenged by coloured voters – but this time, with the required two-thirds majority backing it, the Act was upheld. Only one Appellate Division judge, O D Schreiner, dissented, arguing that the legislation had been passed in a manner which attempted to circumvent the provisions of the South Africa Act.

In the end, however, the Nationalists won – and Harris and his fellow voters had to be content with a separate voters' roll that led first to special representatives in parliament, then to a 'Coloured Persons Representative Council' and finally to the House of Representatives in the tricameral parliament of P W Botha (see page 472).

'working class revolution'

The ideological leader of the NEUM was Dr Goolam H Gool, a medical doctor descended from an old-established Cape Indian family, and brother-in-law of Cissie Gool, the daughter of Abdullah Abdurahman. Gool was a disciple of Leon Trotsky, one of the founders of Bolshevism in Russia who had argued for a permanent revolution of the working class proletariat – earning the hatred of Stalin, who forced him to leave Russia in 1929 and had him murdered while exiled in Mexico in 1940.

The Trotskyite base of the NEUM ensured that its leadership base remained among a tightly knit intelligentsia who were determined to maintain the Marxist line that there was no difference between the working class white man and the working class black man. 'We, the non-European oppressed, must never confuse the European worker . . . with the European ruling class.' The real ally of the white worker, they argued, was the black worker. The Trotsky faction had no desire 'to replace the white *Herrenvolk* (master race) by a black *Herrenvolk*'. This view was decidedly to the left of the African National Congress (ANC) whom they dismissed as 'quislings' and 'collaborators' who were 'unprincipled' and 'unprepared', describing mass action organised by the ANC and its allies as 'spectacular stunts'. The ANC reacted to these jibes with cool indifference,

regarding the movement as unrepresentative and unimportant.

The NEUM preferred a programme of non-collaboration and boycotts – aimed not only at 'white' institutions, such as the 1952 Van Riebeeck Festival, but also at ANC activities.

The hardline attitude of the Anti-CAD faction in the NEUM made it extremely difficult for other political organisations to collaborate with an organisation dedicated to non-collaboration. Those who did not toe the party line became increasingly unwelcome – including, after a while, the Anti-CAD allies in the NEUM, the All-African Convention, which grew increasingly despondent with what was described as the never-never land of dialectic theory. The immediate problem, members of the convention argued, was how to create equality with the whites. The Anti-CAD faction, however, saw only 'class oppression and denied the reality of colour oppression'.

The differences simmered on until 1958 when the Africans re-wrote the last sentence of point seven of the 10-point programme to read: 'Our programme demands the lawful acquisition of land within the Capitalist society of which we are a part.' To the Trotskyites from the Anti-CAD this was rank heresy and an 'acceptance of the *status quo*'. After a bitter war of words, the Anti-CAD group pulled out of the NEUM in 1959.

BENNY KIES *edited and wrote most of the NEUM's newspaper, 'The Torch'.*

With the anti-CAD faction out of the picture, the African group under the leadership of Isaac Tabata formed the All-African People's Democratic Union, which retained its communist ideals. A government crackdown on the organisation in the 1960s forced many of its leaders – including Tabata – overseas. Others were imprisoned on Robben Island. The union went into decline after failing to persuade the Organisation of African Unity to recognise it as a liberation movement.

The Unity Movement itself was resurrected as the New Unity Movement in 1985.

Shots that echoed around the world

On 6 April 1959, exactly 307 years after Jan van Riebeeck landed in southern Africa,
300 former members of the African National Congress (ANC) met in Soweto
to form the Pan-Africanist Congress (PAC). Led by the charismatic Robert Sobukwe,
the new organisation launched its first major assault on apartheid – a campaign against the Pass laws
– on 21 March 1960. Sixty-nine people died in the southern Transvaal township of Sharpeville
when police opened fire on protesters. A few days later 30 000 PAC supporters
marched on the Caledon Square police station in Cape Town.

EARLY MORNINGS ON THE HIGHVELD are chilly – even in summer. And on 21 March 1960, as the first rays of sunshine slanted across the monotonous rows of houses in Vereeniging's Sharpeville township, hundreds of workers, collars turned up against the cold, headed for the Seeiso Street terminus to board the buses that would take them to work at the nearby steel mills and factories in the Vaal triangle.

Talk that morning was not the usual banter about friends and weekend revelries. Instead there was whispered apprehension about a crudely typewritten document that had been circulated in the township four days earlier, calling for a general work stoppage in the Vereeniging area on Monday, 21 March. Tension was palpably in the air.

As the early morning commuters began arriving at the bus terminus, they were met by members of the newly formed Pan-Africanist Congress (PAC), who urged them to heed the stayaway call. Some workers drifted off, others waited for buses that never came: their drivers had been warned the day before not to report for duty.

Countdown to upheaval

Compared with other African townships, Sharpeville could almost be described as a model township. Named after Vereeniging's mayor, John Sharpe, when it was established in 1942, it now housed some 21 000 people in homes that contained running water, sanitation and, in some cases, bathrooms.

And yet, as the 1950s ended, residents were far from happy. Unemployment, particularly among the township's large population of young work-seekers, was rife; there were not enough high school places to accommodate Junior Certificate holders, and strict influx control measures prevented youngsters from moving to the Witwatersrand to seek work. Added to this was the relative newness of the community: most of the residents had moved to the new township from a nearby area called Top Location. But not all had been able to afford the higher rents; and those who could not had been shipped back to the 'homelands' – much to the anger of the relatives and friends they had left behind.

POTLAKO LEBALLO (left), one of the leading Africanists in the ANC, joined Robert Sobukwe (right) in forming the breakaway Pan-Africanist Congress after both had been barred from the second day of the 1958 ANC Transvaal provincial congress by stick-wielding loyalists.

THE PAC EXECUTIVE *in September 1959. Front row, left to right: A B Ngcobo, Robert Sobukwe, A P Mda (not a member), P K Leballo and H S Ncgobo. Back row: J D Nyaose, E Mfaxa, Z B Molete, P Molotsi, S T Ngedane and H Hlatswayo.*

All this made the residents of Sharpeville – and the nearby African townships of Bophelong, Boipatong and Evaton – receptive to the message of the PAC.

Founding of the PAC
The massive anti-Pass campaign initiated by the PAC, and launched on 21 March, had its origins in the organisation's breakaway from the African National Congress (ANC) late in 1958. The split had been developing since the foundation of the Congress Youth League (CYL) under the leadership of Anton Lembede in 1944. Lembede had argued for the adoption of an Africanist philosophy to enable Africans to regain their sense of self-worth – even if this meant a ban on cooperation with other groups that had thrown their weight behind the liberation struggle (see page 363).

But by the time the CYL had gained ascendancy in the ANC in 1949, many members – including Nelson Mandela, Walter Sisulu and Oliver Tambo – had been won over to the idea of a liberation struggle and future democracy in which the contribution of non-Africans would also be welcomed. Although a small bloc continued to argue for the adoption of Africanist principles, their appeals were overwhelmingly rejected by their colleagues.

Ironically, it was the arrest of many of the ANC's top activists on charges of treason (see page 389) that led to the revival of the fortunes of the Africanists: with many of the ANC's leaders languishing in prison, day-to-day leadership of the organisation passed into the hands of less experienced members. By the end of 1957, serious dissension had broken out within the ranks of the Transvaal ANC, which the Africanists – led by Potlako Leballo and Robert Sobukwe – were quick to exploit. At the national conference of the organisation in December of that year, they proposed a motion of no-confidence in the Transvaal executive which, although it was defeated, led to the calling of a special meeting in February 1958 at which the grievances of dissident branches were discussed. The meeting was chaotic; fistfights broke out and

Leballo's call for regional executive elections – backed by a majority of delegates – was ignored by the chairman. Two months later, the Transvaal ANC's call for a stayaway to coincide with the white general election flopped badly. With Leballo and Josias Madzunya (a flamboyant Africanist from Orlando) making capital of the latest disaster, the national leadership met secretly in May, expelled them both from the ANC, and took control of Transvaal affairs. Meanwhile, in the run-up to the general election, the government had imposed a ban on meetings of more than 10 Africans, and this temporarily denied the Africanists a chance to press home the advantage.

The crunch came in November 1958, at a Transvaal provincial congress at which office-bearers were to be elected. With Africanists planning to run their own candidate for regional president, a major test of strength loomed. In a speech that set the tone for the meeting, national president Albert Luthuli warned delegates against the 'racial extremism' the Africanists represented. Thereafter, speakers were heckled and fistfights threatened to break out on several occasions. The first day of the session ended with a decision that only accredited delegates would be permitted to attend the following day, when the elections were to be held. The next morning, dissident delegates were faced by a phalanx of stick-wielding loyalists, determined to keep them out. Rather than settle the matter violently, the Africanists conferred outside the hall and decided to leave the ANC to form their own movement. The PAC was formally established on 6 April 1959.

'Africa for Africans'
The agenda for the first meeting – in a shabby communal hall in the township of Orlando, Soweto – began with the preamble: 'Today, three hundred and seven years ago began the act of Aggression against the Sons and Daughters of Afrika [the arrival of Jan van Riebeeck at the Cape], by which the African people were dispossessed of their land, and subjected to white domination. As it was here, and on this day that it began, it is imperative that it should be here, and on this day that it should be buried.' Placards reading 'Africa for Africans'; 'Cape to Cairo'; 'Morocco to Madagascar'; and 'Imperialists quit Africa', lined the walls. Greetings from Kwame Nkrumah of Ghana and Sékou Touré of Guinea were read out.

Sobukwe, a 35-year-old lecturer at the University of the Witwatersrand, was elected president and Leballo national secretary. Sobukwe, the natural ideological successor to Lembede, was convinced of the strategy of boycott politics and determined not to allow the principles of African nationalism to be compromised by cooperation either with white liberals or with the limited political institutions created by the white authorities for Africans. He was elected national secretary of the CYL in 1949, but faded into the background as the ANC began to enhance its popularity during the early 1950s (see box).

Described as a sincere idealist with a clear, incisive mind, he taught in Standerton in the eastern Transvaal during this period – which is why he was sidelined – then moved to Johannesburg where he re-entered the fray and subjected the ANC's leadership to sharp attacks.

The PAC set itself a target membership of 100 000, to be achieved by July 1959; but by August, the figure had reached only 27 000. The new movement also committed itself to the implementation of the Programme of Action drawn up by the CYL and accepted by the ANC in 1949. Sobukwe believed the programme was more than a strategy simply to move the ANC towards a militant posture; that it embodied – a long-term scheme to help Africans shake off their mentality of defeat and acquiescence, but that this had been ignored by the ANC leadership.

The PAC's first major effort in 1959 was the 'status campaign', aimed at persuading whites to refrain from calling Africans 'kaffir' or 'native' and other racially derogative terms, on pain of boycott and picketing. The campaign faltered and as the year wore on the leadership realised that it would have to pull off a major activist coup if it was to attract a substantial following. Sobukwe also believed that the mood among Africans was ripe for a bold initiative against apartheid. African leadership had hung back too long for fear of failure or of antagonising whites; the PAC,

Robert Sobukwe and the 'United States of Africa'

In 1949 a young man in his final year addressed the graduating class at the University College of Fort Hare in the eastern Cape. He called on his African audience 'to carry with you into the world the vision of a new Africa, an Africa reborn, an Africa rejuvenated, an Africa recreated, young Africa...'.

Robert Mangaliso (meaning 'wonderful') Sobukwe was born in the small Cape town of Graaff-Reinet in 1924. His father was a labourer and his mother had no formal education. He won a scholarship to the Methodist boarding school at Healdtown in the eastern Cape, and from there he went to Fort Hare, where generations of young Africans were politicised, and where he joined a branch of the African National Congress (ANC) Youth League established at the university by Godfrey Pitje, a prominent Youth Leaguer and later its president.

After Fort Hare he worked as a teacher in Standerton in the eastern Transvaal – but lost his job when he spoke out in support of the Defiance Campaign in 1952. He returned to teaching and in 1954 became an instructor in African languages at the University of the Witwatersrand where he soon began to criticise the ANC for allowing itself to be dominated by 'liberal-left multi-racialists'. He ardently believed in an 'Africanist' future for South Africa, rejecting the idea of working with whites.

On a public platform, 'the Prof', as he was affectionately known to his friends and colleagues, could be a charismatic speaker, but he was a self-effacing man who was surprised when chosen to head the PAC at its inaugural congress. But his ability as a speaker, his shining intelligence and his deep-rooted duty-bound commitment to his cause had already marked him out as a natural leader.

When he resigned his university post in order to present himself for arrest (for not carrying a Pass), he issued an impassioned call to 'sons and daughters of the soil' to fight 'for the noblest cause on earth, the liberation of mankind'. He accused the authorities of 'fighting to entrench an outworn, anachronistic, vile system of oppression', while the PAC represented 'progress'. 'They represent decadence. We represent the fresh fragrance of flowers in bloom; they represent the rancid smell of decaying vegetation. We have the whole continent on our side. We have history on our side. We will win! Forward then, to independence now, tomorrow the United States of Africa.'

On the morning of 21 March – the date he had set for the start of his anti-Pass law demonstration, Sobukwe

SOBUKWE *put the Africanists' case to* ANC *members during their 1958 Transvaal congress. The next day he was barred from the meeting.*

rose at 2 am, made a few last-minute arrangements for the safety of his family, and left his Mofolo home at 6 am to walk the 8 kilometres to Orlando police station, where he planned to present himself for arrest. As he set out in the cold early morning, small groups of men joined him from the neighbouring areas of Phefeni, Dube and Orlando West.

By the time he reached the police station, Sobukwe was at the head of a small crowd – most of whom were arrested, including Sobukwe himself. He was sentenced to three years in jail – after which he was kept in 'preventative detention' on Robben Island for a further six years. When finally released, he was restricted by a banning order that prevented him from playing any active political role. He died in 1978.

however, had no such qualms. It would set an example . . . .

The Pass laws had long been a particular source of frustration and humiliation for millions of Africans – and it seemed to both the ANC and the PAC that action in defiance of them might provide the long-sought trigger for popular resistance.

Thus Sobukwe proposed an anti-Pass campaign to begin ahead of a similar campaign called for by the ANC – on 21 March instead of the ANC's date of 31 March – in which PAC leaders themselves would play a prominent part. The slogan would be: 'No bail, no defence, no fine.' Sobukwe put it this way: 'I will lead you, I will be in front. The thing is for the mothers to put food away, put money away, we will call you. We may not come back from where we are going to. Passes, permits, that is their waterpipe. [We will] close that waterpipe.'

For Sobukwe himself, that statement was prophetic. The plan was announced in December, the same month in which the ANC announced its own campaign. As the organisers moved out to promote their anti-Pass action, the signs seemed auspicious: momentum was gathering for an international trade boycott of South Africa; British Prime Minister Harold Macmillan had made his famous speech in which he warned that the winds of African nationalism were blowing everywhere in Africa; there was an upsurge of resistance   riots in Durban claimed the lives of nine policemen and there were violent reprisals against 'collaborators' in Pondoland.

In Cape Town, the PAC campaign had surprising appeal – more than 2 000 Africans gave Sobukwe an enthusiastic welcome at Langa. When the ANC announced 31 March as the starting date of its campaign, the PAC knew it would have to begin earlier to capture the initiative.

The police open fire
On 16 March, Sobukwe informed the Commissioner of Police that the PAC would begin 'a sustained, disciplined, non-violent campaign' on the Monday five days hence, and two days later he announced the date at a Press conference: 21 March. He told the Press: 'I have appealed to the African people to make sure that this campaign is conducted in a spirit of absolute non-violence, and I am quite certain they will heed my call. If the other side so desires, we will provide them with an opportunity to demonstrate to the world how brutal they can be.'

Despite the PAC's optimism, the campaign began with every indication that it would prove to be yet another spectacular failure. But for the events at Sharpeville, it might have gone relatively unnoticed. The PAC decided that all African men were to leave their Passes at home and present themselves for arrest. As the prisons filled up, the country would grind to a halt and Passes would be abolished. Full 'freedom' for Africans in South Africa would have been won by 1963 when the whole continent would have been 'liberated' from its colonial masters.

HOW THE PEOPLE *of Johannesburg received their first news of the shooting at Sharpeville – the 'Star' on Monday, 21 March 1960. The final toll was 69 dead and 180 injured.*

BRITISH PRIME MINISTER *Harold Macmillan warns the South African Parliament of the 'winds of change' in Africa.*

But liberation was still a long, long way off, as the people of Sharpeville were about to discover . . . .

By 10 o'clock a crowd estimated at between 3 000 and 5 000, and described by eyewitnesses as expectant and cheerful, had gathered in the centre of Sharpeville. At the same time, about 4 000 people from the nearby townships of Bophelong and Boipatong began a march to Vanderbijlpark police station. At Evaton, about 18 kilometres from Sharpeville, 20 000 people assembled outside the police station. Both groups were dispersed – in Vanderbijlpark by a baton charge that left one person dead, and by low-flying jets at Evaton.

In Sharpeville the jets were welcomed with a waving of hats. One of the crowd, Tom Petrus, later recalled: 'The aeroplanes were flying high and low. The people were throwing their hats to the aeroplanes. They thought the aeroplanes were playing with them.'

Meanwhile, the police were growing increasingly jittery. Reinforcements were called for, and by lunchtime about 300 policemen, most of them facing a crowd situation for the first time, had arrived in the township. At 1.15 pm a scuffle broke out outside the wire fence surrounding the police station. In the tussle that followed a portion of the fence was trampled and a police officer pushed over. The front rank of the crowd moved forward, pushed by curious onlookers from behind.

It was then that police opened fire, apparently spontaneously and without any order having been given to do so. The front rank of the crowd immediately turned to flee, but could not get through the crush of people behind. Panic gripped the people as they tried to escape – most of those killed were later found to have been shot in the back.

Among the wounded was Adam Malefane, whose right leg was hit by nine sten gun bullets. He spent more than three years in hospital after the shooting – and was left a cripple with three bullets lodged in his knee. But he did not regret his decision to join the Pass law protest. 'The reference book was like a rough chain on our necks,' he said many years later.

Press reports described the scene: a policeman atop a Saracen armoured car swung his sten gun in a wide arc, raking the crowd. Bodies lay scattered about in grotesque positions, strewn in the road and on the pavement. The wounded fled into back yards and side streets. Little children ran like rabbits. One by one, the guns stopped. The

SHARPEVILLE, *21 March 1960: 'Most of the bodies were strewn on the road . . . one man who had been lying still, dazedly got to his feet, staggered a few yards, then fell in a heap . . . . One by one, the guns stopped.'*

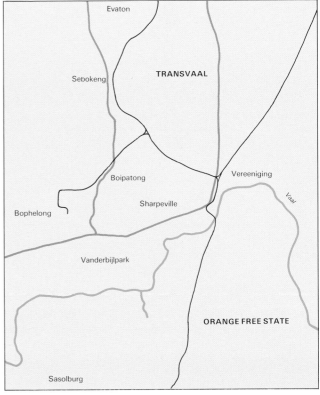

WHILE THE CROWD *gathered at Sharpeville, 4 000 Africans left Bophelong and Boipatong for the Vanderbijlpark police station, and a further 20 000 people assembled at Evaton.*

police stepped out from behind the wire, stunned and disbelieving. Then the ambulances came. Later, two truckloads of bodies were taken to the mortuary.

In a few terrifying moments, the people of Sharpeville had learned that flesh and blood were no match for guns and bullets. Sixty-nine of them had been killed, and a further 180 wounded.

A day of mourning

News of the Sharpeville 'massacre' was received with horror in South Africa and around the world. Luthuli called on Africans to observe 28 March as a day of mourning, and there was a massive stay-at-home as a result. Panicky whites rushed to arm themselves, and gunshops in the Transvaal and the Cape quickly sold out. Share prices plunged on the Johannesburg Stock Exchange as investors began a wave of selling sparked by the general upheaval;

TEARS FLOWED *when 34 of those who had died at Sharpeville were buried by the Rev Z M Voyi of the Anglican Church.*

'The people thought they'd heard fire crackers'

Eyewitness accounts of the shooting at Sharpeville speak of the disbelief that greeted the opening shots – and then the terror as the bullets sliced through the crowd.

One of them was Tom Petrus, who later recounted the shooting in a book published by Ravan Press called 'My Life Struggle'. 'The aeroplanes were flying high and low. The people were throwing their hats to the aeroplanes. They thought the aeroplanes were playing with them. They didn't realise that death was near . . . . Fortunately for me, they [the police] could not shoot on the side where I was standing. That is how I managed to get away. People were running in all directions . . . some couldn't believe that people had been shot, they thought they had heard fire crackers. Only when they saw the blood and dead people, did they see that the police meant business.'

The assistant editor of 'Drum' magazine, Humphrey Tyler, arrived in Sharpeville shortly before the shooting. 'We went into Sharpeville the back way, behind a big grey police car and three Saracens. As we drove through fringes of the township many people shouted the Pan-Africanist slogan "Izwe Lethu", which means "Our Land", or gave the thumbs up "freedom" salute and shouted "Afrika!". They were grinning, cheerful, and nobody seemed to be afraid . . . . There were crowds in the streets as we approached the police station. There were plenty of police, too, wearing more guns and ammunition than uniforms . . . . An African approached . . . and said he was the local Pan-Africanist leader. He told [us] his organisation was against violence and that the crowd was there for a peaceful demonstration . . . . The crowd seemed perfectly amiable. It certainly never crossed our minds that they would attack us or anybody . . . . There were sudden shrill cries of "Izwe Lethu" – women's voices it sounded – from near the police, and I could see a small section of the crowd swirl around the Saracens and hands went up in the Africanist salute.

'Then the shooting started. We heard the chatter of a machine gun, then another, then another. There were hundreds of women, some of them laughing. They must have thought the police were firing blanks. One woman was hit about ten yards from our car. Her companion, a young man, went back when she fell. He thought she had stumbled. Then he turned her over and saw that her chest had been shot away. He looked at the blood on his hand and said: "My God, she's gone!"

'Hundreds of kids were running, too. One little boy had on an old blanket coat, which he held up behind his head, thinking, perhaps, that it might save him from the bullets. Some of the children, hardly as tall as the grass, were leaping like rabbits. Some were shot, too. Still the shooting went on. One of the policemen was standing on top of a Saracen, and it looked as though he was firing his sten gun into the crowd. He was swinging it around in a wide arc from his hip as though he were panning a movie camera. Two other officers were with him, and it looked as if they were firing pistols.

'Most of the bodies were strewn on the road running through the field in which we were. One man who had been lying still, dazedly got to his feet, staggered a few yards, then fell in a heap. A woman sat with her head cupped in her hands. One by one the guns stopped. Before the shooting, I heard no warning to the crowd to disperse. There was no warning volley. When the shooting started it did not stop until there was no living thing in the huge compound in front of the police station.

'The police have claimed they were in desperate danger because the crowd was stoning them. Yet only three policemen were reported to have been hit by stones – and more than 200 Africans were shot down. The police also have said that the crowd was armed with "ferocious weapons" which littered the compound after they fled.

'I saw no weapons, although I looked very carefully, and afterwards studied the photographs of the death scene. While I was there I saw only shoes, hats and a few bicycles left among the bodies. The crowd gave me no reason to feel scared, though I moved among them without any distinguishing mark to protect me, quite obvious with my white skin. I think the police were scared though, and I think the crowd knew it.'

THOUSANDS OF PEOPLE *rest on the banks of De Waal Drive during the march on Cape Town. Tension mounted as the estimated 30 000 marchers set out from their homes in Langa and Nyanga, heading for Caledon Square police station.*

foreign consulates were flooded with enquires about emigration, and the government introduced legislation to outlaw the ANC and the PAC. Serious rioting now shook Johannesburg's townships and, nationwide, all police leave was cancelled as patrols and arrests were stepped up.

Although a commission of enquiry was held into the events at Sharpeville, what actually happened is still subject to sharp dispute. Only a few of the central facts are clear: no order to shoot was given, no warning shots were fired, and the firing continued for up to 30 seconds as the crowd fled.

It is obvious, though, that the nerve of some of the young policemen had suddenly snapped after hours of tension as the crowd, estimated at between 3 000 and 20 000, grew.

The mood of the demonstrators was also disputed: sympathetic witnesses described the people as calm, peaceful, even friendly, and certainly unarmed. The police, however, disagreed: the crowd, they argued, had been hostile, aggressive and armed with sticks and stones.

The report of Mr Justice P J Wessels, who led the commission of enquiry, was inconclusive: pointing to the contradictory evidence from either side, he said it was impossible to ascertain with any measure of accuracy when the order to fire was given, although it appeared that the police officer in command had immediately tried to halt the firing. 'It was clear that some time elapsed between the giving of the order to cease fire and the actual stopping thereof,' the Judge remarked.

The march on Cape Town

On the eve of the Sharpeville shooting, a 23-year-old university student and branch organiser for the PAC in Cape Town, Philip Kgosana, addressed 5 000 'sons and daughters of the soil' in meetings at Langa and Nyanga on the Cape Flats, and called on them to heed the anti-Pass law protest. 'How long shall we starve amidst plenty in our fatherland?' he asked. 'How long shall we be a rightless, voteless and voiceless majority in our fatherland? This is the choice before us: we are either slaves or free men.' The next morning, 21 March, a crowd of 6 000 men gathered in the rain outside the bachelor quarters at Langa in preparation for a march to Langa police station in order to invite arrest for leaving their Passes at home. After being warned by police that a march would be regarded as an attack on the police station, Kgosana asked the crowd to disperse, calling on them to reconvene at 6 pm to hear 'word from the national office [of the PAC]'.

In the meantime, to ensure that no one attempted a march on the police station, PAC pickets were ordered to keep demonstrators at a safe distance.

A smaller crowd, including many women, also gathered at Nyanga and a party of volunteers set out for Philippi police station, where they were arrested. Meanwhile, the police station at Langa was reinforced with Saracen armoured cars and more men armed with sten guns, riot sticks and revolvers. Later that day, news of the Sharpeville massacre reached the township.

Kgosana travelled to Cape Town for a meeting with a leading white liberal and son of a former Governor-General, Patrick Duncan, who told him: 'You have poked the bees but you must be careful. Anything can happen tonight.' Kgosana, according to Duncan, was only too aware of the volatility of the situation and the 'ever-present possibility of violence erupting'.

While Kgosana was in Cape Town, a new crowd of 6 000 gathered in Langa late that afternoon in anticipation of the 6 pm meeting – despite warnings issued from loudspeaker vans banning meetings in the area. At 5.45 pm the police arrived and, after giving an order to disperse, made two baton charges. When the crowd retaliated by throwing stones, the police opened fire, killing two people and forcing the rest to flee.

A POLICEMAN *holds a loudspeaker aloft as Philip Kgosana appeals to the marchers to go home peacefully.*

Recalling the moment he arrived back at Langa station, Kgosana later told the magazine 'Drum': 'As we emerged from the subway I saw soldiers with sten guns lining the fence. Suddenly I heard a volley of shots. I stopped as though a thunderbolt had hit me. Another volley, then another, and the crackle of isolated shots. I felt a great sorrow and confusion. What could have happened?

'I ran towards the shooting. I met a woman who had been hit in the arm. Her hand was swollen and she wore no shoes. She walked very fast. I asked anxiously: "Hei, Mamma, what happened?"

'"Police, my son, police…we were sitting quietly and they fell upon us with batons." She walked away very fast.

'Again a volley rang out – koko, koko, koko, koko, thu-khu, thu-khu. And another volley. I felt that every bullet was felling a man. Ra ta ta ta ta ta, thu-khu. Oh, our people are being finished! I felt like crying. I felt like bursting. I was panting with frightened anger. I cut through the fleeing crowd, as the shooting stopped. I called out: "What happened? How many have been killed?"

'Fortunately the police were firing high, but even so a friend's sister-in-law told me that one person had been killed. I felt relief…but there was still a commotion going on. People cut electric wires, pulled down poles, set a telephone booth, the permit office and the general administration buildings on fire.'

Suddenly a fellow PAC worker warned Kgosana that the police had ordered the crowd to disperse in three minutes. He had argued that the time was not enough… while he

Leading a march on Cape Town

It was the day that Cape Town held its breath – and for a moment the future of South Africa seemed to rest on the young shoulders of a 23-year-old University of Cape Town student who had been propelled into the public eye by a massive police crackdown that had left him the senior Pan-Africanist Congress (PAC) leader on the Cape Flats.

And as 30 000 Africans from Langa and Nyanga began marching to the city centre to protest against police action, Philip Kgosana, dressed in blue running shorts and a frayed brown jacket splattered with mud, appeared at the head of the march, taking control and insisting that the marchers behave peacefully.

A few days earlier, on the eve of the anti-Pass campaign that had led to the Sharpeville shootings, Kgosana had sternly admonished his followers against violence: 'We are not leading corpses to a new Africa,' he said.

The son of a preacher, Kgosana was born in 1936 at Makapansgat near Hammanskraal, nearly 60 kilometres outside Pretoria. As a child he spent more time herding cattle than attending school, but he eventually completed his schooling and persuaded the Institute of Race Relations to give him a grant to attend the University of Cape Town, enrolling in 1959. Living in Langa, with virtually no money, he often had to walk the 8 kilometres to the university.

Intelligent and a forceful speaker, he gravitated to the Africanists and at a PAC meeting in Johannesburg in January 1960 was made regional secretary for the western Cape, abandoning his university studies to become a full-time organiser. It was a fateful choice: 'I realised I had come to the crossroads. If I were to do my duty to my party and my people, it would mean that I would have to neglect my university career.'

After his arrest on 30 March 1960, Kgosana was allowed out on bail so that he could travel, under strict conditions, to the Transvaal to see his family for Christmas. He used the opportunity to flee the country, seeking exile first in Basutoland (Lesotho) and then in Tanzania. In April 1994, while working for the United Nations in Botswana, he returned to South Africa to vote.

PHILIP KGOSANA *returned in 1994 to the scene of his arrest more than three decades earlier.*

was still arguing a policeman hit him on the head with a baton, and firing broke out.

That night the township exploded in rioting as black policemen's homes were attacked, the municipal offices burnt down, telephone lines cut and roads blocked in order to keep out fire tenders. 'At 9 pm we . . . listened to the radio. We heard the news that over 60 had been killed at Sharpeville, and about 140 injured . . . our riot was also mentioned. As we entered Langa we were stopped. There were two Saracens and a fire engine at the entrance. Torches flashed in our faces.'

Early the next morning when police raided hostels in Langa and beat up many of the occupants, Kgosana went into hiding. 'We hid in a nearby yard,' he said, 'but the police flushed us out. We scattered and ran with the police after us. I managed to jump over a fence and dived into some tall grass.' He was spotted by a woman who made him tea – and when he introduced himself, she said: 'Goodness, my son, you are brave.' Later that afternoon, he emerged for another meeting with Duncan.

The following day he was a guest for dinner at Duncan's home, along with luminaries such as Thomas Ngwenya of the ANC and tobacco magnate Anton Rupert. According to Duncan, it was a 'useful and friendly meeting', although Rupert, a government supporter, was apparently heavily patronising, comparing immature African political development to unripe fruit. Nevertheless, the meeting fell into line with Kgosana's own expressed desire to put pressure on industrialists who would then appeal to the government to lift the Pass laws so that workers could return to work.

The following day – Thursday, 25 March – a PAC regional executive member, Wilson Manetsi, left Langa with 100 volunteers to present themselves for arrest at Cape Town's Caledon Square police station – which prompted an even bigger number, estimated at between

2 000 and 5 000, to gather in front of the police station the next morning, with Kgosana and three of his PAC colleagues at their head. A meeting was held with police chief Ignatius Terblanche, who was told by one of the PAC men that the people outside were ready to surrender themselves for arrest. Terblanche, however, said he had no intention of arresting anybody – and went on to announce that for the following month no one would have to show their Passes in the Cape Town area. Kgosana, who had earlier been arrested, was released just after noon and carried off shoulder high by the crowd. That evening, the Pass law suspension granted by the police chief was extended to cover the whole country.

With the weekend looming, the PAC concentrated on getting food supplies into the strike-torn townships, and arranging for the funerals of the victims of Tuesday's shootings – which took place at Langa in the presence of 50 000 mourners. No police were present – and the crowd was controlled by the PAC using a public address system organised for them by Terblanche.

State of emergency

On Wednesday morning, the government declared a state of emergency and 1 500 people were arrested in countrywide swoops. In Langa, police broke into several houses and shot at those attempting to escape. It was this last act that probably triggered what happened next – an apparently spontaneous gathering of people from Nyanga and Langa who began walking – and then marching 12 abreast – towards the centre of Cape Town.

When Terblanche heard they were coming he fell to his knees in prayer – while troops and police resorted to more practical measures, digging in machine-gun emplacements around Parliament while a helicopter whirred ominously overhead. Equally surprised was Kgosana, who was still in bed when he heard that the men were on

The strike continued sporadically for another 10 days – and then police, reinforced by the army and navy, invaded the townships and crushed the strike that had paralysed Cape Town industry for several days. Food deliveries to Nyanga and Langa were stopped by police, who used sticks, batons, crowbars, guns and armoured cars to beat township residents into submission. The final crushing stroke came on Thursday, 7 April, when police arrested 1 500 people. By the following Monday the strike was virtually over.

Marching on Durban

While most PAC activity was centred on Johannesburg and Cape Town, Durban, too, had its share of upheaval when, on 31 March and 1 April 1960, thousands of Africans set out from Cato Manor along various routes to try to reach the city centre. Most of them were driven back by police – and armed white civilian onlookers who fired into the crowd – although one group of about 1 000 marched through the main shopping area to the central jail to demand the release of ANC activists detained on 30 March. Unrest continued in the area for the next week or so after the ANC had called for a 10-day work stoppage. What would prove to be the last peaceful mass demonstration organised by the congresses prior to their being declared illegal organisations was over.

Throughout the country, strikes were swiftly and brutally broken, thousands of Africans were rounded up for the most minor offences, and political activists were arrested in droves. On 8 April, nine days after Kgosana's dramatic march and 18 days after Sharpeville, the government banned the ANC and PAC. Sobukwe, who had been arrested on 21 March, was jailed for three years, then held until 1969, orders for his detention being renewed annually in terms of a special clause – known as the 'Sobukwe clause' – in the government's new emergency powers.

Although the unrest was not a serious attempt to overthrow the government, it convinced many activists of the need for a programme of armed insurgency.

The events of the last 10 days of March 1960 were a watershed in the history of the African liberation struggle: non-violent protest and civil disobedience had failed to move the Nationalist Government, and by the end of 1960 peaceful, non-violent protest was seen to have accomplished nothing: instead the ANC and the PAC were forced underground, making it impossible for them to pursue such forms of protest in future.

Before being outlawed, both organisations sent leaders overseas to set up offices in exile. Oliver Tambo was driven over the border into Bechuanaland (Botswana) by a sympathetic white magazine editor named Ronald Segal to head the ANC's external mission. In June 1961 he and internal ANC leaders met to consider a proposal for a campaign of violent protest, to be carefully controlled to cause minimum bloodshed. The ANC decided to retain its official policy of non-violence, but to set up a military wing, *Umkhonto we Sizwe* (the Spear of the Nation), which, unlike the ANC proper, would be open to non-Africans. At roughly the same time a movement dedicated to violent insurrection was formed among members of the PAC (see page 408).

OLIVER TAMBO *was driven over the border into Bechuanaland (now Botswana) to head the* ANC's *external mission.*

the march. He was given a lift to the head of the procession near the railway line between Athlone and Pinelands, and immediately asked those in the front why and where they were marching. He was told that they were protesting against the police raids of that morning – and that their destination was Caledon Square. After a brief discussion, Kgosana persuaded them to head, instead, for the Houses of Parliament.

Nationwide, African activists were convinced that the hour of liberation was at hand, that the pressure of strikes and protests must eventually gain sufficient momentum to bring the NP Government to its knees. Now, close to noon on the streets of central Cape Town, all hope, all fear focused on the marchers. Yet they themselves were peaceful, cheerful and unthreatening; they were obeying a strict injunction against violence and of disrupting traffic. Thousands more joined the marchers at Mowbray station – and the long procession, 30 000-strong, then headed along De Waal Drive and down towards the Roeland/Buitenkant Street intersection – where, in answer to a request by the Detective Head Constable of Cape Town, Kgosana agreed to call off the march to Parliament and head for Caledon Square instead.

Kgosana again met Terblanche – who promised to arrange a meeting between him and the Minister of Justice, J M Erasmus, on condition that the marchers returned home. Kgosana agreed, and the marchers walked back the way they had come. But when he arrived for the promised meeting, he was promptly arrested.

Fighting fire with fire

By the end of 1960, the stayaways, the boycotts, the pressure of moral rectitude, growing international dismay and the horror of Sharpeville had failed to sway the Nationalist Government from its chosen course of apartheid. Many African activists now reasoned that the only avenue left was to fight fire with fire. A wave of sabotage followed, organised by *Umkhonto we Sizwe*, the newly formed military wing of the African National Congress (ANC), and acts of terror, orchestrated by *Poqo*, the armed wing of the Pan-Africanist Congress (PAC).

FROM EARLY MORNING they queued – endless lines of defeated, shuffling men whose short fire of resistance to apartheid had died with the flames of their burning Passes and the bullets of Sharpeville in the heady days of March, 1960. Their brief dream of halcyon freedom was over – their sobering return to harsh reality was only just beginning.

All over the Highveld and at various government offices in the western Cape, the eastern Cape and Natal the picture was the same: thousands of Africans waiting to apply for new Passes to replace the ones they had burnt so confidently only weeks before in gleeful response to calls by the ANC and PAC for protest against the Pass laws.

Watching them were the forces of law and order – the police – who had moved so swiftly and decisively to crush the protest movement after the declaration of a state of emergency on 30 March. Strikes were broken, crowds were fired on, the ANC and the PAC were banned in April and 18 000 people arrested by early May. Parliament and the white public were told that the flashes of black popular dissent had been ignited by agitators bent on fomenting a communist revolution by stirring the passions of normally 'law-abiding, peace-loving, unsophisticated Bantu'. In dismissing the ANC and the PAC as unrepresentative of African sentiments, a Nationalist MP told the House of Assembly that '99 percent of the Bantu people support the policy of apartheid'.

In an attempt to keep the fires of revolt burning, the newly banned ANC issued a statement committing itself to the continuation of the struggle, and calling for a week-long stayaway to begin on 19 April. But their call was ignored. The will of blacks to resist had given way to their need to survive the growing harshness of the apartheid state.

Sharpeville, nevertheless, precipitated a major economic crisis. Share prices on the Stock Exchange tumbled dramatically and many fortunes were wiped out; the currency came under enormous pressure as confidence crashed and foreign investors began a stampede out of their South African holdings. In 18 months – from January 1960 to June 1961 – foreign reserves dropped from R315 million to R142 million. Even the mighty Anglo-American Corporation was forced to borrow heavily from United States banks.

But both the economy and the government were far more resilient than foreign investors believed: among the measures introduced by the state were the imposition of new controls on imports in order to make up balance of payments deficits; a ban on the repatriation of profits earned by foreign investors; and the enactment of new controls on the export of capital. The result was a rapid build-up of reserves of private capital, which in turn led to the expansion of economic activity and a rise in share prices.

By the end of 1961, the crisis had passed; immigration began to pick up, emigration slowed down, and the major financial institutions which had picked up shares at rock-bottom prices began to reap the reward.

The treason trial (see page 389), together with the state of emergency and its concomitant arrests and bannings, had effectively raked off the leadership of the black resistance movement. Those who escaped the security net, among them Oliver Tambo, were forced to slip out of South Africa to begin the long task of organising resistance from abroad. It was a time for all the players in the South African drama to take stock.

The state of emergency was lifted in stages between May and the end of August 1960. But resistance by the rural peasantry of Pondoland in the eastern Cape continued; at issue were high taxation, government conservation measures and unpopular headmen. After more than two dozen people had been murdered, homesteads burnt and some white motorists stoned, the government moved in troops and declared a state of emergency over Pondoland.

HUTS BURN *in Pondoland, Transkei, on the road between Flagstaff and Bizana during violent protest against high taxation and unpopular headmen. More than 24 people were killed and hundreds made homeless in the unrest.*

VETERAN *political campaigner Helen Suzman (left) helps erect a poster urging whites to vote against the formation of a republic during the referendum of October 1960. After a heated campaign of posters and political rallies, the answer was a narrow 'yes'. On 31 May the following year, Charles Robberts Swart became the first President of the new republic, promising to 'do justice unto all and to devote myself to the well-being of my people'.*

Moves towards a republic

In a referendum in October 1960, whites voted by 52 percent to establish a republic, thus bringing to fruition the cherished dream of Nationalist Afrikanerdom – a final break with British imperialism. At first Prime Minister Hendrik Verwoerd had declared South Africa's intention to remain within the Commonwealth. But when he arrived at the Commonwealth conference in mid-March to a barrage of criticism over his government's apartheid policies, he withdrew the Union's request for continued membership and broke all ties with the Commonwealth.

By now even traditional allies began to distance themselves from South Africa – and in April 1961, at the United Nations, Australia and the United Kingdom lined up for the first time behind a United States resolution calling on member states to consider what action they might take to bring about an end to apartheid.

Picking up the pieces

With the lifting of the emergency, African liberals and former members of the now banned ANC and PAC began slowly to pick up the pieces of the resistance which had been shattered by the state in the preceding months. In December 1960, at a conference in Orlando, a start was made at re-establishing unity after the ANC-PAC rupture, and a call was made for a national convention to press for constitutional change. But the differences which had led to the original ANC-PAC split again emerged – and when a conference which gave rise to the formation of a National Action Council (headed by Nelson Mandela) was held in Pietermaritzburg late in March 1961, it was dominated by former ANC members. Even its tactics were similar to those of the banned organisation: thus its first action was a call on the government to establish a national convention with

'sovereign powers' by 31 May, failing which a strike and widespread demonstrations would be held.

As the deadline drew closer, tens of thousands of pamphlets announcing plans for a three-day strike and a massive display of 'non-cooperation' were distributed. As a new wave of fear began to spread through white communities, the government moved quickly to meet the new threat: a ban was slapped on all gatherings; the police presence in African townships was stepped up; helicopters patrolled likely trouble-spots; contingency arrangements were made for the manning of essential services; and up to 10 000 people were detained. These measures were effective, and the first day of the strike, 29 May, was a disappointment to Mandela. The next day he called off the campaign.

A switch to violence

For nearly 80 years, African, coloured and Indian leaders of all political persuasions had addressed white governments with fervour and compassion, seeking by peaceful, legitimate means to gain participation and representation in the government of South Africa. Now it seemed to many black activists that the society created by decades of segregation and apartheid was inherently violent, that perhaps only violence itself could destroy the will of whites to govern by force and to remake a non-racial society based on internationally accepted democratic principles. And yet 'inter-racial' violence held the risk of creating horrendous scars and of pushing the country towards civil war. The decision to adopt violent struggle was therefore taken only after much soul-searching by men who considered themselves both principled and patriotic.

As white republicans celebrated their first days free of the last shackles of the now-faded British Empire, black

South African leaders reached the conclusion that peaceful protest against those shackles that bound their own liberty had been explored to no avail. At a secret meeting of the ANC's national executive in June, Mandela presented a memorandum arguing that the time had come for Africans to go over to armed struggle as the means to their end. The document was 'carefully considered' and the executive finally agreed that, although the ANC would not abandon the policy of non-violence, it would not discipline those of its members who decided to do so.

The president of the ANC, Dr Albert Luthuli, was kept informed of these developments, but the fact that he was confined to his home at Groutville in Zululand meant that there was little he could do to exercise a restraining influence on the membership. In October 1961, a few days after the Nationalists won their fifth term of office with 105 of the 160 seats in parliament, it was announced in Norway that Luthuli had won the Nobel Peace Prize. His restriction order was lifted for just long enough to enable him to receive his award.

With tacit approval by the ANC that its members could initiate an armed struggle, Mandela, other ANC cadres and members of the now-underground South African Communist Party acquired Lilliesleaf Farm in Rivonia, some 30 kilometres north of Johannesburg. There these members of the national high command of the armed wing, to be known as Umkhonto we Sizwe (Spear of the Nation), set up

ALBERT LUTHULI *pictured with Senator Robert Kennedy of the USA. Kennedy was invited to South Africa in 1966 by the National Union of South African Students* (NUSAS).

their operational headquarters and began to establish small regional networks, many of whose members were, it is now believed, drawn from the ranks of the South African Congress of Trade Unions. The smallest operational unit was the cell, comprising four men. In theory, policy was set by the high command while the cells chose targets, which were approved by the regional commands. In its early days, Umkhonto concentrated on economic sabotage and political targets, attempting to avoid or postpone action which would endanger human lives.

The first attacks began on 15 and 16 December in Durban, Johannesburg and Port Elizabeth. Umkhonto expressed the hope that the bombings would 'bring the government and its supporters to their senses before it is too late, so that the government and its policies can be changed before matters reach the desperate stage of civil war'. The targets were Bantu Administration offices, post offices and other government buildings, electrical and railway installations and equipment. During the next 18 months, 200 such attacks were carried out. But lives were nevertheless at risk as undisciplined cell-members attacked policemen and collaborators. Mandela slipped out of the country in January 1962 and began preparations and training for guerrilla warfare, undergoing a course at a training camp in Algeria. He returned home on 20 July and was arrested while driving through Natal on 5 August. (In 1986, nearly a quarter of a century after Mandela's incarceration, a retired American Central Intelligence Agency (CIA) operative who had been stationed in Durban under diplomatic cover at the time, disclosed that he had given the police the tip-off which led to Mandela's capture. The CIA has never confirmed or denied the claim.)

A SMILING *Nelson Mandela in 1961. He was born into the royal house of the Tembu in what is now Transkei.*

The terror of *Poqo*

If the ANC's leadership had been severely affected by the emergency, the PAC's had been decimated, which partially explains the nihilistic violence generated from within certain quarters of the latter movement. If the ANC's *Umkhonto* cadres were guerrillas, the PAC's *Poqo* members were driven by an apparent hatred of whites and prepared to kill at random. *Poqo* means 'standing alone' in Xhosa, which in many ways characterised the movement and its members: these were small, isolated bands of men, mostly unemployed and living in the towns, whose only real connection with the PAC was an ill-defined support for its leader Robert Sobukwe and their embracement – sharpened by the brutality of their urban experience – of the cruder strains of separatism espoused by the independent African churches at the turn of the century.

These groups were centred mainly in the western Cape and Transkei, and were formed after a power struggle in the underground PAC during 1961, in which those with strong links to migrant labour in the hostels emerged victorious. The organising of cells followed these lines: groups of up to 10 men who came from the same rural area often shared accommodation and worked together. A pamphlet distributed in the Cape Town township of Nyanga in December 1961 summed up their intentions: 'We are starting again Africans . . . we die once. Africa will be free on 1 January. The white people shall suffer, the black people will rule. Freedom comes after bloodshed. *Poqo* has started. It needs a real man. The Youth has weapons so you need not be afraid. The PAC says this.'

Potlako Leballo, who had been jailed with co-founder Sobukwe and other PAC leaders in 1960, was released from prison in May 1962. Having been born in Maseru, capital of the British protectorate of Basutoland, he was able to return there and immediately set about trying to re-organise the PAC. But the first *Poqo* groups were already acting independently of any central command. At 2.30 am on 22 November 1962, 250 men armed with pangas, axes and other makeshift weaponry, marched out of the Mbekweni township near Paarl and formed two groups, one to attack the nearby prison and the other the police station. A bus driver spotted them approaching the sleeping town and raised the alarm, and police intercepted the second group advancing down Main Street towards the police station. Shops were attacked and up to 100 men advanced on the police station. As they approached, the police opened fire and killed two; the others scattered and joined the second group marching down Loop Street towards the prison. With hope of a successful attack now gone, the *Poqo* insurgents attacked three houses, killing a man and a woman and wounding three others. By 5 am, the attackers were in full retreat as police reinforcements arrived on the scene.

Then, on 5 February 1963, five whites – including a woman and two young girls – were attacked and killed as they lay sleeping at the roadside at the Mbashe River Bridge in Transkei. Both these events – the latter in particular – sent a chill down the spine of white South Africa.

Leballo, meanwhile, was making plans for a general uprising in April. He sent messages to PAC cells within South Africa, many of which were intercepted and their recipients arrested; the police were thus well informed on the progress of the PAC's planning and were able to nip any major insurrection in the bud by rounding up thousands of PAC supporters and suspects. Leballo had not been able to resist the temptation to boast; he had declared at a press conference in March that he had more than 150 000 PAC members poised to give a 'knock-out blow' to white South Africa when he gave the word. Shortly afterwards, a PAC emissary from Leballo was arrested while in possession of letters earmarked for PAC cadres and, when Basutoland police raided the PAC headquarters, membership lists were found and passed on to the South Africans.

Hundreds were arrested in the massive crackdown which followed. At the same time, the PAC leader Robert Sobukwe, who was due to be released in May following his arrest on the day of the Sharpeville shootings, was held in detention under special legislation. Although isolated incidents of terror and murder were to continue for a while, the PAC was effectively smashed.

The government hits back

On the very day of the announcement that ANC president Luthuli had won the Nobel Peace Prize, Justice Minister John Vorster served notice that the government was contemplating tough legislative measures 'to limit the freedom of speech and movement of agitators'.

MINISTER *of Justice John Vorster gave the police increased powers and introduced strict legislation aimed at curbing the activities of the opponents of apartheid.*

Much of the police's success in breaking the back of the first efforts by the black resistance to launch an armed struggle was related directly to the reorganisation of the police force under Vorster and the passage through parliament of tough security legislation. The government was anxious to avoid declaring another state of emergency for fear of upsetting the newly restored but fragile confidence of international investors and drawing further diplomatic fire. What eventually followed was the Sabotage Act of June 1962, which gave the Minister extensive powers to restrict the liberty of political activists, enabling him to place 'communist agitators' such as veteran campaigner Helen Joseph, and Walter Sisulu, under house arrest.

The Act also required new newspapers to deposit large sums of money which would be forfeited if the publication was later banned; it defined a large number of activities which could be constituted as dangers to public safety and health, law and order; even trespass and the illegal possession of a weapon fell within the ambit of this law, which carried a minimum sentence of five years' imprisonment and a maximum of the death penalty; and the onus was on the accused, once it had been established that he had been guilty of the offence, to prove that he had acted without political motivation.

'Ninety-day' Act

More was to follow. In 1963, Vorster introduced new legislation with the specific intention of crushing *Umkhonto we Sizwe* and *Poqo*. This was the General Law Amendment or 'Ninety-day' Act, in terms of which any commissioned police officer was given the power to detain a suspect without a warrant for his arrest, on suspicion of political activities, and to hold him – without access to a lawyer – for 90 days for questioning.

The two men responsible for the development of South Africa's security machine – John Vorster and Hendrik van den Bergh – had come a long way together. Both had been members of the *Ossewabrandwag* and had been interned together at Koffiefontein during the war years. Towards the end of the 1920s, the South African Police had appointed members of its Criminal Investigation Department to maintain a watching brief on security matters and groups which the government regarded as politically suspect. During the Second World War, this special branch had cooperated closely with Military Intelligence, then transferred its attentions in the post-war years to the black resistance movement. But, being poorly staffed, its success in this area of activity was at best limited.

When Vorster became Minister of Justice in 1961, one of his earliest steps was to promote Van den Bergh to the head of the Security Police. Vorster then used the political machinery at his disposal to create vast new powers for the Security Police which, armed with real teeth, were at last able to come to grips with the perceived 'revolutionary' threat of the black political movements. The partnership was extremely successful, and Van den Bergh ultimately rose to became Vorster's chief security advisor – secretary for state intelligence after the latter succeeded to the premiership when Verwoerd was assassinated in 1966. Thereafter, the Bureau of State Security became the para-

FORMER OSSEWABRANDWAG *member Hendrik van den Bergh was promoted by Vorster to head the security police.*

mount co-ordinator of all state intelligence and counter-intelligence activities. Together, these two men loomed larger than life over the security apparatus of the state for nearly two decades, until both fell from grace over the Information scandal in the late 1970s (see page 452).

The police swoop

One of Van den Bergh's protégés, and perhaps the most intelligent and cunning security officer of the Nationalist era, Johan Coetzee, had infiltrated one of his agents, Gerard Ludi, into *Umkhonto we Sizwe*. Acting on his information, police surrounded Lilliesleaf Farm in Rivonia on 11 July 1963. When they burst in, they found virtually the whole leadership of *Umkhonto*: Walter Sisulu, who had skipped bail after facing a six-year jail term, Govan Mbeki, Raymond Mahlaba, Ahmed Kathrada, Lionel Bernstein of the Congress of Democrats and Bob Hepple, a lawyer. At the moment the police came through the door, the six men were studying Operation Mayibuye, an *Umkhonto* proposal for guerrilla war, insurrection and revolution. Hundreds of incriminating documents were found, more arrests followed, including that of Dennis Goldberg, a Cape Town engineer and Congress of Democrats leader; Arthur Goldreich, who lived on the farm; Harold Wolpe, the lawyer who had used SACP funds to buy the farm; and others. Goldreich and Wolpe later bribed their prison guards and made a spectacular escape.

Mandela the 'black pimpernel'

As the new decade of the 1960s dawned, it seemed to the members of the African National Congress (ANC) that the freedom they had sought for so long must be close.

Three of them, in particular, were determined to take a stronger line in opposing government policies – Oliver Tambo, Walter Sisulu and Nelson Mandela. All of them had come up through the ranks of the ANC's Youth League and were now holding leadership positions on the ANC's national executive.

Coincidentally, all three had been born in Transkei, Tambo and Sisulu into modest peasant families, and Mandela into the royal house of the Tembu. Both Mandela and Tambo studied law, and even worked as partners in an ill-fated legal practice in Johannesburg in 1952. Mandela spent two years at the University of Fort Hare before being expelled for his part in a student protest. He moved to Johannesburg where he studied law, first by correspondence and then at the University of the Witwatersrand.

Tambo had also been expelled from Fort Hare – after a student strike in 1949. He then taught at a prestigious African school in Johannesburg called St Peter's – clearly having an inspirational effect on many of his pupils who later joined him as members of the ANC's Youth League, of which he was a founder member and became treasurer.

While Mandela was a commanding figure, Tambo struck a more austere note, described as 'characteristically silent and thoughtful'. He was also a puritanical Christian. Mandela was more forceful, but could also be remote. Nevertheless, he became a pragmatic and astute strategist.

Very different to both of them was Walter Sisulu, described by Tom Lodge in 'Black Politics in South Africa since 1945' as a 'dour-looking figure: short, stocky, often hidden in the folds of a wide-lapelled overcoat, bespectacled and with a habit ... of biting his bottom lip in between making terse polemical statements'.

Sisulu also had a very different background to that of his colleagues. Born into a poor peasant household near Engcobo, he worked as a labourer in East London and Johannesburg before a spell on the gold mines. Originally a believer in racially exclusive nationalism, he became a firm advocate of alliance between non-African political groups. He became secretary-general of the ANC.

For nearly 10 years from the early 1950s, Mandela had been forced increasingly to lower his profile as the government harassed him and other leading ANC figures through banning orders and jail sentences. He made a single public appearance between 1952 and his eventual appearance in the dock in 1962, when he received his first long jail term. But in the 28 months between Sharpeville and his arrest, Mandela cut a dramatic, almost swashbuckling resistance figure as he went underground and stayed on the run, so much so that he was dubbed by the Press as the 'Black Pimpernel'. Forced to abandon his wife, Winnie, and his children, Mandela travelled in disguise throughout South Africa, acting as chief spokesman for the ANC, giving interviews to the Press and even British television, meeting with influential, sympathetic white opinion-makers, and trying to re-organise the ANC as an underground movement as well as mobilising activists for the establishment of *Umkhonto we Sizwe*.

In January 1962, six months after persuading the national executive of the ANC to accept the formation of *Umkhonto* and barely a month after the launch of the armed wing's first attacks, Mandela slipped abroad for six months. He met African leaders who pledged support for armed struggle, as well as the leaders of the British Labour and Liberal parties – visits which greatly enhanced his international reputation and broadened the interest which his later trial attracted throughout the world. He also began to study guerrilla warfare, undertook a training course at a camp in Algeria, and began setting up study and training opportunities for young ANC members abroad.

Appearing in court during the so-called 'Rivonia trial', Mandela made a statement from the dock which has become one of the central documents of justification for armed struggle. He denied that the ANC was a communist organisation but said the association between the two movements was based on the communists' acceptance of Africans as equals, and described himself and his ANC colleagues as African patriots.

Finally, he said: 'During my lifetime I have dedicated myself to this struggle of the African people. I have fought against white domination, and I have fought against black domination. I have cherished the ideal of a democratic and free society in which all persons live together in harmony and with equal opportunities. It is an ideal which I hope to live for and to achieve. But if needs be, it is an ideal for which I am prepared to die.'

IN 1952 *Mandela practised law with Oliver Tambo in Johannesburg.*

TAMBO *was described as 'characteristically silent and thoughtful'.*

MOSES KOTANE, *general secretary of the South African Communist Party, was named a co-accused in his absence at the Rivonia trial. His communist links helped him organise funding for the ANC from Eastern bloc nations.*

Ten defendants were brought to trial in October 1963, charged with recruiting guerrillas with the intention of violently overthrowing the state, furthering the objectives of communism, and seeking foreign funds for these purposes. Twenty-four co-conspirators were listed, including Oliver Tambo, J B Marks, Moses Kotane and Alfred Nokwe, who had all left the country. All were defended by Braam Fischer, who would himself later be jailed for his role in the Communist Party and would remain in prison until he contracted cancer, and the authorities released him to die at home.

All the accused pleaded not guilty, claiming that the government should be on trial as it was the government, not the ANC, which was responsible for the situation in

---

One man's war against apartheid

A young member of the South African Communist Party was given five minutes to decide whether or not to join *Umkhonto we Sizwe*, the newly formed military wing of the African National Congress at its formation in December 1961.

David Kitson, who spent 20 years in jail for his part in the sabotage that followed, recalled that moment in an interview with the magazine 'African Perspective', published in 1984.

'They needed me,' remembered Kitson, 'because I was a mechanical engineer and... had served in the army during the war as a Sapper, and knew about... demolitions.' Instead of five minutes, however, Kitson said he would give them his decision the next day.

The answer was yes.

Kitson was working at the time for a large Johannesburg engineering company – and his office became a clearing house for *Umkhonto*. 'People would phone me – there was a whole battery of phones serving this firm, so it was difficult for anybody to monitor them, and I don't think I was even suspected.' Kitson passed on messages – either on the telephone or in person.

His main job, however, was as a technical advisor to *Umkhonto we sizwe*. 'We had to consider how to perform various demolition operations, and how to make various timing devices for explosives and the like. People would come from training in the Soviet Union and China, and we would find out from them what they had learnt there and see if we could apply it to our local practice.... Among the things that we considered... were how to make

Molotov cocktails, how to make hand grenades of the jam-jar type... which could be made from bits of tin and wood and the like by ordinary people. We learnt from the Chinese that gunpowder was considered the people's weapon because anybody could make it.... However, we got quite a lot of dynamite because people used to steal it for us.... And of course various targets were blown up or attempts were made to blow them up....'

Later, Kitson joined the logistics committee, a sub-committee of the national high command of *Umkhonto*, with the job of figuring out the logistical problems of conducting a guerrilla war, such as clothing, medical requirements and armaments. 'The aim of *Umkhonto* was to engage in various acts of sabotage, with great care being taken not to cause any injury or loss of life.'

The police raid on Lilliesleaf Farm in Rivonia decimated *Umkhonto*'s leadership. Kitson, however, escaped – because he was ill in bed with influenza. He remembers the day of the raid vividly: 'I felt bloody miserable because it seemed everybody had been caught.'

Before long he was helping to organise an escape route in order to get wanted people out of the country. 'People would arrive in Johannesburg and we would hide them somewhere while we found out whether they were kosher or not, what their credentials were, and if we were satisfied we would assist them to leave the country.'

Meanwhile Kitson was also helping to re-establish *Umkhonto*, starting up a new national high command with three other members. 'Our atti-

tude now was that each branch had to be self-sufficient. We would provide the general policy and the idea of the target we should attack, and teach them how to make gunpowder and explosives and how to make devices which could be used to time the explosion of gunpowder....'

With the Rivonia trial in progress, however, they did not wish to do anything that might jeopardise the outcome of the trial. 'However, this didn't mean that all acts of sabotage were excluded... and we diverted our attention to blowing railway lines up.' They were careful, however, to avoid derailing trains, merely forcing them to stop. Other targets, he said, included 'the apparatus of apartheid like the Bantu commissioners' offices... and economic targets... to persuade the people in power that they had to start dealing with us'.

Umkhonto also discussed the elimination of state witnesses at the Rivonia trial, but this was decided against because of the 'bad effect it might have upon the trial'.

A few weeks after the end of the Rivonia trial Kitson was arrested in his office and spent the next few days under interrogation 'with 12 police at a time giving me a go.... I was kept awake and standing. This just went on until I said something and I finally decided that I had better say something before I broke down completely and told them everything....'

During the interrogation period, said Kitson, he was held in solitary confinement and allowed no reading matter other than the Bible. Found guilty of sabotage, he was sentenced to 20 years in jail. After his release, he left South Africa to settle in London.

South Africa. However, documents handed in at the trial detailed a plot by four groups of 3 000 armed men to arrive by sea and to be joined by 7 000 local guerrillas to embark on a 'massive onslaught on selected targets' – while a political body was set up in a neighbouring state eventually to become the provisional government of the country.

The Deputy Attorney-General of the Transvaal, Dr Percy Yutar, told the court that the trial was 'a classic case of the intended overthrow of the government of a country by force and violence, with the military and other assistance of foreign countries'. He said it was a 'great pity that the rank and file of Africans... have been duped by false promises of free bread, free transport, free medical services, free housing and free holidays to have embarked upon a policy of violence'.

On 12 June, two days after the United Nations Security Council called on the South African Government to end the trial and release the defendants, the judge sentenced Mandela and eight of the others to life imprisonment. Most of them were flown immediately to Robben Island to begin their sentences.

But the violence was not yet completely over: on 24 July, John Harris, a former Liberal who had joined the African Resistance Movement – formed by radical liberals and Trotskyites – exploded a bomb on Johannesburg railway station, killing a woman, cruelly disfiguring another, and injuring dozens more. He was sentenced to death and hanged. Resistance, both violent and non-violent, had finally been crushed, its leaders were in jail, its activists scattered, and the people on whose behalf it had been waged would remain cowed by the might of the security forces for another decade.

POLICE *on guard outside the Pretoria Supreme Court during the trial of Nelson Mandela and other* ANC *activists who had been arrested at Lilliesleaf Farm, Rivonia, on 11 July 1963.*

AT 4.27 PM *on 24 July 1964 Johannesburg's 'Rand Daily Mail' newspaper received an anonymous telephone call warning that a time bomb was set to explode in the main concourse of the Johannesburg station in six minutes' time. Right on schedule, at 4.33 pm, the bomb exploded, injuring 23 people, one fatally. Six hours after the blast, police arrested a 27-year-old schoolteacher named Frederick John Harris at his home in Hamberg near Roodepoort and charged him with murder and sabotage. Harris, who had been banned under the Supression of Communism Act in January 1964, was a member of the African Resistance Movement and chairman of the South African Non-racial Olympic Committee (*SANROC*). *He was sentenced to death and went to the gallows singing the American civil rights song 'We shall overcome'.*

Swinging with the 'Jazz Maniacs'

The 'Boston Stars', 'Gay Gaieties', 'Manhattan Brothers', 'Synco Fans', 'Jazz Maniacs' and 'Pitch Black Follies'.

If you think these were American jazz groups from the 1930s and '40s you'd almost be right: All of them were, in fact, South African – and they arose from an obsession with American music, particularly black American music, that dominated African popular culture in the cities, particularly Johannesburg, before, during and after the Second World War. And it took root in South Africa after the demise of the indigenous *Marabi* sound.

It is hardly surprising that South African musicians should have looked to American jazz and harmony for inspiration – in many ways, American blacks had to make the same difficult transition from a rural to a city environment, adapting the traditional African rhythms that had accompanied them on the slave ships first into blues and then into jazz. In addition, Africans were quick to notice that the one area where many underprivileged American blacks had earned recognition and respect was through their ability to make music.

Nowhere was this urge to make music stronger than in Sophiatown, the west Rand suburb where freehold land-ownership and a jostling, ambitious community set the pace of African urban life for three decades before the arrival of the apartheid bulldozers at the end of the 1950s (see page 427). In shebeens (illegal drinking houses) such as 'Aunt Babe's', 'The House on Telegraph Hill' and 'The Back of the Moon' customers could listen to the latest jazz recordings from the USA – and to the home-grown musicians who tried their best to copy them.

When not entertaining the drinkers, bands such as the 'Merry Blackbirds' stomped their way through wedding receptions, funerals and birth celebrations, while the guests wore American-cut 'zoot suits' and mouthed American slang. Apart from listening to music, urbanised Africans keenly watched black American singer Lena Horne croon her way through films such as 'Stormy Weather' and 'Black Velvet'. To sound and look like an American was 'hep'.

The movies brought a new dimension to the music of Sophiatown – vaudeville, a song and dance routine that could hold a concert audience enthralled for an entire evening, such as 'Africa', featuring the 'Pitch Black Follies', or the 'Synco Fans' variety troupe backed by the 'Synco Beats Band'.

The outbreak of war provided an enormous boost for African musicians when the military hired the best jazz bands to entertain the troops, thus exposing African talent to white audiences. One of the most successful was 'Zonk', a variety company made up of members of the South African Native Military Corps and organised by Lieutenant Ike Brooks. The company was an immediate hit with the soldiers and, after the war, began a series of concert tours of South Africa featuring veteran horn players Elliot 'Bob' Twala and David Platter.

Hitting the big time

Although the obsession with all things American took a stranglehold on urbanised Africans, newcomers to the city still clung to the more basic music of their rural roots – and the jive of New York mixed with traditional African dance steps to produce the *tsaba-tsaba*, a wildly energetic dance that inspired local composers to create music to fit the whirling feet, culminating in August Musururgwa's classic 'Skokiaan', which topped the American hit parade as 'Happy Africa' in 1954. According to talent scout Walter Nhlapo, the music had 'the spirit of Africa in it . . . an indispensable part of our musical and dance culture'.

For the first time, indigenous African music had hit the international big time, and more was about to follow. A favourite instrument of African youngsters had long been a cheap, six-hole German metal flageolet nicknamed the 'penny whistle'. Now, with the music of American jazzmen such as Benny Goodman and Artie Shaw ringing in their ears and the tradition of *tsaba-tsaba* and other African rhythms in their feet, the young virtuosos used this humble instrument to develop '*kwela*', an internationally recognised sound.

Kwela was racey, fast and fun, but it was also simple, unsophisticated and rooted in the working class. Gradually, however, the rough edges were honed down, the saxophone began to take over from the lightweight penny whistle, and the result was so-called '*kwela*-jazz', produced by the nimble fingers of players such as Spokes Mashiyane, the 'Jazz Maniacs' and Ntemi Piliso and his

DRESSED *in a double-breasted tuxedo, Peter Resant, leader of the 'Merry Blackbirds', was the epitome of a sauve 1930s band leader.*

MULTI-TALENTED *jazz musi-*
cian Dollar Brand, who later
changed his name to Abdul-
lah Ibrahim (above), rose to
fame playing at the Odin
Cinema in Sophiatown
(right) with legendary sax-
ophonist Kippie Moeketsi
(below). Brand, together with
other stars such as singer
Miriam Makeba (left), later
left South Africa to work
abroad.

'Alexandra All-Star Band'. Nevertheless, many players, such as Aaron Lerole, still preferred the penny whistle because they could 'make it talk any sound' they wanted.

The new music soon earned a new name, 'mbaqanga' (Zulu for African maize bread), which by the mid-1950s was shouldering aside the older, large jazz bands – and attracting the commercial attention of local record companies. Among the performers who worked in the studios were Kippie Moeketsi, who played alto with Mackay Davashe's 'Shantytown Sextet', and Miriam Makeba, who formed an all-woman group called the 'Skylarks', with Letta Mbulu, Abigail Kubheka and Mary Rabotapa.

Despite the immense success of the recordings, however, the musicians at first received very little financial reward. Spokes Mashiyane, famed mbaqanga saxophonist and penny whistler whose records sold in their tens of thousands, received a one-off payment of between R15 and R100 for each recording – before he finally concluded a royalty agreement with Gallo Records in 1958.

While mbaqanga captured the musical headlines, the innovative African musicians began to gather at Sophiatown's Odin Cinema, where regular Sunday evening jazz sessions led to the emergence of the 'Jazz Epistles', with Dollar Brand on piano, Kippie Moeketsi on alto, Jonas Gwangwa on trombone, Hugh Masekela on trumpet, Johnny Gertse on guitars and Early Mabuza on drums.

More encouragement came from the newly formed Union Artists, which helped to organise the African Music and Drama Association at Dorkay House – a cultural melting pot that in 1959 produced the smash hit musical 'King Kong', based on the life of heavyweight boxing champion Ezekiel 'King Kong' Dhlamini. With a score by Todd Matshikizi, and leading roles sung by Nathan Mdledle and Miriam Makeba, the show was a dramatic statement about African township life that captivated audiences both in South Africa and overseas. Another star of the show was 10-year-old Lemmy Mabaso, who electrified audiences with his dazzling kwela solos on penny whistle.

The fame of 'King Kong' spawned a string of successors – ranging from the African jazz musical 'Phiri', produced by the Dorkay House-based Phoenix Players in 1972, to 'Ipi Tombi', produced by Bertha Egnos in 1974. 'Ipi Tombi' proved immensely successful among audiences in South Africa, Britain and Australia, but angered purists who accused it of being an 'inauthentic burlesque of African . . . life' that polished 'apartheid's international image'.

New directions

As the shows went from strength to strength, a new musical form was beginning to emerge, borrowing heavily from traditional Zulu music, with the underlying rhythms of mbaqanga to give it commercial appeal. This was simanje-

PENNY WHISTLER *Lemmy Mabaso (above) almost stole the show when he appeared in the original production of 'King Kong' in Johannesburg. The show was revived in 1979 with Eddie Tagoe playing the lead role (left).*

manje (Zulu for now-now), a melodious, moving sound led by a deep-voiced bass that sounded like a goat. Pioneering the new music was the group 'Black Mambazo', with Zeph Nkabinde developing the distinctive 'goat' voice.

In 1955 the government's bulldozers moved into Sophiatown – and, in the words of the township's Anglican priest, Father Trevor Huddleston, South Africa lost 'not only a place but an ideal'. From now on music would have to find a new area in which to grow – and after many false starts it began to take root in the townships of Soweto. In 1961 a series of jazz festivals sponsored by South African Breweries in Soweto gave jazz artists the chance to show their talent to a wider audience and compete for prizes. In 1962 the first prize went to Kippie Moeketsi and the 'Jazz Epistles', while the following year, Chris MacGregor's 'Blue Notes' won with 'Pondo Blues'.

Violence and the closure of traditional venues in terms of the Separate Amenities and Group Areas Acts dogged the musicians, many of whom decided to continue their careers overseas. Pianist Dollar Brand (Abdullah Ibrahim) left South Africa in 1962, returning at the end of the decade to work with his old partner Kippie Moeketsi on the enormously successful long-playing record 'Manenberg' before leaving South Africa once again for the USA. Others who went into exile included Hugh Masekela, Miriam Makeba, Letta Mbulu, Dudu Pukwana and Louis Moholo.

ONE OF THE BIGGEST *international hit musicals to come out of South Africa was 'Ipi Tombi', written by Bertha Egnos and her daughter Gail Lakier. The show opened at the Brooke Theatre, Johannesburg, in 1974 to wild applause from the audience and a chorus of criticism from musical purists.*

High noon of Afrikaner nationalism

With the rebellion of the early 1960s suppressed, it seemed to the arch-deacons
of Afrikaner nationalism that what they had struggled for 60 years to achieve had finally come to pass.
They had won their republic and had laid a foundation for the prosperity of their people
that would far surpass that of the halcyon days of the Boer states. English-speaking whites, too,
were able to share in the prosperity – harsh labour laws created an ideal climate
for an economic boom unparalleled in the nation's history, leaving the Afrikaner government
to pursue its dream of an all-white South Africa with renewed vigour.

AN AIRLINE passenger travelling over Johannesburg's northern suburbs in the late 1960s could not have failed to notice scores of bright blue squares, ovals and rectangles dotting the spacious gardens of the homes hundreds of metres below him. The sight of so many swimming pools moved one observer, American writer Bill Johnson, to comment: 'At some point around 1970 white South Africans overtook Californians as the single most affluent group in the world.'

However, had the plane swung towards Cape Town, a different sight would have greeted our traveller: south of the city, frequently hidden beneath a blanket of smog from thousands of wood stoves, lay Johannesburg's south-western townships (Soweto); ignored, silent, quiescent, smouldering. In a land of stark contrasts, this must surely have been the starkest of all.

Although the 1960s had opened to the sound of gunfire as black activists presented the most serious threat yet to white domination, the rebellion had been crushed within three years, its leaders jailed or exiled and its followers demoralised and cowed. The haemorrhage of foreign capital precipitated by Sharpeville and the emergency had been staunched, and was soon to be replaced by an infu-

sion of new capital on an unprecedented level. Moreover, the last political links with once-imperial Britain had now been severed, and Prime Minister Hendrik Verwoerd was honing the policy of apartheid in the vain hope of creating an 'all-white' South Africa and of creating a stability that international investors would find irresistible.

Small wonder, then, that whites – enjoying the fruits of their political supremacy and economic good fortune – gave the government a free hand to move ahead with the most ambitious aspect of its programme of social engineering: the creation of a series of satellite states that would give Africans limited political rights without impinging on the safety of the white republic (see page 425).

From peasant to worker

South Africa, internationally a highly ranked economic power, had begun to industrialise relatively late; and by the early 1960s, the process was barely 80 years old and had been imposed on a largely landed, peasant society only by major structural changes to society.

Traumatic though this period was, there were plenty of historical precedents for the rapid transformation of the people from peasant to working class. However, where the

A STUDY IN CONTRASTS: *the blue waters of swimming pools twinkle amid the lush, wooded gardens of Johannesburg's northern suburbs (left), while woodsmoke wreaths around dun-coloured houses in the African township of Tembisa near Pretoria (above).*

workers of most other industrialised nations were able to secure a comfortable balance between the demands of pure capitalism and an improved lifestyle, in South Africa successive laws made this almost impossible to achieve except for skilled artisans.

Between 1920 and 1960, the economy had grown at more than four percent a year, but had come to a halt after Sharpeville as investors and immigrants took fright and fled. While the flight of capital took South Africa's reserves to dangerous lows by the end of 1961, the slide was reversed at that point. Immigration returned to its usual high level, and then grew; in 1960 the white population had numbered about 3-million, a figure which stood at more than 4,5-million some 14 years later.

The boom years

It was a time when apartheid, while drawing steadily increasing fire from the international community, hardly bothered the investment community and its major bankers; South Africa was just too good an opportunity to miss, particularly when its government appeared to be able to guarantee the security of an investment that, at current rates of economic growth, could be recovered within five to six years. Rates of return on capital often ran as high as 15-20 percent.

The statistics are impressive and demonstrate a resilience and doggedness on the part of the government and white South Africa that not only pulled the country's economy back from the brink, but then turned it round and created one of the world's major economic success stories of the 1960s. By 1963, the economy had righted itself; its growth rate over the period 1960-70 averaged nearly six percent a year, a rate never before achieved and one second only to Japan's. Imports rose by 109 percent between 1958-62, while exports (excluding gold) rose 135 percent. Foreign investment, which had been valued at R3-billion in 1963, had risen to R7-billion by 1972 – an increase of about 230 percent; this was the fuel that fired the boom, accounting for more than two-thirds of the country's economic growth and bringing with it a vital injection of new technology. Nearly half of South Africa's imports now consisted of capital goods, the machinery that would drive growth to new heights.

Enter Germany and France

The pattern of South Africa's exports now also began to change: in 1962, trade with Britain had accounted for 29,6 percent of South African imports and almost a third of exports; by 1972, imports from and exports to Britain had dropped to 20,9 percent and 26,4 percent respectively. Over the same period, exports to Africa almost tripled and imports rose by about 250 percent. The most significant features of this shifting pattern of trading relations were, however, the special relationships that developed with West Germany and France.

In the wake of the devastation of the Second World War, West Germany had undergone a revival similar to that of Japan; by the Sixties its powerful industrial machine had become the engine of the new European Economic Community (EEC) and was steadily opening up new markets in the East European bloc for its sophisticated, high-technology capital equipment. Thus the Federal Republic was the perfect new trading partner for South Africa, in view of the latter's own roaring economic expansion. Between 1965 and 1972, West German investment in South Africa rose from a mere R70-million to a staggering R1,5-billion, overtaking that of the United States (US), which for years had held the second slot after Britain as a source of foreign investment. In 1974, West Germany actually outstripped Britain as the single highest source of South African imports. More than R2,8-billion in new investment poured into South Africa in the period 1967-72, of which almost 60 percent was brand-new investment from the EEC. By contrast, the increased investment by British and US companies was a result of profits re-invested in their South African subsidiaries.

German equipment poured into every sector of the economy, into the burgeoning industrial parastatals, into South Africa's rapidly increasing defence installations, and even into the budding atomic research programme. Much of West Germany's penetration of the South African economy occurred, curiously, during the early years of the new Social Democratic Government in Bonn. By a happy coincidence, West Germany was not yet a member of the United Nations and was thus able to evade much of the flak being generated in that organisation against trade links with South Africa.

The story of the development of France's political and military relationship with South Africa has its origins in the foreign policy of French President Charles de Gaulle. He was determined that France would pursue its foreign policy independently of those of the two major superpower blocs; it was for this reason that he pulled France out of the North Atlantic Treaty Organisation. This required of De Gaulle that he create a strategic third focus of power in the international game, and he set about establishing a series of special relationships with those countries of second ranking – including the People's Republic of China, Israel, Pakistan, Iran, Brazil – and South Africa. The key to this programme was the creation of a series of dependencies on France, without the country jeopardising its own freedom of movement by becoming similarly dependent

THE PURCHASE *of Mirage F1 fighters from France mirrored stronger economic links between Pretoria and Paris.*

on its second-string 'allies'. When Britain's Labour Government announced in 1964 that it would discontinue its supply of arms to South Africa once existing commitments had been met, France stepped into the breach.

Guns, not butter

Pretoria, meanwhile, had not been slow to use the chance provided by the boom of the 1960s to build up its defence capability. Where the defence budget had been estimated by international sources to be a mere $63-million at the time of Sharpeville, that had been increased 600 percent – to $375-million – by 1964. This figure nearly doubled again to reach $692-million in 1973, and broke through the $1-billion mark two years later. On the other hand, the economy was growing so fast that defence spending as a proportion of gross national product declined in the first years of the 1970s.

By 1975, France had supplied to the South African Defence force nearly 120 helicopters of various types, three submarines, more than 60 Mirage fighter-bombers and a range of other equipment and technology. But the most important deal struck was the French agreement to permit South Africa's Atlas Corporation to manufacture Mirages under licence. By 1980, French technology, with Israeli assistance, had given South Africa nuclear power and – probably – a nuclear weapon capability (which the government has consistently refused to confirm). From 1966, the new Minister of Defence was P W Botha; under his command, the country's arms industry began rapidly to decrease its reliance on arms imports, developing a domestic arms manufacturing industry through ARMSCOR, which by the late 1970s was in a position to export arms.

Cashing in

With the economy's rate of growth almost without equal during this period, and with healthy balance of payments surpluses and the currency strong, the country secure against the threat of internal rebellion, and the workforce compliant, South Africa's credit-worthiness was second to none, and the government took this record to the international finance market. It was able to borrow millions more to expand the parastatals. At the same time, Afrikaner financial institutions, which had led the rush to buy up shares at the rock-bottom prices of the period immediately after Sharpeville, were now immeasurably stronger. And the government had no compunction about expanding the state and semi-state institutions and departments to absorb increasing numbers of Afrikaners into the Civil Service, thus guaranteeing their political loyalty.

Vorster takes over

The economic boom gave the Afrikaner-run republic a kind of respectability that won over many of the English-speaking whites who had voted overwhelmingly against the formation of a republic. However uncomfortable they may have felt about the strident rhetoric of Afrikaner nationalism and apartheid, or about being excluded from political office, many now seemed content simply to enjoy the fruits of the boom.

Just how far this support had grown was illustrated in the general election of 1966, when the National Party won 21 seats from the Opposition, the biggest gain since the 1953 election, cornering 126 of the 170 House of Assembly seats. A few months later, however, the leader of the party, Hendrik Verwoerd, was dead – stabbed by a parliamentary messenger, Dimitri Tsafendas, who was later found to be insane.

Verwoerd's successor was the man who had successfully put down the African revolt of the early Sixties, Justice Minister John Vorster, who immediately made it clear that he planned to continue to implement the ideological apartheid dream of his predecessor.

VERWOERD'S KILLER, Dimitri Tsafendas, was born in Lourenço Marques (Maputo) some time between 1918 and 1921, the illegitimate son of a Greek father and a Mozambican woman. At school he was nicknamed 'Blackie' for his fuzzy hair and dark complexion, and was shunned by the white community. A superb linguist, he lived in Germany, Canada, the United States, Greece, France, Turkey, Portugal, Iran, Ghana, Angola and South Africa, where he was hired as a parliamentary messenger less than a month before he plunged a dagger four times into Verwoerd on 6 September 1966. At his summary trial the following month he was found to be insane and declared a State President's prisoner.

The Afrikaner who was born in Holland

The man who more than any other was to embody the Afrikaner dream of apartheid was not an Afrikaner by birth, but a full-blooded Hollander who was born in Amsterdam and spent part of his childhood in Rhodesia (now Zimbabwe).

Hendrik Frensch Verwoerd was the son of a deeply religious shopkeeper whose decision to migrate to South Africa in 1903, two years after Hendrik's birth, was prompted by a sympathy for the suffering of Afrikaners in the South African War. The Verwoerd family settled in South Africa for 10 years before moving to Bulawayo in Rhodesia, where Hendrik's father became an assistant evangelist for the Dutch Reformed Church. Four years later they moved again – to Brandfort in the Orange Free State (today more famous as the one-time home of the fiery ANC activist Winnie Mandela) where the young Hendrik proved an able scholar. He then proceeded to study psychology at Stellenbosch University and later gained an MA and a doctorate in philosophy.

He turned down a scholarship to Oxford, preferring to continue studying psychology in Germany, where Nazism was just beginning to rise to a troubled surface. In Hamburg he married a fellow student from his Stellenbosch days, and returned to his old university in 1928 to become professor of sociology and social work. During the dark days of the Depression, he became active in social work among poor whites.

His work with the Afrikaner poor drew him into politics – and in 1937 he was offered the editorship of 'Die Transvaler', with the added job of helping to rebuild the National Party (NP) in the Transvaal. Verwoerd revealed himself to be a staunch republican – earning the friendship of Nationalist leader J G Strijdom – and expressed himself strongly in favour of racial segregation by attacking the United Party's policy of 'pampering, levelling and living together'. In 1938 he published a poster against mixed marriages, depicting a black man and a white woman living in poverty. The Jews also came in for sharp criticism – because the important professional positions they held were seen as a menace to the jobs of Afrikaners.

During the Second World War, 'Die Transvaler' was accused by the Johannesburg 'Star' of taking a pro-Nazi stand – which prompted Verwoerd to sue the 'Star's' owners for libel. The judge, however, ruled against him, accusing his newspaper of being a very useful addition to the German propaganda service.

After the war, Verwoerd's republican sentiments came to the fore again when he issued instructions that 'Die Transvaler' totally ignore the visit to South Africa of Britain's royal family in 1947. The following year he left his editor's desk to take a seat as a Nationalist member of the Senate, rising to Cabinet level in 1950 as Minister of Native Affairs. He was responsible for moving 80 000 Africans from Sophiatown, Martindale and Newclare to the newly established southwestern townships of Johannesburg (Soweto). He was also in charge of African education, which he believed should be suited to the 'economic life of South Africa'.

He became Prime Minister in 1958, realising his republican dream two years later when a white referendum narrowly supported his plea for a republic – 'the day on which prayers are answered . . . the arrival of the republican dawn . . . the sun breaking through the morning mist'.

Verwoerd's conception of apartheid changed after he assumed the leadership of the NP. It was not because they were inferior that Africans were disqualified from participating in the South African political system, he now began to claim, but rather because they were not really South African. Under the NP, he promised, the different African 'nations' living in the republic would be given political rights in their own 'homelands'. This represented a change in emphasis for the NP – for, to previous Prime Ministers Daniel Malan and J G Strijdom, no-strings-attached baasskap was the only recipe for the maintenance of (white) Afrikaner power.

Verwoerd probably did most to hone away some of the rough edges of apartheid. In relentlessly pushing his separate 'nations' theory, he argued that contact between 'groups', would hinder their evolution into 'nationhood'. Certainly, his preparedness to 'guide' Africans to 'self-determination' once he considered them

VERWOERD *at the Rand Show in 1961 – before the first attempt on his life.*

ready for such a step, won him many new white supporters.

Protest at his apartheid policies was dismissed with an almost patronising incomprehension, as if the Africans were unaware of the favours he was bestowing on them. At a huge gathering at Meyerton, only a few kilometres from Sharpeville (where 69 Africans had died in a hail of police bullets just days before) Verwoerd reassured a cheering crowd that the 'black masses of South Africa' were 'orderly and peace-loving. They are loyal to the government and administration of the country . . . . The groups of people seeking their own gain are small and they make use of mass psychology at mass gatherings, and by threats and other means are sometimes the cause of the trouble . . . . We do not intend to be perturbed about what is done and said in the outside world in all ignorance.'

Verwoerd cheated death once – surviving two shots in the face from a would-be assassin at the Rand Show on 9 April 1961 – only to die at the hands of a deranged knifeman in the House of Assembly in 1966.

State President Nico Diederichs said in his memory: 'He was above all the one person who could . . . indicate the road ahead . . . and lay the most important foundations for putting his policy into practice.'

'No more black South Africans'

The decolonisation of Africa in the early 1960s led apartheid theoreticians to seek a way
to harness the cry for independence to the preservation of white power in southern Africa.
The result was a plan to transform the country's existing African areas into states in which
Africans would exercise full political rights. All it needed was the will to put the plan
into operation – a massive example of social engineering that seemed to bring
the ultimate dream of apartheid within reach at last: an Afrikaner-run republic with,
in the words of one-time Cabinet Minister Connie Mulder, 'no more black (African) South Africans'

THE LORRIES came very early in the morning, while Jamangile Tsotsobe (not his real name) and his family were still asleep. Within seconds pandemonium was spreading through the tiny African community, jolted from its sleep, as the dreadful cry went from house to house: the GG trucks had arrived.

Tsotsobe had lived in the small settlement of Colchester a few kilometres north-east of Port Elizabeth for 30 years, working as a gardener while his family grew in size from six children to 12. They had enough food to eat and were friendly with their neighbours. Colchester was similar to thousands of so-called 'black spots' scattered throughout South Africa: poor, but with a fair sense of community spirit built on good neighbourliness and long years of sharing good times, and bad times, together.

Then one day the khaki-suited men of the Bantu Administration Board arrived and told the startled villagers that they were going to be moved to a place called Glenmore on the edge of Ciskei. The people of Colchester, however, decided they would rather stay where they were than move to an unknown destination – despite the promises of a free home and work at one of the many industries supposedly established in the area.

For days the fear of removal hung heavy over the settlement – and then, almost without warning, the blow fell. In seven days, they were told, the GG (government) lorries would come and take them away. The axe fell at dawn: the Administration Board men, supported by police, shouted at the villagers to get out of their homes – while demolition teams went to work in a systematic destruction of houses that had stood for years. Some of the villagers scrambled for their pigs and livestock, while others tried to rescue their furniture; some houses were demolished before the contents could be removed – and many villagers lost everything. Finally, after the dust and the shouting had subsided, the convoy was ready. The men rode on the back of the trucks hanging on to the few belongings they had been able to save, while buses were provided for the women and children.

After a long, weeping journey they reached Glenmore, a settlement of 500 structures in a fenced-off camp beneath the dry hills of the Great Fish River valley 40 kilometres from Grahamstown and 200 from Port Elizabeth. The buses and trucks were unloaded, and each family given a tiny three-roomed wooden home with a mud floor and asbestos roof – many of them so draughty that the new inhabitants had to fill up the cracks with mud. Dazed and bewildered, they moved their broken furniture into their new homes, wondering what they had done to deserve such a fate.

For 70-year-old Tsotsobe it was the worst nightmare imaginable, something so incomprehensible that years later he still shook his head at the memory of it. How could a man be forced to leave his house, his work and his friends? The only explanation he could think of was the extraordinary one that he was not really a man at all!

And yet the old man was just one of an estimated 3,5-million people who were forced to move in one of the most ambitious and widespread examples of social engineering in recent history.

The dreaded Section 10

It was one thing to redraw the map of South Africa to a master plan devised in Pretoria; it was another to ensure that it stayed that way.

Fortunately for the planners, the groundwork had been laid down long before the days of the National Party – by the two Land Acts of 1913 and 1936, the Pass laws and the Black Urban Areas Act of 1945 (as amended). Under this latter Act, the government was able to decide which Africans could legally stay in 'white' South Africa, and which could not.

As far as the regulations were concerned 'white' South Africa was divided in two: rural areas and urban (officially 'prescribed') areas.

Africans in rural areas could stay legally only if they had been lawfully recruited by a farmer. A labour control board decided how many Africans could live on a particular piece of land – in effect, a quota system.

The situation in urban areas was dependent on whether or not the African had rights under Section 10 of the Black (Urban Areas) Act. There were three of these: birth; continuous employment for 10 years for the same employer (not 10 annual contracts) or continuous residence for more than 15 years.

The last two qualifications could be invalidated if the African was convicted of a crime carrying a jail sentence of at least six months or a fine of R500.

Without Section 10 qualifications, Africans could stay in 'white' areas for only 72 hours – after which they would be liable to arrest and possible deportation to the 'homeland' of their 'ethnic' origin.

The ultimate dream

While it had long been recognised that the economic interdependence of white and black in South Africa was more or less inevitable, apartheid was forced now to develop an ideological thread that would permit white South Africa the continued use of the massive supply of African labour, dispose of the surplus as required, and simultaneously create some kind of political outlet for Africans. In a sense, 'grand' apartheid rested on two pillars: migrant labour and the 'homelands' policy. It was thus imperative that the rapidly increasing rate of African urbanisation not only be halted but reversed. More than that, the government would now try to complete the task of unscrambling the South African ethnic omelette – even if it meant creating 'racial' differences between 'nations' where none, or hardly any, in fact, existed. In the end, went the theory, South Africa would have no African citizens; they would exercise political rights only in the 'Bantu' states, whether or not they lived in them or had ever been there, according to their ethnic classification.

Foreign Affairs Minister Eric Louw explained the policy to the General Assembly of the United Nations in 1959: 'The Act for the promotion of Bantu self-government [passed in that year] provides the means for the different Bantu territories to progress along the road toward self-government, and eventually to form part of a South African commonwealth, together with the Union of South Africa, which will during the intervening period act as the guardian of the emergent Bantu self-governing states . . . . It follows recent trends and developments in the African continent, and aims at progressively giving the Bantu control of his own homeland.'

The chairman of the Bantu Affairs Commission made it clear in 1968 that the government did not view all 'Bantu as one single people', but as several. They were, he said, 'divided by language, culture and traditions into several peoples or nations . . . . Fortunately for each of these peo-

ple or nations, history left to them within the borders of the present Republic large tracts of land which serve as their homelands. The Government's policy is, therefore, not a racial policy based on the colour of the skin of the inhabitants of the Republic, but a policy based on the reality and the fact that within the borders of the Republic there are found the White nation and several Bantu nations. The Government's policy is, therefore, not a policy of discrimination on the ground of race or colour, but a policy of differentiation on the ground of nationhood of different nations, granting to each self-determination within the borders of their homelands – hence this policy of separate development.'

A few years earlier, in 1961, Verwoerd had been far more succinct when he told parliament that the policy would buy the white man 'his freedom and right to retain domination in what is his country, settled for him by his forefathers'. Areas of African settlement within so-called 'white' South Africa would be designated either as belonging to one or other 'homeland', or their inhabitants simply uprooted and moved to the 'homelands'.

Nationalists, increasingly under fire as the details of forced removals came into public and international view, tried to put milder constructions on their policy without actually changing it. T N H (Punt) Janson told parliament in 1973: 'We should get away from the idea that these homelands could be regarded as dumping grounds for people whom we do not want in white South Africa . . . . However, by the same token and even more so I think it must be realised . . . that with 60 000 or 70 000 odd people coming on to the labour market each year from the Bantu reserves, the white areas should not be regarded as the dumping grounds for the surplus labour which comes from the Bantu homelands. This is a fact which has to be faced. Therefore we are committed to develop these homelands to the fullest of our ability and to the fullest of the potential of these homelands.'

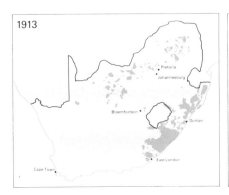

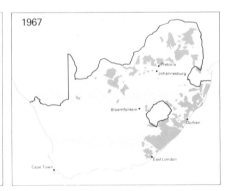

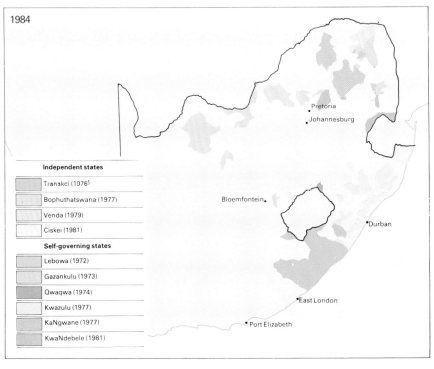

Independent states

Transkei (1976[1])

Bophuthatswana (1977)

Venda (1979)

Ciskei (1981)

Self-governing states

Lebowa (1972)

Gazankulu (1973)

Qwaqwa (1974)

Kwazulu (1977)

KaNgwane (1977)

KwaNdebele (1981)

THE NATIVES' LAND ACT *of 1913 and the Natives' Trust and Land Act of 1936 divided South Africa into 'white' (including coloured and Indian) and African areas, leading through 'consolidation' to the concept of independent 'nations' for Xhosa, Venda, Zulu and so on. Africans outside the 'homelands' without Section 10 rights were moved to the 'homeland' with which they could be ethnically linked.*

Making the theory work

While the planners and theoreticians plotted over their maps in Pretoria, Bantu Administration Board workers fanned out across the country with instructions to make the new political geography work.

Hardly any African was safe as the planners bulldozed their way through long-established settlements, driving victims from their ancestral lands and disrupting what remained of fragile urban and rural economies. In the cities, the Group Areas axe fell on whole communities, much as had happened to Sophiatown in the 1950s, as the government moved against mixed communities.

Despite a chorus of international outrage, the policy remained in place for more than 25 years, during which time at least 3,5-million people were the victims of forced removal; by 1980 a similar number of people were living, it was calculated, in the so-called closer settlements – vast labour dormitories situated on the edges of the new 'homelands', as close as the political geography permitted them to come to the industrial heartlands.

During the 1960s, the policy was pursued with a single-mindedness that bordered on the ruthless. In this period, according to an estimate by the South African Institute of

Race Relations in 1972, at least 1 820 000 Africans were removed from their homes or 'endorsed out' of (ordered to leave) urban areas, while a further 600 000 coloured, Indian and Chinese people – and nearly 40 000 whites – were moved in terms of the Group Areas Act.

Racial domination was not the only rationale behind forced removals. Many had their roots in white farming – fears of African competition in agriculture and the need to create sufficient labour for white farms, while removing 'surplus' Africans to the Reserves: during the 1960s, more than a million people were removed from so-called 'black spots' in rural areas – African-owned and African-settled land surrounded by white-owned land.

A second category of removals involved moving the families of workers living in townships adjacent to 'homelands' inside the 'homeland', even if it meant moving the entire township. This latter option was also achieved simply by redrawing the boundaries of the 'homeland' concerned. A third type of removal was effectively an extended version of the second type, in terms of which people evicted from old urban locations were removed to resettlement camps on the borders of the 'homelands'. A fourth category of removals, which ap-

'Cool down and take your things'

It's no good looking for Sophiatown on a modern street atlas of Johannesburg – because you won't find it. Along with Cape Town's District Six, Sophiatown – once described as the 'Chicago of South Africa' – has ended in the wastepaper bin of history; scrubbed off the map by the bulldozers of apartheid.

The story of Sophiatown began in 1897 with a speculator called Herman Tobiansky who bought 237 acres of land 7 kilometres west of the city, and named it after his wife, Sophia. It was the city fathers who inadvertently decided Sophiatown's future: first they built a sewerage disposal works nearby, which put whites off buying plots in the area; and then, after the First World War, they built a municipal location called Western Native Township next door.

Giving up his dream of a white suburb, Tobiansky decided to sell his plots off to Africans – and Sophiatown was born.

What made Sophiatown so different was that it happened naturally – there was no municipal ordinance, no superintendent, no wire fences and no permission needed for Africans to live there. You just bought a home according to the best of free market principles and moved in. It was almost as if apartheid had never existed – so much so, that many white 'bohemians' arrived to settle in the suburb, rubbing shoulders with a creative community that included leading journalists, musicians, writers and, of course, politicians.

When the Nationalists came to power in 1948 they hated Sophiatown. It stood for everything they believed was wrong with South Africa; and when Hendrik Verwoerd became Minister of Native Affairs he decided that Sophiatown had to go.

Thoroughly alarmed, the residents decided to stand firm – they organised the Western Areas Protest Committee and planned a one-day work stoppage for 12 February 1955, the day on which the removals were due to start. Forewarned, the government moved two days early – on 10 February – and sent in 2 000 police armed with machine guns, rifles and knobkerries. With no answer to this show of force, the first 110 families reluctantly moved to Meadowlands, now part of Soweto.

SOPHIATOWN *in February 1955 – with defiance scrawled on the walls. Most of the families owned their own land, as this 1910 deed of sale shows.*

The rest followed within a few years, the residents classified according to the dictates of the Population Registration Act, and sent to the appropriate 'Bantu', 'coloured', 'Indian' or 'white' area.

One of them, Jane Dakile, then a teacher at St Cyprian's Anglican School, remembers the day on which they came for her: Thursday, 10 November 1958, at half past five in the morning. There were five white men rattling the gate and shouting in Afrikaans 'Maak julle oop! Maak julle oop!' ('Open up! Open up!').

Her husband, preparing to go to work, watched in horror as two lorries pulled up outside the house. 'Before we had even opened the front door, I just heard the hammer on the pillar of the verandah . . . a big sound that made me wonder if I was dying. That sound went right into my heart and I shall never forget it.'

The men told Dakile: 'Whether you like it or not, you are going . . . . Cool down and take your things.'

'We had to take everything and throw it outside. Imagine taking your washing, just as it is, a chair just as it is – that's how [they] removed [us] . . . . I felt such pity for my hus-band . . . because he had built that house with his . . . bare hands. That house was our one and only little kingdom. We had freedom there in Sophiatown and that day I felt we were losing our rights . . . my friends in the yard and that old spirit of the people I lived with.'

Finally everything was piled into the lorries – and one of the men took Dakile and her baby by car to Meadowlands – and her new home. 'It was not very nice. It was just bricks, very cold, with no middle doors, only the outside doors. The houses were put together like trains.'

'Drum' magazine reporter Benson Dyantyi took a last walk through Sophiatown after the bulldozers had moved in: 'She looks like a bombed city . . . the few citizens who remain are hounded out of their houses for not possessing permits . . . hundreds sleep on verandahs, live with friends and live in the ruins . . . and the rains are coming.'

Today, the land that once throbbed to the rhythm of African jive is a neat suburb of modern houses and trim gardens. It is called Triomf (Triumph) – which, for the social engineers in Pretoria, it undoubtedly was.

No more Africans, 'for their own good'

Secretary for Native Affairs Dr Werner Eiselen was adamant that his plan to denude the western Cape of Africans was for their own good.

Speaking in 1954, he warned that Africans in the city quickly became part of a common black working class. 'The African who works in a hotel or boarding house associates on an equal, and very soon, an intimate footing with the female coloured servants. Their respective quarters are often situated close together and it is usually only a matter of time before cohabitation takes place. Under such conditions, the Native, who today is received and welcomed as an honest and trustworthy worker, must in time learn the less estimable "city tricks". In consequence he will no longer be a desirable type of worker.'

In order to preserve African innocence, Eiselen drew a line near the Fish River in the eastern Cape and declared that no Africans would be allowed to live permanently to the west of it, except those with Section 10 (see page 424) rights – and even their stay was only to be temporary.

Removals began almost at once – with Pass law swoops taking place at random – while the government vetoed plans by the Cape Town City Council to build new family housing at the African township of Langa, ordering bachelor hostels to be erected

in their place (taken over later by the Bantu Administration Board).

The next step was against the various African 'squatter' communities that had sprung up around Cape Town. First on the list was the largest and oldest at Windermere, near Maitland. Coloured people were separated from Africans – who were then screened according to Section 10. Those who failed the test were sent eastwards, while those who succeeded in persuading the authorities to let them stay were resettled in other parts of the Peninsula. Many families were separated – husbands sent to bachelor quarters, and their families to various destinations in the east.

By the time he resigned in 1960 to take up a new post in Bophuthatswana, Eiselen could look back on a job well done. The squatter camps had been largely destroyed and the migrant system put in place. And yet, Africans remained drawn to jobs in the western Cape, and their numbers began to grow again – until in 1962 the Nationalist newspaper 'Die Burger' called for a new campaign to remove them: 'It must be made [quite] clear that the party's policy is being carried out.' The local *Afrikaanse Sakekamer* (Chamber of Commerce) went even further: 'If whites cannot remove the Bantu from the Western Cape, our apartheid policy will never succeed.'

The new plan was an ambitious one – the removal of 100 000 Africans and their replacement in the work force by coloured people. Pass law swoops were stepped up – and greater control was enforced over the movement of Africans. Employers wanting to hire Africans had to prove to the Labour Department that no coloured person could be found to do the job. In addition, African women were forbidden to seek work in the western Cape. At Langa between 1951 and 1953 there were three men to every woman, while by 1970 this figure had grown to 10 men to one woman. The number of Pass arrests during the same period soared.

Nevertheless, grinding poverty in the 'homelands' made it inevitable that more and more Africans would find their way into the western Cape – and new squatter communities sprang up at places such as Werkgenot and Modderdam, near Bellville South, and Crossroads, Unibel and KTC near D F Malan airport.

In 1976 the law against squatters was amended to allow a Bantu Administration Board official to post an eviction order seven days before the demolition of a dwelling. In addition, no landowner could allow squatters

SHACKS BLAZE *at Modderdam as a front-end loader goes into action.*

on his land without official approval. A year later, after a long battle, all restraint was removed with the passing of the Prevention of Illegal Squatting Act, which made it possible to flatten a dwelling without any prior notice whatsoever – unless the occupier could prove he had title to the land on which it stood (Africans were not allowed to own land outside the 'homelands').

Removals at Modderdam

In that same year the government decided to act against the giant squatter community at Modderdam. First to go was the squatters' church, St John's, on 25 June 1977. Then coloured squatters were issued with pink eviction notices on 1 July, with orders to dismantle their houses and to take them to the nearby Rifle Range camp where they would receive a plot for R8 a month rental. Five days later, Africans received their notices warning that dwellings would be destroyed and the occupants screened under Section 10: 'legal' families would go to an emergency camp; 'illegal' families to the rural areas; 'legal' men and 'illegal' women divided between the local bachelors' quarters and villages in the eastern Cape.

Despite promises of solidarity, most of the coloured residents began dismantling their dwellings over the next two or three weeks – moving the building material to the Rifle Range on the back of Cape Divisional Council lorries. The next day, 8 August, a yellow front-end loader arrived, escorted by police who announced that demolitions would begin in 15 minutes. Chaos broke out as the squatters ran for their possessions, carrying wardrobes, beds, tables, chairs, suitcases, blankets, dishes and foodstuffs towards the road. Then the front-end loader went into action, lifting a shanty into the air and dropping it in a pile of corrugated iron and wooden beams, going on to demolish 10 more before becoming stuck in the mud. A tractor sent to pull it out also stuck fast, while the watching crowd jeered.

The next day dawned cold and overcast – and the police and municipal officials set to work with a will. First they checked that the shanties were free of booby-traps (some were rumoured to have holes dug un-

IN THE EARLY *1980s Crossroads was the largest settlement in the western Cape.*

derneath them), and then the front-end loader moved in. By afternoon tensions were rising on both sides – and Africans began arming themselves with stones, bottles, broken glass and knives, facing police armed with clubs, guns and dogs. Suddenly a fight broke out between a squatter dog and a police dog – and within seconds a man raised his knobkerrie and rushed a policeman. A major outbreak of violence was prevented only by the intervention of a squatter leader who appealed for calm.

No sooner had the crowd dispersed than a fire broke out – whether by accident or design was unclear – covering the camp with smoke and mingling with teargas fired by police in order to break up minor skirmishes. The night was long and hard – as thousands of homeless residents queued at soup kitchens and tried to shelter under plastic sheeting donated by church and other groups.

The next afternoon – while a northwesterly storm battered what remained of the camp – fires again broke out as two front-end loaders arrived. As the trucks moved in, an Anglican churchman with a long record of helping the squatters, the Reverend David Russell, suddenly lay down in front of the first truck. He was quickly arrested – and the camp closed to all whites except for a few volunteers and journalists. As the afternoon wore on, the officials worked quickly and efficiently, smashing shack after shack until nearly all had gone.

Over the next few days the 10 000 people who had once lived at Modderdam gradually disappeared – but only 60 rail passes had been issued. The rest had dispersed: to other camps, such as Unibel and KTC, and church halls, the African townships of Langa, Nyanga and Guguletu and some to the eastern Cape.

The demolitions continue

With Modderdam demolished, the government turned its attention to the 1 500 squatters remaining in Werkgenot, flattening the camp on 25 August – and arresting a church worker, Dr Margaret Nash, who walked in front of police with a white cross held high in her hand. As a final, mute protest at the demolitions, five families moved into tents in the grounds of St George's Cathedral in the centre of Cape Town.

Even right-wing theology students at the Afrikaans-language University of Stellenbosch were dismayed. In a letter to 'Die Burger', they wrote: 'God forgive us, because we know not what we have done.' The Secretary for Bantu Affairs, Willem Cruywagen, responded by saying he was sorry about what had happened at Modderdam, but 'we did not have any other way . . . the longer you wait the worse the problem becomes . . . .'

And worse, from the government's point of view, it was soon to be. From tiny beginnings, the squatter camp of Crossroads was to grow into the largest in the western Cape.

WHILE AFRICANS *living in 'white' South Africa were liable to be removed to their ethnic 'homeland', there still remained the problem of how to separate the four main 'race' groups – African, coloured, white and Indian – still living in the 'white' portion. This was achieved by the Black Urban Areas Act – which restricted eligible Africans (with Section 10 rights) to designated townships – and the Group Areas Act, which carved up towns and cities into white, coloured and Indian areas. The task of drawing up the demarcation between areas was entrusted to groups such as the one pictured at work in Cape Town in 1964.*

plied to the western Cape, was the declaration of this region as a coloured labour preference area, involving the removal of Africans to what the government deemed their ancestral 'homelands' in the eastern Cape in order to promote jobs for coloured workers. Consolidation – an effort to improve the patchwork appearance of the emerging 'Bantu states' in order to increase their credibility – provided a fifth factor that motivated forced removals. And finally, hundreds of thousands of so-called 'illegals' in urban areas were 'endorsed out' to the 'homelands' and rural resettlement ghettos.

A battery of laws

The government, intent on giving its intentions the respectability of legislative approval, was armed with a battery of nearly 20 laws under which the various types of removal could be effected. Included was the Prevention of Illegal Squatting Act, which empowered officials to demolish structures without prior notice to the occupants or owners. In terms of the National States Constitution Act, Bantustan borders could be adjusted to include or excise land at will, in order to accommodate the removals.

One of the harshest – and perhaps least known – laws was the Black Prohibition of Interdicts Act, which prevented the victims of removal from petitioning the courts, even if it could be shown that the government had acted beyond its powers in authorising or effecting a removal. Courts were forbidden to issue orders restraining the government from carrying out its intentions. And, should the community begin political action to resist, officials were able to call on the full policing and security apparatus of the state; activists could be detained, meetings banned, and

removals enforced at gunpoint. Moreover, where the army was brought in, no news of the removals could be published in terms of the laws preventing the disclosure of military movements. Several removals were executed by the army as full military operations, with all the accompanying codes and secrecies.

For people who considered themselves law-abiding and peaceful, the situation became a nightmare: to challenge the law was almost impossible; every legal loophole was closed as soon as it was found, to the extent that sympathetic lawyers became almost wary of using such loopholes for fear of disclosing them to the authorities.

Putting on a happy face

In time, the government – sensitive to criticism but determined not to budge in principle – changed the language of its rationale. Nowhere is this clearer than in the general circulars issued in 1967 and 1982. The 'settling of nonproductive Bantu resident in European areas' in 1967, became, in 1982, the 'settlement of families and workers from the white areas of the Republic of South Africa in national and independent black states'.

In 1967, it was 'accepted government policy that the Bantu are only temporarily resident in the European areas of the Republic, for as long as they offer their labour there'. By 1982, the language had been revised: 'In pursuance of the government's policy of developing national states and bringing them to full independence, the policy in practice is that blacks should be able to live and work in such states to the maximum extent.'

Nowhere was this attitude more marked than in the name of the ministry whose job it was to carry out the

IT TOOK LESS than three hours to move people from Sophiatown to Meadowlands (now part of Soweto) in February 1955. The police arrived at 5.30 am, waking many residents with three loud knocks on the front door (top left). The families were quickly ordered to load their belongings onto government trucks (above), which took them to the new settlement of Meadowlands (left), often arriving before 8.00 am.

removals. By 1981 it had become the Ministry of Co-operation and Development, headed by Dr Piet Koornhof. In that year he wrote to the Moderator of the Presbyterian Church in South Africa, the Right Reverend J B Hawk-ridge, regarding the people of Mgwali in the 'white' corridor between Transkei and Ciskei. His comments are typical of government reaction to criticism of the removals policy: 'The resettlement of Black people,' Koornhof wrote, 'is resorted to in order to ensure their national unity, to protect their ethnic and political interests and to improve their living conditions and standard of life . . . .

'In resettling a community every endeavour is made to ensure that work opportunities in the resettlement area are comparable with those in the area from which the resettlement is undertaken . . . .

'Resettlement is made as attractive as possible in order to obtain the cooperation of the people concerned, and to achieve this, the Department . . . undertakes the development of residential areas prior to resettlement. This entails the supply of treated water by pipeline to central points throughout the area where water is obtainable from taps; the provision of temporary prefabricated houses for each family and in addition tents are available if required to ena-

ble people to complete their own dwellings in their own time; the provision of sanitary facilities, schools, a clinic and the provision of roads in the area.

'Before resettlement is undertaken the improvements of the people (such as buildings, cattle kraals, fences, etc.) are valued by the Department of Cooperation and Development, and the people receive fair compensation for all such improvements. In addition they are permitted to take any serviceable materials such as doors, windows, corrugated iron, thatch grass etc., (for which they have already been compensated) with them to the resettlement area. Such materials are transported by the Department free of charge.

'As far as land belonging to the people to be resettled is concerned, this is usually valued by the Department of Community Development and the land owners are paid the market value thereof. Payment of the compensatory land (which will be of at least an equivalent agricultural or pastoral value to that of their own land) is withheld from this amount. Should compensatory land (with title deeds), however, not be required, the amount offered for a person's land is paid out to such a person in cash.

'As land owners are given compensatory land (if required) they are free to take whatever livestock they have

HUTS AT WEENEN, *Natal, blaze after the authorities had ordered residents to leave in 1958. Ironically, Weenen (Afrikaans for 'weeping') got its name after a party of Voortrekkers were killed there by Zulu in 1838.*

with them. However, non-land owners are settled in closer settlements and are not allowed to take livestock with them to the resettlement area, as provision is not made for the grazing of such stock . . . . '

While government officials claimed that the policy was being executed in consultation and cooperation with – and even with the approval of – affected communities, it became clear that this was not usually the case.

A fighting retreat

The inhabitants of communities scheduled for removal often found themselves the victims of arbitrary decisions taken by officials; they were generally poor and ill-educated, and unable to avail themselves of legal help or even to comprehend fully the meaning of the notices evicting them from their homes. Even so, many communities fought fierce legal battles to preserve their rights, and every battle was different.

It would begin as rumour. People nearby had been removed, and they were obviously next; a government official had been seen visiting the chief. Then the village would be notified; a notice in the 'Government Gazette' would authorise the removal, then officials would come to the village to address its people. Sometimes, particularly in the rural 'black spots' on or near white farms, the people would not be told at all. In actions reminiscent of the worst abuses of the late 1920s, farmers and police would on occasion combine to drive Africans off 'white' land, bulldozing and burning huts.

Communities deemed by statute to be no more than squatter camps usually had no warning at all, other than the rumble of the bulldozers and – in more tense situations – the barking of police dogs. The time of coming was at dawn, whatever the weather.

In more established settlements, a typical signal of what was to come was the arrival of a GG truck. Officials would climb down with paint and brushes, and begin daubing each house with a number. The number identified the occupants and whatever compensation was due to them, and also served to indicate the number of people in the community. The numbers also effectively froze the community; maintenance and extensions of properties came to halt, and new structures or new inhabitants were readily identifiable and usually forbidden.

On visiting the resettlement area of Kwaggafontein in KwaNdebele north-west of Pretoria, 'New York Times' correspondent Joe Leyleveld described it thus: 'GG: the initials are the first two letters of the official licence plates on the government trucks used to move blacks out of white areas. Throughout the rural Transvaal and Natal, it has become the universal shorthand among blacks for the white government, its pervasive authority, and its arbitrary ways . . . . GG is as predictable as natural calamity. GG scoops you up when you least expect it and drops you somewhere you have never seen, leaving it to you to patch together the torn and ragged pattern of a life. And, like natural calamity, it evokes depression and resignation, rather than resentment.'

A woman who was moved from the Tsitsikamma reserves to Elukhanyweni in Ciskei said: 'This thing came so sudden upon us that I cannot tell you what happened . . . they came with guns and police and with all sorts of things. We had no choice, the guns were behind us. They did not say anything, just threw our belongings in. We did not know, we still do not know this place. And when we came here they dumped our things. We can do nothing.'

Periodically, the public was given glimpses of what was going on. A report in the 'Sunday Tribune' in 1977 described the scene at a Cape Town squatter camp: 'An eye-smarting hell of teargas and snarling dogs, of laughing officials and policemen, of homeless families crouched pitifully with their meagre possessions beside the road.'

The following year, this report of a government attack on the now internationally renowned Crossroads squatter camp near Cape Town appeared in the 'Rand Daily Mail': 'I saw docile squatters . . . dragged by their clothing and beaten with batons and sticks during the second raid in less than six hours. Passes were grabbed by the police and other officials and thrown to the ground or temporarily confiscated. Ten policemen were injured when they were stoned in an earlier raid . . . . A squatter had been shot dead and soon a baby was to die on his mother's back as they were trampled by panic-stricken squatters attempting to escape yet another teargas attack.'

Not that guns, dogs, teargas and bulldozers were the only means of coercion or of breaking a community's will to remain on its land: schools and shops were closed, all renovations were forbidden to the extent that once-habitable dwellings deteriorated over time into slums (enabling the authorities to declare them as such and order them demolished), bus services were halted, officials even made illegal threats to withhold pensions and work permits and drought relief payments. In rural 'black spots', residents were warned not to plant crops and told that they would not be compensated for these crops if they were moved before harvest. On the other hand, the housing built by government contractors in the new townships provided a tempting incentive to those battling it out against the authorities under the miserable conditions of community decay. Even then, the promises held out to African communities by way of inducement to move were frequently broken; the facilities they were promised – schools, clinics, even 'freedom' – often simply never materialised.

Accepting the inevitable

Bantustan leaders, despite their apparent opposition to the programme, were forced to accept the situation; their own power and authority rested on the theory of separate black nations. As such, they too participated in removals and harassed communities of different 'ethnic' identity to that of the 'homeland' in which they lived; they became Pretoria's local agents, described by one researcher as 'ethnic policemen'. Certainly there was little they could do to resist the central government, but there were hidden benefits to cooperation.

The story of the removal of the Batlokwa and Makgato from their home at Sekgosese 50 kilometres north of Pietersburg, many of whose members had been moved four times since the 1940s, is typical. 'After discovering that many people didn't like to go, or refused the removals, they started to take them by force. Dogs were around, biting people, boys were taken to hospitals because they were just roaming about. If they get a person here, for instance the owner of the house, a man, they just get it, they get hold of that person. The truck stands here at the door of the house. They just get those chains and break the house, take everything. While holding you. So that you mustn't run away . . . . Other men take all your things, your properties in the truck and then they get you into the truck too . . . . '

By the 1980s, up to 20 percent of South Africa's people had been directly affected by the loss of their homes and the destruction of their communities.

The city that lost its soul

If you had stood in the late 1980s on the slopes of what is now called Zonnebloem, you would have seen open, grassy stretches of prime real estate close to the Cape Town city centre. Although many had snapped up the vacant land, very few wanted to develop it. So the land stood for many years as a mute testimony to the Group Areas Act – the law that divided up urban land according to the skin colour of its occupants.

Zonnebloem hides an ugly piece of apartheid history: the elimination of a community of 55 000 people in the name of 'orderly progress'. Streets that once echoed to the laughter of children and the cry of a snoek horn were struck dumb. District Six, once the soul of Cape Town, has been celebrated in books, photographs and even a record-breaking musical.

The area received its name in 1867 when it became the last of six districts created by the Municipal Board Amendment Act. Soon it gained a reputation as a crime-ridden slum – attracting drunken sailors and the women who lived off them. In 1901 bubonic plague broke out – and the police forced tenants from the area at gunpoint to an emergency camp where the garden suburb of Pinelands now stands. Most people moved back later – and the old, rough-and-tumble way of life went on.

But if there was crime, there was also a strong sense of community – that flourished in the crowded alleyways and streets of the picturesque suburb. The main thoroughfare, Hanover Street, became a colourful market by day, and a dangerous, shadowy world of criminals and wild characters at night.

In 1966 the government declared District Six a white group area, and over the next 15 years the soul of the city was extinguished as one house after another was razed, the inhabitants relocated to the new townships of the Cape Flats. One of them, Fuad Petersen, found himself uprooted to Mitchell's Plain, 30 kilometres from the city, near the False Bay coast. 'When we were evicted from District Six,' he said, 'we lost more than our home. We lost neighbours and friends whom we could rely on in times of sickness or other misfortune. The government gave us another home, but it couldn't give us a sense of belonging.'

A few kilometres south of District Six lies Harfield Village, a chic, yuppie suburb carved out of the old community of Lansdowne. As the coloured families were being moved out, a large graffiti slogan appeared on the wall of two adjoining houses, reading 'The Group is killing my people.'

DISTRICT SIX *before the axe fell.*

Luanda or bust...

In April 1974 the last dictator in western Europe, Marcello Caetano, was toppled in Lisbon – and the end to the colonial wars in Angola and Mozambique was in sight. The coup, however, was a disaster for the government of South Africa, bringing the forces of change that much nearer. The response was detente, a policy that sought accommodation with the new regimes, boding ill for white Rhodesia. Detente, however, had hardly started when Angola erupted in a blood war of succession, with Cuba, backed by Moscow supporting one side, and South Africa backed by France and the USA, the other.

THE COUNCIL chamber in the United Nations General Assembly was only half full that June afternoon of 1974 when the South African representative, Pik Botha, began to speak. Once he started, however, those members who were present could hardly believe their ears. Could this really be a high official of the apartheid government talking about 'reprehensible' incidents between white and black in his country?

'We do have discriminatory laws,' proclaimed Botha. 'But it is not because the whites in South Africa have any *herrenvolk* [master race] complex. We are not better than the black people, we are not cleverer than they are . . . we shall do everything in our power to move away from discrimination based on race or colour.'

The world was equally amazed when a few days later the Prime Minister, John Vorster, said: 'Give South Africa six months – give us a chance by not making the road any harder than it is already. If you give South Africa a chance you will be surprised where we stand.'

End of the old order

A more informed observer, however, would not have been surprised at South Africa's apparent about turn. Just two months before – in April 1974 – the last fascist regime in Europe had been toppled in a coup d'état: and with it, South Africa's most important guarantee of protection from cross-border attacks on the white south.

For years white South Africans had been protected from what they considered a hostile black Africa by a *cordon sanitaire*, a ring of buffer states controlled by whites. These included South West Africa/Namibia, Rhodesia/ Zimbabwe and the two huge territories controlled by Portugal that flanked the sub-continent on both the Atlantic and Indian Ocean seaboards – the colony of Angola and the overseas province of Mozambique.

It was these two territories, Angola to the west and Mozambique to the east, that were now in imminent danger of falling to the black freedom movements – in fact their continued existence had been one of the main reasons for the Lisbon coup that toppled Prime Minister Marcello Caetano. The Portuguese people had made it plain they could no longer afford to have one foot in Africa and the other in Europe – and they chose Europe.

Portugal had ruled the two territories, together with Guinea-Bissau further north, for hundreds of years, locked to a colonial empire that increasingly hung around its neck like a cumbersome, expensive, bleeding millstone. Under Caetano's predecessor, Antonio Salazar, the colonial policy had been strengthened – particularly by his decision to stay out of the Second World War – and thousands of Portuguese peasants had fled the impoverished economy of their homeland for the lure of greener pastures in Africa. By 1974 there were 350 000 in Angola and 200 000 in Mozambique – and with the MPLA in Angola and Frelimo in Mozambique poised to take over the countries for which they had fought for so long, most of them were now making plans to leave.

PORTUGUESE TROOPS *keep watch while a white settler loads his truck before fleeing Luanda ahead of independence.*

The final nail in the coffin of the Portuguese empire was delivered, unintentially, by France, which finally agreed to open the doors to British membership of the Common Market on 1 January 1973 – along with Denmark, Ireland and Norway. Having lost these traditional trading partners behind the high tariff walls of the European Community, Portugal's already tottering, antiquated economy virtually collapsed – and expensive empires were no longer viable. If Caetano could, or would, not pull Portugal out of Africa, someone else would have to – namely the military, which had already suffered so badly trying to defend Portuguese rule in the colonies. Finally they acted – and with Caetano out of the picture, the dates were set for independence: June 1975 for Mozambique and November 1975 for Angola.

Panic in the south

Up until the moment of Caetano's fall from grace in Lisbon, South Africa's buffer policy had been fairly straightforward: to prevent neighbouring states from becoming sanctuaries for guerrilla movements, and to provide material aid to these countries, but not to become involved in large-scale military actions outside its own borders.

It was a policy based on sound common sense: with a restless population to keep under control at home, it would be sheer folly to become bogged down in a long foreign war. And when Prime Minister John Vorster's advisors sat down to try to swallow the indigestible news from Lisbon, it soon became clear that there was only one course of action they could follow: if the new governments – whatever they turned out to be – could not be beaten in Angola and Mozambique, they would have to be joined, if not literally, then at least figuratively. Vorster forgot about the 'evil Marxists' and 'murdering terrorists', and declared that a 'black government in Mozambique holds no fears for us whatever . . . . I wish them well.'

Words were quickly put into action when South Africa refused a tacit cry for help from white settlers in Mozambique and Angola as they staged a brief revolt against the inevitable. This was an ominous decision indeed for the white Rhodesians, who now realised that South Africa would no longer support them. South Africa, forced into a long-term view of the realities of the southern African situation, had decided it would prefer even a moderately hostile black regime as a neighbour to protracted military action. Indeed, South Africa was willing to assist in the decolonisation of Rhodesia, and even Namibia, in an effort to win black friends in southern Africa.

As international isolation increased, South Africa needed all the friends it could find. The country was still reeling from the shock of the Arab oil embargo of 1973, the massively increased import bill for oil, the British arms embargo and the looming pull-out of the Royal Navy from Simon's Town. Internally it was faced with swelling inflation and a wave of violent strikes by black workers, which lasted between 1972-4 and caused a sharp decrease in the inflow of funds from foreign investors, a drastic increase in the balance of payments deficit (which rose to R1 700-million in 1975), an erratic and downward movement in the gold price and a devaluation of the rand. South Africa

SAMORA MACHEL *of Mozambique established an uneasy relationship of mutual courtesy with Pretoria.*

had run out of options; it needed a settlement in Rhodesia, even at the cost of a white government, and it needed to swallow its pride and welcome Samora Machel's Frelimo Government in Mozambique and whichever government finally took over in Angola.

A helping hand for Mozambique

Both Mozambique and South Africa realised that whoever was in power in their countries, economically they were bound together like Siamese twins. Cooperation was vital: there was the important port of Lourenco Marques, now Maputo, the Cahora Bassa hydro-electric scheme and migrant labour for the mines. The mating dance that followed was filled with displays of quite extraordinary mutual courtesy and aid. Samora Machel, the new leader, declared that economic ties with South Africa would not be cut and that Mozambique would not allow itself to be used as a base for guerrillas. 'We do not pretend to be saviours or reformers of South Africa. That belongs to the people of South Africa,' he said.

South Africa responded to these ringing phrases by sending a contingent of top railway and harbour officials to Maputo to sort out problems on the rail and harbour network, along with a package of technical experts, locomotives, rolling stock, spares and signalling equipment. There was a steady flow of emergency food supplies and a most telling incident in 1976 when Frelimo troops crossed the border into South Africa and were captured. South Africa immediately handed them back, saying their incursion had been nothing more than a mistake. Naturally, white Rhodesians, and many white South Africans, looked on such actions aghast. So did France and the USA, along with a number of black African states: peace and cooperation between South Africa and its new Marxist neighbours were not necessarily in their best interests . . . .

The Angolan nightmare begins

Unlike Mozambique, which had only one liberation movement, Angola had at least three, each in conflict with the other, and backed in turn by the USA, France, the Soviet Union and China with support from South Africa, Zaïre, Nigeria, Zambia, Tanzania and other African countries.

Topping the league was the Marxist MPLA, founded in 1957 and supported primarily by the Soviet Union. At the time of the Portuguese coup in 1974, it was headed by a taciturn doctor and poet named Agostinho Neto whose leadership was about to be challenged by a former professional soccer player named Daniel Chipenda. Although it had the advantage of being in control of the capital, Luanda, it did not have enough support to be a unifying force in the country. In addition, its strong Moscow ties made it highly unpopular with the USA, not to mention most of the white Portuguese settlers.

The MPLA's strongest contender was the FNLA, a more centrist organisation that had built up a considerable fighting force with funds and equipment from the American Central Intelligence Agency (CIA) and China, which wanted to counter Moscow's MPLA-supported influence in the region. Running the show was Holden Roberto, brother-in-law of Zaïre's capricious right-wing ruler Mobuto Sese Seko, an entrepreneur who had managed to filter a sizeable chunk of the CIA's funds into his own pocket and who ran a string of taxi firms and gambling casinos over the Zaïrean border in Kinshasa.

Last of the three was UNITA, formed in 1966 by a Swiss-educated lawyer named Jonas Savimbi who had broken away from Roberto's FNLA in 1964 over Roberto's acceptance of Chinese funds. Although by 1974 it had only a few hundred guerrillas to its name – as opposed to around 6 000 in the MPLA – UNITA had support from Zambia and Zaïre and a wide following in the south among the Ovimbundu people.

A fourth, much smaller contender, was a separatist movement for the oil-rich enclave of Cabinda called the FLEC. This tiny piece of Angola was (and still is) completely cut off from the rest of the country by a chunk of Zaïre, which not only made it a prime target for the covetous eyes of oil-starved France, the FLEC's main backer, but also aroused US corporations determined to hold on to their prospecting rights in the enclave. The rivalry between France, represented by the French oil company ELF, and the USA, represented by the Gulf Oil company, was to play a major role in the civil war that followed. At a time of spiralling oil prices following the 1973 'Yom Kippur' war between Israel and the Arab states, Cabinda's oil offered a glittering prize – which brought the French Secret Service, the SDECE, in large numbers to the region.

Against this patchwork of rival interests there started a powerplay of outlandish intrigue and diplomatic sleight of hand in which South Africa was to emerge the loser.

Round one to the MPLA

In November 1974 – a year before final independence was due for Angola – French mercenaries, almost certainly with their government's backing, struck, leading a rebellion by the FLEC seeking autonomy for Cabinda. Por-

WHILE *the MPLA controlled the area around Luanda, the FNLA – supported mainly by Zaïre – held sway in the north-east, with UNITA relying on South Africa in the south.*

tuguese troops, with MPLA backing, rushed to the rescue, and the remnants of FLEC were forced to flee to Zaïre.

Cabinda, it seemed, was not going to be a piece of *gâteau* after all – especially while the MPLA remained top dog in Angola – and France now realised that it would have to make more powerful friends than the tiny and defeated FLEC; which meant currying favour with the only effective opposition to the MPLA – Roberto's FNLA and Savimbi's UNITA. There was, of course, one other counter – the most powerful one of all – South Africa, a regional power with more than enough firepower, if it chose, to settle the matter once and for all. While French money and arms were poured into the two independence movements, the French Government organised a 'friendly' meeting between Savimbi and South African Bureau of State Security (BOSS) representatives in Paris.

Support for Savimbi also came from Zambia's leader, Kenneth Kaunda, whose dislike of Marxism was matched only by his faith in God. A meeting was arranged between Savimbi and the socialist leader of Tanzania, Julius Nyerere, after which Savimbi flew to Peking where the Chinese, still anxious to prevent a Moscow-controlled Angola, promised to give him arms.

While Savimbi was still jockeying for international support, Roberto acted, sending his estimated 15 000 FNLA troops southwards towards Luanda in a well-disciplined armoured column, intending to steal a march on the MPLA by filling the vacuum left by the Portuguese – despite the fact that all three guerrilla groups had signed a unity agreement in the Kenyan city of Mombasa only days before. The CIA smoothed the way by supplying money to buy up Luanda newspapers and television stations.

For a couple of months the two organisations maintained the farce of supporting a provisional government – during which the uneasy MPLA alliance of Neto and

DESPERATELY WORRIED *at the advances made by the Marxist* MPLA *forces in Angola, Kenneth Kaunda (above) of Zambia told* US *President Gerald Ford that he was pinning his hopes on* UNITA *leader Jonas Savimbi (right, with stick).*

Chipenda came unstuck. Chipenda was expelled – and immediately joined the rival FNLA, becoming vice-president to Roberto in April.

Moscow retaliated by shipping arms to the MPLA who were further boosted by the arrival of the first Cuban advisers. In early April a vicious clash between the MPLA and the FNLA left 20000 dead. In that same month, a concerned Kaunda flew to Washington where he told President Gerald Ford that Zambia, Tanzania and Botswana were backing UNITA.

Kuanda's news could hardly have surprised Ford, or his Machiavellian Secretary of State, Henry Kissinger – for the past few months the USA had been using the CIA to pour aid into the FNLA, despite advice from Kissinger's Africa experts that the MPLA could not be defeated. Their advice was well founded: by July the MPLA were once more in control of the capital, and very rapidly extending control over the rest of the country. For the anti-MPLA grouping of FNLA, UNITA and their Western allies, the time had come to use the only option left to try to prevent a Cuban-backed MPLA takeover when independence was formally declared in November – South Africa.

A carrot for South Africa

France was particularly keen on South African military intervention in the region. If the combined UNITA/FNLA forces could defeat the MPLA, the chances of an FLEC breakaway in Cabinda would be almost guaranteed – and the French would obtain indirect control of the oil enclave.

South Africa, however, its delicate detente policy still in its infancy, was uneasy about military intervention in other African countries. Scare talk of a Marxist government on her doorstep was anything but an inducement to send in her army – after all, look what had been achieved in Mozambique, which also had a Marxist government. A more delectable carrot had to be found to persuade South Africa to commit its troops to Angola – and France had a very irrisistible carrot indeed: armaments.

A few weeks after Valéry Giscard d'Estaing's election in June 1974, the French announced they were selling Daphne submarines to South Africa. Quick to spot the possibilities of the French action leading to the eventual expulsion of Gulf Oil from Cabinda, Washington countered with an offer to supply helicopters and spotter aircraft. An outraged Afro-Arab bloc had barely got its protest together when France came back with a number of Mirage F1 fighter aircraft. Then, in a ridiculous auction for South Africa's favours, the USA declared that it would supply South Africa with enriched uranium for its proposed nuclear power stations. France topped that one, too, by disclosing that a French consortium was tendering for the construction of further nuclear plants in South Africa.

Faced with such overwhelming temptations, South Africa, failing to understand that Washington's pleas did not have the backing of Congress, advanced troops into Angola. They went only as far as Cunene, however, and stopped, ostensibly to guard the Cunene dam. The fact that the US-backed FNLA simultaneously started advancing from the north was a clear indication, especially in view of the republic's refusal to give military assistance to UNITA, of a Pretoria-Washington pact. Paris was miffed, and on a visit to Zaïre in August Giscard d'Estaing announced that France would no longer sell weapons to Pretoria.

By August, Roberto's offensive had run out of steam – and his troops were on the run from the victorious MPLA. With defeat staring the West in the face – and the deadline for independence only three months away – Pretoria agreed to assist the UNITA forces in the south, moving in troops to protect the UNITA stronghold of Huambo, east of Benguela. UNITA then formally declared war on the MPLA.

THE FEARSOME 'Stalin organ' rocket launcher used by Cuban-MPLA militia against South African forces in Angola.

Rhodesia nears the last act

As early as 1974 the Rhodesian High Command had realised that the guerrilla war was not just a passing insurrection caused by a handful of 'agitators'. Increasing numbers of people were giving their support and sympathy to the guerrillas, and many security force leaders were starting to realise that it was a war they were not going to win.

Clearly the looming independence of Mozambique and Angola would make the position for the government of Ian Smith even more vulnerable, as both nations would join other Frontline states in offering support to the Zimbabwe nationalists. Both John Vorster and Kenneth Kaunda seized the opportunity to initiate peace talks – for a Rhodesian settlement was important to both of them. With pressure from South Africa on Smith to release nationalist leaders, including Robert Mugabe, the first settlement talks were held in October 1974. Within a few days the talks disintegrated, both sides claiming they had been forced into talks they did not want. Vorster and Kaunda were disappointed but determined that another attempt should be made. Vorster underlined the importance he attached to a settlement when he stated publicly: 'The alternative is too ghastly to contemplate.'

More pressure was applied to Smith, mainly by the withdrawal of 2 000 South African police from Rhodesia, where they had been helping the Rhodesian security forces, and another meeting took place at Victoria Falls on 25 August 1975, chaired by Kaunda and Vorster, at which Smith and the black nationalists again tried to hammer out a deal. This time Joshua Nkomo indicated that he was willing to reach a compromise, and when Vorster returned to South Africa he was optimistic. Within a few days, however, Smith announced that the talks had been a failure – Rhodesia still had a few more years of agony to endure before peace would prevail (see page 470).

There was deep anger in the South African Cabinet, but there was a limit to the amount of pressure that could be applied to Smith – already conservative critics in South Africa were accusing Vorster of 'betraying the white man in Africa'. But attention was, temporarily, soon to be sharply averted from Rhodesia, with the invasion of Angola only two months later.

Trying to beat the deadline

The primary object of all the anti-MPLA forces – which now included the involvement of many countries in Europe – was to prevent an MPLA victory before independence day on 11 November 1975. South Africa finally agreed to a full-scale attack in the form of a formidable column comprising South African, UNITA and FNLA troops, codenamed 'Zulu', which began the drive north to Luanda on 23 October. The attack was a devastating series of victories: Sa da Bandiera, Moçamedes (now Namibe), Lobito and, by 5 November, Benguela. Then began the advance on Luanda itself, and by 9 November the 'Zulu' column was within 12 kilometres of the capital and commenced long-range bombardment.

By that time the first major contingent of Cuban troops had arrived and, backed by heavy Soviet artillery, including the fearsome 'Stalin Organ', a 40-barrel rocket launcher, held the 'Zulu' offensive in check, destroying much of Roberto's FNLA army in the process. The South African troops withdrew to Novo Redondo but once again came under devastating MPLA fire, losing four men captive.

The 'Zulu' commander radioed Pretoria for reinforcements, but with the spectre of a protracted campaign hanging over the government's head, these were refused. Presumably Pretoria was aware of the huge build-up of Cubans, along with heavy mortars, armoured cars, tanks and MiG 21s in Luanda, and realised the only effective resistance would be to send in the South African Air Force, plus at least another infantry battalion. To enter into a battle on such a scale, against largely unknown forces in a theatre thousands of kilometres from base, and all in the face of world condemnation, was a risk South Africa was not prepared to take – for any reward. Despite pleas from African states such as Zambia and Zaïre to remain in Angola after independence, South Africa's mind was made up. This attitude was strengthened when on 18 December the US Senate put a stop to any further US aid to anti-MPLA forces in Angola.

After weeks of dithering, South Africa started to withdraw in January 1976. In February the Organisation of African Unity (OAU) finally recognised the MPLA as the official government, and by March South Africa had withdrawn across the Namibian border. The whole exercise had cost Pretoria dearly: the detente policy with Africa was up in smoke, the military had lost face, there was a large communist presence on the doorstep and France had been lost as a supplier of weapons. South Africa's involvement in the Angolan morass was conducted in great secrecy, so much so that South Africans were not told about Operation Zulu until it was almost over. The role played by the USA was, if anything, even less clear. What does seem fairly certain is that South Africa misunderstood the confusing signals coming from Washington – going along with CIA operations against the MPLA without realising that they did not have the backing of the US Congress, including the Senate, which finally halted US involvement by stopping aid to the anti-MPLA forces in Angola.

In fact it was hard to imagine a more signal disaster than the one that now faced the South African Government: Malawi, Botswana and Lesotho temporarily stopped

A CONVOY *of armoured cars, jeeps and trucks crosses the Cunene River between Angola and Namibia: South African forces were pulled out of Angola early in 1976.*

recruitment to the mines; South African tourists suddenly found themselves unwelcome in Mauritius; and, worst of all, all hope of a rapprochement with the MPLA similar to the deal that had been struck with Frelimo in Mozambique was shattered by suspicion and fear. From now on, the MPLA would cling to Moscow – and Cuba – in an atmosphere of deep mutual mistrust.

While the world railed against Pretoria for its decision to intervene in Angola, Kissinger quickly isolated himself from any direct contact with the South Africans in a massive cover-up that partially remains to this day. His only consolation was to veto the victorious MPLA's application for United Nations membership – just as he had earlier vetoed a similar application by Vietnam. The shift in the regional balance of power was now decidedly against South Africa – and the vexing problem of Rhodesia loomed larger than ever (see box).

ANGOLA'S *warring factions signed a unity agreement in Mombasa in June 1975 – which broke down almost before the ink was dry. Heading the table is Kenya's President Kenyatta with, on his left (from left) Agostinho Neto (MPLA), Jonas Savimbi (UNITA) and Holden Roberto (FNLA).*

The Israeli connection

So it was that by the first half of 1976 South Africa found itself with few friends in the outside world. One of them, and a very important one, was Israel. Trade between the two countries had grown to around R100-million a year, consisting mainly of coal and uranium for Israel and arms for South Africa – of critical importance after the French arms ban. There was also a strategic advantage to the Israel-South Africa link. At this time almost the entire eastern seaboard of Africa was controlled by left-wing states, most of them sympathetic to the Soviet Union. The only conservative regime was in Kenya, which had a history of good relations with Israel. A discreet but definite bond between these three countries was built up and became apparent during the famous Entebbe raid in July 1976, when Israel staged its dramatic rescue of hijacked hostages from Idi Amin's Uganda. Kenya provided the refuelling stop at Nairobi and Pretoria offered landing rights and back-up, were they to be required.

Another important friend was Iran, which supplied South Africa with more than a third of all its oil. Iran continued to supply oil in the face of the Arab oil boycott, one of the reasons being its substantial interest in the South African state oil refinery, NATREF. Another was the ambitious plans of its ruler, the Shah, to control the Indian Ocean. South Africa had also made advances to Paraguay, fêting President Alfredo Stroessner and providing the country with credit in order to obtain South African goods. Vorster visited Uruguay and secret envoys were sent to Red China in an effort to open up trade.

But without the backing of the USA, Britain or France, even unofficially, South Africa faced severe problems. When Jimmy Carter was elected US President in 1976, the South African Government despaired. 'It will be exactly the same as if the Marxists had taken over,' declared Vorster. Soon, however, he had something far more serious to worry about than the republic's foreign relations. The lid of repression at home was about to blow off in the dusty streets of Soweto . . . .

Resistance, negotiation and reconstruction 1976-

'Deeply concerned Afrikaans medium controversy black schools. Position Soweto very serious.'
Telegram dated 25 May 1976, from Fred van Wyk, director of the South African Institute of Race Relations, to MP René de Villiers.

On 16 June 1976 the bitter resentment of millions of black people at the injustices of apartheid burst forth in an event that became widely acknowledged as the turning point for white rule. While the immediate cause of the Soweto revolt was a protest at the use of the Afrikaans language in black schools and the inferior system of 'Bantu education', the unrest that had been simmering over the past few years boiled over into more than 200 towns and cities across South Africa over the next 15 months.

The defiance against the state – and the often brutal moves by the security forces to crush the revolt – had far-reaching repercussions. Youths fleeing the townships swelled the armies of the liberation movements in exile, the international clamour for South Africa's economic isolation grew deafening, and black opponents of the National Party (NP) Government had a taste of the power that mass action could exert.

Before relative calm was restored to the country in 1978, another crisis confronted the government – this time from within its own ranks. Details emerged of a multimillion rand attempt to whitewash South Africa's policies both at home and overseas. The Information scandal, as it became known, precipitated the resignation of Prime Minister John Vorster and a struggle for the premiership. The new leader, P W Botha, emerged with a policy of 'Total Strategy', a concerted effort to defuse insurrection by creating an African middle class (which meant scrapping the Pass laws) and to halt African National Congress (ANC) incursions from neighbouring states by trying to create a buffer – or 'constellation' – of states economically dependent on Pretoria.

In order to make these reforms possible, Botha widened his own powers, becoming State President under a new constitution that further entrenched apartheid by extending parliament to include three racially distinct houses: for whites, coloured people and Indians. The retention of white control and the exclusion of Africans led to widespread rebellion in 1984 that attracted international sympathy and solidarity on an unprecedented scale. Horrified by television images of South African state forces in tough action against blacks, the world began to impose a new wave of sanctions.

The government's response to the unrest was to impose a state of emergency, while the economy slowed down and the reform process came to a virtual standstill. As the country slumped deeper into recession and violence, new and ominous voices began to be heard in the deepest corridors of power – those of the so-called securocrats: army and police specialists whose growing influence began to supplant even that of the Cabinet. Normal legal processes were increasingly by-passed as activists simply 'disappeared'. Fear stalked an already fearful land.

The liberation movements – and the ANC in particular – were, nevertheless, making strides. Insurgents infiltrated the country, launching acts of sabotage, and also making contact with internal dissidents, who intensified their actions at home to defy the state. But, in spite of the growing support for the ANC inside the country and internationally, its tactics were bringing it no closer to assuming power.

The government, on the other hand, had become the polecat of the world because of its refusal to relinquish apartheid – but was still militarily strong enough to cling to power. Many senior Cabinet members by now accepted the failure of apartheid and the need for change. Botha, who had started with some reforms, seemed unwilling, however, to grasp the nettle and finally abolish apartheid. The task would have to fall to someone else ....

The chance came on 2 February 1989, when Botha suddenly resigned as leader of the NP after suffering a mild stroke, but retained the presidency. Elected in his place was F W de Klerk, whose subsequent rivalry with Botha for the presidency ended sensationally with a televised capitulation by Botha.

Soon after coming to power, De Klerk met jailed ANC leader Nelson Mandela. Then, on 2 February 1990, De Klerk lifted the restrictions on the previously banned ANC, Pan-Africanist Congress and South African Communist Party, and announced the repeal of all apartheid legislation. A few days later he released Mandela to a cheering world.

The stalemate had been broken and talks could begin on shaping a new future for South Africa.

While the political leaders sat down to resolve their differences on constitutional issues, the legacy of oppression fanned the flames of internecine violence as black fought black for supremacy in the townships. Violence came, too, from the white ultra-rightists whose place in the sun had been dramatically over-shadowed by De Klerk's initiatives, and from remnants in the security forces who continued their 'dirty war' in a bid to wreck the negotiations.

In spite of a laborious talks process that exacted compromises from both main parties – the NP Government and the ANC – and of the posturing and politicking, the parties to the talks finally arrived at a deal for a post-apartheid government: an election was held for a five-year Government of National Unity that would run the country while simultaneously writing a new constitution.

At the end of the tricameral parliament era – a decade in which nearly 20 000 people had lost their lives in political violence – a new order came into being. On 9 May 1994, the ANC took up the majority of seats in parliament, ending its 82-year struggle against white domination.

Parliamentary politics

1976	Anti-squatting laws tightened.
	Internal Security Act.
	Transkei becomes first 'independent home-land' (Bophuthatswana follows suit in 1977, Venda in 1979 and Ciskei in 1981).
1978	Auditor-General exposes misuse of funds by Department of Information; B J Vorster resigns as Prime Minister; P W Botha succeeds Vorster
1980	Republic of South Africa Constitution Fifth Amendment Act.
1983	Conservative Party formed.
	Republic of South Africa Constitution Act.
	White referendum on new constitution.
1984	Last sitting of whites-only Westminster-style parliament.
	Elections held for House of Representatives and House of Delegates.
	New constitution comes into force.
1985	Botha's 'Rubicon' speech causes outcry.
1985-6	State of emergency in 36 magisterial districts; heavy censorship on media reports of political protest.
1986	Prohibition of Political Interference Act, Prohibition of Mixed Marriages Act and Section of Immorality Act repealed; Pass laws repealed
1987	Conservative Party becomes official Opposition after House of Assembly elections.
	Coup in Transkei.
1988	South African troops put down attempted coup in Bophuthatswana.
1989	P W Botha suffers stroke; resigns as leader of replaced by F W de Klerk.
	Democratic Party formed.
	Botha meets Nelson Mandela in Cape Town.
	Botha resigns as State President; succeeded by De Klerk.
	NP wins general election with reduced majority
	De Klerk meets Mandela.
1990	De Klerk unbans ANC, PAC, SACP; lifts restrictions on UDF and COSATU; releases Mandela.
	Military coups in Ciskei and Venda.
	Groote Schuur Minute signed by the government and the ANC.
	State of emergency lifted in all provinces except Natal; four months later lifted in Natal and Separate Amenities Act repealed.
	Pretoria Minute signed by the government and the ANC.
	De Klerk visits USA.
	NP opens its doors to all races.
1991	Native Land and Trust Act, Group Areas Act, Population Registration Act repealed.
	National Peace Accord signed.
	'Inkathagate' scandal exposed.
	Convention for a Democratic South Africa (CODESA) comes into being.
1992	Almost 70 percent of white South Africans vote 'Yes' in a referendum to test reform initiatives
	CODESA II collapses.
	Record of Understanding signed by the government and the ANC.
	Government suspends senior military men suspected of sabotaging negotiations.
1993	'Own affairs' administrations of tricameral parliament phased out.
	De Klerk announces six nuclear bombs built secretly in 1980s have been dismantled.
	Negotiating Council begins drafting interim constitution; sets date for democratic election
	De Klerk awarded Nobel Peace Prize jointly with Mandela.
	Transitional Executive Council sits for first time.
1994	Ultra-right launches bombing campaign in run-up to election.
	Tricameral parliament sits for last time.
	NP defeated in election by ANC.
	Government of National Unity constituted.
	'Homelands' reincorporated.

Economic changes; foreign affairs

1976   Soweto riots and aftermath cause deep economic slump, increased international isolation (including calls for sanctions), flight of foreign capital.

1977   M T Steyn becomes Administrator-General of Namibia; repeals Pass laws and discriminatory Acts.
UN arms embargo becomes mandatory.

1978   UN Resolution 435 provides for UN-supervised elections in Namibia; unsupervised elections boycotted by SWAPO.

1979   South Africa launches 'constellation of states' policy in bid to block ANC cross-border raids.
Riekert and Wiehahn commissions bring about important changes in labour field; Industrial Conciliation Act.
Zimbabwe-Rhodesia set up under Abel Muzorewa.
Lancaster House settlement for Zimbabwe-Rhodesia; Governor Lord Soames supervises run-up to new elections.

1980   Robert Mugabe's ZANU-PF wins British-supervised elections; Zimbabwe-Rhodesia becomes Zimbabwe.
Southern African Development Coordination Conference formed to counter economic influence of South Africa.

1981   Cuban withdrawal from Angola first linked to Namibian independence.

1983   SWAPO-Democrats and Democratic Turnhalle Alliance form Namibian Multi-Party Conference (MPC) with other parties.

1984   Lusaka Conference on Namibian independence.
South Africa signs Nkomati Accord with Mozambique.

1985   Namibian MPC forms transitional government.
Financial crisis sparked by foreign banks' decision to suspend loans to South Africa; rand slumps against foreign currencies; disinvestment campaign begins; UK and USA adopt employment codes for their companies operating in South Africa.
White South African businessmen and newspaper editors meet ANC leaders in Zambia.

1986   South African raids on alleged ANC bases in Zimbabwe, Zambia, Botswana as Commonwealth Eminent Persons Group arrives for 'final' negotiations.
Chief Leabua Jonathan toppled in Lesotho coup; ANC leaves Lesotho.
President Samora Machel dies in plane crash.
Stepped-up sanctions campaign in USA.

1988   Angola/Namibia peace talks in various capitals; agreement on Namibian independence signed in New York.
Era of economic reform initiated: African middle class grows; privatisation of state-owned enterprises mooted.

1989   Organisation of African Unity's ad hoc committee on southern Africa issues Harare Declaration approving ANC's position for negotiating with South African Government.
Soviet Union sends diplomatic mission to South Africa after breaking off relations in 1956.

1990   Namibia becomes independent.

1991   USA lifts sanctions against South Africa.

1992   Japan lifts sanctions against South Africa.
Republic opens diplomatic relations with former eastern bloc countries.
De Klerk visits Nigeria.
South African sportsmen and sportswomen take part in Olympic Games for first time since 1960.
Business loses R250-million in countrywide strike in wake of Boipatong massacre.

1993   UN lifts sanctions (except on arms) against South Africa.

1994   South Africa transfers control of Walvis Bay and the Penguin Islands to Namibia.
After installation of ANC government, UN lifts remaining embargoes; Republic readmitted to Commonwealth and UN General Assembly; becomes member of Organisation of African Unity, Non-Aligned Movement and regional economic forum.

Extra-parliamentary politics

1976   Report of Theron commission on coloured people tabled.
Secondary schoolchildren march in Soweto in massive protest against use of Afrikaans; hundreds killed in violence.
Schools unrest spreads to western Cape; first members of 'Class of '76' leave South Africa for training in armed resistance.

1977   Winnie Mandela banished to Brandfort.
Steve Biko dies in detention.
17 organisations and two newspapers banned.

1978   Sobukwe dies.

1979   Council of Unions of South Africa (CUSA) and Federation of South African Trade Unions (FOSATU) formed.
Azanian People's Organisation (AZAPO), Azanian Students' Organisation (AZASO) and Congress of South African Students (COSAS) formed.
Wave of stayaways in western Cape.

1980   Thousands take part in boycotts of schools and universities; protests over bus fares, wages and rent.
SASOL refinery sabotaged.
ANC breaks with Chief Mangosuthu Buthelezi.

1982   Koeberg nuclear power station sabotaged.
National Union of Mineworkers (NUM) founded.

1983   National Forum inaugurated by 'Africanists'.
Car bomb at SAAF headquarters in Pretoria kills 19.
United Democratic Front (UDF) formed.

1984   Violent African response to new constitution.
Anglican Bishop Desmond Tutu awarded Nobel Peace Prize.

1985   Police kill more than 20 mourners in Langa near Uitenhage after Sharpeville commemoration.
Congress of South African Trade Unions (COSATU) launched.
Proposed march from Athlone to Pollsmoor prevented by police.
Clerics issue Kairos document.

1986   About 1,5-million blacks stage May Day stayaway.
Pass laws abolished.

1987   Dakar meeting between PFP and ANC leaders.

1988   Three-million workers strike in protest at Labour Relations Amendment Act.
17 anti-apartheid organisations, including UDF, effectively banned; COSATU restricted.

1989   Hunger strike by political detainees.
Defiance campaign.
Harare Declaration issued.
Anti-apartheid demonstrations permitted in major South African cities.
Walter Sisulu and seven other long-term political prisoners released.
Pan-Africanist Movement (internal wing of PAC) launched.

1990   Nelson Mandela released; later elected deputy president of ANC.
Groote Schuur Minute signed.
Mandela on world tour.
Fighting between Inkatha and ANC supporters spreads to Transvaal townships.
SACP holds first public rally.
Pretoria Minute signed.
PAC president Zephania Mothopeng dies; succeeded by Clarence Makwetu.

1991   UDF disbands.
Political exiles return.
Winnie Mandela found guilty of kidnapping; sentenced to six years (reduced to fine and suspended sentence on appeal).
ANC holds first national conference since banning in 1960:
Nelson Mandela elected ANC president.
Huge anti-VAT stayaway by workers.
CODESA begins.
National Peace Accord signed.

1992   ANC and allies launch mass action campaign.
At least 45 people slain in attack at Boipatong on East Rand.
Ciskei soldiers open fire on ANC demonstration in Bisho, killing 29 people.
Record of Understanding signed.

1993   Violent protests follow assassination of SACP leader Chris Hani.
ANC chairman Oliver Tambo dies.
Commission finds evidence of past human rights abuses in ANC detention camps.
Negotiators draw up new interim constitution.
Nelson Mandela awarded Nobel Peace Prize jointly with F W de Klerk.
PAC suspends armed struggle; joins election.

1994   ANC wins first democratic election; Mandela installed as President.

'Down with Afrikaans'

On a winter's day in 1976 more than 20000 pupils from the African township complex of Soweto began a protest march against a Bantu Education Department regulation that Afrikaans be used as one of the languages of instruction in secondary schools. Several hours later, police and youths were engaged in running street battles all over the dusty township. During the next few weeks dozens of other black townships across the country were involved in the most serious revolt against the white state since the Defiance and anti-Pass campaigns that peaked in 1960.

ON 25 MAY 1976, Fred van Wyk, the director of the South African Institute of Race Relations, sent an urgent telegram to Progressive Reform Party MP René de Villiers: 'Deeply concerned Afrikaans medium controversy black schools,' it said. 'Position Soweto very serious. Could you discuss matter with Minister...?'

De Villiers, a former editor of the country's biggest daily newspaper, 'The Star', immediately tried to set up an interview with one of the ministers responsible for the administration of 'Bantu' affairs, even though he must have realised that he did not stand a chance.

How could one dyed-in-the-wool liberal belonging to a small English-speaking opposition party possibly hope to influence a coterie of ministers determined to follow to the last jot and tittle the native policies of the greatest Afrikaner nationalist ideologue of them all – Hendrik Frensch Verwoerd?

De Villiers tried his best, but the man he got to see – Deputy Minister of Bantu Administration and Development, and of Bantu Education, Andries Treurnicht – did not share his concern. 'I'm not aware of any real problem,' he insisted throughout the brief interview.

It was a statement that was later deservedly preserved for posterity: because a little more than three weeks after Treurnicht's glib assurance, Soweto took the lead in a countrywide rebellion that shook white South Africa to the core. And although the uprising was eventually put down – at a cost of hundreds of lives and millions of rands in damage – South African society would never be the same again. Soweto 1976 proved to be a turning point – for the government, for Africans and for the white liberal establishment: it brought to an end almost two decades of African political inactivity, it gave rise to a generation of black consciousness-inspired activists determined to fight their own battles, and it forced the government to look beyond the use of brute force to safeguard what it saw as the 'right of whites to self-determination'. But more than that, it cleared the decks for the battle between African and Afrikaner nationalism.

Countdown to conflict

The main cause of the protests that started in African schools in the Transvaal at the beginning of 1975 was a directive from the Bantu Education Department that Afrikaans had to be used on an equal basis with English as one of the languages of instruction in the department's secondary schools.

It was not a new rule. Verwoerd had thought of it more than 20 years earlier – in 1953 – when he devised his Bantu Education package. But in the context of *baasskap*, even Verwoerd was capable of errors of judgment; and when the language clause proved to be unworkable

PROGRESSIVE REFORM PARTY MP *René de Villiers (right) tried to warn Deputy Minister of Bantu Education Andries Treurnicht (left) of the growing tide of resentment against the use of Afrikaans as a joint medium with English at African schools. Treurnicht, however, insisted that he was 'not aware of any real problem'.*

due to a shortage of teachers, a lack of Afrikaans text-books and a grudging acceptance that pupils would have immense difficulty in coping with three languages as mediums of instruction, it was quietly forgotten by the white bureaucrats who ran African education.

In 1974, however, the Secretary for Bantu Education, Dr Hennie van Zyl, died and in the shake-up that followed his death, the dour Bantu Education Minister, M C Botha, decided to reintroduce the 50-50 ruling.

Botha had no reason to believe there would be objections. After all, the system he administered had been designed specifically to condition Africans to accept the role of menials in a white man's country.

Bantu education – with its overcrowded classrooms, inadequately trained teachers and separate, inferior universities – was meant to shatter morale. And for many years it did precisely that (see page 379).

But in the late 1960s and early '70s it began to show distinct signs of wear and tear. Influenced by events outside South Africa – the death throes of colonialism in Africa, the rise of 'Black Power' in the USA and a growing worldwide antagonism towards apartheid – African students began to kick against the system.

Rise of black consciousness

Aware that they were the moral and intellectual equals of white students, but that they were the pawns in the racial and economic policies of the white government, African students began uniting under a new and highly significant banner: black consciousness (see box).

Black consciousness was a new way of looking at the world. Liberation, its proponents argued, would come about only when Africans threw off their shackles of fear and their feelings of inferiority, and conducted their own political campaigns instead of relying on white liberals to map out their strategies for them. Whites, they argued, were far too enmeshed in the system of apartheid ever to make reliable allies.

Black consciousness engendered a new sense of pride in millions of Africans: blackness became something to be proud of, to be defiant about and worth fighting for.

And so the message was spread – by students in the rural-based tribal colleges to younger brothers and sisters in the townships. Soon 'BC' became the rallying cry of an entire generation.

The pot begins to boil

Of all the government officials, Bantu Education Minister M C Botha was probably best qualified to read the danger signs in the storm that began to blow over African education. In 1943, when the Nationalists were in opposition, Botha, then secretary of a special *Afrikaner Broederbond* educational committee, had prepared an instruction that urged 'churches to encourage parents to refuse to send their children to schools where [United Party] government policy had been introduced.

'Where a minister is unsympathetic,' he had urged, 'a strong personality in the church council or congregation should take the lead; each member of a school committee should undertake responsibility for ten or so par-

MINISTER *of Bantu Education M C Botha pressed for the implementation of Afrikaans as a medium of instruction.*

ents and children and persuade them to be ready to strike at a given moment.'

Now, Botha was a cabinet minister, and he chose *kragdadigheid* (literally, brute force) to crush opposition to government policies.

Thus, in February 1976, two members of the Meadowlands Tswana School Board were sacked for defying his instruction to use Afrikaans in schools. A few days later the remaining seven members of the board resigned in protest and over the next few weeks the situation deteriorated rapidly.

On 24 February Junior Certificate pupils at Thomas Mofolo Secondary clashed with their principal over the issue and on 17 May a class boycott was started at Orlando West Junior Secondary after a circuit inspector had turned down a request for a meeting. By 25 May the number of boycotting schools had risen to six. On 27 May an Afrikaans teacher at Pimville Higher Primary was stabbed and police were stoned when they tried to arrest a youth in connection with the assault.

Education authorities reacted to the growing unrest with a warning that they would not hesitate to shut down boycotting schools, expel pupils who had absented themselves for more than 10 days at a stretch and transfer teachers. But, if anything, their hard-line stance made matters worse.

At Belle Higher Primary pupils stoned school buildings and clashed with classmates who had returned to lessons; at Naledi High pupils twice clashed with police; at Emthonjeni pupils refused to write their social studies examination in Afrikaans, while Orlando West Junior Secondary was faced with a full-scale boycott of the entire June examinations.

On 11 June Van Wyk sent another telegram to De Villiers, who again spoke to Treurnicht. The Minister, however, disagreed that there had been an escalation of the dispute. He had reason to believe, he assured De Villiers, that the matter would be amicably settled.

Five days later, the storm broke....

CROWDS THRONG *a Soweto street on 16 June 1976 in a massive protest at the use of Afrikaans on an equal basis with English as a medium of instruction at African schools. As more and more students joined the demonstration, a teargas grenade was thrown into the crowd, followed by a single shot, a rain of stones and more shots. Out of the panic and chaos that followed, a student emerged carrying a fatally injured 13-year-old schoolboy named Hector Petersen – and a newspaper photographer, Sam Nzima, took this dramatic picture (below), which came to symbolise internationally the tragedy of 16 June.*

'Afrikaans is a tribal language'

On 13 June delegates representing all the secondary schools in Soweto elected an action committee to plan a protest march through the township, to be followed by a mass rally at the Orlando football stadium.

Secrecy was the byword in the hectic preparations that followed: it needed just one indiscreet word within earshot of one of the many *impimpi* (informers) to scuttle the plan, organisers repeatedly stressed at clandestine meetings. But they need not have worried. In the three days that they flitted in and out of schools to issue their hurried instructions, thousands of lips remained sealed.

The march had been set for Wednesday, 16 June at 7 am. But by 6 o'clock hundreds of pupils were already gathered at the more than a dozen assembly points. The mood of the crowd was relaxed, even jovial, when marshalls began handing out tattered pieces of cardboard on which were scrawled slogans such as 'Down with Afrikaans', 'Bantu Education – to hell with it', and 'Afrikaans is a tribal language'.

At precisely 7 o'clock, the first group of singing, chanting pupils began marching towards Orlando . . . .

Clashes with the police began almost immediately: at White City in Jabavu, shots were fired at two schoolboys hurrying to catch the marchers, while at Dube Vocational College a teargas canister was thrown into a contingent of marchers. Later, several African policemen were put to flight when they tried to turn back another group.

Shortly before 9 am, a senior pupil addressed a crowd of several thousand outside Orlando West Junior Secondary: 'Brothers and sisters,' he said, 'I appeal to you – keep calm and cool. We have just received a report that the police are coming. Don't taunt them, don't do anything to them. Be cool and calm. We are not fighting.'

Within minutes of his appeal, a contingent of police vans and cars arrived and about 50 policemen emerged from their vehicles to form an arc in front of the crowd, which began singing '*Morena Boloka Sechaba sa heso*' (God Save our Nation).

The shooting begins

The upheaval that swept through Soweto began when a single teargas canister was hurled amidst the singing, placard-waving crowd. This was followed by a single shot, a wave of panic, a rain of stones, more shots and yet more stones.

Sophie Tema, a journalist with the newspaper 'The World', described how, out of the chaos, she saw a group of children emerge carrying a critically wounded youth. His name was Hector Petersen, he was 13 years old, and he was covered in blood. She rushed him to a nearby

Black and proud – the origins of black consciousness

In the years that followed the banning in 1960 of the African National Congress and the Pan-Africanist Congress, African students began to look increasingly towards the multiracial National Union of South African Students (NUSAS) as a vehicle through which to express their political aspirations.

At first glance, it seemed a good move: in the early 1960s, the white NUSAS leadership tended to identify strongly with black causes.

But in 1964, in the face of strong opposition by rank-and-file members to some of its more 'radical' policies, NUSAS dipped sharply to the right, confining itself to symbolic multiracial activities. It was the beginning of a period of deep frustration for the small black membership who, unable to articulate their grievances adequately, allowed themselves to be co-opted into the new, no-risks style of NUSAS politics.

However, South African politics is never static for long, and in 1967 a group of black students began seriously to analyse their political predicament. The prime mover in this regard was a young Natal University medical student named Steve Biko.

Born in King William's Town in the eastern Cape in 1947, Biko had been introduced to politics as a teenager in 1963 when an older brother had been arrested as a suspected *Poqo* member and jailed for nine months. Biko himself had been questioned by the police regarding his brother. Expelled by Lovedale High School because of his brother's activities, he was sent to St Francis College at Mariannhill in Natal, and then enrolled at the black medical section of Natal University.

A vastly talented political analyst, he was soon elected to the Students' Representative Council of the university, which in turn drew him into the activities of NUSAS.

At the NUSAS congress in 1968, Biko and a group of friends began to draw black students into a candid discussion on their second-class role within the union. Later, at a University Christian Movement meeting in Stutterheim, he began actively to promote the idea of an all-black university movement.

In July 1969 the South African Students' Organisation (SASO) came into being with Biko as president. Although the new organisation was committed to a philosophy of black consciousness, it did not immediately reject the liberalism of NUSAS. Officials were only too aware that many members still held lingering loyalties towards the multiracial union. But by 1970 Biko felt confident enough to launch a series of attacks on white liberal thinking: 'The integration they [liberals] talk about ... is artificial ... a one-way course, with the whites doing all the talking and the blacks the listening,' he claimed in an article in the August edition of the SASO 'Newsletter'.

And he also had some harsh words for Africans who had been drawn into the 'come-around-to-tea' circuit: 'One sees a perfect example of what oppression has done to the blacks. They have been made to feel inferior for so long that for them it is comforting to drink tea, wine or beer with whites who seem to treat them as equals. This serves to boost up their own ego to the extent of making them feel slightly superior to those blacks who do not get similar treatment from whites. These are the sort of blacks who are a danger to the community.'

To Biko, a true liberal was a white person who directed all his energies into educating other whites and preparing them to accept a future system of majority rule. Until this came about, blacks had to go it alone, he argued.

Black consciousness had an immediate appeal for thousands of black South Africans. Although it was not an organisation, it spawned a number of bodies that espoused its philosophy. By 1972 a Black Peoples' Convention had been set up to act as an umbrella body to co-ordinate its adherents.

In 1977, however, black consciousness was dealt a series of devastating body blows: in September of that year, Biko died after 26 days in police detention; and in October, Justice Minister Jimmy Kruger banned 17 organisations and two newspapers ('World' and 'Weekend World'), all of which he claimed supported black consciousness.

THE IDEOLOGICAL *leader of black consciousness, Steve Biko.*

---

clinic in her car, but he was certified dead on arrival. Later, the photograph of Petersen being carried away became a symbol of the tragedy that was 16 June.

The police, meanwhile, heavily outnumbered by the furious crowd, retreated towards Orlando East, giving the demonstrators a chance to collect their casualties – at least two dead and more than a dozen wounded.

As news of the shooting spread, pupils began erecting barricades across the dusty streets. By noon, hundreds of police reinforcements had been rushed to the area. But there was little they could do to stop the crowds that attacked the property and employees of the West Rand Administration Board (WRAB). Two WRAB employees were murdered by angry crowds; later, smoke billowed over the township as offices and vehicles belonging to the board were put to the torch. Other targets included WRAB-controlled beerhalls and bottlestores. Hundreds of cases of beer were removed from these

JUSTICE MINISTER *Jimmy Kruger (above)
slapped a ban on all outdoor public
meetings in an effort to quell the spreading unrest – which continued unabat-
ed as chanting schoolchildren in Soweto
and elsewhere confronted anxiously
watching police (right).*

premises and broken on the pavements by pupils chanting 'less liquor, better education'.

The next day the government closed the schools,
poured more police reinforcements into the area and
placed the army on alert. But in the continuing violence
hundreds of people were killed and 143 vehicles and 139
buildings destroyed.

As news of the shooting began appearing on television screens and in newspapers in the rest of the world,
South Africa's economy, already showing signs of
decline after the post-Sharpeville boom years, took a
devastating knock: gold shares dropped by an average
of 75 cents on the London stock exchange, while De
Beers diamond shares fell nearly 15 cents. Big business
reacted to these developments with alarm. Of the net foreign capital inflow of R800-million during 1976,
R536-million consisted of short-term loans. With growing horror businessmen realised that if Soweto was to
follow the pattern of the Sharpeville unrest in 1960, overseas borrowing would become appreciably more difficult
and the economy would suffer a downturn.

Government reaction

On 17 June, Treurnicht dealt with the Afrikaans language controversy in a speech in Windhoek, Namibia:
the government, he said, was prepared to be as accom-
modating as possible as far as the use of Afrikaans at African schools was concerned.

But in the next breath, he added: 'In the white areas
of South Africa [Soweto was deemed to be part of 'white'
South Africa], where the government erects the buildings, grants the subsidies and pays the teachers, it is our
right to decide on language policy. The same applies to
schools in areas where there is no compulsory education. Why are pupils sent to schools if [our] language
policy does not suit them?'

That same day in parliament, Justice Minister Jimmy
Kruger accused the University Christian Movement of

having 'initiated a polarisation between black and white
and the development of black power consciousness'.

'The other question one has to ask oneself,' Kruger
continued, 'is why the young people walked with their
fists in the air? Why do they walk with upraised fists?
Surely this is the sign of the Communist Party?'

On 18 June, Prime Minister John Vorster broke his silence with a typically tough speech: 'The government
will not be intimidated,' he told parliament. 'Orders
have been given to maintain order at all costs.'

The first step was a ban, in terms of the Riotous Assemblies Act, on all outdoor public meetings except bona
fide sports events. Later, in analysing the nature of what
he referred to as 'so-called black grievances', Kruger
said: 'Many [grievances] . . . are far-fetched. Some are
impractical and some are real. But I have not found any
grievances that would indicate that Bantu Administration has flopped on the job.'

The spontaneous unrest of Africans throughout the
country appeared to suggest otherwise.

Of course, it was not so much Afrikaans as the whole
system of Bantu education (and ultimately apartheid)
that was the bone of contention for African students. This
was apparent even before the outbreak of unrest. For instance, at the entrance of one Soweto school, pupils had
daubed a slogan that read 'Enter to learn, leave to serve'.
And during the protests a pamphlet addressed to parents stated:' . . . you should rejoice for having given birth
to this type of child . . . a child who prefers to die from
a bullet rather than to swallow a poisonous education
which relegates him and his parents to a position of perpetual subordination.' On the same theme, a Press statement released by the Soweto Students' Representative
Council shortly after its formation in August 1976, stated: 'Twenty years ago, when Bantu Education was introduced, our fathers said: ''Half a loaf is better than no
loaf.'' But we say: ''Half a gram of poison is just as killing as the whole gram.'''

The last journey of Stephen Bantu Biko

Late on the night of 18 August 1977 banned eastern Cape political activist Steve Biko was detained at a police roadblock that had been especially set up for him on the outskirts of Grahamstown. Twenty-six days later he was dead – from massive head injuries sustained in a room at security police headquarters in central Port Elizabeth.

Justice Minister Jimmy Kruger, who announced the death in a rambling statement on the morning of 13 September, clearly believed that Biko had died as a result of a hunger strike: '. . . since 5 September,' he said, 'Mr Biko refused his meals and threatened a hunger strike . . . . The District Surgeon was called in on 7 September after Mr Biko appeared to be unwell . . . [but] he could not find anything wrong.'

The rest of the statement detailed further doctors' visits, a suspicion by both police and medical men that Biko might have been feigning illness and, finally, a 1 120-kilometre dash by Land Rover to get the ill man to a prison hospital in Pretoria.

Kruger, who had a reputation as a hawk, reached new heights the next day at the Transvaal Congress of the National Party: 'I am not glad and I am not sorry about Mr Biko . . . . He leaves me cold,' he told an appreciative audience of cabinet ministers, MPs and other pillars of the party. Later a delegate from Springs, capturing the mood of the gathering, drew roars of laughter when he praised the Minister for granting Biko 'his democratic right to starve himself to death'.

'Inciting blacks to cause riots'
Elsewhere in the country, mainly in the African townships, news of the death of the black consciousness leader was greeted with shock – shock that turned to anger when the story of Biko's final days unfolded at an inquest that opened in Pretoria on 2 November 1977 . . . .

Not formally charged with committing a crime, Biko had been held under Section 6 of the Terrorism Act that allowed for the indefinite detention, for the purposes of interrogation, of any person either thought to be a 'terrorist', or who had information regarding the activities of 'terrorists'.

It was a detention that security police justified by claiming that at the time of his arrest he was on his way to Cape Town to distribute 'inflammatory' pamphlets . . . 'inciting blacks to cause riots'.

On 19 August, after spending the night in a police cell in Grahamstown, he was taken to the Walmer police station in Port Elizabeth where he was held, naked, 'in order to prevent him from hanging himself with his clothes'.

On 6 September, still naked, but now also in leg irons, he was taken to security police headquarters where a five-man team headed by Major Harold Snyman began interrogating him.

What happened there became the subject of a series of heated exchanges between Sydney Kentridge, counsel for the Biko family, and members of the security police.

'He bumped his head against a wall'
The autopsy had revealed the cause of death as a blow (or blows) to the head, struck with enough force almost certainly to have rendered Biko unconscious.

Snyman's explanation was that Biko had bumped his head against a wall during a struggle. He had jumped up with a 'wild look' in his eyes after being confronted with evidence that linked him to riots, arson and boycotts – and it had taken five men to restrain him, said the major.

If this were so, countered Kentridge, why was it not mentioned in any of the 28 affidavits made by police and doctors involved?

Kentridge was particularly scathing in his criticism of the conduct of doctors Ivor Lang, Benjamin Tucker and Colin Hersch, all of whom admitted making incorrect diagnoses. The police, he claimed, faced with allegations that they had assaulted Biko, had closed ranks and entered into a conspiracy of silence into which the doctors had allowed themselves to be drawn.

They had gone along with a police theory that Biko was feigning when it must have been obvious that he

STEVE BIKO'S *coffin is carried through the Victoria Stadium in King William's Town under the flag of the Black People's Convention.*

was, in fact, gravely ill. And even when they were finally moved to suggest that he be taken to hospital, they allowed him to be placed naked in the back of a police Land Rover for a journey of more than 1 000 kilometres to Pretoria. There, said Kentridge, Biko 'died a miserable and lonely death on a mat on a stone floor of a prison cell'.

'We don't work under statutes'
A telex sent by the head of the Port Elizabeth security branch, Colonel Piet Goosen, to Pretoria, cast further doubts on police evidence: describing the events leading to Biko's death, the telex mentioned an injury 'inflicted on' Biko at 7 am on 7 September. Recalled to the stand, Goosen explained 'inflicted on' as a play on words.

Earlier, in another clash with Goosen, Kentridge asked the security police chief who had given him the authority to keep a man in chains for 48 hours.

'I have the full power to do it to ensure a man's safety,' he replied.

'I am asking you to give the statute,' insisted Kentridge.

'We don't work under statutes,' said Goosen.

'Thank you very much,' answered Kentridge. 'That is what we have always suspected.'

The Chief Magistrate of Pretoria, Marthinus Prins, said that Biko's death had probably been caused by head injuries sustained in a scuffle with security police. 'The available evidence does not prove that the death was brought about by any act or omission involving or amounting to an offence on the part of any person.'

Business responds to strife in the cities

URBAN FOUNDATION *leaders Harry Oppenheimer of Anglo-American (left), Jan Steyn, a former judge who became Chief Executive Officer of the foundation, and tobacco magnate Anton Rupert (right).*

In 1976, at the height of the country-wide unrest, Harry Oppenheimer and Anton Rupert, the two giants of South Africa's English and Afrikaans business worlds, met at a London hotel to seek ways and means of persuading the government to encourage the growth of an African middle class, as an ally for the whites and a bulwark against socialism.

The result was the launch, in March 1977, of the Urban Foundation (UF) – an organisation dedicated to creating opportunities for Africans in areas such as home-ownership and education.

Previously, business had shown little interest in more enlightened policy; many had benefited from apartheid legislation, especially labour control. But as the 1980s saw intensified conflict in the cities, increased pressure from abroad, and an extended economic crisis, business leaders expressed an increasingly vocal desire for reform. Pointing out that Africans were integral to South African society, they called for the scrapping of discriminatory laws, and insisted that the many Africans who could not afford to compete in the marketplace should be given a minimum access to facilities.

From the outset, the UF was active in the fields of job-training schemes, literacy work, and pre-school and adult education. Its major contribution, however, has been in the area of housing and urban policy. Led by former Supreme Court Judge, Jan Steyn, the UF played a key role in per-suading the government to introduce the 99-year leasehold scheme which permitted a form of African home-ownership in townships within white South Africa. Following this breakthrough, it was also a leading light in the granting of loans by corporations to African white-collar workers.

But in the 1980s the UF was viewed by many blacks as an arm of P W Botha's 'total strategy' – and much of its work was conducted outside the public eye.

By the 1990s, the political climate had so changed that the UF was able with considerable fanfare to unveil its proposals on urbanisation. The proposals dealt with housing, land usage and ownership, the urban economy, and town and regional planning. They have had considerable influence on local and central authorities, the private sector, and some academics – but some critics charged that the UF was replacing race bars with economic barriers and had failed to redress the imbalances of apartheid.

Many of the recommendations have subsequently become government policy, including the scrapping of discriminatory legislation governing land ownership and control, abandonment of the decentralisation policy, and the acceptance of informal settlement as a feature of city life.

By 1990, there were an estimated 5-7 million squatters in South Africa and the government acknowledged that 70 percent of blacks could not afford to pay R10 000 for a house. Concern for what amounted to a huge housing crisis with major social, economic and political implications led the government to establish with an initial grant of R2-billion the Independent Development Trust (IDT) under the leadership of Jan Steyn.

The IDT expressed its aim as black economic empowerment and much of its thinking has been underpinned by the UF's perspectives. Wary of rejection by the extra-parliamentary movement, however, the IDT first conducted a series of negotiations with community organisations and political parties.

The IDT's initial grants focused on land ownership. R1,56-billion or 61 percent was allocated to housing on the basis of site-and-service. The IDT set up a capital subsidy scheme, granted funds for development of informal settlements and looked at establishing a finance corporation to fund housing for the poor.

At the same time several service organisations with links to black communities also examined housing and land issues. While they lacked the funds available to the UF and IDT, their research was fed into the policy of civic organisations, trade unions and political organisations, such as the ANC. Thus all parties to the negotiated settlement were fully informed on urban policy issues.

A SCHOOL *built jointly by Africans and the Urban Foundation.*

The unrest spreads

Unrest was not confined to Soweto. Less than two weeks after the first clashes between police and pupils, violence had spread like wildfire – first to neighbouring townships on the Reef, and then further afield. By August at least 80 black communities throughout the country had vented their anger.

In Cape Town, 30 people died in unrest that broke out on 11 August in the African townships of Langa, Guguletu and Nyanga. Then, in a significant development at the beginning of September, coloured pupils and students from the Western Cape universities and training colleges joined the protests. Thirty more deaths were reported in the violence that followed.

In Soweto the initial violence burnt itself out within a few days, but calm was not restored to the township until the beginning of 1978. Certainly, for the remainder of 1976 and the whole of 1977, clashes between police and pupils, the burning of schools and beer halls and the mass detention of suspected activists became a regular part of the black experience.

Swopping books for AK-47s

Although in the end guns triumphed over stones and burning barricades, the sullen peace that returned to the townships merely signalled the beginning of a new phase of African resistance to apartheid.

The Soweto uprisings brought to maturity a new generation of Africans who believed in their own worth and their right to equal treatment. Having acquired a taste for battle, hundreds of them began slipping over South Africa's borders into neighbouring states to join the banned nationalist movements, the African National Congress (ANC) and the Pan-Africanist Congress (PAC).

Although the majority of volunteers were black consciousness adherents, most ended up in the training camps and schools of the 'non-racial' ANC (the PAC, at that stage, was wracked by internal squabbles and, in fact, existed only in name).

Appreciably strengthened by this unexpected influx, the ANC began stepping up its low-level and often badly executed campaign of insurgency. Within a year of the countrywide rebellion of the young, the first groups of the class of '76 – now armed with the ubiquitous AK-47 machineguns, limpet mines and hand grenades – began slipping back into the country.

The best intelligence system in Africa

In many ways, the South African security forces proved more than equal to the new challenge. Boasting one of the most effective intelligence-gathering systems in the world (thanks to a vast national and international informer network), the police and army were able to crush many of the ANC's most carefully planned campaigns.

Certainly, when the then head of the Security Police, General Johan Coetzee, claimed in an interview with 'New York Times' journalist Joseph Lelyveld that there was little he did not know about what was going on in the ANC, he was probably speaking the truth. And yet – despite the fact that setbacks outnumbered successes – guerrillas

were occasionally able to evade the security net long enough to carry out acts of sabotage. And in this respect the attack early in 1980 on the oil-from-coal refinery at Sasolburg in the Orange Free State was probably the most spectacular. Six storage tanks were set ablaze by a three-man ANC team – and several days later a thick pall of smoke was still drifting over Johannesburg, more than 80 km away. The sabotage of construction work on the Koeberg nuclear power station was also noteworthy.

The making of a guerrilla

The ANC was well aware that a military victory over the state's security forces was out of the question. The chief purpose of its hit-and-run raids was psychological – to shatter the morale of government supporters and to increase its own backing in the townships.

To a certain extent, it succeeded in its latter aim. But the cost, in terms of lives lost, was awesome. Between 1976 and the ANC's suspension of the armed struggle in 1990, many of the young people who fled South Africa to join *Umkhonto we Sizwe* were either caught or killed.

What drove so many young South Africans to take up arms against the National Party Government? Sometimes answers were given at the tail-end of treason trials. And, almost always, the words which cropped up were 'poverty' and 'humiliation'.

In 1978, Mosima Gabriel 'Tokyo' Sexwale, one member of the class of '76, addressed a Pretoria Supreme Court judge shortly after his conviction on a charge of high treason: 'Now that I have been convicted,' he said, 'I want to explain my actions so that you ... should understand why I chose to join the struggle for the freedom of my people.... It was during my primary school years that the bare facts concerning the realities of South African society and its discrepancies began to unfold before me. I remember a period in the early 1960s, when there was a great deal of political tension, and we often used to encounter armed police in Soweto.... I remember the humiliation to which my parents were subjected by whites in shops and in other places where we encountered them, and the poverty.

'All these things had their influence on my young mind ... and by the time I went to Orlando West High School, I was already beginning to question the injustice of the society ... and to ask why nothing was being done to change it,' said the young activist.

'It is true that I was trained in the use of weapons and explosives. The basis of my training was in sabotage, which was to be aimed at institutions and not people. I did not wish to add unnecessarily to the grievous loss of human life that had already been incurred. It has been suggested that our aim was to annihilate the white people of this country; nothing could be further from the truth. The ANC is a national liberation movement committed to the liberation of all the people of South Africa, black and white, from racial fear, hatred and oppression,' he told the court.

'I am married and have one child, and would like nothing more than to have more children, and to live with my wife and children with all the people in this country. One day that might be possible – if not for me, then at least for my brothers.'

Old wine in new bottles

At the beginning of the 1970s, the South African Government faced a growing crisis: calls for an arms embargo against the Republic had gathered support at the United Nations; disinvestment as a means of forcing South Africa into isolation was being hotly debated in the United States; while, elsewhere in the West, trade unions were stepping up campaigns to disrupt South African trade, air links and postal services. The government responded to this onslaught on its racial policies by trying to serve up the old wine of apartheid in new bottles – by placing more stress on the 'separate development' aspects of its policies.

THE YOUNG MAN who was ushered into Prime Minister John Vorster's office one October morning in 1973 was anything but nervous. Vorster, and his Minister of Finance, Nico Diederichs, studied him carefully. He was lean, fit and well turned out in impeccably tailored clothes. He shook hands confidently, with an easy smile and urbane manner.

Vorster was normally suspicious of outsiders. It was common knowledge among his inner circle of advisors that he rarely granted audiences to Public Service officials and that he did not entertain new schemes and ideas from subordinates lightly. Yet the Prime Minister could not ignore the fact that the man who sat in the upright chair across his desk had come with the highest possible recommendations: General Hendrik van den Bergh, Vorster's trusted right-hand man and head of the secretive Bureau for State Security (BOSS), had described him as 'one of the most intelligent men I have ever met'. Connie Mulder, the Transvaal leader of the National Party (NP) – and Vorster's heir apparent – was so impressed with the man's grasp of current affairs that he had personally arranged this meeting with the Prime Minister.

For the next hour, Vorster listened with growing interest as the visitor outlined a scheme that would alter the destinies of each man in that room and send shock waves through the NP and its leadership – and, indeed, through South Africa itself.

Vorster's fateful choice

The young man was Eschel Rhoodie who, at the age of 38, had recently been appointed Secretary for Information (the senior post in Mulder's high-profile Department of Information). His promotion followed a 15-year stint marked by distinguished service as a senior press and information attaché – at South African embassies and missions in cities as far afield as Canberra, Washington, New York and The Hague.

While overseas, Rhoodie had been appalled by what he considered to be one-sided reporting and double standards applied to South Africa by the international press. Having observed the rising repugnance for apartheid and the threat of increasing sanctions and ostracism, he had formulated a plan to counter these dangers. As he outlined his ideas to Vorster and Diederichs, his sincerity and grasp

DR ESCHEL RHOODIE, *the dynamic young Secretary for Information whose plans to counter the negative media image of the South African Government were to shake the National Party to its core.*

ONE OF *the first steps taken by the Department of Information was the publication of an English-language newspaper sympathetic to the government. After some R14-million of taxpayers' money had been spent, 'The Citizen' was launched early in 1976.*

of world politics, and the international media, deeply impressed the two older men. What was needed, he explained, was a 'drastic programme of psychological and propaganda warfare' to emphasise South Africa's strategic importance, its anti-communist stand and its potential as a haven for capitalism on a continent that had gone socialist.

To improve South Africa's image throughout the Western world, Rhoodie proposed a campaign to influence sympathetic politicians and editors and to counter anti-apartheid groups and what they considered communist-inspired organisations. Pulling no punches about the unorthodox methods he intended to use, he left Vorster in no doubt as to what he was asking.

At the end of his address he turned to Vorster and said: 'Mr Prime Minister, I would not like to operate under a misconception. Are we in agreement that we are not talking about the intensification of the current Department of Information activities, but, in fact, about the launching of a separate, no-holds-barred propaganda war, free of any government rules or regulations? Is that the case?'

Vorster looked at him from beneath his shaggy eyebrows and nodded. 'Yes, I understand perfectly. Very well, it is in order for you to go ahead.'

A radical change of tactics

Before his meeting with the Prime Minister, Rhoodie had completed several secret surveys and trial projects (costing some R3-million) for the Department of Information. But when the Cabinet approved a detailed five-year operation on 19 March 1974 many millions more were placed at his disposal. In fact, about R74-million was transferred by the Treasury to the top-secret weapons procurement fund of the Minister of Defence, P W Botha. Rhoodie was then able to draw on this fund to implement the projects approved by a Cabinet committee of Vorster, Diederichs and Mulder.

Starting a newspaper on the home front

High on the list of Rhoodie's priorities was the acquisition of an English-language newspaper. At first he tried to purchase the controlling shares of South African Associated Newspapers (the owners of the 'Sunday Times' and 'Rand Daily Mail'). The attempt failed, but that did not worry Rhoodie unduly: he simply decided to establish his own independent newspaper.

Of course, the fact that money was no object helped: drawing on its vast resources, the department deposited about R14-million into the business account of a 'straw man' – a leading businessman named Louis Luyt – who announced early in 1976 that he was starting a new English-language daily, 'The Citizen'.

Although the editor, Johnny Johnson, was a high-ranking former employee of the anti-government 'Sunday Times', the new newspaper took a pro-government stance in its editorial columns. According to Rhoodie, 'The Citizen' was set up to counter the anti-government 'Rand Daily Mail', which many of the foreign press corps looked to for information about South Africa.

At first, it seemed unlikely that the newspaper would pose any danger to the long-established 'Rand Daily Mail'. To begin with, its circulation was dismal, far less than the budgeted 80 000 copies a day. To add to its problems, advertisers were aghast to read allegations in the 'Rand Daily Mail' that some 30 000 copies were being dumped and destroyed each night. With actual circulation hovering at around 50 000, advertising fell away.

In a bid to rescue the project, the department sacked Luyt and, from 14 February 1978, appointed J van Zyl Alberts and Hubert Jussen, the publisher of 'To The Point' magazine, to head the newspaper. Later, 'The Citizen' was purchased by the Afrikaner-run publishing company Perskor – but not before some R35-million of taxpayers' money had been used to keep it going.

A dangerous expansion

With a large budget, Rhoodie's men prowled the world, trying by fair means or foul to win friends and influence people, countries and organisations. Some of the department's 184 projects, conceived and executed under a cloak of secrecy, had a measure of success. Others ended in failure or disarray.

In 'Operation Bowler Hat', British MPs from both the Conservative Party and the Labour Party were drawn onto the Info payroll.

The British-based trade press house Morgan Grampian was a notable purchase – the plan being to launch a series of publications from there to win the hearts and minds of the British public. Moves were also made to buy 'The Investor's Chronicle' and the French publications 'L'Express' and 'Paris Match'.

Under the auspices of front organisations such as the Foreign Affairs Association and the Southern African Freedom Foundation, set up in a dozen countries abroad and in South Africa, hundreds of VIPs visited the Republic.

In Europe, the department set up massive public relations networks, foundations and research institutes. In Norway, a right-wing magazine funded directly from

Playing the game of sports boycotts

BASIL D'OLIVIERA *returned to South Africa in the late 1980s to assist with the development of cricket among disadvantaged communities.*

For the young cricketer from Cape Town it was a dream come true – the pinnacle of a cricketing career that had begun on the dusty playgrounds of a city 10 000 km to the south. Batting for England in a crucial final test match against Australia at the Oval in 1968, Basil d'Oliviera hit a magnificent 158 runs to virtually secure his place in the team scheduled to tour South Africa later that year.

As he journeyed to his home in Worcestershire after the match, D'Oliviera could hardly have imagined the effect his performance would have on international sport ....

To begin an incredible sequence of events, he was left out of the touring party. Then, as a bitter debate over his omission raged across the cricketing world, the selectors, stung by accusations of racism, were thrown a lifeline: all-rounder Tom Cartwright withdrew from the side with a back injury and the man from Cape Town was promptly called up as a replacement.

Just one question remained unanswered: D'Oliviera had been classified by the apartheid machinery in Pretoria as 'coloured'. Would the NP allow him to play in the same team as white Englishmen against an all-white South African team?

Prime Minister John Vorster gave his answer shortly after the announcement of D'Oliviera's inclusion. Addressing a public meeting in Bloemfontein, Vorster solemnly declared: '...We are not prepared to receive a team thrust upon us by people whose interests are not the game, but to gain political objectives which they do not even attempt to hide. The team, as it stands, is not the team of the MCC selection committee but of the political opponents of South Africa.' The MCC immediately cancelled the tour.

Vorster's shot in the foot was to cost a generation of South African sportsmen and women any hope of international competition. It also marked the beginning of a concerted international effort to ban South African participation in international sport – both overseas and within the Republic's own borders.

Even without the D'Oliviera incident, South Africa's participation in international sport seemed doomed. In 1968 – the same year that Vorster stopped the cricketer from coming to South Africa – several African countries threatened to boycott the forthcoming Olympic Games in Mexico City if South Africa competed. The response of the International Olympic Committee was almost a foregone conclusion: South Africa was excluded – and two years later in 1970 expelled altogether from the Olympic movement.

Thereafter, the African bloc, often with the support of other non-aligned countries, began forcing the Republic out of many international competitions simply by indicating that it would withdraw if South Africa was included. This action was later extended to cover countries that maintained sporting links with South Africa. In 1976, 21 countries boycotted the Montreal Olympics in protest against participation by athletes from New Zealand, whose rugby team had toured South Africa.

This action made it clear that any sporting links with South Africa meant risking international sporting isolation – and with the Commonwealth Games looming in Edmonton in 1978, few countries were prepared to take this risk. At a meeting at Gleneagles, Scotland, in June 1977, a new agreement was forged. All member countries of the Commonwealth were asked to cut all 'future sporting contacts of any significance between Commonwealth countries or their nationals and South Africa while that country continues to pursue the detestable policy of apartheid'.

Later in the year, the General Assembly of the United Nations passed the 'International declaration against apartheid in sports', calling on member countries to stop all sporting contacts with South Africa.

Both declarations left the more democratic members of the Commonwealth with a dilemma: while their governments supported the boycott, they did not believe they should interfere with an individual sportsman's rights to play where and with whom he chose. However, the sporting bodies in these countries – notably Britain and New Zealand – were only too aware that any breaking of the boycott calls could lead to their own isolation.

The South African response was twofold: first, efforts were made to open sport to all; secondly, a series of 'unofficial' tours was arranged in place of 'official' tours. At the same time individual sportsmen were offered enormous amounts of cash to play in South Africa.

Not surprisingly, sport reform was part of P W Botha's 'Total Strategy' and – despite the apartheid laws – mixed teams received government blessing to tour. However, this so-called 'normalisation' did nothing to take the sting out of the international boycott – simply because the policy of apartheid itself remained in force. 'No normal sport in an abnormal society' became the clarion call of the South African Council on Sport (SACOS), which forbade its members any participation in the government's open sports policy. Even to be seen watching cricket from the stands at Newlands or Ellis Park usually meant disqualification from one of its dozens of affiliates.

Despite the boycott, some official tours – particularly rugby tours – went ahead. In 1980 French and British teams toured South Africa, and the South Africans toured

Chile, Uruguay and Paraguay. In 1981 an Irish team toured South Africa and the Springboks visited New Zealand in a highly controversial, demonstration-plagued tour that cost the New Zealand Government R4-million in police security – and the venue of the next Commonwealth Conference, which was switched from Auckland to the Bahamas in protest.

Cricket tours, too, continued – but on an unofficial basis. In 1982, 15 English cricketers, said to have been paid £50 000 each, participated in an unofficial tour that later led to their being suspended from test cricket for three years.

In 1982, an attempt to arrange a series of matches by an international soccer team fell into disarray when three of South Africa's foremost teams – Kaizer Chiefs, Moroka Swallows and Orlando Pirates – refused to have anything to do with the tourists.

One other attempt was made by South Africa to end the boycotts: the establishment through Eschel Rhoodie's Department of Information of the Committee for Fairness in Sport. The committee died with the Information Department, and its place in the pro-South African lobby was taken by the Freedom in Sport organisation.

In the early 1990s, the unbanning of the ANC led to unity talks among sports administrators, followed by the formation of single, national, non-racial controlling bodies for the majority of previously conflicting sports bodies. Unity earned organisations such as the United Cricket Board of South Africa an almost immediate invitation to return to international sport.

THE SPRINGBOK RUGBY TOUR *of New Zealand in 1981 was greeted by vociferous protest.*

AS THE *'Info scandal' spread, John Vorster resigned as Prime Minister for health reasons.*

Pretoria proved so successful that in 1976 the editor formed his own political party (also with funds from Pretoria) and had four MPs elected.

In the USA, Rhoodie used publisher John McGoff to purchase the California-based 'Sacramento Union'. Earlier, McGoff's bid for the 'Washington Star' had failed. The Info Department also acquired a 50 percent interest in the international TV news agency UPITN-TV, which it hoped to bias in favour of the Republic. Money was donated to political campaigns everywhere, including those of Jimmy Carter in the USA, James Mancham in the Seychelles and Bishop Abel Muzorewa in Rhodesia.

Although it was common knowledge in government circles that the Department of Foreign Affairs and its Minister, Pik Botha, were becoming increasingly irritated by the activities of the Department of Information, someone else was studying Rhoodie's lavish operations with a baleful eye: Auditor-General and former Secretary for Information Gerald Barrie.

Lifting the lid

Barrie began an audit of the Info Department's books at the start of 1977, and in February 1978 tabled a report in parliament criticising extravagant trips abroad and the use of funds without Treasury approval.

Just why he chose this moment to unmask the secret operations of the Info Department has long been a subject of debate, but Rhoodie later claimed that Barrie was prompted by *verligte* (liberal) Nationalist rivals from the Cape. Their aim, he said, was to discredit Information Minister Connie Mulder and, eventually, Vorster himself – the first steps in what was later referred to as P W Botha's 'creeping coup d'etat'. According to Rhoodie, Barrie had

HENDRIK VAN DEN BERGH *(above), who resigned as security chief during the 'Info scandal'.*
CONNIE MULDER *(left) meets Governor Ronald Reagan of California in 1974.*

been aware of the secret funding since 1970, when Barrie himself had proposed to Vorster that a weekly news magazine called 'To the Point' be secretly funded.

Whatever his motivation, Barrie's report was the first trickle in a flood of revelations, speculation, accusations and counter-accusations that began to engulf anyone who had had anything to do with the department.

In a shake-up that followed an investigation by the Public Service Commission, two senior department officials were sent into early retirement – with a golden handshake worth five extra years' service.

Although more leaks from frightened officials in the Public Service followed, these were quickly quashed by government officials, despite increasingly awkward questions being asked by Opposition MPs in parliament.

A top-secret memorandum from the Auditor-General to Vorster, which found its way into the hands of the opposition 'Sunday Express' newspaper, started the flood. Speculation continues to this day about who leaked this vital document. (Rhoodie later claimed that it was a member of the Cabinet intent on destroying Mulder – and his chances for the premiership – once and for all.)

The crunch for Mulder came when Opposition MP Harry Schwartz asked in parliament whether any government or state funds were involved in the running of 'The Citizen'. The next day, Mulder replied that the state had not provided funds for the newspaper. It was this blatant untruth, which Mulder later claimed he was forced into by Vorster, that robbed him of the chance of becoming Prime Minister later that year.

In August 1978, the Department of Information was reconstructed as the Bureau for Information and Rhoodie retired with a golden handshake.

By then, the strain was beginning to show on Vorster and in September that year he announced his resignation for health reasons – adding, however, that he would be available, if chosen, for the office of State President.

Who's next for Prime Minister?

Vorster's resignation pushed the power play for the premiership into high gear. As Transvaal leader of the party, Mulder – the favourite to take over the reins – commanded 80 of the 172 caucus votes as well as the backing of the outgoing Prime Minister (against the 55 caucus votes of his chief rival, the Minister of Defence and Cape leader of the NP, P W Botha).

The first salvo of the leadership contest was fired by the Mulder camp in the form of a Press leak to a government-supporting newspaper. When news of the Information scandal first broke, Vorster had appointed a BOSS auditor named Loot Reynders to investigate the secret expenditure by the Department of Information. Now, shortly before the caucus elections, a report in 'Die Transvaler' claimed that Reynders had found no irregularities.

More shocks were on the way, however.

A Pretoria attorney named Retief van Rooyen, a secret collaborator of Rhoodie's and head of an Information Department front company named Thor Communicators, read the report and contacted Foreign Affairs Minister Pik Botha with an offer of new information about the use of secret funds. Botha immediately set off with Van Rooyen to Cape Town to tell his story to P W Botha and on the way collected Alwyn Schlebusch, the NP leader in the Orange Free State. The three Ministers confronted Vorster, who admitted that Van Rooyen's story – including details regarding the funding of 'The Citizen' – was true.

The next day, after the story had been repeated to the Cabinet, Mulder was asked to quit the race for the premiership. Although he refused, the P W Botha camp had another ace up its sleeve: Pik Botha.

During his time as Ambassador to the United Nations, and as Minister of Foreign Affairs, Botha had become immensely popular among white South Africans. The results of a conveniently timed opinion poll commissioned by the Sunday paper 'Rapport' (owned by the Cape-based

MINISTER *of Foreign Affairs Pik Botha was the vote-splitting card that gave P W Botha the premiership.*

Nasionale Pers) showed that a huge majority of white South Africans favoured Pik Botha as the next Prime Minister. Urged on by these findings, Botha joined the premiership fray, even though he was the most junior Minister in the Cabinet and had refused to challenge Mulder that year as leader of the party in the Transvaal.

Pik Botha's entry was the vote-splitting card that P W Botha needed to ensure his election. In the first round, voting was P W Botha 78; Mulder 72; and Pik Botha 22. The second and final round gave P W Botha 98 votes and Mulder 74.

P W Botha takes over

Botha's first step as Prime Minister was to distance himself and his Cabinet as far as possible from the Information affair, even if it meant having to offer the public scapegoats. First to go was Van den Bergh, whose past dealings with Botha had been fractious, to say the least. He resigned the day Botha became Prime Minister and, according to Rhoodie, was officially ostracised by the government both in South Africa and abroad.

After telling the nation that he would 'uphold a clean administration' and that he would resign if any of his Ministers knew about the secret funds, Botha summarily suspended the Mostert Commission (to whom Retief van Rooyen had first broken the news about 'The Citizen') after an argument with Judge Anton Mostert about disclosing evidence of secret funding of 'The Citizen'. Mostert ignored Botha's instructions and called a Press conference at which he disclosed Van Rooyen's evidence.

Botha then turned his attention to Mulder, forcing him to resign from the Cabinet and then as leader of the NP in the Transvaal. He appointed Mr Justice Rudolph Erasmus to head a three-man commission of inquiry, which found that, while Botha's 'hands were clean in every respect', Mulder was 'incompetent, lax and negligent'. Two months after the report of the Erasmus Commission, Botha

was able to force Mulder to quit parliament altogether, and the following year he was expelled from the NP. In June 1979, the Erasmus Commission announced that, contrary to its earlier findings, Vorster had actually known all about the funding of 'The Citizen' and other secret projects. Botha almost immediately forced Vorster to resign as State President.

The last person to suffer from the Info Department fallout was Rhoodie himself, who, on seeing reports in the European Press, returned to South Africa from a business trip to France to give evidence to the Erasmus Commission. After testifying, he and his wife returned to France. But with the hunt for scapegoats now in full cry, the government, giving the impression that Rhoodie had fled South Africa, asked the French to arrest and extradite him to face charges of fraud involving the secret funds. The extradition was granted in terms of an 1876 Anglo-French treaty, but Rhoodie later claimed it was a 'dirty little deal between France and South Africa in order to protect the skins of the politicians in Pretoria'.

After being convicted, Rhoodie was later cleared of all charges by the Appellate Division of the Supreme Court.

Despite a massive attack by the pro-Botha Afrikaans-language Press on Rhoodie's activities, P W Botha decided to retain 32 of the projects that were started by the disgraced Department of Information.

A new broom

With Mulder and Vorster out of the way, P W Botha began to implement a new policy to deal with a host of economic and political problems. After 1979 South Africa faced a deep economic decline, increased international isolation (including stepped-up international sanctions and the tightening of the sports boycott), a flight of foreign capital, a rising tide of black opposition and industrial strife.

Clearly, if the government was to come to grips with these problems without giving way on the fundamental issue of white hegemony, a drastic rethink of NP policy would be needed. Such a rethink had been going on for some time (particularly in intellectual circles in the Broederbond), and what eventually emerged was a change of emphasis that shook the party to its roots.

The reform that split the NP was driven to a large extent by the capitalist institutions that had been conceived out of Afrikaner resentment at the English control of business almost 50 years earlier. Chief among them was the insurance and banking giant SANLAM, born out of a Broederbond scheme in the 1930s to win Afrikaner rights through playing the English-speakers at their own game – big business. By 1981 SANLAM had become the second largest conglomerate, with assets worth nearly two-thirds the value of all foreign investment in the country. Only Anglo American remained ahead. Others from the top eight companies in South Africa were the Volkskas banking group and the tobacco and liquor giant, the Rembrandt Group.

The men at the top of these major corporations were different in class and thought from the farmers and blue-collar workers who had looked to the NP for salvation from English-speaking exploitation and black domination. They realised that a new deal was needed to make the

Industrial unrest and reform

Modern South Africa is dominated by sprawling industrial cities which, with their mines, factories, dormitory suburbs and townships, are the physical expression of a key feature of South African history – 'proletarianisation', a jaw-breaking mouthful that simply means the transformation of a landed peasant class into a landless working class.

Khoikhoi, *trekboer*, 1820 settler, Zulu, Sotho and Indian alike were affected by this process that had been going on in Western society for centuries and which gave rise to what is known today as the modern capitalist state.

In South Africa, however, proletarianisation was accompanied by ongoing state suppression of workers' rights, which prevented the majority of the labour force – the black workers – from making material gain or achieving personal and political freedom. The capitalist state that emerged in South Africa depended on the price of labour being kept low, not by market forces but by coercion.

The collective bargaining system

The traditional method to balance employers' interests against workers' demands is known as collective bargaining – a process regulated by law.

The Labour Relations Act, which governs collective bargaining in South Africa, was drafted in 1924 as a consequence of the 1922 miners' strikes. It was amended in 1956 to allow for the setting up of industrial councils or conciliation boards: only after disputes had been fully investigated by a board or council could workers legally go on strike.

The Act had one major weakness, though: the majority of the workforce was excluded from collective bargaining and labour law. African workers could not legally negotiate or, unless complex conditions were met, go on strike. Only white unions were formally recognised by the Industrial Registrar.

In October 1972, dissatisfaction among black workers with continuing low wages in the face of spiralling inflation led to a wave of strikes that began in Durban – where 60 000 manufacturing workers won a 15-18 percent pay rise. By 1973, the strikes had spread into Natal, the Transvaal and the eastern Cape, despite attempts by employers to forestall industrial action by granting their workers pay rises. Strike action reached a climax in September 1973 at the Western Deep Levels Mine at Carletonville, near Johannesburg, when police fired on a crowd of strikers, killing 12.

The rebirth of black trade unionism

Despite phenomenal growth, the unions' fight for factory-level recognition initially met with scant success (by 1979, black unions were recognised at only four factories). Undeterred, however, unionists continued to call (mainly illegal) strikes. It became increasingly noticeable, too, that many of the strikes were being called to express growing political frustration.

As worker stayaways increased, the state found itself caught in a cleft stick: although it was quite prepared to arrest or ban strike leaders, it was well aware of the negative effect that this type of action had on overseas investment (which in 1972 was down 35 percent on 1971 figures).

Faced with a dramatic drop in profits and productivity, some employers began suggesting to the state that industrial militancy might best be controlled by including African workers and their unions in the industrial relations process.

In 1977, the government appointed Professor Nic Wiehahn to head a commission of inquiry into industrial relations. Two years later his report convinced parliament of the need to extend labour legislation to cover African workers.

A second commission of inquiry (headed by Dr Piet Riekert), which recommended more freedom of movement and choice of workplace for African workers, led to the landmark abolition of the Pass laws by P W Botha's government in 1986.

The extension of labour law to cover African workers did not result in an immediate flood of registration applications by black trade unions. Indeed, for a long time the question of whether to register proved a prickly subject in the ranks of the emergent unions. Nevertheless, by the late 1980s the unions were using the new legislation to such advantage that, in an attempt to curb the trade union movement, the government would try to roll back labour's gains by amending the Labour Relations Act.

Building worker unity

With the 1973 strikes having signalled the rebirth of black trade unionism in South Africa, the next two decades were dominated by the efforts of the new union movement (not always successfully) to build worker unity, increase organisational strength and grapple with political and economic policy issues. At the same time employers and the government sought ways to live with these developments.

In April 1979, 12 unions formed the non-racial Federation of South African Trade Unions (FOSATU). By the end of 1981, FOSATU had become the largest union federation in the country with 95 000 members in 387 factories.

In 1980, another federation, the black consciousness supporting Council of Unions in South Africa (CUSA) was launched with nine affiliates representing about 30 000 members. Although it remained considerably weaker than FOSATU, CUSA took the lead in organising mineworkers and launched the National Union of Mineworkers (NUM) in 1982. Within two years, the NUM had built up a membership of over 100 000 to become the most powerful union in the country.

UNIONIST *Emily Hlatywayo at a meeting of clothing workers.*

NIC WIEHAHN *urged the government to allow black unions to register.*

The turbulence that rocked South Africa in the late 1970s and 1980s pushed the unions into an increasingly political role. Community organisations linked up with the unions during the boycott of Fattis and Monis products in 1979 – and in the same year strikers at the Ford motor plant were supported by the Port Elizabeth Black Civic Organisation (PEBCO). In the 1980s, more overtly political unions such as the South African Allied Workers' Union (SAAWU) argued that the shop-floor demands of workers could not be separated from their daily lives and political problems. These unions aligned themselves to township civic organisations, shared the political perspectives of the African National Congress (ANC) and joined the United Democratic Front (UDF).

While FOSATU tried to guard its independence and keep its distance from the 'populists', it could not remain totally aloof. A sign of greater politicisation was the countrywide work stoppage in February 1982 by 100 000 workers to protest the death in detention of Food and Canning Workers' Union organiser Neil Aggett. Furthermore, the UDF-led revolt in 1984 against the tricameral parliamentary system directly affected both the unions and their members.

The birth of COSATU

Several trade union blocs were formed in the 1980s, following a series of unity talks. Marked by deep conflict and mistrust, the talks nevertheless culminated at the end of 1985 in the formation of the Congress of South African Trade Unions (CO-SATU), a giant federation representing about half-a-million workers.

Not everyone came to the party, however: CUSA and the recently formed Azanian Confederation of Trade Unions (AZACTU) remained outside, forming their own federation, the National Council of Trade Unions (NACTU) in 1986. Significantly, CUSA's biggest affiliate, the NUM, joined COSATU.

Meanwhile, the Trade Union Council of South Africa (TUCSA) died largely unlamented in December 1986, abandoned by most workers on account of its conservative policies.

COSATU, which was structured as a federation of independent affiliates, maintained a policy of non-racialism and aligned itself with the UDF and later with the ANC and the South African Communist Party (SACP). NACTU, although officially non-aligned, unofficially veered between black consciousness and Africanism. The two federations remained distant from each other until the late 1980s.

In 1986, a third union group with different political loyalties was launched: backed and funded by Inkatha, the United Workers Union of South Africa (UWUSA), signalled its entry into the labour field by launching a series of bitter attacks on COSATU. The tension between UWUSA-Inkatha on the one hand and COSATU-UDF/ANC on the other soon erupted into internecine violence that wracked first Natal and subsequently the Transvaal.

The formation of COSATU was accompanied by a massive wave of strikes, with 1985 seeing the highest number of strikes in 10 years. A May Day stayaway in 1986 was supported by more than 1,5-million people countrywide. In 1987, the May Day stayaway rose to 2,5-million. The strike wave continued into the 1990s, affecting every sector of the economy from agriculture to education.

Marches and stayaways did not, however, always translate into victories for workers: for instance, what the NUM dubbed '21 days that shook the Chamber' ended with the demands of the workers not being met and 50 000 miners being dismissed.

Although the 1986 State of Emergency hit the unions hard, there were limits to the degree of repression the government could use. Employers did not want a return to wildcat strikes and faceless leadership; they needed unions and union leaders to keep collective bargaining on track. COSATU's shop-floor structures also stood the federation in good stead and by mid-1987 its leaders reported that it could continue to function and grow despite the emergency.

COSATU's first 18 months saw many political and organisational differences between the federation's affiliates come to the fore. Simplistically termed workerist-populist, these divisions translated into three union blocs defined in terms of their relationship with the UDF and ANC. Tensions also existed within many of the unions formed in terms of COSATU's principle of 'one industry, one union'. Political conflict also bedevilled NACTU with Africanists, adherents of black consciousness and proponents of various brands of socialism vying for power and resisting pressure to merge with one another. By 1988, however, the labour movement was under such attack that unions and even the two major federations were forced to put aside their differences to fight the government's new labour-law proposals.

The crisis for the unions began when the government, alarmed by the heightened industrial militancy, proposed amendments to the Labour Relations Act (LRA). The bill that became law in September 1988 was described by unionists as the greatest threat ever faced by organised labour. The Labour Relations Amendment Act included clauses that allowed employers to sue unions for loss of profit resulting from industrial action and imposed unwieldy restrictions on strike action.

For more than two years the anti-LRA campaign by COSATU, NACTU and other independent unions consisted of a two-pronged strategy of negotiations with employers and the state coupled with mass action, including stayaways. And it worked ....

The labour legislation was again amended in 1991 and 1993 as employers and the government conceded to union demands that went beyond revoking the amendments to encompass changes to the mechanisms governing industrial disputes as well as extending the law to cover previously unprotected workers.

country more secure, more palatable internationally and in a better position to develop the free-market system that capitalism demanded. Although white domination and the objective of an eventual capitalist system were not in question, the method of securing and extending them was.

Increasingly these business leaders found common cause with the powerful Defence Force intelligence community and the Broederbond, both of which had come to realise that Hendrik Verwoerd's dream of 'no black South Africans' was militarily and intellectually indefensible.

'Total Strategy'

The plan conceived by P W Botha, General Magnus Malan (the Minister of Defence) and a new breed of 'securocrats' was called 'Total Strategy' in response to 'Total Onslaught'. Its aim was to fight foreign pressure, improve and expand the African middle class as a counter to the radical activists in the townships and remove the ANC from South Africa's borders by destabilising neighbouring countries such as Zambia, Zimbabwe and, particularly, Mozambique, where the ANC had offices and training facilities.

The Broederbond think-tank and white Afrikaner business organisations urged the NP to adopt a more central position in white politics – a position that rejected both the Progressive Federal Party concept of a qualified franchise for all South Africans and the Conservative Party concept of continued white government. Botha proposed a 12-point plan that, in effect, would largely abolish so-called 'petty' apartheid while expanding and entrenching 'geopolitical' apartheid, which was designed to give more power to compliant black leaders and their followers in the independent 'homelands', using them as allies in the repression of the ANC and other proscribed organisations.

As the policy began to take effect, some of the more blatant aspects of petty apartheid began to crumble, with discriminatory signs vanishing from public places, leading eventually to significant concessions such as the repeal of

the Mixed Marriages Act (which had prohibited marriage between white and black), of laws preventing sexual intercourse between blacks and whites (1985), and of the Pass laws in 1986.

Despite a lukewarm reception overseas, Botha's 1983 reforms constituted a sufficient break with the past to antagonise many right-wing whites, whose vision of the future remained doggedly entwined with the Verwoerdian dream of a South Africa with no black citizens. They regarded Botha's declared intent of establishing a multiracial parliament for whites, coloured people and Indians and his talk of 'power sharing' as a total deviation from established Nationalist policy. In February 1982 the conservative MPS walked out of the NP caucus and in March Andries Treurnicht resigned from the Cabinet to establish the Conservative Party.

In an effort to retain the support of the disaffected whites, the government extended the already bloated public sector, which was 80 percent Afrikaans-speaking. At the same time, however, the state made a tentative move towards the privatisation of state-owned industries such as SASOL (the oil-from-coal process), with the promise of more privatisation to come. It was a promise that took several years to fulfil.

While much grassroots Afrikaner support dwindled in the face of the new power-sharing policy (even though Africans were totally excluded), the decreased emphasis on ideological apartheid endeared Botha's policies to many English-speaking whites, who had never been comfortable with either the strident rhetoric of Afrikaner nationalism or the daunting prospect of one man, one vote.

As ANC attacks increased and sanctions started to bite, there was a swing away from the old concept of government by a Cabinet answerable to parliament, towards the State Security Council, a statutory body whose permanent members were joined by securocrats from the army and police, co-opted by the State President.

THE ATTACK *by the ANC on the SASOL oil-from-coal installation in the OFS prompted greater action against the organisation.*

Creating an African middle class

Central to the wishes of the securocrats and the NP was the formation of a large African middle class that would, it was felt, be a natural counter to ANC-espoused Marxism, while forming a dependable counter-force to unrest. In this respect, the reports of two commissions – one investigating the highly restrictive labour laws and the other the free movement of African workers – were eagerly awaited.

Both investigations – by the Wiehahn and Riekert commissions – brought forth important changes. Wiehahn's proposals that Africans be brought into the industrial conciliation process and that job reservation be scrapped were adopted, as was Riekert's plea for the abolition of the Pass laws. Other important moves to help in the creation of an African middle class were contained in legislation passed in 1986 in favour of black urban freehold rights, the nurturing of small businesses among Africans, the establishment of free trading areas for all races and the introduction of all-black municipalities as well as multiracial provincial and regional councils.

Undermining the ANC

Meanwhile, the 'constellation' concept had encountered heavy weather. When first mooted, the idea was to extend Pretoria's influence and economic assistance not only to the self-ruling national states within South Africa's boundaries, but also to the neighbouring states such as Zimbabwe, Malawi, Botswana, Lesotho and Swaziland. This, it was predicted, would create a strong anti-Marxist, ANC-free zone around South Africa.

The need for a 'constellation of states' became much greater after the Soweto uprising of 1976 and the consequent stepped-up incursions into South Africa by the ANC's military wing, *Umkhonto we Sizwe.* Two attacks in particular had worried the government: those on the SASOL installation in the Orange Free State and on the Koeberg nuclear power station on the Cape west coast.

When the new policy was launched in 1979, the government pinned its hopes on a Zimbabwe – then on the last legs of white rule – run by Bishop Abel Muzorewa. But when free elections were finally held under the Carrington settlement plan for Zimbabwe, the Bishop lost resoundingly to the Marxist Robert Mugabe, who went on to help found the Southern African Development Coordination Conference (SADCC) with the specific aim of reducing economic dependence on South Africa.

The 'constellation' plan took a new turn from the mid-1980s, when the South African Government began applying a carrot-and-stick approach to neighbouring states: it began offering economic assistance in return for helping to flush out ANC operatives, while at the same time threatening, and carrying out, punitive strikes against alleged ANC targets in countries that refused to cooperate.

Yielding to outside pressure

Botha had another reason for seeking reform: the increasing foreign intervention in white South African decision-making in the form of sanctions and disinvestment was beginning to hurt the economy and create large-scale unemployment.

As early as 1974 a British parliamentary committee had called for a 'code of practice' for British companies operating in South Africa and which would press for African job advancement, put an end to wage and other discrimination at work and recognise African unions. This was followed in 1976 by the Sullivan Code, initiated in the USA by civil rights leader the Reverend Leon Sullivan, who had earlier urged US companies to withdraw from South Africa. He now spelled out his 'Sullivan Principles' urging US firms to remove discrimination in the workplace. Noticeably, he did not at first call for the recognition of trade unions – which inevitably led to charges that Sullivan had made the position of black workers in US companies worse. He gradually raised the standard of his code, finally abandoning it in 1987. The code, however, remained as a statement of principles.

Another code followed hard on the heels of Sullivan – this time from the European Economic Community, which asked companies to recognise unions, combat migrant labour and institute various other reforms in the workplace. Despite criticism, the codes helped to improve the lot of workers in companies that implemented them. These codes were the precursors of a new wave of international action aimed at Pretoria, ranging from economic sanctions to total divestment.

Freedom for Africa's last colony

Between April and July 1915, a few months after the start of the First World War,
43 000 South African troops occupied what was then known as German South West Africa.
Four years later, the newly created League of Nations gave South Africa a mandate
to rule the territory – a mandate that continued as the League dissolved into the chaos
of the Second World War. In 1966 the General Assembly of the United Nations (UN),
the League's successor, revoked the mandate. But it was only in 1990 – after more than
two decades of fighting – that Namibia was at last able to shed its tag of the 'last colony in Africa'.

ONE DAY IN 1932 a five-year-old boy stared into the sky in awe as the first aircraft he had ever seen – a South African bomber returning from a raid on a nearby village – swept low over his parents' tiny home in Ongandjera, western Ovamboland.

Sam Nujoma never forgot the roar of the aircraft, nor the news later that day that more than 200 villagers had died in an air strike on the headquarters of a rebel chief named Ipumbu. The horror of the attack lit the flame of a political consciousness which, over the next six decades, would earn him international recognition as one of Africa's most enduring fighters against colonialism.

In 1985, more than 50 years after the incident, Nujoma, now the leader of the South West African People's Organisation (SWAPO), told a Press conference in Lusaka, Zambia: '[South Africa] will have to continue to buy more jet fighters and helicopters and tanks ... [for] SWAPO is deeply rooted in the Namibian masses. We have been fighting for 19 years and the people are still with us. We will fight for another 19 years to free Namibia.'

In the midst of a war of independence which was marked by short, deadly bursts of fighting, long periods of uncertainty and tiny glimmers of hope, Nujoma could hardly have imagined then just how tantalisingly close his country was to freedom ....

A history of oppression

As with dozens of other countries around the globe, the foundation of modern Namibia was shaped by a series of painful, bloody experiences at the hands of colonial powers.

In 1884, at the tail end of Europe's great 19th century carve-up of the 'dark continent' (the so-called 'scramble for Africa'), late-starter Germany 'claimed' South West Africa – and proceeded to rule it with an iron hand.

It was a trying time for the black inhabitants of the territory – especially in 1904, when Lothar von Trotha, who signed his correspondence 'the great general of the mighty Kaiser', issued a *Vernichtungsbefehl* (extermination order) against the Herero people: 'Every Herero, whether found armed or unarmed, with or without cattle, will be shot. I shall not accept any more women and children,' he vowed – and over the next few months his wishes were carried out with chilling efficiency.

'This bold enterprise,' boasted one contemporary source, 'shows up in the most brilliant light the ruthless energy of the German High Command in pursuing their beaten enemy. No pains, no sacrifices were spared in eliminating the last remnants of ... resistance.'

For almost a year, the Kaiser's forces crisscrossed the countryside in a relentless hunt for victims. In 1905, when

A GROUP *of Herero photographed in 1904 after the issuing by the German General von Trotha of a* Vernichtungsbefehl *(extermination order) against the Herero people. A German officer later commented that the 'solemn silence of the territory echoed with the death-rattle of the dying, the shrieks of maddened people'. Only 16 000 out of an estimated 60 000 to 80 000 Herero survived the German onslaught.*

the operation ground to a halt, about 16 000 of an estimated 60 000 to 80 000 Herero were left – and of these 14 000 were in concentration camps. The Nama people also felt the wrath of the authorities: it is estimated that up to half the Nama population (between 15 000 and 20 000) was wiped out.

The outbreak of the First World War signalled the end of German rule in South West Africa. Between April and July 1915 South African troops occupied the territory – to the immense relief of the indigenous people. But, long before the cessation of hostilities, the joy of the people had turned to growing disillusionment.

A hollow victory

For the many black communities spread across the vast, dry land, South African rule soon proved to be almost as oppressive as that of Germany.

And yet, in 1920, when the Union Government was rewarded for its prompt occupation of South West Africa with a League of Nations mandate (a 'sacred trust of civilisation'), it promised 'to promote to the utmost, the material and moral well-being, and the social progress of the inhabitants of the territory'.

Of course, what the South African authorities really wanted was annexation – and in the decade after the end of German rule the Union Government, confident that it would eventually acquire the territory, worked hard to stamp its authority on South West Africa.

When the Natives' Trust and Land Act was applied to the new territory, for example, it ensured that the best land and stock went either to white South African settlers or (in many cases) to the original German occupiers. By contrast, land set aside for the indigenous people was generally of poor quality – as Herero leader Hosea Kutako pointed out when he was offered 80 000 ha of Omaheke sandveld: the area, he commented ruefully, 'is a desert where no human being has ever lived before'.

The unequal division of land, compounded by the effects of racist legislation such as the Pass laws, master and servant laws, and contract labour laws, made rebellion by the indigenous people inevitable. In 1922, after a revolt by the KwaNyama section of the Ovambo people had been easily put down, the tiny, impoverished Bondelswarts community of the Warmbad region in the south of the country rebelled.

The Bondelswarts rebellion

The Bondelswarts, members of the original Khoisan residents of the area, were among the first of South West Africa's indigenous people to suffer the consequences of settler expansionism.

Having fought, often against overwhelming odds, to defend their possessions against German and South African settlers, they had become a landless people, depending almost entirely on hunting for survival.

And yet, to the labour-hungry white farmers (and their representatives in government), hunting – no matter how precarious an occupation it might have been – still allowed the Bondelswarts too much independence. Something drastic had to be done to push them into the wage labour market, and in 1922 a new regulation was promulgated to achieve precisely this ....

Well aware of the importance of hunting dogs to the Bondelswarts, the authorities announced a stiff hike in the tax on these dogs: in future it would be £1 for one dog, but £10 for five dogs.

The Bondelswarts were furious – and they became more furious still when two of their leaders, Jacobus Christian and Abraham Morris, who had fled to South Africa to escape the Germans, were arrested when they returned to the territory. As tempers simmered, Gysbert Hofmeyr, the Administrator of South West Africa, decided to wield the big stick.

But matters went hopelessly awry ....

To begin with, an air attack, supposedly ordered to machine-gun Bondelswarts flocks, killed 100 people, of whom the majority were women. Then Hofmeyr ordered his troops to pursue (and attack) those Bondelswarts males who had fled into the mountains. Despite the accusations of brutality which reverberated through the corridors of the League of Nations, Union Prime Minister Jan Smuts later added fuel to the flames of anger by publicly defending Hofmeyr.

Although, like other uprisings in the past, the Bondelswarts rebellion was quickly put down, the costs incurred by South Africa (in terms of international goodwill) were considerable.

Squabble at the UN

After the Bondelswarts revolt, life in the territory continued much as before, with the aspirations of indigenous people again being ignored when South West Africa was granted partial self-government based on a system of adult white suffrage in 1926.

This independence-of-sorts started an economic boom, with both the Union Government and overseas investors

HERERO CHIEF *Clemens Kapuuo and his followers file past the grave of their late chief Hosea Kutako in August 1973.*

pumping large sums of money into the country. In addition, white farmers were given generous subsidies; mines were opened; the fishing industry was developed; and educational, residential and recreational facilities were provided for the settlers.

But the South African Government still hankered after annexation ....

In 1945, when the League of Nations was about to be dissolved without provision being made for mandated territories, South Africa tried again: this time the Union Government announced that the South West African people themselves would decide their future. While white participants opted overwhelmingly for inclusion into South Africa, the government-appointed African chiefs (the representatives of the indigenous people) first wanted one question answered: if they voted for incorporation, would they continue to enjoy the protection of the British king?

'Of course,' they were assured. Happy with the reply, the chiefs instructed their followers to vote Yes.

With the people of South West Africa seemingly fully behind him, Smuts travelled to the newly established UN to formalise the takeover.

There would be 'no departure whatsoever from the fundamental principles of promoting the moral and material well-being of the inhabitants which have characterised the administration of the mandate', Smuts promised members.

But no one would believe him – and after his request had been rejected by 37 votes to 0 (with nine abstentions), the UN General Assembly called for the formation of a Trusteeship Committee to guide former mandated territories to independence.

Before the end of the 1940s, however, a dramatic shift in the political allegiances of white South Africans was set to cast a dark shadow over the future of South West Africa.

The National Party's 1948 triumph

In 1948 the National Party (NP) defeated the United Party (UP) in a South African election – and immediately announced that it wanted South West Africa to be officially incorporated as a fifth province of South Africa.

BLACK POWER *salutes go up in Windhoek's Katatura township in 1975 – the year the Turnhalle conference first met.*

Adopting a hardline stance from the outset, the NP not only rejected UN trusteeship of the territory but also decided to stop sending situation reports as was required under the original League of Nations mandate.

In 1950, amid growing anger over South Africa's attitude, the UN General Assembly took the matter to the newly created International Court of Justice, which, in 1951, delivered a verdict that shocked member states: South Africa, said the court, was entitled to rule South West Africa in terms of the original mandate and there was no legal obligation for it to place the territory under UN trusteeship. It added, however, that it would be illegal for South Africa to annex the territory, change its status or refuse to submit regular reports.

Despite the setback to its annexation plans, the government of Daniel Malan reacted to the court's ruling by extending some of its recently introduced apartheid laws – including the Prohibition of Mixed Marriages Act and the Immorality Act – to South West Africa. In 1959, with the NP's policy of social engineering rapidly gaining momentum, thousands of residents of Windhoek's 'Old Location' were ordered to move to the newly established township of Katatura, far outside the capital city.

The instruction sparked widespread opposition – and when more than 30 000 people began boycotting buses and beerhalls in the township, the South African Government moved swiftly to crush the revolt. On the night of 10 December, police gave a large crowd that had gathered inside the location five minutes to disperse. According to Hosea Kutako, the 81-year-old Herero chief, the announcement was made without a loudhailer. 'Those in front, who tried to leave, were pushed forward by those at the back who were inquisitive to see what was going on,' he said. At the end of the five minutes, the police fired, killing 13 people and injuring 52.

As a mood of sullen peace returned to the township, one of the main organisers of the protest vowed to step up the campaign for the liberation of his country. His name was Sam Nujoma.

The new black leaders

In the 1950s a new generation of indigenous leaders emerged – bitterly opposed to South Africa's continued presence in the territory. Andimba (Herman) Toivo ja Toivo was one of them. Born in Umgungundhu in Ovamboland in 1924, he had attended a local Anglican mission school and had qualified as a teacher before joining the Union forces during the Second World War. After the war, he had taught briefly before quitting to become (at various times) a railways policeman, a contract labourer, and a clerk at a manganese mine.

Sam Nujoma, who became a full-time activist after working as a steward for South African Railways and as a clerk in Windhoek, was another of the Young Turks, as was the Herero leader, Clemens Kapuuo (who was assassinated, allegedly by SWAPO insurgents, in his shop in Katatura township outside Windhoek in 1977).

In another important development, British clergyman Michael Scott (the UN representative of Herero chief Hosea Kutako), Mburumba Kerina and Samuel Witbooi based

ORGANISED RESISTANCE *to the South African administration of Namibia began in 1958, when Andimba Toivo ja Toivo (right) founded the Ovamboland People's Organisation, which in 1960 changed its name to the South West African People's Organisation (SWAPO) under the presidency of Sam Nujoma (left). Toivo ja Toivo was imprisoned on Robben Island, while Nujoma escaped from police custody and fled to Dar-es-Salaam in Tanzania.*

themselves at the UN headquarters in New York, where they worked tirelessly (and, for the most part, successfully) to expose the nature of South Africa's rule.

A new political alliance

Two years before the Katatura protests, Toivo ja Toivo had assisted in the founding of South West Africa's first extra-parliamentary opposition group, the Ovamboland People's Congress (OPC), in a barber shop in Cape Town.

The new organisation (which was renamed the Ovamboland People's Organisation, or OPO, in 1958) made an immediate impact among migrant miners and fish cannery workers.

The OPO's popularity increased even further after Toivo ja Toivo had successfully smuggled (in a copy of 'Treasure Island') a tape containing harrowing details about the migrant labour system to UN lobbyist Kerina. Shortly afterwards, Toivo ja Toivo was arrested in Cape Town and deported to South West Africa. After he was again arrested, in Tsumeb, he was restricted to Ovamboland, where he campaigned energetically to build up the grassroots support of the OPO.

After initially backing a merger with the newly established South West African National Union (SWANU) in 1959, Nujoma and several other OPO stalwarts in 1960 formed the South West African People's Organisation (SWAPO), with Nujoma as its first president. In the same year, Nujoma slipped across the border into Botswana en route to Dar-es-Salaam in Tanzania.

Back to the International Court of Justice

While activists such as Toivo ja Toivo and Nujoma were organising opposition to the South African presence in South West Africa, the UN continued condemning South Africa's rule of the territory. In 1960, Ethiopia and Liberia, the only two African members of the General Assembly who had also been members of the League of Nations, took the matter to the International Court ....

The judges took five years to hand down a verdict – and even then it was not a unanimous one. With the Australian president of the court, Sir Percy Spender, exercising his casting vote, the court ruled that it had no power to decide the dispute.

Although reaction to the decision was predictable – ranging from joy on the NP side to anger from the South West African lobbyists – the most significant response came from SWAPO: in a terse statement released from its headquarters in Dar-es-Salaam, the organisation said: 'We have no alternative but to rise in arms and bring about our own liberation ....'

It was the beginning of war.

'South Africa has robbed us of our country'

The first groups of guerrillas entered the country from the north – and within three years were striking at targets as far south as Grootfontein. It quickly became apparent, however, that both sides faced a long, painful struggle for control of the land.

With its anti-insurgency methods improving all the time, South Africa responded to SWAPO's early incursions with a devastating raid on a guerrilla base at Omgulambashe. A large number of insurgents were captured and valuable documents seized in the attack. Information

MEMBERS *of the Democratic Turnhalle Alliance get down to business under the chairmanship of Dirk Mudge.*

gleaned from the prisoners and documents led to the arrest of several SWAPO sympathisers, including Toivo ja Toivo.

But despite a steady increase in the number of South African police pushed into the campaign, SWAPO continued to intensify its activities.

At his trial in the Pretoria Supreme Court in 1967, Toivo ja Toivo spoke at length about his support for the armed struggle: 'Violence,' he said, 'is truly fearsome – but who would not defend his property and himself against a robber? And we believe that South Africa has robbed us of our country .... When I consider my country, I am proud that my countrymen have taken up arms for their people and I believe that anyone who calls himself a man would not despise them ....

'Only when we are granted our independence will the struggle stop. Only when our human dignity is restored to us ... will there be peace between us.'

He was jailed for 20 years.

An end to the UN mandate

In October 1966, the UN General Assembly resolved unanimously to end the mandate; cancelled South Africa's right to 'administer the territory'; and placed South West Africa under UN supervision. In 1969, a new resolution called for the immediate withdrawal of the South African administration.

But South Africa had other plans for the territory ....

Ignoring both UN resolutions, the NP Government tried instead to implement the recommendations of the so-called Odendaal Report, which called for the 'Balkanisation' of South West Africa into 12 'self-governing homelands with unlimited possibilities for self-development and fulfilment [for the different groups] on their own native soil'.

In terms of the recommendations, 39 percent of the (poorest quality) land was earmarked for the indigenous people, while the best, including land on which the mines were located, was to remain in white hands. In another move that raised the hackles of the international community, the South African authorities passed the South West Africa Act of 1969 which increased Pretoria's administrative control and moved South West Africa a step closer to becoming a 'fifth province' of the Republic.

In 1971 first the UN Security Council and then the International Court of Justice backed the General Assembly's decision to revoke the mandate. A few years later, the General Assembly declared SWAPO the 'sole, authentic voice' of the country it now called Namibia.

A buffer state

In 1974, when the UN again demanded that South Africa give up the territory, the government's response was surprisingly guarded – but for good reason: the former white buffer states of Mozambique and Angola were on the verge of winning independence from Portugal (see page 434) and the government of Ian Smith faced a major war in Rhodesia. Detente was the new catchword as the government of Prime Minister John Vorster struggled to come to grips with the new realpolitik of the region.

In an attempt to appease its critics at the UN, the South African Government called a conference of Namibian political parties in 1975 at the Turnhalle Building in Windhoek, with the aim of creating a constitution that would lead to independence by the end of 1978. A blueprint for an interim government was developed and a multiracial Democratic Turnhalle Alliance (DTA) set up under the leadership of Dirk Mudge.

The plan had one major flaw, however: it excluded SWAPO – and it was because of this that both the UN and the Organisation of African Unity (OAU) rejected the proposal.

Nevertheless, a contact group – the so-called 'Big Five' – consisting of representatives of the United States, Canada, Britain, France and West Germany, was set up to try to keep the doors of negotiation open.

A major problem for the peace brokers was Pretoria's refusal to have any dealings with SWAPO. Even though it was common knowledge that SWAPO enjoyed majority support in Namibia, the South African Government was adamant that it would not negotiate with a 'terrorist organisation'. Another difficulty was the fact that the 'Big Five' often did not see eye-to-eye with other members of the UN Security Council.

On 7 September 1978, South Africa's Defence Minister P W Botha re-emphasised his government's attitude towards SWAPO when he told a cheering Orange Free State Congress of the National Party: 'We are not prepared to hand over South West Africa to Marxism and chaos .... We are prepared to negotiate with the world. We have shown it through the Prime Minister's almost painful patience. We will negotiate with the UN Secretary-General, but if they expect us to hand over South West Africa to Marxism, we say there is no further point in talking.'

Shortly after Botha's hardline speech, Prime Minister Vorster announced that elections would be held in December that year, in which SWAPO clearly would not participate. The announcement caused an uproar at the UN and the speedy departure of the contact group to Pretoria for more talks. In an agreement of sorts, the South African

THE SOUTH AFRICAN DEFENCE FORCE *in action against SWAPO bases inside Angola. SWAPO responded to the attacks by digging its bases into camouflaged underground bunkers.*

THE WAR *against SWAPO guerrillas was generally conducted in close secrecy – with only occasional snatches of information being given to the Press. In 1982 South African leaders gave a rare briefing to members of the Press invited to tour the 'operational area' (never closely defined, but agreed to include northern Namibia and southern Angola). From left, they are Minister of Foreign Affairs Pik Botha, Prime Minister P W Botha and Minister of Defence Magnus Malan.*

Government conceded that the December election might be followed in 1979 by a UN-supervised one.

On 29 September 1978, at its 2 087th sitting on the subject, the UN Security Council adopted Resolution 435, requiring that free elections in Namibia be held under UN supervision. The 'Big Five' had persuaded South Africa to agree to the plan in April: South Africa would withdraw its armed forces from Namibia; all political prisoners would be released; a ceasefire declared; a transitional government installed under the direction of the Administrator-General of South West Africa; and elections held under the supervision of a UN commissioner.

The South African Administrator-General, Mr Justice M T Steyn, had meanwhile repealed the Pass laws and some other discriminatory legislation. To many observers, it seemed that a settlement for an independent Namibia was finally in sight.

But squabbles arose again. One source of dispute was the future of Walvis Bay, which had been annexed by Britain in 1878 and which was regarded by the South African Government as South African territory and not part of the original mandate. Disagreement arose later over the size of the UN military force and the methods of ensuring a ceasefire among SWAPO forces.

Meanwhile, in the absence of SWAPO, the DTA swept the field in the December elections.

Rhodesia crumbles

Even as settlement hopes were fading in Namibia, the last white-ruled buffer state to the north – Rhodesia – finally bowed to the inevitable: on 4 March 1980, Robert Mugabe's ZANU-PF won British-supervised elections, and Zimbabwe arose from the ashes of Rhodesia.

It was a sobering moment for those who, having chosen to ignore the obvious pointers to a Mugabe victory, believed to the end that the conservative Bishop Abel Muzorewa would carry the day (see box). Almost overnight, South Africa found itself surrounded by three Marxist states that could be used as springboards for guerrilla attacks by the African National Congress (ANC) or SWAPO against South Africa or Namibia.

Mugabe's victory was also a major setback to the new plan of Prime Minister P W Botha (who had replaced Vor-

ster in the wake of the Information scandal) to create a constellation of southern African states economically dependent on Pretoria and pliant enough to be persuaded to expel the ANC.

In a bid to counter Botha, Mugabe assumed a leading role in the formation of the Southern African Development and Coordinating Conference (SADCC), which tried to break the economic dependence of the frontline states on South Africa.

Stepping up the pressure

In Namibia, meanwhile, SWAPO began stepping up its incursions from southern Angola, occasionally penetrating deep into the south of the country. The South African Defence Force (SADF) responded with frequent sorties into Angola in 'hot pursuit' of SWAPO guerrillas.

Of major concern to the South African Government was the fact that, despite mounting losses, SWAPO continued to spread its influence among the indigenous people.

In 1981, General Charles Lloyd of the SADF touched on this subject during an interview with the British Broadcasting Corporation: 'We can actually destroy our military enemy,' he said, 'but this is not to say we will destroy SWAPO. SWAPO is in the minds of the people. Bullets kill bodies, not minds ....'

Nevertheless, counter-insurgency operations, particularly the secret operations of a plain-clothes unit named *Koevoet* (Crowbar), were widely condemned. Headed by a former South African security policeman named 'Sterk' (Strong) Hans Dreyer and consisting of black Namibians as well as many former members of the Rhodesian army, *Koevoet* acquired a fearsome reputation among northern villagers as an SADF killing machine.

As the war (and the accusations and counter-accusations of atrocities) increased in intensity, secrecy became the byword of South African operations against SWAPO fighters – which made it extremely difficult for observers to obtain an objective view of the war.

But sometimes the veil of secrecy was fleetingly lifted: in the early 1980s, for example, Trevor Edwards, a former lance corporal in the SADF, threw some light on the modus operandi of the South Africans in a BBC interview: his unit's main job in southern Angola, he said, was to 'take an area and to clear it. We killed everything ... we killed cattle, we killed goats and we killed people. Half the time the civilians don't know what is going on.'

A mercenary working for South Africa, who was captured in southern Angola, a Captain Belmundo, later told an international commission of inquiry: 'We had precise instructions to destroy schools, hospitals and houses, and to wipe out the civilian population and its cattle.'

SWAPO responded to repeated South African raids by going underground – literally. In a bid to avoid detection from the air, its units took to living in bunkers, with interlinking tunnels and secret openings.

But this did not stop South Africa from continuing its raids into Angola.

The Angolan connection

Angola paid a heavy price for allowing SWAPO to use its territory as a springboard for attacks into Namibia.

At first, South African security forces reacted to major SWAPO incursions with 'hot pursuit' operations. But later, as the SADF sought to administer a blow that would not only crush SWAPO but also deal a blow to the Marxist MPLA Government of Angola, several pre-emptive strikes were launched deep into Angola. Thus, 'Operation Smoke-shell' was completed with the SADF claiming that it had captured 350 tons of armaments; 'Operation Protea' saw the SADF claim control of large parts of southern Angola; and in 'Operation Daisy', 'Operation Askari' and 'Operation Treurwilger' hundreds of SWAPO guerrillas were reported killed.

When SWAPO turned 25 in 1985, it appeared to have little cause for celebration. For, rocked by the ferocity of the SADF-led onslaught, the scale of operations of SWAPO's military wing, the People's Liberation Army of Namibia (PLAN), had been drastically reduced to minor acts of sabotage in remote areas of northern Ovamboland.

In June 1985, General George Meiring, the head of the South West Africa Territory Force, announced boldly: 'We are ... winning this war.'

The Angolan connection – especially the status of thousands of Cuban soldiers who had been shoring up the MPLA Government since before independence – was cast into a major stumbling block to political settlement in Namibia. 'Cuban linkage' – the withdrawal of Cuban soldiers from Angola in return for UN-supervised elections – had first been mooted by the US State Department in 1981. South Africa, too, became an avid supporter of 'linkage'.

Inside the territory, meanwhile, new political alliances were being forged ....

Formation of the Multi-Party Conference

In 1984, Moses Katjiuonga of SWANU, Andreas Shipanga of the SWAPO-Democrats (a breakaway group from SWAPO) and Dirk Mudge's DTA, together with the white National Party of South West Africa, the coloured Labour Party and the Rehoboth Liberated Democratic Party, formed the Namibian Multi-Party Conference (MPC).

Although the merger threw together politicians whose views were significantly left-of-centre with others who were decidedly right-wing, members were united on one crucial issue: they all hated SWAPO. Dedicating itself to reform and an equitable independence, the MPC hoped to attract the support of 'moderate' Namibians. But even though it acknowledged Resolution 435 as the only acceptable plan for Namibian independence, its exclusion of SWAPO and the fact that it was backed by South Africa made it unacceptable to many Namibians.

In 1984, shortly after releasing a statement of principles (a 'Declaration of Fundamental Rights'), the MPC set off on a West African tour in a bid to drum up African support.

In June 1985, Pretoria permitted it to form a 'transitional government of national unity'.

Perhaps not surprisingly (given the wide differences in the political perceptions of its members), the achievement of unity proved a major obstacle for the new government. Members struggled to reach agreement on a new constitution, and whether it was 'group rights' or 'individual rights' that needed protection. Their failure, also, to reach consensus on matters such as 'open' schools cost the MPC Government dearly in terms of black support.

While the MPC was striving to be all things to all Namibians, far to the north the SADF was involved in a battle with Angola's army – FAPLA – and its Cuban allies that would have a bearing on Namibia's future.

The Battle of Cuito Cuanavale

In mid-1987, in response to an urgent plea for help from Jonas Savimbi's UNITA movement, the SADF provided troops and munitions to back his attempt to stop Angolan Government troops from capturing the UNITA-held town of Mavinga in the province of Cuando Cubango. The Angolans, who had been hoping to use Mavinga as a rear base for an attack on the UNITA stronghold of Jamba, retreated to the town of Cuito Cuanavale, where several battles raged between FAPLA-Cuban troops and the UNITA-SADF forces.

Both sides agreed that the Battle of Cuito Cuanavale was the turning point in the war. The Angolans and Cubans boasted they had inflicted a humiliating defeat and put South African losses in one 45-day period at 140 men. SADF chief General Jannie Geldenhuys, in a book on the events, put the death toll from September 1987 to April 1988 at 4 785 Cuban-FAPLA soldiers and 31 South Africans. He ascribed the discrepancy to Cuba's need to save face if it was to give in to demands for withdrawal from Angola.

South Africa, too, was keen to end its involvement in Angola. It did not want to be involved in a 'Vietnam' of its own, with its young men returning from a military adventure in a foreign land in body bags.

The prospects for the withdrawal of South Africans and Cubans from the military stalemate in Angola, coupled with growing economic difficulties in South Africa, appreciably increased the chances of a political settlement in Namibia.

The final countdown

The breakthrough for all the parties involved in the dispute came in May and July 1988, when representatives of South Africa, Angola and Cuba (with the USA as mediators and the Soviet Union as observers) held a series of talks in London, Cairo, Washington, the Cape Verde islands and

CITIZENS OF WINDHOEK *took to the streets on 21 March 1990 as the last colony on the African continent became independent.*

Brazzaville. Agreement was reached on a set of 14 'essential principles to establish peace in the south-western region of Africa'. Chief among these, as far as the Namibian dispute was concerned, was South Africa's agreement to implement Resolution 435 in return for, among other guarantees, a phased Cuban withdrawal from Angola. (The Republic had originally demanded a complete Cuban withdrawal before it would agree to the terms of the resolution.)

Another crucial area of agreement – aimed specifically at preventing the ANC from establishing military bases in a future independent Namibia – was the acceptance by all the parties 'of the responsibility of states not to allow their territory to be used for acts of war, aggression, or violence against other states'.

In August 1988, peace talks went a step further when South Africa, Angola and Cuba signed the Geneva Protocol, from which arose an unofficial agreement between South Africa and SWAPO that a ceasefire in northern Namibia would begin on 1 September. (The South African Government would not sign a formal peace treaty, because it refused to accept that it had fought a war against SWAPO.)

On 22 December, Cuba, Angola and South Africa committed themselves to two interlocking accords, providing for independence for Namibia and the withdrawal of the 50 000 Cuban troops from Angola.

But less than four months later, Namibia was rocked by yet another crisis.

A storm before the calm
April 1, 1989 started off as a day of celebration for thousands of black Namibians. With SWAPO and South African troops confined to their bases, with UN Special Representative Martti Ahtisaari and the first UN peacekeeping troops in town to oversee the implementation of Resolution 435, the long wait for freedom seemed to be coming to an end at last. In Windhoek, hundreds of dancing, ululating SWAPO supporters were gathered in the city centre, awaiting the arrival of thousands more from the townships of Katatura and Khomasdal.

Earlier that morning a SWA police patrol and a group of SWAPO insurgents, some carrying ground-to-air missiles and rocket launchers, had fought a pitched battle in remote northern Namibia. More clashes followed over the next few days – and, as tempers flared, Pik Botha, the volatile South African Foreign Minister, threatened to kick the UN out of Namibia if it did not do something 'to bring SWAPO to its senses'. With British Prime Minister Margaret Thatcher and Angolan President Eduardo dos Santos adding their voices to those condemning SWAPO, the South Africans persuaded Ahtisaari to release some soldiers from their bases. By the end of April, about 350 people – including 315 SWAPO insurgents – had been killed.

But despite the deaths and the threats from South Africa to expel the UN, there was no turning back this time. Both SWAPO and the government of the Republic regarded the peace process in Namibia as too important for it to be allowed to fail.

Free at last
Elections for a Namibian Constituent Assembly were held from 8 to 13 November 1989 – and although SWAPO, with 41 seats (to the 21 of the DTA), won comfortably, it failed to gain the two-thirds majority that would have given it the sole right to draw up a constitution.

In February 1990, the new constitution, the product of the input of all the country's political parties, was released to almost universal approval. Hailed as the most democratic constitution in Africa, it guaranteed all its citizens the franchise and basic human rights, and limited the powers of government.

On 21 March 1990, at 12.20 am, the South African flag was lowered and the new nation's flag raised. Speaking before the official handover, South Africa's new president, F W de Klerk, said: 'I stand here as an advocate for peace. The season of violence has passed for Namibia and for the whole of southern Africa.'

In his address, Namibian president Sam Nujoma paid tribute to the thousands who had perished in the fight for independence, adding: 'We are here to celebrate the dawn of a new era. To the Namibian people, the realisation of our most cherished goal, the independence of our country, is a fitting tribute to the heroism with which our people fought for this day.'

Four years later, in March 1994, South Africa also handed over control of Walvis Bay to Namibia.

The moment of truth for white Rhodesia

'Good morning, this is the Zimbabwe Broadcasting Corporation. The time is seven o'clock. Here is the news read by Mandy Mundawarara.

'Zimbabwe will become a new state from midnight tonight. Ceremonies to mark the occasion will be held at Rufaro Stadium. Among the ceremonies will be a royal salute, the lowering of the Union Jack, and the raising of the Zimbabwe flag. It will be followed by the blessing of the new flag and the swearing in of President-elect, Mr Banana, and Prime Minister-elect, Mr Mugabe.'

It was 17 April 1980, a day of rejoicing for the followers of Robert Mugabe, who had fought for more than a decade to end the illegal regime of Ian Smith. For tens of thousands of Zimbabwean whites, however, it was the final curtain in a drama whose last act had begun six weeks previously, when Mugabe won the country's British-supervised election.

Mugabe's victory at the polls was also the moment of truth for the South African Government of P W Botha, which, up until that moment, had firmly believed that the victor would be the rightist Bishop Abel Muzorewa. Like so many leaders in history, the white governments of Rhodesia and South Africa had fallen for their own propaganda – reading and hearing what they wanted to believe rather than the simple truth that the Africans wanted their favourite as the new Prime Minister of Zimbabwe.

This refusal to comprehend the aims of the Zimbabwean guerrillas led indirectly to the downfall of white Rhodesia. From a military point of view the Rhodesian security forces were stronger and far better equipped than the guerrillas. On conventional battlefields the Rhodesian army would have won in a matter of weeks. The 'bush war' was something else. An American veteran of the Vietnam War in the Rhodesian army summed it up: 'We thought we'd win because we were superior in firepower and training. We thought they were bad soldiers. But they won. It doesn't matter how and it doesn't have to be militarily. The Rhodesian High Command really didn't understand counter-insurgency warfare . . . you've got to look at it in terms of the people supporting the gooks. It does no good to justify it in your own terms. That's just self-righteous. And that's really what the Smith government was doing all along – looking at the African as a household pet. But he's like white people and you've got to look at his motivation. That's where the white government failed – in never really understanding the enemy or how to fight him.'

The Rhodesian propaganda war started in the early 1970s. Books, cartoons, jokes, radio and TV programmes extolling the invincibility of the white army and deriding the 'terrs' were part of daily life. Africans were saturated with blood-curdling leaflets and films warning them of the horrors that would be visited on them by 'communists, Marxist-Leninists and criminal terrorists'.

The Rhodesian Broadcasting Corporation (RBC) broadcast programmes in English and Shona detailing the barbarisms committed by 'terrorists', offering rewards for reporting their presence and protection by the Rhodesian army. Ironically the only people who listened to these broadcasts were whites. The African people listened to Radio Mozambique and the Voice of Zimbabwe – one of the most popular programmes was the regular talk show by Mugabe. As a Patriotic Front supporter said after the election: 'Every kid had Mugabe fever. Everybody could see that Comrade Mugabe was talking sense.' A well-known black RBC broadcaster, Ben Musoni, later remembered: ' . . . the whole country was behind the freedom fighters.'

As it became apparent to the High Command and the Psychological Operations Unit that their propaganda in the rural areas was not having the desired effect, they tried other methods – some atrocious, others ludicrous. At one point the army airdropped leaflets from helicopters purporting to come from the spirit mediums of the people, and advising them to support the government.

While whites in the Department of Information composed these messages in all seriousness, convinced they would influence 'simple tribesmen', the Africans were simply nonplussed. As one told his captors: 'We have never had instructions from spirit mediums in a helicopter. We have never had a typewritten message from a spirit. When did a spirit have a typewriter?'

On the more grisly side, Combined Operations found that showing footage of 'kills', mounds of dead guerrilla bodies, had a 'good effect'

AFRICANS *wait to vote at Ruwa near Salisbury (now Harare) in the British-supervised 1980 elections that ended white rule in Rhodesia.*

on white morale. As big kills became increasingly difficult inside the country, the High Command made raids across the border, where there were easier targets and the chance for footage of mass kills, such as the training and refugee camps in Zambia and Mozambique.

By the late 1970s the High Command realised it was not going to win, and the government moved towards an internal settlement. It proclaimed that 'free and fair' elections would be held and, for a brief spell, even unbanned the Patriotic Front. But the man white Rhodesia wanted in power was Muzorewa. Under his leadership the whites would retain indirect power and privilege and be able to tell the world that this was 'what the people wanted'. The Patriotic Front was summarily banned again. Amid intense international lobbying, a vast advertising campaign and elaborate stage management of the voting – as well as heavy military and police supervision – the people duly voted in Muzorewa as Prime Minister, and in June 1979 the new state of Zimbabwe-Rhodesia was born.

But the world was not buying the election. Neither was the Patriotic Front, and nor were the people. For them, little had changed. The war carried on, sanctions remained, the oppression continued and the international community refused to recognise Zimbabwe-Rhodesia.

Very quickly and painfully it became apparent that new elections would have to be held, and talks were held under the chairmanship of the British Foreign Secretary, Lord Carrington, at Lancaster House in London to hammer out an accord for a new election. The British Government appointed a temporary Governor, Lord Soames, to oversee a ceasefire in the run-up to the election set for March 1980.

When at last Mugabe returned from Mozambique for the election, a phenomenal crowd turned out to welcome him in Salisbury – more than the entire white population of Rhodesia. Still the penny did not drop. The governments of Rhodesia and South Africa gave Mugabe – at best – the

MUGABE *salutes the huge crowd that greets him on his return from exile.*

chance of winning about 35 of the 80 seats. Money poured in from right-wing sources around the world to back Muzorewa's campaign. There was radio, Press and TV advertising on an unprecendented scale, aircraft, helicopters, bands, contingents of cars and trucks and the entire military wing of the security forces behind Muzorewa's United African National Council.

Other participants in the poll, apart from Mugabe's Zimbabwe African National Union-Patriotic Front party, were Ndabaningi Sithole's Zimbabwe African National Union and Joshua Nkomo's Zimbabwe African People's Union-Patriotic Front. A massive anti-Mugabe propaganda campaign was launched and two assassination attempts were carried out. Advertisements portrayed

Mugabe as a power-mad communist dictator, a 'black Hitler', a monster and mass-murderer. At the same time the electorate was continually assured that it was impossible for Mugabe to win.

But on 4 March, 'The Herald' newspaper said it all with a banner headline reading 'Massive win for Mugabe – 57 seats go to ZANU (PF)'. Muzorewa had gained three seats, and Joshua Nkomo's Patriotic Front 20. It was a landslide.

When John Meiring, a member of Ian Smith's Psychological Operations Unit, heard the news, his 'ass fell on the ground with a thud that could be heard round the room. I mean, I knew there'd be guys who'd vote for Mugabe – but not f . . . ing 90 percent of the black electorate! I went straight to the bar and had a double.'

SIGNING *the Lancaster House agreement (from left): Lord Carrington, Sir Ian Gilmore, Joshua Nkomo and Robert Mugabe.*

Three into one won't go

By 1977, increasing unrest, hostile frontline states and a broadening international campaign had become major problems for the South African Government. In a bid to find a political solution that would take into account Afrikaner fears of *swart gevaar* (black threat), Prime Minister John Vorster appointed Minister of Defence P W Botha to plan a new constitution. The result was implemented in 1984, six years after Botha had taken over the reins of government: a three-house parliament divided on apartheid lines that angered right-wing Afrikaner politicians and convinced many Africans that violence was the only way to obtain political rights.

O N A BLUSTERY MID-WINTER'S day in July 1984 the Speaker of the House of Assembly in Cape Town brought to an end the final sitting of the last whites-only parliament in South Africa.

For 74 years, members representing white voters had met in a striking, red-brick building that had first been used on 15 May 1885 by the Legislative Assembly of the Cape of Good Hope.

Out of this building had come the great cornerstone Acts of apartheid, such as the Natives' Land Acts, the Natives' (Urban Areas) Act, the Population Registration Act, the Separate Registration of Voters Act and the Group Areas Act. Now, parliament had added one more: the Republic of South Africa Constitution Act, which, though it entrenched apartheid in the constitution, also allowed coloured and Indian members into the parliament chambers for the first time.

When parliament reassembled on 3 September, the halls and corridors that had once echoed to the impassioned rhetoric of *swart gevaar* now hosted coloured and Indian parliamentarians in a new, expanded and – to most people – incomprehensible method of government known as the tricameral system.

As the newly elected coloured and Indian members sat down for the first time inside the building that most of them had previously seen only from the outside, the smouldering fuse of African bitterness at being excluded from any say in the running of the country ignited an explosion of violence comparable with that of the darkest days of June 1976.

If, as the government had insisted to the whole world and the white population, the new system signalled reform, something had gone horribly awry.

The root of the problem was this: while the establishment of the tricameral parliament allowed coloured and Indian people into central government, it also entrenched grand apartheid by requiring that they be elected from separate voters' rolls and segregated into separate chambers. It therefore failed to satisfy critics who believed that apartheid had to be scrapped rather than reformed. Moreover, the majority party in the white chamber remained in charge of the running of the country, while Africans were excluded altogether.

In terms of the apartheid master plan, Africans were expected to participate in the political structure of the 'homeland' to which they could be ethnically linked (although in 1984 the government stated that the question of African 'participation' would be next on the agenda and mooted a National Statutory Council for Africans). It was for these reasons that most blacks – including many sympathetic coloured and Indian people – decisively rejected the new dispensation.

In the eyes of these opponents of apartheid, the abandonment of the Westminster system – despite the fact that the old House of Assembly had remained the preserve of white members only – had thrown away the last semblance of a parliament where, in theory at least, blacks could one day sit shoulder-to-shoulder with whites in a non-racial democracy. More disillusioned than ever, many blacks – and some white liberals – began throwing in their lot with extra-parliamentary groups.

The Botha era

When P W Botha became Prime Minister in 1978, continuing internal unrest, economic depression and a ring of hostile neighbouring states were casting a wide pall over the future of white South Africa.

Although he acted quickly to counter the internal and external threats to his government, many of his messages seemed confusingly contradictory: on the one hand, he regularly called on white South Africans faced with new circumstances to 'adapt ... or die'; on the other hand, he warned those clamouring for fundamental change that there would not be one person, one vote in parliament for as long as he was in charge of the government.

Despite his reluctance to make a clean break with the past, many of the alterations he made to NP policy (tentative and unworkable as some of them might have been) raised the hopes and fears of millions of South Africans. Certainly, by the time he was forced out of office by his Cabinet colleagues in August 1989, he had unwittingly taken South Africa to the threshhold of a new era ....

Afrikaner nationalism in a changing world

In his first four years as Prime Minister, Botha worked tirelessly to show the world that apartheid had a 'caring face'.

In 1979, in explaining to his compatriots why the hardline policies of his predecessors, Hendrik Verwoerd and B J Vorster, had to be amended, he said: 'The world does not remain the same, and if we as government want to act in the best interests of the country in a changing world, then we have to be prepared to adapt our policy to those things that make adjustment necessary. Otherwise we die.' This gave rise to a catchphrase which became a rallying cry for reform: 'Adapt or die.'

Of course, like Verwoerd and Vorster, Botha believed that political power had to remain in white hands. But, in order to maintain that power, he was prepared to make a trade-off: a relaxation of laws governing social and economic apartheid in return for continued white control of the Republic.

In order to convince the majority of his white constituency to support this strategy, Botha adopted a two-pronged political approach: on the one hand, using every opportunity to educate whites about the necessity for change; on the other hand, insisting that Africans had to exercise their political rights in their respective 'homelands'. Yet, while billions of rands were spent on attempts to make the 'homelands' system viable, his administration also pumped vast amounts into urban black education and housing.

Of course, it was Botha, too, who tried to draw the coloured and Indian communities into his tricameral parliamentary system ....

Afrikaner nationalists and coloured people

For hundreds of years, the relationship between the white Afrikaner (formerly Dutch-speaking) community and coloured people had been one of master and servant.

In the majority of cases, they spoke the same language, worshipped at the same (albeit segregated) church and shared a cultural understanding. Yet, within eight years of the 1948 election that brought the NP to power, coloured people in the Cape were removed from the common voters' roll (see page 392) and placed on a separate roll.

At first the disenfranchised voters were represented in parliament by white MPs. Later the government created the Coloured Persons' Representative Council (CRC), a legislative body with minor powers which was never accepted by the majority of coloured people. The CRC was abandoned in 1980 after the majority political party in it, the Labour Party, refused to cooperate with the government.

In the early 1970s, the state appointed a commission of inquiry to investigate the political, economic and social development of the coloured people.

In mid-1976, the commission chairperson, retired Stellenbosch University academic Erika Theron, tabled a report that recommended, among other things, the abolition of the Mixed Marriages Act and section 16 of the Immorality Act (which prohibited sexual intercourse between whites and blacks). The report also called for the opening of certain amenities to coloured people and, significantly, the establishment of some type of direct representation for coloured people in parliament – even if the Westminster style of government that had existed in South Africa for more than 100 years had to be altered to accommodate the country's multiracial society.

Although the report of the Theron Commission was clearly in accord with the *verligte* (enlightened) thinking of the Afrikaner capitalists, the Vorster Government reacted cautiously to the Theron report, stating in a White Paper that 'any recommendations to the effect that direct representation be granted to coloureds in the existing parliamentary, provincial and local institutions is … not acceptable'.

The door was not completely shut, however. Having rejected direct representation for the coloured community in parliament, the government appointed a Cabinet committee under the chairmanship of Minister of Defence P W Botha to investigate how coloured people could be accommodated in a future constitution. Later, the terms of

Blueprint for the tricameral parliament

The 1983 Constitution Act made allowance for the South African Parliament to consist of three legislative houses: the House of Assembly (178 seats) for whites; the House of Representatives (85 seats) for coloured people; and the House of Delegates (45 seats) for Asians.

The objective of the constitution, according to the then Minister of Constitutional Affairs, Chris Heunis, was to 'accommodate the coloured people and Indians without detracting from the self-determination of the whites'.

With this in mind, allowance was made for legislation to be divided into 'general affairs' which applied to all groups and dealt with matters such as defence, foreign affairs, justice, police and transport; and 'own affairs', which applied only to specific groups, and covered education, culture, health, community development and local government.

In terms of the Act, 'own affairs' legislation had to be enacted only by the house concerned, whereas 'general affairs' Bills needed the support of all three houses before they could be passed to the State President for assent. If the houses could not agree together on a Bill, the Bill had to go to the President's Council for a final decision.

The 60-member President's Council consisted of 35 members nominated by the three houses and 25 members (of which 10 had to come from opposition ranks) appointed by the State President.

The new constitution effectively made State President P W Botha both the formal and the executive head of state and commander-in-chief of the South African Defence Force.

THE TRICAMERAL *parliament first met in a joint sitting in January 1985. It was bitterly opposed by many who favoured a non-racial state.*

reference of the committee were expanded to include an investigation into the political future of the 800 000 Indians living in South Africa, whose place in the sun had long been under threat from the NP's official policy of repatriation to India.

In September 1978 Botha became Prime Minister, and almost immediately unfurled his flag of reform, sending a clear signal to South Africa and the world that, as far as he was concerned, all was not well in the South African polity. Botha launched his policy of Total Strategy, designed to take the sting out of internal unrest by creating an African middle class, and to spike the guns of the African National Congress (ANC) by forcing it out of surrounding territories.

A new constitution

Crucial to Total Strategy was constitutional reform. In June 1980 parliament passed the Republic of South Africa Constitution Fifth Amendment Act, which abolished the upper house of parliament (the Senate) and replaced it with a multiracial President's Council, consisting of 60 white, coloured and Asian (Indian and Chinese) nominated members. The Council was charged with creating a new constitution that would give expression to coloured and Indian political ambitions.

After two years of debate – during which it heard constitutional experts from all over the world – the Council proposed an executive that would ultimately give Botha more powers: an electoral college consisting of 50 white, 25 coloured and 13 Indian members would elect an executive State President who would combine the portfolios of both Prime Minister and State President for a period of seven years.

The recommendations in a second report provided the basis for the proposals that were presented to parliament in July 1983 for a new constitution that would split a future parliament into three houses: for whites, coloured people and Indians.

A right-wing split

The long debate on power sharing among the white, coloured and Indian communities raised tempers among far-right members of the white House of Assembly.

It had always been clear that Botha's policy of Total Strategy would alienate some traditional NP supporters. Botha and his advisers were well aware that in order to win new allies outside the ruling class, the NP would have to draw resources from the white sector and call into question the fundamental policy of the white power-base upon which the policy of apartheid had been built.

The leader of the anti-reformist group in the government was Andries Treurnicht, the Transvaal leader of the NP and a lucid, stylish orator with an enormous following among blue-collar workers, public servants and farmers, especially in the Transvaal.

Throughout 1980 and 1981, Treurnicht and his supporters used every opportunity to snipe at the proposals. In February 1983, 22 members of the NP abstained or voted against 'power sharing' – and Botha ran out of patience. Furious at this snub, he gave the rebel MPs a week to sign a motion of confidence in his leadership. Only six agreed – and the other 16 (including Treurnicht) were expelled from the party.

The far-right rebels wasted no time in organising themselves. Within a month they had launched the Conservative Party (CP) – with Treurnicht as leader. Old enemies of the reformists – including Botha's once-powerful rival for the premiership – had now found a new home.

The proposal to allow coloured and Indian people into parliament made the right-wing split almost inevitable. The NP had won the 1948 general election by claiming that the lukewarm reforms of General Jan Smuts's United Party would eventually lead to black rule. The fact that the Botha Government had no intention of letting this happen made little difference to the supporters of the CP, who believed that the 'germ' of 'racial integration' was being introduced into South Africa by the new proposals.

DR ANDRIES TREURNICHT *(right) and the* MP *for Nigel, Hannes Visagie (left), show the chairman of the Johannesburg Pen Club, Daan de Kock (centre), the first edition of the Conservative Party's newspaper, 'The Conservative', after they were expelled by P W Botha for failing to come to heel over opposition to the new constitution.*

CHIEF REFERENDUM OFFICER *Gerrie van Zyl announces the results of the 1983 referendum from the Union Buildings in Pretoria. Insets show 'Yes' and 'No' posters, which appeared all over the country during the referendum.*

Going to the people

The formation of the CP drew clear battle lines between supporters and opponents of the new proposals.

The split between the NP and its right-wing opponents also made the proposals more respectable for many English-speaking whites; after all, if the 'lunatic fringe' of Afrikanerdom rejected the constitution, they argued, it probably had some merit. (Furthermore, the proposed system was so difficult to understand, and so theoretical, that most citizens were unable to adjudge it anyway.)

While the debate continued, the government acted. On 31 August 1983, the constitutional guru, Minister of Constitutional Development and Planning Chris Heunis, guided through parliament the Republic of South Africa Constitution Act – and three weeks later it was signed into law by State President Marais Viljoen. Despite its easy victory in parliament, however, the government still felt uneasy. Just how much support had the right wing been able to glean? Would whites show their dislike of the proposals by voting the government out of power at the next opportunity? There was only one way to find out: on 2 November 1983 the government held a referendum to ask the white electorate: 'Are you in favour of the implementation of the new constitution as approved by parliament?'

The referendum was the most hotly debated issue in white South African politics since the 1960 referendum asking whites whether or not they were in favour of a republic.

Calling on voters to say 'No', Frederik van Zyl Slabbert, the leader of the Progressive Federal Party, argued that the proposal further entrenched apartheid and excluded Africans. Instead of promoting goodwill, he added, it would lead to further discontent and conflict. 'The tragedy of South Africa,' said Slabbert, 'is that at a time when the voters have come to acknowledge the need for such reform, the National Party has come forward with a plan that is so defective and ill-conceived that, if implemented, will set back the process of reform for at least a decade.'

Harry Oppenheimer, the doyen of the country's business community and chairman of the giant Anglo-American group, in announcing his intention to vote 'No', warned that Africans bitterly resented and universally condemned the constitution, which had been introduced without 'reference to their opinions, their problems and their rights'.

Many other business leaders, however, announced their support for the proposals – as did newspapers such as the 'Sunday Times' and the 'Natal Mercury' and the magazine the 'Financial Mail', which told readers that, while the new constitution was flawed, it was better than the dispensation that existed at present. Other newspapers – including the 'Cape Times', the 'Rand Daily Mail' and the 'Pretoria News'(which described the proposal as a 'Machiavellian design to place the National Party permanently in the driving seat with a multiracial collection of passengers for cosmetic effect') – urged their readers to vote 'No'. 'The Star' of Johannesburg sat on the fence, urging readers not to vote in the referendum at all.

The churches also waded into the constitutional debate, with the English-language churches calling on parishioners to reject the new proposals. Desmond Tutu, the Anglican Dean of Johannesburg (and general secretary of the South African Council of Churches), urged rejection, arguing that the proposals had been conceived without the participation of the real leaders of South Africa. Methodists rejected the new constitution because it was 'alien to the reconciling Gospel of Jesus Christ' and would lead to further 'polarisation, unrest and violent conflict'. In a pastoral letter signed by Archbishop Denis Hurley of Durban, the Southern African Catholic Bishops' Conference attacked the proposals because 'two-thirds of the population' had been disregarded. Only the major Afrikaans church, the Dutch Reformed Church, refused to take a positive stand – which was hardly surprising, given the fact that secular Afrikanerdom had clearly split over whether or not to support Botha's plan. However, more than 200 ministers representing the Dutch Reformed Church and its sister Afrikaans churches were less reticent, rejecting the proposed constitution because, they argued, Christian values would be undermined by power sharing with Hindus and Muslims.

On 2 November whites made up their minds: in a 76 per cent turnout, almost 66 percent (1 360 223) voted 'Yes'; 33,5 percent (691 557) 'No'; and 0,5 percent (10 669) spoilt their papers. It was a heady moment for Botha.

To vote or not to vote

With the support of the majority of whites in its pocket, the government set about trying to sell the concept to the very constituency it was supposed to appease – the coloured

COLOURED PEOPLE *cast their ballots in the August 1984 House of Representatives election – despite widespread violence and a boycott of coloured schools. Only about 30 percent of the registered voters – about two-thirds of those eligible to register – voted.*

and Indian voters. In both communities an inevitable schism opened between those who saw their chance for advancement through the new constitution and those who rejected it and chose the road of extra-parliamentary activity instead to continue the fight for political rights for all black South Africans.

The coloured Labour Party, which had earlier scuttled the CRC by refusing to cooperate with the government, had already made its decision. At a meeting in Eshowe in Natal, in January 1983, only nine of the 300 delegates voted against the new constitution. Those who supported participation argued that they saw it as a stepping stone towards a one-man, one-vote government. Labour Party leader the Reverend Allan Hendrickse, an eastern Cape Congregational Church minister who had once spent 60 days in detention for political activities against the government, said he believed the NP had undergone a change of heart and should be given a chance.

The Indian community needed a little more urging – and in order to whip up support, Botha met Indian political leaders at the Durban City Hall, while Indian opponents of the constitution held a rival meeting later in the day to organise a boycott of the forthcoming elections. When the talking was over, the South African Indian Council, under the leadership of Amichand Rajbansi, agreed to take part in elections for the new parliament. Major opposition to participation was led by the Natal Indian Congress – several members of which were detained by security police.

As the election days loomed – 22 August 1984 for the coloured voters and 28 August for Indians – the government urged coloured and Indian people to register as voters, but only about two-thirds made the effort. The turnout on the election days was even more dismal, with only about 30 percent of coloured people who had registered casting a vote, and 20 percent of Indians. Far from

disheartened, the government blamed intimidation and pre-election violence for the poor showing.

Predictably, the election winners were Hendrickse's Labour Party and Rajbansi's National People's Party – and both were given places in the new Cabinet as Ministers without portfolio. Botha, who had meanwhile become executive State President, rewarded them at the first session of the new parliament by repealing section 16 of the Immorality Act and the Mixed Marriages Act, along with the Prohibition of Political Interference Act, which had been intended to segregate political parties.

Opposition outside parliament

While Hendrickse and Rajbansi were fêted in parliament, opposition to apartheid moved more determinedly than ever outside it. Even while the new proposals were being discussed, two new extra-parliamentary groupings were launched to oppose the new dispensation: the ANC-aligned United Democratic Front (UDF) and the black consciousness-supporting National Forum.

The idea of a 'united democratic front' against the proposed new constitution was first mooted on 22 January 1983 at a conference called by the Transvaal branch of the anti-South African Indian Council Committee. The idea received enthusiastic support in the western Cape from organisations such as the Federation of Residents' Associations and the Cape Areas Housing Action Committee as well as from trade union groups throughout the country.

At its founding conference, Allan Boesak, the president of the World Alliance of Reformed Churches, said: 'Our response to the crisis facing us is … the politics of refusal, which has within it both the Yes and the No …. While we say "Yes" to this struggle, we say "No" to apartheid, racial segregation and economic exploitation of the oppressed masses in South Africa …. In order to do this we need a united front ….'

'ALL, HERE AND NOW'. *When the United Democratic Front (UDF) was launched in August 1983 to oppose the tricameral constitution, Allan Boesak received a tumultuous welcome.*

The UDF was officially launched on 20 August 1983 in the Mitchell's Plain suburb of Rocklands, near Cape Town. A crowd estimated at between 6 000 and 15 000 roared its approval as some of the country's foremost anti-apartheid activists mounted the podium: veteran ANC member Archie Gumede told the throng that he found inspiration in Moses, who had led the children of Israel out of Egypt; veteran trade unionist Frances Baard said the rally reminded her of a song she used to sing at school – 'land of hope and glory, mother of peace'; Aubrey Mokoena, secretary of the Transvaal Branch of the Release Mandela Campaign, called on the crowd to 'remember our leaders on Robben Island and to pray, but when we pray we must not do so like the missionaries who said we must close our eyes while they pulled the land from under our feet. I would like to call upon you to pray like revolutionaries with your eyes open ....'

The biggest cheer of the day was reserved for Boesak, who spoke to the crowd about 'three little words, words that express so eloquently our seriousness in this struggle: "all, here and now". We want *all* our rights, we want them *here* and we want them *now*.'

The UDF in particular attracted the support of hundreds of political, unionist and social groupings across the country, which moved Boesak to declare: 'The time has come for white people in this country to realise that their destiny is inextricably bound with our destiny and that they shall never be free until we are free.'

Not since the Congress Alliance in 1955 had the government been confronted with such massive unified opposition. By 1984 the UDF had the support of some 600 organisations and an estimated 3-million people. Among union members were the Council of Unions of South Africa, the General and Allied Workers' Union, the South African Allied Workers' Union, and the Motor Assemblers and Component Workers' Union. The UDF's first major or-

ganised protest was the 'Million Signatures Campaign' against the new constitution and they also campaigned to dissuade voters from participating in the coloured and Indian elections.

The government moved swiftly to try to suppress the movement: UDF offices were raided, meetings banned and leaders detained under the Internal Security Act. Within a year, 45 of the 80 UDF leaders were in jail, with the Minister of Law and Order, Louis le Grange, linking the organisation with the ANC and the South African Communist Party.

The formation of the National Forum

While the UDF campaigned for a unified, non-racial opposition to apartheid, the flame of black consciousness that had been articulated by Steve Biko still burned in the hearts of members of the Azanian People's Organisation (AZAPO), under the leadership of people such as vice-president Saths Cooper and secretary-general Muntu Myeza. ('Azania' comes from the old Greek name for the east African coast.)

Released from Robben Island in 1983, Cooper joined intellectual Neville Alexander, whose five-year banning order had been lifted in 1979, in formulating a response to the constitution.

Two months before the UDF was launched, the National Forum (NF) was inaugurated in June 1983 at a meeting in Hammanskraal near Pretoria by AZAPO and other groups which shared its views.

The NF vision of a future South Africa was radically different from that held by the UDF. The UDF links with the ANC came under attack from NF affiliates such as AZAPO, which criticised the Freedom Charter (see page 388) for preserving group rights and recognising minority rights. Cooper, the convenor of the NF, accused the UDF of perceiving the liberation struggle in South Africa as simply an anti-apartheid or civil rights movement rather than a revolutionary campaign designed to restructure society completely by overthrowing the established 'racist/capitalist' order. Alexander told the founding conference that whites who wanted to contribute to the struggle had their place, but that the future leaders of South Africa had to come from the African working class. The NF concluded its deliberations at Hammanskraal with the release of a 'Manifesto of the Azanian People' that called for non-collaboration with 'the oppressor and his political instruments'.

This combination of black consciousness and left-wing revolutionary theory brought the National Forum only lukewarm support – and the organisation never managed to organise anything like the mass following attracted by the UDF. Nevertheless, AZAPO remained strong among African intellectuals.

Following an outbreak of violence between UDF and NF supporters at the University of the North in Turfloop, a wave of petrol bombing and tyre executions ('necklacings') swept through different parts of the country. In an appeal for peace, 'City Press' editor Percy Qoboza called on the two organisations to 'come together and … identify who their real enemy is'. Bishop Tutu also tried to act as a peacemaker, but his attempts to call the rival factions together in a bid to halt the fighting met with only limited success.

An explosive reaction

On the day that the new constitution came into force – 3 September 1984 – alarming news flashed round the country: nine people had been killed in unrest in and around Sharpeville, the township where 69 opponents of apartheid had been killed by police bullets 24 years earlier. Most had been killed in clashes with the police, but at least three were murdered because of their association with the white administration. The deputy mayor of

POLICE *keep a watchful eye on Germiston's Katlehong township in March 1985 after a call by the local Action Committee for a rent boycott until African councillors resigned.*

Sharpeville had been hacked to death on his front doorstep, while two other men had been burned to death after being trapped in their cars.

Behind the unrest was a government decision to establish African-run councils for many of the urban townships – a logical product of Total Strategy (which intended giving certain Africans the privilege of councillor status in order to set them up as a buffer against grassroots unrest). The councils, however, proved immensely unpopular, with many townships simply choosing their own community organisations to run affairs instead.

Voting for the official town councils was sluggish – with only 14 percent of registered voters bothering to vote in Sharpeville.

Popular or not, the new councils were charged by the government with the almost impossible task of financing their affairs from whatever rents could be squeezed from the impoverished township residents. While the immediate cause of the Sharpeville unrest was a rent increase, the fact that it occurred on the first day of the tricameral parliament was enough for anti-government activists to fan the flames of revolt as hard as they could, and within weeks rioting had broken out in many areas of the Vaal triangle and in the eastern and western Cape. A new, powerful weapon had been added to the anti-government arsenal: the rent boycott.

The Durban six

Trouble of a very different kind was brewing in Natal – where, four days later, on 7 September, the Supreme Court in Pietermaritzburg ordered the release of seven UDF members who had been detained on the eve of the coloured and

BISHOP DESMOND TUTU *(right) pictured with newspaper editor Percy Qoboza (left) and Nelson Mandela's daughter, Zinzi.*

'Hell' in Church Street

As the bells of the Church Square clock rang out at 4.30 on Friday afternoon, 20 May 1983, office workers in Pretoria's Church Street outside the Nedbank Building housing the headquarters of the South African Air Force, began queueing at bus stops to go home. Two passersby walked into a coffee bar and asked the owner, Bettie Coetzee, for soft drinks. As she bent down behind the soft drink dispenser to pour the drinks, a blinding red flash filled the shop. For a split second Mrs Coetzee thought the lights in the shop had short-circuited. Before she could look up, however, there was a thunderous explosion. The counter and the dispenser both disintegrated and flung Mrs Coetzee to the floor beneath a pile of debris. When she lifted her head to stare dazedly around her, she saw the two customers lying across the rubble in front of her – covered with blood and clearly dead.

Fire engines, police cars and ambulances rushed to the scene. People lay dying and wounded on the pavements and streets, smoke coiled out of burning shop fronts and cars blazed. A survivor described it as 'a scene from hell'. As firemen and paramedics sifted through the carnage, the grisly toll began to mount. By seven o'clock that evening more than a dozen dead had been found and some 180 people had been taken to hospitals around Pretoria. As a stunned nation counted the cost, the Minister of Defence, Magnus Malan, said the

THE NEDBANK BUILDING *in Pretoria blazes after the bomb attack in 1983.*

government would not hesitate to launch pre-emptive attacks on ANC bases, and that same night the Defence Force launched a devastating attack on five alleged ANC bases in Maputo, claiming to have killed 64 ANC members. Mozambique, on the other hand, claimed that six civilians had been killed.

By Sunday a clearer picture had emerged. The blast had been caused by a 60-kilogram bomb hidden in a stolen car and detonated prematurely, killing the two bombers, identified as Bakayi Maseko and Freddy Shongwe, both connected to the ANC. According to an ANC statement from Lusaka claiming responsibility for the blast, the intended target had been the South African Air Force offices. A spokesman expressed 'regret' at the loss of civilian life.

Indian elections in an effort to spike the guns of the UDF in its calls for an election boycott. Law and Order Minister Louis le Grange promptly issued orders for their redetention – but not quickly enough; six evaded the police net, emerging from hiding a week later at the door of the British Consulate on the sixth floor of a building in Durban. Once inside, they announced that they were staying.

The six were Archie Gumede, one of the 1956 Treason trialists; George Sewpersadh, a veteran of the 1950s Congress Alliance; Billy Nair, an ex-Robben Island prisoner; Paul David, who had spent 17 years on the banned list; and Mewa Ramgobin and Mooroogiah Naidoo, executive members of the Natal Indian Congress.

While consulate staff moved in mattresses, the diplomatic notes began flying between London and Pretoria – and the international Press converged on Durban for one of the biggest stories of the year. With Britain refusing to accede to demands by Pretoria to expel the six from the

consulate, South Africa hit back by breaking its promise to return to England for trial four alleged South African arms runners arrested earlier that year in Coventry.

On 6 October, Ramgobin, Sewpersadh and Naidoo made a bid for freedom, and were immediately re-arrested by waiting police. On 12 December, the remaining 'guests' decided to leave, following the withdrawal against Gumede and David of notices under section 28(1) of the Internal Security Act. Gumede and David were taken away in a police van, while Nair was allowed to go free, and was carried shoulder high from the building by supporters.

Nobel Prize for Tutu

Shortly after the consulate drama, South Africa was again in the international spotlight when Tutu was awarded the Nobel Peace Prize. Although his achievement was virtually ignored by the state-run electronic media, his views

THE TWENTY-FIFTH *anniversary of the Sharpeville massacre was tragically recalled in the shooting of more than 20 people at Langa township, outside Uitenhage.*

on the crisis in South Africa were eagerly sought by international television companies. Tutu, who had become leader of the South African Council of Churches in 1978, incensed the government by his outspoken opposition to apartheid and his continued support for economic sanctions as a lever for political change. In 1984 a commission of inquiry into the South African Council of Churches charged that the council was no longer a religious organisation but one that identified itself with the 'liberation struggle' and supported sanctions against the country.

Many South African churchmen had long believed that apartheid was contrary to the teachings of Christ, but they also believed in Christ's message of peace. Reconciling the two in the troubled townships became increasingly difficult – and at the end of 1985, 151 clerics from 16 church groups issued the so-called Kairos document calling on Christians to 'participate in the struggle for liberation' by supporting civil disobedience campaigns, consumer boycotts and strikes.

Tutu's call for sanctions made him unpopular with many white Anglicans, but he explained his actions by calling on 'dear white fellow-South Africans' to hear the '*cri de coeur* we utter ... we too are just ordinary human beings. We too love to be with our wives every day. We too want our children to rush out to meet us as we come back from work. We too would like to live where we can afford it .... We want to have a new kind of South Africa, where we all, black and white, can walk together ... into the glorious future which God is opening up before us ....'

The violence spreads

While Tutu continued his efforts to calm the inflamed passions of many blacks, the spiral of violence that had greeted the new constitution began to spread ominously

across the land. At the same time workers and students staged mass stayaways in the Vaal triangle.

The suddenness and enormity of the unrest caught the government off guard and it responded by sending in the army. In the early hours of 23 October 1984, 7 000 troops in armoured trucks rolled into Sebokeng township near Vereeniging. Systematically, they began a door-to-door search of the 20 000 houses before moving on to Sharpeville and Boipatong.

The violence, however, continued to spread across the country – to Natal and the eastern Cape, where increasing unemployment coupled with fairly high levels of education among Africans had created an explosive mixture of bitterness and frustration.

Another tragedy occurred after the Port Elizabeth Black Civic Association, a UDF affiliate, had called for a work stayaway to commemorate the 21 March 1985 killings at Sharpeville. At Uitenhage, near Port Elizabeth, a crowd estimated by police at between 3 000 and 4 000 began marching out of the nearby Langa township towards the white area to attend a funeral. About 1,5km outside the township, police in armoured Casspirs opened fire on the crowd, killing more than 20 people.

As condemnation in South Africa and around the world began pouring in, the government appointed Mr Justice Donald Kannemeyer as a one-man commission of inquiry into the shooting.

Although Kannemeyer rejected as 'outright fabrication' a claim by the Minister of Law and Order, Louis le Grange, that the crowd had been armed with petrol bombs and stones, he did not blame the police directly for the shootings, but criticised senior officers for allowing their men to patrol the area without riot control weapons – and only live ammunition.

On 26 March – a few days after the shootings – church leaders, including Tutu, were arrested in Cape Town after a service to remember the Langa dead. They were released the next day. The people of the eastern Cape, however, showed little restraint in their reaction to the killings – scenes of unparalleled ferocity chilled the nation and the world as youngsters turned against anyone or anything with links to the white administration. The most vulnerable targets were those people who had agreed to take part in the government's scheme to promote African town councils, and many died horribly. T B Kinikini, the last remaining councillor in the Kwanobuhle township, was beaten to death together with one of his sons and two nephews. Their bodies were then doused with petrol and set on fire. In the same period, the infant son of a council secretary was burned to death after a petrol bomb attack on her home.

Crisis at the schools

In 1976, and again in 1980, black schools became a flashpoint for revolt against the apartheid system. Youngsters, who had grown up under a system that many of their parents had accepted as a permanent part of their lives, wanted nothing to do with apartheid and were ripe for the kind of rhetoric that flared up under the Azanian Students' Movement (the student wing of AZAPO) and the UDF-affiliated Congress of South African Students (COSAS) ....

On the same day that coloured voters went to the polls – 22 August 1984 – 60 000 pupils (80 percent of the coloured pupil population) boycotted classes. Eleven of the country's coloured teacher-training colleges were also closed as a result of the stayaway. School unrest reached boiling point in the Vaal triangle when a 15-year-old schoolgirl died after being run over by a police Land Rover during a demonstration outside her school in Atteridgeville near Pretoria.

Apart from the wider political connotations, the bitterness felt by black pupils was partly a result of the inferior standard of education they received when compared with whites. Although state spending on African education increased dramatically under the Botha administration (from R68,84-million in 1978 to R237-million by mid-1985), the South African Institute of Race Relations reported that in the period 1982-83 R1 385 was spent on educating every white pupil, compared with R871 for every Indian, R593 for every coloured pupil and R192 for every African schoolchild. Africans were particularly bitter that in many areas their education system was still rooted in the Verwoerdian theory of preparing them only for manual work.

The rise of COSATU

The new constitution also sparked a mammoth stayaway in October 1984 by some 800 000 workers at key parastatal industries such as the oil-from-coal corporation SASOL and the steel mills at ISCOR. Behind these strikes lay a new militancy among black trade unionists that had been brewing since the official recognition given African trade unions following the recommendation of the Wiehahn Commission in 1979 (see page 458).

In October 1984 the UDF-linked Congress of South African Students, which had organised the boycott of schools in protest at the new constitution, gained trade union support in a Transvaal Regional Stayaway Committee. A pamphlet issued by the committee called for, among other demands, the withdrawal of security forces from the townships, the release of detainees and the democratic election of students' representative councils.

The stayaway that followed was immensely successful, despite allegations of intimidation.

In Atteridgeville hardly anyone went to work or to school. Over the entire Reef area some 400 000 pupils stayed at home, temporarily closing 300 schools. It was the biggest mass stayaway that the South African public had ever seen – and its combination of pupil and worker action made it even more significant.

WORKERS *hail the founding of the Congress of South African Trade Unions (COSATU) in Durban in December 1985. The new federation of trade unions represented half-a-million South African workers.*

The stayaway also brought to a head industrial action by the newly formed National Union of Mineworkers (NUM) under the leadership of a lawyer named Cyril Ramaphosa. By 1984, at the start of a new round of pay negotiations, the union had a membership of thousands and had won recognition from various mining companies.

In 1985 the NUM was one of the key movers behind the launch of the Congress of South African Trade Unions (COSATU), which brought together more than 30 non-racial unions, including the Federation of South African Trade Unions (FOSATU). The new umbrella organisation, with Elijah Barayi as president and Jay Naidoo as general secretary, represented more than half-a-million workers. Barayi told the founding rally: 'If they [the government] don't abolish the Pass laws within six months, we'll burn our Pass books.' (In April 1986 President Botha announced the abolition of the Pass laws, while at the same time proclaiming stricter anti-squatting measures.)

Mandela and the ANC

Since the Soweto uprisings of 1976 the ANC had been developing a two-pronged strategy: acts of sabotage and violence through its fighting arm, *Umkhonto we Sizwe*, and the encouragement of internal unrest.

In a broadcast over ANC Radio from Addis Ababa, the organisation called for the people to 'render South Africa ungovernable'. Meanwhile, the charismatic leader of the ANC, Nelson Mandela, was incarcerated just 26 km from parliament itself in Pollsmoor Prison, south of Cape Town.

The status of Mandela provided Botha with a headache: if he released Mandela unconditionally, his government stood to lose an unacceptable amount of face. But if Mandela died in prison, the ANC leader would become a martyr. The government had offered him freedom before – on condition that he return to his birthplace in Transkei and stay there. The offer had been refused, however.

Towards the end of 1984, veteran Progressive Federal Party MP Helen Suzman arranged a meeting between Mandela and a visiting member of the European Parliament, Lord Bethell. According to Lord Bethell, Mandela had indicated a willingness to call a halt to violence if the ANC were legalised. Botha reacted by announcing in parliament that his government was prepared to release Mandela provided he forswore violence. Again Mandela refused, and in his reply, read out by his daughter Zinzi Mandela to a huge gathering at the Jabulani amphitheatre outside Johannesburg, stated that he did not want violence but the opportunity for the ANC to negotiate with the government for a fair and free country.

Watching from the KwaZulu capital of Ulundi were Chief Mangosuthu Buthelezi and his Zulu-based Inkatha movement. Although Buthelezi had always been adamant that Mandela's release was a prerequisite for talks with the government about a peaceful internal settlement, there was little love lost between his organisation and the ANC. Buthelezi, who had been a member of the ANC before it was banned in 1960, now found himself branded as a puppet by the ANC and other black activists inside South Africa for accepting the leadership of the KwaZulu 'homeland',

THE ILL-FATED *Pollsmoor march in 1985 ended in the suburb of Crawford near Cape Town, when police waded into a small group of determined marchers.*

while his Inkatha movement was branded as a Zulu nationalist organisation that cooperated with the government in an effort to secure power for itself. Yet Buthelezi enjoyed considerable support among whites, particularly for his anti-sanctions stand, his support for the concept of free enterprise, and his proposal for a Bill of Rights.

State of emergency

By the end of March 1985 unrest had reached such a pitch that the government had to augment the fully stretched police force with the army. But the unrest did not abate and, in fact, took an ominous turn with random attacks on Africans alleged to be 'informers'. In July, Bishop Tutu intervened when a young man who had been dragged from his car was about to be murdered by an enraged crowd in Duduza township on the east Rand. His quick thinking saved the man's life – and shocked Tutu so deeply that he announced that he would consider leaving South Africa to live elsewhere unless such incidents stopped.

On the evening of Saturday, 20 July 1985 P W Botha announced that a state of emergency would be imposed on 36 magisterial districts from midnight – the first time since the Sharpeville crisis of 1960 that such a measure had had to be resorted to. The violence, however, still did not stop – and areas that had previously been relatively peaceful exploded into unrest.

In the Durban area trouble was sparked by the murder of a leading civil rights lawyer, Victoria Mxenge, who was gunned down as she was getting out of her car in Umlazi township, her murder raising fears of the existence of a right-wing 'death squad'. Her funeral led to confrontation between the UDF and Inkatha – and within four days 50 people had been killed. Hundreds of buildings were burnt, including a school and a literary complex dedicated to the memory of Mohandas Gandhi.

A few days after the start of the Durban unrest, UDF patron Allan Boesak announced a mass march on Pollsmoor Prison near Cape Town to demand the release of Mandela. The government responded quickly by detaining Boesak and sealing off Athlone Stadium – the departure point for the marchers. Nevertheless, an attempt was made to start the march without Boesak, and after several warnings to the demonstrators to disperse, police waded in to the crowd – including several nuns – with quirts. Over the next two days, 30 people died in the unrest that flared up in the African and coloured areas around Cape Town. In a bid to stop the violence, the government closed nearly half the coloured colleges and schools in the western Cape.

The state of emergency gave the government vastly increased powers to detain anyone suspected of fomenting violence, and within three months the police held more than 5 000 people. Organised political meetings were banned, leaving funerals as the main expression of black bitterness. By October at least 685 people had been killed – nearly 500 in police action. Some 20 000 people had been injured and 14 000 arrested for public violence.

Many leaders, such as the eastern Cape activists Matthew Goniwe, Fort Calata, Sparrow Mkhonto and Sicelo Mhlauli, were mysteriously murdered. And state repression of student organisations and UDF support groups was intensified.

The popularity of the ANC among blacks became clear after a Transvaal newspaper conducted a public opinion poll showing that more than 56 percent of its respondents wanted Mandela as their leader. In addition, ANC slogans and pamphlets were passed around freely, freedom songs were sung in public and the ANC flag unfurled at funerals.

P W Botha – the 'hawk' of reform

Before 1978 no one would have guessed that Pieter Willem Botha would one day become the most powerful man ever to emerge in South African politics – Executive State President in a constitution he claimed was necessary to bring about a reform of the apartheid system. In fact, without some careful behind-the-scenes manoeuvring during the election of the new National Party (NP) leader in 1978 – after the retirement of Prime Minister John Vorster in the wake of the Information scandal – Connie Mulder would have become the new Prime Minister, not Botha (see page 456). The fact that the crown went to Botha revealed his ambition, determination and dogged willpower to get his own way. Time and again during his tenure at the helm of the NP he proved to be a tough, uncompromising opponent.

Both Botha's parents were anti-British during the South African War, and his mother had hidden from Imperial forces in a cave for three months before being captured and sent to a concentration camp, where two of her children died. His father, a *bittereinder*, broke his rifle in disgust when the Boer forces surrendered.

Botha was born in 1916, and his interest in politics began early – in 1936 he quit university without obtaining a degree in order to work for the NP. In 1946 he was appointed the party's information officer, coordinating the publicity campaign that culminated in the party's victory at the polls in 1948 – in which he won the seat for George, a picturesque town on the southern Cape coast. As Minister of Community Development, he was responsible for the removal of coloured people from District Six in Cape Town.

In 1966 he became Minister of Defence and soon earned a reputation as a hardliner with a short temper and an admonishing finger. For 12 years he worked hard at the Department of Defence, arguing the case in the Cabinet for sending South African troops into Angola in 1975 in an unsuccessful bid to ensure UNITA participation in the new government.

Following the wide acceptance of his constitutional proposals in the 1983 referendum, Botha visited nine European countries in order to try to convince European leaders that he was serious about instituting reforms in South Africa – and to persuade them to tone down their criticism of his government. His tour brought a howl of protest from European anti-apartheid demonstrators.

As part of his Total Strategy policy, Botha also held talks with the leader of Mozambique, Samora Machel, which led to the Nkomati Accord of 16 March 1984, in which both countries agreed not to allow their territory to be used as a springboard for hostile forces to attack the other. Mozambique agreed to expel the ANC from its territory, while South Africa agreed to cease support for the Mozambican guerrilla organisation, RENAMO. Speaking at the meeting, Botha told the Mozambican delegation: 'We are both African countries, inhabited by African peoples whose past and future are firmly entrenched in the southern part of the African continent. We are of Africa.'

Despite his impassioned words, however, Botha's Nkomati Accord was not a success – particularly as far as Mozambique was concerned. Although South Africa largely achieved its aim of removing the ANC from Mozambique, guerrilla activity by RENAMO increased considerably, amid accusations in Maputo and the United Nations that South Africa had continued to aid the rebels.

P W BOTHA *of South Africa and Mozambican President Samora Machel at the signing of the Nkomati Accord in March 1984.*

Stumbling at the Rubicon

In July 1985, after a storm of international protest at the government's imposition of a state of emergency in 36 magisterial districts, Foreign Minister Pik Botha promised that P W Botha would announce a major programme of reform on 15 August in Durban. Instead of reforms, however, Botha warned the world not to 'push us too far'. After the rand plunged and loan repayments were frozen, the emergency was lifted in March 1986, only to be reimposed in June as violence continued. As the political and economic crisis intensified, P W Botha became locked in a struggle to retain power ....

FORTY-NINE YEARS before the birth of Jesus Christ, an ambitious Roman general stood on the bank of a small river in northern Italy and struggled to make up his mind. Julius Caesar knew that if he crossed the Rubicon River, his bid to win the imperial throne would precipitate a civil war throughout the Roman Empire; there would be no turning back.

Two thousand years later, on 15 August 1985, the State President of South Africa, P W Botha, ascended the podium of the Durban City Hall to deliver a speech that his countrymen and the world had been assured by Foreign Minister Pik Botha would signal a radical change of direction by the government, a major swing to reform in order to defuse the appalling spiral of violence that had gripped the country since the imposition of the new tricameral parliament the previous year.

The South African media had compared it with Caesar's river crossing: it was to be South Africa's Rubicon, a change of heart from which there would be no turning back. In millions of homes around the country – and around the world via a satellite television link-up – people waited for the President to deliver a message of hope ....

PW BOTHA's speech in the Durban City Hall in August 1985 sent shock waves through South African financial circles.

No end in sight

By mid-August 1985, the state of emergency that had been imposed the previous month had failed to stem the unrest. It had, however, increased the strain on the Republic's already precarious international relations: France had announced a freeze on new investment in South Africa; member nations of the European Economic Community (EEC) had recalled their ambassadors for consultations; and the USA, which had already recalled its ambassador, had refused to accredit the new South African ambassador in Washington.

Then, early in August at a meeting in Vienna, Foreign Minister Pik Botha had told the US national security adviser, Robert McFarlane, that President Botha would announce far-reaching reforms in a major policy speech on 15 August.

Television cameramen, photographers and reporters from some 33 countries gathered at the Durban City Hall, while an estimated 300-million people in the Republic and around the globe tuned in to see if Botha would announce the type of changes that South Africa and the world had been waiting for.

Instead of the statesman of reform, however, they saw a truculent Botha warning the world not to 'push us too far' and making it clear that he was not prepared to lead 'white South Africans and other minority groups to abdication and suicide'.

There were several reasons for Botha's turnaround: shortly before his speech, Chase Manhattan, one of the world's largest banks, had unexpectedly called in all outstanding loans to South Africa and refused to make new loans to the South African private sector. An angry Botha had interpreted this as an attempt to coerce his government into negotiations.

Also bothering Botha on the eve of his address was the discomforting progress of the far-right CP opposition. In May 1985, the National Party (NP) had narrowly avoided defeat at the hands of the Conservative Party (CP) in a by-election in the formerly safe NP seat of Harrismith in the Orange Free State. The result had caused misgivings about the government's policy directions among NP parliamentarians and provincial councillors, especially those representing conservative rural constituencies.

Looming on the horizon were five more parliamentary by-elections, dubbed by the media as a 'mini-general election'. To add to Botha's problems, the squabbling groups

CLASHES BETWEEN witdoeke *(vigilantes) and* amaqabane *(comrades) left many people homeless in the sprawling settlements of Crossroads , near Cape Town.*

on the far right were trying to unite (which threatened to alter dramatically the nature of the hustings in the 'mini-general election'). Previously, competing far-right candidates had split the far-right vote in elections and by-elections, allowing the Nationalists to retain seats they would otherwise have lost.

Botha thus faced a difficult choice. On the one hand, he could take a bold leap across the 'Rubicon', which the CP would exploit as a further capitulation to foreigners and which could also have adverse consequences for the party in an important test of white opinion; on the other hand, he could return to more certain ground with a rallying call to the party faithful. Botha, a quintessential party man, chose the latter course.

Certainly, his 'Rubicon' speech had all the makings of an election campaign address: Botha was at his most defiant, and it was the first of many NP speeches in the weeks before the 'mini-general election' that were aimed at rallying white opinion behind the government in the face of a hostile world.

The by-elections took place on 30 October 1985 – and with the unity efforts of the far right coming to nothing, the NP retained four of the five seats (with vastly reduced majorities in three of them). It lost the fifth seat, Sasolburg, to the *Herstigte Nasionale Party*, the original far-right breakaway party (and the most strident of them).

The international monetary community quickly made its feelings towards Botha's speech painfully clear: by 27 August, a panic run on the rand had pushed the value of the South African currency down from an already depressed 52 US cents to below 33 cents. The government's reaction was to close the money markets and the stock exchange for a week to give Reserve Bank Governor Gerhard de Kock time to try to persuade leading international banks to reschedule the nation's debts. The answer, however, was a polite, but firm, 'No', and when the markets reopened, Finance Minister Barend du Plessis had no choice but to announce a four-month freeze on foreign debt repayments.

Over the weeks that followed, events went from bad to worse: the United States immediately imposed limited economic sanctions, while condemnations of Pretoria's harsh regime filled newspapers in all the major capitals of the world. The nightly scenes of violence on television screens brought howls of revulsion and protest.

The explosion of unrest was indeed dramatic: in 1984, there had been 149 deaths and 651 unrest-related injuries; in 1985, 824 people died and 2 615 were injured in unrest-related incidents. Of the 955 people who were killed in political violence between 1 September 1984 and 24 January 1986, 628 had died as a result of action by 'state bodies'.

Not getting the picture

Increasingly, the government began to realise that, even if the bad news could not be stopped, the efforts of the messengers – the television news cameras that followed every police action – could be halted. The final straw for the government came in Athlone near Cape Town in late 1985, when a cameraman filmed police as they emerged shooting from crates on the back of a lorry which had been stoned by protesters. Three people were killed. (An inquest in March 1988 held the police responsible for their deaths.) After lambasting foreign correspondents for 'paying blacks to incite unrest', Botha barred all camera teams from unrest areas.

The violence, however, continued – in mid-November 1985, 19 people died after police had fired on a crowd of 50 000 in Mamelodi, near Pretoria. But this time there were no cameras – and no reporters. All information about the tragedy was issued by the police.

By this time many of the townships around the country had become virtually ungovernable. Community committees began to take over municipal duties such as rubbish collection and the staffing of day hospitals. The earlier African National Congress (ANC) tactic of making the townships 'ungovernable' was being replaced by that calling for 'semi-liberated zones' controlled by 'street committees', the composition of which varied considerably from area to area. In some instances, street committees were held accountable to area committees, which, in turn, were answerable to zonal committees. In many areas even petty criminals were dealt with by the committees and in some townships crime was almost eradicated.

Sometimes, however, the system led to excesses: those who did not join the system voluntarily were victimised; refusal to attend meetings could lead to accusations of being an informer – and, in some cases, to death. As more experienced leaders were detained by the government, so the committee structures often came to be run by less democratically minded residents. Occasionally the power vacuum left by the detention of community leaders was filled by gangs of thugs, who subjected their communities to reigns of terror. Their behaviour was denounced by Zwelakhe Sisulu, son of jailed ANC leader Walter Sisulu and editor of the Roman Catholic-funded newspaper 'New Nation'. People's power, he said, was not the setting up of kangaroo courts by bands of youths who handed out punishment 'under the control of no one, with no democratic mandate from the community'. True people's power, he said, could be achieved only when the leaders had a mandate from the community and were under the democratic control of the people.

It became difficult to know which 'semi-liberated zones' were run with a 'mandate from the people' and which were not. In many areas the excesses of kangaroo courts and summary murders of people alleged to be 'collaborators' led to the emergence of 'vigilantes' – conservative groups who wanted a return to the old order in the townships. Violence intensified around the country.

In the sprawling squatter community of Crossroads, near Cape Town, police denied that they helped the 'vigilantes' to drive out radical young activists (known as 'comrades') opposed to removals to the nearby township of Khayelitsha.

There was another reason for the violence: over the years, a handful of self-appointed squatter leaders had built up huge personal fortunes by forcing residents in areas under their control to pay a fee for being led – a kind of 'protection' payment. When the formation of branches in squatter areas by the United Democratic Front (UDF) began threatening the autocratic rule of some of these leaders, they responded with ruthless violence in a bid to retain their power.

More trouble flared up at Alexandra on 15 February 1986. This African township north-east of Johannesburg remained a 'black spot' in the government's removal programme – almost surrounded by white suburbs and once destined by the social engineers in Pretoria for the bulldozer. As a result, the township had been left to decay into a slum with no running water, sewerage or electricity and with potholed roads.

The man who had played a leading role in persuading the government to stay its hand with forced removals was a local church minister, the Reverend Sam Buti. Despite his efforts, Buti was regarded by many activists as a collaborator because of his membership of the government-sponsored Alexandra Town Council. The firebombing of Buti's house signalled the start of a war between 'comrades' and 'vigilantes', with peace being restored only after the government had sent troops and police in armoured cars into the area.

PROTESTS IN RURAL *areas, such as Mbekweni near Paarl, were often vented on beer halls.*

Unrest in rural areas

Unrest also spread to rural areas – near towns such as Cradock and Uitenhage in the eastern Cape, and Paarl and Worcester in the western Cape.

In the Transvaal, trouble arose when the government announced plans to incorporate Moutse, a crowded area inhabited by some 120 000 Northern Sotho-speaking people, into KwaNdebele, the Nbebele-speakers' 'homeland' north of Pretoria. On 1 January 1986, 30 people were killed when fighting broke out among people from the two areas. On 14 May, police had to escort members of the KwaNdebele Cabinet from their homes during 'anti-independence' protests by inhabitants of the 'homeland'.

In Lebowa in the eastern Transvaal, a mass grave containing more than 30 murder victims was uncovered after protests against the government of Cedric Phatudi. In the Winterveld area of Bophuthatswana, 11 people were killed when police opened fire on a crowd of protesters.

The upwelling of violence in the rural areas flowed from the frustrations of poverty and unemployment, which were far more pressing in those areas than in the cities. The far-reaching Second Carnegie Inquiry into Poverty and Development in Southern Africa had found, for instance, that 93 percent of the country's poor were in rural areas, that 1,43-million people in the 'homelands' had no income, and that almost 9-million people in the 'homelands' were living below the breadline. In the final report of the inquiry (the work of researchers at 22 universities throughout southern Africa), published on 24 January 1989, it was noted that the average income of a black family in a rural area was about half that of a black family in one of the cities. The report also drew attention to the chronic overcrowding in the rural areas: in 1980, the average population density in the Transvaal was 11 people per square kilometre, but it was 29 in Bophuthatswana, 65 in Lebowa, 74 in Gazankulu, 63 in KaNgwane, and 193 in KwaNdebele. In Natal, population density on white farms was 22 per square kilometre, but in rural areas of KwaZulu it was 76.

Several sparks were thrown into this rural tinderbox: between December 1984 and December 1985, the inflation rate stood at 18,4 percent, the highest in 66 years. The official estimate of black unemployment was 652 835 in 1985, but other estimates put it at 3-million for the country as a whole (which meant drastically reduced remittances to rural relatives from workers in the urban areas).

In many rural areas, bus-fare increases (of up to 40 percent in one instance) following a hike in the fuel price precipitated bus boycotts, protest marches and the stoning, fire-bombing and hijacking of buses (which inevitably led to confrontations with the police).

The state of emergency was lifted on 7 March 1986, more in response to international pressure than to an improvement in the level of violence. During the eight months that it lasted, 750 people were killed and almost 8 000 detained (2 000 of them under the age of 16). Psychologists expressed alarm at the effect of the unrest on township youth, fearing a generation of youngsters hardened to violence like those of Beirut and Belfast.

Rings of fire

On 13 April 1986, just over a month after the lifting of the state of emergency, leading activist Winnie Mandela told a huge crowd at Kagiso near Krugersdorp that 'the time for speeches and debate has come to an end'. The year 1986, she said to loud applause, would see the 'liberation of the oppressed masses of this country. We work in the white man's kitchen. We bring up the white man's children. We could have killed them at any time we wanted to. Together, hand in hand with our sticks and our matches, with our necklaces, we shall liberate this country.'

Her use of the word 'necklaces' caused an outcry – with most people concluding that she was referring to a new and devastating form of killing that was primarily reserved for many victims of what became known as 'black-on-black' violence – especially those suspected of collaboration. The 'necklace' was a rubber tyre filled with petrol and forced over the victim's head and shoulders, trapping his arms against his side. It was then set alight. Although Mandela later denied that her speech was a call on Africans to use the 'necklace' against whites, the damage was done – and at every opportunity the government used her exuberant outburst to score propaganda points against the ANC.

The 'necklace' was not the only new form of protest – another that spread across the country in 1986 was the consumer boycott in which blacks refused to buy anything from white-owned businesses. Although boycotts had been used with limited success before, the wave of boycotts that now swept around the country began in the eastern Cape after troops had moved into the troubled townships around Port Elizabeth and Uitenhage. This was, claimed the organisers, the surest way of drawing white attention to black grievances.

There were, however, many reports of coercion by activists trying to enforce the boycott: shoppers were turned back at bus depots and train stations, goods purchased at

FREED RIVONIA *trialist Govan Mbeki gets a helping hand from Winnie Mandela after his release.*

white-owned shops were confiscated, and in some cases it was reported that shoppers had been forced to drink cooking oil as punishment for breaking a boycott.

In the eastern Cape, where the boycott forced many smaller businesses to the wall, the local Chamber of Commerce urged the authorities to begin negotiations with black leaders.

The call for people's power was echoed by a similar cry for 'people's education' – and at a meeting of the newly formed National Education Crisis Committee in Durban in March 1986, Dr Beyers Naude, general secretary of the South African Council of Churches, speaking under a banner reading 'People's education for people's power', called for an end to segregated education.

The second emergency

By May 1986 the government was feeling increasingly besieged by the continuing spiral of violence and harsh criticism of its rule from overseas. Looming ever closer was 16 June, the 10th anniversary of the start of the Soweto uprising in 1976 – and reports of a planned stayaway and mass protests. As far as the government was concerned, Soweto could not be allowed to explode again.

As the 16 June deadline approached, Minister of Law and Order Louis le Grange tried to rush through parliament two security Bills giving the government new powers to counter the planned stayaway. When the coloured and Indian houses of the tricameral parliament refused to pass the Bills, they had to be sent to the President's Council for a decision. By then, however, it was obviously going to be too late for them to be promulgated. In the early hours of 12 June, hundreds of activists were detained in a countrywide swoop. At the same time, Botha signed a nationwide state of emergency far more stringent than its predecessor: journalists were banned from unrest areas, all reports of unrest were issued by the newly formed Bureau for Information and any information that promoted illegal strikes, boycotts, banned organisations or sanctions were labelled 'subversive'.

The bureau issued a daily 'unrest report' throughout 1987, before passing on this chore to the public relations department of the police. Although serious incidents of unrest continued, there was a gradual decrease in the number of killings in certain areas.

In February 1988 the government barred several organisations, including the UDF, the Detainees' Parents Support Committee and the Free Mandela Campaign, from taking part in any activity other than routine organisational tasks such as bookkeeping. The Congress of South African Trade Unions (COSATU), which had stated its intention to confront questions of 'national liberation', was also banned from any non-trade union activity.

On a more conciliatory note, the government released one of the Rivonia trialists, Govan Mbeki, in November 1987, but banned him a few weeks later.

Violence continued to plague the sprawling rural townships around Pietermaritzburg in Natal, where supporters of the UDF and the Zulu-based Inkatha movement battled for control of the area.

Tackling the ANC

South African Defence Force (SADF) raids against neighbouring states were part of PW Botha's Total Strategy to clear the region of ANC bases. Those countries that wanted an economic helping hand from South Africa were likely to receive it, on condition that they rid their territory of the ANC – otherwise it was made clear that the SADF would do it for them. The Nkomati Accord of March 1984 had closed Mozambique to the ANC. A series of raids into Botswana had achieved much the same result – ANC leader Oliver Tambo was forced to withdraw his representatives from the Botswana capital Gaborone in response to a request from Botswana. Lesotho, however, became increasingly obdurate as the Youth League of the ruling Basotho National Party of Chief Leabua Jonathan showed more and more solidarity with ANC members stationed in the country. Irked by Jonathan's refusal to expel the ANC, the South African Government instituted an economic blockade against the landlocked country. Within three weeks, on 20 January 1986, Jonathan was toppled by Major-General Metsing Lekhanya in a virtually bloodless coup. A few days later, after ANC representatives had left Maseru for Zambia, the blockade was lifted.

In Angola and Mozambique tensions simmered on, with South Africa openly supporting the UNITA movement led by Jonas Savimbi in Angola, and being accused of supporting RENAMO rebels against the FRELIMO Government of Mozambique, despite giving many assurances, most notably in the Nkomati Accord, that it would not do so. In October 1986 relations with Mozambique deteriorated even further when a Soviet plane carrying President Samora Machel home from a conference in Zimbabwe crashed in the eastern Transvaal, killing all on board. The new Mozambican President, Joaquim Chissano, accused South Africa of engineering the crash, but this was strongly denied by Pretoria.

South Africa appeared to pursue two policies towards the former Portuguese colonies. On the one hand, Pik Botha's Department of Foreign Affairs groped towards some kind of settlement that would see pro-Pretoria governments established in the two territories, while, on the other hand, the SADF pursued a policy of destabilisation in the two territories. Railways and roads between the coastal ports and the inland frontline states of Zimbabwe, Botswana and Zambia were regularly disrupted, forcing these states to use channels of communication through South Africa. Destabilisation by the SADF was designed to undermine the Southern Africa Development Coordination Conference – formed by the frontline states to end economic dependence on South Africa – and make it impossible for them to impose economic sanctions. South Africa also tried to use its railway network as an economic stick with which to force the frontline states to expel the ANC from their territories.

An international outcry

With powerful voices in the USA joining the cry for international sanctions against Pretoria, the ANC began enjoying a new surge of support around the world.

The US Government's involvement in southern Africa was complicated by the lack of a clear policy direction. In 1986, while the Republican administration of President Ronald Reagan was trying to pursue a policy of 'constructive engagement' with South Africa, the Democrat-controlled Congress was pushing a comprehensive sanctions package through the Senate. The legislation banned new US investments in and loans to South Africa, withdrew landing rights on American soil for South African Airways and banned imports of uranium, coal, textiles, iron, steel and agricultural products. Institutions such as universities and pension funds began selling off their shares in companies with South African connections, while large corporations began closing down their South African operations. Companies such as General Electric, General Motors, IBM, Coca-Cola and Warner Communications saw little point in arguing the case for staying in the country – their small turnovers in South Africa were not worth the political flak at home.

Calls for sanctions also came from the Commonwealth and from the EEC (which imposed a ban on the sale of gold Kruger rands in Europe and on the importation of South African coal). While the pro-sanctions lobby argued that sanctions would bring a peaceful end to the unrest, equally fierce arguments claimed that they would prolong apartheid by forcing the government to retreat into the laager and adopt a siege mentality with a siege economy. Among the supporters of sanctions was the newly elected Anglican Archbishop of Cape Town, Desmond Tutu, who argued that 'when the ladder falls over, it is those at the top who get hurt most ....'

A struggling economy

The sanctions campaign, the stagnation in the area of constitutional reform, and the continuing unrest, wreaked havoc on the South African economy. In 1986 the country experienced a negative growth rate of 1,7 percent. In the same year 48 American companies disinvested or closed shop, while unemployment continued to rise rapidly. Over the decade which began with the 1976 Soweto uprising, some 291 000 jobs were lost in the manufacturing and construction industries alone. All sectors of the economy,

THE SOUTH AFRICAN *Defence Force rushed to the aid of the Bophuthatswana Government, which was threatened by a short-lived coup attempt in February 1988.*

except mining and the public service, showed a decline in the numbers employed since June 1985. At the end of the first half of 1988, Minister of Finance Barend du Plessis announced a net capital outflow of R2,7-billion, which the Governor of the Reserve Bank, Gerhard de Kock, said was 'principally the result of the country's strained international relationships'. In 1988 the giant parastatal electricity supplier, Eskom, announced the impending closure, or mothballing, of 13 of its power stations and by the middle of 1990 the Chamber of Mines estimated that sanctions and disinvestment since 1985 had caused a cumulative foreign exchange loss of R40-billion.

At the same time the latter part of P W Botha's term of office was marked by a consolidation of the trade union movement, after the formation in 1985 of COSATU. With trade unions increasingly becoming the vehicle for expressing political aspirations, about 2 700 trade unionists were detained in 1986, which led to protest strikes across the country. Minister of Manpower Pietie du Plessis announced that there had been 793 strikes in 1986 – more than at any time in the previous 10 years.

A swing to the far right

The anti-sanctions argument that economic action against South Africa would prompt a swing to the far right was given new impetus by the results of the white general election in May 1987. Although the NP won comfortably, the Progressive Federal Party (PFP) was ousted as the official Opposition in the House of Assembly by the far-right CP. The defeat of the parliamentary left was blamed on, among other things: a meeting in Dakar the previous year between PFP and ANC leaders, which the government used to great effect by linking the PFP leadership to an ANC-bogey campaign waged by the state-controlled television; the

sudden resignation and rejection of parliament by PFP leader Van Zyl Slabbert in favour of extra-parliamentary opposition; an election pact between the PFP and the rump of the old United Party, the New Republican Party (NRP); and the appearance of three left-of-centre independent candidates, former NP member Wynand Malan, former South African Ambassador to Britain Denis Worrall and Stellenbosch academic Esther Lategan. Malan was the only successful candidate, taking the Randburg seat from the NP, while Worrall failed narrowly to beat Constitutional Affairs Minister Chris Heunis in the Helderberg constituency in the Cape. Analysts argued that whites who sought reform but distrusted the PFP leadership because of its alleged ANC ties soothed their consciences by voting for the independents.

The NP was voted back into power for its unyielding stand on national security, its ability to stand up to foreign interventionists and its promise of reforms that would not endanger white security. In the process it became the centrist party in South African white politics, attracting large-scale English-speaking support.

The swing to the far right was a rejection of reform altogether – the response to a simple message of white power that found eager listeners among blue-collar white workers, public servants and farmers. The NP's reform programme, said CP leader Treurnicht, had put the country on the road to eventual black rule.

'We'll do it our way'

With its majority secure in the House of Assembly, the government continued doggedly with its efforts to reach agreement on some kind of power sharing with Africans. At the same time, action by the security forces against extra-parliamentary opposition made it plain that expressions of black grievances would be allowed only in the institutions that the government had set up – and even these experienced problems.

In 1987 the leader of the coloured Labour Party, the Reverend Allan Hendrickse, went for a much-publicised swim on a whites-only beach near his home in the eastern Cape and incurred the wrath of President Botha.

The plan to create national states also ran into problems as apparent corruption led to two coups in a row in Transkei; and South Africa had to intervene early in 1988 to reinstate President Lucas Mangope in Bophuthatswana. Ciskei had earlier suffered internal paroxysms as members of the ruling Sebe family fell out among one another. (In 1990, Ciskei's 'president-for-life' Lennox Sebe was removed in yet another coup.)

A new local tier of government – provincial executives and regional services councils – was gradually introduced to replace the provincial councils that had been swept away as part of the Botha Government's constitutional reform programme, threatening the autonomy of liberal municipalities such as the one in Cape Town.

But one of the most significant changes of the 1980s was the creeping militarisation of the country, with the armed forces and police beginning to play an increasingly assertive role in the day-to-day administration of affairs. In March 1986, the government acknowledged the existence

Thousands back a defiance campaign against apartheid

In July 1989 the Congress of South African Trade Unions (COSATU), acting on behalf of an alliance of anti-apartheid groups known as the Mass Democratic Movement (MDM), called on various opponents of the government to support a campaign of defiance against apartheid.

Launched on 2 August (12 days before the resignation of State President P W Botha), the campaign took the form of a series of national protests to force the desegregation of hospitals, beaches and public transport, as well as a massive worker stayaway in protest against the tricameral elections of 6 September 1989.

The response of the South African Government, under acting State President F W de Klerk, was significant: in the weeks leading up to the elections, some protest was met by police dogs and quirts, hundreds of activists were detained and, on election night itself, 23 people were killed in western Cape townships.

A BLAZE OF BANNERS *symbolised the disparate forces which made up the Mass Democratic Movement (MDM) – on the march in Durban in September 1989.*

Immediately after the elections, however, the State Security Council and the Cabinet gave the go-ahead for tens of thousands of people to participate in a march through central Cape Town. Later, similar marches were held in all the major centres of the Republic.

Workers to the fore

The defiance campaign was one of several civil disobedience offensives launched by anti-apartheid groups inside South Africa to back an ANC call early in 1989 for a 'Year of Mass Action': in February, hundreds of political detainees had been released following a highly publicised hunger strike; and in March, representatives of COSATU and their erstwhile rival, the National Council of Trade Unions (NACTU), had committed themselves to a joint programme of action to protest against the Labour Relations Amendment Act, which had been vigorously opposed even

before its promulgation in September 1988.

Later, in a massive show of solidarity with the participants of the defiance campaign, more than 3-million workers stayed away from work on election day.

The defiance campaign of 1989 suggested many parallels with the one of 1952. On both occasions volunteers deliberately broke laws that were deemed offensive. In the 1950s the biggest issues were the hated Pass laws, the Group Areas Act and the existence of separate amenities. Although some of those laws had been repealed by August 1989, the organisers still felt that apartheid had not been eradicated in state institutions.

The result was six weeks of defiant activity that rocked De Klerk's new regime. However, by the time the marches of mid-September were under way, a new era of constitutional process had been initiated by the Nationalist Government.

of a National Security Management System. Under the system, 12 Joint Management Centres (JMCs) had been set up in major urban areas of the country. The government claimed that the JMCs were created to identify sources of unrest and conflict in their early stages. There were 60 JMC sub-committees and more than 400 mini-JMCs at a local government level, spreading the system into the furthest reaches of the country. The Secretary to the State Security Council, Lieutenant-General Pieter van der Westhuizen, said that the JMC system was a plan that had grown out of the concept of a 'total strategy' in response to the 'total onslaught' on South Africa.

The entire JMC structure was dominated by the police and the army, who were empowered to take decisions on matters that previously were the preserve of elected

bodies. Furthermore, they operated in secret and were not publicly accountable, being answerable only to the State Security Council. They were criticised as an 'alternative government' and as manifestations of a 'creeping military takeover', and they were also seen as evidence of the government's seeking to impose solutions arbitrarily.

There were several important reforms in 1986. The central business districts of major cities were opened to trading by all races; hotels and restaurants were freed from having to seek permission before serving black people; the Influx Control Act was repealed, and the Black Communities Development Amendment Act of 1986 gave freehold property rights to Africans in townships attached to 'white' cities. But these reforms were primarily administrative in effect – there was a hiatus in constitutional

'THE BATTLE *of the bald eagles' is how the 'Weekly Mail' dubbed the showdown between President P W Botha (right) and the newly elected leader of the National Party, F W de Klerk (left) in 1989.*

moves to address the aspirations of the black majority. The proposed National Statutory Council, which would have given Africans a consultative 'chamber' within the apparatus of government, never got off the ground because it was rejected by even those 'moderate' blacks willing to participate in the tricameral system.

At the same time there were clear indications that the government viewed the expansion of the African middle class as the ultimate aim of its efforts to stimulate growth and control inflation.

However, the campaign against inflation petered out with continuing profligate expenditure by state departments, and as the economy continued to stagnate and the government failed to make headway in addressing the political hopes and frustrations of the black majority, an air of crisis developed. Something had to give somewhere – and soon. The fateful change did come soon – and from a most unexpected quarter ....

The end of an 'Imperial Presidency'
At about 2 am on 18 January 1989, President Botha awoke to discover that he had suffered a stroke. The following day, Chris Heunis, one of the President's staunchest political allies, who had succeeded him as Cape leader of the NP, was sworn in as acting State President.

Amid rising speculation that his illness would force him to retire, Botha sent a letter to the NP caucus that sparked an acrimonious power struggle. In the letter Botha stated that he wished to separate the offices of leader of the NP and Head of State and that, accordingly, he was tendering his resignation as leader of the party but would stay on as Head of State. At the same time, however, he failed to spell out where the powers of the party leader would end and those of the Head of State begin; and the proposed division was doubly disconcerting to the NP, because this would have been the first time since the party came to power in 1948 that its leader was not also head of the government.

P W Botha had not consulted the Cabinet, the NP hierarchy or the party caucus and there was uncertainty about how to proceed. But the four provincial leaders, after deliberating for an hour, decided on an immediate caucus vote for the new party leader. Those nominated as candidates were F W de Klerk, the Transvaal leader; Chris Heunis, the Cape leader; Pik Botha, the Minister of Foreign Affairs; and Barend du Plessis, the Minister of Finance. Pik Botha was eliminated in the first round of voting and Heunis, P W Botha's favoured choice, in the second. In the third round, De Klerk won with 69 votes to Du Plessis's 61. But for De Klerk the triumph of the moment was tinged with uncertainty, and that afternoon he told a Press conference that the separation of the office of party leader from that of the Head of State would demand of himself and P W Botha a 'special relationship'. Such a relationship seemed improbable. Aside from P W Botha's irascible nature and imperious style, Nationalists reported that the two men had clashed in the past and, in what was a foretaste of things to come, P W Botha did not congratulate De Klerk on his election as party leader.

Newspapers pointed out that the new division of power was bound to lead to a clash of interests, especially over the delay in setting a date for the next general election. As new party leader, De Klerk would want the endorsement of the white electorate, yet the constitution placed the power to call an election in the State President's hands.

Meanwhile, Botha continued to recuperate at his private holiday home at the Wilderness, making occasional sorties to Cape Town to 'attend to correspondence'. On 4 March Nationalist mouthpieces published an interview with Botha, the purpose of which was to make it clear that he had no intention of stepping down. But the odds were mounting against him. '*Die Burger*', mouthpiece of the NP in the Cape and for decades one of Botha's most helpful media allies, reported for the first time that his decision to resume his duties was being seriously challenged inside the party and that without executive powers De Klerk was severely handicapped as party leader. A stubborn Botha, determined to cling to power, went on television on 12 March to declare that he could not understand all the fuss about his health. In response to demands for a general election, he said that a new delimitation of constituencies would have to take place first.

In an atmosphere of growing crisis, the all-powerful federal council of the NP met in Cape Town on the following day and threw down the gauntlet. It overwhelmingly endorsed De Klerk's election as party leader and added in a statement: 'At this stage of our constitutional development it is, in principle, in the best interests of the country and the NP that the national leader of the NP, as the majority party in the House of Assembly, should fill the office of State President.' Botha ignored the party's implied censure of his decision to stay in office and when he returned to work on 15 March he entered the debating chamber in parliament in a jovial mood, chatting amicably to those around him. He kept up the guessing game by acknowledging that he would retire, but without saying when, and by announcing that there would be a general election, though without setting the date.

This heavily compromised the NP. With its back against the wall in its fight with the far right, and losing support among its *verligte* supporters to the emerging Democratic Party (DP), its destiny was in the hands of a man who was no longer party leader and who was in open conflict with the party hierarchy. Moreover, its leader would have to face an election without executive powers and, constitutionally, without a guarantee that he would even be in a future Cabinet – a situation that had never arisen in the four decades of NP rule. With tension continuing to mount, Botha called a general election on 6 September.

The beginning of the end of Botha's political career came in early August, when the NP announced that De Klerk, in his capacity as party leader, would meet President Kenneth Kaunda of Zambia on 28 August. Botha was furious, believing that De Klerk had usurped his position as Head of State. He sent a fax from Tuynhuys saying that 'in terms of the rules governing overseas journeys by Ministers' he had not been made 'aware' of any such meeting. The long-suffering De Klerk, angry at what seemed to be a public scolding, replied by fax, asking Botha to meet a deputation of Ministers. On 10 August 1989, Botha met members of the Cabinet at Tuynhuys as a phalanx of journalists waited outside. It was, De Klerk remarked, 'a heartsore day' as Botha was confronted by his erstwhile colleagues, many of whom had been his protégés. By then he had antagonised them all, and a large number of the party's rank and file, by refusing to quit and by making life as 'difficult as possible for his successor. He was entirely isolated and, after a brief walk in the gardens of Tuynhuys, the once all-powerful Botha, whose term in office had been described as 'The Imperial Presidency', recorded a television address which was broadcast that night.

His statement ran: 'It is evident that after all these years of my best efforts for the National Party and for the government of this country, I am being ignored by Ministers serving in my Cabinet. I consequently have no choice but to announce my resignation.'

'Most difficult' election

A beleaguered NP went into the elections with a leader who had not yet had a chance to prove himself, and who had just suffered a torrid political mauling at the hands of his former leader – and with the economy in deep recession. It was described as the most difficult general election the NP had ever faced, not least because one of the biggest handicaps confronting it was the fact that there had not been a redelimitation of constituencies in recent years. The existing delimitation gave undue representation to white voters in rural and semi-rural constituencies that were heavily supportive of the far right, while voters in the burgeoning urban constituencies, where the NP had been making headway for decades, were underrepresented. But changing this outdated arrangement under the new regime was easier said than done.

The tricameral constitution included new delimitations among those matters that had to be agreed to by a clear majority in all three parliamentary chambers. A defiant Labour Party majority in the House of Representatives, however, had made it clear that it would reject any moves for a new delimitation so long as the Group Areas Act remained in force. Labour also refused to allow an amendment to the constitution that would have permitted Botha to delay an election until 1992.

Rather than compromise, the petulant Botha abandoned the whole idea of delaying the election and getting a new delimitation, even though he knew that an early election would greatly benefit the far right.

During the election campaign De Klerk remained an enigma. While he promised 'a drastically different South Africa', he gave no specifics and from the furious denunciation by NP speakers of the liberal DP's overtures to the ANC there was no hint that he would soon be following the same path. He spoke of 'group rights' and of the 'protection of minorities', leading many to assume that while the NP leadership may have changed, the party's obsession with 'group' concepts and its historic antipathy to the ANC and other liberation movements were unchanged.

As was widely predicted, the NP fared badly in the election. It lost 29 seats, 17 to the CP and 12 to the newly formed DP, the latter's gains being a reflection of the frustration that had been growing among more enlightened voters at the failure of the Botha administration to proceed with political reform. The NP majority in parliament was cut from 80 to 20 in what was the biggest election setback it had suffered since 1948. But De Klerk had won the mandate from the white electorate that he needed to give credence to his leadership.

Dismantling the Botha machine

De Klerk began stamping his own leadership style on the country almost immediately after the NP's victory. The most significant change in his reshuffled Cabinet was the appointment of former Broederbond chief Dr Gerrit Viljoen to the post of full-time convener of negotiations. Less conspicuously, he also began to reduce the huge influence of the security establishment on the day-to-day running of the country. The National Management System, with its hundreds of ancillary bodies (JMCs) around the country,

AWB LEADER *Eugene Terre'Blanche re-emerged in the 1980s as a controversial spokesman for the ultra-right.*

was brought under Cabinet control and the Bureau for Information, which had often been used for government propaganda under his predecessor, was downgraded. De Klerk also cut back on the role of the President's Council, the body used by Botha to draw up the failed tricameral constitution.

Although the state of emergency continued, there was a clear shift from repression to tolerance, a shift signalled by De Klerk's personal intervention to allow a mass march through the streets of Cape Town, an event that was later duplicated in towns and cities across the country.

On 10 October 1989, eight of South Africa's most prominent political prisoners, including five men sentenced to life imprisonment at the conclusion of the Rivonia Trial, one of the great political trials of the 1960s, were released. Among them were ANC leader Walter Sisulu and Jeff Masemola of the Pan-Africanist Congress (PAC). De Klerk's words in announcing their release set the tone of his hectic first year in office: 'Most South Africans are tired of confrontation and wish to speak to one another about the road of prosperity and justice for all.'

Although Nelson Mandela, the world's most celebrated political prisoner, was not among those freed, the national consensus was that he would be released sooner rather than later.

The ANC reacted cautiously to De Klerk's peace overtures, with its newly released leaders speaking of a willingness by Mandela and the rest of their leadership to take part in negotiations if the right conditions existed. While they praised the new State President's announcement that the government wished to get negotiations 'off the ground' in the next five years, they pointed to the continued imprisonment of Mandela and others, the continuing state of emergency and the bans on the ANC, the PAC and other organisations.

Reaction of the far right

As a new political climate haltingly came into being, resistance to change from the far right grew fiercer. The ultra-right wing *Boerestaat Party* and the *Afrikaner Weerstandsbeweging* (AWB) met De Klerk in Pretoria and, after voicing their opposition to the release of ANC prisoners, appealed to him to restore the Boer republics that had existed before 1902. After the meeting De Klerk wryly declared that he did not believe the policies of the far right were realistic or that far-right groups represented many Afrikaners.

On 16 November 1989, De Klerk angered the far right even further, but won substantial praise from elsewhere in the country and from abroad when, in an address to the President's Council, he announced that the Separate Amenities Act, in terms of which public amenities such as beaches, parks and swimming pools were racially segregated, would be repealed as soon as possible. He also announced that all beaches would be opened to all races forthwith. Opposition from municipalities controlled by the CP continued, however, which led to sporadic confrontations at previously segregated amenities.

Death squads

The first whiff of scandal during De Klerk's early months in office emerged with sensational allegations by a former security policeman, Butana Almond Nofomela, who was facing execution for murder. He alleged that police 'death squads' had assassinated leading ANC members and well-known dissidents – allegations supported by statements from a white former security policeman, Dirk Coetzee. Amid calls for a judicial commission of inquiry, the government appointed the Attorney General of the Orange Free State, Tim McNally, to investigate the claims, but eventually bowed to public pressure and appointed Supreme Court Judge Louis Harms to head a commission of inquiry into allegations of murder and 'dirty tricks' by the state's security apparatus (see page 501).

At about the same time, the government announced further curbs on the power and influence of the security services, cutting the compulsory military call-up from two years to one and announcing huge cutbacks in the size of the armed forces.

De Klerk meets Mandela

On 13 December 1989, De Klerk convened a meeting at Tuynhuys with Mandela. Also present were Minister of Justice Kobie Coetsee and the Minister charged with getting negotiations started, Dr Gerrit Viljoen. It was officially announced that follow-up talks would take place in the new year as optimistic forecasts of an imminent breakthrough came from world capitals. As the 1980s drew to a close, there was wide praise from around the globe for De Klerk's 'first 100 days'.

Even so, when he entered parliament for its official opening on 2 February 1990, few people anticipated that he was about to set in motion a process that would fundamentally change the political climate in South Africa and put the country on a turbulent path towards power sharing and international rehabilitation ....

'The time for negotiation has arrived'

When F W de Klerk was elected head of the National Party (NP) in February 1989,
it was thought he might side with the right wing of the party. But, after his inauguration
as State President six months later, he jolted the country – and the world –
first by unbanning liberation organisations and then by releasing Nelson Mandela, the world's
most famous political prisoner, after 27 years of incarceration. Although these moves earned
De Klerk wide praise, on the negative side he also had to answer charges that his government
was involved in a dirty tricks (and assassination) campaign against its opponents ....

IN THE LATE MORNING of 2 February 1990, Frederik Willem de Klerk, State President of the Republic of South Africa, mounted the podium in the large chamber of Parliament in Cape Town – and began a speech that was to alter the course of his country's history.

Watched by a huge contingent of local and foreign journalists, and a television audience of millions, he started his dramatic address slowly and predictably, repeating the fashionably reformist line that 'only a negotiated understanding among the representative leaders of the entire population [will] ensure lasting peace', and promising that the process of negotiation would be given the highest priority and that a constitutional dispensation would be created in which every inhabitant of the country would enjoy equal rights.

What millions of South Africans were waiting for, however, was proof of a fundamental break with the race-based policies of the past.

About three-quarters of the way through the address, it came: De Klerk reminded his audience that he had promised during his inauguration to give attention to the most important obstacles in the way of negotiation. He went on: 'Today I am able to announce far-reaching decisions in this connection ....'

To gasps of astonishment from the media throng – and from thousands of listeners throughout the country – De Klerk announced the lifting of the restrictions on the previously banned organisations the African National Congress (ANC), the Pan-Africanist Congress (PAC) and the South African Communist Party (SACP), adding that people currently serving prison sentences 'merely because they were members of one of these organisations ... would be identified and released'.

Pausing just long enough to allow the stunned media corps to catch its breath, De Klerk added that major changes would be made to security regulations – the chief among which would be the scrapping of the media and education emergency regulations; the lifting of the restrictions on 33 organisations with links to the ANC and the PAC; and amendments to the security emergency regulations governing visual material of unrest scenes.

Turning to the status of the jailed ANC leader Nelson Mandela, De Klerk said: 'I wish to put it plainly that the government has taken a firm decision to release Mr Mandela unconditionally. I am serious about bringing this matter to finality without delay.'

'Taken my breath away'

Both supporters and opponents of the government were rocked by De Klerk's announcement – it was one of the most far-reaching policy shifts ever made by the NP.

Democratic Party (DP) leader Zach de Beer greeted the speech with 'a marvellous sense of relief', while Transvaal Indian Congress president Cassim Saloojee said: 'Now we know F W de Klerk is serious.'

Describing the President's announcement in parliament as 'the most encouraging and hopeful sign of change since the apartheid tragedy began', Bishop Stanley Mogoba of the Methodist Church said: 'Mr De Klerk's speech is the strongest sign yet that the years of protest and pressure are bearing fruit.'

Desmond Tutu, the Anglican Archbishop of Cape Town, remarked: '[De Klerk] has taken my breath away.'

The news was relayed by church leader Allan Boesak to Nelson Mandela, who had been moved from Pollsmoor Prison to a house in the Victor Verster Prison complex, where he was recovering from tuberculosis. According to Boesak, Mandela described De Klerk's announcement as 'courageous and bold'.

But members of the far right were furious: Conservative Party (CP) leader Andries Treurnicht stated that the President had made 'a most revolutionary speech', while Eugene Terre'Blanche, the formidable leader of the quasi-military, ultra-right *Afrikaner Weerstandsbeweging* (AWB), said incredulously: 'Just don't tell me that. No, oh no, it can't be true.'

The metamorphosis of F W de Klerk

As South Africans of all political persuasions began to digest the astounding implications of the State President's announcement, many wondered if he had previously been misrepresented as a conservative. Or did some political metamorphosis take place after he had acquired the awesome powers that P W Botha had so assiduously accumulated over the years?

To some extent he had been misrepresented; but he had also changed in response to the realities around him. As far back as 1985 he had made some of the most enlightened policy statements of his time but was given scant credit for having done so. Among other things, he publicly conceded the failure of 'grand' apartheid at a time when the ideology was still supported by many in his party. In the same year, he also faced the brunt of the far right's attacks by introducing in parliament the repeal of the Prohibition of Mixed Marriages Act and of the section of the Immorality Act that had prohibited sexual intercourse between people of different race groups.

These were hardly the actions of an arch-conservative. But, at the same time, as leader of the NP in the Transvaal, where the biggest challenge from the far right had come, De Klerk had often appeared to appeal to conservative sentiment, especially when he had declared his support for the concept of 'group rights', a term widely regarded as a euphemism for apartheid. Certainly, his public image was sufficiently conservative to engender the general surprise that greeted his announcement of the unbanning of liberation organisations and the release of Mandela.

The realities that had brought about at least part of the change in the NP's official stance in dealing with the African majority had begun to impinge on the country by the time De Klerk took over the reins of power from P W Botha. His tour of European capitals in June 1989, and his earlier meeting with President Kenneth Kaunda of Zambia, must have impressed upon him the impatience of the international community at the rate of progress towards real change in the country, and the growing belief that sanctions were the only instrument left that could facilitate such change. South Africa was in turmoil and it was widely conceded even within the NP that the existing political order – the tricameral parliament – was a costly failure.

The economy, too, was in deep trouble, with the value of the rand having dropped to unprecedented levels, even against the currencies of southern African states. Foreign debt repayments were a huge burden on the treasury, unemployment was rising alarmingly, foreign companies were leaving and sanctions were biting.

At the same time, the human resources of the country had become badly depleted through a brain drain and as a result of four decades of apartheid which, the International Labour Organisation estimated, had cost South Africa some R78-billion to implement.

The President who transformed the National Party

Few political leaders have had so political a background as Frederik Willem 'FW' de Klerk, who was born in Mayfair, Johannesburg, on 18 March 1936. For three generations before his birth, members of his family had been involved in politics and had held public office.

One of his great-grandfathers, Jan van Rooy, of Bethulie in the Orange Free State, was a senator. His grandfather, Willem de Klerk, twice stood as a candidate in elections for the House of Assembly. FW's father, Jan de Klerk, was a teacher who became secretary of the National Party (NP) in the Transvaal and a member of the party's provincial executive. Later, he became President of the Senate and a member of the Cabinet. And FW's uncle, Hans Strijdom, was the second NP Prime Minister.

The young Frederik Willem began showing a keen interest in politics as a child, and by the time he matriculated at the *Hoërskool Monument* in Krugersdorp in 1953, he was a prominent figure in the school debating society and had also played roles in dramatic society productions.

He enrolled at Potchefstroom University, where one of his most distinctive facial features – a slightly streamlined nose – was acquired in an accident while playing hockey. He became vice-chairman of the Students' Representative Council and editor of the university newspaper, and graduated *cum laude* with a BA LLB degree. He was not a bookworm, nor especially accomplished at sport, but he took his politics seriously.

Soon after graduating, he married fellow student Marike Willemse, the daughter of a psychologist.

De Klerk served his articles with a Pretoria firm of attorneys before setting up practice as an attorney in Vereeniging, where he later became NP Member of Parliament. On 3 April 1978, Prime Minister John Vorster gave De Klerk his first Cabinet appointment – as Minister of Posts and Telecommunications. Later portfolios included Sport and Recreation, Mineral and Energy Affairs, Internal Affairs, and Education.

Meanwhile, he had risen rapidly within the party, becoming a co-deputy chairman in the Transvaal, a position that enabled him to make a successful bid for the provincial leadership in 1982. On 2 February 1989, when former President P W Botha resigned as NP leader, De Klerk was elected in his place. After a bruising power struggle, Botha resigned as President and De Klerk took over on 20 September 1989.

During his four-and-a-half years as State President, De Klerk set about dismantling apartheid – receiving praise both at home and abroad for his role in steering the country towards a multiracial democracy. The transition reduced his role and that of his party, but when he conceded on 2 May 1994 that the ANC had won the election, he was able to say: 'All South Africans are now free.'

He was inaugurated as Deputy Vice-President on 10 May 1994.

STATE PRESIDENT *F W de Klerk and his wife Marike. The couple married on 11 April 1959 soon after graduating from Potchefstroom University.*

Compounding the problem, the legacy of 'Bantu education' meant that half the adult population of the country was illiterate, while half the number of pupils at African schools were boycotting classes. Industry and mining simply could not obtain the skilled manpower needed for expansion. Only 23 000 artisans were being trained when, according to the estimates of the mining industry, 100 000 artisans should have been in training.

No system, and no ideology, could long endure the economic pressures that faced the country when De Klerk came to office.

Shortly after the NP victory at the polls in 1989, De Klerk already began to give pointers to the fact that his presidency would be very different from those of his predecessors. His changes included the Cabinet reshuffle to give Dr Gerrit Viljoen the job of full-time convener of negotiations, as well as the reduction of the role of the National Security Management System and the Bureau for Information. These two arms of the government – along with the now down-scaled President's Council – had played an important role during the Total Strategy era.

Release of Mandela

Following the 2 February 1990 unbannings, there was a flurry of speculation around the world that the release of Mandela himself was imminent.

The speculation was vindicated at a Press conference addressed by De Klerk in Cape Town, on 10 February 1990, at which he said that Mandela would be released the following day. Two meetings had taken place between De Klerk and Mandela to discuss his release and, De Klerk said, he was satisfied that the ANC leader was 'committed to a peaceful solution and to a peaceful process' in South Africa.

In spite of the wide anticipation of Mandela's release, the news still caused wild excitement. Within hours of the State President's announcement, dozens of journalists began to converge on Cape Town for what was billed as the 'story of the year'.

Indeed, Mandela was described in reports in many parts of the world as 'the prisoner of the century'.

A legend steps forth

Mandela's release was a moving historical experience for the thousands who gathered outside the Victor Verster Prison on 11 February.

People danced and gave clenched-fist salutes as they waited for the heavy gates to open. Then, after a number of false alarms, he appeared, a tall, gaunt, greying man of 71, with dignified bearing and an expansive smile, the hero of millions whom the world had not seen for 27 years (in terms of the Prisons Act, not even old photographs of him could be published).

Many well-wishers stood on the sides of the highway between Paarl and Cape Town and on overhead bridges as the convoy of cars bore Mandela and his party to the centre of Cape Town, where a huge and excited crowd had poured onto the Grand Parade in front of the old City Hall waiting to see the man and hear him speak. They had begun assembling many hours earlier and, after his arrival, had to wait in the hot summer sun for three-and-a-half hours before he appeared on the great balcony from where statesmen and kings had addressed the people in times past. (See page 504.)

Mandela followed up his public appearances in Cape Town with mass rallies in Johannesburg and other centres, and after a brief rest at his Soweto home, he flew to Lusaka for a long-awaited meeting with the ANC in exile. It was an emotional visit as he embraced friends and colleagues he had not seen in almost three decades.

At a meeting of the ANC's national executive, Mandela was elected deputy president, a designation which he is said to have wished for as a sign of deference to the organisation's president in exile, Oliver Tambo, then recuperating at a clinic in Sweden after a stroke.

Trouble in the townships

An ominous development following the unbanning of restricted groups and the release of Mandela and other political prisoners was the increased levels of violence in many parts of the country, most gruesomely in the crowded townships of the Transvaal industrial heartland, where more than 700 people died in unrest during the first eight months of the year.

In Natal and KwaZulu, the ANC and its allies in the United Democratic Front (UDF), and the country's largest trade union federation, COSATU, were locked in a bitter feud with the traditionalist Zulu organisation Inkatha, headed by Chief Mangosuthu Buthelezi.

In the 'independent homeland' of Bophuthatswana, South African troops were rushed in to quell widespread unrest in March.

South African Defence Force (SADF) troops were also deployed in Ciskei following a coup there. Earlier, a coup had brought a military government into power in Transkei, the first 'homeland' to have gained its 'independence' back in 1976. The new Transkeian leader, Major-General Bantu Holomisa, made public overtures to the ANC and told President De Klerk bluntly at their first meeting on 11 January 1990 that the Transkei 'homeland' was a failed political experiment.

The problems in Transkei and Ciskei were a reflection of general instability and political tension in many of the 'homelands', and police were also sent to help quell unrest in Gazankulu and Venda.

The crumbling of the 'homeland' governments and their wish – with the notable exception of the government of Bophuthatswana – to be reincorporated into South Africa, was the practical outcome of what De Klerk himself had warned of in a speech to parliament in 1985: that 'grand' apartheid had failed and that the 'homelands' policy should be abandoned.

As if to underline the failure, the majority of leaders of non-independent 'homelands' withdrew from scheduled talks with De Klerk and his government in April, amid the government's allegations that the leaders had been pressurised and intimidated by the ANC. Only KwaZulu and QwaQwa showed up for the talks. The failure of the 'homelands' was a signal of the ANC's resurgence of power and influence after its unbanning.

STATE PRESIDENT *F W de Klerk and* ANC *deputy president Nelson Mandela address a media conference after a first round of 'talks about talks' between the government and the* ANC *at the Groote Schuur estate, Cape Town, on 5 May 1990. Both groups expressed a commitment to combatting violence and intimidation 'from whatever quarter' and to working towards a 'peaceful process of negotiation'.*

The Groote Schuur Minute

Apart from the release of Mandela and the unbanning of the ANC, the PAC and the SACP, one of the most talked-about events of 1990 was heralded with an announcement on 18 March that the first formal 'talks about talks' between the ANC and the government would take place on 11 April. But at the end of March, dozens of residents of the township of Sebokeng near Vereeniging were killed or injured in clashes with the police. Accusing the government of the 'unprovoked killing and maiming of defenceless demonstrators', the ANC called off the talks. The police denied using unprovoked violence, claiming they had been attacked by an unruly mob. As an anxious country wondered whether the peace process would continue, De Klerk (after a meeting with Mandela) appointed a judicial commission to investigate the Sebokeng killings. The Goldstone Commission later vindicated Mandela and the ANC by finding that the police had indeed not been attacked and that inexperienced and badly disciplined policemen had been responsible for the fatal shootings.

Meanwhile, De Klerk announced a major deployment of troops in Natal in response to the continuing violence in that region, and, as a conciliatory gesture to the ANC, the government granted temporary indemnity to all ANC exiles who would be involved in talks with the government. Agreement was also reached between De Klerk and Mandela at a meeting in Cape Town on 5 April that a new date would be set for an ANC-government meeting.

On the afternoon of 2 May 1990, as more than 250 journalists from around the world stood by, South Africa's two most powerful political leaders, each backed by teams of negotiators, met for their first 'talks about talks' in the historical Groote Schuur manor house.

The meeting took place with the two sides facing one another across a 30-seat dining room table in an elegant reception room. The South African team included Foreign Affairs Minister Pik Botha, Minister of Constitutional Development Dr Gerrit Viljoen, Minister of Justice Kobie Coetsee, and Minister of Law and Order Adriaan Vlok. The ANC team included internal leader Walter Sisulu, secretary-general Alfred Nzo, international affairs director Thabo Mbeki and general secretary of the SACP Joe Slovo.

Ostensibly the objective of the three days of 'talks about talks' was to identify obstacles to formal negotiations and to work out a *modus operandi for* overcoming them. The first part of the meeting lasted four hours, and it was followed by a private dinner at which delegates were free to establish personal contact with their counterparts in an informal social atmosphere. Security legislation, the return of exiles, troops in the townships, political prisoners, the state of emergency, the ANC's 'armed struggle', sanctions and the need to end violence were the main topics discussed.

At a joint Press conference on 5 May, De Klerk and Mandela announced that broad agreement, encapsulated in the Groote Schuur Minute, had been reached on issues that stood in the way of negotiations, and announced the establishment of a joint working group whose job it would be to look into the issue of political prisoners and the ANC's demand for their release, and also into immunity from prosecution for returning exiles. The working group was given a deadline of 21 May to complete its work. A clearly satisfied Mandela told the Press conference: 'At the end not only are we – the ANC and the government – closer together, but we are all victors – South Africa is the victor.'

International praise for De Klerk

Buoyed by the success of the Groote Schuur talks, and after signing into law a hastily approved Indemnity Bill giving him the power to grant indemnity from prosecution to ANC exiles, De Klerk departed on an 18-day tour of nine European countries, including Britain, France, West Germany and Switzerland. He was the first South African Head of State able to do so 'through the front door' in decades and he was received with encouraging words and accolades. The thrust of his message to European leaders was that the process towards a new and democratic South Africa was 'irreversible', and while sanctions were not on the formal agenda for talks, they arose directly and indirectly in every country the State President visited.

After their meeting in Dublin on 27 June, European Community leaders applauded what they called 'important changes' in South Africa and, although they did not announce the lifting of sanctions, British Prime Minister Margaret Thatcher declared: 'Trade is increasing, investment is increasing and I believe restrictions on South Africa will continue to be eased.'

Although the maintenance of the cultural, sporting and academic boycotts was considered unnecessary, Mandela and the ANC leadership were still opposed to the lifting of economic sanctions. When Mandela set off on a world tour on 9 June, he expressed the hope that the occasion would be 'a long journey of thanksgiving and rededication'. But he found himself forced to argue in a number of countries for economic sanctions to be kept in place.

End of the state of emergency

In June 1990, the state of emergency was lifted in all areas of the country except strife-torn Natal. De Klerk also announced steps to bolster police force numbers by 10 000 in the following 12 months, and disclosed plans to improve police pay. In a seeming sop to the restive far-right wing, he also said that increased use would be made of national servicemen in the police force and that SADF units would be more widely deployed in unrest areas.

Right-wing protests at the changes taking place in the country had meanwhile been increasing in their level of anger, and in June 1990 the police announced the arrest of 11 far-right activists in connection with an alleged plot to assassinate De Klerk, Mandela and other prominent players in the process towards change.

De Klerk met far-right leaders in Pretoria on 26 June. It was one of several meetings he had with them during the year, but on this occasion he issued a stern warning that anarchy would not be allowed 'under any circumstances'.

'Until final victory' – last stand for a white minority

Sorry baas, daardie baas roep jou.' (Sorry, boss, that boss is calling you.) These were the words with which unemployed Simon Mukondeleli distracted and disarmed a fanatical gunman on Tuesday afternoon, 15 November 1988.

Barend Hendrik Strydom, then 23 years old, a member of the ultra-right Afrikaner Weerstandsbeweging (Afrikaner Resistance Movement, or AWB) and a self-confessed member of the Wit Wolwe (White Wolves), had spent 15 minutes on a wild shooting spree in the centre of Pretoria. Six black people died instantly, while a seventh died in hospital – and sixteen were injured. Strydom showed no signs of remorse at his trial, demanding that the government arrest such 'communists as Archbishop Desmond Tutu and [later Democratic Party leader] Dennis Worrall'.

Strydom was one of several ultra-rightwingers convicted of murder during a period that saw an increase in random brutality against blacks.

The ultra-right claimed a long history going back to the Great Trek of the 1830s. Their forefathers had played leading roles in the Boer commandos of the South African War and some of their elder statesmen had been members of the Ossewabrandwag. Many of their aspirations were met by the triumph of the National Party (NP) in 1948, but with the NP's slow retreat from purist Afri-

kaner nationalism, the ultra-right re-emerged as a distinct bloc.

The AWB, the most prominent group, was formed in 1973 as a militant offshoot of the Herstigte (Reconstituted) Nasionale Party (HNP). Its leader, Eugene Terre'Blanche, a former bodyguard of Prime Minister B J Vorster, had stood as an HNP candidate in the 1971 elections, but later dismissed parliamentary democracy as a 'British-Jewish invention designed to weaken Afrikanerdom'.

With its neo-Nazi insignia, marching songs, public display of small arms, and a powerful orator in Terre-'Blanche himself, the AWB enjoyed much media coverage. Estimates of its membership varied from 50 000 to 100 000. Although it never contested an election, it managed to gain at least five seats in the Conservative Party (CP) parliamentary caucus. Like the CP, the AWB and other ultra-right groups drew support mainly from blue-collar white workers, the bureaucracy and farmers. All felt that their lifestyles and economic privilege were being threatened by what they saw as concessions to the black majority.

A plethora of activists

In the early 1980s disputes raged inside the Broederbond concerning the inclusion of blacks in the legislature. In 1982 its chairman, Professor Carel Boshoff, resigned from his post in

AWB SUPPORTERS march into Church Square, Pretoria, during the 150th anniversary celebrations of the Great Trek in 1988.

protest against the triumph of 'inclusionists'. He went on to set up the Afrikaner Volkswag (People's Watch) as a think-tank for far-right organisations. During the 150th anniversary celebrations of the Great Trek in 1988 the Volkswag was instrumental in organising a programme separate from that of the rival, pro-government Federasie van Afrikaanse Kultuurverenigings (Federation of Afrikaans Cultural Societies, or FAK).

A more shadowy group was formed under biochemist Professor Johan Schabort in 1984. Called the Blanke Bevrydingsbeweging (White Liberation Movement, or BBB), its policy called for the 'repatriation' of all black people in 'white South Africa' to their 'homelands', the expulsion of

He cautioned them against organising themselves into commandos and other quasi-military organisations which were beyond state control. But the government drew further attacks from these quarters two days later when it opened six more residential areas to all races.

In their anger and frustration at not being able to force De Klerk into calling another general election, the right-wingers launched a strategy of breaking up NP political meetings, including those addressed by De Klerk and members of his Cabinet.

More talks about talks

At a surprise meeting between De Klerk and Mandela in Pretoria on 20 July 1990, it was agreed that the 'talks about talks' between the government and the ANC would be resumed on 6 August in Pretoria. But within days of the announcement, doubts about whether or not the deliberations would take place arose when De Klerk, commenting on the arrest of more than 40 ANC insurgents and the seizure of arms caches, warned that no one would be allowed to 'sneak in through the back door and try to seize power in the country by force'.

Among those detained after 'Operation Vula' were Mac Maharaj, a leading member of the SACP and also a member of the ANC's national executive. His detention reflected unease in government circles at the ANC's links with the SACP – and especially with the inclusion of SACP general secretary Joe Slovo in the ANC's negotiating team. On 1 August Mandela and De Klerk were again trying to pour oil on troubled waters; after a three-hour meeting, the ANC leader emerged to say that their discussions had taken place in 'a cordial spirit'.

The next round of 'talks about talks' took place in the Old Residency in Pretoria as scheduled on 6 August, De Klerk and Mandela each being accompanied by eight senior advisors. The upshot was a major step towards reconciliation – the announcement by the ANC that it would suspend its armed struggle with immediate effect. The

South African Jews, and the return of Indians to India. It believed implicitly in the 'superiority of the white master race' and denied the events of the Holocaust.

Other right-wing groups formed at this time included the *Boerestaat Party* of Robert van Tonder and Piet 'Skiet' Rudolph (1988), and the *Vereniging van Oranjewerkers* (Union of Orange Workers), which colonised the small village of Morgenzon in the eastern Transvaal as the hopeful forerunner of an Afrikaner 'homeland'.

In January 1989 Eugene Terre-'Blanche squashed a threat to his leadership of the AWB as a result of an alleged relationship with journalist Jani Allan. In the ensuing fallout, three executive members established the *Blanke Vryheidsbeweging* (White Freedom Movement, or BVB). Its press releases were typical of ultra-right demands: 'We simply want our own state where we can live under our own economic, educational and other systems with our own national symbols .... We will fight undermining influences such as humanism, liberalism and the political machinations of foreign powers, and particularly the money powers ....'

As reform gathered momentum after 1990, fringe right-wing groups mushroomed – at the end of 1993 they were said to number as many as 80, six of which were thought to be 'dangerous'.

MEMBERS OF THE AWB *practise hand-to-hand combat as part of their preparations to 'defend* volk *and fatherland'.*

Call to arms

Talk of violence abounded. Terre-'Blanche said in 1988 that his people would continue to 'prepare for the night when in violence the AWB will claim what is rightfully theirs' – and they made no bones about their intentions with the running of training camps and the open display of arms. Police estimated that 15 000 AWB men were trained in the use of weapons.

In 1989, Jan Groenewald of the BVB vowed: 'A real freedom movement will ensure that the struggle continues, until final victory ....'

Apart from banning the tiny BBB in the wake of Strydom's killing spree and prosecuting individuals with links to the AWB and other groups, the state took few steps against the ultraright – partly, it was suggested, because the organisations had many sympathisers in the security forces. These accusations surfaced again when, on 23 June 1993, an armoured vehicle burst dramatically into the venue for constitutional negotiations – opening the way for more than 200 rightwingers, many in AWB uniforms, to occupy the premises, assault staff and damage property. None of the protesters was arrested on the day (although several were charged later).

The occupation of the World Trade Centre was triggered by the negotiators' decision to hold multiracial elections on 27 April 1994. In a last-ditch effort to prevent the elections from taking place, rightwingers went on a bombing spree – setting off an estimated 40 blasts in the first four months of 1994 at targets that included political party offices and venues earmarked for polling.

THE MEETING BETWEEN *F W de Klerk and US President George Bush in Washington in September 1990 was described as a 'triumph' by the South African Government.*

'ceasefire' was contained in a joint statement – the Pretoria Minute – and was acclaimed as a historic truce. While there was a tenuous 'peace' between the government and the ANC – threatened periodically by assertions by ANC personalities that the 'armed struggle' had not been abandoned – violence flared up with a vengeance in African townships on the Witwatersrand.

A horrifying new characteristic of the latest wave of violence was the emergence of unidentified groups of terrorists (loosely described as a 'third force' by the ANC) who began a random series of massacres of innocent people. Some of the victims were caught at all-night vigils in the townships; others were attacked without protection as they rode to work on suburban trains.

Off to the United States

By September 1990, when De Klerk departed for an official working visit to the USA (the first by a South African president), the deployment of troops in the townships and the introduction of curfews had brought an uneasy calm to the townships.

It was a more successful trip than he could have expected. For one thing, the threatened mass protests by anti-apartheid activists who had organised the immensely successful Mandela tour failed to materialise. Instead, only a handful of protesters showed up, indicating that De Klerk's initiatives had dramatically improved his public standing internationally.

Furthermore, he was given a cordial welcome by US President George Bush and was able to make an important impact on American public opinion by addressing the prestigious National Press Club, whose meetings are broadcast live by hundreds of radio stations across the USA and Canada, and by granting interviews with major television networks.

Brown – and proud to be Nat

On 19 October 1990, the National Party (NP), whose name had long been synonymous with 'apartheid', opened its doors to people from all race groups.

Since the late 1970s, the NP had been steadily shedding its image as the torchbearer of Afrikaner nationalism and adopting the mantle of middle-class social democracy, and the move to broaden its base seemed perfectly logical.

Not surprisingly (given its atrocious race-relations record), there was no initial rush for NP membership cards in black communities. What was surprising was the subsequent growth in support for the NP in coloured and Indian areas, considering the massive support during the 1980s in these communities for the United Democratic Front (UDF) and the 80 percent stayaway from the tricameral elections in 1984. By 1992, however, polls indicated 62 percent of coloured people and 59 percent of Indians supported the NP.

State President F W de Klerk's reforms allowed the NP to redefine itself not as an ethnically based organisation but as a party of the centre, favouring free enterprise, property rights and safeguards for minorities.

The NP's growth in coloured and Indian communities was attributed by political observers partly to De Klerk's image as a reformer and partly to the militant public image of the African National Congress (ANC) and its political allies.

In the tussle that began for the support of coloured and Indian voters (who made up roughly 12 percent of the total), the first casualty was the Labour Party (LP), which had maintained a stranglehold on the coloured House of Representatives since its inception in 1984.

By 1991 a steady stream of LP MPs were defecting to the NP. Soon after the opening of parliament in January 1992, Nationalists in the house, under the leadership of Jac Rabie, entered into an agreement with independent MPs to topple Labour from power.

The ethnic parties of the tricameral era took their final bow after the 1994 elections. Several of the 'brown nats' were elected to public office under the NP banner, particularly in the western Cape, where the coloured vote was decisive in securing an NP victory. The LP – having decided it would disband after the poll – fought the election under the ANC banner, gaining five seats in the national parliament.

FORMER LABOUR MP *Abe Williams (right), on the 1994 campaign trail with Hernus Kriel, later joined the Cabinet under the NP banner.*

Death squads, dirty tricks and the 'third force'

Butana Almond Nofomela made a confession in October 1989 from Pretoria Central Prison's Death Row that not only saved him from the gallows the next day, but also set in motion a train of events that would have far-reaching consequences for the security establishment.

Nofomela, a former security policeman who had been sentenced to death for the murder of a white farmer, claimed that he and three colleagues had hacked to death activist attorney Griffiths Mxenge in 1981.

Although Nofomela's confession was denied by the police, the extra-parliamentary UDF reiterated its long-held belief that the government was financing death squads in a campaign to eliminate left-wing opponents of the state.

Poisoning, shooting and stabbing

Then, while newspapers were dusting off the files of unsolved political murders, a police captain named Dirk Coetzee stepped forward with new allegations.

'I was in the heart of the whore,' Coetzee told the weekly newspaper, '*Vrye Weekblad*', 'I was the commander of a South African death squad' (of which Nofomela was a member).

Coetzee outlined a horrifying saga of a small band of killers who – with no apparent regard for the law – had wandered the length and breadth of southern Africa, poisoning, shooting and stabbing anyone singled out as a risk to state security.

Bowing to increasing national and international pressure, President F W de Klerk appointed Supreme Court Judge Louis Harms to probe 'murder and acts of violence allegedly committed with political motives'.

The hearings of the Harms commission began sensationally with a disclosure that the South African Defence Force (SADF) ran a covert branch known as the Civil Cooperation Bureau (CCB).

Witnesses told the commission that the CCB spied not only on opponents of the government, but also on the security police, the National Intelligence Service and Military Intelligence (MI).

Other evidence was equally bizarre: on one occasion, the judge was told, CCB operatives had arranged for a monkey foetus to be attached to the property of the Anglican Archbishop, Desmond Tutu. Another operative had transported a limpet mine with which to blast the Early Learning Centre in Athlone near Cape Town. It was also claimed that a gangster had been paid to assassinate civil rights lawyer (later Minister of Justice) Dullah Omar, as well as Gavin Evans, the journalist son of Anglican Bishop Bruce Evans.

In November 1990, the commission issued a report that rejected Coetzee's allegations, absolved the police from death squad activities and condemned the activities of the CCB. It could not, however, determine who was responsible for dozens of political murders and disappearances over the previous two decades.

In the section of his report dealing with the CCB, Judge Harms pointed out that several individual members of the bureau had refused to divulge important information. Several CCB documents had also 'disappeared'.

The shadowy CCB would surface again in court proceedings, as well as during the investigations of the later Goldstone Commission of Inquiry into political violence ....

Purge of the generals

On 11 November 1992, investigators for Judge Richard Goldstone – acting on a tip-off – raided the offices of a company that turned out to be a front for an MI unit called the Directorate of Covert Collection (DCC). They seized files which they said detailed a campaign, led by the CCB, to discredit the ANC, which by then was negotiating with the NP Government.

De Klerk responded by appointing a senior military officer, Lieutenant-General Pierre Steyn, to look into the DCC's activities. Although Steyn's report was not made public, his investigations led to a 'purge' in which 16 senior officers lost their jobs at the end of 1992.

Another purge followed in March 1994 – this time among police generals – after the Goldstone Commission found what it called 'a horrible network of criminal activity'.

Then, in quick succession, two courts made findings in inquiries into the deaths of government opponents in the 1980s ....

'Permanent removal'

On 28 May 1994, people in the public gallery of the Supreme Court in Port Elizabeth groaned as Eastern Cape Judge President Neville Zietsman said he could not directly link any specific person to the deaths of four Cradock activists in 1985. The four – Matthew Goniwe, Fort Calata, Sicelo Mhlauli and Sparrow Mkhonto – had been stabbed and burnt beyond recognition while returning from a UDF meeting.

During a lengthy inquest, full of dramatic twists and revelations, evidence had been led of a controversial military signal sent 20 days before their deaths. The signal, from Brigadier Joffel van der Westhuizen (later Lieutenant-General and chief of MI), called for the 'permanent removal from society' of Goniwe and Calata.

The judge found that security force members had killed the Cradock Four, but evidence to link the signal and the murders was lacking, as was proof of who had done the killing.

In June 1994, another long-awaited court finding was made: Namibian Judge Harold Levy found that the assassination in September 1989 of Anton Lubowski, a Namibian advocate and executive member of the South West African People's Organisation (SWAPO), had been the deed of an Irishman working on a project initiated by the CCB.

As Namibia sought extradition of the CCB men named by the judge, the new South African Government had already announced a 'truth commission' that would, among other things, look into crimes committed during apartheid's 'dirty war'.

* It was not only the NP Government that was haunted by its past. In November 1992, a damning report by the human rights body Amnesty International described abuse, torture and execution of prisoners in ANC camps in Angola, Tanzania, Uganda and Zambia over the previous 10 years. The report said the victims were mostly genuine ANC members imprisoned because of grievances or differences in policy. 'This pattern of gross abuse was allowed to go unchecked for many years, not only by the ANC's leadership in exile, but also by the governments of the frontline states,' Amnesty said.

A MEMBER *of the AWB sprays teargas at a police dog handler during the 'Battle of Ventersdorp' in August 1991. The sight of police and right-wingers in head-on clashes shocked many South Africans.*

Overall, the De Klerk visit contrasted sharply with the hero's welcome given to Mandela during his visit; but it was a tenuous harbinger of the change in global perspectives of South Africa, following almost a year of breathtaking change.

And yet, despite the euphoria, some reminders of the old-style NP way of doing things continued to surface ....

The 'Inkathagate' scandal

In July 1991, the 'Weekly Mail' newspaper reported that the South African Police had given taxpayers' money to Mangosuthu Buthelezi's Inkatha Freedom Party (IFP) to help the Zulu nationalist organisation oppose the ANC.

The 'Weekly Mail' claimed that, shortly after the release of Mandela, the security police had given the IFP at least R250 000 to enable it to organise anti-ANC activities. Such activities included rallies intended as a show of strength. The violence that erupted after one of these rallies – on 25 March 1990 – became known subsequently as the 'Maritzburg War'.

Quoting from top-secret police documents, the newspaper reported that Buthelezi 'was very emotional and expressed extreme gratitude' for the extent of the financial assistance provided. Buthelezi later denied all knowledge of the 'donation'. 'I'd need my head read to take on the ANC with such a minuscule amount,' he said.

As the row escalated, the IFP repaid the R250 000, South African Foreign Minister Pik Botha admitted that he had arranged the donation (on the grounds that the IFP opposed sanctions) and calls were made for the resignation of Minister of Law and Order Adriaan Vlok.

Appearing on national television, Botha declared: 'If I must do it again, I will do it again – exactly like this.'

The Battle of Ventersdorp

Besides having to contend with accusations that it had not abandoned its 'dirty tricks' campaigns (see page 501), the De Klerk Government faced continued threats of violence from far-right sources.

Certainly, whites in some rural areas regarded De Klerk as the most hated public figure in South Africa.

In August 1991, De Klerk decided to take the fight to his right-wing opponents. A subsequent NP announcement that he would address a rally in Ventersdorp, the home town of militant *Afrikaner Weerstandsbeweging* (AWB) leader Eugene Terre'Blanche, was greeted with outrage by local right-wingers.

On Friday, 9 August, the night of the rally, more than two thousand heavily armed men and women of the AWB's *Wenkommando* began gathering in the town. They were faced by a large police contingent. Some of the AWB members wore plaster casts around their left arm to fend off police dogs; others, anticipating hand-to-hand combat, wore steel arm guards sharpened at both ends. They were determined to storm the NP rally.

Shortly after De Klerk arrived by helicopter that evening, AWB members started marching towards the hall. At 7.30pm, a violent street battle between police and AWB members began raging.

Two minibuses transporting black passengers were attacked by the enraged mob. Soon afterwards, when a bakkie carrying more blacks was attacked, the terrified driver drove straight into the mob, running down two AWB men. Shouting, 'kill them, kill them', the mob fell upon the passengers of the bakkie. The police drove back the crowd. An ambulance carrying a nurse wearing an AWB insignia arrived, but refused to pick up the injured blacks.

NELSON MANDELA *with his ANC delegation at the opening of the Convention for a Democratic South Africa in 1991. The CODESA emblem, showing the sun shining on the Republic's black and white people, symbolised the ideal of a 'New South Africa'.*

By 8pm De Klerk started addressing his rally. When the meeting ended, he and his wife Marike were driven out of Ventersdorp in the back of a Nyala police riot vehicle.

The event at Ventersdorp proved to be another turning point in the history of South Africa: it was the first time, under NP rule, that the police had been given orders to use force against white, predominantly Afrikaner, lawbreakers. (In October 1993, Terre'Blanche and 10 fellow right-wingers involved in the event were convicted of public violence.)

CODESA

Despite opposition from the far right and accusations from the left that it was secretly supporting a 'third force' intent on destabilising the country, the government continued the process of searching for a negotiated political settlement in South Africa.

In December 1991, the government and 18 other parties (the CP and the PAC were notable absentees) making up the Convention for a Democratic South Africa (CODESA) signed a Declaration of Intent incorporating the guiding principles of a new democratic order in South Africa.

Central to the document was a commitment by all the parties involved 'to bring about an undivided South Africa with one nation sharing a common citizenship, patriotism and loyalty, pursuing amidst our diversity freedom, equality and security for all, irrespective of race, colour, sex or creed; a country free from apartheid or any other form of discrimination or domination'.

Notwithstanding several hiccups that arose mainly because of political posturing by some of the bigger groups, the participants were able to reach a surprising degree of consensus on several ticklish issues that arose during initial discussions.

The referendum

Early in 1992, the NP was thrashed in a by-election that had been called in Potchefstroom after the death of former Minister of Law and Order Louis le Grange.

With the CP baying for a general election, De Klerk gambled again: white voters would be given the opportunity, in a referendum, to state whether they supported the reform process that he had initiated in February 1990.

As voting day drew nearer, many feared the worst. But, backed by the DP, big business and a host of show business and sporting personalities in a high-profile campaign, the pro-reform camp swept to a stunning victory. In a turnout of almost 80 percent of registered white voters, 68,7 percent of the electorate voted 'Yes'. De Klerk's gamble had paid off in generous terms. His stature among whites and blacks had been elevated; he had strengthened his party's hand at the negotiation table; and the claims of the right wing had been decisively squashed.

The Johannesburg newspaper 'Weekly Mail' said in the aftermath of the referendum: 'Pinch yourself, South Africa – democracy is coming within months.' But the process of finding a new constitution would take some time ....

VOTERS IN CAPE TOWN *wait patiently to cast their votes in the 1992 referendum. More than 68 percent of white South Africans backed F W de Klerk's reform initiatives.*

Democracy or destruction?

The unbanning of the major anti-apartheid groups in February 1990 was so unexpected that it left a momentary vacuum in extra-parliamentary opposition. Within weeks, however, the battle was on to win the hearts and minds of the people – a battle that spilled violently out of the political arena and into township streets as a host of organisations, including the African National Congress (ANC), Pan-Africanist Congress (PAC) and the newly constituted Inkatha Freedom Party (IFP), vied for power. As the leaders avowed democracy, many of their followers fought pitched battles in Natal and Transvaal, while allegations of a destructive 'third force' of security force personnel added fuel to an already dangerous fire. Real peace seemed as elusive as ever.

A BUZZ OF EXCITEMENT swept through the 4 000-strong crowd as a brown sedan, escorted by three helicopters, came slowly into view. Convinced that the big moment had at last arrived, the crowd edged forward. When the car reached the outer security gates of the Victor Verster Prison, it stopped – and for a few seconds everyone, even the police and the marshalls with their walkie-talkies, seemed to hold their breath. Then a door opened and a photographer, his voice shaking with emotion, shouted: 'He's walking ... he's walking to his freedom!'

It was precisely 4.16pm on Sunday, 11 February 1990, and ANC leader Nelson Mandela was about to savour his first seconds of freedom ....

With his wife, Winnie, holding his hand, and with members of the National Reception Committee flanking him, the man who had spent 27 years in jail, started walking towards the prison gates. Beaming at the crowd, he acknowledged their loud cheers with a clenched fist salute. Then he turned back towards his car. Minutes later he was being whisked off to Cape Town, where more than 100 000 ANC supporters and well-wishers were waiting to see and hear him.

Several hours later, when he stepped onto the great balcony of the old City Hall, he was greeted by tumultuous applause.

'Viva Mandela, viva,' the crowd chanted as he began his address by thanking 'friends, comrades and fellow South Africans' for their 'tireless and heroic sacrifices [which] have made it possible for me to be here today'.

'The mass campaigns of defiance and other actions of our organisation [the ANC] and people can only culminate with the establishment of democracy.'

'Amandla,' they roared as he urged all South Africans to embark on 'decisive mass action to destroy apartheid'.

But the biggest ovation of all was reserved for his announcement that the armed struggle would continue.

'Our resort to the armed struggle in 1960 with the formation of the military wing of the ANC, *Umkhonto we Sizwe*, was a purely defensive action against the violence of apartheid. The factors which necessitated the armed struggle still exist today. We have no option but to continue. We express the hope that a climate conducive to a negotiated settlement will be created soon so that there may no longer be the need for the armed struggle.'

New challenges

In many respects, the euphoria that accompanied Mandela's release was tempered by the knowledge that the myriad problems plaguing black political organisations remained unresolved.

In townships throughout the country, violent rivalries involving rank-and-file activists forced political leaders to spend an inordinate amount of time trying to resolve conflict among groups: when charterists (ANC supporters) and non-charterists (mainly PAC supporters) were not squaring up to one another, ANC and Inkatha supporters had to be kept apart. Often, however, the cause of violence was simply random thuggery, the outcome of years of brutalisation under apartheid.

FLANKED BY HIS WIFE *Winnie and leading activist Cyril Ramaphosa, ANC leader Nelson Mandela savours his first minutes of freedom.*

PANIC-STRICKEN PROTESTERS *in Sebokeng township in the Vaal triangle try to flee after police had been ordered to fire on* *them. At least eight people died and more than 350 were injured in this incident at the end of March 1990.*

The Congress waiting in the wings …

'You cannot win at the negotiating table what you've not already won on the battlefield.'

This is how Pan-Africanist Congress (PAC) general secretary Benny Alexander justified the refusal in 1990 of his organisation to join multi-party negotiations with the South African Government. In an interview with a financial magazine in July 1990, Alexander said: 'Our task is to intensify the struggle until the cost [to the government] for turning its back on the PAC becomes so ghastly to contemplate that it will call a face-saving conference to give us what we have already won on the battlefield.'

Four years later, the PAC had been drawn into the negotiations – and the abandonment of the armed struggle – without scoring that battlefield victory. And, although political analysts had never taken seriously the PAC's claims that it would 'shock' everybody in the 1994 election, the party did even more poorly than expected. Its estimated support in 1992 of five percent of the population translated into 1,25 percent of the votes polled.

Since its unbanning in 1990, the PAC had been eclipsed by its long-time rival, the ANC. Its capitulation on negotiations and the armed struggle lost it some ground among its radical supporters, led to tensions inside the organisation and left few differences between its policies and those of the ANC. In fact, in March 1994, PAC president Clarence Makwetu – in mooting an election pact with the ANC – conceded as much in an interview.

A long fight for survival

After being banned in 1960, the PAC fought a long battle for survival in various African countries – although many of its problems were self-inflicted: for instance, it had been forced to shut down its training camps at Kinkuza in Zaire and Kumasi in Ghana after rank-and-file members had revolted against sub-standard living conditions and poor training methods. Personality conflicts also took their toll – and at one stage became so bad that the Zambian Government decided to appeal to the Organisation of African Unity to withdraw recognition and suspend its funding of the organisation.

The death of its founder, Robert Sobukwe, in South Africa in 1975 sparked a messy leadership crisis, with several top officials being expelled for corruption or for being 'CIA spies'. It was only in the 1980s, when the chairmanship was taken over by Johnson Mlambo, that the organisation began showing signs of revival.

In the run-up to the 1994 election, the PAC was again beset by problems: it was slow in putting together its manifesto and for five months its campaign came to a virtual standstill amid reports that it was broke. Its policies of redistribution of land and wealth to Africans, attacks on civilians by its armed wing, the Azanian People's Liberation Army (APLA), and supporters' chants of 'One settler, one bullet' made it too radical to attract financial backing.

When it did abandon the armed struggle at the end of 1993, the decision was openly criticised by officials – two of whom were suspended from the organisation as a result.

In the wake of the PAC's thrashing at the polls, political analysts warned that the ANC landslide was partly a vote against apartheid, and that the PAC could regain its support if the ANC failed to meet the aspirations of blacks. Kaizer Nyatsumba, political correspondent of 'The Star' newspaper, lamenting the PAC's poor showing, wrote: 'A voice to the left of the ANC is sorely needed in parliament to forever remind the ANC-led government of its responsibility to the black masses as well.'

THE PAC'S *Benny Alexander, Clarence Makwetu, Patricia de Lille and Barney Desai lead a protest march.*

The ANC's Harare Declaration

In July 1989, the ANC, the Congress of South African Trade Unions (COSATU) and the United Democratic Front (UDF) drew up a document setting up the principles they believed should form the basis of a new constitution, their pre-conditions for negotiation and a programme of action for achieving them.

Known as the Harare Declaration, it was accepted by the Organisation of African Unity's *ad hoc* committee on southern Africa and by the United Nations.

The document set up five demands for achieving a climate of negotiation:
* The unconditional release of all political detainees and prisoners;
* The lifting of all bans and restrictions on organisations and people;
* The removal of troops from the townships;
* The end of the state of emergency; and
* The cessation of all political trials.

The signatories to the declaration also outlined a number of principles on which they believed a new constitution should be based. Among these were:
* The formation of a united, democratic and non-racial state;
* Common and equal citizenship and nationality for all South Africans;
* The right of participation in the government and administration of the country on the basis of a universal suffrage exercised through one person, one vote;
* The right of everyone to form or join any political party (provided that the party concerned does not try to further racism);
* An entrenched Bill of Rights;
* A legal system guaranteeing equality before the law;
* An economic order promoting the well-being of all South Africans; and
* A democratic South Africa respecting the rights, sovereignty and territorial integrity of all countries.

In a bid to establish a united front against apartheid, Mandela called on extra-parliamentary groups in the townships to join hands against the government. But while some non-ANC activists recognised his potential as a catalyst to bring about unity, the response of others was decidedly lukewarm.

One of the sceptics, Benny Alexander, the general secretary of the Pan-Africanist Movement (the then internal wing of the PAC), said: 'There is no individual messiah in the land. A solution to the country's problems lies with the action of the toiling masses.' Another left-wing representative, Jean Pease of the Cape Action League (CAL), agreed: 'CAL has problems with building up one person into a unifier.' And so, with unity continuing to prove elusive – and with some leaders admitting that they had lost control over their supporters – protracted unrest in black townships sent the death rate soaring.

It was only in April 1991, more than a year after Mandela's release, that the ANC and the PAC – together with several smaller organisations (but not the Inkatha Freedom Party) – were able to agree on the formation of a 'Patriotic Front'

to confront the government. However, since the ANC was now committed to the process of negotiations, the ideological gulf between the two organisations became so wide as to make the agreement almost worthless.

The ANC's policies under the spotlight
On 2 March 1990, when Mandela was elected ANC deputy president at a meeting of the National Executive Committee (NEC) in Lusaka, Zambia, he reiterated the organisation's commitment to negotiations with the government.

Nevertheless, he was acutely aware that the ANC could not afford to alienate its chief constituency – the masses of rightless, often desperately poor township residents. Thus, at the end of March 1990, when dozens of people were killed and injured by police during a demonstration at Sebokeng near Vereeniging, he immediately broke off planned talks with the government. It was only after State President F W de Klerk announced the appointment of a commission of inquiry into the shootings that the discussions, which were later formalised as the Groote Schuur Minute, were again put on track.

In another departure from established policy (and one that caused consternation in the ranks of the more radical members of the organisation), Mandela (with the backing of the NEC) began a process of dialogue with 'homeland' leaders in an attempt to draw them away from the government's sphere of influence.

In broad terms, ANC policy with regard to a new constitution for South Africa was based on the Harare Declaration (see box), which had been drawn up in 1989 by the ANC, UDF and COSATU.

While the constitutional guidelines simply mentioned the ideal of an economic order benefiting all South Africans, closer questioning by nervous white economists elicited a reply that caused concern: the ANC was committed to nationalising key industries.

It was a recipe for disaster, argued business leaders and members of the government, pointing to the economic woes of countries where nationalisation had been rigidly applied – the rapidly disintegrating communist bloc in eastern Europe. The ANC stood firm, however: there had to be some state intervention, Mandela insisted during an address to 300 business leaders in May 1990. Claiming that fewer than 10 corporations controlled almost 90 percent of the shares listed on the Johannesburg Stock Exchange, he pointed out that if South Africans were genuinely interested in ending the old social order and bringing in a new one, this concentration of economic power would have to change.

Mandela added that the ANC was strongly opposed to privatisation and believed that the disposal of state industries had to be held over until a truly representative government was in place. Privatisation, he said, would reinforce the over-concentration of wealth in the hands of a powerful few.

Over the next few months, however, following warnings that many Western industrialists would be loath to invest in a country that might nationalise their assets, executive pronouncements on the issue appeared to become less dogmatic.

A GROUP OF *Inkatha supporters armed with 'traditional' weapons leave a rally in Thokoza township south of Johannesburg. Clashes between Inkatha and* ANC *supporters on the Witwatersrand left scores dead in the early 1990s.*

A world tour

In June 1990, Mandela set off on a world tour of 13 countries in Africa, Europe and North America, with a central message for his hosts: while conceding that the changes introduced by State President De Klerk were encouraging, he argued that the process towards a truly democratic constitution was still not sufficiently advanced to be regarded as either 'irreversible' or as worthy of such a major reward for De Klerk as the lifting of sanctions.

Although the majority of his hosts assured him that sanctions would not be lifted until there had been further 'significant progress' along the road of negotiations, the economic giants of Europe and North America were more circumspect, refusing to commit themselves beyond an assurance that they would objectively review sanctions on an ongoing basis.

Wherever he went, Mandela was met by massive crowds. From Paris to Geneva, from Bonn to the European Parliament in Strasbourg, from Rome and the Vatican to Ottawa, and then on to New York, Boston, Washington, Atlanta, Miami, Detroit and other American cities, the ANC deputy president was cheered and fêted by political leaders, popular entertainers and exiled South Africans.

On 20 June, at a ticker-tape parade in New York, close to a million people thronged the streets to welcome him. On 26 June, after talks in Washington, both he and President George Bush said that they had reached agreement 'on almost all issues' regarding South Africa. Later, Mandela was given standing ovations when he addressed a joint sitting of both houses of the US Congress.

On 4 July, Mandela met the Western leader least sympathetic to his call for continued sanctions, British Prime Minister Margaret Thatcher, before returning home via the Organisation of African Unity headquarters in Addis Ababa, and talks with heads of state in Uganda, Kenya and Mozambique. On his return to Johannesburg on 18 July, some 45 days after setting out, Mandela was greeted by euphoric crowds. But his triumphant procession was soured by yet more carnage in the townships.

Death on the rails

On 13 July 1990, a heavily armed gang boarded a train on the Soweto-Johannesburg line and started shooting and stabbing passengers at random.

It was the start of a new campaign of terror. Over the next few months, dozens of commuters were killed or injured in similar, apparently motiveless, attacks. One of the worst assaults occurred on 13 September 1990, when 26 people died and more than 100 were injured in an attack on a train between Jeppe and Benrose stations.

Accusations by some survivors that the attackers were Zulu-speakers sparked a series of tit-for-tat attacks on hostels housing Zulu migrant workers, which in turn led to numerous clashes between ANC and Inkatha supporters. The dismal success rate of the police in trying to apprehend the culprits led to charges (from ANC sources in particular) that a 'third force' was responsible for the killings.

Stung by these accusations, the police began a campaign of surprise stop-and-search checks on peak-hour trains, confiscating a number of weapons such as knives and pangas. But when the police scaled down the frequency of their searches, the attacks began again. Police records showed that from mid-1990 to March 1994 more than 600 people had died and more than 1 400 had been injured in train attacks.

The SACP comes in from the cold

Just as communism was showing signs of terminal decline in the Soviet Union, the South African Communist Party (SACP) was making a successful re-entry into mainstream South African politics. On 29 July 1990 almost 50 000 supporters celebrated the relaunch of the SACP at Soccer City Stadium outside Johannesburg. Guest speaker Mandela described the event as 'an important day in the political history of our country ... which should give hope to everyone who calls himself or herself a democrat'.

The ANC, said Mandela, was not a communist party, but 'as a defender of democracy it has fought and will continue to fight for the right of the SACP to exist'.

COMMUNIST PARTY LEADER *Joe Slovo, the former 'Public Enemy No 1' of the South African Government, became a key figure in the negotiating process in the early 1990s.*

SACP general secretary Joe Slovo told the crowd that his party was committed to peaceful negotiations. Answering charges by the government that communists were using the ANC while following a 'secret agenda', Slovo stressed that all SACP members who held leadership posts in the ANC enjoyed the confidence of the ANC and that it was an insult to non-communist ANC leaders such as Chief Albert Luthuli, Oliver Tambo and Mandela to suggest that they had been manipulated against their will by communists.

Slovo was referring to the arrest on 24 July of more than 40 ANC insurgents, including leading SACP member Mac Maharaj, and the confiscation by the police of several arms caches. According to the police, 'Operation Vula' was an SACP plot to overthrow the government by force. (The ANC argued that the operation, which had been planned before the start of its talks with the government, was intended to set up underground structures within the country.)

The NP's threatened break-off of talks with the ANC in protest at the inclusion of Slovo in the ANC team was averted when Mandela emerged from a meeting with De Klerk and announced that the next round of 'talks about talks' would take place in Pretoria on 8 August. Discussions between the two teams led to an agreement by the ANC to suspend its armed struggle.

However, not all talks between the two sides proceeded as smoothly as this ....

Prison hunger strike

Towards the end of April 1991, the delicate negotiations between the government and the ANC reached deadlock over the question of the unconditional release of political prisoners. On the one hand, the ANC claimed that anyone jailed for opposing the state (in whatever way) was a political prisoner and therefore qualified for release. On the other hand, the government contended that those convicted and sentenced for offences such as the bombing of civilian targets or the murder of policemen were guilty of ordinary criminal offences.

On 1 May 1991, political prisoners throughout South Africa began refusing food and lawyers representing them told reporters: 'Their intention is to continue [with a hunger strike] until they are released or until they die.'

By 9 May an edgy government had freed 40 hunger-strikers, but as pressure mounted for the release of the remaining strikers (estimated at 236), the state dug in its heels. Towards the end of May, amid reports that many of the prisoners were in a serious condition, the ANC warned that it would break off talks with the government if any of the hunger-strikers died.

On 7 June, the 36th day of fasting for 14 of the remaining 31 refusing to take food, Mandela appealed to the strikers to call off their fast.

'We are convinced that the point which the hunger-strikers wished to convey to the government has been conveyed: that all political prisoners must be released immediately and unconditionally,' the ANC deputy leader said in a statement.

By the middle of June most of the original group of hunger-strikers were again taking food. However, some people whom the ANC described as political prisoners would remain in jail until a new government was formed.

The ANC executive under fire

Simmering tensions between former UDF members of the ANC and some external stalwarts of the NEC (who, because of the postponement of elections until July 1991, continued to hold the top leadership positions in the organisation) surfaced at a special Consultative Conference in December 1990.

Younger members of the ANC who had struggled (and, indeed, suffered) through the darkest days of P W Botha's two states of emergency were particularly incensed over the reluctance of some of the 'external' group to 'dirty their shoes' in the townships. Furthermore, the 'internal' group contended that the apparent indifference of 'external' members to the immense problems facing ordinary black families was losing the ANC valuable support.

Members of the NEC sat grim-faced as delegates lambasted them for these and other 'tactical errors', such as the suspension of the armed struggle, consultations with 'homeland' leaders and the suggestion that De Klerk was 'a man of integrity'.

The angry mood of delegates was highlighted by their treatment of International Affairs head Thabo Mbeki (tipped by many as the 'logical' successor to Mandela). A paper drawn up by Mbeki, calling for the ANC's policy on sanctions to be applied with more tactical skill, was rejected without even being discussed.

Delegates claimed that the De Klerk Government was not committed to a democratic South Africa but wanted to retain white domination in a new form.

Ironically, the ANC was reaping what it had sowed in the mid-1980s, when it had called for townships to be made 'ungovernable'. Many of the activists who had answered this call now found it difficult to accept the decision to negotiate with a government that they had learnt to hate.

In his closing address, a clearly shaken Mandela admitted that the NEC had made mistakes in the course of its duties. But he added icily: 'Our organisation has in the past dealt with a variety of weaknesses and mistakes on the part of our membership as well: factions and cliques, men and women who used the platforms of the organisation for unprincipled discussions, who played to the gallery, whose aims in meetings of this nature are to prove how revolutionary they are – who have no idea whatsoever of working in a mass movement, who are totally incapable of putting forward constructive ideas and who are quick to pull down what others have built.'

Mandela said that, while there were certain suggestions that he and other NEC members fully accepted – such as that there should be no discussions on a new constitution until all obstacles to negotiation had been removed – there were other arguments that they rejected completely: specifically the one which suggested that the ANC should not be speaking to the government. 'The overwhelming majority of our people generally and the delegates here in particular support negotiation between the ANC and the government,' he said.

The volatile chief Mangosuthu Buthelezi

'Bull ... it's all bull ... I am a Christian and all my life I have been committed to the precepts of Christianity.' Chief Mangosuthu Buthelezi, president of the Inkatha Freedom Party (IFP) and Chief Minister of KwaZulu, was reacting to allegations that Inkatha supporters were instrumental in the violence that plagued the Midlands of Natal in the 1980s and early '90s.

Dominated by Zulu-speakers, the Inkatha National Cultural Liberation Movement was founded by Buthelezi in 1975 at the instigation of the then exiled ANC. It was hoped that Buthelezi would keep the flame of resistance alive in the region – but the ANC leadership had failed to take Buthelezi's character into account.

Mangosuthu Buthelezi was born on 27 August 1928 in Mahlabatini to Chief Mathole and Princess Magogo Zulu, granddaughter of King Cetshwayo. While registered for a BA degree in Bantu Administration at the University of Fort Hare, he became an active member of the ANC Youth League and rose to national prominence in 1970 when he was elected chief executive officer of KwaZulu.

The rise of Inkatha
At the time of its formation Inkatha was intended largely to be a cultural organisation – black consciousness was in the ascendant – but as time wore on it became a formidable power base for Buthelezi himself. In 1990 he claimed a paid-up membership of 1,8-million, but this included all civil servants and students in the 'homeland', whose membership was compulsory.

When Bophuthatswana opted for 'independence' in 1977 under the 'grand' apartheid scheme of Balkanisation, Buthelezi refused to lead

KwaZulu in the same direction. He consistently argued for a non-racial multiparty democracy based on the principles of a free-market economic system. When he refused to support the armed struggle or economic sanctions, however, he lost much support from the ANC/UDF/COSATU alliance but gained the interest of white politicians and the media.

Falling out
Buthelezi's estrangement from the broader liberation movement became evident in the 1980s. He withdrew from the Release Mandela Campaign in 1980, denouncing it as 'an exceptionally clever and deliberate ploy to undermine present-day black leadership and bring about unbridgeable divisions in the black community'.

His alienation from the anti-government alliance continued when he used Inkatha forces in 1982 to crush latent student boycotts in the region, and when he helped to set up the United Workers' Union of South Africa (UWUSA) in 1986 as a rival to COSATU. (The standing of Inkatha and Buthelezi were dented when it was later disclosed that the South African Government had sponsored both UWUSA and Inkatha.)

In the 1990s, the rivalry between Inkatha and the ANC and its allies was turned to the IFP's advantage. Former Inkatha general secretary Oscar Dhlomo said in an interview in 1990: 'Buthelezi has skillfully utilized ANC blunders to his advantage. He is now able to claim, thanks to the ANC, that anyone who demands the dismantling of the KwaZulu Government is challenging not only the Zulu nation but also the Zulu king.'

During multiparty negotiations, Buthelezi insisted on the Zulu mon-

archy's being entrenched in the new constitution, as well as on greater guarantees of regional autonomy. This created a stand-off that threatened the participation of his followers – and those of his nephew, King Goodwill Zwelithini – in the 1994 election. But a last-minute compromise brought the IFP into the election – a week before polling day.

In the national elections, the IFP emerged as the third strongest party with 2,06-million votes (10,5 percent). Most of its support, it would seem, came from KwaZulu/Natal, where the IFP polled 1,8-million votes (50,3 percent) to give it the majority in the new regional legislature.

Buthelezi was appointed Minister of Home Affairs in the new national Cabinet.

KWAZULU CHIEF MINISTER *Mangosuthu Buthelezi was one of the fiercest critics of the ANC during negotiations for a new South African constitution.*

AFTER 25 YEARS *in exile, trade unionist Ray Alexander (left) and her husband, Professor Jack Simons, are greeted by an old friend, women's movement activist Frances Baard, at Jan Smuts Airport, Johannesburg, on 2 March 1990. The return of exiles was one of the cornerstone demands of the* ANC, PAC *and* SACP, *following their unbanning in February 1990.*

The search for answers

At the end of its first year as an unbanned organisation, the ANC could look back on several successes: it had, for instance, cemented its support in black townships across the country, often under extremely difficult conditions; it had demonstrated great skill in acting as both a political organisation (in its talks with the government) and a liberation movement (in its relationship with its grassroots support); and it had kept together a disparate number of organisations and individuals.

But ultimately it was judged by many on the basis of one glaring failure: it could not stop the horrific violence in the townships ....

The violence had hurt the ANC badly: it had reduced the organisation's capacity to organise and expand its activities in unrest ravaged areas and had slowed down to a trickle an initially promising recruitment campaign in white, coloured and Indian communities.

The biggest beneficiary of the unrest was the governing NP, which, by advertising itself as a party for moderates (especially after October 1990, when it opened its doors to all races), began to gain the support of coloured and Indian people.

The ANC was convinced that security structures were responsible for much of the violence: 'Evidence of police collusion … abounds,' the ANC claimed, adding that the government was 'talking peace on the one hand while colluding in the war against its opponents on the other. In this way, they hope to exact from the liberation movement compromises that will leave the system of apartheid essentially unchanged.'

At first such claims were generally rejected as outrageous by the government and as far-fetched by most media commentators. In April 1992, however, at a murder trial in the Supreme Court in Pietermaritzburg of a police station commander and four 'special policemen', the accusations were shown to have some weight.

Finding the accused guilty of 11 murders in the rural Natal township of Trust Feed, Judge Andrew Wilson described the 1988 massacre as the final event in a planned security force operation to disrupt the community, oust an established residents' association and give Mangosuthu Buthelezi's Inkatha organisation control of the area.

Evidence was that senior policemen and Inkatha members had planned and executed the killings – and had then engineered a cover-up.

The station commander, Captain Brian Mitchell (who was later sentenced to death for his part in the massacre), told the court that members of the police's riot unit had, on previous occasions, assisted Inkatha by unlawful means to take over areas. He added that the entire force of 'special policemen' was created as part of a counter-revolutionary (anti-UDF/ANC) strategy.

Clearly, in the new political climate of negotiation, the government faced a major problem: having allowed its security forces to conduct a no-holds-barred campaign against liberation movements such as the ANC, it had to find a way to re-employ them for peaceful purposes. (The problem was not confined to the government: the ANC and, indeed, Inkatha, faced the same difficulty.)

The ANC congress

The perception among a core of radical activists that the ANC had failed to do enough to protect its township supporters fuelled rumours of wholesale changes to the NEC at the ANC congress in Durban in July 1991.

But, while new faces were indeed voted in, a far more significant development was the often brutally frank self-examination by delegates of ANC structures: for instance, dealing with 'problems hampering growth', long-serving secretary-general Alfred Nzo (who later lost his position to National Union of Mineworkers leader Cyril Ramaphosa) listed factionalism, cliquism, ignorance, complacency, confusion at the Johannesburg head office and 'little creativity or variety in campaigns' as serious obstacles to the success of the organisation.

There was, however, also some praise for the organisation: in his opening address, Mandela claimed that it had been ANC pressure which had forced the government to repeal racist legislation, which had set in motion the process leading to the repatriation of exiles and which had secured the release of political prisoners.

But he warned: 'We will experience many things for the first time … [and] are bound to make mistakes and experi-

ence failures. [But] we must make sure that we recognise these quickly, assess them, criticise ourselves where necessary, learn what has to be learnt and emerge from these stronger and better able to carry out our historic mission.'

In December 1991, the ANC reiterated its commitment to negotiation when it joined 18 other parties (including the NP) in forming the Convention for a Democratic South Africa (CODESA). To millions of South Africans, this event signalled a new beginning ….

A 'deadly brew' that killed thousands

By the beginning of 1991 battles to the death were being fought in many parts of South Africa. In Natal and in the industrial heartland of the Transvaal, in particular, villages and township streets had become battlefields, inhabitants were being shot, hacked and burnt to death by the scores, homes and possessions were being burnt, and thousands of people had been displaced by the turmoil.

While political parties blamed their rivals, directly or indirectly, for the 'undeclared war', analysts tried to make sense of the carnage.

'Probably no other aspect of the South African conflict has elicited more divergent explanations and misinterpretations than the ongoing political violence,' wrote authors Heribert Adam and Kogila Moodley.

Violence had been a feature of the South African way of life for a long time. And the killing did not stop when President F W de Klerk's reforms (including the unbanning of the liberation movements) were announced on 2 February 1990 – it increased. The next month, 458 people died in what was categorised as political violence. Before that the figure had never risen above 200 a month. What should have been the start of an era of peace turned instead into what Reuters journalist Rich Mkhondo described as 'A time for weeping'.

Explanations for the rise in the bloodshed abounded. Adam and Moodley wrote: '[The political violence] is variously attributed to (1) De Klerk's double agenda and unreformed police; (2) a "third force" of right-wing elements in the security establishment, bent on derailing the government's negotiation agenda; (3) the Inkatha/ANC rivalry, engineered by an ambitious [Chief Mangosuthu] Buthelezi who fears being sidelined

rather than treated as an equal third party; (4) the ANC's campaign of armed struggle, ungovernability, and revolutionary intolerance; (5) ingrained tribalism, unleashed by the lessening of white repression that resulted in "black-on-black" violence; (6) the legacy of apartheid in general, migrancy, hostel conditions, and high unemployment among a generation of "lost youth" ….'

Arguing against any single-cause explanation, they added: 'Regardless of peace accords signed at the top [by political leaders], antagonistic groups at the bottom often act violently, independent of leadership control. Such behaviour has, in particular, been undertaken by elements of the official security establishment, linked to right-wing agendas of destabilising the negotiation process.'

There was no shortage of initiatives to try to halt the violence. In January 1991, ANC leader Nelson Mandela and IFP leader Chief Mangosuthu Buthelezi held a peace summit, calling on supporters to 'cease all attacks against one another with immediate effect'. The violence intensified. They met again on Good Friday – but the violence continued.

Churches and business stepped in and – on 14 September 1991 – organised a summit on violence, attended by 24 organisations including the government, the IFP and the ANC. Delegates signed a 33-page National Peace Accord, in terms of which committees were set up to monitor a code of conduct for political parties and security forces operating in the townships. In addition, Judge Richard Goldstone was appointed to head a standing commission of inquiry into violence and intimidation.

But the peace accord also failed to halt the violence. Deaths attributed

A VICTIM *of the violence in Natal, killed three weeks before the 1994 election.*

to political violence climbed from 2 706 in 1991 to 3 347 in 1992 and 3 706 in 1993 (an average of more than ten a day). In the darkest month, July 1993, a staggering 547 people lost their lives – nearly 18 for every day of the month.

'The minute one steps back from our culture of violence, its causes as numerous as its injuries, one notices again the enormous shadow cast by the most fundamental social and economic problems,' wrote Mkhondo of Reuters. 'Millions of blacks are caught in a spiral of landlessness, homelessness, unemployment, and poverty. Add to that a clash between modern political structures and traditional tribal ones. Mix in a struggle for hegemony in the region between major political players. Stir in the security forces in all their guises …. Add faceless, apparently trained killers such as the "third force", etc. Sprinkle all that with ancient and recent political or social grudges and you get a deadly brew.'

Shaping up to the future

Hillbrow – Johannesburg's enigmatic inner-city suburb – has had many moods: it could be vibrant and jaunty one day, ugly and distant the next. In its heyday in the 1970s and '80s, its sprawling flatland used to be primarily a transit area – providing shelter for all and sundry. Hobos, adolescent runaways and gangsters nestled in its dark alleys; elderly white pensioners with nowhere else to go clung to the security of an area they had inhabited for decades; newly weds and swinging singles, attracted by the 24-hour entertainment circuit and its proximity to the city, used it as a first stop in the housing ladder; and, for foreign immigrants and rural migrants alike, it was a pitstop before entering the metropolis proper.

Although the pace in the '90s continued to be frenetic, Hillbrow did sometimes show a mellow side: in several parts of the suburb, butcher shops and greengrocers slowly replaced slot machine arcades and sex aid outlets, and the parks started filling with children.

The original 'grey' area

Affectionately known as 'The Brow', Hillbrow was South Africa's first area to 'open' naturally. By the early 1970s, long before the government repealed the Group Areas Act, black and white lived there in reasonable harmony.

Hillbrow's residents were not merely pensioners forced to live amid slum and squalor. Thousands chose to live there because they were black and affluent or white and cosmopolitan. No other suburb in South Africa offered such a vast concentration of coffee shops, cafés, high-class record shops and bookstores (coupled with unlimited shopping hours).

Furthermore, blacks and whites could walk around arm-in-arm without inhibition – the majority of residents had largely outgrown apartheid's obsession with skin colour – and there were numerous instances of 'corridor friendships' (superficial chats between neighbours across

the colour bar before they bolted their respective doors for the night). Although communities tended to stick together – Rastafarians, Hare Krishnas, Yugoslavians, Hungarians, Portuguese, Afrikaners, coloured people, Italians, Hindus, punk rockers and skinheads – each to his own, the melting pot of clashing cultures was by the early 1990s, by and large, no longer on the boil.

Early years

Hillbrow survived as a quiet residential suburb from the time of its proclamation in 1894 until the 1920s, when property speculators moved in to erect flats and five-storey buildings. Unprecedented building development took place in the 1950s to cope with the post-war housing shortage. With the influx to Johannesburg – which had by then become South Africa's industrial centre – landlords erected scores of ugly and impersonal apartment blocks.

Largely because of the immigrant population, the suburb developed its distinctly continental flair. Beatniks gave way to hippies during the 1960s and Hillbrow became a haven for flower children with peace and happiness billowing like marijuana smoke from the balconies.

But then, a mass exodus of South Africans after the 1976 Soweto uprising had a negative impact on Hillbrow – until speculators found a ready market of black people trying to escape the ravages of township life. The removal of rent control and the introduction of the Sectional Titles

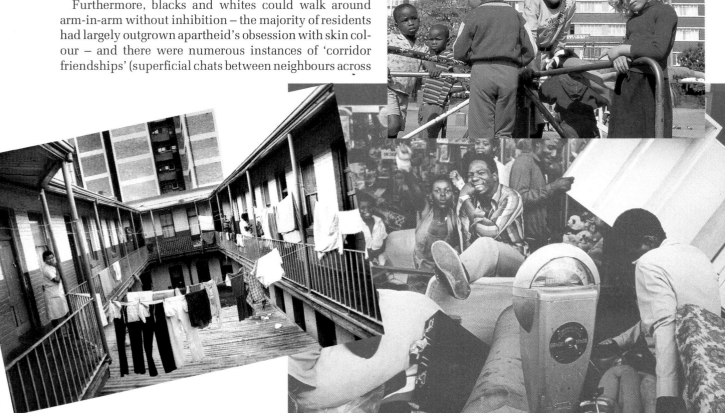

Act led to soaring rentals (and left tenants with no legal recourse). At first the new black tenants, unable to obtain leases legally, lived furtively under constant threat of eviction. But as movement into the area gathered momentum, their presence became more obvious and the tenants themselves grew more confident.

'Before the mid-1980s,' recalled one of the area's first black tenants, 'we were afraid to walk the streets at night for fear of harassment. Today (1992) there is much more confidence. Black people are treated with more respect in Hillbrow – for it is acknowledged that they belong here.' (By 1993, the ratio of black to white for the roughly 32 000 inhabitants was believed to be about 50:50.)

Inner city decay

Barring a few incidents, racial tension did not run high, but crime was part of the way of life in Hillbrow. Research on vagrancy by Dr Denise Bjorkman, commissioned by the National Party and Inkatha during 1991, showed that 46 percent of people living and working in Hillbrow had been the victims of some form of crime. At least 59 percent of these incidents – including mugging, bag snatching and rape – had been unreported.

As night fell on the 'brow of the hill', the sleazy giant changed from residential jungle to reckless reveller. Then the elderly hid behind bars and the more than 3 000 children who lived in box-like apartments with balconies went to sleep. The underworld of drug dealing, escort agencies, teenage prostitution and night clubs took over.

Street children huddled along the pavements, sniffing glue and directing headlights approaching in the haze to suitable parking places in return for handouts of small

change. Approximately one in every five apartment blocks housed a shebeen (a place where alcohol is sold illegally). In the vicinity of a popular chain store, suspect white envelopes changed hands and near corner shops street merchants peddled marijuana to the less affluent.

As a residential area, it was worlds apart from Johannesburg's other suburbs. Smells of urine and rotten food wafted from the dingy gutters, and most apartments were overcrowded, poorly looked after and dilapidated.

Some claimed that, because dwellings were rented out, maintenance was slipshod and less pride was taken in the surroundings. Others blamed the run-down look of the place on unscrupulous landlords making a 'quick buck' at the expense of black tenants. Some blamed it on a lack of foresight on the part of planners and yet others said it was because the population was so transient – residents were estimated to stay for an average of only four years. And yet, the housing problems of the residents of Hillbrow (and other inner-city suburbs) were minuscule when compared with the problems of another product of a changing South Africa: the urban squatter ....

THE MANY FACES *of Hillbrow visible within a short walking distance of one another. While children played together in parks around the suburb (top left), inner city decay (far left) and evictions (bottom left) remained a constant threat for many of the more than 30 000 inhabitants of the area. Although racial tensions began to ease noticeably with familiarity (right), unemployment (below) had yet to be overcome by the early 1990s.*

Rush to the cities

Some called them new pioneers; others viewed them as interlopers and a threat. They were the 5- to 7-million people crammed into shacks built from iron, wood and plastic in thousands of informal settlements dotted around South Africa's cities and towns. Their presence was evidence of continuing urbanisation that forecasters predicted would see three-quarters of the country's black population living in urban areas by the next century.

Newcomers, former hostel dwellers and those squeezed out from overcrowded accommodation in servant's quarters and townships flocked to squatter settlements. Often their welcome from their neighbours in brick houses was less than warm, while white and black local and regional authorities struggled to deal with their presence. Most were desperately poor. Officials estimated in the early 1990s that about 70 percent of black people could not afford to buy a house that cost as little as R10 000.

From actively discouraging squatting, the authorities therefore swung to providing site-and-service schemes for the new arrivals on the periphery of towns and cities. But the problem of how to integrate the cities' poorest inhabitants with the wealthy white municipalities still remained a major challenge.

There was plenty of poverty among the new arrivals – and a high unemployment rate, poor facilities and political insecurity made life difficult in the myriad squatter settlements. However, where there were people there was life, and squatter settlements were often marked by exuberance and innovation in addition to crime, malnutrition and a range of socio-economic ills and hardships.

Maud Ngwenya, one of an estimated 400 000 people living in Khayelitsha, a huge dormitory township outside Cape Town, epitomised the resilience and vigour that many squatters shared: 'I came to the city in the 1980s to find my husband, a migrant worker,' she recalled.

'But I never found him – and so, with my three children I joined a community living in the bush near Crossroads [a squatter camp that came to symbolise the determination and desperation of African people to remain in the city].'

Having lived through Bantu Administration Board harassment, she said she felt so excited when the Pass laws were abolished in 1986 that she went to St George's Cathedral in Cape Town with other members of her community 'to show people that we are here to stay'.

In 1984, she moved to Khayelitsha, which was then a small place with not many houses and shacks. 'I was waiting for a house,' she explained.

IN THE ABSENCE *of formal housing, informal settlements (above, below left) became a feature of urban life in the 1990s. These settlements in turn produced informal schools, such as that at Thembalihle at Inanda, near Durban (below right).*

SQUATTERS *in Hout Bay on the Cape Peninsula (above) live cheek-by-jowl with upmarket homeowners.*

Enoch Madywabe, chairperson of the Western Cape United Squatters Association, also vividly recalled the struggle of Cape Town's squatters to remain in the area: 'The first sign that the authorities accepted us as permanent was when they said we could stay in one big plastic settlement. Later, we took a blanket covered with lice to the Administration Board's office and the officials said we could build a few more shacks.'

By the early 1990s, Cape Town's squatter communities, like many camps elsewhere in the country, resembled mini-cities. Despairing of ever getting housing, some squatters invested a small fortune in their shacks. George Mamile of Site C in Khayelitsha was proud of his double-storey house, which had a facebrick facade, an upstairs balcony and cosy wood panelling inside. It cost him about R15 000 to build.

Meanwhile, entrepreneurs who formed part of a vibrant informal sector did a roaring trade in building materials. Zinc sheets, windows, doors – in fact anything that came to hand – were the staple of many small businesses.

However, like everything else in these settlements throughout South Africa, small businesses were vulnerable to the vicissitudes of the prevailing political climate.

INFORMAL *business, as evidenced by these hawkers at a bus and taxi terminus in Langa, near Cape Town (left and below) was a growth industry in the 1990s – generating R6-billion in income and creating more than three million jobs by 1993.*

Clashes between rival political groups (notably Inkatha and the African National Congress), infighting between local squatter leaders (whom many people dubbed warlords), taxi wars and other conflicts resulted in massacres, arson and a steady flow of refugees.

Across the great divide

Not all black people had to cope with the problem of finding a place to stay: the relaxation of the Group Areas Act (followed by its scrapping in 1991) offered Africans and coloured people the opportunity to buy homes in previously whites-only areas. For many of these 'pioneers' (especially for coloured people in the western Cape) moving meant a nostalgic return to areas from which they had been uprooted by the Group Areas Act.

In most instances – especially in high-income areas – the gentle influx of new black faces caused hardly a stir. Dr Nono Makhudu, a clinical psychologist, took up residence in 1990 in a townhouse in the plush Johannesburg suburb of Sandton. 'I find life fine and I like it here,' she said. 'I have been received very well by neighbours although there were one or two who were unsociable. One moved out when we moved in.'

In some cases, however, the problems were bigger ....

In December 1991 bank employee Ms P S Dube bought a 1 000 square metre plot for R30 000 in the Johannesburg suburb of Winchester Hills and built a modest R43 000 house on it. The neighbours in what had previously been classified a 'white' suburb seemed little perturbed by the colour of Dube's skin. What bothered them was that, unlike the rest of the neighbourhood, she failed to develop a manicured garden, and promptly moved in with her par-

AFTER SOME INITIAL STALLING,
white government schools in urban areas
slowly became multiracial. In the rural areas
(top right), however, conditions remained desperate.

ents, her lover, and six children. At least one neighbour claimed that Dube's tiny house had devalued the worth of his own property.

In the Pietermaritzburg suburb of Wembley, Benard Zikalala caused a stir in September 1991 when he threw a lavish party and proceeded – in traditional African style – to slaughter two sheep, a goat and an ox on the premises. The subsequent public debate drew heated remarks from some who wished for a return to the Group Areas Act.

In towns further away from the major centres, reactions on the part of conservative residents were more militant. In the middle of 1991 the Nkabinde family were harassed by a teenage gang when they moved into a double-storey house in Newcastle, Natal. The gang revved their motorcycles outside the house and hurled stones through the front windows and onto the roof. Later the youths took to painting slogans on the walls.

But generally, the upward mobility of blacks passed without comment from their white neighbours. Indeed, lucky families such as the Mashabas of Heatherdale, north of Pretoria, were fêted by their neighbours: they moved in next door to Minister of Foreign Affairs Pik Botha, who – in defiance of hostile Conservative Party sentiment – hosted a cocktail party for the newcomers.

A new mix at the schools

Another bastion of racial exclusivity to tumble was that of education, where many people argued that if the principle of mixed suburbs was accepted, why not mixed schools?

Although private schools had been 'open' for a number of years, with few problems, the government agonised for a long time over whether to open state schools to all. Eventually, it threw the ball into the court of white parents: 'You decide,' was the gist of what it said.

The result came as a pleasant surprise to those supporting a single, non-discriminatory educational system. Many schools in the larger urban areas voted 'Yes' – subject to strict entry requirements (these concerned mainly the age and academic ability of the applicants). Despite initial nervousness all round, 'open schools' were quickly adjudged a great success – bearing in mind, of course, that the number of black children who enrolled at these (still technically white) schools was a tiny percentage of the total black schoolgoing population.

Most black parents who enrolled their children at 'open' schools cited superior resources and amenities, better qualified teachers and the prospect of uninterrupted schooling as reasons for having done so. Despite

BLACK OWNERSHIP *increased in the taxi industry (above), while informal she-beens (left) continued to flourish.*

the fact that in the early 1990s the numbers and physical condition of black schools, as well as the standard of teaching, were slated as woefully inadequate for the majority of pupils, the annual figures for new matriculants continued to spiral: between 1978 and 1988, the number of black matriculants rose from just over 14 000 to almost 125 000. By contrast, the number of white matriculants increased from 46 000 to only 66 000.

The rise of the minibus taxi industry

Another feature of the 'New South Africa' was the growth of the minibus taxi industry, a development described by author and commentator Clem Sunter as an 'economic miracle created for blacks by blacks'.

By the mid-1990s, when an estimated 100 000 of these taxis were in operation throughout the Republic, the industry was said to be worth about R4,5-billion and responsible either directly or indirectly for 500 000 jobs.

However, its rise to prominence did not come easily: officials of the South African Black Taxi Association (SABTA), who had spent much of the 1970s trying to persuade the government to deregulate the industry, said the turning point came only in 1979, when the state decided to allow nine-seater minibuses to operate as taxis. There was a major scare in 1983 when a government commission recommended that new curbs be introduced to protect bus operators and established taxi services. By then, however, more than 500 000 people were using minibuses daily and there was little the government could do to reverse the process.

Another informal business area that showed impressive economic growth was shebeens. By the mid-1990s there were 30 000 to 40 000 of these informal drinking places in African townships with a total annual income estimated at R1-billion to R1,5-billion.

MUSIC LOVERS *were thrilled to see the return of international stars such as Hugh Masekela (top) and Paul Simon (above).*

The opening of international doors

Although many white South Africans watched the disintegration of economic and racial barriers with a wary eye, there were some welcome spin-offs for them too: the most obvious one was a return to international sport (from which their sportsmen and women had been barred, because of apartheid, for more than a generation).

In 1992 a United Cricket Board of South Africa team was fêted in India, reached the World Cup semi-finals in Australia and was thrashed in the West Indies. As national sporting bodies previously kept apart for racial reasons began forming united, non-racial controlling bodies, more and more invitations for South Africans to participate in international competitions began pouring in.

Cultural barriers also tumbled in the early 1990s – and South Africans were able to welcome former exiles such as jazz artists Abdullah Ibrahim and Hugh Masekela, and singers Miriam Makeba and Letta Mbulu, as well as international superstars such as American singer Paul Simon.

517

No easy walk to freedom

The start of negotiations for a new constitution heralded a period of jostling for position as the main parties – the African National Congress (ANC) and the National Party (NP) – engaged in an unlikely dual role. On the one hand, they acted jointly to try to pull the talks out of one stalemate after another; on the other, they knew they would be opponents in a coming election for a post-apartheid government. And, all the while, several smaller parties, in a fierce battle to carve out some political ground for themselves, threatened the progress being made towards the new order ....

AT EXACTLY 19 minutes past noon on 10 May 1994, centuries of white rule in South Africa ended when the Chief Justice swore in Nelson Rolihlahla Mandela as President. Then, to the wildly cheering crowd before him on the lawns of Pretoria's Union Buildings, Mandela proclaimed: 'The time for healing the wounds has come. The moment to bridge the chasms that divide us has come – the time to build is upon us.

'We have triumphed in our effort to implant hope in the breasts of the millions of our people. We enter into a covenant that we shall build a society in which all South Africans, both black and white, will be able to walk tall ... a rainbow nation at peace with itself and the world.'

With Mandela, on a special bullet-proof stage, were his two deputy presidents: ANC stalwart Thabo Mbeki; and F W de Klerk, the former NP State President who had led the country during its transition to democracy.

The dignified state occasion was conducted with a military decorum that contrasted sharply with widespread fears less than a month earlier that the country would be plunged into chaos as its citizens went to the polls in South Africa's first democratic election. Only last-minute negotiations had averted almost certain civil war ....

Divisions from the start
The differences that lay behind the threat of war – and which would come close to sabotaging the April 1994 election – had already been apparant more than two years earlier at the first session of the Convention for a Democratic South Africa (CODESA I), at which the majority of South Africa's political parties signed the Declaration of Intent on 22 December 1991, committing themselves to a multiparty democracy in a unitary state.

Some parties boycotted CODESA altogether. These included the Conservative Party (CP), which said it would not attend until the 'independence of the white nation' was guaranteed. Along with other white right-wing parties, they would make their demands for a white, Afrikaner *volkstaat* (homeland) with increasing vehemence.

The Pan-Africanist Congress (PAC) – which had formed a 'Patriotic Front' with the ANC and its allies to give the NP Government a 'knock-out blow' – stayed away too, saying it was clear that the government and the ANC were initiating all the decisions and the talks were a charade.

And while the Inkatha Freedom Party (IFP) was there, party leader Chief Mangosuthu Buthelezi had already fired the first verbal shots in his war to retain his regional power in the KwaZulu 'homeland': he decided to stay away from the talks after failing to get extra delegations for the Zulu king and for the KwaZulu administration.

The IFP and the 'independent homeland' of Bophuthatswana were the only two parties taking part in CODESA I which did not sign the Declaration of Intent. The IFP said the declaration appeared to rule out a federal system; and Bophuthatswana wanted its citizens to decide on reincorporation into South Africa.

THE LEADERS OF THE *Government of National Unity gathered outside Tuynhuys in Cape Town: President Nelson Mandela (centre) with his two deputies, Thabo Mbeki (left) and F W de Klerk.*

ANC MARCHERS scattered for cover as Cis-kei soldiers opened fire on them at the Bisho Stadium in September 1992. The massacre, in which 29 people were killed, proved a turning point in the process leading to a new constitution.

CODESA I nevertheless elected five working groups to come to grips with the main areas of negotiations, such as the principles for a new constitution, arrangements for an interim government, the future of the 'homelands', and a set of target dates for the establishment of a democracy.

The signatories to the declaration undertook 'to work to heal the division of the past, to secure the advancement of all, and to establish a free and open society based on democratic values where the dignity, worth and rights of every South African are protected by law'.

Fine words and fine intentions. But trouble lay ahead. When the delegates met for the second time, in May 1992 in a plenary session called CODESA II, talks collapsed over arguments about majority rule, power sharing and the future of regional powers.

In addition to the disputes over what form the 'New South Africa' would take, the talks were being conducted against a backdrop of ever-increasing violence (see page 511). Then, as CODESA II collapsed, an attack came that would have far-reaching repercussions for the country.

The Boipatong massacre
During the night of 17 June 1992 about 200 men from the KwaMadala hostel in Vanderbijlpark, Transvaal, went on a rampage in the nearby Slovo Park squatter camp in Boipatong, killing 15 people, mainly women and children, and injuring many more. Within a week the death toll had risen to at least 45 as some of the injured died in hospital.

One of the survivors, Simon Moloi, telling his story to journalist Rich Mkhondo, recalled how he and his pregnant wife had gone to bed about 10pm. Five minutes later they heard gunshots and screams from their neighbour.

'I went to the door to see what could be going on. I saw two men chopping my neighbour with axes .... I and my wife decided to run and hide in a swamp. I never had a chance to get dressed, so I fled with my underpants .... We had to go through a barbed wire fence to reach the swamp. I tried to lift the fence so that my wife could creep under it, but because of her pregnancy, she could not.

'The attackers were hot on our heels. My wife pleaded with me not to leave her behind. With bullets ricocheting in the ground past me, I had no choice but to run away, hoping they were looking for me and would not hurt a pregnant woman. I spent the night in the cold swamp. In the morning ... I found [my wife] still lying under the fence but covered with a blanket. I lifted the blanket and saw it

was her. She had been shot and hacked. That is how I lost my pregnant wife.'

Visiting the battered township the day after the massacre, Mandela said that, after what he had seen, 'I am convinced we are not dealing with human beings but animals. We will not forget what Mr De Klerk, the National Party and the Inkatha Freedom Party have done to our people. I have never seen such cruelty.'

While most people shared his horror at the attack, ANC supporters were not the only victims of the violence. In fact, when 17 of the killers were sentenced in June 1994, Judge J M C Smit said that each of them, all members of the IFP, had been victims of cruel attacks in the past. He sentenced the attackers to between 10 and 18 years' jail.

Rolling mass action
Among the implications of the outcry over the Boipatong massacre was that it gave impetus to the 'rolling mass action' campaign announced earlier by the ANC and its allies, the South African Communist Party (SACP) and the trade union grouping COSATU. Aimed at sweeping the government from power, the series of work stoppages, sit-ins and marches had begun on the day before the massacre. It carried on throughout July and culminated in a two-day stayaway by millions of black workers on 3 and 4 August that hit the already reeling economy hard. The strike ended with mass marches around the country in which 200 000 people were reported to have taken part. The biggest procession was to the Union Buildings in Pretoria, where Mandela told his supporters as well as the government that it was urgent that the negotiations begin again.

But before that could happen, the ANC alliance's campaign of mass action in the 'homelands' ran into trouble. During a march on the Ciskei capital of Bisho on 7 September 1992, Ciskei soldiers opened fire on defiant members of the crowd who had broken through a razor-wire barrier intended to prevent them from leaving the Bisho Stadium. After three minutes of shooting, 29 people lay dead. Another 200 were injured.

The killings strengthened the growing realisation among ANC leaders that they had to start talking again. Condemnation of Ciskei leader Brigadier Oupa Gqozo and his soldiers was mixed with criticism of ANC leaders for their handling of the march. The ANC realised it could no longer go on paying the costs of the mass action, and nor could the masses, who needed to go back to work.

Chris Hani: a soldier who died when the war was over

'I've come to accept that many personal sacrifices have been made in the struggle for liberation. I've lived with death for most of my life. Nobody wants to die. I want to live in a free South Africa ... I'm prepared to lay down my life for it.'

These words were spoken by Chris Hani in an interview three years before the South African Communist Party (SACP) general secretary was gunned down on 10 April 1993 in the driveway of his Boksburg home by a Polish immigrant, Janusz Waluz.

Hani had given his bodyguards the Easter weekend off, and had gone out briefly on the morning of Easter Saturday to buy newspapers.

As he got out of his car in his driveway, a red sedan pulled up behind him. Waluz walked up to him, raised a pistol and fired four shots into Hani's body at point blank range. One shot was fired from so close that an incriminating splatter of Hani's blood was left on Waluz's shirt.

Waluz fled, but he did not get far. A neighbour of Hani's, Retha Harmse, was driving past when she saw Waluz firing. As Waluz drove off, she noted his registration number, then sped home. Her husband, Daan, alerted the police.

Fifteen minutes later Waluz was arrested 10km from the Hani home. He was still in his car – and so was the murder weapon.

Hani's death plunged the country into uproar. South Africa's foreign exchange rate and its share market slumped. On the day set aside for memorial services, thousands of people marched in cities and townships around the country, and in Cape Town, Port Elizabeth, Durban and Pietermaritzburg marchers went on an orgy of looting, stoning and torching of trains and private vehicles, and petrol bombings. The South African embassy in Umtata, Transkei, was attacked and badly damaged. More than 70 people lost their lives.

Hani's funeral, redolent of a state affair and the biggest in South African history, was televised live by SABC television – the first time a former 'enemy of the state' was accorded this treatment.

Chris Martin Thembisile Hani was born on 28 June 1942 at Cofimvaba, Transkei. He joined the ANC Youth League in 1957 while still at school at Lovedale Institute in Alice, and was later suspended from Fort Hare University because of his involvement in politics. He graduated from Rhodes University in Grahamstown with a BA in Latin and English.

In 1962 he joined the ANC's armed wing, *Umkhonto we Sizwe* (MK), and became a member of the western Cape leadership. Later the same year he was arrested under the Suppression of Communism Act and sentenced to 18 years in jail. When an appeal against his conviction failed, he fled the country to undergo military training.

The man of action was also a man of literature, and whenever he was in the field as an MK guerrilla he was said always to have the selected works of Shakespeare in his backpack. He occasionally wrote poetry and short stories.

In 1973, he was elected to the ANC's national executive committee and was instructed to slip back into South Africa to establish a political infrastructure for the ANC in the Cape. He was moved to Lesotho in 1981, then later recalled to Zambia, where he was appointed deputy commander of MK, taking over from Joe Slovo in 1987 as Chief of Staff.

Hani returned to South Africa with his wife and three daughters after the ANC was unbanned in 1990. At the end of the next year he took over from Slovo as general secretary of the SACP, handing over the reigns of MK to Siphiwo Nyande in April 1992.

Hani was an activist, a tough soldier, and a committed socialist. He played a key role in keeping the ANC/SACP/COSATU alliance in the negotiations. His experience of the armed struggle made his later pleas for peace and political tolerance more credible: he had lived through the alternative.

CHRIS HANI, *guerrilla leader who joined the search for peace.*

The NP government, too, was ready to start talking. The violence was chipping away at foreign sympathy and the NP knew that as long as the stalemate continued, foreign investment would remain blocked, the economy would not recover, and confidence in the government would continue to wane.

As tension and gloom enveloped the country after Bisho, Mandela said that the country's political leadership had to pull it out of the quagmire. De Klerk responded by offering to hold a summit and Mandela accepted.

Negotiating behind the scenes

During the preparation for the summit, two men emerged who would have an impact on talks almost as profound as that of their respective leaders. On the ANC side was its secretary-general, Cyril Ramaphosa, a man with an education in law and a formidable reputation as a negotiator. The former proponent of black consciousness had risen to prominence in the 1980s after forming the powerful National Union of Mineworkers (NUM), where he had honed his skills as a strategist. His government counterpart, Roelf Meyer, a lawyer, was elected to parliament in 1979 and later served as Minister of Defence. But it was as the NP's chief negotiator during the talks that this quiet and unassuming politician really came into his own.

In September 1992 Ramaphosa and Meyer embarked on 19 days of behind-the-scenes meetings. Less than three weeks later, the government and ANC met – on 26 September – and signed the Record of Understanding. The success of the talks between Meyer and Ramaphosa

AGREEMENTS THRASHED OUT *by Cyril Ramaphosa (left) and Roelf Meyer (right) in bilateral meetings often faced heavy weather at the multiparty negotiations forum.*

encouraged both the ANC and the government, and further bilateral meetings were held between the two men during which they began seriously to negotiate the details of a settlement. Their task was made easier by the development of a personal chemistry between them. They were described by a journalist as 'the most unlikely Tweedledum and Tweedledee of negotiations'.

Said Meyer of his rapport with Ramaphosa: 'We effectively managed to conduct a relationship which was not necessarily based on friendship, but a good working relationship. It resulted in an attitude of which we could say not only that we could resolve problems, but that there was not a problem we could not resolve.'

The Record of Understanding

The deal brokered by the two negotiators provided for the release of more political prisoners; and the government agreed to fence and patrol some of the hostels and to prohibit the carrying and display of dangerous weapons.

The ANC's aim had been to gain the release of people jailed for acts committed in pursuit of liberation, but the right wing was quick to demand that its members should also be covered by the amnesty. So, while the freed prisoners included people such as the ANC's Robert McBride, who had killed three women outside a Durban bar in a car bomb blast, among others who went free was rightwinger Barend Strydom, who had killed seven black people at random one afternoon in Pretoria (see pages 498-9).

The Record of Understanding was the compromise CODESA could not have achieved. But only two parties had reached it – albeit the two with the strongest support. The smaller parties felt left out. The IFP's Buthelezi and the white right wing made it clear that they would not give up without a fight. But others also realised that their best hope lay in trying to limit the power of a future central government and promote the powers of regions, where they had their power bases.

A month after the signing of the Record of Understanding, therefore, a new and rather unlikely alliance emerged: the Concerned South Africans Group (COSAG). Its 19 organisations included the largely black IFP and the KwaZulu Government; the governments of the 'independent homelands' of Ciskei and Bophuthatswana; the ultra-right-wing, white CP; and the *Afrikaner Volksunie* (Afrikaner People's Union, a CP breakaway group).

Ambush in rural Natal

By March 1993, the bilateral talks between the government and the ANC had made real progress towards agreement on several procedural issues. But before full multiparty talks could resume again, 20 more people were slain in the already violence-ravaged KwaZulu/Natal.

Early on the morning of 2 March 1993, a group of gunmen ambushed a *bakkie* (pick-up truck) in the Table Mountain area near Pietermaritzburg, spraying the vehicle with rifle and AK-47 fire. Their victims were six children – three of them the sons of an IFP branch chairman – whose bodies lay sprawled among their bloodied school suitcases in the back of the *bakkie*. Two ANC members were arrested in connection with their deaths.

Within a few days, 14 more people had died in a series of retaliatory attacks. Joining the wide condemnation of the bloodshed, SACP leader Chris Hani told the South African Institute of Race Relations: 'We visited the areas worst hit [by the violence]. It hit us in the face like a cold blizzard when we saw the destruction of villages, the stopping of ordinary life ....'

Three weeks later, Hani, too, was to fall victim to an assailant's bullets (see box).

After an 11-month break in multiparty talks, representatives of 26 parties sat down together on 1 April 1993 at the World Trade Centre, the cavernous convention centre near Jan Smuts Airport outside Johannesburg that had been the venue for CODESA. This was the forum that would become known as the Negotiating Council and would thrash out the final deal for the new order.

The talks were suspended on 10 April as the country reeled from the response to the assassination of Hani. His murder, of which senior CP member Clive Derby-Lewis and Polish immigrant Janusz Waluz were later convicted, prompted an upsurge of violence and a fresh wave of stayaways by black workers. Then, as talks resumed and negotiators began discussing the date for democratic elections, the militant right wing gave vent to its feelings in a demonstration that took everyone by surprise ....

Storming of the World Trade Centre

Early on the morning of 25 June 1993 about 2 000 members of a new right-wing umbrella body, the *Afrikaner Volksfront* (Afrikaner People's Front, or AVF) and the *Afrikaner Weerstandsbeweging* (Afrikaner Resistance Movement, or AWB) – many of them armed – demonstrated outside the gates of the World Trade Centre. They were registering their rejection of the election date and demanding that Afrikaners be given a white *volkstaat*. When they encountered little security outside the centre, they broke through the gates and, ignoring the police, began moving in on the building. Police ordered the doors to be locked.

Then, to howls of approval from the protesters, men in black uniforms drove an armoured car through the plate-glass frontage of the building, and hundreds of protesters

MILITANT RIGHTWINGERS *stormed the talks venue in June 1993. AWB leader Eugene Terre'Blanche (with beard, above) was among those in the vehicle that crashed into the building (right).*

poured into the centre. Delegates, journalists and diplomats barricaded themselves in offices as more than 200 of the protesters – most of them wearing the red-and-black Swastika-style insignia of the AWB – occupied the negotiating chamber. They painted slogans on the walls, smashed computer terminals, name plates and glasses.

Eventually the ebullient rightwingers left the building, having caused damage estimated at R700 000. They gathered outside to light fires and hold *braais* (barbecues), and were told by AWB leader Eugene Terre'Blanche: 'This is the beginning of protest. We don't want war, but we don't want peace under the heel of communism.'

Talks train speeds up

The majority of the parties at the Negotiating Council, however, felt differently, and when they decided early in July that South Africa's first democratic election would be held on 27 April 1994, the ANC's Cyril Ramaphosa said: 'The democracy train is on track to its ultimate destination. This is one train that will not and cannot be derailed.'

Once again, several parties felt that they were being taken for a ride and the representatives of the CP, the IFP and the KwaZulu Government walked out.

The agreement made provision for the process to be followed in arriving at a democratic order, and for the establishment of a mini-government, to be known as the Transitional Executive Council (TEC), on which representatives of all parties to the talks would serve. The central and 'homeland' governments would still run South Africa on a day-to-day basis, but the TEC would keep a close watch on developments, operating like a Cabinet and meeting regularly to discuss South Africa's transition to democracy in the period between the adoption of the interim constitution and the election.

Arguments on consensus

The IFP's Buthelezi, increasingly angered by the failure of COSAG to alter the course of the talks, decided to take his fight to court. At issue was the way in which the Negotiating Council had arrived at the agreement: by 'sufficient consensus', a controversial principle established during CODESA I. The concept was that, if agreement by all parties could not be reached, 'sufficient consensus' would do. Only the NP and the ANC seemed to understand fully the meaning of the term, which they said was that a small minority could not be allowed to overturn broad agreement on a point. Cynics, however, said there was no doubt about its real meaning: there was 'sufficient consensus' whenever the NP and the ANC agreed.

Buthelezi and the KwaZulu Government failed in their attempt to have a court overturn the major agreements of the Negotiating Council – the election date and the go-ahead for negotiators to write a constitution. But a thwarted Buthelezi was soon to prove a dangerous obstacle to the coming election.

Deadline fever

On 26 July 1993 the first draft of the interim constitution was tabled. The CP, which pulled out of the talks because there was no provision for a *volkstaat*, described the proposals as 'the completion of the communist revolution'.

But discussion of the document, and a host of other issues, went ahead without the participation of the CP, the IFP and the KwaZulu Government. The negotiators were working against time to finalise agreements to allow the election to take place on the scheduled date.

In September parliament sat to pass four Bills: to provide for the TEC, and for independent electoral, media and broadcasting commissions charged with ensuring that the election would be free and fair. COSAG members with parliamentary representation argued furiously against the legislation in the House of Assembly, realising that the Bills were paving the way for the acceptance of the interim constitution. They were, however, passed with comfortable majorities.

Bophuthatswana and Ciskei walked out of the talks on 7 October, and on the same day they joined their COSAG partners and the AVF in a new coalition: the Freedom Alliance, a formal political movement committed to 'self-determination', the rejection of a unitary state in favour of a federal state in which regions would determine their own boundaries, and the holding of elections only once a final constitution had been drawn up.

The 'last mile to freedom'

In mid-October it was announced that De Klerk and Mandela had jointly been awarded the Nobel Peace Prize, and congratulatory calls flooded in from around the world. But before the two leaders could travel to Norway to collect the prize in December, there were several months of gruelling negotiations to get through.

On 16 November, Mandela and De Klerk met for an 11th-hour session to try to nail down final agreements before the crucial meeting of political leaders on 17 November to ratify the interim constitution. While they spoke, workmen at the World Trade Centre were laying acres of red carpet and assembling a horseshoe of seats and tables.

As the two leaders completed their four hours of talks, a tired but elated Meyer announced that the two major parties had 'moved forward in tandem on all remaining outstanding constitutional issues'.

The next day, Ramaphosa and Meyer were closeted in an office discussing the finer details of the agreements between Mandela and De Klerk. Negotiators were nervous, remembering the collapse of CODESA II.

At 3pm Ramaphosa and Meyer emerged to announce their package. This included: the repeal of legislation that recognised the independence of the 'homelands'; greater guarantees for an independently selected constitutional court that would be charged with upholding the constitution; Cabinet decision-making by consensus or, if necessary, a simple majority; a deadlock-breaking mechanism for the writing of the final constitution after the election; a single ballot paper for both the central and regional governments (the TEC later changed this to two ballot papers); safeguards on the boundaries of the regions; and approval for regions to adopt their own constitutions.

These agreements were then tabled at the Negotiating Council. The smaller parties felt that, once again, they had been bypassed and were being presented with a *fait accompli* to rubber-stamp. The deadline for the session to reach agreement was already hours old, but the debate raged on, with the government and ANC teams doing their best to convince their partners to go along with the deal.

They succeeded soon after midnight (see box). Finally, in the early hours of 18 November 1993, the bleary-eyed delegates, scores of diplomats and a phalanx of journalists from across the globe gathered to hear the Negotiating Council chairman, Mr Justice Ismael Mohammed, congratulate the negotiators. 'This is the breaking of the dawn for a nation wrestling with its soul. No force can stop or delay our emancipation from our shameful racist past, blighted by the ravages of apartheid .... This is the last mile to freedom.'

On 22 November, the tricameral parliament met in Cape Town for what was believed would be the last time: to ratify the interim constitution, despite angry resistance from members of the Freedom Alliance. (In fact, the parliament sat again just 24 hours before the election to allow for the participation of the IFP.)

Foundation for a new order

In the early hours of 18 November 1993, a group of bleary-eyed negotiators, politicians, secretarial staff and journalists looked at each other in awe. Some wept openly. After months of backbreaking effort, a plenary session of the multiparty negotiating forum at the World Trade Centre in Kempton Park had endorsed the 158-page founding document of democracy for South Africa.

It was a birthday present of a lifetime for the ANC's chief negotiator, Cyril Ramaphosa, whose 41st birthday was celebrated at an impromptu party in the cafeteria half an hour later. The singing of 'Happy Birthday' was led by the NP's Roelf Meyer, with whom Ramaphosa had over the months established a close relationship. A beaming Ramaphosa said: 'The important thing is to wish not me but the country happy birthday because we have given birth to something which will allow us all to build a democracy.'

It was not ideal, it was not what everybody had wanted. But as the 'Weekly Mail' put it: 'After three years of filibustering and compromise, a deal finally emerges, inelegant and flawed ... but our last, best hope for peace.'

The 13-chapter interim constitution provided for:
• A three-tier system of government (national, provincial and local).
• A national president, and deputy presidents from parties polling more than 20 percent in a vote based on proportional representation.
• A multiparty Cabinet comprising representatives of parties with at least five percent support.
• A 400-member national assembly consisting of 200 representatives from the parties' national lists of candidates and 200 from provincial lists in nine regions.
• Nine regional legislatures, each with a premier.
• A senate with 10 representatives from each of the nine provinces.
• The final constitution to be drafted – according to principles laid down by the Negotiating Council – by the national assembly and senate sitting together as the constitutional assembly.
• An independent judiciary.
• A Bill of Rights that can be adjudicated by the country's courts.
• Representation for traditional leaders.
• A single national defence and police force.
• Universal adult franchise.
• Eleven official languages.

THE NEW FLAG *(left) was hoisted at the Castle in Cape Town on the eve of the 1994 election – alongside those of earlier administrators of the Cape.*

The PAC's armed struggle

When the TEC sat for the first time two weeks later, on 7 December 1993, the ink was barely dry on a peace pact that officially ended the PAC's armed struggle. The agreement reached with the NP Government cleared the way for the PAC to take part in the TEC. But it had not come easily....

On 2 March 1993, just days before the planning conference for the Negotiating Council was due to begin, Law and Order Minister Hernus Kriel led a government delegation to Gaborone, the capital of Botswana, for talks with the PAC's Willie Seriti and the commandants of the organisation's armed wing, the Azanian People's Liberation Army (APLA). The main topic was the armed struggle.

During the talks, Romero Daniels, APLA's chief political commissar, told journalist Neil Lewis: 'We will go on until the political objectives of the PAC are realised.' APLA's 'legitimate' targets, he said, were 'the colonial settler system and the symbols thereof', such as the South African Police and the South African Defence Force (SADF). 'Children, women and so on, they are not our target really because we are attacking those who defend the system itself .... So we can't take a child here or a woman there who has no relevance whatsoever to the status quo.'

However, an alarming number of attacks on 'soft' targets – including murders of white families on remote farms and the mowing down of patrons at a number of eastern Cape hotels and restaurants by gunmen – were being attributed to APLA, and the NP said it would not support the PAC's attendance at the multiparty negotiations. When the talks started on 1 April 1993, the PAC took part in spite of the government's stand.

Less than two months later, on 25 May, about 200 PAC members, including most of the national executive, were arrested by police in a countrywide pre-dawn swoop ordered by Kriel. Criticism rained on the government, and not just from the PAC. The government justified its action by saying one could not negotiate and conduct an armed struggle at the same time, but the ANC's Ramaphosa responded that it was unacceptable that the government could negotiate and simultaneously act as 'our jailers'.

Kriel was summoned to the World Trade Centre to account for his decision, the first time a Cabinet Minister had had to explain his actions to a body outside parliament. The arrests were defended by President De Klerk, who said: 'As important as negotiations may be, we must also bring murder and violence to an end.'

With the talks in jeopardy, the PAC and the government held a series of bruising meetings to thrash out a solution to the crisis. The PAC decided to return to the talks, but tension between it and the government continued. At the end of June, after the publication of an interview with APLA commander Sabelo Phama calling for an intensification of the armed struggle, the government terminated its bilateral talks with the PAC and said it would ask the Negotiating Council to limit PAC involvement in the talks.

Death at prayer

Then, on Sunday 25 July, in the middle of evening service, gunmen burst into St James Church in Kenilworth, Cape Town, lobbing grenades and firing automatic rifles. Two minutes later the church was a shambles, with pews splintered, bodies slumped on the floor, limbs shattered and blood soaking into the carpet. Eleven people, including two children, died and police reported 55 were injured.

Amid the general outcry over the attack, newspapers received calls from men claiming to be APLA members who had been responsible for the deaths.

Barely a month later, during a militant protest by school pupils in the black Cape Town township of Guguletu, a white American student, Amy Biehl, who was giving friends a lift home, had her car stopped and stoned by a hostile crowd of youths. When she got out of the car to flee, she was chased and hacked to death. The pupils' protest had been called by the PAC's student wing, the Pan-Africanist Students' Organisation (PASO), and members were widely thought to be responsible for the killing.

The PAC officially denied responsibility for both attacks, but it was coming under increasing pressure at home and abroad to end the armed struggle.

A bungled raid

In October, the government and APLA agreed to meet to discuss the violence, but before the meeting took place the South African Defence Force (SADF) raided what was said to be an APLA 'safe house' in Umtata, capital of Transkei. All five occupants were killed. But instead of battle-hardened cadres, they turned out to be two children aged 12, and three teenagers. Three were the children of the owner of the house, PAC member Sicelo Mpendulo.

Defence Minister Kobie Coetsee said the objective of the raid, to disrupt APLA plans for more attacks in South Africa, had been achieved. Asked why children had been shot, he said those killed 'appeared in the middle of the night to be grown up'.

The raid, believed to have been a massive blunder on the part of the security forces, was widely condemned. The PAC said it would continue to take part in the talks at the World Trade Centre, but would continue its armed struggle 'just like the regime'.

In fact, breakthrough was around the corner. Early in November, Kriel met APLA's Phama in Harare, where broad agreement was reached on the need for a peace pact. In Pretoria on 5 November 1993 the government and the PAC formally agreed to begin work immediately towards implementing their pact on 'a moratorium on violence'.

The end of the sanctions era

Among the many implications of the progress at negotiations was the United Nations (UN) decision to lift non-mandatory sanctions on 8 October 1993 and its ban on oil exports in December. US sanctions were ended on 23 November 1993 when President Bill Clinton signed the South Africa Democratic Transition Support Act.

Moves to ease the economic isolation of South Africa started soon after De Klerk announced Mandela's release in February 1990. The first major breakthrough came in August 1991, when South Africa, while still in the midst of an effective standstill on a large portion of its foreign debt, reaccessed the international capital markets with a DM400-million eurobond issue. But as the government

THE LABOUR MOVEMENT *kept up the pressure on the NP Government with massive demonstrations, such as this one in Cape Town in 1992 against value added tax.*

was completing negotiations with a Swiss bank for a loan, CODESA II collapsed and the Boipatong massacre took place, an event that reverberated through the world's banking halls. The Swiss bank pulled out of the negotiations; the financial rand collapsed overnight; the Johannesburg Stock Exchange (JSE), which had been showing signs of life, moved downwards; tourists and potential investors by the thousands cancelled visits.

The financial markets were further weakened when the ANC, with the cooperation of COSATU, launched the 'rolling mass action' campaign in mid-1993 with industrial action as its key weapon. The strike in the wake of the Boipatong massacre brought the economy to a virtual halt. The same political anger from ANC supporters, with a concomitant reaction from the international financial markets, followed the murder of the SACP's Chris Hani.

Throughout the negotiating period, the ANC and COSATU used the strike weapon to place direct and indirect pressure on the NP as well as the 'homelands'. Their intention was to get business to put pressure on the government to avoid strike action. COSATU was also active in resisting government efforts to increase value added tax (VAT) unilaterally in November 1991, and again to resist fuel price increases in 1993. Its message was that the government no longer owned the process and labour had to be consulted.

The lifting of the remaining trade embargoes was not the only good news for the economy in 1993. After being in deep recession for four-and-a-half years as a result of sanctions and one of the worst droughts to ravage the country, the economy started to mend in the summer of 1992-93 with good agricultural harvests.

The average rate of growth in the gross domestic product for 1993 had moved back into a positive 1,2 percent. The end of 1993 also saw a recovery in the gold price, which briefly pushed past the $400 an ounce mark for the first time in three years. With an election in sight, international investors started to look to the potential of the JSE, and the two factors combined to push the JSE to repeated new records. On 3 January 1993 the market capitalisation of shares listed on the JSE was R501-billion – a year later it was R737-billion.

In August 1993, the National Econonic Forum met, bringing together representatives of business, labour and government. The forum started to contribute to a better understanding of problems almost immediately. More and more senior ANC spokesmen publicly accepted the need to adopt growth policies through disciplined fiscal and monetary policies, while business started to accept the need for the ANC's Reconstruction and Development Programme, which it unveiled during its election campaign and which was later endorsed as official policy by the new government.

However, international financial markets and potential foreign investors continued to treat the country with caution because of the turmoil of the election run-up and the lack of clarity on fiscal and monetary policy from the ANC, which only three years earlier had been vociferous in its support of socialist principles, including nationalisation.

Last gasp of the 'homelands'

As the election campaign went into full swing at the beginning of 1994, 'homeland' residents finally regained their South African citizenship on 1 January. The territories would be reincorporated on the day of the election.

The administrations of two of the 'independent homelands' – Ciskei and Bophuthatswana – were still holding out against reincorporation, but they were not counting on the fact that their own civil servants would join the clamour to become part of the new dispensation.

Early in January, Ciskei's leader Brigadier Oupa Gqozo broke with the Freedom Alliance and announced that his 'homeland' would take its seat in the TEC because it had been 'forced' to do so to protect the rights of Ciskei's citizens. The ANC-dominated TEC, he said, was making decisions that directly affected Ciskei, and he feared that the 2 000 members of the Ciskei Defence Force would become unemployed if he did not join the transition process.

The Government of Bophuthatswana, which had been targeted for mass action by the ANC, collapsed in March 1994 to cheers from masses of ANC supporters, but the three days of arson, looting and bloodshed that accompanied the event sent jitters through South Africa.

A WELTER OF LOOTING, *arson and bloodshed accompanied the collapse of the Bophuthatswana Government in mid-March 1994, and scenes such as this prompted many whites to stockpile emergency rations in the run-up to the national election.*

The TEC had suspended a R216-million loan to Bophuthatswana, sparking off tension between the 'homeland' government and its civil service and army, who feared for their jobs and pensions if the territory was not reincorporated. By late February about 1 000 people, mainly nurses and health care workers, were on strike, to be joined in early March by other civil servants and retailers.

At a crisis meeting on 7 March the Bophuthatswana Cabinet decided against registering for the election, and the immediate response was an outbreak of rioting in Mafikeng. As rioting spread, a defiant Lucas Mangope, leader of the 'homeland', announced he would fight reincorporation 'even if I am left with only 50 troops'.

But by 10 March he had disappeared and newspapers speculated that he had fled. There was looting and mayhem as thousands of jubilant people took to the streets, saying they had toppled him. Street battles raged between security forces and rioters in Mafikeng and the capital, Mmabatho, and many police deserted their posts to join the people, waving ANC flags and dancing in the streets.

By the end of the next day, newspapers estimated between 45 and 70 people had been killed in clashes and more than 300 wounded. Among the dead were three white AWB members from a contingent of armed right-wingers who had rushed in to try to bolster the 'homeland' administration, and three blacks apparently shot by roving whites in Mafikeng's main street.

Mangope announced that he would recommend that his government take part in the election, but it was too late. The South African Government and the TEC, which had sent in the SADF during the riots to defend the South African embassy, replaced Mangope with two administrators. They soon defused tension by announcing that civil servants' salaries, pensions and privileges were guaranteed.

Meanwhile, damage of more than R200-million had been caused to buildings, cars and private property. Retailers were estimated to have lost stock worth R40-million.

In Ciskei in early March, tensions similar to those in Bophuthatswana were rising, with prison warders striking and civil servants warning they might turn to 'Bophuthatswana-style' civil disobedience if their pensions were not paid out before reincorporation.

Police took 42 people hostage at the Bisho police college, prompting the Ciskei Government to ask officially for South African assistance to maintain control. Again the TEC responded by ordering the replacement of Gqozo by two administrators.

The SADF also took control of key points in the Lebowa 'homeland' to prevent damage and looting as thousands of civil servants continued a strike.

As one newspaper commentator put it on 24 March: 'Apartheid chickens are coming home to roost with a vengeance as one squalid and despotic homeland fiefdom after another crashes in the dust and the extent and consequences of maladministration, corruption and eccentric rule become more evident .... But by far the greatest problem is presented by KwaZulu.'

The 'KwaZulu crisis'

Days after the signing of the Record of Understanding between the government and the ANC in September 1992, the IFP's Buthelezi told 10 000 people at a Shaka Day rally that the agreement was an attempt 'to wipe us off the face of the earth as Zulus'. He warned that any attempt in terms of the 'Understanding' to disarm the Zulus and fence hostels would be defied. He added: 'President De Klerk signed an agreement with the ANC while knowing full well that I would oppose it vehemently – and in doing so Mr De Klerk has made a fundamental mistake .... I am appalled and disgusted and so is the IFP and the KwaZulu Government ....'

In the event, the hostels were not fenced, and when Buthelezi led huge marches with thousands of people brandishing traditional weapons, they were not prosecuted. However, when the IFP announced that it would not rejoin the talks unless the ANC's armed wing was disbanded, both the ANC and the government made it clear that, while they wanted the IFP to join the negotiations, any decision by parties to stay away was up to them.

As negotiations dragged on to try to bring the Freedom Alliance into the election, the Zulu monarch entered the fray. On 16 December 1993, the anniversary of the defeat of the Zulus at the Battle of Blood River (see pages 118-9), King Goodwill Zwelithini aligned himself with Buthelezi, telling 10 000 subjects to defend KwaZulu 'with their lives'. In mid-February, in what one commentator described as an obstacle that 'appears to render peaceful elections near impossible', the king demanded that KwaZulu/Natal be declared an independent sovereign state.

Two weeks later, on 1 March, De Klerk pleaded with parties considering secession or violence 'to turn back before it is too late'. Buthelezi responded the next day that he wanted a Zulu kingdom separate from the rest of South Africa. He added, ominously, that the KwaZulu Government could not be held responsible for the Zulu nation's anger if elections proceeded without this demand being met.

When the Government of Bophuthatswana collapsed in mid-March, commentators predicted it could be a dress-rehearsal for far greater confrontation in KwaZulu/Natal. As if to underline the warning, there were clashes that weekend between ANC and IFP supporters in Umlazi, near Durban, that left five people dead. Just 40 days before the election, newspaper headlines reflected the general gloom: 'Hope for free and fair Natal poll fading' ... 'Confrontation looms' ... 'KwaZulu crisis'.

On 24 March, the ANC prepared to launch 'rolling mass action' in the territory as the IFP placed all its strongholds in Natal on alert. Violence, always simmering, escalated with the deaths of 16 people and the torching of 40 houses.

De Klerk met Mandela in Pretoria for urgent discussions about the volatile situation. More than 2 000 public servants, pupils and traditional leaders marched through the streets of Ulundi in support of the IFP.

Then came Bloody Monday....

Clashes in Johannesburg's streets

Tens of thousands of people – estimates ranged from 20 000 to 50 000 – marched through the streets of Johannesburg on 28 March 1994. Conspicuously armed with traditional weapons, they had come to support the Zulu King's call for sovereignty.

But, just before midday, when a large part of the crowd was outside the ANC headquarters, there was a clash between marchers and ANC security guards. Shots were fired, and police reported eight people killed. There were clashes elsewhere in the city and by the end of the day at least 53 people were dead – 18 of them killed in the city centre – and hospitals had treated more than 250 injured. Among the dead were two policemen and a traffic officer.

In spite of the government declaring unrest areas in parts of the Transvaal and a state of emergency in the whole of KwaZulu/Natal, more than 300 people died nationwide in the next three weeks.

In a bid to end the stalemate, De Klerk, Mandela and Buthelezi held a peace summit, but Buthelezi's insistence on delaying the election was irreconcilable with Mandela's position that the April date was 'sacrosanct'. A seven-man team of international mediators, including the USA's Henry Kissinger and Britain's Lord Carrington, flew in –

and almost as swiftly flew out again as the parties failed to agree on the terms of reference. They left behind Kenyan academic Professor Washington Jalang'o Okumu, who held private talks with Buthelezi.

A last-ditch plan was made for a second summit with the IFP. Seldom in South African history, political studies lecturer Professor David Welsh wrote of Buthelezi, had so many hopes and fears been concentrated so largely on one man of 'conspicuously volatile temperament'.

De Klerk, Mandela and Buthelezi emerged from the second summit – just a week before the election – wreathed in smiles: the IFP would take part in the poll. De Klerk said: 'This agreement, I believe, removes one of the last main causes for tension and violence .... I thank God that we have reached agreement at this late stage.'

Shares on the JSE rocketed and there was jubilation in Ulundi, capital of KwaZulu, as thousands of IFP supporters gave Buthelezi a hero's welcome. On 25 April, a mere 24 hours before South Africans went to the polls (special votes were cast on 26 April), parliament met to amend the interim constitution to give effect to the agreement that had brought the IFP in: the recognition of the kingdom of KwaZulu and the protection of the institution of the Zulu monarch, his status and his constitutional role.

On the ground, remarkably, there was peace. Two people died in KwaZulu/Natal in the three days after the IFP's registration to vote, compared with 54 the previous week and about 220 in the first two weeks of April.

The election was on track.

Right-wing terror campaign

The threat of bloody insurrection in KwaZulu/Natal had been averted, but the ultra-right wing would make one more attempt to sabotage the election ....

On Sunday, 24 April, a 70-90kg car bomb exploded in central Johannesburg, near the headquarters of the ANC and PAC, killing nine people. One of the dead was Susan

INKATHA'S CHIEF *Mangosuthu Buthelezi (with glasses) and King Goodwill Zwelithini (to the left) lead a huge Zulu rally.*

Keane, an ANC election candidate. A witness said that moments before the blast he had seen two white men running down the street, one carrying something under his jersey.

Six polling stations around the country were bombed on that same day, and more blasts went off the next day, the eve of the election. The toll from the two-day bombing spree attributed to ultra-rightwingers reached 21 dead and more than 170 injured.

This was not the only violence in the run-up to the poll. At the end of March, the Human Rights Commission reported that election-related violence had claimed the lives of 111 people and left 402 injured between 10 and 28 March. The casualty rate had been exacerbated by riots by prisoners who were demanding the franchise (all except those convicted of murder, rape and robbery were eventually permitted to vote) and by the casualties during the 'Bloody Monday' march in Johannesburg.

Apart from the ever-present violence, the election campaign was characterised by its hectic pace, mass rallies around the country, accusations of intolerance as opponents waged power battles – and the panic stockpiling of provisions by a number of people who feared that the country would be engulfed by the kind of chaos that had accompanied the fall of Bophuthatswana.

Just 20 minutes after the polls opened on 26 April for special votes, a powerful car bomb exploded in the international departures area at Jan Smuts Airport, injuring 13 people and causing structural damage to the building. A white man had been seen running from a vehicle which started to smoke and then exploded.

Police swooped on rightwingers, arresting more than 30 thought to be linked to the sabotage campaign.

Peace 'breaks out'

The airport blast was to be the last major, violent incident before – as newspapers put it – peace broke out. After years of bloody mayhem, South Africa entered an unprecedented – and unexpected – period of peace, patience and goodwill as nearly 20-million people cast their votes in the country's first democratic election (see box).

After four days of voting, and innumerable problems during the counting process, Judge Johann Kriegler, head of the Independent Electoral Commission (IEC), finally announced at 2pm on 6 May that the election had been 'substantially free and fair'.

The ANC had won 62,65 percent of the votes, giving it 252 seats in the 400-seat National Assembly, but not the two-thirds majority that would have allowed it to rewrite

---

The 1994 election: South Africa's 'mission impossible'

'I am very happy this day has come,' said Miriam Mqomboti, a 93-year-old woman who came to cast her vote on 26 April 1994 at a polling station at Guguletu, an African suburb of Cape Town. 'I never thought it could happen here. I came to Cape Town from Transkei when I was 18 and after this long time, I thought I would never be able to vote.'

It was the first day of voting, set aside for the elderly and the infirm, and for South Africans abroad. Although the queues were long, spirits were high. But the problems that were to dog the rest of the election had already begun to surface as ballot papers ran short and some polling stations failed to open ....

Judge Johann Kriegler, head of the Independent Electoral Commission (IEC) told journalists after the election: 'I had been told that you couldn't organise an election in less than a year – preferably two. And that to try to run an election without a voters' roll was very close to lunacy.'

But he and his fellow commissioners – along with more than 200 000 specially employed staff – tackled the task in just four months. The IEC had been set up in December 1993 to

ensure that the April election would be 'substantially free and fair' – and the task proved as difficult as had been predicted.

No one knew how many potential voters there were (the IEC 'guesstimated' there were 22,7-million who would qualify), nor how they were distributed around the country. Millions did not even have adequate identity documents and the majority had never voted before. Some were illiterate. Some saw witchcraft in the plan to mark their hands with invisible ink to indicate they had voted. Some lived in areas so remote they were unreached by roads.

Negotiators had agreed only two months before the election to allow two ballot papers – one for the national legislature and one for regional representation. Then, just a week before polling, the IEC had to find an extra 700 polling stations in Kwa-Zulu/Natal to accommodate the IFP's late decision to take part – and had to add stickers with the party's name, logo and a colour picture of its leader to the 80-million ballot papers.

If the IEC workers, the election monitors and local and international observers were feverishly busy, so

were the parties. Only five of the 28 parties taking part had previous electioneering experience, but even they had never fought an election on the basis of proportional representation, and certainly not one of this size.

The first day of voting for most of the population dawned on 27 April, and voters came in their millions. Then they waited – and waited. Queues snaked around polling stations, and then around again as people stood for hours – in some cases all day – in hot sunshine in most of the country. In the western Cape they stood in the rain. As one analyst said, it was the day on which millions of South Africans learned to do something for the first time – black South Africans learnt what whites already knew: how to vote; white South Africans learnt what blacks already knew: how to wait.

Problems abounded. The IFP stickers had not arrived at all the polling stations. At some stations the ballot papers did not arrive in time. Others closed early when they ran out of voting material. Some failed to open.

At the end of the day, IEC officials did a rethink. Voting hours were extended, and the army was called in to the constitution single-handedly. The NP had won 20,4 percent (82 seats), entitling it to the appointment of a vice-president in the five-year post-election government, and had taken the Western Cape region. Third was the IFP (10,5 percent, or 43 seats), which had also gained the majority in KwaZulu/Natal.

Fourth was the Freedom Front (FF) – a party formed a scant two months earlier by General Constand Viljoen, a former SADF chief and leader of the AVF, who defied many of his right-wing colleagues by registering for the election. A clause in the interim constitution provided for future negotiations if there was proof at the poll of 'substantial support' for a *volkstaat*. The FF polled 424 555 votes (2,2 percent), giving it nine seats in parliament.

Among the 'casualties' of the election were the liberal Democratic Party (DP), which polled only 1,73 percent (seven seats), and the PAC with 1,25 percent (five seats). The remaining two seats went to the African Christian Democratic Party, which received 0,5 percent of the vote.

Speaking at a victory celebration at the ANC's election headquarters in Johannesburg, Nelson Mandela, the man who had emerged from prison to lead his party to power, said: 'I regard it as the highest honour to lead the ANC at this moment in history. To the people of South Africa and the

world who are watching ... this is a joyous night for the human spirit. This is your victory too .... You have shown such a calm, patient determination to reclaim this country as your own.'

Coming in from the cold

In the euphoric days after the installation of the new government, pledges of financial aid came flooding in and, with astonishing rapidity, South Africa was formally welcomed back in the international community. On 25 May 1994, the Republic became the 53rd member of the Organisation of African Unity. The country also joined the Non-Aligned Movement and in June was readmitted to the Commonwealth after an absence of more than 30 years. The UN lifted its remaining embargo (on arms) and the country took up the seat at the world body it had vacated more than 20 years earlier.

Tough times lay ahead, but now there was a chance for South Africa to become a beacon of hope for the continent. As Mandela said at his inauguration: 'There is no easy walk to freedom. We know it well that none of us acting alone can achieve success. We must, therefore, act together as a united people, for national reconciliation, for nation building, for the birth of a new world.'

A DAY OF PEACE *dawned as millions of South Africans queued patiently to make their mark in the country's first all-inclusive election.*

deliver a further 5,6-million newly printed ballot papers to remote areas. Polling officers were told to be flexible: if no official stamps were available, officials should sign the ballots; if the invisible ink ran out, they should sign the voters' identity documents; if there were no more ballot boxes, full boxes could be emptied into post office bags. President De Klerk placed virtually the entire Air Force at the disposal of the IEC.

Over most of the country the next day's balloting was considerably quieter, but in six former 'homelands' the voting had to be extended for another day.

And the problems did not end when voting stopped. For days South Africa held its breath as ballot boxes

were ferried from 9 000 polling stations to around 700 central counting stations. Heads down and fingers flying, thousands of counting officers got busy. But in several places counting was delayed by mix-ups with ballot boxes, a strike by counters for more pay, and confusion over who was employed to count. Results began trickling through on 1 May, but four major counting centres were way behind schedule, and accusations were flying of major fraud and irregularities.

Already battling to keep its date with parliament, which was due to elect the new president on 6 May, the hapless IEC discovered early on 4 May that a mysterious trend was developing – votes for the NP, the IFP and the

FF were progressively increasing by thousands. Problems had arisen with the IEC's computer system. Now a backup system had to be used to reflect accurate tallies – and it was much slower. Parliament would have to wait until 9 May – a nailbiting 24 hours before the inauguration ceremony – to elect the president.

The major parties met behind the scenes to iron out the disputes, which were particularly heated in KwaZulu/Natal. Finally, almost a week after voting had ended, a tired Judge Kriegler appeared on television to announce the outcome. Afterwards, he quipped: 'We said at the start it was mission impossible, and we were just too dumb to realise it. But you know what? It worked.'

Glossary

activist One who takes direct and often militant action to achieve an end, especially a social or political one.

African Specifically, a member or descendant of any of the peoples of Africa. (Note that, in order to avoid confusion, 'African' in this book means a Bantu-language speaker.)

Africanism/Africanist philosophy Preaches that blacks should organise together to promote their interests. The philosophy has taken several forms since the 1850s, when it was first propounded by Xhosa missionary Tiyo Soga (p 151). The doctrine was adopted at the turn of the century by independent African churches (p 285), in the late 1940s by the CYL (p 364), at the end of the 1950s by the PAC (p 399) and in the 1970s by the black consciousness movement (p 447).

African League of Rights (ALR) Marxist-run political body founded in 1929 to serve as a popular front for black liberation (p 342).

African Mineworkers' Union (AMWU) Labour union formed in 1941 to campaign against the migrant labour system and to fight for improved working conditions for African miners (p 357).

African National Congress (ANC) Oldest surviving political organisation in South Africa, it was founded in 1912 as the South African Native National Congress (SANNC) and renamed in 1923. Initially a moderate, even conservative organisation, it opted for an armed struggle against the NP regime after being banned in 1960. Unbanned in 1990, it came to power after the 1994 election.

African People's (formerly Political) Organisation (APO) Organisation for middle-class coloured people, founded in 1902 to strive for equality with whites. By 1912 the largest black political movement in the country (p 276).

African Resistance Movement (ARM) 1960s sabotage group formed by a small number of white activists. Its best-known member was John Harris, hanged in 1965 for detonating a bomb at Johannesburg station (p 415).

Afrikaanse Taal en Kultuur Vereniging (ATKV) Language and Cultural Association established by the Broederbond to promote the Afrikaans language and culture (p 335).

Afrikaner White native of South Africa whose mother tongue is Afrikaans.

Afrikaner Bond 'League of Afrikaners'; Cape colonial political organisation between 1880 and 1911 that originally sought to promote Afrikaner interests but later broadened its base in order to attract coloured and African supporters.

Afrikaner Broederbond 'Afrikaner Brotherhood'; highly influential but exclusively Afrikaner secret society formed in 1918. It did most to secure and maintain Afrikaner control in important areas of government, culture, finance and industry (p 334).

Afrikaner Party Small OFS-based party formed in 1940 after Barry Hertzog's split with the HNP. It moved closer to the HNP after Hertzog's death in 1942 and helped the Nationalists win the 1948 general election.

Afrikaner Volksfront (AVF) 'People's Front';

founded in 1993, it was an umbrella body for several right-wing groups.

Afrikaner Volkswag 'People's Watch'; a think-tank for far-right groups, founded in 1982 by Professor Carel Boshoff, son-in-law of former Prime Minister Hendrik Verwoerd.

Afrikaner Weerstandsbeweging (AWB) 'Resistance Movement'; formed in the 1970s as a paramilitary ultra-right-wing organisation striving for a Boer state based on the old Afrikaner republics (pp 498-9).

agterryer Attendant (on horseback), (coloured) batman, mounted servant, musket-bearer, who accompanied Boers on their journeys or into battle (p 246).

AK-47 Kalashnikov rifle, the standard infantry weapon of former Eastern bloc countries; popular with guerrilla movements.

All-African Convention (AAC) Established in 1935 by prominent African and coloured politicians in a vain bid to halt the passage of the so-called 'Hertzog Bills' (p 338). Some of its members later helped to establish the Non-European Unity Movement (NEUM).

All-African People's Democratic Union (AAPDU) Marxist political alliance formed in 1959 by an African group in the NEUM; its leaders were driven into exile or imprisoned after a government crackdown in 1960.

alluvial diggings Diggings for diamonds or gold in the alluvium of mud, silt and sand deposited by flowing water on flood plains, in river beds and in estuaries.

amabutho System in which active northern Nguni men were called up on an age-grade basis for military service, to control elephant hunting in the chiefdom or to engage in cattle-raiding; the Zulu army was built upon this system (pp 81, 85).

Amafelandawonye or **Amafela** 'The Diehards'; women's protest movement that took root in the Herschel district, eastern Cape, in the 1920s (p 324).

amakhanda Zulu royal homesteads (p 81).

amandla 'Power'; a slogan shouted while raising a clenched fist.

amaqabane Comrades; radical, young and often undisciplined township activists with loose ties to the UDF and ANC. The storm-troopers of township protest in the 1980s, they were blamed by the state for the murders of government representatives such as policemen and community councillors.

Andries-Ohrigstad see Ohrigstad.

anglicisation Part of Alfred Milner's strategy to 'pacify' the Boers of the Transvaal and OFS after 1902 by re-educating their children through the medium of English (p 269).

apartheid Literally 'separateness, distinctness'; 'racial' separation at all levels; official NP Government policy from 1948 until the early 1990s (p 376).

Arme Blanke Verbond 'Poor White Alliance'; founded in 1917 to improve the lot of poor whites (p 332).

armed struggle Policy of guerrilla warfare aimed at attaining political power.

ARMSCOR The Armaments Corporation of South Africa; established in 1964 to reduce dependence on overseas weapons suppliers.

asina 'mali 'We have no money'; slogan used in 1950s African bus boycott (p 391).

assegai Stabbing spear which the Zulu under Shaka made a potent weapon of war.

astrolabe Navigational instrument consisting of a graduated circular disc with a movable sighting device, used to measure the altitude of stars and planets.

Australopithecus africanus Southern ape of Africa; inhabited eastern and southern Africa between 1- and 3-million years ago (p 17).

Australopithecus robustus Robust southern ape, seemingly bigger-toothed and more heavily built than *A. africanus* (p 16).

Azania Ancient name for east African coast; favoured by black consciousness-supporting groups such as AZAPO as a new name for a 'liberated' South Africa.

Azanian Confederation of Trade Unions (AZACTU) An umbrella organisation of trade unions supporting the principles of black consciousness. It was formed in 1984. In 1986 it merged with the Council of Unions of South Africa (CUSA) to form the National Council of Trade Unions (NACTU).

Azanian People's Liberation Army (APLA) In 1968 it succeeded *Poqo* as the armed wing of the PAC. It rose to prominence in the 1990s.

Azanian People's Organisation (AZAPO) Black-consciousness organisation founded in 1978 to spread the idea of a future socialist republic of Azania to the masses. It found the going tough, however, and its main supporters appeared to be small pockets of black intellectuals and urban petite bourgeoisie.

Azanian Students' Movement (AZASM) Student wing of AZAPO.

azikwelwa 'We will not ride'; slogan used by African bus boycotters in the 1950s (p 391).

baasskap Literally 'mastership, domination' (as of a master over his servant). In the South African context it means the total domination of whites over blacks (p 370).

bakkie Light truck.

balance of payments Figures showing the balance between a nation's earnings from abroad and its spending abroad. If the value of imports exceeds that of exports, a deficit balance results; if exports are worth more than imports, there is a surplus balance.

Bambatha rebellion Short-lived uprising by dissident Zulu against the imposition of a £1 poll tax promulgated by the Natal authorities in 1905 to push more Africans into wage labour. The rebels, led by the Zondi chief, Bambatha, were routed by the Natal army early in 1906 (p 286).

bandolier Soldier's broad shoulder belt with small pockets or loops for cartridges (p 116).

Bantu Literally 'people'; term used by pre-1976 NP Governments to describe the country's African population. Anthropologists still use the word to describe the language of those African people who migrated southwards from central Africa hundreds of years ago (pp 62-7).

Bantustan Area for Africans which was to be given self-government and eventual independence. A vogue word during the Verwoerdian era, it was later scrapped from the Nationalist vocabulary in favour of 'homeland' or 'self-governing state'.

Basutoland Region between the Orange and Caledon rivers in which Moshoeshoe built up his Sotho kingdom; annexed by the British in 1868; became the independent state of Lesotho in 1966.

Bechuanaland Tswana settlement area caught up in the political power-play of the British, Boers and Germans in the 1880s. The British in 1885 divided the territory into Bechuanaland Protectorate (Botswana since 1966) and the colony of British Bechuanaland (p 220), which became part of the Cape.

bittereinder 'Die-hard' or 'bitter-ender'; used in the South African War to describe a Boer soldier who chose to continue fighting the British even when it became apparent that all was lost (p 259) (*see also* hensopper).

black Person whose skin colour is not white. However, apartheid ideology refers only to Africans as 'blacks', and coloured, Indian and African people together as 'non-whites'. This book uses mainly the first definition.

Black Circuit Name given to the Circuit Court of 1812 because of the way it went about collecting evidence of brutality by white colonists against their black servants.

black consciousness Ideology developed primarily by black students after 1968 that blacks (African, Indian and coloured) had to liberate themselves psychologically from the effects of institutionalised racism and white liberalism. This implied a rejection of all 'white' values and the inculcation of a positive 'black' world view (p 447).

'black-on-black' violence Used mainly by the authorities to describe violence against African 'collaborators' by black opponents of government policy and among supporters of different political groupings (p 487).

Black People's Convention (BPC) Umbrella body set up in 1972 to coordinate the activities of adherents of black consciousness.

black spot Land settled or owned by Africans and surrounded by or contiguous with predominantly 'white' residential, industrial or agricultural areas; in terms of 'grand' apartheid, 'black' spots had to be eliminated (p 378).

'black threat' election *see* swart gevaar election.

Blanke Bevrydingsbeweging (BBB) Extreme right-wing group founded by Professor Johan Schabort. Its policies included 'repatriation' of all Africans to their 'homelands'; the expulsion of Jews from South Africa and the return of Indians to India (pp 498-9).

Blanke Volkstaat Party Far-right party founded by Eugene Terre'Blanche in 1979.

Blanke Vryheidsbeweging (BVB) Far-right organisation formed in 1989 by dissident members of the AWB following a rumpus over Eugene Terre'Blanche's alleged relationship with journalist Jani Allen (pp 498-9).

Bloemfontein Conference Negotiations between Kruger and Milner in 1899 in an effort to prevent war between Britain and the SAR.

Bloemfontein Convention Agreement between the British and the Boers in 1854, enabling the latter to establish a republic between the Orange and Vaal rivers (p 143).

Boer 'Farmer'; descendant of any of the Dutch or Huguenot colonists who settled in southern Africa. The word is often used dis-

paragingly in referring to Afrikaners.

Boeren Beschermings Vereniging 'Farmers' Protection Society'; established in 1878 to protect the interest of Dutch-speaking farmers. It merged with the *Afrikaner Bond* in 1883 (p 197).

Boerestaat Party Far-right party founded by Robert van Tonder and Piet 'Skiet' Rudolph in 1988 (pp 498-9).

Boipatong 'Place of shelter'; African township established in 1955 near Vanderbijlpark, Transvaal.

Bondelswarts Small chiefdom of Nama origin settled at Warmbad in South West Africa. It rebelled against the Union in 1922 and the Smuts Government used aircraft to subdue the rebels (p 463).

Bophelong African township established in 1949 near Vanderbijlpark, Transvaal.

Bophuthatswana see 'homeland'.

Bosjesmans hottentotten Term used by the early Dutch settlers at the Cape to describe the indigenous population (pp 20-5).

bride-wealth (lobola) Money, property or services given by a prospective bridegroom to the father of his bride in order to establish his marital rights (p 64).

British Indian Association (BIA) Transvaal-based organisation of Indians established by Mohandas Gandhi in the early 1900s to fight proposed evictions of Indian traders from 'white' business centres (p 275).

British Kaffraria That part of the eastern Cape between the Keiskamma and Kei rivers annexed in 1847 and administered separately from the Colony under the Governor as High Commissioner (p 133). In 1866 it was incorporated into the Cape Colony.

Broederbond see Afrikaner Broederbond.

broedertwis Disagreement between brothers; a fraternal quarrel (p 296).

Bulhoek massacre In 1921 police were sent to evict members of a religious sect, the Israelites, from government land near Queenstown; they opened fire, killing 183 (p 326).

Bureau for State Security (BOSS) Security police bureau established in 1969 by John Vorster and Hendrik van den Bergh, who became its head. It was disbanded and replaced by the National Intelligence Service after Vorster's fall from grace in 1978.

burgher Dutch term meaning citizen.

bushveld Area of low altitude in northeastern Transvaal, having scrub vegetation. Also known as the lowveld.

Butha Buthe Literally 'place of lying down'; Moshoeshoe established his first fortified stronghold atop this mountain.

bywoner Tenant farmer. The term was applied in the late 19th and early 20th centuries to a poor white sharecropper employed by another white farmer (pp 197, 332).

cadre A nucleus of trained personnel, especially in a military or political organisation, around which a larger organisation can be built and trained.

Caledon Square Block containing the divisional headquarters of the police and magistrates' courts in central Cape Town.

Camdeboo Region in the Karoo near Graaff-Reinet which was one of the first places in the interior to be settled by colonists.

Cape Action League Strongly socialist group aligned to the New Unity Movement. Made up mainly of radical middle-class members

of the coloured community, it strove for a South Africa under a working-class leadership. By the 1990s it had been swallowed up by Workers for a Socialist Azania.

Cape Areas Housing Action Committee United Democratic Front-aligned umbrella body of civic organisations active in coloured and African townships in the 1980s.

Cape Native Convention Cape branch of the South African Native Convention, established by J T Jabavu in 1909 to promote Africans' interests after the terms of Union had become known (p 283).

Cape of Good Hope Cape south of Cape Town and next to Cape Point, named by Portuguese explorers in the 15th century; British colony extending north to the Orange River and east to the Natal border, 1795-1910; after 1910, a province of South Africa.

Cape of Good Hope Punishment Act Law passed in 1836 to extend British jurisdiction to 25 degrees south latitude (p 114).

capitalism Economic system characterised by a free competitive market with private and corporate ownership of production and distribution means, and directed to the accumulation and reinvestment of profits.

Carnegie Commission (1) Inquiry held 1928-32 into the 'poor white' problem in South Africa, assisted by a grant from the Carnegie Corporation, New York (p 332).

Carnegie Commission (2) Inquiry held in the 1980s into poverty in southern Africa. The report, compiled by researchers at 22 universities throughout southern Africa, found, among other things, that almost 9-million people in the 'homelands' were living below the breadline.

chiefdom Area over which a chieftain (or chief) is head or leader; the extent of a chieftain's power or influence.

chieftain or **chief** Head or leader of a clan or group of clans.

Ciskei see 'homeland'.

Civil Cooperation Bureau (CCB) Shadowy wing of the South African Defence Force exposed during the investigation by the Harms Commission into politically motivated killings; it waged a series of illegal campaigns against opponents of the government; formally dissolved in 1990 (p 501).

'civilised labour' policy State labour policy that sought to protect poor white workers by guaranteeing them work at the expense of black competitors (pp 333, 340).

CODESA (Convention for a Democratic South Africa) The vehicle agreed upon by the main political organisations in South Africa (with the exception of the CP and the PAC) to guide the country to a new, non-racial dispensation (*see also* Declaration of Intent). Its first plenary session (in December 1991) became known as CODESA I, and the second (in May 1992) as CODESA II. It was succeeded by the Negotiating Council (*see below*).

Colesberg Kopje Hillock near present-day Kimberley, site of an enormously rich diamond pipe which became the 'Big Hole'.

colour bar Reservation of certain categories of work for people of a particular race (p 306).

coloured Person of mixed descent.

Coloured Advisory Council (CAC) Government-established advisory body ostensibly intended to alleviate poverty among coloured people from 1943.

Coloured People's Congress (CPC) see Coloured People's Organisation.

Coloured People's Organisation (CPO) Political organisation formed in 1953 (later renamed the CPC) to fight government efforts to remove coloured people from the common voters' roll in the Cape.

Coloured Persons' Representative Council (CRC) Came into being in 1968 and could draft legislation, subject to government approval, on matters of finance, local government, education and community development affecting coloured people.

Committee for Fairness in Sport Organisation set up in the late 1970s with financial backing from the Department of Information to lobby for South Africa's re-entry into international sport. It enjoyed little success.

Communist Party of South Africa (CPSA) Political party formed in 1921 in Cape Town to promote Marxist socialism; outlawed under the Suppression of Communism Act of 1950, and re-formed underground as the South African Communist Party (SACP) in 1953; unbanned in 1990.

compound Enclosure or living quarters in which African mineworkers are housed; usually attached to a mine (pp 175, 202).

comrades see amaqabane.

Concerned South Africans Group (COSAG) Alliance of parties of the white right wing and those governing the 'homelands'; formed in 1992 to unite against ANC and NP agreements in constitutional negotiations. Predecessor of the Freedom Alliance (see below).

Congress Alliance Agreement in 1953 between the ANC, SAIC, Coloured People's Congress and South African Congress of Trade Unions following the Defiance Campaign to work towards the Congress of the People (see below) and the adoption of the Freedom Charter (p 387).

Congress of Democrats Marxist organisation attracting many former members of the CPSA after its banning in 1950 (p387).

Congress of South African Students (COSAS) Black organisation affiliated to the UDF.

Congress of South African Trade Unions (COSATU) Umbrella trade union body formed in 1985 and representing some 1,3-million black workers by 1994 (p 481).

Congress of the People Gathering held at Kliptown, south of Johannesburg, in June 1955 to adopt the Freedom Charter (p 387).

Congress Youth League (CYL) Youth wing of the ANC, founded in 1943 (p 364).

Conquered Territory Large tract of Sotho land claimed by the OFS in the Treaty of Thaba Bosiu (1866) (p 161).

Conservative Party (CP) Ultra-right-wing white political party formed after the split in the NP in 1982 over the new constitution. Refused to take part in the 1994 election.

constellation of states Proposal first made in 1978 to create an economically dependent, anti-Marxist, ANC-free zone around South Africa. Part of Total Strategy (p 460).

constructive engagement Policy of US President Ronald Reagan's Republican administration based on the belief that maintaining ties would positively influence reform in South Africa.

'coolie' labour Unskilled indentured labour imported from India to work on Natal sugarcane plantations (pp 222, 273).

cordon sanitaire Literally 'sanitary line'; a series of buffer states, especially when protecting a nation from infiltration or attack.

Council of Non-European Trade Unions (CNETU) Formed in 1936, it emerged as a powerful African labour grouping (p 357).

Council of Unions of South Africa (CUSA) Group of African trade unions aligned to black-consciousness political organisations; formed in 1980. In 1986 it merged with AZACTU to form NACTU.

Crossroads Squatter community on the Cape Flats south of Cape Town.

Declaration of Intent Document signed in December 1991 at CODESA I, committing signatories to a multiparty democracy in a unitary state, regular elections, separation of legislative, administrative and judicial powers, an independent judiciary, and the supremacy of the constitution.

Defiance Campaign Attempt in 1952 by groups opposed to apartheid to overburden law-enforcement machinery by contravening discriminatory legislation; ended in the banning of most ANC leaders; led to the formation of the Congress Alliance (p 283).

De Kaap Dutch name for the settlement at Cape Town.

Democratic Party Left-of-centre (in the South African context) political party formed in 1989 from the Progressive Federal Party, elements of the New Republic Party and the Independent Party.

Democratic Turnhalle Alliance (DTA) Political grouping in Namibia formed under Dirk Mudge by parties involved in the 1975 Turnhalle Conference in Windhoek (p 466).

Detainees' Parents Support Committee Group of parents and others who strove during the late 1980s and the '90s for the release of children detained without trial.

detente Diplomacy; relaxing of tensions, especially between nations; specifically John Vorster's policy of 'promoting friendship with South Africa's neighbours', in particular post-colonial Mozambique.

'De Zuid Afrikaan' Dutch-Afrikaans newspaper which did much to develop Afrikaner language and nationalism (p 195).

'Die Afrikaanse Patriot' First Afrikaans newspaper, published in the late 19th century (pp 196-7).

Difaqane Sotho term for the upheavals affecting Sotho communities living on the highveld in the 1820s and early 1830s (see Mfecane).

Directorate of Covert Collection Shadowy Military Intelligence unit uncovered in 1992 by Goldstone Commission (p 501).

direct reduction smelting Method of producing iron first used by Iron Age metal-workers.

disinvestment campaign Instituted by foreign opponents of apartheid, it put pressure on the NP Government by encouraging investors to withdraw from South Africa.

District Six Former (mainly coloured) residential and commercial area at the foot of Table Mountain in Cape Town proclaimed a white area in 1966. Its buildings were demolished and its inhabitants forcibly resettled on the Cape Flats (p 433).

Doctors' Pact 1950 declaration of cooperation between African and Indian political leaders opposed to apartheid (p 384).

dominee Church minister.

Dominion Party Political party founded in 1934 by dissatisfied English-speaking, pro-British SAP members; strongly in favour of preserving the unity of the British Empire and the status of the Union as a dominion within it.

dopper coat Worn by 19th-century Boers, black, high-collared, knee-length and buttoned all the way up.

Doppers (1) Group of religious fundamentalists in the north-eastern Cape Colony characterised by certain beliefs and customs (eg their dress); (2) Members of the Calvinist *Gereformeerde Kerk*.

doppie Small shell or percussion cap; bullet casing.

dorp Small town or village.

drift Ford or river crossing.

drostdy Office or residence of a magistrate (*landdrost*) at the Cape, 1685-1828.

Dutch East India Company Trading company which established a refreshment station at the Cape of Good Hope, 1602-1795; dissolved in 1798.

Early Iron Age From 3 000 years ago to 800-900 years ago in Africa.

Early Stone Age In Africa from 2,5- to 3-million years ago to about 70 000 years ago.

eeufees Centenary (celebrations), particularly of the Great Trek (pp 336-7).

emergency regulations These extend the powers of the executive and restrict the jurisdiction of the courts.

End Conscription Campaign Organisation campaigning against compulsory military conscription.

endorse out To endorse the reference book (Pass) of an African, requiring him to leave a particular area and return to his 'homeland'.

entrenched clause Clauses of the South African constitution of 1909 which could be amended only by a two-thirds majority vote of parliament (p 271).

eolith Literally 'dawn stone'; a stone produced under natural conditions (as opposed to a man-made tool) which could be used for a variety of purposes (p 18-19).

Erasmus Commission Headed by Judge Rudolph Erasmus, it was appointed in 1978 by Prime Minister P W Botha to investigate the Department of Information.

Ethiopian Church Independent (separatist) African Christian Church founded by former sugar-cane labourer Mangena Mokone in 1892 in Pretoria (p 285).

eurobond Mechanism for raising short- or medium-term finance, particularly for international trade, in a foreign currency held on deposit in Europe.

European Economic Community (EEC) Economic association of several countries in Western Europe; also known as the Common Market. Succeeded by the European Union.

Fagan Commission Appointed by the UP Government in 1946 to inquire into the laws relating to Africans in urban areas, migrant labour and other matters (pp 371-2).

FAPLA Name of the official armed forces of the People's Republic of Angola.

federal state One in which authority is shared by a central government and regional governments with some autonomy.

Federasie van Afrikaanse Kultuurverenigings (FAK) 'Federation of Afrikaans Cultural Societies', founded at a national language and cultural conference in 1929; based on the 'Christian national' principles of the Afrikaner *volk* (p 335).

Federation of South African Trade Unions (FOSATU) Non-racial trade union federation affiliated to the UDF. A later amalgamation gave rise to COSATU.

field-cornet (veldkornet) Military, administrative and judicial officer during the 19th century.

financial rand Foreign exchange mechanism to allow overseas investment at a discount on the normal rate of exchange.

FLEC 'Front for the Liberation of the Enclave of Cabinda', which fought unsuccessfully for independence for this oil-rich enclave of Angola in 1975.

FNLA 'National Front for the Liberation of Angola'; a rightist nationalist movement which fought first the colonial Portuguese and then unsuccessfully the rival MPLA in Angola in 1974-6 (p 436).

Food and Canning Workers' Union Founded in 1941 under Ray Alexander. Well known for its factory floor organisation and militant struggles for wages and recognition. Founder member of COSATU in 1985.

Franchise Action Committee Formed in 1951, it tried unsuccessfully to prevent the removal of coloured people from the Cape common voters' roll.

free burghers Employees of the Dutch East India Company who were freed of their duties and allowed to farm on their own; they were joined later by settlers.

Freedom Alliance Coalition that succeeded COSAG (*see above*); formed in 1993 to fight for federal principles at constitutional negotiations.

Freedom Charter Document propounding a non-racial society, liberty and individual rights, adopted by the Congress of the People at Kliptown outside Johannesburg in 1955 (p 388).

Freedom Front (FF) Formed by former SADF chief General Constand Viljoen in 1994, two months before the April election, to test support for an Afrikaner *volkstaat*.

Freedom in Sport British-based organisation that campaigned for South Africa's re-entry into the international sporting arena.

Free Mandela Campaign Organisation, affiliated to the UDF, campaigning for the unconditional release of Nelson Mandela from jail.

frontline states African states bordering or close to South Africa: Angola, Botswana, Lesotho, Malawi, Mozambique, Swaziland, Tanzania, Zambia and Zimbabwe.

Fusion Union of Smuts's South African Party and Hertzog's NP leading to the formation of the United South African Party in 1934 (pp 344-7).

Gazankulu *see* 'homeland'.

Genootskap van Regte Afrikaners, Die 'Society of Real Afrikaners'; founded in Paarl in 1875 'to stand for our Language, our Nation and our Country' – to promote the Afrikaans language and culture (pp 196-7).

Gesuiwerde Nasionale Party 'Purified National Party'; formed in 1934 by breakaway NP members (led by D F Malan) who rejected fusion between the NP and the SAP; became the HNP in 1940; won the 1948 general election; changed its name to NP in 1951 (p 348).

Glen Grey District east of Queenstown and west of the Indwe River, added to the Cape Colony after the eighth frontier war in 1852 and set aside for Thembu occupation; in 1894 Cecil Rhodes' Glen Grey Act was first applied to it (p 206).

gold exchange standard Linking of paper money to gold (p 333).

Goldstone Commission A judicial commission appointed by President F W de Klerk to investigate politically inspired violence (pp 497, 511).

Goringhaicona Literally 'children of the Goringhaiqua'; Khoikhoi who roamed the beaches of southern Africa in search of (sea) food and called *Strandlopers* by the Europeans (pp 43-4).

Government of National Unity Government voted into office in 1994 in terms of the interim constitution agreed to by the Negotiating Council. Its mandate was to govern the country for five years and write a post-apartheid constitution.

'Graham's Town Journal, The' First newspaper outside Cape Town, it was the mouthpiece of the British settlers in the eastern frontier districts; first published 1831.

'grand' apartheid Creation of a totally 'white' South Africa devoid of all African citizens – who would become citizens of the self-governing 'homeland' to which they could be ethnically linked (Zulu, South Sotho, etc).

Great Trek Migration of thousands of Dutch-speaking farmers (mainly from the eastern Cape) intending to set up their own independent republic outside the borders of the Cape Colony (p 114).

Great Wife African chief's most elevated wife, who bears the chief's heir.

Griqua People of mixed European, Khoikhoi and other ancestry who settled originally in Griqualand West in the early part of the 19th century, and later in Griqualand East around Kokstad.

Griqualand West Area of southern Africa in the northern Cape north of the Orange River; it was settled after 1803 by the Griquas; annexed by the British in 1871; incorporated into the Cape in 1880 (pp 166-7).

grondwet Constitution.

Groote Schuur Minute Agreement encompassing progress on the release of political prisoners and return of exiles, signed by the government and the ANC after the first formal talks between the two organisations at the Groote Schuur manor house in Cape Town in 1990.

gross domestic product (GDP) Total value of goods and services produced within a country during a given period, excluding income derived from investments abroad (in which case it becomes the gross national product).

group areas Areas set aside for exclusive occupation by a particular 'race' group in terms of the Group Areas Act, 1950 (p 376).

hamba kahle Xhosa term for 'proceeding carefully'.

Handhawersbond 'Defence League'; founded in 1930 by Gert Yssel and a group of idealists to uplift the Afrikaner, support Afrikaner entrepreneurs and strengthen Afrikaans cultural and language organisations. It petered out after 1935 (p 348).

Harare Declaration Document compiled in 1989 by the ANC, UDF and COSATU outlining their terms for talks with the government and their proposals for a new constitution.

Harms Commission Official inquiry (1989) into murder and violence committed with political motives. It uncovered the existence of the CCB (p 501).

heemraden Council of notables who assisted the *landdrost* to dispense justice under the Dutch administration.

Helpmekaar movement An Afrikaner mutual assistance movement that resulted from the pressing financial needs of the 1914 rebels in the OFS and Transvaal.

hensopper Literally 'hands-upper', quitter; in the South African War it referred to one (usually a lower-class Boer) who pressed for an end to hostilities or who surrendered (*see also bittereinder*) (p 257).

Herenigde (Reunited) National Party (HNP) Political party formed after Barry Hertzog and D F Malan agreed to join forces to oppose the Smuts Government after the outbreak of the Second World War. It won the 1948 general election and was renamed the National Party (*see below*) in 1951 (p 348).

Herero rebellion Rebellion by Herero Africans against German rule in South West Africa, 1904-7 (pp 217, 462).

Herrenvolk Master race.

Herstigte Nasionale Party (HNP) Reconstituted National Party; far-right political party formed in 1969 by a breakaway group from the NP.

Het Volk 'The People'; a Boer political party established in the Transvaal in 1905 to fight for self-government; it won the 1907 election (p 270) and, under Louis Botha, formed the first responsible government administration in the Transvaal.

highveld High-altitude, summer-rainfall grassland region of the Transvaal and OFS, lying at 1 200-1 800 metres above sea level.

'homeland' Region where members of a particular African language group (eg Zulu, Xhosa, Tswana) were offered self-government by the NP administration. The 'homeland' system with its 10 'ethnic' areas was the backbone of 'grand' apartheid (p 378). Four opted for 'independence': Transkei (for Xhosa-speakers); Bophuthatswana (Tswana-speakers); Venda (Venda-speakers); and Ciskei (also Xhosa-speakers). The other six were: Gazankulu (Shangaan-speakers); KaNgwane (South African Swazi-speakers); KwaNdebele (Ndebele-speakers); KwaZulu (Zulu-speakers); Lebowa (northern Sotho-speakers); and QwaQwa (southern Sotho-speakers). The 'homelands' were scrapped in 1994 (*see also* national states).

Homo erectus (erect man) Name of an extinct species of man represented by Old World fossils belonging to the Middle Pleistocene epoch; *H. erectus* evolved from the group of hominids called *Homo habilis* (p 17).

Homo habilis (handy man) Species of extinct man representing a stage between *Australopithecus* and *Homo erectus* and more like human beings (p 17).

Homo sapiens (wise man) Modern man; the only extant species of the genus *Homo* (p 17).

Hotnotstaal Literally 'Hottentots' language'; derogatory reference to Afrikaans (p 299).

Hottentot (1) Used by Dutch settlers to describe the pastoral people (Khoikhoi) of southern Africa. (2) Sometimes used as a derogatory description of a coloured person.

House of Assembly; House of Delegates; House of Representatives Chambers of tricameral parliament (1984-1994) representing white, Indian and coloured voters respectively.

Huguenots French refugees who settled in southern Africa in 1688 after fleeing France to avoid religious persecution.

'Ilanga lase Natal' 'The Sun of Natal'; Natal's leading African newspaper in the 1940s (p 384).

Iliso Lomzi Vigilance association which led organised resistance by rural Africans in the eastern Cape in the 1920s, staging boycotts and pickets to highlight bread-and-butter issues (p 324).

illicit diamond buying (IDB) Legislation makes it an offence to buy uncut diamonds without a licence – thus creating effective control of the price and distribution of diamonds. Contravention carries a stiff fine or jail term.

Imbumba Eliliso Lomso Ontsundu 'Union of Native Vigilance Associations'; formed in 1887 to protect African interests (p 208).

imizi Zulu homesteads (p 81).

impimpi Township informers (p 442).

'Imvo Zabantsundu' 'Native Opinion'; a Xhosa newspaper first published in King William's Town in 1884 (p 208).

inboekseling African child kidnapped by Transvaal Boers in the 1850s-70s and 'indentured' into virtual slavery (p 146).

indaba Zulu for 'topic'; a meeting to discuss a serious matter.

Independent ANC Breakaway group formed by ANC 'radicals' and communist sympathisers in the western Cape in 1930 (p 327).

Independent Board of Inquiry into Informal Repression Body set up by the South African Council of Churches to investigate politically inspired violence.

Independent Development Trust Body set up with an initial state grant of R2-billion to tackle South Africa's housing crisis.

Independent Electoral Commission Set up in December 1993 to organise South Africa's first election for all races and to ensure that the election was 'substantially free and fair'.

Independent Party Formed in 1988 by former South African ambassador to Britain Dennis Worrall (p 488).

Indian Congress see South African Indian Congress.

induna Zulu official who ensured that the king's orders were carried out (p 84).

Industrial and Commercial Workers' Union (ICU) Started as a union among dockworkers in Cape Town in 1919 and spread countrywide to become the largest African resistance movement in the 1920s under the leadership of Clements Kadalie (p 320).

influx control Regulations controlling the movement of Africans out of the Reserves/'homelands' into 'white' South Africa (p 424).

Inkatha Zulu national and cultural movement led by Chief Mangosuthu Buthelezi; opened its doors to all races as the Inkatha Freedom Party (IFP) in 1990 (p 509).

'Inkathagate' Scandal involving government cash handouts to Inkatha to finance its anti-ANC programmes (p 502).

'Inkululeko' 'Freedom'; newspaper of the Communist Party of South Africa, edited in the 1940s by Edwin Mofutsanyana (p 362).

International Court of Justice Court established in The Hague, Netherlands, to settle disputes between member states of the United Nations.

Iron Age The age during which iron was worked by man, from about 3 000 years ago in Africa (see Early Iron Age, Later Iron Age).

ISCOR Iron and Steel Industrial Corporation, established as a public utility in 1927 to develop the country's own smelting industry (pp 346-7). It was privatised in 1989.

'Isigidimi Sama-Xosa' 'Xhosa Express'; a newspaper established by Lovedale College in the eastern Cape in 1881 (p 208).

isiqataviku see skokiaan.

Israelites African religious sect active in the early 1920s at Bulhoek near Queenstown in the eastern Cape (p 326).

izindlu Zulu huts (p 81).

'Izwe Lethu' 'Our Land'; a slogan of the Pan-Africanist Congress (p 403).

'Izwi Labantu' 'Voice of the People'; newspaper established in 1898 and edited by A K Soga (p 208).

job reservation Regulations reserving certain jobs exclusively for workers of a particular group (white, coloured, etc). Used primarily to prevent employers hiring lower-paid Africans to undertake work done by whites (p 306), but also to enforce 'grand' apartheid in the western Cape, which became a 'coloured preference area' (p 428).

Joint Management Centre (JMC) Branch of the National Security Management System; the 12 JMCs' boundaries roughly corresponded with South Africa's military districts.

kaffir-farming Letting of land to Africans; creation of pools of African labour on Transvaal farms in the late 19th century, which were made available to mine recruiting agencies for a large commission (pp 331-2).

Kaffraria see British Kaffraria.

Kairos document Drafted in 1985 by 152 leading churchmen, it argued that Christians faced by unjust laws were obliged to rebel.

kakebeenwa Voortrekker wagon shaped like the jawbone of an ox.

kangaroo court Unofficial court set up by township activists to try those whom they saw as 'offenders'.

KaNgwane see 'homeland'.

kappie Large bonnet worn by Voortrekker women (pp 114, 124).

Kat River Settlement Established in 1829 by government official Andries Stockenström and settled by Khoikhoi, freed slaves and 'other persons of colour' north of Fort Beaufort as a buffer between European settlers and Xhosa (p 134).

Keate award Decision by court of arbitration headed by Lieutenant-Governor of Natal Robert Keate in 1871 after a three-way tussle between the South African Republic, Orange Free State and Griqua chief Nicolaas Waterboer to control the diamond fields. The court decided in favour of Waterboer – and the region became the British colony of Griqualand West (p 168).

khaki election General election held during wartime in 1943 (p 348).

Khoikhoi 'Men of men'; herders who inhabited large areas of southern Africa (p 20).

Khoisan The collective name for Khoikhoi (herders) and San (hunter-gatherers) (p 20).

kimberlite Type of rock in which diamonds may be found. Also called blue ground.

Kindergarten Alfred Milner's team of Oxford-educated young administrators brought from England in an attempt to build the Transvaal Colony into a British dominion. Named because of their youth (p 266).

kleurlinge(n) Literally 'coloureds'; Dutch term for 'people of colour' (p 246).

kloof Mountain pass, gorge or ravine.

knecht Farm foreman or, under the Dutch East India Company, a slave supervisor, usually an unskilled European labourer or soldier of the lowest rank (p 53).

knobkierie Type of stick used as a club.

Koevoet Police unit accused of using unconventional methods against SWAPO guerrillas and sympathisers in pre-independence Namibia; disbanded in 1992.

kommissie trek Small, exploratory trek undertaken in the 1830s ahead of the main trekker groups.

'Koranta ea Becoana' 'Bechuana Gazette', established in English and Tswana in 1901 and edited for a time by Sol T Plaatje (p 290).

kragdadigheid Literally using 'brute force' to achieve (political) goals.

krans Sheer rock face, precipice or cliff.

kruithoring Powderhorn or flask used to charge a firearm with gunpowder (p 116).

krygsraad Council of war; court martial.

KwaNdebele see 'homeland'.

KwaZulu see 'homeland'.

kwela Literally 'jump up'; musical style derived from African rhythms and American swing, popularly played on the penny whistle.

kwela-jazz More sophisticated kwela, with the saxophone replacing the penny whistle.

laager Camp defended by a circular formation of wagons lashed together to protect people and animals inside. More recently, the term refers to the political attitude of isolationism against a hostile environment.

Labour Party (1) Political party founded in 1910 and representing mainly English-speaking white workers. (2) Political party representing coloured people in the House of Representatives in the tricameral parliament (see below).

Labour Relations Amendment Act Attempt by the government to curb trade unions by, among other things, allowing employers to sue unions for loss of profits resulting from industrial action and imposing restrictions on strike action. The legislation was again amended after two years of protests and negotiations by unions (pp 458-9).

landdrost Magistrate (p 73).

landdrost en heemraden Administrative courts set up by the Dutch East India Company at the Cape in 1685. The landdrost was the ex officio chairman of the heemraden, who assisted him with boundary, ownership and other disputes. The office was replaced by that of magistrate in 1827 (p 73).

Later Iron Age Began some 800-900 years ago in southern Africa.

Later Stone Age Began some 20 000 years ago in southern Africa (p 19).

League of Nations Association formed in 1920 to preserve world peace. It fell apart in 1946.

Lebowa see 'homeland'.

leningplaatsen 'Loan places'; roughly 20-hectare farms granted by the Dutch East India Company on loan to colonists (mainly trekboers) for a fixed period.

Liberal Party Left-of-centre political party formed in 1953 by, among others, Alan Paton, advocating political equality for all. It never secured a parliamentary seat and was dissolved in 1968 when its non-racial membership was prohibited by law.

liberation doctrine Methods and efforts by which oppressed people plan to achieve their liberation.

lobola *see* bride-wealth.

location Township for Africans usually situated near a 'white' area.

London Convention Treaty between Britain and the Transvaal in 1884 abolishing the supervision granted to Britain over the region by the Pretoria Convention of 1881.

Long Tom Nickname for a gun used by the Boers in the South African War (p 241).

lowveld Low-lying area east of the great escarpment in the eastern Transvaal.

mahatma Literally 'great soul' or sage. Title conferred on Mohandas Gandhi (p 279).

Mandaat(en) Mandate(s) or authority(-ies) issued as exchequer bills for services to the state (p 148).

mandated territory Overseas territory taken from Germany during the First World War and administered from 1920 under the League of Nations (p 464).

mandoor Foreman, headman; slave overseer at the Cape who was himself a slave (p 52).

Manifesto of the Azanian People Issued by black-consciousness adherents in 1983, setting out their vision of a future South Africa.

Marabi African township music which developed during the 1920s and '30s and expressed the defiance of slum-dwellers in the face of adversity (p 358).

martial law Permits the executive branch of government to suspend civil liberties to maintain order through military intervention.

Marxism Political and economic ideas of Karl Marx and Friedrich Engels in which the concept of class struggle plays a primary role both in analysing Western society in general and in understanding its allegedly inevitable development from bourgeois oppression under capitalism to a socialist society and thence to communism.

Marxist One who believes in or follows the ideas of Marx and Engels (*see* Marxism *above*).

mass action Campaign of strikes and other industrial action, sit-ins, marches, etc.

Mass Democratic Movement Loose alliance of anti-apartheid groups during the 1980s.

mbaqanga Zulu for 'African maize bread'; a type of music popular among urban Africans in the 1940s and '50s (p 418).

meester Master, schoolmaster (often itinerant).

Mfecane Upheaval in south-eastern Africa in the early 1800s believed to have been caused by increasing population pressures and dwindling resources, and leading to internecine warfare among various African groups. Some historians now dispute that the *Mfecane (Difaqane)* occurred.

Middle Stone Age Estimated to have started about 2,5-million years ago and continued until 20 000 years ago in southern Africa.

migrant labourer Person who moves (or is forced to move) from one part of the country to another in search of employment, often for a fixed period.

mixed marriage Union between a white and a black (African, coloured or Indian) person; outlawed between 1949 and 1985.

MK Nickname of *Umkhonto we Sizwe*, the armed wing of the ANC.

MPLA 'Popular Movement for the Liberation of Angola'; founded by Agostinho Neto in 1957. It took over the government of Angola in 1975 (p 436).

Multi-Party Conference *see* Namibian Multi-party Conference.

Nagmaal Holy Communion in Afrikaans churches.

Namibian Multi-Party Conference Political association of SWAPO-Democrats, Turnhalle Alliance and others seeking an equitable independence for Namibia (p 468).

Natalia, Republic of Set up by Natal Voortrekkers in 1838 and annexed by Britain in 1843 (pp 154-5).

Natal Indian Congress (NIC) Founded in 1894 to strive for Indian rights (p 274).

Natal Native Congress Branch of the South African Native National Congress, forerunner of the ANC.

National Convention 1908-9 conference of states in southern Africa to negotiate union (p 271).

National Council of Trade Unions (NACTU) Black consciousness-supporting union federation that came about in 1986 after the amalgamation of AZACTU and CUSA.

National Economic Forum Launched in 1992 as a policy planning body representing labour, employers and government.

National Education Crisis Committee (NECC) Made up of prominent community leaders across the spectrum campaigning for fundamental change to South Africa's race-bound educational system.

National Forum Association of black-consciousness organisations formed in 1983 to oppose the tricameral parliament (p 477).

National Intelligence Service South Africa's 'spy' network. Replaced the Bureau for State Security in 1978.

nationalisation Putting an industry, service or resource under state control.

Nationalists Members or supporters of the National Party.

National Party (NP) Political party formed by Barry Hertzog in 1914 to represent Afrikaner interests. Fused with Smuts and the SAP in 1934 to form the UP; emerged as the HNP after Hertzog had split with Smuts over whether to enter the war against Germany and linked up with D F Malan's 'Purified' Nationalists. Came to power in 1948 and renamed NP in 1951. Relaunched in 1990, opening its membership to people of all races. Lost power to the ANC in 1994.

National Peace Accord 33-page document signed in September 1991 by 24 political parties, committing themselves to a code of conduct that prohibited provocation and intimidation by political parties in townships and governed the behaviour of security forces. It also brought into being a Peace Secretariat with legal powers (p 511).

National People's Party Indian political party represented in the House of Delegates in the tricameral parliament.

National Reception Committee Group of ANC supporters entrusted with the task of seeing that the release of Nelson Mandela in February 1990 went off smoothly.

National Security Management System An elaborate political-military apparatus devised by P W Botha to counter anti-government activity (*see* Joint Management Centre).

national states Territories set aside for occupation by members of a particular language group (Zulu, Xhosa, South Sotho, and so on). Originally called 'Reserves', they were given a measure of self-government by apartheid theorists (such as Hendrik Verwoerd) who wanted to remove all Africans from 'white' South Africa. Four (Transkei, Ciskei, Venda and Bophuthatswana) later chose 'independence' (recognised only by South Africa and each other) (p 426). The territories were reincorporated into South Africa in 1994 (*see* 'homeland').

National Union of Mineworkers (NUM) Launched by CUSA in 1982, this predominantly black union later affiliated to COSATU. It boasted a membership of 270 000 in 1993.

National Union of South African Students (NUSAS) Association of mainly English-speaking liberal student bodies founded in 1924; linked up with the Congress of South African Students in 1991 to form the South African Students' Congress.

Native Labour Passport Document entitling an African to seek work in a 'white' area (p 293).

Natives' Representative Council (NRC) Established in 1936 after the last Africans were removed from Cape voters' roll. Abolished in 1951 (p 342).

necklace Rubber tyre filled with petrol, forced over a victim's head and shoulders, and then set alight.

Negotiating Council Multiparty forum that drafted the interim constitution in terms of which South Africa held its first election in which people of all races voted in 1994.

New Democratic Movement Political party founded in 1987 by former NP member Wynand Malan.

New Republic Shortlived republic declared by a group of Boers under Lukas Meyer in Natal in 1884.

New Republic Party (NRP) Political party formed by a group of mainly Natal politicians after the demise of the UP in the mid-1970s. Disbanded in 1987.

Nguni Zulu- and Xhosa-speaking people (p 62).

Nkomati Accord 1984 agreement between South Africa and Mozambique undertaking not to harbour aggressors against each other.

'Nkosi Sikelel' iAfrika' 'God Bless Africa'; composed by Enoch Sontonga in 1897 (p 209). It became the anthem of the ANC and, after the 1994 election, the national anthem along with *'Die Stem'*.

No Man's Land Between the Cape Colony and Natal, settled by the Griqua from 1862 and subsequently annexed by Britain. Now Griqualand East (p 190).

Non-European Unity Movement (NEUM) Formed in 1943 by, among others, opponents of the Coloured Affairs Department. Remained ideologically aloof from other resistance movements, adhering strictly to

Trotskyite principles (p 396).

Northern Nguni Bantu-speakers settled mainly in what is now Natal and Swaziland (pp 63, 65-6).

Northern Sotho Bantu-speakers settled in the Transvaal (pp 63, 66).

Ohrigstad Capital of Boer statelet (later replaced by Lydenburg) established in the eastern Transvaal in 1845 (p 144).

oorstroming Act of being inundated or overrun.

opstal Homestead, farm building.

Orange River Colony Name given to the OFS when it was annexed by Britain after the Boers had been defeated in the South African War in 1902.

Orange River Sovereignty Area of Transorangia (across the Orange River) over which Britain proclaimed sovereignty (1848-54).

Oranje Unie 'Orange Union'; political organisation formed to achieve self-government for the Orange River Colony after the South African War (p 270).

Ordinance 50 of 1828 Guaranteed all Cape Colony 'Hottentots and other free persons of colour' the same freedom and protection before the law as whites (p 97).

Organisation of African Unity (OAU) Association of African states formed in 1963 to fight colonialism and promote unity in Africa. South Africa became a member in 1994.

Ossewabrandwag 'Ox-wagon sentinel'; an organisation of Afrikaners formed in 1939 in opposition to South Africa's declaration of war on Germany. It carried out acts of sabotage against the Smuts Government (p 353).

'ostrich palace' Gracious home in the Oudtshoorn district built around the height of the ostrich feather boom (p 227).

Ovamboland People's Congress (OPC) Founded in Cape Town in 1957 (p 465), it was the forerunner of the Ovamboland People's Organisation (OPO), which became the South West African People's Organisation (SWAPO).

Pact (Government) Successful agreement between the Labour and National parties designed to defeat the SAP at the 1924 general election; government formed after the election (p 318).

Pan-Africanist Congress (PAC) Established in 1959 by breakaway Africanist members of the ANC under the presidency of Robert Sobukwe (pp 399, 505).

Pan-Africanist Movement Formed in 1989 as an 'internal wing' of the then banned PAC.

paramount chief Chief of greatest significance; supreme ruler.

Paranthropus robustus Fossils found at Sterkfontein, Transvaal, later reclassified as *Australopithecus robustus* (p 16).

parastatal Semi-state institution or industry established and run in consultation with the state.

Pass *see* reference book.

passenger Indians Indians who came to Natal at their own expense after 1870, as opposed to indentured labourers. They came to form a professional/business class (p 225).

passive resistance Non-violent resistance by means such as fasting, peaceful demonstration or non-cooperation.

Patriotic Front Anti-apartheid coalition formed in 1991 to present a united front during multiparty negotiations.

Patriots Burghers sympathetic to Adriaan van Jaarsveld who demanded the resignation of the magistrate at Graaff-Reinet in 1785 (p 73).

peasants Small farmers, tenants and labourers in areas where they are the main labour force in agriculture.

penny *see* shilling.

penny whistle Cheap metal flageolet favoured by players of *kwela* music (*see above*).

people's education Alternative to 'Bantu education' in order to prepare children for a post-apartheid society.

People's Liberation Army of Namibia (PLAN) The armed wing of the South West African People's Organisation (SWAPO) during its guerrilla war against South African forces.

petite bourgeoisie Member of a class that includes small businessmen, skilled manual workers and low-ranking white-collar staff.

'petty' apartheid Enforced segregation of public amenities such as benches, beaches, buses and trains (*see* 'grand' apartheid).

Phalaborwa hoe Diamond-shaped tool dating from the Early Iron Age in north-eastern Transvaal (p 31).

phylloxera Vine-root disease that almost destroyed the Cape's wine industry in 1885 (p 229).

placaat Dutch proclamation or edict.

platteland Literally 'flat land'; countryside, rural areas away from the cities.

plattelander Person living in the *platteland*.

Poqo Xhosa for 'standing alone'; the military wing of the Pan-Africanist Congress (p 411). Forerunner of APLA.

Port Elizabeth Black Civic Organisation (PEBCO) Spearheaded by Thozamile Botha, Henry Fazzie and Edgar Ngoyi, PEBCO was at the forefront of a number of anti-government protests during the mid-1980s.

power sharing Vague concept of whites 'sharing' government with South African blacks, without necessarily relinquishing control.

President's Council Chamber of the tricameral parliament, heavily weighted in favour of the 'white' house, which had final power to pass or veto legislation.

Pretoria Convention Treaty signed between Britain and Transvaal Boers in 1881 making the Transvaal a self-governing state subject to certain conditions (p 199).

Pretoria Minute Second round of talks between the government and the ANC in August 1990; main issues arising from the negotiations were a commitment by the ANC to suspend its armed struggle and a pledge by the government to begin releasing political prisoners from 1 September 1990.

privatisation Putting government industries, services or resources under private control.

proletarian An industrial wage earner; manual labourer.

proportional representation System of representation in government whereby the parties are allocated seats in proportion to the percentage of votes they win.

Province of Queen Adelaide Land between the Keiskamma and Kei rivers in the eastern Cape; annexed by the Cape authorities in 1835 and handed back to the Xhosa soon afterwards (p 106).

quitrent System of land tenure introduced by the Dutch East India Company in 1732 which guaranteed farmers occupation for at least 15 years, after which the land reverted back to the company (p 57).

QwaQwa *see* 'homeland'.

radio-carbon dating Technique for determining the age of fossils, etc (p 18).

ramkie Four-stringed, guitar-like instrument brought to the Cape by Malabar slaves (p 61).

Rand Short for Witwatersrand, the goldbearing 'Ridge of white waters' upon which Johannesburg is built.

rand Principal unit of South African currency. There are 100 cents in one rand.

randlord Witwatersrand mining magnate (p 203).

realpolitik Statesmanship based on political reality as opposed to moral stance.

Reconstruction and Development Programme ANC policy document unveiled during the 1994 election campaign. Adopted as official government policy after the poll, it provided for socio-economic upliftment, especially for blacks.

Record of Understanding Document, signed by the ANC and the NP Government on 26 September 1992, providing for the release of political prisoners, fencing of migrant labour hostels and a ban on carrying traditional weapons. It also covered procedural issues relating to the transition towards a new government.

Reef, the Another name for the Witwatersrand, derived from the vein or 'reef' of goldbearing ore.

reference book 96-page document carried by all Africans in 'white' South Africa after 1952. It had to be carried at all times and produced on demand. Specifically, it detailed residence and working rights. Scrapped in 1986 (p 377).

referendum To put an issue to the direct vote of the electorate.

Renamo Nickname for the National Resistance Movement of Mozambique, opposed to the country's Marxist government.

Reserve Land set aside for African occupation. Later called 'Bantustan', 'homeland', 'national state' or 'self-governing state'.

Resolution 435 1978 resolution by the UN demanding the withdrawal of South African forces from Namibia and the holding of UN-supervised elections.

Riekert Commission Appointed in the 1970s to inquire into the utilisation of manpower. Its recommendations led to the abolition of the Pass system (p 458).

rinderpest Literally 'cattle pest'; acute contagious viral disease of cattle (p 228).

Rivonia trial The trial at which eight *Umkhonto we Sizwe* leaders, including Nelson Mandela, Govan Mbeki and Walter Sisulu, were sentenced to life imprisonment for plotting to overthrow the government.

Rooi Luisies 'Red Lice'; derogatory reference to the soldiers (who wore red flashes) who volunteered to serve beyond the country's borders in the Second World War (p 349).

Rubicon A river in northern Italy serving as the boundary between Italy and Cisalpine Gaul; Julius Caesar broke the law that a general might not lead his army out of the province to which he had been posted when he crossed it (and precipitated a civil war) in 49 BC. Today, it means the point of no return.

Rudd concession Agreement between British 'protectors' of Bechuanaland and the Ndebele king, Lobengula, giving mineral rights over his territories to a group led by Rhodes (p 218).

San Hunter-gatherers indigenous to southern Africa known to the Dutch as 'Bushmen'. A few still survive in the more remote regions of the Kalahari and in Namibia.

Sand River Convention 1852 convention at which the British told Voortrekkers north of the Vaal River that they were no longer British subjects and could rule themselves (p 142).

SANLAM South African National Life Assurance Company; Afrikaner insurance company founded in 1918 by William Hofmeyr as a counter to the English stranglehold on big business (pp 335-6).

sanna Matchlock or flintlock musket.

SANTAM South African National Trust and Assurance company; created with capital provided by western Cape farmers to provide short- and long-term assurance (p 336).

SASOL Parastatal industry established in 1950 to manufacture petroleum from coal.

satyagraha Literally 'the force which is born of truth and love'; philosophy upon which Mohandas Gandhi's passive (non-violent) resistance campaigns were based (p 275).

scheduled areas Areas in which African land-ownership was restricted in terms of the Natives' Land Act 1913. The Act barred Africans from buying land except from other Africans or in existing Reserves (p 292).

'school' Africans Western-educated or mission-educated Africans (p 153).

Section 10 rights Section 10 of the Black (Urban Areas) Act 1945 granted exceptions to the general rule forbidding Africans to reside outside the Reserves (p 424).

segregation Policy of racial separation.

Selborne Memorandum 1907 document which examined the desirability of forming a united South Africa (p 281).

self-governing states see national states.

separate development Name that attempted to glamorise apartheid by insisting that it fostered the development of each 'racial' and African language group.

servants' revolt Uprising of Khoisan living in the Zuurveld in 1799 (p 96).

sextant Instrument used in navigation, consisting of a telescope through which a sighting of a heavenly object is taken, with protractors for determining its angular distance above the horizon (p 35).

shebeen Place where liquor is sold, usually without a legal licence (p 416).

shilling Unit of currency before decimalisation. There were 12 pennies (12d) to a shilling, and 20 shillings (20s) to a pound (£1).

simanje-manje Zulu for 'now-now'; style of 1950s music (pp 418-9).

sirdar Foreman among Natal Indian sugar plantation workers (p 224).

skokiaan; isiqataviku 'Kill me quick'; home-brewed alcoholic beverage (p 358).

socialism Social system in which the means of producing and distributing goods are owned collectively and political power is exercised by the whole community.

sofasonke Literally 'we shall all die together'; name given to James Mpanza's

squatter movement on the Witwatersrand after 1944 (p 356).

South African Broadcasting Corporation (SABC) State-owned national radio and television broadcaster.

South African Bureau of Racial Affairs (SABRA) NP 'think-tank' on racial affairs.

South African Coloured People's Organisation Continued the work of the Franchise Action Committee formed in 1951, organising protests against group areas removals.

South African Communist Party (SACP) Formed underground in 1953 as the successor of the banned Communist Party of South Africa. It was unbanned in 1990.

South African Congress of Trade Unions (SACTU) Labour federation formed in 1955 and closely associated with the ANC. Dissolved in 1990.

South African Council of Churches (SACC) Formed in 1968, the SACC's mission was to foster black leadership in the mainstream (particularly Anglican and Methodist) churches. It was a major factor in the revival of mass protest in the late 1970s and the '80s.

South African Council on Sport (SACOS) Umbrella sporting body adhering strictly to non-racialism with the slogan 'No normal sport in an abnormal society'; campaigned extensively for South Africa's expulsion from international sport.

South African Defence Force (SADF) Made up of four commands: army, navy, air force and medical services. Renamed South African National Defence Force in 1994.

South African Indian Congress (SAIC) Founded in 1920 to secure Indian rights. Co-operated with the ANC during the Defiance Campaign (p 383) and co-sponsored the Congress of the People.

South African Native Affairs Commission (SANAC) Set up by Alfred Milner under the chairmanship of Sir Godfrey Lagden, it advocated in 1905 the political and territorial separation of whites and Africans (pp 280, 312).

South African Native Congress (SANC) African political organisation founded in 1898 to strive for African rights.

South African Native Convention African response objecting to proposals for Union made at the 'white' convention in 1909 (p 282).

South African Native National Congress (SANNC) Established by Africans at a conference in Bloemfontein in January 1912; later renamed the African National Congress (pp 288-95).

South African Party (SAP) Political party representing white English- and Afrikaans-speaking South Africans from 1910 until it 'fused' with the National Party in 1934.

South African Republic (SAR) First unified Boer republic north of the Vaal River, 1860-1902.

South African Students' Organisation (SASO) Black-consciousness university movement formed in 1969 with Steve Biko as president (p 447).

Southern African Development Coordination Conference (SADCC) Association of frontline states aimed at reducing economic dependence on South Africa. Later renamed Southern African Development Community.

Southern Nguni Bantu-speakers occupying the broad coastal strip of what is now Natal,

Transkei and Ciskei (p 64).

Southern Sotho Language spoken by Africans in the general area of the OFS and Lesotho (pp 66-7).

South West African People's Organisation (SWAPO) Formed in 1960 under Sam Nujoma and dedicated to democratic independence for Namibia (p 464).

Soutpansberg Boer statelet established in the far northern Transvaal in 1848; joined the SAR in 1860 (p 144).

Soweto Acronym for 'south-western townships'; a contiguous group of African townships south-west of Johannesburg.

Spoorbond Union of Railwaymen established by the Broederbond in 1934.

stad City.

state of emergency Suspension of certain civil liberties in order to strengthen the arm of the executive in controlling a perceived threat to the state.

State Security Council Founded by P W Botha, it was granted powers in 1980 to create a network of regional and local committees that would bring together the police, the SADF and civilians to coordinate state security (see National Security Management System).

status campaign Initiated by the PAC in 1959 in a bid to persuade whites not to refer to Africans in derogatory terms, on pain of boycott or picketing (p 400).

status quo Agreement between Chamber of Mines and white miners that the existing ratio (c 1920) of blacks to whites in certain jobs would not be changed (pp 306, 307).

Stone Age Period of human development identified by the use of stone implements; in Africa, from about 2,5- to 3-million years ago until modern times in certain cultures.

stormjaers 'Stormtroopers'; military wing of the Ossewabrandwag (see above) which waged a campaign of urban terror in opposition to South Africa's involvement in the Second World War (p 349).

Strandlopers Literally 'beach walkers'; see Goringhaicona (p 349).

subsistence farming Most of the produce is consumed by the farmer and his family, leaving little or nothing to be marketed.

Sullivan Principles Drawn up by US civil rights worker Leon Sullivan in 1976 for US firms operating in South Africa (p 461).

SWAPO see South West African People's Organisation.

SWAPO-Democrats A group of Namibians under Andries Shipanga which broke with SWAPO in 1978.

swart gevaar Literally 'black threat' or 'black peril'; fear by white South Africans that they would be 'swamped' by the African majority (p 312).

swart gevaar election 1929 general election, fought on the issue of white fear of blacks (p 338).

swartskut Literally 'black shot'; African servant of the Boers taught to shoot for ivory in malaria zones (p 147).

Telanthropus capensis Humanoid fossils found at Sterkfontein (p 16).

Thaba Bosiu 'Mountain of the Night'; impregnable fortress home of Moshoeshoe, founder of the Basotho nation (p 139).

third force Loosely used to indicate right-wing elements inside the security forces suspected of perpetrating or fomenting violence to sabotage political change (p 501).

Tomlinson Commission Reported in 1954 on the rehabilitation of the African Reserves as an essential element of separate development policy (p 378).

Total Onslaught In the opinion of the P W Botha regime, the campaign by the international community to isolate South Africa in order to force it in the direction of a one-person, one-vote democracy.

Total Strategy Initiated by the military in 1977 to counter external threats by creating a 'constellation of southern African states' and to quell internal unrest by expanding the African middle class (p 460).

tot system Part-payment of farm labourers with wine.

Trade Union Council of South Africa (TUCSA) Trade union federation run on racial lines, which folded in 1986.

Trades and Labour Council (TLC) Essentially white grouping of trade unions formed in 1927.

Transitional Executive Council (TEC) Mini-government representing all parties involved in negotiations for a post-apartheid government; set up at the end of 1993 to oversee the transition to democracy.

Transkei Territory east of the Kei River, settled by Xhosa chiefdoms and administered as a district of the Cape (*see also* 'homeland').

Transorangia North of the Orange River.

Treason Trial of 156 ANC members and others following the civil disobedience campaigns of the early 1950s.

treaty system Between the Cape Colony and Xhosa chiefs to try to bring order to the eastern districts, 1836-44 (p 106).

trekboer/trekker Nomadic pastoral farmer, usually of Dutch extraction.

trekgees Literally 'trekking spirit'; wanderlust of semi-nomadic trekboers.

tricameral parliament Government representing white, coloured and Indian (but not African) voters in racially segregated houses; created in 1984 and superseded by the Government of National Unity in 1994 (*see above*).

Trotskyism Theories of communism advocated by Leon Trotsky and his followers, who argued for the permanent worldwide revolution of the working classes.

Trotskyite Follower of the theories of Leon Trotsky (*see above*).

tsaba-tsaba Traditional African musical rhythm (p 416).

Tsonga Bantu-speakers who occupied land north of Kosi Bay and in the 19th century expanded to the eastern Transvaal (p 67).

tung'umolomo Literally 'the shutting of mouth'; denying the vote.

Tuynhuys Official Cape residence of the State President of South Africa.

uitlander Alien, foreigner; particularly a Briton living in the South African Republic in the 1890s.

Umkhonto we Sizwe Literally 'the spear of the nation'; military wing of the ANC established soon after the organisation was banned in 1960 (p 410).

Union Buildings Complex of buildings built after 1910 to house the main offices of the central government.

UNITA 'National Union for the Total Independence of Angola'; pro-Western movement fighting the MPLA Government in Angola.

unitary state One in which the central government holds authority.

United Cricket Board of South Africa National cricket body that came about as a result of the merger between the predominantly white South African Cricket Union and the black South African Cricket Board. The formation of the board led to the almost immediate opening of international doors to South African cricketers.

United Democratic Front (UDF) Extra-parliamentary, non-racial political alliance of various organisations striving for a democratic South Africa; established in 1983 and dissolved in 1991.

United Party (UP) Political party that emerged after 'Fusion' between the South African Party and the National Party in 1934 (p 346); dissolved in 1977.

United Workers' Union of South Africa (UWUSA) Trade union organisation affiliated to the Inkatha movement.

Universal Declaration of Human Rights Pledge by member states of the United Nations to guarantee not only civil rights such as life, liberty and freedom from arbitrary arrest, but also social rights such as the rights to work and to an education; adopted by the UN General Assembly in December 1948.

unrest areas In terms of state of emergency regulations, the government could declare 'unrest areas', allowing security forces special powers in those areas.

Urban Foundation Organisation founded in 1976 by business conglomerates from both the English- and Afrikaans-speaking sectors to encourage the creation of an African middle-class society.

Vaal triangle Area surrounding the largely industrial towns of Sasolburg, Vereeniging and Vanderbijlpark in the Transvaal.

vastrap Up-tempo music accompanying *boer* folk dances and typically played on a small concertina.

veldkornet *see* field-cornet.

Venda *see* 'homeland'.

Vereniging van Oranjewerkers 'Union of Orange Workers'; ultra-right political organisation (pp 498-9).

verligte 'Enlightened person'; used during the apartheid era to indicate a member or supporter of the NP who advocated reform.

vierkleur Four-coloured flag (red, white, blue and green) of the Transvaal and SAR.

vigilante Person who takes the law into his own hands, particularly a conservative African township dweller.

VOC *Vereenigde Oost-Indische Compagnie* – *see* Dutch East India Company.

volk People, nation.

volksgemeenskap People's community.

volkskapitalisme People's capitalism, referring to the Afrikaners' bid for a greater share in the nation's wealth.

volksleier National leader.

volksraad 'People's assembly'; parliament.

volkstaat 'People's state'; word used by ultra-rightwingers in the 1990s for the white, Afrikaner homeland they espoused.

Voortrekkers Literally 'front trekkers'; vanguard of Boers who trekked out of the Cape Colony in the 1830s to set up an independent republic away from British rule (pp 124-5).

vrijgelaten swarte Literally 'freed black'; African freed from slavery or bondage.

Vrijkorps 'Free Corps'; group of German-supporting Afrikaners who raided South Africa from South West Africa in 1914 (p 302).

wakis 'Wagon chest'; kist in which trekkers carried their valuables while on trek.

Warden Line (1849) Line fixed by Major Henry Warden determining the boundary between Basutoland and the former Orange River Sovereignty.

War of the Axe Seventh frontier war, sparked off in 1846 by the arrest of a Xhosa who had been caught stealing an axe from a shop, who was 'rescued' by his friends and whom Chief Sandile refused to return to the authorities (pp 108-9).

War Veterans Torch Commando Offshoot of the largely white Civil Rights League, made up initially of mainly white ex-servicemen opposed to D F Malan's NP and the removal of coloured people from the Cape voters' roll.

Wenkommando 'Victory Commando'; military-style designation for ordinary members of the *Afrikaner Weerstandsbeweging* (*see above*).

Western Sotho (Tswana) Branch of Bantu-speakers occupying the southern and western Transvaal (p 67).

West Rand Administration Board (WRAB) Board that began administering African townships in the West Rand, Transvaal, in 1971.

'White South Africa First' 1924 election slogan of the Pact formed between Hertzog's NP and Creswell's Labour Party, aimed at winning support from white labour (p 318).

Wiehahn Commission Inquiry (1977-9) into industrial relations; led to the scrapping of job reservation and the inclusion of Africans in the industrial conciliation process (p 458).

Witdoeke One of the factions among the residents of the squatter camp of Crossroads in the 1980s, so named for the white scarves they wore as identification.

Witwatersrand Literally 'ridge of white water'; rocky ridge of gold-bearing ground situated in the southern Transvaal and discovered in 1886 by George Harrison, a British immigrant (pp 200-1).

Wit Wolwe The name claimed by white ultra-rightwingers responsible for attacks on black civilians.

Ystergarde Armed wing of the *Afrikaner Weerstandsbeweging* (*see above*).

ZANU-PF Zimbabwe African National Union-Patriotic Front; liberation movement led by Joshua Nkomo, who formed a pre-election 'Patriotic Front' alliance with ZANU's Robert Mugabe. However, they contested the polls as separate parties (p 470).

Zionist Church Separatist church that blends traditional African and Christian beliefs and rituals in a new religious form.

Zonnebloem *see* District Six.

Zulu Collective name assumed by the majority of northern Nguni people of south-east Africa after the rise to power of Shaka in the 19th century.

Zuurveld 'Sour veld'; region of good grazing land west of the Fish River in the eastern Cape.

Index

Page reference are in *italics* where subjects appear in illustrations and/or captions and, usually, in the main text on the same page. **Bold** has been used where the subject is the central figure or theme in a separate box.

N

Bibliography

Abbreviations:
CHA – Cambridge History of Africa
CUP – Cambridge University Press
CAS – Centre for African Studies
DP – David Philip
IHSA – Cameron and Spies (editors) *Illustrated History of South Africa* (Johannesburg, Jonathan Ball, 1986)
JB – Jonathan Ball
JAH – *Journal of African History*
JSAS – *Journal of Southern African Studies*
WUP – Wits University Press
OUP – Oxford University Press
SAHJ – *South African Historical Journal*
SAIRR – *South African Institute of Race Relations*
UCT – University of Cape Town

Part 1
Africa the cradle of man
Mason, Revel 'The Earlier Stone Age and the Transvaal' in *South African Archaeological Bulletin No 17*; Tobias, Philip 'Man's Past and Future' in *Raymond Dart Lectures No 5* (WUP, 1969); Tobias, Philip *Essay on the life and work of Professor Raymond Dart* (WUP, 1984); Tobias, Philip 'The Dawn of the Human Family in Africa' in *IHSA*

San hunter-gatherers and Khoikhoi herders
Birmingham, D; Marks, Shula 'Southern Africa' in *CHA Vol 3* (CUP, 1977); Bredenkamp, Henry 'The Origin of the Southern African Khoisan Communities' in *IHSA*; Clark, J D *The Prehistory of Africa* (London, Thames & Hudson, 1969); Elphick, Richard *Khoikhoi and the Founding of White South Africa* (Ravan, 1985); Hausman, Alice Jane *Holocene Human Evolution in Southern Africa: The Biocultural Development of the Khoisan* (unpublished D.Phil Thesis, State University of New York, 1980); Inskeep, Richard; Clark, J D in *Perspectives on the Southern African Past* (CAS, UCT, 1979); Inskeep, Richard 'The Bushmen in Prehistory' in *The Bushmen – San Hunters and Herders of Southern Africa* (1978); Malherbe, C *Men of Men* (Pietermaritzburg, Shuter & Shooter, 1984); Marks, Shula ' ''Bold, Thievish, and not to be Trusted'': Racial Stereotypes in South Africa in Historical Perspective' in *History Today Vol 31* (August, 1981); Marks, Shula; Gray, Richard 'Southern Africa and Madagascar' in *CHA Vol 4* (CUP, 1971); Parkington, J E 'Stone Age Populations' in *Perspectives on the Southern African Past* (CAS, UCT, 1979); Peires, Jeff *The House of Phalo* (Ravan, 1981); Robertshaw, P T 'The Origins of Pastoralism in the Cape' in *SAHJ No 10* (1978); Tobias, Phillip (editor) 'The San – an Evolutionary Perspective' in *The Bushmen – San Hunters and Herders of Southern Africa* (1978); West, Martin 'The San and Khoi People' in *Perspectives on the Southern African Past* (CAS, UCT, 1979); Willcox, A R *The Rock Art of South Africa* (Johannesburg, Thomas Nelson & Sons, 1963); Wilson, M L 'Khoisanosis: The question of separate identities for Khoi and San' in Singer and Lundy (editors) *Variation, Culture and Evolution in African Populations* (WUP, 1986); Wright, J B *Bushmen Raiders of the Drakensberg* (1971)

The Iron Ages
Birmingham, David; Marks, Shula 'Southern Africa' in *CHA Vol 3* (CUP, 1971); Clark, J D *The Prehistory of Africa* (London, Thames and Hudson, 1969); Denbow, J R *Iron Age Economics* (D.Phil Thesis, Indiana University, 1983); Ehret, C 'Cattle Keeping and Milking in Eastern and Southern African History: The Linguistic Evidence' in *JAH* (1967); Fagan, Brian *Southern Africa in the Iron Age* (London, Thames & Hudson, 1965); Hall, Martin *Early Farming Communities of Southern Africa: A Population Discovered* (South African Historical Society, University of Durban-Westville, 1981); Hall, Martin *The Changing Past: Farmers, Kings and Traders in Southern Africa* (DP, 1987); Inskeep, Richard *Perspectives on the Southern African Past* (CAS, UCT, 1979); Maggs, T M *Iron Age Communities of the Southern Highveld* (Pietermaritzburg, Natal Museum, 1976); Maylam, Paul *A History of the African People of South Africa from the Early Iron Age to the 1970s* (DP, 1986); Oliver, Roland; Fagan, Brian 'The Emergence of Bantu Africa' in *CHA Vol 2* (CUP, 1978); Phillipson, D W *The Later Prehistory of Eastern and Southern Africa* (London, Heinemann, 1977); Robertshaw, P T 'The Origins of Pastoralism in the Cape' in *SAHJ No 10* (1978); Van der Merwe, N J *The Iron Age: A Prehistory of Bantu-Speaking South Africans* (CAS, UCT, 1979)

The first contact
Boxer, C R (editor) *The Tragic History of the Sea: 1589-1622* (CUP, 1959); Parry, J H *Europe and the Wider World 1415-1715* (Hutchinson University Library, 1949); Wolf, Eric *Europe and the People without History* (University of California Press, 1982); Wilson, Monica; Thompson, Leonard (editors) *A History of South Africa to 1870* (DP, 1982)

The Dutch come to stay
Boxer, C R *The Dutch Seaborne Empire* (London, Hutchinson, 1965); Boëseken, A J 'The Arrival of Van Riebeeck at the Cape' in C F J Muller (editor) *500 Years: A History of South Africa* (Pretoria, Academica, 1969); Guelke, Leonard 'The White Settlers, 1652-1780' in Elphick and Giliomee (editors) *The Shaping of South African Society 1652-1820* (Cape Town, Longman, 1979); Schutte, Gerrit 'Company and Colonists at the Cape' in Elphick and Giliomee (editors) *The Shaping of South African Society 1652-1820* (Cape Town, Longman, 1979); Picard, Hymen *Cape Epic* (Howick, Khenty Press, 1977)

Part 2
Khoikhoi and colonists
Bredenkamp, Henry 'The Pre-colonial and Colonial Khoikhoi – from Fragile Independence to Permanent Subservience' in *IHSA*; Elphick, Richard *Khoikhoi and the Founding of White South Africa* (Ravan, 1985); Elphick, Richard 'The Khoisan to the 17th Century' in Elphick and Giliomee (editors) *The Shaping of South African Society 1652-1820* (Cape Town, Longman, 1979); Elphick, Richard; Shell, R 'Intergroup Relations: Khoikhoi, settlers, slaves and free Blacks 1652-1795' in Elphick and Giliomee (editors) *The Shaping of South African Society 1652-1820* (Cape Town, Longman, 1979); Marks, Shula 'Khoisan resistance to the Dutch in the 17th and 18th Centuries' in *JAH Vol 13* (1972); Marks, Shula; Gray, Richard 'Southern Africa' in *CHA Vol 4* (CUP, 1971); Penn, Nigel *The Frontier in the Western Cape, 1700-1740* (conference paper, 1984)

Settlers and slaves
Armstrong, J C 'The Slaves 1652-1795' in Elphick and Giliomee (editors) *The Shaping of South African Society 1652-1820* (Cape Town, Longman, 1979); Freund, William 'The Cape Under the Transitional Governments, 1795-1814' in Elphick and Giliomee (editors) *The Shaping of South African Society 1652-1820* (Cape Town, Longman, 1979); Ross, Robert *Cape of Torments – Slavery and Resistance in South Africa* (Routledge & Kegan Paul, 1983); Van Zyl, J 'Die Slaaf in die Ekonomiese Lewe van die Westelike Distrikte van die Kaap Kolonie 1795-1834' in *SAHJ No 10* (1978); Worden, Nigel *The Distribution of slaves in the Western Cape During the 18th Century* (CAS, UCT, 1979); Worden, Nigel *Cape Slave Emancipation and Rural Labour in a Comparative Context* (CAS, UCT, 1983); Worden, Nigel *Rural Slave Ownership in the Stellenbosch and Drakenstein Districts of the Cape Colony during the 18th Century* (unpublished seminar paper)

Trekboers and Khoisan
Guelke, Leonard 'The White Settlers 1652-1780' in Elphick and Giliomee (editors) *The Shaping of South African Society 1652-1820* (Cape Town, Longman, 1979); Guelke, Leonard 'Frontier Settlement in Early Dutch South Africa' in *Annals of the Association of American Geographers Vol 66*; Guelke, Leonard; Shell, R 'An Early Colonial Landed Gentry: Land and Wealth in the Cape Colony 1682-1731' in *Journal of Historical Geography* (1983); Penn, N G *The Frontier in the Western Cape 1700-1740* (conference paper, 1984); Ross, Robert 'The Rise of the Cape Gentry' in *JSAS Vol 9 No 2* (April, 1983)

Life of the times: 18th century Cape Town
Bickford-Smith, V *Cape Town on the Eve of the Mineral Revolution (c1875): Economic Activity and Social Structure* (UCT History Department, 1985); Botha, Graham *Social Life and customs during the Eighteenth Century* (Cape Town, Struik, 1970); De Kock, Victor *Those in Bondage: An Account of the Life of the Slave of the Cape in the days of the Dutch East India Company* (Cape Town, NG Kerkpers, 1950); Ross, Robert *Cape of Torments – Slavery and Resistance in South Africa* (Routledge & Kegan Paul, 1983); *South African Heritage: From Van Riebeeck to 19th Century Times* (Cape Town, Human & Rousseau, 1965)

African societies in the 17th and 18th centuries
Hammond-Tooke, W D 'Descent Groups, Chiefdoms and South African Historiography' in *JSAS Vol 11 No 2* (1985); Marks, Shula; Gray, Richard 'Southern Africa 1600-1790' in *CHA Vol 4* (CUP, 1975); West, Martin 'The Bantu-Speaking People' in *Perspectives on the Southern African Past* (CAS, UCT 1979); Wilson, Monica 'The Nguni People, The Sotho, Venda and Tsonga' in Wilson and Thompson (editors) *A History of South Africa to 1870* (DP, 1985); Maylam, Paul *A History of the African People of South Africa from the Early Iron Age to the 1970s* (DP, 1986); Thompson, Leonard (editor) *African Societies in Southern Africa: Historical Studies* (London, Heinemann, 1969)

Raids, war and rebellion in the eastern Cape
Bundy, Colin 'The Frontier Revisited' in *Remaking the Past* (UCT Department of Adult Education and Extra Mural Studies, 1986); Elphick, Richard 'The Khoisan to 1770' in Elphick and Giliomee (editors) *The Shaping of South African Society 1652-1820* (Cape Town, Longman, 1979); Giliomee, Herman 'The Burgher Rebellions on the Eastern Frontier 1795-1815' in Giliomee and Elphick (editors) *The Shaping of South African Society 1652-1820* (Cape Town, Longman, 1979); Giliomee, Hermann 'The Eastern Frontier 1770-1812' in Elphick and Giliomee (editors) *The Shaping of South African Society 1652-1820* (Cape Town, Longman, 1979); Maclennan, Ben *A Proper Degree of Terror* (Ravan, 1986); Muller, C F J *500 Years: A History of South Africa* (Pretoria, Human & Rousseau, 1975); Newton-King, Susan; Malherbe, V C *The Khoikhoi Rebellion in the Eastern Cape (1799-1803)* (CAS, UCT, 1981); Peires, Jeff *The House of Phalo* (Ravan, 1981); Wilson, Monica 'Cooperation and Conflict – The Eastern Cape Frontier' in Wilson and Thompson (editors) *A History of South Africa to 1870* (DP, 1982); Wyndlam Smith, K *From Frontier to Midlands – A History of the Graaff-Reinet District* (Institute of Social and Economic Research, Rhodes University, 1976)

Part 3
The rise of the Zulu kingdom
Cobbing, Julian 'The Ndebele State' in Jeff Peires (editor) *Before and After Shaka – Papers in Nguni History* (Grahamstown, Rhodes University, 1981); Cobbing, Julian *The Case Against the Mfecane* (Wits University African Studies Institute, 1984); Du Buisson, Louis *The White Man Cometh* (Johannesburg, Jonathan Ball, 1987); Lye, W F *The Sotho Paramount Chief and the Difaqane* (African Studies Association, Denver, 1971); Lye, W F; Murray, C *Transformations on the Highveld: The Tswana and the Southern Sotho* (DP, 1980); Maylam, Paul *A History of the African People of South Africa from the Early Iron Age to the 1970s* (DP, 1986); Parsons, Neil *A New History of Southern Africa* (London, Macmillan, 1984); Sanders, Peter *Moshoeshoe – Chief of the Sotho* (DP, 1976); Thompson, Leonard *Survival in Two Worlds – Moshoeshoe of Lesotho 1786-1780* (Oxford, Clarendon Press, 1975); Thompson, Leonard 'Cooperation and Conflict: The Highveld' in Wilson and Thompson (editors) *A History of South Africa to 1870* (DP, 1982)

Upheaval in southern Africa
Cobbing, Julian 'The Ndebele State' in Jeff Peires (editor) *Before and After Shaka – Papers in Nguni History* (Rhodes University, 1981); Cobbing, Julian *The Case Against the Mfecane* (Wits University African Studies Institute, 1984); Lye, W F *The Sotho Paramount Chief and the Difaqane* (Denver, 1971); Lye, W F; Murray, C *Transformations on the Highveld: The Tswana and the Southern Sotho* (DP, 1980); Maylam, Paul *A History of the African People of South Africa from the Earliest Iron Age to the 1970s* (DP, 1986); Parsons, Neil *A New History of Southern Africa* (Macmillan, 1984); Sanders, Peter *Moshoeshoe – Chief of the Sotho* (DP, 1976); Shillington, Kevin *The Colonisation of the Southern Tswana* (Ravan, 1985); Thompson, Leonard *Survival in Two Worlds – Moshoeshoe of Lesotho 1786–1870* (Clarendon Press, 1975); Thompson, Leonard 'Cooperation and Conflict: the Highveld' in Wilson and Thompson (editors) *A History of South Africa to 1870* (DP, 1982)

Boer, Brit and Khoisan
Attwell, Michael *South Africa: Background to the Crisis* (London, Sidgwick & Jackson, 1986); Bundy, Colin 'The Imperial Factor: Crucial Variable in the Historical Equation' in *Remaking the Past* (UCT Department of Adult Education and

Extra-Mural Studies, 1986); Atmore, Anthony; Marks, Shula 'The Imperial Factor in South Africa in the 19th Century: Towards a Reassessment' in *Journal of Imperial and Commonwealth History Vol 3* (1974); Bryer, Lynne; Hunt, Keith *The 1820 Settlers* (Cape Town, Don Nelson, 1984); Davenport, Rodney 'The Consolidation of a New Society' in Wilson and Thompson (editors) *A History of South Africa to 1870* (DP, 1985); Davenport, Rodney *South Africa: A Modern History* (Johannesburg, Macmillan, 1987); Giliomee, Hermann; Elphick, Richard 'The Structure of European Domination at the Cape 1652-1820' in Elphick and Giliomee (editors) *The Shaping of South African Society 1652-1820* (Cape Town, Longman, 1984); Mockley, S M E *The Story of the British Settlers of 1820 in South Africa* (Cape Town, Juta, 1948); Newton-King, S 'The Labour Market of the Cape Colony 1807-1828' in Marks and Atmore (editors) *Economy and Society in Pre-Industrial South Africa* (Harlow, Longman, 1985); Picard, Hymen *Cape Epic* (Howick, Khenty Press, 1977); Sachs, A 'Enter the British Legal Machine' (University of London Institute for Commonwealth Studies, 1969-70)

The attack on Xhosa independence
Bundy, Colin *The Rise and Fall of the South African Peasantry* (Berkeley, University of California Press, 1979); Coplan, David *In Township Tonight!* (Ravan, 1985); Davenport, Rodney *South Africa: A Modern History* (Johannesburg, Macmillan, 1987); Giliomee, Hermann 'The Eastern Frontier 1770-1812' in Elphick and Giliomee (editors) *The Shaping of South African Society 1652-1820* (Cape Town, Longman, 1979); Hutchinson, B 'Some Social Consequences of 19th Century Missionary Activity among the South African Bantu' in *Africa Vol 27* (London, OUP, 1957); Maclennan, Ben *A Proper Degree of Terror* (Ravan, 1986); Peires, Jeff *The House of Phalo* (Ravan, 1981)

Causes of the Great Trek
Atmore, Anthony; Marks, Shula 'The Imperial Factor in South Africa in the 19th Century: Towards a Reassessment' in *Journal of Imperial and Commonwealth History Vol 3* (1974); Denoon, Donald *Southern Africa since 1800* (London, Longman, 1972); Du Bruyn, J T 'The Great Trek' in *IHSA*; Elphick, Richard; Giliomee, Hermann *The Shaping of South African Society 1652-1820* (final chapter)(Cape Town, Longman, 1979); Konya, Phyllis 'A Day of a Voortrekker Youth' in Hans Rooseboom (editor) *The Romance of the Great Trek* (Pretoria, Society of Historical Knowledge, 1949); Muller, C F J *500 Years: A History of South Africa* (Pretoria, Academica, 1981); Muller, C F J *A Pictorial History of the Great Trek* (Cape Town, Tafelberg, 1978); Newton-King, S 'The Labour Market of the Cape Colony 1807-1828' in Marks and Atmore (editors) *Economy and Society in Pre-Industrial South Africa* (London, Longman, 1985); Sachs, A 'Enter the British Legal Machine' (Collected Seminar Papers on the Societies of Southern Africa in the 19th and 20th Centuries Vol 1, University of London Institute for Commonwealth Studies, 1969-70); Thompson, Leonard *The Political Mythology of Apartheid* (New Haven & London, Yale University Press, 1985); Venter, C *The Great Trek* (Cape Town, Don Nelson, 1985); Walker, Eric *The Great Trek* (London, 1934)

The Great Trek
Davenport, Rodney *South Africa: A Modern History* (Johannesburg, Macmillan, 1987); Delius, Peter; Trapido, Stanley 'Inboekselings and Oorlams: The Creation and Transformation of a Servile Class' in *JSAS Vol 8 No 2* (1982); Delius, Peter *The Land Belongs to Us – the Pedi Polity, the Boers and the British in 19th century Transvaal* (Berkeley & Los Angeles, University of California Press, 1984); Du Bruyn, J T 'The Great Trek' in *IHSA*; Muller, C F J *500 Years: A History of South Africa* (Pretoria, Academica, 1981); Sanders, Peter *Moshoeshoe – Chief of the Sotho* (DP, 1975); Thompson, Leonard 'The Difaqane and its Aftermath' in Wilson and Thompson (editors) *A History of South Africa to 1870* (DP, 1982)

Life of the times: Settlers and Voortrekkers
Dugmore, Henry Hare *Reminiscences of an Albany Settler* (Grahamstown, Grocott & Sherry, 1958); Du Preez, Sophia *History, Homes and Customs of the Voortrekkers (National Cultural History and Open-Air Museum No 4, 1974);* Muller, C F J *A Pictorial History of the Great Trek* (Cape Town, Tafelberg, 1978); Rooseboom, Hans (editor) *The Romance of the Great Trek* (Pretoria, Society of Historical Knowledge, 1949); Venter, C *The Great Trek* (Cape Town, Don Nelson, 1985)

Cape liberalism
Bundy, Colin *The Rise and Fall of the South African Peasantry* (Berkeley & Los Angeles, University of California Press, 1979); Davenport, Rodney *South Africa: A Modern History* (Johannesburg, Macmillan, 1987); Davenport, Rodney 'The Cape Colony: The Consolidation of a New Society' in Wilson and Thompson (editors) *A History of South Africa to 1870* (DP, 1985); Lewsen, Phyllis 'Cape Liberalism in its Terminal Phase' in D Hindson (editor) *Working Papers in Southern African Studies* (1983); Lewsen, Phyllis 'The Cape Liberal Tradition – Myth or Reality?' in *Race* Vol 13 (1971); Trapido, Stanley 'The Friends of the Natives' in Marks and Atmore (editors) *Economy and Society in Pre-Industrial South Africa* (London, Longman, 1985); Trapido, Stanley 'Liberalism in the 19th and 20th Centuries in *Societies of Southern Africa Vol 4* (1974); Rich, P 'Segregation and the Cape Liberal Tradition' in *Societies of Southern Africa Vol 10* (1981)

Wool and warfare on a troubled frontier
Dubow, S *Land, Labour and Merchant Capital – The experience of the Graaff-Reinet District in the Pre-Industrial Rural Economy of the Cape 1852-1872* (CAS, UCT, 1982); Kirk, T 'The Cape Economy and the expropriation of the Kat River Settlement 1846-1853' in Marks and Atmore (editors) *Economy and Society in Pre-Industrial South Africa* (London, Longman, 1985); Le Cordeur, Basil 'The Occupation of the Cape 1795-1854' in *IHSA*; Mabin, Alan *The Course of Economic Development in the Cape Colony 1854-1899 – A Case of Truncated Transition* (Economic History Conference Paper, Economic History Society of South Africa, 1984) Peires, Jeff *The House of Phalo* (Ravan, 1981); Peires Jeff 'The Late Great Plot: The Official Delusion Concerning the Xhosa Cattle Killing 1856-1857' in *History in Africa Vol 12* (African Studies Association, University of California, 1985); Ralston, R D 'The Xhosa Cattle Sacrifice 1856-1857: The Messianic Factor in African Resistance' in *Profiles of Self-Determination – African responses to European Colonialism* (Northridge, California State University Foundation, 1976); Wilson, Monica 'Cooperation and Conflict: The Cape Eastern Frontier' in Wilson and Thompson (editors) *A History of South Africa to 1870* (DP, 1985)

Beyond the Orange River
Harington, A L *Sir Harry Smith – Bungling Hero* (Cape Town, Tafelberg, 1986); Le Cordeur, Basil 'The Occupation of the Cape 1795-1854' in *IHSA*; Ross, Robert *Adam Kok's Griquas* (CUP, 1976); Sanders, Peter *Moshoeshoe – Chief of the Sotho* (DP, 1975); Thompson, Leonard *Survival in Two Worlds – Moshoeshoe of Lesotho 1786-1870* (Oxford, Clarendon Press, 1975); Thompson, Leonard 'Cooperation and Conflict: The Highveld' in Wilson and Thompson (editors) *A History of South Africa to 1870* (DP, 1985)

Boers and Africans in the Transvaal
Agar-Hamilton, J A I *The Road to the North – South Africa 1852-1880* (London, Longmans, Green & Co, 1937); Bonner, P L *Aspects of the Political Economy of the Transvaal 1846-1873* (1977); Bonner, P L *Kings, Commoners and Concessionaires* (CUP, 1982); Delius, Peter *The Land Belongs to Us* (Berkeley & Los Angeles, University of California Press, 1984); Delius, Peter 'Migrant Labour and the Pedi, 1840-80' in Marks and Atmore (editors) *Economy and Society in Pre-Industrial South Africa* (London, Longman, 1985); Harries, Patrick 'Kinship, Ideology and the Nature of Pre-Colonial Labour Migration' in Marks and Rathbone (editors) *Industrialisation and Social Change in South Africa* (London, Longman, 1982); Harries, Patrick *Industrialisation, Legislation and Internal Colonialism: the Emergence of Ethnicity amongst the Tsonga Speakers of South Africa* (CAS, UCT, 1983); Trapido, Stanley *Aspects in the Transition from Slavery to Serfdom – The South African Republic 1842-1902* (unpublished paper, 1975); Trapido, Stanley *The Long Apprenticeship: Captivity in the Transvaal 1843-1881* (African Studies Institute Conference Paper, 1976); Trapido, Stanley 'Reflections on Land, Office and Wealth in the South African Republic 1850-1900' in Marks and Atmore (editors) *Economy and Society in Pre-Industrial South Africa* (London, Longman, 1985); Wagner, R 'Zoutpansberg: the Dynamics of a Hunting Frontier 1848-1867' in Marks and Atmore (editors) *Economy and Society in Pre-Industrial South Africa* (London, Longman, 1985); 'The Community that Died in a Cave' in *New Nation* (September 1987)

Xhosa and missionaries
Bundy, Colin *The Rise and Fall of the South African Peasantry* (Berkeley & Los Angeles, University of California Press, 1979); Maclennan, Ben *A Proper Degree of Terror* (Ravan, 1986); Mayer, P *Black Villagers in an Industrial Society* (Cape Town, OUP, 1980); Peires, *Jeff The House of Phalo* (Ravan, 1981); Williams, D *Umfundisi – A Biography of Tiyo Soga 1829-71* (Cape, Lovedale Press, 1978)

Mpande, Natal and the Shepstone system
Brooks, E M; Webb, C A *History of Natal* (Durban, University of Natal Press, 1965); Etherington, N 'Labour Supply and the Genesis of South African Confederation in the 1870s' in *JAH Vol 20* (1979); Slater, Henry 'Land, Labour and Capital in Natal: The Natal Land and Colonisation Company 1860-1948' in *JAH Vol 16* (1975); Slater, Henry 'The Changing Patterns of Economic Relationships in Rural Natal 1838-1914' in Marks and Atmore (editors) *Economy and Society in Pre-Industrial South Africa* (London, Longman, 1985); Thompson, Leonard 'The Zulu Kingdom and Natal – The British Colony' in Wilson and Thompson (editors) *A History of South Africa to 1870* (DP, 1985); Trapido, Stanley 'Natal's Non-Racial Franchise 1856' in *African Studies Vol 22* (1963); Welsh, David *The Roots of Segregation: Native Policy in Colonial Natal 1845-1910* (OUP, 1971)

The end of an epoch
Atmore, A 'The Passing of Sotho Independence' in Leonard Thompson (editor) *African Societies in Southern Africa* (London, Heinemann, 1969); Bundy, Colin *The Rise and Fall of the South African Peasantry* (Berkeley & Los Angeles, University of California Press, 1979); Campbell, W B 'The South African Frontier 1865-1885 - A Study in Expansion' in *Archives Year Book for South African History* (Office of the Chief Archivist, 1959); Etherington, N 'Labour Supply and the Genesis of South African Confederation in the 1870s' in *JAH Vol 20* (1979); Marks, Shula; Atmore, Anthony (editors) Introductory chapter to *Economy and Society in Pre-Industrial South Africa* (London, Longman, 1985); Thompson, Leonard 'The Highveld – Afrikaner Republics and African States 1854-1870' in Wilson and Thompson (editors) *A History of South Africa to 1870* (DP, 1985)

Part 4
The discovery of diamonds
Kallaway, Peter 'Labour in the Kimberley Diamond Fields' in *South African Labour Bulletin Vol 1 No 7* (UCT Press, November/December 1974); Mabin, Alan *The Making of Colonial Capitalism: Intensification and Expansion in the Economic Geography of the Cape Colony, South Africa 1854-1899* (Thesis, Simon Fraser University, 1984); Marks, Shula; Rathbone, Richard (editors) *Industrialisation and Social Change in South Africa* (London, Longman, 1982); Roberts, Brian *Kimberley: Turbulent City* (DP, 1976); Turrell, Rob *The 1875 Black Flag Revolt on the Kimberley Diamond Fields* (JSAS, 1981); Turrell, Rob *Capital and Labour on the Kimberley Diamond Fields 1871-1890* (London Institute of Commonwealth Studies, 1985)

Confederation – the first attempts
Atmore, Anthony; Marks, Shula 'The Imperial Factor in South Africa in the 19th Century: Towards a Reassessment' in *Journal of Imperial and Commonwealth History Vol 3* (1974); Davenport, Rodney *South Africa: A Modern History* (Johannesburg, Macmillan, 1987); Etherington, N A 'Why Langalibalele Ran Away' in *Journal of Natal and Zulu History Vol 1* (1978); Etherington, N A 'Labour Supply and the Genesis of South African Confederation in the 1870s' in *JAH Vol 20* (1979); Etherington, N A 'Theories of Imperialism in Southern Africa Revisited' in *African Affairs Vol 81 No 324* (1982); Manson, A 'A People in Transition: The Hlubi in Natal 1848-1877' in *Journal of Natal and Zulu History Vol 2* (1979); Thompson, Leonard, Wilson, Monica (editors) *The Oxford History of South Africa Vol 2* (OUP, 1971)

Painting the map red
Burman, Sandra 'Masopha' in Christopher Saunders (editor) *Black Leaders in Southern African History* (London, Heinemann, 1979); Colenbrander, Peter 'An Imperial High Commissioner and the making of a War' in *Reality, A Journal of Liberal and Radical Opinion* (January 1979); Davenport, Rodney *South Africa: A Modern History* (Johannesburg, Macmillan, 1987); Delius, Peter *The Land Belongs to Us: The Pedi Polity, the Boers and the British in 19th century Transvaal* (Ravan, 1983); Guy, Jeff 'Cetshwayo' in Christopher Saunders (editor) *Black Leaders in Southern African History* (London, Heinemann, 1979); Guy, Jeff *The Destruction of the Zulu Kingdom* (Ravan, 1982); Guy, Jeff 'The British Invasion of Zululand: Some Thoughts for the Centenary Year' in *Reality, A Journal of Liberal and Radical Opinion* (January 1979); Laband, J; Wright, *King Cetshwayo ka Mpande* (Pietermaritzburg, Shuter and Shooter, 1980); Maylam, Paul *A History of the African People of South Africa from the Early Iron Age to the 1970s* (DP, 1986); Ross, Robert *Adam Kok's Griquas: A Study in the Development of Stratification in South Africa* (CUP, 1976); Sanders, Peter *Moshoeshoe, Chief of the Sotho* (London, Heinemann, 1975); 'Statement from a Zulu Deserter' in *Zulu War Album* (Killie Campbell Africana Library)

Republic reborn
Adam, Heribert; Giliomee, Hermann *Ethnic Power Mobilized* (London, Yale University Press, 1979); Davenport, Rod-

ney *The Afrikaner Bond 1880-1900* (UCT, 1960); Delius, Peter *The Land Belongs to Us* (Ravan, 1983); Muller, C F J *500 Years: A History of South Africa* (Pretoria, Academica, 1981); Ransford, Oliver *The Battle of Majuba Hill: The First Boer War* (London, John Murray, 1967); Van Jaarsveld, Floors *The Awakening of Afrikaner Nationalism* (Cape Town, Human & Rousseau, 1961)

The discovery of gold
Callinicos, Luli *Gold and Workers – 1886-1924* (Ravan, 1980); Hobart Houghton, D 'Economic Development 1865-1965' in Wilson and Thompson (editors) *The Oxford History of South Africa Vol 2* (OUP, 1971); Innes, Duncan 'The Exercise of Control in the Diamond Industry of South Africa' in T Adler (editor) *Perspectives on South Africa* (Wits University African Studies Institute, 1977); Jeeves, Alan 'The Control of Migratory Labour on the South African Gold Mines in the Era of Kruger and Milner' in *JSAS Vol 2 No 1* (October 1975); Johnstone, F A *Class, Race and Gold: A Study of Class Relations and Racial Discrimination in South Africa* (London & New York, Routledge and Kegan Paul, 1976); 'Labour in the Kimberley Diamond Fields' in *South African Labour Bulletin Vol 1 No 7* (November/December 1974); Murray, M J (editor) *South African Capitalism and Black Political Opposition* (Massachusetts, Shenkman, 1982); Murray, M J 'The Development of Capitalist Production Process: The Mining Industry, the Demand for Labour and the Transformation of the Countryside, 1870-1910' in Murray (editor) *South African Capitalism and Black Political Opposition* (Massachusetts, Schenkman, 1982); Turrell, Rob 'Kimberley: Labour and Compounds 1871-1888' in Marks and Rathbone (editors) *Industrialisation and Social Change in South Africa* (London, Longman, 1982); Van Onselen, Charles *Studies in the Social History of the Witwatersrand 1886-1914 – New Babylon* (Ravan, 1982)

The changing face of African society
Bundy, Colin 'Mr Rhodes and the Poisoned Goods' in Beinart and Bundy (editors) *Hidden Struggles in Rural South Africa* (Ravan, 1987); Bundy, Colin 'A Voice in the Big House' in Beinart and Bundy (editors) *Hidden Struggles in Rural South Africa* (Ravan, 1987); Coplan, David *In Township Tonight!* (Ravan, 1985); Etherington, Norman *Preachers, Peasants and Politics in South-East Africa 1835-1880* (London, Royal Historical Society, 1978); Harries, P 'Kinship, Ideology and the Nature of Pre-Colonial Labour Migration' in Marks and Rathbone (editors) *Industrialisation and Social Change in South Africa* (London, Longman, 1982); Jeeves, Alan 'The Control of Migratory Labour on the South African Gold Mines in the era of Kruger and Milner' in *JSAS Vol 2 No 1* (October 1975); Karis, T; Carter G M (editors) *From Protest to Challenge: A Documentary History of African Politics in South Africa 1882-1964 Vol 1* (Hoover Institution Press, 1972); Lacey, M *Working for Boroko: The Origins of a Coercive Labour System in South Africa* (Ravan, 1981); Maylam, Paul *A History of the African People of South Africa from the Early Iron Age to the 1970s* (DP, 1986); Odendaal, André *Vukani Bantu! The Beginnings of Black Protest Politics in South Africa to 1912* (DP, 1984); Odendaal, André *African Political Mobilisation in the Eastern Cape, 1880-1910* (Thesis, Cambridge, 1986); Webster, Eddie (editor) *Essays in Southern African Labour History* (Ravan, 1983)

Life of the times: The 'Naughty Nineties'
Van Onselen, Charles *Studies in the Social and Economic History of the Witwatersrand 1886-1914: New Babylon* (Ravan, 1982)

The colonial zenith
Bley, Helmut 'Social Discord in South West Africa' in Gifford and Roger Louis (editors) *Britain and Germany in Africa – Imperial Rivalry and Colonial Rule*; Keet, D L *The Annexation of Pondoland* (Thesis, UCT, 1964); Kienetz, A *Nineteenth Century South West Africa as a German Settlement* (Xerox University Microfilms, 1976); Lewin, E *The Germans and Africa* (Cassel & Co, 1915); Peters, M T *British Government and the Bechuanaland Protectorate 1885-1895* (Thesis, UCT, 1947); Phimister, I R 'Rhodes, Rhodesia and the Rand' in *JSAS*; Phimister, I R *The Making of Colonial Zimbabwe: Speculation and Violence 1890-1902* (Unpublished seminar paper, African Studies Institute, Wits University, 1982); Sillery, A *Founding a Protectorate – A History of Bechuanaland 1885-1895* (The Hague, Mouton, 1965); Sillery, A *Botswana – A Short Political History*

Indian South Africans
Arkin, A J *The Contribution of Indians to the South African Economy* (Institute for Social and Economic Research, University of Durban-Westville, 1981); Bhana, S; Brain, J B *Movements of Indians in South Africa 1860-1911* (SA Historical Society Conference Papers, 1985); Bhana, S; Pachai, B *A Documentary History of Indian South Africans* (DP, 1984); Huttenback *Gandhi in South Africa – British Imperialism and the Indian Question 1860-1914* (1971); Meer, Y S (editor) *Documents of Indentured Labour: Natal 1851-1917* (Institute of Black Research, 1980); Palmer, Mabel *The History of Indians in Natal* (OUP, 1971); Swan, Maureen *Gandhi: The South African Experience* (Ravan, 1985)

Life on the land
Ballard, C *The Great Rinderpest Epidemic in Natal and Zululand* (Wits African Studies Seminar, 1984); Brink, J *The Ostrich Trade in the Little Karoo* (UCT History Department, 1977); Bundy, Colin 'The Transkei Peasantry c1890-1914: Passing though a period of stress' in Parsons and Palmer (editors) *The Roots of Rural Poverty in Central and Southern Africa* (London, 1977); *Forced Removals in South Africa* (Surplus Peoples' Project Vol 1, Cape Town, 1983); *Land Tenure in Natal Before Union* (Surplus Peoples' Project Vol 4, Cape Town, 1983); Scully, Pam *Whining Farmers: Stellenbosch District 1870-1900* (UCT History Department, 1986); Trapido, Stanley *Putting a Plough to the Ground: A History of Tenant Production on the Vereeniging Estates 1890-1920* (Wits University African Studies Seminar, 1984); Trapido, Stanley 'Landlord and Tenant in a Colonial Economy' in *JSAS Vol 5 No 1* (1978); Van Onselen, Charles 'Reactions to Rinderpest in Southern Africa 1896-1897' in *JAH Vol 13 No 3* (1972)

South African Republic before the war
Blainey, G 'Lost Causes of the Jameson Raid' in *The Economic History Review Vol 18* (1965/66); Butler, J *The Liberal Party and the Jameson Raid* (London, OUP, 1968); Davenport, Rodney *South Africa: A Modern History* (Johannesburg, Macmillan, 1987); De Kiewiet, C W *A History of South Africa – Social and Economic* (London, OUP, 1957); Delius, Peter 'Abel Erasmus: Power and Profit in the Eastern Transvaal' in Beinart, Delius and Trapido (editors) *Putting a Plough to the Ground* (Ravan, 1987); Mendelsohn, Richard 'Blainey and the Jameson Raid: The Debate Renewed' in *JSAS Vol 6 No 2* (April 1980); Marais, J S *The Fall of Kruger's Republic* (London, OUP, 1961); 'The Randlords in 1895: A Reassessment' in *The Journal of British Studies Vol 11 No 2* (May 1972); Wilson, Monica; Thompson, Leonard *The Oxford History of South Africa Vol 2* (London, OUP, 1975)

Causes of the South African War
Bransky, Dennis *The Causes of the Boer War: Towards a Synthesis*; De Kiewiet, C W *A History of South Africa – Social and Economic* (London, OUP, 1957); Hobson, J A *The War in South Africa: Its Causes and Effects* (James Nisbet & Co, 1900); Le May, G H L *British Supremacy in South Africa 1899-1907* (OUP, 1965); Marais, J S *The Fall of Kruger's Republic* (London, OUP, 1961); Marks, Shula; Trapido, Stanley 'Lord Milner and the South African State' in Bonner (editor) *Working Papers in Southern African Studies Vol 2* (Ravan, 1981); Porter, A N *The Origins of the South African War: Joseph Chamberlain and the Diplomacy of Imperialism 1895-99* (Manchester University Press, 1980); Warwick, P (editor) *The South African War* (London, Longman, 1980)

South African War: the formal war
Alhadeff, Vic *A Newspaper History of South Africa* (Cape Town, Don Nelson, 1976); Davenport, Rodney *South Africa: A Modern History* (Johannesburg, Macmillan, 1987; Kruger, Rayne *Goodbye Dolly Gray* (London, Cassell & Co, 1983); Lee, Emanoel *To The Bitter End* (Harmondsworth, Viking, 1985); Packenham, Thomas *The Anglo-Boer War* (London, Weidenfield & Nicolson, 1979); Pretorius, F *The Anglo-Boer War of 1899-1902* (1985); Reitz, Deneys *Commando: A Boer Journal of the Boer War* (London, 1929); Spies, S B *Methods of Barbarism* (Cape Town, Human & Rousseau, 1977); Warwick, P; Spies S B (editors) *The South African War* (1980)

South African War: the informal war
Lee, Emanoel *To The Bitter End* (Harmondsworth, Viking, 1985); Nasson, Bill *Black South Africans in the Cape Colony and the South African War* (D.Ph Thesis, African Studies Library, 1983); Nasson, Bill; John, J M M 'Abraham Esau: A Calvinia Martyr in the Anglo Boer War' in *Social Dynamics* (1985); Nasson, Bill *Moving Lord Kitchener: Black Military Transport and Supply Work in the South African War 1899-1902, with particular reference to the Cape Colony* (Journal of Imperial and Commonwealth History, 1986); Packenham, Thomas *The Anglo-Boer War* (London, Weidenfield & Nicolson, 1979); Pretorius, F *The Anglo-Boer War of 1899-1902* (1985); Plaatje, Sol *The Boer War Diary of Sol T Plaatje* (J Comaroff, 1973); Spies, S B *Methods of Barbarism* (Cape Town, Human & Rousseau, 1977); Warwick, P; Spies S B (editors) *The South African War* (1980); Warwick, P *Black People and the South African War* (1983)

Part 5
The aftermath of war . . .
Davenport, Rodney *South Africa: A Modern History* (Johannesburg, Macmillan, 1987); Garson, N G 'Het Volk: The Botha-Smuts Party in the Transvaal 1904-11' in *The Historical Journal Vol 9 No 1*, (UCT, 1966-7); Levy, Norman *Problems of Acquisition of Labour for the South African Gold Mining Industry: The Asian Labour Alternative and the Defence of the Wage Structure* (Centre for Southern African Studies, University of York); Marks, Shula; Trapido, Stanley 'Lord Milner and the South African State' in Bonner (editor) *Working Papers in Southern African Studies* (Ravan, 1981); Richardson, Peter *Chinese Mine Labour in the Transvaal* (London, Macmillan, 1982); Richardson, Peter *Coolies, Peasants and Proletarians: The Origins of Chinese Indentured Labour in South Africa, 1904-1907* (University of York); Spies, S B 'Reconstruction and Unification, 1902-1910' in *IHSA*; Thompson, Leonard *The Unification of South Africa, 1902-1910* (London, 1960); Ticktin, David *White Labour's Attitude, 1902-1910, towards the Importation of Indentured Chinese Labourers* (UCT, 1972)

Indian and coloured protest movements
Bhana, S; Brain, J B *Movements of Indians in South Africa 1860-1911* (1985); Bhana, S; Pachai, B *A Documentary History of Indian South Africans* (DP, 1984); Huttenback *Gandhi in South Africa – British Imperialism and the Indian Question 1860-1914* (1971); Lewis, Gavin *Between the Wire and the Wall* (DP, 1987); Naidoo, G R 'Indians' 100-year Saga' in *Drum* (November, 1960); Palmer, Mabel *The History of Indians in Natal* (OUP, 1971); Roux, Edward *Time Longer Than Rope* (Madison, University of Wisconsin Press, 1964); Swan, Maureen *Gandhi: The South African Experience* (Ravan, 1985); Van der Ross, Richard *The Rise and Decline of Apartheid* (Cape Town, Tafelberg, 1986)

The rise of modern African politics
Davenport, Rodney *South Africa: A Modern History* (Johannesburg, Macmillan, 1987); Karis, T; Carter G M (editors) *From Protest to Challenge: A Documentary History of African Politics in South Africa 1882-1964* (Hoover Institution Press, 1972); Lewis, Gavin *Between the Wire and the Wall* (DP, 1987); Marks, Shula *Reluctant Rebellion: The 1906-8 Disturbances in Natal* (London, OUP, 1970); Odendaal, André *Vukani Bantu! The Beginnings of Black Protest Politics in South Africa to 1912* (DP, 1984); Odendaal, André *African Political Mobilisation in the Eastern Cape, 1889-1910* (Thesis, Cambridge, 1986); Roux, Edward *Time Longer Than Rope* (Madison, University of Wisconsin Press, 1964); Welsh, David *Origins of Segregation: Native Policy in Colonial Natal 1845-1910* (Cape Town, OUP, 1971)

The founding of the ANC
Coplan, David *In Township Tonight!* (Ravan, 1985); Davenport, Rodney *South Africa: A Modern History* (Johannesburg, Macmillan, 1987); Karis, T; Carter G M (editors) *From Protest to Challenge: A Documentary History of African Politics in South Africa 1882-1964* (Hoover Institution Press, 1972); Odendaal, André *Vukani Bantu! The Beginnings of Black Protest Politics in South Africa to 1912* (DP, 1984); Plaatje, Sol *Native Life in South Africa* (Ravan, 1982); Roux, Edward *Time Longer Than Rope* (Madison, University of Wisconsin Press, 1964); Simons, H R; Simons, R E *Class and Colour in South Africa* (Harmondsworth, Penguin, 1969); Willan, Brian *Sol Plaatje: South African Nationalist 1876-1932* (University of California Press, 1984); Walshe, A P *The Rise of African Nationalism in South Africa: The African National Congress, 1912-52* (London, 1952)

A split in Afrikanerdom
Alhadeff, Vic *A Newspaper History of South Africa* (Cape Town, Don Nelson, 1976); Davenport, Rodney *South Africa: A Modern History* (Johannesburg, Macmillan, 1987); Hancock, Sir William *Smuts: 2 Vols* (CUP, 1962); Hobart Houghton, D; Dagut, J (editors) *Source Material of the South African Economy: 1860-1970* (OUP, 1972); Hofmeyr, Isabel *Building a Nation from Words: Afrikaans Language, Literature and 'Ethnic Identity' 1902-1924* (Wits University, 1984); Ingham, Kenneth *Jan Christiaan Smuts: The Conscience of a South African* (JB, 1986); Johnstone, Frederick *Class, Conflict and Colour Bars in the South African Gold Mining Industry 1910-26* (Institute of Commonwealth Studies, University of London); Johnston, Hazel *Hertzog and Botha: The Genesis of the Division between them and the Origins of the Nationalist Party 1910-1914* (BA Hons. extended essay, UCT, 1958); Krüger, D W *South African Parties and Policies 1910-1960* (Cape Town, Human & Rousseau, 1960); Ticktin, David *The White Labour Movement in South Africa 1902-1910 and Working Class Solidarity* (Conference on Southern African Labour History, Wits University African Studies Institute, 1976)

Miners and the 1922 strike
Alhadeff, Vic *A Newspaper History of South Africa* (Cape Town, Don Nelson, 1976); Bloch, Robin 'The High Cost of Living: The Port Elizabeth "Disturbances" of October 1920' in *Africa Perspective No 19* (1981); Bonner, P L 'The 1920 Black Mineworkers Strike: A Preliminary Account' in Bozzoli (editor) *Labour, Townships and Protest: Studies in the Social History of the Witwatersrand* (Ravan, 1979); Bonner, P L 'The Transvaal Native Congress 1917-1920: The Radicalisation of the Black Petty Bourgeoisie on the Rand' in Marks and Rathbone (editors) *Industrialisation and Social Change in South Africa: African Class Formation, Culture and Consciousness 1870-1930* (London, Longman, 1982); Davies, Rob 'The 1922 Strike and the Political Economy of South Africa' in Bozzoli (editor) *Labour, Townships and Protest: Studies in the Social History of the Witwatersrand* (Ravan, 1979); Johnstone, Frederick *Class, Conflict and Colour Bars in the South African Gold Mining Industry 1910-1926* (Institute of Commonwealth Studies, University of London); Roux, Edward *Time Longer than Rope* (Madison, Wisconsin University Press, 1964); Simons, H J; Simons, R E *Class and Colour in South Africa* (Harmondsworth, Penguin, 1969); Walshe, Peter *The Rise of African Nationalism in South Africa: The African National Congress 1912-1952* (London, Hurst & Co, 1970); Yudelman, David *The Emergence of Modern South Africa: State, Capital and the Incorporation of Organised Labour on the South African Gold Fields, 1902-1939* (DP, 1983)

The foundations of apartheid
Cell, John *The Highest Stage of White Supremacy* (CUP, 1982); Davenport, Rodney *South Africa: A Modern History* (Johannesburg, Macmillan, 1987); Davenport, Rodney 'The Triumph of Colonel Stallard: The Transformation of the Natives' (Urban Areas) Act between 1923 and 1937' in *The SAHJ* (November 1970); Horrell, Muriel 'Principal Legislative Measures Affecting Race Relations, 1909-1948' in *South African Institute of Race Relations Yearbook* (1966); Kinkhead-Weekes, B *The Development of Popular Resistance Among Local Africans, 1918-1935* (UCT, History Department, 1985); Legassick, Martin *The Rise of Modern South African Liberalism: Its Assumptions and Social Base* (African Studies Faculty, University of Sussex, 1975); Legassick, Martin *The Making of South African 'Native Policy', 1903-1923* (Institute of Commonwealth Studies, University of London); Proctor, A 'Class Struggle, Segregation and the City: A History of Sophiatown 1905-1940' in Bozzoli (editor) *Labour, Townships and Protest: Studies in the Social History of the Witwatersrand* (Ravan, 1979); Rex, John 'The Plural Society: The South African Case' in *Race Vol 12 No 4* (London, Institute of Race Relations, 1971); Rich, Paul *Ministering to the White Man's Needs: The Development of Urban Segregation in South Africa, 1913-1923* (Wits University History Workshop, 1978); Saunders, Christopher 'The Creation of Ndabeni, Urban Segregation, Social Control and African Resistance in Cape Town' in *Studies of the History of Cape Town Vol 1* (UCT, 1979); Swanson, Maynard 'The Sanitation Syndrome: Bubonic Plague and Urban Native Policy in the Cape Colony 1900-1909' in *JAH Vol 18 No 3* (1977); Yudelman, David *The Emergence of Modern South Africa: State, Capital and the Incorporation of Organised Labour on the South African Goldfields, 1902-1939* (DP, 1983)

Rural resistance and 'black peril'
Beinart, William 'Amafelandawonye (The Die-hards): Popular Protest and Women's Movements in Herschel District in the 1920s' in Beinart and Bundy *Hidden Struggles in Rural South Africa* (Ravan, 1987); Bradford, Helen 'A Taste of Freedom: Capitalist Development and Response to the ICU in the Transvaal Countryside' in Bozzoli (editor) *Town and Countryside in the Transvaal* (Ravan, 1983); Bradford, Helen *Lynch Law and Labourers: The ICU in Umvoti, 1927-1928* (Wits University History Workshop, 1984); Bradford, Helen 'Strikes in the Natal Midlands: Landlords, Labour Tenants and the ICU' in *Africa Perspective No 22* (1983); Bradford, Helen *The Industrial and Commercial Workers' Union of Africa in the South African Countryside, 1924-1930* (Ph.D Thesis, Wits University, 1985); Bundy, Colin 'Land and Liberation: The South African National Liberation Movements and the Agrarian Question, 1920s-1960s' in *Review of African Political Economy No 29* (1984); Edgar, Robert *The Fifth Seal: Enoch Mgijima, the Israelites and the Bulhoek Massacre, 1921* (Ph.D Thesis, University of California, 1977); Edgar, Robert *Garveyism in Africa: Dr Wellington and the 'American Movement' in the Transkei, 1925-40* (Institute of Commonwealth Studies, University of London); Hofmeyr, Willie 'Rural Popular Organisation and its Problems: Struggles in the Western Cape, 1929-1930' in *Africa Perspective No 22* (1983); Roux, Edward *Time Longer Than Rope* (Madison, Wisconsin University Press, 1964); Simons, H J; Simons, R E *Class and Colour in South Africa* (Harmondsworth, Penguin, 1969)

Poor whites and Afrikaner nationalism
Alhadeff, Vic *A Newspaper History of South Africa* (Cape Town, Don Nelson, 1976); Callinicos, Luli *Working Life 1886-1940* (Ravan, 1987); Giliomee, Hermann *Ethnic Power Mobilised* (London, Yale University Press, 1979); Albertyn, J R; Rothmann, M E *The Poor White Problem in South Africa – Report of the Carnegie Commission, Part 5: Sociological Report* (Stellenbosch, Pro Ecclesia, 1932); Bundy, Colin 'Vagabond Hollanders and Runaway Englishmen: White Poverty in the Cape Before Poor Whiteism' in Beinart; Delius; Trapido (editors) *Putting a Plough to the Ground* (Ravan, 1986); Giliomee, Hermann 'Constructing Afrikaner Nationalism' in *Journal of Asian and African Studies Vol 18* (1983); Harrison, David *The White Tribe of Africa* (Johannesburg, Macmillan, 1981); Keegan, Tim *Lapsed Whites and Moral Panic: An Aspect of the South African Ideological Crisis* (UCT, 1979); Le Roux, Pieter *Poor Whites: Second Carnegie Inquiry into Poverty and Development in Southern Africa* (Conference Paper, UCT, 1984); O'Meara, Dan *Volkskapitalisme: Class, Capital and Ideology in the Development of Afrikaner Nationalism 1934-1948* (Ravan, 1983); O'Meara, Dan 'White Trade Unionism, Political Power and Afrikaner Nationalism' in Webster (editor) *Essays in South African Labour History* (Ravan, 1978); O'Meara, Dan 'The Afrikaner Broederbond 1927-1948: Class Vanguard of Afrikaner Nationalism' in *Journal of South African Studies Vol 3 No 2* (April 1977); *South Africa's Yesterdays* (Cape Town, Reader's Digest, 1981); Wilkins, Ivor; Strydom, Hans *The Super Afrikaners* (Johannesburg, Jonathan Ball, 1978)

The assault on the Cape franchise
Ballinger, Margaret *From Union to Apartheid: A Trek to Isolation* (Cape Town, Juta, 1969); Bonner, Philip *The Decline and Fall of the ICU – A Case of Self-destruction?*; Davenport, Rodney *South Africa: A Modern History* (Johannesburg, Macmillan, 1987); Karis, T; Carter, G M (editors) *From Protest to Challenge: A Documentary History of African Politics in South Africa 1882-1964 Vol 2 – Hope and Challenge* (Hoover Institution Press, 1972); Lacey, Marian *Working for Boroko: The Origins of a Coercive Labour System in South Africa* (Ravan, 1981); O'Meara, Dan *Volkskapitalisme: Class, Capital and Ideology in the Development of Afrikaner Nationalism 1934-1948* (Ravan, 1983); Roux, Edward *Time Longer than Rope* (Madison, Wisconsin University Press, 1964); Tatz, C M *Shadow and Substance in South Africa: A Study in Land and Franchise Policies Affecting Africans, 1910-1960* (Pietermaritzburg, University of Natal Press, 1962); Walshe, Peter *The Rise of African Nationalism in South Africa: The African National Congress 1912-1952* (London, Hurst & Co, 1970)

Economic recovery – and the Second World War
Attwell, Michael *South Africa: Background to the Crisis* (London, Sidgwick & Jackson, 1986); Davenport, Rodney *South Africa: A Modern History* (Johannesburg, Macmillan, 1987); Harrison, David The White Tribe of Africa (Johannesburg, Macmillan, 1981); Natrass, Jill *The South African Economy, Its Growth and Change* (OUP, 1981); Roberts, M; Trollip, A E G *The South African Opposition 1939-1945* (London, 1947); *South Africa's Yesterdays* (Cape Town, Reader's Digest, 1981); Stultz, Newell *Afrikaner Politics in South Africa, 1934-1948* (University of California Press, 1974); Vatcher, W H *White Laager – The Rise of Afrikaner Nationalism* (London, 1965); Wilson, Monica; Thompson, Leonard *The Oxford History of South Africa Vol 2* (London, OUP, 1975); Yudelman, David *The Emergence of Modern South Africa: State, Capital and the Incorporation of Organised Labour on the South African Gold Fields* (DP, 1983)

Life of the times: Second World War
South Africa's Yesterdays (Cape Town, Reader's Digest, 1981); Roux, Edward *Time Longer Than Rope* (Madison, Wisconsin University Press, 1964)

Africans and the cities
Callinicos, Luli *Working Life 1886-1940* (Ravan, 1987); Coplan, David 'The Emergence of an African Working Class Culture' in Marks and Rathbone (editors) *Industrialisation and Social Change: African Class Formation, Culture and Consciousness 1870-1930* (London, Longman, 1982); Coplan, David *In Township Tonight!* (Ravan, 1985); 'Goodbye Shebeens' in *Drum* (August, 1961); Hirson, B *Reorganization of African trade unions in Johannesburg 1936-1942*; Koch, Eddie *Without Visible Means of Subsistence*; Lodge, Tom *Black Politics in South Africa Since 1945* (Ravan, 1983); Ngcobo, Duke 'The Sofasonke Story: From Death Cell to Success' in *Drum* (September, 1961); Roux, Edward *Time Longer Than Rope* (Madison, Wisconsin University Press, 1964); Simons, H J; Simons, R E *Class and Colour in South Africa 1850-1950* (Harmondsworth, Penguin, 1969); Stadler, Alf 'Birds in the Cornfields' in Bozzoli (editor) *Labour, Townships and Protest: Studies in the Social History of the Witwatersrand* (Ravan, 1979); Stein, M *Black Trade Unionism during the Second World War: The Witwatersrand Strikes of December 1942*

The new black activists
Davenport, Rodney *South Africa: A Modern History* (Johannesburg, Macmillan, 1987); Feit, Edward 'Generational Conflict and African Nationalism in South Africa: The African National Congress, 1949-1959' in *African Historical Studies Vol 5 No 2* (African Studies Centre, Boston University, 1972); Gerhart, Gail *Black Power in South Africa: The Evolution of an Ideology* (University of California Press, 1978); Giffard, Chris *'The Hour of Youth has Struck!': The African National Congress Youth League and the Struggle for a Mass Base, 1943-1952* (BA Honours Economic History, UCT, 1984); Lodge, Tom *Black Politics in South Africa since 1945* (Ravan, 1983); Lodge, Tom *Class Conflict, Communal Struggle and Patriotic Unity: The Communist Party of South Africa during the Second World War* (Wits University African Studies Institute, 1985); O'Meara, Dan *The 1946 African Mineworkers' Strike and the Political Economy of South Africa* (University of Sussex); Roux, Edward *Time Longer Than Rope* (Madison, Wisconsin University Press, 1964); Simons, H J; Simons, R E *Class and Colour in South Africa 1850-1950* (Harmondsworth, Penguin, 1969); Walshe, Peter *The Rise of African Nationalism in South Africa: The African National Congress 1912-1952* (London, Hurst & Co, 1970)

Part 6
The vote for apartheid
Alhadeff, Vic *A Newspaper History of South Africa* (Cape Town, Don Nelson, 1976); Hancock, Sir William *Smuts: 2 Vols* (London, CUP, 1962); Harrison, David *The White Tribe of Africa* (Johannesburg, Macmillan, 1981); Ingham, Kenneth *Jan Christiaan Smuts: The Conscience of a South African* (JB, 1986); Legassick, Martin 'Legislation, Ideology and Economy in Post-1948 South Africa' in *JSAS Vol 1 No 1* (OUP, 1974); Luthuli, Albert *Let My People Go* (London, Collins, 1962); Matthews, Z K *Freedom For My People* (DP, 1981); O'Meara, Dan *Volkskapitalisme: Class, Capital and Ideology in the Development of Afrikaner Nationalism 1934-1948* (Ravan, 1983); Stultz, Newell *Afrikaner Politics in South Africa, 1934-1948* (University of California Press, 1974)

A decade of division (1948-58)
Attwell, Michael *South Africa: Background to the Crisis* (London, Sidgwick & Jackson, 1986); Carter, G *The Politics of Inequality* (London, Thames & Hudson, 1958); Davenport, Rodney *South Africa: A Modern History* (Johannesburg, Macmillan, 1987); Harrison, David *The White Tribe of Africa* (Johannesburg, Macmillan, 1981); Horrell, Muriel *Laws Affecting Race Relations in South Africa* (Johannesburg, SAIRR, 1978); Karis, T; Gerhart, G M (editors) *From Protest to Challenge: Documents of African Politics in South Africa, 1882-1964 Vol 3 – Change and Violence, 1953-1964* (Hoover Institution Press, 1977); Legassick, Martin 'Legislation, Ideology and Economy in Post-1948 South Africa' in *JSAS Vol 1 No 1* (1974); Lodge, Tom *Black Politics in South Africa since 1945* (Ravan, 1983); Modisane, Bloke *Blame Me on History* (Johannesburg, A D Donker, 1986); Roux, Edward *Time Longer Than Rope* (Madison, Wisconsin University Press, 1964); Wilkins, Ivor; Strydom, Hans *The Super Afrikaners* (Johannesburg, Jonathan Ball, 1978)

ANC and defiance
Carter, G *The Politics of Inequality* (London, Thames & Hudson, 1958); *For Freedom in South Africa: Statements by Chief Albert J Luthuli on Receipt of Nobel Peace Prize in December 1961* (United Nations Centre Against Apartheid); Karis, T; Carter, G (editors) *From Protest to Challenge: Documents of African Politics in South Africa 1882-1964 Vol 2 – Hope and Challenge 1935-1952* (Hoover Institution Press, 1973); Lodge, Tom *Black Politics in South Africa Since 1945* (Ravan, 1983); Luthuli, Albert *Let My People Go* (London, Collins, 1962); Roux, Edward *Time Longer Than Rope* (Madison, Wisconsin University Press, 1964); Suttner, Raymond; Cronin, Jeremy *30 Years of the Freedom Charter* (Ravan, 1986)

Apartheid and the Cape franchise
Carter, G *The Politics of Inequality* (London, Thames & Hudson, 1958); Davenport, Rodney *South Africa: A Modern History* (Johannesburg, Macmillan, 1987); Lewis, Gavin *Between the Wire and the Wall* (DP, 1987); Lodge, Tom *Black Politics in South Africa* (Ravan, 1983); Tayal, Maureen *Ideology in Organised Indian Politics, 1880-1948* (Wits University African Studies Institute, 1983); Van der Ross, Richard *The Rise and Decline of Apartheid* (Cape Town, Tafelberg, 1986); Walshe, Peter *The Rise of African Nationalism in South Africa: The African National Congress 1912-1952* (London, Hurst & Co, 1970)

PAC and the Sharpeville shootings

A Précis of the Reports of the Commissions appointed to enquire into the Events occurring on 21 March 1960 at Sharpeville and Langa (SAIRR); Alhadeff, Vic *A Newspaper History of South Africa* (Cape Town, Don Nelson, 1976); Gerhart, Gail *Black Power in South Africa: The Evolution of an Ideology* (University of California Press, 1978); Karis, Thomas; Carter, Gwendolen M (editors) *From Protest to Challenge: A Documentary History of African Politics in South Africa 1882-1964* Vol 3: Karis, Thomas; Gerhart, Gail M 'Challenge and Violence 1953-1964' (Hoover Institution Press, 1977); Kgosana, Philip 'A 20-year-old Student Leads the March on Cape Town' in *Drum* (October, 1960); Lelyveld, Joseph *Move Your Shadow – South Africa Black and White* (London, Michael Joseph, 1985); Lodge, Tom *Black Politics in South Africa Since 1945* (Ravan, 1983); Nkoana, Matthew 'Robert Mangaliso Sobukwe, new Africanist Leader and Political Tough-Talker' in *Drum* (May, 1959); Roux, Edward *Time Longer Than Rope* (Madison, Wisconsin University Press, 1964); Petrus, Tom *The Story of My Life* (Ravan)

The swing to violence

Davenport, Rodney *South Africa: A Modern History* (Johannesburg, Macmillan, 1987); Gerhart, Gail *Black Power in South Africa* (University of California Press, 1978); 'Interview with David Kitson' in *Africa Perspective No 25* (1984); Johnson, R W *How Long Will South Africa Survive?* (Johannesburg, Macmillan, 1977); Karis, Thomas; Carter, Gwendolen M (editors) *From Protest to Challenge: A Documentary History of African Politics in South Africa 1882-1964* Vol 3: Karis, Thomas; Gerhart, Gail M 'Challenge and Violence 1953-1964' (Hoover Institution Press, 1977); Lambert, Rob *Black Resistance in South Africa 1950-1961: An Assessment of the Political Strike Campaigns* (Institute of Commonwealth Studies, University of London, 1981); Lodge, Tom *Black Politics in South Africa Since 1945* (Ravan, 1983); Roux, Edward *Time Longer Than Rope* (Madison, Wisconsin University Press, 1964); Sachs, Albie 'The Instruments of Dominion in South Africa' in Thompson, L M; Butler, J (editors) *Changes in Contemporary South Africa*: (University of California Press, 1975)

Life of the times: Making South African music

Coplan, David *In Township Tonight!* (Ravan, 1985)

The Sixties' boom

Alhadeff, Vic *A Newspaper History of South Africa* (Cape Town, Don Nelson, 1976); Beyers C J (editor-in-chief) *Dictionary of South African Biography Vol 4* (Pretoria, Human Sciences Research Council, 1981); Davenport, Rodney *South Africa: A Modern History* (Johannesburg, Macmillan, 1987); Hanlon, J *Apartheid's Second Front: South Africa's War Against Its Neighbours* (Harmondsworth, Penguin, 1986); Hepple, Alexander *Verwoerd: Political Leaders of the 20th Century* (London, Pelican, 1967); Johnson, R W *How Long Will South Africa Survive?* (Johannesburg, Macmillan, 1977)

'National States' and forced removals

Baldwin, A 'Mass Removals and Separate Development' in *JSAS* (1975); Bundy, Colin 'The Past and Present: Towards an Understanding' in *Remaking the Past* (UCT Department of Adult Education and Extra-Mural Studies, 1986); Desmond, Cosmas *The Discarded People: African Resettlement in South Africa* (London, Penguin, 1971); Duncan, Sheena 'Exclusion – the Heart of Apartheid' in *South Africa – A Land Divided* (Black Sash, 1982); Innes, Duncan *Disqualified: A Study of the Effects of Uprooting the Coloured People of South Africa* (London, Africa Publications Trust, 1975); Johnson, R W *How Long Will South Africa Survive?* (Johannesburg, Macmillan, 1977); Lodge, Tom 'The Destruction of Sophiatown' in Bozzoli, B (editor) *Town and Countryside in the Transvaal* (Ravan, 1983); Modisane, Bloke *Blame Me on History* (Johannesburg, A D Donker, 1986); Nash, M; Charlton, N (editors) *An Empty Table? Churches and the Ciskei Future* (Johannesburg, SA Council of Churches, 1981); Platsky, L; Walker, C *The Surplus People – Forced Removals in South Africa* (Ravan, 1985); Proctor, A 'Class Struggle, Segregation and the City: A History of Sophiatown, 1905-1940' in Bozzoli, B (editor) *Labour, Township and Protest* (Ravan, 1979); Pinnock, Don *Breaking the Web: Economic Consequences of the Destruction of Extended Families by Group Areas Relocations in Cape Town* (Cape Town, Second Carnegie Inquiry into Poverty and Development in Southern Africa, 1984); Silk, A *A Shanty Town in South Africa: The Story of Modderdam* (Ravan, 1981); Stein, Pippa; Jacobson, Ruth *Sophiatown Speaks* (Johannesburg, Junction Avenue Press, 1986)

Detente and desperation

Bench, B 'Constructive Engagement: The Confused Art of Regional Foreign Policy' in *South African Review 2* (Ravan, 1984); Davenport, Rodney *South Africa: A Modern History* (Johannesburg, Macmillan, 1987); Crest, J 'Mozambique: A Decade of Independence' in *South African Review 3* (Ravan, 1986); Hanlon, J *Beggar Your Neighbours* (1986); Hanlon J *Apartheid's Second Front : South Africa's War Against Its Neighbours* (Penguin, 1986); Vale, Peter 'The Botha Doctrine: Pretoria's Response to the West and to its Neighbours' in *South African Review 2* (Ravan, 1984)

Part 7
Soweto and black consciousness

Attwell, Michael *South Africa: Background to the Crisis* (London, Sidgwick & Jackson, 1986); Brooks, Alan; Brickhill, Jeremy *Whirlwind Before the Storm* (London, International Defence and Aid Fund for Southern Africa, 1980); Davies, Rob; O'Meara, Dan; Dlamini, Sipho *The Struggle For South Africa* (London, Zed Books, 1984); Frederickse, Julie *South Africa: A Different Kind of War* (Ravan, 1986); Harrison, David *The White Tribe of Africa* (Johannesburg, Macmillan, 1981); Kane-Berman, John *Soweto: Black Revolt, White Reaction* (Ravan, 1978); Lee, Marshall; Magubane, Peter *Soweto* (Lansdowne, Citadel Press, 1983); Pollack, Luis *The Inquest into the Death of Stephen Bantu Biko – A Report to the Lawyers' Committee for Civil Rights* (February, 1978); *Steve Biko, A Short History* (UCT Projects Committee, SRC Press, 1977)

Misinformation and Total Strategy

Baskin, Jeremy *Striking Back: A History of COSATU* (Ravan, 1991); Bundy, Colin 'The Past and Present: Towards an Understanding' in *Remaking the Past* (UCT, 1986); Cawthra, Gavin *Brute Force – The Apartheid War Machine* (London, International Defence and Aid Fund, 1986); Cooper, C; Ensor, L *PEBCO, a Black Mass Movement* (SAIRR, 1981); Davies, Rob; O'Meara, Dan 'The State of Analysis of the Southern African Region: Issues Raised by South African Strategy' in *Review of African Political Economy No 29* (1985); Devereaux, S *South African Income Distribution 1900-1980* (South African Labour and Development Research Unit, UCT School of Economics, 1983); Friedman, Steven *Building Tomorrow Today: African Workers in Trade Unions 1970-1984* (Ravan, 1987); Frost, M 'Collective Sanctions in International Relations: an Historical Overview of Theory and Practice' in *South Africa and Sanctions: Genesis and Prospects* (SAIRR, 1979); Johnson, W R *How Long Will South Africa Survive?* (Johannesburg, Macmillan, 1977); Maré, G 'The New Constitution: Extending Democracy or Decentralising Control?' in *South African Review 3* (Ravan, 1986); Ramsamy, Sam *Apartheid – The Real Hurdle: Sport in South Africa and the International Boycott* (London, International Defence and Aid Fund, 1982); Rhoodie, Eschel *The Real Information Scandal* (Oribis SA (Pty) Ltd, 1983); South African Institute of Race Relations Survey of Race Relations (1978); *Update No 1 – South Africa in the 1980s* (London, Catholic Institute for International Relations, 1984); Vale, Peter 'The Botha Doctrine: Pretoria's Response to the West and to its Neighbours' in *South African Review 2* (Ravan, 1984); Vale, Peter 'Comment' in *South Africa and Sanctions: Genesis and Prospects* (SAIRR, 1979)

Namibian independence

Bench, B 'Constructive Engagement: The Confused Art of Regional Foreign Policy' in *South African Review 2* (Ravan, 1984); Crest, J 'Mozambique: A Decade of Independence' in *South African Review 3* (Ravan, 1986), Davenport, Rodney *South Africa, A Modern History* (Johannesburg, Macmillan, 1987); Du Preez, Max 'Namibia: A Future Displaced' in *South African Review 3* (Ravan, 1986); Frederickse, Julie *None But Ourselves, Masses versus the Media in the Making of Zimbabwe* (Ravan, 1982); Geldenhuys, Jannie *Dié Wat Wen: 'n Generaal se Storie uit 'n Era van Oorlog en Vrede* (Van Schaik, 1993); Hanlon, J *Beggar Your Neighbour* (Catholic Institute for International Relations, 1986); Hanlon, J *Apartheid's Second Front: South Africa's War Against Its Neighbours* (Penguin, 1986); Herbstein, Denis; Evenson, John *The Devils Are Among Us – The War for Namibia* (London, Zed Books, 1989); Moss, G *Introduction to South African Review 3* (Ravan, 1986); Soggot, D *Namibia: The Violent Heritage* (1986); 'South Africa and its Peripheries' in *South African Review 3* (Ravan, 1986); *UN Resolution 435 – 10 Years Later* (SA Pressclips, 1988); Vale, Peter 'The Botha Doctrine: Pretoria's Response to the West and to its Neighbours' in *South African Review 2* (Ravan, 1984); Vigne, R *A Dwelling Place of Our Own – The Story of the Namibian Nation* (1975); *Keesing's Record of World Events* Vol 40 No 3 (UK, Longman, 1994)

Tricameral parliament

Barrell, Howard 'The United Democratic Front and National Forum: Their Emergence, Composition and Trends' in *South African Review 2* (Ravan, 1984); Bench, Bryan 'Constructive Engagement: The Confused Art of Regional Foreign Policy' in *South African Review 2* (Ravan, 1984); Bundy, Colin 'South Africa on the Switchback' in *New Society* (1986); Coleman, M; Webster, D 'Repression and Detentions in South Africa' in *South African Review 3* (Ravan, 1986); Collinge, Jo-Anne 'The United Democratic Front' in *South African Review 3* (Ravan, 1986); De Villiers, F *Bridge or Barricade: The Constitution – A First Appraisal* (SAAN, 1983); Frederickse, Julie *South Africa – A Different Kind of War* (Ravan, 1986); Hanlon, J *Beggar Your Neighbour* (Catholic Institute for International Relations, 1986); Haysom, Nicholas 'The Langa Shootings and the Kannemeyer Commission of Enquiry' in *South African Review 3* (Ravan, 1984); Lodge, Tom 'From Nkomati to Kabwe, the African National Congress January 1984 - June 1985' in *South African Review 3* (Ravan, 1986); Lodge, Tom; Nasson, Bill *All, Here and Now: Black Politics in South Africa in the 1980s* (Cape Town, DP, 1991); Maré, G 'The New Constitution: Extending Democracy or Decentralising Control?' in *South African Review 3* (Ravan, 1986); Plaut, Martin 'The Political Significance of COSATU' in *Transformation 2* (1986); Race Relations Survey (SAIRR, 1986); Schrire, Robert *Bridge or Barricade: The Constitution – A First Appraisal* (SAAN, 1983); Schrire, Robert *Adapt or Die: The End of White Politics in South Africa* (USA, Ford Foundation, 1991); *Upfront No 6*, various articles (1987); 'White Election – The Crucial Issue is Black Politics' in *Work in Progress 47* (1987); 'The Last White Election' in *New Era* Vol 1 No 2 (1987); Weaver, Tony 'The President's Council' in *South African Review 1* (Ravan, 1983); *The Politics of Opposition* (SA Pressclips)

Conflict and coercion

Barrell, Howard 'The United Democratic Front and National Forum: Their Emergence, Composition and Trends' in *South African Review 2* (Ravan, 1984); *Black Wednesday* (Cape Town, SA Pressclips, 1988); Coleman, M; Webster, D 'Repression and Detentions in South Africa' in *South African Review 3* (Ravan, 1986); Collinge, Jo-Anne 'The United Democratic Front' in *South African Review 3* (Ravan, 1986); 'Focus on Wiehahn' in *South African Labour Bulletin* (August, 1979); Frederickse, Julie *South Africa – A Different Kind of War* (Ravan, 1986); Gilliomee, Hermann; Adam, H *The Rise and Crisis of Afrikaner Power* (DP, 1979); *Incorporation and Re-incorporation: The Homelands System Faces Collapse* (Cape Town, SA Pressclips, 1990); Leach, Graham *South Africa* (London, Routledge & Kegan Paul, 1986); Lodge, Tom; Nasson, Bill *All, Here and Now: Black Politics in South Africa in the 1980s* (Cape Town, DP, 1991); *Negotiations: ANC vs NP – Will They Talk?* (SA Pressclips, 1989); Race Relations Survey (SAIRR, 1986); *Repression in a Time of Reform: A Look at Events in the Transvaal since August 1984* (United Democratic Front, Black Sash, Transvaal Indian Congress, Transvaal Anti-PC, JODAC, DESCOM, DPSC, HAP, November 1984); Rok, Ajuhi *Wiehahn and Riekert: New Mechanism for Control and Oppression of Black Labour and Trade Unions* (Institute of Labour Studies, 1981); Schrire, Robert *Adapt or Die: The End of White Politics in South Africa* (USA, Ford Foundation, 1991); Slabbert, Frederik Van Zyl *The Last White Parliament* (JB, 1986); *The Politics of Oppression: United Democratic Front-National Forum* (SA Pressclips, 1983/1984); *The 1989 Detainees' Hunger Strike* Vol 1 (SA Pressclips, 1989); *Death Squads* (SA Pressclips, 1990)

Dismantling apartheid

Adam, Heribert; Moodley, Kogila *The Negotiated Revolution: Society and Politics in Post-Apartheid South Africa* (Johannesburg, JB, 1993); Harber, Anton; Ludman, Barbara (Editors) *Weekly Mail & Guardian A-Z of South African Politics: The Essential Handbook* (Penguin Books, 1994); Laurence, Patrick *Death Squads: Apartheid's Secret Weapon* (Penguin Forum Series, 1990); Lodge, Tom; Nasson, Bill *All, Here and Now: Black Politics in South Africa in the 1980s* (Cape Town, DP, 1991); Minnaar, Anthony; Liebenberg, Ian; Schutte, Charl (editors) *The Hidden Hand: Covert Operations in South Africa* (Pretoria, Human Sciences Research Council, 1994); Schrire, Robert *Adapt or Die: The End of White Politics in South Africa* (USA, Ford Foundation, 1991); Uys, Stanley 'The Retreating Right' in *The Times Literary Supplement* (London, The Times Supplements, 1 April 1994); Race Relations Survey (SAIRR, 1992/93, 1993/94); *Mandela Comes Home; Right-wing; Right-wing Attacks; ANC Unbanned; Apartheid Dead? – F W's Speech, Reaction and Comment; F W de Klerk; Incorporation and Re-incorporation: The Homelands System Faces Collapse; Inkatha Scandal* Vol 1 and 2; *Sanctions, Disinvestments and Boycotts; Death Squads* (All SA Pressclips); various newspaper articles

The battle for hearts and minds

Adam, Heribert; Moodley, Kogila *The Negotiated Revolution: Society and Politics in Post-Apartheid South Africa* (Johannesburg, JB, 1993); Ellis, Stephen; Sechaba, Tsepo

Comrades Against Apartheid – The ANC and the South African Communist Party in Exile (London, James Currey, 1992); Harber, Anton; Ludman, Barbara (editors) *Weekly Mail & Guardian A-Z of South African Politics: The Essential Handbook* (Penguin Books, 1994); Kane-Berman, John *Political Violence in South Africa* (SAIRR, 1993); Lodge, Tom; Nasson, Bill *All, Here and Now: Black Politics in South Africa in the 1980s* (Cape Town, DP, 1991); Mkhondo, Rich *Reporting South Africa* (London, James Currey; USA, Heinemann, 1993); Schrire, Robert *Adapt or Die: The End of White Politics in South Africa* (USA, Ford Foundation, 1991); *SA Barometer Vol 4, No 22; Vol 5 No 16; Vol 6, No 23* (Johannesburg, WM Publications, 1990, 1991, 1992); *Race Relations Survey* (SAIRR, 1992/93, 1993/94); ANC Conference Vol 1, 2, 3; *ANC Unbanned; Apartheid Dead? – FW's Speech, Reaction and Comment; Congresses, Conferences and Position Statements in 1990; F W de Klerk; Hunger Strike; Incorporation and Re-incorporation: The Homelands System Faces Collapse; Inkatha in 1990; Mandela Comes Home; SACP Unbanned* (All SA Pressclips); various newspaper articles

Life of the times: The many faces of a changing South Africa
Kane-Berman, John *South Africa's Silent Revolution* (Johannesburg, SAIRR, 1991); various newspaper articles

The handover of power
Adam, Heribert; Moodley, Kogila *The Negotiated Revolution: Society and Politics in Post-Apartheid South Africa* (Johannesburg, JB, 1993); Friedman, Steven (editor), Centre for Policy Studies (research) *The Long Journey: South Africa's Quest for a Negotiated Settlement* (Ravan, 1993); Harber, Anton; Ludman, Barbara (editors) *Weekly Mail & Guardian A-Z of South African Politics: The Essential Handbook* (Penguin Books, 1994); Kane-Berman, John *Political Violence in South Africa* (SAIRR, 1993); Mkhondo, Rich *Reporting South Africa* (London, James Currey; USA, Heinemann, 1993); *Race Relations Survey* (SAIRR, 1992/93, 1993/94); various newspaper articles

Picture credits

Picture credits for each page read from top to bottom, using the top of the picture as the reference point. Where the tops of two or more pictures are on the same level, credits read from left to right.

Every effort has been made to trace the copyright holders of photographs reproduced in this publication. The publishers will be most grateful for any information that would trace the copyright holders of any photographs reproduced in this book for which copyright is not credited.

Abbreviations
ALM Albany Museum, Grahamstown
AM Africana Museum, Johannesburg
BC Barnett Collection, *The Star*
BPA Bailey's African Photo Archives, Johannesburg
CA Cape Archives, Cape Town
CL Cory Library, Rhodes University, Grahamstown
DB *Die Burger*
HW History Workshop Photo Archives, University of the Witwatersrand, Johannesburg
INCH Institute for Contemporary History, University of the Orange Free State, Bloemfontein
KC Killie Campbell Africana Library, Durban
LHM Local History Museum Collection, Durban
MHM South African National Museum of Military History, Johannesburg
RD Reader's Digest
SAL South African Library, Cape Town
SAM South African Museum, Cape Town
SU Source Unknown
TA Transvaal Archives, Pretoria
TS *The Star*
UNISA Documentation Centre, University of South Africa, Pretoria
UWC Mayibuye Centre, University of the Western Cape, Bellville South
VM Voortrekker Museum, Pietermaritzburg
WF William Fehr Collection, The Castle, Cape Town
Wits University of the Witwatersrand, Johannesburg

Front cover Nelson Mandela: INPRA/SYGMA.

PART 1
5 Brooks Kraft, SYGMA. **6** Fanie Jason. **14** Frank Herholdt. **15** David Panagos, courtesy Transvaal Museum. **16** AM. **17** RD. **19** SAM. **20** Anthony Bannister. **21** SAM. **22** AM. **23** All W J van Rijssen, courtesy SAM. **24** Both SAM. **25** *Sketches of some of the various classes and tribes inhabiting … Southern Africa*, SAL. **27** Both Archaeology Department, Wits. **28** Illustration, RD. **29** Anthony Bannister. **30** Archaeology Department, Wits. **31** Archaeology Department, Wits; Rooiberg Tin Mine and Mrs J Boyd Harvey; Archaeology Research Unit, Wits, courtesy the Director, R J Mason; Archaeology Research Unit, Wits, courtesy the Director, R J Mason. **33** CA. **34** AM. **35** Greenwich Maritime Museum, London; Professor Eric Axelson. **36** WF. **37** WF; AM; CA; CA; AM.

PART 2
42 AM. **43** South African Cultural History Museum, Cape Town. **44** AM. **45** Both AM. **46** *The age of firearms*, SAL. **47** RD. **48** SU; Library of Parliament. **50** RD. **51** The VOC Collection of Mercedes-Benz, South African Cultural History Museum, Cape Town. **52** Grey Collection, SAL. **55** SU. **57** Simon's Town Museum; AM. **58** Both AM. **60** CA; South African Cultural History Museum, Cape Town. **61** Both AM. **64** Jean Morris; AM. **65** AM. **66** Both AM. **67** Both Jean Morris. **69** CA. **70** David Steele, Photo Access; John Paisley, Photo Access. **71** AM. **72** CA. **73** AM. **74** AM. **75** AM.

PART 3
80 AM. **81** AM. **82** Zimbabwe National Archives, Harare. **84** AM. **85** Both Jean Morris. **86** CA; *Diary of Henry Francis Fynn*, SAL. **87** LHM; AM. **88** AM. **89** AM. **90** AM. **92** AM. **93** Both AM. **94** SU. **95** CA; Library of Parliament. **96** Illustration, RD. **97** Port Elizabeth Library; AM; King George VI Art Gallery, Port Elizabeth; AM. **98** AM. **99** SU; WF. **100** *The Cape of Good Hope Government Gazette*, 25 July 1828, SAL; ALM; AM. **101** *The History of the South African College*, SAL; AM; *The South African Journal*, January-February 1824, SAL. **102** AM. **103** Brian Aldridge; AM; ALM. **104** ALM. **105** ALM. **106** CA. **107** WF; AM. **108** CA; AM. **109** ALM; AM. **110** *Historia*, SAL. **111** VM. **112** TA. **113** *The Graham's Town Journal*, 2 February 1837, SAL. **114** LHM. **116** AM. **117** SU; VM. **118** Illustration, RD; David Steele, Photo Access. **120** LHM. **121** CA; LHM. **122** ALM; WF; ALM. **123** David Bristow; SU. **124** VM; AM; VM; VM. **125** VM. **126** AM. **128** *The South African Commercial Advertiser*, 30 June 1849, SAL; *Old Cape Houses*, SAL; AM. **129** Iconographic Department, SAL. **130** Both *Eastern Province Herald*, 10 August 1852, SAL. **132** AM. **133** Iconographic Department, SAL. **134** AM; SAL. **135** CA; AM; CL. **136** King George VI Art Gallery, Port Elizabeth; ALM. **137** CL; WF. **138** *Tribes and Kingdoms*, SAL. **139** *Moshweshwe of Lesotho*, SAM. **140** CA. **141** Bensusan Museum of Photography, Johannesburg; CA. **142** CA. **143** AM. **145** *Prehistory of the Transvaal*, Wits University Press. **147** AM. **148** CA; AM. **149** *Lydenburgse Eeufeesgedenkboek*, SAL; TA. **150** South African Missionary Museum, King William's Town. **151** AM. **152** SAM. **153** AM. **154** AM. **155** AM; LHM. **156** CA. **157** *Emigrants Guide to Port Natal*, Grey Collection, SAL; AM. **158** AM. **159** CA; TA; *Contrere Vol 1*, January 1877, SAL. **160** CA; Central Archives, Pretoria. **161** Natal Archives, Pietermaritzburg.

PART 4
166 AM. **167** De Beers; *The Story of the Cape to Cairo Railway and River Route: from 1887 to 1922*, Volume 1, SAL. **168** CA; *The Microcosm*, SAL; CA. **169** CA. **170** AM; CA. **171** De Beers. **172** Illustration, RD; CA. **173** David Steele, Photo Access; CA. **174** AM; De Beers; SU. **175** Both CA. **177** CA. **178** LHM. **179** CA. **180** Both CA. **181** AM; CA. **182** South African Cultural History Museum, Cape Town. **183** LHM. **184** AM. **185** AM. **186** David Steele, Photo Access; Illustration, RD. **187** Map net, RD; LHM. **188** AM. **189** KC; AM; LHM. **190** SAM; *Reminiscences of Life in South Africa*, SAL. **191** AM; CA. **193** Both Library of Parliament. **194** CA. **195** AM. **196** AM; *Die Afrikaanse Patriot*, 15 January 1876, SAL; AM. **197** *Standard Encyclopaedia of Southern Africa*; CA. **198** AM; TA. **199** AM; CA. **200** BC. **201** AM. **202** Both AM. **203** AM. **204** Both AM. **205** *The Diggers' News*, 24 February 1887, SAL; RD. **207** HW. **208** *Isigidimi Sama-Xosa*, 2 January 1882, SAL; AM. **209** Iconographic Department, SAL; CA; SAL. **210** University of Cape Town Libraries. **211** *Hidden Struggles*, SAL. **212** AM; RD; AM. **213** BC. **214** AM; CA. **215** BC; AM. **216** Both *Südwes Afrika*, SAL. **218** *Among the Matabele*, SAL; AM. **219** RD; BC; BC. **220** *Tribes and Kingdoms*, SAL; Iconographic Department, SAL. **221** Both CA. **222** LHM. **223** CA. **224** LHM. **225** *Portrait of Indian South Africans*, SAL. **226** AM. **227** Gordon Douglas; *South African Ladies' Pictorial*, SAL. **228** SU. **229** AM. **231** SU; AM. **232** CA. **233** Peter Culverwell Antiques. **234** CA; Iconographic Department, SAL. **235** Iconographic Department, SAL; CA. **236** Both BC. **237** Both BC. **239** Simon's Town Museum; Greenwall Collection. **240** AM. **241** CL; CA. **242** AM; TA. **243** AM; SU. **244** BC. **246** CA. **247** LHM; CA. **248** *The South African War*, SAL; KC; CL. **249** SU. **250** Illustration and map, Marshall Editions Limited; CA. **251** AM; Map net, Marshall Editions Limited. **252** Both AM. **253** CA; CA; Greenwall Collection. **254** BC. **256** AM. **257** Both CA. **258** Both *Cape Times Weekly*, 13 March 1901, SAL. **259** CA. **260** CA. **261** Greenwall Collection; South African Cultural History Museum, Cape Town; Greenwall Collection; Greenwall Collection; Greenwall Collection; Greenwall Collection.

PART 5
267 CA; AM. **268** Dr Oscar Norwich; CA; Dr Oscar Norwich. **269** *Some Reminiscences*, SAL; CA. **270** CA; AM; *Cape Times*, 31 May 1910, SAL. **271** Postage stamp reproduced under Government Printer's Copyright Authority 8893 of 5.7.1988; SU. **272** UWC. **273** AM. **274** AM. **275** AM. **276** AM. **277** UWC; *Between the Wire and the Wall*, SAL.

278 LHM. **279** LHM; Natal Archives, Pietermaritzburg. **280** *The African Yearly Register*, SAL; *Imvo*, 11 March 1903, SAL. **281** *The African Yearly Register*, SAL. **282** LHM. **283** Department of Public Relations, University of Fort Hare. **284** *Illustrated London News*, 4 August 1909, SAL. **285** AME Church. **286** LHM. **287** KC; AM; LHM. **288** *Gatsha Buthelezi*, SAL. **289** AM; *The African Yearly Register*, SAL. **290** Both SU. **292** *South African Recollections*, SAL. **293** AM; Grey Collection, SAL. **295** *South African Who's Who*, 1923, SAL; UWC. **296** CA; AM. **298** DB, 6 October 1915, SAL; Manuscript Department, University Library, Stellenbosch. **299** TA; *Die Brandwag*, 15 November 1910, SAL; *Die Brandwag*, 15 June 1910, SAL. **301** CA; *The Capture of De Wet*, SAL. **302** *The Pictorial*, SAL. **303** CA; *The History of the South African Forces in France*, SAL; MHM; CA. **305** AM; Dr Oscar Norwich; TS. **307** *Who's Who in the Union Parliament*, SAL. **308** CA; AM; AM; AM. **309** AM; CA; CA; TS; CA; AM. **310** HW. **311** HW. **313** AM; CL. **314** Iconographic Department, SAL. **315** *The African Yearly Register*, SAL. **317** *Report of the Local Government Commission*, 1921, SAL; TA. **318** United Party Archives, Unisa, Pretoria. **319** INCH. **320** *The African Yearly Register*, SAL. **321** *The Workers Herald*, 14 October 1926, SAL. **322** Both UNISA. **323** *Philosophy and Opinion of Marcus Garvey*, SAL. **324** *Hidden Struggles*, SAL. **325** HW; *Worcester Standard*, 27 March 1930, SAL. **327** AM. **328** Iconographic Department, SAL. **329** *Carnegie Commission Report 1936*, SAL. **330** *Carnegie Commission Report 1936*, SAL; *Carnegie Commission Report 1936*, SAL; *Andrew Murray na 100 Jaar*, SAL. **331** City Council of Pretoria. **332** City Council of Pretoria. **334** INCH; CA. **335** *Afrikaanse Kultuuralmanak*, SAL. **336** *Afrikaanse Kultuuralmanak*, SAL; SU; SU. **337** SU; KC. **339** Department of Public Relations, University of Fort Hare; *From Protest to Challenge*, SAL. **340** UNISA; MHM. **341** UWC; *Drum*, June 1952, SAL. **342** Both HW. **344** *Outspan*, SAL. **345** AM; *The Star*, 4 September 1939, SAL. **346** *Iscor News*, April 1936, SAL; City Council of Pretoria. **347** MHM. **348** City Council of Pretoria; MHM. **349** SU. **350** All AM. **351** MHM; Postage stamp reproduced under Government Printer's Copyright Authority 8893 of 5.7.1988; SU; SU; MHM. **352** LHM; AM. **353** *South African Industry and Trade*, SAL; LHM; AM; MHM. **354** Both SU. **355** HW. **356** HW; BPA. **357** BPA; UWC. **358** AM; *In Township Tonight!*, SAL; HW. **359** UWC. **360** AM; *Natal Mercury*, 28 May 1948, SAL. **362** UWC. **363** BPA. **364** Both BPA. **365** Both UWC.

PART 6

370 DB; *Pretoria News*. **371** BPA. **372** SU. **373** AM. **374** *Outspan*, SAL. **375** TS. **376** SU. **377** DB; Associated Press, Johannesburg. **378** DB, 20 May 1957, SAL. **379** BPA; UWC. **380** DB. **381** TS; UWC. **382** BPA. **384** SU. **385** Both *Drum*, October 1952, SAL. **386** *Drum*, October 1952, SAL. **387** BPA. **388** *Drum*, April 1957, SAL. **389** UWC; *Drum*, September 1957, SAL. **390** TS; *Drum*, February 1957, SAL; BPA. **391** BPA; UWC. **392** CA. **395** KC; TS. **396** *Drum*, April 1954, SAL. **397** *Drum*, March 1960, SAL. **398** *Drum*, April 1960, SAL. **399** *From Protest to Challenge*, SAL. **400** BPA. **401** *Cape Times*; TS, 21 March 1960. **402** UWC. **403** *Drum*, May 1960, SAL. **404** *Drum*, October 1960, SAL. **405** *Drum*, February 1961, SAL; *The Argus*. **406** *Drum*, October 1960, SAL. **407** BPA. **408** *Drum*, January 1961, SAL. **409** TS; AM. **410** AM; BPA. **411** TS. **412** SU. **413** Both BPA. **414** *From Protest to Challenge*, SAL. **415** TS; *Rand Daily Mail*, 26 July 1964, SAL. **416** BPA. **417** *In Township Tonight!*, SAL; BPA; BPA; BPA. **418** Both TS. **419** Human Sciences Research Council, Pretoria; SU. **420** Both Herman Potgieter. **421** Herman Potgieter. **422** TS, 7 September 1966; SU. **423** *Cape Times*. **425** TS. **427** BPA; *Drum*, February 1955, SAL. **428** Derek Carelse. **429** Glynn Griffiths, Photo Access. **430** SU. **431** All BPA. **432** *Drum*, June 1958, SAL. **433** Jean Morris. **434** TS. **435** Argus Africa News Service. **437** SU; TS. **438** TS. **439** Both TS.

PART 7

444 Both TS. **445** TS. **446** Both TS. **447** *Christian Science Monitor*. **448** *The Argus*; TS. **449** TS. **450** TS; Peter John. **452** DB. **453** *The Citizen*, 7 September 1976, SAL. **454** *The Argus*. **455** Both *The Argus*. **456** TS; SU. **457** SU. **458** TS. **459** DB. **460** Peter John. **461** TS. **462** AM. **463** TS. **464** TS. **465** Rashid Lombard; SU; Central Archives, Pretoria. **466** TS. **467** TS. **469** Guy Tillim, SouthLight. **470** TS. **471** SU; TS. **473** Cape Times Collection, SAL. **474** TS. **475** All TS. **476** SU. **477** *The Argus*. **478** Both TS. **479** TS. **480** *Eastern Province Herald*. **481** TS. **482** Cape Times Collection, SAL. **483** SU. **484** TS. **485** Dave Hartman, SouthLight; Peter John. **486** Grassroots Publications. **487** TS. **489** Eric Miller, SouthLight. **490** Adil Bradlow. **491** Adil Bradlow. **493** TS. **495** *The Argus*. **497** South African Communication Service. **498** Adil Bradlow. **499** Johan Kuus, SIPA Press. **500** South African Communication Service; *The Argus*. **502** Johan Kuus, SIPA Press. **503** South African Communication Service; South African Communication Service; *The Argus*. **504** Jacques Witt, SIPA Press. **505** Herbert Mabuza, SIPA Press; Fanie Jason. **507** Johan Kuus, SIPA Press. **504** South African Communication Service. **509** Johan Kuus, SIPA Press. **510** Anna Zieminski. **511** Jon Jones, SYGMA. **512** Anna Zieminski; Graeme Williams, SouthLight; Eric Miller, SouthLight. **513** Graeme Williams, SouthLight; Joao Silva, SouthLight. **514** Fanie Jason; Grassroots Publications; Rafs Mayet, SouthLight. **515** All Fanie Jason. **516** Graeme Williams, SouthLight; Joao Silva, SouthLight; Adil Bradlow; Paul Weinberg, SouthLight. **517** All Fanie Jason. **518** *The Argus*. **519** Adil Bradlow, SouthLight. **520** Fanie Jason. **521** *The Argus*. **522** Patrick du Noirmont, SouthLight; Steve Hilton-Barber, *Weekly Mail*. **523** *The Argus*. **525** Fanie Jason. **526** Fanie Jason. **527** Fanie Jason. **529** Henner Frankenfeld, SouthLight; *The Argus*.

Colour separations and reproduction by Unifoto (Pty) Ltd, Cape Town. Printing and binding by Cape & Transvaal Book Printers, Parow, Cape.